ARCTIC OCEAN

N. Cape
Novaya Zemlya
Severnaya Zemlya
New Siberian Is.

Baltic Sea
L. Ladoga
North European Plain
Ob
Yenisey
Lr. Tunguska
West Siberian Plain
Lena
Aldan
Kamchatka

Europe
Carpathian
Danube
Don
Volga
Ural Mts.
Irtysh
Angara
Sayan Mts.
Baikal
Stanovoy Ra.
Amur
Sea of Okhotsk

Black Sea
Caucasus
Elbrus 5642
Aral Sea
Syrdarya
Amudarya
L. Balkhash
Tian Shan
Altai
Gobi Desert
Hwang-ho
Sakhalin
Hokkaido

Apennines
Anatolia
Mt. Ararat 5165
Caspian Sea
Great Caucasus
Pamirs
Tarim Basin
Kunlun Shan
Qilian Shan
North China Plain
Korea
Sea of Japan
Yellow Sea
Japan
Mt. Fuji 3776

Mediterranean Sea
Dead Sea ▼403
Tigris
Euphrates
Zagros Mts.
Hindu Kush
K2 8611
Plateau of Tibet
Mt. Everest 8850
Gonga Shan 7556
East China Sea

Isthmus of Suez
Libyan Desert
Nile
Arabia
The Gulf
Sulaiman Ra.
Indus
Thar Desert
Himalaya
Yangtze
Si
China
Taiwan
PACIFIC
Wake

Tibesti
Red Sea
Rub' al Khali
Ganges
India
Deccan
W. Ghats
E. Ghats
Bay of Bengal
Indo-China
Mekong
Hainan
Mariana Is.

Sahara
Africa
L. Chad
White Nile
Blue Nile
Socotra
C. Guardafui
Arabian Sea
C. Comorin
Ceylon
Str. of Malacca
South China Sea
Philippine Is.
Guam
Mariana Trench 11022
Marshall Is.

Mt. Cameroon 4095
Ethiopian Highlands
Somali Peninsula
Sumatra
Kinabalu 4101
Celebes Sea
Caroline Is.

Congo
Congo Basin
L. Turkana
Mt. Kenya 5199
Seychelles
INDIAN
Borneo
Celebes
Moluccas
Sunda
OCEAN
New Guinea
Nauru
Puncak Jaya 5029
Gilbert Is.

Kasai
L. Victoria
Kilimanjaro 5895
Java Sea
Banda Sea
Bismarck Arch.
Solomon Is.

L. Tanganyika
Comoros
OCEAN
Java Trench 7450 ▼
Java Is.
Timor
Torres Str.
C. York
Ellice Is.

Cabango
L. Malawi
Zambezi
Cocos
Coral Sea
New Hebrides
Fiji Is.

Orange
Mozambique Chan.
Madagascar
Pic Boby 2658
Mauritius
Réunion
Hamersley Ra.
MacDonnell Ra.
Australia
New Caledonia

Kalahari Desert
Drakensberg
Great Victoria Desert
Great Divide
Darling

Cape of Good Hope
Great Australian Bight
C. Leeuwin
Murray
Great Divide
Mt. Kosciuszko 2237
Bass Str.
Tasman Sea
North I.
New Zealand

Crozet Is.
Kerguelen
Tasmania
Aoraki-Mt. Cook 3753
South I.

SOUTHERN OCEAN

en Maud Land
Enderby Land
Queen Mary Coast
Wilkes Land
South Magnetic + Pole

Antarctica
Victoria Land
Ross Sea

om Greenwich

PHILIP'S
NATURE
ENCYCLOPEDIA

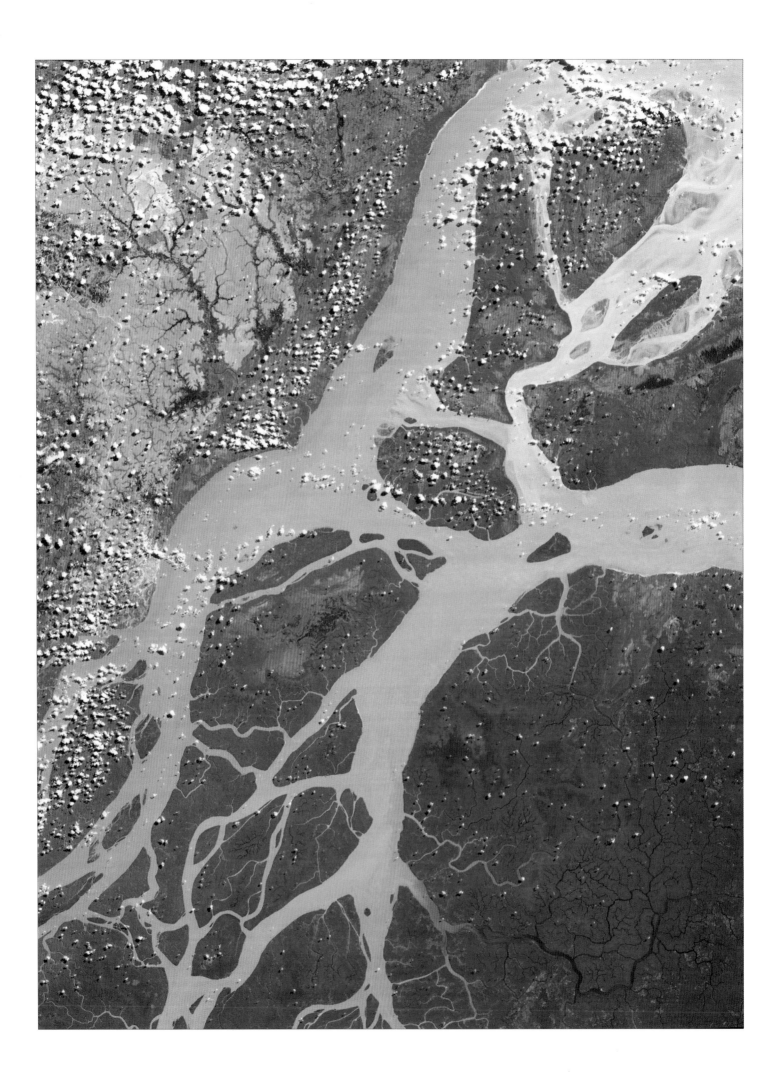

PHILIP'S

NATURE

ENCYCLOPEDIA

CHANCELLOR
PRESS

Philip's Nature Encyclopedia

First published 2001 by Philip's,
an imprint of Octopus Publishing Group Limited

This edition published 2003 by Chancellor Press,
an imprint of Bounty Books, a division of
Octopus Publishing Group Ltd,
2-4 Heron Quays, London E14 4JP

Copyright © 2001 Philip's

COMMISSIONING EDITOR Robin Rees
Canopus Publishing Limited

SENIOR EDITOR Frances Adlington

EXECUTIVE ART EDITOR Mike Brown

EDITORIAL ASSISTANT Rachel Lawrence

PRODUCTION Sally Banner

ISBN 0 7537 0758 6

Printed by Oriental Press, Dubai

▲ **The barn owl** is a skilful and silent flier. As in all birds, the main muscles used for flight are located at the base of, and below, the wings. The positioning of these heavy muscles ensures that the bird's centre of gravity is below the level of the wings, making it aerodynamically stable.

Frontispiece
This satellite image shows the River Amazon near the town of Macapá, Brazil. At this stage the river is more than 6000km (3700mi) from its farthest source, and it has almost reached the Atlantic Ocean. It is up to 75km (50mi) wide at this point. The complexity of channels, islands and tributaries can be clearly seen, as can the clouds floating above the forest. The Amazon discharges 15% of all the fresh water introduced into the oceans by all the Earth's rivers.

PREFACE

The original meaning of "Natural History" was the description and classification of all the phenomena in the material world. Nowadays, it is commonly understood to cover the sciences that deal with the Earth and the diversity of life on Earth. The Philip's *Nature Encyclopedia* has been created, with this definition in mind, for secondary school and college students, for natural history enthusiasts, and for everyone who is curious about the planet we share with so many other species. Written by leading experts in the fields covered, the Encyclopedia presents more than 6500 entries in A–Z order, with nearly 1000 lively colour illustrations.

The selection of entries has been made with the help of a panel of distinguished academics and teachers. In the Earth sciences (geology and related subjects) and life sciences (biology and related subjects), the selection reflects modern subject divisions. Care has been taken to ensure that terms relating to examination syllabuses are included, so that students can use the Philip's *Nature Encyclopedia* as a complement to their textbooks.

With an estimated 3.5 million species of beetle alone to be found on Earth, no reference work on natural history can ever provide complete coverage at individual species level. Our choice of which species of animals and plants to include is based upon what non-specialists might reasonably find in the wild, or encounter in the media. With international travel now so readily accessible, we have taken care to ensure that this coverage is global.

The team of authors responsible for creating this work includes academics from the universities of Cambridge, Bristol and Sheffield and the Open University in the United Kingdom, and Villanova, Pennsylvania, in the United States. They are recognised specialists in their fields and expert communicators; several are best-selling authors in their own right.

A–Z content

More than 6500 articles are arranged from A to Z in the main body of the encyclopedia. They can be divided into four broad categories – Earth sciences, life sciences, flora and fauna, and biographies. Approximately 1000 articles on Earth sciences cover the origins of the Earth, atmosphere, interior, surface, oceans, rocks, minerals, fossils and geological time. The 1500 articles on life sciences include classification and terms, plant physiology, plant morphology, reproduction, genetics, evolution, cellular biology, molecular biology, ecology, environment and conservation. There are approximately 4000 articles on flora and fauna, encompassing amphibians, reptiles, fish, bacteria, fungi, invertebrates, birds, mammals and plants. In addition there are 150 concise biographies of the most distinguished scientists in the history of Earth and life sciences.

Chronology

The Philip's *Nature Encyclopedia* also features an extensive chronology of science. Organized into five main areas – farming and food, biology, chemistry, physics and medicine – the timeline spans twelve thousand years, from 10,000 BC to the present day.

Ready Reference

Supplementing the main body of the Philip's *Nature Encyclopedia*, the Ready Reference section provides hard facts and statistics in tabular form. Earth data includes lists of the most devastating earthquakes and volcanoes, the composition of the atmosphere, and the Earth's largest lakes, highest mountains and longest rivers. Also detailed in this section are the topical issues of global warming, gases implicated in climate change and holes in the ozone layer. The complicated subject of taxonomy is clarified with the help of tables and diagrams. A very wide range of conservation issues is covered, including threatened species, rarest trees and protected areas, as well as milestones in conservation history. The information has been provided by UNEP - World Conservation Monitoring Centre, which is part of the United Nations Environment Programme. There are also units and conversion tables. Addresses and websites are provided for some of the world's natural history museums and arboretums in order that those whose appetites have been whetted by the Encyclopedia can further their knowledge.

Cross-references

The Philip's *Nature Encyclopedia* has more than 10,000 cross-references, indicated by SMALL CAPITAL letters, which take the reader from one article to other related articles. For example, "inspiration" includes cross-references to GILLS, LUNGS, EXPIRATION, GAS EXCHANGE and RESPIRATION.

Nomenclature

Individual species are presented under their common names, but their entries include the technical Latin names to species level. Closely related groups of animals are usually presented together, unless an animal is more likely to be looked up under a different name. For example, many beetles appear under the headword "beetle" ("beetle, ambrosia", "beetle, bacon" and so on), but the stag beetle article appears under "s", with a cross-reference from "beetle, stag".

Current scientific terms and classification systems are used, with cross-references from old terms that are likely to be looked up. Metric units are used throughout, with corresponding imperial measurements in brackets.

▲ **The African elephant** is the largest land mammal; a big male may stand at nearly 4m (13ft) tall and weigh more than 7 tonnes. The tusks continue to grow throughout the animal's life.

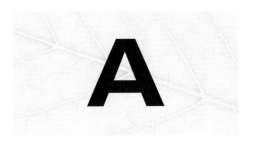

A

aardvark
Nocturnal, bristly haired mammal of central and s Africa. It feeds on termites and ants, which it scoops up with its sticky 30cm-long (12in) tongue. Length: up to 1.5m (5ft); weight: up to 70kg (155lb). It is the only representative of the order TUBULIDENTATA.

aardwolf (ardwolf)
Mammal found on the open grassy plains of s and E Africa. It is yellowish with black stripes and a black-tipped tail. Usually solitary, the aardwolf feeds on termites and insect larvae at night. Head-body length: 55–80cm (22–31in); tail: 20–30cm (8–12in). Family Hyaenidae; species *Proteles cristatus*.

abaca (manila hemp)
High quality fibre obtained from the fibrous, sheathing leaf bases of the plant of the same name. A relative of the banana, abaca is native to the Philippines and is cultivated in Southeast Asia and South America. The curved fruit, which is 5–8cm (2–3in) long, is full of seeds and not edible. Height: to 6.1m (20ft). Family Musaceae; species *Musa textilis*.

abalone (ormer)
Gastropod MOLLUSC with a single, flattened, spiral shell perforated by a row of respiratory holes. Abalones are found in the shallows of rocky shores. They are edible. Length: to 30cm (12in). Family Haliotidae; species include *Haliotis rufescens*.

abdomen
In vertebrates, that portion of the body between the chest and the pelvis containing the abdominal cavity and the abdominal viscera, including most of the digestive organs. In arthropods the abdomen is the posterior part of the body, containing the reproductive organs and part of the digestive system.

abiotic factors
Various non-living factors – favourable or harmful – that contribute to the ENVIRONMENT of living things.

They include the atmosphere, climate, geology, amount of light and temperature of the ECOSYSTEM.

abir
Scented powder used in worship by Hindus. It has as its main ingredient the RHIZOME of the GINGER LILY, a member of the ginger family native to Nepal. The plant spreads by means of rhizomes and often forms dense stands. It is grown as a hothouse ornamental for its strongly perfumed flowers. Family Zingiberaceae; species *Hedychium spicatum*.

ablation
Measure of glacial loss through melting, evaporation, wind erosion or calving (the formation of icebergs). The term is sometimes used in geomorphology to mean the loss of surface soil or rock by wind or water action. *See also* ACCUMULATION; EROSION

abrasion
Mechanical wearing down of rock surface by the dragging of rock particles across it. Agents of abrasion are the bed load of streams, rock debris at the base of glaciers, and sand transported by waves. *See also* EROSION

abscission
Deliberate shedding of a part of a plant. Commonly occurring with fruit and leaves, it is controlled by abscisic acid and other growth substances. An abscission layer of cells forms in an abscission zone at the base of the part. As these cells break down, the part falls off the plant, usually dislodged by the wind or rain.

abyssal
Term to describe oceanic features occurring at great depths, usually more than *c*.3000m (*c*.10,000ft) below sea level. Abyssal **plains** cover *c*.30% of the Atlantic and nearly 75% of the Pacific ocean floors. They are covered by deposits of biogenic oozes, formed by the remains of microscopic plankton, and nonbiogenic sediments (red clays). The gradient is less than 1:1,000, except for the occasional low, oval-shaped abyssal **hills**. The plains are characterized by stable temperatures from $-1°C$ to $5°C$ (30–41°F) and the relative absence of water currents. The abyssal **zone** is the deepest area of the ocean. It receives no sunlight, so there are no seasons and no plants, but there are many forms of life, such as glass SPONGES, CRINOIDS (sea lilies) and BRACHIOPODS (lamp shells).

acacia
Any member of a group of evergreen shrubs and trees that are widely distributed in tropical and subtropical regions. Acacias have compound leaves and yellow or white flowers. Australian species are known as WATTLES. Height: 1.2–18m (4–59ft). Family Leguminosae; genus *Acacia*.

acanthocephalan
See SPINY-HEADED WORM

acanthus
Perennial plant with thistle-like leaves, found in Africa, the Mediterranean region, India and Malaysia. It has lobed, often spiny leaves and white or coloured flower spikes. The pattern of the leaves in a stylized form is a common classical architectural motif. Family Acanthaceae.

accentor
Small, rather drab-coloured, perching bird with streaked grey or brown plumage, found mainly in

Asia and Europe. The 12 species include the hedge accentor (or hedge sparrow or dunnock), a common European garden bird, and the alpine accentor, which lives in rocky mountain sites. Length: 15–18cm (6–7in). Family Prunellidae.

acclimatization
Temporary adjustment of an organism to a new environment, climate or circumstance. It involves a gradual, natural change in physiology allowing an organism to exploit new regions, but, unlike EVOLUTION, it does not involve any genetic change.

accretion
Continually growing or building up; a term used to describe certain modes of geological DEPOSITION.

accumulation
Addition of snow and ice to a GLACIER. It usually occurs near the head of the glacier where the air temperature is well below freezing. Snow from avalanches and precipitation falls onto the glacier and becomes compressed under its own weight, forming ice. *See also* ABLATION

acer
See MAPLE

acetylcholine (ACh)
Chemical compound released by certain nerve cells. It serves as a transmitter in the NERVOUS SYSTEM. Acetylcholine is involved in the transmission of impulses across the junction (synapse) between nerve cells and between nerve and muscle cells, triggering the contraction of muscles.

achene
Type of FRUIT that contains only one seed. It is a dry, indehiscent fruit (that is, it does not open spontaneously) formed from a single CARPEL, with the seed separated from the wall of the fruit. Examples include members of the BUTTERCUP family and CLEMATIS. Winged achenes are called SAMARAS.

achocha
Annual, strong-smelling, vigorously growing vine, native to Mexico and Central America. It has lobed leaves and small flowers, which produce an oblong, softly prickly and yellowish-white fruit. Family Cucurbitaceae; species *Cyclanthera pedata*.

acid rain
See feature article, page 3

▲ **aardvark** Found throughout much of Africa, the termite-eating aardvark (*Orycteropus afer*) is a shy, nocturnal animal. Its presence may be detected by the large burrows it digs, using the hoof-like claws on its front feet.

▲ **aardwolf** A predominantly solitary creature, the aardwolf (*Proteles cristatus*) resembles the hyena, which affords it some protection from other animals, although it does not have the hyena's strong jaws and teeth. In Afrikaans, the name aardwolf means "earth wolf".

acid rock

Any IGNEOUS ROCK that contains a high proportion (more than 66%) of silica. The main silica mineral is QUARTZ, but some FELDSPARS are also quite rich in silica. Acid igneous rocks are usually light in colour. The most common type is GRANITE. SOIL produced by the WEATHERING of acid rocks is generally infertile.

aconite

Flowering plant of the genus *Aconitum*. Its roots provide the ALKALOID aconitine, which is used in medicine; in ancient times it was used as a poison. Species of *Aconitum* include MONKSHOOD and WOLFSBANE. Family Ranunculaceae.

acorn worm (hemichordate)

Marine invertebrate. It feeds on detritus and dwells in burrows or in the shelter of other underwater debris. The number of acorn worm species is small, but they are notable for being closely related to the ECHINODERMS (phylum Echinodermata) and the CHORDATES (phylum Chordata). Phylum Hemichordata; class Enteropneusta.

acouchi

Small rodent that is native to Central and South America. It is dark reddish or greenish with paler yellow underparts and a white-tipped tail. It feeds on roots, grass and berries in the undergrowth of forests. There are two species. Head-body length: 32--38cm (13–15in); tail: 5–7cm (2–3in). Family Dasyproctidae; genus *Myoprocta*.

acquired characteristic

Feature that develops during the lifetime of an organism. The enlarged muscles of a manual worker are an example of an acquired characteristic. Because they are not genetically controlled, these acquired traits cannot be passed on to offspring – that is, they cannot be inherited (although the French naturalist Jean Baptiste LAMARCK incorrectly thought that they could).

actinobacterium

Type of BACTERIUM that is able to degrade a variety of organic compounds and is therefore important in the process of mineralization. Some, such as *Frankia*, are able to fix nitrogen; others, for example *Streptomyces* and *Arthrobacter*, produce many of the antibiotics used in medicine. *See also* NITROGEN-FIXING BACTERIUM

actinomycete

Any member of the major group of bacteria the Actinomycetes. The group comprises more than 500 species and is the source of most antibiotics.

action potential

Change that occurs in the electrical potential between the outside and the inside of a nerve fibre or muscle fibre when stimulated by the transmission of a NERVE IMPULSE. At rest the fibre is electrically negative inside and positive outside; this is called **resting potential**. When the nerve or muscle is stimulated, the charges are momentarily reversed.

activator

Agent that accelerates or augments chemical activity; for example, certain impurities increase luminescence. Some ENZYMES require an activator to function; for example, thrombokinase, which is important in blood clotting, is activated by calcium ions.

active transport

Energy-requiring process by which molecules or ions are transported across the membranes of living CELLS against a concentration gradient. It is particularly important in the uptake of food across the gut lining, in the reabsorption of water and salts from the urine in the kidney before excretion, in secretion of substances from gland cells, in the transmission of nerve impulses, and in the uptake of minerals by the plant root. The energy is supplied by the chemical ADENOSINE TRIPHOSPHATE (ATP), which is broken down by an enzyme at the site of active transport to form adenosine diphosphate (ADP), with the release of energy.

► **addax** Highly prized by hunters for its meat and skin, the addax (*Addax nasumaculatus*) is an endangered species. It has a well-developed sense of hearing, but it lacks the speed to flee successfully from danger.

Active transport enables cells to maintain an internal chemical environment that is of a different composition from that of their surroundings.

adaptation

See feature article

adaptive radiation

EVOLUTION of different forms of living organisms from a common ancestral stock as different populations adapt to different environmental conditions or modes of life. Eventually the populations may become so different that they constitute separate SPECIES. If, for instance, a species becomes distributed over several types of surroundings, in time the populations of each area may develop specialized features suited to the new environment. For example, the many different kinds of finches in the Galápagos Islands diversified to specialize in different kinds of food, feeding methods and habitats. *See also* ADAPTATION

addax

Endangered horse-like ANTELOPE found in dry regions of N Africa. The addax is highly adapted to living in deserts and can survive without drinking, obtaining its water from leaves and grasses. Distinguished by long spiral horns in both sexes, it is pale in colour with a long black-tipped tail. Height: 95–115cm (37–45in); length: 150–170cm (59–67in). Family Bovidae; subfamily Hippotraginae; species *Addax nasomaculatus*.

adder

Any of numerous species of heavy-bodied, venomous SNAKES with wide, triangular heads. The European VIPER (*Vipera berus*) is called an adder in Britain and is the country's only poisonous snake. The PUFF ADDER (*Bitis arietans*) is a large African viper, and the death adder (*Acanthophis antarticus*) is a dangerous Australian elapid.

adenine

Nitrogen-containing, organic base of the PURINE group found combined in the NUCLEIC ACIDS. In DNA adenine pairs with the pyrimidine base THYMINE.

adenosine diphosphate (ADP)

Nucleotide chemical involved in energy-generating reactions during cell METABOLISM. ADP consists of

---

ADAPTATION

Adjustment by a living organism to its surroundings. Animals and plants adapt to changes in their environment through variations in structure, reproduction or organization within communities. Some such changes are temporary (ACCLIMATIZATION), whereas others may involve changes in the genetic material (DNA) and be inherited by offspring (EVOLUTION). The word is also used to describe a particular characteristic, of body size, shape, colour, physiology or behaviour, that fits an organism to survive in its environment.

► **The various honeycreepers** of Hawaii evolved from one species of bird now long extinct (centre). Over millions of years the honeycreepers evolved different methods of feeding. This ensured the island's various habitat niches could be exploited, resulting in less competition among the birds and therefore allowing more to survive. The main adaptation was the dramatic change in the shape of the beaks. A few species evolved beaks best suited to feed on nectar (1), others feed purely on insects (2), while some feed on fruit (3) or seeds (4).

Acid rain is RAIN that is highly acidic because of sulphur oxides, nitrogen oxides and other air pollutants dissolved in it. Normal rain is slightly acidic, with a pH of 6. (The pH scale ranges from 1 for extremely acidic to 14 for extremely basic or alkaline, with 7 being neutral.) Acid rain may have a pH value as low as 2.8.

Many aquatic organisms live in waters exposed to acid rain and the resulting corrosive environment means that they are unable to survive. Acid rain also eats away at the surfaces of buildings. In the European forests, the trees are extremely vulnerable. Damage to forests by acid rain is affecting more than half of all trees in the Czech Republic, Slovakia, Germany, Greece, the Netherlands, Norway, Poland and Britain.

An important air pollutant is tetra-ethyl lead, which is added to petrol to prevent engine-knocking. It is emitted by exhaust pipes and concentrates in air and dust. It is especially harmful

in cities, where it can build up in the inhabitants' blood. Lead in the blood can cause stomach pains, headaches, irritation, coma and death. Very low levels of lead can even affect the brains of growing children. There is growing international pressure to ban the use of leaded petrol, but lead is only one of the harmful substances regularly pumped into the air as a by-product of our industrialized society.

The comparatively recent and rapid industrialization of many parts of the world has added tremendous quantities of acidic pollutants to the atmosphere. The result has been lifeless lakes, dying forests and contaminated soils. FOOD CHAINS may be disrupted within forests as the leaves of damaged trees become deficient in calcium through LEACHING processes. Leaves are

eaten by caterpillars, which, in turn, are eaten by nesting birds. These birds produce very thin and easily damaged eggshells, or even no eggs at all, and the bird population accordingly declines. Acid rain can contaminate supplies of drinking water by dissolving and thus liberating toxic metals in the soil. The corrosion of underground drinking water pipes is another source of danger. One very serious consequence is the harm caused to the liver and kidneys of young children by an accumulation of high levels of copper.

Since the early 1980s some progress has been made in tackling acid rain. A number of industrially based countries have signed international agreements to reduce emissions of sulphur and nitrogen oxides, especially from large coal-fired power stations. Environmentalists have strongly suggested, however, that such promised reductions do not go far enough. Soils and lakes of many regions are now so acidified that the situation will remain problematical for many years to come.

▲ **Most sulphur** (1) leaves factory chimneys as the gaseous sulphur dioxide (SO_2), and most nitrogen (2) is also emitted as one of the nitrogen oxides (NO or NO_2), both of which are gases. The gases may be dry deposited – absorbed directly by the land, by lakes or by the surface vegetation (3). If they are in the atmosphere for any time, the gases will oxidize (gain an oxygen atom) and go into solution as acids (4). Sulphuric acid (H_2SO_4) and the nitrogen oxides will become nitric acid (HNO_3). The acids usually dissolve in cloud droplets and may travel great distances before being precipitated as acid rain. Catalysts such as hydrogen peroxide, ozone and ammonium help promote the formation of acids in clouds (5). More ammonium (NH_4) can be formed when some of the acids are partially neutralized (6) by airborne ammonia (NH_3). Acidification increases with the number of active hydrogen (H^+) ions dissolved in an acid (7). Hydrocarbons emitted by, for example, car exhausts (8) will react in sunlight with nitrogen oxides to produce ozone (9). Although it is invaluable in the atmosphere, low-level ozone causes respiratory problems and also hastens the formation of acid rain. When acid rain falls on the ground it dissolves and liberates heavy metals and aluminium (Al) (10). When it is washed into lakes, aluminium irritates the outer surfaces of many fish; their gills can become clogged with mucus and they die. As acid rain falls or drains into the lake the pH of the lake falls. Each drop of 1 point on the pH scale means that acidity has increased tenfold. Experiments indicate that minnows and shrimps disappear when the pH reaches 6. At pH 5.6 the exoskeletons of crayfish soften and become overrun with infestation. All that is left is a clear lake with a lush carpet of green algae and moss. Forests suffer the effects of acid rain through damage to leaves, the loss of vital nutrients, and the increased amounts of toxic metals liberated by acids, which damage roots and soil microorganisms.

A

the PURINE base ADENINE linked to the sugar D-ribose, which in turn carries two phosphate groups. It is formed by the hydrolysis of ADENOSINE TRIPHOSPHATE (ATP) – with the release of energy – or the phosphorylation of ADENOSINE MONOPHOSPHATE (AMP) – which requires the input of energy; both reactions are catalysed by ENZYMES.

adenosine monophosphate (AMP)
Nucleotide chemical involved in energy-generating reactions during cell METABOLISM. AMP consists of the PURINE base ADENINE linked to the sugar D-ribose, which in turn carries a phosphate group. It is formed by the HYDROLYSIS of ADENOSINE TRIPHOSPHATE (ATP) – with the release of energy – catalyzed by ENZYMES.

adenosine triphosphate (ATP)
NUCLEOTIDE chemical consisting of ADENINE, D-ribose and three phosphate groups. Found in all plant and animal CELLS, it is fundamental in the biochemical reactions required to support life. In animal respiration, ATP can be broken down through the process of HYDROLYSIS, coupled with PHOSPHORYLATION, to form ADENOSINE DIPHOSPHATE (ADP) and phosphate, or ADENOSINE MONOPHOSPHATE (AMP) and pyrophosphate. In either case, the reactions, which are catalysed by ENZYMES, yield large amounts of energy. The energy is used either to turn simple molecules into more complex ones required by individual cells, or to control an activity such as muscle contraction. Conversely energy is used up when ATP is indirectly synthesized from ADP and AMP by complex biochemical reactions known as the electron chain system during the KREBS CYCLE. In plants, ATP is also synthesized during PHOTOSYNTHESIS.

adiabatic process
Thermodynamic change without any gain or loss of heat or mass into or out of a system during expansion or compression of the gas or fluid composing the system. Truly adiabatic changes must take place in short time intervals so that the heat content of the system remains unchanged, or else the system must be perfectly insulated (a practical impossibility). *See also* ISOTHERM

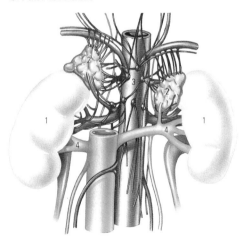

▲ **adrenal gland** Located just above the kidneys (1), the two adrenal glands (2) are well supplied with blood entering from the aorta (3), and from the tributaries of the renal arteries (4). Each gland consists of an outer layer (the cortex) and a central medulla.

The cortex produces steroid hormones, hormones involved in maintaining water-balance, and small quantities of sex hormones. The medulla produces adrenaline and noradrenaline, both of which prepare the body for an emergency or stress situation.

adipose tissue (fatty tissue)
Connective tissue made up of body cells that store large globules of fat.

admiral
Any of several species of brown BUTTERFLY from various genera found worldwide. Admiral caterpillars feed on various plants, including stinging nettles (*Urtica* spp.) and honeysuckle (*Lonicera* spp.). Like MONARCH butterflies, adult admirals may migrate over long distances. Adult body length: *c*.3cm (*c*.1in); wingspan: *c*.9cm (*c*.4in). Family Nymphalidae; genera include *Vanessa* and *Limenitis*; species include *Vanessa atalanta* (red admiral) and *Limenitis camilla* (white admiral).

adrenal gland
One of a pair of small endocrine glands situated on top of the KIDNEYS. They produce many STEROIDS that regulate the blood's salt and water balance and are concerned with the metabolism of carbohydrates, proteins and fats. They also produce the hormones ADRENALINE and NORADRENALINE, which are closely involved in preparing the body to meet conditions of stress, such as pain, shock, intense cold or physical danger. *See also* ENDOCRINE SYSTEM

adrenaline (epinephrine)
Hormone that is secreted by the medulla of the ADRENAL GLANDS; it is important in preparing a body's response to stress. Adrenaline has widespread effects in the body, increasing the strength and rate of heart beat and the rate and depth of breathing, diverting blood from the skin and digestive system to the heart and muscles, and stimulating the release of glucose from the liver to increase energy supply by promoting increased respiration. Synthetic adrenaline is used medicinally in some situations, especially in the resuscitation of patients in shock or following cardiac arrest.

adventitious root
ROOT that grows in an unusual place on a plant. Normally roots grow underground at the base of a plant, but some plants produce roots from their stems and branches. With IVY, for example, adventitious roots provide nourishment and enable the plant to cling onto other plants or buildings for support.

aeolian formation
Structure created by wind-transported material. It may be a dune on a riverbank, ripple marks in sand, or the growth phase of dune building. The term can also can be used to describe shapes carved in rock by the wearing away of softer materials. *See also* BUTTE

aerobe
Minute organism that usually grows only in the presence of free atmospheric oxygen. Some aerobes can, however, remain alive even in the absence of oxygen and are called facultative ANAEROBES.

aerobic
Connected with or dependent on the presence of free OXYGEN or air. An aerobic organism can only function normally in the presence of oxygen and depends on it for breaking down glucose and other foods to release energy. This process is called aerobic RESPIRATION. *See also* ANAEROBIC

aestivation
State of prolonged inactivity in some animals that occurs during a period of hot weather or drought. Bodily activities such as feeding, movement and respiration slow down, and the animal expends very

▲ **agaric** The fly agaric (*Amanita muscaria*) is often found under birch trees with which it forms a mycorrhizal (symbiotic) association. Its unmistakable red cap (pileus), with pyramidal white scales, protects the delicate spore-bearing layer (hymenium) on the gills.

little energy; in this respect, it is similar to dormancy. Aestivation occurs in some insects, snails and lungfish. In botany, the term aestivation describes the way petals and sepals are arranged in a flower bud. *See also* HIBERNATION

afara
Wood from a large hardwood tree native to tropical W Africa. The timber has commercial value for export and is used for furniture. The name *Terminalia* comes from the Latin *terminus*, referring to the way the leaves are borne on the tips of the shoots. Family Combretaceae; species *Terminalia superba*.

African eye worm
NEMATODE worm that is a PARASITE of human blood. It is transmitted by a biting fly. The nematodes migrate just below the surface tissues and can sometimes be seen moving in the eye. African eye worms are known to cause large swellings on the skin and lymphatic enlargement. Phylum Nematoda; species *Loa loa*.

African giant snail
See SNAIL, AFRICAN GIANT

African marigold
Popular garden plant, once thought to be native to Africa, but in fact a member of a group found from New Mexico and Arizona to Argentina. It is a stout annual growing to *c*.0.6m (*c*.2ft) in height with pinnately divided, gland-bearing leaves and large, yellow to orange, solitary flower heads. Family Compositae; species *Tagetes erecta*.

African oak
One of a large family of trees, shrubs and herbs with a tropical distribution; it includes a number of hothouse ornamentals. Two tree species in the genus *Lophira*, both commonly called African oak, have timber of commercial value. Family Ochnaceae; genus *Lophira*.

African violet
Tropical, African, flowering house plant, with velvety, rounded leaves that grow in spreading rosettes

around purple, white or pink blossoms with yellow stamens. The stems and undersides of the leaves are often purple. Propagation is by leaf cuttings or crown division. Height: 10–15cm (4–6in). Family Gesneriaceae; genus *Saintpaulia*.

African walnut

One of a family of trees, shrubs, climbing plants and lianas, native to the tropics worldwide but mostly concentrated in Africa and Asia. The African walnut is named after its walnut-like fruits, which are eaten fresh, boiled or roasted. The timber is used for building houses. Family Olacaceae; species *Coula edulis*.

agamid

Any of *c*.350 species of diurnal LIZARD that inhabit Africa (except Madagascar), Asia and Australasia. They have granular or spiny skin and well-developed limbs. Many agamids, for example the FRILLED LIZARD and MOLOCH, have spines, horns, crests, dewlaps or frills on their heads and bodies. Length: 7.5–100cm (3–39in). Family Agamidae.

agaric

Any member of the Agaricales order of FUNGI, which includes edible mushrooms, ink caps and the poisonous AMANITA. Their spores are borne on the surface of gills or pores on the under-surface of the cap.

Agassiz, Alexander (1835–1910)

US marine zoologist, b. Switzerland. He was influential in the development of modern systematic zoology. In the 1870s Agassiz published a major study of echinoderms. In 1874 he succeeded his father, Louis AGASSIZ, as curator of the Harvard Museum of Natural History. Agassiz was also a mining engineer, serving as president of a successful copper mine.

Agassiz, Louis (Jean Louis Rodolphe) (1807–73)

Swiss naturalist. Between 1833 and 1843, Agassiz published a highly influential study of extinct fish. He did further research into the fossils of echinoderms. Agassiz's other major field of study concerned the movement of glaciers. In 1840 he published his theory that an ice age had once covered most of N Europe. Moving to the United States, Agassiz became (1847) professor of zoology at Harvard University. He continued to study fish and established (1859) a museum of zoology at Harvard.

agate

Microcrystalline form of QUARTZ with parallel bands of colour. Extracted from rock cavities, it is regarded as a semiprecious stone and is used for making ornaments and jewellery. Hardness *c*.6.5; r.d. *c*.2.6.

agave

Succulent, flowering plant found in tropical, subtropical and temperate regions. Agaves have narrow, lance-shaped leaves clustered at the base of the plant, and many have large flower clusters. The flower of the well-known century plant (*Agave americana*) of SW North America grows up to 7.6m (25ft) in one season. The century plant was thought to flower only once in 100 years, but it in fact flowers every 20–30 years. Other species are SISAL (*A. sisalana*) and MESCAL (*Lophophora williamsii*), the fermented sap of which forms the basis of the liqueur tequila. Family Agavaceae.

agglomerate

Coarse volcanic rock that includes both rounded and angular fragments in a fine matrix, thus combining the characteristics of CONGLOMERATES and BRECCIAS.

aggregate

Material such as sand, crushed and broken stone, pebbles and boiler ashes, used to form concrete by mixing with cement, lime, gypsum or other adhesive. It provides volume and resistance to wear.

agnathan

Member of the Agnatha class or subphylum of jawless fish. Only the LAMPREY and the HAGFISH live today, but many fossil species date from as long ago as 450 million years.

agouti

Common name for members of the genus *Dasyprocta*. Found in forests and thick brush of Central and South America, these rodents feed on fruit and succulent plants. Head-body length: 41–62cm (16–24in); tail: 1–3cm (0.4–1in). Family Dasyproctidae. *See also* ACOUCHI; PACA

agrimony

Perennial herb that is distributed throughout Europe to the Middle East and North Africa; it has been introduced into North America. Found along roadsides, hedgerows and in grasslands, agrimony has small yellow flowers, which are clustered in long upright spikes. It is fragrant when crushed. Valued for its medicinal properties, agrimony contains 5% tannin, which may be responsible for its wound-healing properties. Family Rosaceae; species *Agrimonia eupatoria*.

airglow

Faint permanent glow of the Earth's IONOSPHERE. It is thought to result from the recombination of molecules, such as oxygen and nitrogen, that have been ionized by ultraviolet radiation from the Sun and probably by cosmic-ray and solar-wind particles. *See also* ATMOSPHERE

air mass

Large body of the ATMOSPHERE that is nearly uniform horizontally in temperature, pressure and vapour content and therefore in weather effects. High and low pressure zones on weather maps correspond to air masses, covering large areas horizontally although only a few miles vertically. FRONTS, or frontal zones, occur between air masses, and it is the movement of the fronts that brings changes in the weather. Air masses are often classified in terms of origin as polar (cold) or tropical (warm), maritime (wet, over oceans) or continental (dry, over land). *See also* CIRCULATION, ATMOSPHERIC

air pressure

See ATMOSPHERIC PRESSURE

▲ **agouti** The ground-dwelling agouti is a shy rodent capable of moving quickly if pursued by a predator. Agoutis live in monogamous pairs; the female gives birth in a burrow made of boulders and leaves on the forest floor.

air sac

In birds, one of the many thin-walled sacs connected to the lungs or inside cavities in the bones. Air sacs improve the efficiency of air ventilation in the lungs and contribute to the lightness of the bones. In insects, air sacs connected to the tracheae (breathing tubes) improve GAS EXCHANGE by increasing the surface area available for RESPIRATION.

akee (akye)

Tropical tree native to W Africa, grown for its fruit. At the base of each seed is a white fleshy aril which is edible when cooked. It is named after seaman William Bligh, British commander of the ship *Bounty*. Height: to 12.2m (40ft). Family Sapindaceae; species *Blighia sapida*.

akialoa

One of a group of unusual FINCHES found only on the Hawaiian Islands. It has a long, down-curved bill with which it probes for insects. It also gathers nectar with its long tongue. The akialoa inhabits the mountain rainforests of the island of Kauai, where it is close to extinction. Length: 19cm (7in). Family Fringillidae; species *Hemignathus obscurus*.

akiapolaau

One of a group of unusual FINCHES found only on the Hawaiian Islands. The akiapolaau has perhaps the strangest of all bills, with the upper, curved, mandible much longer than the lower. It hammers on bark with its lower mandible then uses the upper to probe for food. It is highly endangered. Length: 14cm (6in). Family Fringillidae; species *Hemignathus munroi*.

akohekohe

One of a group of unusual FINCHES found only on the Hawaiian Islands. The akohekohe is rather colourful, with a bright red neck patch. It is found only on the island of Maui and feeds on insects and nectar. Length: 18cm (7in). Family Fringillidae; species *Palmeria dolei*.

albacore

Long-finned, fast-swimming TUNA found worldwide in tropical and temperate waters. It is cigar-shaped, with a large tail sharply divided into two lobes and a long pectoral fin. An important food and game fish, it is sold as "white meat tuna". Length: to 130cm (51in); weight: 18–36kg (40–80lb). Family Scombridae; species *Thunnus alalunga*.

albatross (mollymawk)

Oceanic bird famed for having the longest wingspan of any living bird, thus enabling it to glide for hours with barely a wing beat. The albatross eats on the wing and only comes to land to breed. There are thirteen species worldwide, nine of which live in the Southern Hemisphere. Length: 71–117cm (28–46in); wingspan: 203–324cm (80–128in). Family Diomedeidae.

albatross, black-browed

Large albatross with blackish-brown tail and upper wings, and white head, lower back and wing linings. The dark streak above the eye gives it a frowning appearance. It breeds in Southern Hemisphere oceans. Length: 81–86cm (32–34in); wingspan: 229cm (90in). Family Diomedeidae; species *Diomedea melanophris*.

albatross, Laysan

Albatross that is similar in plumage to the black-browed albatross but with broader black margins on its under wings and a dark spot in front of the eye.

A

▲ **albatross, Laysan** When breeding, the Laysan albatross (*Diomedea immutabilis*) is commonly found on the islands around Hawaii. Like most albatrosses, the female lays a single egg in November, which is incubated by both sexes for several months, hatching in January. Between July and October, it stays at least 20–30km (12–19mi) offshore.

The Laysan albatross is often seen following ships in the N Pacific Ocean. Length: 81cm (32in); wingspan: 203cm (80in). Family Diomedeidae; species *Diomedea immutabilis*.

albatross, royal

Albatross that is pure white except for its wings, which have black tips and a thick black trailing edge. The closed bill of the royal albatross has a black cutting edge. It is found mainly around the seas of New Zealand, but stragglers occasionally reach s Australia and s South America. Length: 122cm (48in); wingspan: 305cm (120in). Family Diomedeidae; species *Diomedea epomophora*.

albatross, sooty

Sooty brown albatross with a white ring round its eye and a long, wedge-shaped tail. It is the bird into which

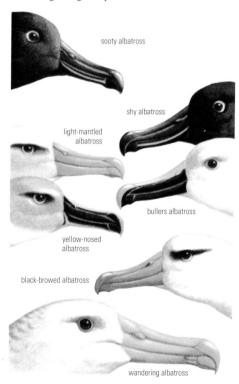

sooty albatross

shy albatross

light-mantled albatross

bullers albatross

yellow-nosed albatross

black-browed albatross

wandering albatross

▲ **albatross** Shown here are the heads and beaks of seven of the 13 species of albatross. Most are of the genus *Diomedea*, apart from the light-mantled and sooty albatrosses, which belong to the *Phoebetria* genus.

ancient seafarers believed the souls of drowned sailors passed, as mentioned in Samuel Taylor Coleridge's "The Rime of the Ancient Mariner". Length: 81cm (32in); wingspan 198cm (78in). Family Diomedeidae; species *Phoebetria fusca*.

albatross, wandering

Albatross that is pure white except for its wings, which have black tips and a black trailing edge. Its bill and legs are flesh coloured. The wandering albatross has the longest wingspan of any bird, and takes five years to reach maturity. It is found throughout Southern Hemisphere oceans. Length: 110–120cm (43–47in); wingspan: 324cm (128in). Family Diomedeidae; species *Diomedea exulans*.

albatross, waved

Albatross that is dusky brown except for its white head and neck, yellow bill and bluish-white legs. It is the only albatross found within the tropics, breeding on the Galápagos Islands and wintering over the Humboldt Current off Ecuador and Peru. Length: 89cm (35in); wingspan: 208cm (82in). Family Diomedeidae; species *Diomedea irrorata*.

albedo

Fraction of light or other radiation that is reflected from a surface. An ideal reflector has an albedo of 1; those of real reflectors are less. The albedo of snow varies from 0.45 to 0.90; that of the Earth viewed from satellites is 0.35. Much has been deduced about the surfaces of planets by comparing their albedos with those of known substances.

albumin

Type of water-soluble protein occurring in animal tissues and fluids. It coagulates if heated. Principal forms are egg albumin (egg white), milk albumin and blood albumin.

alder

Any member of the genus *Alnus*, which comprises deciduous trees native to the Northern Hemisphere and w South America. Alders are characteristically found in wet ground and along streamsides. Some species are planted as ornamentals. They are wind-pollinated, with male and female flowers borne in separate catkins. Alders are able to fix atmospheric nitrogen by means of root nodules containing bacteria. Family Betulaceae; species include *Alnus glutinosa* (the European alder), *Alnus rubra* (the red alder) and *Alnus rugosa* (the speckled alder).

alderfly

Any of the species within the family Sialidae of the primitive order of winged insects Megaloptera. Adult alderflies have large, highly reticulated wings but are not strong fliers. The larvae are aquatic predators with obvious abdominal gills. Adult body length: 1.5–3.5cm (0.6–1.4in). Family Sialidae.

alethe

Any of six species of small songbird, related to the THRUSH, found in tropical forests of central Africa. One of the commonest species of alethe is the fire-crested alethe, which has a bright orange-red crest. Other species include the white-chested alethe and the cholo alethe. Length: 16cm (6in). Family Muscicapidae; genus *Alethe*.

alewife

Fish, related to the HERRING, that occurs in the N Atlantic Ocean. It tends to migrate into fresh waters to spawn. Some landlocked populations occur, and the alewife has been introduced into North America's Great Lakes. It is commercially important as fresh, salted or smoked fish. Length: to 40cm (16in). Family Clupeidae; species *Alosa pseudoharngus*.

alfalfa (lucerne)

Leguminous, perennial plant from sw Asia. It has spiral pods and pale mauve to violet, clover-like flowers. Like other LEGUMES, it has the ability to enrich the soil with nitrogen and is often grown by farmers and then ploughed under. It is a valuable fodder plant. Height: 0.5–1.2m (1.5–4ft). Family Leguminosae; species *Medicago sativa*.

algae

Large group of essentially aquatic photosynthetic organisms that belong to the kingdom PROTOCTISTA. Algae are found in salt and fresh water throughout the world. They are a primary source of food for molluscs, fish and other AQUATIC ANIMALS. Algae are directly important to humans as food (especially in Japan) and as fertilizers. They range in size from unicellular microscopic organisms, such as those that form green pond scum, to huge brown seaweeds more than 45m (150ft) long. *See also* CHLOROPHYTE; CHRYSOPHYTE; CYANOBACTERIUM; PHAEOPHYTE; RHODOPHYTE

algal bloom

Sudden increase in the amount of ALGAE growing in fresh water. The common species involved are CYANOBACTERIA (blue-green algae), although other types of PHYTOPLANKTON may also rapidly grow in numbers. It is usually caused by an increase in nitrates and other nutrients in the water, often from artificial fertilizers washed off nearby fields or from effluent containing sewage. Algal blooms often occur in lakes, and may be prolific enough to prevent light from reaching the lower depths of the water. They are a factor in EUTROPHICATION.

alimentary canal (gut)

Digestive tract of an animal that begins with the

▲ **alderfly** The European alderfly (*Sialis lutaria*) is c.20mm (c.0.08in) in length. As with other endopterygotes, its larva changes into a pupa, or chrysalis, which may lie dormant for many months before being transformed into an adult fly.

▲ **alfalfa** Due to its extremely long roots, up to 15m (49.2ft), the alfalfa plant is capable of withstanding extreme weather conditions, relying on food and water sources deep in the ground. It is a rich source of vitamins and minerals.

mouth, continues through the OESOPHAGUS to the STOMACH and INTESTINES, and ends at the anus. It is c.9m (c.30ft) long in humans. *See also* DIGESTION; DIGESTIVE SYSTEM

alkaloid
Member of a class of complex, nitrogen-containing, organic compounds found in certain plants. Some alkaloids are bitter and highly poisonous substances. Many are used as drugs; examples include codeine, morphine, nicotine and quinine.

alkanet
Bristly, perennial herb native to Europe, grown in gardens and also found as an escape on waste ground. The terminal inflorescences are composed of showy, purplish-violet flowers, which are tubular, opening out to 7–15mm (0.3–0.6in) across. Family Boraginaceae; species *Anchusa officinalis*.

allantois
Sac-like membrane that grows from the hindgut in the embryos of birds, mammals and reptiles. It is involved in respiration and the absorption of nutrients (in mammals); in birds and reptiles it acts as a bladder for the storage of waste products within the egg. *See also* PLACENTA

allele
One of two or more alternative forms of a particular GENE. Different alleles may give rise to different forms of the characteristic for which the gene codes;

for example, different flower colour in peas is due to the presence of different alleles of a single gene. *See also* DOMINANT; HEREDITY; MENDEL, GREGOR JOHANN; RECESSIVE

alligator
Broad-snouted, crocodilian REPTILE found only in the United States and China. The American alligator, *Alligator mississippiensis*, is found in SE United States; it grows up to 5.8m (19ft) long. The almost extinct, smaller Chinese alligator, *Alligator sinensis*, is restricted to the Yangtze-Kiang river basin. Length: up to 1.5m (5ft). Family Alligatoridea. *See also* CAYMAN; CROCODILE

alligator gar
Bony GAR fish found in the backwaters, lakes and bayous of the Mississippi River basin and the Ohio River of the United States and in NE Mexico. Its long, cylindrical body is covered with bony, diamond-shaped, flat plates. It has a "snout studded with teeth, and vertebrae resembling those of reptiles. It is considered a sport fish. Length: to 3m (10ft); weight: to 45kg (100lb). Family Lepisosteidae; species *Lepisosteus spatula*.

alligator lizard
See LIZARD, ALLIGATOR

alligator turtle
See TURTLE, ALLIGATOR SNAPPING

allium
See ONION

allspice (pimento)
Aromatic tree native to the West Indies and Central America. The fruits are used as a spice, in perfume, and in medicine. Height: up to 12m (40ft). Family Myrtaceae; species *Pimenta officinalis*

alluvial fan
Generally fan-shaped area of ALLUVIUM (water-borne sediment) deposited by a river when the stream reaches a plain on lower ground, and the water velocity is abruptly reduced. Sand, silt and gravel are the main constituents of the alluvium, with the coarser material deposited near the head of the fan. Organic matter is also transported, making the soil highly fertile. Valuable minerals such as cassiterite (tin ore, SnO_2), diamonds, gold and platinum are often found in alluvial fans.

alluvium
Fine mud or silt that is deposited by RIVERS. Alluvium accumulates on river beds but can be spread over large areas of a river valley at times of flood. All rivers have some alluvium deposits, but large rivers such as the Mississippi or Amazon have alluvial plains that are several kilometres wide. Alluvial deposits at the foot of steep mountains often accumulate in a triangular or cone shape rather like an inland DELTA.

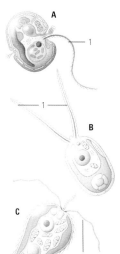

◄ **algae** Many unicellular (single-celled) algae are said to be motile, that is they move in response to changes in their environment, in particular to light. This is achieved with tail-like flagella (1) which propel them through the water. The illustration shows three types of algae. (A) *Gonyaulax tamarensis*, (B) *Chlamydomonas* and (C) *Prymnesium parvum*. Algae have been found in rocks over 2700 million years old. They are a vital source of oxygen.

almond
Small tree native to the E Mediterranean region and SW Asia; also the seed of its nut-like fruit. Family Rosaceae; species *Prunus dulcis*.

aloe
Any member of a genus of plants native to S Africa, with spiny-edged, fleshy leaves. They grow in dense rosettes and have drooping red, orange or yellow flower clusters. Family Liliaceae; genus *Aloe*.

alp
Area of grassland vegetation high up on the side of any mountain range. The alpine pasture is used by grazing animals in the summer but is snow-covered in winter. Alp is also the name given to a high mountain.

alpaca
See LLAMA

alpine newt
See NEWT, ALPINE

alpine poppy
Perennial POPPY native to the Alps, with blue-green lobed leaves and almost stemless flowers. The petals are white with a yellow or pink to orange base. The plant is grown as an ornamental. Family Papaveraceae; species *Papaver alpinum*.

alternation of generations
Two-generation cycle by which plants and some algae reproduce. The asexual diploid SPOROPHYTE form produces haploid SPORES, which in turn grow into the sexual (GAMETOPHYTE) form. The gametophyte produces the egg cell, which is fertilized by a male gamete to produce a diploid ZYGOTE, which grows into another sporophyte.

altruism
Principle of acting for the welfare or interests of

▶ **alligator gar** The alligator gar (*Lepisosteus spatula*) is a member of the Holostei, a group of actinopterygians that lived in the Triassic 225 million years ago. Its thick scales probably differ little from those of its ancestors. Like them, it has a short symmetrical tail, which is a forerunner of the homocercal tail of teleosts.

A

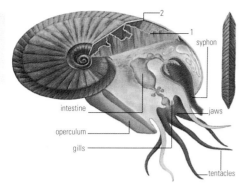

▲ **ammonite** Ammonites had a soft anatomy, similar to that of the modern nautilus, which lives in the open end of its shell. As the animal grew it secreted more and more shell and moved forward into the new part, walling off the old section with a septum (1). The walled-off chambers were used for buoyancy, being supplied with air from a tissue filament or siphuncle (2), which connected all the chambers. The septa met the shell wall in suture lines that had identifiable patterns for each species and became increasingly complex as the group advanced.

someone else. The word was coined by the French philosopher Auguste Comte (1798–1857) from the Italian *altrui*, meaning others. It is used in biology to describe the behaviour of an animal that enhances the prospects of survival or reproduction of another individual at the expense of its own interests. Most cases of altruism among animals involve close relatives or young, with whom the animal shares many GENES. So it is, in effect, perpetuating its own genes in the process.

alum root
Any of a group of perennial herbs native to North America. Some members of the group, for example coralbells, are grown for their ornamental flowers. The leaves form a basal rosette, from which slender spikes bearing sprays of small, bell-shaped flowers arise; the garden forms often have pink or red flowers. The root is supposedly astringent. Family Saxifragaceae; genus *Heuchera*.

alveolus
One of a cluster of microscopic air sacs that open out from the alveolar ducts at the far end of each bronchiole in the lungs. The alveolus is the site for the exchange of gases between the air and the bloodstream, and its walls contain a network of capillary blood vessels. *See also* GAS EXCHANGE; RESPIRATORY SYSTEM

alyssum
Large group of annual and perennial herbs, mostly native to the Mediterranean region. A few members of the group are grown as rock-garden and border plants, owing to their low, branching growth habit and their small but showy flowers. The name alyssum derives from the Greek word for madness, as alyssum plants were supposed to stop hydrophobia. Family Brassicaceae; genus *Alyssum*.

amanita
Any member of the large, widely distributed *Amanita* genus of FUNGI. Amanitas usually have distinct stalks and the prominent remains of a veil in a fleshy ring under the cap and at the bulbous base. They include some of the most poisonous fungi known, such as the DEATH CAP. Phylum Basidiomycota; family Amanitaceae.

amaranth
Large group of annual herbs with a wide distribution. Some amaranths are well-known weeds, for example pigweed; others are grown for the ornamental colours of their leaves and inflorescences. Young leaves and stems can be cooked and eaten as a vegetable. Native North Americans cultivated amaranth plants for their small seeds, which were ground into a nutritious flour. Family Amaranthaceae; genus *Amaranthus*.

amaryllis
Any member of the genus *Amaryllis*, which consists of a single species of bulbous plant, *Amaryllis belladonna*, the belladonna lily, which has several trumpet-shaped, pink or white flowers. Amaryllis is also the common name for *Hippeastrum*, a bulbous houseplant. Family Amaryllidaceae.

amazon
Any member of a genus of medium-sized, colourful PARROTS found in South and Central America. Their feet have two toes pointing forwards and two pointing backwards. They are popular cage birds. In the wild amazons gather in groups in the treetops where they feed on seeds, fruits and flowers. Length: 35–45cm (14–18in). Family Psittacidae; genus *Amazona*.

amazon, red-crowned
Stocky green parrot whose entire crown is red; the female amazon's head is less red. In flight it has a square red patch on the inner wings. The red-crowned amazon flies, usually in pairs, with quick, rather duck-like, shallow wing beats. It is found only in NE Mexico. Length: 30cm (12in). Family Psittacidae; species *Amazona viridigenalis*.

amazon, yellow-crowned
Stocky green parrot. The adults are of two types: northern birds, which have entirely yellow heads; and southern birds, which have only a yellow forehead and neck. They may prove to be different species. Like other amazons, the yellow-crowned amazon has a square red patch on its inner wings. It is found from Mexico to Brazil. Length: 30–38cm (12–15in). Family Psittacidae; species *Amazona ochrocephala*.

amber
Hard, yellow or brown, translucent FOSSIL resin, mainly from pine trees. Amber is most often found in alluvial soils, in lignite beds or around sea-shores, especially near the Baltic Sea. The resin occurs as rods or as irregular nodules, sometimes with embedded fossil insects or plants. Amber can be polished to a high degree and is used to make necklaces and other items of jewellery.

amberfish (amberjack)
Marine, fast-swimming food and game fish found in tropical and subtropical waters. It is blunt-headed, blue and silver with a bronze stripe along its side. The young have bright golden bands along the sides. Length: 1.5–1.8m (5–6ft); weight: 54kg (120lb). Family Carangidae; species *Seriola dumerli*.

ambrosia fungus
Fungus that lives in association with ambrosia BEETLES; the beetles bore into sapwood and introduce fungal spores, which grow on the walls of the tunnels to produce a white or creamy mould. Spores of the ambrosia fungus form the chief food of the developing beetle larvae. Phylum Basidiomycota; species include *Monilia ferruginea*, *Ambrosiella sulcati* and *Graphium*.

American ash (White Ash)
Tree that is native to E North America but is grown for ornament and shade in the United States and Europe. The American ash grows rapidly and has a symmetrical shape. The leaves turn a clear yellow or purple in the autumn. The wood can be used for tool handles, oars and furniture. Height: to 37m (120ft). Family Oleaceae; species *Fraxinus americana*.

American hog plum (tallow wood)
Tropical tree with hard, yellow-pink wood. It is found in South America, where it has been used as a substitute for sandalwood. The American hog plum's

◄ **amazon** Brilliantly coloured amazons and macaws gather in large groups in the treetops of the Amazon forest region of Peru. They are most active in the relative cool of the mornings and evenings, when they fly to and from their feeding grounds. Amazons are noisy birds, with squawky calls.

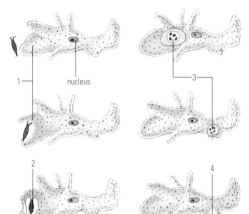

▲ **amoeba** In order to move, an amoeba pushes out projections called pseudopods (lit. fake foot) from its body. Cytoplasm – the fluid content of the cell – flows into the pseudopod, constantly enlarging it until all the cytoplasm has entered and the amoeba as a whole has moved. Pseudopods are also used in feeding: they move out to engulf a food particle (1), which then becomes enclosed in a membrane-bound food vacuole (2). Digestive enzymes enter the vacuole, which gradually shrinks as the food is broken down (3). Undigested material is discharged by the vacuole and left behind as the amoeba moves on (4).

fruits are bitter owing to the presence of prussic acid. Family Olacaceae; species *Ximenia americana*. **American hog plum** is also the name given to a graceful tree found throughout the tropics. It is cultivated for its edible fruit, which is ovoid and yellow, with a large stone. Height: to 18m (60ft). Family Anacardiaceae; species *Spondias mombin*.

American mastic
Evergreen tree with graceful, pendulous branches, native to the American tropics. The fruits are small, round and rose-coloured, hanging in dense clusters; they have been used to make an alcoholic beverage in Peru and Chile. The tree also produces a gum resin. Height: to 6m (20ft). Family Anacardiaceae; species *Schinus molle*. *See also* PEPPER TREE

amethyst
Transparent, violet variety of crystallized QUARTZ, containing more iron oxide than other varieties. It is found mainly in Brazil, Uruguay, Ontario, Canada and North Carolina, United States. Amethyst is valued as a semiprecious gem and can be made synthetically.

amino acid
Organic acid containing at least one carboxyl group (COOH) and at least one amino group (NH_2). Amino acids are of great biological importance because they combine together to form PROTEINS. Amino acids form peptides by the reaction of adjacent amino (NH_2) and carboxyl (COOH) groups. Proteins are polypeptide chains consisting of hundreds of amino acids. About 20 amino acids occur in proteins; not all organisms are able to synthesize all of them. **Essential amino acids** are those that an organism has to obtain ready-made from its environment. There are ten essential amino acids for humans: arginine, histidine, isoleucine, leucine, lysine, methionine, phenylalanine, threonine, tryptophan and valine.

ammonite
Any member of the order Ammonitida, an extinct group of shelled cephalopod MOLLUSCS. Most ammonites had a spiral shell, and they are believed to be related to the nautiloids, the only surviving form of which is the PEARLY NAUTILUS. They are common as FOSSILS in marine rocks.

amnion
Membrane or sac that encloses the EMBRYO of a reptile, bird or mammal. The embryo floats in the amniotic fluid within the sac.

amniote
VERTEBRATE whose EMBRYO has an AMNION and ALLANTOIS. The amniote group comprises the reptiles, birds and mammals.

amoeba
Microscopic, almost transparent, single-celled PROTOZOA of the phylum Rhizopoda. Amoebas have a constantly changing, irregular shape. Found in ponds, damp soil and animal intestines, they consist of a thin outer cell membrane, a large nucleus, food and contractile VACUOLES and fat globules. They reproduce by binary FISSION. Length: up to 3mm (0.1in). Species include the common *Amoeba proteus* and *Entamoeba histolytica*, which causes amoebic dysentery. Genus *Amoeba*.

amphibian
See feature article, pages 10–11

amphibole
Any of a large group of complex rock-forming minerals characterized by a double-chain silicate structure (Si_4O_{11}). They all contain water as OH^- ions and usually calcium, magnesium and iron. Found in IGNEOUS and METAMORPHIC ROCKS, they form wedge-shaped fragments on cleavage. Their orthorhombic or monoclinic crystals are often needle-like or fibrous. Common varieties are HORNBLENDE, tremolite, actinolite and anthophyllite. Some varieties are used in commercial asbestos.

amphioxus (lancelet)
Marine, fish-shaped animal found off sandy shores in warm seas. An invertebrate, it has a well-developed NOTOCHORD instead of a true backbone. The amphioxus has no distinct head region or brain and no heart. It has rudimentary eyes and tentacles round its mouth for straining food from water. Reproduction is sexual with fertilization occurring externally. Length: up to 8cm (3in). Subphylum Cephalochordata; genus *Branchiostoma*.

amphipod
Any member of the Amphipoda order of CRUSTACEANS. Most amphipods are found in marine waters, but some inhabit fresh water and a few, such as the BEACH FLEA, are semi-terrestrial. There are *c.*4600 species, many of which are brightly coloured and all of which have laterally compressed bodies. Some are parasitic. Length: 0.1–14cm (0.04–6in).

amphisbaenid (worm lizard)
Cylindrical, usually legless, burrowing reptile found in tropical America and Africa. Amphisbaenids resemble earthworms and have rings of scales around their bodies and tails. They have no external ear openings. Some species have short front legs. Length: 20cm (20in). Formerly regarded as lizards, the 100 species are now classified as a Squamata suborder. Family Amphisbaenidae.

amphiuma
Large, elongate, aquatic SALAMANDER with vestigial limbs. There are one-, two- and three-toed species. Amphiumas are native to the SE United States, where they live in ponds, ditches and slow-flowing creeks. They respire using both lungs and gills. Females brood their eggs until they hatch into gilled larvae. Length: to 116cm (46in). Family Amphiumidae; genus *Amphiuma*.

amphoteric
Term used to describe a substance that has both acidic and alkaline properties. Aluminum hydroxide is a typical amphoteric compound. It behaves like the base $Al(OH)_3$ when it reacts with acids (to form aluminum salts); it behaves like the acid H_3AlO_3 when it reacts with alkalis (to form aluminates). Zinc hydroxide is also amphoteric. Amino acids can also be regarded as amphoteric because they contain both an acid $-COOH$ group and a basic $-NH_2$ group.

amylase
Digestive ENZYME secreted by the salivary glands (salivary amylase) and the pancreas (pancreatic amylase). It aids DIGESTION by breaking down STARCH into MALTOSE (a disaccharide) and then GLUCOSE (a monosaccharide).

amylose
POLYSACCHARIDE carbohydrate made up of around 300 GLUCOSE molecules linked by 1–4 GLYCOSIDIC BONDS to form an unbranched helical chain. It has a total RELATIVE MOLECULAR MASS of up to 50,000 and stains deep blue with IODINE. It typically makes up around 20% of STARCHES.

anabolism
Energy-requiring process in which living organisms synthesize complex MOLECULES from simpler ones. *See also* CATABOLISM; METABOLISM

anaconda
Large, constricting BOA of South America, the longest (up to 9m/30ft) and heaviest (up to 500kg/1100lb) snake in the world. Anacondas are mainly aquatic and are found chiefly in swamps. They feed on birds and small mammals. Females give birth to up to 75 live young. Family Boidae; species *Eunectes murinus*. *See also* PYTHON

anaerobe
Minute organism that grows only in the absence of free atmospheric oxygen. Anaerobic bacteria can be a hazard in food preservation because they can multiply in foods even in a vacuum. *See also* AEROBE

anaerobic
Connected with the absence of oxygen or air or not dependent on oxygen or air for survival. An anaerobic organism, or **anaerobe**, is a microorganism that can survive by releasing energy from GLUCOSE and other foods in the absence of oxygen. The process by which it does so is called anaerobic RESPIRATION. Most anaerobes can survive in oxygen but do not need it for respiration. *See also* AEROBIC

▲ **amphisbaenid** Feeding on insects and worms, the amphisbaenid spends the majority of its time underground, for which it is well adapted. It has scales over its eyes and a wedge-shaped snout for burrowing.

A

▲ **anchovy** A member of the herring family, the tiny anchovy is fished mainly in the Mediterranean. It is cured, using a fermentation process. The American anchovy (*Engraulis encrasicholus*) belongs to the Engralidae family.

anaphase
Stage or stages in CELL DIVISION. In MITOSIS, anaphase occurs when chromatids (from the CHROMOSOMES) separate and go to each end of the spindle. In MEIOSIS, there are two anaphases. In the first, paired chromosomes separate and move apart. In the second, the chromatids separate and move to the poles of the spindle, as in mitosis.

anapsid
Any member of the subclass Anapsida, the most primitive subclass of the REPTILES. Anapsids date back 250 million years. They are characterized by an absence of both openings (fossae) and arches (apses) in the region of the skull near the temples. Present day representatives of the anapsid group include the TURTLES and TORTOISES.

anchovy
Commercially valuable food fish found worldwide in large shoals in temperate and tropical seas. There are more than 100 species. Length: 10–25cm (4–10in). Family Engraulidae.

andalusite
One of many crystalline forms of aluminum silicate, occurring in contact METAMORPHIC ROCK and in other deposits. It is mined commercially in the United States, Kazakstan and South Africa to make temperature-resistant and insulating porcelains.

andesite
Fine-grained, intermediate volcanic rock, found most frequently in recent or ancient continental margin areas. It is largely composed of finely crystalline FELDSPARS, with occasional larger crystals called PHENOCRYSTS. Andesite is chemically and mineralogically similar to DIORITE.

androecium
Male part of a FLOWER. It comprises the STAMENS, each of which consists of a two-lobed, pollen-carrying ANTHER on a thin stalk called a FILAMENT. *See also* GYNOECIUM

anemone (sea anemone)
Marine animal related to coral and commonly seen on CORAL REEFS and rocky shores. Most anemones attach themselves to the surface on which they live by means of a pedal disc and remain exposed, but some burrow or secrete a mucous tube before becoming SESSILE. At the opposite end of the body to the pedal disc is the oral disc, which is surrounded by tentacles used in feeding. Because many anemones, such as the **dahlia anemone**, are highly coloured and splay their tentacles radially, they are sometimes called flowers of the sea. The **ball anemone** has reduced tentacles, while others, for example the **snakelocks anemone**, have many well-developed tentacles. The highly invaginated tentacles of the **plumose anemone** resemble feathers. Phylum Coelenterata/Cnidaria; class Anthozoa; order Actinaria.

◀ **anemone** The white wood anemone (*Anemone nemorosa*) is found in European and Asian woodland. Like all anemones, what appear to be petals are actually sepals. In Greek mythology, anemones grew from the blood of Adonis. In Chinese mythology, they represent death. Anemones contain the poison anemonin.

anemone (windflower)
Perennial plant found worldwide. Anemones have sepals resembling petals, and many stamens and pistils covering a central knob; two or three deeply toothed leaves appear in a whorl midway up the stem. Many are wild flowers, such as the wood anemone (*Anemone nemorosa*). There are 120 species. Family Ranunculaceae. *See also* BUTTERCUP; SEA ANEMONE

anemonefish
See CLOWNFISH

anemophily
Type of POLLINATION that relies on the wind to carry the pollen. Most grasses and many trees have anemophilous flowers, which lack scent and nectar, and have small or nonexistent petals. Male and female flowers are usually separate, as with the catkins of many trees, which bloom before the trees come into leaf.

angelfish
Tropical fish found in the Atlantic and Indo-Pacific oceans. It is popular as an aquarium fish because of its graceful, trailing fins and beautiful markings. Length: 2–10cm (1–4in). Family Cichlidae.

angelica
Plant of the CARROT family; it grows in northern temperate regions and in New Zealand. Garden angelicas (*Angelica archangelica*) grow to 1.5m (5ft) in height and have greenish flowers. The stems, usually crystallized, and oil from the roots and seeds, have culinary uses. Family Apiaceae/Umbelliferae.

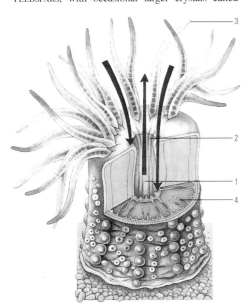

▲ **anemone** The sea anemone supports itself by circulating water around its central cavity (1). Water is drawn in down *siphonoglyphs* (grooves) (2) at the side of the cavity; it is expelled up the centre. The tentacles (3) can be withdrawn by individual retractor muscles (4).

A mphibians are members of the class Amphibia, which comprises egg-laying vertebrates, whose larval stages are usually spent in water but whose adult life is normally spent on land. Amphibians have smooth, moist skin and are ECTOTHERMIC (cold-blooded). Larvae breathe through GILLS, but the adults of most species have LUNGS. All adults are carnivorous; most larvae are herbivorous. There are three living orders: Urodela (NEWTS and SALAMANDERS); Anura (FROGS and TOADS); and Apoda or CAECILIANS.

Some 370 million years ago the first creatures to leave the seas and walk on land were the amphibians. They pioneered the use of lungs for full-time air breathing and were the first vertebrates to have true legs, tongues, ears and voice boxes. The increase in body area covered by the nerve cells led to those cells invading the brain: a step to intelligence. Today there are c.4000 species of amphibian.

Despite being cold-blooded, and therefore particularly at the mercy of their environment, amphibians are found on all the continents

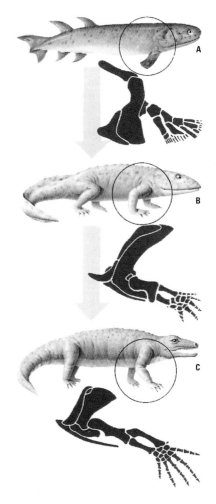

▲ **The evolution of** the pentadactyl limb can be partly traced through the fossil record. The basic design was already present in lobe-finned fish such as *Eusthenopteron* (A). Adapting to the terrestrial environment, the limb rotated downwards and away from the body. In the first known amphibian, *Ichthyostega* (B), the limb is still compact and the body close to the ground. *Seymouria* (C) developed more extended limbs, which provided greater articulation and ground clearance.

except Antarctica, from the tropics to north of the Arctic Circle. Many features distinguish the amphibians from other vertebrates. They have a three-chambered heart, paired lungs (which are reduced or absent in some salamanders and caecilians), a flattened skull, and teeth that can bend inwards.

Unlike reptiles, amphibians have not developed waterproof skins. In fact, many species supplement lung breathing with GAS EXCHANGE through their skins, which must be kept moist for this purpose. The lining of the mouth is moist and well supplied with capillaries; it can also function in gas exchange. A few aquatic salamanders retain their larval external gills in the adult, and a few terrestrial forms have no lungs at all. The senses also had to adapt to life on land. Eyelids and eye-moistening glands evolved, as did true ears (with outer eardrums and two middle-ear bones, neither of which are found in fish ears) for detecting sound vibrations in air. At the same time, the voice box and vocal sacs evolved – amphibians were the first vertebrates to have a larynx. For the sense of smell, internal nostril openings, called nares, allow air to be taken into the lungs while the mouth is closed or when only the external nares are above water. This can also help when the amphibian is avoiding land predators.

Amphibians have retained many of their adaptations to the aquatic life. When moving, many amphibians retain an undulating, fish-like motion, except for the frogs and toads, which evolved long hind limbs for hopping on land or kicking out to swim. Also, many frogs and toads still discharge unfertilized eggs into the water, where sperm is then shed on to them for fertilization to occur. Amphibians have kept their streamlined shape, and many species have webbed feet for locomotion in water. Their inability to generate internal body heat confines them to the warmer parts of continents, but many species survive considerable cold by reducing their metabolic rates. Amphibians are surprisingly common in deserts and other arid regions. They avoid overheating by burrowing in the day and emerging at night. Their main problem is the unpredictable water supply.

Certain species can store up to half their body weight in the bladder. Some frogs and toads are remarkably tolerant of water loss: the Western spadefoot toad can withstand up to 60 per cent reduction in its body water. Another adaptation is to retain urea in the blood, thus permitting the uptake of water by osmosis from even apparently dry soils. Most terrestrial frogs have a patch of skin rich in blood capillaries in the pelvic region, which takes up water when sitting on damp earth. *See also* METAMORPHOSIS

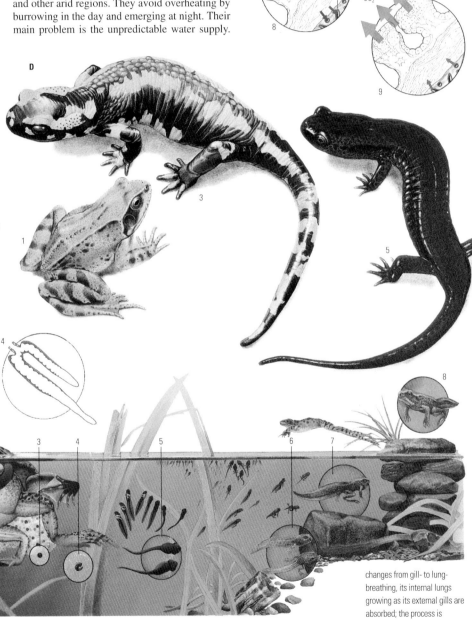

▶ **Modern amphibians** (D) display considerable variance in the adaptation of their respiratory systems to the terrestrial environment. Only a few aquatic forms retain their gills when adult. The common frog (1) has complex lungs (2) with intricate infolding of the vascular cavity walls. In more advanced four-legged animals, the lungs usually provide the animal's total oxygen requirement during active behaviour. The fire salamander (3) has much simpler respiratory organs. Its tubular lungs (4) have little infolding with which to increase their surface area. For this reason the lungs can be considered as auxiliary, as oxygen is also obtained through gas exchange over the whole of the body surface. As a result, the fire salamander requires a moist environment; it only ventures into the open at night when it is cooler – thereby reducing water loss – and also under very humid conditions. The dusky salamander (5) is a *plethodont*, one of a family of lungless salamanders found in North America, for which all respiration takes place through surface gas exchange. This is only possible if the surface is kept moist by secretions from mucous glands (6). Exchange takes place via a dense capillary network just below the skin surface (7). Dissolved oxygen enters and is absorbed into the blood (8). Carbon dioxide waste from the blood passes out of the body through a reverse process (9). All amphibians make some use of surface exchange. Many frogs can meet their total respiratory requirement in this way while inactive in cool and moist conditions. Surface exchange is much less important to other vertebrates, and is usually insignificant. In humans, for example, surface exchange accounts for less than 1 per cent of respiration.

▲ **Amphibians undergo metamorphosis** (E). When common frogs mate, fertilization and egg laying occur in water (1). Within an hour, the jelly around the egg swells to produce frogspawn (2). The eggs develop (3) and produce embryos (4) that hatch, as long-tailed tadpoles with external feathery gills, six days after fertilization (5). Mouths and eyes develop later and the tails become powerful means of propulsion. Hind legs are well formed by week eight (6); meanwhile, the tadpole has changed from a herbivore to a carnivore. Via an intermediary gill and lung stage, the tadpole changes from gill- to lung-breathing, its internal lungs growing as its external gills are absorbed; the process is complete when the gills fully disappear at month three, by which time the forelegs are developed (7). Metamorphosis is complete when the young frog (8) loses its tail.

A

angiosperm
See feature article

angiotensin
Peptide in the blood that increases blood pressure by inducing contraction of narrow blood vessels.

anglerfish
Any of 300 species belonging to the order Lophiiformes. Anglerfish are found in all marine temperate and tropical environments from the shallow littoral zone to the abyssal plain. They are characterized by a specialized dorsal fin spine (bioluminescent in some species), which is used as a lure to attract prey. Species of anglerfish include the goosefish, *Lophius americanus*.

anglesite
Sulphate mineral, a form of lead sulphate ($PbSO_4$). It is usually found together with cerussite in hydrothermal veins as an alternation product of GALENA. Its crystals are usually orthorhombic, and can be tabular or prismatic. It can be colourless, white or grey. Hardness 2.5–3; r.d. 6.4.

angwantibo (golden potto)
Slow, climbing PRIMATE that is found in the dense rainforests of central Africa. It is light reddish and feeds on insects and sometimes fruit. When faced with danger, the angwantibo rolls up into a ball. It is solitary, except during the breeding season. Head-body length: *c*.24cm (*c*.9in); tail: 1cm (0.4in). Family Lorisidae; species *Arctocebus calaberensis*.

anhinga
See DARTER

anhydrite
Mineral form of CALCIUM SULPHATE ($CaSO_4$); it is usually found in SEDIMENTARY ROCKS in salt beds. Its crystals are orthorhombic and usually occur in large deposits. Anhydrite has a glassy or pearly lustre and is colourless when pure. Hardness: 3–3.5; r.d. 3. *See also* GYPSUM

ani
Any of three species of woodland bird, related to the CUCKOO, found in Central and South America. Anis forage in loose flocks, often following livestock as they search for disturbed insects. They roost and nest in groups, with older young helping to rear the new chicks. Several females lay in the same nest, resulting in a clutch of up to 30 eggs. Length: 34cm (13in). Family Cuculidae; genus *Crotophaga*.

animal
Living organism of the kingdom Animalia, usually distinguishable from members of the plant kingdom (Plantae) by its: power of locomotion (at least during some stage of its existence); a well-defined body shape; limited growth; its feeding exclusively on organic matter; the production of two different kinds of sex cells; and the formation of an embryo or larva during the developmental stage. Higher animals, such as the VERTEBRATES, are easily distinguishable from plants, but the distinction becomes blurred with the lower forms. Some one-celled organisms could easily be assigned to either category. Scientists have classified about a million different kinds of animals in more than twenty phyla. The simplest (least highly evolved) animals include the PROTOZOA, SPONGES and CNIDARIANS. Other invertebrate phyla include ARTHROPODS (ARACHNIDS, CRUSTACEANS and INSECTS), MOLLUSCS (shellfish, OCTOPUS and SQUID) and ECHINODERMS (SEA URCHINS and STARFISH). Vertebrates belong to the chordata phylum, which includes FISH, AMPHIBIANS, REPTILES, BIRDS and MAMMALS.

animal behaviour
See ETHOLOGY

animal classification
Systematic grouping of animals into categories based on shared characteristics. The first major CLASSIFICATION was drawn up by Aristotle. The method now used was devised by the Swedish botanist Carolus LINNAEUS in the 1750s. Each animal is given a two-part Latin name (*see* BINOMIAL NOMENCLATURE), the first part indicating its GENUS, the second (with the first) its SPECIES. A species is composed of animals capable of interbreeding in nature. A genus includes all similar and related species. The FAMILY takes in all related genera, and an ORDER is made up of all related families. Similar orders are grouped in a CLASS, and related classes make up a PHYLUM. More than twenty separate phyla comprise the animal KINGDOM. For example, the DOG is classified in phylum Chordata; class Mammalia; order Carnivora; family Canidae; genus *Canis* and species *Canis familiaris*. *See also* Ready Reference, pages 462–63

animal kingdom
Members of the group Animalia, one of the five KINGDOMS into which, in one system of CLASSIFICATION, all living organisms are divided. In this system, the other kingdoms are Prokaryotae, Protoctista, Fungi and Plantae.

ANGIOSPERM

Any of *c*.250,000 species of plant belonging to the phylum Angiospermophyta, which produce FLOWERS, FRUITS and SEEDS. Angiosperms include most herbs, shrubs, many trees, fruits, vegetables and cereals. Their seeds are protected by an outer covering – angiosperm means "plant with enclosed seeds". Angiosperms are further subdivided into two classes, MONO-COTYLEDONS (Monocotyledonae) and DICOTYLE-DONS (Dicotyledonae). Many flowering plants are used for food and timber and in medicine. *See also* CONIFEROPHYTE

▶ **Sexual reproduction in** angiosperms begins with the production of gametes. Male pollen grains are made in the anther's (1) four pollen sacs (2), which are packed with *microsporocyte* cells (3). The microsporocytes are surrounded by a layer of nutritive cells which is known as the *tapetum* (4). Each microsporocyte goes through two *meiotic* (chromosome-reducing) divisions to form first a two-cell *dyad* (5), then a *tetrad* of cells (6), which splits into four *microspores* (7). Each microspore divides mitotically (normally) to form a *generative nucleus* (8) and a *tube cell nucleus* (9), around which a thick, sculptured wall (10) develops. This is now the mature pollen grain. When the mature anther splits open (11) the pollen grains (12) are released to pollinate another plant. The female gametes originate in the *ovaries* (13). Within each ovary are one or more ovules (14), which will eventually develop into seeds. They are surrounded by two protective layers of tissue, the *integuments* (15), and have a small opening, the *micropyle* (16). An ovule consists of a single *megasporocyte* (17), which divides meiotically to produce four *megaspores* (18). Only one of these develops further (19) – by mitotic divisions through two (20), four (21) and finally eight nuclei. Around these eight nuclei are formed the contents of the mature *embryo sac* (22): the *antipodal cells* (23) and the *synergid cells* (24) which eventually disintegrate; the *endosperm mother cell* (25) with two *polar nuclei* (26); and the *egg cell* (27). When the pollen grain germinates on the stigma (28), a thread-like *pollen tube* (29) grows down the *style* (30) into the *ovary* (31), led by the tube cell nucleus. The generative nucleus divides into two *sperm nuclei* (32), which follow down the pollen tube and enter the embryo sac through the micropyle. One fuses with the egg, fertilizing it, making a *zygote* (33). The other fuses with the two polar nuclei (34), producing the *primary endosperm cell* (35), which develops into the *endosperm* (36), the seed's food supply tissue. As the endosperm tissue develops a multicellular structure (37), the young embryo (38) divides and grows (39). The mature embryo is surrounded by a seed coat (the *testa*) (40) – formed from the integuments – and has all the parts of a young seedling: the *cotyledon* (41), *plumule* (42) and *radicle* (43).

A

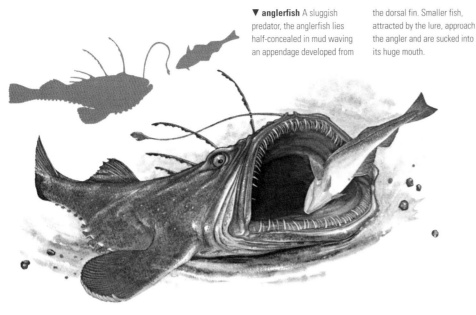

▼ **anglerfish** A sluggish predator, the anglerfish lies half-concealed in mud waving an appendage developed from the dorsal fin. Smaller fish, attracted by the lure, approach the angler and are sucked into its huge mouth.

anion
ION that is negatively charged. It is attracted to the anode during electrolysis.

anise
Annual herb that is native to Egypt and widely cultivated for its small, ridged, liquorice-flavoured seeds. Its flowers are small and white. Height: up to 76cm (30in). Family Apiaceae/Umbelliferae; species *Pimpinella anisum*.

ankylosaurid
Armoured ORNITHISCHIAN DINOSAUR that lived from the mid-Jurassic to the end of the Cretaceous period. Ankylosaurids, such as the *Ankylosaurus*, had thick bony plates and knobs together with spikes on the back and head for protection from predators. They were medium to large dinosaurs, with massive and powerful hind legs supporting a stiff tail that ended with a large bony club. Length: up to 10m (33ft).

annatto
Shrub or small tree with oval leaves and pink or rose-coloured flowers approximately 5cm (2in) across. It is native to tropical America but widely distributed throughout the tropics. A reddish-yellow dye, also called annatto, is extracted and prepared from the pulp around the seeds and used for colouring food-stuffs. Height: to 9.2m (30ft). Family Bixaceae; species *Bixa orellana*.

annelid
Member of the Annelida phylum of segmented worms. All have encircling grooves that usually correspond to internal partitions of the body. A digestive tube, nerves and blood vessels run through the entire body, but each segment has its own set of internal organs. Annelids form an important part of the diets of many animals. The three main classes are POLYCHAETA, marine worms; OLIGOCHAETA, freshwater or terrestrial worms; and Hirudinea, LEECHES.

annual
Plant that completes its life cycle in one growing season, such as SWEET PEA, SUNFLOWER and WHEAT. Annual plants overwinter as seeds. *See also* BIENNIAL; PERENNIAL

annual ring (growth ring)
Concentric circles visible in cross-sections of woody stems or trunks. Each year the CAMBIUM layer produces a layer of XYLEM, the vessels of which are large and thin-walled in the spring and smaller and thick-walled in the summer, creating the contrast between the rings. The number of rings can be used to determine the approximate age of trees; the thickness of these rings reveals the environmental conditions during a tree's lifetime.

anorthosite
Coarse-grained, basic IGNEOUS ROCK that forms deep underground and in DYKES and INTRUSIONS. It is composed mainly of FELDSPAR, with some olivine and pyroxene. Usually light in colour, anorthosite may have bands of darker minerals.

anseriform
Member of the bird order Anseriformes, which includes DUCKS, GEESE and SWANS (family Anatidae), together with the SCREAMERS (family Anhimidae), a small group of primitive South American wading birds.

ant
Insect that occurs in most terrestrial habitats, from subpolar tundra to tropical rainforest. Approximately 10,000 of the estimated 15,000 ant species have been named, and the ecological importance of ants is renowned. They routinely contribute more than one quarter of the animal biomass in an ecosystem (well in excess of that contributed by all vertebrates) and also make up approximately three quarters of the total insect biomass on Earth. Ants are social insects, having co-operative brood care, overlapping generations and distinct reproductive castes. Adult body length: 0.5–40mm (0.02–1.6in). Order Hymenoptera; family Formicidae.

ant, army (driver ant)
Highly predacious ant found in tropical and subtropical parts of the world. It travels in huge armies when hunting for food or migrating. Family Formicidae; subfamily Dorylinae.

ant, carpenter
Large black ant that makes its home in galleries in damp wood; it is found throughout the world. The carpenter ant feeds on honeydew from aphids and not on the wood in which it lives. Family Formicidae; genus *Camponotus*.

ant, driver
See ANT, ARMY

ant, honey
Any of several species of ant found worldwide. They live on sweet juices from plants and plant-sucking insects such as aphids. A number of young honey ants serve as storage vessels for plant nectar and honeydew, which they feed back to the workers in times of shortage. Family Formicidae; genera include *Myrmecocystus*, *Leptomyrmex* and *Plagiolepis*.

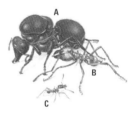

▶ **ant, leaf-cutter** Most ant societies are made up of different types of ant known as castes. Shown here are the queen (A), soldier (B) and small worker (C) of the leaf-cutter species *Atta caphalotes*. Females develop from fertilized eggs and males from unfertilized eggs. Nutrition determines whether a female becomes a queen or worker. First generation larvae are fed entirely by the queen's saliva. Mating takes place in flight, after which the male dies. The queen proceeds to lay eggs for the remainder of her life (up to 15 years).

ant, leaf-cutter (parasol ant)
Large ant that cuts and transports bits of leaves to its nest. The beds of macerated leaves are used to grow the fungi on which the ant lives. Leaf-cutter ants live in large colonies in sometimes enormous underground nests. Family Formicidae; genus *Atta*.

ant, parasol
See ANT, LEAF-CUTTING

ant, slave-making
Any of many species of ant well known for raiding the nests of other ant species. Slave-making raids take various forms. The queen of a slave-making species may enter the nest of another species, kill the existing queen, and then exploit the labours of the remaining workers. Slave-making workers also go on raids to remove the larvae and pupae from besieged nests in order that the adults that later emerge become workers within the slave-makers' colony. Family Formicidae; species include *Formica sanguinea*.

ant, weaver
Any member of the genus *Oecophylla*. Weaver ants dwell mainly on plants and take their common name

▶ **ankylosaurid** The *Scolosaurus* lived in the upper Cretaceous and was one of the last heavily armoured dinosaurs. It was a squat, four-legged creature with a compact mosaic of armour over its back. Its tail spikes were probably used as a defence against predators.

▶ **anteater, giant** The giant anteater (*Myrmecophaga tridactyla*) is found in South America, particularly in the swampy regions of the Chaco in Argentina. It uses its claws to rip open termite mounds before scooping up the termites with its long tongue.

from the fact that they join living leaves together to make nests. The leaves are bonded with a silk produced and applied by larval ants, which are carried by adult ants. Family Formicidae.

ant, white
See TERMITE

ant, wood
Various species of ant found in temperate woodland habitats. Their nests can contain up to half a million individuals. Wood ants undertake little actual tunnelling in wood and their nests are located below the ground surface. They are carnivorous, and workers spend much of their time scavenging and predating upon other insects. Family Formicidae; main genus *Formica*.

antbird
Small, rather long-legged bird found in the woodlands and forests of Central and South America. Males and females frequently have very different plumages. Antbirds often follow columns of army ants in order to feed on the insects that the ants disturb. There are *c*.50 species of antbird. Length: 11–15cm (4–6in). Family Formicariidae (part).

antbird, bare-crowned
Antbird with mainly black plumage. The males have a bright blue patch of bare skin on the crown and encircling the eye. The females fare brown with the bare blue skin only round the eyes. Bare-crowned antbirds are found in dense thickets from Honduras to Colombia. Length: 15cm (6in). Family Formicariidae; species *Gymnocichla nudiceps*.

antbird, dusky
Terrestrial, wren-like, slaty-black antbird. It has tiny dots of white on its wings. The females, like many species of antbird, are dark brown above and reddish-brown below. Dusky antbirds search for worms and insects in thickets at the edge of forests from Mexico to the Amazon basin. Length: 15cm (6in). Family Formicariidae; species *Cercomacra tyrannina*.

anteater
Toothless, mainly nocturnal, insect-eating mammal that lives in swamps and savannas of tropical America. It has a long, sticky tongue and powerful claws. There are four species – the giant anteater, the lesser anteater, the two-toed anteater and the silky anteater. Family Myrmecophagidae. *See also* EDENTATE

anteater, giant
Solitary animal that inhabits the savanna and scrubland of Central and South America. It has long,

▶ **antelope, sable** Herds of sable antelope are found in the woodlands of Zimbabwe. The herds vary in size but usually consist of many females and young and one male. They mainly feed on grass but also browse on other vegetation, especially in the dry season. They never stray far from water.

coarse, grey hair and a black stripe along its side. It has two strong, hook-like claws on each hand, which it uses to rip open ants' nests. It extracts the occupants with its long, thin tongue, which is covered with tiny spines and sticky saliva. Though it walks on its knuckles, the giant anteater can amble at 14m (46ft) per minute. It is an endangered species. Head-body length: 100–120cm (39–47in), tail: 70–90cm (28–35in). Family Myrmecophagidae; species *Myrmecophaga tridactyla*.

antechinus
Small, mouse-like MARSUPIAL found in Australia and New Guinea. It is also the common name given to several other species of DASYURID, including the sandstone antechinus (*Parantechinus bilarui*) and the little red antechinus (*Dasykatula rosamondae*). Mostly insectivorous, the antechinus also feeds on earthworms, spiders, small lizards and fruit. Family Dasyuridae; genus *Antechinus*.

antelope
Even-toed, horned UNGULATE (hoofed mammal) belonging to the family Bovidae of the order Artiodactyla.

antelope, pygmy
Solitary species of antelope that inhabits dense forests in central Africa. Head-body length: 50–58cm (20–23in); tail: 4–5cm (*c*.2in). Subfamily Antilopinae; species *Neotragus batesi*.

antelope, roan
Antelope that inhabits open grassland in central and

s Africa. It is brown-black with white underparts. The roan antelope has a white face with black stripes. Both males and females have long horns. Head-body length: 190–240cm (75–94in); tail: 37–48cm (15–19in). Subfamily Hippotraginae; species *Hippotragus equinus*.

antelope, royal
Shy dwarf antelope that lives in dense forest in North Africa, between Sierra Leone and Ghana. It is reddish-brown with white underparts. The males have short horns. Head-body length: 45–55cm (18–22in); tail: 4–4.5cm (*c*.2in). Subfamily Antilopinae; species *Neotragus pygmaeus*.

antelope, sable
Antelope that generally inhabits wooded country in central and s Africa. It is dark in colour with long ribbed horns. Head-body length: 197–210cm (78–83in); tail: 38–46cm (15–18in). Subfamily Hippotraginae; species *Hippotragus niger*.

antenna
Long sensory organ (usually of touch and smell) on the heads of insects and most other ARTHROPODS. Insects have a single pair of antennae, crustaceans generally have two pairs. The antennae of crustaceans are sometimes used for attachment or locomotion.

anthelion
Phenomenon in which there appears to be a second Sun in the sky opposite the real Sun. The "ghost" Sun is at the same altitude as the real Sun and is caused by the refraction of sunlight by small crystals of ice in the atmosphere. In polar regions, the faint halo sometimes seen fringing the shadow of an object cast onto fog or a bank of cloud is also called an anthelion.

anther
Element of a FLOWER that produces, contains and distributes the POLLEN (which contains the male GAMETES, or sex cells). The pollen is formed within two chambers called pollen sacs, and the chambers themselves are located in two lobes. Together with its connecting FILAMENT, the anther forms a STAMEN. *See also* POLLINATION

antheridium
Male sex organ of FUNGI and various primitive plants. As well as in fungi, antheridia are found in ALGAE, BRYOPHYTES (LIVERWORTS and MOSSES), PTERIDOPHYTES (CLUB MOSSES, FERNS and HORSETAILS) and CYCADS. They produce male GAMETES (sex cells) called antherozoids. These move independently in a film of water to the female gametes to achieve fertilization.

anthracite
Form of COAL consisting of more than 90% carbon. It is relatively hard and black, with a metallic lustre. Anthracite burns with the hot nonluminous flame of complete combustion. It is the final form in the series of fuels: peat, lignite, bituminous coal and black coal. *See also* FOSSIL FUEL

antibiotic
Substance that is capable of stopping the growth of, or destroying, BACTERIA and other microorganisms. Many antibiotics are themselves produced by microorganisms (bacteria and moulds). Antibiotics are germicides that are safe enough to be swallowed or injected into the body. The introduction of antibiotics, from about the time of World War 2, has revolutionized medical science, making possible the virtual elimination of once widespread and often fatal diseases, including typhoid fever, plague and cholera. Some antibiotics are selective – that is, effective against specific microorganisms; those effective against a large number of microorganisms are known as broad-spectrum antibiotics. Some important antibiotics are penicillin, the first widely used antibiotic, streptomycin and the tetracyclines and cephalosporins. Because some bacteria have now become resistant to certain antibiotics, there is a constant search for new ones.

antibody
See feature article

anticline
Arch-shaped FOLD in rock strata, closing upwards. Unless the formation has been overturned, the oldest rocks are found in the centre with younger rocks symmetrically on each side of it.

anticoagulant
Substance that prevents or counteracts coagulation, or clotting. Anticoagulants are used to treat and prevent diseases caused by blood clots, such as thrombosis. HEPARIN is a commonly used blood anticoagulant. The saliva of blood-sucking animals, such as leeches, often contains anticoagulants.

anticodon
Triplet of organic bases on a TRANSFER RNA molecule. During PROTEIN SYNTHESIS it combines with a complementary sequence of three bases, the CODON, on a strand of MESSENGER RNA. Each transfer RNA molecule carries a specific AMINO ACID. When a series of transfer RNA molecules are lined up according to the codon sequence on the messenger RNA, the amino acids link together to form a POLYPEPTIDE.

anticyclone
Area of high atmospheric pressure around which air circulates. The circulation is clockwise in the Northern Hemisphere and anti-clockwise in the Southern Hemisphere. Anticyclones are often associated with settled weather conditions. In middle latitudes, they bring periods of hot, dry weather in summer and cold, often foggy, weather in winter.

antigen
Any substance or organism that is recognized as "foreign" by the IMMUNE SYSTEM. The presence of an antigen triggers the production of an ANTIBODY, part of the body's defence mechanism against disease. The antibody reacts specifically with the antigen and neutralizes it, causes it to destroy itself, or attracts LEUCOCYTES to carry out the destruction.

antirrhinum (snap dragon)
Any of *c*.50 herbaceous species native to the Northern Hemisphere and abundant in North America. Popular garden plants, they have showy, tubular, two-lipped flowers, often in terminal spikes, of white to red or purple. Family Scrophulariaceae; genus *Antirrhinum*.

ant lion
Any larva belonging to the NEUROPTERAN family Myrmeleontidea, found in most parts of the world. Ant lions are carnivorous, with large, sickle-shaped jaws. Most species dig pits in dry sand where they lie waiting for ants and other insects to fall in. Family Myrmeleontidea. *See also* LACEWING

antpitta
Short-tailed, stocky, long-legged bird found in the forests of Central and South America. A solitary bird, it hops about on the forest floor hunting for invertebrate prey. There are *c*.45 species. Length: 11–19cm (4–7in). Family Formicariidae (part).

antpitta, giant
Antpitta that inhabits the Andean slopes of Ecuador and s Colombia. It rakes the forest floor for slugs and giant earthworms (*Rhynodrylus*), which it chops into segments to eat. The giant antpitta's plumage is leaf green above with a white eye-ring, and chestnut-buff below. Length: 19cm (7in). Family Formicariidae; species *Grallaria gigantea*.

antpitta, scaled
Antpitta that is found from central Mexico to Peru. It hops over the forest floor, flicking leaves and debris with its bill in its search for insects and worms. Almost tailless, it has a scaly pattern above, buff throat and cinnamon underparts. It is very reticent. Length: 20cm (8in). Family Formicariidae; species *Grallaria guatimalensis*.

antshrike
Medium-sized bird found in lowland forests of Central and South America. Some species have striking, barred plumage. Antshrikes can be quite aggressive, sometimes chasing other birds to rob them of their food. There are *c*.45 species. Length: 14–17cm (6–7in). Family Formicariidae (part).

antshrike, barred
Antshrike found in secondary scrub and clearings from Mexico to Argentina. The transversely barred, black-and-white plumage of the male is unmistakable; the female's plumage is bright cinnamon above and tawny below, with strong black streaks on the cheeks and neck. Length: 15cm (6in). Family Formicariida; species *Thamnophilus doliatus*.

antshrike, slaty
Antshrike found in humid lowland forests from the Caribbean to Brazil. The male is slaty blue-grey with a black cap and white spotted wing bars; the female is olive-brown above and paler below, with buff wing bars. The bill is hooked. Length: 15cm (6in). Family Formicariida; species *Thamnophilus punctatus*.

ant-thrush
Medium-sized, ground-feeding bird found in the forests of Central and South America. Its short tail is often cocked as it hops about amongst the leaf-litter. There are *c*.10 species. Length: 18cm (7in). Family Formicariidae (part).

ANTIBODY

Protein synthesized in the blood by LYMPHOCYTES in response to the entry of "foreign" substances or organisms (antigens) into the body. Each episode of bacterial or viral infection prompts the production of a specific antibody to fight the antigens in question. After the infection has cleared, the antibody remains in the blood to fight off any future invasion. This process is a significant part of the body's IMMUNE SYSTEM.

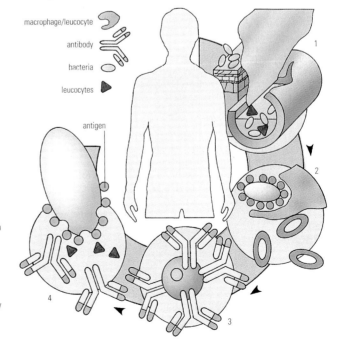

macrophage/leucocyte
antibody
bacteria
leucocytes
antigen

▶ **When bacteria enter** the blood stream at the site of a wound (1), macrophages (leucocytes) engulf some (2) and carry them to the lypmh nodes (3), where B-cells (blue) produce antibodies to bind with the unique antigen proteins on the surface of the invading bacteria (4). When the antibodies released into the blood stream attach themselves to the bacteria they stimulate certain leucocytes to destroy them.

► **aphid** The greenfly (*Aphis* sp.) occurs in enormous numbers, and the 2000 or species probably inflict more damage on crops than any other insect pest. Their remarkable power of reproduction is due to the fact that the females are parthenogenetic, that is they can produce young without fertilization by a male.

ant-thrush, black-faced
Dark ant-thrush found in humid lowland forests from Mexico to the Amazon basin. It behaves like a small RAIL, furtively walking along the forest floor with its cocked-up tail. It has a black throat and patches of pale blue skin round the eyes. The sexes are similar. Length: 18cm (7in). Family Formicariida; species *Formicarius analis*.

antwren
Small, active bird found in the forests of Central and South America. The antwren is constantly on the move, seeking out insects and other small invertebrates from the leaves of forest trees and vines. There are *c*.55 species. Length: 10–14cm (4–6in). Family Formicariidae (part).

antwren, dot-winged
Small antwren, superficially similar to the slaty antwren; it is found from Mexico to Amazonian Brazil. The males are wholly black with white wing bars; the females are similar but reddish-brown below. The dot-winged antwren searches in trees for insects. Length: 10cm (4in). Family Formicariidae; species *Microrhopias quixensis*.

antwren, slaty
Small, short-tailed antwren found in humid forests from Mexico to Peru. The male is slaty blue with a black chest and white wing bars; the female is olive-brown above and paler below. The slaty antwren often hangs upside down like a chickadee or tit and flocks with other birds. Length: 10cm (4in). Family Formicariidae; species *Myrmotherula schisticolor*.

anus
Opening at the end of the ALIMENTARY CANAL in most animals, through which waste material and undigested food are passed from the body in the form of feces. *See also* DIGESTIVE SYSTEM

aorta
Principal ARTERY in the body of higher vertebrates. In humans, the aorta leaves the left ventricle of the HEART, carrying freshly oxygenated blood, and descends the length of the trunk, finally dividing to form the two femoral arteries that serve the legs. *See also* CIRCULATORY SYSTEM

aoudad
See SHEEP, BARBARY

Apache beads (yerba mansa)
Aquatic plant found in sw North America. Its aromatic, STOLON-bearing rootstock was once used by Native North Americans to make cylindrical necklace beads. An infusion of the rootstock in water is said to ease malarial and dysenteric conditions. Family Saururaceae; species *Anemopsis californica*.

apalis
Any member of a genus of warblers found in the forests of s Africa. The apalis is an active, insect-eating bird, with green, grey or brown plumage and a long, rather narrow tail. Length: *c*.12.5cm (*c*.5in). Family Cisticolidae; genus *Apalis*.

apatite
Phosphate mineral, usually found as calcium phosphate associated with hydroxyl, chloride or fluoride ions. It occurs in igneous rocks and sedimentary deposits, as prismatic or tabular hexagonal crystals, as granular aggregates or in massive crusts. It is usually too soft for cutting and polishing, but there are two gem varieties. Hardness: 5; r.d. 3.1–3.4.

apatosaur (formerly brontosaurus or brontosaur)
Any member of the *Apatosaurus* genus of herbivorous DINOSAURS. Apatosaurs date from the Jurassic and early Cretaceous periods. They had long necks and tails. The apatosaurs' small heads had eyes and nostrils on the top so that they could remain completely immersed in water. Length: 21m (70ft); weight: to 30 tonnes.

aphid
Any of almost 4500 species of insect, most of which are renowned for their prodigious rates of reproduction. Feeding on the phloem of agricultural and ornamental plants, aphids are some of the most important insect pests. Many species alternate between sexual and asexual modes as well as alternating between host plant species. A single species may utilize drastically different host plants at different times and the feeding sites (such as roots or leaves) on these plants may be very different. An aphid species may also have several different morphological types; some even possess soldiers and exhibit social behaviour. Order Hemiptera; superfamily Aphidoidea; families Anoeciidae, Aphididae, Drepanosiphidae, Greenideidae, Hormaphididae, Lachnidae, Mindaridae, Pemphigidae, Phloeomyzidae and Thelaxidae.

aphid, bean (blackfly)
Aphid that is a widely distributed pest of crops such as beans, carrots, beets, corn and squashes. It clusters in large numbers around the stems and undersides of leaves and its feeding eventually results in the drying and deterioration of the host plants. Like other aphids, it may also be an important vector for plant viruses. Family Aphididae; species *Aphis fabae*.

aphid, cotton
See COTTON APHID

aphid, woolly
Member of a number of aphid families that are so called because they produce white wax strands which trail from the dorsum of their abdomens.

aphotic
Describing a region in which there is no light. In the

► **apple** Grown predominantly in temperate regions since prehistoric times, the apple is thought to be native to the Caucasus. China and the United States (particularly Washington state) are the world's largest producers of apples. Its juice is fully fermented to make vinegar.

seas and oceans, the aphotic zone exists at depths below which light does not penetrate, generally below 1500m (5000ft).

apocrine gland
In mammals, type of sweat-producing GLAND usually associated with hair follicles. In humans, apocrine glands are restricted mainly to the armpits and groin. In response to sex and stress stimuli, they secrete a liquid that is quickly decomposed by bacteria and produces an unpleasant smell. *See also* ECCRINE GLAND

apodiform
Member of the bird order Apodiformes, which includes HUMMINGBIRDS (suborder Trochili) and SWIFTS (suborder Apodi). Among the most aerial and aerobatic of all birds, they have certain wing structures in common. Their weak feet make them unable to walk or hop.

apostlebird
One of two species of Australian mudnester. It has soft, grey plumage and inhabits woodland and scrub in E Australia. Apostlebirds are very social, and the young may stay with their parents for up to four years. Length: 35cm (14in). Family Corcoracidae; species *Struthidea cinerea*.

appendix
Finger-shaped organ, *c*.10cm (*c*.4in) long, found in some mammals. It is located near the junction of the small and large intestines, usually in the lower right part of the abdomen. It has no known function in humans but can become inflamed or infected causing appendicitis.

apple
Common name for the most widely cultivated fruit tree of temperate climates. Developed from a tree native to Europe and sw Asia, apple trees are propagated by budding or grafting. From the flowers, which require cross-pollination to produce a desirable fruit, the fleshy fruit grows in a variety of sizes, shapes and acidities; it is generally roundish, 5–10cm (2–4in) in diameter, and a shade of yellow, green or red. A mature apple tree may yield up to 1cu m (30 bushels) of fruit in a single growing season. Europe produces 50–60% of the world's annual crop, and the United States 16–20%. Family Rosaceae; genus *Malus*.

apple berry
Evergreen, climbing, shrubby plant that is native to Tasmania. The apple berry is grown for its creamy white to purple flowers and edible, blue berries. Family Pittosporaceae; species *Billardiera longiflora*.

apple maggot (railroad worm)
Black and yellow spotted FLY. It is a serious pest of apples and blueberries throughout North America. The larvae leave brown trails through the inside of the fruit. Length: 4–6mm (0.16–0.24in). Order Diptera; family Tephritidae; species *Rhagoletis pomonella*.

apricot
Tree that originated in China and is now cultivated throughout temperate regions. It is a large, spreading tree with dark green leaves. The apricot tree's white blossoms bear yellow or yellowish-orange edible fruit, with a large stone. Family Rosaceae; species *Prunus armeniaca*.

apterygiform
Member of the bird order Apterygiformes, which

A

contains only the family Apterygidae, comprising the three species of KIWI.

apterygote
Any member of the subclass Apterygota, which comprises small, wingless insects, found worldwide. It includes the order Thysanura, of which the SILVER-FISH is a member. Apterygotes have elongated scaly bodies, long antennae and bristle-like appendages on the lower abdomen.

aquarium
Name given to a water-filled container used to display aquatic plants and animals. Aquariums vary in size from small circular or rectangular tanks used to contain goldfish to vast oceanaria containing millions of gallons of sea-water in which organisms as large as DOLPHINS and SHARKS are kept. The first public aquarium was opened at the London Zoo in Regent's Park in 1853. The name is also used for institutions that exhibit aquatic life.

aquatic animal
Animal that predominantly lives in water and has evolved to an aquatic existence. Most have adapted to obtaining oxygen from the water by means of specialized structures, such as GILLS, but some aquatic animals, such as WHALES, are air-breathing.

aqueous humour
Watery fluid that fills the eyeball between the lens and the CORNEA. It serves a double purpose: to nourish the eyeball and to refract light rays, so helping them to focus on the retina. *See also* VITREOUS HUMOUR

aquifer
Porous, permeable rock, often sandstone or limestone, that stores and transmits water. Much of the world's population obtains its water supply through ARTESIAN WELLS drilled into aquifers.

aquilegia (columbine)
Any member of a large genus of herbaceous perennials native to the north temperate regions. Many aquilegia are cultivated for their showy flowers, the petals of which have long, backward-pointing, nectariferous spurs. The flowers cover a wide range of colours, and hybrid varieties have extended the combinations of colours even further. Family Ranunculaceae; genus *Aquilegia*.

Arabian jasmine
Climbing shrub native to India and cultivated for its perfume. It has double, white, fragrant flowers, up to 2.5cm (1in) across, in few to many-flowered clusters. Height: up to 1.5m (5ft). Family Oleaceae; species *Jasminum sambac*.

arabis (rock-cress)
Small, annual, biennial and perennial herbs found in temperate regions, a few of which are cultivated in borders and rock-gardens. The white or purple flowers of the arabis are often small but are borne in profusion over a prolonged period. Family Brassicaceae; genus *Arabis*.

aracari
Brightly coloured, large-billed bird belonging to the TOUCAN family, found in the rainforests of South America. Aracaris are generally smaller and more slender than toucans and have a green back and bright red rump. They forage in the trees for fruit and make loud, rattling calls. Length: 35cm (14in). Family Ramphastidae; genus *Pteroglossus*; there are *c*.10 species.

arachnid
ARTHROPOD of the class Arachnida, which includes the SPIDER, TICK, MITE and SCORPION. Arachnids have four pairs of jointed legs, two distinct body segments (cephalothorax and abdomen) and chelicerate jaws (consisting of clawed pincers). They lack antennae and wings.

aragonite
Carbonate mineral, calcium carbonate ($CaCO_3$). It is formed under special conditions, generally in caverns and hot springs. Present-day MOLLUSC shells are formed of aragonite. It readily converts to CALCITE (another mineral of $CaCO_3$). Aragonite occurs as orthorhombic system groups of needle-like crystals or massive deposits. Its appearance is glassy white. Hardness 3.5–4; r.d. 2.9.

araguaney
Ornamental, evergreen, tropical tree. The showy flowers, produced in terminal clusters, have the tubular, trumpet-like shape characteristic of this family. Family Bignoniaceae; genus *Tabebouia*.

aramina
Tough, yellowish-white fibre; it is longer lasting than jute and is used as a substitute in various industries. The aramina plant occurs as a weed in tropical countries and is cultivated commercially in Brazil and Congo, where its main use is for making coffee sacks. Family Malvaceae; species *Urena lobata*.

arapaima (pirarucu)
One of the largest freshwater fish. It occurs in the Amazon River system and is also popular as a food fish, cultured successfully in ponds. The arapaima has a swim bladder that is used as a lung, allowing it to breathe air. Length: to 2.5m (8.2ft). Family Osteoglossidae; species *Arapaima gigas*.

araucaria
Any member of a group of tall, evergreen trees from South America, Australia and the South Pacific Islands. The araucaria group includes the MONKEY-PUZZLE (*Araucaria araucana*) and the NORFOLK ISLAND PINE (*Araucaria excelsia*), which are grown outside in subtropical regions as ornamentals. The leaves are scale-like and stiff, arranged in spirals. Family Araucariaceae; genus *Araucaria*.

arbor vitae
Common name for five species of tree or shrub of the genus *Thuja*. They are resinous, evergreen CONIFERS of the CYPRESS family and are native to North America and E Asia. They have thin outer

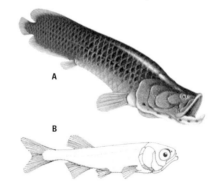

▲ **arapaima** The arapaima (A) is characterized by a bony tongue used to crush and digest prey. Its ability to breathe air gives it an advantage over more slow-moving fish in areas where the oxygen level in the water is low. A possible ancestor of the arapaima, Lycoptera (B), is also shown.

▲ **archaeopteryx** The earliest known recognizable bird, the archaeopteryx dates from the upper Jurassic period. The presence of wings and feathers define it as a bird, but the skeleton is quite reptilian. The wings, instead of being the specialized flying limbs of modern birds, were really elongated forelimbs, complete with claws. The tail resembles a lizard's and the skull had teeth. The small breastbone shows it was a poor flyer.

bark, fibrous inner bark and flattened branches. Family Cupressaceae.

arbutus
Any member of a group of evergreen trees or shrubs native to W North America, Canary Islands and the Mediterranean, some of which are grown ornamentally. The bark is characteristically smooth and reddish, peeling off in thin strips. The fruits are round, warty and orange or red, hence the common name strawberry tree for the *Arbutus unedo* species. Family Ericaceae; genus *Arbutus*.

Archaea (formerly archaebacteria)
One of three domains of living organism (Archaea, BACTERIA and EUKARYA). They only superficially resemble ordinary bacteria. Archaea form a coherent group with two main branches – METHANOGENIC BACTERIA and SULPHUR BACTERIA.

Archaean
Subdivision of PRECAMBRIAN geological time, from about 4000 to 2500 million years ago.

Archaebacteria
See ARCHAEA

archaeopteryx
Any member of the genus *Archaeopteryx*, comprising the first known BIRDS. They were about the size of a crow and fully feathered. Fossilized skeletons indicate that archaeopteryx were more like reptiles than modern birds; their beaks had pronounced jaws with teeth. They were probably capable only of weak flight. Archaeopteryx date from the upper JURASSIC period.

archegonium
Flask-shaped female sex organ of all plants except algae. BRYOPHYTES (liverworts and mosses), Lycopodophyta (CLUB MOSSES), Sphenophyta (HORSETAILS) and Filicinophyta (FERNS) all have archegonia. Female GAMETES (ova) develop in the base of the flask. At fertilization the cells forming the "neck" of the flask disintegrate to allow male gametes (antherozoids) to enter. *See also* ANTHERIDIUM; PROTHALLUS

A

▲ **archerfish** Its uniquely shaped mouth enables the archerfish to propel water as far as 1m (3.3ft). It shoots water at insects on overhanging plants, knocking them into the water. Its colourful markings make it a popular aquarium fish.

archerfish
Fish that is found in brackish waters of Southeast Asia and Australia. It is yellowish-green to brown with dark markings. It catches its insect prey by spitting water "bullets". Length: up to 20cm (8in). Family Toxotidae.

archipelago
Originally a lake or sea, such as the Aegean Sea, that contains numerous islands. The term is now generally used for a group of islands.

archosaur
Member of an ancient and major grouping (Archosauria) of reptiles; it includes the CROCODILES, PTEROSAURS, BIRD ancestors and DINOSAURS. The archosaurs dominated life on Earth for 180 million years from late TRIASSIC times to the end of CRETACEOUS times. The only extant order of archosaurs is the Crocodylia.

Arctic fox
See FOX, ARCTIC

ardwolf
See AARDWOLF

arenaceous
Describing something that is associated with SAND; most commonly used to describe types of SEDIMEN-TARY ROCK. In botany, an arenaceous plant is one that thrives in sandy soil; while in zoology, arenaceous animals live in sand. The shells of some microscopic animals, which consist mainly of sand particles, are also described as being arenaceous.

arête
Sharp ridge formed by EROSION where the heads of two GLACIERS meet. An example is the Matterhorn on the Swiss-Italian border.

argali
Wild SHEEP from the mountains of E central Asia. A gregarious animal, it has large ridged horns that spiral outwards. The argali is the largest species of sheep; it stands 127cm (50in) at the shoulder. Family Bovidae; subfamily Caprinae; species *Ovis ammon*.

argentite (silver glance)
Mineral that is an important ore of silver. It is dark grey and consists of silver sulphide (Ag_2S). Argentite occurs in veins, often together with native silver, in parts of Germany, Mexico and the United States.

argillaceous
Describing something that consists of very fine grains, such as those associated with CLAY, SHALE or SILT. Argillaceous rocks, such as kaolinite, are SEDI-MENTARY ROCKS, the particles of which are similar in size to those of clay or silt.

arkose
Comparatively young, medium-grained SEDIMENTA-RY ROCK resembling sandstone, consisting of QUARTZ with up to 30% FELDSPAR. It forms in marine and freshwater sediments and continental deposits, usual-ly from the breakdown of GRANITE. It is pale grey to pinkish in colour.

armadillo
Heavily armoured mammal found in South, Central and S North America. The armadillo's armour consists of bands of stiff, horny material separated by flexible skin. Although armadillos belong to the order Edentata (meaning "with all the teeth removed"), they all have simple peg-like teeth. Family Dasypodidae.

armadillo, giant
Largest of the armadillos, found in most of South America. The dark brown, giant armadillo inhabits forested areas near water, where it eats termites and other invertebrates. It will also take snakes and car-rion. Head-body length: 75–100cm (30–39in); tail: 45–50cm (18–20in). Family Dasypodidae; species *Priodontes maximus*.

armadillo, nine-banded (common long-nosed armadillo)
Armadillo with nine movable bands in its armour. The only armadillo to extend its range into the United States, it is found in Texas, as well as Central and South America. It inhabits areas with shady cover and feeds on invertebrates as well as small reptiles and amphibians. Head-body length: 24–57cm (9–22in); tail: 12.5–48cm (5–19in). Family Dasypodidae; species *Dasypus novemcincuts*.

armadillo, pink fairy
Smallest armadillo species. It inhabits the grasslands and sandy plains of central Argentina. It is pale pink and feeds mainly on ants and their larvae. Head-body length: 8–12cm (3–5in); tail: 3–3.5cm (*c*.1in). Family Dasypodidae; species *Chlamyphorus truncatus*.

armadillo lizard
See LIZARD, ARMADILLO

army ant
See ANT, ARMY

armyworm
Larva of a NOCTUID moth. Armyworms travel in hordes and are notorious for destroying all crops in their path. The best-known species is *Pseudaletia unipuncta*, which is orange-, brown- and yellow-striped. Outbreaks of this caterpillar occur annually in parts of the E United States. Length: 38mm (1.5in). Family Noctuidae.

arnica
Large genus of perennials of the DAISY family, native to the Northern Hemisphere. An oil obtained from the species *Arnica montana* was formerly used for treating sprains. Family Compositae.

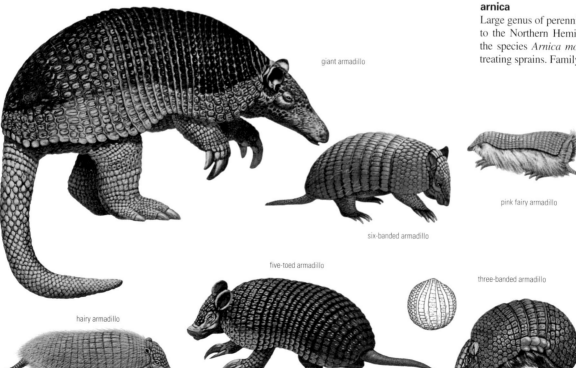

giant armadillo

pink fairy armadillo

six-banded armadillo

five-toed armadillo

three-banded armadillo

hairy armadillo

◄ **armadillo** The 21 species of armadillo are among the most abundant and widespread of South American mammals. Uniquely protected by plates of bone joined with skin, a few of them, such as the three-banded armadillo (*Tolypeutes matacus*), can roll themselves into defensive balls when threatened. But most escape predators by rapid burrowing. Armadillos vary considerably in size from the giant armadillo (*Priodontes giganteus*), 1.5m (5ft) in length, to the pink fairy armadillo (*Chlamyphorus truncatus*), which is less than 12cm (5in) long and spends most of its life underground. Armadillos are regarded as pests in some areas, but they do help to rid crops of harmful insects and other small animals.

aroid
Any plant of the ARUM family, a large group of plants that are found worldwide but are particularly prevalent in the tropics. Aroids mostly grow in wet or shady habitats. They have considerable economic importance: many are cultivated as ornamentals or as food sources, for example TARO, due to their edible starchy corms. Family Araceae.

arrack
Liquor produced from the sap of various species of palm in tropical Asia. Sap is collected from the upper part of the stems or unopened flowerheads; this toddy has a sugar content of about 14% and, when fermented, produces an alcoholic beverage. Family Palmae; genera *Arenga*, *Borassus*, *Caryota* and *Cocos*.

arrowgrass
Small, perennial, rhizome-bearing plant, found in wet and marshy habitats of temperate and cold regions. Arrowgrass plants have a rosette of basal linear leaves and wind-pollinated flowers in a terminal raceme. The leaves of sea arrowgrass, *Triglochin maritima*, are edible. Family Juncaginaceae; genus *Triglochin*.

arrowhead
Group of aquatic herbs named after the arrowhead-like leaf shape of some of the species. Rooted in mud, they produce leaves that may be held above the water surface, floating or submerged. Their flowers are showy with white or pinkish petals. Some species produce edible tubers. Family Alismataceae; genus *Alisma*.

arrow-poison frog
See FROG, ARROW POISON

arrowroot
Tropical and subtropical perennial plant found in wet habitats of America and some islands of the West Indies. Its leaves are lance-shaped and the flowers are usually white. The ground roots are used in cooking. Family Marantaceae; species *Maranta undinaceae*.

arrowworm
See CHAETOGNATH

arsenopyrite (iron arsenide-sulphide, FeAsS)
Sulphide mineral, the major ore of arsenic. It is found with precious metal ores in high-temperature veins. It occurs as monoclinic system, prismatic crystals or granular masses. It is a metallic white-grey. Hardness 5.5–6; r.d. 6.

artery
One of the BLOOD vessels that carry blood away from the HEART. The pulmonary artery carries deoxygenated blood to the lungs, but all other arteries carry oxygenated blood to the body's tissues. An artery is usually protected and embedded in muscle. Its walls are thick, elastic and muscular and they pulsate with the heartbeat. A severed artery causes major haemorrhage.

artesian well
Well from which water is forced out naturally under pressure. Artesian wells are bored where water in a layer of porous rock is sandwiched between two inclined layers of impervious rock. The water-filled layer is called an AQUIFER. Water flows up to the surface because parts of the aquifer are higher than the wellhead and the water is under great pressure.

arthropod
Any member of the largest animal phylum, Arthropoda. Living forms include CRUSTACEA,

◀ **arrowroot** The island of St Vincent in the West Indies is the main source of arrowroot (*Maranta arundinacea*).The plant has rhizomes that produce a light starch used in food preparation.

ARACHNIDS, CENTIPEDES, MILLIPEDES and INSECTS. Fossil forms include the extinct TRILOBITE. The species (numbering well over one million) are thought to have evolved from ANNELIDS. All have a hard outer skin of chitin, which is attached to the muscular system on the inside, and is periodically shed (ECDYSIS) during growth. The body is divided into segments, modified among different groups, with each segment originally carrying a pair of walking or swimming jointed legs. In some animals some of the legs have evolved into jaws, sucking organs or weapons. Arthropods have well-developed digestive, circulatory and nervous systems. Land forms use trachea for respiration.

artichoke (globe artichoke)
Tall, thistle-like, perennial plant, cultivated for its large, edible, immature flower heads. It is native to the Mediterranean region and has spiny leaves and blue flowers. Height: 0.9–1.5m (3–5ft). Family Asteraceae/Compositae; species *Cynara scolymus*. A different plant, the JERUSALEM ARTICHOKE, is grown for its edible tubers. Family Asteraceae/Compositae; species *Helianthus tuberosus*.

artificial insemination
Method of inducing pregnancy without sexual intercourse by injecting sperm into the female genital tract. Artificial insemination of livestock allows proven sires to impregnate many females at low cost. *See also* ARTIFICIAL SELECTION

artificial selection
Breeding of plants, animals or other organisms in which the parents are individually selected by humans in order to perpetuate certain desired traits and eliminate others from the captive population. By this means, most of our domestic crops, livestock and pets have arisen. The many breeds of dog have been developed by artificial selection. Crops such as wheat have been altered by artificial selection over thousands of years. Artificial selection can be accelerated today by techniques such as plant tissue culture, in which selected plants can be cloned and grown directly into new plants without having to wait for seed production and germination. ARTIFICIAL INSEMINATION is another method of artificial selection. In the near future the cloning of livestock embryos may also be possible. GENETIC ENGINEERING is the ultimate advance in artificial selection, allowing humans to combine specific sequences of DNA in order to combine desired genes. *See also* CLONE

artillery plant
Plant native to tropical America, cultivated as an ornamental for its fine, dense foliage. It is also known as the gunpowder or pistol plant because of the artillery-

like discharge of puffs of pollen from the stamens, when planted in a sunny location. Family Urticaceae; species *Pilea muscosa*.

artiodactyl
Any member of the Artiodactyla order of mammals, characterized by hoofs with an even number (two or four) of toes. Artiodactyls are all herbivores. The order includes GIRAFFES, HIPPOPOTAMUSES, DEER, CATTLE, PIGS, SHEEP, GOATS and CAMELS. They are mostly of Old World origin and range in size from the 3.6kg (8lb) mouse deer to the 4.5-ton hippopotamus.

arum
Any member of a genus of low-growing herbs with arrow-shaped leaves native to Eurasia. The inflorescence consists of a spathe sheathing the male and female flowers, which are produced on a central column that is adapted for a complex pollination mechanism using flies as pollinators. The inflorescences of many Arum species emit a fetid odour to attract flies. Family Araceae; genus *Arum*.

arum lily
Plant with smooth, shining leaves and fragrant flowers. The flowers are characteristic of the ARUM genus, with a creamy white spathe up to 25cm (10in) long. Native to South Africa, the arum lily is often grown as an ornamental in gardens, where it makes large conspicuous clumps. Family Araceae; species *Zantedeschia aethiopica*.

asafetida (oleo-gum-resin)
RESIN that is derived from stout perennial herbs of Iran and Afghanistan. It is obtained as a milky juice that exudes from cuts made at the base of the stem or the top of the root during the rainy season. Asafetida has a strong and unpleasant odour; it is used for flavouring food products and has medicinal properties. Family Apiaceae; species *Ferula asafoetida* and related species.

asbestos
Group of fibrous, naturally occurring, silicate minerals used in insulating, fireproofing, brake lining and in astronaut suits. Several types exist, the most common being white asbestos. Many countries have banned the use of asbestos, as it can cause lung cancer and asbestosis, a lung disease.

ascidian (sea squirt)
Marine animal that is part of a group known as tunicates. It lives attached, sponge-like, to seaweeds or rocks and filters its food and oxygen from the sea water. Phylum Chordata; subphylum Urochordata; class Ascidiacea. Length: 0.2–25cm (0.08–10in).

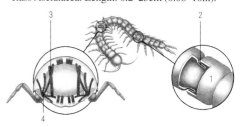

▲ **arthropod** The most numerous invertebrates (animals without a backbone) are the arthropods (joint-legged animals), such as the centipede. They owe their success to the exoskeleton that covers their bodies and allows the development of jointed limbs. Body segments are encased in a rigid protein cuticle (1) and body flexibility is permitted by an overlapping membrane (2). The strength of the exoskeleton ensures that muscles (3) can be anchored to the inside of the cuticle. Groups of muscles (4) are used to move the legs.

▶ **ash** The white ash (*Fraxinus americana*) of E North America grows to 41m (135ft) in height. The leaves of the ash are distinctive in being split into many small leaflets, giving the impression of very fine foliage.

ascomycete
Any member of the Ascomycota phylum of FUNGI. Ascomycetes are characterized by the formation of **asci**, which are enlarged, commonly elongated, cells in which eight spores are formed. Examples of ascomycetes include YEASTS, TRUFFLES, and blue and green MOULDS.

asexual reproduction
Type of reproduction that does not involve the union of male and female reproductive cells. Asexual reproduction occurs in several forms: FISSION – simple division of a single individual, as in BACTERIA and PROTOZOA; BUDDING – growing out and eventual splitting off of a new individual, as in HYDRA; SPORE formation, as in FUNGI; VEGETATIVE REPRODUCTION – in which a plant sends out runners that take root to form new plants, as in STRAWBERRIES, or new plants grow from organs such as BULBS. *See also* SEXUAL REPRODUCTION

ash
Group of mainly deciduous trees, usually having winged fruits and leaves made up of many small leaflets. The wood is elastic, strong and shock-resistant, and is widely used for furniture. Ash trees are native to temperate regions. Species include: manna ash, *Fraxinus ornus*, the flowering ash of S Europe and Asia Minor; the European ash, *Fraxinus excelsior*, which grows to 45m (148ft) tall; and *Fraxinus floribunda*, a native of the Himalayas. Family Oleaceae; genus *Fraxinus*. The mountain ash of Europe and Asia (*Sorbus aucuparia*) comes from a different family.

ash, volcanic
Fine particles of LAVA thrown up by a volcanic explosion. The cone of compound VOLCANOES consists of built-up layers of ash and lava.

asilid (robber-fly)
Large predatory FLY. The asilid catches other insects in flight and uses its piercing mouthparts to suck internal fluids and soft structures from its prey. Order Diptera; family Asilidae.

asity
Small bird with bright, metallic plumage and a curved bill; it resembles the sunbird. Asities are found only in Madagascar, where they feed on insects as well as nectar gathered from bright flowers. They weave hanging nests suspended from a branch. Family Philepittidae; there are four species.

asparagus
Perennial plant that is native to Asia and Africa. Asparagus has a tuberous or fleshy root, scale-like leaves and small greenish flowers. *Asparagus officinalis* is grown widely for its edible, tender shoots. Family Liliaceae.

asparagus fern
Plant related to the familiar edible asparagus, often used for its decorative foliage. The leaves are reduced to scales and both scales and branches are closely spaced on tall, climbing stems to make frond-like sprays. There are a number of cultivated varieties. Family Liliaceae; species *Asparagus plumosus*.

aspen
One of three species of tree of the genus *Populus*, with toothed, rounded leaves. Closely related to poplars, the aspens are native to temperate Eurasia, North Africa and North America. Height: to 30m (100ft). Family Salicaceae.

asphodel
Small group of Mediterranean plants, some of which are grown as garden ornamentals. The flowers are borne in long spikes above rush-like leaves. The yellow asphodel, *Asphodeline lutea*, is mentioned in Greek writings and its starchy tubers were used as food by the Greeks. Family Liliaceae; genera *Asphodelus* and *Asphodeline*.

aspidistra (cast-iron plant)
Any member of the genus *Aspidistra*, a group of durable house plants native to Asia, with long, broad, arching leaves. Height: to 91cm (36in). Family Liliaceae; species include *Aspidistra elatior*.

asplenium (spleenwort)
Any member of the genus *Asplenium*, a large group of ferns found worldwide, some of which are cultivated in gardens or as pot plants. The fronds may be simple or divided to various degrees and some are evergreen. Family Polypodiaceae; species include *Asplenium nidus* (bird's nest fern).

ass
Close relative of the domestic HORSE and ancestor of the donkey. There are two species of ass. Order Perissodactyla; family Equidae.

ass, African
Ass found in the rocky deserts of NE Africa. It is the smallest member of the horse family. The African ass is pale coloured with a dark stripe along its back and sometimes a shoulder cross. Head-body length: 200cm (79in); tail: 42cm (17in). Family Equidae; species *Equus africanus*.

ass, Asiatic (onager)
Ass found in the desert steppes of Asia. It is larger than the African ass. The Asiatic ass is reddish brown but paler in the winter. It has a prominent stripe along

▲ **ass, Asiatic** The wild Asiatic ass (*Equus hermionus*) has been displaced by domestic livestock on to the most barren pastures in its native N Iran. In addition to overhunting, this has made the Asiatic ass an endangered species.

▲ **assassin bug** The most common species of assassin bug is the kissing bug (*Mindarus* sp.). These nocturnal creatures tend to inhabit cracks in buildings or vegetation and seek out humans or other warm-blooded creatures at night.

its back. Head-body length: 210cm (83in); tail: 49cm (19in). Family Equidae; species *Equus hermionus*.

assassin bug (kissing bug)
Brown to black BUG found in South and Central America, Mexico and Texas. It bites human beings and rodents, usually near the mouth, and is a carrier of Chagas' disease. Length: 2.5–3.3cm (1–1.3in). Order Heteroptera; family Reduviidae; genera *Triatoma* and *Rhodinus*.

assegai wood
Strong, durable wood from a tree of tropical S and E African origin. It is used for making furniture, agricultural implements, and bobbins and shuttles for weaving. Assegai wood has also been used by Zulu peoples for spears and by early settlers in Africa for making wagons. Family Cornaceae; species *Curtisia dentata*.

assimilation
Process by which an organism uses substances taken in from its surroundings to make new living protoplasm or to provide energy for metabolic processes. It includes the incorporation of the products of food digestion into living tissues in animals, and the synthesis of new organic material by plants during photosynthesis.

aster
See MICHAELMAS DAISY

asthenosphere
Weak zone within the EARTH's upper MANTLE, extending from 100 to 700km (60–450mi) below the surface. It is detected by a slowing of seismic waves passing through the mantle.

astrobiology
See EXOBIOLOGY

atavism
Reversion by an organism to a characteristic of its ancestors after an interval of at least one generation in which the trait was absent. The term is no longer in scientific use since the reappearance of ancestral traits is now understood to be the expression of RECESSIVE genes.

atmosphere
See feature article

atmospheric pressure
Downward force that is exerted on a specified area by the ATMOSPHERE because of its weight (gravitational attraction to the Earth or other body). It is measured by barometers and usually expressed in units of millibars (mb). Standard atmospheric pressure at sea level is 1013.25mb. The column of air above 1cm² (0.15in²) of Earth's surface has a mass of about 1kg (2.2lbs).

atoll
Ring-shaped REEF of CORAL enclosing a shallow LAGOON. An atoll begins as a fringing reef surround-

ing a slowly subsiding island, usually volcanic. As the island sinks the coral continues to grow upwards until eventually the island is below sea level and only a ring of coral is left at the surface.

atom
See feature article, page 22

atrium (auricle)
Either of the two upper chambers of the four-chambered HEART. They are comparatively thin-walled since they only pump blood down into the muscular VENTRICLES of the heart. The term is also used for various other chambers in animals.

Attenborough, Sir David Frederick (1926–)
English naturalist and broadcaster. He was controller of BBC2 television (1965–68). Since 1954 Attenborough has travelled on zoological and ethnographical filming expeditions, which have formed the basis of such landmark natural history series as *Life on Earth* (1979), *The Living Planet* (1984), *The Trials of Life* (1990) and *The Private Life of Plants*

(1995). In the *State of the Planet* (2000) he investigated how human beings have affected the environment. He was knighted in 1985.

attrition
Type of EROSION in which the particles produced by the erosive process go on to erode each other. The process may take place in water, where sand particles in the river's load erode each other, or where pebbles on a beach tumble against each other. Eventually particles affected by attrition become completely rounded.

aubergine (eggplant)
Plant that is grown for its large purple fruits, up to 25cm (10in) long, which are eaten as vegetables. A member of the POTATO family, the aubergine has very large, hairy leaves, spiny stems and small, lilac-coloured, seven-petalled flowers. In its native India and China it grows as a perennial, but commercial varieties are grown as annuals in Europe and North America. Family Solanaceae; species *Solanum melongena*.

▶ **aubergine** Although hardy and relatively insensitive to pests, aubergine plants (*Solanum melongena*) grow slowly and are damaged by cold temperatures. The fruits are high in fibre and carbohydrates and contain potassium, calcium and vitamins A and B. The fruits are shades of red, yellow or purple, but the purple variety is the most common.

aubrieta
Any member of a small group of low-growing perennial plants distributed from the E Mediterranean region to Iran. Popular rock garden plants, aubrietas form spreading mats with small, colourful, rose or purple flowers. A number of varieties have been developed. Family Brassicaceae; genus *Aubrieta deltoidea*.

ATMOSPHERE

Envelope of gases surrounding the Earth. It shields the planet from the harsh environment of space, while the gases it contains are vital to life. About 95% by weight of the Earth's atmosphere lies below 25km (15mi) altitude; the mixture of gases in the lower atmosphere is commonly called air. The atmosphere's composition by weight is: nitrogen 78.09%, oxygen 20.9%, argon 0.93%, 0.03% carbon dioxide, plus 0.05% of hydrogen, other gases and varying amounts of water vapour. The atmosphere can be seen as concentric shells; the innermost is the TROPOSPHERE, in which dust and water vapour create the clouds and weather. The STRATOSPHERE extends from 10–55km (8–36mi) and is cooler and clearer and contains ozone. Above, to a height of 70km (43mi), is the MESOSPHERE in which chemical reactions occur, powered by sunlight. The temperature climbs steadily in the THERMOSPHERE, which gives way to the EXOSPHERE at about 400km (250mi), where helium and hydrogen may be lost into space. The IONOSPHERE ranges from about 80km (50mi) out to 1000km (625mi), the start of the Van Allen radiation belts.

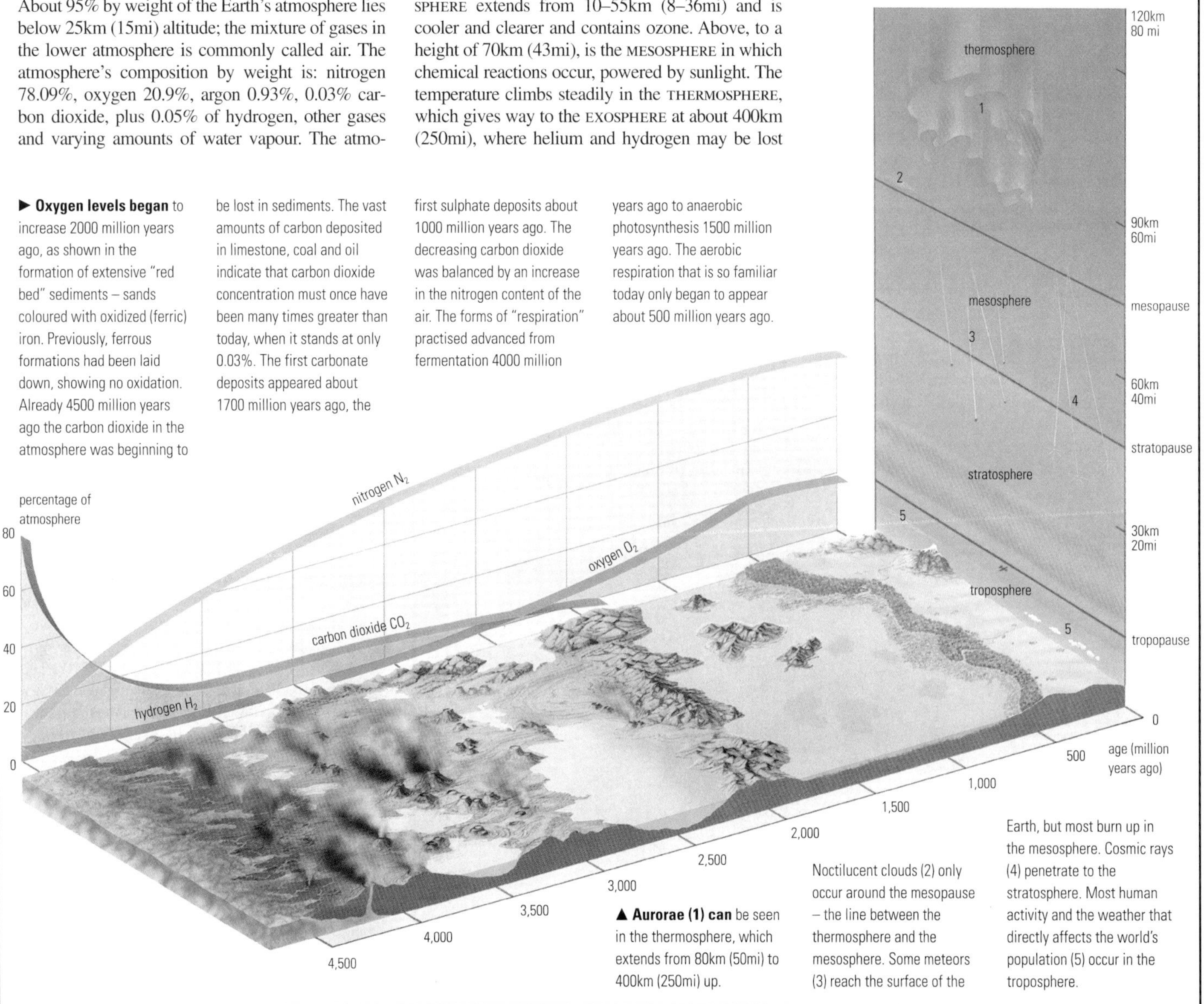

▶ **Oxygen levels began** to increase 2000 million years ago, as shown in the formation of extensive "red bed" sediments – sands coloured with oxidized (ferric) iron. Previously, ferrous formations had been laid down, showing no oxidation. Already 4500 million years ago the carbon dioxide in the atmosphere was beginning to be lost in sediments. The vast amounts of carbon deposited in limestone, coal and oil indicate that carbon dioxide concentration must once have been many times greater than today, when it stands at only 0.03%. The first carbonate deposits appeared about 1700 million years ago, the first sulphate deposits about 1000 million years ago. The decreasing carbon dioxide was balanced by an increase in the nitrogen content of the air. The forms of "respiration" practised advanced from fermentation 4000 million years ago to anaerobic photosynthesis 1500 million years ago. The aerobic respiration that is so familiar today only began to appear about 500 million years ago.

percentage of atmosphere

80
60
40
20
0

nitrogen N₂
oxygen O₂
carbon dioxide CO₂
hydrogen H₂

age (million years ago)
500
1,000
1,500
2,000
2,500
3,000
3,500
4,000
4,500

120km 80 mi
thermosphere
1
2
90km 60mi
mesosphere
mesopause
3
60km 40mi
4
stratopause
stratosphere
5
30km 20mi
troposphere
tropopause
5
tropopause
0

▲ **Aurorae (1) can** be seen in the thermosphere, which extends from 80km (50mi) to 400km (250mi) up.

Noctilucent clouds (2) only occur around the mesopause – the line between the thermosphere and the mesosphere. Some meteors (3) reach the surface of the Earth, but most burn up in the mesosphere. Cosmic rays (4) penetrate to the stratosphere. Most human activity and the weather that directly affects the world's population (5) occur in the troposphere.

A

auditory nerve
Bundle of nerves that carry impulses related to hearing and balance from the inner EAR to the brain.

auditory ossicles
Three small bones in the middle EAR. They transmit vibrations from the eardrum to the COCHLEA in the inner ear.

Audubon, John James (1785–1851)
US ornithologist and artist. His remarkable series of some 400 watercolours of birds, often in action, was published in *Birds of America* (1827–38). It is an important record of the species of birds that were known in North America at that time.

auger shell
Any member of a family of marine snails with conical shells. The snail has a sting on its foot, which it uses to paralyse its prey before consuming it. Phylum Mollusca; class Gastropoda; order Neogastropoda; family Terebridae.

auk
Squat-bodied sea bird of colder Northern Hemisphere coastlines. The flightless great auk (*Pinguinus impennis*), or Atlantic penguin, became extinct in the 1840s. Height: 76cm (30in). The razorbill auk (*Alca torda*) is the largest of the living species. Family Alcidae.

auk, little (dovekie)
Smallest member of the AUK family. Blackish brown above and white below, it is distinguished by its small size and short, stout bill. The little auk breeds on islands in the North Atlantic and nearby Arctic Ocean. It winters at sea further south and is often driven inland by gales. Length: 20cm (8in). Family Alcidae; species *Plautus alle*.

auricula
Plant of the *Primula* genus; it is native to the European Alps. The auricula's leaves are thick and oblong in shape, and the primrose-like flowers are borne above the leaves in a many flowered umbel. Cultivated forms are available in a wide range of colours; some varieties are dusted with a white mealy covering. Family Primulaceae; species *Primula auricula*.

aurora
Sporadic display of coloured light in the night sky, usually green, caused by charged particles from solar flares interacting with atoms and air molecules in the Earth's upper ATMOSPHERE. The charged particles from the Sun are attracted by the Earth's magnetic field into zones called VAN ALLEN RADIATION BELTS. Auroras occur in polar regions and are known as aurora borealis, or "northern lights", in the Northern Hemisphere, and aurora australis in the Southern Hemisphere.

Australian bower plant
Ornamental woody vine native to tropical Australia. Its attractive white or pinkish flowers can be up to 5cm (2in) long. The fruit forms a woody pod up to 10cm (4in) in length. Its seeds are winged. Family Bignoniaceae; species *Pandorea jasminoides*.

Australian cherry
Tree of the SANDALWOOD family. Its scale-like leaves give it a superficial resemblance to some conifers. Most members of the family are semi-parasitic: they are able to manufacture their own food but they also require a host from which they obtain water and minerals. The fruits of the Australian cherry tree are edible. Family Santalaceae; species *Exocarpos cupressiformis*.

◀ **avocado** A member of the laurel family, the fruit of the avocado tree (*Persea americana*) contains a single large seed surrounded by pale green flesh. It was probably first cultivated by the Aztecs; Mexico is the world's largest producer.

Australian laurel
Small tree that is distributed from New South Wales, Australia, to Tasmania. It is grown as an ornamental for its glossy, evergreen foliage and fragrant, creamy flowers. The genus name, *Pittosporum*, comes from the Greek for pitch (*pittos*) and seed, referring to the resinous coating round the seeds. Height: to 24m (79ft). Family Pittosporaceae; species *Pittosporum undulatum*.

Australian sassafras
Tree native to New South Wales, Australia. Aromatic oils extracted from the leaves and bark are used locally for making perfumes. Family Monimiaceae; species *Doryphora sassafras*.

australopithecine ("southern ape")
Any member of a group of ancient and extinct human relatives who lived in Africa from around four million to one million years ago. They gave rise to our human ancestors, of the genus HOMO, more than two million years ago. The australopithecines evolved from an ancestor shared with the higher apes. They walked upright. Height: 1–1.6m (3.3–5.2ft).

autolysis
Process in which a tissue, cell or part of a cell self-destructs. The process is brought about by ENZYMES that act on cells, produced by LYSOSOMES within the cell itself, normally after the cell has died.

autonomic nervous system (ANS)
In mammals, the part of the body's NERVOUS SYSTEM that regulates the body's involuntary functions. In conjunction with the peripheral nervous system it helps prepare the body for action or rest by regulating functions such as heartbeat, digestion and sweating. The ANS is divided into the sympathetic nervous system and the parasympathetic nervous system.

autosome
CHROMOSOME that is not a sex chromosome. In human beings there are 23 pairs of chromosomes, of which 22 pairs, the autosomes, are identical in both sexes. *See also* HETEROSOME

autotroph
Organism that manufactures its own organic food from simple inorganic chemicals in a process known as **autotrophic nutrition.** Green plants are typical autotrophs; they make sugars by PHOTOSYNTHESIS from carbon dioxide and water using the energy of sunlight. In FOOD CHAINS, autotrophs make up the PRIMARY PRODUCERS, providing energy (as food) for organisms higher up the chain. *See also* HETEROTROPH

autumn crocus
Plant, native to Europe and N Africa, that produces a few leaves in spring and large purple flowers, up to 10cm (4in) across when fully expanded, in the autumn. The ALKALOID colchicine is obtained from the dried corm and seed. Family Liliaceae; species *Colchicum autumnale*.

auxin
PLANT HORMONE produced mainly in the growing

ATOM

Smallest particle of matter that can take part in a chemical reaction, every element having its own characteristic atoms. The atom, once thought indivisible, consists of a central, positively charged NUCLEUS orbited by negatively charged ELECTRONS. The nucleus (identified in 1911 by British physicist Ernest Rutherford) is composed of tightly packed PROTONS and NEUTRONS. It occupies a small fraction of the atomic space but accounts for almost all of the mass of the atom. In 1913 Danish physicist Niels Bohr (1885–1962) suggested that electrons moved in fixed orbits. The study of quantum mechanics has since modified the concept of orbits: the Heisenberg uncertainty principle says it is impossible to know the exact position and momentum of a subatomic particle. The number of electrons in an atom and their configuration determine its chemical properties. Adding or removing one or more electrons produces an ION.

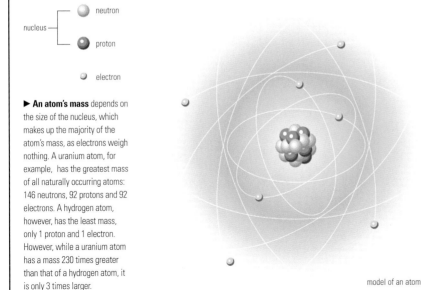

nucleus — neutron

proton

electron

▶ **An atom's mass** depends on the size of the nucleus, which makes up the majority of the atom's mass, as electrons weigh nothing. A uranium atom, for example, has the greatest mass of all naturally occurring atoms: 146 neutrons, 92 protons and 92 electrons. A hydrogen atom, however, has the least mass, only 1 proton and 1 electron. However, while a uranium atom has a mass 230 times greater than that of a hydrogen atom, it is only 3 times larger.

model of an atom

► **avalanche** A great mass of snow and rock can be seen moving rapidly down this mountain slope, which is part of the Rockies mountain range, in Colorado, United States. Avalanches damage whatever is in their path and much research has been done into methods of predicting when they will happen. Avalanche control also involves the intentional triggering of an avalanche before too much snow has been able to accumulate.

tips of plant stems. Auxins accelerate plant growth by stimulating cell division and enlargement, and by interacting with other hormones. Actions include the elongation of cells (by increasing the elasticity of cell walls, allowing the cells to take up more water) in GEOTROPISM and PHOTOTROPISM, and fruit drop and leaf fall. Synthetic auxins are the basis of rooting powders and selective weedkillers.

avalanche
Sudden mass movement of rock, sediment, ice or snow downslope, often have devastating effect on anything living in its path. Such catastrophic failures may occur on any overloaded slope above or below water. The mass of material can accelerate up to 400km per hour (250mph), travelling tens of kilometres from their source.

Avalonia
Small crustal PLATE consisting of parts of the maritime states of North America, England, Wales, SE Ireland and parts of W Europe. It split from GONDWANALAND early in ORDOVICIAN times and collided with LAURENTIA during SILURIAN times.

avens
Any member of a group of perennial herbs from cold and temperate regions, many of which are grown in gardens. The leaves are mostly present as a basal rosette. The flowers may be solitary or clustered on tall stems, yellow, white or red in colour, and showy in the ornamental forms. Family Rosaceae; genus *Geum*.

aviary
Large cage or similar container used to keep and display BIRDS.

avocado
Evergreen, broad-leafed tree native to the tropical New World. The name is extended to its green, pear-shaped fruit. Avocados have a high oil content and a nutty flavour. Weight: 200g (7oz) but exceptionally up to 2kg (4.4lb). Family Lauraceae; species *Persea americana*.

avocet
Any of four species of graceful wading bird, with black-and-white plumage, long legs and a remarkable upturned, narrow bill. The avocet feeds by swishing its bill from side to side through shallow water, filtering out small aquatic invertebrates. Length: 45cm (18in). Family Recurvirostridae; genus *Recurvirostra*.

avocet, red-necked
Avocet that is found in Australia and Tasmania. It has a bright, rusty coloured head and neck and the typical long, fine, upturned bill. As with other avocet

species, the red-necked avocets are noisy and aggressive when nesting, chasing off passers-by with their sharp, needle-like bills. Length: 40–46cm (16–18in). Family Recurvirostridae; species *Recurvirostra novaehollandiae*.

axil
Angular space between a growing leaf, bract or branch and the stem that it grows from. Buds or shoots that grow in axils are known as axillary buds or shoots.

axolotl
Permanently aquatic SALAMANDER that retains gills and other larval features throughout its life. The name axolotl is sometimes incorrectly applied to gilled adult forms of tiger salamanders, but it is correctly given to *Ambystoma mexicanum*, a species from the Mexican plateau. Albinism is common in axolotls. Length: *c*.25cm (*c*.10in). Family Ambystomatidae; genus *Ambystoma*.

axon
Part of a nerve cell, or NEURONE, that carries a nerve impulse beyond and away from the cell body, such as an impulse for movement to a muscle. There is typically only one axon per neurone, and it is generally long and unbranched. It is encased by a fatty, pearly MYELIN SHEATH in all peripheral nerves and in all central nerves except those of the brain and spinal cord. Axons in peripheral nerves are covered by an additional delicate sheath, a neurilemma, which helps to regenerate damaged nerves. *See also* NERVOUS SYSTEM

aye-aye
Largest species of nocturnal PRIMATE. It has coarse dark hair, a big bushy tail and large naked ears. The aye-aye taps on dead wood to find insect larvae and then uses its greatly elongated middle finger to draw out its food. It climbs trees in the rainforests of Madagascar. Head-body length: 40cm (16in); tail: 42cm (16.5in). Family Daubentoniidae; species *Daubentonia madagascariensis*.

azalea
Any of certain shrubs and small trees of the genus *Rhododendron*, found in temperate regions of Asia and North America. Mostly deciduous, azaleas have leathery leaves and funnel-shaped red, pink, magenta, orange, yellow or white flowers, which are sometimes variegated. Family Ericaceae.

azurite
Basic copper carbonate mineral found in the oxidized parts of copper ore veins, often as earthy material with MALACHITE. The crystals are blue, brilliant and transparent. In the past azurite gemstones were used as pigments in wall paintings. Hardness 3.5–4; r.d. 3.77–3.89.

◄ **aye-aye** The only remaining member of the Daubentoniidae family, the aye-aye (*Daubentonia madagascariensis*) is an endangered species, mainly due to deforestation in its native Madagascar. It is a reclusive and solitary creature.

B

babaco
Small, tropical tree native to Ecuador and Colombia. It is cultivated in Latin America for the sweet, juicy envelope that surrounds its seeds. The tree is sparingly branched with soft wood. All parts of it contain a milky latex. Family Caricaceae; species *Carica pentagona*.

babbler
Small or medium-sized perching bird that is found mainly in Africa, s Asia and Australasia. A single species, the WREN-TIT, lives in North America. Most babblers are thrush-like and have rather drab, grey or brown plumage. Their calls are loud and musical. There are *c*.250 species. Length: 10–25cm (4–9in). Family Timaliidae.

babbler, common
Babbler with a long, graduated tail, short wings and a stout, curved bill. It is mainly brownish with darker streaks. The common babbler is often seen hopping on the ground with its tail raised or flying to cover in low, laboured flight. Length: 22cm (9in). Family Timaliidae; species *Turdoides caudatus*.

babbler grey-crowned
Largest species of babbler. It has big white eyebrows bordering a pale grey crown and pale yellow eyes. Found in scrubby woodland in Australia, it is now becoming uncommon around towns and cities, seemingly unable to adapt to disturbance of its habitat. Length: 30cm (12in). Family Timaliidae; species *Pomatostomus temporalis*.

babirusa
Wild PIG found in the tropical rainforests of various Indonesian islands. It has pale skin with sparse hair. One of its two pairs of tusks grows upwards through the muzzle, curving towards the forehead. A specialized herbivore, the babirusa feeds on fruit and grass. Head-body length: 85–105cm (33–41in); tail: 27–32cm (11–13in). Family Suidae; species *Babyrousa babyrussa*.

baboon
Any of several species of large MONKEY found in

Africa. Baboons are social animals, and they travel in families or groups led by old males. They are quadrupeds. Family Cercopithecidae.

baboon, gelada
One of the largest baboon species. It is heavily built and has a naked area of red skin on its chest and a red rump. It inhabits open rocky grassland in the mountains of Ethiopia. The gelada has a very precise finger grip and can pick the best blades of grass. The social organisation of geladas is very complex. Head-body length: 50–74cm (20–29in); tail: 32–50cm (13–20in). Family Cercopithecidae; species *Theropithecus gelada*.

baboon, hamadryas
Baboon found in rocky desert areas of NE Africa. It feeds on anything edible, from plant material to small animals. The male has a silver-grey cape over its shoulders and a red face. Head-body length: 76cm (30in); tail: 61cm (24in). Family Cercopithecidae; species *Papio hamadryas*.

baboon, savanna
Baboon of which there are four subspecies – the olive baboon, yellow baboon, Guinea baboon and chacma baboon. Savanna baboons are found in open grassland near trees across much of s and E Africa. Their colour varies geographically from reddish to greenish. Although mostly terrestrial, savanna baboons will climb trees to sleep and to search for the plant material on which they feed. They also prey on small animals, including young antelope. Head-body length: 56–79cm (22–31in); tail: 42–60cm (17–24in). Family Cercopithecidae; species *Papio cynocephalus*.

baby's breath
Tall perennial with widely spaced branches and pale blue-green leaves and stems. It is native to Europe and N Asia. Baby's breath is cultivated in gardens for its tiny, white flowers, which are produced in many branched, delicate inflorescences, sometimes including up to 1000 flowers. Family Caryophyllaceae; species *Gypsophila paniculata*.

bachelor's buttons
Alternative name for several different plants, including CORNFLOWER and FEVERFEW.

backcross
Offspring of a first-generation HYBRID and either of its parents. Backcrosses are used by biologists as a means of testing the GENOTYPE of the hybrid.

bacteria
See feature article

▲ **badger** The Eurasian badger (*Meles meles*) of s China lives in sizeable family groups in large burrows known as setts. Setts have a complex network of tunnels and chambers, each serving a particular function.

bacteriology
Scientific study of BACTERIA. These single-celled organisms were first observed in the 17th century by the amateur microscopist Anton van LEEUWENHOEK, but it was not until the researches of Louis PASTEUR and later Robert KOCH that bacteriology was established as a scientific discipline.

bacteriophage
Virus that lives on and infects BACTERIA. It has a protein head, containing a core of DNA, and a protein tail. Since its discovery in 1915, it has been important in the study of GENETICS.

badger
Any of a group of about nine species of rather bulky carnivorous mammals belonging to the WEASEL family. Badgers are mainly nocturnal and most live in underground burrows. They feed mainly on worms, insects, roots, seeds and fruits. Most badgers are dark coloured, with black and white face markings. Family Mustelidae (part).

badger, American
Badger found from s Canada to Mexico. A nocturnal carnivore, it feeds on small mammals, carrion and invertebrates. It is grey-reddish with a central white face stripe. Head-body length: 42–72cm (17–28in); tail: 10–16cm (4–6in). Family Mustelidae; species *Taxidea taxus*.

badger, Eurasian
Badger native to Europe. It is a nocturnal carnivore. The Eurasian badger is mostly grey-black but its head and ear tips are white, with black stripes running through the eyes. A well-defined social group shares a complex burrow system or sett. Head-body length: 56–90cm (22–35in); tail: 11–20cm (4–8in). Family Mustelidae; species *Meles meles*.

badger, honey (ratel)
Badger that inhabits open dry savanna in Africa and parts of Asia. Its back is pale in colour, with darker underparts and legs. Capable of climbing trees, it feeds on honey and has been known to prey on domestic poultry. Head-body length: 60–70cm (24–28in); tail: 20–30cm (8–12in). Family Mustelidae; species *Mellivora capensis*.

badlands
Eroded, barren plateau in an arid or semi-arid area characterized by steep gullies and ravines. Because of the lack of adequate vegetation (due to climate or human intervention), the rainwater runs off very quickly and erodes soft and exposed rock. The best-known examples are the badlands of sw South Dakota and NW Nebraska, United States.

Baer, Karl Ernst von (1792–1876)
Estonian embryologist. His discovery of the mam-

▶ **babirusa** The tusks of the strange pig-like babirusa (*Babyrousa babyrussa*) grow from its lower jaw and pierce its upper lip. A shy animal, it usually hunts at night, foraging in swampy areas and along river banks in the jungle. It can swim and is a fast runner.

Bacteria are one of three domains of living organisms (ARCHAEA, Bacteria and EUKARYA). Simple, unicellular, microscopic organisms, bacteria lack a clearly defined nucleus and most are without CHLOROPHYLL. Many species are motile, swimming by means of whip-like FLAGELLUM. Most multiply by FISSION. Under adverse conditions many can remain dormant inside highly resistant spores with thick, protective coverings. Bacteria may be AEROBIC or ANAEROBIC. Although pathogenic bacteria are a major cause of human disease, many bacteria are harmless or even beneficial to humans, providing an important link in FOOD CHAINS, by decomposing plant and animal tissue and converting free nitrogen and sulphur into amino acids and other compounds useful to plants and animals. Some contain chlorophyll and carry out PHOTOSYNTHESIS. *See also* ACTINOBACTERIUM; CYANOBACTERIUM; ENTEROBACTERIUM; HALOBACTERIUM; LACTOBACTERIUM; METHANOGENIC BACTERIUM; NITROGEN-FIXING BACTERIUM; NON-SULPHUR BACTERIUM; SULPHUR BACTERIUM

B

▼ **Bacteria occur in** three basic shapes and forms: spherical forms called cocci (A), rod-like bacilli (B), and spiral spirilla (C). Cocci can occur in clumps known as staphylococci (1), groups of two called diplococci (2) or chains called streptococci (3). Unlike cocci, which do not move, bacilli are freely mobile; some are termed peritrichous and use many flagellae (4) to swim about, whereas other monotrichous forms (as seen below) use a single flagellum (5). Bacilli can also form spores (6) to survive unfavourable conditions. Spirilla may be either cork-screw-shaped spirochaetes like Leptospira (7), or less coiled and flagellated, such as Spirillum (8) (magnification × 5000).

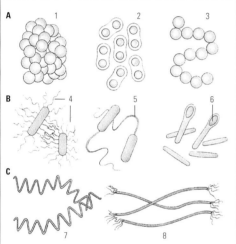

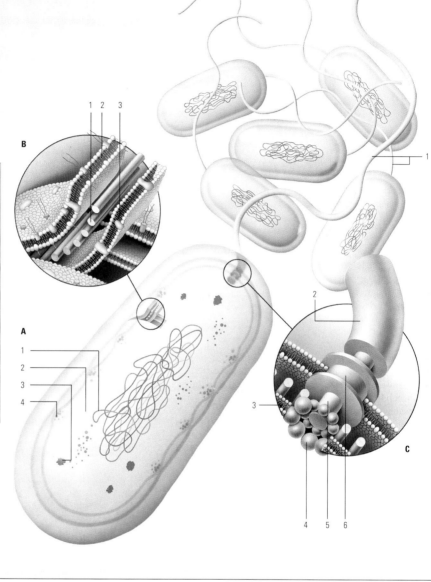

► **Bacteria (A) have** no nucleus; instead, they have a nucleoid (1), a single loop of DNA. This carries the genes, chemically coded instructions that define the bacterium. The average bacterium has about 3000 genes, compared to a human's 100,000. The cytoplasm (2) also contains glycogen (food) granules (3) and ribosomes (4), which give the cytoplasm a grainy appearance and are the site of protein production. In many bacteria the cytoplasm also contains minute genetic elements called plasmids. Most, but not all, bacteria have rigid, protective cell walls (B). There are two main types. One has a single thick (10–50nm) layer. Bacteria with this type of cell wall are called Gram-positive, because they stain bright purple with the Gram stain. Gram-negative bacteria, as shown, have a thinner wall (1) with an extra layer of proteins and lipids on the outside (2). This type of cell does not stain purple, a basic distinction useful in medicine. The defensive cells of the body recognize bacteria by their cell walls. A cell membrane (3) surrounds the cytoplasm. It is a few molecules thick, made of proteins and lipids, and is the barrier at which a living cell controls what enters and leaves it. Some bacteria move (C) using flagella (1) whirled about by a hook (2). The motion is powered by a flow of protons across the cell membrane (3), which rotates a disc of protein molecules (4) in the membrane. A rod (5) connects this protein "rotor" to the hook via another disc (6), which seals the cell wall.

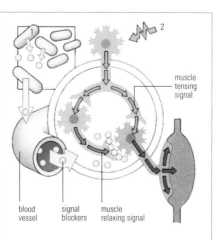

◄ **Before the advent** of effective sanitation and the discovery of antibiotics, recurrent epidemics of serious bacterial diseases swept Europe. The symptoms of many bacterial diseases are caused by toxic proteins (called toxins) produced by the bacteria. Botulinum toxin, produced by the food-poisoning bacterium *Clostridium botulinum*, is one of the most powerful poisons known. Tetanus toxin, produced by the related *Clostridium tetani* (1), can infect deep, dirty wounds. When a nerve impulse (2) tenses a muscle cell, the toxin blocks the relaxing part of the signal so the muscle stays tensed (the reason why tetanus is sometimes called lock-jaw). Most of the real killers among bacteria are now under control in the developed world, where tuberculosis is rare and diphtheria seldom a problem. In the developing world, however, bacterial diseases still take a dreadful toll.

blood vessel   signal blockers   muscle relaxing signal

muscle tensing signal

B

▲ **bamboo** Woody members of the grass family, bamboos can vary in height from a few centimetres to several metres. While most bamboo grows in dense clumps in tropical regions, some species, such as

Arundinaria alpina (shown here), grows on mountainsides and can withstand cold conditions. Though hollow, bamboo is surprisingly strong for its weight; it is used sometimes for building houses and making furniture.

malian ovum, described in *On the Mammalian Egg and the Origin of Man* (1827), established that mammals developed from eggs. Further research led to his discovery of the notochord and the functions of other embryonic tissues. Baer's research was published in *On the Development of Animals* (two volumes, 1828, 1837).

Bailey, Liberty Hyde (1858–1954)
US botanist. He helped to establish horticulture as an applied science through the systematic study of cultivated plants. His work had an important influence on the development of genetics and plant pathology. Bailey founded and directed the Bailey Hortorium at Cornell University, United States. Among his most influential publications are *The Standard Cyclopedia of Horticulture* (1914) and *Manual of Cultivated Plants* (1923).

balata
Non-elastic type of RUBBER obtained from the LATEX of a tree native to Trinidad and South America. It contains *c*.50% GUM. Balata was used in the past for machine beltings because it grips tightly and does not stretch. It has also been used as a substitute for CHICLE. Height: 30m (100ft). Family Sapotaceae; species *Mimusops balata*.

bald cypress (swamp cypress)
Deciduous tree that grows in shallow water in the SE United States. It loses its feathery, light green needles in autumn. Just above the water line, there is a woody growth on the roots. Height: to 4.6m (15ft). Family Taxodiaceae; species *Taxodium distichum*.

balloon fish
PUFFERFISH with thick spines that become erect when the fish fills itself with water as a defence. It is found in coastal coral reefs of the Gulf of California, the Gulf of Mexico and the Caribbean. Length: to 46cm (18in). Family Diodontidae; species *Diodon holocanthus*.

balloon flower
Perennial plant native to China; it is often cultivated as a garden ornamental. It is named after the bal-

loon-like shape of the flower buds before the flowers open. The large, saucer-shaped flowers, which may be blue, lilac or white, are followed by decorative fruits. Family Campanulaceae; species *Platycodon grandiflorum.*

balloon-fly (dance-fly)
Small, predatory FLY. It uses its piercing mouthparts to feed on other insects. The name is derived from the structure that males create as courtship gifts for females: shiny spheres of white silk, which often contain prey items, are presented to females prior to mating. Order Diptera; family Empididae; there are many species.

balloon vine
Annual or biennial climber found in tropical and subtropical regions throughout the world. The white flowers are followed by inflated, bladdery, three-angled fruit capsules *c*.2.5cm (*c*.1in) across. Height: to 3m (10ft). Family Sapindaceae; species *Cardiospermum halicacabum.*

ball python
See PYTHON, BALL

balm
Resin from a BALSAM plant; also the name of various aromatic plants, particularly those of the genera *Melissa* and *Melittis*, both belonging to the family Lamiaceae/Labiatae.

balsa
Lightweight wood obtained from a South American tree. It is used for modelling and for building rafts. Family Bombacaceae; species *Ochroma lagopus*.

balsam
Aromatic RESIN obtained from plants; or healing preparations, especially those with benzoic and cinnamic acid added to the resin; or balsam-yielding trees, such as the BALSAM FIR and balsam poplar. The name is also given to many species of Balsaminaceae, which are plants of moist areas, with pendent flowers. *See also* IMPATIENS

balsam apple
Slender, annual climber with unbranched tendrils and lobed leaves. It is native to the Old World tropics. Balsam apple is cultivated for its oval, orange fruits, which may be up to 8cm (3in) long, sometimes with a warty skin. The fruit is said to have purgative properties, but it can be eaten after careful washing and cooking. Family Cucurbitaceae; species *Momordica balsamina.*

balsam fir
Evergreen tree native to NE North America. It has flat needles and cones *c*.6cm (*c*.2in) in length. It is often grown for pulpwood and Christmas trees. Height: to 21m (70ft). Family Pinaceae; species *Abies balsamea.*

bamboo
Tall, tree-like GRASS native to tropical and subtropical regions. The hollow, woody stems grow in branching clusters from a thick rhizome; the leaves are stalked blades. It is used in house construction

BANANA

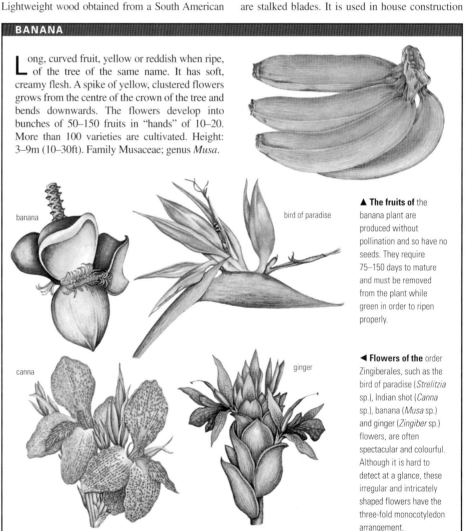

Long, curved fruit, yellow or reddish when ripe, of the tree of the same name. It has soft, creamy flesh. A spike of yellow, clustered flowers grows from the centre of the crown of the tree and bends downwards. The flowers develop into bunches of 50–150 fruits in "hands" of 10–20. More than 100 varieties are cultivated. Height: 3–9m (10–30ft). Family Musaceae; genus *Musa.*

banana

bird of paradise

canna

ginger

▲ **The fruits of** the banana plant are produced without pollination and so have no seeds. They require 75–150 days to mature and must be removed from the plant while green in order to ripen properly.

◄ **Flowers of the** order Zingiberales, such as the bird of paradise (*Strelitzia* sp.), Indian shot (*Canna* sp.), banana (*Musa* sp.) and ginger (*Zingiber* sp.) flowers, are often spectacular and colourful. Although it is hard to detect at a glance, these irregular and intricately shaped flowers have the three-fold monocotyledon arrangement.

and for household implements. Some bamboo shoots are eaten. The pulp and fibre can form a basis for paper production. Height: to 40m (131ft). There are *c*.1000 species. Family Poaceae/Gramineae; genus *Bambusa*.

banana
See feature article

bananaquit
Active bird that inhabits damp woodland, swamps and parkland in Central and South America. It has a narrow, down-curved bill and yellow, grey and white plumage. It feeds on insects, spiders and nectar. The bananaquit is related to the American wood WARBLER. Length: 10cm (4in). Family Parulidae; species *Coereba flaveola*.

bandicoot
Rabbit-sized MARSUPIAL with a pointed muzzle, native to Australia and New Guinea. All bandicoots dig for invertebrates and also eat fruit and seeds. Many species are endangered, either due to overgrazing of their habitat by sheep and cows or due to introduced predators, such as foxes.

bandicoot, greater rabbit-eared (greater bilby, dalgyte)
Sole living representative of the family Thylacomyidae, found only in Australia. Unlike other bandicoots, it digs its own spiralling burrows. It has blue-grey fur and very long ears. It feeds on insects and their larvae. Head-body length: 29–55cm (11–22in); tail: 20–29cm (8–11in). Family Thylacomyidae; species *Macrotis lagotis*.

bandicoot, short-nosed (quenda, Southern brown bandicoot)
One of three species of short-nosed bandicoot. It has brown fur with hints of orange on its back, paler underneath. Head-body length: 30–35cm (12–14in); tail: 10–15cm (4–6in). Family Peramelidae; species *Isoodon obesulus*.

bandy-bandy
Nocturnal, egg-laying, black-and-white-banded SNAKE found in E and N Australia. It feeds chiefly on blind snakes. When disturbed the bandy-bandy throws its body into loops held high off the ground. Length: to 1m (39in). Family Elapidae; species *Vermicella annulata*.

baneberry
Any member of a small group of upright, perennial herbs found on rich woodlands in the north temperate zone of North America. The stem bears large divided leaves and at the top a dense flower cluster of small white flowers. The shiny red or white berries are highly poisonous. Family Ranunculaceae; genus *Actaea*.

Banks, Sir Joseph (1743–1820)
English botanist. He was the senior scientist of the group that sailed to Tahiti with Captain James Cook aboard HMS *Endeavour* in 1768. At Botany Bay, Australia, in 1770, Banks collected examples of plants hitherto unknown in Europe, including the shrub BANKSIA, named in his honour. On his return, he helped set up the Royal Botanic Gardens at Kew, London, and financed international plant-collecting expeditions. In 1778 Banks became president of the Royal Society.

banksia
Any of *c*.70 species of flowering shrubs and small

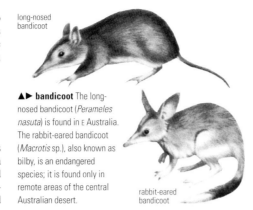

▲▶ bandicoot The long-nosed bandicoot (*Perameles nasuta*) is found in E Australia. The rabbit-eared bandicoot (*Macrotis* sp.), also known as bilby, is an endangered species; it is found only in remote areas of the central Australian desert.

long-nosed bandicoot

rabbit-eared bandicoot

trees found in Australia and New Guinea. Their evergreen leaves are long and leathery, and they bear tube-shaped heads of yellowish or reddish flowers. The genus was discovered by Sir Joseph BANKS. Family Proteaceae; genus *Banksia*.

banyan
Evergreen tree of E India. The branches send down aerial shoots that take root, forming new trunks. Such trunks from a single tree may form a circle up to 100m (330ft) across. Height: to 30m (100ft). Family Moraceae; species *Ficus benghalensis*.

baobab
Tropical tree native to Africa. It has a stout trunk containing water storage tissue, and short, stubby branches with sparse foliage. Fibre from its bark is used for rope. Its gourd-like fruit has edible pulp. Height: to 18m (60ft); trunk diameter: to 12m (40ft). Family Bombacaceae; species *Adansonia digitata*.

bar
Unit of pressure; the pressure created by a column of mercury 75.006cm high at 0°C (32°F). It is equal to 10^5 pascals. Standard atmospheric pressure (at sea level) is 1.01325 bars, or 1013.25 millibars.

Barbary sheep
See SHEEP, BARBARY

Barbary macaque
See MACAQUE, BARBARY

barbel (barb)
CARP-like freshwater fish of W Asia and S central Europe. A game and food fish, it has an elongated body, flattened underside and two pairs of fleshy mouth whiskers (BARBELS). It is a strong swimmer, well adapted to fast-flowing rivers. Length: 50–90cm (20–35in); weight: 16kg (35lb). Family Cyprinidae; species *Barbus barbus*.

barbel
Whisker-like appendage attached to the upper or lower jaw of a fish. It is covered by taste buds, allowing a fish to locate food in bottom sediments. Barbels are characteristic of many fish, including CATFISH and GOATFISH.

barberry
See BERBERIS

barbet
Any of *c*.80 species of brightly coloured perching birds related to the woodpecker. Barbets have large heads and large, stout bills. Despite their bold plumage they can be difficult to see, feeding in the tops of trees. They feed mostly on fruit, especially figs. Barbets are found in Africa and Asia. Length:

13–35cm (5–14in). Family Capitonidae; there are several genera, including *Megalaima*, *Trachyphonus* and *Lybius*.

barbet, blue-throated
Medium-sized, bright green barbet with a blue face, throat and upper breast and a black and red crown. Like many Asiatic barbets, it has a persistent, monotonous and loud "took-a-rook" call during the breeding season. It feeds mainly on figs in forest groves, often near habitation. Length: 23cm (9in). Family Capitonidae; species *Megalaima asiatica*.

barbet, coppersmith
Common green barbet found in Asia. It is small, with a crimson forehead and breast and yellow patches around the eye and throat. Its call is a loud, metallic and monotonous "tuk tuk", which is very familiar throughout Asian woodlands. Length: 17cm (7in). Family Capitonidae; species *Megalaima haemacephala*.

barbet, great
Largest species of barbet. It has a bluish head and red under-tail feathers. Its breast and back are brown; its tail and wings are green. The great barbet occurs in groups of five or six but may congregate in parties of 30 or more in fruit-laden trees. Length: 35cm (14in). Family Capitonidae; species *Megalaima virens*.

barbet, red and yellow
African barbet with brilliant, unmistakable plumage. It has a red head, an orange-red bill, yellow underparts and an orange and red rump; its black back and tail are spotted white. The red and yellow barbet has a loud cackling call, uttered in duet. Length: 25cm (10in). Family Capitonidae; species *Trachyphonus erythrocephalus*.

barbet, red-faced
African barbet with a red face and throat, brown back, white underparts and short bristles at the base of its heavy grey bill. It is found in woods and cultivated areas. Length: 15cm (6in). Family Capitonidae; species *Lybius rubrifacies*.

barbet, yellow-fronted
Medium-sized, mainly green barbet. It has a yellow forehead and crown and a short yellow stripe from the base of its bill; the sides of its face and throat are blue. The yellow-fronted barbet is found only in broadleaved forests and well-wooded gardens in Sri Lanka. Length: 21cm (8in). Family Capitonidae; species *Megalaima flavifrons*.

barchan
Crescent-shaped DUNE found in sandy DESERTS throughout the world where the wind is constant in speed and direction. Barchans also occur fairly frequently in coastal regions; they are quickly shifted by the wind, particularly when small.

barite
See BARYTE

bark
Outer protective covering of a woody plant stem. It is made up of several layers. The CORK layer, waxy and waterproof, is the thickest and hardens into the tough, fissured outer covering. Lenticels (pores) in the bark allow gas exchange between the stem and the atmosphere. *See also* CAMBIUM; DENDROCHRONOLOGY

bark bug
Any member of a family of insects within the true

B

bug order Hemiptera. They feed on the fungus growing on the bark of trees. Bark bugs are usually camouflaged to resemble the bark surface. They are dorso-ventrally flattened, with lateral lobes extending from their thoraxes and abdomens. Order Hemiptera; family Aradidae.

barklouse
Any member of the Psocoptera order within the class Insecta. Barklice are detritivores, feeding on fungi, algae and dead plant matter with their chewing mouthparts. As well as occurring on bark and other plant surfaces, they are sometimes found in libraries, but they generally cause little or no damage. Adult body length: 1–5mm (0.04–0.2in). Order Psocoptera. *See also* BOOKLOUSE

barley
Cereal GRASS native to Asia and Ethiopia, cultivated perhaps since 5000 BC. Three cultivated species are: *Hordeum distichum*, commonly grown in Europe; *H. vulgare*, favoured in the United States; and *H. irregulare*, grown in Ethiopia. Barley is eaten by humans and many other animals, and is used to make malt beverages. Family Poaceae/Gramineae.

barnacle (cirriped)
CRUSTACEAN that lives mostly on rocks and floating timber. Some barnacles live on whales, turtles and fish without being parasitic, although there are also parasitic species. The larvae swim freely until ready to become adults, when they settle permanently on their heads; their bodies become covered with calcareous plates. Two main types are those with stalks (**goose barnacles**) and those without (**acorn barnacles**). Subclass Cirripedia.

barn owl
See OWL, BARN

barracouta (snake mackerel)
Marine fish found in tropical and temperate waters; it is a deep-sea fish. The barracouta is a commercial food fish. It has a laterally compressed body, two dorsal fins and an elongated lower jaw filled with sharp teeth. Length: 1m (3.3ft); weight: 4–10kg (9–22lb). Family Gemphylidae; species *Thyrsites atun*.

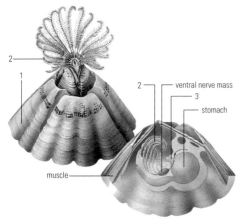

▲ **barnacle** Lying on its back, the barnacle is protected by a strong box of calcareous (calcium-based) plates (1). When the tide is out and it needs to avoid drying, the barnacle folds its limbs away inside. When the tide is in and it is ready to feed, the topmost hinged plates open and it kicks its legs about in the water. Each limb divides near its base into two separate branches or *cirri* (2), each bearing a dense array of tiny bristles (*setae*) that filter food particles from the water. After being waved about briefly in the water, the limbs are withdrawn and pulled towards the mouth (3).

barracuda
Marine fish found in tropical Atlantic and Pacific waters. Known to attack people, the barracuda has a large mouth with many large, razor-sharp teeth. It is long, slender and olive green. Length: usually 1.2–1.8m (4–6ft); weight: 1.4–22.7kg (3–50lb). The great barracuda of the Florida coast grows to 2.5m (8ft). Family Sphyraenidae; there are 20 species.

barrel cactus
Barrel-shaped CACTUS found in North America. Most have stout, hooked spines and obvious ribs. The flowers, which vary in colour, are usually fragrant. Smaller species with showy blooms are often kept as houseplants. Family Cactaceae; genera *Ferocactus* (height: to 3m/10ft) and *Echinocactus* (height: to 0.6m/2ft).

barrier reef
Long, narrow CORAL REEF lying some distance from and roughly parallel to the shore, but separated from it by a deep LAGOON. The Great Barrier Reef off the coast of Queensland, NE Australia, is the most famous.

Bartram, John (1699–1777)
US botanist, the first in North America to hybridize flowering plants. Bartram travelled the American colonies extensively, often with his son William, collecting plant specimens. The botanical gardens that he established near Philadelphia were internationally famous.

baryte (barite or heavy spar)
Barium-containing mineral, the chief ore of the metal. Barite consists of barium sulphate ($BaSO_4$). It usually occurs as white crystals, although it may be brown, grey or yellow, and is often found in association with lead or zinc ores. Because of its high density, barite is used to make muds for lubricating and cooling oil-well drilling equipment. It is also used in the chemical industry for paper-making, rubber manufacture and high-quality paints. Hardness 3–3.5; r.d. 4.5

basal metabolic rate (BMR)
Minimum amount of energy required by the body to sustain basic life processes, including breathing, circulation and tissue repair. It is calculated by measuring oxygen consumption. Metabolic rate increases well above basal metabolic rate (BMR) during vigorous physical activity, fever or under the influence of some drugs (including caffeine). It falls below BMR during sleep, general anaesthesia or starvation. BMR is highest in childhood and decreases with age.

basalt
Hard, fine-grained, basic IGNEOUS ROCK; it may be an intrusive or extrusive rock. Its colour can be dark green, brown, dark grey or black. If it originally solidified quickly it can have a glassy appearance. There are many types of basalt with different proportions of elements. It may be vesicular (porous), because of gas bubbles contained in the lava while it was cooling, or compact. If the vesicles are subsequently filled with secondary minerals, such as quartz or calcite, it is called amygdaloidal basalt. Basalts are the main rocks of ocean floors; on continental areas they form the world's major lava flows, such as the Deccan Trap in India.

base pair
Combination of two nitrogen-containing organic bases in a molecule of DNA. There are four bases in DNA: ADENINE, CYTOSINE, GUANINE and THYMINE.

▲ **bass** Large numbers of sea bass (*Dicentrarchus labrax*) are found in the NE Atlantic Ocean, but they also inhabit estuaries, rocks and reefs around the British Isles, for example. Their diet typically consists of shrimps, crabs and small fish, although larger bass may prey on species of whiting or cod.

Using hydrogen bonds, adenine always pairs with thymine, and cytosine always pairs with guanine. The pairs form the "rungs" of the double-helix structure of DNA and form the basis of the GENETIC CODE. RNA also has base pairs, but URACIL replaces thymine.

basic rock
Any IGNEOUS ROCK that contains a low proportion of silica (less than 55%). The main minerals, which include OLIVINE, PYROXENE and PLAGIOCLASE FELDSPAR, are ferromagnesian. Basic igneous rocks are generally dark in colour, such as BASALT and GABBRO, and are associated with the VOLCANISM of OCEANIC CRUST.

basidiomycete
Any member of the Basidiomycota phylum of FUNGI. Basidiomycetes include the jelly fungus, the BIRD'S NEST FUNGUS, the BRACKET FUNGUS, the ear fungus and MUSHROOMS. They reproduce through sexual spores (basidiospores) produced by a specialized cell called the BASIDIUM.

basidium
Cell that produces SPORES (basidiospores) used in sexual reproduction by certain types of FUNGI of the phylum Basidiomycota (BASIDIOMYCETES). Basidia are cylindrical or club-shaped, often grouped to form the external fruiting bodies (gills) of BRACKET FUNGI, MUSHROOMS and PUFFBALLS. Each basidium produces four spores.

basil
Common name for a tropical plant of the MINT family, the leaves of which are used for flavouring. It has white or purple flowers. Family Lamiaceae/Labiatae; species *Ocimum basilicum*.

basket flower
Perennial, bulb-forming plant found in the Andes mountains in Peru and Bolivia. It has several strap-shaped leaves and large, white flowers, up to 10cm (4in) across, in clusters of two to four. The anther filaments are joined to make a funnel-shaped cup structure with spreading fringed lobes. Family Amaryllidaceae; species *Hymenocallis calathina*. **Basket flower** is also the name given to a stout, rough-textured, annual plant distributed from Missouri and Louisiana, United States, to Mexico. Its solitary, daisy-like flower head is 7–13cm (3–5in) across. The flowers are pinkish to purple or sometimes white. Family Asteraceae; species *Centaurea americana*.

bass
Any of several bony fish, both freshwater and marine, not all closely related. Together they make up a valuable commercial and sport fish. They include the white, black, striped, rock and calico basses. The three main bass families are Serranidae, Moronidae and Centrarchidae.

bass, striped
Important game and food fish of the United States, found in coastal and estuarine waters of the Atlantic and Pacific oceans and the Gulf of Mexico. It ascends rivers to spawn. The striped bass is related to the white bass and white perch. The largest size that it is known to have reached is 57kg (125lb) in weight, 1.8m (6ft) in length. Family Percichthyidae or Moronidae; species *Morone saxatilis*.

basswood (American linden)
Tree with deeply furrowed bark and heart-shaped leaves, native to North America. The flowers are pendulous and sweetly scented. The wood has been used for furniture, and the tough inner bark as fibre for mats and ropes. Height: to 36m (120ft). Family Tiliaceae; species *Tilia americana*.

bastard breadnut
Tree of the mulberry family, mostly distributed in the tropics and subtropics. Members of this family produce a milky sap that contains latex. The bastard breadnut is useful for its edible fruit. Family Moraceae; genus *Pseudolmedia*.

bastard bullet tree
Member of a family of trees native to Central and tropical South America. It is the only member of economic importance: its durable, reddish-brown hardwood is used locally for construction. Family Houmiriaceae; species *Houmiria floribunda*.

bat
Any member of the only group of MAMMALS to have developed true flight. There are *c*.950 species in 19 families. Many bats use ECHOLOCATION to hunt their prey. They inhabit all areas of the world, except high mountainous areas and the most northerly and southerly latitudes.

bat (flying fox)
Any member of the group of mammals known as the Old World fruit bats; they are found in tropical and subtropical regions from Africa to Australia. The genus includes some of the largest bats, with wingspans of up to 2m (6.6ft). Their diet consists mainly of ripe fruit, but they will also take other plant material and insects. Old World fruit bats have drab brown fur, but some are brightly coloured, for example silver or red. Head-body length: 17–41cm (7–16in); they have no tail. Family Pteropodidae; genus *Pteropus*.

bat, blossom
Bat that inhabits wet, tropical forests in Australia and Indonesia, where it feeds on nectar and pollen. Head-body length: 5–7cm (2–3in). Family Pteropodidae; genera *Synonycteris* and *Macroglossus*.

bat, bulldog (fisherman bat)
Bat that is found near water in tropical or subtropical Central and South America and nearby islands. It may be found near lakes, streams or the sea. Bulldog bats have sharp claws on long legs for catching fish. The males have yellow or orange fur. Family Noctilionidae; genus *Noctilio*.

bat, disc-winged (New World sucker-footed bats)
Bat that is found in the tropical forests of South America. It has circular suckers on short stalks that extend from its wrists and ankles. Each one of these suckers can support the whole weight of the bat, gripping to the smooth surfaces of the large furled leaves in which the bat roosts. Head-body length: 3–5cm (1–2in); tail: 2–3cm (*c*.1in). Family Thyropteridae; genus *Thyroptera*.

bat, false vampire
Bat that is found in tropical regions of the Old World. False vampire bats feed on small vertebrates, spiders and insects. Unlike true vampire bats, which only suck the blood of their prey, false vampire bats eat the whole animal. They are among the largest of bat species and have very big ears. Head-body length: 6–14cm (2–6in). Family Megadermatidae. **New World false vampire bats** inhabit Central and South America. They are the largest bats to be found in the Americas. Family Phyllostomatidae.

bat, free-tailed
Bat that lives in warm and tropical regions worldwide. It is called "free-tailed" because its tail extends beyond the membrane stretched between its legs. Some species roost in groups numbering millions, others are solitary. They all feed on insects. Head-body length: 4–13cm (3–5in); tail: 1.5–8cm (0.6–3in). Family Molossidae.

bat, funnel-eared
Small insectivorous bat that lives in Central America, N South America and nearby islands. It has long fur and slender wings. The ears are large and funnel shaped. Head-body length: 3.5–5.5cm (1.4–2.2in); tail: 5–6cm (*c*.2in). Family Natalidae; genus *Natalus*.

bat, ghost
Bat that is found near water in Central and South America. It is unusual in being white or very pale in colour. It has large eyes, a short tail and small, round ears. Head-body length: 5–8cm (2–3in); tail: 1.2–2.5cm (0.5–1in). Family Emballonuridae; genus *Dicliduras*. The **Australian ghost bat** belongs to the family known as false vampire bats. It is very pale in colour and has no tail. As well as ECHOLOCATION, the Australian ghost bat uses its big eyes to identify its prey, which includes large insects and any small vertebrates, including other bats. It is found in a variety of habitats in N Australia. Head-

body length: 6–14cm (2–6in). Family Megadermatidae; species *Macroderma gigas*.

bat, ghost-faced
Bat found in SW United States, through Central America to Brazil. Unlike the ghost bat, the ghost-faced bat is usually reddish to dark brown. Its ears are round, meeting across its forehead. Its face is flattened and sculptured so that sounds bouncing off its prey are reflected into its ears. It feeds on flying insects, such as moths. Head-body length: 4–8cm (2–3in); tail: 1.5–3.5cm (0.6–1.4in). Family Mormoopidae; species *Mormoops melophylla*.

bat, horseshoe
Any of more than 60 species of bat found throughout Europe, Africa and Asia, mostly in tropical regions, with a few in more temperate areas. Horseshoe bats use the complex, horseshoe-shaped skin formation around their noses to direct sounds emitted through the nostrils as part of an ECHOLOCATION system. Their broad wings make them highly manoeuvrable for catching flying prey close to the ground. Head-body length: 3–11cm (1–4in); tail: 2.5–4.5cm (1–1.8in). Family Rhinolophidae; genus *Rhinolphus*.

bat, Kitti's hog-nosed (bumblebee bat)
Brown to reddish-grey species of bat, found in W Thailand. It is the smallest of all bats, possibly the smallest mammal in the world. It has relatively large ears, a pig-like nose and no tail. It roosts in small groups and is insectivorous. Head-body length: *c*.3cm (*c*.1in). Family Craseonycteridae; species *Craseonycteris thonglongyai*.

bat, leaf-nosed (trident bat)
Insectivorous bat that is found in tropical regions of Africa and Asia. Leaf-nosed bats are mostly drab grey-brown, but some are more brightly coloured. Head-body length: 2.5–14cm (1–6in); tail: 0–6cm (0–2in). Family Hipposideridae.

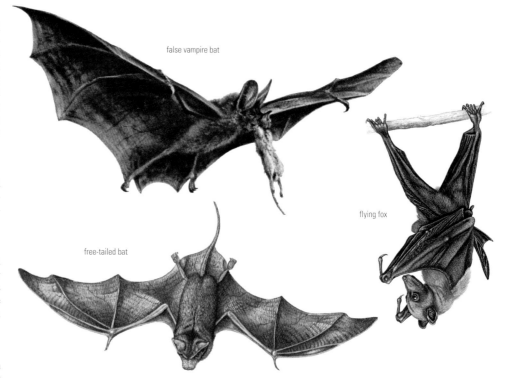

false vampire bat

flying fox

free-tailed bat

▲ **bat** The fierce-looking Linneas false vampire bat (*Vampyrum spectrum*) is the largest of the New World bats. Like other false vampire bats, it is tailless with a characteristic "horn" of skin on its snout and large ears. Several species of free-tailed bat hunt in large groups. The Mexican free-tailed bat (*Tadarida brasiliensis*) will travel up to 25km (40mi) in search of food. It can eat up to half its body weight in insects in one night. The grey-headed flying fox (*Pteropus poliocephalus*) of Australia grows to 40cm (16in) and has a wingspan of more than 1m (3.3ft). Flying foxes feed in groups on a variety of wild and cultivated fruits.

bat, long-eared

Bat that belongs to the family known as common or vesper bats. They are found in parts of Europe, Africa and Asia. Their ears can be almost as long as their bodies, but some tuck them away under their wings when resting. Long-eared bats are brown with paler underparts. Head-body length: 4–7cm (2–3in); tail: 3.5–5.5cm (1.4–2.2in). Family Vespertilionidae.

bat, mouse-tailed

Insectivorous bat that is found in dry, treeless regions from North Africa to the Middle East and Asia. It has a long tail, large ears and a pig-like nose. Mouse-tailed bats often congregate in large roosts. Head-body length: 5–9cm (2–4in); tail: 4.3–7.5cm (1.7–3in). Family Rhinopomatidae.

bat, sheath-tailed

Bat that is found worldwide, including on many islands in the Indian and Pacific oceans. Most species live in the tropics, and those that live in cooler climates may hibernate. Sheath-tailed bats are insectivorous, some catching their prey on the ground, but they may also feed on fruit. Head-body length: 3–10cm (1–4in); tail: 0.5–1.3cm (0.2–0.5in). Family Emballonuridae.

bat, short-tailed

Rare bat found in New Zealand and adjacent islands. Its varied diet includes fruit, nectar and insects. Not a particularly good flier, it hunts for most of its food on the ground. Short-tailed bats are unusual in having thumb and toe claws, which they use for running, climbing and burrowing for food. Head-body length: 6–8cm (2–3in); tail: 1.8cm (0.7in). Family Mystacinidae.

bat, slit-faced (hollow-faced bat)

Bat found in tropical regions from Africa to Indonesia. It has large eyes, broad wings and a tail with a split end. Its prey items are mostly insects, either terrestrial ones or those at rest on vegetation or walls. The bat's name derives from the groove that divides its complex nose structure. Head-body length: 4–8cm (2–3in); tail: 4–8cm (2–3in). Family Nycteridae; genus *Necteris*.

bat, spear-nosed

Bat with a spear-shaped extension on its nose and widely separated ears, native to Central and South America. It lives in a variety of habitats. All species are gregarious. Its food may include small vertebrates, insects, nectar and pollen. Head-body length: 7.5–13cm (3–5in); tail: 1–2.5cm (0.4–1in). Family Phyllostomatidae; genus *Phyllostomus*.

bat, sucker-footed

Bat found in Madagascar. It differs from other sucker-footed bats in that the adhesive discs on its wrists and ankles are not on short stalks. Head-body length: 5–6cm (c.2in); tail: 4.5–5cm (c.2in). Family Myzopodidae; species *Myzopoda aurita*. The disc-winged bat of South America (*see* BAT, DISC-WINGED) is sometimes referred to as the sucker-footed bat.

bat, thumbless

Any member of two genera of poorly known bats found in tropical Central and South America. The thumbless bat is brown-grey with a very small, insignificant thumb and funnel-shaped ears. It feeds on insects. Head-body length: 3–6cm (1–2in); tail: 2–3.5cm (c.1in). Family Furipteridae.

bat, vampire

Any of three species of bat native to tropical and subtropical areas of Central and South America. Using very sharp teeth, the vampire bat cuts small, painless incisions in the skin of mammals and birds and uses a specially shaped tongue to lap up blood. Head-body length: 6–9cm (2–4in); it has no tail. Family Desmodontidae.

bat, vesper (common bat)

Any of c.300 species of bat found throughout the world. Most species are insectivorous, catching their prey in flight, but some species of the genus *Myotis* catch fish. Some species are solitary, but others roost in colonies numbering more than a million. Head-body length: 3–10cm (1–4in); tail: 2.5–7.5cm (1–3in). Family Vespertilionidae.

bateleur

Colourful, long-winged, short-tailed EAGLE found in the sub-Saharan savannas of Africa. Its unusual flight, characterized by its habit of tilting from side to side, in the manner of a trapeze artist, explains its common name, which comes from the French for tightrope walker. The bateleur feeds on small mammals and reptiles, including snakes, and also takes carrion. Length: 60cm (24in). Family Accipitridae; species *Terathopius ecaudatus*.

Bates, Henry Walter (1825–92)

British naturalist. Bates' work on NATURAL SELECTION in animal MIMICRY lent support to Charles DARWIN's theory of EVOLUTION. Bates collected more than 8000 previously unrecorded species of insects during 11 years (1848–59) in the Amazon region. He recounted his experiences in *The Naturalist on the River Amazon* (1863).

Bateson, William (1861–1926)

British biologist. He founded and named the science of GENETICS. Bateson translated much of Gregor MENDEL's pioneering work on inheritance in plants, thus bringing it recognition. By his own experiments, Bateson extended Mendel's theories to animals and provided a foundation for the modern understanding of HEREDITY.

batfish

Any of 60 species of the family Ogcocephalida; a type of ANGLERFISH. Its highly specialized body is flattened and covered with spines. A poor swimmer, it uses its fins to "walk" along the seafloor. Some species of batfish occur in shallow water, but the majority are found at depths of 200–1000m (660–3300ft). Batfish are distributed in all tropical and subtropical regions. Order Lophiiformes

bat-fly

Member of either or two families of the true FLY order. They are wingless, with elongate, well-developed legs. Bat-flies are exclusively ectoparasites of bats. Order Diptera; families *Nycteribiidae* and *Streblidae*.

batholith

Huge mass of IGNEOUS ROCK at the Earth's surface that has an exposed surface of more than 100sq km (40sq mi). A batholith may originate as an intrusive igneous structure that has been gradually eroded to become surface material. Most batholiths consist of GRANITE rock types and are associated with the orogenesis (mountain-building phases) of PLATE TECTONICS.

bathyal zone

Region of the ocean floor from the edge of the CONTINENTAL SHELF, about 133m (436ft) in depth, to about 2000m (6560ft), where the ABYSSAL plain begins. Only a feeble light penetrates to the upper layers of this zone.

bathysphere and bathyscaphe

Manned vehicles for deep-sea exploration. The **bathysphere**, invented by Otis Barton and William BEEBE in the United States, had steel walls and thick, toughened glass windows through which underwater observations could be made. Used mainly during the 1930s, it was released from a surface vessel and was lowered on a steel cable to depths of more than 900m (3000ft). The **bathyscaphe** was invented by Swiss physicist August Piccard (1884–1962); it was first used in 1948. It consists of a bathysphere slung below a tank called a float. The whole device can be sunk or made buoyant in a controlled manner, while propellers move the craft horizontally. In January 1960

▼ **bathyscaphe** The *Trieste* was August Piccard's second bathyscaphe. It consisted of a steel observation gondola slung below chambers containing ballast or gasoline. To descend, various chambers filled with water. To ascend, the ballast was released into the water until the craft reached the surface.

Piccard and Don Walsh of the US Navy made a descent in the bathyscaphe *Trieste* to a depth of 10,916m (35,810ft) (approximately equivalent to the altitude of commercial jets) in the Pacific Ocean's Mariana Trench off the island of Guam. This record still stands.

bauhinia
Any member of a large group of tropical trees, shrubs and some climbers. The leaves may be entire or characteristically cleft into two lobes or distinct leaflets; the flowers range in colour from white to red, purple or yellow. Bauhinia is named after the 16th-century herbalists John and Caspar Bauhin, because the twin leaflets suggest two brothers. Family Caesalpiniaceae; genus *Bauhinia*.

bauxite
Rock from which nearly all aluminium is extracted. Bauxite is a mixture of several minerals, such as diaspore, gibbsite, boehmite and iron. It is formed by prolonged weathering and leaching of rocks containing aluminium silicates. Large deposits occur in the United States, France, Hungary, Guyana, Jamaica, Surinam, Italy, Greece, Russia, Azerbaijan and Kazakstan.

bay
Tree or shrub of the LAUREL family. The leaves of some varieties are used to flavour food. In classical tradition, head wreaths of bay leaves were awarded as tokens to conquerors. Family Lauraceae; species *Laurus nobilis*.

bay bar
Ridge of SEDIMENT that is deposited across the mouth of a bay. It is usually attached to the shore at each end. The deposit may be carried to the bar by LONGSHORE DRIFT, or it may be carried there by a river. When it grows large enough it may completely block the bay from the ocean, so that a DELTA forms on the landward side as further deposits pile up.

bayberry
Deciduous shrub that is native to the E United States. The bluish-white berries are covered with a thick layer of wax, which can be removed by boiling in water and used for the manufacture of candles. Height: to 3m (10ft). Family Myricaceae; species *Myrica pennsylvanica*.

bay rum
Aromatic tree from tropical West Indies, Venezuela and Guyana. It has leathery leaves and white flowers. The leaves yield an essential oil, known as bay oil or oil of myrcia, used in perfumery. The oil was formerly distilled with rum to make bay rum. Height: to 7.6m (25ft). Family Myrtaceae; species *Pimenta racemosa*.

baza (cuckoo falcon)
Small bird of prey, related to the KITE. There are five species of baza, found in Africa, Southeast Asia and Australia. The crested baza is found in the sw Pacific, New Guinea and NE Australia. Bazas have a notched bill, bright yellow eyes and a crest at the back of the head. Length: 40cm (16in). Family Accipitridae; genus *Aviceda*.

beach
Sloping zone of the shore that extends from the low-water line to the limit of the highest storm waves. The beach is covered by SEDIMENT, sand or pebbles. The sediment is derived from coastal EROSION or river ALLUVIUM.

beach flea
See SANDHOPPER

beach grass (marram grass)
Perennial grass that spreads by means of underground stems. It is found around the coasts of Europe on sand dunes, where it binds and consolidates drifting sand. It is sometimes cultivated in connection with soil conservation projects. Beach grass can be used for thatch, baskets, brooms and mats. Family Poaceae; species *Ammophila arenaria*.

beaded lizard
See LIZARD, BEADED

Beadle, George Wells (1903–89)
US geneticist. During his study of mutations in the bread mould *Neurospora crassa*, he and Edward TATUM found that genes are responsible for the synthesis of enzymes and that these enzymes control each step of all biochemical reactions occurring in an organism. For this discovery they shared with Joshua LEDERBERG the 1958 Nobel prize for physiology or medicine.

Beagle, HMS
British survey ship that carried Charles DARWIN as the ship's naturalist. HMS *Beagle* left England in December 1831 and for five years explored parts of South America and the Pacific islands. Darwin's observations formed the basis for his theory of EVOLUTION of species by NATURAL SELECTION.

bean
Name given to several leguminous plants and their seeds. Rich in protein, the seeds are commonly used for human or animal food. Varieties include BROAD BEAN (*Vicia faba*), FRENCH BEAN (*Phaseolus vulgaris*) and SOYA BEAN (*Glycine max*). The name is also applied to the seeds of non-leguminous plants that have a bean-like shape, for example COFFEE.

bean weevil
Stout-bodied, dull grey or brown BEETLE found worldwide. It lays eggs on bean pods and the hatched larvae bore into the beans. The bean weevil can breed all year round in stored dried beans. Length: up to 5mm (0.2in). Family Bruchidae; species *Acanthoscelides obtectus*.

bear
Member of a group of large carnivores. Bears are bulky and powerful, with large paws armed with sharp claws. They can catch and kill other mammals, birds and fish, but also eat a wide range of vegetable food. They have poor sight and only fair hearing, but an excellent sense of smell. Family Ursidae; there are seven species.

bear, American black
Bear distributed from Mexico to Alaska, but found predominantly in the north of this region. The American black bear actually comes in a variety of colours, from white to blue and black. Subspecies include the kermodes and glacier bear. They are omnivorous animals, feeding mainly on plant material but also taking carrion, fish and young hoofed mammals. Length: 130–180cm (51–71in). Family Ursidae; species *Ursus americanus*.

bear, Asian black
Bear that is similar to but slightly smaller than the American black bear. It inhabits mountainous, forested areas between Iran and Japan. It may be black, brown or reddish, with a distinctive v-shaped pale patch on the chest. It has larger ears than other bears. Like the American black bear, this Asian species is omnivorous but feeds mainly on plant material. Length: 140–170cm (55–67in). Family Ursidae; species *Selenarctos thibetanus*.

bear, grizzly (brown bear)
Most widespread species of bear. It is found in NW North America, from Scandinavia across Russia, and in mountainous areas elsewhere in Europe. Grizzly bears vary greatly in colour (from cream to black) and in weight. The white-tipped ends of the long hairs on their shoulders give them a grizzled appearance, hence their name. Length: 200–280cm (80–110in). Family Ursidae; species *Ursus arctos*.

bear, polar
Bear found in polar regions; it is the largest terrestrial carnivore. The polar bear feeds on seals and occasionally birds, eggs and whales. It is completely at home in the water, having partially webbed feet for swimming. Length: 200–300cm (80–120in). Family Ursidae; species *Ursus maritimus*.

bear, sloth
Bear found mainly in lowland forests of E India and Sri Lanka. It has a long, shaggy coat and long, curved claws, which allow it to hang upside down from branches like a sloth. Primarily nocturnal, this dark-coloured bear feeds on termites and other insects with its long tongue; it will also eat plant material and carrion. Length: 150–190cm (60–75in). Family Ursidae; species *Melursus ursinus*.

bear, spectacled
Bear that lives in forested mountainous regions of South

▲ **bear, spectacled** This bear (*Tremarctos ornatus*) is found in the Andes and is the only bear species of South America. Its distinctive facial markings vary from one animal to the next. An adept climber, it will ascend a 30m (98ft) palm, tear off the branches and descend to the ground to eat the leaves.

▶ **bedbug** The common bedbug is found all over the world, infesting houses and beds. Its bite causes irritation but, unlike other parasites, carries no disease.

America, as far south as Bolivia. It may be black or dark brown, with pale rings around the eyes like huge spectacles. It is omnivorous, feeding on small mammals, leaves and fruit. Length: 130–210cm (51–83in); females are much smaller. Family Ursidae; species *Tremarctos ornatus*.

bear, sun

Small, omnivorous bear found in Southeast Asia; it is the smallest species of bear in the world. It has a short, black coat with a crescent-shaped yellow mark on its chest and a light grey or orange muzzle. Its diet consists primarily of insects, such as bees and termites, but it also eats honey, fruit and small vertebrates. Length: to 120cm (47in). Family Ursidae; species *Ursus malayanus*.

bearberry

Trailing or creeping evergreen shrub native to cool regions of North America and Europe. The flowers are small, pink and lantern-shaped, produced in terminal clusters; the fruits are bright red berries, which, as the name suggests, are eaten by bears. The plant has also had many medicinal uses. Family Ericaceae; species *Arctostaphylos uva-ursi*.

beardtongue

Any member of a large group of herbaceous and shrubby perennials native to North America, many of which are grown as ornamentals, with various cultivars now available. The colourful flowers are produced in terminal racemes. The name "beardtongue"

refers to the fifth, sterile stamen, which is often bearded. Family Scrophulariaceae; genus *Penstemon*.

beard worm

See POGONOPHORAN

bear grass

Plant that is found in open woodlands and clearings of the W United States. The tiny, cream-coloured flowers are produced in a large, dense, elongated head above a clump of long, narrow, basal leaves. The leaves are traditionally used by Native North Americans to weave garments and baskets. Family Liliaceae; species *Xerophyllum tenax*.

bear's breech

Herbaceous perennial native to the Mediterranean region, grown in gardens as an ornamental and found naturalized along roadsides and railway banks. The leaves are produced in a basal rosette and the large white or purplish flowers are produced in sturdy spikes up to 1m (39in) tall. Family Acanthaceae; species *Acanthus mollis*.

Beaufort wind scale

Range of numbers from 0 to 17 representing the force of winds, together with descriptions of the corresponding land or sea effects. The Beaufort number 0 means calm wind less than 1km/h (0.62mph), with smoke rising vertically. Beaufort 3 means light breeze, 12–19km/h (8–12mph), with leaves in constant motion. Beaufort 11 is a violent storm, 103–117km/h (64–72mph), and Beaufort 12 is a hurricane, 118+km/h (73+mph), with devastation. Beaufort 13–17 indicates the force of the hurricane. The scale is named after its inventor, British Admiral Sir Francis Beaufort (1774–1857).

beaver

Either of two species of largely aquatic mammals.

They are some of the largest of the rodents. Beavers have flattened tails, which help them steer when swimming, and large chisel-like teeth for gnawing wood. Family Castoridae.

beaver, Canadian (North American beaver)

Large rodent that is found across North America from Canada to N Mexico. It has a distinctive, paddle-shaped, scaly tail and webbed hind feet. The Canadian beaver spends much of its time in the water, feeding on trees and aquatic plants and building dams across streams. Head-body length: 80–120cm (31–47in); tail: 25–50cm (10–20in). Family Castoridae; species *Castor canadensis*.

beaver, European (Asiatic beaver)

Rodent that was common throughout Europe and N Asia until the end of the 19th century, when it was hunted almost to extinction. The European beaver population, although still vulnerable, is now recovering. The animals live in burrows along wooded streams, rivers or small ponds. They build fewer dams than the North American species and are mainly nocturnal. Head-body length: 70–100cm (28–40in); tail: 30–40cm (12–16in). Family Castoridae; species *Castor fiber*.

beaver, mountain (boomer, sewellel)

Fully terrestrial, primitive rodent that is found in SW Canada and W United States; it is not closely related to other beaver species. The mountain beaver spends most of its life underground in burrows, from which it emerges only at night to collect vegetation for food, which may be stored in the burrow. Head-body length: 30–41cm (12–16in); tail: 2.5–4cm (1–2in). Family Aplodontidae; species *Aplodontia rufa*.

becard

Any of 16 species of birds that belong to the tyrant flycatcher family, found mainly in South and Central America. They feed mostly on insects, which they catch in flight. Becards inhabit dry scrub and open woodland. Length: 15cm (6in). Family Tyrannidae; genus *Pachyramphus*.

bêche de mer

See SEA CUCUMBER

bed

Layer of SEDIMENTARY ROCK greater than 1cm (0.4in) in thickness, representing a single episode of sediment deposition. The original sediment of a bed is usually deposited in a horizontal sheet.

bedbug

Broad, flat, wingless insect found worldwide. It feeds by sucking blood from mammals, including human beings. Bedbugs usually gorge themselves at night and remain hidden during the day. Length: to 6mm (0.24in). Order Heteroptera; family Cimicidae; species *Cimex lectularius*.

bedding plane

Dividing line between two different strata of SEDIMENTARY ROCK. A bedding plane generally indicates a slight change of rock type; each stratum would have been deposited over a period of years, and then consolidated to form a layer of rock.

bedrock

Solid rock that occurs below the soil and any REGOLITH (rock fragments). It is the C or D horizon in a soil profile (*see* SOIL HORIZON). On hillsides the bedrock may be only a few centimetres below the

---

BEE

Insect distinguished from other members of the order Hymenoptera, such as ants and wasps, by the presence of specially adapted hairs, with which they collect POLLEN; all bees feed their young NECTAR and pollen. Although the HONEYBEE and BUMBLEBEE are

social insects living in well-organized colonies, many other bee species are solitary. Found worldwide, except in polar regions, they are important pollinators of flowers. Entomologists recognize *c*.12,000 species, but only the honeybee provides the honey that we eat.

worker   queen   drone

▶ **The nest of** the honeybee consists of a number of wax combs suspended in a shelter, such as a hollowed-out tree. The cells of the outer edges of the comb (1) contain nectar mixed with saliva, which the workers fan with their wings to evaporate excess water before the cell is capped with wax; this mixture eventually turns into honey. Other cells are used to contain reserves of pollen (2). Developing larvae (3) in open cells are kept clean by worker bees to prevent fungal infestations. They are fed by young workers with

regurgitated food, and with honey and pollen from the storage cells. When a newly formed worker emerges from its cell it is fed regurgitated pollen and nectar from another worker (4). Its vacated cell is thoroughly cleaned and re-used. The queen (5), surrounded by a retinue of workers, rests on a group of capped cells, each of which contains a worker pupa. Eggs (6) are laid by the queen in the centre of the comb. When new queens are needed, the workers construct extra large cells at the edge of the comb (7) in order to accommodate them.

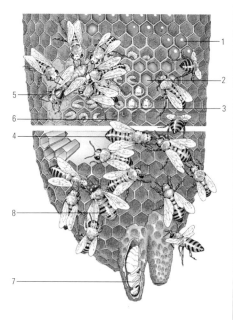

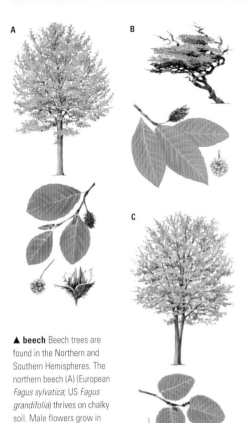

A B C

▲ **beech** Beech trees are found in the Northern and Southern Hemispheres. The northern beech (A) (European *Fagus sylvatica*; US *Fagus grandifolia*) thrives on chalky soil. Male flowers grow in clusters, separate from the female. The Antarctic beech (B) (*Nothofagus antarctica*) grows to 30m (100ft) and is found in the Andes, SE Australia and New Zealand. It differs from its northern cousin in being an evergreen species. The eastern beech (C) (*Fagus orientalis*) grows up to 36m (120ft) high and is found at lower elevations than the northern.

surface, whereas on prairies and plains it may be several metres down.

bedstraw

Any member of a large group of slender herbaceous plants found worldwide. The stems are often square in cross-section, producing small leaves in whorls; the tiny, four-petalled flowers may be yellow or white, produced in leaf axils or in terminal heads. The plants were once used for making bedding. Family Rubiaceae; genus *Galium*.

bee

See feature article

bee, bumble-

See BUMBLEBEE

bee, carder

Any of several species of BUMBLEBEE. As with other bumblebees, carder bees make nests that last for just one season in which the mated queen overwinters. Carder bees bite hairs from plants such as yarrow (*Achillea millefolium*) and use these in the construction of the cells of their nests. Carder bees are named after the process of carding used in textile production, in which a raw fibrous material is drawn out. Adult body length: 15–30mm (0.6–1.2in). Family Apidae.

bee, carpenter

Yellow and black to metallic-coloured bee. Found worldwide, it makes its nest in plant stems or wood. Larger carpenter bees resemble bumblebees in appearance. Family Apidae; subfamily Xylocopinae. Length: 6–25mm (0.2–1in).

bee, cuckoo

Social bee that is parasitic on BUMBLEBEES. There are no worker cuckoo bees, instead the bumblebee workers rear the young cuckoo bees. Cuckoo bees usually resemble their host but have less dense hair on their abdomens. Females have no pollen baskets and emerge after their host in the spring. Adult body length: 3–28mm (0.1–1.1in). Family Anthophoridae; genus *Psithyrus*.

bee, honey-

See HONEYBEE

bee, leaf-cutter

Bee that cuts semicircular notches in leaves to form egg cells within a nest. After mating in spring, solitary females lay between 35 and 40 eggs in a two-month lifespan. In North America, leaf-cutter bees are the favoured pollinators of alfalfa and oil seed rape because they are more efficient than honeybees. Adult body size: *c.*11mm (0.4in). Family Megachilidae; genus *Megachile*.

bee, mason

Solitary bee. After mating in spring, females build nests made from saliva and mud or plant fibre. The nests are usually built in aggregations. Adult body size: *c.*10mm (*c.*0.4in). Family Megachilidae; genus *Osmia*.

bee, mining (digger bee)

Member of the *Andrena* genus of bees. Solitary females excavate tunnels in soil. Branches are then dug off the tunnel and an egg, pollen balls and nectar are placed in each. With a relatively low fecundity, mining bees produce only one or two generations per year. Adult body size: *c.*10mm (*c.*0.4in). Family Andrenidae; genus *Andrena*.

bee, orchid

Tropical bee that gets its name from its pollinatory association with the orchid flower. It can travel up to 50km (30mi) a day pollinating flowers along a particular route. Orchid bees are among the most brilliantly coloured insects found in the Western Hemisphere. Adult body size: 8–30mm (0.3–1.2in). Family Apidae; genus *Euglossa*.

bee, solitary

Any of a group of non-colonial bees. After mating, the female constructs a nest with about 10 brood cells containing nectar and pollen. An egg is laid in each cell and the female dies before the nymphs emerge. Individual bees are solitary, but the females may make their nests close together. The activity of the solitary bee coincides with flower bloom, and after pollination the bee dies. Family Apidae; species include the hornfaced bee *Osmia cornifrons*.

bee, stingless

Any of a large group of highly social bees in which the sting is atrophied. The bees carry pollen and nectar, with the exception of species of *Lestrimellita*, which destroy nests of other species and steal pollen. Some species of *Trigona* obtain protein from dead animal flesh, which they collect and store in their nest. Subfamily Meliponinae; two tribes – Meliponini (containing genus *Melipona*) and Trigonini; there are 10 genera; species include *Melipona panamica*.

Beebe, Charles William (1877–1962)

US naturalist and explorer. He was the curator of ornithology (1899–1919) at the New York Zoological Gardens and director of tropical research (1919–52) at the New York Zoological Society. He led explorations in Central and South America, the West Indies and the Far East. Beebe also made undersea descents of 1000m (3300ft) in his invention, the BATHY-SPHERE. His numerous books include *Galápagos* (1923) and *Beneath Tropic Seas* (1928).

beech

Tree that is found in the Northern Hemisphere (genus *Fagus*) and the Southern Hemisphere (genus *Nothofagus*). Beeches have wide-spreading branches, smooth grey bark, and alternate, coarse-toothed leaves. Male flowers hang from thin stems; pairs of female flowers hang on hairy stems and develop into triangular, edible nuts enclosed by burs. The American beech (*Fagus grandifolia*) and the European beech (*Fagus sylvatica*) are important timber trees; their wood is used for furniture and tool handles. Height: to 36m (118ft). Family Fagaceae; there are 10 species.

bee-eater

Brightly coloured, long-winged, long-tailed, land bird. It feeds and nests in colonies. The adults have elongated central tail feathers and sharply pointed wings. Bee-eaters perch, watching for flying insects, and swoop, with long glides, to capture their prey. Family Meropidae; main genus *Merops*; there are 23 species.

bee-eater, Australian (rainbow bird)

Bee-eater that is found in open country throughout Australia. It has colourful plumage, with green back and forewing and copper-coloured flight feathers. It occasionally plunges into water after prey. Length 23–28cm (9–11in). Family Meropidae; species *Merops ornatus*.

bee-eater, carmine

Bee-eater that is found in wooded and bush country in Africa, often in gardens and along roadsides. Its combination of vivid, carmine pink plumage, green face and forehead and a dark mark through the eyes is distinctive. Length: 40cm (16in). Family Meropidae; species *Merops oreobates*.

bee-eater, European

Bee-eater that has harlequin plumage, mainly blue-green, with a chestnut head and back and a yellow rump and throat. In flight it has a conspicuous chestnut colouring under its wings. The European bee-eater often feeds at a great height so that only its far-carrying and distinctive "*prrritt*" call indicates its

▲ **bee-eater, carmine** Found in central Africa, this colourful, slender bird (*Merops oreobates*) nests in large tunnelled colonies in cliffs, usually near riverbanks.

B

► **beet** Several varieties of beet have been cultivated for different purposes. The beet root shown here is used in cooking; it is most often pickled or made into soup. Another variety, swiss chard, is grown for its edible leaves. Sugar beet is grown throughout the world and is an important source of sugar. The mangold is one of the oldest types of beet and is used as fodder for livestock.

presence. Length: 28cm (11in). Family Meropidae; species *Merops apiaster*.

beefwood (she-oak, Australian pine)
Any member of the *Casuarina* genus; a group of trees that are native to Asia, Australia and Polynesia, and widely naturalized elsewhere. Beefwood trees are grown ornamentally for their unusual foliage, which consists of long, drooping green, scale-like structures instead of leaves, and cone-like fruits. The name alludes to the red colour of the wood. Family Casuarinaceae.

beet
Vegetable that is native to Europe and parts of Asia and is cultivated in most cool regions. Its leaves are green or red and edible, although it is generally grown for its thick red or golden root, known as beetroot. Some varieties are eaten as a vegetable, others are a source of sugar, and some are used as fodder. Family Chenopodiaceae; species *Beta vulgaris*. *See also* SUGAR BEET

beetle
COLEOPTERAN insect characterized by horny front wings that serve as protective covers for the membranous hind wings. These protective sheaths are often brightly coloured. Beetles are usually stout-bodied, and their mouthparts are adapted for biting and chewing. They are poor fliers but (like all insects) are protected from injury and drying up by an EXOSKELETON. Beetles are the most numerous of the insects. More than 250,000 species are known, and new ones are still being discovered. Most species feed on plants, some prey on small animals, including other insects, whereas others are scavengers. Beetles undergo complete METAMORPHOSIS. Order Coleoptera. *See also* LADYBIRD; SCARAB BEETLE; WEEVIL

beetle, ambrosia
Wood-boring beetle, often considered a pest of various horticultural and ornamental plants, including peach and cherry trees. Adult females tunnel in the bark and wood of the host and create galleries in which the larvae mature. Adult body length: *c*.5mm (*c*.0.2in). Family Scolytidae; genus *Xylosandrus*.

beetle, bacon
Carpet beetle that is renowned for attacking dried foodstuffs, including bacon. Adults have a fine layer of yellow hairs on their ventral surface. A yellow band of hairs also extends onto the basal region of their dark brown elytra (wing cases). Adult body length: 10mm (0.4in). Family Dermestidae; species *Dermestes lardarius*.

beetle, bark (engraver beetle)
Small, brown to black beetle that tunnels through the inner bark and wood of trees. The tunnels of some

species form characteristic patterns, resembling engravings. Family Scolytidae.

beetle, bloody-nosed
Large, black, flightless leaf beetle. It gets its name from its habit of secreting a blood-red fluid if disturbed. Adult body length: 20mm (0.8in). Family Chrysomelidae; species *Timarcha tenebricosa*.

beetle, bombardier
See BOMBARDIER BEETLE

beetle, bruchid (seed beetle)
Member of a family of beetles that is widespread and common in both tropical and temperate regions. They are sometimes destructive pests of stored products, particularly legumes. Adult bruchid beetles lay their eggs inside seeds, and several larvae can mature there by feeding on the cotyledons contained within. Adult body length: 1–18mm (0.04–0.7in). Family Bruchidae.

beetle, buprestid
Member of a family of beetles known as jewel beetles. Many species are very brightly coloured and patterned, often with a cuticle that is iridescent or metallic in appearance. Buprestids are herbivorous; the larvae often tunnel in wood or other plant matter. Most species are tropical. Adult body length: 10–50mm (0.4–2in). Family Buprestidae.

beetle, burying (carrion beetle)
Medium-sized beetle found in temperate regions. It digs under the carcasses of small animals, burying them, and then lays its eggs in them. Family Silphidae; genus *Necrophorus*.

beetle, cardinal
Any of several species of beetle, mostly of the genus *Pyrochroa*, which are predatory on other insects. The cardinal beetle takes its name from the fact that the adults are bright scarlet – the colour of the robes often worn by cardinals. Adult body length: 12–15mm (0.5–0.6in). Family Pyrochroidae; main genus *Pyrochroa*.

beetle, carpet
Small beetle with brightly coloured scales. The larvae are extremely destructive, feeding on rugs, upholstery, stored clothing and other textile products. Adult body length: *c*.3mm (*c*.0.1in). Family Dermestidae; genera *Anthrenus* and *Attagenus*.

beetle, carrion
See BEETLE, BURYING

beetle, churchyard
Beetle that is sometimes found in church graveyards. It is one of the largest of the darkling family, and like many others in the family is flightless. Adult body length: *c*.20mm (*c*.0.8in). Family Tenebrionidae; species *Blaps mucronata*.

beetle, click (skipjack)
Any member of a large family of beetles, comprising more than 7000 species. Click beetles are elongate beetles of extremely varied coloration. Both adults and larvae are herbivorous and can be destructive to crops. An adult click beetle has a process on its thorax which neatly fits into a notch and catch mechanism located on its abdomen. This mechanism allows the insect to jump some distance, with an accompanying clicking sound, when it is disturbed. Adult body length: 2–20mm (0.08–0.8in). Family Elateridae.

beetle, Colorado
See COLORADO BEETLE

beetle, darkling
Member of a large family of beetles which vary greatly in shape and size. Most darkling beetles are black or very dark brown. They are found in nearly all terrestrial habitats, and some are adapted for dry conditions such as deserts and grainstores. When threatened, some species of darkling beetle can produce noxious chemicals. Adult body length: 2–45mm (0.08–1.8in). Family Tenebrionidae; genera include *Tenebrio* and *Tribolium*. *See also* BEETLE, CHURCHYARD; BEETLE, FLOUR; BEETLE, MEALWORM

beetle, deathwatch
See DEATHWATCH BEETLE

beetle, diving
Predacious aquatic beetle that is found worldwide. It has thread-like antennae and long hind legs adapted for swimming. It is one of the most ferocious freshwater carnivores. Adults and larvae feed on insects, tadpoles and small fish. Family Dytiscidae; genus *Dytiscus*.

beetle, dor
Stout, DUNG BEETLE with legs modified for digging. Female dor beetles excavate burrows under dung, then haul dung inside and lay eggs on it. In this way, they assist in the return of nitrates to the soil. The dor beetle known as the lousy watchman (*Geotrupes stercorarius*) is often infested with mites. Adult body length: 5–42mm (0.2–1.7in). Family Scarabaeidae; species include *Geotrupes stercorarius* and *Typhaeus typhoeus*.

beetle, drug-store
Small, hairy, brown beetle that attacks stored products. The larvae eat biscuits, bread, flour and drugs, particularly opiates. The beetles legs are short and can be drawn into special grooves. Adult body length: 1–8mm (0.04–0.3in). Family Anobiidae; species *Stegobium paniceum*.

beetle, dung
See DUNG BEETLE

beetle, engraver
See BEETLE, BARK

beetle, flea
Any of several small beetles found worldwide. Their enlarged hindlegs make them excellent jumpers. Flea beetles feed on leaves, and some are regarded as serious pests of crops. Family Chrysomelidae.

beetle, flour
Type of darkling beetle that is a pest of flour, cereal, dried fruit and chocolate products. Flour infested by the flour beetle's larvae is grey in colour and often turns mouldy. The female flour beetle can squeeze into tightly secured food packets, where it lays several hundred eggs, which require a high temperature (above 18°C/64°F) to develop. Adult body length: *c*.3mm (*c*.0.1in). Family Tenebrionidae; genus *Tribolium*.

beetle, fungus
Beetle that mostly feeds inside fruiting bodies of large fungi, fungus-infected rotting wood or stored produce. The elytra (wing cases) are usually a metallic black, green or blue, and in many species the head, pronotum (covering of the prothorax) and legs are reddish-brown. Adult body length: 3–25mm

(0.1–1in). Family Erotylidae; genera *Triplax*, *Dacne*, *Tritoma* and *Triplax*.

beetle, fur
Dull-coloured scavenger beetle; it is covered in hairs. It has short, club-ended antennae, which can be hidden in grooves on the underside of the thorax. Larvae of the fur beetle family are extremely hairy and sometimes called "woolly bears". Fur beetles feed on furs, carpet, stored grain and bird's nests. Adult body length: 10mm (0.4in). Family Dermestidae; genus *Attagenus*.

beetle, furniture
See FURNITURE BEETLE

beetle, grain-borer
Small beetle that feeds on grain and is a serious pest in grain stores. The grain-borer beetle is brown with blunt teeth on the sides of its thorax. Adult body length: *c*.3mm (*c*.0.1in). Family Silvanidae; species *Oryzaephilus surinamensis*.

beetle, harlequin
Brightly coloured longhorn beetle that is found in South America. The adults have extremely long antennae and feed on pollen or nectar. Their larvae are wood-boring and their burrows are large, with a circular cross-section. Harlequin beetles sometimes damage trees. Family Cerambycidae; species *Acrocinus longimanus*.

beetle, Hercules (rhinoceros beetle)
Tropical American SCARAB BEETLE. The male Hercules beetle has two horns – a long one on the head and a shorter one on the thorax. Length (including horn): to 160mm (6.3in). Family Scarabaeidae; species *Dynastes hercules*.

beetle, hide
Dull-coloured, hairy scavenger beetle; it is closely related to the fur beetle. The larvae of this family are sometimes called "woolly bears". The beetle's short, club-ended antennae can be hidden in grooves on the underside of the thorax. It feeds on hides and fur as well as stored foods. Adult body length: 10mm (0.4in). Family Dermestidae; species *Dermestes maculatus*.

beetle, Japanese
Beetle that is native to E Asia; it was accidentally introduced in North America in *c*.1916. Adults are greenish-bronze with coppery brown elytra (wing cases). Japanese beetles are serious crop pests, feeding on fruits and leaves of a great variety of plants. Eggs are laid in borrows 30–100mm (1–4in) deep. The cream-coloured to brown larvae feed primarily on grass roots and soil humus. Adult body length: 13mm (0.5in). Family Scarabaeidae; species *Popillia japonica*.

beetle, jewel
Brilliantly coloured beetle, the wing cases of which are sometimes used in embroidery and jewellery. They are distributed worldwide but are primarily tropical. The larvae chew wood, and many species are serious pests of trees. Adults feed on nectar or foliage and in some instances fungi. Adult body length: 2–65mm (0.08–2.6in). Family Buprestidae; genera *Melanophila*, *Anthaxia* and *Agrilusi*.

beetle, June (flower chafer)
Large green beetle found in North America. It is a serious farm and garden pest: the adults eat the leaves and fruit of many plants, and the stout, dirty-white larvae injure the roots of grasses, garden vegetables and ornamentals. Adult body length: *c*.25mm (*c*.1in). Family Scarabaeidae; species *Cotinus nitida*.

beetle, larder
Any member of a family of beetles often found in indoor food stores. They infest foods with a high protein content, such as dried meats and dead animals. There are many species of larder beetle and they are most active in spring, when they can be found outside. Adult body size: *c*.7mm (*c*.0.3in). Family Dermastidae.

beetle, leaf
Any member of a family of small, oval, leaf-feeding beetles. Many, including the COLORADO BEETLE, are yellow with black markings. They are important pests on potato crops. Adult body length: *c*.12mm (*c*.0.5in). Family Chrysomelidae.

beetle, longhorn
Any of numerous species of wood-boring beetles found worldwide, especially in the tropics. It has long antennae (up to twice the body length), long legs and a cylindrical body. The coloration varies according to the species, with some beetles resembling wasps or ants. The larvae have strong jaws and can cause great damage to trees. Adult body length: 3–150mm (0.1–6in). Family Cerambycidae.

beetle, May (June bug)
Any member of a genus of medium-sized, stout SCARAB BEETLES. The May beetle is brownish with shiny elytra (wing cases). It feeds on flowers and tree foliage. The larvae, known as white grubs, eat the roots of various crops and are one of the most destructive soil pests facing farmers. Adult body length: 13–25mm (0.5–1in). Family Scarabaeidae; genus *Phyllophaga*.

beetle, mealworm
Medium-sized darkling beetle that infests grain products such as flour. The larvae, known as mealworms, are bred as food for birds and insectivorous pets. Length: *c*.32mm (*c*.1.3in). Family Tenebrionidae; genus *Tenebrio*.

beetle, Mexican bean
Brown or yellow LADYBIRD beetle with 16 black spots on its elytra (wing cases). It feeds mainly on beans and is one of the few harmful ladybird beetles. Adult body length: 8–10mm (0.3–0.4in). Family Coccinellidae; species *Epilachna varivestis*.

beetle, minotaur
Beetle that breeds on rabbit and sheep dung, which it buries up to a depth of 150cm (60in). The adults are sexually dimorphic, with the male possessing three horns and females only two. The minotaur beetle is mostly active at night and is a strong flier. Adult body size: *c*.20mm (*c*.0.8in). Family Geotrupidae; genus *Typhaeus*.

beetle, net-winged
Any member of a family of beetles that are characterized by raised networks of lines, resembling netting, on their wingcases. The bright colour of the beetles advertises their acidic taste. Net-winged beetles are not fussy eaters and will predate insects and suck plant juices. Adult body size: *c*.7mm (*c*.0.3in). Family Lycidae.

beetle, oil (blister beetle)
Beetle that gets its name from the cantharidin layer that it secretes, which causes painful blisters on contact with skin. Larvae climb to flower-heads and attach to passing bees whereupon they parasitize their nests. Adult oil beetles are commonly found in alfalfa flowers. Adult body size: *c*.15mm (*c*.0.6in). Family Meloidae; genus *Lytta*; species include *Lytta vesicatoria* (Spanish fly).

beetle, pollen
Member of a family of small, scavenging, black beetles, which usually possess compact, three-segmented antennae. Pollen beetles swarm all over flower heads in the summer looking for pollen to eat. Adult body size: *c*.5mm (*c*.0.2in). Family Nitidulidae; genus *Meligethes*.

beetle, potato
See COLORADO BEETLE

beetle, rose (rose chafer)
Small, long-legged, tan SCARAB BEETLE that is found in E United States. It feeds on the fruit and foliage of grapes, peaches, roses and other fruit. The rose beetle's larvae burrow underground, where they feed on roots. Adult body length: 8–12mm (0.3–0.5in). Family Scarabaeidae; species *Macrodactylus subspinosus*.

beetle, rose chafer
Beetle that is found on a number of flowers including roses, which they are said to damage. The wing-shields (elytra) are a golden-green colour, sometimes coppery. The larvae are found in rotten stumps, leaf mould, old compost heaps and sometimes wood ant nests. Populations of rose chafer beetles have declined over the last twenty years. Adult body size: *c*.23mm (*c*.0.9in). Family Scarabaeidae; genus *Cetonia*.

◄ **beetle, Hercules** The fierce-looking Hercules beetle (*Dynastes hercules*) is the largest species of beetle. It is capable of picking up and throwing other males with its horn when defending territory or female beetles.

beetle, rove
Any member of a family of small, slender beetles distributed worldwide. They are found chiefly near decaying plant and animal matter. The rove beetle has short elytra (wing cases), which cover its functional wings. When distressed, it ejects a foul-smelling fluid from its abdomen. Family Staphylinidae.

beetle, scarab
See SCARAB BEETLE

beetle, screech
Beetle that, when disturbed, produces a loud squeak by rubbing the tip of its abdomen against a file under its wing-case. The screech beetle's aquatic larvae breathe through gills and are believed to feed mainly on tubifex worms. Adult body size: *c*.8mm (*c*.0.3in). Family Hygrobiidae; genus *Hygrobia*.

beetle, snapping
See BEETLE, CLICK

beetle, soldier
Any of a large group of fast-moving carnivorous beetles. They are usually narrow and elongated, with soft bodies. Their elytra (wing cases) are soft and often covered in short, downy hair. Many species are black and red, hence the beetle's common name. Their larvae are ground-dwelling. Superfamily Cantharoidea; family Cantharidae; species include *Cantharis rustica*.

beetle, spider
Beetle that has a rounded body and long legs, hence its common name. It inhabits birds' and other animals' nests and mainly scavenges insects. Several species of spider beetle are pests of stored material, such as grain and fabric. Family Ptinida; species include *Ptinus fur*.

beetle, stag
See STAG BEETLE

beetle, stone
Tiny, reddish-brown to black beetle; it is covered in long hairs. It has an ant-like body and a head with a distinct neck. Its elytra (wing cases) are oval and shiny and cover the abdomen. The family is closely related to the Staphylinidae. Some species of stone beetle feed on soil-dwelling mites; others live in ant or termite nests. They are nocturnal and typically found in moist, concealed spaces. Family Scydmaeidae; species *Eusphalarem*.

beetle, tiger
Any member of a family of active, usually strikingly coloured, medium-sized beetles. Adults and larvae prey on other insects. They are found worldwide, but most commonly in subtropical or tropical regions. Adult body length: 10–20mm (0.4–0.8in). Family Cicindelidae.

beetle, tobacco (cigarette beetle)
Beetle that attacks stored products, including tobacco. The eggs are white and laid on tobacco. The small (*c*.4mm/0.2in) larvae bore through the leaves to pupate in the damaged material. Adult tobacco beetles are red-brown, oval and good fliers. Their heads bend downwards, giving them a hump-backed look. Adult body length: 2–3mm (0.08–0.1in) Suborder Polyphaga; superfamily Bostrichoidea; family Anobiidae; genus *Lasioderma*.

beetle, tortoise
Small, oval beetle, with a distinctive tortoise-shaped appearance. The larvae are elongate-oval, flattened and covered in thorny, branched spines. Excrement, cast skins and other debris are collected on the larva's back, and when full, the tail curls over the back. If a predator attacks the larva, it releases its load. Both larvae and adult tortoise beetles are leaf-feeders. Family Chrysomelidae; species include *Plagiometriona clavata*.

beetle, wasp
Beetle that is black with yellow stripes, thus mimetically resembling a wasp. It also taps its antennae and moves like a wasp. The larvae tunnel in trees and other plants. Family Cerambycidae; species *Clytus arietis*.

beetle, water
See BEETLE, DIVING; BEETLE, WATER SCAVENGER; BEETLE, WHIRLIGIG

beetle, water scavenger
Oval, dark-coloured, aquatic beetle that is found in marshy fresh water worldwide. The adult eats decaying plant and animal matter. The larvae are carnivorous, feeding not only on other insects but also on other water scavenger larvae. The adult beetle is distinguished from the diving beetle by its club-shaped antennae. Adult body length: to 50mm (2in). Family Hydrophilidae.

beetle, whirligig
Medium-sized, dark-coloured water beetle often seen resting or gyrating in groups on the surface of a still pool. They prey on small insects and dive underwater when attacked. The larvae hatch underwater and have fringed gills; they leave the water to pupate. Family Gyrinidae.

beetroot
See BEET

begonia
Any member of the genus *Begonia*, which includes plants, shrubs and trees native to tropical America and Southeast Asia. Begonias make popular houseplants, with their white, pink or red flowers. There are three types: **rex**, with ornamental leaves of green, red and silver; **rhizomatous**, with fleshy, creeping stems and glossy leaves; and **basket**, with trailing stems and brightly coloured leaves. Family Begoniaceae; species include *Begonia semperflorens*.

behavioural ecology
Study of the complex relationship between environment and animal behaviour. This involves drawing on the disciplines of natural history to study the adaptive features of an organism within its habitat. Human behaviour is similarly studied. *See also* ADAPTATION; ECOLOGY; ETHOLOGY

beira
Rare dwarf ANTELOPE found in dry, rocky regions of Somalia and Ethiopia. The beira has a reddish-grey back with a distinctive dark band along its sides. It has very large ears and a long, white tail. Males have short, straight horns. Head-body length: 70–85cm (28–33in); tail: 14–20cm (6–8in). Family Bovidae; subfamily Antilopinae; species *Dorcatragus megalotis*.

belemnite
Member of an extinct group (order) of CEPHALOPODS that appeared in the Jurassic period (213–144 million years ago) and lived through the Cretaceous period (144–65 million years ago), with a few persisting into the early part of the Tertiary period (65–2 million years ago) up to about 45 million years ago. Entirely marine creatures, belemnites were characterized by a bullet-shaped, cylindrical shell.

belladonna
See DEADLY NIGHTSHADE

bellbird
Any of four species of the genus *Procnias* (family Cotingidae), native to the forests of Central and South America, or an Australian species belonging to the genus *Oreoica* (family Muscicapidae). They are all named after their loud resonating calls, which echo through the trees.

bellbird, crested
Bellbird species that is common throughout the interior of Australia. It is best known for its remarkable calls, which can differ between individuals and between districts. Brown above and whitish below, the male bellbird has a white forehead and throat and a slender black crest and breast band. Length: 20–23cm (8–9in). Family Muscicapidae; species *Oreoica gutturalis*.

bellbird, three-wattled
Bellbird species, the survival of which is threatened because its native habitat, forests in Central America, is being destroyed. The male bellbird is chestnut-brown with a white hood and has strange, black, leech-like wattles on its bill. The female bellbird is olive-green above and yellow below. The bellbird's call is a remarkably resonant "*bonk bonk*". Length: 25–30cm (10–12in). Family Cotingidae; species *Procnias tricarunculata*.

bellflower
Plant native to northern temperate regions and tropical mountains. It has bell-shaped flowers, alternate leaves and milky sap. Bellflowers are now widely cultivated. Family Campanulaceae; genus *Campanula*; there are 250–300 species.

beluga
See STURGEON; WHALE, WHITE

Benioff zone
Area of deep-focus EARTHQUAKES that dips from the Earth's surface to a depth of about 700km (450mi). The zone is thought to indicate areas of active SUBDUCTION of the Earth's tectonic plates. *See also* PLATE TECTONICS

benitoite
Glassy, blue to violet mineral, barium titanium silicate ($BaTi(SiO_3)_3$), found in San Benito, Texas, United States. It forms hexagonal system, tabular, triangular crystals and is a valuable gem when transparent and without flaws. Hardness 6-6.5; r.d. 3.6.

Bentham, George (1800–84)
British botanist. His classification of gymnosperms (seed plants) provided a foundation for modern systems of CLASSIFICATION. With William Hooker (1785–1865) Bentham wrote the multi-volume *Genera Plantarum* (1862–83), a definitive work in its time. His other works include *Handbook of British Flora* (1858).

benthos
Flora and fauna of the seabed. The fauna includes sedentary forms such as SPONGES, crawling animals such as CRABS and SNAILS, burrowing animals such as worms, and countless BACTERIA.

berberis (barberry)
Any member of a genus of *c.*450 species of shrubs native to temperate regions. The bark and wood are yellow, the stems are usually spiny, and the golden flowers give way to sour, blue berries. The stamens are sensitive to touch. It is a host for the plant diseases rust, especially those that attack cereal crops. Family Berberidaceae; genus *Berberis*.

bergamot orange
Dwarf form of the SEVILLE ORANGE, with oblong leaves and small, white, very fragrant flowers. The tree is cultivated for bergamot oil, which is made from the peel of the pear-shaped, pale yellow fruit, and oil of neroli, made from the blossom, both of which are used in perfumery. Family Rutaceae; species *Citrus aurantium* var. *bergamia*.

bergschrund
Deep, wide crevice or a series of parallel narrow crevices in a GLACIER. It is produced by tension within the ice, often at the point where the moving ice pulls away from the rock slope at the head of the glacier CIRQUE.

berm
Narrow ridge of debris above the foreshore. During storms, extra large waves carry debris up the beach so that it forms a narrow horizontal shelf or ridge above the normal high-water mark.

Bermuda buttercup
Perennial plant that is native to South Africa; it has become naturalized in Bermuda and elsewhere. The three-leafleted leaves and bright yellow flowers on long stalks arise from a short underground stem above a deep main bulb. The tuberous underground parts of the Bermuda buttercup are used as a vegetable in s Europe and North Africa. Family Oxalidaceae; species *Oxalis pes-caprae*.

Bermuda grass
Perennial grass from Europe and Asia, now spread worldwide. A creeping grass, it spreads by means of extensive networks of RHIZOMES and STOLONS. Its species name, "*dactylon*", refers to the three to five dactyls (fingers) of the inflorescence. Bermuda grass is used as a lawn and pasture grass in warm climates; it has become an invasive weed and roadside cover in some areas. Family Pooaceae; species *Cynodon dactylon*.

Bernard, Claude (1813–78)
French physiologist. His research was primarily concerned with metabolism and neurology. Bernard defined the role of the pancreas in digestion, the role of the liver in regulating blood sugar levels and carbohydrate stores, and the regulation of blood supply by vasomotor nerves. His work was important in establishing how a body maintains its constant internal conditions despite a changing external environment. In 1860 Bernard published his influential *An Introduction to the Study of Experimental Medicine*. He was elected to the Académie française in 1868.

berry
Many-seeded, fleshy FRUIT in which the wall has a skin-like outer covering (exocarp). The exocarp is often brightly coloured in order to attract birds and other animals, which ingest the fruit and so help disperse the digestive-resistant seeds. The middle layer (mesocarp) of the berry is thick and succulent while the inner layer (endocarp) is membranous. Examples include many fruits regularly eaten by humans, such as tomatoes, gooseberries, blackcurrants and grapes. The term is also applied to eggs of many CRUSTACEA, including CRAYFISH and LOBSTER.

berrypecker
Small, brightly coloured bird that is found only in the dense mountain forests of Papua New Guinea. Length: 15cm (6in). Species include the painted berrypecker and the fan-tailed berrypecker. Family Melanocharitidae.

beryl
Mineral, beryllium aluminium silicate. Its crystals are usually prisms of the hexagonal system. Gemstone varieties are aquamarine (pale blue-green) from Brazil; emerald (deep green) from Colombia; and morganite (pink) from Madagascar. Cut stones have little brilliance, but are valued for their intense colour. Hardness 8; r.d. 2.6–2.8.

betel nut
Tall, slender PALM native to Malaysia, but widely cultivated wherever the nuts are used. The hard seed is sliced, rolled in betel pepper leaves and mixed with lime to form the traditional masticatory of the East; the betel habit has a long history and was first described in 340 BC. Height: to 23m (75ft). Family Arecaceae; species *Areca catechu*.

betony
Herbaceous perennial, native to moist fields, open woodlands and hedgerows of Europe and North Africa. It has aromatic leaves and small purple flowers clustered in a terminal spike. It has been considered a panacea for all ills since ancient times and is used as a home remedy. Family Lamiaceae; species *Stachys officinalis*.

betta
See FIGHTING FISH

bettong (woylie)
Common name for several species of RAT KANGAROO found in grasslands and woodlands of Australia. It eats plant material and insects. Woylie refers in particular to the species *Bettongia penicillata*. Head-body length: 28–45cm (11–18in); tail: 25–33cm (10–13in). Family Potoroidae.

bichir
Any of 10 species of fish confined to the freshwaters of central and w tropical Africa and the Nile River system. The bichir has an elongated body with a characteristic series of dorsal finlets and fleshy pectoral fins. Length: to 1m (39in). Family Polypteridae; genus *Polypterus*.

biennial
Plant that completes its life cycle in two years, producing flowers and seeds during the second year; an example is the ONION. It is different from an ANNUAL, which germinates, flowers, fruits and dies in one season, and a PERENNIAL, a plant that lives for three years or more.

bignonia
Any member of a genus of woody, tendril-bearing climbers mostly from tropical N South America, although one species is native to SE United States. Bignonia are grown as ornamentals for their beautiful, trumpet-shaped flowers, which can be up to 9cm (3in) across, with flaring lobes of various colours. Height: to *c.*15m (*c.*50ft). Family Bignoniaceae; genus *Bignonia*.

bilberry (blueberry or whortleberry)
Deciduous evergreen shrub native to N Europe and E North America. It produces a small, dark purple fruit. Family Ericaceae; genus *Vaccinium*.

bilby
See BANDICOOT, GREATER RABBIT-EARED

bile
Bitter, yellow, brown or green, alkaline fluid that is secreted by the LIVER of vertebrates and stored in the GALL BLADDER. Important in DIGESTION, it enters the duodenum via the bile duct. The bile salts it contains emulsify fats, allowing easier digestion and absorption, and neutralize stomach acids. Its

◄ **benthos** The flora and fauna of the seabed can be brilliantly colourful, especially in tropical regions, as demonstrated by the nudibranch *Hypselodoris bullockii* shown here, which is found from the Maldives to Thailand and Australia. The water temperature, salinity and depth all affect the type and abundance of animals and plants found on the seabed.

B

▲ **bindweed** Black bindweed (*Polygonum convolvulus*), shown here, is commonly found in cultivated fields in Europe. It trails along the ground or, like field bindweed (*Convolvulus arvensis*), twines itself around crops.

colour comes from the breakdown products of erythrocytes (red blood cells).

binary fission
See FISSION

bindweed (convolvulus)
Climbing plant with white or pink trumpet-shaped flowers. Family Convolvulaceae; species include *Calystegia sepium* (hedge bindweed) and *Convolvulus arvensis* (field bindweed).

binomial nomenclature
System of categorizing organisms by giving them a two-part Latin name. The first part of the name is the GENUS and the second part (together with the first part) the SPECIES. For example, *Homo sapiens* is the binomial name for humans; *Homo* is the genus and *Homo sapiens* is the species name. The system was developed by the Swedish botanist Carolus LINNAEUS in the 18th century. *See also* CLASSIFICATION; TAXONOMY

binturong (bear cat)
Carnivorous mammal found in the dense rainforests of Southeast Asia and Indonesia. It is a very good climber and has a thick, prehensile tail. Black with long white whiskers, the binturong feeds at night, on fruit and small animals. Head-body length: 60–95cm (24–37in); tail: 60–90cm (24–35in). Family Viverridae; species *Arctictis binturong*.

biochemical oxygen demand (BOD)
Chemical test for determining the level of pollution of water by organic matter. Two equal samples of water are taken, and the first is treated chemically to "mop up" any dissolved oxygen. Both samples are then incubated in the dark for some days, after which the second sample is given a similar chemical treatment. This allows the amount of "mopped-up" oxygen to be measured. The difference between the two measurements represents the amount of oxygen that has been used up by living and dead organic matter in the water during the period of storage.

biochemistry
Science of the chemistry of life. Biochemistry attempts to use the methods and concepts of organic and physical chemistry to investigate living matter and systems. Biochemists study both the struc-

ture and the properties of all the constituents of living matter (such as FATS, PROTEINS, ENZYMES, HORMONES, VITAMINS, DNA, CELLS, MEMBRANES and ORGANS) together with the complex reactions and pathways of these in METABOLISM.

biodegradable
Property of a substance that enables it to be decomposed by microorganisms. The end result of the decomposition is stable, simple compounds, such as water and carbon dioxide. This property has been designed into products such as plastics to aid refuse disposal and reduce pollution.

biodiversity
Wide variety of plant and animal species, genetic strains and the ECOSYSTEMS that support them. The maintenance of biodiversity is a major aim of conservationists concerned about ecological stability and biological research. It is estimated that less than 10% of the Earth's surface is host to nearly 75% of its species. Many of the world's most species-rich habitats, such as RAINFORESTS and WETLANDS, are also the most threatened by human development.

bioelectricity
Electricity generated in plants and animals. In animals bioelectricity is associated with nerve impulses and muscle contractions. Different electric potentials are built up within the organism by the process of ionic separation across a membrane. Some fish have electric organs that create more powerful external currents used for sensing or to stun prey.

biogas
Fuel gas derived from the decomposition of biological material. It is a mixture consisting mainly (up to 60%) of METHANE, which is combustible, with some carbon dioxide. It is formed by the ANAEROBIC breakdown – termed FERMENTATION – of waste matter such as domestic and agricultural sewage. The waste is contained in a digester where it is acted on by METHANOGENIC BACTERIA.

biogenesis
Biological principle maintaining that all living organisms derive from parent(s) generally similar to themselves. This long-held principle was originally established in opposition to the idea of SPONTANEOUS

BIOLOGICAL CLOCK

Internal system in animals and plants that relates behaviour to certain rhythms. Functions, such as growth, feeding or reproduction, coincide with certain external events, including day and night, tides and seasons. This innate sense of timing makes some animals feed during the day when food is available and they can see best. These "clocks" seem to be set by environmental conditions, but if organisms are isolated from these conditions, they still function according to the usual rhythm. If conditions change gradually, the organisms adjust their behaviour gradually. *See also* BIORHYTHM; CIRCADIAN RHYTHM

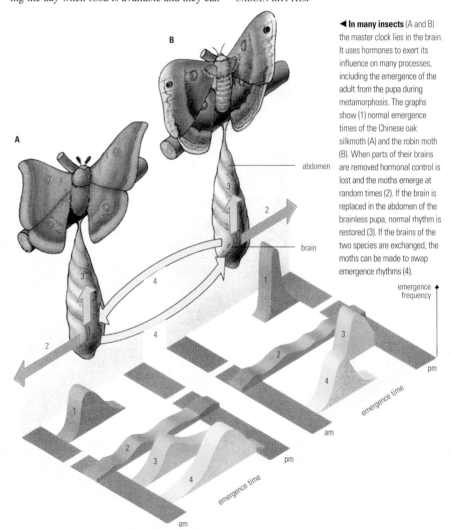

◄ **In many insects** (A and B) the master clock lies in the brain. It uses hormones to exert its influence on many processes, including the emergence of the adult from the pupa during metamorphosis. The graphs show (1) normal emergence times of the Chinese oak silkmoth (A) and the robin moth (B). When parts of their brains are removed hormonal control is lost and the moths emerge at random times (2). If the brain is replaced in the abdomen of the brainless pupa, normal rhythm is restored (3). If the brains of the two species are exchanged, the moths can be made to swap emergence rhythms (4).

GENERATION of life. On the whole, it still holds good, despite variations in individuals caused by MUTATIONS, HYBRIDIZATION and other GENETIC effects.

biogenetic law (recapitulation theory)
Principle that the stages that an organism goes through during embryonic development reflect the stages of that organism's evolutionary development.

biogeography
Study of the geographical distribution of plants and animals.

biological clock
See feature article

biological control
Use of biological methods to control pests. Usually the term describes the deliberate introduction of a PARASITE or other natural enemy of the pest; it is often preferred to the use of chemical pesticides. Examples include the introduction of ladybirds to kill scale insects on citrus crops in the United States, and the use of cactus moth caterpillars to control prickly pear cactus on Australian farmland. In another method, successfully employed to control screw worm flies that parasitize cattle, male flies sterilized by radiation are released into the natural population to produce a reduction in the fly population (because of the preponderance of sterile matings). Parasitic wasps are also commercially available to gardeners to control white fly and aphids in greenhouses. Care has to be taken with biological control so as not to upset the natural ecological balance.

biological fuel
Fuel that is derived directly from PHOTOSYNTHESIS and is, therefore, renewable. Plant material can be converted by bacterial FERMENTATION into fuels such as METHANE, methanol and ethanol. The process can use discarded parts of food plants or plants that have no food value. The gasohol programme in Brazil uses sugar cane waste to produce motor vehicle fuel. Animal manure, human sewage and other domestic and industrial wastes can be converted into useful fuels such as methane using BIOGAS digesters. *See also* FOSSIL FUEL

biology
Science of life and living organisms. Its branches include botany, zoology, ecology, physiology, cytology, genetics, taxonomy, embryology and microbiology. These sciences deal with the origin, history, structure, development and function of living organisms, their relationships to each other and their environment, and the differences between living and non-living organisms.

bioluminescence
Production of light, with very little heat, by some living organisms. Its biological function is varied: in some species, such as FIREFLIES, it is a recognition signal in mating; in others, such as SQUID, it is a method of diverting predators for protection; and in deep-sea ANGLERFISH it is used as a lure to attract prey. The light-emitting substance (luciferin) in most species is an organic molecule that emits light when it is oxidized by molecular oxygen in the presence of an enzyme (luciferase). Each species has different forms of luciferin and luciferase.

biomass
Total mass (excluding water content) of the plants and/or animals in a particular place. The term is often

BIOTECHNOLOGY

Use of biological processes for medical, industrial or manufacturing purposes. Humans have long used yeast for brewing and bacteria for products such as cheese and yogurt. Biotechnology now enjoys a wider application. By growing microorganisms in the laboratory, new drugs and chemicals are produced. GENETIC ENGINEERING techniques of cloning, splicing and mixing genes facilitate, for example, the growing of crops outside their normal environment, and the production of vaccines to fight specific diseases. Hormones are also produced, such as insulin for treating diabetes.

ripe tomato

new variety

◄ **In a ripe** tomato, rotting is caused by an enzyme formed by the copying of a gene in the plant DNA (1) in a messenger molecule mRNA (2). The mRNA is changed into the enzyme (3), which damages the cell wall (4). In a genetically altered tomato, a mirror duplicate of the gene that starts the process is present (5). The result is that two mirror-image mRNA molecules are released (6) and they bind together preventing the creation of the rotting enzyme. The result is longer-lasting tomatoes. Introducing the necessary DNA through the rigid cell wall is accomplished by using a bacteria (7) that naturally copies its own DNA onto that of a plant. It is easy to introduce the mirror DNA (8) into the bacteria and once the bacteria has infected the cell the DNA is transferred (9). All cells then replicated have the new DNA in their chromosomes and can be grown to create the new variety of plant.

used to refer to the totality of living things on Earth; or those occupying a part of the Earth, such as the oceans. It may also refer to plant material that can be exploited, either as fuel or as raw material for an industrial or chemical process.

biome
Natural and extensive community of animals and plants (FAUNA and FLORA), the make-up of which is determined by the type of soil and the climate. There is usually distinctive, dominant vegetation and characteristic climate and animal life. Ecologists divide the Earth (including the seas, lakes and rivers) into ten biomes. *See also* ECOSYSTEM

bionomics
Study of the relationships of an organism (or a population of organisms) to its living and non-living environment. *See also* ECOLOGY

biophysics
Study of biological phenomena in terms of the laws and techniques of physics. Techniques include those of X-ray diffraction and spectroscopy. Subjects studied include the structure and function of biological molecules, the conduction of electricity by nerves, the visual mechanism, the transport of molecules across cell membranes, muscle contraction (using electron microscopy) and energy transformations in living organisms.

biorhythm
Any regular pattern of changes in METABOLISM or

activity in living things. These are usually synchronized with daily, monthly, seasonal or annual changes in the environment. Examples of daily, or circadian, rhythms are the opening and closing of flowers, feeding cycles of animals during the day or the night, the response of marine organisms to the tides and, in humans, changes in body temperature and blood pressure. Monthly changes include the MENSTRUAL CYCLE in some female primates. Annual rhythms include HIBERNATION, MIGRATION and reproductive activity. The internal mechanism of these rhythms (sometimes referred to as the BIOLOGICAL CLOCK) is not yet fully understood.

biosphere (zone of life)
Portion of the Earth from its CRUST to the surrounding ATMOSPHERE, encompassing and including all living organisms, animal and plant. It is self-sufficient except for energy and extends a few kilometres above and below sea level.

biosynthesis
Process in living CELLS by which complex chemical substances, such as PROTEINS, are made from simpler substances. A GENE "orders" a molecule of messenger RNA to be made, which carries the genetic instructions from the DNA. On the RIBOSOMES of the cell, the protein is built up from molecules of amino acids, in the order determined by the genetic instructions carried by the messenger RNA.

biotechnology
See feature article

B

biotite

Common mineral of the MICA group. It is a silicate of aluminium, iron, potassium and magnesium. Its colour ranges from greenish-brown to black. Its lustrous, monoclinic-system crystals are opaque to translucent, and cleave to form flexible sheets. Biotite is found in IGNEOUS ROCK (such as granite), METAMORPHIC ROCK (such as schist and gneiss) and SEDIMENTARY ROCK.

bipedal (lit. having two feet)

Ability to walk on two legs, as do humans. The trait may have developed in early humans because it enabled them to see over the grassland vegetation in which they developed. Whatever the reason, it freed the use of the forelimbs from locomotion, enabling them to be used to manipulate various implements.

birch

Any of c.40 species of trees and shrubs native to cooler areas of the Northern Hemisphere. The double-toothed leaves are oval or triangular with blunt bases and are arranged alternately along branches. The smooth, resinous bark peels off in papery sheets. Male catkins droop, whereas smaller female catkins stand upright and develop into cone-like clusters with tiny, one-seeded nuts. Species include the grey, silver, sweet and yellow birches. Height: up to 30m (98ft). Family Betulaceae; genus *Betula*.

bird

See feature article, pages 42–43

bird cherry

Deciduous shrub or tree native to the woods and scrubs of Europe and Asia. Several cultivars have been developed as ornamentals for streets and gardens. The fragrant white flowers are clustered along elongated terminal racemes. The bitter fruit is shiny black, round and berry-like. Height: to 18m (60ft). Family Rosaceae; species *Prunus padus*.

bird-eating spider

See SPIDER, BIRD-EATING

bird louse (chewing LOUSE)

Any of c.3000 species of small, flattened insects of the order Mallophaga. They are distinguished from the sucking lice in that they do not suck blood and are not such harmful transmitters of disease. Bird lice have mouths designed for chewing and are found on the feathers, skin or hair of their hosts. Despite their name, more than 300 species of bird lice are parasites of mammals.

bird of paradise

Solitary, rather crow-like forest bird, named after its very beautiful and elaborate, colourful plumage. The males establish territories, called "leks", where they display with complex mating dances to attract mates. Birds of paradise inhabit the forested highlands of Papua New Guinea and neighbouring islands; a few species are found in N Australia. Family Paradisaeidae; there are 45 species.

bird of paradise, blue

Endangered species of bird of paradise from central New Guinea. It has extraordinary plumage with feathery, bright-blue plumes, combined with two long streamers that arch over its body in an upside-down display. Length: 30cm (12in). Family Paradisaeidae; species *Paradisaea rudolphi*.

bird of paradise, king

Relatively small species of bird of paradise. The male's plumage is bright red above and pure white beneath. Two plumes extend from the tail in a lyre shape. It is found mainly along rainforest edges in New Guinea. Length: 16cm (6in). Family Paradisaeidae; species *Cicinnurus regius*.

bird of paradise, king of Saxony

Bird of paradise found on New Guinea. Its plumage is mainly dark, with a yellow breast, but the head is adorned with two very long, arching plumes, up to 50cm (20in) in length. Length: 22cm (9in). Family Paradisaeidae; species *Pteridophora alberti*.

bird of paradise, magnificent

Bird of paradise from NW New Guinea. The male has dark, rather iridescent plumage, with a golden back and two spiral tail plumes. The female is mainly brown and barred. The male displays on low branches. Length: 17cm (7in). Family Paradisaeidae; species *Diphyllodes magnificus*.

bird of paradise, raggiana

Bird of paradise found in the rainforests of New Guinea. The adult male has a trailing mass of bright orange plumes, a green chin and a yellow crown and nape; the female is a dull brown. The males indulge in a communal display, including a sequence in which the birds hang upside down. Their flight is rather clumsy. Length: 32cm (13in). Family Paradisaeidae; species *Paradisaea raggiana*.

bird of paradise, ribbon-tailed

Bird of paradise from New Guinea; it was first described in 1939. The male has long, mainly white, trailing tail feathers, up to c.1m (c.40in) long. Length: 35cm (14in). Family Paradisaeidae; species *Astrapia mayeri*.

bird of paradise, sickle-crested

Bird of paradise found in high-level cloud forests of New Guinea. It has a crest adorned with fine plumes. The male's plumage is bright orange-red above and dark beneath. Length: 25cm (10in). Family Paradisaeidae; species *Cnemophilus macgregorii*.

bird of paradise, superb

Bird of paradise that inhabits the rainforests of New Guinea. The male is black, with iridescent blue, wing-like breast feathers, which fan out into a shield, and a velvety cape around the nape. The female is dull-coloured. Length: 25cm (10in). Family Paradisaeidae; species *Lophorina superba*.

bird of paradise, twelve-wired

Long-billed bird of paradise from the New Guinea highlands. The male has iridescent blue and bright yellow plumage, with twelve, long, narrow, wire-like plumes, which are spread forwards during the display. Length: 25cm (10in). Family Paradisaeidae; species *Seleucidis melanoleuca*.

bird of paradise flower

Perennial plant native to South Africa and cultivated widely for its brilliantly coloured, curiously shaped flowers. The condensed flower spike is enclosed in a boat-shaped, stiff, green and pink sheath, from which the orange and blue flowers arise in succession. Family Musaceae; species *Strelitzia reginae*.

bird of prey

Bird that usually has a sharp, hooked beak and curved talons with which it captures its prey. Two orders of birds fit this description: the Falconiformes (HAWKS, FALCONS, EAGLES, VULTURES and SECRETARY BIRD); and the Strigiformes (OWLS).

bird sanctuary

Aviary or natural habitat that is kept primarily as a refuge for birds that might otherwise be in danger of extinction.

bird's head

One of a large group of perennial herbaceous or woody climbers found in tropical and warm temperate forests and scrublands of Eurasia and the Americas. Bird's head is cultivated for its curiously shaped and coloured flowers and its variegated foliage. Family Aristolochiaceae; species *Aristolochia ornithocephala*.

bird's nest

FUNGUS that gets its name from its nest-like fruiting body, which, when mature, forms a deep cup 4–8mm (0.16–0.3in) across; the membranous cover sloughs off to expose several off-white 1–2mm (0.04–0.08in) "eggs" containing the spores. Bird's nest fungus colonizes wood, twigs and other vegetable remains, often with several fruiting cups together. Phylum Basidiomycota; species *Crucibulum laeve*.

bird's nest orchid

Saprophytic ORCHID native to Britain and Ireland; it has no chlorophyll. It is found amongst leaf-litter in woods, often beechwoods on calcareous soils. Its brownish leaves are small and scale-like and its flowers pale brown. Height: to 50cm (20in). Family Orchidaceae; species *Neottia nidus-avis*.

birth (parturition)

Bringing forth of live, partly or fully formed offspring. All mammals (except the echidna and the platypus), some reptiles and sharks, and various insects and other invertebrate animals give birth to live young (*see* VIVIPARITY). All birds, most reptiles, amphibians and fish, and the majority of insects lay eggs from which the live young later emerge. This process is called hatching (*see* OVIPARITY). In humans, birth involves the delivery of the FETUS at the end of pregnancy. There are three stages in this process. First, contractions of the uterus begin and the cervix dilates in readiness; the sac containing the amniotic fluid ruptures. In the second stage the contractions strengthen and the baby is propelled (usually head first) through the birth canal. The third and final stage, once the baby has been born, is the expulsion of the placenta and fetal membranes, together known as the afterbirth.

birthwort

Fetid, herbaceous perennial distributed from Europe to N Asia, occasionally introduced into the wild in North America and Britain. It has large, heart-shaped

B

leaves. Its curiously shaped, yellow flowers consist of a curved tube with an oblong limb at the end. Long cultivated as a medicinal plant, it has been used as an aid in childbirth. Family Aristolochiaceae; species *Aristolochia clematitis*.

bishop

Dumpy, brightly coloured bird of the WEAVER family, found in Africa. Bishops inhabit grassland, savanna and woodland, although some are found near water. Their plumage is red, yellow or black, depending on the species. They usually nest in loose colonies. Of the several species, the red bishop (*Euplectes orix*) is one of the most common. Length: 12–14cm (5–5.5in). Family Ploceidae; genus *Euplectes*.

bishop's-weed

See GROUND ELDER

bison

Two species of wild OX that formerly ranged over the grasslands and open woodlands of most of North America and Europe. Family Bovidae; genus *Bison*.

bison, American

Bison native to North America, sometimes inaccurately known as buffalo. Its head, which cannot be raised to shoulder level, is broad and massive and it has a prominent shoulder hump. It lives in small groups and feeds mainly on grass. Females give birth to usually one calf in May after a gestation of nine months. Once numbered in millions, the American bison was hunted almost to extinction in the 19th century by white settlers. It is now a protected species. Height (males): *c*.200cm (*c*.80in); weight (males):

c.900kg (*c*.1980lb); females are much smaller. Family Bovidae; species *Bison bison*.

bison, European (wisent)

Bison native to the woodlands of Europe. Reduced to two herds by the 18th century, it now survives in protected areas. It is more massive and has a shaggier coat than the American bison. Length: to 350cm (138in); height: to 300cm (118in); weight: to 1350kg (2980lb). Family Bovidae; species *Bison bonasus*.

biting midge (punkie)

Any member of the *Culicoides* genus of ceratopogonid MIDGES. The biting midge is a small fly with piercing mouthparts, with which it feeds on the blood of vertebrates, including humans. The larvae mature in water-logged soils. Adult body size: 2–7mm (0.08–0.3in). Order Diptera; family Ceratopogonidae; genus *Culicoides*.

bitter aloe

Any member of a large group of Old World tropical and South African plants of the genus *Aloe*. They have stiff, basal rosettes of spiny-edged, fleshy leaves. The showy red or yellow flowers are clustered on tall stems above the leaves. A bitter laxative drug is made from the juice of certain aloe leaves. Family Liliaceae.

bitterling

Deep-bodied, freshwater fish native to Asia Minor and central Europe. The female deposits her eggs in the mantle cavities of clams and mussels for hatching. Length: to 7.5cm (3in). Family Cyprinidae; species *Rhodeus sericeus*.

▲ **bison** The American bison (*Bison bison*) was almost hunted to extinction by European settlers who wanted to free the land for farming and deprive some of the Native Americans of their herds. Strict conservation programmes subsequently have ensured the survival of large numbers of this animal in protected areas.

bitter melon

Twining vine with deeply lobed leaves, native to tropical Asia. Its fruits are oblong, up to 20cm (8in) long, green or orange-yellow and covered with blunt warts; they split open when mature to display seeds with scarlet arils. The fruits are used as a vegetable in pickles and curries. Family Cucurbitaceae; species *Momordica charantia*.

bittern

Stocky bird of the HERON family, found in reedbeds and marshland. It has highly camouflaged, brown-streaked plumage. When disturbed, it stands stiffly erect, with its bill pointed skywards, and is extremely difficult to see. Bitterns feed on small fish, amphibians and invertebrates, which they catch with their dagger-like bills. Length: 64cm (25in). Family Ardeidae; main genus *Botaurus*.

bittern, American

Brown-streaked, skulking bittern. It has a diagnostic black streak down the sides of its neck and dark wing tips. The American bittern often feeds in the open. Despite its typically slow, ponderous flight, it migrates annually to Europe from North America. Length: 60–75cm (24–30in). Family Ardeidae; species *Botaurus lentiginosus*.

bittern, Australasian

Bittern found in SE Australia, Tasmania and New Zealand. Darker than most bitterns, it has camouflaged plumage that resembles old leaves. It is often called "boomer" because of its unusual call, which is thought to have inspired Native Australian legends. The bittern is partly nocturnal but will feed by day. Length: 66–76cm (26–30in). Family Ardeidae; species *Botaurus poiciloptilus*.

bittern, European

Very shy, owl-like bittern. The European bittern is more often heard than seen, uttering a low mooing or "booming" song like a distant foghorn or cow. Confined to large reedbeds, it only feeds in the open in hard weather. This species is becoming rare in Europe due to drainage of its habitat. Length: 70–80cm (28–31in). Family Ardeidae; species *Botaurus stellaris*.

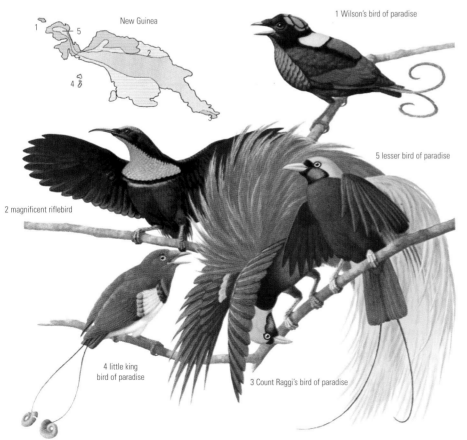

New Guinea

1 Wilson's bird of paradise

5 lesser bird of paradise

2 magnificent riflebird

4 little king bird of paradise

3 Count Raggi's bird of paradise

▲ **birds of paradise** The Paradisaeidae family of birds is descended from a crow-like species which migrated from Asia to New Guinea in prehistoric times. The male bird of paradise performs an elaborate courtship display, which involves ruffling the feathers on his neck and breast; some species, like the king bird of paradise, also have elongated tail feathers for attracting females. In preparation for a display which may last for several hours, the male clears an area on the ground, using the branches of young sapling as perches. The female builds the nest and raises the chicks.

irds are feathered vertebrates making up the class Aves; there are c.8600 species. They occupy most natural habitats, from deserts and tropics to polar wastes. They are ENDOTHERMIC (warm-blooded). All birds are remarkably similar in basic structure, in that their body-plan evolved primarily as an adaptation for flight. Even the flightless species evolved from ancestors that could fly, and therefore they share many typical features. Birds' bones are light and strong, and the skeleton has the form of a rigid box, with a large breastbone, or sternum. They have forelimbs modified as wings, hindlimbs for walking and jaws elongated into a toothless beak. The really unique feature of birds, however, is their covering of feathers. No other vertebrates have these extraordinary outgrowths, which, in all their modifications, provide birds with many attributes.

Birds lay EGGS (usually in NESTS), incubate the eggs and care for young. As a group they feed on seeds, nectar, fruit and carrion, and hunt live prey ranging from insects to small mammals, although individual species may be very specialized in their diet. Sight is the dominant sense, smell the poorest. Size ranges from the bee HUMMINGBIRD, 6cm (2in) long, to the wandering ALBATROSS, whose wingspread reaches 324cm (128in). The 2.5m (8ft) tall OSTRICH is the largest of living birds, but several extinct flightless birds were even bigger.

Of the 27 orders of birds, the perching birds (Passeriformes) include more species than all others combined. There are several groups of large flightless birds, including the ostrich, RHEA, EMU, CASSOWARY, KIWI and PENGUIN. Birds are descended from theocodonts (reptiles); the first fossil bird, ARCHAEOPTERYX, dates from late Jurassic times. *See also* ANSERIFORM; APODIFORM; APTERYGIFORM; CAPRIMULGIFORM; CHARADRIIFORM; CICONIIFORM; COLUMBIFORM; CUCULIFORM; GALLIFORM; PASSERIFORM; PICIFORM; PROCELLARIIFORM; PSITTACIFORM; STRIGIFORM; and individual species

clavicle
scapula
pelvic girdle
femur
pygostyle
tarsus

tibia
coracoid
humerus
sternum

radius
ulna
carpals
carpometacarpus

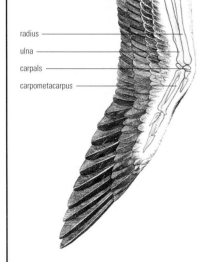

◀ **The skeleton of** an albatross (A) shows how birds are perfectly adapted for flight. The structure of many of a bird's bones (B) is designed to be light but strong. The bones of the wings, for example, are hollow but have supporting "struts" (1) to provide strength. The modified forelimbs (wings) differ most radically from a human's arms in the hand and wrist region. The bird's "fingers" have fused together forming a narrow structure called the carpometacarpus, which increases wingspan and improves lift. The wrist bones of birds (carpals) are strong and flexible. This improves mobility and enables birds to make aerial manoeuvres. The fused clavicles, the scapula and coracoid ensure that the base of the wings is kept in position away from the body. The deep sternum provides a good anchor point to which are attached the powerful pectoralis muscles used in flight. As well as being attached to the pelvic girdle, a bird's vertebrae, apart from those of the neck, are fused together, providing a strong but light frame specialized for flight. The bones of a bird's skull (C and D) have a honeycomb structure to reduce weight.

FILTER FEEDING

Flamingoes feed by lowering their heads into the water so that their bills are upside down (1). Its crooked shape allows the front half of the bill to lie horizontally in the water (2). Tiny hook-like lamellae (3) strain food as the water is pumped through them by a backward and forward motion of the tongue. Protuberances on the tongue (4) scrape the particles of food off the lamellae for ingestion as the tongue moves back and forth.

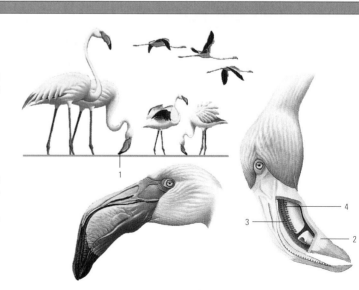

B

EGGS

A hen's fertilized ovum moves from the ovary (1) into the enlarged head of the oviduct (2). First it passes along the main section of oviduct, or magnum (3), the walls of which add layers of egg white (albumen). After about three or four hours, it enters another section, called the isthmus (4), where the egg and shell membranes are deposited. The shell itself forms over the egg in a wider section of the oviduct just beyond the isthmus. This is called the uterus (5), or shell gland, and the process of shell formation takes about 20 hours. The egg is laid through the cloaca (6), by contractions of the vagina.

Eggs vary enormously in shape and size:
1) wood warbler
2) dunnock
3) blackbird
4) tawny owl
5) Egyptian vulture
6) emu
7) ostrich

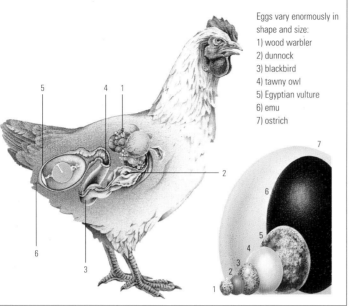

NESTS

Weaver birds live in warm regions of Europe, w Asia and North Africa. The weaver birds' nest is built by the male. Using no adhesive, he loops, twists and knots leaf strips to make an enclosed hanging structure. Starting with a ring attached to a forked twig (1), he gradually adds a roof and entrance (2). When the finished nest is accepted by the female, she inserts soft, feathery grass tops or feathers to make a thick, soft lining around the egg chamber base. "Weaving" the nest is a little misleading, since the green leaves used are rarely over three times the bird's length. Young male birds' first nests tend to be untidy; gradually, however, they learn how to make neater and better nests, using good vision and well-coordinated head movements to direct claws and beak to manipulate the nest material. The leaf fastenings the bird uses include half-hitch knots and slip knots.

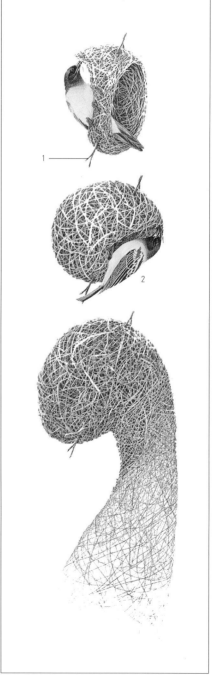

▲ **Many birds (A)** show astonishing range, quality and agility in their singing. A bird's respiratory system is very complex; its relatively small lungs (1) are supplemented by connected unmuscled air-sacs (2) filled or emptied by the chest muscles. To sing, a bird first closes a valve in one of the two bronchi (3) between the lung and syrinx (4, and enlarged B), or voice box, allowing it to compress air in the sacs. Air pressure in the clavicular sac (5) surrounding the syrinx (B) forces (6) very fine tympanic membranes (7) into the bronchial passage (8), briefly closing it. Muscles in the syrinx (9) then tense (10 and 11), opposing air pressure in the sac and pulling the membrane back to reopen the bronchial passage. Air rushes across the tensed membrane, vibrating it in song. As tension grows, so the song's pitch rises, just as a drum's note rises as its skin gets tenser — though the bird's song is more versatile. (Each pair of syrinx muscles of songbirds works independently, allowing different notes to be sung in each bronchial passage or a note in one and nothing in the other.) The highly tenses muscles at (11) produce a higher note than at (10), where the muscles create less tension across the membrane. If the membrane is too taut it stops vibrating, letting air pass through silently.

B

▲ **blackcurrant** An ingredient in desserts and drinks, blackcurrants are widely grown in the UK. It is a less popular crop in North America, where the cultivation of one species (*Ribes nigrum*) has led to the spread of white-pine blister rust.

bittern, little
Small, skulking bittern that ranges from Europe, parts of Africa, through Asia to Australia. It has a dark back and crown, cream underparts and prominent whitish wing patches. It may climb about the reeds like a giant warbler. Length: 30cm (12in). Family Ardeidae; species *Ixobrychus minutus*.

bitter-root
Small, herbaceous plant native to w North America; it is the state flower of Montana. It has deep pink to white flowers on short stalks within a rosette of narrow, succulent leaves. It was first collected by Meriwether Lewis, of the Lewis and Clark expedition, and is named after him. Family Portulacaceae; species *Lewisia rediviva*.

bittersweet
See NIGHTSHADE

bivalent
Describing a pair of HOMOLOGOUS CHROMOSOMES formed during MEIOSIS

bivalve
Any animal of the class Bivalvia. Bivalves have a shell with two halves or parts hinged together. The term most usually applies to a class of molluscs – Pelecypoda or Lamellibranchiata – with left and right shells, such as CLAMS, COCKLES, MUSSELS and OYSTERS. Bivalve can also refer to animals of the phylum Brachiopoda (BRACHIOPOD) with dorsal and ventral shells.

Bjerknes, Vilhelm Friman Koren (1862–1951)
Norwegian meteorologist. He laid the foundation of a revolution in weather forecasting by applying theories of fluid forces and motions to the circulation of the atmosphere with the development of air masses, fronts and cyclones.

blackband iron ore
Thin seam of dark-coloured iron ore that occurs in layers of coal. Historically it was important to the development of iron and steel industries and often accounted for the location of smelters near coal mines. Once the blackband ore was exhausted, iron ore had to be imported and it became more economical to locate steel works near ports.

black bear
See BEAR, AMERICAN BLACK; BEAR, ASIAN BLACK

blackberry (bramble)
Fruit-bearing bush native to northern temperate regions. The prickly stems may be erect or trailing, the leaves oval and toothed, and the blossoms white, pink or red. The edible berries are black or dark red. Family Rosaceae; genus *Rubus*.

blackbird
Familiar European garden and woodland song bird of the THRUSH family. The male is mat black with a yellow-orange bill; the female is speckled dark brown. Length: 25cm (10in). Family Turdidae; species *Turdus merula*. **Blackbird** is also the name given to a number of similar Asiatic species in the thrush family, such as the grey-winged blackbird. Family Turdidae; genus *Turdus*.

blackbird, red-winged
North American bird more closely related to ORIOLES than thrushes. Males are glossy black with red shoulder patches. The females and young are heavily streaked grey-brown. In winter, red-winged blackbirds roam in immense flocks, which cause considerable damage to crops. Length: 22cm (9in). Family Icteridae; species *Agelaius phoeniceus*.

blackbuck
GAZELLE that inhabits semidesert or open woodland in India and Pakistan; it is one of the fastest land mammals. Male blackbucks can be very dark and have long, spiral horns; females are paler with no horns. Blackbucks live in herds numbering up to about fifty. Head-body length: 100–150cm (40–60in); tail: 10–17cm (4–7in). Family Bovidae; subfamily Antilopinae; species *Antilope cervicapra*.

blackcap
WARBLER that is found in Europe, Asia and Africa. It takes its name from the jet black cap of the male; the female's cap is chestnut brown. The blackcap has a pleasant song – a jangly warble ending in a fluted, high-pitched phrase. Blackcaps are common in European woodland and also in gardens with tall trees. Those birds breeding in the northern part of the range usually migrate south for the winter. Length: 14cm (5.5in). Family Sylviidae; species *Sylvia atricapilla*.

blackcurrant
Shrub found in woods and along shady streamsides in N Europe, central and N Asia. The lobed leaves are scented when crushed, and the small greenish-white flowers hang in clusters, producing round black fruits. The medicinal properties of the leaves and fruits were recorded in 17th-century English herbals. Family Grossulariaceae; species *Ribes nigrum*.

black earth
See CHERNOZEM

black-eye
Small, insectivorous bird that inhabits high-mountain heathlands in Borneo. It belongs to a family known as WHITE-EYES, most of which have a white ring surrounding the eye, but in this particular species, the eye is set in a black patch. Length: 11cm (4in). Family Zosteropidae; species *Chlorocharis emiliae*.

black-eyed Susan
Herbaceous, perennial, twining plant from tropical Africa; it is now naturalized widely in the tropics and is also grown as an ornamental. The striking, trumpet-shaped flowers have black or purple centres and yellow, orange or pale-cream petals. Black-eyed Susan gets its scientific name from the Swedish botanist Carl Thunberg. Family Acanthaceae; species *Thunbergia alata*. **Black-eyed Susan** is also the name given to a hairy, herbaceous, biennial plant found in the fields, prairies and open woods of E United States. Its daisy-like flower heads have a conical brown centre and showy, golden-yellow ray flowers. Family Asteraceae; species *Rudbeckia hirta*.

blackfish
Name given to several different fish. A freshwater fish from Siberia and Alaska, species *Dallia pectoralis*, is sometimes known as blackfish. A number of dark-coloured marine fishes, including sea BASS, are called blackfish, as are small toothed WHALES of the genus *Globicephala*.

blackfly
See APHID, BEAN

black gum
Deciduous tree that is native to swamps and damp ground in E North America; it is grown as an ornamental in North America and Europe. Its leaves turn brilliant orange and red in autumn. The wood has been used to make wheel hubs, boxes, bowls and baskets. Height: to 30m (100ft). Family Nyssaceae; species *Nyssa sylvatica*.

black henbane
Poisonous, unpleasant-smelling, annual or biennial herb, native to Europe, Asia and North Africa; it has been introduced into North America. It produces bell-shaped, purple-veined, yellow flowers on terminal spikes. Black henbane has a long history of medicinal use; it contains the powerful alkaloids hyoscyamine and scopolamine. Family Solanaceae; species *Hyoscyamus niger*.

black Jack
Annual herb that is native to South America and spread widely as a sometimes noxious weed; it is a member of the bur-marigold group. Its leaves are opposite and pinnate, and the achenes possess two or sometimes three characteristic bristles. Family Asteraceae; species *Bidens pilosa*.

black oak
Deciduous tree native to E North America. Its leaves, which are a dark, shiny green above, can be up to 25cm (10in) long. Acorns are half enclosed by a cup fringed with loose scales around the edge. The bark is used as a source of tannin and the yellow dye quercitron. Height: 23m (75ft). Family Fagaceae; species *Quercus velutina*.

black smoker
See HYDROTHERMAL VENT

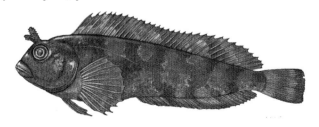

◀ **blenny** Like other species of blenny, the tompot blenny (*Blennius gattorugine*) lives in rocky areas in shallow water and is frequently encountered by divers. It has a set of sharp teeth and feeds on a variety of small animals that live on the sea bed.

◀ **black wattle** Flowering by a roadside in Queensland, Australia, is the black wattle (*Acacia decurrens*). The name wattle is applied to many Australian acacia trees. It comes from Anglo-Saxon and recalls the early English settlers' use of the trees' timber to make their "wattle and daub" huts.

Commonly called the hollow ball of cells stage, it occurs at or near the end of CLEAVAGE and precedes the GASTRULA stage. The blastula stage in mammals is known as a blastocyst or germinal vessel.

blazing star (gayfeather)
Herbaceous perennial native to North America. Its stiff, narrow leaves and rose-purple or white flowers are produced on tall, showy spikes or racemes in late summer or autumn; some species are grown as ornamentals. Family Asteraceae; genus *Liatris*.

bleeding heart
Any of five species of DOVE that are native to Southeast Asia. Rather dainty birds, bleeding hearts take their name from the bright red patch on their chests, which gives the impression that the bird is injured. This red patch is used during courtship displays. Length: 28cm (11in). Family Columbidae; genus *Gallicolumba*.

bleeding heart
Ornamental plant native to Japan; it is grown in gardens for its attractive flowers and foliage. The soft, compound leaves and pale green stems are somewhat fleshy. Bleeding heart produces drooping racemes of pink and white, heart-shaped flowers. Height: to 0.6m (2ft). Family Fumariaceae; species *Dicentra spectabilis*.

blenny
Marine fish that is found in shallow and offshore waters of all tropical and temperate seas. Often scaleless, with a long dorsal fin, it is olive green with varicoloured markings. Length: to 30cm (12in). Family Blenniidae.

blackthorn (sloe)
Tree or shrub of the ROSE family. It bears white flowers early in the year and has small plum-like fruits (sloes) and long black thorns. Family Rosaceae; species *Prunus spinosa*.

black walnut
Deciduous tree that is native to central and E United States; it is grown as an ornamental in Europe. Black walnut's dark brown wood is used to make furniture, musical instruments and boats. The nut meats are regarded as superior in flavour to English walnut. Height: to 30m (100ft). Family Juglandaceae; species *Juglans nigra*.

black wattle
WATTLE tree native to Australia. It has reddish bark under a fissured surface. Its leaves are made up of 30–60 pairs of tiny leaflets, and the small, globose, pale yellow flowers are clustered into heads of 20–30. Black wattle is a source of wattle bark, used in tanning leather. Height: to 15m (50ft). Family Mimosaceae; species *Acacia decurrens*.

black widow spider
See SPIDER, BLACK WIDOW

blackwood (Australian blackwood)
ACACIA tree native to Australia and grown as an ornamental. The cream to yellow flowers are produced in small clusters. The wood is hard and close-grained and therefore suitable for furniture, cabinet work and musical instruments. Height: to 15m (50ft). Family Mimosaceae; species *Acacia melanoxylon*.

bladder
Large, elastic-walled organ in the lower abdomen in which URINE is stored. Urine passes from each KIDNEY by way of two narrow tubes (called ureters) to the bladder, where it is stored until it can be voided. When pressure in the bladder becomes too great, nervous impulses signal the need for emptying. Urine leaves the bladder through a tube called the URETHRA.

bladder nut
Any member of a small group of deciduous shrubs or small trees native to temperate regions of the Northern Hemisphere; some species are grown as ornamentals. They have smooth, striped bark and white flowers, which are produced in terminal clusters. The fruit consists of two or three lobes and is inflated and membranous. Family Staphyleaceae; genus *Staphylea*.

bladderwort
Any member of a group of carnivorous, aquatic plants found in ponds or slow-moving water in Europe, Asia and North and South America. The finely divided leaves bear minute bladders, which trap and then digest small aquatic organisms. The two-lipped, yellow flowers are borne on stems above the water. Family Lentibulariaceae; genus *Utricularia*. *See also* INSECTIVOROUS PLANT

blastula
Stage in the development of the EMBRYO in animals. The blastula consists of a hollow cavity (blastocoel) surrounded by one or more spherical layers of cells.

BLOOD

Fluid that circulates through the body carrying oxygen and nutrients to all cells and removing wastes such as carbon dioxide. In a healthy human, blood constitutes *c*.5% of the body's total weight; by volume, it comprises *c*. 5.5 litres (11.6 pints). It is composed of a colourless, transparent fluid called PLASMA in which are suspended microscopic ERYTHROCYTES (red blood cells), which make up nearly half the blood volume; LEUCOCYTES (white blood cells); and PLATELETS. The type of ANTIGENS present on the surface of the erythrocytes determines the blood group.

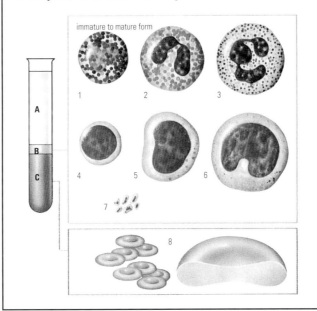

immature to mature form

◀ **Spun in a** high-speed centrifuge, blood separates out into plasma (A), layers of leucocytes and platelets (B) and erythrocytes (C). Fluid plasma, almost 90% water, contains salts and proteins. Three main types of leucocytes (shown in magnification) are: polymorphonuclearcytes (1–3), responsible for the destruction of invading bacteria and the removal of dead or damaged tissue; small and large lymphocytes (4 and 5), which assist in the body's immune system; and monocytes (6), which form a further line of the body's defence. Platelets (7) are vital clotting agents. Erythrocytes (8) are the most numerous; they are concerned with the transport of oxygen around the body.

B

blewit
FUNGUS with a mushroom-shaped, brown-capped fruiting body and a stem that is slightly bulbous at the base; the flesh is bluish-lilac in colour. Field blewit is found in pastureland, while wood blewit inhabits woodland and gardens; both are edible and have a strongly perfumed taste and smell. Phylum Basidiomycota; genus *Lepista*.

blind fish (blind cave fish)
Any of several species of pale-coloured, freshwater fish found mainly in cave waters of North America. Some species are blind, others are partly sighted. Their lack of proper sight is compensated for by the possession of tactile organs elsewhere on the body. Length: up to 13cm (5in). Family Amblyopsidae; species include *Amblyopsis spelaeus*. Also family Characidae; species include *Anoptichthys jordani*.

blind lizard
See LIZARD, BLIND

blind snake
See SNAKE, BLIND

block mountain
Uplift that is the result of block faulting. This is one type of FAULT in which the crustal portions of the Earth are broken into structural blocks of different elevations and positions.

blocky lava
Surface of hot molten LAVA covered with a "skin" of large angular lava blocks formed by the break-up of a solidified surface of a lava flow. Blocky lavas are characteristic of high viscosity lavas with relatively high silica content.

blood
See feature article, page 45

bloodberry
Upright herb native to tropical and subtropical America; it has been introduced into Asia, Australia and Africa. The plant has spreading branches with oval leaves and racemes of white or rosy-coloured flowers. The small, scarlet berries are used as a source of red dye. Height: from 0.3–0.9m (1–3ft). Family Phytolaccaceae; species *Rivina humilis*.

bloodroot
Herbaceous perennial native to E North America. It flowers in spring with a solitary, lobed, basal leaf and a single, white flower with a golden-orange centre. A red juice from the underground stem was traditionally used by Native North Americans as a dye for baskets, clothing and war paint, and as an insect repellent. Family Papaveraceae; species *Sanguinaria canadensis*.

blood vessel
Closed channel that carries blood throughout the body. An ARTERY carries oxygenated blood away from the heart; these give way to smaller arterioles and finally to tiny capillaries deep in the tissues, where oxygen and nutrients are exchanged for cellular wastes. The deoxygenated blood is returned to the heart by way of the VEINS.

bloodwood
Tree of the EUCALYPTUS family, native to Australia. It has rough bark, formed in distinct, small flakes. It flowers in terminal, flat-topped clusters or corymbs. The tree's common name refers to the presence in veins or pockets in the timber of a red gum, which exudes when the bark is cut. Family Myrtaceae; genus *Corymbia*.

bloodworm
Larva of several species of NON-BITING MIDGE. Bloodworms contain the red pigment HAEMOGLOBIN, which is also the oxygen-carrying pigment found in mammalian blood. Order Diptera; family Chironomidae; genus *Chironomus*.

bloom
Powdery or waxy covering on the surface of fruits such as plums and grapes. The term is also used to describe ALGAL BLOOM, which is the rapid, often seasonal increase in the population of ALGAE in lakes and seas. More generally, the term bloom applies to flower blossom or to the state of a plant in flower.

blowfish
See PUFFERFISH

blow-fly
See BLUEBOTTLE

blow hole
In geology, hole in a cliff or cave through which seawater spurts at high tide. Blowholes are formed by EROSION. Initially, waves acting on a JOINT or other line of weakness in a cliff face carve out a cave. Continued HYDRAULIC ACTION by pounding waves on the roof of the cave forms a sort of chimney. Eventually this breaks through the surface of the ground near the edge of the cliff. At high tide, incoming waves force water out of the top of the blowhole. In biology, blowhole refers to the nostrils (single or double) of whales, situated towards the back of the skull.

blubber
Layer of subcutaneous fat that surrounds the bodies of many aquatic mammals. The fat, a feature of WHALES and SEALS, acts as an energy store and insulating layer to prevent the loss of heat to cold water. During the days of mass international whaling, blubber was rendered down by boiling and used as a source of oil for many applications, all of which can now be supplied by synthetic substances.

bluebell
Spring-flowering plant native to European woodlands. It grows from a bulb and bears a drooping head of bell-shaped flowers. Height: 20–50cm (8–20in). Family Liliaceae; species *Hyacinthoides non-scripta*.

blueberry
See BILBERRY

bluebird, Asian fairy
Bird that inhabits moist, broad-leaved, evergreen forests in Southeast Asia; it is a member of the BROADBILL family. The male has glistening, violet-

◄ **bluebell** A spring-flowering bulb, the bluebell (*Endymion nonsciptus*) is a monocotyledon. The bulb is a storage organ for the plant and provides a means of vegetative reproduction.

blue upper parts and black underparts; the female is entirely dull blue-green. They feed on nectar and fruit in the treetops. Length: 25cm (10in). Family Eurylaimidae; species *Irena puella*.

bluebird, eastern
Bird that inhabits rural woodlands, farms and gardens in North America; it is member of the THRUSH family. The male is deep blue above with a chestnut throat and breast. The female is duller and greyer. There has been a recent decline in the eastern blackbird population due to competition for nest sites from introduced species such as the starling. Length: 18cm (7in). Family Turdidae; species *Sialis sialis*.

bluebonnet
Any of several species of LUPIN native to North America. The leaves are digitate with several narrow leaflets. Showy, bluish lavender or purple flowers are produced in terminal spikes. Family Fabaceae; species include *Lupinus sericeus*.

bluebottle (blow-fly)
Black or metallic blue-green FLY, slightly larger than, but similar in habits to, the HOUSE-FLY. The larvae (maggots) usually feed on carrion and refuse containing meat. Adult length: 6–11mm (0.2–0.4in). Order Diptera; family Calliphoridae; genus *Calliphora*.

bluebuck
Large ANTELOPE that was hunted to extinction at the beginning of the 19th century. It was closely related to, but slightly smaller than, the sable and roan antelopes. Found in South Africa, the bluebuck had a blue-grey back and long, backwardly curving horns. Family Bovidae; subfamily Hippotraginae; species *Hippotragus leucophaeus*.

blue butterfly
See BUTTERFLY, BLUE

blue crab
See CRAB, BLUE

bluefish
Predatory marine fish that is found in most tropical and temperate seas. Fished widely for food and sport, the bluefish has an elongated blue-green body and a large mouth with sharp teeth. Length: 1.2m (4ft). Family Pomatomidae; species *Pomatomus saltatrix*.

bluegrass
Slender, annual or perennial grass native to temperate and cold regions of the world. It has spikelets in open or dense panicles and narrow leaf blades. Bluegrass is of great importance for its forage value, and several species are cultivated for pastures and lawns. The most important species is Kentucky bluegrass (*Poa pratensis*). Family Poaceae; genus *Poa*.

blue-green alga
See CYANOBACTERIUM

bluethroat
Small, active bird belonging to the THRUSH family; it is closely related to the NIGHTINGALE. The bluethroat is found in Europe, Asia and W Alaska. The male has a bright blue patch on its throat in the breeding season. Bluethroats feed mainly on small insects. They have a musical, rather high-pitched song. Length: 14cm (6in). Family Turdidae; species *Luscinia svecica*.

bluff
Steep slope at the side of a bend in a river. A bluff

boa The boa constrictor (*Constrictor constrictor*) is found in many areas of South America. It feeds on birds and small mammals, such as rats and agoutis, which it kills by restricting their ability to breathe.

forms on the outside of a MEANDER by the erosive action of the slow-moving river water. Some bluffs are as much as 100m (330ft) tall.

blusher
FUNGUS that has a rosy brown to flesh-coloured cap to its fruiting body; the stem is white and flushed with the cap colour. The flesh, especially in the stem, gradually turns pink when bruised or exposed to air. Blusher fungus is common in coniferous and deciduous woodland; it is edible if cooked but poisonous if eaten raw. Phylum Basidiomycota; species *Amanita rubescens*.

B-lymphocyte
See LYMPHOCYTE

boa
Large, constricting SNAKE. The boa constrictor (*Constrictor constrictor*) of the American tropics can grow to 3.7m (12ft) in length. The iridescent rainbow boa, the emerald tree boa and the rosy boa are smaller species. Most boa species are tree-dwellers, but the rubber boa of the w United States is a burrowing species. Family Boidae. *See also* ANACONDA; PYTHON

boa, tree
Any of four species of tropical American arboreal SNAKES with broad heads and muscular bodies; they are often patterned in bright, bold colours. The tail is prehensile and is used to anchor the snake to tree branches while it strikes at and swallows its prey. The tree boa uses heat-sensitive labial pits to detect its warm-blooded prey. Length: to 2m (6.6ft). Family Boidae; genus *Corallus*.

boar, wild
Dark-coloured PIG that is found in woodland across central and s Europe, North Africa and central and s Asia. Young boars are paler with white stripes. Wild boars are even-toed, hoofed mammals. They are omnivorous, rooting around with their snouts for roots and tubers and also eating insects, small mammals and carrion. Head-body length: 90–180cm (35–71in); tail: 30–40cm (12–16in). Family Suidae; species *Sus scrofa*.

boatbill
Bird that lives in the rainforests of Queensland, Australia, and New Guinea; it belongs to the monarch flycatcher family. The boatbill has an unusual flattened bill and feeds mainly on flies and other invertebrates. The male boatbill has a dark head and back and a bright yellow chest. Length: 12cm (5in). Family Muscicapidae; species *Machaerirhynchus flaviventer*.

bobbing gnat
Any of several species belonging to the CRANE-FLY

family that habitually bob up and down on their long legs. Order Diptera; suborder Nematocera; family Tipulidae.

bobcat
See CAT, BOB-

bobolink
Common bird found from s Canada to central United States; it belongs to the American ORIOLE family. The female has a dull, sparrow-like plumage; the male is mainly black, with white patches on the wings and rump and a buff-coloured nape. It is named after its bubbling song, which has phrases sounding like "bobolink". It winters in South America. Length: 17cm (7in). Family Icteridae; species *Dolichonyx oryzivorus*.

bobwhite
Type of QUAIL found in open coniferous forests in the United States and Mexico. It is named after its characteristic call. The bobwhite feeds mainly on the seeds of grasses and shrubs. Like most quails, it has a mottled brown, cryptic plumage, which makes it hard to spot until it takes flight. Length: 25cm (10in). Family Phasianidae; species *Colinus virginianus*.

Bock, Hieronymus (1498–1554)
German botanist. He constructed a system of plant classification based on physical characteristics of plants and similarities between them. He published his detailed descriptions and illustrations of German plants in the *New Kreuterbuch* (1539), which was a great improvement on any of the earlier herbals.

bog (peat bog)
Spongy, wet soil, consisting of decayed vegetable matter. It develops in a depression with little or no drainage, where the water is cold and acidic and almost devoid of oxygen and nitrogen. Unlike a MARSH, a bog rarely has standing water, but plants such as cranberry and the carnivorous sundew readily grow there.

bogbean
Perennial, aquatic or bog plant native to Europe, central and N Asia and North America. It has long been valued for its tonic and fever-reducing properties. The thick, glossy, trifoliate leaves and pink and white flowers with fringed petals are borne on long stalks above the water level. Family Menyanthaceae; species *Menyanthes trifoliata*.

bog myrtle (sweet gale)
Deciduous shrub found in North America, Europe and Asia. It has strongly aromatic leaves. The flowers, which are produced in stiff catkins before the leaves open, are reduced to stamens in the male flowers, or styles in female flowers, without a perianth. Height: to 1.5m (5ft). Family Myricaceae; species *Myrica gale*.

Bohr effect
Effect of carbon dioxide concentration on the oxygen dissociation curve for HAEMOGLOBIN. As the carbon dioxide concentration increases the curve is displaced more to the right, which means that the haemoglobin more readily releases its oxygen. The more active a tissue is the more carbon dioxide it produces and so the haemoglobin releases its oxygen at the time of its greatest need. This effect is important in maintaining the activity of muscles during periods of exercise.

boldo
Hardwood timber from an evergreen tree native to Chile. It has leathery leaves and small flowers in clusters, which produce edible fruit. Aromatic oils from the leaves and bark are used medicinally, and the bark is also a source of dye. Family Monimiaceae; species *Peumus boldus*.

boletus
Any member of the *Boletus* genus of terrestrial FUNGI. Their spore-bearing parts are tubes instead of the usual gills. There are many species, all of which have a fleshy cap on a central stem and many of which are edible. Some poisonous kinds have red tube mouths. Phylum Basidiomycota; species include *Boletus edulis*, the edible cep.

boll weevil
Small, black or grey BEETLE that is common in the United States. Both adults and larvae feed on cotton plants, especially the bolls, and can cause serious crop damage. Length: 6mm (0.24in). Family Curculionidae; species *Anthonomus grandis*

bollworm
Larva of various species of MOTH found in many areas where cotton is grown. The bollworm is cream or slightly pink in colour and feeds mainly on the green cotton bolls, causing considerable damage. Length: 12mm (0.5in). Order Lepidoptera; families include Gelechiidae and Noctuidae; there are various species.

bomb, volcanic
Piece of solid material, usually cooled LAVA, that is ejected by a VOLCANO. Volcanic bombs are usually greater than 32mm (1.3in) in diameter but can be much larger.

bombardier beetle
Ground BEETLE found in North America and Europe. It has a reddish body with dark blue or black wings. The bombardier beetle fights off predators by bom-

▲ **boletus** Devil's boletus (*Boletus satanas*) is a poisonous fungus; its bulbous cap can grow to the size of a football. It is found along the w coast of North America and in Europe, for example in chalk beech-woods in s Britain.

B

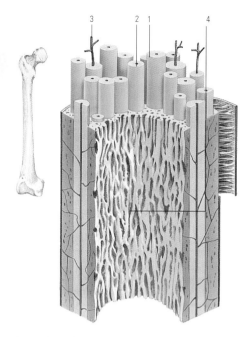

▲ **bone** A magnified cross-section of bone shows that it is composed of rod-like units (1), which have a central channel (2) containing blood vessels (3). These are surrounded by concentric layers of collagen fibres, each arranged in a different direction from those in adjacent layers. Calcium salt crystals and bone cells (4) are embedded between the fibres.

barding them with an irritating gas. Each discharge of gas makes a sound like a tiny popgun. Family Carabidae; genus *Brachinus*.

bonding
Process by which a CHEMICAL BOND is formed.

bone
In vertebrates CONNECTIVE TISSUE that forms the skeleton of a body, protects its internal organs, serves as a lever during locomotion and stores calcium and phosphorus. Bone is composed of a strong, compact layer of COLLAGEN and calcium phosphate, and a lighter, porous inner spongy layer. The inner layer contains marrow, in which erythrocytes and some leucocytes are produced.

bonefish
Any of two or more species of silvery white, spindle-shaped fish, characterized by a conical snout. The bonefish occurs in coastal tropical waters, often around mangroves in the Atlantic and Pacific oceans. Length: to 105cm (41in). Family Albulidae; species include *Albua vulpes*.

boneset
Herbaceous perennial that is native to North America. It has hairy foliage and dense, flat-topped clusters of white flowers. The leaves are united at their bases to surround the stem. Dried leaves are used to make boneset tea. Family Asteraceae; species *Eupatorium perfoliatum*.

bongo
ANTELOPE found in the lowland forests of E, central and W Africa. It is the largest of the forest antelopes. The bongo is chestnut red or darker, with narrow, pale stripes on its body and a white chevron between its eyes. Both sexes have twisted horns, up to 100cm (40in) long in the males. They feed on leaves. Head-body length: 220–235cm (87–93in); tail: 24–26cm (9–10in). Family Bovidae; subfamily Bovinae; species *Tragelaphus euryceros*.

bonito
Speedy, streamlined, tuna-like fish found in all warm and temperate waters, usually in shoals. Bonitos are blue, black and silver. They are highly valued as food and game fish. The ocean bonito (*Katsuwonus pelamis*) is also called skipjack tuna or bluefin. Family Scombridae.

bontebok
ANTELOPE that grazes the open grasslands of South Africa. It is purplish brown with white patches on its face, belly and legs. Both sexes have slightly curving horns up to 51cm (20in) long. The bontebok, originally considered a subspecies of *Damaliscus dorcas*, has recently been reclassified as *Damaliscus pygarus*. Head-body length: 140–160cm (55–63in); tail: 30–45cm (12–18in). Family Bovidae; subfamily Hippotraginae.

bony fish
See FISH

bonytongue
Any of the freshwater fish in the superorder Osteoglossomorpha. Among the 217 species is the ARAPAIMA, one of the largest freshwater fish. Bonytongues are so named because their tongues have teeth that bite against teeth on the roof of the mouth. They are found in North America and are also widely distributed in the Southern Hemisphere.

booby
Large oceanic seabird. Adept at soaring, it feeds by plunging, dart-like, into surface waters to catch fish or squid. It has white plumage, long, rather narrow wings and a dagger-shaped bill. Length: *c*.75–90cm (*c*.30–35in). Family Sulidae; there are 9 species, some of which are also known as GANNETS.

booby, Abbott's
Booby that is found only on Christmas Island in the E Indian Ocean. There are *c*.2000 pairs of this highly endangered bird, which nests under the canopy of forest. Family Sulidae; species *Sula abbotti*.

booby, brown
Booby distributed across many of the tropical oceans. It breeds in rather small colonies mainly around the Indian Ocean and on Pacific islands. Family Sulidae; species *Sula leucogaster*.

booby, masked (blue-faced booby)
Booby with bright white plumage, a dark, bluish face mask and a dark trailing edge to the wings. It nests on oceanic islands in colonies that may number thousands. Family Sulidae; species *Sula dactylatra*.

booby, Peruvian
Booby that lives along the coast of Peru and Chile. They nest in highly concentrated colonies, where their droppings solidify into GUANO. They are depen-

▲ **bonito** The oceanic bonito (*Katsuwonus pelamis*), also known as skipjack tuna, is a tuna fish weighing up to *c*.25kg (*c*.55lbs) and measuring up to 90cm (35in). It is found in warm waters worldwide and feeds on anchovies, sardines and squid.

▲ **booklouse** Small, soft-bodied insects, booklice like dark, damp environments and feed on dry organic matter. They are not true lice as they do not bite or live on animals. They can be a pest, however, if they infest materials or food.

dent on the shoals of anchovetta fish that occur in the fertile HUMBOLDT CURRENT. Many boobies die when food stocks are depleted by the warmer water brought by the EL NIÑO phenomenon. Family Sulidae; species *Sula variegata*.

booby, red-footed
One of the most common and widespread species of booby. It ranges over all tropical seas. The adult booby can be brown or white, depending on the race, but its feet are always bright red. It nests mainly in trees. Family Sulidae; species *Sula sula*.

booklouse (bookworm)
Transparent to white, usually wingless insect found worldwide. Booklice feed on moulds in hot, humid, dusty places, such as shelves and books. Length: to 5mm (0.2in). Order Psocoptera; genus *Liposcelis*.

boomslang
Slender-bodied, arboreal SNAKE of sub-Saharan Africa. It is rear-fanged and has a potent venom that prevents its victim's blood clotting. The boomslang feeds chiefly on birds, which it ambushes by remaining motionless in the branches of trees. When disturbed, it inflates its neck region. Length: to 1.5m (5ft). Family Colubridae; species *Dispholidus typus*.

bootlace worm (ribbon worm)
Any member of the phylum Nemertea. Bootlace worms occur mainly in the shallow parts of temperate marine waters but some species are found in the tropics. Some species are aquatic, and some are terrestrial. Bootlace worms move by means of slow undulations of the body. They catch prey with the aid of an eversible (capable of being turned inside out) proboscis.

borage
Hairy, annual plant native to S Europe. It has rough, oblong leaves and drooping clusters of pale blue flowers. It is cultivated as a food and a flavouring. Height: up to 60cm (24in). Family Boraginaceae; species *Borago officinalis*.

boreal
CLIMATE ZONE between 60 and 40 degrees north; there is a large annual temperature range, from cold snowy winters to warm summers. The vegetation is BOREAL FOREST and also hemlock, herbs, lichens and mosses.

boreal forest
Large area of tree-covered land occupying the northern and mountainous parts of the Northern Hemisphere. The trees are typically coniferous, mainly firs and spruces. Its northern edge is bordered by frozen TUNDRA.

bornite (peacock ore, Cu_5FeS_4)
Common copper mineral, a copper iron sulphide. It

generally occurs in masses and sometimes as crystals (cubic system) in intrusive igneous rocks and metamorphic rocks. It is opaque and bronze with an iridescent purple tarnish. Hardness 3; r.d. 5.0.

botanic garden

Large garden preserve for display, research and teaching purposes. Wild and cultivated plants from all climates are maintained outdoors and in greenhouses. Although organized gardens date from ancient Rome, the first botanic gardens were established during the Middle Ages. In the 16th century, gardens existed in Pisa, Bologna, Padua and Leiden. Aromatic and medicinal herbs were arranged in rows and still exist in the Botanic Garden of Padua. The first US botanic garden was established by John BARTRAM in Philadelphia in 1728. Famous botanic gardens include the Royal Botanic Gardens in Kew, near London (established 1759), the New York Botanic Gardens in the Bronx (established 1891) and the Missouri Botanical Gardens in St Louis (established around 1860). *See also* Ready Reference, pages 470–71

botany

Study of plants and algae, including their classification, structure, physiology, reproduction and evolution. The discipline used to be studied in two halves: lower (non-flowering) plants, which included the algae (now in the kingdom Protoctista), moss and ferns; and higher (seed-bearing) plants, including most flowers, trees and shrubs. Botany also studies the importance of plants to people.

bot-fly

See feature article

bo tree (bodhi tree, peepul)

Large tree that is native to India, where it is regarded as a sacred tree. The bo tree's leaves are unusual in having a terminal projection or "drip tip", which is sometimes more than half the length of the

remainder of the oval leafblade. Family Moraceae; species *Ficus religiosa*.

bottlebrush

Any member of a large group of shrubs and trees native to Australia; they are planted as ornamentals in warm regions or grown in glasshouses. The flowers, which are clustered near the ends of branches, resemble a bottle brush, with long, colourful, orange or red stamens forming the "brush". Family Myrtaceae; genera *Callistemon* and *Melaleuca*.

bottle gourd

Annual vine, probably native to Old World tropics but now widespread in warm climates. It is cultivated for its thin-shelled fruits, which are used as receptacles, utensils, bird-houses and decoration. The bottle gourd's showy white flowers, which are solitary and short lived, produce fruits of many shapes and sizes with a hard, durable shell. Family Cucurbitaceae; genus *Lagenaria*; species include *Lagenaria vulgaris* (calabash gourd).

bottle tree

Tree that is native to Australia and grown as an ornamental in warm regions. The bottle tree has a strangely shaped, swollen trunk. Family Sterculiaceae; species *Brachychiton rupestris*.

bougainvillea

Any member of a group of tropical, woody vines native to South America; they are often grown as garden plants. The flowers have purple or red bracts. The genus was named after the French navigator Louis de Bougainville. Family Nyctaginaceae; genus *Bougainvillea*.

boulder clay *See* TILL

Bowen, Norman Levi (1887–1956)

Canadian petrologist and mineralogist. His contributions to the study of the origins, structure and chem-

◄ **bowerbird** The tooth-billed bowerbird (*Scenopoeetes dentirostris*) is found in NE Australia. As with other bowerbird species, the male builds a bower as part of a courtship ritual and the females lay their eggs in nests nearby.

istry of igneous rocks were outstanding. Much of his research was done at the Carnegie Institute in Washington, D.C., where he established his reputation with *The Later Stages of the Evolution of the Igneous Rocks* (1915). Bowen's most important book is the influential *The Evolution of Igneous Rocks* (1928).

bowerbird

Stocky, medium-sized bird found in the forests of New Guinea and N and E Australia. Bowerbirds take their name from the often elaborate courtship bowers constructed by the male birds to entice the females, almost as an extension of, or substitute for, gaudy plumage. Length: 20–36cm (8–14in). Family Ptilonorhynchidae; there are 18 species.

bowerbird, golden

Bowerbird that lives only in highland rainforest around the Atherton Tableland of Queensland, Australia. It has yellow and green plumage. It builds a large bower like a maypole, with additions of flowers, moss and fruits. Family Ptilonorhynchidae; species *Prionodura newtoniana*.

bowerbird, great grey

Largest species of bowerbird; it inhabits woodland in N Australia but is sometimes seen in suburban gardens. Like most bowerbird species, it is a fine mimic, not only of other bird calls but also of other sounds in their surroundings. The great grey bowerbird feeds primarily on insects and fruit. Family Ptilonorhynchidae; species *Chlamydera nuchalis*.

bowerbird, satin

Bowerbird found in E Australia. It is probably the most famous of all the bowerbirds, mainly because of its highly intricate bower. The bower typically consists of a "stage" and an "avenue" made of twigs, decorated with colourful objects such as feathers and flowers. The male is a shiny blue-black, the female grey-green. Family Ptilonorhynchidae; species *Ptilonorhynchus violaceus*.

bowerbird, vogelkop gardener

Bowerbird that is found in the mountain rainforests of New Guinea. Its plumage is a dull yellow-brown, but its bower is quite spectacular – a tented structure adorned with moss, fruits and flowers. Family Ptilonorhynchidae; species *Amblyornis inornatus*.

Bowman's capsule (renal capsule)

Funnel-shaped end of a NEPHRON in a KIDNEY. It has special epithelial cells (podocytes) that allow fluid filtered from the blood to pass into the nephron, from where it eventually passes into the pelvis of the kidney as urine. There are about a million Bowman's capsules in each human kidney.

box

Evergreen tree or shrub found in tropical and temperate regions in Europe, North America and W Asia. The shrub is popular for topiary; boxwood is used for musical instruments. The 100 species include English (or common) *Buxus sempervirens* and the larger *Buxus balearica*, which grows to 24m (80ft). Family *Buxaceae*.

BOT-FLY

Any member of several families of stout, hairy, black-and-white to grey FLY. Its larvae are parasites of livestock, small animals and humans. The horse bot-fly (family Gasterophilidae) lays its eggs on the hair of the front legs or face of a horse. With licking, the eggs hatch and the larvae pass into the horse's stomach, where they cause much damage. The deer bot-fly

(family Oestridae) is capable of flying at 80km/h (50mph), making it one of the swiftest insects. The human bot-fly (family Cuterebridae) is found in the tropics. The adult female attaches an egg to a blood-sucking insect, such as a mosquito. The egg hatches, and when the mosquito bites a human, the larva enters the body. Order Diptera.

▶ **The families of** bot-flies, Cuterebridae, Oestridae and Gasterophilidae, are parasitic on humans, sheep and horses respectively. The life cycle of the common horse bot-fly (*Gasterophilus intestinalis*) begins (1) as eggs are glued by the adult to the hairs, usually on the front legs of the horse. The stimulus of the moisture and friction provided by the horse's tongue when cleaning itself near the eggs causes the larvae to emerge and attach themselves to the animal's tongue and lips. The larvae pass to the stomach (2) where they attach themselves to the walls. The fully developed larvae release their hold on the walls and pass out with excrement (3). The larvae pupate in the ground and emerge as adults (4).

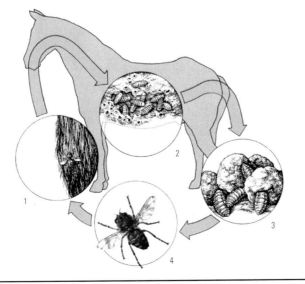

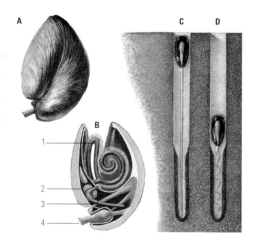

▲ **brachiopod** The marine animal known as a brachiopod, or lampshell, lives in holes in mud flats. It comprises (A) a hinged shell and a stalk with which it grips the rocks. The cross-section (B) shows: the lophophore (1), which bears ciliated tentacles for feeding; digestive gland (2); mouth (3); and stalks (4).

When feeding, *Lingula* (C), which resembles fossil forms of 500 million years ago, rests at the surface of its burrow using feathery cilia to filter water for food particles. When disturbed, its stalk contracts, drawing the animal into the burrow (D), out of sight and reach of its potential predator.

box elder
Large tree native to North America. It has pinnate leaves and pendulous, yellowish-green flowers. Box elder is drought resistant but grows rapidly in moist soil, making it useful for retaining banks and screens. The wood has been used for paper pulp and wooden ware. Height: 22m (70ft). Family Aceraceae; species *Acer negundo*.

box jellyfish (sea wasp, jimble, cubomedusan)
Any member of the order Cubomedusae, closely related to true JELLYFISH. Box jellyfish swim free in all tropical seas. They are characterized by a swimming bell that is square in cross-section, from which trail the long tentacles with which they paralyse and kill their prey. The neurotoxins released by the nematocysts (stinging cells) of the tentacles are extremely potent; the sting of box jellyfish can be extremely painful or even fatal to humans. Phylum Coelenterata/Cnidaria; class Cubozoa; order Cubomedusae.

box turtle
See TURTLE, BOX

boysenberry
Large BERRY fruit that is dark purplish-red to black when ripe, resembling a loganberry. It originated as a hybrid between blackberry and raspberry. It is named after the US horticulturalist Rudolph Boysen, who developed it in *c*.1935. Family Rosaceae; genus *Rubus*.

brachiopod (lamp shell)
Any of *c*.260 species of small, bottom-dwelling, marine invertebrates of the phylum Brachiopoda. They are similar in outward appearance to BIVALVE molluscs, having a shell composed of two valves; however, unlike bivalves, there is a line of symmetry running through the valves. Brachiopods live attached to rocks by a pedicle (stalk), or buried in mud or sand. Most modern brachiopods are less than 5cm (2in) across.

bracken
Persistent, weedy FERN that is found worldwide. It has an underground stem that can travel 1.8m (6ft) ; it sends up fronds that may reach 4.6m (15ft) in height in some climates. The *typica* variety is widespread in Britain. Family Dennstaedtiaceae; species *Pteridium aquilinum*.

bracket fungus (shelf fungus)
Any member of a large family of common arboreal fungi that have spore-bearing tubes under the cap. Bracket fungi are usually hard and leathery or wood-like and have no stems. They often cover old logs, and their parasitic activity may kill living trees. Some are edible when young. Phylum Basidiomycota; family Polyporaceae.

braconid
Small parasitic WASP. It lays its eggs inside other insects and the larvae feed on and mature inside the living host. Braconid wasps are especially known for, and are sometimes reared for, their ability to control populations of pest insects. Adult body length: 3–15mm (0.1–0.6in). Order Hymenoptera; family Braconidae.

bract
Modified leaf found on a flower's stalk or base. Bracts are usually small and scale-like. In some species, such as the POINSETTIA, they are large and brightly coloured.

braided river (braided stream)
Network of small, shallow interlacing rivers. It forms when a river deposits sediment, causing it to divide up into new channels, which then redivide and rejoin, resembling a braided cord.

brain
See feature article

brain fungus (cauliflower fungus)
Fungus that has a subglobose, cauliflower-like fruiting body composed of flattened lobes on a short, thick stem. It is pale brown to buff in colour, darkening with age. Brain fungus can be found at or near the base of conifer trees and is edible when young. Phylum Basidiomycota; species *Sparassis crispa*.

bramble
Any member of a large group of scrambling shrubs that are native to the Northern Hemisphere. They have well-developed prickles and arching stems that are able to root at the tips. The black fruits of the bramble consist of many tiny fleshy drupes, each with a pip, exemplified by the BLACKBERRY. Family Rosaceae; genus *Rubus*.

branching
Growth extension of vascular plants. A branch develops from the stem and consists of the growth

BRAIN

Mass of nerve tissue that regulates all physical and mental activity; it is continuous with the spinal cord. It weighs about 1.5kg (3.3lb) in an adult human (about 2% of body weight). The human brain has three parts – the HINDBRAIN, MIDBRAIN and FOREBRAIN. The hindbrain is where basic physiological process-es such as breathing and the heartbeat are coordinated. The midbrain links the hindbrain and the forebrain. The forebrain is the seat of all higher functions and attributes (personality, intellect, memory, emotion), as well as being involved in sensation and initiating voluntary movement.

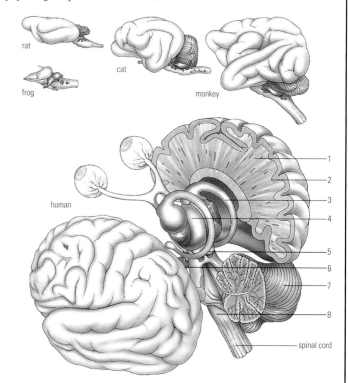

▶ **The vertebrate brain** has three major structural and functional regions – the forebrain, the midbrain and the hindbrain. In primitive animals, such as amphibians, the forebrain is concerned with smell, the midbrain with vision and the hindbrain with balance and hearing. In higher animals, such as rats, cats, monkeys and humans, parts of the brain have adapted to meet the needs of the organism. Most notably, part of the forebrain, the cerebrum (1), developed into a complex, deeply fissured structure. It comprises large regions concerned with association, reasoning and judgement. Its outer layer, the cortex (2), contains areas that coordinate movement and sensory information. The limbic system (3) controls emotional responses, such as fear. The thalamus (4) coordinates sensory and motor signals, and relays them to the cerebrum. The hypothalamus (5), along with the pituitary glands, controls the body's hormonal system. Visual, tactile and auditory inputs are coordinated by the tectum (6), part of the midbrain. In the hindbrain, the cerebellum (7) controls the muscle activity needed for refined limb movements and for maintaining posture. The medulla (8) contains reflex centres that are involved in respiration, heartbeat regulation and gastric function.

▲ brassica Cabbage (A) broccoli (B), cauliflower (C) and Brussels sprouts (D) are all varieties of the same Brassica species (*Brassica oleracea*), although they differ greatly in appearance. Curly endive (H), chicory (I), lettuce (J) and curly kale (E) all belong to the Asteraceae family and are used in salad. Also in this family is the artichoke (G), of which the heart and fleshy parts of the scales (leaves) are edible. Spinach (F) belongs to the family Chenopodiaceae. Brassicas are usually hardy plants and some species are capable of withstanding cold winters.

from the previous year (branchlet) together with new growth (twig). New twigs are produced during the next season of growth, both from the terminal bud at the end of the twig and from lateral buds in leaf axils along it.

brassica
Any member of a group of herbaceous annuals, biennials and perennials native to north temperate areas of the Eastern Hemisphere. Many brassicas are important food crops, for example CABBAGE, BROCCOLI, CAULIFLOWER and TURNIP. The characteristic yellow, four-petalled flowers give rise to slender pods with globular, yellowish-brown or black seeds, which are economically important for mustards and oils. Family Brassicaceae; genus *Brassica*.

Brazil nut
Seed of an evergreen tree of the same name. The Brazil nut tree, which is native to South America, has leathery leaves and grows to a height of c.41m (c.135ft). Its flowers produce a thick-walled fruit, 10–30cm (4–12in) in diameter, which contains 25–30 large seeds. Family Lecythidaceae; species *Bertholletia excelsa*.

breadfruit
Tree of the FIG family, native to Malaysia but widely grown in the tropics, particularly Polynesia, for its edible fruit. The thick, leathery, lobed leaves may be 0.6m (2ft) or more in length. The prickly, melon-sized, usually seedless fruits can be cooked and eaten as a vegetable. Height: 15m (50ft). Family Moraceae; species *Artocarpus altilis*.

breadnut
Type of BREADFRUIT that produces fruit containing seeds. The fruit rind is covered in fleshy spines, and the brownish seeds are 2.5cm (1in) or more in length and up to 2.5cm (1in) in diameter. Eaten after boiling or roasting, the seeds are said to resemble chestnuts. Family Moraceae; species *Artocarpus altilis*. **Breadnut** is also the name for a tall tree from tropical America. It has a dense, wide crown and leathery leaves. The round, yellow fruits, about 2.5cm (1in) in diameter, are used roasted or boiled and made into paste for human food, or roasted for coffee. The breadnut timber is used by carpenters and cabinetmakers. Family Moraceae; species *Brosimum alicastrum*.

breadroot (Indian turnip)
LEGUME from the upper Missouri and Rocky Mountain region of the United States. The root was regarded as a luxury by the Native American tribes of Kansas and Nebraska, eaten roasted when fresh or dried and stored for winter use. Family Fabaceae; species *Psoralea esculenta*.

bream
Freshwater fish of E and N Europe. Its stocky body is green-brown and silver. Anglers prize the bream for its tasty flesh. Length: 30–50cm (12–20in); weight: 4–6kg (9–13lb). Family Cyprinidae; species *Abramis brama*.

breathing
Process by which air is taken into and expelled from the LUNGS for the purposes of GAS EXCHANGE. When mammals breathe in (inhale), the intercostal muscles raise the ribs, increasing the volume of the THORAX and drawing air into the lungs. During breathing out (exhalation), the ribs are lowered, and air is forced out through the nose, and sometimes also the mouth.

breccia
SEDIMENTARY ROCK that is formed by the cementation of sharp-angled fragments in a finer matrix of the same or different material. It can also refer to rock formed by movements of the crust (fault breccia) and to volcanic rock from a vent (volcanic breccia). *See also* CONGLOMERATE

briar
Heath plant native to the Mediterranean region. Large woody nodules, which form on the roots and at the base of the stem, are cured and boiled to produce the material traditionally used in the manufacture of pipes for smoking. Family Ericaceae; species *Erica arborea*.

Bridges, Calvin Blackman (1889–1938)
US geneticist. He helped to prove the chromosomal basis of HEREDITY and sex. His work with Thomas Hunt MORGAN on the FRUIT FLY (*Drosophila*) proved that inheritable variations could be traced to observ-

▲ bream The common bream (*Abramis brama*) is often found swimming in large shoals in slow-flowing lakes or ponds. It feeds mainly on plankton, water fleas and sometimes molluscs.

▲ bristlehead The Bornean bristlehead (*Pityriasis gymnocephala*) lives in lowland forest, often near peat swamps, and feeds on insects and sometimes small vertebrates, such as lizards. Although rarely seen, it has a loud call.

able changes in the chromosomes. These experiments resulted in the construction of "gene maps".

brill
FLATFISH that is similar to and related to the TURBOT. The brill is fished for food. Unlike the turbot, it lacks tentacles. Family Scophthalmidae; species *Scophthalmus rhombus*.

brilliant
Special cut of certain gemstones, such as diamonds, with FACETS to enhance the internal reflection of light within the crystal. It serves to increase the fire or brilliance of the gemstone.

bristle-bill
Any of three species of BULBUL, found in tropical forest, mainly in W and central Africa. The bristle-bill has a musical, thrush-like song and spends much of its time hunting amongst tall trees for insects, especially ants. Its bill, which is fairly long and deep, has stiff bristles at its base. Length: 20cm (8in). Family Pycnonotidae; genus *Bleda*.

bristlebird
Any of three species of Australian WARBLER. It is found mainly in thick scrub, where, being rather shy, it is hard to spot. Bristlebirds have brown plumage, long legs and a long tail, which is often cocked upwards. They are mainly insectivorous, hunting for food amongst leaves and vegetation on the ground. Their common name is a result of the stiff bristles at the base of their beaks. Length: 22cm (9in). Family Sylviidae; genus *Dasyornis*.

bristlefront
Either of two species of forest bird in the TAPACULO family, found in South America. Its plumage is dark and slaty, and there is a prominent tuft of bristly feathers on its forehead, just above the base of the bill. Bristlefronts hunt low amongst trees, banks and boulders for their insect prey. Their song is loud, with clear, rather silvery notes. Length: 19cm (7in). Family Rhinocryptidae; genus *Merulaxis*.

bristlehead
Highly unusual and rare species of bird that lives in the rainforests of Borneo. It is classified in a family of its own and there is only the one species. In build, the bristlehead resembles a rather dumpy shrike. It has a heavy bill, hooked at its tip, and the top of its head is covered in bristly feathers. Its dark body contrasts with a bright red head and neck and yellow crown. Length: 25cm (10in). Family Pityriasididae; species *Pityriasis gymnocephala*.

B

bristlemouth

Any member of the family Gonostomatidae, including the very abundant genus *Cyclothone*. Bristlemouth fish occur at mesopelagic depths (200–1000m/660–3300ft) in the tropical regions of oceans worldwide. They carry out daily vertical migrations. Bristlemouths have characteristic patterns of bioluminescent light organs and many change their sex from male to female as they age. Length: 2–30cm (1–12in).

bristletail

See SILVERFISH

bristleworm

Marine segmented worm. It may be actively predacious, and some species are toxic to humans. If touched, small, sharp bristles bearing toxin become imbedded in the skin and cause irritation and pain. Phylum Annelida; class Polychaeta; order Amphinomida. The term "bristleworm" is also sometimes used to refer to polychaetes in general. *See also* FIREWORM

brittle fracture

Sudden break at a point just beyond the elastic strength of a material. Most rock materials deform by brittle fracture at normal pressures and temperatures.

brittle star (serpent star)

Marine ECHINODERM that has a small, central, disc-shaped body and up to twenty (though typically five) long, sinuous arms. The arms break off easily, sometimes as a means of escaping a predator, and are replaced by REGENERATION. The brittle star feeds mainly on decaying matter and plankton. Phylum Echinodermata; class Ophiuroidea; genera include the phosphorescent *Amphiopholis* and *Ophiactis*; most common species *Amphipholis squamata*.

broad bean

Important food LEGUME grown in the north temperate regions and the higher altitudes of some subtropical regions. The plants are erect with grey-green leaves. The large seed pods bear seeds of high protein content. Large-seeded varieties are used as human food and small-seeded varieties for animal feed. Family Fabaceae; species *Vicia faba*.

broadbill

Small or medium bird with a rather short, broad beak, found in Africa and parts of Asia. Its head is relative-

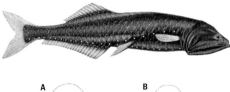

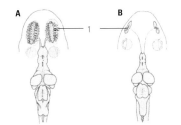

▲ **bristlemouth** A very common fish, the bristlemouth has a series of light organs on its belly which compensate for its poor eyesight. The male bristlemouth (A) uses large olfactory organs (1), which are far more developed than those of the female (B), to detect pheromones secreted by the female during the breeding season.

ly large, with big eyes, and the bill opens to reveal a wide gape. Some species have colourful male plumage. Family Eurylaimidae; there are 14 species.

broadbill, African

Broadbill found in many parts of central Africa, as far south as Angola. It prefers bush country or open woodland, where it hunts mainly for insects, often taken in flight. Its display flight involves rapid wing vibrations, which produce an audible trilling sound. Length: 13cm (5in). Family Eurylaimidae; species *Smithornis capensis*.

broadbill, lesser green

Broadbill found in the forests of Borneo, Thailand and Sumatra. Both sexes have green plumage, which blends well with the foliage of the forests, though that of the male is brighter. They often feed in small groups. Length: 20cm (8in). Family Eurylaimidae; species *Calyptomena viridis*.

broccoli (It. sprouts)

Variety of CABBAGE cultivated for its edible, immature flowers. It is the same variety (*Brassica oleracea botrytis*) as the CAULIFLOWER. Winter broccoli has large white heads. Sprouting broccoli (calabrese) has tiny green or purple flower buds which gather in compact heads. Family Brassicaceae/Cruciferae.

brocket

Small, solitary DEER found in mountain and forest undergrowth in Central and South America. Young animals have spotted coats. The antlers of the adults are simple spikes. Family Cervidae; subfamily Odocoilinae; genus *Mazama*.

brocket, brown

Brocket found in open forests from Mexico to Argentina. Shoulder height: 35–61cm (14–24in). Family Cervidae; species *Mazama gouazoubira*.

brocket, dwarf

Brocket found in certain areas of N Bolivia and Peru. Shoulder height: 35cm (14in). Family Cervidae; species *Mazama chunyi*.

brocket, little red

Brocket found in Venezuela, Ecuador and Peru. Shoulder height: 35cm (14in). Family Cervidae; species *Mazama rufina*.

brocket, red

Brocket that is found from Mexico to Argentina. It has a reddish coat with paler underparts and is a good swimmer. Shoulder height: 71cm (28in). Family Cervidae; species *Mazama americana*.

brolga

CRANE that inhabits swamps, wet meadows and shallow water in Australia. It is tall, with grey plumage and bright red markings on its head. It feeds on roots, underground stems and seeds, as well as invertebrates, including insects and molluscs, and small vertebrates. Like most cranes, brolgas display to each other with graceful dances and leaps. Length: 120cm (47in). Family Gruidae; species *Grus rubicundus*.

bromeliad

Any of 1700 species of the PINEAPPLE family (Bromeliaceae). Most are native to the tropics and subtropics and, besides the pineapple, include many of the larger EPIPHYTES of trees of the rainforests.

bronchus (pl. bronchi)

One of two branches into which the trachea or

▲ **bromeliad** Many bromeliads, such as *Aechmea fasciata*, are epiphytes (air plants), plants that use other plants for support but are not parasitic. Its broad leaves catch water as it drips through the canopy of the tropical forest.

windpipe divides, with one branch leading to each of the lungs. The bronchus divides into smaller and smaller branches, called bronchioles, which extend throughout the lung, opening into the air sacs or alveoli. The bronchi are supported and kept open by rings of cartilage.

Bronowski, Jacob (1908–75)

British biologist and writer. He lectured at many US universities and, in 1967, was made a fellow of Jesus College, Cambridge. Among his books are *Science and Human Values* (1958), *Nature and Knowledge* (1969) and three studies of William Blake. His celebrated BBC television series on man's intellectual history was published as *The Ascent of Man* (1973).

brontosaurus

See APATOSAUR

bronzewing

Any of three species of DOVE found in forest and scrub over large parts of Australia. It has a brownish back and bright, reflective wings. Bronzewings fly fast and sometimes move in flocks of thousands. They feed on the ground, mainly on seeds. Length: 30cm (12in). Family Columbidae; genus *Phaps*.

broom

Any of various deciduous shrubs of the PEA family (Fabaceae/Leguminosae). They have yellow, purple or white flowers, usually in clusters. Many belong to the genus *Genista*, which gave its name to the Plantagenate kings of England (Latin, *Planta genista*), who used the broom as their emblem.

broom corn

Type of SORGHUM that has been cultivated in Italy and other countries in Europe for centuries, and in the United States since 1797, for its specialized inflorescences. The long, straight branches of the flower head form a large, wiry tuft, which is used in making brooms and brushes. Family Poaceae; species *Sorghum bicolor*.

broomrape

Any member of a group of plants distributed in temperate Europe and Asia; they are parasitic upon the roots of other plants. They produce no chlorophyll and their leaves are reduced to scales. The two-lipped, tubular flowers are produced on spikes above ground. Some species of broomrape are serious pests on agricultural crops such as beans and peas. Family Orobanchaceae; genus *Orobanche*.

Brown, Robert (1773–1858)

Scottish botanist. The naturalist on Matthew

Flinder's voyage to Australia (1801–05), Brown returned to England with valuable botanical collections of thousands of new species. He described the flora of Australia in *Prodomus Florae Novae Hollandiae et Insulae Van Diemen* (1810). Brown's studies enabled him to outline the difference between gymnosperms and angiosperms. He is best known for establishing, in *A Brief Account of Microscopical Observations* (1828), that minute particles suspended in a liquid or gas are continuously in motion. This motion has since been called **Brownian movement**.

brown alga
See PHAEOPHYTE

brown cabbage tree
Tropical or subtropical tree found on low islands in the Pacific Ocean. Glandular fruits are dispersed by animals. The light, soft wood is used for canoes, and the leaves can be used as a vegetable. Family Nyctaginaceae; species *Pisonia grandis*.

brown coal
See LIGNITE

brown rot
Any of various chiefly fungal plant diseases that are characterized by DECAY and browning of tissues. The worst cause of brown rot is the fungus *Monilivia fructicola*, which attacks peaches and other stone fruits after harvesting.

brown snake
See SNAKE, BROWN

browser
Herbivore that feeds on twigs, leaves or scanty vegetation, often moving from one source of food to another in short succession. An example of a browsing animal is a GIRAFFE.

brucite
Mineral form of magnesium hydroxide ($Mg_3(OH)_6$); it is derived from periclase. The crystals are either glassy or waxy, can be white, pale green, grey or blue, and occur in fibrous masses or plate aggregates. Brucite is found in serpentine, schists and other metamorphic rocks. It is used to make magnesia refractory materials.

Brunfels, Otto (1488–1534)
German botanist. His *Living Pictures of Herbs* (1530–40) helped move botany towards becoming a modern science. The text, a record of the properties of plants, was distinguished by accurate descriptions and detailed drawings.

brushtail possum
See POSSUM, BRUSHTAIL

brush-turkey
Bird that belongs to the mound-builders group; it is a close relative of the MALLEE FOWL and resembles a turkey in general build and plumage. It inhabits coastal areas in E Australia. The brush-turkey lives mainly on the ground in scrubland and uses its powerful feet to grub about for insects and seeds. It covers its eggs with a large mound which acts like a compost heap, heating up as it decays. The male attends to the mound, regulating the temperature as the eggs develop. Length: 70cm (28in). Family Megapodiidae; species *Alectura lathami*.

Brussels sprout
Cultivated plant that appeared in *c*.1750 in Belgium and spread to other N European countries. Originally grown only in gardens, the Brussels sprout is now widely grown as a market garden crop for its enlarged axillary buds, which are cooked and eaten as human food. Family Brassicaceae; species *Brassica oleracea* var. *gemmifera*. *See also* BRASSICA

bryony
Either of two unrelated plants, both of which are climbers in hedgerows in Europe and elsewhere. White bryony (*Bryonia alba*) is a member of the GOURD family (Cucurbitaceae); it has large, hand-shaped leaves. Black bryony (*Tamus communis*) is a member of the YAM family (Dioscoreaceae); it has heart-shaped leaves.

bryophyte
Any member of the phylum Bryophyta – small, green, rootless, non-vascular plants, including MOSSES and LIVERWORTS. Bryophytes grow on damp surfaces exposed to light, including rocks and tree bark, almost everywhere from the Arctic to the Antarctic. There are *c*.24,000 species.

bryozoan
See MOSS ANIMAL

buckeye
Tree of the horse-chestnut group, native to the United States. It is grown for shade and as an ornamental. Its striking and fragrant flowers can be yellow, pink or white. The leaves are compound with radiating leaflets. Its often prickly fruits contain shiny brown nuts. Family Hippocastanaceae; genus *Aesculus*.

buckthorn
Deciduous, usually spiny shrub found in hedgerows, scrub and open woods of Europe, North Africa and W Asia. The highly purgative bark and berries have been used as laxatives for centuries, but are not now recommended for human use. Height: to 8m (26ft). Family Rhamnaceae; species *Rhamnus cathartica*.

buckwheat
Herbaceous annual native to central Asia; it is cultivated widely in China, North America and parts of Europe for its fruits. These fruits are ground into a nutritious flour for making cakes and breads, or, as in Japan, doughs and noodles. Beer can also be brewed from the grain. Family Polygonaceae; species *Fagopyrum esculentum*.

buckwheat tree
Shrub or small tree native to wetlands in SE North America. The attractive white flowers are followed by four-winged fruits. Its reddish-coloured autumnal foliage makes it useful as an ornamental. Family Cyrillaceae; species *Cliftonia monophylla*.

bud
Small swelling or projection consisting of a short stem with overlapping, immature leaves covered by scales. Leaf buds develop into leafy twigs, and flower buds develop into blossoms. A bud at the tip of a twig is a terminal bud and contains the growing point; lateral buds develop in leaf axils along a twig.

budding
Method of ASEXUAL REPRODUCTION that produces a new organism from an outgrowth of the parent. HYDRAS (small, freshwater polyps), for example, often bud in spring and summer. A small bulge appears on the parent and grows until it breaks away as a new individual.

buddleia
Any member of a group of flowering shrubs, often conspicuous because of the butterflies attracted to its purple or yellow flowers. Buddleias used to be classified as members of the logania family, native to the tropics, but are now considered to be a separate family, the Buddlejaceae. Genus *Buddleia*.

budgerigar (parakeet)
Small, brightly coloured seed-eating PARROT native to Australia. A popular pet, it can be taught to mimic speech. The sexes look alike, but the coloration of the cere (a waxy membrane at the base of the beak) may vary seasonally. Length: 19cm (7in). Family Psittacidae; species *Melopsittacus undulatus*.

▼ **budgerigar** This popular species (*Melopsittacus undulatus*) of parakeet is often found in large flocks, such as this one at a waterhole near Alice Springs, central Australia. Wild budgerigars have just the one plumage, but caged varieties can be many different colours.

buffalo

Any of several massive, horned mammals; also a misnomer for the North American BISON. The ox-like Indian, or water, buffalo (*Bubalus bubalis*), found in Southeast Asia and the Indian Subcontinent, is often domesticated for milk and hides. It has a dull black coat and large horns. Height: 1.5m (5ft); weight: up to 800kg (1800lb). The African, or Cape, buffalo (*Syncerus caffer*) inhabits scrub and open woodland in sub-Saharan Africa. It is similar in appearance to the Indian buffalo but with characteristically curved horns. Height: 1.5m (5ft); weight: up to 900kg (2000lb). Family Bovidae.

buffalo berry

Upright, deciduous, thorny shrub native to central and N North America. It has silvery young growth. Its scarlet or yellow fruits are used to make jelly. It is named after English botanist John Shepherd (1764–1836). Family Eleagnaceae; species *Shepherdia argentea*.

buffalo fish

Freshwater fish found in large rivers of the Mississippi Valley, United States; it is a member of the SUCKER family. The buffalo fish is brownish to bluish-green and lives and feeds at the bottom of rivers. There are several species. The bigmouth buffalo fish can reach a length of 90cm (35in) and a weight of 30kg (66lb). Family Catostomidae; species *Ictiobus cyprinellus* (bigmouth) and *Ictiobus bubalus* (smallmouth).

buffalo grass

Grey-green grass with curly leaf blades, native to North America. It is one of the most important grazing grasses of the uplands of the Great Plains region. Early settlers used the grass sod to make sod houses. Height: up to 15cm (6in). Family Poaceae; species *Buchloe dactyloides*.

buffer solution

Solution to which a moderate quantity of a strong acid or a strong base can be added without making a significant change to its pH value (acidity or alkalinity). Buffer solutions usually consist of either a mixture of a weak acid and one of its salts, a mixture of an acid salt and its normal salt or a mixture of two acid salts.

bufflehead

North American DUCK, related to the GOLDENEYE. The breeding male has a high, domed, black forehead, with a white patch on the back of the head; it shows a large, white wing-patch in flight. Buffleheads are usually seen in small groups on pools, lakes and rivers; in winter they may also be found on estuaries and coastal waters. Length: 35cm (14in). Family Anatidae; species *Bucephala albeola*.

▲ **bulb** As well as serving as underground storage organs, bulbs may also provide flowering plants with a means of vegetative reproduction. In spring, the flower bud (1) and young foliage leaves (2) develop into a flowering plant using the food and water stored in the bulb's fleshy scale leaves (3). When the flower has died, the leaves live on and continue to make food, which is transported downwards to the leaf bases. These swell and develop into new bulbs. Axillary buds (4) may develop into daughter bulbs, which break off to form new independent plants.

Buffon, Georges Louis Leclerc, Comte de (1707–88)

French naturalist. From 1739, as keeper of the Jardin du Roi (now Jardin des Plantes) in Paris, Buffon began to collect data for *Histoire naturelle* (1749–1804), a popular compendium of natural history and geology. Only 36 of the 44 volumes were published before his death. He was elected to the Académie française in 1753.

bug

Any member of the INSECT order Hemiptera, although in the United States any insect is commonly called a bug. True bugs are flattened insects that undergo gradual or incomplete METAMORPHOSIS, have two pairs of wings, and use piercing and sucking mouthparts. Most species, such as the greenfly, feed on plant juices, although a number attack animals and are carriers of disease.

bugle

Perennial, creeping plant native to Europe, Asia and North Africa and naturalized in North America. Found in damp woods and fields, it is also grown as a garden plant. Its purple flowers are borne on spikes. The bugle has been valued for centuries as a wound healer. Family Lamiaceae; species *Ajuga reptans*.

bugloss

Wild flowering plant native to Europe and naturalized in E North America; it is a member of the BORAGE family. It has bright, purplish-blue flowers.

Height: *c*.40cm (*c*.16in). Family Boraginaceae; genera *Lycopsis* and *Echium*; species include *Echium vulgare* (Viper's bugloss).

bulb

Food storage organ consisting of a short stem and swollen scale leaves. Food is stored in the scales, which are either layered in a series of rings, as in the ONION, or loosely attached to the stem, as in some LILIES. Small buds between the scale leaves give rise to new shoots each year. New bulbs are produced in the AXILS of the outer scale leaves. *See also* ASEXUAL REPRODUCTION

bulb-fly

Any of several species of HOVERFLY. They are considered pests. The bulb-fly lays its eggs on the stem of, or in the soil near, bulb-producing plants, such as daffodils, lilies, tulips and narcisci. Maggots hatch from the eggs and tunnel into the bases of the bulbs, where they feed, killing or damaging the plant. Adult body length: *c*.20mm (0.8in). Order Diptera; family Syrphidae.

bulbil

Small, BULB-like structure that grows on a plant. Bulbils may develop above the ground at the base of a plant or on stems from an axillary bud, or they form instead of flowers (as with some onions). Bulbils that become detached and fall to the ground can develop into new plants, and so function as a method of ASEXUAL REPRODUCTION.

bulbul

Any of numerous species of medium-sized songbird, native to Africa and Asia. They have rather drab plumage but musical calls. Family Pycnonotidae; there are *c*.125 species.

bulbul, black

Bulbul that inhabits forests from S India through Southeast Asia, at altitudes of up to 3000m (10,000 feet) in the Himalayas. It utters a wide range of bell-like or squeaking calls. Length: 23cm (9in). Family Pycnonotidae; species *Hypsipetes madagascariensis*.

bulbul, black-collared

Bulbul that lives in the savannas and woods of central Africa. It is rather small, with a pale underside and a dark chest band. It has a rather shrike-like upright stance. Length: 15cm (6in). Family Pycnonotidae; species *Neolestes torquatus*.

bulbul, chestnut-eared

Bulbul that is native to Japan, S China and Taiwan; it often visits gardens and bird feeders. It has slaty blue plumage and a long tail. Length: 27cm (11in). Family Pycnonotidae; species *Hypsipetes amaurotis*.

bulbul, garden (common bulbul)

Bulbul that is common in central and North Africa. It has a dark grey head, dark back, wings and tail and a white underside. It utters musical, bubbling calls, and is often quite tame. Length: 18cm (7in). Family Pycnonotidae; species *Pycnonotus barbatus*.

bulbul, long-billed

Bulbul that lives in lowland forests of Borneo and Sumatra. Its rather long bill is hooked at the tip. In addition to the usual bulbul diet of fruit, it also eats insects. Length: 18cm (7in). Family Pycnonotidae; species *Setornis criniger*.

bulbul, red-whiskered

Bulbul that is found from India to China, in jungle,

► **buffalo** The African buffalo (*Syncerus caffer*) is usually found in open areas near jungle, or wallowing in swampy ground. With horns up to 1m in width, it can be extremely aggressive if attacked or wounded. Due to hunting and the destruction of its natural habitat, the numbers of African buffalo have declined severely. A smaller subspecies of cape buffalo, inhabiting the forests of central and w Africa, is reddish brown with smaller horns.

woodland and also gardens. Its head has a jaunty crest and there is a red patch on the cheeks and under the tail coverts. Length: 20cm (8in). Family Pycnonotidae; species *Pycnonotus jocosus*.

bulbul, striated green
Bulbul that inhabits jungles and forests of the Himalayas, at altitudes of up to 3000m (10,000ft). Small flocks call almost constantly as they move about amongst the trees. Length: 20cm (8in). Family Pycnonotidae; species *Pycnonotus striatus*.

bulbul, white-cheeked
Bulbul found in the Himalayan region. It lives in forests and scrubland, but may also be seen around villages, in gardens and on balconies. It is an active bird with a range of pleasant calls. Length: 20cm (8in). Family Pycnonotidae; species *Pycnonotus leucogenys*.

bullace (damson)
Small tree of the group that includes the common PLUM; it is known only in cultivation or as an escape. It has densely hairy, often spiny twigs. Its small, dark purple, ovoid fruits have flattened stones and are usually borne in clusters. Family Rosaceae; species *Prunus domestica* ssp. *insititia*.

Bullard, Sir Edward Crisp (1907–80)
English geophysicist. He is noted for his work in geomagnetism, especially his theory of the geomagnetic dynamo, based on convective motion in the Earth's core. An early supporter of the theory of plate tectonics, he produced a computer-generated map matching the continental shelves of Africa and South America.

bullfinch
Large, plump FINCH of Europe and Asia. It is common in woodland and gardens, where it likes to feed on buds, making it unpopular in orchards. The male has a striking pink breast and grey-blue back; both sexes have a white rump. Length: 15cm (6in). Family Fringillidae; species *Pyrrhula pyrrhula*.

bullfrog
FROG that is found in streams and ponds in the United States; it is green or brown and breeds in the spring. The bullfrog is the largest North American frog and can jump long distances. It gets its name from its loud bass voice. Length: up to 20cm (8in). Family Ranidae; genus *Rana*.

bullhead
Freshwater CATFISH, native to the E United States. Now farmed as food, it has been introduced in Europe and Hawaii. It has four pairs of fleshy mouth whiskers and a square tail. Length: to 61cm (24in); weight: to 3.6kg (8lb). Family Ictaluridae; species include *Ictalurus natalis* (yellow bullhead) and *Ictalurus nebulosus* (brown bullhead).

bull rout (father lasher)
Short-spined, marine fish, common in the E Arctic and Atlantic oceans. It has a large head and lacks a swimbladder. A voracious predatory fish, it feeds on crustaceans and the eggs and larvae of commercial fish. Family Cottidae; species *Myoxephalus scorpius*.

bull snake
See SNAKE, BULL

bulrush (red mace)
Aquatic, perennial reed of the CATTAIL genus; it is found rooted in the mud of swamps, slow rivers and ponds throughout North America, Europe and Asia. The cylindrical inflorescence contains male flowers

◄ **bunting** The black-headed bunting (*Emberiza melanocephala*) is found in SE Europe and SW Asia. This species grows to about 16cm (6in) in length.

at the tip and female flowers below; it ripens into a characteristic brown, felt-like cylinder. Height: c.2m (80in). Family Typhaceae; species *Typha latifolia*. In North America, **bulrush** usually refers to species of the *Scirpus* genus of the SEDGE family. Family Cyperaceae.

bulrush millet
Annual GRASS grown in semi-arid regions of Africa and India. The white, yellow or grey seeds or grain are eaten in the same way as rice or ground into a flour for porridge. The green plant is used as fodder. Family Poaceae; species *Pennisetum typhoides*.

bumblebee (humble bee)
Robust, hairy, black BEE with broad yellow or orange stripes. Bees of the genus *Bombus* live in organized groups in ground or tree nests, where the fertile queen lays her first eggs after the winter hibernation. These eggs become worker bees. Later, the queen lays eggs to produce drones (males) and new queens, which develop before the colony dies. The cycle is then repeated. The cuckoo bee (genus *Psithyrus*) lays its eggs in the nests of *Bombus* bees, which rear them. Length: up to 2.5cm (1in). Order Hymenoptera; family Apidae.

bunting
Any of c.280 species of small, seed-eating birds; the group also includes the American sparrows. Buntings are found mainly in Europe and Asia, although the Lapland bunting also occurs in America. In plumage they range from brown and grey to yellow and green, and many also have striking black-and-white markings. Family Emberizidae (part).

bunting, indigo
Bunting found in E North America. The breeding male is entirely blue; the female is a drab brown. The indigo bunting is a close relative of the painted bunting. Length: 14cm (6in). Family Emberizidae; species *Passerina cyanea*.

bunting, Lapland
Bunting that breeds around the Arctic tundra, but winters further south, often on coastal marshes. The breeding male has a black-and-white face and a chestnut nape. Length: 16cm (6in). Family Emberizidae; species *Calcarius lapponicus*.

bunting, painted
North American species; it is more closely related to the GROSBEAK than to other buntings. The male is very pretty, with red, blue and green plumage. Length: 16cm (6in). Family Emberizidae; species *Passerina ciris*.

bunting, reed
Marshland bird found in Europe and Asia. It has a

pleasant, lilting song, usually delivered from a reedbed or nearby scrub. Length: 16cm (6in). Family Emberizidae; species *Emberiza schoeniclus*.

bunting, snow
Beautiful bunting that breeds in the tundra around the Arctic, where its white plumage gives good camouflage. It breeds as far north as Greenland. Length: 16cm (6in). Family Emberizidae; species *Plectrophenax nivalis*.

burbot
Bottom-dwelling, freshwater COD found in colder waters of Asia, North America and Europe. It is a slender, brown fish and spawns in winter. Length: to 110cm (43in); weight: to 16kg (35lb). Family Gadidae; species *Lota lota*.

burdock
Tall, herbaceous biennial native to Europe and Asia and naturalized widely in North America. Its purple flowers are produced in round heads and encased in overlapping stiff scales with hooked tips; the whole head sticks to any fur or clothing that comes into contact with it and thus the seeds are dispersed. Family Asteraceae; genus *Arctium*.

Burgess Shale
See feature article, page 56

burnet
Perennial plant native to north temperate regions. Its leaves are used to give a cucumber-like flavour to salads. Long-stamened, pink flowers are borne on tall stalks. Family Rosaceae; genus *Sanguisorba*.

burning bush
Strong-smelling plant that is native from S Europe to N China. Grown in gardens as an ornamental, it produces large showy flowers in terminal heads. Burning bush is so-called because vapours produced by oil glands give a flash of light if a burning match is held under the flower cluster on a still, hot evening. Family Rutaceae; species *Dictamnus albus*. **Burning bush** is also the name of a deciduous shrub or tree native to North America. It has elliptic leaves and purple flowers in slender-stalked clusters. The fruit is deeply four-lobed and scarlet; the seeds are brown with a scarlet aril. Height: to 7.6m (25ft). Family Celastraceae; species *Euonymus atropurpureus*.

bur reed
Any member of a small group of aquatic or semi-aquatic, herbaceous perennials, found mainly in the temperate and arctic zones of the Northern Hemisphere. The flowers are crowded in characteristic round heads, with male and female flowers in separate heads. Stands of the plant provide shelter and food, in the form of seeds, for wildfowl. Family Sparganiaceae; genus *Sparganium*.

burrowing toad
See TOAD, BURROWING

burying beetle
See BEETLE, BURYING

◄ **burbot** Nocturnal bottom-dwelling fish, burbots (*Lota lota*) are found at depths of up to 200m (656ft). Suited to well-oxygenated water, burbot populations have declined in areas of water pollution.

bush baby (galago)

Nocturnal PRIMATE that is found in the forests of sub-Saharan Africa. It is so called because its plaintive cries sound like those of a human baby. The bush baby's strong hind legs enable it to leap from branch to branch; its long tail provides balance. All bush baby species have excellent senses of smell and hearing and very large, forward-facing eyes. It feeds on fruit and insects. Family Lorisidae; subfamily Galaginae.

bush baby, Allen's

Bushbaby that lives mostly in the lower branches of tropical forests. It has a thick, red-grey coat. Head-body length: 20cm (8in); tail: 25cm (10in). Family Lorisidae; species *Galago alleni*.

bush baby, lesser (Senegal bush baby)

Bushbaby that inhabits dry forests and rainforests across Africa; there are several subspecies. The lesser bush baby has a pale grey coat. Head-body length: 16cm (6in); tail: 23cm (9in). Family Lorisidae; species *Galago senegalensis*.

bush baby, needle-clawed

Two species of bushbaby, both of which have long, pointed nails used for gripping branches. Head-body length: 30cm (12in); tail: 29cm (11in). Family Lorisidae; species *Galago elegantulus*. Head-body length: 16cm (6in); tail: 23cm (9in). Family Lorisidae; species *Galago inustus*.

bush baby, thick-tailed

Largest bushbaby species. It sometimes eats small vertebrates as well as fruit and insects. Head-body length: 32cm (13in); tail: 44cm (17in). Family Lorisidae; species *Galago* or *Otelumur crassicaudatus*.

bushbuck

Smallest species of spiral-horned ANTELOPE. Often solitary, it is found throughout sub-Saharan Africa in a wide variety of habitats with dense cover. Its short coat varies from bright chestnut to dark brown, with white stripes and spots and some white face markings. The male bushbuck's long horns are straight apart from one twist near the base. Head-body length: 115–145cm (45–57in); tail: 20–24cm (8–9in). Family Bovidae; subfamily Bovinae; species *Tragelaphus scriptus*.

bush-cricket

See CRICKET, BUSH-

bushmaster

Largest pit VIPER, found in Central America and N South America. It has long fangs and large venom glands. It is pinkish and brown with a diamond pattern. Length: up to 3.7m (12ft). Family Viperidae; subfamily Crotalidae.

bush-shrike

Any of *c*.16 species of chunkily built, medium-sized African birds of the SHRIKE family. Their ample bills are hooked at the tip. Despite having vivid plumage, with red, green and yellow markings, bush-shrikes are quite secretive and can be hard to spot. Some species live in rainforest, others inhabit more open scrubland. They feed on invertebrates and small vertebrates. Some species have a loud, bell-like, whistling call. Length: 20–25cm (8–10in). Family Laniidae (part).

bush-shrike, fiery-breasted

Bush-shrike that lives in rainforest in W and central Africa. It is vividly coloured, with a bright red breast, blue head, green back and tail, and a black and yellow tail tip. Length: 25cm (10in). Family Laniidae; species *Malaconotus cruentus*.

bush-shrike, four-coloured

Bush-shrike found in bush and forests of E and S Africa, mainly towards the coast. It is mostly green, with a red chin, black neck-band and patches of yellow. The male has a bell-like call. Length: 20cm (8in). Family Laniidae; species *Telophorus quadricolor*.

bushtit

Only member of the long-tailed TIT family to be found in North America, where it inhabits open woodland and is a common garden visitor. It is mostly buff-coloured, with a tiny beak and a long, narrow tail. Length: 11cm (4in). Family Aegithalidae; species *Psaltriparus minimus*.

bushy poppy

Stiff leafy shrub with whitish bark. It is native to

BURGESS SHALE

Layer of siltstone in a quarry in Yoho National Park in E British Columbia, Canada. Discovered in 1909 by US scientist Charles D. Walcott, it contains a large number of FOSSILS of animals that lived in the CAMBRIAN period, more than 500 million years ago. The fossils and the silt that covered them accumulated at the foot of an undersea cliff. The silt has preserved traces of many of the soft bodies of sea creatures, which normally do not survive. The fossils include the oldest known chordate (*Pikaia*), a worm-like creature that is the forerunner of all animals with backbones. The Burgess Shale fossils also include a number of kinds of animals that have completely vanished, and apparently do not belong to any of the approximately 32 phyla of animals that are known today.

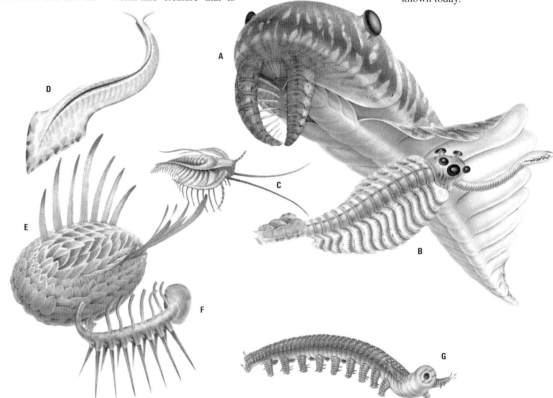

▶ **The Burgess shale** organisms provide a fascinating glimpse of marine life 570 million years ago. These creatures lived during the Cambrian explosion, a period of intense evolutionary diversification when the ancestors of probably all the modern animal groups we know today came about. The majority (perhaps 90%) of those organisms became extinct, and with them many experiments in animal design. *Anomalocaris* (A) was the largest of the Burgess shale creatures, at over 2ft (0.6m) long, with powerful circular jaws that crunched up trilobites. *Opabinia* (B) was a strange animal with a bizarre vacuum-like frontal nozzle. *Marella* (C), an arthropod, was the first – and most abundant – creature found in the Burgess shale. *Pikaia* (D), a worm-like animal, is significant among all the Burgess organisms because it is the first known chordate. *Wiwaxia* (E) was covered in plates and spines, which presumably acted as protection against predators. If *Hallucigenia* (F) existed as an independent organism, it was probably a bottom dweller, supported by its peculiar struts and feeding with its many tentacles. It has been suggested, though, that it may simply be part of a larger, undiscovered creature. *Aysheaia* (G) was probably a parasite, living and feeding on ancient sponges on the seabed.

California and NW Mexico, where it is found in dry parts of the coastal ranges and mountains. It is grown ornamentally for its bright, golden-yellow flowers, which are 2.5–5cm (1–2in) across. Height: to 3m (10ft). Family Papaveraceae; species *Dendromecon rigida*.

bustard
Any of *c.*22 species of medium or large ground-dwelling birds. They have strong legs and long necks and their grey, brown and white plumage blends well with their habitat of scrub or open grassland. They take a range of food, including fruit, seeds and shoots, as well as insects and small vertebrates. Family Otididae.

bustard, Australian
Bustard that inhabits plains, grasslands and open woodlands in N and central Australia. The male makes loud booming calls when displaying. Length: 80–120cm (31–47in). Family Otididae; species *Choriotis australis*.

bustard, crested
Bustard of the African savanna. The male has an amazing display flight in which it takes off vertically to a height of *c.*30m (*c.*100ft). Length: 50cm (20in). Family Otididae; species *Eupodotis ruficrista*.

bustard, great
Bustard found scattered in parts of North Africa, the Iberia Peninsula, E Europe and Russia. Although not the tallest bustard, it is the bulkiest; it is one of the world's heaviest flying birds – the male can weigh as much as 18kg (40lb). Length: 75–105cm (30–41in). Family Otididae; species *Otis tarda*.

bustard, houbara
Bustard that is found mainly in the semideserts of Africa and Asia. It roams in small flocks. This species is particularly threatened by hunting. Length: *c.*60cm (*c.*24in). Family Otididae; species *Chlamydotis undulata*.

bustard, kori
Bustard that lives mainly in the savannas of E Africa, particularly in Kenya, where it stalks majestically amongst the grasses. Its loose neck feathers give it a thick-necked appearance. Length: 76–100cm (30–39in). Family Otididae; species *Ardeotis kori*.

bustard, little
Small bustard that lives in sometimes large flocks in grassland and farmland of North Africa, S Europe and parts of Asia. The black-and-white neck plumage of the male is puffed out during display, which is accompanied by a strange, hollow, trilling sound. Length: *c.*43cm (*c.*17in). Family Otididae; species *Tetrax tetrax*.

bustard, Vigors'
Bustard that inhabits stony grassland in S Africa. The Vigors' bustard has rather plain, sandy coloured plumage. Length: *c.*60cm (*c.*24in) Family Otididae; species *Eupodotis vigorsii*.

busy Lizzie
Perennial plant with fleshy stems, elliptical leaves and large, flat flowers with a long spur. The popular garden plant, which has brightly coloured, white through red and orange flowers, is a hybrid between two species native to tropical E Africa. The ripe fleshy pods burst suddenly when touched. Family Balsaminaceae; species *Impatiens holstii* x *Impatiens Sultanii*. *See also* IMPATIENS

butte
Isolated, flat-topped, steep-sided hill. It is formed when a remnant of hard rock overlies and protects softer rock underneath from being worn down, while the surrounding areas continue to be eroded. It is most often found in arid areas, particularly in the plains of the W United States.

buttercup
Herbaceous flowering plant found worldwide; the many species vary considerably but usually have yellow or white flowers and deeply cut leaves. Family Ranunculaceae; genus *Ranunculus*.

buttercup tree
Tropical tree native to India; it is sometimes grown as an ornamental in dry areas. The leaves are palmately lobed and the large yellow flowers are borne in clusters. The colourless sap is fragrant, and in older trees an amber-coloured gum with medicinal value may be obtained. Family Cochlospermaceae; species *Cochlospermum religiosum*.

butterfish
Marine fish found along Atlantic and Pacific coasts. A favourite sport fish, it is silvery-grey or blue with dark spots. Length: 30cm (12in); weight: 0.5kg (1.2lb). Family Stromateidae; species include Atlantic *Peprilus triacanthus* and California pompano *Peprilus simillimus*.

butterfly
Day-flying INSECT of the order Lepidoptera. The adult has two pairs of often brightly coloured, scale-covered wings. The female lays eggs on a selected food source and the larvae (CATERPILLARS) emerge within days or hours. The larvae have chewing mouthparts and often do great damage to crops until they reach the "resting phase" of the life cycle, the pupa (chrysalis). Within the pupa, the adult (imago) is formed, with wings, wing muscles, antennae, a slender body and sucking mouthparts. *See also* METAMORPHOSIS

butterfly, admiral
See ADMIRAL

butterfly, angelwing
Common name for several North American species of brown butterfly. The usual larval-host plants are stinging nettles (*Urtica* spp.). Adult body length: *c.*30mm (*c.*1.2in); wingspan: *c.*90mm (*c.*3.5in). Family Nymphalidae; genus *Polygonia*; species include *Polygonia satyrus*.

butterfly, birdwing
Large, colourful butterfly found in tropical regions. It has highly patterned and scalloped wings. Adult body length: 50–100mm (2–4in). Family Papilionidae; genus *Ornithoptera*.

butterfly, blue
Any of many species within the butterfly family Lycaenidae, but particularly those within the subfamily Plebeiinae. Blues are small, erratic flyers with bright or iridescent blue coloration on the dorsal surface of the wings. Adult body length: 10–30mm (0.4–1.2in). Family Lycaenidae.

butterfly, brimstone
Yellow butterfly commonly seen feeding on meadow flowers in Europe and elsewhere. Its life is long, often up to nine months. The brimstone butterfly is named after its deep yellow coloration, which is close to that of sulphur (formerly known as brimstone).

▲ **buttercup** The creeping buttercup (*Ranunculus repens*) is native to North America and Europe and is often found in lawns and gardens. It is considered a pest by many gardeners as it inhibits the growth of nearby plants.

Adult body length: *c.*30–40mm (*c.*1.2–1.6in). Family Pieridae; species *Gonepteryx rhamni*.

butterfly, brown
Any of many species within the butterfly family Nymphalidae. Most have brown bodies and wings as well as a series of eyespots towards the edges of their wings. Like most butterflies, adult browns are nectar feeders. They commonly frequent meadows and lightly wooded areas. Adult body length: 20–80mm (0.8–3.1in). Family Nymphalidae.

butterfly, cabbage white
See CABBAGE WHITE BUTTERFLY

butterfly, clouded yellow
Butterfly with yellow wings featuring minute spots of grey. The larvae feed on legumes, and the adults frequent grassy regions. Adult body length: 30–50mm (0.1–0.2in). Family Pieridae; genus *Colias*.

butterfly, copper
Any of several species of butterfly of the genus *Lycaena*. Many of the caterpillars feed on dock or sorrel (*Rumex* spp.), and the adults are small but aggressive defenders of the flowers, which they exploit for their nectar. The dorsal surface of the wings is covered in iridescent copper scales. Coppers are closely related to the blue butterflies. Family Lycaenidae.

butterfly, dead-leaf (leaf butterfly)
Butterfly native to the tropics of S Asia. When a dead-leaf butterfly rests on a twig, its folded wings look like withered leaves. Adult body length: 70–90mm (2.8–3.5in). Family Nymphalidae; genus *Kallima*.

butterfly, fritillary
See FRITILLARY

butterfly, hairstreak
Any of a group of butterflies in the family Lycaenidae. Hairstreaks are grey and brown, often

B

with antennae-like extensions to their hindwings. They are found in open areas on every continent, especially in the tropics. Hairstreaks have a quick, erratic flight. Adult body length: 15–25mm (0.6–1in). Family Lycaenidae; genus *Strymon*.

butterfly, monarch
See MONARCH BUTTERFLY

butterfly, morpho
Large butterfly noted for the brilliant blue metallic lustre of the upper surfaces of the male's wings. The females are more dull in colour and have broader wings. The larvae are plant feeders. They are found in the American tropics. Adult body length: 50–110mm (2–4.3in). Family Nymphalidae; genus *Morpho*.

butterfly, mourning cloak (Camberwell beauty)
Large butterfly found in Europe, North America and Asia. It is mainly dark brown, but has bright blue spots and a strip of yellow along each lateral wing margin. The larvae feed on various host trees, including elms, poplars and willows, at the beginning of spring. Unusually, it is the adults that overwinter. Adult body length: 5–7mm (0.2–0.3in). Family Nymphalidae; species *Nymphalis antiopa*.

butterfly, painted lady (thistle butterfly)
Widely distributed butterfly, found in Europe and Africa. It has brown, black, orange and white wing markings. Its caterpillars feed on thistles or nettles. Adult body length: 20–40mm (0.8–1.6in). Family Nymphalidae; species *Vanessa cardui*.

butterfly, peacock
See PEACOCK BUTTERFLY

butterfly, purple emperor
Large European butterfly; the upper wings of the male have an iridescent, purple sheen. Wild populations are often confined to large oak forests. The eggs are laid over the summer and the larvae hibernate on sallow twigs. Adult body size: *c*.25mm (*c*.1in); forewing span: *c*.70mm (*c*.3in). Family Nymphalidae; genus *Apatura*.

butterfly, satyr
Brown and grey butterfly that usually has eyespots on its wings. The veins of the front wings are typically swollen at the wing base. It generally inhabits woodlands. Adult body length: 20–30mm (0.8–1.2in). Family Satyridae; genus *Neonymphia*.

butterfly, skipper
See SKIPPER

butterfly, sulphur
Medium-sized, orange or yellow butterfly. Its wings are bordered or otherwise marked with black. White

▲ **butterfly, viceroy** This species (*Limenitis archippus*) inhabits marshes, riverbeds and wet meadows, especially where willow, poplar and aspen trees occur. The species is increasingly threatened because of habitat loss.

members of the family are called WHITES. Adult body length: 20–50mm (0.8–2in). Family Pieridae; species include *Callidryas eubule*, which is the common yellow butterfly of E United States.

butterfly, swallowtail
See SWALLOWTAIL BUTTERFLY

butterfly, thistle
See BUTTERFLY, PAINTED LADY

butterfly, tortoiseshell
See TORTOISESHELL BUTTERFLY

butterfly, viceroy
Large butterfly that has orange-brown wings with black veins and borders. It is noted for its MIMICRY of the MONARCH BUTTERFLY. The viceroy can be distinguished from the monarch by its smaller size and a transverse black band on its hind wings. Family Nymphalidae; species *Limenitis archippus*.

butterfly, white
Common, white butterfly with mainly white wings. Its host plants are usually members or relatives of the genus *Brassica*. It deposits its eggs on the undersides of leaves; the caterpillars feed on the leaves and pupate on the host plant, sometimes damaging crops. Family Pieridae; genus *Pieris*.

butterfly, zebra longwing
Butterfly that is found in tropical areas of S North America, the West Indies, Central America and N South America. It gets its common name from the striped pattern of the adults. The eggs are laid mainly on passion vine. The white caterpillars have long black spines on each segment and a pale yellow head. The adults feed on nectar and pollen and produce a creaking sound when alarmed. Family Heliconiidae; species *Heliconius charitonius*.

butterfly fish
Tropical marine fish, a brightly coloured and conspicuous member of coral reef communities. It has a compressed body and, in some species, an extended snout. Length: 15–20cm (6–8in). Family Chaetodontidae; species include *Chaetodon ocellatus* (common butterflyfish). The name butterfly fish also refers to the freshwater BONYTONGUE *Pantodon* of Africa. Family Pantodontidae.

butterfly flower
See BUDDLEIA

butternut (white walnut)
Tree with grey, deeply fissured bark, native to E North America. Its young twigs and oblong, ridged fruit are sticky and hairy. The fruit husk is used to dye cloth yellow; the wood is used for furniture and church altars. Height: to 30m (100ft). Family Juglandaceae; species *Juglans cinerea*.

butterwort
Any member of a large group of carnivorous bog plants that trap and digest insects in a sticky secretion on their leaves. They bear single white, purple or yellow flowers on a leafless stalk. The sides of the leaves roll over to enclose the insect while it is digested. Family Lentibulariaceae; genus *Pinguicula*. *See also* INSECTIVOROUS PLANT

buttonquail (hemipode)
Small bird that is quail-like in appearance; it is closely related to the crane. Buttonquails live mainly in Asia and Australia, except for the little buttonquail

(Andalusian hemipode), which is found in North Africa and, rarely, s Spain. Buttonquails eat insects and seeds. The male incubates the eggs. Length: 14cm (6in). Family Turnicidae; genera *Turnix* and *Ortyxelos*; there are 15 species.

buttonwood (American plane)
Tall, round-headed, deciduous tree native to North America, found from Maine to Minnesota and south to Florida and Texas. Its creamy-white bark peels off in small plates, which become brown and fissured on old trunks. The buttonwood tree is used for shade, and its wood for boxes, furniture and charcoal. Height: to 52m (170ft). Family Platanaceae; species *Platanus occidentalis*.

buzzard
Broad-winged bird of prey. True buzzards are those that belong to the genus *Buteo*, although many of these are known as hawks in North America. True buzzards are medium-sized birds with short, rather fan-shaped tails; there are *c*.26 species. Non-*Buteo* birds of prey that are also called buzzard include: the lizard buzzard of Africa (*Kaupifalco monogrammicus*); the grasshopper buzzard and relatives (genus *Butastur*); and also the turkey vulture (*Cathartes aura*) of North and South America, which is locally called "buzzard".

buzzard, Eurasian
Common European bird of prey. It inhabits woodland and farmland and takes invertebrates, such as worms, as well as small rodents and rabbits. Length: *c*.55cm (*c*.22in). Family Accipitridae; species *Buteo buteo*.

buzzard, grasshopper (buzzard-eagle)
Bird of prey; it is rather HARRIER-like in outline, with a long tail. It breeds south of the Sahara desert. It sometimes gathers in flocks following swarms of insects. Length: *c*.42cm (*c*.17in). Family Accipitridae; species *Butastur rufipennis*.

buzzard, honey
Bird of prey that is more closely related to the KITE than to the true buzzard. Honey buzzards have small, rather pigeon-like heads and long tails. They feed partly on bees, wasps and their grubs. Length: *c*.56cm (*c*.22in). Family Accipitridae; species *Pernis apivorus* (Western honey buzzard).

buzzard, jackal
Buzzard that is common in much of E and S Africa. It takes its common name from its dog-like yelping call. One race of this species is known as the augur buzzard. Length: *c*.50cm (*c*.20in) Family Accipitridae; species *Buteo rufofuscus*.

buzzard, long-legged
Buzzard that lives mainly in dry steppe and semi-deserts, from North Africa to Asia. Length: *c*.55cm (*c*.22in). Family Accipitridae; species *Buteo rufinus*.

buzzard, rough-legged (rough-legged hawk)
Buzzard that inhabits the northern tundra. It eats small mammals, such as voles and lemmings, and moves south in the winter. Length: *c*.55cm (*c*.22in). Family Accipitridae; species *Buteo lagopus*.

by-the-wind sailor
Any of several species of marine hydromedusae of the genus *Velella*. They have a sail-shaped float, which is held above water and permits the animal to sail at an angle to the wind. By-the-wind sailors feed on other small marine animals, which they catch with the tentacles that trail from their floats. Phylum Cnidaria; class Hydrozoa; order Chondrophora.

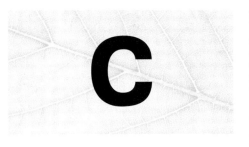

C

cabbage
Low, stout vegetable of the genus *Brassica*. Members include BRUSSELS SPROUTS, CAULIFLOWERS, BROCCOLI, KOHLRABI and TURNIPS. They are all biennials, producing "heads" one year and flowers the next. The common cabbage (*Brassica oleracea capitata*) has an edible head and large, fleshy leaves. Cabbage species grow in temperate regions. Family Brassicaceae/Cruciferae.

cabbage root-fly
Either of two species of FLY that are renowned pests of crops such as cabbage, turnips and rape. The cabbage root-fly usually lays its eggs in the soil near to the roots of the host plant. The larvae hatch and tunnel into the soft root tissues, causing extensive damage, which often results in the plant's death. Adult body length: 7mm (0.3in). Order Diptera; family Anthomyiidae; species *Delia radicum* and *Delia brassica*.

cabbage tree
Name given to many types of trees that are characterized by massive heads of leaves. Cabbage trees are found in different genera, including: in Africa *Anthocleista*, *Vernonia* and *Cussonia*; in New Zealand *Cordyline*; and in the West Indies *Andira*. Cabbage trees are sometimes planted for shelter belts.

cabbage white butterfly
Species of BUTTERFLY, the green caterpillar of which is a common pest on cabbage plants. The female adult is almost completely white except for black spots on its wings; the male has no forewing spots. Family Pieridae; species *Pieris brassicae*.

cabbage whitefly
Any of several species of small, sucking bug; they are not flies. Adult cabbage whiteflies have functional wings and are quite mobile. The nymphs live under waxy coverings and feed on sap in the leaves and shoots of their host plants. Cabbage whiteflies are considered pests of brassicas such as cabbage, cauliflower and broccoli. Adult body length: 3–5mm (0.1–0.2in). Order Hemiptera; family Aleyrodidae; genus *Aleyrodes*.

cacomistle
Either of two species belonging to the genus *Bassariscus* of the RACCOON family, found in Central America and S United States. Both species are grey or brown with white patches above and below each eye and on the cheeks. Nocturnal predators, cacomistles feed on lizards and small mammals as well as insects, fruit and nuts. The North American cacomistle is also known as the ringtailed cat or ringtail. Head-body length: 31–38cm (12–15in); tail: 31–44cm (12–18in). Species *Bassariscus astutus*. The other species of cacomistle is *Bassariscus sumichrasti*. Head-body length: 38–50cm (15–20in); tail: 39–53cm (16–21in). Family Procyonidae.

cactus
Any of more than 2000 species of succulent plants, found particularly in hot desert regions of the Western Hemisphere. A cactus has long roots, which are adapted to absorb moisture from desert terrains. Stems are usually spiny, cylindrical and branched. Cactus flowers are usually borne singly in a wide range of colours. Height: from 2.5cm (1in) to more than 15m (50ft). *See also* XEROPHYTE

caddis fly
Any of several thousand moth-like insects of the order Trichoptera. Adult caddis flies have long, many-jointed antennae and hold their typically hairy wings tent-like over their bodies. Caddis flies usually live near fresh water and feed on nectar and plant juices. The larvae, known as caddis worms, live in water and often build underwater cases or nests. They are a popular food of many fish. Length: to *c.*2.5cm (*c.*1in).

caecilian
Elongate, limbless, burrowing or aquatic amphibian. Caecilians have robust skulls, small eyes that may be covered by skin or bone, and a pair of sensory tentacles. The *c.*160 species are distributed throughout tropical America, Southeast and S Asia, and in wetter areas of W and E Africa. Length: 11–152cm (4–60in). Order Gymnophiona.

caecilian, lungless
Fully aquatic caecilian that is found in cold montane streams in N South America; it lacks both gills and lungs. The lungless caecilian is the largest vertebrate to rely on its skin as its chief GAS EXCHANGE surface. Length: 73cm (29in). Family Typhlonectidae; species *Atretochoana eiselti*.

caecum
Dilated pouch at the junction of the small and large intestines, terminating in the appendix. It has no known function in humans. In rabbits and horses, the caecum contains large numbers of microorganisms that help to break down the cellulose cell walls of the

▲ **cactus** The cactus form is generally cylindrical or spherical to reduce surface evaporation. Few cacti (1,2,3,4,7,10) have leaves, but many have sharp thorns or spines to discourage animals from eating them. The cactus form may be seen in other desert plants (11,12), but most have succulent (5,8,9) or reduced (6) leaves.

plants they eat, thus making more nutrients available to their hosts.

cahow (Bermuda petrel)
Small to medium-sized PETREL with grey-blue and white plumage. Its distribution is limited to Bermuda. It was once abundant, then thought to be extinct, and was later rediscovered. Length: 33–36cm (13–14in). Family Procellariidae; species *Pterodroma cahow*.

caiman
See CAYMAN

calabash gourd
See BOTTLE GOURD

calabash tree
Tree that is native to tropical America. Its gourd-like berries are attractive to ants and thus ward off herbivores. The hard shells of the fruit are used for bowls and scoops. Young fruits can be pickled for eating. In

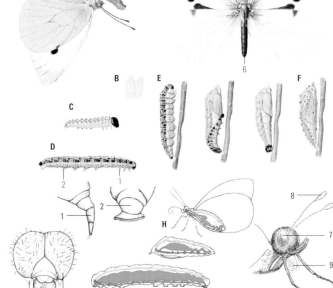

► **cabbage white butterfly** The complete metamorphosis of this species begins with the female (A) laying her eggs (B) on the underside of leaves in batches of 100 or more. The eggs hatch into the first stage larva or caterpillar (C). The larva moults successively and after four moults is fully grown (D). It has three pairs of "true" legs (1), which represent the butterfly's legs, and four pairs of prolegs (2). It also has claspers at the end of the abdomen and mandibles for chewing. The head bears rudimentary eyes (3) and antennae (4). After the fifth moult (E), the caterpillar's skin hardens to form the case of the pupa or chrysalis (F), in which the tissues of the caterpillar reorganize to form the butterfly (G). The butterfly's thorax (6) bears two pairs of wings and three pairs of legs. The head has large, compound eyes (7), clubbed antennae (8) and also a coiled proboscis (9). The internal systems (H), including those of the nerves (red), blood (yellow) and digestion (blue), have become more complex at each stage. Soon after emergence from the chrysalis, the adult butterflies mate.

Nicaragua the seeds are cooked and made into drink. Family Bignoniaceae; species *Crescentia cujete*.

calabrese
See BROCCOLI

calcareous
Describing a rock that is rich in calcium carbonate ($CaCO_3$). CHALK is a common calcareous rock, as are other LIMESTONES, although these may also contain many other minerals. Soils that develop on such rocks are also termed calcareous.

calceolaria (slipper flower)
Any member of the genus *Calceolaria*, a large group of herbs and shrubs mostly native from Mexico to Peru and Chile. Many, including hybrids, are cultivated for their showy flowers. The flowers are usually yellow or purple and irregularly spotted, with a large, inflated, slipper-like lower lip. Some plants are used as medicine locally. Family Scrophulariaceae; genus *Calceolaria*.

calcite
Mineral, calcium carbonate ($CaCO_3$). Calcite is a major constituent of CALCAREOUS SEDIMENTARY ROCK, especially LIMESTONE. The crystals are in the hexagonal system and vary in form from tabular (rare) to prismatic or needle-like. Calcite is usually glassy white but it may be red, pink or yellow. Calcite reacts with dilute hydrochloric acid. Hardness 3; r.d. 2.7.

calcium carbonate
($CaCO_3$) White compound, insoluble in water, that occurs naturally in such forms as MARBLE, CHALK, LIMESTONE and CALCITE. It also forms the shells of molluscs. Crystals are in the hexagonal system and vary in form from tabular (rare) to prismatic or nee-dle-like. Calcium carbonate is used in the manufacture of cement, iron, steel and lime, to neutralize soil acidity, and as a constituent of antacids.

caldera
Large CRATER formed when a VOLCANO collapses due to the migration of the MAGMA under the Earth's crust. The caldera of an extinct volcano, if fed by floodwater, rain or springs, can become a CRATER LAKE.

California redwood
Conifer that grows to more than 100m (330ft); it is one of the tallest trees. Species *Sequoia sempervirens*. Its close relative from California is the less common big tree or giant sequoia (*Sequoiadendron giganteum*), the heaviest tree in the Western world. Sequoias live to be more than 4000 years old. Family Taxodiaceae.

California poppy
Plant that is native to w North America; it is the state flower of California. It has yellow flowers in the wild but is cultivated in a white or pink form. Colourless latex from the California poppy is mildly narcotic and is used by Native Americans to treat toothache. Family Papaveraceae; species *Eschscholzia californica*.

calla lily
Any of several species belonging to the genus *Zantedeschia*. The calla lily is an attractive, usually white-flowered, tropical plant. It is cultivated as an ornamental, used widely in floristry. The ARUM LILY is perhaps the best-known calla lily. Family Araceae; genus *Zantedeschia*.

callus
Protective mass of undifferentiated plant cells formed at the site of a wound in a woody plant.

▶ **Californian redwood**
Giant sequoias
(*Sequoiadendron giganteum*), close relatives of the California redwood, are only found on the western slopes of the Sierra Nevada, California, usually in scattered groves. The giant sequoias shown here grow in Mariposa Grove. These trees are exceeded in height only by the California redwoods. In girth, they are probably the largest trees, with diameters at the base reaching 8m (25ft) in some cases.

Callus tissue is also formed at the base of cuttings as they start to take root. Callus tissue is important as the starting point for TISSUE CULTURE of plants.

calumba
Climbing plant grown in tropical Africa. The dried root is used locally as a tonic. Family Menispermaceae; species *Jateorhiza columba*.

Calvin, Melvin (1911–97)
US chemist. Calvin conducted experiments using radioactive carbon-14 as a trace to label carbon dioxide and to track the process by which plants turned it into glucose by means of PHOTOSYNTHESIS. The series of reactions that take place during photosynthesis are known as the CALVIN CYCLE. Calvin received the Nobel Prize for chemistry in 1961.

Calvin cycle
Sequence of reactions that takes place during the dark stage of PHOTOSYNTHESIS. The overall effect of the cycle is the REDUCTION of carbon dioxide to form carbohydrate. First, an ENZYME (ribulose bisphosphate carboxylase) causes carbon dioxide to combine with ribulose bisphosphate to form a six-carbon compound that quickly decomposes to give two molecules of glycerate 3-phosphate (a three-carbon compound). Then, after being changed to glyceraldehyde 3-phosphate, this re-forms ribulose bisphosphate with the release of the sugars fructose and glucose. The whole cycle takes place in the CHLOROPLASTS in leaves or other green parts of the plant. It was worked out, using radioactive tracers, by Melvin CALVIN.

calyptura
Rare bird of the South American rainforests; the smallest member of the COTINGA family. It is often called the kinglet calyptura because of its superficial resemblance to a kinglet. The calyptura is a secretive bird and is difficult to observe. Length: 7.5cm (3in). Family Cotingidae; species *Calyptura cristata*.

calyx
SEPALS of a flower, taken as a group. Usually green in colour, the calyx protects the flower when it is a bud. When the flower opens, it surrounds the CARPELS, PETALS and STAMENS, and forms the outer whorl of the PERIANTH.

camaroptera
Any member of a genus of small, short-tailed WARBLERS with dull plumage. They are found in broadleaved woodlands of central, E and S Africa. Camaropteras have rather long bills and feed on insects and spiders. Family Sylviidae; genus *Camaroptera*.

camass (camash, quamash)
North American plant, some species of which have edible bulbs. Other species are cultivated as ornamentals. Family Liliaceae; species include *Camassia quamash* (common camass) and *Zigadenus glauca* (white camass).

Camberwell beauty
See BUTTERFLY, MOURNING CLOAK

cambium
Layer of cells parallel to the surface of stems and roots of plants that divides to produce new cells to allow for growth in diameter of the stem and roots. Once a plant cell has differentiated, it is unable to divide again. To allow for growth, certain bands of cells remain undifferentiated, retaining their ability

C

to divide. The cambium is made up of such cells. There are two main types of cambium, the **vascular cambium** and the **cork cambium**. The vascular cambium produces new PHLOEM on the outside and XYLEM on the inside, leaving narrow bands of thin-walled cells which allow nutrients and gases to diffuse to the centre of the plant. The cork cambium forms a cylinder just below the EPIDERMIS; it produces cork cells to replace the epidermis, which ruptures as the stem and root expand, forming the bark and the corky outer layer of the older root. *See also* MERISTEM

Cambrian
Earliest period of the PALAEOZOIC era, lasting from *c*.590 million to 505 million years ago. The rocks of this period are the earliest to preserve the hard parts of animals as fossils. Cambrian rocks contain a large variety of fossils, including all the animal phyla with the exception of the vertebrates. At that time the animals lived in the seas, while the land was barren. The commonest animal forms were trilobites, brachiopods, sponges and snails. Plant life consisted mainly of seaweeds.

camel
See feature article

camouflage
Means by which some animals blend in with their natural environment, usually by resembling their surroundings in form and/or colour. Camouflage enables animals to conceal themselves from their prey or to protect themselves from predators. The LEAF INSECT is a notable example. It is flat and green and the female has large leathery forewings with markings that resemble a pattern of leaf veins. Camouflage is a form of MIMICRY.

campion
Common name given to species belonging to the genus *Silene*. Red campion (*Silene dioica*) is found in the woods and hedges of Europe and North America. Other species include sea campion (*Silene maritima*) and moss campion (*Silene acaulis*). Family Caryophyllaceae.

Canadian pondweed
Aquatic plant that is native to North America. Canadian pondweed was first recorded as an alien in England in 1847 and is now widespread, found in most kinds of ponds, canals, dykes, rivers and streams where the soil is fertile. The flowers appear on the water surface. Family Hydrocharitaceae; species *Elodea canadensis*.

canary
Small FINCH with yellow-brown plumage, closely related to the serin. In the wild, it is found exclusively on the Canary Islands. It feeds on seeds and some invertebrates. The popular caged varieties mostly have yellow plumage. Length: 13–15cm (5–6in). Family Fringillidae; species *Serinus canarius*.

canary-bird flower
See CANARY CREEPER

canary creeper (canary-bird flower)
Creeping annual native to the Andes in Ecuador and Peru. It has yellow flowers with fringed petals. It is a popular garden plant. Family Tropaeolaceae; species *Tropaeolum peregrinum*.

Canary Island ivy
Attractive and ornamental species of IVY. In sunny

CAMEL

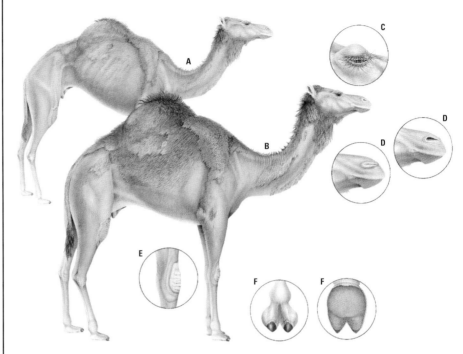

Large, hump-backed, UNGULATE mammal. There are two species – the two-humped **Bactrian** (*Camelus bactrianus*) of central Asia and the single-humped Arabian **dromedary** (*Camelus dromedarius*). The camel's broad, padded feet and ability to travel several days without water make it a perfect desert animal. It feeds on coarse vegetation, such as dry grass, thorny plants and twigs. Camels can carry up to 270kg (600lb) and cover *c*.50km (*c*.30mi) a day. Family Camelidae.

▲ **A laden dromedary** camel can walk across a scorching desert for eight days without drinking or eating. In times of adversity, the animal relies on the reserves of fat stored in its prominent hump. It is able to lose one quarter of its body weight without harmful effects (A); but when food and water are available, it can regain its full weight in just two or three days (B), and it is capable of drinking 150 litres (33 gallons) of water at a time. Among its other adaptations to desert life, the dromedary camel has soft fur that traps a layer of air, helping it to stay cool during the day and warm at night. Long eye lashes (C) shield the camel's eyes from wind-blown sand, as do the nostrils, which can be opened and closed at will (D). Hard knee pads protect the animal when it kneels on the scorching sand (E), and its toes are joined together by a fleshy pad, which acts as a snow shoe (F), preventing the camel from sinking into the sand.

---

situations, it can grow to a height of *c*.5m (*c*.16ft). Family Araliaceae; species *Hedera canariensis*.

Cancer, Tropic of
Line of latitude, 23.5° north of the Equator, that marks the northern boundary of the tropics. It indicates the farthest north position at which the Sun appears directly overhead at noon. The Sun is vertical over the Tropic of Cancer on about 21 June, the summer SOLSTICE in the Northern Hemisphere.

candlefish (eulachon)
Marine SMELT of inshore temperate waters or cold seas of the Northern Hemisphere. During the spawning season candlefish have such oily flesh that Native Americans used to dry them in order to burn them as torches. Length: 30cm (12in). Family Osmeridae; species *Thaleichthys pacificus*.

candle tree
Tree that bears on its trunk edible fruits up to 1.3m (4.3ft) long. It is native to Panama. Family Bignoniaceae; species *Parmentiera cereifera*.

candlewood
Tropical American tree, found particularly in Cuba. The wood is resinous, and torches of it burn with a pleasant smell. Several species have wood that is hard and takes a beautiful polish. Candlewood is widely used for timber, incense and oil to the extent that supplies in Jamaica are now depleted. Family Rutaceae; species *Amyris balsamifera*.

candytuft
Plant with umbrella-like flower heads that have outer petals longer than inner. It has some medicinal uses, but is largely used by florists and grown in gardens. Family Cruciferae; species *Iberis amara*.

canestero
Any of a group of *c*.20 species of rather secretive, small- to medium-sized birds. They have dull plumage and slender bills. Canesteros are widely distributed across South America, where they are found chiefly in arid areas and open country. They feed mainly on insects. Family Furnariidae.

canine
Any one of four sharp "stabbing" TEETH in the frontal dentition of most mammals. In humans they are also called eyeteeth.

canker disease
Disease in which areas of plant tissue die; it usually attacks fruit or forest trees that have been weakened by injury. It can be caused by various agents but most commonly by fungi such as *Nectria galligena*, which attacks apple and pear trees.

C

canna
Tropical American and West Indian perennial plant belonging to the only genus of the family Cannaceae. The plant has a tuberous rhizome (underground stem) from which arise large, broad leaves and large, conspicuous, orange or yellow flowers. Starch from the rhizome of *Canna edulis* is used in infant and invalid diets; the black seeds are often used as beads. Other species have been developed as ornamental plants for heated greenhouses. Family Cannaceae; species include *Canna edulis* and *Canna indica*.

cannabis
Common name for the Indian hemp plant *Cannabis sativa* and for the dried plant or extracted resin when used as a psychotropic drug. The drug produces a sedative effect sometimes allied with a feeling of well-being. It is highly carcinogenic and can induce mild psychosis. It has been shown to relieve the symptoms of some illnesses, such as multiple sclerosis. Family Cannabaceae.

cannonball tree
Tree that is native to wet tropical regions of South America. It is grown as an ornamental for its waxy, sweet-smelling, red and yellow flowers, which are borne on the branches and trunk. The flowers are followed by spectacular spherical fruits up to 20cm (8in) in diameter. Family Lecythidaceae; species *Couroupita guianensis*.

cantaloupe
Type of MELON belonging to the cucumber family; it is found in tropical regions. Cantaloupe plants are climbers, bearing tendrils and yellow flowers. The family contains a number of major food crops. Family Cucurbitaceae; species *Cucumis melo*.

Canterbury-bell
Tall, biennial plant native to N and central Italy and SE France. It is an alien in the British Isles, where it is commonly grown in gardens. Escaped plants have established themselves on railway banks in S England. It produces blue flowers in May and June. Many cultivated forms and colour varieties have been produced. Family Campanulaceae; species *Campanula medium*.

canvasback
Medium-sized diving DUCK, closely related to the European POCHARD. The male canvasback is grey-black with a brick-red head; the female is dull brown. It is found in North America, as far south as the Gulf of Mexico. Canvasbacks feed mainly on invertebrates, with some vegetable material. Length: 46–53cm (18–21in). Family Anatidae; subfamily Aythyinae; species *Aythya valisineria*.

canyon
Deep, narrow depression in the Earth's crust. Land canyons are the result of EROSION by rivers of comparatively recent origin flowing through arid terrain. Marine canyons may be formed when a river-bed and the surrounding terrain is submerged, or by turbulence produced by deep-water currents.

Cape box
Evergreen shrub of South Africa. The wood is prized by engravers and is used for carving, inlaying furniture and for making musical instruments. Family Buxaceae; species *Buxus macowani*.

Cape gooseberry
Member of the same widespread family as the potato, tomato and tobacco plant. It is native to tropical

► **capybara** Although clumsy on land due to its webbed feet, the capybara (*Hydrochoerus hydrochoeris*) is an excellent swimmer. A herbivore, it lives in colonies in swamps and near rivers in tropical South America.

regions and produces small, edible fruits. Family Solanaceae; species *Physalis peruviana*.

Cape heath
South African ornamental shrub. It belongs to the widespread family Ericaceae, which includes heathers and rhododendrons. Cape heath became popular towards the end of the 19th century as a plant for cool glasshouses. Family Ericaceae; genus *Erica*.

Cape honeysuckle
Popular garden shrub, native to tropical regions; it is no relation to true HONEYSUCKLE (*Lonicera*). Cape honeysuckle has bright orange flowers and is attractive to hummingbirds, particularly in tropical America. Family Bignoniaceae; species *Tecomaria capensis*.

Cape jasmine
Tropical climbing shrub; it is native to China and widely cultivated for ornamental use and as a hedging plant. Perfume from the flowers is used in fragrance manufacture and to scent Chinese tea. The fruits are used in dyes, in emetic, stimulant and diuretic medicines, and to cure jaundice and kidney and lung troubles. The leaves are crushed with sugar to cure fever and are used as poultices. Family Rubiaceae; species *Gardenia jasminoides*.

capelin
Marine SMELT of the Northern Hemisphere oceans. It mainly feeds on plankton. The capelin is an important food source for other fish, sea birds and marine mammals. It is also an important food fish, caught in nets in coastal waters. Length: to 23cm (9in). Family Osmeridae; species *Mallotus villosus*.

Cape pondweed
Freshwater aquatic plant native to South Africa; it has become naturalized in S Australia, South America and W Europe. Cape pondweed can survive dry periods as a dormant TUBER. It has edible flower spikes and makes a decorative aquarium plant. Family Aponogetonaceae; species *Aponogeton distachyos*.

caper
Shrub native to Sicily and other Mediterranean countries. It is known for its flower bud, which is often pickled in vinegar and used as a condiment or to make sauces. Family Capparidaceae; species *Capparis spinosa*.

capercaillie
Largest member of the GROUSE family. Male capercaillies are blue-black and turkey-like in shape; females are speckled mainly grey. The capercaillie lives in conifer forests from N Europe into Asia. It feeds on conifer shoots, berries and invertebrates. Length: 60–87cm (24–34in). Family Phasianidae; subfamily Tetraoninae; species *Tetrao urogallus*.

capillary
Smallest of BLOOD vessels, connecting ARTERIES and VEINS. Capillary walls consist of only a single layer of cells, so that fluid containing dissolved oxygen and other nutrients (as well as carbon dioxide and other wastes) can pass easily between the blood and surrounding tissues.

Capricorn, Tropic of
Line of latitude, 23.5° south of the Equator, which marks the southern boundary of the tropics. It indicates the farthest south position at which the Sun appears directly overhead at noon. The Sun is vertical over the Tropic of Capricorn on about 22 December, which is the summer SOLSTICE in the Southern Hemisphere.

caprimulgiform
Member of the bird order Caprimulgiformes, the best-known representative of which is the NIGHTJAR. Caprimulgiform birds are typically nocturnal, wide-mouthed insect-eaters, with incessant, distinctive calls. An Australian family, the OWLET-NIGHTJARS, provides some evidence of a link with the owls. Other members of the order include the South American OILBIRD.

capsicum
See PEPPER

capsid bug
Member of a family of true BUGS. Most capsid bugs are harmless to human interests, but some are crop pests because of the high densities in which they sometimes feed. Capsids have sucking mouthparts and most are herbivores. Some, however, are predators of other insects and, as such, may even be considered beneficial if they can assist in controlling other insect crop pests. Adult body length: 2–10mm (0.08–0.4in). Order Hemiptera; family Miridae (sometimes called Capsidae).

capsule
In botany, a dry type of FRUIT that releases its SEEDS when it ripens. The capsule is formed by the fusion of several CARPELS, which may split apart to allow the seeds to scatter. Other types of capsules have a lid that opens, or holes through which the seeds escape. The SPORE-containing structures of MOSSES and LIVERWORTS are also called capsules. In zoology, the sticky layer that surrounds the cell walls of some bacteria is called a capsule, as are various other surrounding structures, such as the sheath of connective tissue surrounding the bones in a joint and the membranous envelope surrounding the kidneys and spleen.

capuchin monkey
See MONKEY, CAPUCHIN

capybara
Largest living RODENT, native to Central and South America. It is semi-aquatic with webbed feet, a large, nearly hairless, body, short legs and a tiny tail. Length: 1.2m (4ft). Family Hydrochoeridae; species *Hydrochoerus hydrochoeris*.

caracal (desert lynx, African lynx)
Small CAT found in a wide variety of habitats across Africa and through to Asia. Caracals are mainly active at twilight, hunting small mammals and birds. Red-brown or yellow-grey in colour, they are distinguished by black tufts on their ears. Head-body length: 55–75cm (22–30in); tail: 22–23cm (c.9in). Family Felidae; species *Felis caracal*.

caracara
Any of a group of approximately nine species of large and distinctive birds of prey. They are found in South America and S North America. Caracaras are named after their call. They feed on a variety of prey, including beetles, snakes, young birds and carrion. Family Falconidae.

caracara, yellow-headed

Caracara that is found from Panama to N Argentina. It moves about in small groups in open country, hunting for insects and other small prey. Length: c.40cm (c.16in). Family Falconidae; species *Milvago chimachima*.

carapace

Back of the SHELL of certain animals. The shield-like part of the skeleton that covers and protects the head and thorax of crabs and other crustaceans is called a carapace, as is the dorsal (upper) part of the shell of a tortoise or turtle. In a tortoise, the carapace is made up of bony plates joined to the backbone and ribs, covered by an outer horny layer.

caraway

Biennial herb that is native to Eurasia. It is cultivated for its small, brown, seed-like fruits, which are used for flavouring foods. It has feathery leaves and white flowers. Family Apiaceae/Umbelliferae; species *Carum carvi*.

carbohydrate

Organic compound that is composed of CARBON, HYDROGEN and OXYGEN; it is a constituent of many foodstuffs. The hydrogen and oxygen atoms are in the ratio of 2:1, as they are in water (H_2O). The simplest carbohydrates are the SUGARS, which usually have five or six carbon atoms in each molecule. GLUCOSE and FRUCTOSE are MONOSACCHARIDES, naturally occurring sugars; they have the same formula ($C_6H_{12}O_6$) but different structures. One molecule of each combines with the loss of water to make SUCROSE ($C_{12}H_{22}O_{11}$), which is a DISACCHARIDE. Sucrose also occurs naturally in SUGAR CANE and SUGAR BEET. Starch and cellulose are POLYSACCHARIDES – carbohydrates consisting of hundreds of glucose molecules linked together in a chain. *See also* SACCHARIDE

carbon (symbol C)

Common, nonmetallic element of group IV of the periodic table. Carbon forms a vast number of compounds, which, with hydrogen (hydrocarbons) and other nonmetals, form the basis of organic chem-istry. Until recently, it was believed there were two crystalline carbon allotropes (distinct physical forms): GRAPHITE and DIAMOND. In 1996 a third type, buckminsterfullerene ("buckyballs"), was discovered, the molecules of which are shaped like geodesic domes. Various amorphous (noncrystalline) forms of carbon also exist, such as COAL, coke, charcoal, soot and lampblack. Amorphous carbon has many uses, for example as pigment for inks and as a filler for rubber for tyres. Synthetic forms of carbon include carbon fibre. The radioactive isotope ^{14}C is used for CARBON DATING of archaeological specimens. Properties: at.no. 6; r.a.m. 12.011; r.d. 1.9–2.3 (graphite), 3.15–3.53 (diamond); m.p. c.3550°C (c.6422°F); sublimes at 3367°C (6093°F); b.p. c.4200°C (c.7592°F); most common isotope ^{12}C (98.89%).

carbonate

Salt of carbonic acid (H_2CO_3). It is formed when carbon dioxide (CO_2) dissolves in water, as when rain falls through the air. Carbonic acid is an extremely weak acid and both it and many of its salts are unstable, decomposing readily to release carbon dioxide. Nevertheless, large parts of the Earth's crust are made up of carbonates, such as CALCIUM CARBONATE and DOLOMITE.

carbonation

Process of chemical EROSION of rocks by rainwater containing carbon dioxide. When carbon dioxide gas in the atmosphere dissolves in rainwater, it forms carbonic acid. This will dissolve CALCAREOUS rocks such as CHALK and LIMESTONE. The dissolved chemicals can drip into CAVES where they may form STALACTITES and STALAGMITES.

carbon cycle

Circulation of CARBON in the BIOSPHERE. The carbon cycle is a complex chain of events. The most important components of the cycle are the taking up of carbon dioxide from the atmosphere by green plants during PHOTOSYNTHESIS, and the return of carbon dioxide to the atmosphere by the RESPIRATION and eventual DECOMPOSITION of animals that eat the plants.

carbon dating (radiocarbon dating)

Method of determining the age of organic materials by measuring the amount of radioactive decay of an ISOTOPE of carbon, carbon-14 (^{14}C). This radio-isotope decays to form nitrogen, with a half-life of 5730 years. When a living organism dies, it ceases to take carbon dioxide into its body, so that the amount of ^{14}C it contains is fixed relative to its total weight. Over the centuries, this quantity steadily diminishes. Refined chemical and physical analysis is used to determine the exact amount remaining, and from this the age of a specimen is deduced.

carbon dioxide (CO_2)

Colourless, odourless gas that occurs in the ATMOSPHERE (0.03%) and as a product of the combustion of FOSSIL FUELS and RESPIRATION in plants and animals. It is taken up by green plants in PHOTOSYNTHESIS. In its solid form (dry ice) it is used in refrigeration; as a gas it is used in carbonated beverages, fire extinguishers and provides an inert atmosphere for welding. If inhaled in large amounts, carbon dioxide can cause suffocation. Research indicates that its increase in the atmosphere leads to the GREENHOUSE EFFECT and GLOBAL WARMING. Properties: m.p. −56.6°C (−69.9°F); sublimes −78.5°C (−109.3°F).

Carboniferous

Fifth geologic period of the PALAEOZOIC era, lasting from 360 to 286 million years ago. The Carboniferous is divided into two series; the Lower Carboniferous is characterized by marine limestones with a coral-rich fauna; the Upper Carboniferous is dominated by river and deltaic sediments containing coal seams formed from extensive swampy forests of conifers and tree ferns. In North America, the Lower Carboniferous is known as the Mississippian period and the Upper Carboniferous as the Pennsylvanian period.

cardamom

Perennial plant native to tropical Asia. It has dark green leaves and small yellow flowers. It is best known for the pungent spice made from its red-brown seeds, which are contained within pods. Cardamom is a member of the GINGER family. Family Zingiberaceae; species *Elettaria cardamomum*.

cardinal

Any member of a family of small- to medium-sized, bunting-like birds that are confined to North and Central America. Family Fringillidae.

cardinal, northern

Small cardinal. The male is scarlet with a black throat; the female is a dull olive brown. Highly successful in North America, it is found in a variety of habitats. The northern cardinal feeds on large seeds and grain and also some insects. Length: 20–23cm (8–9in). Family Fringillidae; species *Pyrrhuloxia cardinalis*.

cardinal, red-crested

Small cardinal with a light-grey back, white underside and neck collar, and a crimson head and crest. It is found in low vegetation alongside rivers across s South America. It feeds mainly on seeds but also some insects and small fruits. Length: 19cm (7.5in). Family Fringillidae; species *Paroaria coronata*.

cardinal flower

Tropical plant of the LOBELIA family. It has scarlet flowers and is cultivated for ornamental use in herbaceous borders. Family Lobeliaceae; species *Lobelia cardinalis*.

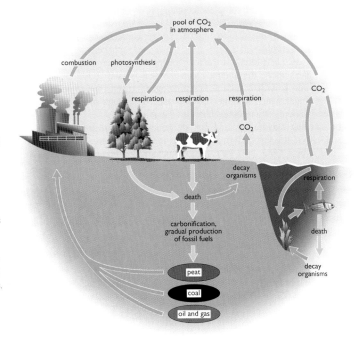

► **carbon cycle** Elemental carbon is in constant flux. Gaseous carbon dioxide (CO_2) is first incorporated into simple sugars by photosynthesis in green plants. These sugars may be broken down (respired) to provide energy, a process that releases CO_2 back into the atmosphere. Alternatively, animals that eat the plants also metabolize the sugars and release CO_2 in the process. Geological processes also affect the Earth's carbon balance, with carbon being removed from the cycle when it is accumulated within fossil fuels such as coal, oil and gas. Conversely, large amounts of carbon dioxide are released into the atmosphere when such fuels are burned.

C

carnation

Slender-stemmed, herbaceous plant native to Europe. The carnation has narrow leaves and swollen stem joints. It produces several dense blooms, ranging from white to yellow, pink and red, with serrated petals. Family Caryophyllaceae; species *Dianthus caryophyllus*.

carnivore

In the wider, ecological sense of the term, a carnivore is any animal that eats other animals. In the narrower, taxonomic sense, it is any member of the order of flesh-eating mammals (Carnivora). Mustelids – WEASELS, MARTENS, MINKS and the WOLVERINE – make up the largest family. The cats are the most specialized killers among the carnivores; DOGS, BEARS and RACCOONS are much less exclusively meat eaters; and CIVETS, MONGOOSES and their relatives also have a mixed diet. Related to the civets, but in a separate family, are the HYENAS, large dog-like scavengers. More distantly related to living land carnivores are the SEALS, SEA LIONS and WALRUSES; they evolved from ancient land carnivores, which gave rise to early weasel- or civet-like forms. Extinct carnivores include the SABRE-TOOTH CATS, which died out during the Pliocene epoch 2 million years ago.

carnivorous plant

See INSECTIVOROUS PLANT

carnosaur

Member of a group of large THEROPOD dinosaurs, ranging from early Jurassic age forms, such as *Dilophosaurus*, to the late Cretaceous TYRANNOSAURS. Carnosaurs were characterized by large skulls and teeth.

carnotite

Secondary vanadate mineral, potassium uranium vanadate ($K_2(UO_2)_2(VO_4)_2 . nH_2O$), an ore of uranium and radium. It is important for nuclear energy. Carnotite occurs in Australia, Congo and the Colorado Plateau, United States, as yellow-green crusts or cavity fillings in sandstone and in fossilized wood. It is finely crystalline (monoclinic), dull or earthy. Hardness 2; r.d. 3–5.

caroa

Member of the PINEAPPLE family; it is native to Brazil. Caroa is grown for its fibre, which is used in cloth and net-making. Family Bromeliaceae; species *Neoglaziovia variegata*.

Carolina allspice

Tree with large fragrant flowers; it is native to SE

► **carnation** Native to the Mediterranean region, carnations (*Dianthus caryophyllaceus*) are a species of pink. A great number of hybrids have been developed to be grown in gardens in many temperate regions.

▲ **carp** The carp (*Cyprinus carpio*) is an omnivorous, bony fish belonging to the order Cypriniformes. It has a large body usually covered evenly with scales (top), but these may be missing in cultivated types such as the mirror carp (bottom).

United States, south from Virginia. The original plants were collected in South Carolina, hence the plant's common name. The leaves, wood and roots have a pleasant camphor-like fragrance and the dried aromatic bark is used as a substitute for cinnamon. Height: to *c*.3m (*c*.10ft). Family Calycanthaceae; species *Calycanthus floridus*.

carotene

Plant pigment that is converted to vitamin A by the liver. It occurs in various fruits and vegetables (such as carrots).

carp

Freshwater fish native to temperate waters of Asia. It has been introduced to the United States and Europe. The carp is an important food fish. It is brown or golden and has four fleshy barbels (mouth whiskers). It is omnivorous, feeding mainly on submerged vegetation. The mirror carp, a domesticated variety of carp, has only a few scales; the leather carp, another variety, has none. Length: to 1m (39in). Family Cyprinidae; species *Cyprinus carpio*.

carpal

In humans, one of the small bones in the wrist.

carpel

Female reproductive element of a FLOWER. A carpel consists of a STIGMA (which receives pollen), a STYLE and an OVARY (containing ovules). A group of carpels make up the GYNOECIUM, the complete female reproductive structure within a flower.

carrageen (carragheen)

RHODOPHYTE (red alga) found in shallow waters of warm seas, particularly the Indian Ocean. When boiled it sets into jelly. It is used as a setting agent known as agar-agar, which is commercially produced and marketed in porous transparent sheets used in jellies, for carrying flavourings and for thickening soups and sauces. It is eaten all over the world in ice creams and sweets. Other uses for carrageen include laxatives and cement. Family Rhodophyceae; species *Chondrus crispus*.

carrot

Herbaceous, generally biennial, root vegetable, cultivated widely as a food crop. The edible, orange taproot is the plant's store of food for the following year. The plant is topped by delicate fern-like leaves and white or pink flower clusters. Family Umbelliferae; species *Daucus carota*.

carrot-fly

FLY that is a pest of carrots, and occasionally, of other taproots. It lays its eggs at the base of the car-

rot shoots; the larvae tunnel extensively in the taproots, which lie beneath the soil surface. The tunnelling causes rotting and rust-like stains, making the vegetables inedible. Adult body length: 7–10mm (0.3–0.4in). Order Diptera; family Psilidae; species *Psila rosae*.

carrying capacity

Maximum stable size of a population that can be maintained in a particular environment. Beyond the carrying capacity, certain factors limit further population growth. Such factors include predation, disease, availability of food, light, water, oxygen and shelter.

Carson, Rachel Louise (1907–64)

US writer and marine biologist. Carson is best known for her popular books on marine ecology. *The Sea Around Us* (1951) won a National Book Award. *Silent Spring* (1962) directed public attention to the dangers of agricultural pesticides and was a pioneering work in the development of the environmental movement. Carson's other works include *Under the Sea Wind* (1941) and *The Edge of the Sea* (1955).

cartilage (gristle)

Flexible supporting tissue made up of the tough protein COLLAGEN. In the vertebrate embryo, the greater part of the SKELETON consists of cartilage, which is gradually replaced by BONE during development, except in areas of wear such as the ends of bones and the INTERVERTEBRAL DISCS, where caps of cartilage help to protect the bone below. In humans, cartilage is also present in the larynx, nose and external ear, and rings of cartilage help to support the windpipe (TRACHEA) and BRONCHUS.

cartilaginous fish

See FISH

cashew

Evergreen shrub or tree grown in the tropics. It is important for the nuts it produces, which grow at the end of fleshy stalks called cashew apples. The wood is used for boxes and boats and produces a gum similar to gum arabic. Height: to 12m (39ft). Family Anacardiaceae; species *Anacardium occidentale*.

casparian strip

Distinctive, waterproof band of suberin that runs around the radial and transverse walls of the endodermal cells of plant roots. It ensures that the passage of water and solutes into the plant's vascular tissue takes place through the cytoplasm of endodermal cells, which are able to regulate the movement of the water and solutes into the XYLEM.

cassa-banana

Perennial LIANA native to tropical America. It is cultivated both as an ornamental and for its edible,

◄ **cashew** Grown in tropical regions, the cashew (*Anacardium occidentale*) bears bean-shaped nuts which form beneath an apple-like fruit. They have an inner and an outer shell, which are removed before roasting.

► **cassava** Grown widely throughout the tropics, cassava (*Manihot utilissama*) is one of the world's most important tuber-producing plants. A processed form of meal is produced from its roots and used as a cereal substitute.

C

fragrant fruit, which is used for preserves and for scenting linen. Family Cucurbitaceae; species *Sicana odorifera*.

cassada wood
Tree that belongs to a family of temperate and tropical trees and shrubs, some of which are cultivated as ornamental garden plants. It grows mainly in the West Indies. Cassada wood trees are important for their useful, tough wood. Family Staphyleaceae; species *Turpinia occidentalis*.

cassava (manioc)
Tapioca plant native to Brazil. It is a tall, woody shrub, with small, clustered flowers. A valuable cereal substitute is made from its tuberous roots. Height: up to 2.7m (9ft). Family Euphorbiaceae; species *Manihot esculenta*.

cassiterite
Translucent black or brown mineral, tin oxide (SnO_2); the major ore of tin. It occurs in PLACER DEPOSITS, chiefly in the Malay peninsula, and in pegmatites and other INTRUSIVE IGNEOUS ROCKS. It takes the form of short, tetragonal, prismatic crystals, or masses and radiating fibres. Hardness 6–7; r.d. 7.

cassowary
Any of a family of three species of large, heavy-bodied birds. They are all flightless and forest-dwelling. Cassowaries have black plumage and bright blue heads, with a bony helmet or casque. They have powerful hind claws and can run surprisingly fast, at speeds of up to 50km/h (30mph). Cassowaries are found exclusively in Australia and New Guinea. Family Casuariidae.

cassowary, double-wattled
Largest cassowary. It is found in New Guinea and N Australia. It has two long, pinkish wattles and eats soft fruit, berries, insects and some vegetable matter. Length: 140–150cm (55–59in). Family Casuariidae; species *Casuarius casuarius*.

cassowary, dwarf
Smallest cassowary. It is found on the islands of New

Guinea and New Britain (Papua New Guinea). It feeds on soft fruit, berries, insects and some vegetable matter. Length: 99–102cm (39–40in). Family Casuariidae; species *Casuarius bennetti*.

casts and moulds
Common mode of FOSSIL preservation in which the surrounding sediment replicates the surface topography and sometimes fine details of a fossil shell or bone. The original fossil material may be lost or replicated by another material during FOSSILIZATION.

casuarina
Any member of a genus of trees and shrubs found mainly in Southeast Asia and the W Pacific region. They are adapted to dry habitats. Casuarinas are tall trees with a weeping habit. They have peculiar, scale-like leaves forming sheaths on the stems; the flowers are small and wind-pollinated. Casuarina wood is extremely hard and is valued for furniture manufacture. Family Casuarinaceae; genus *Casuarina*; species include *Casuarina equisetifolia* and *Casuarina stricta*.

cat
Carnivorous, often solitary and nocturnal mammal of the family Felidae, ranging in size from the rare Siberian TIGER to the domestic cat. It has specialized teeth and claws for hunting, a keen sense of smell, acute hearing and sensitive vision. It balances well using its long tail (only the Manx cat is tailless). Cats all have fully retractile claws, except for the CHEETAH. One of the first animals to be domesticated, cats have appeared frequently in myth and religion. Order Carnivora.

cat, bob- (red lynx)
Red-brown cat with dark stripes and spots, distributed from s Canada throughout the United States to Mexico. It prefers rough, rocky ground with trees. It is active at twilight, when it hunts rodents, small mammals and large ground birds. Head-body

▲ **cat, bob-** A solitary and territorial creature, the bobcat (*Felis rufus*) has become increasingly threatened following the introduction of hunting restrictions on other types of lynx. Its pelt is highly sought after by hunters.

length: 62–76cm (24–30in); tail: 10–20cm (4–8in). Family Felidae; species *Felis rufus*.

cat, jungle
Cat that inhabits a variety of habitats from dry forest to reed beds, though rarely jungle. It is found from Egypt through sw Asia to India. It feeds on rodents and frogs, usually during the day. Sandy-brown or red-grey in colour, it sometimes has dark stripes on its face, legs or tail. Head-body length: 60–75cm (24–30in); tail: 25–35cm (10–14in). Family Felidae; species *Felis chaus*.

cat, margay (tigrillo)
Cat that inhabits forest and scrubland between N Mexico and N Argentina, where it hunts small arboreal mammals and birds. An excellent climber, it is yellow-brown with dark spots and stripes. Head-body length: 45–70cm (18–28in); tail: 35–50cm (14–20in). Family Felidae; species *Felis wiedi*.

cat, wild
Nocturnal cat, distributed from w Europe to India and Africa. It is brown with dark stripes and a black-tipped tail. It hunts small mammals and birds. Wild cats are related to the domesticated cat, which has been introduced worldwide. Head-body length: 50–80cm (20–31in); tail: 28–35cm (11–14in). Family Felidae; species *Felis sylvestris*.

catabolism
Process in which living organisms break down complex MOLECULES into simpler ones with the liberation of ENERGY. *See also* ANABOLISM; METABOLISM

catalase
ENZYME that breaks down the hydrogen peroxide produced by living cells during METABOLISM into oxygen and water. Because hydrogen peroxide is highly toxic, it is important that it does not accumulate in cells. Catalase is, therefore, one of nature's fastest acting enzymes: one molecule of catalase is capable of breaking down millions of hydrogen peroxide molecules every minute.

catalpa
Ornamental tree of North America and the West Indies. It has heart-shaped leaves, white or purple flowers and bean-like fruit pods containing many seeds. Common catalpa (*Catalpa bignonioides*) is also called the Indian bean. Height: to 18m (60ft). Family Bignoniaceae.

catalyst
Substance that speeds up the rate of a chemical reaction without itself being consumed. Many industrial processes rely on catalysts; for example, the Haber process for manufacturing ammonia uses iron as a catalyst. Metals or their compounds catalyze by adsorbing gases to their surface, forming intermediates that then readily react to form the desired product while regenerating the original catalytic surface. The METABOLISM of all living organisms depends on biological catalysts called ENZYMES. Without these catalysts most reactions would happen so slowly that life would not be possible.

cataract
Term usually applied to that section of a rapidly flowing river where the running water falls suddenly in a sheer drop. When the drop is less steep, the fall is known as a cascade.

catbird, grey
Small- to medium-sized bird; it has all grey plumage

C

except for a black cap and tail with reddish-brown under-tail coverts. It is found in North and Central America. The grey catbird forages on the ground for insects and berries. Its alarm call sounds like a kitten, hence its name. Length: 22–24cm (c.9in). Family Mimidae; species *Dumetella carolinensis*.

catchfly
Common name for certain species of the genus *Silene*, a large group of flowering plants found widely in the Northern Hemisphere. Certain other species of this genus are known as CAMPION. Family Caryophyllaceae; genus *Silene*.

catena
Variation on the vertical profile of soils derived from the same parent material, usually resulting from topographic changes, such as a hillslope, which controls other soil-forming factors such as microclimate and drainage. *See also* SOIL PROFILE

caterpillar
Worm-like larva of a BUTTERFLY or MOTH; it has a segmented body, short antennae, simple eyes, three pairs of true legs and chewing mouthparts. Nearly all feed voraciously on plants and are serious crop pests. Order Lepidoptera.

catfish
Any of *c.*2500 species of fish belonging to the order Siluriformes; they are found in tropical and subtropical waters. Catfish are typically slow-swimming and scaleless. They have fleshy barbels on their upper jaws, sometimes with venomous spines. Most species of catfish live in fresh water and can be farmed. Length: up to 3m (10ft). Order Siluriformes; families include Ictaluridae, Siluridae and Clariidae.

catfish, walking
Catfish that is capable of breathing air. It uses the spines in its pectoral fins like a pair of crutches to walk over land when river channels and lakes dry up. The walking catfish occurs in Africa and Asia and has been introduced into fish ponds in Florida, SE United States, where thriving populations have become established. Family Clariidae; species include *Clarias batrachus*.

cation
ION that is positively charged. It is attracted to the cathode during electrolysis.

catmint (catnip)
Common name given to a purple-flowered species of

Nepeta, a plant genus that occurs widely in dry, temperate areas. Its mint-like smell is irresistible to some cats. Catmint is popular as a garden and container plant. Family Labiatae; species *Nepeta cataria*.

cat's claw
Perennial herb growing in sandy pinelands, fields and woods of North America. It is closely related to the SENSITIVE PLANT, sharing the same characteristics of curling and drooping when touched. It gets its Latin name from Thomas Nuttall (1786–1859), the American plant collector who discovered it. Family Leguminaceae; species *Schrankia nuttallii*.

cattail
Any member of the genus *Typha*, found in temperate and tropical localities. A tall, aquatic plant, it grows in shallow, freshwater habitats, such as reed-swamps, lakes, rivers and ponds. Family Typhaceae; genus *Typha*; species include *Typha latifolia* (BULRUSH).

catworm
Any of several species of marine and estuarine POLYCHAETES. Catworms are segmented worms, which actively burrow in sediment by means of an eversible (capable of being turned inside out) proboscis. They are predacious on small invertebrates. Phylum Annelida; class Polychaeta.

cauliflower
Form of CABBAGE with a short, thick stem, and large, lobed leaves. Edible white or purplish flower clusters form tightly compressed heads. Family Brassicaceae; species *Brassica oleracea botrytis*.

cave
See feature article

cave fish
See BLIND FISH

cavy (wild guinea pig)
Herbivorous rodent from which the domestic GUINEA PIGS are descended. It is native to South America. Small with dark fur, cavies live in burrows and often form large colonies for protection. Family Caviidae; species *Cavia aperea*.

cayman (caiman)
Any of several species of reptile belonging to the ALLIGATOR family, found in Central America and N and E South America. They include: the small, heavily armoured smooth cayman (*Paleosuchus trigonatus*) and dwarf cayman (*Paleosuchus palpe-*

brosus); the spectacled cayman (*Caiman crocodilus*); and the large, fierce black cayman (*Melanosuchus niger*). Family Alligatoridea.

ceanothus (New Jersey tea, Californian lilac)
Any member of the *Ceanothus* genus, native to North America. It is frequently grown in gardens, where it prefers warm, sheltered sites. Species vary from prostrate, mat-forming shrubs to tall bushes. It has abundant and attractive powder-blue flowers. Family Rhamnaceae; genus *Ceanothus*.

celandine
Any of several different plants that are known as celandine. **Greater celandine** is common to Europe; it has serrated leaves, yellow flowers and narrow seed pods. Its yellow sap was used to cure warts. Family Papaveraceae; species *Chelidonium majus*. **Lesser celandine** is a low-growing plant with bright yellow flowers in spring. It is common in the United States, Britain, Europe and w Asia. Family Ranunculaceae; species *Ranunculus ficaria*.

celery
Biennial plant native to the Mediterranean region. It is widely cultivated for its long stalks, which are used as a vegetable. Its fruits are used as food flavouring and in medicine. Family Apiaceae/Umbelliferae; species *Apium graveolens*.

celery-fly
Pestiferous FRUIT-FLY. It lays its eggs directly on to the leaves of celery and other umbelliferous plants. The larvae tunnel inside the leaves and the result is a sick and under-developed plant. Adult body length: 7–9mm (0.3–0.4in). Order Diptera; family Tephritidae; species *Euleia heraclei* (sometimes placed in the genera *Acidia* or *Philophylla*).

celestial equator
Great circle on the CELESTIAL SPHERE, lying midway between the CELESTIAL POLES in the same plane as the Earth's Equator.

celestial poles
Two diametrically opposite points at which the extension of the Earth's axis meets the CELESTIAL SPHERE. The celestial sphere rotates about a line through the celestial poles.

celestial sphere
Imaginary sphere of infinite radius used to define the positions of celestial bodies as seen from Earth, the centre of the sphere. The sphere rotates, once in 24 hours, around a line that is an extension of the Earth's axis. The position of a celestial body is the point at which a radial line through it meets the surface of the sphere. The position is defined in terms of coordinates, such as declination and right ascension or altitude and azimuth, which refer to great circles on the sphere, such as the CELESTIAL EQUATOR or the ecliptic.

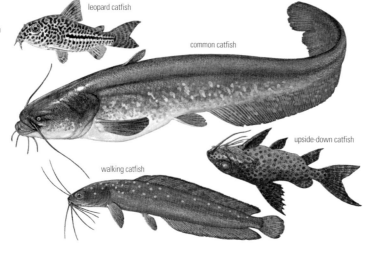

► **catfish** The common catfish (*Parasilurus asotus*) is just one member of a large and varied family of fish with whisker-like barbels. The Leopard catfish (*Corydoras julii*) lives in tributaries of the Amazon. The upside-down catfish (*Synodontis nigriventris*) is native to Africa and habitually swims upside-down. The walking catfish (*Clarias batrachus*) is capable of travelling across land. Some catfish have venomous spines on their fins which can be used against predators.

leopard catfish

common catfish

upside-down catfish

walking catfish

celestine
Mineral, strontium sulphate ($SrSO_4$), with distinctive pale blue or white, glassy, orthorhombic crystals, sometimes occurring in fibrous masses. It is found chiefly in SEDIMENTARY ROCK and also as gangue material in ore veins. There are deposits in Britain, Sicily and the United States. It is an important source of strontium and some of its compounds.

cell
See feature article, pages 68–69

cell division
Process by which living cells reproduce and thereby allow an organism to grow. In EUKARYOTE cells, a single cell splits in two, first by division of the NUCLEUS (occurring by MITOSIS or MEIOSIS), then by fission of the CYTOPLASM. For growth and asexual reproduction, where the daughter cells are required to be genetically identical to their parents, mitosis is used. Meiosis results in daughter cells having half the number of chromosomes (HAPLOID). This type of division results in the production of haploid sex cells or GAMETES, which allows genetic information from two parents to be combined at FERTILIZATION, when the DIPLOID number of chromosomes is restored. *See also* ALTERNATION OF GENERATIONS

cellulose ($[C_6H_{10}O_5]_n$)
POLYSACCHARIDE CARBOHYDRATE that is the structural constituent of the cell walls of plants and algae. Cellulose consists of parallel unbranched chains of GLUCOSE units cross-linked together into a stable structure. It forms the basic material of the paper and textile industries.

cellulose nitrate (nitrocellulose, guncotton)
Organic compound that is made by reacting the natural polymer CELLULOSE with nitric acid. Cordite was chiefly used in the 19th and 20th centuries (together with camphor) to make celluloid – one of the first plastics – or as a propellant explosive (also called cordite).

Celsius, Anders (1701–44)
Swedish astronomer who invented the CELSIUS, or centigrade, temperature scale in 1742. He was a strong supporter of the introduction of the Gregorian calendar. In 1733 he published a collection of 316 observations of the AURORA Borealis made by himself and other astronomers.

Celsius
TEMPERATURE SCALE based on the freezing point of water (0°C) and the boiling point of water (100°C). The interval between these points is divided into 100 degrees. The name "Celsius" officially replaced "centigrade" in 1948. Degrees Celsius are converted to degrees FAHRENHEIT by multiplying by 1.8 and then adding 32. The scale was devised by Anders CELSIUS.

Cenozoic
Most recent era of geological time, beginning about 65 million years ago and extending up to the present. It is subdivided into the TERTIARY and QUATERNARY periods. It is the era during which the modern world with its present geographical features and plants and animals developed.

centaury
Any plant of the genus *Centaurium* of the GENTIAN family. They are mainly native to temperate Northern Hemisphere regions. Garden varieties are small plants with flat clusters of reddish flowers. Family Gentianaceae; genus *Centaurium*.

centigrade
See CELSIUS

centipede (lit. hundred-legged)
Any member of the class Chilopoda of the phylum Arthropoda. Centipedes have jointed legs and a distinct head bearing a pair of long ANTENNAE. Their bodies are composed of up to 200 segments, each bearing a single pair of legs. Nocturnal and often blind, they are generally small, although some tropical species may be 30cm (12in) long. All centipedes are carnivorous, feeding mainly on rotten animal food, and they live in moist, dark situations. They possess poison claws and fangs, which are used to protect themselves. Native British species are harmless, but some tropical species can be dangerous to humans. There are around 3000 species of centipede worldwide. *See also* ARTHROPOD; CHILOPOD

central nervous system (CNS)
In some advanced INVERTEBRATES, a neural pathway along which are located clusters of NEURONES called ganglia, which are involved in the movement of limbs, wings and so on. In VERTEBRATES, the central nervous system is that part of the NERVOUS SYSTEM that comprises the brain and spinal cord; it is connected to the PERIPHERAL NERVOUS SYSTEM, a branching network of sensory and motor nerves. In humans, the CNS coordinates all neural activity including that producing movement, thought, emotion and REFLEX ACTIONS. *See also* AUTONOMIC NERVOUS SYSTEM (ANS)

centriole
Dense body consisting of MICROTUBULES near the nucleus of a cell. It occurs in all cells except those of ANGIOSPERMS and the sperm cells of FERNS and CONIFEROPHYTES. During CELL DIVISION centrioles reproduce before the rest of the cell and move to each pole to form the SPINDLE.

centromere
Part of a CHROMOSOME that appears only during CELL

CAVE

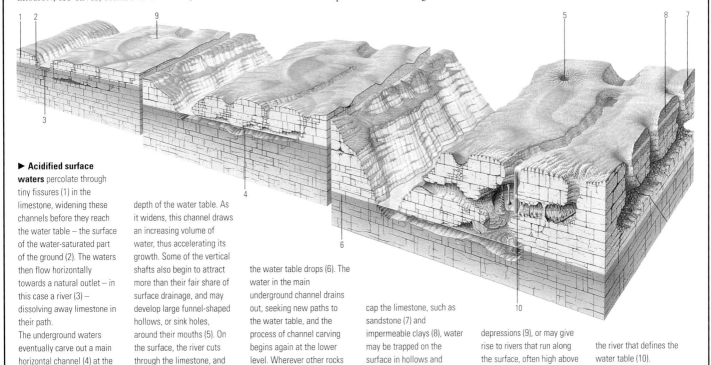

Natural underground cavity. The various kinds of cave include: **coastal caves**, formed by wave EROSION; **ice caves**, formed in GLACIERS; and **lava caves**. By far the largest caves are formed in LIMESTONE rocks by water dissolving the calcium carbonate. As water seeps downwards through the soil it passes over decaying organic matter, which gives off carbon dioxide. This gas dissolves in the water to form carbonic acid, which dissolves the rock.

▶ **Acidified surface waters** percolate through tiny fissures (1) in the limestone, widening these channels before they reach the water table – the surface of the water-saturated part of the ground (2). The waters then flow horizontally towards a natural outlet – in this case a river (3) – dissolving away limestone in their path.
The underground waters eventually carve out a main horizontal channel (4) at the depth of the water table. As it widens, this channel draws an increasing volume of water, thus accelerating its growth. Some of the vertical shafts also begin to attract more than their fair share of surface drainage, and may develop large funnel-shaped hollows, or sink holes, around their mouths (5). On the surface, the river cuts through the limestone, and the water table drops (6). The water in the main underground channel drains out, seeking new paths to the water table, and the process of channel carving begins again at the lower level. Wherever other rocks cap the limestone, such as sandstone (7) and impermeable clays (8), water may be trapped on the surface in hollows and depressions (9), or may give rise to rivers that run along the surface, often high above the river that defines the water table (10).

A cell is the basic unit of which all plant and animal tissues are composed. The cell is the smallest unit of life that can exist independently, with its own self-regulating chemical system. Most cells consist of a MEMBRANE surrounding jelly-like CYTOPLASM with a central NUCLEUS. The nucleus is the main structure, in which DNA is stored in CHRO-MOSOMES. Animal cells vary widely in shape. An ERYTHROCYTE (red blood cell), for instance, is a biconcave disc, whereas a NEURONE has a long fibre. The cells of plants and algae are enclosed in a cell wall, which gives them a more rigid shape. Bacterial cells also have a cell wall, but they do not have nuclei or chromosomes; instead, they have a loop of DNA floating in the cytoplasm. More advanced cells (those that have nuclei) often have other membrane-bounded structures inside the cell, such as MITOCHONDRIA and CHLOROPLASTS.

All animal cells are remarkably similar in structure. Of the millions of different species of animal, from the simple sponge to the complex mammal, the cells of which they are made share much the same basic internal organization. The human body is made of 10 million million cells, and while each cell has its own specific function to perform, they have to cooperate and communicate to ensure the body survives.

Modern microscopy has revealed the complexity of the internal structure of animal cells. Some structures are responsible for maintaining the shape of the cell, others assemble and transport complex molecules, and yet more are involved with the essential processes of cell division. Different cell processes occur within different types of compartment, called organelles. Many organelles are common to both plant and animal cells, but the most

significant difference is that animal cells do not contain chloroplasts and are therefore unable to perform photosynthesis, obtaining their energy rather from digested food.

Plant cells come in a great variety of shapes and sizes, and not all cells contain all the features in the "typical" cell illustrated here. However, they all have an inflexible cellulose cell wall on the outside of the membrane. The earliest plant cells are thought to have formed more than 1000 million years ago, when cells that fed on the nutrients of the primeval seas were colonized by bacteria capable of photosynthesis. Over time the bacteria lost their independence and developed into chloroplasts. The sugars resulting from photosynthesis can be broken down by mitochondria, releasing energy to fuel the cell's activity, or can be used as a source of carbon for larger molecules from which new plant material is made. The presence of structures that produce and store food is another feature that distinguishes plant cells from animal cells.

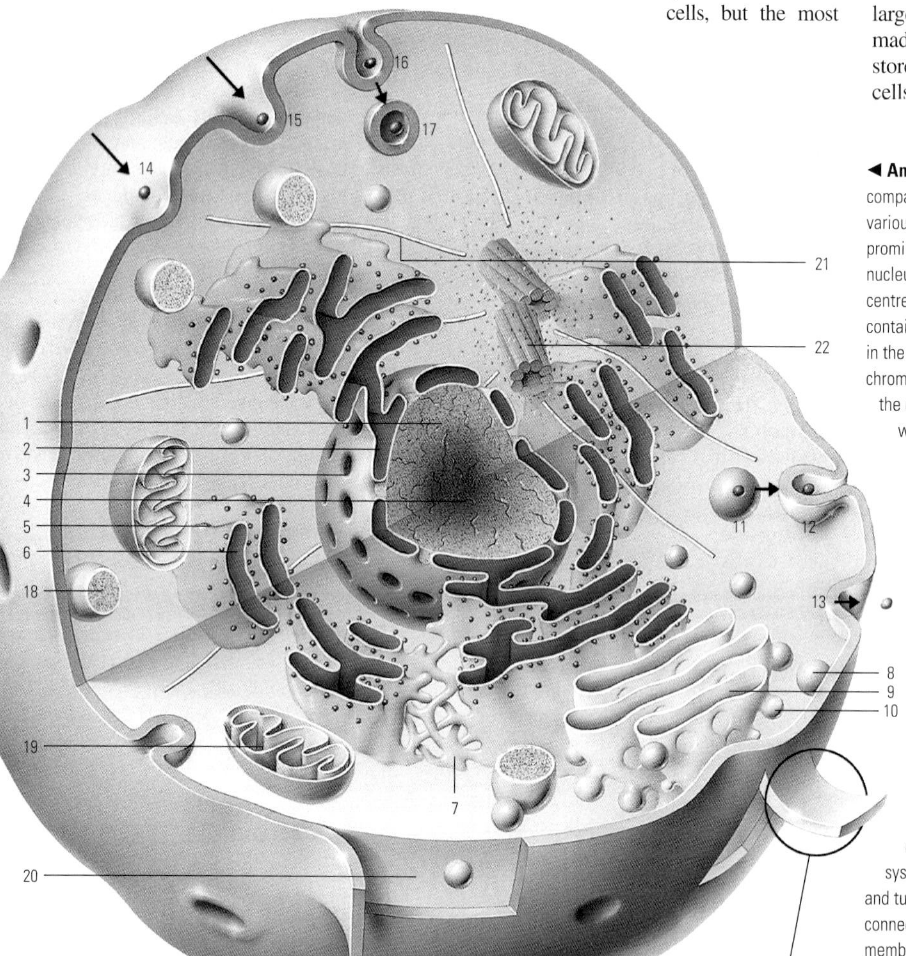

◄ **Animal cells are** compartmentalized into various organelles. The most prominent of these is the nucleus (1), the information centre of the cell, which contains the genetic material in the form of long thread-like chromosomes. It is bounded by the nuclear membrane (2), which has many pores (3) to allow communication between the nucleus and other parts of the cell. In the centre of the nucleus is the nucleolus (4), which is responsible for the production of ribosomes. The ribosomes (5) are the cell's protein factories and are found studded on the outer surface of the rough endoplasmic reticulum (6). This is a system of flattened sacs and tubes of membrane connected to the nuclear membrane. It brings the messenger RNA molecules –

which direct protein synthesis – to the ribosomes. Lipids are also produced here and form part of the cell membrane. The smooth endoplasmic reticulum (7) – connected to the rough – produces small membranous spheres called vesicles (8) These transport proteins to the Golgi body (9), which modifies, sorts and packs many large molecules into other vesicles, which bud off the body (10). They are then sent to other organelles or secreted from the cell. The fusion of such vesicles with the cell membrane allows particles to be transported out of the cell (exocytosis) (11–13). Similarly, particles can be brought into the cell (14–17) in vesicles (endocytosis). Molecules entering the cell may be broken down by enzymes found in special vesicles, called lysosomes (18). The mitochondria (19) are the powerhouses of the cell, using oxygen and food to generate energy (as ATP), which is then used in many metabolic processes. The majority of these processes are chemical reactions taking place in the aqueous medium of the cytoplasm (20). Running through the cytoplasm is a matrix of protein filaments (microtubules, 21) known as the cytoskeleton, which acts like scaffolding, giving the cell shape, and also providing a system for transport and movement. The cytoskeleton originates at the centrioles (22), which also help the chromosomes line up during cell division.

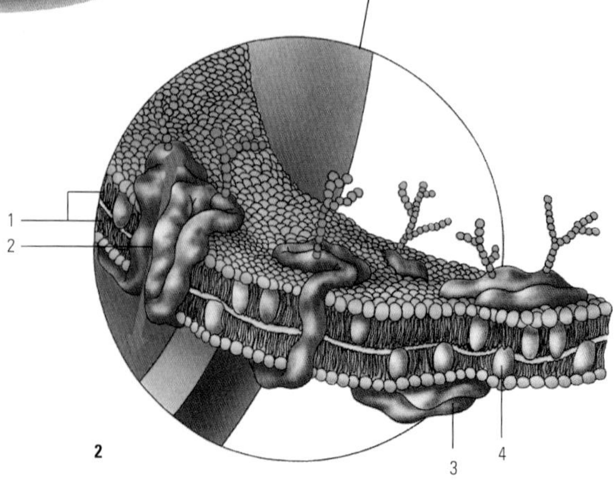

► **The cell membrane** is a thin, two-fold layer of lipid molecules (1) that surrounds the cytoplasm of all cells. Very few molecules can pass through the cell membrane unaided. Special transport proteins and protein-lined channels (2) in the membrane let through sugars, amino acids and essential ions such as sodium and calcium. Other proteins (3) act as receptors for chemical signals, and provide a chemical signature that allows recognition by other cells, particularly of the immune system. Cholesterol molecules (4) are important for the membrane's stability, although too many can cause the membrane to seize up.

PROTON POWERHOUSE

Cells are powered primarily by energy released from adenosine triphosphate (ATP) as it becomes adenosine diphosphate (ADP). ATP is made in the mitochondria (1) by recycling ADP. The first step is to split pyruvate (2) – a fuel molecule derived from glucose in the cytoplasm – into carbon dioxide, hydrogen and high-energy electrons. These electrons pass along a line of proteins in the inner membrane (3), giving them energy to pump out protons (4) into the intermembrane space (5). As more protons are pumped out, a pressure builds up in the space, forcing protons back across the membrane. But the protons can only flow back into the matrix via the ATP generator (6) – the enzyme

ATP synthetase – and as they do so they drive round the blades of this turbine, producing ATP (7).

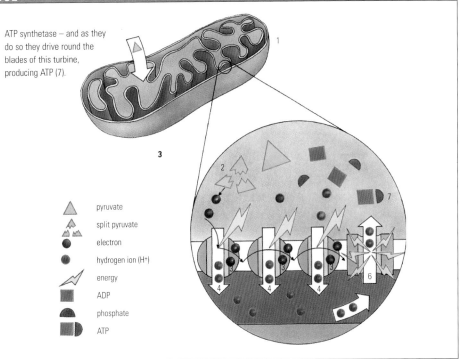

△	pyruvate
🔺🔺	split pyruvate
●	electron
●	hydrogen ion (H⁺)
⚡	energy
■	ADP
◗	phosphate
▰	ATP

PLANT CELLS

The most prominent feature of a plant cell is the nucleus (1), which contains the cell's genetic material or DNA, normally arranged in thin strands called chromatin (2). Messenger molecules copied from the DNA pass through pores in the nuclear membrane (3); they then attach themselves to ribosomes (4), where they direct the synthesis of new cell proteins. Ribosomes are anchored to parallel membranes – the endoplasmic reticulum (5) – that form a maze-like network in the cell.

Endoplasmic reticulum may lack ribosomes, in which case it is called smooth endoplasmic reticulum (6). Plant cells additionally contain chloroplasts (7) and enzyme-containing microbodies (8).

The solution of biological molecules outside the nucleus is the cytoplasm (9), which is connected to adjacent cells by plasmodesmata (10). Mitochondria (11), lysosomes (12) and Golgi bodies (13) are common to all cells, as are the microfilaments and microtubules (14) that form the cell's internal skeleton.

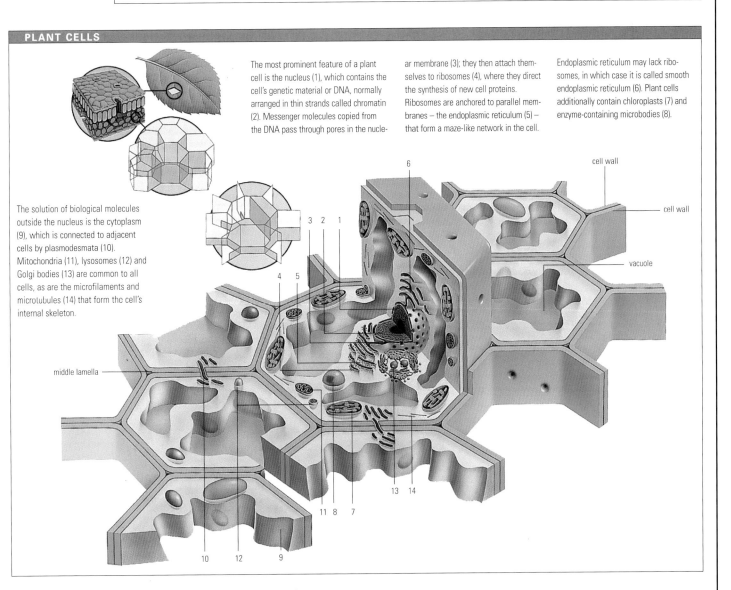

cell wall

cell wall

vacuole

middle lamella

C

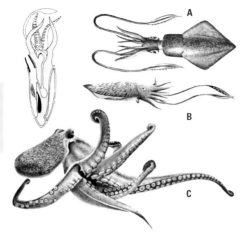

▲ **cephalopod** The squid (A), cuttlefish (B) and octopus (C) are all swimming molluscs of the Cephalopoda class. They have advanced, powerful eyes. Their tentacles are lined with sucker pads, which are used to catch fish and small crustaceans. The horny jawed mouth is powerful enough to break up their prey before it is digested in the gut.

DIVISION. When chromosomes shrink during MEIOSIS or MITOSIS, the centromere appears as a narrowing that contains no genes. It connects the chromosomes to the SPINDLE fibres.

centrosome

Region in a cell where MICROTUBULES are broken down and assembled during CELL DIVISION. Located alongside the nucleus, the centrosome contains two CENTRIOLES. At METAPHASE, the centrioles separate and the two regions of the centrosome containing them move to opposite sides of the cell as the microtubules form a SPINDLE between them. The spindle eventually divides the chromosomes into the two daughter cells. *See also* HAPLOID

cephalochordate

Any member of the subphylum Cephalochordata. A cephalochordate is a small marine animal that looks and swims rather like a fish but has no head or paired fins. Cephalochordates are related to vertebrates, having a NOTOCHORD throughout their lives. Their method of filter-feeding is, however, much more like that of invertebrates. They inhabit shallow, temperate and tropical seawater. Subphylum Cephalochordata. *See also* AMPHIOXUS

cephalopod

Any of more than 600 species of predatory marine MOLLUSC of the class Cephalopoda, including SQUID, NAUTILUS, OCTOPUS and CUTTLEFISH. Each has eight or more arms surrounding the mouth, which typically has a beak. The nervous system is well developed, permitting great speed and alertness; the large eyes have an image-forming ability equal to that of vertebrates. Most squirt an inky fluid to alarm attackers. Cephalopods move by squirting water from their mantle edge. Their heavily yolked eggs develop into larval young that resemble the adults. Members of this class vary dramatically in size from 4cm (1.5in) to the giant squid, which may reach 20m (65ft).

ceratopsian

Member of a group of *c.*20 species of rhinoceros-like, horned, plant-eating DINOSAURS of late Cretaceous times. Ceratopsians included *Protoceratops*.

cereal

Flowering plant of the family Graminae usually grown for the STARCH present in its seeds. Once dried, the seeds, which contain around 75% CARBOHYDRATE and 10% PROTEIN, are easily stored. Many varieties are grown commercially including WHEAT, BARLEY, RICE, MAIZE, OATS, RYE, MILLET and SORGHUM. Around 1800 million tonnes of cereal are produced worldwide each year, 75% of which are wheat, maize and rice. It is likely that wheat was the first plant to be grown by humans for food, its history stretching back some 10,000 years.

cerebellum

Part of the BRAIN, often known as the "little brain", which is located at the base of the CEREBRUM. It is involved in maintaining muscle tone, balance and coordinated movement.

cerebral cortex

Deeply fissured outer layer of the CEREBRUM. The cortex, also known as the "grey matter", is the most sophisticated part of the BRAIN, responsible for the appreciation of sensation, for initiating voluntary movement, and for all higher functions, such as the emotions and intellect.

cerebral hemispheres

Lateral halves of the CEREBRUM, the largest parts of the BRAIN and the sites of higher thought. Because nerve fibres cross over from one cerebral hemisphere to the other, the right side controls most of the movements and sensation on the left side of the body, and vice versa. Damage to the cerebral hemispheres often produces personality changes.

cerebrum

Largest and most highly developed part of the BRAIN, consisting of the CEREBRAL HEMISPHERES separated by a central fissure. It is covered by the CEREBRAL CORTEX. It coordinates all higher functions and voluntary activity.

cerussite (white lead)

Mineral form of lead carbonate ($PbCO_3$). It forms in oxidized regions of mineral veins, particularly of GALENA. Its prismatic or needle-shaped crystals (orthorhombic) are usually colourless or white, but may be green or grey with a resinous or vitreous lustre. Cerussite is mined as lead ore in Mexico; it is also used as a white pigment. Hardness: 3–3.5; r.d. 6.6.

cetacean

Any member of the order Cetacea of aquatic mammals found in all oceans and some rivers. The larger cetaceans are WHALES, the smaller ones are PORPOISES or DOLPHINS. Cetaceans are streamlined, with a pair of front flippers and horizontal tail flukes. Their bodies are insulated by a thick layer of BLUBBER. Length: from 1.5m (4.9ft) to more than 30m (100ft); weight: from 36kg (80lb) to 100 tons.

Ceylon olive

Tropical tree that bears succulent fruits and seeds. It grows in E Asia. Family Elaeocarpaceae; species *Elaeocarpus serratus*.

CFC

Abbreviation of CHLOROFLUOROCARBON

chachalaca, plain

Medium to large bird, related to the guan and the curassow. It is similar in appearance to a half-size turkey. The plain chachalaca is dark above and light brown below. It is found in brushy woodland from Texas, United States, to Nicaragua. It is a ground feeder, eating vegetation, fruit, insects and worms. Length: 46cm (18in). Family Cracidae; species *Ortalis vetula*.

chaetognath

Any member of the phylum Chaetognatha, which includes arrowworms – small marine animals that are not at all closely related to any other group. Chaetognaths are between 3mm and 10cm (0.1–4in) long and have narrow bodies, with bristly jaws for seizing their prey, usually plankton. Although invertebrate animals, they swim like fish, by means of fins. They are HERMAPHRODITE. Some species are useful INDICATOR SPECIES for marine biologists because they are sensitive to the temperature, salinity and depth of the water in which they live.

chafer

Any of a large number of beetles, particularly of the SCARAB BEETLE family (Scarabaeidae), that feed on the leaves of plants. They include the GARDEN CHAFER, PINE CHAFER and rose chafer BEETLE.

chaffinch

Small FINCH found in Europe, North Africa and w Asia. The male has a pink breast and light blue head, and the female is dull brown; both sexes have two white wing flashes. A woodland bird, the chaffinch is also common in gardens and parkland. It feeds on seeds, insects, buds and berries. Length: 15cm (6in). Family Fringillidae; species *Fringilla coelebs*.

chaffinch, blue

Small FINCH found in pine forests in mountainous parts of the Canary Islands. The male is slate blue and the female is brown; both sexes lack the white wing flash of the chaffinch. It feeds on seeds and insects. Length: 16cm (6in). Family Fringillidae; species *Fringilla teydea*.

chalcanthite

Mineral consisting mainly of hydrated copper sulphate ($CuSO_4.5H_2O$), although it is rarely used as a source of copper. It occurs as greenish-blue triclinic crystals

◀ **ceratopsian** The Styracosaurus lived in the Cretaceous period and, like all ceratopsians, was equipped with armour that served as protection against therapods, such as the carnivorous Tarbosaurus. Ceratopsians were characterized by a head shield and varying numbers of horns. The Styracosaurus also used its limbs when under attack, the hind limbs carrying the weight of the body and the fore-limbs able to turn quickly to face an attacker.

► **chameleon** With a curled tail and agile toes that divide into two and three digits, the chameleon is well-adapted to grasping branches. The males of some species have well-developed horns on their heads which are sometimes used for fighting other males.

or as fibrous veins or stalactites. It is soluble in water and has a nauseating taste. Hardness 2.5; r.d. 2.25.

chalcedony

Microcrystalline form of QUARTZ. When cut and polished, it is used by gem engravers. It is waxy and lustrous; there are white, grey, blue and brown varieties. Chalcedony is often coloured by artificial methods. Some varieties contain impurities giving a distinctive appearance, such as AGATE (coloured bands), ONYX (striped) and bloodstone (dark green with red flecks).

chalcid

Any member of the cosmopolitan insect superfamily Chalcidoidea. Most species are black or yellow. They are predators on or parasites of other insects. Some chalcid larvae benefit humans by feeding on insect crop pests. Like some other hymenopterans, some chalcid species are so small as to be hyperparasites (parasites of parasites). Order Hymenoptera.

chalcocite

Dark grey, metallic, soft mineral, copper sulphide (Cu_2S); one of the chalcocite group. It is a major ore of copper, found mainly in sulphur deposits. The crystals occur in orthorhombic granular masses, or rarely in prismatic form. Hardness 2.5 to 3.0; r.d. 5.7.

chalcopyrite (copper pyrites)

Opaque, brass-coloured, copper iron sulphide

($CuFeS_2$); the most important copper ore. It is found in sulphide veins and in IGNEOUS and certain META-MORPHIC ROCKS (*see* CONTACT METAMORPHISM). The crystals are tetragonal but often occur in masses. Hardness 3.5–4; r.d. 4.2.

chalk

Porous, fine-grained rock, mainly composed of CAL-CAREOUS skeletons of marine microorganisms, especially COCCOLITHS and FORAMINIFERA. It varies in properties and appearance; pure forms, such as CAL-CITE, contain up to 99% calcium carbonate. It is used in making putty, plaster and cement, and harder forms are occasionally used for building.

chameleon

Arboreal LIZARD, found chiefly in Madagascar, Africa and Asia. It is notable for its ability to change colour. The compressed body has a curled, prehensile tail. It has bulging eyes that move independently. Length: 17–60cm (7–24in). Family Chamaeleontidae; genus *Chamaeleo*; there are 80 species.

chamois

Nimble, goat-like RUMINANT that lives in mountain ranges of Europe and W Asia. It has coarse, reddish-brown fur with a black tail and horns. Its skin is made into chamois leather. Length: up to 130cm (51in); weight: 25–50kg (55–110lb). Family Bovidae; species *Rupicapra rupicapra*.

chamomile (camomile)

Low-growing, yellow- or white-flowered herb. Several species are cultivated as ground cover. Flowers of the European chamomile (*Chamaemelum nobile*) are used to make herbal tea. Family Asteraceae; genus *Chamaemelum*.

chanterelle

Medium-sized, edible, fleshy, terrestrial mushroom. It occurs in beech and oakwoods in autumn. It has a bright yellow, funnel-shaped cap with prominent gills continuing down the stem. Phylum Basidiomycota; family Cantharellaceae; species *Cantharellus cibarius*.

chanting goshawk

Either of two similar species of BIRDS OF PREY. The chanting goshawks are found in Africa, where one is

▲ **char** The arctic char (*Salvelinus alpinus*) has the most northerly distribution of any freshwater fish. Its large body size makes it a popular sport and food fish, although its population is threatened by over fishing.

largely distributed in the east and the other in the west. Family Accipitridae.

chanting goshawk, dark

Large bird of prey. It is grey with a barred underside and pink cere (a swelling at the base of the upper beak) and legs. It is found in bushveld and broadleaved woodlands of Africa, with a rather easterly distribution. It hunts by waiting in trees. It feeds on small animals, lizards, insects and birds. Length: 50–56cm (20–22in). Family Accipitridae; species *Melierax metabates*.

chanting goshawk, pale

Large bird of prey, very similar to, but paler than, the dark chanting goshawk. It is found in arid parts of NW, equatorial and S Africa and SW Arabia. It hunts from a perch and also by stalking on the ground. Its food includes small animals, lizards and insects. Length: 53–63cm (21–25in). Family Accipitridae; species *Melierax canorus*.

chaos theory

Theory that attempts to describe and explain the highly complex behaviour of apparently chaotic or unpredictable systems that show an underlying order. The behaviour of some physical systems is impossible to describe using the standard laws of physics. This is because the mathematics needed to describe these systems is too difficult for even the largest supercomputers. Such systems are sometimes known as "non-linear" or "chaotic" systems, and they include complex machines, electric circuits and natural phenomena such as the weather. Nonchaotic systems can become chaotic, as when smoothly flowing water hits a rock and becomes turbulent. The lack of an adequate description means that a standard prediction of their behaviour is also impossible. Chaos theory provides mathematical methods needed to describe chaotic systems, and even allows some general prediction of a system's likely behaviour. Chaos theory also shows, however, that even the tiniest variation in the starting conditions of a system can lead to enormous differences in the state of the system some time later. Thus because it is impossible to know the precise starting conditions of a system, accurate prediction is also impossible.

char

Any of several species of freshwater game fish belonging to the genus *Salvelinus* of the SALMON family. The arctic char (*Salvelinus alpinus*) is found in North America and N Europe, mainly in the Arctic Ocean, from where it moves into fresh water to breed. North American species include: the lake TROUT (*Salvelinus namaycush*), which is found in

◄ **chanting goshawk, pale** The pale chanting goshawk (*Melierax canorus*) inhabits open plains and thorn bush. Usually found singly or in pairs, they have a distinct home range, centred on a group of trees. They hunt on the ground and are fast runners. Chanting goshawks are named after the distinctive singing calls they make during the breeding season.

C

C

▲ **cheetah** Also known as the hunting leopard, the cheetah (*Acinonyx jubatus*) is well adapted to catching its prey of antelope, hares and some species of birds, such as guinea fowl and young ostriches. It has long legs, a supple but strong back and well-developed eyesight. It is distinguished by its pattern of solid black spots, a striped tail and a dark line running from the inner eye to the mouth.

cold, deep lakes; the brook trout (*Salvelinus fontinalis*), which inhabits cold rivers, streams and lakes; and the Dolly Varden or bull trout (*Salvelinus malma*), which is found in fresh and salt water in North America and E Asia. Family Salmonidae.

characin
Any member of a family of more than 885 species of subtropical and tropical freshwater fish found in Central and South America and Africa. The family is extremely diverse, its members including the carnivorous PIRANHAS, the herbivorous pacus, silvery silver dollars, colourful TETRAS and BLIND FISH. They are related to catfish and minnows. Many characins are popular aquarium fishes. Family Characidae.

charadriiform
Member of the bird order Charadriiformes. They are found in most areas of the world and many are shore-dwellers. Charadriiform birds include GULLS, TERNS, GUILLEMOTS, PUFFINS, PLOVERS, CURLEWS, SNIPE and PHALAROPES, and the South American JACANAS and SHEATHBILLS.

charlock (wild mustard)
Abundant, annual, arable weed that occurs throughout temperate regions of the world. Charlock grows best in chalky and clay soils and will not tolerate shade. The yellow flowers appear in the summer and are pollinated by bees and flies. Family Brassicaceae (Cruciferae); species *Sinapis arvensis*.

chaste tree
Shrub that is native to s Europe and that has been widely naturalized. The twigs are used in basketwork and the fruits as a pepper substitute. The cultivated variety known as alba has long been considered a symbol of chastity. Family Verbenaceae; species *Vitex agnus-castus*.

chat
Member of a group of small birds found in open country of Europe, Africa and Asia. They are named after their call, which sounds like a loud "*chat*". Mainly insectivores, they are commonly seen on the ground or in low bushes. Chats have a characteristic upright stance, with a flicking tail. Family Turdidae (part). Other species commonly called chat belong to different bird families.

chat, Arnot's
Smallish, black and white bird found in central s Africa. The male has a white crown; the female has a black head and a white throat. They occupy mature, broadleaved (mopane) woodland, mostly living on the ground, where they feed on insects. Length: 46cm (18in). Family Turdidae; species *Thamnolea arnoti*.

chat, crimson
Small species of chat. The male has a crimson crown and belly, black back and white throat; the female is dull brown. The crimson chat is found across Australia, except for the most northerly and eastern parts, in inland hills and mallee heath. It feeds on insects. Length: 10–12cm (4–5in). Family Ephthianuridae; species *Ephthianura tricolor*.

chat, rose-breasted
Small, active bird, a member of the American wood warbler family. It inhabits Amazonian rainforests, often keeping to the canopy, where it hunts for insects. Length: 13cm (5in). Family Parulidae; species *Granatellus pelzelni*.

checkerberry
Cultivated, ornamental shrub. It is native to North America. The checkerberry produces red, berry-like fruits. Like other members of its family, it has aromatic leaves, which yield methyl salicylate, the original medicinal wintergreen. Family Ericaceae; species *Gaultheria procumbens*.

cheetah
Large species of CAT found in hot, arid areas of Africa, the Middle East and India. The cheetah is a long-legged animal with blunt, non-retractable claws. It has a tawny brown coat with distinctive round black spots. Capable of running at more than 95km/h (60mph), the cheetah hunts gazelles and antelopes by sight. Length: body: 140–150cm (55–59in); tail: 75–80cm (30–31in); weight: 60kg (132lb). Family Felidae; subfamily Acinonchinae; species *Acinonyx jubatus*.

chelonian
Member of a large group of reptiles that evolved in late Triassic times. It includes the TURTLES and TORTOISES, both living and fossil. Chelonians have short, wide bodies that are protected above and below by shields of bony plates covered with horny tortoiseshell.

▲ **cherry** Grown for their fruit in many parts of the world, the cherry forms a type of fruit known as a drupe, which takes the form of a single seed surrounded by flesh. Cherries date from Roman times and the one shown is the black Early Rivers variety. The Japanese have a annual national festival to celebrate the arrival of cherry blossom.

▲ **chickadee** The coal tit (*Parus ater*) is a small species of chickadee which mainly inhabits coniferous woodlands. It is a sedentary bird, which comes near human settlements in winter. It is named after the sound of its melodic song.

chemical bond
Any mechanism that holds together atoms to form molecules. There are several types, arising either from the attraction of unlike charges or from the formation of stable configurations through electron-sharing. The total number of bonds that an atom can form is dependent upon its VALENCE. The main types include IONIC BOND, COVALENT BOND and HYDROGEN BOND.

chemolithotrophic bacterium
BACTERIUM that uses the oxidation of inorganic compounds as its principal energy source and carbon dioxide as its main source of carbon. The manner in which the energy is obtained from chemical sources varies with the type of bacterium; examples include *Thermococcus* and *Thermoproteus*, which obtain energy by reducing sulphur.

chemoreceptor
Tiny region on the outer membrane of some biological cells that is sensitive to chemical stimuli. The chemoreceptor transforms a stimulus from an external molecule into a sensation, such as smell or taste.

chemotropism
Growth or movement of a plant or plant part in response to a chemical stimulus. In **positive chemotropism**, the movement is towards the chemical; in **negative chemotropism** movement is away from the chemical. An example occurs during pollination. The ovary releases sugars into the style of the flower, and these act positively to cause pollen to produce a pollen tube that moves down the style.

chernozem (black earth)
Humus-rich type of dark soil typical of the grasslands of the steppes of Eurasia and the prairies of North America. It is prized for its agricultural qualities such as good structure and high nutrient content.

cherry
Widely grown fruit tree of temperate regions, probably native to w Asia and E Europe. Various types are grown for the fruit, which is small, yellow, red or almost black with a round stone. The wood is used in furniture. Height: to 30m (100ft). Family Rosaceae; genus *Prunus*; there are about 50 species.

cherry laurel
Tree that is native to SE Europe and SW Asia. It is most commonly grown as a clipped suburban hedge.

When damaged, cherry laurel leaves produce cyanide, which was widely used in the "killing bottles" of entomologists. Family Rosaceae; species *Prunus laurocerasus*.

chert
Impure, brittle type of FLINT. A cryptocrystalline variety of SILICA, it can be white, yellow, grey or brown. It occurs mainly in limestone and dolomite, although its origin is unknown.

chervil
Annual herb of the PARSLEY family, native to Eurasia; it is cultivated for its aromatic leaves, which are used for food flavouring. Height: to 61cm (24in). Family Apiaceae/Umbelliferae; species *Anthriscus cerefolium*.

chestnut
Deciduous tree native to temperate areas of the Northern Hemisphere. It has lance-shaped leaves and furrowed bark. Male flowers hang in long catkins; female flowers are solitary or clustered at the base of catkins. The prickly husked fruits open to reveal two or three edible nuts. Family Fagaceae; genus *Castanea*; there are four species. *See also* HORSE CHESTNUT

chevrotain
Any of four species, in two genera, of small, nocturnal mammal. Intermediate between pigs and deer, chevrotains are reddish-brown, sometimes with pale spots or stripes. They have short, thin legs and no horns or antlers. Chevrotains inhabit tropical rainforests in Africa, India and Southeast Asia. Head-body length: 44–80cm (17–31in); tail length: 3–14cm (1–6in). Family Tragulidae; genera *Hyemoschus* and *Tragulus* (the MOUSE-DEER).

chiasma
Point at which any two CHROMATIDS of a pair of HOMOLOGOUS CHROMOSOMES are joined. During the first PROPHASE of MEIOSIS the chromatids wrap around each other and form chiasmata. It is at these points that chromatids may break and combine with a different chromatid thus creating variety through the reassortment of ALLELES on the chromatids. It is this variety that is essential to evolution through NATURAL SELECTION. *See also* CROSSING OVER

chiastolite
Variety of andalusite, aluminium silicate (Al$_2$OSiO$_4$), found in METAMORPHIC ROCKS. It has elongated, prismatic crystals, which in cross-section show a black cross on a grey ground. Hardness 7.5; r.d. 3.1–3.2.

chickadee (titmouse)
Any of seven species of small bird found mainly in woodland, but also in gardens, of North America. They are dull coloured with short, stubby bills. Very

► **chick-pea** With pinnate leaves, small red or white flowers and two-seeded pods, the chick-pea plant measures up to 60cm (24in). Valued for their protein content, chickpeas are a staple food in countries such as India. The peas are boiled to make them edible and are sometimes roasted and used as a substitute for coffee beans.

▲ **chimaera** Found in the E Atlantic Ocean and the Mediterranean Sea, the chimaera is characterized by an immoveable upper jaw, which is an integral part of the skull. The male also has an unusual calcified hook on its head, the function of which is unknown.

active birds, chickadees feed on a variety of items, but mainly insects, seeds and nuts. Family Paridae; genus *Parus*.

chickadee, black-capped
Small member of the titmouse family; it is found in Canada and the United States, as far south as North Carolina. It is grey with a black bib and cap. It feeds mostly on insects, with some seeds and nuts. Length: 12–14cm (5–6in). Family Paridae; species *Parus atricapillus*.

chick-pea (dwarf pea, garbanzo, chich or gram)
Bushy annual plant cultivated since antiquity in S Europe and Asia for its pea-like seeds. It is now also grown widely in the Western Hemisphere. Family Fabaceae/Leguminosae; species *Cicer arietinum*.

chickweed
Cosmopolitan weed. It flowers freely all year, producing countless tiny brown seeds. Its Latin name means "little star", a reference to its very small white flowers. Chickweed is fed to chickens and cage-birds and is also used as a salad vegetable. Its characteristic feature is the single line of hairs running down its stem; they catch drops of dew, which are absorbed by the plant against times of drought. Family Caryophyllaceae; species *Stellaria media*.

chicle
Tropical rainforest tree of South and Central America. It produces a milky LATEX, which was used as chewing gum by the Aztecs, long before it was first processed and sweetened for commercial use in the 19th century. Family Sapotaceae; species *Manilkara zapota*.

chicory
Perennial weedy plant, the leaves of which are cooked and eaten or served raw in salads. The fleshy roots are dried and ground for mixing with (or a substitute for) COFFEE. Chicory has bright blue, daisy-like flowers. Height: 1.5m (5ft). Family Asteraceae/Compositae; species *Cichorium intybus*.

chigger (harvest mite or red bug)
Tiny red larva of some kinds of MITES. Adult mites lay eggs on plants, and hatched larvae find an animal host. The animal's mouth parts are borne on a "false head". On humans, chigger bites cause a severe rash and itching. Length: 0.1–16mm (0.004–0.6in). Family Trombiculidae.

Chilean fire bush
Ornamental shrub of South America. It grows in open places from the coast up to the treeline and is

successfully cultivated in other tropical, subtropical and temperate regions. It produces bright red flowers. Family Proteaceae; species *Embothrium coccineum*.

chilli (chili)
Hot, red PEPPER. It is an annual with oval leaves and white or greenish-white flowers that produce red or green seedpods. When dried, the pods are ground. Cayenne comes from the same plant. Height: 2–2.5m (6–8ft). Family Solanaceae; species *Capsicum annuum*.

chilopod
Any member of the class Chilopoda, ARTHROPOD animals that have long, flat, segmented bodies, each bearing one pair of legs. *See* CENTIPEDE

chimaera
Any of 34 species belonging to the order Chimaeriformes; they are related to sharks. Various species are known as spookfish, ghost sharks and elephant fish. Chimaeras are scaleless with a large head, one dorsal spine and a single gill opening. They occur near the ocean bottom in continental shelf waters at depths of up to 2600m (8500ft). Length: to 1.5m (5ft).

chimpanzee
APE that is distributed across W and central Africa. Chimpanzees are principally vegetarian, eating mainly fruit, but some animal food is included in their diet. Order Primates; family Pongidae.

chimpanzee, common
Chimpanzee found in a range of habitats from humid forest to dry savanna. It is dark in colour, although juveniles may have pink skin on the hairless face, hands and feet. Common chimpanzees often use tools, for example to extract termites. Head-body length: 73–83cm (29–33in), females smaller. Family Pongidae; species *Pan troglodytes*.

chimpanzee, pygmy (bonobo)
Chimpanzee that lives only in humid forest. It is not much smaller than the common chimpanzee, but is thinner, with longer arms and a darker, smaller face. It is generally less aggressive. Head-body length: 73–83cm (29–33in), females smaller. Family Pongidae; species *Pan paniscus*.

China grass
Tropical Asian plant. It is cultivated for its long, tough, silky fibres, which are used in rope-making and in the production of ramie (a Chinese linen fab-

▲ **chimpanzee** Like all primates, chimpanzees have large brains capable of mastering complex skills. They have been observed using sticks to "fish" for termites, a skill which the young learn by copying their elders.

C

ric). China grass belongs to the same family as the common stinging nettle, which also contains a small amount of silky fibre, used in Scotland as recently as the 19th century for table and bed linen. Family Urticaceae; species *Boehmeria nivea.*

China jute
Plant of tropical and warm climates. It produces tough fibres, which are widely used in rope-making. Family Malvaceae; species *Abutilon theophrasti.*

China root
Climbing plant of mainly tropical and subtropical regions. Its root yields a substance with stimulant properties. Family Smilaceae; species *Smilax china.*

chinch bug
Small insect with a black body, white wings and red legs. It is a serious pest of grass, corn, wheat and other grain in E and central United States. The chinch bug lays its eggs on the roots or lower stems of grain plants; the larvae feed on plant sap, causing much damage. Length: to 5mm (0.2in). Order Hemiptera; family Lygaeidae; species *Blissus leucopterus.*

chinchilla
Any member of a genus of small, furry RODENTS native to South America. Chinchillas were hunted almost to extinction. They are now bred for their soft fur, which is the most expensive of all animal furs. Length: 23–38cm (9–15in); weight; 450–900g (1–2lb). Family Chinchilidae.

Chinese cabbage
Cultivated form of a species of CABBAGE. It is grown traditionally in the Far East but is now commonly sold in the West. It is popular as a crunchy addition to salads and in stir-fries. Family Cruciferae; species *Brassica rapa*; varieties include *Chinensis* and *Pekinensis.*

Chinese lantern
Ornamental plant, the stems of which bear persistent, inflated, bright reddish orange, lantern-like calyxes around small berries. It is widely used dried in flower arrangements. The family to which the Chinese lantern belongs includes not only many essential vegetables and fruits, such as POTATO, TOMATO, PEPPER and CAPE GOOSEBERRY, but also some poisonous species, such as DEADLY NIGHTSHADE. Family Solanaceae; species *Physalis alkekengi.*

chipmunk
Small, ground-dwelling SQUIRREL native to North America and Asia. It carries nuts, berries and seeds in cheek pouches, to store underground. Active tree-climbers in summer, chipmunks hibernate in winter. Most species are brown with one or more black-bordered, light stripes. Length: 13–15cm (5–6in), excluding the tail. Family Sciuridae; genera *Eutamias* and *Tamias.*

chiropteran
Any member of the order Chiroptera, which contains the 178 genera of BATS. Bats are the only MAMMALS to have true flight (although a few others can glide).

▶ **chinchilla** Found in the Chilean and Bolivian Andes, chinchillas feed on seeds, roots and grasses. They rely on these foods for water as well as nutrients due to the scarcity of drinking water in the rocky terrain which they inhabit.

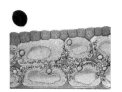

◀ **chloroplast** Found mostly in the cells of plant leaves, chloroplasts absorb sunlight and use it to manufacture special types of sugar. They are able to move about in order to receive the maximum amount of light possible. A section through a leaf reveals that during the day (top) chloroplasts have moved to the outer and inner walls in the direct line of light. During the night (bottom) they move to the inner and side walls only.

A bat's wing is formed by a sheet of skin stretched over a frame of greatly elongated bones. Bats are able to navigate in complete darkness by means of a kind of sonar, which uses echoes of the bat's own supersonic squeaks to locate obstacles and prey. Bats are nocturnal and found in all tropical and temperate regions. Most are small, although they range in wingspan from 25cm to 147cm (10–58in).

chiru (Tibetan antelope)
Endangered species of ANTELOPE that lives in the steppe regions of Tibet, China and India. It is pale with dark markings on the front of its legs and face. The chiru has short ears and a dense coat of soft wool. Males have slightly curving black horns, 50–72cm (20–28in) long. Head-body length: 120–130cm (47–51in); tail: 18–30cm (7–12in). Family Bovidae; subfamily Caprinae; species *Pantholops hodgsoni.*

chitin
Hard, tough substance that occurs widely in nature, particularly in the hard shells (EXOSKELETONS) of ARTHROPODS such as CRABS, INSECTS, SPIDERS and their relatives. The walls of HYPHAE – the microscopic tubes of fungi – are composed of slightly different chitin. Chemically, chitin is, like cellulose, a polysaccharide, derived from GLUCOSE.

chiton (coat-of-mail shell)
MOLLUSC that lives attached to, or creeping on, rocks along marine shores. It is bilaterally symmetrical. Its upper surface has eight overlapping shells, underneath which are a large, fleshy foot and a degenerate head with mouth, gills and mantle. Length: to 33cm (13in). Class Amphineura; order Polyplacophora; family Chitonidae.

chive
Perennial herb, the long, hollow leaves of which have an onion-like flavour used for seasoning. The flowers grow in rose-purple clusters. Family Liliaceae; species *Allium schoenoprasum.*

chlamydia
Small, virus-like BACTERIA that lives as a PARASITE in human beings and animals and causes disease. One strain, *Chlamydia trachomatis*, is responsible for trachoma, the leading cause of blindness in the developing world; it is also a major cause of pelvic inflammatory disease (PID) in women. *Chlamydia psittaci* causes psittacosis, a disease of birds that can be transmitted to human beings. Chlamydial infection is the most common sexually transmitted disease in many developed countries.

chloride shift
Inward diffusion of negatively charged chloride ions into an ERYTHROCYTE (red blood cell) to offset the loss of negatively charged hydrogen carbonate ions. In this way the electrochemical neutrality of the red blood cell is restored. The process is important in the carriage of carbon dioxide in the blood.

chlorofluorocarbon (CFC)
Chemical compound in which the hydrogen atoms of a hydrocarbon, such as an alkane, are replaced by atoms of fluorine, chlorine and sometimes bromine. Chlorofluorocarbons (CFCs) are inert, stable at high temperatures and are odourless, colourless, nontoxic, noncorrosive and nonflammable. Under the trade name of Freons, CFCs were widely used in aerosols, fire-extinguishers, refrigerators and in the manufacture of foam plastics. The two most common are Freon 11 (trichlorofluoromethane, $CFCl_3$) and Freon 12 (dichlorodifluoromethane, CF_2Cl_2). When CFCs are used they slowly drift into the STRATOSPHERE and are broken down by the Sun's ultraviolet radiation into chlorine atoms, which destroy the OZONE LAYER. It often takes more than 100 years for CFCs to disappear from the atmosphere. Growing environmental efforts led to a 1990 international agreement by governments to reduce and eventually phase out the use of CFCs and other chemicals harming the ozonosphere, and to develop safe substitutes.

chlorophyll
Group of green PLANT PIGMENTS present in the CHLOROPLASTS of plants and ALGAE that absorb light for PHOTOSYNTHESIS. There are five types: chlorophyll *a* is present in all photosynthetic organisms except bacteria; chlorophyll *b* in plants and CHLOROPHYTES; and chlorophylls *c*, *d* and *e* present in some algae. It is similar in structure to HAEMOGLOBIN, with a magnesium atom replacing the iron atom.

chlorophyte (green alga)
Any member of the phylum Chlorophyta, a large group of marine and freshwater ALGAE. Chlorophytes have several features that make them more like typical green plants than other types of algae: they have cup-shaped CHLOROPLASTS that contain CHLOROPHYLL *b*; they have cell walls made of CELLULOSE; and they store food in the form of STARCH. Some produce cells with flagella (*see* FLAGELLUM) at some stage in their lives. Chlorophytes range in size from microscopic, single-cell types (some of which have flagella) to large, complex SEAWEEDS.

▲ **chough** Nesting alone or in pairs, choughs build mud-walled nests in tree-tops or cliff crevices. They are known for their whistling calls and aerial acrobatics.

chloroplast

Microscopic green structure within a plant cell in which PHOTOSYNTHESIS takes place. The chloroplast is enclosed in an envelope formed from two membranes and contains internal membranes to increase the surface area for reactions. Molecules of the light-absorbing pigment CHLOROPHYLL are embedded in these internal membranes.

cholla

CACTUS found in desert and semidesert regions of North, Central and South America. It has many-jointed, disc-like stems and lots of minute, readily detached spines. Some species, such as the PRICKLY PEAR, are edible. Other chollas produce cochineal and others are used for living fences. Family Cactaceae; genus *Opuntia*.

chondrite

Commonest kind of stony METEORITE; chondrites make up *c*.80% of all meteorite falls. They are characterized by the presence of small globules of OLIVINE and PYROXENE minerals. As primitive meteorites, chondrites formed *c*.4700 million years ago, at the same time as the Earth.

Christmas cactus

CACTUS that has smooth, flat-jointed stems and bright red, pink or orange flowers, which appear in winter. It is native to Brazil and widely cultivated for ornamental use. Family Cactaceae; species *Schlumbergera bridgesii*.

Christmas rose

Perennial herb found in chalky regions of Europe; it is named after its habit of flowering in December. The flowers are white and turn green after pollination in the wild. Its root is black inside, hence its Latin name. Family Ranunculaceae; species *Helleborus niger*.

cholesterol

White, fatty STEROID. It occurs in large concentrations in the brain, spinal cord and liver. Cholesterol is synthesized in the liver, intestines and skin and is an intermediate in the synthesis of vitamin D and many hormones.

Chondrichthyes

Class of cartilaginous FISH that includes the Elasmobranchii (SHARK, RAY and SKATE) and the Holocephali (CHIMAERA). These marine fish have cartilaginous (composed of CARTILAGE) skeletons, a well-developed lower jaw, paired fins, separate gill openings, no air bladder, bony teeth and plate-like (placoid) scales. The class also includes a number of extinct fossil groups which evolved in late Ordovician times.

chordate

Any member of the phylum Chordata, a large group of VERTEBRATES and some marine INVERTEBRATES that, at some stage in their lives, have rod-like, cartilaginous supporting structures (known as NOTOCHORDS). Invertebrate chordates are divided into three subphyla: Tunicata (SEASQUIRTS); Cephalochordata (AMPHIOXUS); and Hemichordata (ACORN WORMS).

chorion

Outermost of the protective membranes of the embryonic system of birds, reptiles or mammals, or of the insect egg. In birds the chorion is the moist lining between the shell and the ALLANTOIS (the organ for GASEOUS EXCHANGE). In placental mammals the

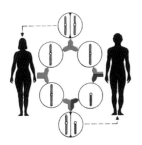

▲ **chromosome** The 46 chromosomes in somatic (non-reproductive) cells contain a single sex-determining pair, which consists of an X and Y chromosome in males, or an XX pair in females. Ova contain only the X chromosome, while spermatozoa contain X or Y chromosomes in equal proportions. At fertilization, therefore, there is a 50% chance of an XX or XY pair being formed.

chorion contributes to PLACENTA formation, and through it the EMBRYO receives nourishment, oxygen and water.

chough

Medium-sized member of the CROW family. It has black plumage, with a scarlet bill and red legs. Frequenting rocks and cliffs in mountainous districts, it is found in w Britain, Spain, the Alps, s Italy, the Balkans and Asia, as far east as China. It feeds mainly on insects, worms and seeds. Length: 39–40cm (15–16in). Family Corvidae; species *Pyrrhocorax pyrrhocorax*.

chough, alpine

Medium-sized member of the CROW family. It is all black with a yellow bill and red legs. The alpine chough frequents rocky regions of high mountains up to the snow line in the Pyrenees, Alps, Balkans and Asia, as far east as China. It feeds on invertebrates. Length: 36–39cm (14–15in). Family Corvidae; species *Pyrrhocorax graculus*.

chough, white-winged

Medium to large bird found in dry woodland of E and SE Australia. It has black plumage and white patches, which are exposed in flight, on its wing feathers. Length: 45cm (18in). Family Corcoracidae; species *Corcorax melanorhamphos*.

chromatid

Either of the two duplicate strands into which each CHROMOSOME in a biological CELL nucleus divides in the first phase of MITOSIS or MEIOSIS (cell division). When the nucleus is about to split, the pairs of identical chromatids are separated by a long fibrous structure made of proteins, called a mitotic SPINDLE. The separated chromatids become identical "daughter" chromosomes of the same kind as those of the parent cell on opposite sides of the nucleus. *See also* CROSSING OVER; HOMOLOGOUS CHROMOSOME

chromatin

Substance that makes up CHROMOSOMES in the nucleus of a cell. It consists of DNA and some RNA, as well as HISTONES and other proteins. In a metabolically active cell nucleus, the chromatin expands to create a region in which MESSENGER RNA (mRNA) may be formed.

chromatography

Name given to a number of techniques of chemical analysis by which substances are separated from one another, identified and measured. Chromatography was invented (1906) by the Russian botanist Mikhail Tsvett (1872–1920). There are several types, all involving a moving phase consisting of a liquid or gaseous mixture of the substances to be separated, and a stationary phase consisting of a material that differentially absorbs the substances in the mixture.

chromatophore

Pigment-containing cell that occurs in the skin of some lower animals. Accumulation or dispersion of granules of pigment in chromatophores under nervous or hormonal stimulation allows some animals, such as CHAMELEONS, to change colour to suit their surroundings. Chromatophores that contain black pigment are called **melanophores**.

chromite

Black, metallic mineral, ferrous chromic oxide ($FeOCr_2O_3$), the only important ore of chromium. It separates from magma when IGNEOUS ROCKS first form, occurring as octahedral crystals and as granular masses. Chromite is weakly magnetic and opaque. Hardness 5.5; r.d. 4.6.

chromosome

Structure carrying the genetic information of an organism, found only in the cell nucleus of EUKARYOTES. Thread-like and composed of DNA, chromosomes carry a specific set of GENES. Each species usually has a characteristic number of chromosomes; these occur in pairs, members of which carry identical genes, so that most cells have a DIPLOID number of chromosomes in every one of their cells, varying from two to more than 300, although most organisms have between 10 and 40 in each cell. GAMETES (sex cells) carry a HAPLOID number of chromosomes. *See also* HEREDITY

chrysalis

Intermediate stage in the life cycle of all INSECTS that undergo complete METAMORPHOSIS (holometabolous insects). The chrysalis is usually covered with a hard case, but some pupae, such as those of the silk moth, spin a silk COCOON around themselves. Within the chrysalis, feeding and locomotion stop and the final stages of the development take place. *See also* PUPA

chrysanthemum

Any member of the genus *Chrysanthemum*, a large group of annual and perennial plants that are native to temperate Eurasia and are now widely cultivated. Centuries of selective breeding have modified the original plain daisy-like flowers, and most species have large white, yellow, bronze, pink or red flower-heads. Family Asteraceae/COMPOSITAE.

chrysoberyl

Oxide mineral, beryllium aluminum oxide ($BeAl_2O_4$). It is found in beryllium-rich pegmatite dykes. Its hexagonal system crystals are prismatic or tabular. It can be transparent green, yellow or brown, but bright yellow-green is most highly valued. Gem varieties include cat's eye and alexandrite. Hardness 8.5; r.d. 3.69.

◄ **chrysanthemum** Native to E Asia, the chrysanthemum, along with the cherry blossom, is the national flower of Japan. Today there are some 200 species cultivated around the world.

► **chub** The European wide-mouth chub (*Squalius cephalus*) is found in well-oxygenated waters with plentiful vegetation. A voracious feeder, it eats insects, plants, other fish and amphibians.

C

chrysophyte (golden-green alga)
Any member of a diverse group of ALGAE ranging from phytoplankton to benthic, intertidal species. Chrysophytes may be unicellular, colonial or filamentous, and the majority are flagella-bearing unicells. Their golden-green colour is due to pigmentation composed of a dominant carotenoid, fucoxanthin, as well as chlorophylls and diatoxanthin. Family Chrysophyceae.

chrysotile
Fibrous serpentine mineral, from which comes most of the world's supply of ASBESTOS. Serpentines are hydrated magnesium silicates ($3MgO2SiO_2.2H_2O$). The variety called chrysotile has crystalline, tubular fibres that are particularly suitable for spinning and weaving into heat-resistant fabrics.

chub
Any of several species of freshwater fish belonging to the CARP family, found in Europe and North America. The European chub (*Leuciscus cephalus*) is grey-brown, with a large head and a wide mouth. Length: 10–60cm (4–24in). Family Cyprinidae. **Chub** is also the name of several species of marine fish found in warm areas of the Pacific Ocean. It has a brightly coloured, oval-shaped body and a small mouth. Family Kyphosidae.

chuckwalla
Flattened, desert-dwelling LIZARD of sw North America. It is dull-coloured, sometimes with red blotches, and has loose side folds of skin. It hides in rocky crevices and, when threatened, inflates its body so that it cannot be moved from the crevice. Length: to 50cm (20in). Family Iguanidae; species *Sauromalus obesus*.

cicada
GRASSHOPPER-like insect that is found in most parts of the world. The male makes a loud sound by vibrating a pair of plates in its abdomen. The female lays eggs in tree branches. The dog-day cicada appears annually in summer. The larvae of the periodical cicada spends 13 or 17 years in the ground; it lives only a week as a winged adult. Length: up to 5cm (2in). Order Homoptera; most species belong to the family Cicadidae.

► **cicada** The life-cycle of a cicada is longer than that of most insects. The female cuts a slit in a twig in which she lays her eggs. When the eggs hatch, the nymphs fall to the ground and burrow into the soil. They remain underground for several years feeding off plant roots and moulting repeatedly, before emerging as adults.

nymph

cicada, periodical
Cicada whose nymphs live underground for 13 or 17 years, depending on the species, surviving on plant root juice. All cicadas in one area emerge rapidly over two weeks in early summer, resulting in astronomical populations of up to 1.5 million individuals per acre. Adult body size: *c*.30mm (*c*.1.2in). Family Cicadidae.

cichlid
Any member of a family of tropical freshwater fish found mainly in South America, Africa and s Asia. Cichlids are popular aquarium fish because of their brilliant colours. Many are mouth breeders, the female harbouring the unfertilized eggs inside her mouth. Family Cichlidae.

ciconiiform
Member of the bird order Ciconiiformes, which comprises *c*.100 species of wading birds. Ciconiiform birds include the FLAMINGO, HERON, IBIS, STORK and SPOONBILL. They have long legs and necks and are found worldwide, except in polar regions.

cilia (sing. cilium)
Small, hair-like structures on cell walls; they are used for propulsion and feeding. Cilia are present in great quantities on some lining cells of the body, such as those along the respiratory tract. The wafting movements of the cilia help to propel foreign particles towards the exterior. Cilia are also found on some single-celled PROTOZOA, some species of which, such as the trypanosome of sleeping sickness, are known as CILIATES.

ciliate
Any one of the *c*.8000 species of the phylum Ciliophora, characterized by hair-like CILIA used for locomotion and food collecting. Ciliates are the largest and the most complex of the PROTOZOA. They are found in both aquatic and terrestrial habitats and many are carnivorous. Ciliates have two nuclei (**macronucleus** and **micronucleus**) and a variety of organelles, such as a cystome (mouth). Subclasses include the Holotrichs (*Paramecium*), Spirotrichs (*Stentor*) and Peritrichs (*Vorticella*).

cinchona
Any member of a genus of evergreen trees native to the Andes and cultivated in South America, Indonesia and the Democratic Republic of Congo. The dried bark of the cinchona trees is a source of QUININE and other medicinal products. Family Rubiaceae; genus *Cinchona*.

cineraria
Originally, a member of the genus *Senecio*, of the daisy family, growing specifically in Africa. The brightly coloured cineraria popular with florists and gardeners are now known as *Pericallis*. Family Compositae; genus (originally) *Senecio*; now cultivated as the species *Pericallis hybrida*.

cinnabar
Deep red mineral, mercury(II) (mercuric) sulphide (HgS), the major ore of mercury. Its crystal system is trigonal. Cinnabar occurs as rhombohedral crystals, often twinned, and as granular masses. It is found in hydrothermal veins and volcanic deposits. The ore is reduced to mercury by roasting. Hardness 2–2.5; r.d. 8.1.

cinnabar moth
See MOTH, CINNABAR

cinnamon
Bushy evergreen tree native to India and Burma and cultivated in the West Indies and South America. The light-brown spice also called cinnamon is made from the dried inner bark of the tree. Its delicate aroma and sweet flavour make it a common ingredient in food. It was also used for religious rites and witchcraft. Family Lauraceae; species *Cinnamomum zeylanicum*.

cinquefoil (Fr. five leaves)
Any member of the genus *Potentilla*; they are named after the way in which the leaflets are usually grouped. The **creeping cinquefoil** (*Potentilla reptans*) grows widely in Eurasia and North America. It has yellow flowers and can be an invasive weed. The red-flowering **marsh cinquefoil** (*Potentilla palustris*) is widespread in boggy areas of Europe, central Asia and N North America. The **arctic cinquefoil** (*Potentilla hyparctica*) grows amongst grasses in polar regions. It is covered in hairs, which protect it from the bright sun and the cold temperatures. Family Rosaceae.

circadian rhythm
Internal "clock" mechanism that normally corresponds roughly with the 24-hour day. It relates most obviously to the cycle of waking and sleeping, but it is also involved in other cyclic variations, such as body temperature, hormone levels, metabolism and mental performance. It can be disrupted by irregular events such as shift-working and jet lag. *See also* BIOLOGICAL CLOCK

circulation
See CIRCULATORY SYSTEM

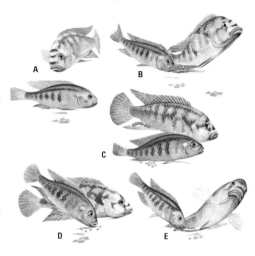

A

B

C

D   E

▲ **cichlid** Mating between mouth-brooding fish like the cichlid is a brief but elaborate encounter. A male cichlid (*Haplochromis burtoni*) approaches the female (A). He brings her into the breeding condition by flashing the set of dummy eggs on his anal fin (B). The female lays her eggs (C) and almost immediately takes them in her mouth (D). Once spawning has taken place, the male again spreads the anal fin. The female attempts to take up these eggs as well (E); instead she takes up the sperm emitted by the male. This involved encounter ensures that all the eggs in the mouth of the female are fertilized.

circulation, atmospheric

Flow of the ATMOSPHERE around the Earth. It is caused by temperature differences in the atmosphere and the rotation of the Earth, which transfers heat from warm zones (the tropics) to cooler zones (towards the poles). The poleward circulation due to convection gives rise to large-scale eddies, such as a CYCLONE and ANTICYCLONE, low-pressure troughs and high-pressure ridges. The eddies also take part in the longitudinal atmospheric circulation around the Earth, with the Earth's rotation maintaining easterly winds towards the Equator and westerly winds towards the poles. Narrow JET STREAMS blow swiftly over middle latitudes in the STRATOSPHERE, moving farther towards the poles during the summer. *See also* CORIOLIS EFFECT; FERREL CELL; HADLEY CELL

circulatory system

See feature article

cirque

Bowl-shaped, steep-sided hollow in a mountain area being glaciated or formerly glaciated. The eroded area is usually cut into the bedrock by repeated freezing and the result of glacial movement. When the ice melts a lake may form in the base of the cirque. Such lakes are known variously as cirque lakes, **corries** (in Scotland) or **cwm** (in Wales). They are often fed by the retreating GLACIER that created them. *See also* EROSION

cirriped

See BARNACLE

cirrocumulus

See CLOUD

cirrostratus

See CLOUD

cirrus

See CLOUD

cisticola

Any member of the *Cisticola* genus, which comprises *c*.30 species of grass or bush WARBLERS. All cisticolas are dull brown, often with streaked plumage. They are mainly found in s Europe, Middle East, Africa and Australia. Family Sylviidae (part).

cisticola, golden-headed

Small warbler found in long grassland around the N and E perimeter of Australia. It is brown with streaked back and wings; the breeding plumage includes an unstreaked golden head. It feeds on insects. Length: 10cm (4in). Family Sylviidae; species *Cisticola exilis*.

cisticola, tink-tink

Tiny warbler with a short tail. The tink-tink cisticola inhabits grassland and marshy ground in central and s Africa. It gets its common name from its loud, metallic call. Length: 9cm (4in). Family Sylviidae; species *Cisticola textrix*.

cisticola, zitting (fan-tailed warbler)

Small warbler, with brown, streaked plumage and a short tail. It is found in grasslands in s Europe, Middle East, Africa and parts of N and NE Australia. It feeds on insects. Length: 10cm (4in). Family Sylviidae; species *Cisticola juncidis*.

cistron

Region of a DNA molecule that unwinds during the TRANSCRIPTION phase of PROTEIN SYNTHESIS. HYDROGEN BONDS between BASE PAIRS in the DNA DOUBLE HELIX break, exposing the bases along both strands. Each base along the transcribing (sense) strand attracts its complementary RNA nucleotide, thus forming a strand of MESSENGER RNA, which is used as a template for forming a specific POLYPEPTIDE.

CITES

Acronym for CONVENTION ON INTERNATIONAL TRADE IN ENDANGERED SPECIES OF WILD FLORA AND FAUNA

citron

Evergreen shrub or small tree of the RUE family, native to Asia. It has short spines and oval leaves. It bears large, rectangular, lemon-yellow fruit. Height: up to 3.5m (11.5ft). Family Rutaceae; species *Citrus medica*.

citronella

Plant that is native to South America; it is found mostly in rainforests but also sometimes on dry, barren soil. Citronella leaves are used locally to make a kind of tea. Family Icacinaceae; species *Citronella gongonha*.

citrus

Group of trees and shrubs of the genus *Citrus* in the RUE family, native to subtropical regions. They

---

CIRCULATORY SYSTEM

Means by which OXYGEN and NUTRIENTS are carried to the body's tissues and CARBON DIOXIDE and other waste products are removed. It consists of BLOOD VESSELS that carry the BLOOD, propelled by the pumping action of the HEART. In humans and other mammals, blood travels to the LUNGS, where, by the process of GAS EXCHANGE, it picks up oxygen and loses carbon dioxide. It then flows to the heart, from where it is pumped out into the aorta, which branches into smaller ARTERIES, arterioles and CAPILLARIES. Oxygen and other nutrients diffuse out of the blood, and carbon dioxide and other tissue wastes pass into the capillaries, which join to form VEINS leading back to the heart. Blood then returns to the lungs and the entire cycle is repeated. This is known as a double circulatory system, because the blood is pumped first to the lungs, and then to the rest of the body. Because the lungs are delicate, the double cycle allows the heart to pump blood strongly through the body without risk of damaging the lungs. In fish and many other animals, there is a single circulatory system, with blood passing through the GILLS and on to the rest of the body without an extra boost from the heart. Both these circulatory systems are closed; the blood remains confined within the blood vessels. Insects and many other invertebrates have an open circulatory system, where the blood flows freely within the body cavity, but passes through a series of open blood vessels and heart(s), the pumping of which maintains a directional flow.

▶ **The system by** which oxygen and nutrients are carried to the body's tissues and carbon dioxide and other waste products removed is called the circulatory system. In human beings and other mammals, blood travels to the lungs, where it picks up oxygen and loses carbon dioxide, before flowing back to the heart. This is known as the lesser (pulmonary) circulation. From the heart it is pumped out into the aorta. The aorta's first two branches, the coronary arteries, subdivide into brachial and carotid arteries. The aorta then runs to the abdomen, with branches to the vertebrae, diaphragm and intercostal muscles. In the abdomen it divides into the common iliac arches to the legs. There are four main branches: gastric to the stomach; splanchnic to the intestine; renal to the kidneys; and splenic to the spleen. The venous blood returns to the superior and inferior venae cavae and thus to the right atrium.

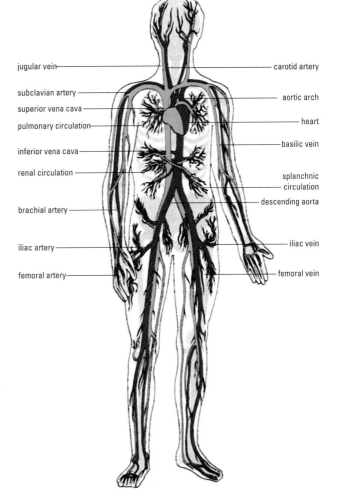

jugular vein — carotid artery
subclavian artery — aortic arch
superior vena cava — heart
pulmonary circulation — basilic vein
inferior vena cava — splanchnic circulation
renal circulation — descending aorta
brachial artery — iliac vein
iliac artery — femoral vein
femoral artery

▲ **citrus** Most fruits belonging to the genus *Citrus* originated in China and Southeast Asia. The fruits are commercially important throughout the world, and some hybrids have been created to increase the number of varieties available. The orange (A) is probably the most economically important and popular citrus fruit. The largest producer is Brazil. It is sweet and contains a great amount of vitamin C. The grapefruit (B) is less sweet; it has been crossed with the tangerine to produce the sweet, juicy fruit known as the ugli (C). The lemon (D) is one of the few citrus fruits to have a sour taste. The world's largest producer of grapefruits and lemons is the United States.

include GRAPEFRUIT, LEMON, LIME, MANDARIN and ORANGE. The stems are usually thorny, the leaves bright green, shiny and pointed. The flowers are usually white, waxy and fragrant. The fruit (hesperidium) is usually ovoid with a thick, aromatic rind. The inside of the fruit is pulpy and juicy, and is divided into segments that contain the seeds. Most citrus fruits contain significant amounts of vitamin C. Family Rutaceae.

civet
Long-bodied, carnivorous mammal with a long, thick tail. Civets are usually solitary and nocturnal. They are related to the WEASEL family. Family Viverridae; there are six subfamilies.

civet, African
Member of the subfamily of true civets. It is found in a wide variety of habitats in tropical Africa. A terrestrial animal, it has an omnivorous diet, which includes small animals, carrion and fruit. The African civet is grey brown with dark spots and stripes and a dark crest along its back. Head-body length: 84cm (33in); tail: 42cm (17in). Family Viverridae; subfamily Viverrinae; species *Civettictis civetta*.

civet, banded palm
Member of the Hemigalinae subfamily of civets; also the name of an individual species within that subfamily. The banded palm civet is carnivorous and semiarboreal and is found in the rainforests of Southeast Asia. It is yellow with brown markings on its body and tail. Its name comes from the broad vertical bands on the side of its body. Head-body length: 53cm (21in); tail: 32cm (13in). Family Viverridae; subfamily Hemigalinae; species *Hemigalus derbyanus*.

civet, large Indian
Civet that is distinguished by its striking, black-and-white body stripes, white tail bands and an erectile crest of dark hair along its back. It is found in India and Southeast Asia. Head-body length: 81cm (32in); tail: 43cm (17in). Family Viverridae; subfamily Viverrinae; species *Viverra zibetha*.

civet, Madagascar
See FANALOKA

civet, Malay (Malayan, oriental or ground civet)
Civet closely related to the large Indian civet. It is found in Southeast Asia. The Malay civet has dark spots and bands across its back and neck, and an erectile crest. Head-body length: 66cm (26in); tail: 43cm (17in). Family Viverridae; subfamily Viverrinae; species *Viverra tangalunga*.

civet, otter
Either of two species of civet found in the rainforests of Southeast Asia. They are adapted for a semiaquatic life, with small ears and thick whiskers. Their feet are less webbed than those of true otters so that they are still adept at climbing trees. They feed on fish. Otter civets are brown with a white throat or underside. Head-body length: 64cm (25in); tail: 17cm (7in). Family Viverridae; subfamily Hemigalinae; genus *Cynogale*.

civet, palm
Member of the Paradoxurinae subfamily of civets found in the forests of India, Southeast Asia and Africa. They are excellent climbers and feed on fruit and small animals, both vertebrates and invertebrates. Head-body length: 50–88cm (20–35in); tail: 46–73cm (18–29in). Family Viverridae; subfamily Paradoxurinae.

cladistics
System of classifying organisms on the basis of homologies, or features shared due to common descent from the same ancestor. Organisms that share several characteristics are put into taxonomic groups known as **clades**. A **cladogram** is a diagram, resembling a sideways family tree, that shows how pairs or groups of clades diverged from common ancestors. Not all taxonomists agree about the validity of cladistics.

clam
Bivalve MOLLUSC found mainly in marine waters. It is usually partly buried in sand or mud. It has a large foot for burrowing. The clam's soft, flat body lies between two muscles for opening and closing the shells. A fleshy part, called the mantle, lies next to the shells. Clams feed on plankton. Phylum Mollusca; class Pelecypoda.

clarkia
Any member of the genus *Clarkia*. It is a sprawling, hairy shrublet, with pink, purplish or white flowers that appear between June and August. There are *c.*40 different species of *Clarkia*, found mostly in w North America but also as far south as Chile. It was named after Captain William Clarke, who explored the Rocky Mountains in 1806. A familiar cottage garden plant, it was introduced to Europe in the 1830s. Family Onagraceae; species include *Clarkia amoena* and *Clarkia unguiculata*.

class
Part of the CLASSIFICATION of living organisms, ranking above ORDER and below PHYLUM. Class names are printed in roman (not italic) letters, with an initial capital; for example Mammalia is the class in which all mammals are found.

classification
Organization of organisms into categories based on appearance, structure, genetic sequence or evolution. The categories, from the most inclusive to the most exclusive, are KINGDOM, PHYLUM, CLASS, ORDER, FAMILY, GENUS, SPECIES and sometimes variety. Some categories also include subphyla, subfamilies and so on. For example, the domestic dog is classified as being kingdom Animalia, phylum Chordata, class Mammalia, order Carnivora, family Canidae, genus *Canis*, species *Canis familiaris*. The five kingdoms classification system divides all living organisms into five kingdoms: Animalia (ANIMAL); Plantae (PLANT); Fungi (FUNGUS); PROKARYOTAE; and PROTOCTISTA. A different classification system, the three domains system, divides living organisms into three higher categories (ARCHAEA, BACTERIA and EUKARYA) called DOMAINS. *See also* BINOMIAL NOMENCLATURE; TAXONOMY; Ready Reference, pages 462–63

Claude, Albert (1899–1983)
US cell biologist, b. Belgium. He shared the 1974 Nobel Prize for physiology or medicine with Christian de DUVE and George PALADE for his pioneering use of the electron microscope to study the detailed anatomy of the cell. Claude also pioneered the use of the centrifuge to separate various components of a cell.

clavicle (collarbone)
Thin, slightly curved bone attached by ligaments to the top of the STERNUM (breastbone); it is present in most vertebrates. In humans, the clavicle and SCAPULA (shoulder blade) make up the shoulder girdle, linking the arms to the axis of the body.

clay
Mineral consisting of hydrous silicates of aluminium and magnesium, including kaolinite and halloysite, usually mixed with some quartz, calcite or gypsum. It is formed by the WEATHERING of surface granite or the chemical decomposition of feldspar. Soft when wet, clay hardens on firing and is used to make pottery, stoneware, tiles, pipes, bricks and moulds, and as a filler for paper, rubber and paint.

cleaner fish
Fish that feeds on parasites found on other fish. Cleaner fish are often found around coral reefs. They establish permanent cleaning stations where larger fish allow the cleaner fish to pick parasites from their body surface, mouth and gills. The cleaner WRASSES of the genus *Labroides* are among the best-known cleaner fish.

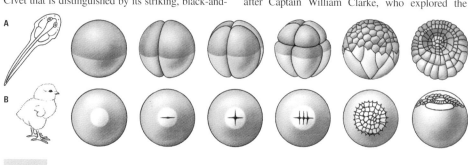

◄ **cleavage** After fertilization, the egg divides many times. The type of division (or cleavage) varies between different animal species, according to the yolk present. Frog eggs (A, top) divide to form some relatively large cells. The large amount of yolk in bird eggs (B, bottom) means that they do not divide; instead cleavage results in a small patch of cells on top of the yolk.

◀ **cliff** A ridge of chalk hills, known as the South Downs, runs through s England. The chalk ridge meets the sea in a series of impressive cliffs. Erosion occurs along joint lines, resulting in pillar-like formations. The section of cliff shown here, near Eastbourne, East Sussex, is known as the "Seven Sisters" after the seven distinct peaks.

cleavage

In embryology, progressive series of CELL DIVISIONS that transforms a fertilized OVUM (egg) into the earliest embryonic stage, called the BLASTULA. The ovum is divided into **blastomeres** (smaller cells), each containing a DIPLOID number of CHROMOSOMES.

cleavage, rock

Formation of definite planes through a rock. It is caused by compression associated with folding and METAMORPHISM. It results in the rock splitting easily parallel to the cleavage. The line of cleavage follows the alignment of minerals within the rock.

cleg-fly (cleg)

Any of several species of HORSEFLY. Adult cleg-flies frequent wet wooded areas and are greyish brown in colour. They often bite mammals, including humans, with their piercing mouthparts. Adult body length: 8–12mm (0.3–0.5in). Order Diptera; family Tabanidae; genus *Haematopota*.

cleistogamous flower

Small, closed, self-fertilizing flower. Cleistogamous FERTILIZATION takes place within a flower that does not open; it enables seed production in the absence of normal cross-POLLINATION. OXALIS and IMPATIENS are examples of such flowers.

clematis

Any member of a genus of perennial, mostly climbing shrubs found worldwide. Many have attractive deep blue, violet, white, pink or red flowers or flower clusters. The leaves are usually compound. Family Ranunculaceae; genus *Clematis*.

cliff

Geological formation consisting of a steep slope, sometimes of exposed rock. Cliffs can be nearly vertical or even overhanging. They may result from the exposure of rock strata due to geological FAULTS (*see* ESCARPMENT) or, as in the case of shore-line cliffs, they may be caused by water and weather EROSION.

climate

Overall WEATHER conditions of a place or region prevailing over a long time. The daily weather records are added together and then averaged out to give a general pattern of the climate. The major factors influencing climate are temperatures, air movements, incoming and outgoing radiation and moisture movements. Climates are defined on different scales, ranging from **macroclimates**, which cover the broad climatic zones of the globe, down to **microclimates**, which refer to the conditions in a small area, such as a wood or a field. *See also* CONTINENTAL CLIMATE; MARITIME CLIMATE; MEDITERRANEAN CLIMATE

climate change

Variation in CLIMATE over a period of time. The geological record of sedimentary rocks and fossils shows that climates have changed throughout the Earth's geological history and will, therefore, continue to do so. During much of the MESOZOIC era, there were no polar ice caps and forests grew in Antarctica. At the other extreme, their have been at least six ICE AGES, one of which, in Precambrian times, may have widely glaciated the Earth. The present may well be a warm phase within the QUATERNARY Ice age.

▼ **climate** This map of Eastern and Western Hemispheres shows the world's main climatic regions. Latitude is a major factor in determining the amount of solar radiation, with the greatest in equatorial regions and the least in polar regions.

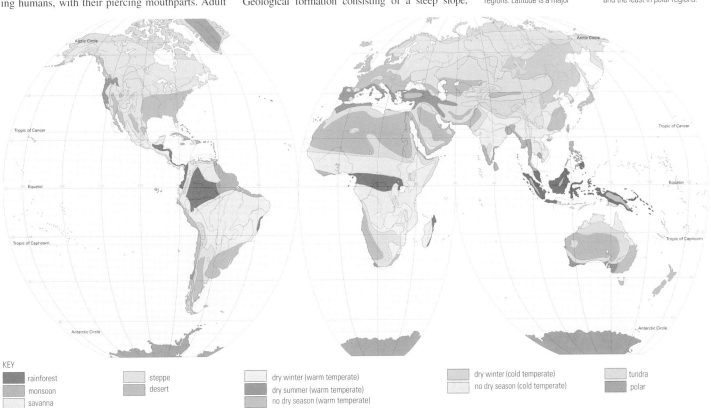

KEY

- rainforest
- monsoon
- savanna
- steppe
- desert
- dry winter (warm temperate)
- dry summer (warm temperate)
- no dry season (warm temperate)
- dry winter (cold temperate)
- no dry season (cold temperate)
- tundra
- polar

climate modelling

Use of a computer to simulate the Earth's climate. Physical data, such as temperature, pressure, wind direction and so on, are manipulated mathematically by a powerful computer to give a model of the Earth's whole climatic system. Researchers can vary various parameters to see what changes occur. In this way they can study the effects of the GREENHOUSE EFFECT and possible GLOBAL WARMING, or what would happen if there was a significant change in the amount of radiation from the Sun. Such modelling can be limited by scientist's understanding of the key factors controlling climates.

climate zones

Regions into which the Earth can be divided on the basis of CLIMATE. The heat the Earth receives from the Sun varies with latitude and time of year. Consequently, climate changes in broad zones, roughly parallel to latitude, from the hot tropics to the cold poles. However, the distribution of oceans and landmasses affects the complex interplay between atmospheric air pressure, temperature and humidity and modifies the basic ZONATION.

climatology

Scientific study of the Earth's climates. **Physical climatology** investigates relationships between temperature, pressure, winds, precipitation and other weather phenomena. **Regional climatology** considers latitude and other geographical factors, such as the influence of large landmasses in the climatic study of a particular place or region.

climax community

In ecology, the stable COMMUNITY that exists at the end of a SUCCESSION. During succession, a series of plants and their associated animal life gradually colonize an area, with newcomers usually displacing many of the species already present. Eventually, at the climax, colonization ceases and a relatively stable community persists in equilibrium with the local conditions.

climbing perch

Small freshwater fish. It is able to breathe air absorbed through the internal lining of its mouth cavity, thus allowing it to travel small distances over land. Native to Southeast and s Asia, the climbing perch has been introduced into North American freshwaters. Family Anabantidae; species *Anabas testudineus.*

clingfish

Any member of the marine fish family Gobiesocidae. The clingfish lives on or near the bottom of all tropical and temperate oceans. It is characterized by a single dorsal fin and, in most species, an adhesive disc on the ventral surface. Family Gobiesocidae; there are *c.*100 species.

clinometer

Hand-held surveying instrument used for measuring slope, elevation or inclination. It is useful in ecological studies for finding out the angle of slope of a hillside or sea-shore and hence its effect on distribution of species.

clint

Flat block of limestone typically 1–2m (3–7ft) across. It is separated from other clints by vertical cracks, called GRIKES, which together form a limestone pavement.

cloaca

Common cavity into which intestinal, urinary and genital tracts open in fish, reptiles, birds and some primitive mammals.

clone

Set of organisms obtained from a single original parent through some form of ASEXUAL REPRODUCTION or by artificial PROPAGATION. Clones are genetically identical and may arise naturally from PARTHENOGENESIS in animals. Cloning is often used in plant propagation (including TISSUE CULTURE) to produce new plants from parents with desirable qualities such as high yield, or from plants that have been genetically engineered. It is now possible to produce animal clones from tissue culture. In 1997 scientists in Scotland announced that they had cloned a sheep. Using nuclear transfer (transfer of a cell NUCLEUS) technology, they produced an embryo from a single udder cell of an adult sheep. The embryo was then implanted into a surrogate mother, and Dolly, an identical twin of the sheep that donated the cell, was born in February 1997. In 1998 Dolly gave birth naturally, thus allaying fears that, as a result of being cloned from an older sheep, she would not be able to reproduce. *See also* ARTIFICIAL SELECTION; GENETIC ENGINEERING

clotting factors

Group of chemicals, largely comprised of plasma proteins, which normally exist in a soluble (inactive) state. When activated, for example by damage to a blood vessel, they produce a cascade effect that leads to the clotting of the blood. The factors are given Roman numerals from I to XII. A lack of factor VIII in certain people causes haemophilia.

cloud

Visible mass of water particles or ice crystals suspended in the lower atmosphere. Clouds are formed when water from the Earth's surface becomes vapour through the process of EVAPORATION. As the water vapour rises into the atmosphere it cools and condenses around microscopic salt and dust particles, forming droplets. Where the atmosphere is cold (below the freezing temperature of water) the droplets turn to ice. There are 10 different classifications of clouds: **cirrus** are high, white and thread-like. They do not give rain, but their presence can be a sign of an approaching DEPRESSION. Cirrus occurs at heights of above 6000m (20,000ft) and sometimes as high as 12,000m (39,500ft). **Cirrocumulus** are high clouds consisting of small patches of ice crystals, often stretched out in a linear form. **Cirrostratus** are white and almost transparent sheets of ice crystals. **Altocumulus** are greyish-white globular clouds found between 2400m (8000ft) and 6000m (20,000ft). **Altostratus** are grey/blue and streaky, often covering the whole sky. They often produce drizzle. **Nimbostratus** are low, thick and dark, and usually shed rain or snow. **Stratocumulus** are masses of white, grey or dark cloud, within which vertical patches of cumulus may cause heavy rain. **Stratus** are low-lying and grey, with thicker examples producing light rain. **Cumulus** are white and fluffy-looking, with a characteristic dome shape. **Cumulonimbus** are vast, towering, dark clouds which generally produce thunderstorms. They have bases almost touching the ground and extend upwards to 75,000ft (22,875m). They can also produce tornadoes. By day, clouds reflect the rays of the Sun back into the atmosphere, keeping the ground cool. At night, clouds trap and re-radiate heat rising from the Earth, keeping surface temperatures warm. There is no real difference between low clouds, which may shroud hills or the tops of skyscrapers, and FOG and MIST, which both form at low level.

cloud cover

Approximate proportion of sky covered by CLOUD

▲ **cloud** The major cloud types have characteristic shapes and occur within broad altitudinal boundaries. Stratus (1) is a low-level cloud, usually featureless and grey. Its base may obscure hilltops or occasionally extend right down to the ground, and because of its low altitude it appears to move very rapidly on breezy days. Stratus can produce drizzle or snow, particularly over hills, and may occur in huge sheets covering thousands of square kilometres. Cumulus (2) clouds also seem to scuttle across the sky, reflecting their low altitude. These small "fleecy" clouds are short-lived, lasting no more than 15 minutes before dispersing. They are typically formed on sunny days, when localized convection currents are set up: these currents can form over power stations or even stubble fires, which may produce their own clouds. Cumulus may expand into stratocumulus (3) or into giant cumulonimbus (4), which are up to 10km (7mi) in diameter. These clouds typically form on summer afternoons: their high, flattened tops contain ice, which may fall to the ground in the form of heavy showers of rain or hail. Rising to middle altitudes, stratus and cumulus cloud (then termed altostratus (5) and alto cumulus (6)), appear to move more slowly because of their greater distance from the observer. Cirrus clouds (7) are named after the Latin for "tuft of hair", which they resemble. Relatively common over N Europe, they sometimes become associated with a jetstream and then appear to move rapidly despite their great height. Cirrocumulus (8) is often present with cirrus cloud in small amounts, while the presence of cirrostratus (9) is given away by haloes surrounding the Sun or Moon.

C

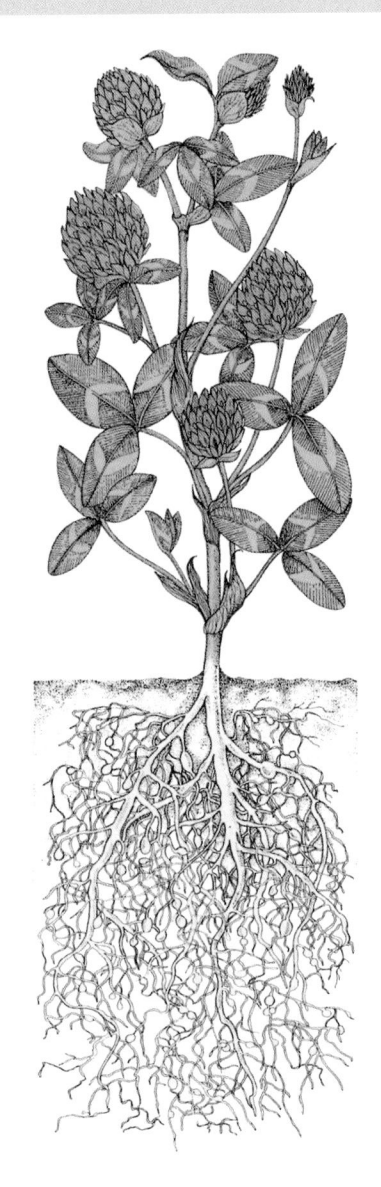

▲ **clover** Of the many species of pasture clover, the most common is red clover (*Trifolium pratense*). White clover (*Trifolium repens*) is often found on lawns, while Alsike clover (*Trifolium hybridum*) is used for hay and as a soil enricher. The bacteria-containing root nodules are clearly visible on the clover shown here.

and overcast. Cloud cover is usually measured visually in eighths (oktas), from scant cloud cover (1 okta) to complete cover (8 oktas).

clove

Tall, aromatic, evergreen tree that is native to the Moluccas. The small, purple flowers appear in clusters; the dried flower buds are widely used in cookery. Oil of cloves is distilled from the stems. Height: to 12m (40ft). Family Myrtaceae; species *Syzygium aromaticum.*

clover

Low-growing, annual, biennial and perennial plants native to temperate regions of Europe but now found throughout warmer regions of the Northern Hemisphere. The leaves have three leaflets, rarely four (considered good luck), and the dense flower clusters are white, red, purple, pink or yellow. Some species are grown as food for cattle. Most species are good nitrogen-fixers, due to the bacteria in their ROOT NODULES, which help to enrich soil. Family Fabaceae/Leguminosae; genus *Trifolium. See also* NITROGEN CYCLE; NITROGEN FIXATION

clownfish (anemonefish)

Member of a group of colourful, tropical DAM-SELFISH. They are found in and around CORAL REEFS, typically living in symbiotic association with sea ANEMONES. Clownfish are popular aquarium fish. Family Pomacentridae; genus *Amphiprion*; there are 27 species.

club moss

Any of *c.*200 species of small, evergreen, spore-bearing plants of the phylum LYCOPODOPHYTA. Unlike the more primitive true MOSSES, club mosses have specialized tissues for transporting water, food and minerals. They are related to FERNS and HORSE-TAILS. The small leaves are arranged in tight whorls around the aerial stems. Millions of years ago their ancestors formed the large trees that dominated CARBONIFEROUS forests.

clubroot disease

Disease of cabbages, cauliflowers, turnips and related plants of the mustard family, characterized by club-like swellings of the roots. It is caused by the fungus *Plasmodiophora brassicae* and can be avoided by using disease-free and disease-resistant plants and uncontaminated soils.

clubtail

Any member of a family of DRAGONFLIES. Clubtail nymphs bury themselves shallowly in the sediments of watercourses and use their extensible masks to catch passing prey. Adult clubtails are often seen flying over the surface of flowing water. They are distinctive for their abdomens, which expand posteriorly into distinct clubs. Adult body length: *c.*80mm (*c.*3in). Order Odonata; family Gomphidae.

cluster-fly

Species of true FLY. Adult cluster-flies are black and are often seen in clusters around human habitations as they search for shelter at the onset of winter. The larvae parasitize earthworms. Adult body length: *c.*7mm (*c.*0.3in). Order Diptera; family Calliphoridae; species *Pollenia rudis.*

cnidarian

Any one of the 9000 species of the phylum Cnidaria (commonly called the **coelenterates**). Marine invertebrates, cnidarians include CORALS, JELLYFISH and SEA ANEMONES. Characterized by a digestive cavity that forms the main body cavity, they may have been the first animal group to reach the tissue level of organization. The cnidarians are radially symmetrical, jelly-like and have a nerve net and one body opening. Reproduction is sexual and asexual; REGENERATION also occurs.

coal

Blackish, CARBON-rich deposit formed from the remains of fossil plants. In the Carboniferous and Tertiary periods, swamp vegetation subsided to form PEAT bogs. Sedimentary deposits buried the bogs, and the increasing pressure and heat produced LIGNITE (brown coal), then bituminous coal, and finally ANTHRACITE if temperature increased sufficiently. This is termed the **coal rank series**; each rank of coal represents an increase in carbon content and a reduction in the proportion of natural gases and moisture. Lignite, which has a low carbon content, is a poorer fuel than anthracite. Most coal seams are inter-stratified with shale, clay, sandstone and sometimes limestone.

coal fish

See POLLACK

coati (coatimundi)

Three species of RACCOON-like rodents of sw United States and South America. Most have long, slender, reddish-brown to black bodies with tapering snouts and long ringed tails. Length: 67cm (26in); weight: 11.3kg (25lb). Family Procyonidae; genus *Nasua.*

cobnut

Edible form of hazelnut found predominantly in temperate regions of the Northern Hemisphere. The trees are used for coppice, especially for firewood, hurdles, legume-poles and wattle-and-daub. Kentish cobs (*Corylus maxima*) are a related species. Family Betulaceae; species *Corylus avellana. See also* HAZEL

cobra

Any of several highly poisonous SNAKES in the family Elapidae, including the MAMBA, CORAL SNAKE, kraits and true cobras. A cobra can expand its neck ribs to form a hood. Found primarily in Africa and Asia, cobras feed on rats, toads and small birds. It is the only snake to make a nest for its young. The **king cobra** (*Ophiophagus hannah*) reaches 5.5m (18ft) in length, and is the largest venomous snake in the world. It is found from China to Southeast Asia. The **Indian cobra** (*Naja naja*) has spectacle-like markings on its hood. Some African species can spit venom into a victim's eyes from more than 2m (7ft), causing temporary or permanent blindness.

coca

Shrub that is native to Colombia and Peru. It contains the ALKALOID drug cocaine. Native Americans chew the leaves. The coca plant has yellow-white flowers, which grow in clusters, and red berries.

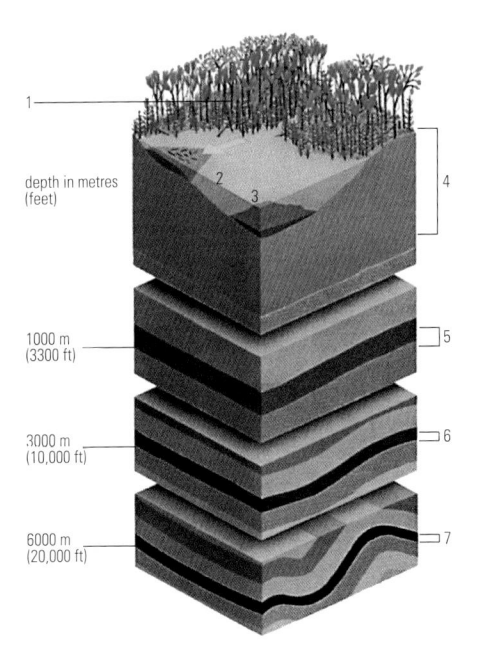

▲ **coal** The process of making coal begins with plant debris (1). Dead vegetation lies in a swampy environment and forms peat (4), the first stage of coal formation. Underwater bacteria remove some oxygen, nitrogen and hydrogen from the organic material. Debris carried elsewhere and deposited by water forms a product called cannel coal (2). Algal material collected underwater forms boghead coal (3). If the dead organic material is buried by sediment, the weight on top of the peat and the higher temperature will turn the peat into lignite (5). With more heat and pressure at increasing depths, lignite becomes bituminous coal (6) and then anthracite (7).

depth in metres (feet)

1000 m (3300 ft)

3000 m (10,000 ft)

6000 m (20,000 ft)

▲ **cockatoo** The palm cockatoo (*Probosciger aterrimus*) is the largest species of cockatoo and also the largest parrot to be found in Australia. Palm cockatoos have a wide repertory of vocalizations and displays, such as that shown here, which they use to communicate and maintain contact with one another in dense forest.

Height: *c*.2.4m (8ft). Family Erythroxylaceae; species *Erythroxylon coca*.

coccolith

Any microscopic, single-celled flagellate of the Coccolithophorida, a class of ALGAE of the phylum Chrysophyta. The cell is covered with round, chalky platelets only one or two thousandths of a millimetre in diameter. Many limestone and chalk cliffs are made up entirely of the remains of such platelets.

coccus

Spherical BACTERIUM with an average diameter of 0.5–1.25 micrometres. Some cocci, such as *Streptococcus* and *Staphylococcus*, are a common cause of infection.

cochlea

Fluid-filled structure in the inner EAR that is essential to HEARING. It has a shape like a coiled shell, and is lined with hair cells that move in response to incom-

▲ **cockchafer** A familiar beetle in Europe, the cockchafer appears in vast numbers every three or four years. It feeds at night on deciduous trees, fruit and flowers, destroying young plants and weakening old ones.

ing sound waves, stimulating nerve cells to transmit impulses to the brain. Different groups of hair cells are stimulated by different pitches of sound, thus helping the brain to analyse the sound.

cochoa

Any member of a genus of three species of birds belonging to the THRUSH family. The green cochoa is found in mountain forests of the Himalayas and other ranges in Southeast Asia. It is green, with a blue head, tail and wing patches. Length: 30cm (12in). Family Turdidae; species *Cochoa viridis* (green cochoa).

cockatiel

Medium-sized PARROT. It is mostly grey, with white wings, a lemon-yellow crest and an orange face patch. The cockatiel is found across Australia, in arid open country near water. It is a popular cage bird. It feeds on fruit, grain and seeds, small insects and nectar. Length: 32cm (13in). Family Psittacidae; species *Nymphicus hollandicus*.

cockatoo

Any of a group of medium- to large-sized PARROTS, mostly black or white in colour and with pronounced crests. Cockatoos are found in parts of Australia, Philippines, Moluccas and New Guinea. Family Psittacidae.

cockatoo, palm

Large parrot with dark plumage, a prominent crest and a massive, down-pointed bill; the female is smaller than the male. The palm cockatoo is found in closed tropical forest in the northern peninsula of Queensland, Australia, and the islands of New Guinea. It feeds on nuts, berries, seeds, fruit and buds. Length: 60cm (24in). Family Psittacidae; species *Probosciger aterrimus*.

cockatoo, red-tailed black

Large black parrot. The male has red flashes in its tail; the female is duller, with yellow patches and bars. The red-tailed black cockatoo inhabits forests, woods and sometimes shrubland in N and E Australia; it is often found in noisy, and sometimes

large, flocks. It feeds on fruit and buds. Length: 63cm (25in). Family Psittacidae; species *Calyptorhynchus magnificus*.

cockatoo, sulphur-crested

Large parrot. It is white with a sulphur-yellow, forward-raised crest and yellow underwings. It is found commonly in a variety of habitats across E and N Australia and New Guinea. It feeds on fruit, nuts, seeds, berries, grain and insects. Length: 45cm (18in). Family Psittacidae; species *Cacatua galerita*.

cockatoo, gang-gang

Medium-sized parrot. The male is grey with a scarlet head and wispy crest; the female is grey with a breast that is barred with pink-yellow. The gang-gang cockatoo is found in the tree-tops in open forest of SE Australia. It feeds on seeds, berries and fruit. Length: 34cm (13in). Family Psittacidae; species *Callocephalon fimbriatum*.

cockchafer (maybug, June beetle)

Any of various species of large SCARAB BEETLES. The larvae are white grubs, which feed on the roots of trees and crops, causing severe destruction. The adults emerge in the spring. Length: to 3cm (1in). Family Scarabaeidae.

cockle

Marine, bivalve MOLLUSC. Its varicoloured, heart-shaped shell has between 20 and 24 strong, radiating ribs. There are *c*.200 recognized species, many of which are edible. Average length: 40–80mm (1.6–3.1in). Class Bivalvia; family Cardiidae; species include *Cardium aculeatum*.

cocklebur

Fruit of a fairly widespread weed belonging to the DAISY family. Cockleburs are covered in tiny hooks, which become attached to animals, particularly sheep, so aiding seed dispersal (but also lowering the value of the fleece). Family Compositae; species *Xanthium strumarium*.

cock of the rock

Gaudy member of the COTINGA family. The male is bright orange with black wings and tail; it has a pronounced orange crest. The cock of the rock is found in mountainous regions of Venezuela, Guyana and N Brazil. Length: 38cm (15in). Family Cotingidae; species *Rupicola rupicola*.

cockroach

Any of more than 4000 species that make up one of the best-known orders of INSECTS. Cockroaches occur worldwide and several species are important pests of humans. Cockroaches are herbivores or omnivorous scavengers; they have well-developed chewing mouthparts. Many cockroaches have wings, and some engage readily in flight. Most species reproduce sexually, but some are capable of parthenogenetic production of female offspring. Eggs are usually laid together in a case called an ootheca. Adult body length: 4–100mm (0.2–4in). Order Blattodea.

◀ **cockle** Bivalves, such as the cockle (*Cardium* sp.), have calcareous shells, the two halves of which are hinged, and can be closed by muscular action.

▲ **cockroach** The large winged Brazilian giant cockroach (*Blaberus giganticus*) has reddish fur and a wingspan of *c*.8cm (*c*.3in). Like the Madagascar hissing cockroach (*Gromphadorina portentosa*), it is occasionally kept as a pet.

cockroach, American

Cockroach that originated in tropical America but is now cosmopolitan. A nocturnal pest, it is closely associated with human dwellings. It feeds widely on vegetable and animal detritus. Adult American cockroaches are reddish brown and have well-developed cursorial (running) legs. Their wings permit short flights. Adult body length: 40–50mm (1.6–2in). Family Blattidae; species *Periplaneta americana*.

cockroach, German (croton bug)

Cockroach that is a widespread pest of human dwellings. It thrives best at the temperatures preferred by humans and readily finds food and water in human dwellings. Some German cockroaches carry bacteria that are pathogenic to humans and can stimulate allergic reactions. Adult females carry between 20 and 50 eggs in their oothecae; the developmental time of German cockroach nymphs is faster than in any other pestiferous cockroach. Adult body length: 12–15mm (0.5–0.6in). Family Blattellidae; species *Blattella germanica*.

cockscomb

Tropical, herbaceous annual with plumed, white to yellow, purple or red flowers. It is commonly cultivated as a house plant. Family Amaranthaceae; species *Celosia cristata*.

cocoa

Powder obtained from the seeds of the tropical American evergreen tree *Theobroma cacao*. The seeds are crushed and some fatty substances are removed to produce cocoa powder. Cocoa is the basic ingredient of chocolate. Family Sterculiaceae.

▲ **cocoa** The cacao tree (*Theobroma cacao*) sprouts pendulous pods 15–35cm (6–14in) long from its branches and trunk. Each pod contains 30–40 beans from which cocoa and chocolate are made.

coco de mer (double coconut)

Slow-growing, tropical palm, with large leaves; it is endemic to the Seychelles. The fruit takes six years to develop and contains between one and three seeds, which, at up to 50cm (20in) in length, are the largest in the world. The coco de mer is now restricted to reserves and is rarely cultivated. Its fruits, which can be very hard and smooth, are used as bowls and can be decoratively carved. Height: to *c*.30m (*c*.100ft). Family Palmae; species *Lodoicea maldivica*.

coconut palm (copra plant)

Tall palm tree native to the shores of the Indo-Pacific region and the Pacific coast of South America; commercially, it is the most important of all palms. It has a leaning trunk and a crown of feather-shaped leaves. **Copra**, the dried kernel of the coconut fruit, is a valuable source of oil used in the manufacture of margarine and soap. The fibrous husk is used for matting. Height: to 30.5m (100ft). Family Arecacae/Palmae; species *Cocos nucifera*.

cocoon

Case or wrapping produced by larval forms of animals (such as some MOTHS, BUTTERFLIES and WASPS) for the resting or pupal stage in their life cycle. Some spiders spin a cocoon that protects their eggs. Most cocoons are made of silk, and those of the domestic silkworms provide most of the world's commercial SILK. *See also* CHRYSALIS; PUPA

cod

Any member of a family of bottom-dwelling, marine fish found in cold to temperate waters of the Northern Hemisphere. It typically refers to the Atlantic cod, *Gadus morhua*, which is one of the most important food fish in Europe and North America. It is also the source of cod liver oil. The Atlantic cod is grey, green, brown or red with darker speckled markings. It has a characteristic configuration of fins, with three dorsal fins and two anal fins. Family Gadidae.

codominance

Form of allelic interaction in which ALLELES express themselves equally in the PHENOTYPE rather than one being dominant and the other recessive. In the snapdragon (ANTIRRHINUM) for example, when a plant with red flowers is crossed with one with white flowers, all the plants produced have the intermediate colour of pink rather than red or white flowers.

codon

Unit of the genetic code in a molecule of DNA or MESSENGER RNA (mRNA). In messenger RNA a codon consists of a triplet of bases that usually specifies a particular AMINO ACID as part of a POLYPEPTIDE chain being built into a protein. Some codons carry instructions (such as "start" and "stop") involved in the process of protein building. *See also* ANTICODON; GENE

coelacanth

Bony fish of the genus *Latimeria*. Thought to have become extinct 60 million years ago, it was found in deep waters off the African coast in 1938. Its scales and bony plates are unlike those of modern fish. The coelacanth is grey-brown, with lobed fins that have fleshy bases. Length: 1.5m (5ft). Family Latimeriidae; species *Latimeria chalumnae*.

coelenterate

Common name for a CNIDARIAN

coenocyte

Type of CELL that has many nuclei. Coenocytes occur

◄ **coconut palm** Their ability to survive in sandy, salty soil makes the coconut palm (*Cocus nucifera*) a common sight close to beaches. The nut is found within an outer skin and thick fibrous layer or husk. A hard shell covers the edible white "meat".

when only the NUCLEUS of a cell divides repeatedly, without division of the whole cell or cell wall. The fibres of striated muscle, for example, are made up of such cells, giving a type of tissue called **syncytium**. Coenocytes are also found in some algae and fungi.

coenzyme

Nonprotein organic molecule, usually containing a vitamin and phosphorus. When combined with an **apoenzyme**, a protein molecule, it activates an ENZYME. A coenzyme always regains its original structure even though it may have been altered during a reaction. The coenzyme NICOTINAMIDE ADENINE DINUCLEOTIDE (NAD) is derived from the vitamin NICOTINIC ACID and acts as a coenzyme to the dehydrogenases that are essential to respiration.

coevolution

EVOLUTION of complementary features in two different species; a result of interaction between the two. Examples include the evolution of predator defences by a prey species, subsequent evolution by the predator of ways to thwart the prey's defences, and so on. In other instances, both species gain from the association and evolve structures or behaviour of mutual benefit. The classical example occurs in plants that are pollinated by insects. The plant's flowers have a colour or smell that attracts insects, and a shape that makes it easy for insects to reach the nectar and in

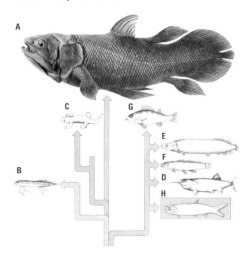

▲ **coelacanth** The only surviving member of the subclass Crossopterygii, the coelacanth (A) exemplifies the significance of fleshy finned fish in evolution. Crossopterygian fish, which include lungfish such as Protopterus (B), are the stock from which all land vertebrates, such as the salamander (C), arose. The illustration shows how the coelacanth relates to other primitive living fossils such as the paddlefish (D), arapaima (E), the bowfin (F) and the present-day bony fish like the perch (G). Palaeoniscus (H), now extinct, is the oldest ray-finned fish, which gave rise to later forms (D,E and F).

▲ **coffee** The Arabian coffee plant (*Coffea arabica*) is the most common kind of coffee plant. It is a small, evergreen tree which can grow to a height of 7.5m (25ft), but is pruned to 3m (10ft) on plantations. Its leaves are *c*.7.5–15cm (*c*.3–6in) long. The white blossoms are followed by tiny green berries, each holding two tough-skinned, greenish beans. The berries ripen to a deep red after six or seven months and are then ready for picking. Instant coffee often uses another species, *Coffea Robusta*.

doing so remove pollen. The insects have evolved to be able to see and smell the flowers, and have mouthparts adapted to reach the nectar.

coffee
Plant and the popular caffeine beverage produced from its seeds (coffee beans). The plants of the genus *Coffea* are evergreen with white fragrant flowers. Native to Ethiopia, coffee plants are now cultivated in the tropics, especially in Brazil (the world's biggest producer), Colombia and the Ivory Coast. Family Rubiaceae.

coffin-fly
True FLY known for its association with human cadavers. Coffin-fly larvae feed on decaying flesh, including human corpses, and several generations may occur in a single coffin. Adult body length: *c*.5mm (*c*.0.2in). Order Diptera; family Phoridae; species *Conicera tibialis*.

Cohn, Ferdinand Julius (1828–98)
German botanist, one of the founders of BACTERIOLOGY. After early work on algae, Cohn began (1868) to study bacteria and was one of the first to classify bacteria according to their morphology. He conducted research into the bacterial causes of infectious disease. Cohn was an early supporter of the work of Robert KOCH.

col
In geology, a low point between two mountain peaks or on an upland ridge. In meteorology, a calm area between two DEPRESSIONS and two ANTICYCLONES.

colchicum
Any member of the *Colchicum* genus of the widespread LILY family, which contains some of the most beautiful plants in the world. The colchicum closely resembles the CROCUS (family Iridaceae) and their families are closely related. **Colchicine**, a substance taken from the dried corms and seeds of *Colchicum autumnalis*, the autumn crocus, is used as a painkiller. It is also used in plant-breeding processes because it causes a doubling of chromosomes. Family Liliaceae; genus *Colchicum*.

cold-blooded
See POIKILOTHERMIC

cold front
See FRONT

coleopteran
Any member of the order Coleoptera, the largest order of the animal kingdom, generally the BEETLES. They are insects that undergo complete METAMORPHOSIS. Most possess two pairs of wings, the forward pair usually being hard covers that fold over the flying pair. More than 350,000 species are known, many of them pests called WEEVILS. Beetles include some of the largest and many of the smallest of all insects. Their larvae are either maggot-like or elongated with six legs.

coleoptile
Protective sheath that covers the shoot from an embryo of a grass SEED. The coleoptile protects the shoot as it forces its way upwards through the soil, and it remains in place until it is split open by the development of the first true leaves. *See also* GERMINATION

coleus
Any member of the *Coleus* genus, belonging to the mint and sage family. They are tropical plants with brightly coloured flowers and striking variegated foliage. They are popular house plants in cooler regions. Some species have edible TUBERS, for example *Coleus rotundifolius*, known as the hausa potato, which is native to India and Southeast Asia. Family Labiatae; species include *Coleus blumei* and *Coleus rotundifolius*.

collagen
Protein substance that is the main constituent of bones, tendons, cartilage, connective tissue and skin. It is made up of inelastic fibres.

collenchyma
Tissue that provides mechanical support to young plant stems. It consists of living cells, the walls of which are thickened with extra CELLULOSE at the corner, thus enabling the cells to resist compression while still being able to extend if required.

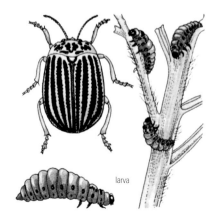

▲ **Colorado beetle** The female Colorado beetle lays yellow eggs on the underside of a leaf. The larvae feed on the leaves before pupating on the ground.

larva

Collenchyma is usually distributed as a thin band just beneath the EPIDERMIS of herbaceous stems.

collision zone
Area of impact between two colliding continental crustal plates following the destruction of an intervening ocean through SUBDUCTION. *See also* CONTINENT; CRUST; PLATE TECTONICS

colon
Part of the large INTESTINE, the digestive tract that extends from the small intestine to the RECTUM. The colon absorbs water from digested food and allows bacterial action for the formation of faeces. *See also* DIGESTIVE SYSTEM

colony
Group of similar animals or plants that live together for mutual benefit. Individuals within the colony perform like or varied functions and may be structurally separated or united.

Colorado beetle
Oval leaf BEETLE that is a major pest of potatoes and other members of the potato family, including the tomato and aubergine. Adult beetles are similar in shape to ladybirds but twice as long. They are yellow with black stripes or spots. Native to w North America, Colorado beetles are becoming established across Europe, despite the use of insecticides such as lead arsenate. Family Chrysomelidae; species *Leptinotarsa decemlineata*.

coltsfoot
Member of the daisy family, native to Europe and E North America. Coltsfoot grows in poor soil and on waste ground. The yellow flowers appear from February, before the hoof-shaped leaves, from which the plant gets its name. The leaves were at one time dried and smoked as a cure for asthma; the scientific name *Tussilago* comes from the Greek *tussis*, meaning "a cough". Family Compositae; species *Tussilago farfara*.

colugo (flying lemur)
Gliding animal that inhabits rainforests and plantations in s Asia, Malaysia and the Philippines. There are two species of colugo, neither of which are closely related to any other living mammals. Colugos have a very large membrane stretched from the neck to the ends of the fingers and toes, which also includes the tail. Mottled brown or grey above and pale underneath, these agile gliders feed on fruit and leaves. Head-body length: 33–42cm (13–17in); tail: 22–27cm (9–11in). Family Cynocephalidae; genus *Cynocephalus*.

columbiform
Member of the bird order Columbiformes, which includes the PIGEONS and DOVES and also the SAND GROUSE. The largest member of the order was the DODO, which is now extinct. Pigeons are the only birds able to suck up water; they are also notable for feeding their young on "pigeon's milk", a white liquid regurgitated from the crop (a distensible part of the oesophagus).

columbine
See AQUILEGIA

columbite
Black oxide mineral of iron, manganese and niobium. Niobium is replaced by tantalum to form tantalite, which has similar properties to columbite but is denser. Columbite and tantalite are found in granite

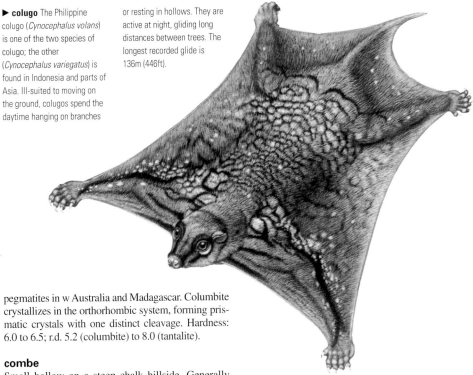

▶ **colugo** The Philippine colugo (*Cynocephalus volans*) is one of the two species of colugo; the other (*Cynocephalus variegatus*) is found in Indonesia and parts of Asia. Ill-suited to moving on the ground, colugos spend the daytime hanging on branches or resting in hollows. They are active at night, gliding long distances between trees. The longest recorded glide is 136m (446ft).

pegmatites in w Australia and Madagascar. Columbite crystallizes in the orthorhombic system, forming prismatic crystals with one distinct cleavage. Hardness: 6.0 to 6.5; r.d. 5.2 (columbite) to 8.0 (tantalite).

combe
Small hollow on a steep chalk hillside. Generally found on an ESCARPMENT, combes are formed when WEATHERING opens up and enlarges a JOINT in the rock. Weathered material that slips down to the bottom of the slope may form a mound known as a combe rock.

comb jelly (sea walnut, sea gooseberry, Venus' girdle)
Any member of the Ctenophora phylum, a small phylum of marine animals. There are c.90 species, some of which are abundant in coastal waters. Comb jellies are considered to be an offshoot of an ancestral medusoid CNIDARIAN. They are radially symmetrical and move using cilia, which are fused in bands to form combs, hence their name. Comb jellies are hermaphroditic and have no form of vegetative reproduction and no sedentary phase. Most species are colourless, bioluminescent and carnivorous, feeding mainly on plankton.

comet
Any member of a group of three species of HUMMINGBIRD, found in South America. Agile birds, they feed on the wing, sucking up nectar with their tube-like tongue. Comets tend to be long-tailed birds. Family Trochilidae.

comfrey
Any plant of the genus *Symphytum* of the BORAGE family, native to Eurasia. Comfreys have small yellow or purple flowers and hairy leaves. Boiled concoctions of *Symphytum officinale* were once used to treat wounds. Family Boraginaceae.

commensalism
Situation in nature in which two species live in close association but only one partner benefits. One of the species (the **commensal**) may gain from increased food supply, or by procuring shelter, support or means of locomotion, but the other (the **host**) neither gains nor loses from the relationship. *See also* MUTUALISM; PARASITE; SYMBIOSIS

community
Naturally occurring group of plants and animals living within a restricted area. Communities are usually named after a prominent physical characteristic or a dominant species.

companion cell
Small, narrow cell in the PHLOEM tissue of flowering plants; it is characterized by dense cytoplasm and a prominent nucleus. Companion cells are associated with the SIEVE TUBE elements alongside which they are situated.

compass plant
Plant native to the prairies of North America. It gets its common name from the way in which the leaves tip vertically, so avoiding the full strength of the midday sun, the surfaces facing north and south. Family Compositae; species *Silphium lacinatum*.

competition
Relationship that exists between two or more organisms or groups of organisms when a shared resource is limited. For example, there may be direct confrontation over the amount of living space, the food supply or the availability of mates. There are two main types of competition: **intraspecific competition** between members of the same SPECIES; and **interspecific competition** between different species. The usual outcome is the classic "SURVIVAL OF THE FITTEST", with at least a temporary reduction in the numbers of the less fit organism, and for this reason competition is a significant force in the process of EVOLUTION.

compound eye
Type of animal eye that consists of many individual **facets**; it is common in adult crustaceans and flying insects. Each facet is an individual visual unit called an **ommatidium**. It has a lens and several light-sensitive cells with nerve fibres that converge to form the optic nerve leading to the animal's brain. The ommatidia in the eyes of day-flying insects each produce a separate image to produce a mosaic of the whole visual field. In night-flying insects, each ommatidium "sees" a large part of the visual field so that individual images overlap to produce a bright view lacking in detail. Compound eyes are made up of from 12 to more than 1000 facets, depending on the species of animal. *See also* SIGHT

conception
Start of pregnancy. The term is used to describe the fertilization of an OVUM (egg cell) by the SPERM, or the implantation of the fertilized ovum in the wall of the UTERUS.

conch
Marine snail. It has a distinctively shaped shell, with an outer whorl extending well beyond the rest of the shell, eventually narrowing to an apex. Conch-type shells are also found in the families Fasciolariidae and Melongenidae. Conch shells are sometimes used as musical instruments. Length: to 300mm (12in). Phylum Mollusca; class Gastropoda; order Mesogastropoda; family Strombidae.

condensation
Formation of a liquid from a gas or vapour, caused by cooling or an increase in pressure. More particularly, it is the changing of water vapour in the air into water droplets, forming mist, cloud, rain or drops on cold surfaces.

condensation nucleus
Small liquid or solid particle, such as dust, on which WATER VAPOUR in the atmosphere begins to condense in tiny droplets or ice crystals, resulting in CLOUD formation.

condensation reaction
Type of CHEMICAL REACTION in which two simple molecules combine to form a third more complex molecule, with the elimination of a simple substance. The molecules of the substance produced are larger than those of the combining molecules, while the eliminated substance (typically ammonia or water) consists of very small molecules. Condensation reactions occur mainly in organic chemistry. An example is the reaction between a ketone and hydroxylamine to produce an oxime and water. A similar process involving monomers can be used to produce a polymer in a type of reaction called condensation polymerization.

condor
Either of two species of New World VULTURE. Condors feed on carrion and are found mainly in mountainous regions. They are the largest of all BIRDS OF PREY. Family Cathartidae (part).

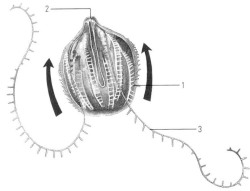

▲ **comb jelly** The free-swimming comb jelly maintains its spherical shape through the presence of water in internal canals that lead off the stomach. These canals provide support for the ctenes (comb plates) (1) with which the comb jelly swims. Each ctene is covered with rows of cilia that beat in rhythmic waves and propel the animal forward. The direction of the effective stroke is away from the mouth (2), so that the animal swims mouth first. Simple muscles provide some control over the tentacles (3).

condor, Andean

Large, vulture-like bird. Its plumage is mainly blue black, with a white collar and a bare head and neck. It has a huge wingspan. This species of condor is found in mountainous parts of South America, along the Andes chain. It feeds mainly on carrion. Length: 110cm (43in). Family Cathartidae; species *Vultur gryphus*.

condor, California

Large, vulture-like bird. The California condor's plumage is mostly black, with white flashes on its wings and a black collar. It has a bare neck and head, which are flame-yellow. Very rare, this species of condor is found only in the coastal mountain region of California, United States. It feeds on carrion, mainly dead cattle, sheep and horses. Length 110cm (43in). Family Cathartidae; species *Gymnogyps californianus*.

conduction, thermal

Transfer of heat from a hot region of a body to a cold region. If one end of a metal rod is placed in a flame, the heat energy received causes increased vibratory motion of the molecules in that end. These molecules bump into others farther along the rod, and the increased motion is passed along until finally the end not in the flame becomes hot.

cone

Conical, spheroidal or cylindrical fruit- or seed-bearing structure borne by CONIFER trees and comprising clusters of stiff, overlapping, woody scales that separate to release seeds from naked ovules developed at their base.

conebill

Small, South American forest bird related to the American wood WARBLER. Conebills forage in the foliage and flowers for their insect prey. Length: *c*.12cm (*c*.5in). Family Parulidae; genus *Conirostrum*; there are 10 species.

cone shell

Any of *c*.500 species of marine snail found in tropical seas. It has a heavy, cone-shaped shell, with vivid markings and colours. Most species feed on small worms or fish and some species can inflict serious or even fatal stings. Length: to 13cm (5in). Phylum Mollusca; class Gastropoda; family Conidae.

conger eel

See EEL, CONGER

conglomerate

SEDIMENTARY ROCK made up of rounded pebbles embedded in a fine matrix of sand or silt, commonly formed along beaches or on river beds.

conifer

See feature article

coniferophyte (gymnosperm)

Any member of the Coniferophyta phylum, comprising CONE-bearing plants that produce neither flowers nor fruits. The seeds are not protected within an OVARY and the leaves are usually needle-like. Examples, which include CONIFERS, FIRS and SPRUCES, are typically large trees of cold northern climates or mountainous regions. The group used to be called Gymnospermae.

conjugation

SEXUAL REPRODUCTION by FUSION of GAMETES. It is characteristic of certain simple animals, lower plants and bacteria. In some ALGAE, for example, a temporary conjugation tube forms a passageway for the contents of one cell to enter another.

Conklin, Edwin Grant (1863–1952)

US biologist. He was professor of biology at Princeton University (1908–33). Conklin is famous for his pioneering research in embryology and for his work in the processes of evolution and heredity. His books include *Heredity and Environment in the Development of Men* (1915).

connective tissue

Type of animal tissue with a supporting and packing function; it helps to maintain a body's shape and hold it together. Connective tissue comprises a small number of cells (such as FIBROBLASTS) and protein fibres within a noncellular substance known as the **extracellular matrix**. BONE, CARTILAGE, SKIN and ADIPOSE TISSUE are all types of connective tissue.

conodont

Member of an extinct group of small, jawless sea creatures whose mouths were filled with several pairs of bony tooth-bars which formed a feeding apparatus. Conodonts are thought to have been CHORDATES, possibly primitive, jawless vertebrates. They evolved in late Cambrian times and became extinct at the end of the Triassic period; their fossil teeth are of considerable use in dating marine strata.

consanguinity

Being descended from the same ancestor; having the same "blood line".

conservation

Term that has come to mean a number of different, if associated, things in the preservation of nature and natural resources. Conservation requires planning and organization to make the best use of resources or to preserve the natural landscape and wildlife. It may involve a combination of: 1) placing restrictions on the use of materials or areas; 2) using alternative materials; 3) providing areas of protection; and 4) applying methods that limit or control the amount of change or damage to the natural environment. The term is also used to describe the preservation, and sometimes renovation, of ancient and historic structures.

constrictor

See BOA

constructive margin

In PLATE TECTONICS, the boundary between two lithospheric plates that are moving apart as new crust is being formed. Constructive margins are associated with shallow-focus EARTHQUAKES, high heat flow, and eruptions and injections of basalt. Characteristically they produce submarine MID-OCEAN RIDGES, although Iceland is an example where a mid-ocean ridge has surfaced above sea level. *See also* LITHOSPHERE

consumer

Organism that obtains its energy from consuming other organisms. Consumers include all animals and

CONIFER

Cone-bearing tree, generally EVERGREEN, such as PINE, FIR and REDWOOD. Some conifers are the Earth's largest plants, reaching heights of up to 99m (325ft). They are a major natural resource of the Northern Hemisphere, particularly in the cooler temperate regions, where they are most abundant.

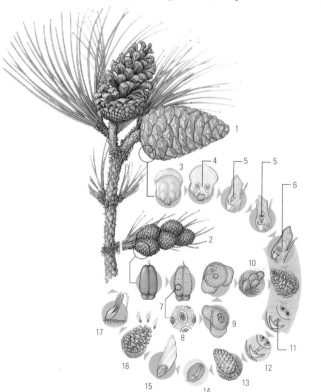

▶ **The reproductive cycle** of the ponderosa pine is typical of many conifers. In summer, the mature tree bears both female cones (1) and male cones (2). A scale from the female cone (3) contains two ovules (4). Within each ovule, a spore cell (5) divides to develop into a female gametophyte (6). A scale from the male cone (7) contains many spores (8). Each of these develops into a male gametophyte within a winged pollen grain (9). This process lasts one year. Pollination occurs early the next summer, when female cones open so that airborne pollen grains enter an ovule. Inside the ovule, the female gametophyte develops two ova (11). Fertilization occurs during the spring of the following year, after the male gametophyte has matured and grown a pollen tube (12), and the cone closes (13). Within the female gametophyte, the fertilized ova (zygote) develops into an embryo (14); and around it, a tough, winged seed case is formed (15). In the autumn of the second year, the female cone opens (16), and seeds are dispersed by wind, ready to germinate (17).

180 million years ago

135 million years ago

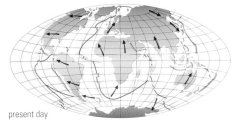

present day

▲ **continental drift** About 200 million years ago, the original Pangaea land mass began to split into two continental groups, which further separated over time to produce the present-day configuration.

fungi and some bacteria. PRIMARY CONSUMERS (HERBIVORES) feed on plants (PRIMARY PRODUCERS), while SECONDARY CONSUMERS (CARNIVORES) feed on PRIMARY CONSUMERS. Where a carnivore feeds on another carnivore it is called a TERTIARY CONSUMER. *See also* FOOD CHAIN; HETEROTROPH; TROPHIC LEVEL

contact metamorphism
Recrystallization of rocks surrounding an igneous INTRUSION in response to the heat supplied by the intrusion. There is no significant increase in pressure and the affected rocks do not melt in the process.

continent
Any one of seven (or six) large land masses on the Earth's surface. The continents are Europe and Asia (or Eurasia), Africa, North America, South America, Australia and Antarctica. They are concentrated in the Northern Hemisphere. They cover about 30% of the Earth above sea level and extend below sea level, forming CONTINENTAL SHELVES. All continents have four components which make up the continental crust: **shields** – areas of relatively level land rising no more than a few hundred metres above sea level and consisting of crystalline rocks that are generally very old, up to 3.8 billion years; **stable platforms** – areas of the continent that have a thin covering of SEDIMENTARY ROCKS, which are generally horizontal; **sedimentary basins** – broad, deep depressions filled with sedimentary rocks formed in shallow seas that sometimes covered parts of the ancient shields or their margins; **folded mountain belts** of younger sedimentary rocks, which typically occur along their margins and consist of long, linear zones of intensely folded and faulted rocks that have been metamorphosed and intruded by igneous and volcanic activity. The continental crust is composed of rocks that are less dense than the basaltic rocks in ocean basins and they appear to be riding on the asthenosphere of the

underlying MANTLE, moving over the surface of the Earth very slowly by CONTINENTAL DRIFT. Its thickness is mainly between 30–40km (20–25mi) except under large mountain chains where thickness can be 70km (45mi). Continental crust is thought to originate from the SUBDUCTION of early crust, causing partial melting that released lighter material that punched up through the crust. This material was too light to be subducted and the continents grew by the collision and fusion of these microcontinents.

continental climate
Type of CLIMATE found in the interior of large continents, that is, hot summers with convectional rainfall and very cold, dry winters, with only light falls of snow. Summer temperatures are about 20°C (68°F), and winter temperatures are −10°C to −20°C (14°F to −4°F) in the coldest months. Total annual precipitation is about 500mm (20in). The natural vegetation consists of grassland. Areas of continental climate are found on the North American prairies, in Poland and Hungary, and on the steppes of Russia. In the Southern Hemisphere there are no areas of real continental climate because the land masses are relatively narrow, so oceanic influences are present throughout. *See also* MARITIME CLIMATE; MEDITERRANEAN CLIMATE

continental crust
See CRUST

continental drift
Theory that the CONTINENTS change position very slowly, moving over the Earth's surface at a rate of a few centimetres per year, adding up to thousands of kilometres over geological time. Until the mid-20th century most scientists believed that the continents were in a fixed position. Early supporters of continental drift claimed that the jigsaw shapes of the present-day continents could be pieced together to form an ancient landmass that at some time in the past split and drifted apart. Evidence for the theory included matching the outlines of continents, rock types, geological structures and fossils. Fossil magnetism in rocks is used to calculate the ancient latitude of continents over time. Continental drift became accepted with the development of PLATE TECTONICS in the 1960s. In recent years continental movement has been confirmed by direct measurements made by global positioning satellites using laser beams. *See also* PANGAEA

continental margin
Region of the ocean floor that lies between the shoreline and the deep-ocean floor. It includes the CONTINENTAL RISE, the CONTINENTAL SHELF and the CONTINENTAL SLOPE.

continental rise
Gently sloping region of the CONTINENTAL MARGIN at the foot of the CONTINENTAL SLOPE. It is an area of thick deposits of sediments carried down by currents off the CONTINENTAL SHELF.

continental shelf
Gently seaward-sloping part of the CONTINENTAL MARGIN between the shoreline and the CONTINENTAL SLOPE, at a depth of about 150m (500ft). A continental shelf can be quite narrow, as, for example, off the W coast of South America, but in places can be more than 150km (90mi) wide – for example, in the North Sea and around Britain. The shallow waters contain rich food for fish, and therefore some of the world's major fishing grounds are on continental shelves. Other areas of continental shelf, such as the North

Sea and the Gulf of Mexico, have been exploited for oil and natural gas.

continental slope
Relatively steep slope in the seabed that lies between the CONTINENTAL SHELF and the CONTINENTAL RISE leading into the areas of much deeper water. In many places the continental slope is cut into by deep submarine canyons.

contour
In cartography, a line on a map joining places of equal elevation. Closely spaced contours indicate a steep slope, few or no contours mean flat or almost flat ground.

A

B

C

D

E

F

▲ **continental shelf** The regions immediately off the land masses are the continental shelves. There are several different sorts. Off areas of North America, such as California, the shelf (A) has deep gorges; they can be caused by river erosion before the land was submerged by the sea, or by turbidity currents. Mud and sediment-laden water often pour out of major estuaries scouring out gorges. Other regions of North America and Europe have shelves with a gentle relief (B), often with sandy ridges and barriers. In high latitudes, floating ice wears the shelf smooth (C) and in clear tropical seas a smooth shelf may be rimmed with a coral barrier like the Great Barrier Reef off E Australia (D), leaving an inner lagoonal area dammed by the reef. Other types of continental shelf often start with a gradual slope, but then drop suddenly. This can be caused by strong offshore currents washing sediment away (E). Continental shelves can also be affected by faulting (F), which disrupts the original shelf.

contractile root

Type of ADVENTITIOUS ROOT that develops from the base of a BULB or CORM. New bulbs or corms form higher in the soil at the tops of the contractile roots, which then shorten to pull the bulbs or corms down to a better level.

contractile vacuole

See VACUOLE

conure

Member of a group of small- to medium-sized parrots. They are rather chunky with very short tails. Conures are found in South America. Family Psittacidae (part).

convection cell

Organized circular flow of fluid, such as air or water, based on thermal changes in density and gravitational attraction, rising away from the heat source and sinking in cooler outer areas.

convection current

In geology, heat generated from radioactivity deep within the Earth's MANTLE causing rock to flow towards the CRUST. At the top of the mantle the rising rock is deflected laterally below the crust before sinking. This mantle convection is thought to be the process driving PLATE TECTONICS. In meteorology, convection is the process by which air that is warmed close to the ground rises because it is less dense than the surrounding air. This can lead to condensation, cloud formation and rain, which is called **convectional rainfall**. It is frequently associated with cumulonimbus clouds and thunderstorms.

Convention on International Trade in Endangered Species of Wild Flora and Fauna (CITES)

Organization founded (1975) to ban trade in ENDANGERED SPECIES and to regulate trade in species that might become endangered. In 2001 its membership included 152 countries. Its secretariat is in Geneva, Switzerland.

convergent evolution

Tendency of several different species to resemble each other and to develop similar characteristics in their attempt to adapt to similar environments. The most commonly cited example is the wings of bats and birds. *See also* EVOLUTION

▼ **copperhead** The North American copperhead (*Agkistrodon contortrix*) is a venomous snake found in E and central United States. It inhabits woodlands and wetlands. It detects its prey, usually mice, lizards, amphibians or insects, using temperature-sensitive pits on each side of its head. It can swallow prey much wider than itself and its gastric juices are capable of digesting bones and fur.

convergent margin

In PLATE TECTONICS, the boundary between two lithospheric plates that are moving towards each other. It can form either a SUBDUCTION margin or a COLLISION ZONE. *See also* LITHOSPHERE

convolvulus

See BINDWEED

Cooloola monster

Highly unusual Australian insect related to the cricket. It was discovered in the late 1970s in Cooloola National Park. It spends most of its life underground, but surfaces on rainy nights to prey on smaller insects. Order Orthoptera; family Cooloolidae; species *Cooloola propator*.

coot

Medium-sized, plump bird found on open water inland. Most species have mainly black plumage and long, lobed toes. They feed on items taken under water, usually vegetation. The group has a cosmopolitan distribution. Family Rallidae; genus *Fulica*.

coot, Eurasian

Medium-sized, plump bird, with black plumage and a bald white face. It is found on open or slow-moving water throughout Europe, Asia, Australia and New Guinea. The Eurasian coot feeds mostly on plant material but also takes small aquatic animals. It is often found in large flocks. Length: 32–39cm (13–15in). Family Rallidae; species *Fulica atra*.

coot, crested (red-knobbed coot)

Medium-sized bird, with black plumage, a bare white forehead and two bright red "knobs" on its head. It is found on open water in Africa and s Spain. The crested coot feeds on aquatic plants and animals. Length: 38–43cm (15–17in). Family Rallidae; species *Fulica cristata*.

Cope, Edward Drinker (1840–97)

US palaeontologist. He discovered approximately 1000 US species of extinct animals, particularly those of the Tertiary period. He also revived the Lamarckian theory of EVOLUTION. *The Vertebrata of the Cretaceous Formations of the West* (1875) and *The Vertebrata of the Tertiary Formations of the West* (1883) are standard references.

copepod

Any marine or freshwater CRUSTACEAN of the subclass Copepoda. Copepods are possibly the most numerous type of animal in the world and are a major component of the marine FOOD CHAIN. Some are parasitic on aquatic animals, especially fish. Their segmented, cylindrical bodies have a single median eye and no carapace. Length: 0.5–2mm (0.02–0.08in);

length of parasitic forms may be more than 30cm (1ft). Class Copepoda; there are *c*.7500 species.

copperhead

Any of various species of snake, so-called because of the colour of their heads. The North American copperhead (*Agkistrodon contortrix*) is a pit VIPER, rarely more than 1m (3ft) long. The Australian copperhead (*Denisonia superba*) is a venomous snake of the COBRA family, often reaching 1.5m (5ft) in length. The Indian copperhead (*Elaphe radiata*) is a rat snake.

copra

See COCONUT PALM

coprolite

Fossilized excretion of many kinds of animals of a great range of sizes, relationships and geological ages. Coprolites are useful to geologists and biologists because they often contain undigested plant seeds and tissues.

coquette

Member of a small group of HUMMINGBIRDS. They are very small and brightly coloured, often with iridescent feathers. Coquettes feed exclusively on nectar, which they suck up through a tubular tongue. They are found in South America, almost entirely within the tropical region. Length: to 6cm (2.4in). Family Trochilidae (part); there are seven species.

coral (anthozoan)

Small marine animal often found in colonies. True corals belong to the class Anthozoa. Phylum Coelenterata/Cnidaria; class Anthozoa.

coral, hard

True coral of the order Scleractinia. Hard corals are responsible for the formation of CORAL REEFS around the world. Most of these corals consist of colonial POLYPS, which are cemented together by the CALCIUM CARBONATE that they secrete. The calcium carbonate persists for many hundreds of years after the polyps have died. The polyps feed on microscopic marine animals, which they catch with tentacles that extend from the tubes they inhabit. **Brain corals** are common, particularly in tropical areas. They are named after their spherical shape and grooved surface, which makes them resemble a mammalian brain. **Leaf corals** form vertically oriented plates, which have a velvety texture when living. **Plate corals** form horizontally oriented tiers. The concave surface of **vase corals** transforms them into shallow receptacles. **Stagshorn corals** are usually large; they vary in morphology from antler-like formations to sprawling plates. **Mushroom corals** have a circular or oval shape; their radiating skeletal walls resemble the underside of a mushroom. Phylum Coelenterata/Cnidaria; class Anthozoa; order Scleractinia.

coral, soft

True coral of the order Alcyonacea. Soft corals are much fleshier than hard corals, although some species do contain mineral sclerites. Soft corals include **finger corals**, which are named after their branched finger-like projections. Phylum Coelenterata/Cnidaria; class Anthozoa; order Alcyonacea.

coral, black

Coral that is found in almost all oceans; it is named after the dark colour of its stiff, spiny skeleton. Black corals are found in several orders, but primarily in the order Antipatharia. Phylum Coelenterata/Cnidaria; class Anthozoa; order Antipatharia.

CORIOLIS EFFECT

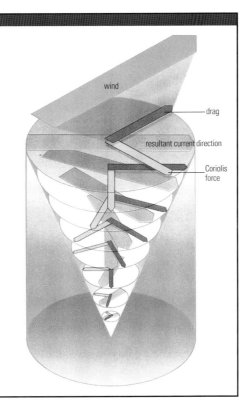

Apparent force on particles or objects due to the rotation of the Earth under them. The Coriolis effect causes objects in motion, including ocean and atmospheric currents, to be deflected towards the right in the Northern Hemisphere and towards the left in the Southern Hemisphere and therefore impacts greatly on the world's WEATHER systems. The direction of water swirling round in a drain or whirlpool demonstrates this effect. It is named after the French mathematician Gaspard Gustave de Coriolis (1792–1843).

▶ **A wind will** tend to drag ocean surface water after it. However, as soon as the water starts to move, the Coriolis effect throws it off at an angle. Each successive thin sheet of water beneath the surface layer begins to move because it is linked by friction to the layer above. But each layer is thrown even farther off course by the Coriolis effect. So the surface current moves at an angle of 45° to the wind at about 2–3% of the wind speed. Lower layers move more slowly, at an increasingly eccentric angle. The resulting vertical profile of the motion is the Ekman spiral. At a depth called the Ekman depth, the water flows in the opposite direction to that of the surface current and at 0.043 times the speed of the surface current.

coral, fire
Coral that inflicts a burning sting on divers that brush against it. It is not a true coral. Phylum Coelenterata/Cnidaria; class Hydrozoa.

coral, gorgonian
Coral that has a flexible internal skeleton. Gorgonian coral is often wispy or bushy in appearance. Phylum Coelenterata/Cnidaria; class Anthozoa; order Gorgonacea.

coralberry
North American ornamental shrub belonging to the HONEYSUCKLE family. It has bright red berries, and its leaves are used locally as medicine. Family Caprifoliaceae; species *Symphoricarpos orbiculata*.

coral fish
Brilliantly coloured tropical fish that lives among CORAL REEFS and similar formations. Its flat, round body, large tail and short fins give it the manoeuvrability that its habitat demands. Coral fish include the BUTTERFLY FISH, ANGELFISH, DAMSELFISH and PARROT FISH. They belong to various families.

coral fungus (coral spot fungus)
FUNGUS with tiny, crowded, coral pink or cinnabar-red pustules and a flask-shaped fruiting body. It is common on dead wood and is not edible. Phylum Ascomycota; species *Nectria cinnabarina*. **Coral fungus** is also the name of two other types of FUNGUS, grey coral fungus (*Clavulina cinerea*) and white or crested coral fungus (*Clavulina cristata*). They produce coral-like fruiting bodies consisting of clumps of densely branched tufts, the tips of which are fringed or crested. The fungi are terrestrial and found in woodlands. Phylum Basidiomycota; genus *Clavulina*.

coral reef
See feature article, pages 90–91

coral vine
Flamboyant, climbing VINE of Central America. It has edible, nutty-tasting TUBERS. Coral vine has bright pink flowers and is a popular garden plant. Family Polygonaceae; species *Antigonon leptopus*.

cordillera
Chain of MOUNTAINS. The term is used particularly of parallel mountain ranges, such as those of the Rockies, Sierra Nevada and Coastal Ranges in w North America or of the Andes in South America.

cordon-bleu
Any member of a small group of finch-like birds belonging to the WAXBILL family. They are small seed-eating birds found in open country in Africa. The electric blue colour of their underparts and much of the face makes them very popular cage birds. Family: Estrildidae (part).

core
Central area of the EARTH from a depth of 2900km (1800mi); it accounts for 16% of the Earth's volume and 31% of its mass. Information about the core is obtained from the measurement of SEISMIC WAVES. These indicate that the outer part of the core is liquid, because shear (S) waves will not travel through it, whereas the inner core from 5150km (3200mi) to the centre of the Earth is interpreted as solid because seismic velocities are lower. It is believed that the change from liquid to solid core occurs because of immense pressure conditions. The core is thought to be composed of iron-nickel alloy (90% iron, 10% nickel). Temperature estimates for the core vary from 4000 to 7000°C. CONVECTION in the iron liquid outer core is thought to be responsible for producing the Earth's magnetic field.

coriander (cilantro)
Strong-smelling herb of the CARROT family, native to the Mediterranean and Near East. The leaves, the seeds and oil from the seeds are used as an aromatic flavouring in foods, medicines and liqueurs. Family Apiaceae/Umbelliferae; species *Coriandrum sativum*.

Coriolis effect
See feature article

cork
Outer, dead, waterproof layer of the BARK of woody plants. The bark of the CORK OAK (*Quercus suber*) is the chief source of commercial cork.

cork oak
Tree that is native to s Europe and North Africa. Every eight to ten years, the thick bark is stripped off trees that are more than twenty years old. The bark is used for insulation, tiles, bottle corks, floats and, when ground, as a constituent of linoleum. Family Fagaceae; species *Quercus suber*.

corm
Fleshy underground stem that produces a plant such as the GLADIOLUS or CROCUS. In most plants, new corms form on top of old ones, which last for one season. They are an important element in forms of ASEXUAL REPRODUCTION.

cormorant
Any member of a family of *c*.32 species of large aquatic birds. Cormorants are long-necked, fish-eating birds, with mostly black plumage. They have short legs, webbed feet and strong, sharply hooked bills. They feed by catching their prey underwater. Family Phalacrocoracidae.

cormorant, Cape
Glossy black marine bird found around the coast of s Africa. It has a yellow patch under its bill and lacks a crest. It feeds on fish and often hunts in small flocks. Length: 64cm (25in). Family Phalacrocoracidae; species *Phalacrocorax capensis*.

cormorant, double-crested
Large, glossy black marine bird with an orange-yellow throat pouch. The double-crested cormorant is found in flocks along the Atlantic coast of North America. It feeds on fish. Length: 76–91cm (30–36in). Family Phalacrocoracidae; species *Phalacrocorax auritus*.

cormorant, flightless
Large, flightless marine bird with glossy black plumage and very small wings. It is found exclusively on the Galápagos Islands, off the coast of South America. The flightless cormorant feeds on fish, octopus and eels. It nests in colonies. Length: 90cm (35in). Family Phalacrocoracidae; species *Nannopterum harrisi*.

cormorant, great
Large, glossy black cormorant. It has a yellow bill and white cheeks. The great cormorant is found in

◀ **cormorant, great** The great cormorant (*Phalacrocorax carbo*) is the largest of the cormorant species. It is found in or near coastal regions of N Europe, Iceland, w Greenland, Africa, Asia, Australia and New Zealand.

C

Coral reefs have been referred to as the rain forests of the sea, and, like rainforests, they are extremely diverse, being home to an enormous variety of animals and plants. They are also ancient – some coral reefs may well have been in existence for 500 million years.

The living reef is composed of a thin veneer of living coral colonies growing on the surface of older, dead coral skeletons. Coral colonies that die or are broken off during storms break down to form sand, which fills the spaces between the frame-building corals. If the land on which the coral is growing sinks, or the sea level rises, the reef continues its upward growth. Eventually, the living reef community may be growing on many hundreds of metres of sold coral rock. The living reef at Enewatak atoll in the Marshall Islands, for example, grows on a base of 1370m (4500ft) of coral limestone, which has been built up on top of a volcanic cone that rises *c*.5000m (16,400ft) above the seafloor.

Reef-building corals do not grow well below 20–30m (70–100ft) because they contain microscopic ALGAE, called zooxanthellae, that require sunlight for PHOTOSYNTHESIS. The association between the coral animal and the zooxanthellae benefits both partners, with the algae deriving nutrients and carbon dioxide from the coral while speeding up the coral's rate of skeleton formation. Other algae, both unicellular and macroscopic, are important to the productivity of reefs, while encrusting, calcareous forms cement loose material together, thus stabilizing the surface of the reef for the colonization of larval corals.

Solitary corals are widely distributed, but do not form reefs, which are best developed in the tropics and subtropics, where water temperatures range between 20°C and 30°C (68°F and 86°F). Although reefs grow well at 18°C (64°F) in the Florida Keys, and above 33°C (91°F) in the Northern Great Barrier Reef of Australia and the Persian Gulf, most reefs grow in areas with water temperatures of around 24°C (75°F).

Corals are actually colonies of tiny individual animals or POLYPS, which secrete a skeleton of calcium carbonate. The colonies grow by adding new individuals, and the growth may take quite different forms in different species. Corals range from the compact brain corals found in areas of high wave energy, through heavy branching and plate corals in the deep water of the reef edge, to smaller, finely branched forms found in more sheltered water behind the reef crest. The most active coral growth is generally on the outer edge of the reef, where water movement is greatest, carrying with it the PLANKTON on which corals feed. In addition to reproducing by simple budding, so increasing the size of the colony, corals also reproduce sexually, producing eggs and larval forms. The larvae are dispersed by currents before settling to form new colonies.

Coral reefs are among the most diverse marine habitats in the world. A single large reef system may support around 200 coral species. About 1000 species of reef-building corals have been described worldwide. The centre of coral diversity is the Southeast Asian region, with some 700 species being found in the Indo-West Pacific, compared with only around 35 in the Atlantic. More than 400 species of hard corals are believed to occur in the Philippines, and as one moves away from this centre of diversity, the numbers of species decline.

The wide diversity in growth forms of different corals provides a multitude of micro-habitats, refuges and food sources for other organisms, the diversity of which is also high: coral reefs are believed to support a third of all living fish species. While some animals, such as the crown-of-thorns STARFISH and the PARROTFISH feed on corals directly, many other animals use the reef as a place of attachment. SEA FANS and SPONGES grow attached to the surface and filter feed on the plankton and suspended matter contained in the surrounding water. Up to 80 per cent of the plankton in the water passing over a reef may be removed by corals and other filter-feeding organisms. In sandy areas SEA CUCUMBERS feed on surface detritus or eat the sand directly, digesting the bacteria and microorganisms that themselves live on dead organic matter. Grazing animals, such as SEA URCHINS and many MOLLUSCS, feed on the film of algae that grows on all dead surfaces of a reef, while small fish crop the fine algal turf and are themselves eaten by predators such as moray EELS. The moray eel is not immune from predation, being eaten by the venomous SEA SNAKE. To avoid predation, many reef animals are brightly coloured, advertising the fact that they are distasteful or poisonous. The bright colours of many other reef animals serve, however, as signals, enabling individuals to recognize members of their own species.

Unfortunately the diverse and beautiful world of the coral reef is as threatened as that of the rainforests. It has been estimated that more than 10 per cent of the world's coral reefs have been degraded beyond recovery by human activity, notably overfishing, fish dynamiting, mining, silt run-off from land erosion and pollution. A further 30 per cent is likely to decline seriously within the next 20 years and it has been suggested that more than 70 per cent of all reefs may collapse ecologically within the next 80 to 100 years.

◄ **Coral reefs grow** in warm waters over 20°C (68°F), thriving at about 24°C (75°F). Reefs grow beyond the tropics in sufficiently warm currents. Corals do not grow in freshwater discharges and cannot grow in water full of sediment, which smothers the fragile reef organisms. Although the optimum depth for growth is a few metres below the surface, where oxygen and sunlight are abundant, coral can grow at up to around 40m (132ft). In ideal conditions, healthy reefs grow up to 25mm (1in) in a year.

. coral reef

◄ **Coral reefs are** the largest structures constructed by living organisms. In reef island situations, typical characteristics arising from the growth of a barrier reef and a fringing reef include a water-covered platform, known as a reef flat, sandy islands and a debris-filled lagoon supporting its own coral life. Beneath the living surface of the reef, dead coral and debris of ancient origin remain as the foundation for the present-day formation. Coral will only grow when it is continuously covered by sea water but at depths where light can penetrate. Only the surface layer of coral on any reef is living since it is in constant contact with the water, food, oxygen and light.

coral and algal debris filling
living coral and calcareous algae
knoll
lagoon
fringing reef
volcanic island
river
sand cay
debris   reef flat
lagoon coral
outer reef coral
breaker zone
reef island
barrier reef
scree

CORAL FORMATION

calcium carbonate

Coral colonies consist of large numbers of polyps, which secrete a skeleton of calcium carbonate. Individual polyps secrete their own theca or cup, into which they can withdraw. Each individual is connected to its neighbour by tissue.

theca or cup

reef flat

reef crest

reef front

▲ **A coral reef** extracts nutrients from the sea and redistributes them through a complex food chain in which every available niche is exploited. The reef front is the fastest-growing area, steeply sloping to the sea bed. Plate coral (1) grows large plates to expose the greatest possible area to the poor light; nurse sharks (2) may lay eggs in

protective coral crevices. Growth at the reef crest is hampered by dry periods at low tide. Behind the seaward side is the sheltered shallow reef flat, home for many fast-growing staghorn corals (3), whose branches raise them above rivals, such as brain coral (4), in the quest for sunlight. Broken-off branches may regrow, spreading the

colony. Home for small fish like the black-backed butterfly fish (5), lower coral parts are mostly dead and algae-covered, food for various invertebrates and the purple-headed parrotfish (6), which bites off bits of coral, ingesting it with the algae and excreting the coral as fine sand, thus building up the shallow water area. Its gaudy colours enable

it to mark out territory and scare off enemies. Like parrotfish, plankton-eating fairy basslets (7) change sex to suit circumstances. Among the world's most venomous animals, olive sea snakes (8) prey on such fish. Cleaner wrasse (9) eat parasites on the skin of other fish. Giant clams (10) eat a mix of filtered food and photosynthetically

produced nutrients from symbiotic algae living in its lips. Gorgonian coral (11) flexes more than most corals, allowing it to survive close to turbulent water surfaces. Sea grass (12) pollinates underwater, with currents carrying the pollen; providing a home for many creatures, it is food for few animals except turtles, urchins and dugongs.

Tubular (13) and vase (14) sponges have chimney-like structures that create updraughts to suck water over their feeding chambers. The male frigate bird's (15) huge red sack is inflated during courtship. Fish eaters, these birds often force others, such as the blue-footed booby (16), to drop prey, catching it as it falls.

C

marine and some inland waters in Africa, Europe, Asia and Australasia. It feeds on fish, which it catches by swimming underwater. Length: 80–85cm (31–33in). Family Phalacrocoracidae; species *Phalacrocorax carbo.*

cormorant, guanay
Large marine bird, with a black back and a white front and underside. It is found around the central Pacific coast of South America, where it nests in very large colonies. The guanay cormorant feeds on fish, such as anchovies, caught on the surface. Its droppings solidify into GUANO, which is often gathered for its high nitrogen content. Length: 76cm (30in). Family Phalacrocoracidae; species *Phalacrocorax bougainvillei.*

cormorant, little black
Cormorant with completely black plumage. It is found in most aquatic habitats in Australia except for the central region. It feeds on fish. Length: 60–65cm (24–26in). Family Phalacrocoracidae; species *Phalacrocorax sulcirostris.*

cormorant, pied
Large aquatic bird. It is white with a black back, back of the neck and top of the head. The pied cormorant is found in waters in and around Australia and New Zealand. It feeds on fish caught underwater. Length: 65–84cm (26–33in). Family Phalacrocoracidae; species *Phalacrocorax varius.*

cormorant, pygmy
Smallest species of cormorant. It has a short, thick neck, long tail, brown back and a white and brown breast. The pygmy cormorant is found in open fresh water with reeds in central and E Europe and in parts of Asia and the Middle East. It feeds on fish and crustaceans. It nests in colonies. Length: 45–55cm (18–22in). Family Phalacrocoracidae; species *Phalacrocorax pygmeus.*

cormorant, red-legged
Handsome bird with bright red legs and mainly grey plumage. It inhabits the coasts of SW South America, usually as isolated pairs or in small groups. Length: 75cm (30in). Family Phalacrocoracidae; species *Phalacrocorax gaimardi.*

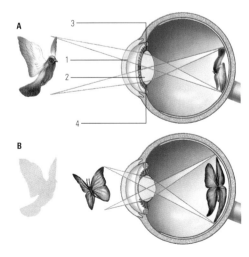

▲ **cornea** Focusing of light rays from distant objects (A) is mainly done by the cornea (1) with a little help from the lens (2). Ciliary muscles (3) encircling the lens relax and stretch ligaments (4), which pull the lens flat. Rays from a near object (B) are bent by a thick lens produced when the ligaments slacken as the ciliary muscles contract. This process, which is called accommodation, is essential for sharp focusing.

corn borer
Any member of a genus of MOTHS known for being important pests of corn (*Zea mays*), as well as other crops such as cotton and sorghum. Its common name, corn borer, comes from the fact that the caterpillars sometimes bore inside the corn stalks as well as the corn ears themselves. The majority of damage and loss of yield is caused by the insects feeding on the young plants. Adult body length: *c.*20mm (*c.*0.8in). Family Pyralidae; genus *Ostrinia.*

corn cockle
Member of the pink and CARNATION family. It has reddish-purple flowers. Corn cockle was once a troublesome weed of grain fields because its seeds became mixed with the corn, thus lowering the quality of the flour. With improved agricultural techniques, the plant is disappearing fast, particularly from Great Britain. Family Caryophyllaceae; species *Agrostemma githago.*

corncrake
See CRAKE, CORN-

cornea
Transparent membrane at the front of the EYE. It is curved and acts as a fixed lens, so that light entering the eye is to some extent focused before it reaches the eye lens.

corn earworm (cotton bollworm)
NOCTUID moth CATERPILLAR that is a serious crop pest in North and South America. It attacks many plants and is a major pest of cotton and corn. Family Noctuidae; species *Heliothis zea.*

cornflower (bachelor's button)
Annual of the composite family common in many parts of Europe. Its leaves are covered in tiny, white hairs and it produces blue flowers. Family Asteraceae/Compositae; species *Centaurea cyanus.*

corolla
PETALS of a flower. The corolla encloses the STAMENS and CARPELS. The petals, which may be free or fused, form the inner whorl of the PERIANTH.

corpus luteum
Mass of yellow tissue formed in the GRAAFIAN FOLLICLE in the OVARY of a mammal after the OVUM (egg cell) is released. If the ovum is fertilized, the corpus luteum secretes PROGESTERONE, a hormone that is needed to prepare the uterus for pregnancy. If the ovum is not fertilized, the corpus luteum becomes inactive.

corrasion
Mechanical EROSION caused by loose material, such as sand or pebbles, during transportation. The material is carried by wind, water or ice, and it scrapes against the bed or sides of the river or glacial valley, or against the cliffs and the shore.

Correns, Karl Erich (1864–1933)
German botanist and geneticist. In 1900 he rediscovered the works of Gregor MENDEL outlining the principles of HEREDITY. Correns conducted experiments to determine the validity of Mendel's laws and helped to provide evidence that proved his theories.

corrie
See CIRQUE

corrosion
Chemical EROSION leading to the disintegration of

◄ **cotton** After rapid flowering, small green seedpods (bolls) develop on the cotton plant. The seeds within the bolls sprout a mass of fine fibrous hairs. When mature, the bolls rupture a soft cloud of cotton erupts. The crop is harvested by hand or machine and then taken to be ginned (separating the seed from the fibres), cleaned, carded and spun into yarn.

rocks, such as by the action of running water or by SOLUTION. It is particularly common in limestone.

cortex
Outer layer of a gland or tissue. Examples include the cortex of the ADRENAL GLANDS; the cerebral cortex or outer layer of the BRAIN; and the cortical layers of tissue in plant roots and stems lying between the BARK or EPIDERMIS and the hard wood or conducting tissues.

cortisone
HORMONE that is produced by the CORTEX of the ADRENAL GLANDS and is essential for carbohydrate, protein and fat metabolism, kidney function and disease resistance. Synthetic cortisone is used to treat adrenal insufficiency, rheumatoid arthritis and other inflammatory diseases, rheumatic fever, asthma, severe allergies and skin complaints. A potent, versatile drug, it can have unwanted side effects such as body swelling.

corundum
Translucent to transparent mineral that exists in many hues, aluminium oxide (Al_2O_3). Corundum is found in IGNEOUS and METAMORPHIC ROCKS, occurring as pyramidal or prismatic crystals in the rhombohedral class and as granular masses. It is the hardest natural substance after DIAMOND. Gemstone varieties are sapphire and ruby. It is used in watches and motors and is an important industrial abrasive. Hardness 9; r.d. 4.

corvid
Any member of the family Corvidae, comprising *c.*100 species of perching birds (birds of the order Passeriformes). The family is commonly known as the CROW family. It includes crows, JACKDAWS, JAYS, MAGPIES, NUTCRACKERS, RAVENS and ROOKS. Crows are agile and aggressive in the air and will often mob birds of prey.

cosmos
Any member of the *Cosmos* genus, belonging to the daisy family. They are tropical plants, found in Mexico and Central America. Various cosmos cultivars are popular as garden plants, some being known as "cosmeas" or "Mexican asters". Family Compositae; genus *Cosmos.*

cotinga
Member of a family of *c.*90 species of fruit-eating birds. They are of diverse size and appearance, and the males often have brightly coloured plumage. Cotingas are found in tropical Central and South America. They are mainly forest-dwelling birds with bell-like calls. Family Cotingidae.

cotinga, lovely
Cotinga found in tropical forests from S Mexico to Costa Rica. The female is a drab brown, but the breeding male is one of the most attractive of birds,

with vivid iridescent blue plumage. Length: 20cm (8in). Family Cotingidae; species *Cotinga amabilis*.

cotinga, snowy
Cotinga found in tropical forests of Honduras, Nicaragua, Costa Rica and Panama. The male is a pure snowy white; the female is pale beneath, with a dove-grey upperside. Length: 20cm (8in). Family Cotingidae; species *Carpodectes nitidus*.

cotoneaster
Any member of a genus of *c*.50 species of deciduous shrubs of the ROSE family, mostly native to China. With small, white flowers and small, red or black, berry-like fruit, they are often cultivated as ornamental plants. Family Rosaceae; genus *Cotoneaster*.

cotton
Annual shrub that is native to subtropical regions. Cotton is widely cultivated in order to make fabric from the fibres that envelop the seeds. Family Malvaceae; genus *Gossypium*.

cotton aphid (melon aphid, cotton louse)
Small, soft-bodied APHID. It is green to black and may be winged or wingless. The cotton aphid feeds on cotton, squashes, melons or lilies, among others, and is known to spread some plant diseases. Length: 3mm (0.1in). Order Hemiptera; family Aphididae; species *Aphis gossypii*.

cotton bollworm
See CORN EARWORM

cottonmouth (water moccasin)
Venomous, semiaquatic SNAKE, native to the swamps of SE United States. It is a pit VIPER, closely related to the North American COPPERHEAD. Adult cottonmouths have broad, brown bands along their bodies. When threatened, the cottonmouth bares its white mouth. They feed on warm-blooded animals. Length: to 1.5m (5ft). Family Viperidae; species *Agkistrodon piscivorus*.

cottonseed
Seed from the COTTON plant; it produces an oil when crushed. Cottonseed contains the bitter pigment gossypol and was considered inedible until the beginning of the 19th century. Successful purifying techniques were eventually developed and it is now widely used in margarine manufacturing, cooking and soap powders. The use of cottonseed in a province of China in the 1930s indicated a link with reduced male fertility due to the gossypol; further experimentation and studies have been carried out. Family Malvaceae; genus *Gossypium*.

cotton spinner
Black SEA CUCUMBER (bêche de mer). It crawls on the surface of ocean sediments and, when threatened, squirts long, white, sticky threads from its anus. Phylum Echinodermata; class Holothuroidea; order Aspidochirotida; family Holothuriidae; species *Holothuria forskali*.

cotyledon
First leaf or pair of leaves produced by the embryo of any ANGIOSPERM (flowering plant). The cotyledon's function is to store and digest food for the embryo plant and, if it emerges above ground, to PHOTOSYNTHESIZE for seedling growth. *See also* DICOTYLEDON; MONOCOTYLEDON

coucal, pheasant
Large, long-legged bird of the CUCKOO family. It has

a black head and breast and a reddish-brown back and tail; it is barred with cream and black. The pheasant coucal is found in scrub and canefields of the N and E perimeter of Australia and in New Guinea. It feeds on insects, lizards and snakes. Length: 60–80cm (24–31in). Family Cuculidae; species *Centropus phasianus*.

couch grass
Name given to a number of different weedy GRASSES. Some species of couch grass are particularly persistent on farmland, where they are extremely difficult to eradicate. Family Gramineae; species include *Elytrigia repens*, *Cynodon dactylon*, *Digitaria didactyla* and *Arrhenatherum elatius* var. *bulbosum*.

cougar
See PUMA

country rock
Rock that has been intruded into by a subsequent igneous INTRUSION.

courgette
See ZUCCHINI

courser, cream coloured
Medium-sized, ground-living bird. It has a creamy, sandy body, with a black and white stripe on its face. The courser is found in arid areas of SW Asia, S Europe, the Middle East and North Africa. It feeds on insects and other invertebrates. Length: 23–26cm (9–10in). Family Glareolidae; species *Cursorius cursor*.

Cousteau, Jacques Yves (1910–97)
French oceanographer. Best known as the co-inventor (with Emile Gagnan) of the aqualung, Cousteau also invented a process of underwater television and conducted a series of undersea living experiments (Conshelf I–III, 1962–65). Many of the expeditions made by his research ship *Calypso* were filmed by him for television and cinema. Although immensely popular around the world with the public, academics accused him of showmanship and questioned the validity of his research. In his later life he became a prominent figure in ecological movements.

covalent bond
Chemical bond in which two atoms share a pair of

electrons, one from each atom. Covalent bonds with one shared pair of electrons are called single bonds; double and triple bonds also exist. The molecules tend to have low melting and boiling points and to be soluble in nonpolar solvents. Covalent bonding is most common in organic compounds.

covellite
Mineral form of copper sulphide (CuS). It occurs with other copper minerals and is mined as an ore. It forms hexagonal, platy crystals, which have a deep indigo blue colour, often tinged with purple. It cleaves into thin, flexible plates. Hardness: 1.5–2.0; r.d. 4.7.

cowbird
Small bird found in temperate North America; it is a member of the American ORIOLE family. Most cowbirds have brownish or grey plumage. They feed on insects, often taken from the backs of cattle, hence their common name. They are parasitic breeders. Length: 20cm (8in). Family Icteridae; genus *Molothrus*.

cowfish
Bony marine fish found in tropical waters on both sides of the Atlantic Ocean. Its triangular body has net-like markings, and it has spines projecting from the top of its head. The cowfish's fused scales form a rigid carapace protecting its body. Length: up to 50cm (20in). Family Ostraciidae; species *Acanthostracian quadricornis*.

cow parsley
Tall plant belonging to the carrot family. It grows abundantly in temperate regions, particularly in hedges, roadsides and wasteland. Its early, white, distinctively smelling flowers are evocative of spring. Family Umbelliferae; species *Anthriscus sylvestris*.

cowpea
Herbaceous climbing plant that belongs to the

▼ **cotton spinner** The cotton spinner (*Holothuria forskali*) is a type of sea cucumber found on rocky areas of the seafloor. On its underside are numerous tube feet, which it uses to walk and to cling on to rocks. It is usually found in areas where sediment collects. It takes in large quantities of sediment, digesting anything of nutritional value and expelling the rest. When attacked the cotton spinner ejects from its anus a mass of cotton-like sticky threads to confuse the predator.

widespread PEA family. It originated in the Old World tropics and was taken to America in *c*.1600. It is now widely distributed throughout tropical and subtropical regions. The cowpea's long pods are eaten as a vegetable and also used as a "green manure", thus returning valuable material to the soil. Cowpea is widely used in the United States as a fodder crop because it is easy to grow and smothers weeds. Fibre can be extracted from its stems and its leaves are used for green dye. Family Leguminosae; species *Vigna sinensis*.

cowrie (cowry)

Marine snail that can be identified by its ovoid, highly polished shell, which has a long, toothed opening and varied markings. The cowrie is found on coral shores. Length: 8–150mm (0.3–6in). Phylum Mollusca; class Gastropoda; family Cypraeidae; there are more than 160 species, including the map cowry *Cypraea mappa*.

cowslip

Either of two species of yellow-flowered herbs. Cowslip most commonly refers to the English PRIM-ROSE native to Europe. Family Primulaceae; species *Primula veris*. The MARSH MARIGOLD of the United States is sometimes known as cowslip. Family Ranunculaceae; species *Caltha palustris*. The term is also sometimes used for the shooting star and the Virginia cowslip.

coyote

Wild DOG that was originally native to w North America. Coyotes have moved into many areas formerly inhabited by wolves in the E United States. Usually greyish-brown, they have pointed muzzles, big ears and bushy tails. Length: 90cm (35in); weight: *c*.12kg (*c*.26lb). Family Canidae; species *Canis latrans*.

coypu
See NUTRIA

crab

Any member of the largest group of DECAPOD CRUSTACEANS. Crabs have flattened bodies that are protected by a hard, plate-like carapace; the abdomen is permanently flexed beneath. Crabs use their legs for swimming, walking and feeding, and their tiny larvae float free in the water. Most crab species are marine. Class Crustacea; subclass Malacostraca; order Decapoda (part).

crab, blue

Swimming crab found along Atlantic and Gulf coasts. It is a scavenger in brackish water near the mouths of rivers. Its body extends on each side to a long, sharp spine. After moulting, the blue crab's shell is soft. Its last pair of legs is flat and oar-like. Adult body length: 15cm (6in). Family Portunidae; species *Callinectes sapidus*.

crab, edible

One of a number of crabs that are eaten as seafood. The edible crab occurs on rocky substrates of shores, especially on the European Atlantic coasts. It scavenges on fish, molluscs, echinoderms and other crustaceans. Its carapace is broad, with teeth on the front margin. The first antennae are folded longitudinally and the flagellum is hairy. Female edible crabs move to deeper water to spawn. Adult body length: 11–13cm (4–5in). Family Cancridae; species *Cancer pagurus*.

crab, fiddler

Small, burrowing crab of the genus *Uca*. Fiddler crabs are found worldwide on sandy beaches and salt marshes. The male has one huge claw, which it holds in front of the body. This pincer is used in courtship

displays and fights with other males. They are poor swimmers and remain in burrows during high tide. Adult body length: to 3cm (1in). Family Ocypodidae.

crab, ghost (sand crab)

Amphibious, fast-moving crab found throughout the world. It lives on sandy beaches and mud flats and is relatively independent of water when mature. Its compact body is protectively sandy coloured. Adult body length: to 5cm (2in). Family Ocypodidae; genus *Ocypode*.

crab, giant spider (Japanese Island crab)

Crab that has the largest leg span of any known arthropod: males are regularly recorded with a 4m leg span (the female is much smaller). The giant spider crab is found in continental shelf areas at depths of 50–300m (160–980ft). It is regarded as a culinary delicacy by the Japanese. Adult body length: 50cm (20in). Family Majidae; species *Macrocheira kaempferi*.

crab, hermit

Small crab found in shallow waters worldwide. Unlike other crabs it has a soft abdomen, which it protects with sea-snail shells. It changes shells as it grows. Some hermit crabs are terrestrial and do not use shells as adults. Family Paguridae.

crab, land

Terrestrial crab found in tropical America, w Africa and Indo-Pacific regions. It has gills in cavities in its shell and breathes air. A forest-floor and swamp scavenger, it migrates to water to breed. Adult body length: 11–30cm (4–12in). Family Gecarcinidae.

crab, pea

Tiny crab that lives commensally with other organisms. Different species of pea crab live in different environments, including in the mantle cavity of oysters or other molluscs, in polychaete tubes or burrows, in branchial cavities of ascidians, in cloacas of sea cucumbers, or in the burrows of other crustaceans. After establishing this commensal habitat, pea crabs moult and their exoskeletons remain soft. Adult body length (females): to 2cm (0.8in); males are smaller. Family Pinnotheridae.

crab, porcelain

Crab with a well-developed tail fan. Porcelain crabs are more closely related to lobsters than to true crabs. They are most abundant in the intertidal zone and in moderate depths of warmer seas. Adult body length: *c*.12mm (*c*.0.5in). Family Galatheidae; genera include *Porcellana*.

crab, robber

Large, agile crab found on tropical islands. The robber crab gets its name from its habit of raiding coconut trees to feed. It spends much time on land and can climb well using its sharp claws. Adult body length: to 45cm (18in). Family Coenobitidae; species *Birgus latro*.

crab, sand
See GHOST CRAB

crab, shore

Crab that is common on Atlantic shores. It is often seen running sideways in shallow water between tides, browsing on molluscs, amphipods, worms and small fish. When threatened, the shore crab rises up and can attack with its pincers. It is widely distributed, from Nova Scotia, E Canada, to Virginia, E United States, and from N Norway to NW Africa.

▶ **crab** There are around 4500 species of crab which vary considerably in size from small species like the Dorset spider crab (*Inachus dorsettensis*) to the robber crab (*Birgus latro*), the largest crab species. The swimming crab (*Micropipus depurator*) has a fourth pair of legs, which are modified as paddles. The broad-clawed porcelain crab (*Porcellana platycheles*) is extremely hairy with huge claws.

Dorset spider crab

robber crab

swimming crab

broad-clawed porcelain crab

crane, black-crowned
One of the most primitive crane species, the black-crowned crane (*Balearica pavonina*) existed in the Eocene epoch. It is the only crane to perch in a tree. It stamps the ground in order to flush out insects to eat and sometimes performs an elaborate dance, involving jumping and flapping its wings.

Adult body length: 8cm (3in). Family Portunidae; species *Carcinus maenas*.

crab, spider
Any of *c*.500 species of marine crab found in the Atlantic and Pacific oceans. Spider crabs have a spiny, sac-shaped carapace that is pointed in front. They have extremely long, thin legs. The Japanese spider crab is the largest species. Family Majidae.

crab apple
Small, sour fruit produced by certain APPLE trees. The various species grow in Europe, North America and Asia. The fruit is used in making preserves and jelly. Family Rosaceae; genus *Malus*.

crab grass
Common name of three species of GRASS native to tropical and warm regions. They are cultivated for food crops, animal fodder and some ornamental use. Family Gramineae; species *Digitaria abyssinica*, *Eleusine indica* and *Panicum hemitomon*.

crake
Aquatic bird with a squat body, short wings and long legs. Its plumage is mostly cryptic to provide camouflage in the marshes and fens that it inhabits. Some crake species, for example the corncrake, are found in drier habitats. Crakes are found on all continents except Antarctica. They belong to the RAIL family. Family Rallidae (part).

crake, American black
Very small crake. It is dark-grey beneath and dark brown streaked with black above, with a black beak. It is found in wetlands in E United States, wintering in South America. It feeds on vegetable matter, insects, molluscs and small fish. Length: 15cm (6in). Family Rallidae; species *Laterallus jamaicensis*.

crake, Baillon's
Very small crake; it is similar to the little crake, but more heavily barred black, with white flanks. Baillon's crake is found in aquatic habitats in SE Europe, w Asia, Africa and Australia. It feeds on insects, larvae, worms, snails and some plant material. Length: *c*.18cm (*c*.7in). Family Rallidae; species *Porzana pusilla*.

crake, corn- (corncrake)
Small crake with cryptic brown plumage. It is found in high grassland, mainly in central and s Europe and w Asia, wintering in s Europe, Africa and Asia. It feeds on insects, worms, snails and seeds. The corncrake has a highly distinctive, repeated, grating call. Length: 27–30cm (11–12in). Family Rallidae; species *Crex crex*.

crake, little
Very small crake species. Its plumage is largely cryptic brown with black barring, and it has a green bill. The little crake is found in reedbeds from s Europe into w Asia, wintering in North Africa. It feeds on small aquatic animals, insects and seeds. Length: 18–20cm (7–8in). Family Rallidae; species *Porzana parva*.

crake, spotted
Small crake. It is mainly brown, with black flecking above and spotted white underparts. It is found in wetlands in Europe and w Asia, wintering in Africa. The spotted crake feeds on insects, snails, aquatic animals and seeds. Length: *c*.23cm (*c*.9in). Family Rallidae; species *Porzana porzana*.

cranberry
Plant of the HEATH family, distributed widely in temperate regions of the Northern Hemisphere. It is a creeping or trailing shrub. It bears red berries with an acid taste; they are used to make sauce and juice. Family Ericaceae; genus *Vaccinium*.

crane
Any of *c*.15 species of long-legged, long-necked, tall birds, most of which are ground-dwelling and migratory. The crane family has a cosmopolitan distribution. Plumage is usually grey or white, often with a patch of bright red on the head. Unlike herons, cranes fly with their necks outstretched. Their food includes insects, seeds, grain and reptiles. Family Gruidae.

crane, black-crowned
Crane with mainly dark grey plumage, white wing patches and a golden crest. It is found on savanna in Africa. Unusually for members of this family, the black-crowned crane often perches in trees. It feeds on seeds, grain, locusts and other insects, and reptiles. Length: 110–130cm (43–51in). Family Gruidae; species *Balearica pavonina*.

crane, common
Crane that is mainly grey, with a white stripe down the back of its neck and a red patch on its crown. It is found on the marshes, bogs and tundra of N Europe and w Asia, migrating to winter in Spain, Africa and India. The common crane feeds on grain, small animals, larvae and vegetable matter. Length: 110–120cm (43–47in). Family Gruidae; species *Grus grus*.

crane, demoiselle
Crane with light grey plumage, white ear tufts and a black breast and "beard". It is found on the marshy areas and steppe of SE Europe, s Russia, w Asia and North Africa, wintering in s Asia and North Africa. It feeds largely on grain, rice and small animals. Length: 90–100cm (35–39in). Family Gruidae; species *Anthropoides virgo*.

crane, sandhill
Small crane. It is mostly light grey, with long black legs and a red patch on its crown. If is found in Arctic Canada and NE Siberia. An omnivore, the sandhill crane feeds on such things as roots, grain, insects and frogs. Length: *c*.100cm (*c*.39in). Family Gruidae; species *Grus canadensis*.

crane, sarus
One of the largest species of crane. It is tall with light grey plumage and a red head and throat. The sarus crane is found in rice plantations and wetlands from s Asia to Australia. An omnivore, it feeds on such items as berries, grain, insects, mice and snakes. Length: *c*.140cm (*c*.55in). Family Gruidae; species *Grus antigone*.

crane, Siberian white
One of the largest cranes. It is white except for black wingtips, a red forehead and pink legs. It is a very rare species, found only in Siberia, from where it migrates in winter to N Asia. It is almost entirely vegetarian, eating shoots, corms, seeds and roots. Length: 120–140cm (47–55in). Family Gruidae; species *Grus leucogeranus*.

crane, whooping
Large, very rare species of crane. It is white, with a red patch on its head and a black moustachial stripe; its legs are dark. It is found in wetlands in NW Canada or, in winter, in s United States and Mexico. The whooping crane is omnivorous, feeding on vegetable matter and aquatic invertebrates. Length: 122–127cm (48–50in). Family Gruidae; species *Grus americana*.

crane-fly (daddy long legs)
Non-biting, true FLY. It has a slender body, long,

crane, whooping This endangered species (*Grus americana*) was on the verge of extinction in the mid-20th century. Its habit of laying two eggs but only rearing one chick has, however, enabled ornithologists to establish captive breeding programmes and numbers have increased.

fragile legs and one pair of wings. The female crane-fly has a specialized abdomen in order to lay eggs beneath the ground. The larvae, known as leather-jackets, live in the soil, where they feed on plant roots and stems, frequently becoming serious agricultural pests. Adult body size: 10–20mm (0.4–0.8in). Order Diptera; family Tipulidae; species include *Tipula simplex*.

cranesbill
Common name for certain species of wild GERANI-UM. Some cranesbill species are grown for ornamental ground cover. Family Geraniaceae.

cranium
Dome-shaped part of the SKULL that protects the BRAIN. The cranium is composed of eight bones that are fused together.

crater
Roughly circular depression in the surface of the Earth, the Moon, or some other planets, usually with steep sides. It is formed either by meteoric impact, when shock waves blast out a hole in the ground, or at the vent of a volcano, when lava is expelled explosively. Space probes have revealed such craters on Mars and Mercury, and on some of the larger asteroids and satellites of other planets.

crater lake
Accumulation of water, usually by precipitation of rain or snow but sometimes ground water, in a volcanic crater (CALDERA). Should an eruption occur, the resulting mud flow (**lahar**) is often more destructive than a lava flow, owing to its greater speed. A noted example is Crater Lake in Crater Lake Park, Oregon, United States. The waters of the lake were formed by precipitation and are maintained solely by rain and snow; there is no outlet.

craton
Stable area of the Earth's CRUST that has not been affected by TECTONIC activity during the previous 1000 million years. Cratons form the SHIELD areas of the Earth's CONTINENTS.

crawfish (crayfish, crawdad, langouste)
Large LOBSTER that lives in the N Atlantic Ocean and the Mediterranean Sea. It is much sought after as a delicacy. The crawfish's hard carapace has numerous sharp spines. It usually lives at 20–70m (66–230ft) depth. Adult body length: to 50cm (20in). Family Palinuridae; species *Palinurus elephas*. The species in this family are known generally as spiny lobsters.

crayfish
Edible, freshwater, ten-legged crustacean found in rivers of temperate regions. They burrow into the banks of streams and feed on animal and vegetable matter. Some cave-dwelling species are blind. They are smaller than LOBSTERS, to which they are related. Length: normally 8–10cm (3–4in). Families Astacidae (Northern Hemisphere), Parastacidae (Southern Hemisphere) and Austroastacidae (Australia).

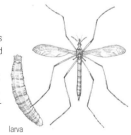

▶ **crane-fly** The hindwings of the crane-fly have evolved into small balancing organs known as halteres. In flight they vibrate with the wings, detecting and helping to correct any deviation from the stable flight path.   larva

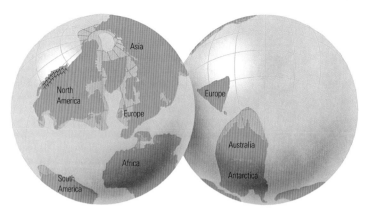

◀ **Cretaceous** The splitting up of Gondwanaland continued during the Cretaceous period. North America broke away from Europe, leaving part of its original mass behind as part of Scotland and Norway. The movement of North America caused the Rocky Mountains to rise.

creep
Slow downward movement of material on the Earth's surface. This slow movement of soil is not associated with EROSION. It may occur on all sorts of slopes including those that are covered with vegetation. The steady downflow of soil and rock carries the vegetation with it. Creep may be caused by the growth of plant roots, the burrowing of small animals or trampling of larger ones, frost movement, or successive drying and wetting leading to shrinkage and swelling of the soil.

creeper, New Zealand
Small brown bird of the Australian warbler family. It takes its name from its habit of creeping about the foliage searching for insects. It is found in the South Island of New Zealand. Length: 13cm (5in). Family Acanthizidae; species *Finschia novaeseelandiae*.

creeper, plain-headed
Small brown bird with a white breast flecked with brown on its flanks. An agile bird, it is adept at clambering on bark. The plain-headed creeper is found in thick forests in mountainous parts of the Philippines. It feeds on insects, often taken from flowers. Length: 15cm (6in). Family Rhabdornithidae; species *Rhabdornis inornatus*.

creeper, spotted grey
Small bird belonging to the treecreeper family. It is dark brown with white spots above, and white with brown barring below. The spotted grey creeper is found in forests and open woodland in Africa and Asia. It feeds on insects, caterpillars, beetles and ants. Length: 13cm (5in). Family Certhiidae; species *Salpornis spilonotus*.

creeping jenny
Yellow-flowering plant native to damp woodland areas of Europe and North America. It is believed by herbalists to alleviate pain. Creeping jenny has become popular in the garden as ground cover and as a decorative edging plant for ornamental ponds. Family Primulaceae; species *Lysimachia nummularia*.

creosote bush
Plant found in Mexico and adjacent areas. Some individual bushes are estimated as being more than 11,000 years old. The twigs of the creosote bush can be steeped in boiling water to yield an antiseptic lotion. The flower buds are pickled and eaten as a caper substitute. Family Zygophyllaceae; species *Larrea tridentata*.

cress
Any of several small, pungent-leaved plants of the MUSTARD family, often used in salads and as garnishes. The best-known species is WATERCRESS. Family Brassicaceae; species *Nasturtium officinale*.

Cretaceous
Last period of the MESOZOIC era, lasting from 144 to 65 million years ago. DINOSAURS flourished until the end of this period, when they died out in a mass extinction that killed off a vast range of vertebrate and invertebrate life forms. The first true placental and marsupial mammals and flowering plants appeared. The chalk rocks of NW Europe were deposited during the Upper Cretaceous.

crevasse
Deep crack in a GLACIER. It is the result of stress within the glacier or the movement of the glacier over uneven terrain.

Crick, Francis Harry Compton (1916–)
British biophysicist. In the 1950s, in association with James WATSON and Maurice WILKINS, he established the double-helix molecular structure of deoxyribonucleic acid (DNA). The discovery of the structure enabled the role of DNA in HEREDITY to be explained. The three were jointly awarded the Nobel Prize for physiology or medicine in 1962. Since 1977 Crick has been a professor at the Salk Institute for Biological Studies, California, United States. His recent neurobiological research has concentrated on the functioning of the brain.

cricket
Any of *c*.2500 species of insect, mostly within the family Gryllidae, closely related to GRASSHOPPERS and katydids. Crickets are usually omnivorous, feeding on plant matter as well as on other insects and detritus. Male crickets sing, day and night, by stridulating (rubbing parts of the forewings together). Adult body length: 3–60mm (0.1–2.4in). Order Orthoptera; main family Gryllidae.

cricket, ant
Very small cricket that lives in ant nests. It stimulates the worker ants to feed it. Adult body length: 3–6mm (0.1–0.2in). Family Myrmecophilidae.

cricket, bush- (long-horned grasshopper)
Cricket that belongs to the long-horned family of

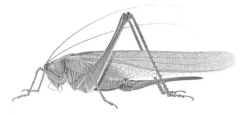

▲ **cricket** The great green bush-cricket (*Tettigonia viridissima*) of S Europe, North Africa and Asia is bright green in colour to blend in well with its surroundings. The chirping of bush-crickets increases with temperature.

GRASSHOPPERS; some species are known as **katydids**. Most bush-crickets are quite large, some being among the largest of the insects. Adults and nymphs are omnivorous, taking small insects as well as plant matter. They are often found on shrubs and bushes, unlike some other grasshoppers. Some bush-crickets are flightless. The males of most species have a high-pitched courtship call, which is produced by rubbing their wing bases together. Adult body length: 30–120mm (1–5in). Family Tettigoniidae.

cricket, camel (cave cricket)
Wingless cricket. Its hunch-backed appearance and preference for moist dark habitats such as caves give rise to its two common names. Adult body length: *c*.20mm (*c*.0.8in). Family Raphidophoridae.

cricket, field
Any of several species of cricket. Field crickets are usually brown or black and tend to be found in sunny, dry grassland sites. Adult body length: 10–30mm (0.4–1.2in). Family Gryllidae; genera include *Acheta* and *Gryllus*.

cricket, house
Any of several species of cricket that are similar in appearance and size to field crickets but are usually lighter in coloration. Family Gryllidae; genus *Acheta*.

cricket, mole
Any of a family of crickets that have specialized digging forelimbs to suit their burrowing lifestyle. They feed on insect larvae and other invertebrates, as well as plant roots. Adult body length: 15–40mm (0.6–1.6in). Family Gryllotalpidae.

cricket, wood
Any of various crickets that inhabit wooded areas. Adult body length: 7–20mm (0.3–0.8in). Family Gryllidae; genera include *Gryllus* and *Nemobius*.

crinoid
Any member of the class Crinoidea, a group of primitive ECHINODERMS that includes the SEA LILY and the feather star. A crinoid's mouth, on a small disc with the other main organs, is surrounded by long feathery arms. It feeds on particles that fall through the water and respires by means of its tube-feet. Crinoids first appeared in the Ordovician period (510 million years ago); fossil crinoids are an important constituent of Palaeozoic limestones.

crinum lily
Bulbous plant found in temperate and tropical regions, with spirally arranged leaves and conspicuous flowers. Many have local medicinal uses. There are many cultivated and ornamental species of crinum lily, which are popular for greenhouses and temperate gardens. There are also several aquatic species, for example *Crinum asiaticum*, which has a layer of cork over the seed to ease water-dispersal. Family Amaryllidaceae; species include *Crinum powellii* and *Crinum asiaticum*.

croaker (drum)
Any of the 250 species of fish belonging to the family Sciaenidae. They are named after their ability to produce sound using muscles that vibrate the swim bladder. Croakers are distributed worldwide, mainly in shallow continental shelf waters of the tropics and subtropics; there are also some freshwater species. Family Sciaenidae.

crocodile
Carnivorous, lizard-like REPTILE found in warm parts of every continent, except Europe. Most crocodiles have a longer snout than ALLIGATORS. All lay hard-shelled eggs in nests. There are about 12 species, including two dwarf species in Africa. The Asian saltwater crocodile (*Crocodylus porosus*) sometimes attacks humans. Length: up to 7m (23ft). Family Crocodylidae.

crocus
Hardy, perennial flowering plant. It is low, with a single, tubular flower. Its grass-like leaves rise from an underground CORM. Family Iridaceae; genus *Crocus*.

crombec
Any of a group of *c*.10 species of small bird belonging to the warbler family. Crombecs are squat and almost tailless, similar in body shape to nuthatches. They are found in open woodland in Africa, where they feed mainly on insects. Family Sylviidae; genus *Sylvietta*.

cross-bedding
Sedimentary structure comprising a series of inclined parallel or near parallel layers within a bed, found mainly in sandstones but also in some limestones and conglomerates. Cross-bedding forms where SEDIMENT is being moved as it is being deposited, building sand dunes, sand waves or ripples. It is useful for interpreting ancient environments because the direction and strength of former currents can be determined from the pattern and type of structure.

crossbill
Small bird of the FINCH family. It has a relatively large head and overlapping mandibles. The crossbill is a specialized feeder, taking the seeds from within pine cones. It is found in Europe, North America and NW Africa. Family Fringillidae; genus *Loxia*; there are four species.

▲ **crocodile** A visual comparison between alligators (A) and crocodiles (B) shows the different shapes of their snouts. Another sign of difference is that the long lower fourth tooth protrudes from the closed jaw of a crocodile. In general, crocodiles are more aggressive than alligators. The gharial (gavial) of the Indian subcontinent (C) has a very elongated jaw shape.

cross breeding
Breeding between individuals of two different SPECIES or distinct varieties of a single species, whether by natural or artificial means, to produce living offspring.

crossing over
During CELL DIVISION, a mechanism by which pairs of HOMOLOGOUS CHROMOSOMES exchange strands (CHROMATIDS) of each chromosome. At the end of the first PROPHASE in MEIOSIS, the diverging chromosomes remain in contact at a number of places, called CHIASMA. Chromatids split and rejoin at each chiasma, with the result that sections of chromatids are exchanged. This alters the distribution of GENES along the chromosomes and so gives rise to genetic variation in the resulting GAMETES. This variation is essential in the process of EVOLUTION.

cross-pollination
Transfer of POLLEN from the flower of one plant to another. The process may be used by plant breeders to hybridize compatible plant species, thus producing "synthetic" varieties. The result of the process is called a HYBRID.

croton
Tropical plant of the genus *Croton*, found particularly in South America, where there are more than three hundred species in Brazil alone. Various species are used for timber and shade-trees, teas, insecticides, tonics and bitters. Croton oil, which comes from the seeds of *Croton tiglium*, is one of the most powerful purgatives known; it is now generally considered unsafe for medicinal use. Family Euphorbiaceae; species include *Croton tiglium* and *Croton megalocarpus*.

croton bug
See COCKROACH, GERMAN

crow
Name given to many members of the Corvidae family, a large family of *c*.112 species of medium to large birds. Most crows are predominantly black with large bills. They are, in general, opportunistic omnivores. Crows are among the most intelligent of all birds and have a cosmopolitan distribution. Family Corvidae.

crow, American
Largest American crow, common throughout most of North America. It is all black, with a long, heavy bill. It often gathers in flocks. Length: 45cm (18in). Family Corvidae; species *Corvus brachyrhynchos*.

crow, carrion
Common, all-black crow that inhabits a variety of open-country habitats, including suburbia, through

C

most of Europe. It is a solitary nester, building its nest high up in trees. The carrion crow is omnivorous. Length: 47cm (18.5in). Family Corvidae; species *Corvus corone*.

crow, jungle
Large crow, with a deep, heavy bill. It is famed for its intelligence and cunning. Jungle crows are found across a wide range through Asia to Japan and the Philippines. Length: 48cm (19in). Family Corvidae; species *Corvus macrorhynchos*.

crow, pied
Crow found in open country throughout tropical Africa and Madagascar. It is mainly black, but with a white or grey-white belly and shoulder. It is omnivorous. Length: 46cm (18in). Family Corvidae; species *Corvus albus*.

crowberry
Evergreen shrub found on heathlands in cool temperate regions of the Northern Hemisphere and s South America. The black berries are used locally for jams and preserves. Crowberry is cultivated for ornamental use in rock and heath gardens. Family Empetraceae; species *Empetrum nigrum*.

crowfoot
Common name given to any BUTTERCUP that grows in water. There are in fact only nine true species of crowfoot, which include the common water-crowfoot, the thread-leaved crowfoot and the river water-crowfoot. They are common in temperate and cold regions of the Northern Hemisphere. Family Ranunculaceae; species include *Ranunculus aquatilis*, *Ranunculus tricophyllus* and *Ranunculus fluitans*. In the United States, crowfoot is the common name given to a species of GRASS that grows in warm regions. Family Gramineae; species *Dactyloctenium aegyptium*.

crown of thorns
Member of a family of shrubs and trees that grow in tropical and warm regions. Most members of the family have thorns, useful timber and edible fruits, which are often dried or used in cough-cures. The crown of thorns is possibly the shrub from which was made the thorn crown said to have been worn by Jesus Christ. Family Rhamnaceae; species *Ziziphus spina-cristi*.

▼ **crystal** Frost on ice crystals, as shown here, illuminates their form. The shape of the ice crystals depends on the temperature at which the crystals formed. The size of the crystals depends on the rate of crystallization.

▶ **cuckoo, Eurasian** The common Eurasian cuckoo (*Cuculus canorus*) is famous for its parasitic behaviour. The female lays its egg in a smaller host's nest. The young cuckoo ejects its smaller nest mates and receives all the attention of its foster parents.

crust
Thin outermost solid layer of the EARTH. The crust represents less than 1% of the Earth's volume and varies in thickness from as little as 5km (3mi) beneath the oceans to about 70km (45mi) beneath mountain chains such as the Himalayas. **Oceanic crust** is generally 7km (4.5mi) thick and basaltic in composition, whereas **continental crust** is mainly between 30–40km (20–25mi) thick and of granitic composition. The crust is defined by its seismicity (the velocity of EARTHQUAKE waves that pass through it). The lower boundary of the crust is defined by a marked increase in seismic velocity, known as the Mohorovičić discontinuity. *See also* MOHO; SIAL; SIMA

crustacean
Any member of the class Crustacea, a class of about 30,000 species of ARTHROPOD. The class includes the DECAPODS (CRABS, LOBSTERS, SHRIMPS and CRAYFISH), ISOPODS (PILL MILLIPEDES and WOODLICE) and many varied forms, most of which have no common names. Most crustaceans are aquatic (marine or freshwater) and breathe through gills or the body surface. They are typically covered by a hard EXOSKELETON. They range in size from the Japanese SPIDER CRAB, which grows to 3m (12ft) across, to the ocean PLANKTON, as small as 1mm (0.04in) in diameter.

crustal plate
See PLATE TECTONICS

cryolite (kryolite)
Brittle, icy-looking, red, brown or black halide mineral, sodium-aluminium fluoride (Na_3AlF_6), found in pegmatite DYKES (Greenland has the only large deposit) and used in aluminium processing. It occurs as crystals in the monoclinic system, occasionally the cubic system, sometimes as granular masses. The crystals are frequently twinned. Cryolite is also a source of aluminium salts and fluorides.

cryptogam
Name given by early botanists to a group of plants that included the BRYOPHYTA (MOSSES and LIVERWORTS) and Filicinophyta (FERNS). The name derives from the fact that these spore-bearing plants do not have prominent organs of reproduction as do the flowering plants. *See also* PHANEROGAM

cryptophyte
Plants that grow on ice or snow. They are mostly BACTERIA and ALGAE but include FUNGI and MOSSES. The presence of some algal SPECIES may colour the ice and snow. For example, some species of chlamydomonas make snow appear red.

crystal
Solid with a regular geometrical form and with characteristic angles between its faces, having limited chemical composition. The structure of a crystal, such as common salt, is based upon a regular 3-D arrangement of atoms, ions or molecules (an ionic or CRYSTAL LATTICE). Crystals are produced when a substance passes from a gaseous or liquid PHASE to a solid state, or comes out of solution by evaporation or precipitation. The rate of CRYSTALLIZATION determines the size of crystal formed. Slow-cooling produces large crystals, whereas fast-cooling produces small crystals.

crystal lattice
Three-dimensional arrangement of atoms, ions or molecules in a crystalline substance. The term is sometimes used in a more restricted sense to denote the diagrammatic abstraction of the pattern in which the atoms, ions or molecules are positioned. *See also* CRYSTAL

crystallization
Process of forming CRYSTALS by a substance passing from a gas or liquid to the solid state (sublimation or fusion) or coming out of solution (precipitation or evaporation). In the fusion method a solid is melted by heating, and crystals form as the melt cools and solidifies. Ice crystals and monoclinic sulphur are formed in this way. Crystallization is an important laboratory and industrial technique for purifying and separating compounds.

crystallography
Study of the formation and structure of crystalline substances. It includes the study of CRYSTAL formation, chemical bonding in crystals and the physical properties of solids. In particular, crystallography is concerned with the internal structure of crystals including substances that were not previously thought capable of forming crystals, such as DNA.

cubomedusan
See BOX JELLYFISH

cuckoo
Name given to some members of a large family (c.140 species) of medium to large birds, many of which are brood parasites. Cuckoos mainly feed on insects, but also in some cases frogs, lizards and other small reptiles. Their plumage is usually dull brown or grey. Family Cuculidae.

cuckoo, channel-billed
Large cuckoo, grey above and white below, with a huge pale bill. It is found in forests and tall trees across Australia, with some birds wintering in New Guinea and Indonesia. It feeds on insects, fruit and figs. Length: 60cm (24in). Family Cuculidae; species *Scythrops novaehollandiae*.

cuckoo, didric
Small cuckoo found in dry woodland, savanna, bush

and suburbia in tropical Africa. The male is coppery green with white wing flashes and breast; the female is brown with white wing flashes. It is a brood parasite. The didric cuckoo feeds on insects, mainly caterpillars. Length: 18cm (7in). Family Cuculidae; species *Chrysococcyx caprius*.

cuckoo, Eurasian
Medium-sized cuckoo. It is grey or reddish-brown, with a white breast barred black. It is best known for the two-tone call of the male in spring. The Eurasian cuckoo is found in woods and open country in Europe and temperate and subtropical Asia, wintering in Africa and India. It is a brood parasite. It feeds on insects, particularly caterpillars. Length: *c*.33cm (*c*.13in). Family Cuculidae; species *Cuculus canorus*.

cuckoo, great spotted
Medium to large, elegant cuckoo. Its grey back is spotted white, and its white breast has a conspicuous crest of light grey. It is found in open country in parts of Africa, SE Europe and Asia. The great spotted cuckoo parasitizes members of the crow family. It feeds on insects. Length: 38–40cm (15–16in). Family Cuculidae; species *Clamator glandarius*.

cuckoo, yellow-billed
Medium-sized cuckoo with a brown back and white underside. It is found in open country in North America and the West Indies, wintering in South America. The yellow-billed cuckoo normally builds its own nest. It feeds on insects, caterpillars, fruit and berries. Length: 30cm (12in). Family Cuculidae; species *Coccyzus americanus*.

cuckoo, Klaas'
Small cuckoo. The male is a bright metallic green above, with a white breast; the female is dull green and heavily barred. The Klaas' cuckoo is found in bushveld and woodland, mainly in E and S Africa. It feeds on insects and caterpillars. Length: 17cm (7in). Family Cuculidae; species *Chrysococcyx klaas*.

cuckoo, fan-tailed
Medium-sized cuckoo. It is dark grey above and fawn below, with a wedge-shaped tail. The fan-tailed cuckoo is found in Australian forests and woodlands away from the arid regions. It feeds on insects and fruit. Length: 24–28cm (9–11in). Family Cuculidae; species *Cuculus flabelliformis*.

cuckooflower
Pink to white, spring-flowering, wild plant that is common in damp pastures and by streams throughout temperate regions. Its name is thought to refer to the time of flowering, April and May, when the cuckoo is around. The edible leaves are often eaten as a substitute for watercress. Family Cruciferae; species *Cardamine pratensis*.

cuckoopint (wake robin or lords-and-ladies)
Tuberous plant native to Europe. It has arrow-shaped leaves and sends up stout SPATHES, each of which unfurls to reveal a SPADIX that gives off a fetid carrion scent, attractive to insects. Red poisonous berries form as the spathe dies off. Family Araceae; species *Arum maculatum*.

cuckoo-roller
Medium-sized bird, classified in a family of its own. The male is grey with a copper sheen above. The female has black bars on its neck and brown underparts spotted with black. The cuckoo-roller is found in forest and brushland in Madagascar and the Comoros, often in small parties. It feeds on

◄ **cucumber** Large, watery fruits are a common feature of the cucumber (*Cucumis sativus*) and its relatives. The plants are generally large and covered in coarse hairs; many species have tendrils that help them climb.

chameleons, locusts, insects and small caterpillars. Length: 43cm (17in). Family Leptosomatidae; species *Leptosomus discolor*.

cuckoo-shrike
Member of a family of *c*.70 species of small- to medium-sized, arboreal birds. They are shrike-like in build, but with cuckoo-like plumage. Cuckoo-shrikes are usually gregarious and are found in tropical regions of Africa, Asia and Australia. Family Campephagidae.

cuckoo-shrike, black
Cuckoo-shrike found in bush and woodland in tropical Africa. The male is black with a yellow patch on its shoulder; the female is black with a yellow back and white underside with black barring. It feeds on insects, caterpillars, fruit and berries. Length: 22cm (9in). Family Campephagidae; species *Campephaga flava*.

cuckoo-shrike, black-faced
Medium-sized cuckoo-shrike found in open woodland and forest in India, Southeast Asia and Australia. It has a black face and grey upperparts and is pale below. It feeds on insects, fruit and berries. Length: 33cm (13in). Family Campephagidae; species *Coracina novaehollandiae*.

cuckoo-shrike, blue
Cuckoo-shrike found from Sierra Leone to the Democratic Republic of the Congo. The male has entirely blue plumage. It is a shy forest bird.

Length: 22cm (9in). Family Campephagidae; species *Coracina azurea*.

cuculiform
Member of the bird order Cuculiformes. A small order, it includes CUCKOOS, ROADRUNNERS, TOURACOS and various related birds.

cucumber
Trailing annual vine covered in coarse hairs; it has yellow flowers. The immature fruit is eaten raw or pickled. Family Cucurbitaceae; species *Cucumis sativus*.

cumacean
Any of many species of small, marine CRUSTACEANS resembling small tadpoles. The cumacean's head is enclosed in a carapace, and the rest of the body is slender. It is found on coastal sediments, mainly in shallow water. Cumaceans feed on organic detritus and very small organisms; they in turn are a major part of the diet of many fish. Length: to *c*.30mm (*c*.1.2in), many species are smaller. Order Cumacea.

cumin
Annual herb native to the Middle East and widely cultivated for its seed-like fruit, which is used as a food flavouring. It has a branching stem and small pink or white flowers. Height: to 15cm (6in). Family Apiaceae/Umbelliferae; species *Cuminum cyminum*.

cumulonimbus
See CLOUD

cumulus
See CLOUD

cupressus
Any member of the genus *Cupressus*, more commonly known as CYPRESS.

cuprite
Reddish-brown, brittle, translucent oxide mineral, cuprous oxide (Cu_2O). It is formed by the OXIDATION of other ores such as copper sulphide and so is commonly found near the surface. It has octahedral, dodecahedral and cubic crystals; it also occurs in grains. Hardness 3.5–4; r.d. 6.1.

curassow
Any of *c*.12 species of medium to large birds found in Central and South America. Most curassows are tree-dwellers in rainforests, where they are frugivores; the larger species, however, are ground feed-

▲ **curassow, great** A poor flier, the great curassow (*Crax rubra*) spends most of its time on the forest floor. The male is mostly black, whereas the female is brown and rust-coloured and has a crest with black-and-white markings.

C

99

curassow, great

C

ers and take insects and frogs as well as fruit. Most species are black with heavy bills, a bright-coloured cere (swelling at the base of the upper beak) and a spiky crest. Family Cracidae (part); genera *Crax* and *Nothocrax*.

curassow, great

Large bird found in forests from Mexico to Ecuador. It has mostly black plumage, with a white belly; its pale bill has an orange-yellow cere. The great curassow feeds on fruit taken from the forest floor. Length: 76–96cm (30–38in). Family Cracidae; species *Crax rubra*.

curassow, nocturnal

Curassow with rusty brown plumage. It utters a cooing song and is mainly active during the night. Length: 66cm (26in). Family Cracidae; species *Nothocrax urumutum*.

curlew

Any of a group of eight species of medium to large shorebirds. Curlews are usually brown above and pale below, with scalloped or flecked plumage and, most noticeably, a long, down-curved bill. Curlews

are often seen on open mudflats at the coast, feeding on aquatic worms. Family Scolopacidae (part); genus *Numenius*.

curlew, Eskimo

Small curlew that is one of the rarest of all birds; it may already be extinct. It bred on the Canadian Arctic tundra and was seen in the E United States, Texas and the Great Plains on its way to its wintering grounds in Argentina. The Eskimo curlew fed on marine worms, grubs, snails and berries. Length: 33–36cm (13–14in). Family Scolopacidae; species *Numenius borealis*.

currawong, pied

Medium to large bird found in E Australia, in open forest, woodland, scrub, agricultural and urban land. It is black with white wing patches, rump and tail tip. Its name comes from one of its strange calls. It is omnivorous, feeding on insects, fruit and young birds. Length: 41–51cm (16–20in). Family Cracticidae; species *Strepera graculina*.

currant

Any of several mainly deciduous shrubs and their

fruits, which are rich in vitamin C. Black, red and white currants are included in the genus *Ribes*; they are popular plants and are cultivated widely. The fruits are used in pies, preserves and syrups. Family Grossulariaceae.

current

Broad, slow drift of moving water, distinguishable from the water surrounding it by differences in temperature and/or salinity. A current can be caused by prevailing winds that sweep surface water along, forming drift currents. Currents are affected by the CORIOLIS EFFECT, by the shape of the ocean bed or by nearby land masses. Currents at a deeper level are the result of variation in density of the water, which in turn varies according to the temperature and salinity.

cuscus (phalanger)

Large, tree-dwelling, nocturnal MARSUPIAL with a

▼ **current** Moving immense quantities of energy as well as billions of tonnes of water every hour, the oceanic currents are a vital part of the great "heat engine" that drives the climatic conditions of the Earth.

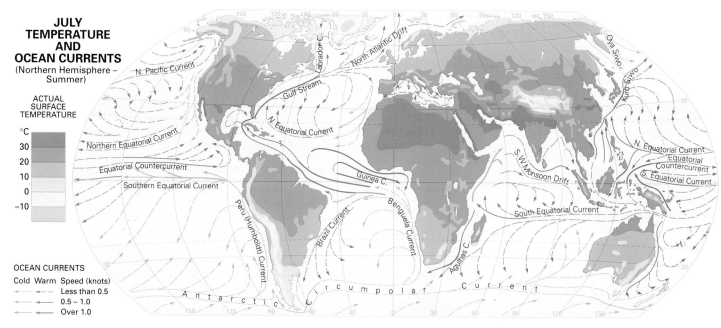

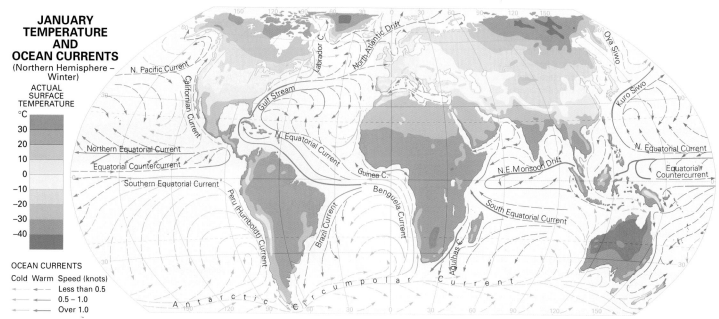

▲ **cuttlefish** The male cuttlefish courts a female (A) by displaying to her, often blushing red as he does so. The two animals then join (B), either side by side or head-to-head, with their tentacles entwined. The male then transfers a package of sperm – known as a spermatophore – to the female's mantle cavity using a modified tentacle, called the hectocotylus, which may then drop off. The male cuttlefish then dies (C), and the female lays her eggs on the sea-bed (D) before she too dies.

long, prehensile tail and sharp claws for climbing. It eats leaves and fruit but will also take eggs and insects. Ten species are found in a range of rainforest and woodland habitats in Australia, New Guinea and neighbouring islands. Head-body length: 34–70cm (13–28in); tail: 30–50cm (12–20in). Family Phalangeridae.

custard apple (soursop, sweetsop)
Large, fleshy, sweet, edible fruit of several species of small tree. Custard apple trees are native to the New World tropics. Family Annonaceae; species include *Annona reticulata* and *Annona squamosa*.

cuticle
Exposed outer layer of an animal. In humans this refers to the EPIDERMIS, especially the dead skin at the edge of fingers. In botany, cuticle refers to the waxy layer on the outer surface of the epidermal cells

▲ **cycad** Like conifers, cycads bear either a female (A) or male (B) cone. However the mobility of the sperm, and thus fertilization, requires a wet environment. The spores develop into gametophytes.

After fertilization, the female cones produce seeds that will grow into sporophytes.

of the leaves and stems of vascular plants. It helps to prevent excessive water loss.

cuttlefish
Cephalopod MOLLUSC related to the SQUID and OCTOPUS. Like squid, cuttlefish swim rapidly by the propulsion of a jet of water forced out through a siphon. They have ten sucker-covered arms on the head, two of which are much longer than the rest. Their flattened bodies contain the familiar chalky cuttlebone. Capable of rapid colour changes, they can also eject blue-black "ink" as a means of protection. Family Sepiidae; species *Sepia officinalis*.

cutworm
CATERPILLAR that attacks plants and crops, cutting through their stems at groundlevel. Some species of cutworm attack the roots of plants. Cutworms are mainly nocturnal. They are usually the larvae of NOCTUID moths belonging to the genus *Agrotis*. Length: to 5cm (2in). Family Noctuidae.

Cuvier, Georges, Baron (1769–1832)
French geologist and zoologist, a founder of comparative anatomy and palaeontology. His scheme of classification stressed the form of organs and their correlation within the body. He applied this system of classification to fossils, and came to reject the theory of the gradual development of the Earth and animals, favouring instead a theory of catastrophic changes. *See also* PUNCTUATED EQUILIBRIUM

cyanobacterium (formerly blue-green alga)
BACTERIUM that is distinguished by the presence of the green pigment CHLOROPHYLL and the blue pigment phycocyanin. Cyanobacteria perform PHOTOSYNTHESIS. Analysis of the genetic material of CHLOROPLASTS shows that they evolved from cyanobacteria by ENDOSYMBIOSIS. Many cyanobacteria perform NITROGEN FIXATION. They occur in soil, mud and deserts; they are most abundant in lakes, rivers and oceans. Some produce toxic blooms.

cycad
Any member of the phylum Cycadophyta, primitive palm-like shrubs and trees that grow in tropical and subtropical regions. They have feathery palm- or fern-like leaves (poisonous in most species) at the top of stout (usually unbranched) stems. In addition to their main roots, cycads also have special roots containing CYANOBACTERIA that carry out NITROGEN FIXATION. Cycads first flourished c.225 million years ago. Most of the 100 or so surviving species are less than c.6m (c.20ft) tall.

cyclamen (sowbread)
Any member of the *Cyclamen* genus, found through-

out the Mediterranean region as far east as Iran. Cyclamens are the only members of the primrose family to have CORMS. The starch-containing corms are often eaten by pigs, hence the common name for the plants. The flowers come in white and pink shades and have petals that are bent backwards; the sticky seeds are often dispersed by ants. Many cultivars (cultivated varieties) make attractive house or garden plants. Family Primulaceae; species include *Cyclamen hederifolium* and *Cyclamen persicum*.

cyclone (low)
System of atmospheric low pressure that occurs when a cold air mass moving s from the Arctic meets a warm air mass moving N from the tropics to form a circulating air mass. A cyclone is characterized by relatively low pressure at the centre, and by counterclockwise wind movement in the Northern Hemisphere and by clockwise motion in the Southern Hemisphere. There are two types of cyclone: the DEPRESSION, associated with temperate latitudes; and the tropical cyclone, which is much more violent but usually affects a smaller area. *See also* ANTICYCLONE

cyclops
Any member of a genus of common, freshwater, predatory, copepod CRUSTACEANS. Transparent and bullet-shaped, the cyclops derives its name from its large median eye. Gravid (pregnant) females carry two large egg sacs. Length: to 1.6mm (0.06in). Order Cyclopoida; genus *Cyclops*.

cymbidium
Any member of the genus *Cymbidium*, which comprises tropical ORCHIDS with large, fragrant flowers. Cymbidiums are widely cultivated for use as buttonholes and as ornamental pot plants. The flowers have had other uses in the past: in China the flowers of one species were infused and used as an eye treatment. Family Orchidaceae; species include *Cymbidium ensifolium* and *Cymbidium virescens*.

cynodont
Member of an extinct group of advanced reptile-like tetrapods, which evolved in late Permian times. Cynodonts were mostly carnivores, such as

◄ **cyclamen** Often cultivated for its pink or white flowers, the cyclamen has distinctive petals that are twisted at the base and bent back.

► **cypress, false** The
Lawson cypress
(*Chamaecyparis lawsonia*) can
grow to a height of 60m
(200ft), and live for up to 600
years. Also known as the
Oregon cedar, this tree is
native to Oregon and
California, United States,
where it is grown for timber
and for its natural beauty.

C

Cynognathus, and include the ancestors of the mammals. They became abundant in the Triassic and died out in late Jurassic times.

cypress

Tall, evergreen tree native to North America and Eurasia. It has scale-like leaves, roundish cones and a distinctive symmetrical shape. The wood is durable and fragrant. It is of value commercially, used for timber and for scenting soap. Height: 6–24m (20–80ft). Family Cupressaceae; genus *Cupressus*; there are *c.*20 species, including *Cupressus lusitanica* and *Cupressus arizonica*.

cypress, false

Any of several species of tree that make up the genus *Chameacyparis*. They are native to North America and E Asia. The cones of the false cypress are smaller than those of the true CYPRESS. Family Cupressaceae; species include *Chameacyparis lawsonia* (Lawson cypress).

cypripedium

Any member of the genus *Cypripedium*, more commonly known as LADY'S SLIPPER.

cytochromes

Proteins containing haem (heme), an iron group, as in HAEMOGLOBIN. They are fundamental to the process of RESPIRATION in all living cells that need atmospheric oxygen.

cytokinin (kinetin or kinin)

Any of a group of PLANT HORMONES that stimulate CELL DIVISION. Cytokinins work in conjunction with AUXINS to promote swelling and division in the plant cells producing lateral buds. They can also slow down the aging process in plants, encourage seeds to germinate and plants to flower, and are involved in plant responses to drought and waterlogging. They are used commercially to produce seedless grapes, to stimulate germination of barley in brewing, and to prolong the life of green-leaf vegetables. Cytokinins, such as zeatin, are derived from ADENINE.

cytology

Study of living CELLS and their structure, behaviour and function. The discipline began with the English scientist Robert Hooke's microscopic studies of cork in 1665, and the various forms of microscope are still the main tools of cytology. In the 19th century, a cell theory was developed which suggested that cells are the basic units of organisms. Recently cytological study has focused on the chemistry of cell components (cytochemistry).

cytoplasm

Jelly-like matter inside a CELL and surrounding the NUCLEUS. Cytoplasm has a complex constituency and contains various bodies known as organelles, which have specific metabolic functions. The proteins needed for cell growth and repair are produced in the cytoplasm. *See also* METABOLISM

cytosine

Nitrogen-containing, organic base. Cytosine was first isolated in 1894. Derivatives of cytosine made in the body are important in cellular METABOLISM and in the formation of RNA and DNA, thus they are vital for the retention of genetic characteristics. *See also* GENE

D

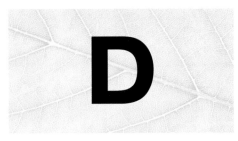

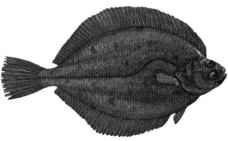

▲ **dab** Living on or near the sea bed, the dab (*Limanda limanda*) feeds on crustaceans. As with all flatfish, the dab's spine twists as it grows, such that its eyes and mouth are on the upperside, which is green with rust-coloured spots; the underside is white.

dab

Marine FLATFISH; a valuable food fish. The upper, "sighted" side is brown with darker spots; the underside is almost white. It is found in the N Atlantic and N Pacific oceans. Length: to 25cm (10in). Family Pleuronectidae; species *Limanda limanda*.

dace

Any of several small freshwater fish of the CARP family. The common European dace (*Leuciscus leuciscus*) is silvery and can grow up to 30cm (12in) long. The Moapa dace (*Moapa coriacea*) is an endangered species. Family Cyprinidae.

daffodil (lenten lily)

Bulbous flowering plant, native to Europe and the Mediterranean region and naturalized elsewhere. Many cultivated varieties have also been naturalized, and there are many ornamental hybrids. The outer sepals of the flower are typically a paler yellow than the trumpet-shaped corona. Family Liliaceae; species *Narcissus pseudonarcissus*.

dahlia

Any member of the *Dahlia* genus, which comprises perennial plants with tuberous roots and large flowers. The common garden dahlia (*Dahlia pinnata*) has been developed into more than 2000 varieties. Height: to 1.5m (5ft). Family Asteraceae/Compositae.

daisy

Any of several members of the family Asteraceae/Compositae, especially the common English garden daisy, *Bellis perennis*. It has long stalks with solitary flower heads, each of which has a large, yellow central disc and small, radiating, white, petal-like florets.

▶ **dahlia** Numbering over 7000 varieties, the dahlia is named after the Swiss botanist Anders Dahl. Most varieties have been developed from the original S American species *Dahlia pinnata*.

Dale, Sir Henry Hallett (1875–1968)

British physiologist who shared the 1936 Nobel Prize for physiology or medicine with Otto LOEWI for discoveries relating to the chemical transmission of NERVE IMPULSES. Dale found that the chemical acetylcholine served to transmit nerve impulses across the tiny gap (SYNAPSE) from one NEURONE to another. His writings include *Adventures in Physiology* (1953) and *An Autumn Gleaning* (1954).

Dam, Carl Peter Henrik (1895–1976)

Danish biologist. In 1934 he discovered vitamin K, the fat-soluble vitamin needed for blood clotting. He isolated it from hempseed and the seeds of other plants, and he also discovered it in liver. For this work, he received the 1943 Nobel Prize for physiology or medicine, which he shared with Edward DOISY. In addition, he examined the roles of other vitamins and lipids.

damping-off disease

Disease of seeds or seedling plants caused by many types of fungi, including species of *Pythium* and *Rhizoctonia*. In the most striking form, known as postemergence damping-off, young seedlings topple over as a result of stem rot at the soil line. Damping-off fungi may also invade a seed before it sprouts (known as germination failure) or attack a seedling before it reaches the soil surface (preemergence damping-off).

damselfish

Tropical and subtropical, marine, perch-like fish. It is common on coral reefs, especially in the Indo-Pacific. CLOWNFISH are damselfish. Many species are brightly coloured. Family Pomacentridae; there are 28 genera and 315 species.

damselfly

Delicate insect resembling and related to the DRAGONFLY. Almost all have a slender, elongated, blue abdomen and a pair of membranous wings that are held vertically over the body when at rest. Length: to 5cm (2in). Order Odonata.

damson

Small tree and its edible fruit. The name is often applied to varieties of PLUM (*Prunus domestica*). The fleshy DRUPE is generally borne in clusters. It has a tart flavour and is often made into jam. Family Rosaceae. The **damson-plum** of tropical America is a separate species, *Chrysophyllum oliviforme*. Family Sapotaceae.

dandelion

Widespread perennial weed, with leaves growing from the base and yellow composite flowers. The dandelion reproduces by means of parachute seeds. The leaves are used in salads, the flowers in winemaking. Family Asteraceae/COMPOSITAE; species *Taraxacum officinale*.

daphne

Any member of a genus of *c.*50 species of deciduous or evergreen shrubs, which grow naturally in habitats ranging from lowland woodland to mountains in Europe, North Africa and S Asia. They have laurel-like leaves and fragrant, long-tubed, four-petalled flowers in colours that range from white through yellow and pink to lilac. Many species are grown in gardens for their flowers, foliage or glossy, spherical fruits. All parts of the plant are poisonous. Family Thymelaeaceae; genus *Daphne*; species include *Daphne laureola* (spurge laurel).

daphnia

See WATER FLEA

dark reaction (light-independent reaction)

One of the two distinct phases of PHOTOSYNTHESIS; the other being the LIGHT-DEPENDENT REACTION. During the dark reaction, which can take place in light or in darkness, carbon dioxide is reduced to carbohydrate (sugars) by means of the CALVIN CYCLE.

darter (anhinga)

Large aquatic bird with a snake-like neck, dagger-shaped bill, long wings and a very long tail. It is an expert diver and hunts fish underwater. It often swims with its body submerged and only its sinuous head and neck above water. The darter is widespread in Asia, Australia and South America. Length: 85–97cm (33–38in). Family Anhingidae; species *Anhinga melanogaster*.

darter

Any of *c.*100 species of freshwater, bottom-dwelling fish found in clear streams of E North America. Darters are slender and brightly coloured and capable of darting quickly through the water. They feed mainly on small aquatic animals. Length: to 23cm (9in). Family Percidae.

darter

Any member of a family of DRAGONFLIES commonly found around ponds. The darter's flight is fast and darting, hence its name. Some species show sexual dimorphism in their coloration, with the males being pale blue. Adult male darters are highly territorial. The females deposit their eggs in water and the larvae are aquatic, feeding in the bottom mud and detritus. Adult wingspan: 45–75mm (1.8–3in). Order Odonata; family Libellulidae; genera *Libellula*, *Sympetrum* and *Orthetrum*.

Darwin, Charles Robert (1809–82)

British naturalist, originator of a theory of EVOLUTION based on NATURAL SELECTION. In 1831 he joined a round-the-world expedition on HMS BEAGLE as the ship's naturalist. The many observations that he made of the FLORA and FAUNA of South America (especially the Galápagos Islands) formed the basis of his work on animal variation. The development of a similar theory by Alfred WALLACE led Darwin to present his ideas to the Linnean Society in 1858, and in 1859 Darwin pub-

▲ **Darwin, Charles Robert** Darwin's theory of evolution by natural selection came to have a huge impact on natural and life sciences. It was highly controversial in his lifetime as it fundamentally challenged orthodox theological thinking.

D

lished *The Origin of Species*, widely accepted as one of the world's most influential science books. Darwin argued that organisms reproduce more than is necessary to replenish their population, creating competition for survival. Opposed to the ideas of LAMARCK, Darwin argued that each organism was a unique combination of genetic variations. The variations that prove helpful in the struggle to survive are passed down to the offspring of the survivors. He termed this process natural selection. Darwin did not distinguish between ACQUIRED CHARACTERISTICS and genetic variations. Instead, NEO-DARWINISM supplemented his ideas with modern research into HEREDITY, especially MUTATION.

Darwin, Erasmus (1731–1802)
British physician, grandfather of Charles DARWIN. His *Zoonomia or the Laws of Organic Life* (1794–96) advanced the theory of EVOLUTION.

Darwinism
See EVOLUTION

dasyurid
Any member of a family of small- to medium-sized, carnivorous marsupials. Most dasyurids are mouse-like, with the exception of the larger QUOLLS, MARSUPIAL CATS and the TASMANIAN DEVIL. They are found in a wide range of habitats, from desert to woodland, throughout Australia, Tasmania and New Guinea. Head-body length: 5–65cm (2–26in); tail: 6–26cm (2–10in). Family Dasyuridae.

date palm
Tree, native to w Asia and North Africa, that produces huge bunches of sweet edible berries known as dates. Like most PALM trees, it has a single, unbranched trunk covered with the scars and remains of old leaves. New leaves, up to 6m (20ft) long, grow as fern-like fronds from the top of the trunk. Date palms are DIOECIOUS, meaning that male and female flowers are produced on separate plants. Height: to 30m (100ft). Family Arecaceae/Palmae; species *Phoenix dactylifera*.

date plum
Spreading, deciduous tree native to China. It has long (*c*.12cm/5in), lance-shaped, glossy, dark green leaves and tiny, bell-shaped, green flowers tinged

▲ **date palm** Now grown as an ornament as well as for its fruit, the date palm has been cultivated for over 4000 years. It bears clusters of as many as 1000 dates which are often dried and contain more than 50% sugar.

▲ **death cap** A mycorrhizal fungus, the death cap (*Amanita phalloides*) lives on the roots of live trees, providing water, nitrogen, phosphates and other nutrients to the vascular cells of the tree roots in exchange for carbohydrates.

with red. The date plum is grown in gardens for its colourful autumn fruits, which look like plums but are inedible. Height: to 10m (33ft). Family Ebenaceae; species *Diospyros lotus*.

datura
Any member of a genus of North American plants with large, trumpet-shaped, sweet-smelling flowers. Some produce useful drugs, others are ornamentals. Thorn apple (*Datura stramonium*) is a poisonous, annual weed, with foul-smelling leaves. Its large, white or violet, trumpet-shaped flowers are succeeded by round prickly fruits. It is the source of a drug used in the treatment of asthma. Family Solanaceae (NIGHTSHADE); genus *Datura*.

Daubenton, Louis Jean Marie (1716–1800)
French comparative anatomist. He assisted Georges BUFFON with *Histoire Naturelle* (1749–1804). His research on mammalian skeletal structure aided the development of comparative anatomy into a special branch of study.

Dawkins, Richard (1941–)
English zoologist. Dawkins studied at the University of Oxford before accepting a teaching post in California, where he remained until returning to Oxford in 1970. He is currently Charles Simonyi Professor of the Public Understanding of Science at Oxford University. Dawkins' first popular science book, *The Selfish Gene* (1976), examines animal behaviour in the context of EVOLUTION, proposing that genes govern behaviour in order to survive. *The Blind Watchmaker* (1986) is an introduction to NEO-DARWINISM.

dawn redwood
Conical, deciduous, coniferous tree that is found in the damp valley forests of central China. In autumn the dawn redwood's broad, soft, bright-green needles turn gold or red-brown and fall. It produces small, light-brown cones. Until its discovery in 1941, the dawn redwood tree was known only from fossils that are two million years old. Height: to *c*.10m (*c*.33ft). Family Taxodiaceae; species *Metasequoia glyptostroboides*.

day flower (widow's tears)
Any member of a genus of plants from s Africa, Asia and the Americas. They are clump-forming annuals or perennials, with lance-shaped leaves. They produce small, saucer-shaped, three-petalled, green or

blue flowers, each of which lasts less than one day. Family Commelinaceae; genus *Commelina*; there are *c*.100 species.

daylily
Any of *c*.15 species of herbaceous, perennial plants that grow from bulbs or rhizomes, producing clumps of long, strap-like leaves and spikes of large, six-petalled flowers, each of which lasts just one day. In the wild, daylilies grow around forest margins in China, Korea and Japan. About 30,000 garden cultivars have been produced. Family Liliaceae; genus *Hemerocallis*.

dead-leaf butterfly
See BUTTERFLY, DEAD-LEAF

deadly nightshade (belladonna)
Poisonous, perennial plant native to Europe and w Asia. It has large leaves, purple flowers and black berries. ALKALOIDS, such as atropine, are obtained from its roots and leaves. Family Solanaceae; species *Atropa belladonna*.

dead man's fingers
Fungus with an irregular, finger-like fruiting body that is 3–8cm (1–3in) high and 1–3cm (0.4–1in) wide. It is black with a wrinkled or roughened surface and white flesh. A common fungus, it usually grows on the stumps of beech trees. It is not edible. Phylum Ascomycota; species *Xylaria polymorpha*.

deadnettle
Any member of a genus of *c*.50 species of low-growing annuals or perennials, which grow in a range of habitats, from dry scrub to moist woodland, from Europe across North Africa to Asia. Deadnettles have square stems and oval or kidney-shaped leaves, the toothed edges of which often have coloured markings. The hooded flowers, borne on leafy spikes, may be white, yellow, pink or purple. Some of the more colourful species are grown in gardens as ground cover. Family Labiatae; species include *Lamium purpureum* (red deadnettle) and *Lamium maculatum* (spotted deadnettle).

deamination
Removal of an amino (–NH$_2$) group from a compound, particularly an AMINO ACID. It takes place in the liver of animals, where enzymes cause the amino group to be converted into ammonia, which is either excreted as it is or converted into urea or uric acid and then excreted in the urine.

death cap (deadly amanita)
Highly poisonous fungus that grows in woodland. It has a yellowish-green cap and a white stem with a drooping ring and sheathed base. If eaten, the poison causes great pain, serious liver damage and, in most cases, death. Phylum Basidiomycota; species *Amanita phalloides*.

deathwatch beetle
Small BEETLE that tunnels through wood. It makes a faint ticking sound once said to presage death. It is the mating signal of the female as it taps against the wood. Length: to 9mm (0.3in). Family Anobiidae; species *Xestobium rufovillosum*.

decapod
CRUSTACEAN belonging to the Decapoda order, which includes CRABS, CRAYFISH, LOBSTERS, SHRIMPS and PRAWNS. Most decapods are marine, with a few freshwater, terrestrial and amphibious exceptions. The first three pairs of thoracic

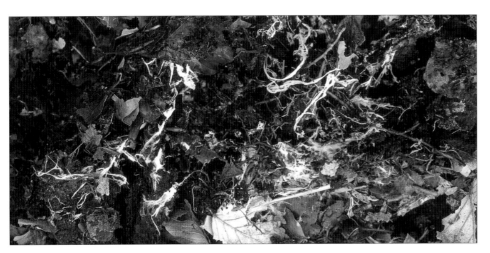

▲ **decay** Fungal mycelia can clearly be seen on the leaf litter. The fungus feeds by secreting digestive enzymes onto the dead leaves and other organic matter and absorbing the soluble products. As a result of this process, the leaves are decomposed into the simpler compounds from which they are made. Thus, vital nutrients are returned to the soil and to the ecosystems that rely on them. Without agents of decay, nutrients would remain in the dead bodies of plants and animals without being returned to the food chain.

appendages are modified, and the remaining five pairs (from which derives the name – Greek *deka* "ten" and *podos* "foot") are legs. Most decapods are predators or scavengers, important in the ecosystem and for food. Order Decapoda.

decay (rot)
Partial or complete deterioration of a substance caused by natural changes. Plant rot, caused by soil-borne bacteria and fungi, can affect any plant part, making it spongy, watery, hard or dry. *See also* DECOMPOSITION

deceiver
Common fungus that is so named because it is variable in appearance and thus difficult to recognize at first sight. The cap may be tawny to brick-red in colour, with a tough, fibrous stem of the same colour. It inhabits heaths and woods and is edible. Phylum Basidiomycota; species *Laccaria laccata*.

deciduous
Term describing the annual or seasonal loss of all leaves from a TREE or shrub; it is the opposite of EVERGREEN.

declination, magnetic (deviation)
Amount by which the direction indicated by a magnetic compass differs from the direction of true north. It arises because the magnetic north pole is not coincident with the true North Pole. As a result, declination varies from place to place on the Earth's surface. Also, because the north magnetic pole slowly moves over time, declination varies from year to year.

► **deer, fallow** These medium-sized deer are often kept in parks or zoos. The females (does) and males (bucks) live separately, except during the autumn mating season. The does usually bear one fawn the following June.

decomposer
Saprophytic FUNGI and BACTERIA that break down the complex organic compounds of dead organisms and waste products into simple components such as carbon dioxide, water and inorganic ions. In so doing, the decomposers contribute to the recycling of nutrients. *See also* FOOD CHAIN; SAPROPHYTE

decomposition
Natural degradation of organic matter into simpler substances, such as carbon dioxide and water. Organisms of decay are usually bacteria and fungi. Decomposition recycles nutrients by releasing them back into the ecosystem.

deep scattering layer (DSL)
Layer between the surface and the bottom of the open ocean that scatters the sound waves from sonar equipment, sending back echoes. It is found in all deep oceans of the world except the Arctic and Antarctic. It rises to the surface at night and sinks again by day. The phenomenon appears to be due to the vertical MIGRATION of deep-living fish.

deer
Even-toed UNGULATE with a graceful body and long legs. In most species males have antlers that are shed every year; they vary from simple spikes to complex branched structures. Females tend to be smaller than males. Young deer are often spotted for camouflage. Family Cervidae.

deer, axis (chital, spotted deer)
Deer that is native to India and Sri Lanka and has been introduced in Australia and the United States. Its coat is reddish with white spots; males have long antlers. Preferring newly sprouting grass, the axis deer is primarily a grazer, living close to tree or shrub cover. Shoulder height: 91cm (36in); tail: 20cm (8in). Family Cervidae; subfamily Cervinae; species *Axis axis*.

deer, fallow
Deer that is native to Europe, Asia Minor and Iran and has been successfully introduced in Australia and New Zealand. Fallow deer prefer woodland but will graze in open grassland close to tree cover. Their coat colour varies widely, but in summer it tends to be brownish with pale spots and pale underneath, grey-brown without spots in the winter. The antlers are palmate or flattened towards the ends. Shoulder height (males): 90–95cm (35–37in). Family Cervidae; subfamily Cervinae; species *Dama dama*.

deer, hog
Unusual member of the deer family. It has a short face and legs and slender antlers. It lives in grasslands in N India and Southeast Asia and has been introduced to Australia. The hog deer is yellow-brown with darker underparts; indistinct spots on its back fade with age. Shoulder height: 66–74cm (26–29in). Family Cervidae; subfamily Cervinae; species *Axis porcinus*.

deer, mule (black-tailed deer)
Large-eared deer found in grassland and woodland in W North America and Central America. It has a white face, tail and throat patches, and a black tip to its tail. In summer, mule deers are red in colour; in winter they are brown-grey. Shoulder height: 92–107cm (36–42in). Family Cervidae; subfamily Odocoilinae; species *Odocoileus hemionus*.

deer, musk
Any of three species of deer, placed in a family of their own. Musk deer inhabit densely forested areas of Asia. They have large, rounded ears, slender hooves and no antlers. Males have long upper canines that form external tusks; they secrete an oily substance used in perfumes. Shoulder height: 50–70cm (20–28in). Family Moschidae; genus *Moschus*; species include *Moschus moschiferus*.

deer, pampas
Shy deer that inhabits the open grassy plains of South America. It is red-brown with white underparts and a dark tail. Shoulder height: 69cm (27in). Family Cervidae; subfamily Odocoiliniae; species *Ozotoceros bezoarticus*.

deer, Père David's
Deer originally from China but now found only in parks and zoos. It is bright red with a dark stripe along its back in the summer, grey in winter. Other features include long branching antlers, a long tufted tail and wide hooves. Shoulder height: 120cm (47in). Family Cervidae; subfamily Cervinae; species *Elaphurus davidiensis*.

deer, red
Deer that is widespread across Europe, into Asia and N Africa; it has been introduced in Australia and New Zealand. It is red-brown in the summer, with a

▲ **deer, pampas** The pampas deer (*Ozotoceros bezoarticus*) is the only mammal of any size to be found on the South American grasslands, although its numbers have seriously declined due to hunting and destruction of its habitat.

D

105

D

▲ **degu** Found in the grasslands of Peru and Chile, degus (*Octodon degus*) live in groups in burrows. When captured, they may escape by shedding the skin of their tails.

longer, greyer coat in the winter. Males have pointed, branching antlers. Family Cervidae; subfamily Cervinae; species *Cervus elaphus*.

deer, roe
Deer found across Europe and Asia. In the summer its coat is red with a white chin and black face band. In the winter it is greyer with a white rump and throat patches. Roe deer are selective browsers found in a range of habitats from open moor to thick woodland. Shoulder height: 64–89cm (25–35in). Family Cervidae; subfamily Odocoilinae; species *Capreolus capreolus*.

deer, sika (Japanese deer)
Deer that is native to Japan and Southeast Asia; it has been semi-tamed in parks. It is chestnut to yellow-brown with white spots along the side of its body in summer; in the winter it is grey-brown. Males have simple antlers. Shoulder height: 65–109cm (26–43in). Family Cervidae; subfamily Cervinae; species *Cervus nippon*.

deer, swamp (barasingha, gond)
Deer found in India and Nepal. It lives in marshy areas but is also found in forests. It is brown with paler underparts. The males' long antlers (up to 100cm/40in) branch into many points near the ends. They graze in herds. Family Cervidae; subfamily Cervinae; species *Cervus duvauceli*.

deer, tufted
Deer found in the mountainous forests of China and Burma. Its coarse coat is dark chocolate brown with paler underparts, ear tips and tail. The male's small, unbranched antlers are hidden in a tuft of dark hair. Shoulder height: 50–70cm (20–28in). Family Cervidae; subfamily Muntiacinae; species *Elaphodus cephalophus*.

deer, water (Chinese water deer)
Deer native to China and Korea, where it inhabits swamps, reedbeds and grassland. It has a golden-brown coat that is paler underneath; in the winter the coat is dull brown. Water deer have no antlers, but both males and females have tusks formed by growth of the upper canines. Shoulder height: 45–55cm (18–22in). Family Cervidae; subfamily Hydropotinae; species *Hydropotes inermis*.

deer, white-tailed
Deer found in North and Central America, and N South America, distinguished by the white underside of its tail. It is red-brown in the summer, grey-brown in the winter, with paler throat, underside and inner ears. White-tailed deer are usually solitary or found in small family groups, which may be larger in the winter. Their branching antlers have many points. Shoulder height: 81–102cm (32–40in). Family Cervidae; subfamily Odocoilinae; species *Odocoileus virginianus*.

deer-fly (gadfly)
Fly with a brown or black body and dark wing markings; it is closely related to the HORSEFLY. The female gives a painful bite and is known to transmit anthrax, tularaemia and loa loa. Length: 7–10mm (0.3–0.4in). Order Diptera; family Tabanidae; genera *Chrysops* and *Tabanus*.

defoliant
Chemical preparation used to remove leaves. It is mostly used for military purposes to remove ground cover. Agent Orange, so called because of the distinctive orange stripe on its pack, was used in the 1960s by the United States to defoliate forests during the Vietnam War in order to expose the Vietcong.

deforestation
Clearing away of forests and their ECOSYSTEMS, usually on a large scale. It may be done to create open areas for farming or building, or to make use of the timber from the trees. There is an immediate danger that the vital topsoil will be eroded by wind (as in the DUST BOWL in the s Great Plains of North America in the 1930s) or, in hilly areas, by rain. Proposals to clear whole regions of the rainforests of Amazonia in Brazil, which play a key role in maintaining the oxygen balance of the Earth, could, if fully implemented, cause an environmental catastrophe. *See also* REFORESTATION

degeneration
Term used to describe the effects disease may have on cells or groups of cells, resulting in loss of function or, in extreme cases, death. In evolution, the term refers to the gradual appearance of a VESTIGIAL STRUCTURE, such as the appendix in humans or the wings of emus, which serve little or no function in the evolved species.

degu
Rodent found in s South America. Its long silky fur is grey-brown on the back and creamy underneath. Large groups inhabit rocky ledges in lowland areas and feed on tubers, roots, bark and cacti. Head-body length: 12–20cm (5–8in); tail: 4–18cm (2–7in). Family Octonontidae; species *Octodon degus*.

dehiscent
Describing a FRUIT or SEED pod that opens spontaneously to release its seeds. Often violent, dehiscence disperses the seeds over a wide area. The explosive release of spores from a SPORANGIUM or pollen from an ANTHER is also described as dehiscence. *See also* INDEHISCENT

Delbrück, Max (1906–81)
US biologist, b. Germany. He shared the 1969 Nobel Prize for physiology or medicine with Alfred HERSHEY and Salvador LURIA for work on reproduction in VIRUSES.

delphinium (larkspur)
Any of *c*.250 species of herbaceous plants native to temperate areas, with spirally arranged leaves and loose clusters of flowers. Petals form a tubular spur. Garden delphiniums are varieties of *Delphinium elatum*. Family Ranunculaceae.

delta
Fan-shaped body of SEDIMENT deposited at the mouth of a river. A delta is formed when a river deposits its sediment load as its speed decreases while entering the sea or a lake, and the waves, tides and currents are not sufficiently strong to carry the material away. The shape and size of a delta is controlled by a combination of factors, including climate, water discharge, sediment load, rate of subsi-dence of the sea or lake, and the nature of the river mouth processes. Most deltas are extremely fertile areas, but are subject to frequent flooding.

deme
Group of individuals that breed with one another within a population of one SPECIES. Although individuals within the deme breed with each other most of the time, they can still breed with individuals of other demes. If demes become separated, the flow of GENES between them may cease and each may evolve along separate lines. If reunited the demes may be incapable of successfully interbreeding and each would then be a separate species with its own GENE POOL. *See also* SPECIATION

demography
Scientific study of human populations, their changes, movements, size, distribution and structure.

demoiselle
Large DAMSELFLY, found mainly in the tropics. It has a metallic-looking, brightly coloured body. The wings of the male are partly covered in a patch of dense colour, often deep blue or purple, which is displayed during agile courtship dances. Adult wingspan: 80–100mm (3–4in). Order Odonata; family Agriidae; genus *Agrion*.

dendrite
Short branching projection from a nerve cell (NEU-RONE). It carries impulses to the cell body and transmits impulses to other nerve cells over short gaps called SYNAPSES. There may be more than one dendrite per neurone.

dendritic drainage
Tree-like branching pattern of streams and their tributaries. The pattern is common in regions where the land is essentially flat and the rock is homogeneous.

dendrobium
Any member of a genus of *c*.1400 species of deciduous or evergreen plants. Some dendrobiums are epiphytic (that is, they grow naturally on tree branches without soil), others grow in the ground. They are found in the rainforests of India, Southeast Asia, New Guinea, Australia and the Pacific Islands. Lance-shaped leaves grow from elongated, stem-like pseudo-bulbs. Dendrobiums produce spikes of showy flowers in a wide range of beautiful colours and shapes. They are grown commercially as greenhouse orchids. Family Orchidaceae; genus *Dendrobium*.

dendrochronology
Means of estimating time by examination of the ANNUAL RINGS (growth rings) in trees. This data can be related to wood used in buildings, for instance. It may also indicate the HYDROLOGY of the region in which the tree grew, thus fixing points in the climatic history of that region. Chronology based on the bristle-cone pine extends back more than 7000 years.

dendron
Major projection that protrudes from a nerve cell (NEURONE) and is concerned with nerve transmission. Found mostly on MOTOR NEURONES, dendrons usually branch into smaller DENDRITES, which chemically transmit NERVE IMPULSES across a SYNAPSE to other neighbouring neurones.

denitrification
Process that chemically reduces ammonia, nitrites or nitrates to yield free nitrogen. Under waterlogged conditions denitrifying BACTERIA change the nitrogen

of ammonia into free nitrogen that enters the atmosphere or soil. *See also* NITROGEN CYCLE

density (symbol ρ)

Ratio of mass to volume for a given substance, usually expressed in SI UNITS as kilograms per cubic metre (kgm^{-3}). It is an indication of the concentration of particles within a material. The density of a solid or liquid changes little over a wide range of temperatures and pressures. **Relative density** (symbol r.d.) or **specific gravity** (symbol s.g.) is the ratio of the density of one substance to that of a reference substance (usually water) at the same temperature and pressure. The density of a gas depends strongly on both pressure and temperature. In ecology, the term density is used to describe the number of organisms per unit area.

dental formula

System for indicating the type and distribution of TEETH in an animal's JAW. Half of each jaw is considered and represented by two sets of four numbers, one set above and one set below a horizontal line. The numbers above the line stand for the upper jaw and the numbers below the line for the lower jaw. The first number in each set stands for the number of incisors, the second number for the canines, the third number for the premolars and the fourth number for the MOLARS. An adult human with a full set of teeth has, in each half of each jaw, two incisors, one canine, two premolars, and three molars. The dental formula is written: $\frac{2\ 1\ 2\ 3}{2\ 1\ 2\ 3}$

Adding all the numbers and multiplying by 2 gives the total number of teeth (32). *See also* DENTITION

dentine

Hard yellow matter of all TEETH. It consists of crystals of calcium and phosphate. Human beings and other higher animals have **tubular** dentine, so called because dentine-producing cells (**odontoblasts**), surrounding the pulp, send out tubules into the dentine; these tubules transmit sensations to the nerve.

dentition

Type, number and arrangement of TEETH (*see* DENTAL FORMULA). An adult human has 32. The incisors are used for cutting; the canines for gripping and tearing; and the molars and premolars for crushing and grinding food. A HERBIVORE has relatively unspecialized teeth. They grow throughout life, to compensate for wear (plant fibres are very tough), and are adapted for grinding. A CARNIVORE has a range of specialized teeth related to killing, gripping and crushing bones. In carnivores, unspecialized milk teeth are replaced by more specialized adult teeth, which have to last a lifetime.

denudation

Wearing away of land by WEATHERING and EROSION. Denudation is a broad term and includes all the natural agencies, such as Sun, rain, wind, rivers, frost, ice and sea, as well as heating and cooling, freezing and thawing, SOLUTION, ABRASION, CORRASION and CORROSION. In addition to weathering and erosion, the removal of material, that is, the transportation, is also part of denudation. Together with DEPOSITION, denudation is the major process which creates the Earth's landscape.

deodar

Conical, evergreen, coniferous tree from the snowy slopes of the W Himalayas, where it has religious significance. Its spreading branches droop or "weep" at their ends. The leaves are bright green needles, *c*.5cm (*c*.2in) long, produced in whorls of between 20 and 30. The bark is very dark brown or black and the cones are held upright. Height: to 33m (108ft). Family Pinaceae; species *Cedrus deodara*.

D

DESERT

Area with a dry CLIMATE; a desert is sometimes defined as having a total annual rainfall of 250mm (10in) or less. The effectiveness of 250mm (10in) of rainfall can vary, however, depending on whether it falls within a short time or over a prolonged period. A desert is almost barren, although there are very few places with absolutely no vegetation – this occurs only on some patches of moving sand dunes or on bare rocky areas. Most deserts contain tufts of grass and scattered, usually thorny, bushes that have the ability to withstand long dry spells. In some deserts there are cactus plants and various species of flowering plant that have a very short life cycle. They spring up quickly after a shower of rain and go through their complete life cycle in a few days before dying and leaving seeds to lie dormant until the next rain. Some deserts contain large areas of sand dunes, but most deserts are rocky. There are bare rock areas, but generally there will be a cover of loose stones with patches of moving sand. The stones and sand are gradually broken down by mechanical WEATHERING and wind action (AEOLIAN FORMATION). The world's major deserts, including the Australian, Kalahari and Sahara, are found in the HORSE LATITUDES, where the permanent high pressure causes drought throughout the year. Deserts occur in various west coast areas, where the influence of cool CURRENTS offshore makes the land even drier, with less than 100mm (4in) rainfall in places; for example, the Atacama Desert in Peru (with the Humboldt Current offshore) and the Namib Desert in S Africa (with the Benguela Current offshore). There are deserts in the middle of the largest continents, where no onshore winds can reach to bring any rainfall; for example, the Gobi Desert in Asia, and the Mojave Desert, Imperial Valley and Death Valley in the United States. Some cold regions are also regarded as deserts because they have less than 250mm (10in) annual precipitation. Antarctica and Greenland are ice deserts, and even the TUNDRA areas of N Canada, N Siberia and elsewhere have some similarities to deserts, although they have cool summers and very cold winters.

▲ **Where rain is** infrequent but heavy, it cuts deep, steep or vertically sided valleys called *wadis* (1), which isolate *buttes* (2) and the larger *mesas* (3). Wadis develop when flash floods widen and deepen random depressions in mountain areas or arid plateaus. Rocky surfaces are much more common than sand seas in the desert. About 30 per cent of Arabian deserts are sand covered, whereas only 1 per cent of desert surface in North America is sandy. Any rain that falls on the mountains may drain into porous rock layers (4) that can stretch many kilometres beneath the desert. Wherever these porous layers come to the surface they give rise to an *oasis* (5). Finding and utilizing water is one of the most urgent problems in the desert, and one ancient solution that is still used is the *qanat* (6). First a head well (7) is sunk down to the porous rock, which may be 100m (300ft) deep. Then a line of ventilation shafts (8) is dug and finally a channel (9) is begun from the *qanat* mouth (10). When the qanat is completed, gravity brings the water to the settlement, and canals (11) take it where it is needed.

D

deoxyribonucleic acid
See DNA

depletion
Special form of depreciation referring to the exhaustion of nonrenewable natural resources (such as oil, minerals or natural gas) as they are exploited for human use. Depletion is usually figured as the percentage of the estimated reserves of the resource that has been used.

deposition
Laying down of material that has been removed by DENUDATION. Most of the material will be SEDIMENT and therefore a possible source of SEDIMENTARY ROCKS when consolidated. After denudation has taken place, the material is transported, sometimes over quite considerable distances, before being deposited. Most of the material will eventually be dumped on the seabed by rivers. However, there will be some deposition on land – for example, SILT on flood plains, TILL deposited by ice, LOESS deposited by wind. Together with denudation, deposition is the major process that creates the Earth's landscape.

depression
Region of low ATMOSPHERIC PRESSURE with the lowest pressure at the centre. It usually brings unsettled or stormy weather. In the Northern Hemisphere, winds circulate counterclockwise in a depression; they circulate clockwise in the Southern Hemisphere. *See also* CYCLONE

dermapteran
Any INSECT belonging to the order Dermaptera, commonly known as the EARWIGS.

dermis
Thick inner layer of the SKIN that lies beneath the EPIDERMIS. Also known as the true skin, it consists mainly of loose CONNECTIVE TISSUE and is richly supplied with BLOOD and LYMPH vessels, nerve endings, sensory organs and sweat glands.

desert
See feature article, page 107

desertification
Process by which a DESERT gradually spreads into neighbouring areas of semidesert, transforming them into true desert. The change may result from a natural event, such as the destruction of vegetation by fire or a slight climatic change, but it occurs most frequently as a result of human activity. In many semiarid areas and dry grasslands, the vegetation becomes overgrazed by domestic animals, so that the land is left bare. Wind and rain then erode the soil, removing any residual fertility, so that no new vegetation can survive. Once the vegetation and soil have gone, the land becomes desert. An additional problem is the use of trees and bushes for firewood by the local people. With an increasing population there is an increasing need for fuel, and so landscapes become depleted of trees. Once it has been destroyed, restoring the land is a long and slow process. Extensive desertification has been taking place in the Sahel, the s edge of the Sahara Desert, and there are also examples in s Africa, India and many other places where there are too many people subsisting on an inadequate landscape.

desman
Either of two rare, poorly known genera of aquatic animals, closely related to MOLES. Desmans have tiny eyes, a long snout and an excellent sense of touch. They have webbed toes and a flattened tail for swimming. Largely nocturnal, they feed mostly on aquatic insects and larvae. Family Talpidae.

desman, Pyrenean
Desman that is found in cold, flowing, mountain streams of s France and N Spain and Portugal. The Pyrenean desman is a solitary animal with a permanent home range. Head-body length: 11–14cm (4–6in); tail: 12–16cm (5–6in). Family Talpidae; species *Galemys pyrenaicus*.

desman, Russian
Desman that is found in the major river basins of sw Russia and Kazakstan. It is similar in many ways to the Pyrenean desman, but may be nomadic and more sociable. It includes fish and amphibians in its diet. Head-body length: 18–22cm (7–9in); tail: 17–21cm (7–8in). Family Talpidae; species *Desmana moschata*.

▲ **desman, Pyrenean** A fast swimmer, the mainly nocturnal Pyrenean desman (*Galemys pyrenaicus*) propels itself with its webbed hind feet. It moves clumsily on land, but is a good climber. It relies on smell rather than sight to find its way.

destructive margin
In PLATE TECTONICS, the boundary between two lithospheric plates (*see* LITHOSPHERE) that are moving towards each other, and where oceanic crust is being recycled into the mantle by SUBDUCTION. Destructive margins can be detected by shallow- to deep-focus EARTHQUAKES (the BENIOFF ZONE), ocean TRENCHES and volcanic ISLAND ARCS. *See also* CONSTRUCTIVE MARGIN

detritus
In geology, sediment deposited by natural forces. It is classed by the size of the particles. In biology, detritus is the organic debris from decomposing plants and animals, normally in the form of small fragments. *See also* DETRITIVORE

detritivore
Animal that feeds on DETRITUS. Detritivores usually differ from DECOMPOSERS in being larger and in digesting food internally rather than externally. Examples include EARTHWORMS, WOODLICE and SEA CUCUMBERS.

deuterium
Isotope (D or ^{2}H) of hydrogen, the nuclei (deuterons) of which contain a neutron in addition to a proton. For every million hydrogen atoms in nature, there are about 156 deuterium atoms. Deuterium occurs in water as D_2O (heavy water), from which it is obtained by electrolysis. Heavy water is used as a moderator in some fission reactors. Properties: r.a.m. 2.0144.

deutzia
Any member of a genus of *c*.60 deciduous shrubs from scrub or woodland areas of the Himalayas and E Asia. The leaves are lance-shaped and toothed. The flowers are five-petalled, white or pink, cup- or star-shaped and often fragrant; they are produced in profusion in spring. Colourful plants, deutzias can be grown in gardens in a shrub border or as specimen plants. Family Hydrangeaceae; genus *Deutzia*; species include *Deutzia gracilis*.

devilfish (manta, horned ray)
Flat-bodied, cartilaginous fish found in tropical and temperate marine waters. It is a surface feeder. Its disc-like body may be blue, black or brown. It has two slender fins on its head and, in some species, a poisonous tail spine. Width: 1–6m (3–20ft). Family Mobulidae; there are four genera. *See also* RAY

devil's coach horse
Large, dark-coloured BEETLE; it is the largest member of the family Staphylinidae. The devil's coach horse has strong, concealed wings. It is found in or near decaying organic matter, including carrion

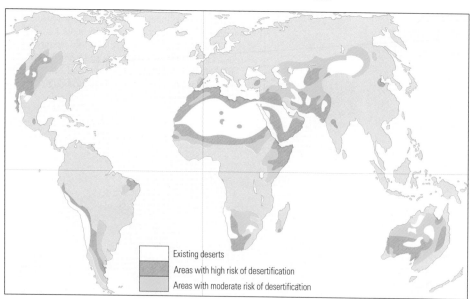

Existing deserts
Areas with high risk of desertification
Areas with moderate risk of desertification

▲ **desertification** The true causes of desertification are complex and still not entirely understood, but it is generally accepted that recent desertification is directly attributable to increased human intervention. On a large scale, the burning of fossil fuel is likely to shift climatic belts and increase areas of desert. More localized problems have occurred due to overgrazing of livestock and ill-planned irrigation processes.

and dung. Length: to 28mm (1.1in). Family Staphylinidae; species *Ocypus olens*.

Devonian

Fourth-oldest period of the PALAEOZOIC era, lasting from 408 to 360 million years ago. It is sometimes called the Age of Fishes. Numerous marine and freshwater remains include jawless FISH and forerunners of today's fish. The first known land vertebrate, the amphibian *Ichthyostega*, appeared at this time. Land animals included SCORPIONS, MITES, SPIDERS and the first insects. Land plants consisted of tall CLUB MOSSES, HORSETAILS and FERNS. In Devonian times much of the British Isles was desert mountain environment or semidesert coastal plains, giving rise to the red rock known as Old Red Sandstone.

De Vries, Hugo (1848–1935)

Dutch botanist. His experimental methods led to the rediscovery (1900) of Gregor MENDEL's laws of HEREDITY and the development of a theory of MUTATION. De Vries argued that GENETIC mutation was the chief engine of EVOLUTION.

dew

Water droplets formed, usually at night, by CONDENSATION on vegetation and other surfaces near the ground. Hoar-FROST is formed when temperatures are below freezing. FOG also deposits moisture on exposed surfaces.

dewberry

Sprawling, deciduous shrub related to the BLACKBERRY or BRAMBLE. It has long, arching stems, with short, weak prickles; its leaves have only three leaflets. The white flowers are 2.5cm (1in) across with five-petals. The blue-black fruits have only a few large segments. Family Rosaceae; species *Rubus caesius*.

dew point

Temperature at which a vapour begins to condense, for example when WATER VAPOUR in the air condenses into clouds as the air becomes saturated with vapour.

dhole

Rare, reddish-brown, wild DOG native to S and Southeast Asia. The dhole hunts in packs, running its prey, usually large mammals, to exhaustion. Length: (without tail) to 1m (3.3ft). Family Canidae; species *Cuon alpinus*.

diagenesis

Physical and chemical processes whereby SEDIMENTS are transformed into solid rock, usually at low pressure and temperature. Pressure results in compaction, forcing grains together and eliminating air and water. Cementation then binds individual particles together by the precipitation of a secondary mineral, commonly an iron oxide, calcite or silica.

diamond

Crystalline form of carbon (C); the hardest natural substance. Diamond is found in kimberlite pipes and in alluvial deposits as cubic system octahedral crystals. It is brilliant, transparent to translucent, colourless or of many hues, including yellow, green, blue and brown, depending on the impurities contained. Bort, a variety of diamond inferior in crystal and colour, and carborondo, an opaque grey to black variety called black diamond, as well as all other non-gem varieties are used in industry. Industrial diamonds are used as abrasives, bearings in precision instruments such as watches, and in the cutting heads

of drills for mining. Synthetic diamonds, made by subjecting graphite with a catalyst to high pressure and temperatures of about 3000°C (5400°F), have been made since 1955, but are fit only for industrial applications. Diamonds are weighed in carats (0.2gm) and in points (1/100 carat). The largest producer of diamonds is Australia. Hardness 10; r.d. 3.5.

dianthus

Any member of a plant genus that comprises more than 300 species of low-growing, evergreen sub-shrubs, perennials, biennials and annuals. Dianthuses include CARNATIONS, PINKS and SWEET WILLIAMS. They are found in the mountains and meadows of Europe, Asia and S Africa. There are tens of thousands of garden cultivars and hybrids. Dianthuses all have long, thin, pointed, often blue- or grey-green leaves, which grow along the stems in opposite pairs. The tube-shaped flowers have five petals and are usually pink or red. Family Caryophyllaceae; species include *Dianthus deltoides* (the maiden pink) and *Dianthus plumarius* (the common pink).

diapause

Time break in the development of an INSECT. During diapause, growth stops and METABOLISM slows down. It occurs because of interruptions in an innate rhythm brought about by unfavourable changes in the environment, possibly because of seasonal changes in climate. In this way, the developing insect survives until conditions improve. *See also* BIOLOGICAL CLOCK

diaphragm

Sheet of muscle that separates the ABDOMEN from the THORAX, the cavity of the chest, in mammals. During exhalation (breathing out) it relaxes and allows the chest to subside; on inhalation it contracts and flattens, causing the chest cavity to enlarge.

diapsid

Member of a major group of animals that are characterized by a pair of openings in the skull immediately behind the eye socket. They first evolved in late Carboniferous times. The group includes the extinct marine reptiles and dinosaurs, plus CROCODILES, LIZARDS, SNAKES and BIRDS.

diatom

Any of a group of tiny, microscopic, single-celled ALGAE (phylum Bacillariophyta) characterized by a shell-like cell wall made of silica. The shell (**frustule**) consists of two halves that fit together like the two halves of a petri dish. Diatom frustules occur in a wide variety of highly symmetrical shapes. Diatoms live in nearly every environment that has water and is exposed to sunlight, including virtually all bodies of salt and fresh water and even soil, damp rocks, tree bark and the undersides of icebergs. Light

can pass through the transparent cell wall and is used for PHOTOSYNTHESIS. The microscopic shells of long-dead diatoms accumulate in, for example, diatomite (kieselguhr), a mineral with abrasive, absorbent and refractory uses.

dibatag (Clark's gazelle)

ANTELOPE that inhabits the grassy plains and scrubland of Ethiopia and Somalia. It has a long neck and a long, thin, black tail, which is held upright when the animal is in flight. It has a red-grey back, pale underparts, and white and chestnut face-markings. The males' horns (15–25cm/6–10in long) point backwards at the base and curve forwards near the tips. Head-body length: 152–168cm (61–67in); tail: 30–36cm (12–14in). Family Bovidae; subfamily Antilopinae; species *Ammodorcas clarkei*.

dibbler

MARSUPIAL MOUSE found in heath vegetation of coastal regions of SW Western Australia. It has distinctive white eye rings and is most active at dusk and dawn. It feeds on insects, small reptiles and nectar. Once thought to be extinct, the dibbler is now considered an endangered species. Head-body length: 14cm (6in); tail: up to 11cm (4in). Family Dasyuridae; species *Parantechinus apicalis*.

dicotyledon

Any member of the class Dicotyledonae within the phylum Angiospermophyta – ANGIOSPERMS (flowering plants). Dicotyledonous plants are characterized by two seed leaves (COTYLEDONS) in the seed embryo. Other general features of dicotyledons include: broad leaves with branching veins; FLOWER parts (sepals, petals, stamens) arranged in whorls of fours or fives; VASCULAR BUNDLES arranged in a ring in the stem and ROOT; and a main central root (TAP-ROOT). There are *c*.250 families of dicotyledons, including the ROSE, DAISY and MAGNOLIA families. *See also* MONOCOTYLEDON

dictyosome

In plants, stacks of GOLGI BODIES.

dicynodont

Member of an extinct group of advanced, plant-eating, reptile-like tetrapods, such as *Dicynodon*, which evolved in late Permian times and survived until the end of the Triassic period. Dicynodonts had two downward-pointing, tusk-like teeth. Many had a horny, turtle-like beak for eating tough plant material.

dieffenbachia (dumb cane, mother-in-law's tongue)

Any member of a genus of *c*.30 evergreen perennials from the tropical forests of North and South America and the West Indies. They have large, oval leaves, often marked with yellow or white patterns, and pro-

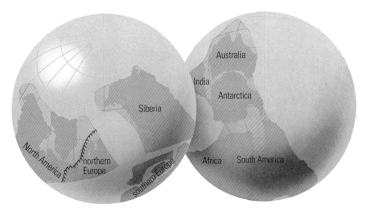

◀ **Devonian** By the Devonian period, North America had collided with N Europe and the sediments between them had been thrust up to form the Caledonian Mountains.

duce creamy inflorescences throughout the year. Dieffenbachias are popular houseplants, and there are many cultivars. All parts of these plants cause severe discomfort if ingested; the sap may irritate the skin. Family Araceae; genus *Dieffenbachia*; species include *Dieffenbachia seguine*.

Dietz, Robert Sinclair (1914–95)
US geophysicist. In 1961 he proposed a theory of SEAFLOOR SPREADING, which was later confirmed. He is also known for his studies of the Moon's physical features and of meteorite impact on rocks.

differentiation
Process by which cells become specialized for different functions during embryonic development.

diffusion
Movement of a substance in a mixture from regions of higher concentration to regions of lower concentration, resulting from the random motion of the individual atoms or molecules. Diffusion ceases when there is no longer a concentration gradient. Its rate increases with temperature, since average molecular speed also increases with temperature. The process occurs quickly in gases and liquids, much more slowly in solids.

digestion
See feature article, pages 112–13

digestive system (alimentary system)
Group of organs of the body concerned with the DIGESTION of foodstuffs. In humans the digestive system begins with the mouth, where the action of teeth and enzymes in saliva begin the process of breaking down the food. It continues with the OESOPHAGUS, which carries food into the STOMACH. The stomach leads to the small intestine, which then opens into the COLON. After food is swallowed, it is pushed through the digestive tract by PERISTALSIS. On its journey, food is transformed into small molecules that can be absorbed into the bloodstream and carried to the tissues. CARBOHYDRATE is broken down to sugars, PROTEIN to AMINO ACIDS, and FAT to FATTY ACIDS and GLYCEROL. Indigestible matter, mainly cellulose, passes into the rectum, and is eventually eliminated from the body (as faeces) through the ANUS.

digitalis
Drug obtained from the leaves of the FOXGLOVE (*Digitalis purpurea*); it is used to treat heart disease. It increases heart contractions and slows the heartbeat.

dihybrid cross
Genetic cross involving two GENES that are carried on separate CHROMOSOMES. Each ALLELE of one gene may combine randomly with either allele of the other gene. In a typical cross involving an organism that is pure breeding for two DOMINANT characters, A and B, and an organism that is pure breeding for two RECESSIVE characters, A and B, the offspring all show the dominant characters only. Interbreeding these offspring produces a 9:3:3:1 ratio of both dominant characters (9), dominant A with recessive B (3), recessive A with dominant B (3), both recessive characters (1). *See also* MONOHYBRID CROSS

dikdik
Any of three species of dwarf ANTELOPE found in NE Africa between Ethiopia and Tanzania, with one species also inhabiting Namibia and Angola. The dikdik's chosen habitat is rocky hillsides with some bushes for cover. Its colour ranges from yellow-grey to red-brown, sometimes with white eye rings. The dikdik's short, backwards-facing horns (4–9cm/2–4in long) are sometimes hidden in tufts of hair. Head-body length: 52–72cm (20–28in); tail: 3–5cm (1–2in). Family Bovidae; subfamily Antilopinae; genus *Madoqua*.

dike
See DYKE

dikkop (stone curlew, thick-knee)
Plover-like bird with large, pale eyes, long legs and camouflaged plumage. It feeds mainly at night. The dikkop breeds on dry open grasslands or the sandbanks of large rivers in Europe, Asia and s Africa. Length: 40–55cm (16–22in). Family Burhinidae; genera *Burhinus* and *Esacus*.

dill
Aromatic annual herb that is native to Europe. Its small oval seeds and feathery leaves are used in cooking. Family Apiaceae/Umbelliferae; species *Anethum graveolens*.

dingo
Yellowish-brown, wild DOG found in Australia; it is probably a descendant of early domestic dogs introduced by Native Australians thousands of years ago. It feeds mainly on rabbits and other small mammals. Height (at shoulder): *c*.61cm (*c*.24in). Family Canidae; species *Canis dingo*.

dinoflagellate
Any member of a group of mostly unicellular, free-living, motile cells. Dinoflagellates form a major component of marine phytoplanktonic communities and are most abundant in tropical and subtropical waters. Some dinoflagellates are bioluminescent (*Noctiluca*), some are toxic (red tides, *Gonyaulax*) and a few are parasitic on fish. Their most unusual features are a distinctive cell shape and two dissimilar flagella, one wrapped around the cell in a groove, the other trailing behind. Division Pyrrhophyta.

dinosaur (Gr. terrible lizard)
Any of a large number of REPTILES that lived during the MESOZOIC era, between 225 and 65 million years ago. They appeared during the TRIASSIC period, survived the JURASSIC and became extinct at the end of the CRETACEOUS. Dinosaurs ranged in size from 80cm (30in) to the 27m (90ft) DIPLODOCUS. Most dinosaur species were egg-laying animals. There were two orders: SAURISCHIAN dinosaurs ("lizard hips") included the bipedal carnivores and the giant herbivores; the ORNITHISCHIAN dinosaurs ("bird hips") were smaller herbivores. The dinosaurs' posture, with limbs vertically beneath the body, distinguishes them from other reptiles. There is evidence that some birds are the living descendants of ornithischians. Many theories are advanced to account for the dinosaurs' extinction. It is possible that, as the climate changed, they were incapable of swift adaptation. A more catastrophic theory is that they died because of the devastating atmospheric effects from the impact of a large meteor. *See also* ANKYLOSAURID; APATOSAUR; CARNOSAUR; CERATOPSIAN; HADROSAURID; HYPSILOPHODONT; IGUANODONT; ORNITHOPOD; SAUROPOD; STEGOSAUR; TYRANNOSAUR

dioecious
Having either female, **pistillate** flowers (with CARPELS only) or male, **staminate** flowers (with STAMENS only) on a plant; but not both. The DATE PALM is an example of a dioecious plant. Completely dioecious plants are rare; it is far more usual for a plant to be predominantly, although not completely, of one sex, for example PLANTAIN (Plantago) and ASH (Fraxinus). *See also* MONOECIOUS

diorite
Intermediate, coarse-grained IGNEOUS ROCK. It is similar to GRANITE in texture but is made up mainly of PLAGIOCLASE FELDSPAR and HORNBLENDE, with BIOTITE or augite. It is usually dark grey.

dip
Steepest angle of a tilted plane of a rock (such as BED, JOINT, CLEAVAGE and FAULT). The dip is measured from the horizontal, 90° being vertical, using a CLINOMETER.

◄ **dingo** A male (standing) and female dingo are shown here. Dingoes are thought to have arrived on the Australian mainland between 3500 and 4000 years ago, probably arriving with sailors from Southeast or s Asia. The oldest fossil so far found dates from *c*.3500 years ago. Dingoes contributed to the extinction (through competition) in Australia of the Tasmanian wolf and Tasmanian devil.

◀ **diplodocus** With a small head and slender teeth, the diplodocus probably grazed in marshes and shallow water. In order to compensate for the small size of its brain, there was a concentration of nerves in the base of its spine which helped it to coordinate its enormous body.

dip, magnetic
See INCLINATION, MAGNETIC

dipeptide
MOLECULE formed when two AMINO ACIDS are combined by a PEPTIDE bond as the result of a CONDENSATION REACTION. *See also* POLYPEPTIDE

diplococcus
Any member of a genus of BACTERIA characterized by gram-positive, spherical cells that grow in pairs. Diplococcus includes the pneumococcus, which causes pneumonia.

diplodocus
Any member of the *Diplodocus* genus of DINOSAURS. It lived during the JURASSIC period, in what is now the N United States. The longest land animal that has ever lived, it had a long, slender neck and tail and was a swamp-dwelling herbivore. Length: up to 27m (90ft).

diploid
Term describing a nucleus or CELL that has its CHROMOSOMES in pairs. Almost all animal cells are diploid, except GAMETES (reproductive cells), which are HAPLOID (containing only a single set of chromosomes). The cells of angiosperms (flowering plants) and gymnosperms (non-flowering plants) are also diploid. Algae and lower plants, such as ferns and mosses, have two generations in their life cycle, one diploid and the other haploid. In a diploid cell, the chromosomes of each pair carry the same GENES. *See also* ALTERNATION OF GENERATIONS

diplopod
Any member of the class Diplopoda, more commonly known as MILLIPEDES.

dipluran
Member of a class and order of small, elongate, slender HEXAPODS. They are whitish in colour, blind and entognathous (that is, having the mouthparts inside the head). Diplurans are represented by two main families: the herbivorous Campodeidae, which are characterized by long cerci (sensory appendages at the tip of the abdomen); and the carnivorous Japygidae, which have short cerci resembling forceps. They are distributed worldwide. Adult body length: *c*.1cm (*c*.0.4in). The largest dipluran belongs to the Australian genus *Heterojapyx*. There are *c*.800 species.

dipper
Compact, thrush-like bird with short wings and tail. It lives along fast-flowing mountain streams worldwide and specializes in swimming underwater to find insects. It has a characteristic white membrane that covers and protects its eyes underwater. Length: 20cm (8in). Family Cinclidae; genus *Cinclus*; there are five species.

dipteran
Any member of the order Diptera, the true flies. Adult flies have soft bodies and one pair of wings, the other being reduced to knob-like **halteres**; they have COMPOUND EYES and sucking mouthparts. They have a complete life cycle: the adult lays eggs that hatch into LARVAE (maggots); these pupate and become adults. Within the Diptera order are many important pests, such as MOSQUITOES, HOUSE-FLIES and others that attack human beings, animals or crops or carry diseases. *See also* INSECT

directional selection
Evolutionary selection that operates towards one extreme in a range of variation. For example, within a population of rabbits there will be a range of fur length. If over a number of years the average environmental temperature falls, those rabbits with the longer length of fur will have the selective advantage of being better insulated from the cold. These individuals will be more likely to survive and breed, which in turn gives rise to offspring with long fur. The mean fur length of the rabbit population will move towards the extreme of longer fur over a number of generations. *See also* DISRUPTIVE SELECTION; EVOLUTION; NATURAL SELECTION; STABILIZING SELECTION

disaccharide
CARBOHYDRATE formed when two SUGAR units are combined by a GLYCOSIDIC BOND as the result of a CONDENSATION REACTION. Examples include MALTOSE (the combination of two GLUCOSE molecules), SUCROSE (glucose and FRUCTOSE) and LACTOSE (glucose and galactose). Disaccharides are sweet, water-soluble, crystalline substances.

discharge (symbol Q)
Measure of waterflow at a particular point, measured in cubic metres per second ($m^3 s^{-1}$). Discharge can be calculated with the formula $Q = V \times A$, where V is the velocity of the water and A the cross-sectional area of the river channel.

discus fish
Any member of the freshwater genus *Symphysodon*. The colourful markings of discus fish make them popular aquarium fish. The young feed on skin secretions produced by the adults. They are related to the JACK DEMPSEY and TILAPIA. Family Cichlidae; species include *Symnphysodon discus*.

displacement
Relative movements on either side of a FAULT. It incorporates the direction of change and the specific amount of the movement. **Lateral displacement** is described as strike slip and strike separation, whereas **vertical displacement** is known as dip slip and dip separation.

disruptive selection
Form of selection that is uncommon but nevertheless important in bringing about evolutionary change. It occurs where an environmental factor takes on a number of distinct forms and separate varieties of a species evolve their own special features to adapt them to each of the conditions. In time the separate varieties may each evolve into a different species. *See also* DIRECTIONAL SELECTION; EVOLUTION; NATURAL SELECTION; STABILIZING SELECTION

disulphide bond
COVALENT BOND between two sulphur molecules. Disulphide bonds commonly occur between

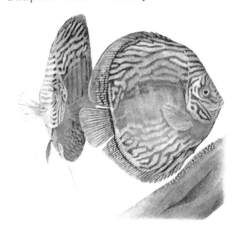

▲ **discus fish** Found in tributaries of the Amazon River, discus fish, like the green discus fish (*Symphysodon* *aequifasciata*) shown here, demonstrate unique parental behaviour, nursing their young in a similar way to mammals.

D

Digestion is the process of breaking down food mechanically and chemically into smaller molecules that can be readily absorbed. Animals use a variety of methods to break up the food mechanically, using hard structures such as a RADULA (snails), MANDIBLES (insects) and TEETH (many vertebrates).

Food has to be broken down to make it soluble allowing it to pass across cell membranes. The chemical breakdown of food is speeded by ENZYMES. Each enzyme works best under different conditions, some preferring an acid environment others an alkaline one. The ALIMENTARY CANAL has evolved to be long enough in many organisms to allow different regions to have different conditions. The stomach region is normally acid, due to the secretion of hydrochloric acid. Mineral salts produced by the LIVER, PANCREAS and ileum wall make the duodenum neutral and the ileum alkaline.

Food is moved along the tubular alimentary canal of animals by a wave of muscular contraction. Muscles in the wall of the gut cause a series of constrictions which pass slowly along. The process is called PERISTALSIS and is aided by mucus produced by the gut wall, which lubricates the movement of food.

The small, soluble molecules that result from digestion are absorbed into the body through the wall of the ileum by DIFFUSION and ACTIVE TRANSPORT. To make this process more efficient the wall of the ileum has a large surface area due to its considerable length (6m/20ft in humans and 45m/150ft in cattle), the folding of its walls, the presence of finger–like projections (VILLI) and the presence of minute cellular outgrowths (MICROVILLI).

SUGARS, AMINO ACIDS and other water-soluble materials, such as MINERALS, enter blood capillaries, whereas FATTY ACIDS and GLYCEROL enter LYMPH vessels. Most of the water that is drunk is absorbed by the stomach. Much water, however, enters the gut as secretions (up to 10 litres per day in humans), and this is reabsorbed in the ileum and colon.

Plant material is relatively tough due to the presence of cellulose. While many invertebrates produce the enzyme cellulase to digest cellulose, no mammal produces this enzyme. Instead HERBIVORES rely on mutualistic microorganisms to do so. Even so digestion is a long and complex process requiring special digestive features, such as flat, ridged teeth to grind the food, jaws that easily move from side to side and teeth that grow continuously to compensate for the wear that occurs in grinding. Herbivorous mammals also have a long alimentary canal to allow longer for digestion and a specialized region to contain cellulose-digesting bacteria, for example the rumen in sheep and cattle and the CAECUM in rabbits.

Carnivores eat meat, which is rich in nutrients. Once captured and ingested, the digestion of meat presents little problem. Many of the adaptations to a carnivorous diet are associated with obtaining food. They include sharp pointed teeth for killing prey and tearing the flesh from the bones, and overlapping upper and lower teeth to slice up the food. Carnivores' other adaptations include: powerful jaw muscles to grip the prey; no side to side jaw movement, which may allow struggling prey to escape; and a short alimentary canal, because food is easily digested.

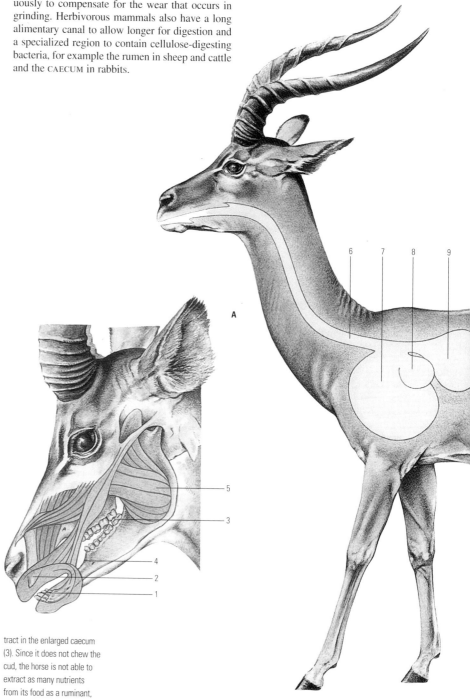

► **The digestive system** of mammalian herbivores can be illustrated by the impala and the horse. The impala (A) is a small but agile ruminant found in the grasslands of central and E Africa. When grazing, it grasps vegetation between its spade-like incisors (1) and a hard upper pad (2) and pulls it up rather than biting it off. The molars (3) are ideal for chewing: ridges on the upper molars fit into grooves on the lower teeth, thereby increasing the grinding area. The gap between incisors and molars (diastema) (4) allows the tongue to mix food with saliva. The powerful masseter muscle (5) moves the jaw up and down, while other facial muscles move it laterally for grinding.
After chewing, food passes down the oesophagus (6) to the largest chamber of the stomach – the rumen (7). Enzymes produced by microbes in the rumen partially break down the food, which is then formed into small balls of cud. The cud is returned to the mouth and chewed at length then reswallowed to let fermentation continue in the rumen and the reticulum (8). Absorption occurs in the third chamber of the stomach – the omasum (9). The remaining food particles proceed through the "true stomach" (10), small intestine (11) and caecum (12), where "normal" digestion takes place.
The horse (B) is a less efficient feeder than the ruminants, as evidenced by the undigested plant material often visible in its faeces. It has a one-chambered stomach (1) in which proteins and sugars are broken down: they are absorbed either in the stomach or the small intestine (2). The cellulose-splitting and fermenting bacteria (similar to those found in the ruminant gut) are located far down the digestive tract in the enlarged caecum (3). Since it does not chew the cud, the horse is not able to extract as many nutrients from its food as a ruminant, and consequently must take in more food to compensate.

▶ **Different enzymes are** produced in different parts of the digestive system, and they work on different types of food, as shown in this table. Enzymes are proteins that function as catalysts in biochemical reactions. They operate within a narrow temperature range. Enzymes also have optimal pH ranges, thus different enzymes function in the varying levels of acidity or alkalinity within the different parts of the digestive system.

TYPE OF ENZYME	EXAMPLE	WHAT THE ENZYME WORKS ON	WHAT IS PRODUCED	WHERE THE ENZYME IS PRODUCED	WHERE THE ENZYME WORKS
carbohydrases (act on carbohydrates)	amylase	starch	maltose	salivary glands	mouth
				pancreas	duodenum
lipases (act on fats and oils)	lipase	fats and oils	fatty acids and glycerol	pancreas	duodenum
proteases (act on proteins)	pepsin	proteins	peptides	stomach wall	stomach
	trypsin	proteins	peptides	pancreas	duodenum
	peptidases	peptides	amino acids	ileum wall	ileum

B

D

DIGESTIVE SYSTEM OF PRIMATES

In primates, the digestion and absorption of food takes place within the digestive tract, a coiled tube some 10m (33ft) long that links mouth to anus. Food is passed down the oesophagus (1) to the stomach (2), where it is partially digested. Chyme is released into the duodenum (3), the first part of 7m (23ft) of small intestine. The duodenum receives bile secreted by the gall bladder (4) in the liver (5), and enzymes secreted by the pancreas (6). Most absorption occurs in the jejunum and ileum, the remaining parts of the small intestine (7). Any residue passes into the caecum (8), the pouch at the start of the large intestine. At one end of the caecum is the 10cm (4in) long vermiform appendix (9). Water is reabsorbed in the colon (10). Faeces form and collect in the rectum (11) before being expelled as waste through the anus (12).

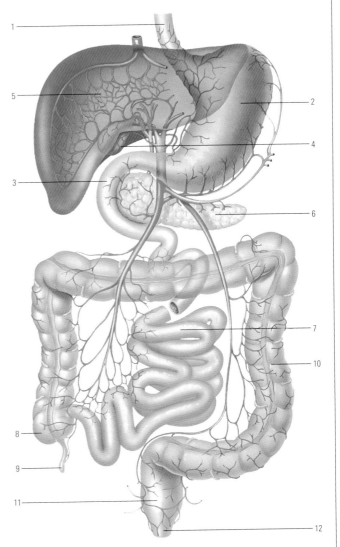

D

► **dock** The curled dock (*Rumex crispus*) of Europe and Asia, is related to sorrel. It gets its name from the wavy margins of its leaves.

molecules of the sulphur-containing AMINO ACID cysteine. They are important in maintaining the structural stability of fibrous PROTEINS.

Ditmars, Raymond Lee (1876–1942)
US naturalist. He was curator of reptiles (1899–1910) and of mammals (1910–1942) for the New York Zoological Park. His many popular books on the biology of reptiles include *The Reptile Book* (1907) and *Snakes of the World* (1931).

diurnal rhythm
See CIRCADIAN RHYTHM

diver (loon)
Goose-sized diving bird with a long, cigar-shaped body. Its legs are positioned to the rear, making it an expert swimmer but clumsy on land. In flight, divers have a hump–backed appearance. They breed on northern lakes, coastal inlets or small tundra ponds and spend the winter at sea. They have distinctive breeding plumages, but in winter they become dark above and whitish below. Length: 53–91cm (21–36in). Family Gaviidae; genus *Gavia*.

diver, black-throated (Arctic loon)
Diver that is between the great northern and red-throated in size. Its summer plumage is most distinctive, with a grey head and a black throat patch on its grey neck. Length: 58–73cm (23–29in). Family Gaviidae; species *Gavia arctica*.

diver, great northern (common loon)
Diver that has a black head and distinctive greyish back and neck markings. It is larger and stouter than the black-throated diver. Its distinctive, eerie, wailing call during the breeding season is evocative of North American lakes in summer. Length: 69–91cm (27–36in). Family Gaviidae; species *Gavia immer*.

diver, white-billed (yellow-billed loon)
Diver that is slightly larger and stouter than the much more common great-northern diver. It has similar plumage but a distinctive, up-tilted, yellow-ivory-coloured bill in all seasons. Length: 76–91cm (30–36in). Family Gaviidae; species *Gavia adamsi*.

diver, red-throated (red-throated loon)
Smallest and slimmest species of diver. In summer it has a red throat patch on its grey neck. At all times, the red-throated diver swims with its head and bill distinctively up-tilted at an angle of 30 degrees. Length: 53–69cm (21–27in). Family Gaviidae; species *Gavia stellata*.

divergent evolution
Situation where the same basic structure evolves to produce organs with different form and function. *See also* CONVERGENT EVOLUTION; EVOLUTION

diving-petrel
Any of a group of four very similar, small, fish-eating seabirds found in the cold currents of the Southern Hemisphere oceans. Diving petrels have short bodies with feet set well back, black upperparts and white underparts. They resemble the AUKS of the Northern Hemisphere but have tube noses that produce a waterproof preening oil. The bill has a distensible pouch to carry food. Length: 18–23cm (7–9in). Family Pelecanoididae; genus *Pelecanoides*.

DNA (deoxyribonucleic acid)
See feature article

DNA hybridization
Method of comparing DNA from different organisms in order to discover genetic relationships between species. Single strands of DNA from each species are placed together and allowed to react. Some strands will "hybridize" to form double strands (the usual structure of DNA) and the extent to which they do so indicates how many base sequences are complementary. This in turn is a a measure of how similar are the genes.

DNA polymerase
Enzyme that acts on the HYDROGEN BONDS that link the base pairs of the DNA double helix, thus separating the two strands of the DNA molecule. As all enzymes are capable of calalysing both forward and reverse reactions, DNA polymerase also causes complementary bases to link to the separated strands, thus producing identical copies of each strand to form two new DNA strands from the original. This process is the basis of semi-conservative DNA replication. DNA polymerase is widely used in aspects of GENETIC ENGINEERING such as gene cloning.

Dobzhansky, Theodosius (1900–75)
US geneticist, b. Russia. An authority on HUMAN EVOLUTION, he was influential in the development of population GENETICS as a separate study. His writings

include *Genetics and the Origin of Species* (1937), *Mankind Evolving* (1962) and *Genetics of the Evolutionary Process* (1970).

dock
Any of more than 200 species of flowering plants native to N United States and Europe. Curled dock (*Rumex crispus*) has scaly brown flowers. Dock leaves are a country remedy for nettle stings. Family Polygonaceae.

dodder
Leafless, parasitic, twining plant. It has a thread-like stem and clusters of small, yellow flowers. It feeds using haustoria (modified roots that enter the host plant). Family Convolvulaceae; species *Cuscuta europaea*.

dodo
Extinct flightless bird that lived on the Mascarene Islands in the Indian Ocean. The last dodo died in *c*.1790. The true dodo (*Raphus cucullatus*) of Mauritius was a heavy-bodied bird with a large head and large hooked bill. Weight: to 23kg (50lb). Family Raphidae.

dog
Domesticated, carnivorous mammal closely related to the JACKAL, WOLF and FOX. Typically it has a slender, muscular body; a long head with a slender snout; small paws, with five toes on the forefeet and four on the hind; non-retractile claws; and well-developed teeth. Smell is the dog's keenest sense; its hearing is also acute. The gestation period is 49 to 70 days; one or more puppies are born. Dogs developed from the tree-dwelling *miacis*, which lived *c*.40 million years ago. The dog was domesticated *c*.10–14,000 years ago. There are *c*.400 breeds. Length: 34–135cm (13–53in); tail: 11–54cm (4–21in); weight: 0.1kg–70kg (0.2–150lb). Family Canidae; species *Canis familiaris*.

dog, African wild (Cape hunting dog)
Dog that is found in a wide variety of habitats between the Sahara and South Africa, although it prefers woodland savanna. The African wild dog is a pack hunter. Its coat is short and dark with irregular white and yellow patches; it has large, rounded ears and a white-tipped tail. Head-body length: 75–100cm (30–40in); tail: 30–40cm (12–16in). Family Canidae; species *Lycaon pictus*.

dog, bush
Dog found in the forests and surrounding areas of Central and South America. It hunts in packs for large rodents and other animals. It has short legs and a compact body with small, round ears; it is an excellent swimmer. Head-body length: 66cm (26in); tail: 13cm (5in). Family Canidae; species *Speothos venaticus*.

◄ **dodder** Like other parasitic plants, dodder (*Cuscuta europaea*) lacks chlorophyll and gains all its nutrients from its host plant. Because it does not photosynthesize, its leaves are reduced and resemble small scales. Dodder seeds germinate in the soil and the young plant forms a temporary anchoring root which sends up slender stems. When these stems make contact with a host plant – in this case glasswort – the roots rot away and the stem wraps itself tightly around the host. This enables the parasite's haustoria (1) to penetrate the host's tissues and make contact with the xylem and phloem, from which it sucks nutrients.

xylem
phloem

DNA (deoxyribonucleic acid) is the NUCLEIC ACID that is the major constituent of the CHROMOSOMES of EUKARYOTE cells and some VIRUSES. DNA is often referred to as the "building block" of life since it stores the GENETIC CODE which functions as the basis of HEREDITY. The molecular structure of DNA was first proposed by James WATSON and Francis CRICK in 1953. It consists of a DOUBLE HELIX of two long strands of alternating sugar molecules and phosphate groups linked by nitrogenous bases. The whole molecule is shaped like a twisted rope ladder with the nitrogenous bases forming the rungs. The sugar is deoxyribose, and the four bases are ADENINE (A), CYTOSINE (C), GUANINE (G) and THYMINE (T). The bases are always paired in the same way: adenine always binds with thymine, guanine with cytosine. This regularity ensures accurate self-replication. During replication the two DNA strands separate, each providing a template for the synthesis of a new strand of RNA (MESSENGER RNA). This process of TRANSCRIPTION, mediated by ENZYMES, results in an identical copy of the original helix. The amount of DNA is constant for all cells of a species of animal or plant. In the process of replication the amount of DNA doubles as the chromosomes replicate themselves before MITOSIS; in the gametes, ovum and sperm (HAPLOID cells), the amount is half that of the body cells (see MEIOSIS). A base and its associated sugar and phosphate are known as a NUCLEOTIDE; the whole chain is a polynucleotide chain. The genetic code is stored in terms of the sequence of nucleotides: three nucleotides code for one specific AMINO ACID and a series of them constitute a GENE.

A single human cell contains 4m (13ft) of DNA packed into a nucleus only 5000ths of millimetre across. In this mass of tangled threads is contained all the information needed to make a human being. DNA directs development and maintains life of an organism by instructing cells to make proteins. The cell's DNA is a vast library of coded commands; the long molecules are packaged into chromosomes on which genes are arranged like beads on a string. Each chromosome is believed to involve more than 100,000 different genes – shorter, functional units of DNA – each representing one of the instructions needed to make and maintain the organism from which it originated. The complete set of genes from a living organism is known as its GENOME, and every cell of that organism carries at least one copy of the basic set. See also BIOTECHNOLOGY; GENETIC ENGINEERING; MUTATION; RECOMBINANT DNA RESEARCH

▼ The structure of DNA is crucial to its role as the cell's information store. The molecule is often called a double helix – a reference to its two spiral "backbones" (1, 2), which are made up of sugar and phosphate units. Linking the two backbones like the rungs of a ladder are the so-called bases (3) – adenine, thymine, guanine and cytosine. Each backbone contributes one base to each rung, and the bases are paired according to strict rules – adenine (light blue) always pairs with thymine (dark blue), and cytosine (red) with guanine (yellow). The sequence of bases along one backbone therefore exactly mirrors, or complements, the sequence on the other; when DNA is replicated in cell division, this property makes base mispairing – which may constitute a damaging mutation – less likely. The bonds between paired bases are relatively weak, allowing the DNA molecule to be "unzipped" prior to the processes of replication or transcription.

DNA is permanently locked into the nucleus. But the machinery for protein synthesis is situated in the cytoplasm – outside the cell membrane. DNA communicates with this machinery through a messenger molecule known as RNA. The messenger RNA (mRNA) is chemically similar to DNA itself, but has a single rather than double backbone, and the base uracil takes the place of the DNA's thymine. When a gene is active, the DNA base sequence corresponding to that gene is transcribed into mRNA. Enzymes in the nucleus "read" the base sequence and assemble a complementary strand of mRNA (4) from the base-sugar phosphate subunits (5). When the whole gene has been transcribed into mRNA, the messenger molecule (6) passes into the cytoplasm via pores in the nuclear membrane (7). The mRNA becomes attached to one or more ribosomes (8) – small cytoplasmic particles that are the sites of protein synthesis. A ribosome moves along the mRNA molecule sequentially passing each three-base "word" that specifies a particular amino acid. Another type of RNA, known as transfer RNA (tRNA) (9), then comes into play. This molecule acts as an adaptor between the three-letter words in mRNA and the amino acids that will be joined together to make a protein. At one end of each tRNA molecule is a sequence of three bases (10), complementary to a particular word on the mRNA: at the other end is the amino acid (11) specified by that word. The appropriate tRNAs plug into the mRNA, and the amino acids they carry are linked together by enzymes. As the ribosome passes along the mRNA strand, the protein chain gradually grows in length (12). A typical protein chain made this way may contain a sequence of between 100 and 500 amino acids linked by enzymes.

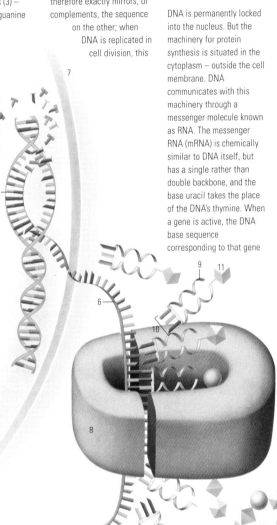

Viewed under a microscope, a chromosome of a dividing cell has a simple cross-like shape (A), which belies the complex way in which it "packages" DNA. Magnifying a small section (B) reveals a tightly coiled strand of chromatin – DNA closely associated with protein. Further enlarging a segment of chromatin (C) shows it to be a tight coil of nucleosomes – bead-like subunits composed of a protein core wrapped by the DNA molecule (D). The protein core is positively charged, allowing it to bind to the negatively charged DNA molecule (E) with its double helix structure (F). It is essential to the organization of the cell that the DNA is condensed. If it was not, the DNA double helix would take up too much space. By keeping DNA in compact bundles, the cell is much better able to manage it, uncoiling certain lengths as the genes contained in them are required.

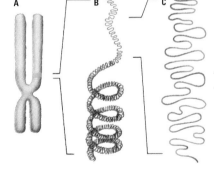

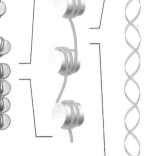

D

dog, raccoon

Dog native to forests in China, Japan and SE Siberia; it is now found across W Europe and Russia as well. In appearance it strongly resembles a raccoon, with a long, grey-brown coat, short, black legs, small, rounded ears, a bushy tail, and black face-markings. It is omnivorous, feeding on small vertebrates, insects and fruit. The raccoon dog is thought to be the only dog that does not bark. Head-body length: 50–60cm (20–24in); tail: 18cm (7in). Family Canidae; species *Nyctereutes procynoides*.

dogbane (Indian hemp)

Any of a group of seven species of perennial herb native to North America. Dogbanes have milky sap, and fibrous bark and leaves. The common dogbane traps insects in a sticky secretion produced at the base of its clusters of pink, bell-shaped flowers. Family Apocynaceae; species *Apocynum cannabinum* (common dogbane).

dogfish

SHARK found in marine waters worldwide. Generally greyish with white spots, it lacks a lower tail lobe. Eggs are laid in cases known as mermaids' purses. Dogfish are divided into two groups: spiny and spineless. A food fish, they are sold as rock salmon. Length: spiny, 0.6–1.2m (2–4ft); spineless, 7.3m (24ft). Suborder Squalidae.

dog rose

Vigorous, climbing, deciduous shrub of European hedgerows. Its long, arching branches bear hooked thorns. The leaves consist of five or seven toothed leaflets. The sweetly scented, pink or white flowers have five flat, heart-shaped petals. The fruits (hips) are oval and glossy red; they were used as a source of Vitamin C during the World War 2. Family Rosaceae; species *Rosa canina*.

dog-violet

Low-growing, perennial plant found in woods, hedgerows and grasslands of temperate Europe, North Africa, W Asia and United States. The blue-violet flowers have five petals, the darkly veined lower one being larger than the others, with a pale spur behind. The fruits are rounded capsules that split into three segments to release the tiny seeds. The leaves are heart-shaped. Family Violaceae; species include *Viola canina* (heath dog-violet), *Viola riviniana* (common dog-violet) and *Viola adunca* (western dog-violet).

dogwood

Any of several small trees and shrubs in the genus *Cornus*. Wild flowering dogwoods are found in deciduous forests. They have small flowers in four large, petal-like, white bracts. Family Cornaceae.

Doisy, Edward Adelbert (1893–1986)

US biochemist. He researched blood buffers, vitamins and metabolism. Doisy also isolated the female sex hormones, oestrone (1929) and oestradiol (1935). He shared the 1943 Nobel Prize for physiology or medicine with Henrik DAM for their analysis of vitamin K.

▶ **dogfish** The lesser spotted dogfish (*Scyliorhinus caniculus*) is a common dogfish found in the Mediterranean Sea. Like the larger spotted dogfish, or nurse hound (*Scyliorhinus stellarius*), it is caught as a food fish.

doldrums

Region of the ocean near the Equator, characterized by calms, and light and variable winds. It corresponds approximately to the belt of low pressure around the Equator.

dolerite

Medium-grained, basic, dark-coloured INTRUSIVE ROCK found in DYKES, SILLS and volcanic plugs.

dolomite

Carbonate mineral, calcium-magnesium carbonate $(CaMg(CO_3)_2)$, found in altered LIMESTONES. It is usually colourless or white. Dolomite is a calcite-like, rhombohedral class, prismatic crystal. It is often found as a gangue mineral in hydrothermal veins, particularly associated with galena and sphalerite. Dolomite is also the name given to a pearly white or pink SEDIMENTARY rock, probably formed by the alteration of limestone by seawater, where 90% or more of the calcite is replaced by calcium magnesium carbonate. Hardness 3.5–4; r.d. 2.8.

dollarbird

Dark greenish-blue bird of the ROLLER family. It has a red bill and deep blue flight feathers with a large white spot. It sallies after flying insects from its perch, often at dusk. The dollarbird has a wide distribution: it is found from India to Southeast Asia to Australia, in forests and often suburbs. Length: 28–30cm (11–12in). Family Coraciidae; species *Eurystomus orientalis*.

dolphin

Mammal that belongs to the order of toothed WHALES; the name commonly refers to those medium-sized marine animals with beak-like snouts, a central, sickle-shaped, dorsal fin and slender, streamlined bodies. Pilot and killer whales belong to the same family, which includes 32 species in 17 genera. River dolphins belong to a different family. *See also* TUCUXI

dolphin, Amazon

Dolphin that lives in the Amazon and Orinoco river systems of South America. It belongs to a more primitive family than its marine relatives. In common with other river dolphins, it has very poor eyesight; it uses ECHOLOCATION in the murky waters. Amazon dolphins feed on fish, shrimps and crabs. They are blue-grey on the back with pink undersides. Length: 208–228cm (82–90in). Family Platanistidae; species *Inia geoffrensis*.

dolphin, bottle-nosed

Most familiar species of dolphin. It is dark grey on the back with a paler underside and has a short beak. It is distributed worldwide, from temperate to tropical, coastal to deep ocean waters. Length: 340–390cm (134–154in). Family Delphinidae; species *Tursiops truncatus*.

dolphin, common

Dolphin with a dark back and pale underside, a prominent yellow band along the sides and black eye stripes. It often dives to feed on squid in deep waters, also taking fish and crabs. Common dolphins some-

times travel in groups, or pods, of several thousand, but they will usually feed in smaller groups. They have a worldwide distribution in tropical and warm temperate waters. Length: 210cm (83in). Family Delphinidae; species *Delphinus delphis*.

dolphin, hourglass

Dolphin found in the cooler waters of the Antarctic Ocean; it is seen off the coast of South America in the winter and all the way to the edge of the icepack in Antarctica in the summer. Its coloration is very distinctive: black on the back, white underneath with two large white side patches on either side of the dorsal fin, connected by a thin white band. Length: 160cm (63in). Family Delphinidae; species *Lagenorhynchus cruciger*.

dolphin, Irrawaddy (snubnose dolphin)

Dolphin found in rivers and inshore waters along the coasts of India and Southeast Asia, extending down to Australia. It is blue-grey, slightly paler underneath, and has a beakless, blunt head, large, bulging eyes and a small, rounded, dorsal fin. Although it can spend its entire life in freshwater, feeding on bottom-dwelling fish and crustaceans in shallow, muddy waters, this dolphin tends to travel across warm, tropical seas. Length: 200cm (80in). Family Delphinidae; species *Orcaella brevirostris*.

dolphin, Peale's (blackchin dolphin)

Dolphin that is found in the coastal waters of S South America. It is dark grey above, white below, with small, dark flippers, a dark nose and eye stripe, and a large dorsal fin. Head-tail length: 200cm (80in). Family Delphinidae; species *Lagenorhynchus australis*.

dolphin, Risso's (grey dolphin)

Dolphin distinguished by the many fine white scars present on the grey backs of the adults. These marks appear to be made by the teeth of other dolphins in the group. Risso's dolphins are found in all tropical and warm temperate seas, usually in small pods of about twelve, although herds of several thousand have been known. Length: 300–400cm (120–160in). Family Delphinidae; species *Grampus griseus*.

dolphin, river

Any of five species of dolphin that inhabit muddy river waters, relying on echolocation rather than vision to hunt for fish and crustaceans. These primitive river dolphins are found in South America, India and Southeast Asia. Species include: the Ganges dolphin (*Platanista gangestica*) of India and Bangladesh; the Indus dolphin (*Platanista minor*) of Pakistan; the whitefin dolphin (*Lipotes vexillifer*) of China; and the Amazon (*Inia geoffrensis*) and La Plata (*Pontoporia blainville*) dolphins of South America. Length: 155–260cm (61–102in). Family Platanistidae.

dolphin, striped

Dolphin found in tropical and warm waters of the Atlantic and Pacific oceans; they have also been seen as far north as Greenland. They are not often seen in coastal waters. Striped dolphins vary in colour, from brown to blue. They all have a series of prominent stripes along the flanks, beginning at the eye and extending towards the tail and flippers. They hunt fish and sometimes squid and shrimp. Length: 240cm (94in). Family Delphinidae; species *Stenella coeruleoalba*.

dolphin fish (mahi mahi)

Large, colourful, oceanic fish found worldwide in

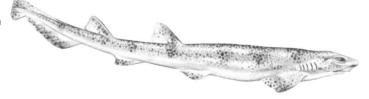

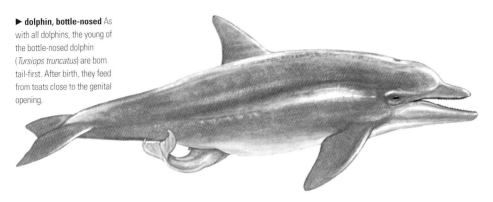

▶ **dolphin, bottle-nosed** As with all dolphins, the young of the bottle-nosed dolphin (*Tursiops truncatus*) are born tail-first. After birth, they feed from teats close to the genital opening.

D

tropical waters. The dolphin fish is a popular food fish. Family Coryphaenidae.

domain

In certain CLASSIFICATION schemes, a category that is recognized as higher than KINGDOM. In these schemes the two subkingdoms of Prokaryotae (Archaebacteria and the Eubacteria) constitute two domains, called ARCHAEA and BACTERIA, while all other living organisms are included in a third domain, the EUKARYA. *See also* Ready Reference, pages 462–63

domestication

Process by which groups or individual wild animals are tamed. Domestication is often for the economic profit of a community, typically for food, production of materials or as a source of labour. Domesticated animals have their food, territory and reproduction controlled and are kept isolated from their wild relatives. There is evidence of the process in the Mediterranean and Near East regions around 12,000 years ago, when dogs were used as hunting partners, watchdogs and companions. It is also possible that our PLEISTOCENE ancestors may earlier have kept animals as companions. Goats and sheep were domesticated around 9000 years ago. The term is also used in connection with plants, a process that probably began around 10,000 years ago with the domestication of wheat in the Middle East.

dominant

In genetics, term that describes the ALLELE of a heterozygous pair of alleles that manifests itself over the other. For example, if an offspring has one allele each for brown eyes and blue eyes, the brown-eyed allele will dominate and manifest itself over the RECESSIVE, blue-eyed allele, although he or she will retain the ability to pass on recessive genes to his or her children. *See also* HETEROZYGOTE; HOMOZYGOTE

donacobius (black-capped mocking-thrush)

Largest member of the WREN family; it resembles a mockingbird more than a wren. The donacobius is black above and white below. It is found throughout South America, especially in tropical rainforests. Length: 25cm (10in). Family Troglodytidae; species *Donacobius atricapillus*.

dopamine

Chemical normally found in the corpus striatum region of the human BRAIN, where insufficient levels are associated with Parkinson's disease. Dopamine is a NEUROTRANSMITTER and a precursor in the production of ADRENALINE and NORADRENALINE. The low levels in Parkinson's disease can be treated by administering the drug L-dopa.

dorado

Tropical, offshore, marine fish. A favoured sport fish, it has a squarish head, forked tail and a long dorsal

fin with rays. Its silvery, blue and yellow colours rapidly fade when it is taken from the water. Length: 150cm (60in). Family Coryphaenidae; species *Coryphaena hippurus* (common dorado) and *Coryphaena equisetus* (pompano dolphin).

dormancy

Temporary state of inaction or reduced METABOLISM. Animals may become dormant by HIBERNATION during winter months when food resources are scarce; dormant plant seeds for a time cease to grow or develop. An organism can return to a fully active state when conditions, such as temperature, moisture or day length, change.

dormouse

Rodent that occurs in Africa, Europe, Asia and Japan; it is similar in appearance to a squirrel. Most dormice are nocturnal and will hibernate in cooler weather. Family Gliridae or Selevinidae.

dormouse, common (hazel mouse)

Dormouse that lives in lowland and mountain forests from Great Britain to w Russia. It feeds on nuts, seeds and berries but may also take birds' eggs and nestlings. It constructs globular, grass-lined nests of shredded bark and leaves. Yellow-brown to red, it has a creamy throat and chest and a pinkish belly, large eyes and small ears. Head-body length: 6–9cm (2–4in); tail: 5–7cm (2–3in). Family Gliridae; species *Muscardinus avellanarius*.

dormouse, desert

Dormouse that is sometimes included in a family of its own. It is found in desert areas of central Asia. It eats insects and spiders, feeding at twilight. Its dense, soft fur is grey above and whitish below, but its tail is naked. Head-body length: 7–9cm (3–4in); tail: 6–8cm (2–3in). Family Gliridae or Selevinidae; species *Selevinia betpakdalensis*.

dormouse, edible (fat dormouse, squirrel-tailed dormouse)

Dormouse that inhabits both lowland and mountain forests across Europe, including the Mediterranean islands, and into Asia. It has large, rounded ears, small eyes and a long, bushy tail. It is an excellent climber, with rough pads on its hands and feet for gripping. It feeds mostly on seeds, fruit and nuts, but also sometimes insects and small birds. Head-body length: 13–19cm (5–7in); tail: 11–15cm (4–6in). Family Gliridae; species *Glis* or *Myoxus glis*.

dormouse, garden (orchard dormouse)

Either of two species of dormouse found in a wide variety of habitats, from swamps and forests to rocky areas and cultivated fields in North Africa through to Lebanon and Turkey. Its short fur is grey-brown, creamy underneath, usually with some black face-markings, and a tufted tail tip. It feeds on fruit, seeds,

nuts, insects and small rodents and birds. Head-tail length: 10–17cm (4–7in); tail: 6–11cm (2–4in). Family Gliridae; genus *Eliomys*.

dormouse, tree (forest dormouse)

Any of three species of dormouse found in dense forests between Europe and Pakistan. The tree dormouse is grey to yellow-brown, paler underneath, and is an excellent tree climber. It may be active throughout the winter in warmer areas, feeding on seeds, fruit, insects, eggs and young birds. Head-body length: 8–13cm (3–5in); tail: 6–11cm (2–4in). Family Gliridae; genus *Dryomys*.

dorsal

Upper surface of an organism – the surface that is turned away from the ground or other support. In an animal that walks on all fours, the dorsal surface is its back. By extension, in all VERTEBRATES it is the surface along which the spine runs. In animals that walk on two legs, such as humans, it is therefore the surface that faces backwards, or the posterior surface. On FISH, the dorsal fin is the main fin running along the top of the body.

dory

See JOHN DORY

dotterel

Small, short-billed, terrestrial PLOVER. It has boldly coloured summer plumage. The female, often with brighter plumage than the male, leads courtship displays; the duller male incubates the eggs. Dotterels breed on dry sandbanks, sparsely vegetated uplands and tundra. They characteristically feed by running for a short distance and then bobbing to pick up food. Length: 16–23cm (6–9in). Family Charadriidae.

double helix

Structure of DNA (deoxyribonucleic acid), the basic store of genetic information in the cells of each living organism. First demonstrated in 1953 by Francis CRICK and James WATSON, the knowledge of the structure of the DNA molecule has since revolutionized biological science.

double refraction

Splitting (refraction) of a beam of light in two as it passes through certain crystal materials, for example CALCITE.

Douglas fir (Oregon pine)

Evergreen, coniferous tree native to the Rocky Mountains of North America. It is grown both for its magnificent appearance and for its timber. The narrow, strap-like needles grow all around the stem. The light-brown, pendulous cones, up to 10cm (4in) long, have long, protruding bracts. Height: to 100m (330ft). Family Pinaceae; species *Pseudotsuga menziesii*.

doum palm

Evergreen tree native to North Africa. It is one of the

▲ **dormouse** Found in Europe and Asia, the edible dormouse (*Glis glis*) usually lives in trees. Its hands and feet are equipped with rough pads to assist in climbing. The dormouse's diet is chiefly vegetarian, but may include insects and small birds. They were once bred for human consumption.

few PALM species to have a branching stem, each branch repeatedly dividing into two until the tree reaches its full height. Each thin branch bears a crown of fan-shaped leaf fronds, up to 80cm (30in) long, at its tip. The tree produces orange-yellow, scented, edible fruits. Height: to 15m (50ft). Family Palmae; species *Hyphaene thebaica*.

dove
Medium-sized, mainly woodland bird, with strong, direct flight. The larger species are usually called PIGEONS. Some doves have sombre plumage, often with iridescent, green-purple neck patches; others have vivid colours. Most doves have a small head, a short bill and a crooning or cooing voice. Length: 15–34cm (6–13in). Family Columbidae.

dove, common ground-
Sparrow-sized dove that is common by arid roadsides in villages and towns from s United States to N South America. It has a scaly head and breast, reddish-brown wing patches, a short, black-edged tail and white under its wings. Length: 15cm (6in). Family Columbidae; species *Columbina passerina*.

dove, diamond (red-eyed dove)
Small, blue-grey dove found in Australia. It is washed brown above, with a red eye ring, fine white spots on its wings and chestnut wing feathers. Highly nomadic, it follows available water, nesting near water in dry scrub and woodland. Length: 19–21cm (7–8in). Family Columbidae; species *Geopelia cuneata*.

dove, inca
Dove that is similar to the common ground dove but with conspicuously scalloped plumage, especially on its belly, and a longer, white-edged tail. The inca dove is often found around towns and villages in cactus and mesquite country, from s North America to N South America. Length: 17–23cm (7–9in). Family Columbidae; species *Scardafella inca*.

dove, mourning
Slim-bodied dove; its long tail tapers to a point and its outer tail feathers have white tips. It is abundant and widespread, found from s Canada to Panama. The mourning dove inhabits farms and meadows and is seen in towns and suburbs. Length: 31cm (12in). Family Columbidae; species *Zenaida macroura*.

dove, namaqua
Small, budgerigar-shaped dove. Its central tail feathers are very long and black, and its primary feathers show a large, red-brown patch in flight. The male has a distinctive black face and upper breast. The namaqua dove spends much of its time on the ground. It lives and breeds in the Gulf States and E

► **dove, mourning** The mourning dove (*Zenaida macroura*) can withstand a variety of climatic conditions and so is found in desert as well as more temperate climates. It is named after its plaintive call.

Africa. Length: 29cm (11in). Family Columbidae; species *Oena capensis*.

dove, peaceful
Small, grey-brown dove, with a blue-grey head and neck, dense black-and-white barring on its neck and upper breast, and chestnut wing linings. It is found in Australia, Malaysia and Indonesia. Sedentary, the peaceful dove is found mainly in open scrub, farmland, parks and gardens, where it sometimes becomes tame. Length: 17–23cm (7–9in). Family Columbidae; species *Geopelia striata*.

dove, rock
Dove that is mainly grey, with a white or grey rump and two short black bars on its secondary wing feathers. The rock dove breeds colonially on mountain ledges and sea cliffs, mainly in Europe, the Middle East and North Africa. It is probably the ancestor of the domestic (and town) pigeon. Pure colonies are becoming rare, because rock doves breed with feral variants. Length: 31–34cm (12–13in). Family Columbidae; species *Columba livia*.

dove, stock
Dove that is similar to the rock dove but darker grey with black wing tips and a grey rump. The stock dove breeds in open woodland and open country with scattered trees in Europe and North Africa. Length: 32–34cm (12–13in). Family Columbidae; species *Columba oenas*.

dove, turtle
Strongly migratory dove, which breeds in Europe and the Middle East and winters in Africa. Its upperparts are mottled chestnut and black, with black-and-white neck patches. It frequents open wooded country. The turtle dove's call is a characteristic purring like the muted ring of a telephone. Turtle dove numbers are declining due to habitat loss and shooting on its migratory routes. Length: 26–28cm (10–11in). Family Columbidae; species *Streptopelia turtur*.

dovekie
See AUK, LITTLE

dove tree
See HANDKERCHIEF TREE

dowitcher
Snipe-like wading bird with a very long, probing bill and a white lower back and rump. It has a characteristic sewing-machine-like feeding action, often submerging its head. There are three dowitcher species worldwide. The long-billed and short-billed dowitchers breed in North America; despite their names, they are best distinguished by flight calls and breast markings. The Asiatic dowitcher, which breeds in Mongolia and winters in Indonesia, lacks the white rump; it is a globally threatened species. Length: 23–25cm (9–10in). Family Scolopacidae; genus *Limnodromus*.

dracaena
Any member of a genus of *c*.40 evergreen shrubs and trees found in forests, scrubs or open slopes of tropical Africa and the Canary Islands, with one species found in South America. The branched stems produce crowns of long, strap-like, glossy leaves. They bear small flowers on long spikes, which are followed by red or yellow berries. Dracaenas are grown as specimen garden plants or houseplants. Family Agavaceae/Dracaenaceae; species include *Dracaena draco* (DRAGON TREE) and *Dracaena sanderiana* (ribbon plant).

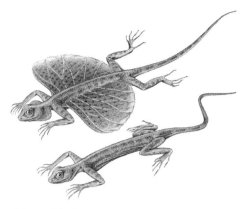

▲ **dragon** Flying dragons feed on ants in the middle layer of the forest, where there are few horizontal branches. They seem to have difficulty moving down a tree, and their evolution of gliding has probably helped them to ensure a reliable food supply with the minimum expenditure of energy, as they run up the trunk after a glide, then launch themselves once more to repeat the process.

draco
See DRAGON

dragon
Name applied to a variety of LIZARDS as well as to a variety of mythical reptiles. In Australia, dragon is the collective name for all agamid lizards, for example WATER DRAGON. It is also used for large monitors, such as the KOMODO DRAGON. The scientific name of the "flying" lizards of s and Southeast Asia is *Draco*, literally dragon. "Flying" dragons glide between trees by expanding skin-covered "wings" supported by ribs. Length: 18–38cm (7–15in). Family Agamidae.

dragonet
Small, colourful, bottom-dwelling, marine fish. It is related to the CLINGFISH, but lacks the adhesive disc on its breast. In most species, the male dragonet differs in appearance from the female. Families: Callionymidae and Draconettidae.

dragonfish
Mid- and deepwater fish found in all major temperate and subtropical oceans, with some species found in subarctic and Antarctic waters. The dragonfish is characterized by its slender body, light organs and hinged teeth. The family includes barbelled dragonfish, scaly dragonfish, scaleless black dragonfish and black dragon fish. Family Stomiidae.

dragonfly
Swift-flying insect of the order Odonata. It has a long, slender, often brightly coloured abdomen and two pairs of large membranous wings. Like the DAMSELFLY, it mates while flying. The carnivorous nymphs are aquatic. *See also* DARTER

dragonfly, emerald
Dragonfly with emerald-green eyes and a metallic-green thorax. The adults feed on other flying insects. Males establish breeding territories, and, after mating, the females lay eggs in water. The emerald dragonfly's larvae are aquatic and predatory. Adult wingspan: *c*.70mm (*c*.3in). Family Corduliidae; species include *Somatochlora hineana* and *Somatochlora metallica*.

dragonfly, emperor
One of the largest European dragonflies. It has a very striking appearance, with a green thorax, bright blue and black abdomen, and large eyes that touch on top

D

of its head. It is usually found around still water. The emperor dragonfly often breeds in small ponds and ditches. The nymphs are aquatic and predatory. Adult wingspan: *c*.85mm (*c*.3.3in). Family Aeshnidae; species *Anax imperator*.

dragonfly, hawker
Largest and most powerful of the world's dragonflies. The hawker dragonfly usually has striking blue or green markings. The adults are territorial. The larvae are aquatic and predatory. Some hawker species are pests around honeybee hives, killing workers and drones. Adult body length: 65–90mm (2.6–3.5in). Family Aeshnidae; genera *Aeshna*, *Anax* and *Brachytron*.

dragonfly, skimmer
Large, slender-bodied dragonfly; its two pairs of wings have an intricate network of veins. The skimmer has very large compound eyes and short, inconspicuous antennae. Its flight is very rapid. The larvae are aquatic and feed on small fish, tadpoles and other aquatic insects. Genus *Orthetrum*.

dragon tree
Slow-growing, widely branching tree from the Canary Islands; when mature, it looks like an inside-out umbrella. Long, lance-shaped leaves grow in tufts and have sharp spines at their tips. In summer, the dragon tree produces long spikes of white-tipped, green flowers, which are followed by large, spherical, orange fruits. Height: to 10m (33ft). Family Agavaceae/Dracaenaceae; species *Dracaena draco*.

drainage basin (catchment area)
Region from which all PRECIPITATION, such as rain and melted snow, flows to a single stream or system of streams. By identifying such a basin, scientists can calculate DENUDATION rates and moisture balances from various hydrological measurements such as EVAPORATION rates. The boundary of a drainage basin is called a WATERSHED. The shape of a drainage basin may help in forecasting river flooding.

drainage network
Relationship between the sizes, frequency, lengths and patterns of streams within a DRAINAGE BASIN. The drainage network can by analyzed in any combination of these variables to help describe the characteristics of a drainage basin.

drainage system
System by which surface water is collected and removed by streams, rivers and lakes. The pattern of drainage is determined by the type of rock and the slope of the land over which the water flows.

drift
In geology, gradual change in the land mass, related to soil CREEP. In oceanography, it indicates slow, oceanic circulation. Sedimentary drift is a general description of surface debris carried by either a river or a glacier. It may also indicate an accumulation such as a snowdrift or sand drift. CONTINENTAL DRIFT is the movement of continents.

drill
Rare BABOON, related to the MANDRILL, which lives in the rainforests of Nigeria and Cameroon. It is dark brown and has a black face with a fringe of white hair. It has a long muzzle with pronounced ridges along its length. The drill lives on the ground, feeding mostly on fruit, seeds and roots, but also on insects and small vertebrates. Head-body length: 70cm (28in); tail: 12cm (5in). Family Cercopithecidae; species *Papio* (formerly *Mandrillus*) *leucophaeus*.

drone-fly
Two-winged fly belonging to the HOVERFLY family. It is black and yellow, resembling a stinging bee, and this MIMICRY provides effective protection from predators. Order Diptera; family Syrphidae; species *Eristalis tenax*.

drongo
Noisy and pugnacious, crow-like perching bird with glossy, black plumage. It has a long, often deeply

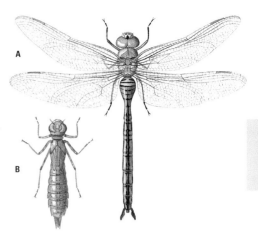

▲ **dragonfly** An incomplete metamorphosis, such as occurs in dragonflies, may be an adaptation to take advantage of different habitats. The adult form (A) of *Anax imperator* is a fast-flying predator on other insects, whereas the nymph (B) is aquatic, preying on a variety of life in freshwater ponds.

forked tail and an upright stance when perched. The drongo twists and turns adroitly in mid-air, catching insects in flight. Adaptable and intelligent, it often deliberately leaves hulled fruits in the path of vehicles so that it can feed on the crushed, exposed pith. It is found in India, Africa, Asia, Australia and Africa. Length: 24–32cm (10–13in), half of which is the tail. Family Dicruridae; genus *Dicrurus*.

drongo, black
Most common species of drongo. It has glossy, blue-black plumage, with a long, deeply forked tail. It is found around open cultivations, villages and suburbs of towns and villages. Length: 28cm (11in). Family Dicruridae; species *Dicrurus macrocercus*.

drongo, racquet-tailed
Either of two species of drongo; they are found in dense, broadleaved, evergreen forests and bamboo jungle. The **lesser racket-tailed drongo** has a tufted forehead and a square-ended tail with flattened, oval, racket-shaped end feathers. Length: 25cm (10in). Family Dicruridae; species *Dicrurus remifer*. The **greater racket-tailed drongo** has a crested head and longer, twisted tail rackets. Length: 32cm (13in). Family Dicruridae; species *Dicrurus paradiseus*.

drowned coast (submerged shoreline)
Coastal strip that has been submerged under the ocean, either because the sea level has risen, or because the land has sunk. Valleys become flooded and hills become islands.

drum
See CROAKER

drumlin
Smooth, oval-shaped mound of glacial TILL, one end of which is blunt, the other tapered. Drumlins usually occur in groups called a "drumlin field" or "drumlin swarm". They are believed to be formed beneath the outer zone of an advancing ice sheet, which deposits and streamlines material. The long axis of a drumlin lies parallel to the direction of the movement of the GLACIER.

drupe (stone fruit)
Any FRUIT that has a thin skin, fleshy pulp and hard stone or pip enclosing a single seed. Examples of drupes include plums, cherries, peaches, olives, almonds and coconuts.

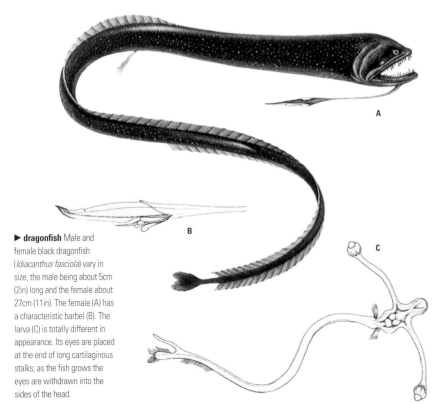

▶ **dragonfish** Male and female black dragonfish (*Idiacanthus fasciola*) vary in size, the male being about 5cm (2in) long and the female about 27cm (11in). The female (A) has a characteristic barbel (B). The larva (C) is totally different in appearance. Its eyes are placed at the end of long cartilaginous stalks; as the fish grows the eyes are withdrawn into the sides of the head.

duck

Waterfowl that is smaller than a swan or goose, with a shorter neck and legs. There are distinct male and female plumages, except during moulting, when the males resemble the females, a situation known as eclipse plumage. The dabbling or "puddle" ducks feed on the surface by upending. They take off by springing directly into flight; in most species a distinctive swatch of bright feathers, the speculum, marks the trailing edge of the secondary wing feathers. Diving ducks swim submerged and need a running start on water for take-off. Order Anseriformes; family Anatidae.

duck, American black

Blackish-brown dabbling duck. It has a pale face and neck and conspicuous pale under wings that are visible in flight. In North America, the American black duck is being replaced by the MALLARD, with which it frequently interbreeds. Length: 58cm (23in). Family Anatidae; species *Anas rubripes*.

duck, canvasback

North American diving duck; it is a prized game bird. It has a chestnut head and neck, pale grey back, and a black breast and tail. Length: 61cm (24in). Family Anatidae; species *Aythya valisneria*.

duck, harlequin

Small duck found in subarctic oceans. The male has a unique blue and white pattern with chestnut belly patches. The harlequin duck breeds by fast-flowing streams and waterfalls; it winters at sea by rocky coasts, often in rough surf where it swims buoyantly with its tail cocked. Length: 38–45cm (15–18in). Family Anatidae; species *Histrionicus histrionicus*.

duck, long-tailed (oldsquaw)

Duck that breeds in the Arctic region and winters in N North America. The male has a long tail and different and distinctive black-and-white plumages in summer and winter. In flight the wings are all dark. Active and noisy, the long-tailed duck has a loud, yodelling, three-part call when breeding. Length: 41–56cm (16–22in). Family Anatidae; species *Clangula hyemalis*.

duck, mallard

See MALLARD

duck, muscovy

Ungainly, goose-sized duck, with uniformly glossy green plumage and white wing patches. It is found in Mexico, Central and South America. It is the ancestor of the farmyard muscovy duck, which is usually black and white with a large patch of red skin

▲ **duck, long-tailed** Known for its musical song, the long-tailed duck is also capable of diving to great depths. Descending to depths of up to 60m (197ft), it can remain submerged for more than a minute.

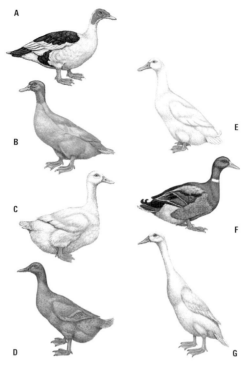

▲ **duck** The various breeds of duck include the Muscovy (A), buff Orpington (B), Aylesbury (C), khaki Campbell (D), Peking (E), Rouen (F) and Indian runner white (G).

between the bill and the eyes. In England, the farmyard muscovy has established feral populations. Length: 58–65cm (23–26in). Family Anatidae; species *Cairina moschata*.

duck, musk

Large, blackish-grey Australian duck. It has a leathery flap under its bill and a stiff, pointed tail. It is awkward on land and seldom flies. The musk duck swims mostly submerged, diving for crabs in shallow water. Its strange nocturnal call, a grunt followed by a shrill whistle, is a familiar sound around the permanent swamps with dense vegetation where it breeds. Length: 47–72cm (19–28in). Family Anatidae; species *Biziura lobata*.

duck, ruddy

Dumpy, large-headed, short-necked diving duck, which often swims with its long tail cocked up. The male has a rich chestnut plumage and a white face. It has been introduced to Europe from North America, where its rapid spread is checked by culling to prevent hybridizing with the globally threatened white-headed duck, to which it is related. Length: 35–43cm (14–17in). Family Anatidae; species *Oxyura jamaicensis*.

duck, steamer

Any of three species of duck, two of which are flightless, found in S South America. Steamer ducks are rather heavily built, with blue-grey and white plumage. The Falkland Islands flightless steamer duck, also known as the loggerhead duck, is darker with bronze patches on its head. Length: 60cm (24in). Family Anatidae; genus *Tachyeres*.

duck, torrent

Any of six South American species found in the very fast mountain rivers of the Andean mountain chain, from Venezuela to Tierra del Fuego. Torrent ducks are slim with long tails; the males have distinctive white heads with a black stripe and red bills. Family Anatidae; genus *Merganetta*.

duck, tufted

Diving duck found in Europe and Asia. The male has white flanks and black upperparts; it is the only waterfowl to have a drooping black crest. The female is brown with a short crest. Tufted ducks breed on still and slow-moving fresh water; in winter they flock on open lakes and reservoirs, rarely on the coast. Length: 40–47cm (16–19in). Family Anatidae; species *Aythya fuligula*.

duck, wood (Carolina duck)

Woodland duck that nests in tree cavities or nest boxes near ponds or rivers in North America; it has been introduced to Europe. The male has unmistakable colourful plumage, with a sleek, iridescent, green crest; the female has a teardrop-shaped eye patch. Length: 47cm (19in). Family Anatidae; species *Aix sponsa*.

duckweed

Perennial herb, one of the smallest of all flowering plants. It consists of a single, rounded, flat, leaf-like THALLUS, less than 5cm (2in) across, which floats on the surface of freshwater ponds, trailing a hair-like root beneath. There are no true leaves and no stem; the minute flowers consist of just the stamens and ovary. There are between 20 and 40 species of duckweed worldwide. Family Lemnaceae; species include *Lemna minor* (common duckweed).

Duffy blood group

Form of BLOOD GROUP in which the gene locus has two ALLELES one of which (Fy-) is common only in W Africa. Its distribution is associated with the form of malaria caused by *Plasmodium vivax*. The parasite normally uses the Duffy antigen on erythrocytes (red blood cells) as a site of attachment before burrowing through the cell membrane. It is less able to attach to Fy- antigen and so individuals with this form of the gene are less prone to contracting malaria. The allele has, therefore, become more prevalent in malarial areas such as W Africa as a result of NATURAL SELECTION.

dugong (sea cow)

Large, plant-eating, aquatic mammal found in shallow coastal waters of Africa, Asia and Australia. Grey and hairless, the dugong has no hind legs, and its forelegs are weak flippers. Length: 2.5–4m (8–13ft); weight: 270kg (600lb). Family Dugongidae; species *Dugong dugon*.

duiker

Small- to medium-sized ANTELOPE found in densely forested areas of Africa. Often both sexes have short, conical horns. Primarily browsers, taking fruit, seeds and shoots, some species are known to stalk and kill small birds. Family Bovidae; subfamily Cephalophinae.

duiker, bay

Nocturnal duiker found in central and W equatorial Africa. It is reddish brown with darker legs and a dark band running down its back from head to tail. Its horns are relatively long, at 5–10cm (2–4in). Head-body length: 70–100cm (28–40in); tail: 8–15cm (3–6in). Family Bovidae; subfamily Cephalophinae; species *Cephalophus dorsalis*.

duiker, black

Duiker that is dark brown or black with a reddish forehead; its tail has a white underside. Its diet includes a lot of fruit, and it has a large mouth. Little is known about the black duiker's habits because it is very shy. Head-tail length: 80–90cm (31–35in); tail:

12–14cm (5–6in). Family Bovidae; subfamily Cephalophinae; species *Cephalophus niger*.

duiker, blue
Smallest species of duiker, found across central Africa. Females are usually larger than males and sometimes have no horns. They are a uniform grey to grey-brown in colour. Head-body length: 50–75cm (20–30in); tail: 7–10cm (3–4in). Family Bovidae; subfamily Cephalophinae; species *Cephalophus monticola*.

duiker, common (savanna duiker, bush duiker)
Only species of duiker to be found in open country. It is red brown or grizzled grey and white underneath; its short tail is black on top. The female is often larger than the male. Usually only the male has horns. Head-body length: 80–115cm (31–45in); tail: 10–20cm (4–8in). Family Bovidae; subfamily Cephalophinae; species *Sylvicapra grimmia*.

duiker, yellow-backed
Largest species of duiker, found only in w Africa. Dark brown or black, it has white or orange hair along its back. It is nocturnal. Young animals are camouflaged with spots. Head-tail length: 115–145cm (45–57in); tail: 11–20cm (4–8in). Family Bovidae; subfamily Cephalophinae; species *Cephalophus sylvicultor*.

dulse
Any of a group of large red SEAWEEDS (genus *Rhodymenia*), especially *Rhodymenia palmata*, that are used as food condiments. Dulses grow chiefly in cold seas of the Northern Hemisphere.

dumortierite
Silicate mineral, hydrous aluminum borosilicate ($Al_8BSi_3O_{19}[OH]$). It is found scattered in METAMORPHIC ROCKS, and occurs usually in fibrous masses,

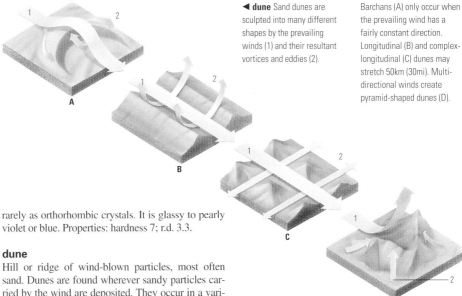

◄ **dune** Sand dunes are sculpted into many different shapes by the prevailing winds (1) and their resultant vortices and eddies (2). Barchans (A) only occur when the prevailing wind has a fairly constant direction. Longitudinal (B) and complex-longitudinal (C) dunes may stretch 50km (30mi). Multi-directional winds create pyramid-shaped dunes (D).

rarely as orthorhombic crystals. It is glassy to pearly violet or blue. Properties: hardness 7; r.d. 3.3.

dune
Hill or ridge of wind-blown particles, most often sand. Dunes are found wherever sandy particles carried by the wind are deposited. They occur in a variety of shapes depending on the direction of the wind, whether or not it is constant, and the surrounding landforms. *See also* BARCHAN; SEIF

dung beetle
See feature article, page 122

dung-fly
Black, yellow or brown, hairy fly that resembles the HOUSE-FLY. The larvae are dung-feeders, and the adults are predatory on small insects. Adults often carry disease-causing organisms on their feet. Adult body length: 3–13mm (0.1–0.5in). Order Diptera; family Scathophagidae; genus *Scathophaga*.

dunite
Coarse-grained IGNEOUS ROCK of colour ranging from light yellowish-green to an emerald green; it is composed almost entirely of OLIVINE. Dunite occurs at Dun Mountain, New Zealand, from where it takes its name.

dunnart
Nocturnal MARSUPIAL MOUSE found in Australia and New Guinea. Dunnarts are pale with slender feet.

They feed on insects, spiders and small vertebrates. Head-body length: 7–12cm (3–5in); tail: 5–13cm (2–5in). Family Dasyuridae; genus *Sminthopsis*; there are *c*.10 species.

duodenum
First section of the small INTESTINE, shaped like a horseshoe and part of the DIGESTIVE SYSTEM. The pyloric sphincter, a circular muscle, separates it from the STOMACH. Alkaline BILE and pancreatic juices are released into the duodenum to aid the DIGESTION of food.

durian
Evergreen tree of Southeast Asia, best known for the creamy white flesh of its long (20cm/8in), spiny fruit or aril. It is grown commercially for its fruits, which have a delicious flavour and a strong but rather unpleasant aroma; they decay rapidly once ripe. The fruits are eaten by people and large animals, including elephants, tigers and tapirs. The flowers are creamy white and the leaves are dark green above and golden beneath. Family Bombacaceae; species *Durio zibethinus*.

dust bowl
Arid landscape that has suffered severe and prolonged drought leading to EROSION by wind and the removal of soil, often exacerbated by overfarming. The Great Plains region of North America was originally prairie grassland but, on being ploughed for cereal crops, it degenerated into dustbowl conditions during the droughts of the 1930s and 1980s. Similar dustbowls are being formed today in Africa due to population pressure and overgrazing.

dust storm
Strong winds that pick up small particles of sediment and dry soil and carry them for considerable distances (hundreds of miles). Stony DESERTS and ablation hollows are formed where there is constant removal of loose material by wind. Where the particles are deposited, wave-shaped bodies called DUNES build up to form sandy deserts. Sediment-laden wind has considerable erosive power and can abrade rocks to produce small grains. *See also* DESERTIFICATION

dusty miller (rose campion)
Biennial plant from SE Europe; it has silver-grey stems and leaves covered by fine wool. Long,

▼ **dugong** The dugong family contains only one species, *Dugong dugon*. The dugong is seen here foraging on the seafloor in the Indo-Pacific region. It feeds on sea grasses, hence its common name of sea cow. Its mouthparts are adapted for pulling up these plants by the roots. Dugongs are large creatures, whose primary predator, apart from humans, is the shark.

D

Small to medium-sized SCARAB BEETLE. Some species form balls of dung as food for their larvae and may roll the balls some distance before burying them. Other species burrow under the dung. Family Scarabaeidae; species include *Geotrupes stercorarius*.

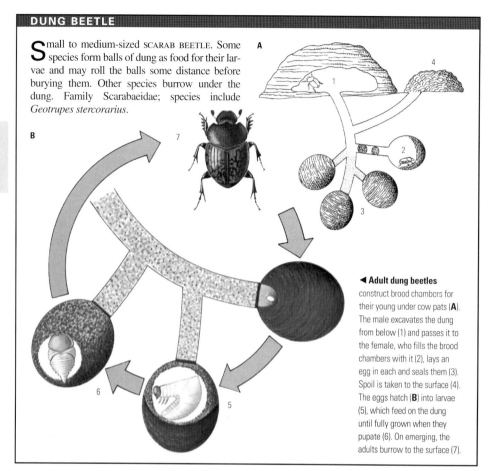

◄ **Adult dung beetles** construct brood chambers for their young under cow pats (**A**). The male excavates the dung from below (1) and passes it to the female, who fills the brood chambers with it (2), lays an egg in each and seals them (3). Spoil is taken to the surface (4). The eggs hatch (**B**) into larvae (5), which feed on the dung until fully grown when they pupate (6). On emerging, the adults burrow to the surface (7).

lance-shaped leaves grow from the base of the plant, those further up the stem are shorter. The purple-red, tubular flowers have five rounded petals. Height: to 80cm (30in). Family Caryophyllaceae; species *Lychnis coronaria*.

Dutch elm disease
Highly infective fungal infection that attacks the bark of elm trees and spreads inwards until it kills the tree. It is spread by beetles whose grubs make a series of linked tunnels in the wood below the bark.

Dutchman's breeches
Clump-forming, woodland perennial native to E North America. The blue-green leaves have three deeply divided leaflets. In early spring arching stems bear arrowhead-shaped, yellow-tipped, white flowers. All parts of the plant may cause discomfort if ingested; contact with the skin may induce allergic reactions. Family Fumariaceae; species *Dicentra cucullaria*.

Dutchman's pipe
Any of *c*.300 species of evergreen or deciduous, climbing perennials found worldwide in moist, tropical and temperate woodlands. The leaves, up to 30cm (12in) long, are heart-shaped, dark green above and lighter beneath. The flowers have no petals but consist of an s-shaped calyx resembling a smoking pipe. Family Aristolochiaceae; species include *Aristolochia macrophylla*.

Dutton, Clarence Edward (1841–1912)
US geologist who developed the principle of isostasy, according to which the level of the Earth's crust is determined by its density. The rise of light materials forms continents and mountains; the sinking of heavy materials forms oceans and basins.

Duve, Christian René de (1917–78)
Belgian cell biologist who shared with Albert CLAUDE and George PALADE the 1974 Nobel Prize for physiology or medicine for a detailed description of the structure and function of the cell and its parts. Analysis of biochemical activity in a cell led him to discover the LYSOSOME, an organelle that acts as the "stomach of the cell".

dyke (dike)
INTRUSION of IGNEOUS ROCK forming a seam that cuts across the structure of the surrounding rock; it is often vertical or near-vertical. The cross-cutting nature indicates that a dyke is younger than the rocks it has intruded. At the edge of a dyke the rock is finer-grained than at the centre, as a result of cooling and solidifying more quickly; this is termed a chilled margin. The rock immediately next to the dyke may be altered by CONTACT METAMORPHISM, for example in intruded limestones there may be a thin zone of marble alongside each dyke.

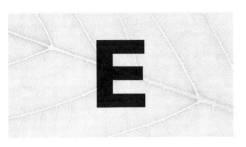

E

eagle

Very large BIRD OF PREY with broad wings and tail, a hooked beak and powerful talons. The eagle's flight is heavy and powerful, and it soars with outspread and upturned wings. Eagles breed in wild mountainous areas, open steppe, prairie or wooded country, according to species. Their large nests, built in trees or on ledges, are often used year after year. Length: 45–95cm (18–37in); wingspan: 150–300cm (60–120in). Family Accipitridae; genera include *Aquila*, *Haliaeetus* and *Hieraaetus*; there are 59 species worldwide.

eagle, African fish-

Eagle that is found in tropical Africa. The adult bird has a white head, short, white tail and chestnut body. Its call is loud, wild and far carrying. Length: 74–84cm (29–33in); wingspan: 200–250cm (80–100in). Family Accipitridae; species *Haliaeetus vocifer*.

eagle, harpy

Large South American eagle. It is black above and white below; its grey head has a conspicuous double crest and it has a broad black chest band. Young birds have pure white heads. The harpy eagle hunts over tropical forest canopy for monkeys and sloths, which it catches with its powerful talons. Length: 85–90cm (33–35in). Family Accipitridae; species *Harpia harpyja*.

eagle, bald

Eagle that is the heraldic symbol of the United States. An adult bald eagle is easily identified by its brown body, white head, white tail and huge yellow bill. In the 1960s and 70s, shooting, loss of habitat and pesticide poisoning seriously reduced the number of bald eagles in the United States; intense recovery programmes have since increased populations. Length: 79–94cm (31–37in); wingspan: 178–229cm (70–90in). Family Accipitridae; species *Haliaeetus leucocephalus*.

▲ **eagle, imperial** During the 20th century, the imperial eagle (*Aquila heliaca*) population declined severely and it is now an endangered species in Europe. Sensitive to changes in its habitat, it is also at risk from being shot while migrating.

eagle, black

Majestic, long-winged and long-tailed eagle; it is dark brownish-black, with distinctive yellow feet and base of bill. It flies with its wings raised in a v shape and with upturned and splayed wing tips. The black eagle is found in broadleaved forests on hills of the Indian subcontinent and Southeast Asia. Length: 69–81cm (27–32in). Family Accipitridae; species *Ictinaetus malayensis*.

eagle, booted

Small species of eagle that exists in three different colour forms: a pale form, most common in Europe, which has strikingly pale underwings; a reddish-brown form, found in the Middle East, which has a dark brown band on its under wing; and a dark form, which is rich dark brown with a pale tail. All booted eagles have a white mark on the leading edge of their wings. They breed in forested areas. Length: 45–53cm (18–21in); wingspan: 100–121cm (40–48in). Family Accipitridae; species *Hieraaetus pennatus*.

eagle, golden

Large eagle that is tawny brown with a paler head. Its flight is majestic and graceful, and it often soars for hours at a time on up-tilted wings. The golden eagle is widely distributed in North America, Europe and Asia. It breeds mainly in mountains, but also in lowland forests and wetlands. Length: 75–88cm (30–35in); wingspan: 204–220cm (80–87in). Family Accipitridae; species *Aquila chrysaetos*.

eagle, imperial

Longest necked of the large *Aquila* eagles. It has a small white patch on its shoulders and a golden buff crown and neck. The distinctive Spanish form has a large white shoulder patch and a white leading edge to its wing. Imperial eagles are found in open plains, deserts, rocky forests and wetlands of s Europe and the Middle East. Length: 72–83cm (28–33in); wingspan: 190–210cm (75–83in). Family Accipitridae; species *Aquila heliaca*.

eagle, martial

Largest African eagle. It has a dark brown head with piercing yellow eyes, and a distinctive crest on its nape. It has a brown back and white underparts, spotted with brown. The martial eagle is widely distributed in savanna and forest edges of sub-Saharan Africa. Its prey includes small antelopes and storks. Length: 83–85cm (33–34in). Family Accipitridae; species *Polemaetus bellicosus*.

eagle, Philippine (monkey-eating eagle)

Huge eagle. It has a long, white head and a massive bill. It is brown above and whitish buff below; its neck feathers are streaked brown like a mane. The Philippine eagle hunts monkeys in the forest canopy. It is a critically endangered species and is found only in the Philippines, where there are perhaps fewer than 200 individuals left due to clearance of their forest habitat. Length: 91cm (36in); wingspan: 200cm (80in). Family Accipitridae; species *Pithecophaga jefferyi*.

eagle, short-toed

Medium-sized, snake-eating eagle. It has long wings, a rounded, owl-like head and almost all white under wings. It often hovers like a huge kestrel. The short-toed eagle is a summer visitor to Europe and the Middle East from sub-Saharan Africa. Length: 62–67cm (24–26in); wingspan: 185–195cm (73–77in). Family Accipitridae; species *Circaetus gallicus*.

◀ **eagle, martial** A predominantly solitary and quiet bird, the martial eagle (*Polemaetus bellicosus*) is commonly seen perched on a large dead tree. It often nests in the same tree for several years and will hunt within a 130sq km (50sq mi) radius. With a wingspan of up to 2.5m (8ft), it spends much of its time on the wing and flies so high that it is difficult to see with the naked eye. The martial eagle is capable of soaring for hours on an updraught, diving at great speed to catch prey. On average, the martial eagle breeds once every 18 months.

eagle, Steller's sea

Fish-eating eagle with a huge, yellow-orange bill. It is brown with white shoulders and a white leading edge to its wings; it has a white, wedge-shaped tail and thighs. The Steller's sea eagle nests in NE Asia and Japan. Length: 66–89cm (26–35in); wingspan: 203–241cm (80–95in). Family Accipitridae; species *Haliaeetus pelagicus*.

eagle, Verreaux's

Eagle that in flight has a distinctive s-shaped curved rear edge to its wings. The adult bird is black with a conspicuous white patch on its wings above and below; it has a pure white lower back and a white v shape on its shoulders. The Verreaux's eagle is found in open wooded country with hills and ravines in the Middle East and E Africa. Length: 80–95cm (31–37in); wingspan: 225–245cm (89–96in). Family Accipitridae; species *Aquila verreauxi*.

eagle, wedge-tailed (eaglehawk)

Eagle that is typical of members of the *Aquila* genus. It is glossy black-brown with tawny feathering on its neck; it has a pale bill, long, diamond-shaped tail and a huge wingspan. Its flight is majestic, with powerful wing beats soaring it to great heights. The wedge-tailed eagle is confined to Australia and Tasmania. Length: 89–106cm (35–42in); wingspan: 250–300cm (100–120in); females are larger than males. Family Accipitridae; species *Aquila audax*.

▶ **eagle, Philippine** Like many eagles, the Philippine, or monkey-eating, eagle (*Pithecophaga jefferyi*) is an endangered species. The destruction of its habitat has meant that young eagles have been unable to disperse easily thus limiting their chances of surviving and reproducing. Attempts to breed the Philippine eagle in captivity have failed, and it continues to be sought after by trophy-hunters and for private zoos.

eagle, white-tailed sea

Enormous, brown, vulture-like, fish-eating eagle. It has broad, parallel-edged wings, a massive bill and a wedge-shaped tail that is white in adults. Its flight is ponderous. The white-tailed sea eagle is found along coasts, lakes and rivers in wild country. It ranges over N Eurasia and Greenland. Attempts are being made at reintroducing the white-tailed sea eagle to Scotland. Length: 66–89cm (26–35in); wingspan: 183–239cm (72–94in). Family Accipitridae; species *Haliaeetus albicilla*.

E

ear

Organ of HEARING and balance. It converts sound waves to nerve impulses that are carried to the BRAIN. In most mammals it consists of the outer, middle and inner ear. The **outer** ear carries sound to the eardrum. The **middle** ear is air-filled, and has three tiny bones (ossicles) that pass on and amplify sound vibrations to the fluid-filled inner ear. The **inner** ear contains the cochlea. Vibrations stimulate tiny hairs in these organs, which causes impulses to be sent via the auditory nerve to the brain. The inner ear also contains SEMICIRCULAR CANALS, which maintain orientation and balance.

Earth

See feature article, pages 126–27

earthcreeper

Small, thrush-sized songbird found in South America. It has a long, slender, down-curved bill; it is usually brown above and pale below. The earthcreeper scurries over rocks and soil in search of insects. It digs tunnels in soft soil to nest. There are nine species, one of which is found only in Bolivia. Length: 20cm (8in). Family Furnariidae; genus *Upucerthia*.

earthquake

See feature article, page 129

Earth sciences

General term used to describe all the sciences concerned with the structure, age, composition and atmosphere of the EARTH. It includes the basic subject of GEOLOGY, with its subclassifications of GEO-

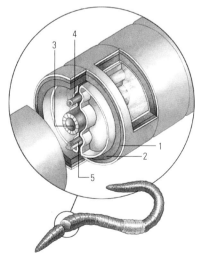

▲ **earthworm** The earthworm's body is formed by a tubular muscle wall consisting of two layers, surrounding fluid-filled segments. The upper layer (1) contains circular muscles that wrap around the body, while the lower layer (2) is made up of longitudinal muscles. The circular muscles provide anchorage, and the longitudinal muscles permit forward movement. The intestine (3), blood vessels (4) and nerve cord (5) run right through the segment walls.

▲ **earwig** The elegant hind wings of the earwig fold up under short wing cases. The male earwig has larger pincers than the female. In addition to trapping and eating insects, the pincers may be used to attack rival males. In defence the earwig can curl its tail like a scorpion and some species have a gland that secretes a foul-smelling liquid when threatened. The earwig takes its name from an unfounded superstition that it crawls into human ears at night.

CHEMISTRY, GEOMORPHOLOGY and GEOPHYSICS; MINERALOGY and PETROLOGY; SEISMOLOGY and VOLCANISM; OCEANOGRAPHY; METEOROLOGY; and PALAEONTOLOGY.

earth star

Any member of a group of fungi that produce star-shaped mature fruiting bodies. The fruiting body develops as a globular structure, then the outer wall splits into several pointed rays, which curve back to reveal a globular spore sac from which the spores escape. Phylum Basidiomycota; genera *Geastrum* and *Myriostoma*.

earthworm

ANNELID with a cylindrical, segmented body and tiny bristles. Most earthworms live in moist soil. Their burrowing aerates the soil, helping to make it fertile. Length: 5cm–33m (2in–11ft). There are several hundred species. Class Oligochaeta; family Lumbricidae; genus *Lumbricus*.

earwig

Slender, flattened, brownish-black insect found in crevices and under tree bark. There are *c*.900 species worldwide. All have a pair of forceps at the hind end. Order Dermaptera; a common genus is *Forficula*.

East, Edward Murray (1879–1938)

US plant geneticist, botanist and chemist whose work influenced the development of hybrid maize. He worked to determine and control the fat and protein content in maize.

easterlies

Winds, such as TRADE WINDS, that blow persistently from the east.

ebony

Hard, fine-grained, dark heartwood of various Asian and African trees of the genus *Diospyros* in the ebony family. The major commercial tree is the macassar ebony (*Diospyros ebenum*) of S India and Malaysia. Family Ebenaceae.

eccrine gland

One of two types of SWEAT GLAND in mammals – the other is the APOCRINE GLAND. Both are found within layers of the SKIN. In humans and some apes, eccrine glands are the more numerous and are distributed generally over the body, not associated only with hair, as are apocrine glands.

ecdysis

In ARTHROPODS, the periodic shedding (moulting) of the cuticle. In insects, the inner portion of the old cuticle is absorbed and it becomes split along certain lines of weakness before being cast off. By swallowing air the insect expands the new soft cuticle, which hardens leaving space for the internal growth of the insect. *See also* ECDYSONE

ecdysone

Hormone that stimulates MOULTING in some animals. Ecdysone is a steroid hormone produced by CRUSTACEANS and INSECTS. By acting at particular sites on genes, it stimulates the production of the proteins that are involved in moulting (ECDYSIS) and METAMORPHOSIS.

echidna (spiny anteater)

Either of two species of MONOTREME, found in Australia, Tasmania and New Guinea. An echidna is a primitive, egg-laying mammal, with a cloaca, spines on the upper body and an elongate snout. Family Tachyglossidae.

echidna, long-beaked

One of the two species of echidna. The dark hairs on its back sometimes hide the usually lighter spines. Its slightly curved, elongate snout makes up two thirds of the length of its head. It feeds on earthworms. It has horny spines on the tip of its tongue but no true teeth. Length: 45–90cm (18–35in). Family Tachyglossidae; species *Zaglossus bruijni*.

echidna, short-beaked

Toothless mammal with long, yellow spines and dark fur. It is a solitary animal, living in temporary shelters in a variety of habitats from woodland to open areas. The short-beaked echidna feeds on ants and termites, which it catches with its long, sticky tongue. Length: 30–45cm (12–18in). Family Tachyglossidae; species *Tachyglossus aculeatus*.

echinoderm

Any member of the phylum Echinodermata, a group of spiny skinned, marine invertebrate animals, which includes SEA URCHINS, SEA CUCUMBERS and STARFISH. Radially symmetrical with five axes, echinoderms have a skeleton of calcareous plates in their skin. Their hollow body cavity includes a complex, internal, fluid-pumping system and tube feet. They reproduce sexually, producing bilaterally symmetrical larvae resembling those of CHORDATES; REGENERATION also occurs.

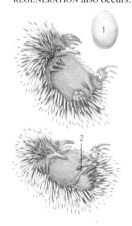

◄ **echidna** An example of a primitive mammal, the echidna (spiny anteater) is classified as a monotreme. Instead of giving birth to live young like other mammals, it lays a tiny egg. The egg (1) is soft-shelled and resembles a reptile's egg. Once the egg is laid, the echidna uses its hind limbs to roll it to a special incubation groove (2). The minute hatchling is about 1.25cm (0.5in) long.

echiuran

See SPOON WORM

echolocation

System of navigation used principally by WHALES and BATS. The animal emits a series of short, high-frequency sounds, and from the returning echo it gauges its environment. Bats and DOLPHINS also use the system for hunting. *See also* SONAR

eclogite

Coarse- to medium-grained METAMORPHIC ROCK consisting mainly of green PYROXENE and red GARNET. A very dense rock, eclogite is formed deep in the Earth's crust under conditions of very high temperature and pressure. It occurs in SCHISTS (Norway) and in diamond-bearing pipes of KIMBERLITE (South Africa).

ecological niche

Position or role any species occupies within its HABITAT. It represents more than a physical area within the habitat because it includes an organism's behaviour and its interactions with its biotic (living) and abiotic (non-living) environment. No two species can occupy the same ecological niche – a condition known as the **competitive exclusion principle**.

ecological pyramid

Bar diagram that is used to indicate the relative numbers of individuals of a species at each TROPHIC LEVEL in a FOOD CHAIN. The length of the bar gives a measure of the relative numbers, BIOMASS or energy of all organisms at that trophic level in the food chain. The overall shape is roughly that of a pyramid, PRIMARY PRODUCERS outnumbering the PRIMARY CONSUMERS, which in turn outnumber the SECONDARY CONSUMERS.

ecology

Biological study of relationships of organisms to their ENVIRONMENT and to one another. The term was coined (1866) by German zoologist Ernst Haeckel (1834–1919). Ecologists study populations (groups of individual organisms), COMMUNITIES (different organisms sharing the same environment), or ECOSYSTEMS (a community and its physical environment). The maximum population that can be sustained by a particular environment's resources is called its CARRYING CAPACITY. The role of a species within its community is termed its ECOLOGICAL NICHE. Within the BIOSPHERE, natural cycles (CARBON CYCLE, HYDROLOGICAL CYCLE, NITROGEN CYCLE and OXYGEN CYCLE) are assisted when the biological diversity of species fill these various ECOLOGICAL NICHES. This diversity produces CLIMAX COMMUNITIES; an extensive climax COMMUNITY is called a BIOME. **Applied ecology** is the practical management and preservation of natural resources and environments.

ecosphere

Similar to BIOSPHERE, the total of all the ECOSYSTEMS of the Earth. The term BIOSPHERE is used solely to indicate the zone of life, but the term ecosphere includes the interaction of living organisms with their abiotic ENVIRONMENT. *See also* ABIOTIC FACTORS

ecosystem

Basic unit in ECOLOGY, consisting of a community of organisms in a physical ENVIRONMENT. Study of these systems is based often on energy flow. The Sun provides the energy that PRIMARY PRODUCERS, such as green plants, convert into food by PHOTOSYNTHESIS. Plants also need ABIOTIC (non-living)

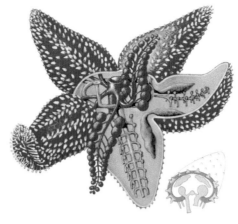

▲ **echinoderm** A starfish feeds by surrounding its prey, eventing its stomach through its mouth and partially digesting the food, which is then taken back into the stomach extensions (red). It moves by means of a water-vascular system (blue) unique to echinoderms. Water enters through the sieve plate (1), and is drawn by tiny hairs through the five radial canals into the many pairs of tube feet (2) armed with suckers. When the ampulla (3) of each tube foot contracts, water is forced into the foot (illustrated in cross-section), which extends (4) and allows attachment to the hard rock. Muscles in the foot then shorten it (5), forcing water back into the ampulla and drawing the starfish forward.

substances from the water and soil to grow. In a typical FOOD CHAIN, HERBIVORES or PRIMARY CONSUMERS, such as rabbits, eat the plants and in turn serve as food for SECONDARY CONSUMERS, such as foxes. DECOMPOSERS, such as BACTERIA, break down dead organic matter into simple nutrients completing the food chain. The chemicals necessary for life are recycled by the processes of the CARBON CYCLE, HYDROLOGICAL CYCLE, NITROGEN CYCLE and OXYGEN CYCLE. Interference with these finely balanced natural processes, such as POLLUTION, climate change or the loss of a species, can disrupt the entire ecosystem.

ecotone

Transitional zone between two adjacent HABITATS.

ecotype

In ecology, variety of a species that has special inherited characteristics that allow it to thrive in a particular HABITAT. In botany, variety of a plant species, the distinguishing characteristics of which are mainly inherited rather than resulting from environmental pressure.

ectoderm

One of three so-called GERM LAYERS of tissue formed in the early development of a fertilized OVUM (egg). It is the outer layer of the BLASTULA and later develops, in most animals, into a skin or shell, a nervous system, lining tissue, parts of some sense organs, and various miscellaneous tissues. The other germ layers are the ENDODERM and MESODERM.

ectoplasm

Outer layer of the CYTOPLASM of a CELL; it is usually semisolid and transparent.

ectothermic (poikilothermic)

Animal whose body temperature fluctuates with the temperature of its surroundings, often referred to as "cold-blooded". REPTILES, AMPHIBIANS, FISH and INVERTEBRATES are cold-blooded. They can control their body temperature only by their behaviour – by moving in and out of the shade, or orienting themselves to absorb more or less sunlight. *See also* ENDOTHERMIC

edaphic factor

Any element or condition pertaining to the SOIL or substratum. Such elements affect the growth of plant species and include particle size, HUMUS content, water retention, air content, mineral composition, MICROORGANISMS, pH and TOPOGRAPHY.

edelweiss

Small, perennial plant native to the Alps and other high Eurasian mountains. It has white, downy leaves and small, yellow flower heads enclosed in whitish-yellow bracts. Family Asteraceae/Compositae; species *Leontopodium alpinum*.

edentate (Lat. with all the teeth removed)

Any of a small order of North and South American mammals found from Kansas, central United States, to Patagonia, s South America. There are *c*.30 species of edentates, including ARMADILLO, SLOTH and ANTEATER. Only anteaters are truly toothless.

Ediacaran

Member of a group of soft-bodied marine organisms that evolved in late Precambrian times and had mostly become extinct by early Cambrian times. It is not yet clear what kinds of organisms they were, although some seem to belong to living groups such as the seapens. They are named after the Ediacara Hills in the Flinders Range of South Australia, where many examples are well preserved.

edmi (Cuvier's gazelle)

Very rare GAZELLE that both grazes and browses in the open forests or rocky semideserts of Morocco, Algeria and Tunisia. The edmi has a dark grey or brown back, a darker side band and distinctive facial markings. Length: 101–125cm (40–49in). Family Bovidae; subfamily Antilopinae; species *Gazella cuvieri*.

eel

Marine and freshwater fish found worldwide in shallow temperate and tropical waters. Eels have snake-like bodies, dorsal and anal fins, and an air bladder at the throat. Length: up to 3m (10ft). Types include freshwater, moray and conger. Order Anguilliformes.

eel, conger

Any of *c*.100 species of true eel that are found in all tropical and subtropical oceans. They are distributed from shallow to deep waters. Conger eels are considered excellent food and sport fish. Family Congridae; species include *Conger conger* (the European conger).

eel, electric

Elongate freshwater fish found in South America. It

▲ **eel** Freshwater eels are related to the carp and have long been valued for their rich flesh. European (*Anguilla anguilla*) and Japanese (*Anguilla japonica*) eels are two of the most widely cultivated types of eel.

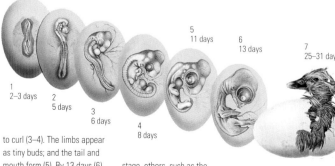

undulated moray

black-spotted moray

▲ eel, moray Moray eels such as the undulated moray (*Gymnothorax undulatus*) and the black-spotted moray (*Gymnothorax favagineus*) are found in tropical seas. They favour rocks and areas of broken ground that provide resting places during the day. Largely nocturnal in their habits, moray eels seldom move during the day except to poke their heads out of their hiding places to snap at passing prey. They can inflict a severe bite.

has an electric organ made up of modified trunk muscle tissue. It can generate an electrical discharge of up to 550 volts at 1 amp, which it uses to stun prey fish or to repel predators. Length: to 2m (6.6ft). Family Electrophoridae; there is only one species, *Electrophorus electricus*.

eel, glass
Life stage of eels of the genus *Anguilla* (European or common eels). The eels spawn in marine water. The leaf-like larvae, known as **leptocephali**, transform into glass eels, so called because they are transparent. Glass eels in turn become **elvers**, which migrate into fresh water. Family Anguillidae.

eel, gulper (pelican eel)
Highly modified black eel found in deep water. It has small eyes and an extraordinarily large mouth, with minute teeth and a distensible pharynx that can accommodate very large prey. Length: to 75cm (30in). Family Eurypharyngidae; species *Eurypharyx pelecanoides*.

eel, moray
Any member of a family of true eels, characterized by small, round gill openings and long, fang-like teeth. Moray eels are common on coral reefs, where they occupy rock crevices. Some species are involved in ciguatera poisoning and others have skin toxins. Length: to 3m (10ft). Family Muraenidae; there are 200 species.

eel, pelican
See EEL, GULPER

eelgrass
One of the few flowering plants to grow submerged in salt water. A perennial herb, it grows in shallow tropical and temperate seas. It has slender stems and strap-like leaves up to 90cm (35in) long. Family Zosteraceae; species *Zostera marina*. **Eelgrass** is also the name given to a similar but unrelated freshwater plant from s Europe and w Asia. Family Hydrocharitaceae; species *Vallisnera spiralis*.

eelpout
Elongate, bottom-dwelling, marine fish found in cold seas. It has a large head and mouth with prominent lips. Length: to 1.1m (3.6ft). Family Zoarcidae.

eelworm
Tiny, thread-like NEMATODE found worldwide in soil, fresh and saltwater. Most species are parasitic and can cause extensive damage to crops. They have been used to control other pests. *See also* ROUNDWORM

effector
Term used for any agent or structure that brings about a physiological response. For example, a MOTOR NEURONE that causes a muscle to contract or a hormone that stimulates a gland to function are both effectors. The target tissues are effector muscles and effector glands.

eft
Chiefly terrestrial, juvenile life stage of the NEWT. Efts are typically rough-skinned and are usually found in forest habitats. After several months to several years, depending on the species, efts return to breeding ponds and complete their development into breeding adults of more aquatic habits. Family Salamandridae.

egg
For egg-laying animals, the female GAMETE (OVUM), once it has been laid or spawned by the mother. The developing EMBRYO is surrounded by ALBUMIN, shell, egg case or MEMBRANE, depending on the species. The egg provides a reserve of food for the embryo in the form of YOLK and protects it from a potentially harmful external environment. For non-egg-laying animals, including almost all mammals, the term egg is synonymous with ovum.

eggplant
See AUBERGINE

eglantine
See SWEETBRIAR

▶ egg A duck embryo grows from a patch of cells on the surface of the egg yolk. The yolk is its food store. First, a network of tiny blood vessels spreads over the yolk and a simple heart develops. The developing embryo (enlarged here for clarity) begins to elongate and develops a vertebral column (1). A head and bulging eye start to form, and the heart folds around into its final position (2). The gut forms, the brain begins to enlarge and the embryo starts to curl (3–4). The limbs appear as tiny buds; and the tail and mouth form (5). By 13 days (6), it is possible to identify the bird from its bill. Some species of bird hatch shortly after this stage, others, such as the mallard duck (7) continue to develop in the egg. Feathers grow, limbs become stronger and the bird hatches with its eyes open and able to see.

1
2–3 days

2
5 days

3
6 days

4
8 days

5
11 days

6
13 days

7
25–31 days

Earth is the third major planet from the Sun, and the largest of the four inner, or terrestrial, planets. From space, the Earth is predominantly the blue of the oceans, plus the browns and greens of its land masses, the white polar caps, and a continually changing pattern of white cloud. Some 70% of the surface is covered by water, and it is this and the Earth's average surface temperature of 13°C (55°F) that make it suitable for life. The continental land masses make up the other 30%. Our planet has one natural satellite, the Moon.

Monitoring the propagation of SEISMIC WAVES from EARTHQUAKES has revealed the Earth's internal structure. Like all the terrestrial planets, there is a dense CORE rich in iron and nickel, surrounded by a MANTLE consisting of silicate rocks. The thin, outermost layer of lighter rock is called the CRUST. The dense metallic core is at high pressure and temperature, whereas crustal rocks are generally cooler and under less pressure. The crust has evolved into two distinct types, oceanic and continental, distinguished by differences in age, thickness, structure, composition, density, behaviour and formation. The inner core rotates at a different rate from the solid outer layers, and this, together with currents in the molten outer core, gives rise to the Earth's MAGNETIC FIELD.

The Earth's ATMOSPHERE is divided into a number of layers according to the way in which its temperature varies with altitude. The TROPOSPHERE contains most of the atmosphere and is where lifeforms are found and weather systems operate. The STRATOSPHERE contains the OZONE LAYER, which absorbs the high-energy ULTRAVIOLET RADIATION from the Sun, which is harmful to life. METEORS occur in the MESOSPHERE, and AURORAS in the THERMOSPHERE. The thermosphere is extremely rarefied, and its high temperature indicates the high kinetic energy of its molecules, rather than its heat content. Ionized atoms and molecules in the mesosphere and thermosphere constitute the IONOSPHERE. Above the thermosphere is the EXOSPHERE, which contains the Earth's MAGNETOSPHERE and VAN ALLEN RADIATION BELTS; it merges into interplanetary space.

The planet Earth probably began in the coming together (accretion) of dust and gas particles around the newly formed Sun about one billion years after the Big Bang, which is thought to have occurred some 20 billion years ago. Extraterrestrial materials, therefore, provide a good way of investigating the Earth's internal structure. METEORITES are thought to be fragmented remains of planet-like bodies only a few tens of kilometres across. The different types of meteorite would then represent different layers in the planetoid structure. IRON METEORITES (siderites) are about 97% metal, mainly nickel-iron, and being so dense would probably represent the Earth's core. Chondrite meteorites are of silicate composition and are thought to represent the lower mantle. Finally, achondrites are also silica based, but with different composition. This type of meteorite may represent fragments of crust and upper mantle.

Earth Data: diameter (equatorial) : 12,756km; mass: 5378 billion billion tonnes; volume: 1803 billion km³; density (water=1): 5.44; orbital period: 365.3 days; rotation period (equatorial): 23h 56m 04s; surface temperature: 290K

E

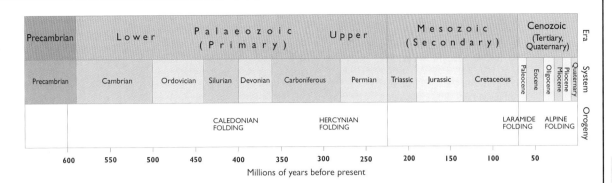

		Palaeozoic					Mesozoic			Cenozoic	
Precambrian	Lower	(Primary)			Upper		(Secondary)			(Tertiary, Quaternary)	Era
Precambrian	Cambrian	Ordovician	Silurian	Devonian	Carboniferous	Permian	Triassic	Jurassic	Cretaceous	Paleocene Eocene Oligocene Pliocene Quaternary	System
			CALEDONIAN FOLDING		HERCYNIAN FOLDING					LARAMIDE FOLDING ALPINE FOLDING	Orogeny

600   550   500   450   400   350   300   250   200   150   100   50

Millions of years before present

▲ **The 4600 million** years since the formation of the Earth are divided into four great eras, further split into periods and, in the case of the most recent era, epochs. The present era is the Cenozoic ("new life"), extending back through the Mesozoic and Palaeozoic to the Precambrian. The geological map of the Earth shows the relative dates of the Earth's continents and landscape features. It reveals, for example, that all the continents were formed during the Precambrian era, and that the Appalachian mountains are much older than the relatively young Himalayan chain.

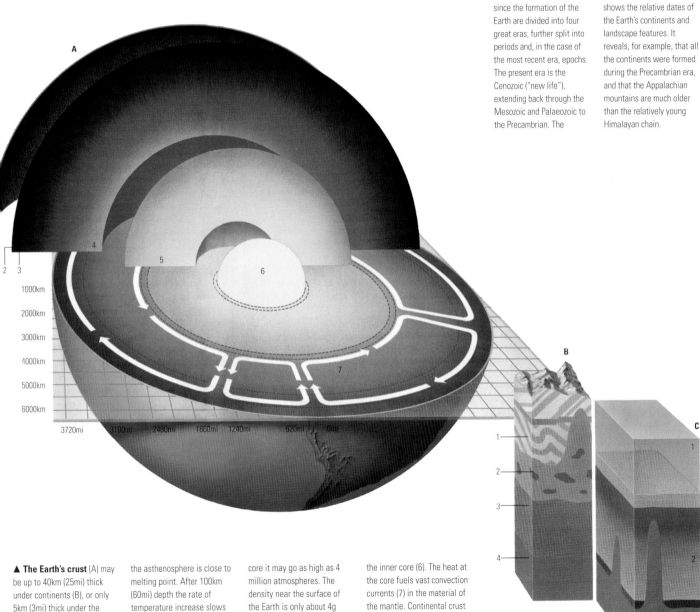

▲ **The Earth's crust** (A) may be up to 40km (25mi) thick under continents (B), or only 5km (3mi) thick under the ocean (C). The crust and the very top of the mantle (A) form the lithosphere (1), which drifts on the plastic asthenosphere (2). The upper mantle (3) stretches down to overlie the lower mantle (4) at 700km (430mi) depth. From the surface the temperature inside the Earth increases by 30°C/km (85°F/mi) so that the asthenosphere is close to melting point. After 100km (60mi) depth the rate of temperature increase slows dramatically. Because we know so little about what happens deep within the Earth, there is a great uncertainty about the temperature of the core. Pressure also increases with depth: already in the asthenosphere the pressure is equal to 250,000 atmospheres. At the Earth's core it may go as high as 4 million atmospheres. The density near the surface of the Earth is only about 4g cm^{-3}, and this does not vary by much more than 30% right down through the lower mantle. The increase in density that does occur is due to closer atomic packing under pressure. There is a leap in density to 10g cm^{-3} in passing to the outer core (5) and a further leap to between 13 and 16g cm^{-3} in the inner core (6). The heat at the core fuels vast convection currents (7) in the material of the mantle. Continental crust is made by many different processes and is therefore difficult to generalize. A typical cross section (B) might well consist of deformed and metamorphosed sedimentary rocks at the surface (1), underlain by a granite intrusion (2). The remaining crust would consist of metamorphosed sedimentary rock and igneous rock (3) reaching to the mantle (4). In oceanic crust (C), ocean sediments (1) overlie a basalt which is pillowed and also chemically altered by sea water. Below this layer (2) the basalt is made up of dykes – small vertical intrusions that are packed so close together they intrude each other. Gabbros are coarse-grained igneous rocks with a very similar composition to basalt. They are sometimes layered.

127

egret

HERON-like wading bird that is mainly white, with occasional dark colour phases. Its long legs, neck and bill enable it to feed in shallow water. The egret's flight is slow, with its neck extended and its legs trailing. In breeding season the legs, face skin and bill often turn orange and the yellow irises turn red. Family Ardeidae.

egret, cattle

Small, white, stocky egret, with a short, stout, yellow bill. In the breeding season it has orange plumes on its crown and back. The cattle egret feeds in pastures on insects disturbed by cattle and antelopes, often picking insects off the animals' backs. It has worldwide distribution and is expanding northwards in Europe; it is now find throughout North America since it became established in Florida in the 1950s. Length: 51cm (20in). Family Ardeidae; species *Bubulcus ibis*.

egret, little

Slim, white egret, with a long, black bill, black legs and yellow feet. In the breeding season it has a long, drooping crest and wing plumes. The little egret breeds in s Europe, Southeast Asia and Australasia. In Europe, its range is expanding northwards, and it has bred in England since the early 1990s. Length: 55–65cm (22–26in). Family Ardeidae; species *Egretta garzetta*.

Ehrenburg, Christian Gottfried (1795–1876)

German biologist, founder of the science of micropalaeontology. Ehrenburg studied at Berlin University and travelled widely as a naturalist, identifying and classifying many terrestrial and marine plants and microorganisms. He advanced the theory of "complete organisms", stating that all animals – even microscopic ones – have complete organ systems; it was later refuted.

Eichler, August Wilhelm (1839–87)

German botanist who developed a system of plant classification that was eventually accepted worldwide. It included the division of plants into four major classes. He helped to edit some 15 volumes on the flora of Brazil and published *Diagrams of Flowers*, a two-volume study of the comparative structure of flowers.

eider

Bulky sea duck of the Northern Hemisphere. An expert diver, it is rare inland. Male eiders are boldly

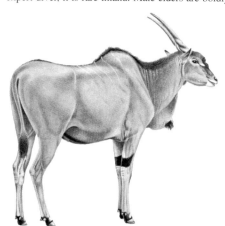

▲ **eland, common** An agile creature, the common eland (*Taurotragus oryx*) is capable of huge leaps and of running at up to 40km/h (25mph). It has been successfully domesticated for its protein-rich milk and low-fat meat.

▲ **eland, giant** The giant eland (*Taurotragus derbianus*) is the largest species of antelope. Threatened to the brink of extinction in the mid-20th century, its numbers have since increased, but it is still hunted for meat and hides.

patterned; the females are mottled brown. The bill usually continues in a straight line from the forehead, and feathers extend well down the upper mandible. Females pluck their own feathers (eider down) to line their nests. Family Anatidae; genus *Somateria*; there are four species worldwide.

ejaculation

Process of emitting fluids, especially SEMEN, from the body. During SEXUAL REPRODUCTION, semen is ejected from the PENIS of male mammals by PERISTALSIS of the wall of the urethra.

eland

Largest living ANTELOPE species; it is native to central and s Africa. Gregarious and slow-moving, elands have heavy, spiral horns. Family Bovidae; there are two species.

eland, common

ANTELOPE found across central, w and s Africa, mostly in game reserves, where it forms large herds in savanna grassland or open woodland. The common eland is tan to reddish, sometimes with pale stripes on the flanks and dark markings on the legs, back and tail. Both sexes have long, almost straight horns, with one or two tight twists. Hanging below the chin is a fold of loose skin known as a dewlap. Head-body length: 200–345cm (79–136in); tail: 60–90cm (24–35in). Family Bovidae; subfamily Bovinae; species *Taurotragus oryx*.

eland, giant

Spiral-horned ANTELOPE found to a small extent in woodland areas of central and w Africa, and in larger numbers in E Africa. It is longer with more slender horns than the common eland. The giant eland is reddish brown in colour with paler body stripes, facial and leg markings; it has a black stripe along its back. It has a dewlap hanging below its chin. Head-body length: 220–290cm (87–114in); tail: 90cm (35in). Family Bovidae; subfamily Bovinae; species *Taurotragus derbianus*.

elder

Shrub or small tree that is found in temperate and subtropical areas. It has divided leaves and clusters of small, white flowers. Its small, shiny, black berries are used for making wine and jelly and in medicine. Family Caprifoliaceae, genus *Sambucus*; there are 40 species.

elecampane

Perennial herb from Europe and w Asia. It has thick, furrowed stems and long (up to 80cm/31in in length), wavy edged, oval leaves. Both the stems and undersides of the leaves are covered with thick, woolly down. Bright yellow, daisy-like flower heads are borne in summer. Elecampane roots are used as an expectorant in medicine. Height: to *c*.2m (6.6ft). Family Asteraceae/Compositae, species *Inula helenium*.

electron

Stable fundamental particle with a negative charge of -1.06×10^{-19} coulomb and a mass of 9.1×10^{-31}kg. Electrons are one of the three primary constituents of the ATOM. They form in shells that surround the positively charged nucleus. In a free electron the total negative charge balances the positive charge of the PROTONS in the nucleus. Removal or addition of an atomic electron produces a charged ION.

electron transport system (electron transport chain)

Sequence of biochemical reactions that transfers ELECTRONS, through a series of carriers, in certain metabolic processes. The electron transport system involves carrier substances that accept electrons and then donate them to the next carrier in the chain, while themselves undergoing a series of OXIDATION-REDUCTION reactions. It forms the last stage of aerobic RESPIRATION in cells, causing hydrogen atoms to combine with oxygen to form water and conserving energy in the form of ADENOSINE TRIPHOSPHATE (ATP). PHOTOSYNTHESIS also involves an electron transfer system.

electrophoresis

Movement of electrically charged colloidal particles through a fluid from one electrode to another when a voltage is applied between the electrodes. Electrophoresis is used in the analysis and separation of colloidal suspensions, especially colloidal proteins; clinical medicine uses electrophoresis to measure protein content of body fluids. It is also used as a means of depositing coatings of one material, such as paint, on another.

elepaio

Rare bird of the FLYCATCHER family. It has a dark brown crown and back. It has white under parts, with its upper breast lightly streaked brown, and white wing bars, rump and tail-tips. The elepaio is an endangered species confined to Hawaii; it is thought that only *c*.1500 birds remain. The elepaio will follow hikers through the forest and can be attracted by imitating its call. It is the guardian spirit of canoe makers. Length: 15cm (6in). Family Muscicapidae; species *Chasiempis sandwichensis*.

elephant

Largest land animal, the only surviving member of the mammal order *Proboscidea*, which included the MAMMOTH and the MASTODON. It is native to Africa

◄ **elder** Native to Europe, the elder grows to a height of 12m (40ft). In early summer, the tree bears clusters of white flowers. The species shown here is the European, or black, elder (*Sambucus nigra*).

An earthquake is a tremor below the surface of the Earth that causes shaking to occur in the CRUST. Shaking lasts for only a few seconds, but widespread devastation can result. There are 150,000 noticeable earthquakes every year, and more than a million can be measured with sensitive apparatus. The human cost is frequently appalling, but the science of earthquake prediction is not exact and the only resource for millions living in areas of high seismic risk is to design better earthquake-resistant buildings.

According to PLATE TECTONICS, earthquakes are caused by the movement of crustal plates, which produces FAULT lines. The main earthquake regions are found along plate margins, especially on the edges of the Pacific, such as the San Andreas fault. A large earthquake is usually followed by smaller "aftershocks". An earthquake beneath the sea can often result in a TSUNAMI. Earthquake prediction is a branch of SEISMOLOGY. Present methods indicate only a probability of earthquake activity and cannot be used to predict actual events. The world's largest recorded earthquake, at Tangshan, China in 1976, killed more than 250,000 people and measured 8.2 on the RICHTER SCALE.

Several kinds of fault in the surface of the Earth commonly lead to earthquakes. The 1985 quake that killed 10,000 people in Mexico City occurred because a SUBDUCTION ZONE – where one tectonic plate slips beneath another – generated a thrust fault when the overlying plate became compressed by the plate subducting under it. The San Andreas fault is the most famous example of a strike-slip fault, where one plate slides laterally past another. But perhaps the most common earthquake-causing fault is exemplified by the devastating Armenian quake of 1988, which occurred on a thrust fault, where one block of earth was driven vertically up above another by compressional forces.

An earthquake's energy is transmitted in the form of three main types of wave: primary/push (P), secondary/shake (S) and longitudinal/surface (L). P and S waves originate from the seismic focus, from where they travel to the surface and cause shaking. On the Earth's surface, they travel as L waves. The surface point directly above the seismic focus is the EPICENTRE, around which most damage is concentrated. Surface waves (L waves) are the largest and most slow-moving and, in shallow earthquakes, transmit the bulk of the energy. The surface waves of particularly strong earthquakes may travel right around the Earth several times and still be measured on seismograms days after the event took place.

Two concepts are commonly used to measure earthquakes: magnitude and intensity. Magnitude represents a measure of the total energy generated in an earthquake; it is calculated by measuring the maximum amplitude of seismic waves involved. Most commonly used now is the Richter scale, which is logarithmic: each unit represents a 10-fold increase in the amplitude of the waves (and nearly a 30-fold increase in the energy generated). The largest earthquakes measure around 8.8 on the Richter scale, but there is no upper limit. However, discrepancies can occur depending on whether S, P or surface waves are measured – surface waves are frequently used because they bear the most direct relationship to ground movement. Intensity, on the other hand, corresponds to the subjective experience of observers near the earthquake, and is a guide to the degree of shaking. The MERCALLI SCALE runs from I (indicating that the event is not felt at all) to XII (the total destruction of land-based objects, ripples in the ground, and people thrown into the air). Sometimes the strain energy is released slowly, so that no sudden rupturing takes place and no earthquake occurs. Instead, rocks slide past each other in a process known as a seismic slip or "CREEP". Faults creep especially where "greased" with a natural mineral lubricant, such as hydrated magnesium silicate (serpentine).

Earthquakes themselves do not usually kill people: it is the collapse of buildings, road and other human artefacts that kills. Considerable destruction is also caused by after effects like fire, flood, landslide and tsunamis. A high standard of construction work, carried out to earthquake-resistant design, is vital. Modern skyscraper designs rely on reinforced frames that can absorb and distribute seismic energy. Some skyscrapers in San Francisco sit on bearings made of layers of steel and rubber, which allow the buildings to shift with ground movement. *See also* Ready Reference, pages 453–54

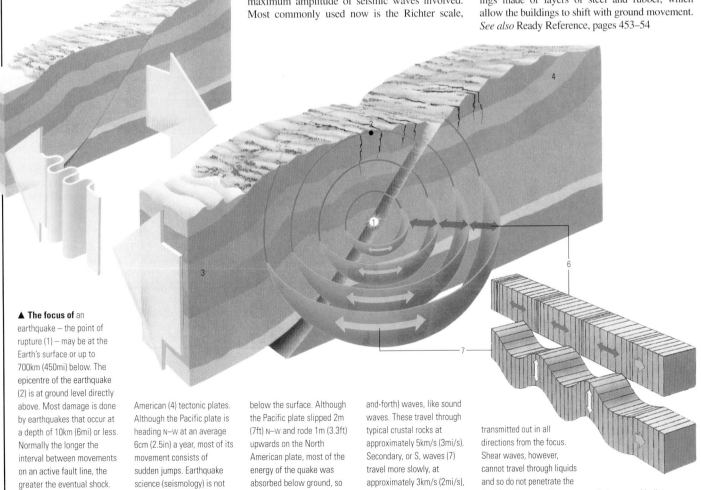

▲ **The focus of** an earthquake – the point of rupture (1) – may be at the Earth's surface or up to 700km (450mi) below. The epicentre of the earthquake (2) is at ground level directly above. Most damage is done by earthquakes that occur at a depth of 10km (6mi) or less. Normally the longer the interval between movements on an active fault line, the greater the eventual shock. The San Andreas fault in California is a 1200km (750mi) boundary between the Pacific (3) and the North American (4) tectonic plates. Although the Pacific plate is heading N–W at an average 6cm (2.5in) a year, most of its movement consists of sudden jumps. Earthquake science (seismology) is not advanced enough to predict such jumps accurately. In the 1989 Loma Prieta quake, the focus was 18km (11mi) below the surface. Although the Pacific plate slipped 2m (7ft) N–W and rode 1m (3.3ft) upwards on the North American plate, most of the energy of the quake was absorbed below ground, so there was only comparatively minor surface cracking (5). Primary, or P, waves (6), are compression-dilation (back-and-forth) waves, like sound waves. These travel through typical crustal rocks at approximately 5km/s (3mi/s). Secondary, or S, waves (7) travel more slowly, at approximately 3km/s (2mi/s), or 7km/s (4mi/s) deeper in the mantle, and are shear (side-to-side) waves. Both of these types of wave are transmitted out in all directions from the focus. Shear waves, however, cannot travel through liquids and so do not penetrate the Earth's molten core. The difference in speed between the waves results in a time lapse between their arrival that grows with distance; this time lapse allows scientists to pinpoint the focus of a quake.

(*Loxodonta africana*) and India (*Elephas maximus*). The tusks, which are elongated upper incisors, are used for digging up roots. The Indian cow (female) elephant has no tusks. The trunk is an elongated nose and upper lip used for drinking and picking up food. The African elephant is taller and heavier than its Indian counterpart. A bull (male) elephant may weigh as much as 7000kg (eight tonnes) and can charge at speeds up to 40km/h (25mph). The African elephant has much larger ears, up to 100cm (40in) in diameter. Elephants are herbivores and browse in herds led by a bull. The cow (female) gives birth to its calf after 18 to 22 months gestation. Elephants live for 60 to 70 years. Indian elephants are used as beasts of burden but do not breed in captivity. The hunting of elephants for the ivory of their tusks saw the population reduce from 1.3 million in 1979 to 600,000 in 1989. A ban on hunting has led to a resurgence.

elephant fish

African freshwater fish. It has a very large brain and an electric organ that produces a weak electric field. Family Mormyridae. **Elephant fish** is also the name sometimes used to refer to cartilaginous CHIMAERAS, which are shark relatives with scaleless bodies, large eyes and elongated tapered tails.

elephant's foot (Hottentot bread)

Deciduous, climbing, perennial plant that is found in South Africa. Elephant's foot grows slowly from an above-ground, woody TUBER, which reaches an enormous size, often 1m (3ft) in height and diameter. The inside of the tuber is fleshy, with a constitution similar to a turnip and a taste resembling that of a yam. Elephant's foot produces heart-shaped, blue-green leaves and tiny, greenish-yellow flowers with dark spots. Family Dioscoreaceae; species *Dioscorea elephantipes*.

elephant-shrew

Mammal with large eyes, long legs and a trunk-like nose; it is widespread across Africa, particularly in s and central areas. Fifteen species of elephant-shrew are found in habitats ranging from lowland forest and desert to mountains. They feed on invertebrates. Elephant-shrews are not closely related to true shrews. Head-body length: 10–39cm (4–15in); tail: 13–26cm (5–10in). Family Macroscelidae.

elm

Any of *c*.45 deciduous trees making up the genus *Ulmus*. They are found in temperate woodlands of the Northern Hemisphere. Their rounded or oval leaves have toothed margins and usually turn attractive golds and reds in autumn. Elms bear clusters of tiny, bell-shaped flowers, which are followed by winged fruits. Height: to 30m (100ft). Family Ulmaceae; genus *Ulmus*; species include *Ulmus americana* (the American white elm) and *Ulmus procera* (the English elm).

El Niño (Sp. Christ child)

See feature article

Elsasser, Walter Maurice (1904–91)

US theoretical physicist and geophysicist. In 1925 Elsasser predicted electron diffraction and, in 1936, neutron diffraction. Elsasser is noted for his investigation of the upper mantle of the Earth; he developed a model of movements within the Earth's mantle and core that would account for the Earth's magnetic properties.

► **elephant-shrew** Found in thickets or forest undergrowth, the forest elephant-shrew (*Petrodromus tetradactylus*) does not build a nest but instead sleeps under vegetation or in empty holes. Its diet consists largely of termites. It makes a cricket-like noise and beats its tail against the ground or raps its hind legs together to signal danger to other elephant-shrews.

embryo

Early developing stage of an animal or plant. In animals, the embryo stage starts at FERTILIZATION and ends when the organism emerges from the egg or from its mother's UTERUS. In mammals, an embryo is sustained through blood supplied by the mother via the PLACENTA. In humans, the embryo is called a FETUS after the first eight weeks of pregnancy. In invertebrate animals the embryo is usually called a LARVA. In plants, the embryo is found in the seed, and the embryo stage ends on GERMINATION. An embryo results when the nuclei of an EGG and a SPERM or male sex cell fuse to form a single cell, called a ZYGOTE. The zygote then divides into a ball of cells called a BLASTULA. The blastula and then the embryo undergoes rapid changes in which the cells differentiate themselves to form features, such as limbs and organs.

embryology

Biological study of the origin, development and activities of an EMBRYO. This science traces the sequence of events from OVUM (egg) to BIRTH, hatching or germination.

emerald

Variety of BERYL, varying in colour from light to deep green and highly valued as a gemstone. The colour is due to the presence of small amounts of chromium but the stone may lose its colour if heated. Emeralds were mined in Upper Egypt in 1650 BC; now they are found mainly in Colombia.

emery

Impure form of the mineral CORUNDUM (aluminium oxide, Al_2O_3). It occurs as dark granules containing MAGNETITE and HAEMATITE. An unusually hard mineral, emery is used as an ABRASIVE.

emigration

Process by which individuals depart from a population. The emigrants may either enter an existing neighbouring population, or, as in the swarming of LOCUSTS and BEES, they may form a new population. Factors such as overcrowding often act as a stimulus for emigration. Unlike the periodic seasonal movements characteristic of MIGRATION, emigration is a non-reversible, one-way process. *See also* IMMIGRATION

emperor penguin

See PENGUIN, EMPEROR

emu

Huge, flightless bird; it is second only to the OSTRICH in size. The emu's plumage varies from pale grey-brown to almost black; the skin of its head and neck is blue. It can run in bursts at speeds of up to 50km/h (30mph). It also swims well. The emu is confined to dry open and cereal country on the Australian mainland. It is found singly and in flocks of dozens or occasionally hundreds. Length: 150–185cm (60–73in). Family Dromaiidae; species *Dromaius novaehollandiae*. *See* illustration, page 132

▲ **elephant** The most primitive ancestor of the elephant is the *Moeritherium* (A), a hog-sized animal that lived during the Eocene epoch. It had a pig-like snout rather than a trunk and the upper and lower tusks were simple, slightly elongated incisor teeth. Eyes and ears raised high on the skull, and short limbs encased in fat, suggest that it wallowed along the fringes of rivers and estuaries. The *trilophodon* (B) lived during the Miocene epoch. It represents a fairly advanced stage in the evolution of elephants. It was a long-jawed mastodon with four flattened tusks and a short trunk, which was probably used for tearing vegetation from bushes and low trees. In later mammoths and elephants (C), the lower jaw shortened and the lower tusks disappeared. The African elephant (D) is the largest land mammal.

emu bush

Any of *c*.180 species of evergreen, perennial shrubs and trees of the *Eremophila* genus, native to Australia. They have attractive, tubular, two-lipped flowers, which can be pink, red, orange, yellow or green. The common emu bush grows to *c*.1.5m (*c*.5ft) in height but has a spreading habit. It has lance-shaped hairy leaves. Family Myoporaceae; species include *Eremophila glabra* (common emu bush).

emu-wren

Either of two species of small, brown Australian wrens. They have long, tufty, cocked tails of only six feathers, which resemble stiff emu feathers. No other known bird has fewer tail feathers. Length: 12–20cm (5–8in). Family Maluridae; genus *Stipiturus*.

enamel

In mammals, hard covering of the crown of the TOOTH; it is the hardest body tissue. Strongest at the biting edges, enamel varies in thickness and density over the tooth.

endangered species

Animals or plants threatened with extinction as a result of such activities as habitat destruction and overhunting. In 1948 the International Union for the Conservation of Nature and Natural Resources (IUCN) was founded in Geneva, Switzerland, to protect endangered species. The IUCN publishes the *Red Data Book*, which currently lists more than 1000 animals and 20,000 plants considered endangered. The CONVENTION ON INTERNATIONAL TRADE IN ENDANGERED SPECIES OF WILD FLORA AND FAUNA (CITES) was signed in 1975. It seeks to prevent international trade in *c*.30,000 species. In the United Kingdom, the Wildlife and Countryside Act (1981) gives legal protection to a wide range of wild animals and plants. In the United States, the Endangered Species Act (1973) gives legal protection to a wide range of wild animals and plants. *See also* BIODIVERSITY; CONSERVATION; ECOLOGY; HABITAT; WETLAND; Ready Reference, page 457–58

endive

Leafy annual or biennial plant that is widely cultivated for its sharp-flavoured leaves. There are two main types: varieties with slender, wavy-edged leaves; and varieties with broad, flat leaves. Family Asteraceae/Compositae; species *Cichorium endivia*.

endocrine system

Body system made up of all the **endocrine glands** (ductless glands), which secrete HORMONES directly into the bloodstream to influence body processes. The endocrine system (together with the AUTONOMIC NERVOUS SYSTEM, and collectively called the **neuroendocrine system**) controls and regulates all body functions. It differs from other body systems in that its ductless glands are not structurally connected to one another. The chief endocrine glands are the PITUITARY GLAND, located at the base of the brain; the thyroid gland, located in the throat; the parathyroid glands, usually embedded in the thyroid; the ADRENAL GLAND, situated on top of the kidneys; specialized cells called the ISLETS OF LANGERHANS in the PANCREAS; and the sex gland or GONAD (TESTIS in males and OVARY in females) and, in pregnancy, the placenta. *See also* EXOCRINE GLAND

endocytosis

Process by which a CELL takes in substances. When a cell's MEMBRANE comes into contact with food, a portion of the cytoplasm surrounds the substance and a depression forms within the cell wall. The food is eventually engulfed into a vesicle, which then moves further into the cell where it meets a LYSOSOME. Within the lysosome are digestive enzymes that break down the food. There are two types of endocytosis: **pinocytosis** is the incorporation and digestion of dissolved substances; **phagocytosis** is the engulfing and digestion of microscopic particles. Phagocytosis is the process by which many PROTOZOA obtain sustenance. In higher animals, PHAGOCYTE cells are an important part of the IMMUNE SYSTEM, helping to expel infectious microorganisms.

endoderm (entoderm)

One of the three so-called GERM LAYERS of tissue formed in the early development of a fertilized OVUM (egg). It is the innermost layer of the three and forms the EPITHELIUM of the liver, pancreas, digestive tract and respiratory system. It is also the inner cell layer of a simple animal body. The other germ layers are the ECTODERM and MESODERM.

endodermis

Inner layer of the cortex in plant roots and some

EL NIÑO

Periodic easing or reversing of the TRADE WINDS over the S Pacific Ocean, causing the warm surface waters that have "piled-up" in the W Pacific to flow back and warm the coastal waters of South America by up to two or three degrees. It occurs around Christmas time, hence its name. El Niño has a dramatic effect on climate patterns in Australia and Southeast Asia and may be implicated in changed rainfall patterns as far away as Africa. In normal years, trade winds blow E to W along the Equator, dragging sun-warmed surface waters into a pool off N Australia and monsoon rains to Indonesia. In the W Pacific, the Humboldt Current pushes the surface waters away from the coast of Peru, bringing cold, nutri-ent-rich water to the surface. This upwelled, nutrient-rich water stimulates the production of phytoplankton and swells the population of anchovies, which themselves are prey to seabirds (such as boobies and brown pelicans), and the Peruvian fishing industry thrives. In an El Niño year, the upwelling ceases and the biological productivity of the area collapses. In 1982–83, for instance, the catch of anchovies was reduced by 60%. In addition, mean sea level along the coast of Latin America may increase by as much as 50cm (20in), causing widespread flooding. Some scientists believe that the frequency and effects of El Niño are increasing. *See also* LA NIÑA

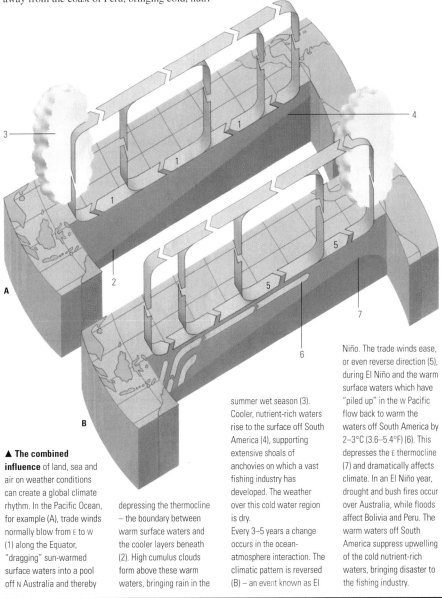

▲ **The combined influence** of land, sea and air on weather conditions can create a global climate rhythm. In the Pacific Ocean, for example (A), trade winds normally blow from E to W (1) along the Equator, "dragging" sun-warmed surface waters into a pool off N Australia and thereby depressing the thermocline – the boundary between warm surface waters and the cooler layers beneath (2). High cumulus clouds form above these warm waters, bringing rain in the summer wet season (3). Cooler, nutrient-rich waters rise to the surface off South America (4), supporting extensive shoals of anchovies on which a vast fishing industry has developed. The weather over this cold water region is dry. Every 3–5 years a change occurs in the ocean-atmosphere interaction. The climatic pattern is reversed (B) – an event known as El Niño. The trade winds ease, or even reverse direction (5), during El Niño and the warm surface waters which have "piled up" in the W Pacific flow back to warm the waters off South America by 2–3°C (3.6–5.4°F) (6). This depresses the E thermocline (7) and dramatically affects climate. In an El Niño year, drought and bush fires occur over Australia, while floods affect Bolivia and Peru. The warm waters off South America suppress upwelling of the cold nutrient-rich waters, bringing disaster to the fishing industry.

E

stems. In roots it is a single-celled layer, with characteristic banding, known as the CASPARIAN STRIP. *See also* PERICYCLE

endometrium
MUCOUS MEMBRANE, well supplied with blood vessels, that lines the UTERUS of mammals. In the latter part of the MENSTRUAL CYCLE of higher primates, it becomes thickened, but if no pregnancy takes place it is shed during menstruation.

endopeptidase
ENZYME that hydrolyses PEPTIDE BONDS in the central region of a POLYPEPTIDE, reducing it to smaller polypeptides. Examples of endopeptidases include PEPSIN and TRYPSIN, both of which are found in the alimentary canals of mammals and the digestive systems of many other animals. *See also* EXOPEPTIDASE

endoplasmic reticulum
Network of membranes and channels in the CYTOPLASM of EUKARYOTE cells (those which contain a nucleus, such as the cells of plants, animals and fungi). The network helps to transport material inside the cell. Parts of the endoplasmic reticulum are covered with minute granules called RIBOSOMES. Where ribosomes are present it is known as a rough endoplasmic reticulum, where they are absent the term smooth endoplasmic reticulum is used. Ribosomes consist of protein and a form of ribonucleic acid (RNA); they are sites of PROTEIN SYNTHESIS.

endoskeleton
Supporting system of bones and cartilage inside the body of an animal. All VERTEBRATES have an endoskeleton. It supports the body and surrounds and protects internal organs. It also provides attachment points for muscles in order to facilitate movement. SPONGES have a type of endoskeleton consisting of a network of rigid or semirigid spicules. *See also* EXOSKELETON

endosperm
Tissue that surrounds the developing EMBRYO of a seed and provides food for growth. It is triploid (each cell has three sets of chromosomes), being derived from the FUSION of one male GAMETE from the germinated pollen grain and two of the HAPLOID nuclei in the embryo sac. *See also* ALTERNATION OF GENERATIONS

endosymbiosis
Mutually beneficial relationship in which one organism lives inside another. For example, bacteria were engulfed by EUKARYOTE cells and formed symbiotic relationships with them, eventually becoming so interdependent that the cells behaved as a single organism: the bacteria became MITOCHONDRIA and CHLOROPLASTS. Mitochondria and chloroplasts have their own small RIBOSOMES, which resemble those of bacteria, and also their own DNA distinct from that of the host cell. *See also* SYMBIOSIS

endothelium
Tissue that lines various body structures; it consists of a thin layer of cells. Like EPITHELIUM, endothelium is made up of plate-like cells. It lines the inner surfaces of blood vessels and the heart; lymphatic vessels are also lined with endothelium.

endothermic (homeothermic)
Describes an animal whose body temperature does not fluctuate as the temperature of its surroundings fluctuates, often referred to as "warm-blooded". Mammals and birds are warm-blooded. They maintain their body temperature through METABOLISM. *See also* ECTOTHERMIC

endothermic reaction
Chemical reaction in which heat is absorbed from the surroundings, causing a fall in temperature. An example of an endothermic reaction is the manufacture of water-gas from coke and steam.

enstatite ($MgSiO_3$)
Orthorhombic mineral of the PYROXENE group, commonly found in ultrabasic IGNEOUS ROCKS such as norites, pyroxenites, gabbros and peridotites. It varies from colourless to yellowish grey, shading to green if iron is present. Hardness 5.5; r.d. 3.2–3.5.

enterobacterium
One of a group of facultatively anaerobic, rod-shaped BACTERIA that are widespread as pathogens of plants, man and other animals, and as saprophytes in soil and water. Their metabolism can be AEROBIC or ANAEROBIC, that is, using oxygen or FERMENTATION respectively, according to conditions. Examples of enterobacteria include *Klebsiella*, which is able to carry out NITROGEN FIXATION, *Salmonella*, *Escherichia* and *Shigella*.

entoderm
See ENDODERM

entomology
Scientific study of INSECTS. The ancient Greeks of the 4th century BC were the first serious entomologists, and Aristotle coined the term from the Greek *entomon*, meaning "insect".

entomophily
POLLINATION of a flower by a pollen-carrying insect. Most entomophilous flowers are scented and brightly coloured, often with nectar, to attract insects. The flowers may have different structures to ensure CROSS-POLLINATION.

entropy
Quantity that specifies the disorder or randomness of a physical system. In thermodynamics, it expresses the degree to which thermal energy is available for work – the less available it is, the greater the entropy. The entropy of the Universe is increasing. Energy can be extracted from a system only as it changes to a less ordered state. According to the second law of thermodynamics, an isolated system's change in entropy is either zero or positive in any process.

environment
Physical and biological surroundings of an organism. The environment covers both non-living factors (ABIOTIC FACTORS), such as temperature, soil, atmosphere and radiation, and living organisms, such as the plants, microorganisms and animals that make up the biotic (living) environment.

environmental impact
Effect of human activity on the ENVIRONMENT. Human activity has evolved high levels of use of manufactured goods, which require sophisticated means of converting raw materials and involve the consumption of water, energy and air, all of which have an impact on the environment. The conversion of raw materials into manufactured goods can never be complete, so there are residues, such as solid wastes, as well as energy waste in the form of heat, noise and vibration. Unused residues discharged into the environment become pollutants.

enzyme (Gk. *zymosis*, in yeast)
Protein that functions as a CATALYST in biochemical reactions. The FERMENTATION properties of yeast cells have long been utilized in brewing alcohol. In 1897 German chemist Edward Büchner (1860–1917) discovered that cell-free extracts of yeasts could ferment sugars to alcohol. In 1926 the US biochemist

◄ **emu** Only one type of emu exists today, the other races having been wiped out by colonizers in the 18th century. They are sociable animals, usually found in small flocks near water. They feed on fruit, seeds and young shoots – the most nutritious parts of the plants. The females are slightly larger than the males. Emus nest among trees or bushes. The males hatch and rear the young, staying with them for several months.

James B. SUMNER was the first person to isolate an enzyme in pure crystal form. He extracted urease from the jack bean and proved that enzymes are protein molecules. In the next decade, PEPSIN, TRYPSIN and chymotrypsin were crystallized. Today, more than 1500 catalysts have been identified, and their AMINO ACID structures revealed through x-ray crystallography. In 1969 scientists first synthesized an enzyme, ribonuclease. Chemical reactions can occur several thousand or million times faster with enzymes than without them. The efficiency of an enzyme is measured in terms of its turnover rate. They operate within a narrow temperature range (usually 30°C to 40°C) and have optimal pH ranges. Many enzymes have to be bound to nonprotein molecules. These include trace elements (such as metals) and COENZYMES (such as vitamins). If a coenzyme is tightly attached to the protein enzyme, the unit is termed a prosthetic group. The lack or malfunction of enzymes can cause a variety of metabolic diseases. Enzymes are widely used in the manufacture of detergents, antibiotics and food.

Eocene
Second of the five epochs of the TERTIARY period, from c.55–38 million years ago. The name implies the "dawn" of life in which the modern families appeared. The fossil record shows members of modern plant genera, including BEECHES, WALNUTS and ELMS, and indicates the apparent dominance of mammals, including the ancestors of CAMELS, HORSES (notably *Hyracotherium*), RODENTS, BATS and MONKEYS. The world climate was warmer than at the present time.

ephedrine
Drug that is chemically similar to ADRENALINE (epinephrine). It stimulates the AUTONOMIC NERVOUS SYSTEM. Once used to treat asthma, it is still found in some cold remedies as a nasal decongestant.

epicentre
Spot on the Earth's surface directly above the focus of an EARTHQUAKE. Depending on the character of the focus, the epicentre may be a small circle or a line.

epidermis
In animals, outer layer of skin that contains no blood vessels; in plants, the outermost layer of a leaf or of an unthickened stem or root. In plants, the outer surface of the epidermis is usually coated in a waxy layer, the CUTICLE, which reduces water loss. The epidermis of leaves and stems may be perforated by pores, called STOMATA, which allow GAS EXCHANGE.

epidote
Orthosilicate mineral, hydrated calcium iron-aluminium silicate ($Ca_2Fe_3(Al_2O)(OH)(Si_2O_7)$ [Si_2O_4]). It is found in METAMORPHIC and IGNEOUS ROCKS as monoclinic system prismatic crystals and fibrous or granular masses. It is typically pistachio green, glassy and brittle. Certain large crystals, 7.5–25cm (3–10in), are collector's items. Hardness 6–7; r.d. 3.4.

epiglottis
In mammals, small flap of CARTILAGE projecting upward behind the root of the tongue. It closes off the LARYNX during swallowing to prevent food entering the airway.

epilimnion
Upper layers of water in a lake. It is warmer than the deeper water. Because light penetrates the epilimnion it can support PHOTOSYNTHESIS and plant life. The water may be disturbed by wind and water currents. *See also* HYPOLIMNION

epinephrine
See ADRENALINE

epiphyte (air plant)
Plant that grows on another plant but is not a PARASITE. Epiphytes usually have aerial roots and produce their own food by PHOTOSYNTHESIS. They are common in tropical forests. Examples are some FERNS, some ORCHIDS, SPANISH MOSS and many BROMELIADS.

epithelium
Layer of cells, closely packed to form a surface or a lining for a body tube or cavity. Epithelium covers not only the SKIN, but also various internal organs and surfaces such as the intestines, nasal passages and mouth. Epithelial cells may also produce protective modifications, such as hair and nails, or secrete substances such as ENZYMES and MUCOUS.

equilibrium
State in which the forces acting to increase a given quantity, such as the number of individuals in a population or the number of species in a COMMUNITY, roughly or exactly balance the forces acting to reduce the same quantity. The term can also be ascribed to a body with a constant temperature; this is known as **thermal equilibrium**.

equilibrium sense (vestibular sense)
Mammalian ability to remain upright in relation to gravity and to detect changes in position and momentum. The principal organs of equilibrium are contained in the inner EAR: the UTRICLE, which transmits orientation information, and the SEMICIRCULAR CANALS, which are concerned with acceleration and deceleration. These systems help humans to locate their bodies in space.

equinox
Either of the two points at which the Sun crosses the celestial equator. The **vernal equinox** (also known as the **spring equinox**) occurs when the Sun crosses the equator from south to north on or near 21 March each year in the Northern Hemisphere. This point is also called the First Point of Aries. The other equinox is the **autumnal equinox**, which occurs on or near 23 September in the Northern Hemisphere when the Sun crosses the equator from north to south. This point is also called the First Point of Libra. At the equinoxes, the Sun rises due east and sets due west.

erection
State of becoming swollen and distended through the accumulation of blood in erectile tissue, such as the penis. The erection of the penis is necessary to allow it to be inserted in the vagina during SEXUAL INTERCOURSE. The condition whereby erection cannot be achieved is known as impotence and can have a variety of causes, both physical and psychological.

eremomela
Tiny, warbler-like songbird found in dry woods, bushland and forest canopy in sub-Saharan Africa. Some species are mostly pale grey above and yellow below; others are brown above and white below, with a chestnut crown. Length: 10cm (4in). Family Sylviidae; genus *Eremomela*.

ergot
Fungus that infects rye, barley, oats and wheat. It produces potent neurotoxic alkaloids, which, if ingested by humans or livestock, may cause ergotism (also known as St Anthony's fire), a disfiguring and often fatal disease. Purified derivatives of the poisonous

alkaloids are used in medicine, for example in the treatment of migraine. Phylum Ascomycota; species *Claviceps purpurea*.

erica (heath)
Any of *c*.700 evergreen shrubs belonging to the *Erica* genus. Some species are found in the wet moorlands and sandy heathlands of s Africa; others are from temperate Europe and Asia. Ericas have narrow, flat leaves and long spikes of bell- or urn-shaped flowers in a variety of colours, from purple, red and pink through white and yellow. They are grown in gardens for ground cover, winter colour or as specimen plants. Family Ericaceae; species include *Erica tetralix* (cross-leaved heath) and *Erica bauera* (bridal or Albertinia heath).

ermine
See STOAT

erosion
Alteration of landforms by the wearing away of rock and soil and the removal of any debris (as opposed to WEATHERING). Erosion is carried out by

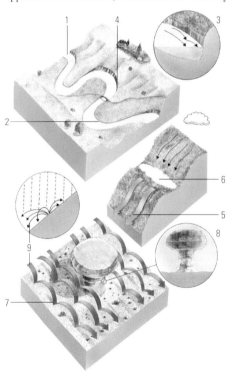

▲ **erosion** The breakdown and transportation of rock due to the action of an outside agent is known as erosion; there are three main forms: river, glacial and wind. Rivers (1) erode their channels through the flow of water and the abrasion of the load they are carrying against the banks and riverbed. Erosion is most forceful at the outside of bends (2), where the banks are undercut (3) often creating cliffs or bluffs (4) down which material moves. Flood surges dramatically increase the power of the river and correspondingly magnify the erosive force. On a smaller scale, rainwater will move material down a hillside (5). Particles of soil are carried by rivulets and the impact of raindrops throws soil down slope. Vegetation reduces such erosion by binding the soil together. Where vegetation is removed, as on tracks (6), erosion is accentuated. In arid conditions wind erosion can carve distinctive features. Sand and stones blown by the wind (7) have the same effect as shot-blasting. Mushroom-shaped formations, pedestals (8), are often the result. They are caused because there is a maximum height at which the erosive sand is carried by the wind as it bounces across the surface (9), and above that height the rock is untouched.

the agents of wind, water, glaciers and living organisms. In **chemical erosion**, minerals in the rock react to other substances, such as weak acids found in rainwater, and are broken down. In **physical erosion**, powerful forces such as rivers and glaciers physically wear rock down and transport it. Erosion can have disastrous economic results, such as the removal of topsoil, the gradual destruction of buildings, and the alteration of water systems. Inland, erosion occurs most drastically by the action of rivers, and in coastal regions by the action of waves. *See also* GEOMORPHOLOGY

erratic

Rock that has been transported some distance from its source by glacial action and is, therefore, unlike the surrounding rocks. The tracing of erratics back to their source can give important information about the movement of ice.

eruption

Release of lava and gas from the Earth's interior to the Earth's surface, either on land or under the sea, and into the atmosphere. *See also* VOLCANO

erythrocyte (red blood cell)

BLOOD cell that carries oxygen around the body. It contains HAEMOGLOBIN, which combines with oxygen to form OXYHAEMOGLOBIN and gives blood its red colour. In mammals erythrocytes are usually disc-shaped and have no nucleus. In other vertebrates they are more oval in shape and contain nuclei. Normal human blood contains an average of 5 million such cells per mm³ of blood, making them the most numerous blood cell. They are manufactured in bone MARROW.

escarpment (scarp)

Steep slope or cliff arising from a flat or gently sloping area, produced by faulting and/or differential EROSION.

esker

Long, narrow ridge of rock formed by a stream flowing under a GLACIER. Subglacial streams and rivers carry gravel and sand that they deposit on the river beds as they tunnel below the ice. When the ice melts, the rivers may move to other channels, leaving the eskers as long ridges 10–25m (30–80ft) high and 5–25m (15–80ft) across; they can be many kilometres long.

esparto (needlegrass, alfa)

Coarse perennial grass, native to Spain and North Africa. It is used to make paper, rope and twine. Height: to 0.9m (3ft). Family Gramineae; genera *Stipa* and *Lygeum*; there are *c*.150 species.

essential oil

Oil found in flowers, fruits or plants. It is the source of their characteristic odour and is widely used in aromatherapy, potpourri and perfumed toiletries. Many are obtained from plants that originate in dry Mediterranean climates. These oils are usually produced by special glands.

estuary

Coastal region where a river mouth opens into the ocean and fresh water from the land is mixed with salt water from the sea. Many estuaries are drowned river valleys, perhaps formed after a rise in sea level at the end of an ice age. They usually provide good harbours and are often breeding grounds for many kinds of marine life. *See also* DROWNED COAST

ethology

Study of animal behaviour, especially in the natural environment, first outlined in the 1920s by Konrad LORENZ and Nikolaas TINBERGEN. Ethologists study natural processes ranging across all animal groups, such as courtship, mating and self-defence. Field observations and laboratory experiments are used.

etiolation

Condition that arises when green plants are grown in the dark. Symptoms include pale yellow leaves, due to the absence of CHLOROPHYLL, and long thin stems, due to the plant growing rapidly in search of light.

eucalyptus (gum tree)

Any member of a genus of evergreen shrubs and slender trees native to Australia and cultivated in warm and temperate regions. They are valuable sources of hardwood and oils. Leaves are blue/white, and they bear woody fruits and flowers without petals. Height: to 120m (400ft). Family Myrtaceae; genus *Eucalyptus*; there are *c*.600 species.

eugenics

Study of human improvement by SELECTIVE BREEDING, founded by British scientist Sir Francis Galton (1822–1911). It proposed the genetic "improvement" of the human species through the application of social controls on parenthood, encouraging parents who are above average in certain traits to have more children, while ensuring those who are below average have fewer. As a social movement, eugenics was discredited in the early 20th century owing to its ethical implications and its racist and class-based assumptions. Advances in GENETICS have given rise to the modern field of genetic counselling, through which people known to have defective genes that could cause physical or mental disorders in offspring are warned of the risks.

Eukarya

One of the three DOMAINS of living organisms: ARCHAEA, BACTERIA and Eukarya. Eukarya are organisms with a true nucleus. *See* EUKARYOTE

eukaryote

Organism whose CELLS have a membrane-bound nucleus, with DNA contained in CHROMOSOMES. Eukaryotes include all animals, plants, fungi and PROTOCTISTS. They have a complex CYTOPLASM with an ENDOPLASMIC RETICULUM; most of them possess MITOCHONDRIA. Most plants and algae also possess CHLOROPLASTS. Other structures specific to eukaryotic cells include MICROTUBULES, GOLGI BODIES and membrane-bound FLAGELLA. In some CLASSIFICATION systems eukaryotes make up the DOMAIN Eukarya. *See also* PROKARYOTE

euonymus

Any of *c*.175 species of the genus *Euonymus*, most of which are found in Asia. They may be deciduous or evergreen shrubs or trees. Some have square stems with flanges (wings) at the corners. The leaves are oval and may have variegated markings or turn bright colours in autumn. The tiny, four-petalled flowers are insignificant, but the pink or red four-lobed fruits, which split open to reveal orange seeds, are attractive in autumn. All parts may cause stomach upset if ingested. Family Celastraceae; species include *Euonymus europaeus* (SPINDLE TREE) and *Euonymus japonicus* (Japanese spindle).

euphorbia (spurge)

Any of *c*.2000 species of the very varied *Euphorbia* genus. They may be annuals or perennials, evergreen or deciduous, herbs, shrubs or succulents. They come from varied habitats worldwide. Most euphorbias have clumps of usually green (but sometimes red or yellow) flowers, which are reduced to the male and female parts surrounded by bracts. The leaves are often lance-shaped, but in succulents they may become spines. All parts of the plant cause discomfort if ingested or in contact with the skin. Family Euphorbiaceae; species include *Euphorbia caput-medusae* (Medusa's head) and *Euphorbia pulcherrima* (POINSETTIA).

euphotic zone

Uppermost layer of the ocean. It is a comparatively shallow zone, where much light penetrates. Many green plants and herbivores are found in the euphotic zone, as well as sea-dwelling mammals.

eurypterid

Member of an extinct group of scorpion-like arthropods, some of which grew to 3m (9.8ft) in length. They lived in both salty and fresh waters from early Ordovician to the end of Permian times.

eutrophication

Process by which a stream or lake becomes rich in nutrients by runoff from the land or by artificial means. Compounds of nitrogen, phosphorus, iron, sulphur and potassium are vital for plant growth in water;

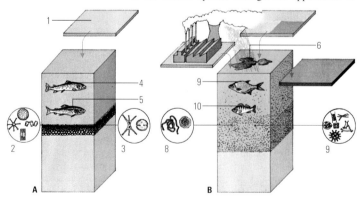

► **eutrophication** Lakes may be classified according to their fertility or productivity. Young oligotrophic lakes (A) become more fertile, or eutrophic, with age as they are efficient traps of nutrients delivered in run-off water from surrounding land (1). This natural process is hastened when the water contains agricultural fertilizers and industrial effluent. Oligotrophic lakes are characterized by clear water, a sandy or pebbly bottom and a low density of algae and plankton (mainly diatoms, 2, and desmids, 3). Typical fish are trout (4) and char (5), which thrive in deep, cold water. In eutrophic lakes (B), nitrate fertilizers and industrial organic effluent (6), which is rapidly broken down to release nitrates, phosphates and potassium, cause a great increase in algal growth, especially green algae (7) (chlorophytes) and cyanobacteria (8). The bottom of the lake becomes muddy, the water becomes turbid, and stagnation eliminates the bottom fish, which are replaced by perch (9) and bream (10). Eventually the algal bloom becomes so important that most of the dissolved oxygen is removed from the water, killing large numbers of fish. The decomposition of large amounts of organic matter will further reduce the oxygen content and a reducing condition exists in which hydrogen sulphide and methane are produced.

Evolution can be defined as the changes that occur across successive generations of organisms. The causes of evolution include NATURAL SELECTION and GENETIC DRIFT. Early work on evolutionary theory was initiated by Jean LAMARCK during the early 1800s, but it was not until the mid-1800s that the theory was considered worthy of argument. Quite independently, Charles DARWIN and Alfred WALLACE developed the same theory on evolution. They observed that organisms produce far more offspring than they need to maintain the size of their population. Yet most populations remain relatively constant in numbers because many die due to predation, disease and starvation. Consequently, individuals are competing with each other to be the one to survive. Each individual has different GENES and is, therefore, distinct from the others. Some individuals will be better suited to survive in the existing conditions – a situation known as SURVIVAL OF THE FITTEST. These "fitter" individuals are more likely to breed and pass their advantageous genes on to their offspring. Over many generations, the individuals with favourable characteristics will build up in number at the expense of those lacking them. In time, more variations will lead to the evolution of a new species. This process is known as natural selection.

Evidence for the theory of natural selection is that dated fossil remains show that life did not arise at once, but as a gradual change from one type of organism into another. Also the structures of different animals or plants show such similarity that it is highly probable they evolved from a common ancestor. The bones in the wing of a bird, the arm of a primate and the paddle of a whale, for example, all show remarkable similarity. Equally, many of the proteins in organisms are fundamentally the same and we all share many common genes.

Species are not evenly distributed around the world. Elephants are found in India and Africa but not in similar habitats in South America. This discontinuous distribution is explained by the theory of evolution. A species originates in a particular area and individuals disperse to avoid overcrowding. As they meet new environments they adapt to the new conditions, but climatic, physical and other barriers prevent them from breeding with their ancestors. A new species is created, which continues to adapt to the new conditions. *See also* NEO-DARWINISM; MENDEL, GREGOR JOHANN; PUNCTUATED EQUILIBRIUM

◄ **The peppered moth** (*Biston betularia*) exists in two forms. The light form, which is camouflaged against lichens on trees, and the melanic form, which is camouflaged against soot-covered buildings. In rural areas the light form is common and the melanic form is rare, whereas the reverse is true in urban environments. The melanic form was a chance mutation, but as the coloration was less conspicuous in urban environments those moths with the mutation flourished because their main predators, birds, could not see them so well. Birds will eat far more of the moths that are conspicuous against their background than those that are camouflaged. The difference in colorations is genetic. It is an interesting example of natural selection: the genetic change becomes common because it improves an organism's chance of survival in a particular location.

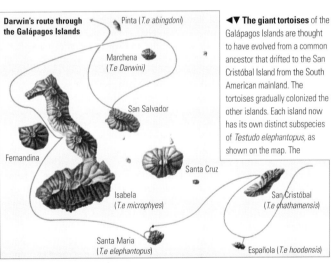

Darwin's route through the Galápagos Islands

Pinta (*T.e abingdoni*)
Marchena (*T.e Darwini*)
San Salvador
Fernandina
Santa Cruz
Isabela (*T.e microphyes*)
San Cristóbal (*T.e chathamensis*)
Santa Maria (*T.e elephantopus*)
Española (*T.e hoodensis*)

◄▼ **The giant tortoises** of the Galápagos Islands are thought to have evolved from a common ancestor that drifted to the San Cristóbal Island from the South American mainland. The tortoises gradually colonized the other islands. Each island now has its own distinct subspecies of *Testudo elephantopus*, as shown on the map. The subspecies evolved different shell shapes, the differences varying according to what best helped the tortoise to flourish in those particular local conditions. According to the principle of survival of the fittest, any adaptation that increased the tortoise's chance of survival was more likely to be passed on to the next generation until all the individuals in the area had that adaptation. As Charles Darwin travelled around the Galápagos, he observed the similarities and differences between the tortoises, and it is this work that inspired him to develop his theory of natural selection.

Testudo elephantopus abingdoni

Testudo elephantopus microphyes

Testudo elephantopus elephantopus

Testudo elephantopus hoodensis

Testudo elephantopus chathamensis

Testudo elephantopus darwini

in excess, however, they overstimulate the growth of surface CYANOBACTERIA and microorganisms, which consume all the available dissolved oxygen.

evaporation

Process by which a liquid or a solid becomes a vapour. The reverse process is CONDENSATION. Solids and liquids cool when they evaporate because they give up energy to the escaping molecules.

evaporite

Mineral deposit of precipitated salts, formed by the evaporation of saline lakes or confined volumes of salt water, usually in previous geological eras. Evaporites are important sources of GYPSUM, ANHYDRITE, rock-salt, sylvite and small amounts of nitrates and borates.

evapotranspiration

Combined processes of EVAPORATION and TRANSPIRATION in which water is transferred from the Earth's surface to the atmosphere. It is a key factor in the HYDROLOGICAL CYCLE. Water or ice is evaporated by the Sun's rays and by the wind, and plants are cooled by transpiration.

evening primrose

Any of various plants of the genus *Oenothera*, many of which are native to w North America. They have yellow, pink or white flowers that open in the evening. Height: 1.8m (5.3ft). Family Onagraceae; genus *Oenothera*.

evergreen

Plant that retains its green foliage for a year or more (DECIDUOUS plants lose their leaves every autumn or dry season). Evergreens are divided into two groups: narrow-leaved (CONIFERS) and broad-leaved. Conifers include FIR, SPRUCE, PINE and JUNIPER. Among the broad-leaved evergreens are HOLLY and RHODODENDRON. Not all conifers are evergreens; exceptions are the deciduous LARCH (*Larix*) and DAWN REDWOOD (*Metasequoia*).

evolution

See feature article, page 135

Ewing, William Maurice (1906–74)

US geophysicist. The first person to take seismic measurements in open seas (1935), he aided understanding of marine sediments and ocean basins. Ewing proposed that earthquakes are associated with central oceanic rifts. He took the first deep-sea photographs (1939).

excretion

Elimination of materials from the body that have been involved in METABOLISM. Such waste materials, particularly nitrogenous wastes, would be toxic if allowed to accumulate. In mammals these wastes are excreted mainly as URINE, and to some extent also by SWEATING. CARBON DIOXIDE, a waste product of metabolism, is excreted mainly through the lungs during BREATHING. Defecation, strictly speaking, is not excretion: faeces consist mostly of material that has never been part of the body. They are eliminated through the ANUS.

exfoliation

Process of WEATHERING in which rock flakes off in small pieces. It is caused by large differences in day and night temperatures, as occur in hot deserts. During the day the rock heats up and expands; dur-

ing the night it cools and contracts. Eventually the rock is weakened by the repeated expansion and contraction, and pieces flake off. The presence of dew or other water hastens the process. Because the rock flakes off like the skin of an onion, it is also known as onion weathering.

exobiology

Branch of science that explores the possibility of life beyond the Earth.

exocrine gland

Gland that releases its secretion onto the surface or into a body cavity. Examples of exocrine glands in the skin include sebaceous glands (which secrete waxy sebum) and sweat glands (which secrete perspiration). Mammary glands are temporary exocrine glands which secrete milk. Exocrine glands in the PANCREAS secrete digestive juices along ducts to the duodenum and intestines. *See also* ENDOCRINE SYSTEM

exocytosis

Process by which material is removed in bulk from a CELL. It occurs in many cells but especially secretory ones. Typically, the GOLGI BODY processes and packages the material to be removed and then forms VESICLES. The vesicles move to the cell surface and fuse with the CELL MEMBRANE, releasing the vesicle contents to the outside. An example is the SECRETION of MILK in the mammary glands. *See also* ENDOCYTOSIS

exopeptidase

ENZYME that hydrolyses the PEPTIDE BONDS on the terminal AMINO ACIDS of POLYPEPTIDES, progressively reducing them to their individual amino acids. Exopeptidases are of two types: aminopeptidases, which work at the end of the polypeptide chain with a free amino (–NH) group; and carboxypeptidases, which work at the end where the amino acid has a free carboxy (–COOH) group. Exopeptidases normally act after ENDOPEPTIDASES have broken up the polypeptides into smaller units, thereby giving the exopeptidase more "free" ends to act upon, thus making DIGESTION more efficient. For this reason exopeptidases are secreted and act later in the digestive process than endopeptidases.

exoskeleton

Protective skeleton or hard supporting structure forming the outside of the soft bodies of certain animals, notably ARTHROPODS and MOLLUSCS. In arthropods, it consists of a thick horny covering attached to the outside of the body and may be jointed and flexible. The exoskeleton does not grow as the animal grows; instead it is shed periodically and the animal generates a new one. *See also* ENDOSKELETON

exosphere

Outer shell in the Earth's ATMOSPHERE from which light gases, including hydrogen and helium, can escape. It lies about 400km (250mi) above the surface of the Earth.

exothermic reaction

CHEMICAL REACTION in which heat is evolved, causing a rise in temperature. A common example is combustion. *See also* ENDOTHERMIC REACTION

expiration (exhalation)

Process by which air (or water in the case of fish) is expelled from the lungs (or gills). In mammals it involves a reduction in the volume of the chest cavity by relaxation of the diaphragm muscles and contrac-

tion of the muscles between the ribs. This "squeezes" the lungs and forces gases out until the pressure in the lungs is the same as atmospheric pressure. Expiration and its opposite process, INSPIRATION, are fundamental in aiding GAS EXCHANGE, part of the complete process of RESPIRATION.

extensor

MUSCLE that makes a limb extend or straighten. *See also* FLEXOR

exteroceptor

See INTEROCEPTOR

extinction

Dying out of a species or population. Extinction is part of the evolutionary process in which species of plants and animals die out, often to be replaced by others. The rate at which extinctions have occurred is very variable. Periods of the Earth's history when extinction rates have been high are called **mass extinctions**. Extinctions brought about by human impact on the environment do not necessarily involve the replacement of extinct species by others. Extinctions can occur locally or globally. **Local extinction** refers to the loss of a species in a particular place, with other populations of the same species possibly, but not necessarily, occurring elsewhere. **Global extinction** is the permanent loss of a species throughout its entire range. *See also* EVOLUTION; PUNCTUATED EQUILIBRIUM

extracellular fluid

Any of various body fluids that exist outside CELLS in body spaces lined with moisture-exuding membranes. Such fluids are also found in blood, in lymph, in various body tissues including muscle, and in the channels and cavities of the brain and spinal cord.

extrusive rock (volcanic rock)

Type of IGNEOUS ROCK formed by MAGMA that has reached the surface of the ground. Extrusive rock generally comes from the vents of VOLCANOES or fissures producing LAVA flows. It cools quickly and is therefore fine-grained or even glassy. The term does not generally apply to PYROCLASTIC rocks.

eye

Organ of SIGHT. It converts light energy to nerve impulses that are transmitted to the visual centre of the brain. Most of the mass of a human eye lies in a bony protective socket, called the **orbital cavity**, which also contains muscles and other tissues to hold and move the eye. The eyeball is spherical and composed of three layers: the sclera (white of the eye), which contains the transparent CORNEA; the choroid, which connects with the iris, pupil and lens and contains blood vessels to provide nutrients and oxygen; and the RETINA, which contains rods and cones for converting the image into nerve impulses. The AQUEOUS HUMOUR (a watery liquid between the cornea and the iris) and the VITREOUS HUMOUR (a jelly-like substance behind the lens) both help to maintain the shape of the eye.

eyebright

Any of several small, annual and perennial plants found in temperate and subarctic regions. They have terminal spikes of white, yellow or purple flowers. Some are hemiparasites, the roots of which form attachments to those of other plants. European eyebright (*Euphrasia officinalis*) was formerly used to treat eye diseases. Family Scrophulariaceae.

F

Fabre, Jean Henri (1823–1915)
French entomologist. He made accurate and important studies of the anatomy and behaviour of insects and arachnids, especially bees, ants, beetles, grasshoppers and spiders. He emphasized the importance of the theory of inherited instincts in insects. Fabre's most important work was embodied in the ten volumes of his *Souvenirs Entomologiques* (1879–1907).

facet
Cut and polished planar surface on a gemstone, often angled to show maximum colour and brilliance.

facies
All the features of a rock or a stratum of rock that show the history of the rock's formation. Geologists often distinguish the age by the facies. The term is also applied to gradations of IGNEOUS ROCK.

Fahrenheit, Gabriel Daniel (1686–1736)
German physicist and instrument-maker. He invented the alcohol thermometer (1709), the first mercury thermometer (1714) and devised the FAHRENHEIT temperature scale. Fahrenheit also showed that the boiling points of liquids vary with changes in pressure and that water can remain liquid below its freezing point.

Fahrenheit
System for measuring temperature based on the freezing point (32°F) and the boiling point (212°F) of water. The interval between them is divided into 180 equal parts. The Fahrenheit scale is still used in the United States for non-scientific measurements. Fahrenheit is converted to CELSIUS by subtracting 32 and then dividing by 1.8.

fairy fly
Minute HYMENOPTERAN; it is one of the world's smallest insects. The fairy-fly can by yellow, dark brown or black. Its wings are very narrow and are fringed with long hairs. Fairy flies are egg parasitoids of other insects and their larvae develop within the host's eggs. Adult body length: 0.2–2mm (0.008–0.08in). Order Hymenoptera; family Mymaridae; genera *Mymar*, *Anagrus*, *Ooctonus*, *Polynema* and *Gonatocerus*.

fairy-wren
Small Australian wren. It has a long, cocked tail. The male bird is extremely colourful, with blue and lilac iridescent plumage, but it moults in winter to resemble the brownish female. Very sociable, fairy-wrens produce three broods a season, and the offspring of the first broods help to feed later broods. Length: 11–14cm (4–6in). Family Maluridae; genus *Malurus*; there are eight species.

falanouc
MONGOOSE-like animal found in the rainforests of Madagascar. Its elongate body is pale- to medium-brown with a lighter underside; it has a long snout and a bushy tail. The falanouc is solitary and preys mainly on invertebrates. Head-body length: 55–60cm (22–24in); tail: 22–25cm (9–10in). Family Viverridae; species *Eupleres goudotti*.

falcon
BIRD OF PREY. It mostly hunts by day and usually catches prey in flight. It has long, pointed wings, a long tail, hooked beak and sharp, curved talons. Female falcons are often larger than males. They nest on ledges or in the abandoned nests of other species. Some species have undergone serious population declines due to habitat loss and pesticide poisoning. Larger species are used by falconers. Family Falconidae.

falcon, aplomado
Grey-backed falcon with a black breast band. It has a striking head pattern of buff eye stripe, black mark through the eye and black moustache. The aplomado falcon is probably extinct in s United States but is found through Central and South America, as far south as Tierra del Fuego, in coastal scrub and arid country. Length: 38–42cm (15–17in). Family Falconidae; species *Falco femoralis*.

falcon, Eleonora's
Rare, slender and powerful falcon, the plumage of which varies from dark, like a peregrine falcon, to blackish brown, like a sooty falcon. Eleonora's falcon breeds in colonies on rocky islands in the Mediterranean Sea and off the coast of Morocco. Its late breeding season coincides with the southward migration of songbirds, which are its major prey item. It winters in Madagascar. Length: 36–40cm (14–16in). Family Falconidae; species *Falco eleonorae*.

falcon, forest-
Hawk-like falcon with a long tail and short, rounded wings. The barred forest-falcon is dark above and finely barred below; the collared forest-falcon is dark above and white below, with a black crescent on its face. Forest-falcons inhabit heavy lowland forests of central South America, where they are often difficult to see, lurking just below the canopy. Length: 32–60cm (13–24in). Family Falconidae; genus *Micrastur*.

falcon, gyr-
Largest species of falcon. It is native to the mountains and tundra of Scandinavia and Arctic regions. The gyrfalcon hunts low to the ground, feeding mainly on ground-dwelling birds. Plumage is a mottled grey-brown. Length: to 61cm (24in). Family Falconidae; species *Falco rusticolus*

▲ **falcon, Eleonora's** During its migration from s Europe to Madagascar, the Eleonora's falcon crosses the path of many small birds migrating from N Europe to Africa. These birds form the falcon's staple diet.

◀ **falcon, lanner** A popular falconry bird, the lanner falcon is a fast and agile flier. It feeds mainly on other birds and is capable of catching small birds in mid-air. It prefers rocky habitats but is also found in the African savanna.

falcon, lanner
Medium-sized falcon. It is dark brown above, paler buff below and has distinct black moustachial stripes. The North African lanner falcon often has a reddish-brown crown and nape. It is found in s Europe and North Africa. Length: 34–50cm (13–20in). Family Falconidae; species *Falco biarmicus*.

falcon, peregrine
Falcon that is widely distributed in Europe, Asia and Australasia. It has a distinctive flight outline, with long, pointed, broad-based wings and a tapered tail. It has black moustache-like streaks on its white cheeks. The peregrine falcon soars to a great height and then stoops on prey at speed. It nests on ledges, cliffs and tall buildings in cities, where it feeds on feral pigeons. It is prized by falconers. Length: 36–48cm (14–19in). Family Falconidae; species *Falco peregrinus*.

falcon, pygmy
Smallest African bird of prey. It is grey above and white below, with black wing tips and tail and a red patch between the eyes and bill. The pygmy falcon typically sits, with an upright stance, on the top of shrubs or trees. It breeds in the old nests of weaver birds. Length: 20–25cm (8–10in). Family Falconidae; species *Polihierax semitorquatus*.

falcon, red-footed
Falcon that is a summer visitor from central Africa to s Europe and central Asia. The male bird is dark grey with chestnut red thighs and under tail covets; its feet and the base of its bill are orange red. The female has a dark grey back and an orange-buff head and breast. Red-footed falcons nest colonially in trees and often roost in flocks on buildings. They feed mainly on large insects. Length: 28–31cm (11–12in). Family Falconidae; species *Falco vespertinus*.

falcon, saker
Large, powerful, broad-winged falcon. It has a brown back and wings, and pale buff head and underparts. It is found in SE Europe and the Middle East. The saker falcon is much prized by Arab falconers, who use it to hunt bustards. Length: 45–55cm (18–22in). Family Falconidae; species *Falco cherrug*.

falcon, sooty
Falcon that resembles the Eleonora's falcon, except for its slate-blue upper parts and darker wingtips and outer upper tail. Its habits are similar to those of the Eleonora's: it breeds in late summer, feeding its young on autumn migrants, and it often feeds at dusk on bats. The sooty falcon breeds on rocky and coral islands along the Red Sea and Gulf coasts. It winters in Madagascar. Length: 32–35cm. (13–14in). Family Falconidae; species *Falco concolor*.

falconet
Tiny FALCON. It preys mainly on insects, which it

F

F

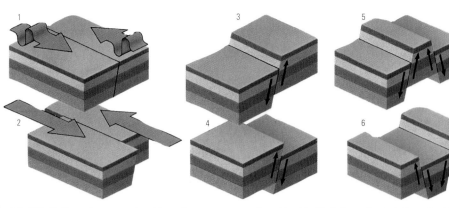

▲ **fault** The Earth's crust is subjected to enormous forces, and the stress creates faults. In a tear fault (1), the stresses cause horizontal movement. The forces build up until they are released in a sudden movement (2), often causing earthquakes. In a normal fault (3), the rocks are pulled apart, causing one side to slip down along the plane of the fault. In a reverse fault (4), the rocks on either side of the fault are forced together. One side rises above the other along the fault plane. In a horst fault (5), the central section is left protruding due to compression from both sides or the sinking of the bracketing rock. A rift valley (6), has a sunken central section, formed either by compression or by the outward movement of the two valley sides.

swoops down on from an open perch. Falconets occasionally take birds larger than themselves by swooping on them like the larger falcons. There are two species of falconet, found in the Himalayan foothills and wooded clearings in the east of the Indian subcontinent. Length 18–20cm (7–8in). Family Falconidae; genus *Microhierax*.

Fallopian tube (oviduct)
In mammals, either of two narrow ducts leading from the upper part of the UTERUS into the pelvic cavity and ending in finger-like projections called fimbriae, which almost encircle each OVARY. After ovulation, an OVUM enters and travels through the Fallopian tube, where FERTILIZATION can occur. The fertilized ovum continues into the uterus, where it becomes implanted.

false gharial
Large, narrow-snouted, freshwater CROCODILE of the Malay Peninsula, Sumatra, Java and Borneo. It strongly resembles the Indian GHARIAL. False gharials have distinct bands on their bodies and tails. They feed chiefly on fish and other small, aquatic vertebrates. Length: to 4m (13ft). Family Crocodylidae; species *Tomistoma schlegelii*.

family
Part of the CLASSIFICATION of living organisms, ranking above GENUS and below ORDER. Family names are printed in Roman (ordinary) letters with an initial capital; for example Felidae is the family of all cats.

fanaloka (Madagascar civet, Malagasy civet)
Animal that inhabits dense rainforest on Madagascar. It is fox-like in appearance and red-grey in colour, with rows of brown dots on its back. Its prey includes many small vertebrates. Head-body length: 47cm (19in); tail: 9cm (4in). Family Viverridae; species *Fossa fossa*.

fantail
Small songbird that is constantly and restlessly searching for insects. Its plumage is blackish-grey above and white or yellow below; its dark tail has bold white edges. Fantails are so called because they erect and spread their tails like a fan, droop their wings, turn from side to side and make frequent sallies after insects, often twisting and looping in the air. They are found in India and the Far East. Length: 13–19cm (5–7in). Family Muscicapidae; genus *Rhipidura*.

fanworm
Marine worm that lives in tubes constructed within marine sediments. It feeds by filtering microorganisms and detritus from the water by means of numerous appendages held in a fan-like array. Phylum Annelida; class Polychaeta.

fat
Semisolid organic substance made and used by plants and animals to store energy. In animals, fats also serve to insulate the body and protect internal organs. Fats are soluble in organic solvents such as ether, carbon tetrachloride, chloroform and benzene. They are triglycerides: esters of one molecule of glycerol connected to three molecules of FATTY ACIDS (carboxylic acids), such as palmitic, lauric and stearic acid, each having 12 to 18 carbon atoms. Research indicates that the consumption of high levels of animal fats can increase the risk of heart disease. Vegetable oils are similar to fats, but they are viscous liquids rather than semisolids and have a higher proportion of molecules with double carbon–carbon (C=C) bonds in the chain – that is, they are unsaturated.

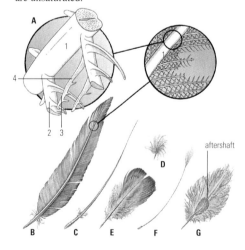

▲ **feather** The structure of a bird's feather (A) shows how barbs (2) extend from the central midrib (1). Barbules (3) project from both sides of the barb, one side of which has tiny hooks (hamuli) (4) which catch on the next barbule. The interlocking construction adds strength and helps the feather to retain its shape. Types of feather include: flight (B); bristle (C); down (D); contour feathers (E), which insulate; filoplumes (F), hair-like feathers that are either sensory or decorative; and body contour feathers (G), which have a smaller feather (aftershaft) growing from the base.

fatty acids
Organic compounds, so called because they are present widely in nature as constituents of fat. They are carboxylic acids containing a single carboxyl group (–COOH). Examples of saturated fatty acids (lacking double bonds in their hydrocarbon chain) are acetic acid and palmitic acid, the latter being a common fat constituent; unsaturated fatty acids (having one or more double carbon–carbon bonds – C=C) include oleic acid. Both saturated and unsaturated fatty acids have molecules shaped like a long, straight chain. *See also* LIPID

fault
Crack or fracture in the Earth's CRUST along which movement has occurred. The movement will be slow and quite small, only a few centimetres, though fault movements often continue for thousands of years. In such cases, uplift or downthrow of hundreds of metres is possible. Faulting is caused by PLATE TECTONICS, when movements in the Earth's crust create stress and tension in the rocks, causing them to stretch and crack. Vertical movements cause normal and reverse faults, and horizontal movements cause tear faults. The vertical change of height on opposite sides of a fault is called the throw, and the horizontal movement is called the heave. Faults often occur in groups and if two or more roughly parallel faults cause a block of land to rise, it is called a HORST or BLOCK MOUNTAIN. If the land sinks between two or more parallel faults, it creates a GRABEN or RIFT VALLEY.

fault plane
Surface along which a FAULT occurs. In a normal fault, caused by tension pulling two masses of rock apart before one mass slips downwards, the fault plane is either vertical or inclined so that the mass moves downward on the dip side of the fault plane.

fauna
Collective name for all the animals that are found in a particular area, or that lived at a particular time.

feather
One of the skin appendages that make up the plumage of birds. Feathers are composed of the fibrous protein KERATIN. They provide insulation and enable flight. They are usually replaced at least once a year.

feather-duster worm
POLYCHAETE worm that dwells in marine sediments; there are numerous species. They are so called because the tentacle masses protruding from the tubes in which they live are reminiscent of a household feather duster. These "dusters" are used in filter feeding. Phylum Annelida; class Polychaeta.

feedback
Mechanism by which homeostatic control of processes is maintained by detectors that operate when a system deviates from a set reference point. The detectors initiate a chain of events to return the system to its set reference point. For example, in some mammals, when the body temperature becomes higher than normal, the feedback mechanism prompts vasodilation and sweating in order to lower the body temperature.

feldspar
Important group of common, rock-forming minerals that contain aluminium, silicon and oxygen, and varying proportions of potassium, sodium and calcium. They are essential constituents of IGNEOUS ROCK. ORTHOCLASE and MICROCLINE are potassium

FERN

Any member of the estimated 9000–15,000 species belonging to the non-flowering plant phylum Filicinophyta. Ferns are extremely diverse in their habitats, in their shapes, and in the ways that they reproduce. Ferns are characterized by their ALTERNATION OF GENERATIONS: the conspicuous SPOROPHYTE, which possesses leafy fronds, stems, RHIZOMES and roots and reproduces by minute SPORES usually clustered on the leaves; and the inconspicuous GAMETOPHYTE, which resembles moss and produces GAMETES (sperm and ova). Fronds unroll from curled fiddle-heads and may be divided into leaflets. Ferns were growing in the Devonian period, some 400 million years ago.

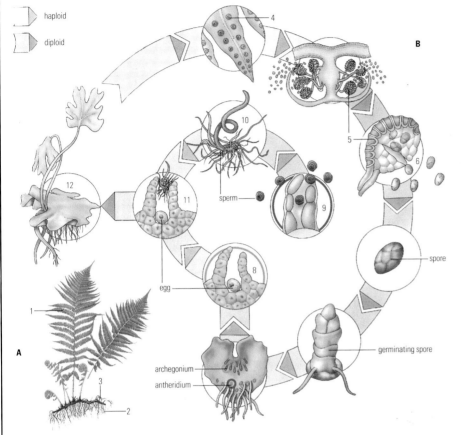

▲ **The dominant sporophytic** form of the lady fern (**A**) has upright leaves (or fronds) (1) and roots (2) that arise from nodes on the underground stem (3). Ferns can reproduce asexually, usually by fragmentation of the underground stem, or sexually, through the formation of the independent, short lived plant – the gametophyte. The sexual process (**B**) begins with meiosis, the results of which are spores. On the underside of fronds, structures called *sori* (4) enclose the *sporangia* (5) in which the spores are formed. After its release (6), a spore germinates into a heart-shaped *prothallus* (the gametophyte) (7), which bears egg and sperm-forming structures – called the *archegonia* (8) and *antheridia* (9) respectively. In wet conditions, the sperm, propelled by their many flagella (10), swim down the neck of the archgonium to fertilize the egg (11). The resulting zygote develops into the new fern plant (12).

---

feldspars of monoclinic and triclinic system crystals, respectively. Members of the PLAGIOCLASE series (sodium and calcium feldspars) have physical properties similar to microcline, but with crystals frequently twinned. Hardness 6–6.5; r.d. 2.5–2.8.

fell
Upland in N England, especially in the Lake District and the Pennines. The fells are areas of rough grazing often used for sheep in summer.

femur
Thigh bone, extending from the hip to the knee of four- and two-legged vertebrates, including humans. It is the longest and strongest bone of the human SKELETON. Its rounded, smooth head articulates with the pelvis at the hip socket.

fen
Flat, low-lying, marshy area. Regions of fen occur in many river valleys where there used to be lakes, and near the coast where land has been reclaimed from the sea by silting. The Fens are an area near the Wash, E England, where the marshes have been drained and the former wetlands have been turned into very arable farmland. There is another large expanse of fenland in Somerset, called the Somerset Levels. Some fen soils are very peaty and acidic, but others are alkaline in character.

fennel
Tall, perennial herb of the PARSLEY family, native to S Europe. The seeds and extracted oil are used to add a liquorice flavour to medicines, liqueurs and foods. It grows to 1m (3.3ft) in height. Family Apiaceae/Umbelliferae; species *Foeniculum vulgare*.

fer-de-lance (lancehead)
Lance-headed pit VIPER that is widely distributed in Central and South America. It has light-coloured diamond markings, edged with black, on a brown ground colour. The fer-de-lance's fast-acting venom is usually fatal to humans. Length: to 2m (6.6ft). Family Viperidae; species *Bothrops atrox*.

fermentation
Energy-yielding metabolic process by which sugar and starch molecules are broken down to carbon dioxide and ethanol in the absence of air (ANAEROBIC respiration); the process is catalysed by ENZYMES, usually in microorganisms such as yeast. Uses of fermentation include bread-making, wine-making, beer-brewing and cheese maturation. The intoxicating effect of crushed fruits stored in a warm place (where they would ferment) may have been known as early as 4000 BC.

fermenting bacterium
BACTERIUM that uses organic compounds in the process of producing energy, utilizing substrates such as carbohydrates, organic acids, amino acids and other nitrogenous compounds. FERMENTATION is relatively inefficient in that glucose is not completely oxidized, as it is in respiration. Fermenting bacteria include *Escherichia coli*, *Lactobacillus*, *Streptococcus* and *Clostridium*.

fern
See feature article

fernbird (matata)
Secretive, pipit-like perching bird found only in New Zealand. It is reddish-brown above, finely streaked with black, and has a white throat, a pale, finely streaked breast and a long, graduated tail. It flies weakly, with its long tail hanging down. The fernbird creeps around the base of dense vegetation looking for insects and grubs. Length: 15cm (6in). Family Sylviidae; species *Bowdleria punctata*.

Ferrel cell
Atmospheric circulation cell lying polewards of the HADLEY CELL. Like the Hadley cell, the Ferrel cell transfers heat and is caused by convection. In the Northern Hemisphere it flows northeastwards and rises upon being warmed in mid-latitudes; as it cools, it flows southeastwards and then descends at the tropics.

ferret
Domesticated POLECAT, often albino or white in parts. Feral populations are present in New Zealand. They are carnivorous. Ferrets have long, slender bodies and thick coats. If alarmed they can release strong-smelling fluid from a scent gland. Males may be twice as large as females. Reports of the domestic ferret go back at least 2500 years. Head-body length (males): 30–50cm (12–20in); tail: 10–19cm (4–7in). Family Mustelidae; species *Mustela putorius furo*.

ferret, black-footed
Rare mammal found on the short grass prairies of

▲ **ferret, black-footed** Now classed as an endangered species, the black-footed ferret has suffered from the cultivation of the North American plains which has destroyed the burrows of its main prey – the prairie dog.

North America. It has yellowish fur with dark markings on its face, back, tail tip and feet. It hunts prairie dogs in their burrows, usually at night, sometimes also taking small rodents or birds. Head-body length: 38–41cm (15–16in); tail: 11–13cm (4–5in). Family Mustelidae; species *Mustela nigripes*.

fertilization
See feature article

fescue
Any member of a genus of between 300 and 400 species of grass found in temperate areas worldwide. Their long, strap-like leaves, which are often blue-green, grow in dense tufts up to 50cm (20in) tall. Family Gramineae/Poaceae; genus *Festuca*; species include *Festuca ovina* (sheep's-fescue) and *Festuca glauca* (blue or grey fescue).

fetus
EMBRYO in a mammal after the main adult features are recognizable. In humans it dates from about eight weeks after CONCEPTION *See also* BLASTULA

feverfew (bachelor's buttons)
Strongly aromatic perennial herb originally from the Balkan region but now found throughout Europe, North and South America. It has yellow and white, daisy-like flowers in many-flowered heads. The leaves are made up of three or five deeply toothed leaflets. It has been used medicinally for centuries as a general tonic for nervous complaints. Height: to 60cm (24in). Family Asteraceae/Compositae; species *Tanacetum parthenium*.

fever-fly
Non-biting MIDGE that is commonly found on and around flowers in spring. It has a black body and sluggish flight. It is distinguished by a small circlet of spines around the tip of the front tibia. Adult body length: *c*.4mm (*c*.0.2in). Order Diptera; family Culicidae; species *Dilophus febrilis*.

fibroblast
Type of living cell found in the CONNECTIVE TISSUES of the body. Fibroblasts are mobilized to restore tissue damaged as a result of injuries. The elongated or irregularly shaped fibroblasts lay down the fibrous protein COLLAGEN and other structural materials of the connective tissues.

fiddler crab
See CRAB, FIDDLER

fieldfare
Large, bold THRUSH. It has a blue-grey head and rump, chestnut back and wings and a speckled breast. It breeds in coniferous and broadleaved

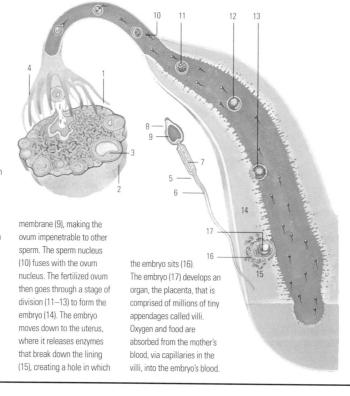

▲ **fig** The common fig tree (*Ficus carica*) bears small pear-shaped receptacles inside which both male (1) and female (2) flowers grow. Once the tree has been fertilized by wasps, the receptacles grow into edible fruits (3).

forests and wooded moorland from Greenland to Siberia; it is sometimes found as a vagrant in Alaska. The fieldfare winters in central and s Europe, where it is found in nervous, noisy flocks on farmland and in town parks. Length: 25cm (10in). Family Turdidae; species *Turdus pilaris*.

field mouse
See MOUSE, FIELD

fieldwren
Lively, small, brown bird with bold, blackish streaking above and below. It carries its tail cocked. The fieldwren is found only in s Australia and Tasmania. It is often seen diving for cover, showing its white-tipped, dark-banded tail. It sings boldly from an exposed perch in open grassy country, dunes and saltpans. Length: 12–14cm (5–6in). Family Pardalotidae; species *Calamanthus fuliginosus*.

fig
Tree, shrub or climber of the MULBERRY family. It grows in warm regions, mainly from the E Mediterranean to India and Malaysia. The common fig (*Ficus carica*) has tiny flowers without petals that grow inside fleshy flask-like receptacles; these become the thick outer covering holding the seeds, the true, edible fruit of the fig tree. Height: to 12m (39ft). Family Moraceae, genus *Ficus*.

figwort
Common name for *c*.3000 plant species of the genus *Scrophularia*. They are perennial herbaceous plants distributed worldwide. Most species have a strong smell and bear small, greenish-yellow or purple flowers. Family Scrophulariaceae.

figbird
Oriole-like bird found only in Australasia. The male is dark green above and below with a black cap; its tail has prominent white tips, and it has a patch of reddish skin around its eyes. The female is duller green and whitish below streaked with brown. The figbird is found in rainforests, eucalyptus and woodlands, often in flocks of between 10 and 50 birds. Length: 26–29cm (10–11in). Family Oriolidae; species *Sphecotheres viridis*.

fighting fish (betta, Siamese fighting fish)
Freshwater tropical fish of Southeast Asia. Males will fight each other until exhausted or injured. In the wild, fighting fish are a dull greenish colour.

FERTILIZATION

Key process in SEXUAL REPRODUCTION during which the nuclei of female and male GAMETES (sex cells) fuse to form a ZYGOTE. The zygote contains the genetic material (CHROMOSOMES) from both parents (*see* HEREDITY). In most animals, the female sex cell is called the OVUM and the male cell SPERM. After fertilization, the zygote begins to divide through a number of stages to form an EMBRYO. Fertilization of the female ovum by the male sperm can be external (outside the body, as in most fish, amphibians and aquatic invertebrates) or internal (inside the body, as in reptiles, birds, mammals and insects). In plants, the male gamete is found in POLLEN, and for most higher plants POLLINATION occurs before fertilization. While most animals and plants undergo **cross-fertilization**, in which the male gamete fuses with the female gamete of another animal or plant, some organisms undergo **self-fertilization**, whereby the male gamete fuses with the female gamete of the same flower or plant, or where an HERMAPHRODITE animal fertilizes itself. *See also* CELL DIVISION; DIPLOID; HAPLOID

▶ **Mammalian fertilization begins** with ovulation, in which an ovum or egg (1) develops in an ovary (2) into a follicle (3). The follicle consists of the ovum, a sac of liquid and follicle cells. The pressure in the follicle increases until it bursts, releasing the ovum into the Fallopian tube (4). During ovulation, oestrogen is produced by the collapsed follicle, which causes the lining of the uterus to thicken and extend its network of blood vessels, from which the ovum will be nourished. Fertilization occurs when sperm (5) are ejaculated from the penis during copulation. The sperm use their tail-like flagella (6), powered by mitochondria (7), to swim up the uterus. The first to reach the ovum penetrates the ovum membrane with enzymes secreted by the acrosomal vesicle (8). This triggers the formation of a membrane (9), making the ovum impenetrable to other sperm. The sperm nucleus (10) fuses with the ovum nucleus. The fertilized ovum then goes through a stage of division (11–13) to form the embryo (14). The embryo moves down to the uterus, where it releases enzymes that break down the lining (15), creating a hole in which the embryo sits (16). The embryo (17) develops an organ, the placenta, that is comprised of millions of tiny appendages called villi. Oxygen and food are absorbed from the mother's blood, via capillaries in the villi, into the embryo's blood.

Selective breeding has produced brilliantly coloured specimens with long, flowing fins, popular in home aquariums. Length: 5–7cm (2–3in). Family Anabantidae; species *Betta splendens*.

fig-parrot

Tiny, bright-green PARROT. It feeds on fruit. The fig-parrot has a large head, a broad, robust bill, a very short, rounded tail and blue wing patches; the males have red cheeks. Fig-parrots creep through the foliage in rainforests and swampy woodlands. They often browse on lichens and fungi on tree trunks. Length: 13–16cm (5–6in). Family Psittacidae; genus *Psittaculirostris*.

filament

Term used generally to describe a thread-like structure. Examples include the stalk of a plant's ANTHER, the HYPHA of a fungus and, in birds, the stalk of a down feather.

filarial worm

Any of a group of parasitic NEMATODE worms. The filarial worms *Brugia malayi* and *Wuchereria bancrofti* are transmitted among humans by mosquitoes. The larvae mature to adulthood in the lymph nodes, where they can cause blockage and swelling. Elephantiasis (swelling of the limbs and other body parts) or other associated complications can result from infection with the filarial worms.

filbert

Small species of HAZEL tree, found from SE Europe to the Caucasus mountains. It has long, heart-shaped leaves. In late winter it produces yellow hanging catkins; edible nuts are formed the following autumn. Height: to 6m (20ft). Family Betulaceae; species name Corylus maxima.

filefish

Tropical marine fish of the Atlantic, Indian and Pacific oceans. It is common in shallow waters, especially on coral reefs. The filefish is characterized by a ball and socket mechanism by which a spine in its dorsal fin can be locked in an erect position. Filefish are related to PUFFERFISH, TRUNKFISH and PORCUPINEFISH. Family Monocanthidae.

filial generation, first (F$_1$)

Genetic term denoting the offspring resulting from a first cross of plants or animals of the parental generation (P$_1$). The use of F$_1$ is normally limited to the offspring of HOMOZYGOUS parents at the start of an experiment.

filial generation, second (F$_2$)

Genetic term denoting the offspring resulting from crossing the individuals of the F$_1$ generation amongst themselves.

filicinophyte

Any member of a phylum of plants that comprises the FERNS. The group displays ALTERNATION OF GENERATIONS, with the SPOROPHYTE being large and dominant while the GAMETOPHYTE stage is a small, free-living PROTHALLUS dependent on water. Fern sporophytes have large leaves, known as fronds, which bear sori on their undersides. Within the sori are groups of SPORE-producing sporangia.

finch

Small songbird with a short, stout bill that is adapted to eating seeds. It has characteristically undulating or dancing flight. Male finches are usually brightly coloured; the females are often duller. Attractive species are sometimes kept as cage birds. In winter, finches often gather in large flocks of several species. They are found in open and arable country. Family Fringillidae.

finch, gold-

See GOLDFINCH; GOLDFINCH, AMERICAN; GOLDFINCH, EURASIAN

finch, Gouldian

One of Australia's most beautiful birds. The male has a black face, a bright green back with a purple rump, a black tail ending in two long fine points, a purple breast patch and a bright yellow belly. It is shy. The Gouldian finch is found near rivers in the wet season, where it feeds on flying insects. Length: 12–13cm (5in). Family Fringillidae; species *Erythrura gouldiae*.

finch, ground

Any of a group of finches found only on the Galápagos Islands. The different species are distinguished by the thickness of their beaks; they overlap in size, however, making identification difficult. Charles DARWIN suggested that all ground finches came from a common ancestor and the various ADAPTATIONS necessary to survive had produced the different species, thus illustrating his theory of EVOLUTION. Length: 15cm (6in). Family Fringillidae; genus *Geospiza*.

finch, house

Finch that is native to W North America and Mexico. It was introduced to E North America in the 1940s, and its population is expanding rapidly. The male house finch is brown above with a red front of head, breast and rump. The female is streaked brown all over. The house finch is found in lowlands up to altitudes of 1800m (6000ft); it is common in urban areas, often shopping precincts. Length: 15cm (6in). Family Fringillidae; species *Carpodacus mexicanus*.

finch, snow

Relatively large alpine sparrow; it is not a true finch. It is brown above and creamy white below, with a grey head; its black-and-white wings and tail are noticeable in flight. The snow finch is found in mountains in Europe and Asia; it winters at lower altitudes, often near buildings. Length: 18cm (7in). Family Passeridae; species *Montifringilla nivalis*.

▲ **finch, zebra** Zebra finches (*Poephila guttata*) are highly gregarious birds, often gathering in large groups numbering up to 100 birds. They are found in much of the interior of Australia and sometimes near the coast. Although the birds can survive for long periods without water, they do not usually stray far from a water source. Zebra finches pair for life and share the incubation of the eggs and the feeding of the young.

finch, woodpecker

Finch that is found only on the Galápagos Islands. It is a light olive green, with underparts streaked white or yellow; its bill is stout and elongated. The woodpecker finch sometimes uses a tool, such as a twig or cactus spine, to extract insects, larvae and spiders from holes. Length: 17cm (7in). Family Fringillidae; species *Camarhynchus pallidus*.

finch, zebra

Small cage bird that has a wax red bill and a vertical white and black mark on its face. The male bird has an orange cheek patch; its white breast is finely barred black and its black tail is barred white. The zebra finch is found in dry open habitats in Australia. Small breeding colonies have established in Europe from escaped cage birds. Length: 10cm (4in). Family Fringillidae; species *Poephila guttata*.

finchbill

Any of a small group of BULBULS. Finchbills are short-necked, short-winged perching birds with longish tails. They have heavy, short, pale bills. The crested finchbill is olive green with a distinctive green crest; the collared finchbill lacks the crest and has a blackish face with a small, white half collar. Finchbills are found in scrub and farmland of Southeast Asia. Length: 23cm (9in). Family Pycnonotidae; genus *Spizixos*.

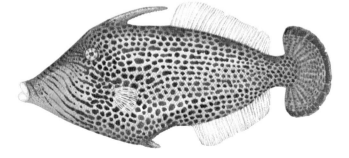

► **filefish** Commonly found in warm pacific waters, filefish, such as the fan-tailed species (*Pervagor spilosoma*) shown here, are named after their roughly textured scales. When alarmed they retreat into coral cavities and erect their fin spines to make themselves immovable.

F

► **fir** The largest Douglas firs, named after the botanical explorer David Douglas, grow to some 90m (300ft) and can live for more than 400 years. In damp conditions, a Douglas fir will grow 1m (3ft) a year for the first 30 years of its life. Douglas firs are not true firs.

finger millet

Drought-resistant GRASS that is productive even in poor soils. It is a staple cereal crop in some parts of Africa and India. The grain or seed, produced in a dense spike at the top of the main stem, is harvested and ground to a meal to make porridge or to be fermented into beer. Family Gramineae; species *Eleusine coracana*.

fir

Any of a number of evergreen trees of the PINE family, native to alpine regions of the Northern Hemisphere. The pyramid-shaped trees are prized for their beauty and fragrance. They have flat needles and cylindrical cones that shed their scales when mature. The North American BALSAM FIR is the source of BALSAM. Height: 15–90m (50–300ft). Family Pinaceae; genus *Abies*. The DOUGLAS FIR is not a true fir.

firebrat

Slender, elongate, brown or tan insect; it is covered in greyish scales. The posterior part of the firebrat's abdomen has three, tail-like filaments. It likes hot habitats and is often found in bakeries, kitchens and heating ducts, hence its common name. Firebrats are distributed worldwide and are often associated with humans. Adult body length: 8–20mm (0.3–0.8in). Order Thysanura; family Lepismatidae; species *Thermobia domestica*.

firebush (flame flower)

Evergreen tree from the Andean forests of South America. The bright scarlet or yellow tubular flowers are borne in showy clusters at the ends of the branches. The deep-green leaves are oblong and leathery. Height: to 10m (33ft). Family Proteaceae; species *Embothrium coccineum*.

firecrown

Either of two South American hummingbirds, the green-crowned (*Sephanoides sephanoide*s) and the Juan Fernandez (*Sephanoides fernandensis*). The male of the latter species is metallic yellow-orange and reddish-brown; the female is metallic blue-green and white. The differences between the two sexes are so marked that two species were described until juveniles of both types were found in the same nest. The Juan Fernandez firecrown is critically endangered, with only *c*.200 pairs left. Length: 10cm (4in). Family Trochilidae; genus *Sephanoides*; there are two species.

firefly

Light-emitting BEETLE found in moist places of temperate and tropical regions. Organs underneath the abdomen give off rhythmic flashes of light in most species. The luminous larvae and wingless females of some species are called GLOW-WORMS. Length: to 25mm (1in). Family Lampyridae; there are *c*.1000 species.

firethorn

Spiny, evergreen shrub found in s Europe, sw Asia, the Himalayas, China and Taiwan. It has oval, glossy, dark green leaves and small, white, five-petalled flowers. Firethorn shrubs are grown in gardens for their bright autumn berries, which range from yellow through orange to scarlet. The seeds can cause stomach upset. Family Rosaceae; species include *Pyracantha coccinea*.

fireworm

Any of several species of BRISTLEWORM, so named because of their ability to bioluminesce. Phylum Annellda; class Polychaeta; order Amphinomida.

firn (névé)

Hard-packed mountain snow that has been converted into granular ice in a mountain GLACIER and, with an accumulation of broken rock materials at its base, digs out round basins called CIRQUES.

fish

See feature article, pages 144–45

fisher (pekan, Virginian polecat)

MARTEN that is found in Canada and w United States. It is brown with darker legs and tail. It has a pale chest, large rounded ears and a bushy tail. An agile tree climber, the fisher feeds on carrion, fruit, nuts and small vertebrates, including porcupines. Head–body length: 47–75cm (19–30in); tail: 30–42cm (12–17in). Family Mustelidae; species *Martes pennanti*.

fish louse

Highly modified ectoparasite of marine and freshwater fish and whales. Fish lice are found worldwide. They have flattened bodies and feed on tissue fluids (especially blood) from the base of fins and gill chamber walls. In the wild, the numbers of fish lice pose no threat to fish, but in hatcheries they can become a problem. Adult body length: 25mm (1in). Order Copepoda; genera include *Argulus*.

fission

Form of ASEXUAL REPRODUCTION found in some single-celled organisms. In **binary fission**, the parent cell, such as a bacterium, diatom or protozoan, simply divides in two to produce two identical daughter cells. **Multiple fission** produces four, eight, or, in the case of some protozoa, more than 1000 daughter cells, each of which develops into a new organism.

fjord (fiord)

Narrow, steep-sided inlet on a sea coast. These deeply cut valleys were formed by glaciers as they moved toward the sea, and then flooded when the ice melted and sea levels rose.

flag

See IRIS

flagellate

Any member of the class Mastigophora. Flagellates are single-celled organisms that possess, at some stage of their development, one or several whip-like structures (FLAGELLUM) for locomotion and sensation. Flagellates are divided into two major groups: the **phytoflagellates** resemble plants, in that they obtain their energy through photosynthesis; the **zooflagellates** resemble animals, in that they obtain their energy through feeding. Most flagellates have a single nucleus. Reproduction may be asexual (FISSION) or sexual.

flagellum (pl. flagella)

Long, whip-like extension of a cell. There may be a single flagellum or a group of them. Many cells, such as SPERM cells and some BACTERIA, PROTOZOA and single-celled ALGAE, beat their flagella as a means of locomotion. In sperm and protozoa, the structure and movement of the flagella resemble those of CILIA, whereas in bacteria, the flagellum has a different structure and a rotary action. *See also* FLAGELLATE

flamingo

Large, pink and white wading bird, with a stout, curved bill. It flies with its wings outstretched and its legs trailing. Noisy and gregarious, flamingos are usually found on extensive shallow lakes or lagoons, where they feed by filtering microorganisms through the top of their bills. They build conical-shaped nests of mud. Family Phoenicopteridae.

flamingo, Andean

Flamingo that is found on Andean lakes, up to an altitude of 4300m (14,000ft) above sea level, in Bolivia, Chile and Argentina. It is the only flamingo species to have yellow legs and feet and, unlike the other species, except the very rare James' flamingo, has no hind toe (hallux). Length: 90–100cm (35–39in). Family Phoenicopteridae; species *Phoenicoparrus andinus*.

flamingo, greater (American flamingo)

Largest species of flamingo. It has a distinctive black and red bill and red legs. The striking contrast of red and black on the wings is visible in flight. The greater flamingo has a worldwide distribution around the latitude of the Tropic of Cancer; in the United States it is occasionally found as far north as Florida. Length: 125–145cm (49–57in); wingspan: 140–165cm (55–65in). Family Phoenicopteridae; species *Phoenicopterus ruber*.

flatbug (fungus bug)

Small, flat, rough, dark-coloured insect. It is usually found under stones or in crevices, where it feeds on fungi and moisture in decaying wood. The flatbug's wings are small but well developed. Adult body length: *c*.5mm (0.2in). Order Heteroptera; family Aradidae; genus *Aradus*.

flatfish

Any of more than 500 species of bottom-dwelling,

◄ **flax** Cultivated in moist, temperate climates, only one of several species of flax (*Linum usitatissimum*) is cultivated for its fibre and rich oil seeds. After harvesting, flax stems are retted (soaked in water) to soften the fibres, which are then spun into yarn.

mainly marine fish found worldwide. Flatfish have a laterally flattened body, with one anal and one dorsal fin. Both eyes are on the same side. The fish lie on their "blind" side, which is generally white. The upper surface is coloured to blend with their surroundings, and some species are able to alter their pigmentation. Examples include HALIBUT, PLAICE, TURBOT, SOLE, DAB and FLOUNDER. Order Pleuronectiformes.

flatworm

Any member of the phylum Platyhelminthes. There are c.14,000 species, all of which are characterized by being unsegmented and dorso-ventrally flattened. Flatworms have no coelom and their gut, where present, is highly branched with only a single opening. The FLUKE is a flatworm.

flavine adenine dinucleotide (FAD)

Organic chemical that carries hydrogen ions in the ELECTRON TRANSPORT SYSTEM. It is important in helping to synthesise ADENOSINE TRIPHOSPHATE (ATP) from the hydrogen ions produced during the KREBS CYCLE. *See also* NICOTINAMIDE ADENINE DINUCLEOTIDE

flavine mononucleotide (FMN)

COENZYME that is synthesised from vitamin B2 (RIBOFLAVIN). It is important in the cellular production of FLAVINE ADENINE DINUCLEOTIDE (FAD), hydrogen carrier of the ELECTRON TRANSPORT SYSTEM, and is therefore involved in the release of energy during RESPIRATION.

flax

Any of c.200 species that make up the plant genus *Linum*. A varied genus, it includes deciduous or evergreen, annual or perennial shrubs and sub-shrubs. Flax plants grow in dry areas of temperate regions of the Northern Hemisphere. They have oval leaves and five-petalled, trumpet-shaped flowers, which are brightly coloured blue, yellow, white or red. Flax has been cultivated to produce linen fibre and linseed oil since prehistoric times. Family Linaceae; species include *Linum usitatissimum* (cultivated flax), *Linum flavum* (yellow or golden flax) and *Linum perenne* (perennial flax).

F-layer (Appleton layer)

Region within the IONOSPHERE of the Earth's atmosphere.

flea

Small, wingless insect. Its hard body is highly flattened laterally. The flea has large hindlegs which enable it to jump great distances. Its mouthparts are modified for piercing the host's skin and for sucking blood. Many species of flea will attack a range of animals. Bubonic plague is caused by a bacterium carried by the rat flea. Adult body length: 2–5mm (0.08–0.2in). Order Siphonaptera; family Pulicidae; species include *Ctenocephalides felis* (cat flea), *Ctenocephalides canis* (dog flea), *Pulex irritans* (human flea), *Xenopsylla cheopis* (rat flea) and *Ceratophyllus* sp. (bird fleas).

fleabane

Any of c.250 species of plants of the genus *Erigeron*; they grow in temperate climates. Most have lance-shaped leaves and daisy-like flowers, with yellow central discs and white, yellow, pink or purple florets. Canada fleabane (*Erigeron canadense*) is dried and used in the treatment of diarrhoea. Height: to 1m (3.3ft). Family Compositae; genus *Erigeron*.

flesh-fly

Any member of the insect genus *Sarcophaga*. Some species are carrion feeding; others are parasitic on insects or vertebrates. Flesh-fly eggs develop and hatch internally; the female flies, therefore, give birth to larvae. If food containing the larvae is eaten, intestinal problems can result. Some species are used to control insect pests. Adult body length: 2–20mm (0.08–0.8in). Order Diptera; family Sarcophagidae; genus *Sarcophaga*.

flexor

MUSCLE that makes a limb bend. A flexor usually has two points of attachment on either side of a joint. For example, the biceps muscle attaches to the forearm and the upper arm. Flexing the biceps causes the arm to bend. Like all flexors, the biceps has an antagonistic ("opposite") muscle called an EXTENSOR that causes the arm to straighten – in this case the triceps.

flicker

WOODPECKER with strong claws, short legs and stiff tail feathers. The flicker is well adapted to climbing tree trunks. The feet of most species have two toes pointing forwards and two pointing backwards. The sharp bill is used to chisel out insects for food, to make nest holes and to "drum" a territorial signal. The flicker's flight is usually deeply undulating. Family Picidae.

flicker, campo

South American woodpecker that specializes in feeding on insects on the ground. It is striking black above, finely barred white and grey; it is finely barred black below. Its face and neck are yellow with thick, black, moustache-like marks and a black cap. Length: 32cm (13in). Family Picidae; species *Colaptes campestris*.

flicker, northern

Common woodpecker of woods and gardens; it ranges from Alaska throughout North America to Nicaragua. The northern flicker has a brown-barred back, spotted under parts, a black crescent bib and, in flight, a conspicuous white rump. It often feeds on the ground. The form with reddish wing linings is called the **red-shafted flicker**. Length: 32cm (13in). Family Picidae; species *Colaptes cafer*.

flight

Movement through the air. The two main requirements to maintain level flight are lift and thrust. The wings of flying animals have a similar shape in cross-section to an aerofoil. Air moves faster over the more highly curved upper surface than over the lower surface. The slower-moving air exerts a higher pressure, resulting in an overall upward force, or lift. Thrust to overcome the resistance of the air, or drag, is provided by the beating of the wings, which are angled to push the animal through the air. *See also* INSECT

flint

Granular variety of QUARTZ (SiO_2) with a fine crystalline structure. Flint is usually smoky brown or dark grey, although the variety known as CHERT is a paler grey. It commonly occurs in rounded nodules and is found in chalk or other SEDIMENTARY ROCKS containing calcium carbonate. Of great importance to early humans during the Stone Age, flint can be flaked, when struck a glancing blow, leaving sharp edges appropriate for tools and weapons; two flints struck together produce a spark that can be used to make fire.

▲ **flounder** The European flounder (*Platichthys flesus*) is found in both fresh and salt water. It grows to a length of 50cm (20in). As with all flounder species, it has a coloured upperside and a white underside.

floodplain

Level land alongside a RIVER consisting of ALLUVIUM deposited by the river when in flood. Such plains usually have extremely fertile soil and are often used, as for example near the Nile River, for intensive cultivation.

flora

Collective term used to describe all the plants that are found in a particular area, or that occurred at a particular time.

florican

Medium-sized, mainly brown bird of semidesert, grassland and scrub. Floricans typically have long legs, stout bodies, long necks and short bills; they are often called BUSTARDS. The two species of the Indian subcontinent are called floricans. The male Bengal florican and the male lesser florican have black heads and breasts, but the lesser florican is smaller and has head plume feathers. The females of both species are drab brown. Length: 46–66cm (18–26in). Family Otidae; species *Sypheotides indica* (lesser florican) and *Houbaropsis bengalensis* (Bengal florican).

flounder

Marine FLATFISH found in the Arctic, Atlantic and Pacific oceans. It is grey, brown or green on the upper, sighted, side; the blind underside is nearly white. It is an important food fish. Length: to 90cm (35in). Order Pleuronectiformes; species include *Platichthys flesus* (European flounder).

flow, solid

Slide, flow or creep of solid, unsuspended material downwards on a slope. The movement within the solid is achieved by rearrangement between or within its particles.

flower

Reproductive structure of all ANGIOSPERMS (flowering plants). It has four sets of organs set in whorls on a short apex (RECEPTACLE). Typically the SEPALS are leaf-like structures that protect the bud; they form the CALYX. The petals, often brightly coloured, form the COROLLA. The STAMENS are stalks (filaments) tipped by ANTHERS (pollen sacs). The CARPELS form the PISTIL, with an OVARY, STYLE and STIGMA. Flowers are bisexual if they contain sta-

F

Classification of fish varies. They are usually divided into three classes: Agnatha, which are **jawless** fish, including the HAGFISH and LAMPREY; Chondrichthyes (**cartilaginous** fish), which includes SHARK, SKATE, RAY and CHIMERA; and the much more numerous Osteichthyes (**bony** fish), including subclasses of soft-rayed fish (LUNGFISH and LOBEFIN), and the very successful teleost fish, such as SALMON and COD. There are more than 22,000 species of bony fish, and they represent about 40% of all living vertebrates. They are divided into 34 orders and 48 families.

All fish are ECTOTHERMIC (cold-blooded), aquatic, vertebrate animals. They are characterized by fins, gills for breathing, a two-chambered heart, and a streamlined body that is almost always covered by scales or bony plates on to which a layer of mucus is secreted. Fish reproduce sexually, and FERTILIZATION may be external or internal. The eggs develop in water or inside the female, according to species. Fish have lateral line organs, which are fluid-filled pits and channels running under the skin of the body. Sensitive fibres link these channels to the central nervous system and detect changes of pressure in the water and changes of strength and direction in currents.

About 75% of all fish live in the sea; the remainder are freshwater species, living in lakes, rivers and streams. A few fish, such as the salmon and EEL, divide their lives between salt and freshwater habitats. The range of habitats is quite extreme: some fish live near the ocean surface, others live at depths of up to 2000m (6600ft). The icefish lives under the polar ice, and desert PUPFISH live in hot springs. Some fish, including the LUNGFISH and walking CATFISH, can even survive long periods on land and are capable of breathing air.

Fish are the most ancient form of vertebrate life. True bony fish (teleosts), which first appeared 175 million years ago, evolved from the shark-like fish of 380 million years ago and the jawless fish of some 460–480 million years ago. However, the evolutionary success of the ear-lier types ensured that they did not succumb to competition and simply die out when "newer" fish evolved; they too continued to evolve. Today most species of fish are "ray-finned" fish, characterized by a single dorsal fin, pectoral fins lined with thin radial bones, scales that grow throughout life, a bony skeleton, and a swim bladder for flotation. They derive from ancestors that appeared some 390 million years ago: they are a "modern" type of fish. Sharks, which are often thought of as relatively primitive, in fact evolved later, between 190 and 135 million years ago.

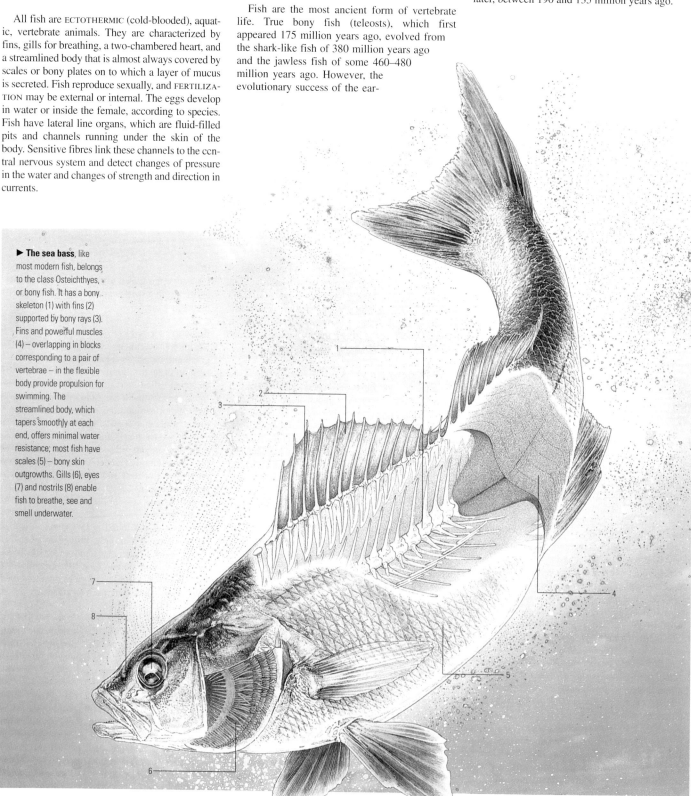

▶ **The sea bass**, like most modern fish, belongs to the class Osteichthyes, or bony fish. It has a bony skeleton (1) with fins (2) supported by bony rays (3). Fins and powerful muscles (4) – overlapping in blocks corresponding to a pair of vertebrae – in the flexible body provide propulsion for swimming. The streamlined body, which tapers smoothly at each end, offers minimal water resistance; most fish have scales (5) – bony skin outgrowths. Gills (6), eyes (7) and nostrils (8) enable fish to breathe, see and smell underwater.

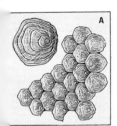

◀ **Fish have different** types of scales depending on whether they are teleosts (bony fish), such as the sea bass on the opposite page, or cartilaginous, such as sharks. Cycloid (or ctenoid) scales (A) are arranged in rows, each one having a series of tiny ring-shaped ridges – growth rings that can show the fish's age. Scales are both a protection and a flexible covering. Because they are translucent, the scales let the pigmentation on the skin of the fish show through from below. Placoid scales (B), found on cartilaginous exoskeletons of sharks, look like tiny, closely spaced teeth. Ganoid scales are another type of scale found on primitive fish, such as the bony gar. These diamond-shaped scales contain ganoin, which gives a silvery, mirror-like look. Some fish, such as certain species of eel and freshwater catfish, have no scales at all.

▶ **A family tree** outlines fish evolution from the most primitive armour-plated fish to modern fish with scales, bony skeletons and paired fins – known as teleosts. The primitive coelacanth and sharks survive, but ray fins and armoured fish are extinct.

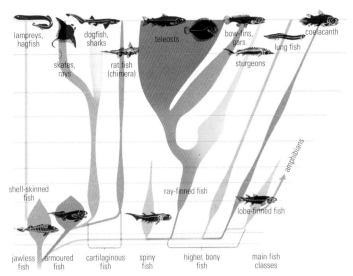

▶ **Fish breathe oxygen** dissolved in water and extracted by gills, which can achieve 80% extraction rates, over three times the rate human lungs can extract from air. Water enters the mouth (1), passes through the gill chamber (2) over the gills (3) and exits via a flap called the operculum (4). Flow is maintained by the pumping action of the mouth, synchronized to the opening and closing of the operculum. The gills are rows of bony rods (5) to which are attached fleshy filaments (6) rich in blood capillaries to absorb oxygen. Each filament has fine secondary flaps (lamellae) (7) to maximize the gas exchange surface area, which, in active fish like mackerel, can be over 10 times the outer body area.

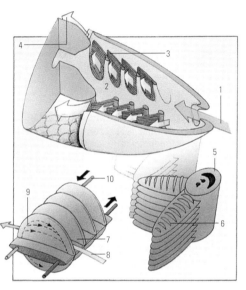

Water (8) passes over the gills against the capillary blood flow (9); this "counter-current flow" ensures water always passes over de-oxygenated blood, maximizing oxygen absorption. Blood vessels (10) circulate the blood.

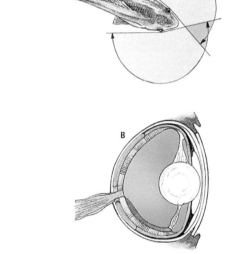

◀ **Fish eyes** (A) are adapted to see underwater. Unlike a human lens, a fish lens (1) is a perfect sphere, which may reduce image distortion. The eyes protrude somewhat to give reasonable all-round vision, but there is very little overlap between each eye's field of vision (B), hence 3-dimensional vision is poor. Fish have no eyelids – there is no need to prevent the eye from drying up – and they also lack pupils that can vary their size. Most fish have some colour vision, but sharks and rays appear to see only in black and white. Unlike those species that live in caves, fish of deep water have functioning eyes, probably used to detect luminous deep-sea creatures.

ANATOMY

There are more than 22,000 species of bony fish. Although they vary in shape and the way they swim, they share many common features. All have a tail with equal upper and lower lobe sizes, which provides neither up nor down thrust. Such fish achieve natural buoyancy by adjusting their density using the swim bladder. The fish can expand or contract the swim bladder by secreting gas into or absorbing gas out of it, thus adjusting the volume and external pressure and counteracting the tendency to sink or to float to the surface.

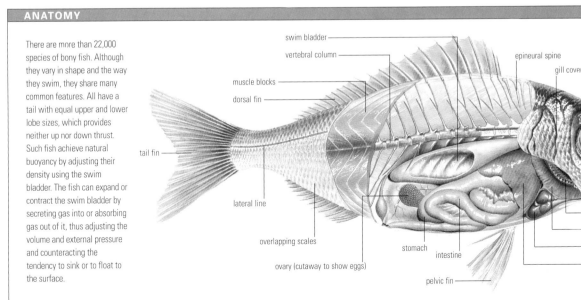

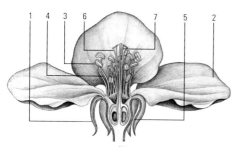

▲ **flower** A typical flower has four main parts: sepals, petals, stamens and carpels. The sepals (1) form a protective covering (the calyx) over the developing flower bud and lie outside the showy petals (2). Each male stamen is made up of an anther (3), which contains the pollen grains, borne on a filament (4). The female carpels, which together form the pistil, are found at the centre of the flower. Each carpel contains ovaries (5), which bear ovules, and a style (6), which supports the stigma (7) – the structure on which pollen is deposited.

mens and carpels, and unisexual if only one of these is present. Reproduction occurs following POLLINA-TION, when POLLEN is transferred from the anthers of one flower to the stigma of a flower of another plant (**cross-pollination**), or to the same flower or flower of the same plant (**self-pollination**). A pollen tube grows down into the ovary where FERTILIZA-TION occurs and a seed is produced. The ovary bearing the seed ripens into a FRUIT containing the seed, and the other parts of the flower wilt and fall.

flowering ash (manna ash)
Bushy, rounded, deciduous tree belonging to the OLIVE family; it grows in s Europe and sw Asia. The pinnate leaves, which have rust-coloured hairs underneath, turn purple-red in autumn. In spring it produces large, showy heads of creamy, white, star-like flowers. A sugary substance, mannite, is collected from cuts made in the bark and used medicinally. Height: to 18m (60ft). Family Oleaceae: species *Fraxinus ornus*.

flowering cherry
Any of more than 200 species of ornamental CHERRY tree found in temperate regions of the Northern Hemisphere, as well as in Southeast Asia and Andean regions of South America. They have pointed, oval, green or purple leaves, which often turn red in autumn. Their white or pink, saucer-shaped, five-petalled flowers are followed by spherical fleshy fruits. Some of the many cultivated varieties of flowering cherry trees have double flowers. Family Rosaceae; species include *Prunus campanulata* (bell-flowered or Taiwan cherry) and *Prunus avium* (wild cherry or gean).

flowering quince (Japanese quince)
Deciduous, twiggy shrub native to the mountains of Japan and China. It bears five-petalled, pink or scarlet, saucer-shaped flowers singly or in clusters. The flowers often appear before the glossy green, oval-toothed leaves. In autumn the flowering quince produces apple-like, edible, aromatic fruits. Family Rosaceae; species *Chaenomeles japonica*.

flowering plant
See ANGIOSPERM

flowering rush (water gladiolus)
Rhizomatous (*see* RHIZOME) perennial plant found at pond margins throughout Europe and w Asia. Its long, twisted leaves turn from bronze-purple to green as they mature. In late summer the flowering

rush produces spikes of rose-pink, cup-shaped, fragrant flowers. Height: to 1.5m (5ft). Family Butomaceae; species *Butomus umbellatus*.

flowerpecker
Tiny perching bird which has a short beak and tail and a long tongue for feeding on nectar. The male is brightly coloured, with blue or scarlet upper parts. Flowerpeckers are very active birds, restlessly searching the tree canopy for the flowers, insects and spiders on which they feed. They often twist and turn when perched. Length: 8–13cm (3–5in). Family Dicaeidae; genus *Dicaeum*.

flowerpiercer
Very small, often rather plain, nectar-feeding tropical bird. It has a slightly upturned bill with a hooked tip. The cinnamon flowerpiercer (*Diglossa baritula*) is blue grey above with a dark grey hood and a cinnamon-coloured belly. It is found in cloud forest and the pine-oak forest zone in Central and South America. Length: 10cm (4in). Family Emberizidae; genus *Diglossa*.

fluke
FLATWORM that is an external or internal PARASITE of animals. Flukes have suckers for attachment to the host. Human infection can result from eating uncooked food containing encysted larvae or from penetration of the skin by larvae in infected waters. The worms enter various body organs, such as the liver, lungs and intestines, causing oedema (swelling) and decreased function. Phylum Platyhelminthes; class *Trematoda*.

fluorite (fluorspar)
Mineral, calcium fluoride (CaF_2). It has cubic system crystals with granular and fibrous masses. It is brittle and glassy and its colour varies; it can be yellow, purple or green and is frequently banded. It is found in mineral veins as a gangue mineral with metallic ores. It is used as a flux in steel production and in the ceramics and chemical industries. The deep-purple banded variety is known as Blue John. Hardness 4; r.d. 3.1.

fluvial
Associated with or relating to a RIVER, for instance environments, deposits and inhabiting organisms.

▶ **flycatcher, paradise** The paradise flycatcher (*Terpsiphone viridis*), like all flycatchers, catches its prey of small insects on the wing. It sits on its perch waiting to dart out after insects, rather than trying to catch them in continual flight.

fluvioglacial
Associated with rivers that are produced by and flow from melting ice. The term can be applied to environments, deposits and inhabiting organisms.

fly
Any member of a large order (Diptera) of two-winged insects. They range in size from MIDGES *c*.1.6mm (*c*.0.06in) long to ROBBER-FLIES more than 76mm (3in) in length. The 60,000–100,000 species are found worldwide. All flies undergo METAMORPHOSIS. A female lays between one and 250 eggs at a time. The larva (MAGGOT) typically lives on rotting flesh or plants. Adult flies have compound eyes and sucking mouthparts. Many are pests and vectors, especially HORSEFLIES, MOSQUITOES and TSETSE FLIES. The common HOUSE-FLY is species *Musca domestica*.

flycatcher
Any member of a huge group of small, mainly woodland songbirds. Flycatchers have broad, flattened bills with short whiskers at the base. They feed on flying insects, which they catch in persistent to and fro sallies, often from the same perch. Flycatchers show a huge variation in plumage, from the very nondescript to spectacularly colourful and contrasting. The main families are Monarchidae, Muscicapidae and Tyrannidae.

flycatcher, Acadian
Any member of the genus *Empidonax*, a group of ten flycatcher species found in North America. They are very difficult to distinguish. All are drab olive-green above and yellowish below, with whitish eye rings and wing bars. The Acadian flycatcher has a rather long, broad-based bill; its call is a soft "*peet*". Length: 15cm (6in). Family Tyrannidae; species *Empidonax virescens*.

flycatcher, boat-billed
Large, kingfisher-shaped flycatcher found from Mexico to Brazil. It has bright yellow underparts, a striking black mask, a white stripe above its eyes, a black crown and a very wide, thick bill. The wings and tail are a dull grey-brown. Length: 22cm (9in). Family Tyrannidae; species *Megarynchus pitangua*.

flycatcher, great-crested
One of a group of six very similar migratory flycatchers found from central United States south to Argentina. It is dark olive above, with a bright lemon-yellow belly and under tail and a bushy grey crest. It is common in central and E United States. The great-crested flycatcher is only reliably distinguished from the brown-crested flycatcher by its voice. Length: 20cm (8in). Family Tyrannidae; species *Myiarchus crinitus*.

flycatcher, paradise
Flycatcher found in Africa. The male has a black head and crest, with white or reddish-brown underparts and enormous tail streamers. The female lacks the long tail feathers. The paradise flycatcher darts out to catch flying insects, the male often whisking his long tail streamers. Length: 30cm (12in), with streamers up to an additional 35cm (14in). Family Muscicapidae; species *Terpsiphone paradisi*.

flycatcher, pied
Flycatcher that breeds in woodlands and parks across Europe and central Asia and winters in central Africa. The male is black above and white below, with distinct white wing bars. Females, juveniles and winter-plumage males are brown above but retain

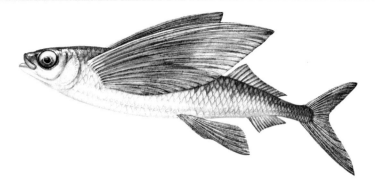

▶ **flying fish** By spreading its large, elongated pectoral fins, the flying fish can make a flight lasting between four and ten seconds. To emerge from the sea it holds its fins close to its body, takes off from the crest of a wave then spreads its fins to climb and glide. It will often, particularly when pursued by a predator, make a number of consecutive glides, beating its tail against the water.

the wing markings. Length: 12cm (5in). Family Muscicapidae; species *Ficedula hypoleuca*.

flycatcher, red-breasted
Small flycatcher. The male has a red throat and upper breast and conspicuous white eye rings; it frequently cocks its tail to show the white sides of the tail base. Females are similar but lack the red throat. The flycatcher is a summer visitor to Eastern Europe, where it breeds in broad-leaved woodlands. Length: 12cm (5in). Family Muscicapidae; species *Ficedula parva*.

flycatcher, royal
Flycatcher that is found in Central and South America. The male has a spectacular, red, fan-shaped crest, which is fringed with black and white; it is erected at right angles to the head. The female has a yellow crest. Royal flycatchers are found in dense undergrowth usually near water in interior forests. They build hanging nests, often under bridges. Length: 15cm (6in). Family Tyrannidae; species *Onychorhynchus coronatus*.

flycatcher, scissor-tailed
Flycatcher that has pearl-grey plumage with dark grey wings and salmon-pink flanks, under tail and wing linings. The adult birds have extremely long, black, outer tail feathers with white tips. The scissor-tailed flycatcher is found in open country. It is a summer visitor to s central United States and winters from central Mexico as far south as Panama. Length: 33cm (13in). Family Tyrannidae; species *Tyrannus forficatus*.

flycatcher, shining
Flycatcher native to Australasia; it is always found near water. The male is entirely glossy jet black. The female has white underparts and glossy black crown and nape, with the rest of its upperparts rich chestnut. Both sexes habitually flick their tails up. The shining flycatcher's wide repertoire of calls varies from mellow whistles to strange croaks. Length: 17–20cm (7–8in). Family Muscicapidae; species *Myiagra alecto*.

flycatcher, spotted
Flycatcher that is mousy brown above and paler below, with brown streaks on its crown, neck and breast. It perches upright and sweeps down on its prey with rather long, pointed wings; it usually returns to the same perch. The spotted flycatcher is a summer visitor to Europe and Asia from Africa. It has become less common in recent years. Length: 14cm (6in). Family Muscicapidae; species *Muscicapa striata*.

flycatcher, vermilion
Flycatcher found from sw United States to Argentina; it lives near water in dry scrub, desert and open savanna. The male has brown upperparts

and a vermilion red crown and underparts. The females and immature birds are grey-brown above, with underparts washed yellow or pink. The male has a butterfly-like, hovering display flight. Length: 12–15cm (5–6in). Family Tyrannidae; species *Pyrocephalus rubinus*.

flycatcher plant
Australian perennial herb; it is the only species in its family. The flycatcher plant has a deep TAPROOT and a short, woody underground stem. It produces buff-coloured flowers. Its lower leaves form pitchers that trap and digest insects. Family Cephalotaceae; species *Cephalotus follicularis*.

flying dragon
See DRAGON

flying fish
Tropical marine fish found in warm waters worldwide. It is dark blue and silver. The flying fish uses its enlarged pectoral and pelvic fins to glide above the water surface for several yards. Length: to 46cm (18in). Family Exocoetidae; species include *Cypselurus opisthopus*.

flying fox
See BAT

flying gurnard
Bottom-dwelling marine fish of tropical and temperate waters. It is characterized by its extremely large, wing-like and, in most species, colourful pectoral fins. It has an elongated body and bony plates on its head. Length: to 50cm (20in). Family Dactylopteridae; species include *Dactylopterus volitans* (Atlantic flying gurnard) and *Dactyloptena orientalis* (Oriental flying gurnard).

flying lemur
See COLUGO

fody
Small, canary-like finch. Individual species are confined to islands in the Indian Ocean; several species are now critically endangered. The Madagascar Fody is pinkish red with dark wings; it has a black mark through its eyes and a very short, black, triangular, finch-like bill. Length: 12cm (5in). Family Fringillidae; genus *Foudia*.

fog
Mass of water droplets immediately above the Earth's surface that reduces visibility to less than 1km (0.6mi). A light fog is called mist or haze. Fog is caused by water vapour condensing as a result of the air becoming cooler. This condensation takes place around particles of dust. There are four main types of fog: **advection fog** develops from air flowing over a surface of a different temperature, for example the steam fog that results from cold air passing over warm water; **frontal fog** forms when warm rain falls through cold air near the ground; **radiation fog** occurs when the ground cools on a still, clear night, and is most common in valleys; **upslope fog** develops when air cools as it ascends a slope. *See also* DEW POINT

fold
Bend in a layer of rock. An upfold is an ANTICLINE; a downfold a SYNCLINE. A monocline (flexure) slopes in one direction only and usually passes into a FAULT. Folds occur as part of the process of PLATE TECTONICS, where rock strata buckle and bend

▼ **fog** The fir trees of Yosemite National Park, California, United States, are shrouded in fog. The various types of fog occur most frequently in autumn and winter, often when mild, damp air flows over cold surfaces or when cold air flows over a warmer surface.

F

under pressure. If the compression is fairly gentle and even, the resulting fold is symmetrical. If the pressure is uneven, then asymmetrical folds will form. In many cases, the folds are pushed over to form recumbent folds. Eventually the rock strata may break under the pressure to form an overthrust or a NAPPE.

foliation

Crude layering of rocks produced under compression. The layering is approximately parallel to the bisecting planes of FOLDS. Foliation often results in the rock splitting because of the parallel orientation of the mineral layers. MICA and SLATE are good examples of foliation.

foliage-gleaner

Any of several species of small, plain, brown or blackish brown songbirds. The foliage-gleaner is an acrobatic feeder around the tips of twigs, rather like a chickadee or a tit. It is found in dense rain and cloud forests from Central America to Brazil. The scaly throated foliage-gleaner (*Philydor variegaticeps*) is characterized by a buff eye stripe and eye-ring. Length: 15–20cm (6–8in). Family Furnariidae; species include *Philydor rufosuperciliatus* (buff-browed foliage-gleaner) and *Philydor rufus* (buff-fronted foliage-gleaner).

follicle

Fruit that splits along one side to release its seeds when it is ripe. It differs from a pod, which splits along both sides. Follicles occur in clusters called **etaerios**. They are found in plants such as DELPHINIUMS and LARKSPUR.

follicle

In zoology, group of cells forming a sac that envelops and protects a structure within it. A hair follicle surrounds and nourishes the root of a hair. A GRAAFIAN FOLLICLE encloses a developing OVUM.

food chain

See feature article

food web

Often complex pattern of interrelating FOOD CHAINS. When created schematically on paper the lines that link the various animals and plants, and that make the individual food chains, form a crisscross pattern resembling a web.

foraminiferan

Any member of the order Foraminiferida, a group of single-celled animals found mainly in marine waters. They have multi-chambered, chalky shells, known as tests, which may be spiral, straight or clustered. Many foraminiferan species remain as fossils and are useful in geological dating. When foraminifera die, their shells sink to the seafloor to form large deposits, the source of chalk and limestone. Test size: from microscopic up to *c*.5cm (*c*.2in). Kingdom Protoctista; order Foraminiferida.

forebrain

One of the three primary parts of the developing BRAIN, clearly distinguishable, together with the MIDBRAIN and HINDBRAIN, in the early embryo. It becomes overlaid in the adult human by the CEREBRAL HEMISPHERES, which are massive developments from the forebrain.

forest

Large area of land covered with a dense growth of trees and plants. Earth's first forests developed *c*.365 million years ago. In the early 1800s forests covered 60% of the Earth; today they account for about 30%. DEFORESTATION is a major environmental concern, since forests make such a vital contribution to Earth's atmosphere and also regulate water flow. Forests have been an important source of timber, food and other resources since prehistoric times. The forest ECOSYSTEM has five basic strata: forest floor, herb layer, shrub layer, understorey and canopy. Forests are classified into three general formations. **Tropical hardwood forests**, including RAINFORESTS, are predominantly EVERGREEN. They account for 7% of the Earth's landmass, but about 50% of the Earth's species. **Temperate hardwood**

forests are mostly DECIDUOUS and are found in temperate climates. **Boreal forests**, consisting mainly of evergreen CONIFERS, lie in the far north.

forget-me-not

Any of *c*.50 species of hardy perennial and annual herbs belonging to the genus *Myosotis*. They are found in temperate regions. The forget-me-not's five-petalled flowers are sky blue but may change colour with age. Family Boraganacea (BORAGE).

forktail

Any member of a small genus of wagtail-like water birds found in the mountains of s Asia. They have bold black-and-white plumage. All species, except for the little forktail (*Enicurus scouleri*), have a long, forked, black-and-white tail. The tail is constantly swayed up and down while the bird walks daintily at the water's edge. Length: 12–25cm (5–10in). Family Turdidae; genus *Enicurus*.

forsythia (golden bells)

Any member of the genus *Forsythia*, a group of hardy, deciduous, garden shrubs. Originally from China, forsythia is now commonly cultivated in temperate regions worldwide. It is grown for its beautiful, four-petalled, bright yellow flowers, which appear in early spring before the lance-shaped leaves. Forsythia is named after the Scottish botanist William Forsyth (1737–1804). Height: to 10m (33ft). Family Oleaceae; species include *Forsythia x intermedia*.

fossa

Largest Madagascan carnivore. An arboreal, nocturnal mammal, it lives mainly in coastal rainforests. It is reddish or dark brown with short legs. A cylindrical tail, large eyes and rounded ears give it a cat-like appearance. Head-body length: 60–75cm (24–30in); tail: 60–75cm (24–30in). Family Viverridae; species *Cryptoprocta ferox*.

fossil

Any direct evidence of the existence of an organism that is more than 10,000 years old. Fossils mostly consist of original structures, such as bones or shells or wood, often altered through MINERALIZATION or preserved as CASTS AND MOULDS. Imprints such as tracks and footprints are known as trace fossils. Leaves are often preserved as a carbonized film outlining their form. Occasionally organisms are totally preserved in frozen soil (such as MAMMOTHS), peat bogs and asphalt lakes, or trapped in hardened resin (such as insects in amber). COPROLITE (fossil excrement) frequently contains undigested and recognizable HARD PARTS. Very few animals and plants that die become fossilized. Since fossils reveal evolutionary changes through time, they are essential clues for geological dating. *See also* FOSSIL, TRACE

fossil, trace

Evidence preserved in rock strata of the activity of organisms. Examples of trace fossil include the footprints of a dinosaur or the toothmarks of a scavenger incised on a FOSSIL bone.

fossil fuels

See feature article, page 150

fossilization

Process by which the FOSSIL remains of dead organisms are recruited to the stratigraphic record. After the decay of the soft body tissues, any remaining HARD PARTS or mineralized body parts that are buried

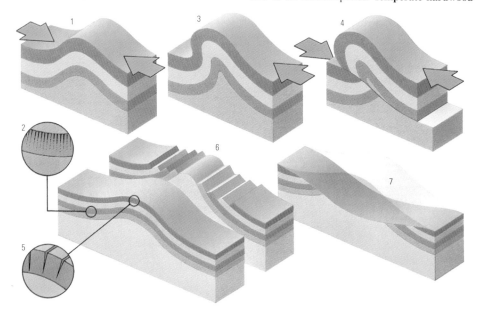

▲ **fold** Tectonic forces warp the Earth's surface and are powerful enough to bend strata of rock. An anticline (1) is created when the rock is pushed upward. When the rock is forced down, a syncline (2) is formed. If the force continues an overfold (3) forms. If the strata are warped too much, they can in effect snap (4) making an overthrust fold or nappe, which is both a fold and a fault. At the top of an anticline, the rocks are "stretched" (5), while at the base of a syncline they are compressed. The extra joints and small cracks at the top of the anticline (6) make it more prone to weathering and erosion. If this process continues, over many thousands of years, an anticline can be eroded to form what appears to be a syncline (7).

A food chain comprises a series of organisms, each organism consuming the previous member of the chain. The Sun's radiation is the ultimate source of energy for all living organisms. Because green plants use the Sun's energy to manufacture food they are called PRIMARY PRODUCERS. Some animals feed on plants to obtain their energy and are called PRIMARY CONSUMERS (HERBIVORES). Other animals feed on herbivores and are called SECONDARY CONSUMERS (CARNIVORES). In this way energy is passed from organism to organism in what is called a food chain.

An example of a food chain is:

oak tree – aphid – ladybird – thrush.

In this food chain the oak tree uses energy from the Sun to photosynthesize. The aphid feeds on the oak tree, the ladybird on the aphid and the thrush, in turn, on the ladybird.

Each feeding level in the chain is called a TROPHIC LEVEL. Food chains are often interconnected to form food webs, such as the one shown here:

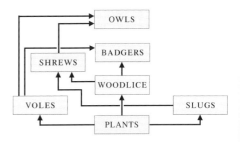

Each organism loses energy in waste materials, as heat or in carrying out living processes such as respiration and movement. As a result, only a small proportion of the available energy is transferred from one trophic level to the next; it is, therefore, rare to find food chains with more than six trophic levels. As a result, the BIOMASS of all the organisms at each trophic level in a food chain is less than it was at the previous one.

Only about 2% of the Sun's energy is converted into chemicals of plant cells. In the rest of the food chain the amount of energy that is passed to the next trophic level is as little as 10% on average. Zooplankton, however, may obtain up to 40% of the energy in the phytoplankton they eat, while many herbivores may obtain only 1% of the plant's energy. It is, therefore, more efficient for humans to eat food that is lower in the food chain, that is, vegetables rather than meat. Similarly, it is more efficient if, for instance, food animals are kept in warm conditions so that they loose less energy. When organisms die they are decomposed by microorganisms, such as bacteria and fungi, which release valuable nutrients for recycling into the food chain.

▲ Lions chase vultures away from their kill in the Masai Mara, Kenya. Lions are secondary consumers, feeding on primary consumers (mammalian herbivores). Vultures are also secondary consumers, but they take advantage of other animals' kills rather than capturing and killing their own food.

▶ Lake food chains begin with algae (1), prey to plankton like *Daphnia* (2), in turn prey to carnivorous plankton like cyclops (3). Minnows (4) reduce the chance of individuals being preyed upon by swimming in shoals. Perch (5), normally pelagic residents, breed in littoral waters, trailing mucus-covered eggs (6). Carp (7), however, are benthic, using whisker-like barbels (8) to find food, such as caddis fly larvae (9), which build armour from plant fragments. Midge larvae (10) are prey for many ducks, fish and birds, particularly when they hatch into vast insect swarms. *Tubifex* worms (11) have oxygen-carrying haemoglobin in their blood and are a rich food source for fish. Underwater plants such as wormwort (12) and Canadian pondweed (13) are both bottom-rooted and photosynthesize in minimal light. Slime on their surfaces is food for the great pond snail (14). The great diving beetle (15) attacks anything from worms to tadpoles (16). Dragonflies (17) eat smaller insects; living underwater as carnivorous nymphs, they reach a last moult stage (18), before emerging as adults. Some lakeland birds, such as the great crested grebe (19) and tufted duck (20), feed by diving for fish, others such as the mallard (21) dabble for plant matter. The osprey (22) catches fish in its talons. Plants such as bulrushes (23) grow near the water's edge and help the slow colonization of the lake by the land. Long stems of lilies (24) convey oxygen to roots at the bottom. Floating plants, like the water soldier (25), have roots taking nutrients directly from the water. A water shrew (26) dives for beetles.

F

Fossil fuels is the term used to describe oil, natural gas and coal – fuels that were formed millions of years ago from the fossilized remains of plants or animals. They are a nonrenewable energy source.

Oil, gas and coal are all formed from the decay of once-living organisms under heat and pressure. More than 80% of the oil and gas currently exploited formed in Mesozoic or Tertiary strata between 180 and 30 million years ago, from marine microorganisms deposited as sediment on the sea bed. The basic components of oil and gas are created when the organic remains are not completely oxidized, leaving a residual mass of carbohydrates, hydrocarbons and similar compounds. As layers of sediment bury this residue, temperature and pressure increase and the liquid hydrocarbons are segregated into pore spaces in the rock. Coal deposits come from many epochs, but primarily the Carboniferous period (360–286 million years ago). The quantity of oil and gas formed depends on temperature and on the speed of subsidence of strata. Ideally up to 3km (2mi) of overlying strata are needed. Gas and oil migrate up – the gas and lighter oils first, with heavier bitumens staying closer to their source – until they are trapped by overlying impermeable rocks.

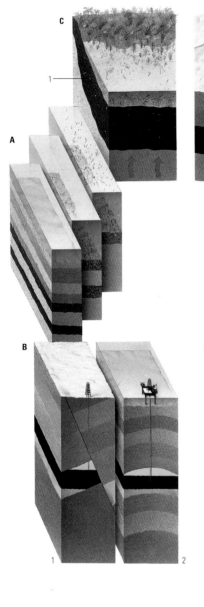

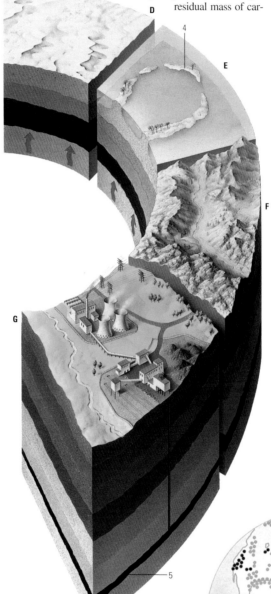

◄ **Oil and gas** are formed as layers of plankton are buried under thick piles of sediment (A). Increasing heat and pressure at depth first cause gas and oils from the bodies of the marine organisms to "link up" into a thick compound called kerogen. As temperature increases with burial, long chains made of hydrogen and carbon atoms break away from the kerogen, giving a viscous heavy oil. With even more heat, valuable light oils and natural gas are formed. The oils accumulate in "reservoir" rocks – permeable rocks such as sandstone which hold the oil like a sponge. To form an oilfield, the oil must be trapped between layers of an impermeable rock, such as shale (B). Faults, where such rock has sheared to form a seal (1), can trap oil and gas, as can convex domes (2). The making of most coal (C–G) was begun in the middle of the Carboniferous period. The Earth's equatorial regions were hot and wet, and lush tropical forests grew in extensive swamps (C). In these types of environment, thick layers of peat were laid down (1): typically they were sandwiched between layers of sediment, such as shale (2), deposited when the waters temporarily retreated. The seas receded during the Permian period and many of the tropical coastal plains turned to desert (D). Other sedimentary rocks, such as sandstones (3), were laid down over the shale and peat. With increasing temperature and pressure, the buried peat began its metamorphosis into coal. Around 150 million years ago (E) the deserts were covered by shallow, tropical seas in which limestone (4) was deposited. Around 50 million years ago, plates of the Earth's crust collided forcing mountains up and further burying the underlying rocks (F). Metamorphism continued, converting coal into high-grade anthracite (5). Today anthracite is found in deep seams up to 30m (100ft) thick.

▶ **The predicted future** life of the world's coal reserves was once put at as low as a few decades, but the real figure is actually nearer 300 years. Some E European countries and the United States have the greatest resources. Western Europe, India, China, Brazil, South Africa and Australia also have large stocks of top-rate coal from the Carboniferous and Permian periods. Brown tertiary lignites can be found in central Europe and the Ukraine. Antarctica also has large unused coal reserves, which could only be exploited at disastrous environmental cost. Estimating oil reserves is very complex as new sources are always being discovered. But some scientists estimate that we have used between a quarter and a tenth of all oil reserves.

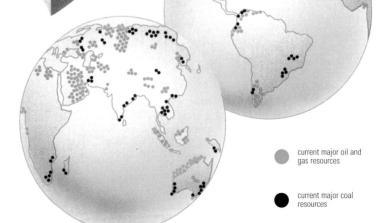

● current major oil and gas resources

● current major coal resources

► **fox, fennec** The kit fox (*Vulpes velox*) and the fennec fox (*Fennecus zerda*) are similar but unrelated desert mammals. The kit fox is from the New World, the fennec from the Old, both have adapted independently but in the same way to desert life. This is a case of convergent evolution – the development of similar characteristics by animals or plants of unrelated species. Both species are nocturnal and live in burrows. They feed on insects, lizards, rodents and birds, which they detect with their large and sensitive ears.

in sediment will have some potential to become fossil. Even after burial, however, physical and chemical changes that occur in the rock strata may alter or destroy the remains. *See also* STRATIGRAPHY

fossil record
Remains of past life preserved in many different ways, from shells and bones to trace FOSSILS and chemical fossils found within sedimentary strata. It records a history of life on Earth stretching back more than 3.8 billion years.

four-eyed fish
Either of two species belonging to the genus *Anableps*; they are found in Mexico and South America. They are the largest of the KILLIFISH. The four-eyed fish does not actually have four eyes, rather its eyes have divided corneas, pupils and retinas, which allow it to focus on objects above and below the water's surface simultaneously. Length: to 32cm (13in). Family Anablepidae; genus *Anableps*; species *Anableps tetrophthalmus* and *Anableps microlepis*.

fox
Small and agile member of the DOG family. Various species are found from the Arctic through to the tropics. Some foxes live in arid desert regions. Foxes are distinguished by sharp features, rather large ears and a long bushy tail. The female fox (vixen) bears four or five cubs. Family Canidae (part); genera *Alopex*, *Dusicyon*, *Otocyon* and *Vulpes*; there are 21 species.

fox, Arctic
Fox found in polar regions of the Northern

► **foxglove** Native to Europe, North Africa and Asia, foxgloves are hardy plants that bear purple and white, or less commonly, golden flowers.

Hemisphere. Two colour variations occur – white (with a grey-brown summer coat) and blue (dark grey in the summer, slightly paler in winter). Arctic foxes are opportunistic carnivores, feeding on invertebrates and small mammals as well as carrion and berries. Head-body length: 46–73cm (18–29in); tail: 25–52cm (10–20in). Family Canidae; species *Alopex lagopus*.

fox, bat-eared
African fox that is distinguished by its huge ears and its black, raccoon-like face mask. Its fur is pale grey or buff with black feet and ear tips. It is unusual in that it feeds mainly on termites. Head-body length: 46–58cm (18–23in); tail: 24–34cm (9–13in). Family Canidae; species *Otocyon megalotis*.

fox, crab-eating
Fox found in dense grassland and open woodland of w and central South America. It is omnivorous, feeding on small animals and fruit. Crab-eating foxes are generally grey-brown with paler undersides, but there is a wide variation in colour. Head-body length: 60–70cm (24–28in); tail: 30cm (12in). Family Canidae; species *Dusicyon thous*.

fox, fennec
Smallest species of fox. It is found in desert regions from North Africa to the Arabian Peninsula. In order to stay cool, it digs long burrows in which it spends the day; it hunts by night. The fennec fox is pale brown with very large ears. Head-body length: 23–40cm (9–16in); tail: 18 30cm (7–12in). Family Canidae; species *Vulpes zerda*.

fox, grey (tree fox)
Omnivorous fox that lives in desert and wooded areas ranging from Canada to Panama. It has mottled grey and red fur and is adept at climbing trees. Head-body length: 50–75cm (20–30in); tail: 30–40cm (12–16in). Family Canidae; species *Vulpes cinereargenteus*.

fox, red
Most common species of fox, widespread throughout Europe, Asia and North America. Its fur is often red or orange, but it varies through to black with a white-tipped bushy tail. Omnivorous, red foxes feed on small mammals, carrion, berries, invertebrates and sometimes fish. Head-body length (males): 67–80cm (26–31in); tail: 40cm (16in). Family Canidae; species *Vulpes vulpes*.

fox, swift
Fast-running fox found in central United States and

s Canada. The swift fox has a mottled grey back, yellow sides and white underparts. Solitary and usually nocturnal, the swift fox digs extensive burrows. It hunts small mammals, birds and insects and will also take berries. Head-body length: 51–53cm (20–21in); tail: 27–28cm (*c*.11in). Family Canidae; species *Vulpes velox*.

foxglove
Hardy plants of the genus *Digitalis*, found in Eurasia. They have long, spiky clusters of drooping tubular flowers. The common biennial foxglove (*Digitalis purpurea*), source of DIGITALIS, is grown for its showy purple or white flowers. Family Scrophulariaceae; genus *Digitalis*.

francolin
Dark, quail-like game bird, belonging to the PHEASANT family. It has a pale face and complex patterns of black or brown chevrons or bars on its underside. The francolin is found in Europe and Asia, often in mountainous regions. Some species, such as the double-spurred francolin of Morocco, are endangered. The black francolin has been introduced into the United States. Length: 31–34cm (12–13in). Family Phasianidae; genus *Francolinus*.

frangipani (pagoda tree)
Shrub or small tree native to tropical America. It is widely cultivated in the Old World tropics for its fragrant white, yellow, pink or red flowers, which are used as offerings in Buddhist temples. A perfume is prepared from the flowers. Frangipani has a poisonous milky sap. Family Apocynaceae; genus *Plumeria*; species include *Plumeria rubra*.

frankincense (olibanum)
Gum resin extracted from the bark of trees of the genus *Boswellia*, found in Africa and parts of the Middle East. Used in religious ceremonies and one of the gifts of the Magi, it is burned as incense. The fine spicy oil extracted from the resin is used as a fixative in perfumes. Family Burseraceae.

free energy
Energy that is available to do work under conditions of constant temperature and pressure.

freesia
Any member of a genus of perennial herbs belonging to the IRIS family, native to South Africa. Species of freesia are widely cultivated for their fragrant yellow, white or pink flowers. They are grown in greenhouses for winter blooming. Family Iridaceae; genus *Freesia*.

◄ **freesia** Cultivated commercially worldwide, freesias thrive in greenhouses or mild climates. Their flowers appear in the spring and are extremely fragrant. The plants grown to a height of 75cm (30in).

French bean

▲ **frog, arrow-poison** The two-toned arrow-poison frog (*Phyllobates bicolor*) is a highly poisonous native of Peru. The rim of its upper jaw is armed with small teeth.

French bean (common, snap, kidney or runner bean)
Leguminous plant originally from Central America and now grown as a vegetable crop throughout America and Europe. It is a climbing annual plant. Its leaves have three leaflets and its flowers are pea-like. The beans are the seeds, which are borne in long, fleshy pods. Many varieties have been developed. Family Leguminosae; species *Phaseolus vulgaris*. See also KIDNEY BEAN

French marigold
Annual garden bedding plant with smooth, purple-tinged stems. Its long leaves are divided into lance-shaped, toothed leaflets. The showy, daisy-like flowerheads are often double; the outer ray-florets, in shades of red-brown, orange or yellow, surround disc-florets of the same or contrasting colours. Family Asteraceae/Compositae; species *Tagetes patula*.

friarbird (leatherhead)
Any of a group of oriole-sized songbirds belonging to the HONEYEATER family. The skin of the friarbird's head is wholly or partly unfeathered. Most species have large, curved, blade-like bills surmounted by a raised ridge or knob. They have an extraordinary range of loud calls. Friarbirds are found in tropical forests, woodlands, wooded scrub and gardens in Australasia. Length: 25–35cm (10–14in). Family Meliphagidae; genus *Philemon*.

Fries, Elias Magnus (1794–1878)
Swedish botanist who developed one of the first systems for the classification of fungi. His system is still a basis for classification.

frigatebird (man-o'-war hawk)
Large, sinister-looking, piratical seabird found in the tropics. Most species are all black, with long, deeply forked tails and long, slender, sharply hooked bills. Male frigatebirds have bright red throat patches, which they inflate into large balloons during display. Length: 89–100cm (35–39in); wingspan: up to 250cm (100in). Family Fregatidae; genus *Fregata*; there are five species worldwide.

frilled lizard
See LIZARD, FRILLED

Frisch, Karl von (1886–1982)
Austrian zoologist. He shared with Konrad LORENZ and Nikolaas TINBERGEN the 1973 Nobel Prize for physiology or medicine for his pioneering work in ETHOLOGY (the study of animal behaviour patterns). He deciphered the "language of bees" by studying their dance patterns (WAGGLE DANCE), in which one bee tells others in the hive the direction and distance of a food source. In his earlier work he showed that fish and bees see colours, fish can hear and bees can distinguish various flower scents.

frit-fly
Small FLY that is a pest of cereal crops. The larvae tunnel into stems and ears of cereals, particularly oats and barley. The female frit-fly's abdomen is characteristically pointed with a rigid ovipositor. Adult body length: 1.5mm (0.06in). Order Diptera; family Tephritidae; species *Oscinella frit*.

fritillary
Common name for several genera of BUTTERFLIES including large fritillaries (silverspots) of the genus *Speyeria* and small fritillaries of the genus *Boloria*. The larvae (caterpillars) are largely nocturnal. Family Nymphalidae.

fritillary
Any of c.100 species of perennial, bulb-forming plants of the genus *Fritillaria*, found in a range of habitats throughout the Northern Hemisphere. A fritillary plant has lance-shaped leaves at the base of its stem and in whorls further along. Its bell-shaped flowers comprise six petal-like sepals, which can be white, yellow through orange to deep red or purple-black, often with a chequered pattern. Family Liliaceae; genus *Fritillaria*; species include *Fritillaria imperialis* (crown imperial) and *Fritillaria camschatcensis* (black sarana).

frog
Any of c.4400 species of tailless, mostly night-active amphibians with short, compact trunks, large heads and often long, powerful hindlimbs. Frogs occur worldwide except in polar regions and are placed into c.28 families. Most frogs pass through an aquatic, TADPOLE, larval stage before metamorphosing into adults, which may be aquatic, terrestrial, burrowing or arboreal (tree-living). Frog tongues are attached at the front of the mouth and flip out forwards to capture live prey, usually insects. Male frogs generally produce complex, species-specific mating calls. Length: 1–30cm (0.4–12in). Order Anura. See also LARVA; METAMORPHOSIS; TOAD

frog, arrow-poison
Small, diurnal, terrestrial frog of tropical Central

▲ **frog** Tree frogs belong to the Hylidae family of frogs and live in forests, high above land predators. Circular pads on the tips of their digits contain glands that secrete a substance that glues them to slippery leaves.

and South America. Its highly toxic skin secretions contain a variety of steroids, alkaloids and other compounds. The secretions were traditionally used by Native Americans to poison arrow tips for hunting monkeys and other game. Most species of arrow-poison frog are brightly coloured, which acts as a warning of their toxicity. Eggs are laid on land and guarded by the male, who carries the tadpoles to water when they hatch. Length: 12–60mm (0.5–2.4in). Family Dendrobatidae.

frog, clawed
Any of a group of flattened, fully aquatic, African frogs with thick, powerful hindlegs and strongly webbed toes that end in claws. The eyes are directed upwards; there are no external eardrums and no tongue, but mechanoreceptive organs are present over the body. One species, the common platanna (*Xenopus laevis*), is widely used in scientific experiments, especially in its albino form. Length: 35–130mm (1.4–5.1in). Family Pipidae; genus *Xenopus*.

frog, Darwin's
Terrestrial frog with an elongate, pointed snout. It is found in the cool temperate forests of s South America. It lays its eggs on land and when they hatch the male takes them into his mouth, where they pass into his vocal sac. The tadpoles develop in this protective environment and are released after they metamorphose. Length: c.3cm (c.1in). Family Rhinodermatidae; species *Rhinoderma darwinii*.

frog, gastric-brooding
Short-snouted, squat-bodied frog with granular skin, strongly webbed feet and prominent bulging eyes. Gastric-brooding frogs occurred along montane streams in Queensland, Australia, but have not been seen since the 1980s and may now be extinct. Females swallow the eggs and development takes place in the stomach, with froglets emerging from the throat. Length: 4–8cm (2–3in). Family Myobatrachidae; genus *Rheobatrachus*.

frog, ghost
Any of five species of frog that live in and around fast-flowing mountain streams in South Africa. The ghost frog's body is somewhat flattened, and its eyes are large and conspicuous. Its toes are webbed and end in expanded pads for climbing. Ghost frog tadpoles have large, sucker-like mouths for holding on to the substrate in the torrents where they live. Length: to 6cm (2in). Family Heleophrynidae; genus *Heleophryne*.

frog, glass
Chiefly tree-dwelling, tropical American frog. The glass frog has little or no pigment in its ventral skin, and its internal organs are visible through the abdomen. The glass frog lays eggs on leaves overhanging streams, and the hatching tadpoles drop to the water below. Length: to 7cm (3in), but usually less than 4cm (2in). Family Centrolenidae; there are c.120 species.

frog, gliding (flying frog)
Tropical tree frog that has expanded webbing between its toes. It is able to make a controlled descent from the canopy by stretching out its limbs and toe webs. The most well-known example is the Bornean "flying" frog, *Rhacophorus nigropalmatus*. Length: to 10cm (4in). Families Rhacophoridae and Hylidae; there are several species.

frog, gold
Tiny, gold-coloured, burrowing frog from the Atlantic

F

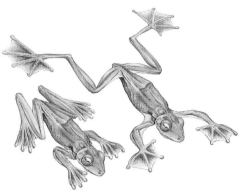

▲ **frog, gliding** Several species of tree-frog from South and Central America, Southeast Asia and Australasia have developed a limited form of flight. They all have large webs of skin between the lengthened toes of their feet. They leap from trees with their hind limbs stretched out, then bring them up close to the body with feet splayed out to extend the gliding membranes as soon as they have achieved a steady glide. Many species can flatten their bodies in flight so that the whole animal provides lift.

forests of Brazil. It has very large eyes and only three functional toes on each foot. Its skull is very bony, and a bony plate covers the vertebrae. Gold frog eggs develop directly, with no free-living tadpole stage. Length: to 16mm (0.6in). Family Brachycephalidae; species *Brachycephalus ephippium*.

frog, goliath
Largest species of frog in the world. An aquatic frog, it is native to w Africa, where it lives in deep pools. It is a powerful swimmer, with long, muscular legs and webbed toes. Length: to 30cm (12in); weight: to 3.3kg (7.3lb). Family Ranidae; species *Conraua goliath*.

frog, harlequin
Brightly coloured, slender-limbed, diurnal frog from Central and South America. Despite its appearance, the harlequin frog is closely related to true TOADS. As with the arrow-poison frog, the bright patterns of the harlequin frog warn of its highly toxic skin secretions. Some species communicate using arm waving signals. Length: 17–63mm (0.7–2.5in). Family Bufonidae; genus *Atelopus*; there are c.60 species.

frog, marsupial
South American tree frog. Females carry fertilized eggs in a pouch on their backs. Depending on the species, the young may hatch as tadpoles or remain in the pouch until metamorphosed. *Gastrotheca marsupiata* is green with dark spots on its back and has striped legs; it reaches a length of up to 8cm (3in). Family Hylidae.

frog, narrow-mouthed
Any of several species of plump-bodied frogs with small, rather pointed heads and small mouths; they have a fold of skin behind their heads. They are found in North and Central America. Narrow-mouthed frogs spend much of their time under cover or in burrows; they feed primarily on ants. Length: 22–40mm (0.9–1.6in). Family Microhylidae; genus *Gastrophryne*.

frog, paradoxical
South American frog with muscular legs and strongly webbed toes. Its eyes are somewhat upward directed and it is virtually fully aquatic. The tadpoles can reach huge sizes (to 25cm/10in), whereas the adults are relatively small, hence their common

name. Length: to 7cm (3in). Family Pseudidae; species *Pseudis paradoxa*.

frog, sedge (reed frog)
Small, mostly tropical frog distributed throughout sub-Saharan Africa. Most species are brightly coloured, and the males make very loud calls for their small size. Sedge frogs live in swampy areas and marshes, where they climb on reeds, sedges and other low vegetation, where they also lay their eggs. Length: 15–40mm (0.6–1.6in). Family Hyperoliidae; genus *Hyperolius*; there are more than 100 species.

frog, Seychelles
Frog that occurs only on the granitic islands of the Seychelles in the Indian Ocean. The eggs of the Seychelles frog are laid on the ground and either undergo direct development or hatch into tadpoles that are carried on the back of the female until metamorphosis. Length: 15–40mm (0.6-1.6in). Family Sooglosidae; there are three species.

frog, tailed
Archaic frog that inhabits cold, fast-flowing streams in the forests of the Pacific Northwest of North America. The skin is somewhat warty and the toes of the hindfeet are relatively thick and short. The "tail" of the adult male is a device for transferring sperm. Tadpoles take several years to metamorphose. Length: 2.5–5cm (1–2in). Family Ascaphidae; species *Ascaphus truei*.

frog, wood
Terrestrial frog found in moist, wooded areas of Canada and NE United States, sometimes far from water. Its colour varies from yellowish to brown and black. It has a dark patch extending backwards from its eyes. Length: to 8cm (3in). Family Ranidae; species *Rana sylvatica*.

frogbit
Either of two species of aquatic perennial herbs found in shallow water areas of Europe, Asia and Africa. The frogbit resembles a small water lily. It has rounded

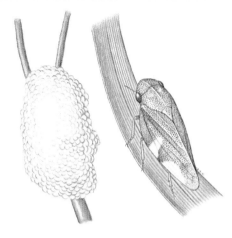

▲ **froghopper** The spittle that protects froghopper larvae (left) is formed from a liquid secreted by the adult (right). It froths up the spittle using air bubbles emitted from its abdomen. This covering protects the young insect from predators and prevents it drying out.

glossy green leaves and bowl-shaped, three-petalled, creamy-white flowers. Family Hydrocharitaceae; species include *Hydrocharis morsus-ranae*.

frogfish
Bottom-dwelling, marine ANGLERFISH found in tropical and subtropical seas (except the Mediterranean). One spine on the frogfish's dorsal fin is modified as a "fishing pole", which is used to attract prey; the "fishing pole" varies in form between species. An example of a frogfish is the sargassum fish (*Histrio histrio*), which lives on floating seaweed in the Sargasso Sea. Family Antennariidae.

froghopper (spittlebug)
Any of various species of small, hopping insects whose eggs and young are covered with a protective frothy mass known as cuckoo spit. Adult froghoppers are triangular and grey, greenish or brown. They feed on plants. Length: to 15mm (0.6in). Order Homoptera; family Cercopidae.

FRONT

Boundary between two AIR MASSES that are of different temperatures or of different densities. **Cold fronts** occur when a relatively cold and dense air mass advances against and beneath a warmer air mass. The upward movement of the warm air usually results in condensation, cloud formation and rainfall. With a **warm front**, the warmer air gradually rises over colder air. As the air rises it cools and forms clouds, usually cumulus or cumulonimbus. Eventually it may give rise to some warm rain, known as frontal rainfall. An **occluded front** is a combination of a warm front and a cold front in a DEPRESSION. It occurs when the cold front catches up with the warm front and undercuts it. The effects of the warm front and the cold front together are to cause heavier and more prolonged rain than either front would yield alone. Cumulonimbus clouds will be found at an occluded front.

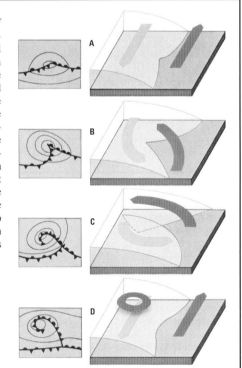

▶ **A front forms** in temperate latitudes where a cold air mass meets a warm air mass (**A**). The air masses spiral round a bulge causing cold and warm fronts to develop (**B**). The warm air rises above the cold front and the cold air slides underneath the warm (**C**). Eventually, the cold air areas merge, and the warm air is lifted up or occluded (**D**).

F

▲ **frogmouth** Like all species of frogmouth, the tawny frogmouth (*Podargus strigoides*) hunts at night, swooping on insects, reptiles or small mammals. It uses its large bill to mangle its prey and make it easier to swallow.

frogmouth
Bird that resembles a cross between a nightjar and an owl. It is named after its broad, hooked bill, which it uses to catch prey at night. It has intricately patterned, camouflaged plumage, with tufts of coarse plume feathers over its bill. During the day, the frogmouth sits immobile, looking like dead wood. It is a Southern Hemisphere bird. Length: 33–58cm (14–23in). Family Podargidae.

front
See feature article, page 153

frost
Atmospheric temperature at Earth's surface below 0°C (32°F). The visible result of a frost is usually a deposit of minute ice crystals formed from dew and water vapour on exposed surfaces. In freezing weather, the "degree of frost" indicates the number of degrees below freezing point. When white **hoar-frost** is formed, water vapour changes from its gaseous state to its solid state, without becoming a liquid. A frost is referred to as white or black, depending on whether or not white hoar-frost is present. Frost can do great damage to crops, and farmers and fruit-growers endeavour to protect their crops against its effects. Frost is also a significant cause of EROSION, of the mechanical WEATHERING of rock masses, and of the upthrusts of ground ("frost heaves") that damage roads.

frozen bodies
Cadavers of animals that died in regions of PERMAFROST and were not consumed by scavengers. The bodies may become frozen solid and be buried by natural processes. Frozen bodies of Ice Age animals, such as MAMMOTH, WOOLLY RHINOCEROS, BISON, HORSE and WOLVERINE, some of which are 80,000 years old, have been recovered from Siberia and Alaska.

fructose (fruit sugar)
Simple, white, crystalline sugar ($C_6H_{12}O_6$) found in honey, sweet fruits and the nectar of flowers. It is a MONOSACCHARIDE. Fructose is sweeter than the DISACCHARIDE sucrose (cane sugar), of which it is a component along with glucose. It is made commercially by the HYDROLYSIS of beet or cane sugar and is used in foods as a sweetener. Its derivatives play a crucial role in providing energy to living organisms.

fruit
See feature article, page 156

fruit-dove
Any of a group of Australasian pigeons. The black-banded fruit-dove has contrasting black, white and grey plumage; other species are multicoloured, but the majority, for example the purple-crowned fruit-dove, are a rich golden green. Fruit-doves are found mostly in deep gullies of tropical forests. Some species are becoming rare. Length: 22–35cm (9–14in). Family Columbidae; genus *Ptilinopus*.

fruit fly (drosophilia)
Common name for any of the flies of the families Tephritidae or Drosophilidae. The Tephritidae family (**peacock flies**) contains *c*.1200 species. They lay their eggs directly in the pulp of fruit. Larvae tunnel their way through the fruit; they are a serious pest of fruit. The Drosophilidae (**pomace flies**) feed mainly on the yeasts of rotting fruit. *Drosophila melanogaster* (a VINEGAR-FLY) is used extensively in GENETIC studies. Order Diptera.

fuchsia
Any member of a genus of shrubby plants found in tropical and subtropical South and Central America and parts of New Zealand. They are widely cultivated. They are named after the German herbalist Leonard Fuchs (1501–66). Fuchsia plants have oval leaves and pink, red or purple, trumpet-shaped, waxy flowers. Family Onagraceae; genus *Fuchsia*; there are *c*.100 species, including *Fuchsia procumbens* and *Fuchsia speciosa*.

fulgorid bug
See LANTERN FLY

fulmar
Seabird with pearl-grey plumage. It superficially resembles a gull but has a tubenose (two nostrils that open together like a tube on top of the bill). The fulmar only returns to land to breed, spending its whole life at sea, flying into the severest storms on stiffly held wings. Length: 46–51cm (18–20in); wingspan: 107cm (42in). Family Procellariidae; genus *Fulmarus*; there are two species worldwide.

fulvetta
Small, warbler-like BABBLER. It is mostly brown or green above, with distinctive white, yellow or grey eye stripes and crown markings. Some species, such as the golden-breasted fulvetta, are contrasting yellow below and grey above. Fulvettas are found mostly in undergrowth in the moist subtropical or alpine forests of Southeast Asia. Length: 10–15cm (4–6in). Family Timaliidae; genus *Alcippe*.

► **frost** White hoar-frost covers the trees and undergrowth in this oak and beech forest in Bavaria, Germany. A hoar-frost occurs when the air is supersaturated with water vapour. At temperatures above freezing point a dew would form, but at temperatures below freezing point interlocking ice crystals form on all the surfaces.

There are *c*.100,000 fungus species. Traditionally regarded as plants, fungi are now usually classified by biologists in a kingdom (Fungi) of their own because they are so different from plants in their structure, in how they grow, and in the way they feed. Fungi include mushrooms, moulds and yeasts.

Unlike green plants, fungi cannot harness the Sun's energy to make their own food and do not, therefore, photosynthesize. Some fungi grow only on simple sugars, using them as sources of carbon, and get their nitrogen in the form of inorganic nitrates or ammonium compounds. Other species release enzymes to digest the complicated molecules present in dead plant and animal matter, turning them into a solution of simple nutrients which can then be absorbed. Still other species are parasitic or symbiotic: fungal PARASITES depend on living animals or plants; SAPROPHYTES utilize the materials of dead plants and animals; and symbionts obtain food in a symbiotic relationship with plants (*see* SYMBIOSIS).

Some fungi are unicellular or consist of only a few cells, but most grow as fine threads (HYPHAE) that extend and branch at their tips, forming a network or MYCELIUM. Although individual hyphae can only be seen under a microscope, the fluffy mycelia of common household moulds are a familiar sight. Hyphae of simple fungi – or ZYGOMYCETES – are no more than continuous tubes of cellular material (cytoplasm) containing many nuclei, all enclosed in a cell wall. In contrast, the hyphae of higher fungi - the BASIDIOMYCETES and ASCOMYCETES - are divided by cross-walls into compartments, and make up the fleshy tissue of a mushroom, toadstool or truffle.

All fungi reproduce by SPORES. A spore is a single cell, often surrounded by a protective coat, from which a new organism can develop. Some simple fungi produce zoospores, which look like tiny sperms and are propelled by one or two whip-like flagella. Fungi that produce zoospores are either aquatic, like the water moulds, or parasitic, living inside the cells of plants and releasing their zoospores into the film of water that covers the surfaces of leaves, stems and roots. Common household moulds produce simple spore-bearing containers (SPORANGIA), which burst when mature, releasing a cloud of minute dust-like spores. When the spores alight on a suitable growing medium, they germinate. From each spore a hypha emerges and rapidly develops into a new mycelium.

Most common higher fungi are basidiomycetes – so called because they produce spores externally in a structure called a BASIDIUM. The club-shaped basidia are borne on short-lived, often conspicuous, fruiting bodies. These fruiting bodies are the toadstools and mushrooms that raise the spores above the soil and leaf litter, thus aiding their dispersal by air currents. The permanent part of the fungus, which can persist for years, is a mycelium that often spreads for many metres through the soil or wood. The morrels, TRUFFLES and YEASTS belong to the third major group of fungi – the ascomycetes. They produce their spores internally in capsules (or asci), which are formed when two hyphae of different "mating type" join. The nuclei of the parent hyphae fuse and divide, giving rise to four or eight spores arranged within the ascus like peas in a pod.

Fungi have had an immense influence on human history – their fermentations give us bread, wine and beer, and many ANTIBIOTICS. On the other hand, fungal infections cause crop failure across the globe. Fungi play a vital role in the natural cycle of life. By decomposing dead animal and plant material they release locked-up nutrients, which can then be recycled in a new generation of plant and animal life.

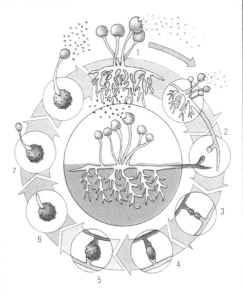

▲ **Like most zygomycetes**, black bread mould feeds by breaking down dead matter. The bulk of the mycelium grows within the food substance – but some hyphae grow upright and swell at their tips, forming sporangia, the organs of asexual reproduction. Numerous spores develop within these swellings: the sporangium wall disintegrates and the spores are dispersed by air currents (1). They germinate and give rise to a new mycelium. Zygomycetes also undergo a sexual process (conjugation). Two hyphae of different "sex" (represented by pink and purple colours) grow towards one another (2), attracted by chemicals released by the mycelia. Once in contact, the tips of the hyphae swell and become cut off by a cross-wall (3). The two adjacent tips, which contain many nuclei, fuse (4) and develop a tough wall (5). The resistant spore then germinates (6), undergoes genetic reshuffling (meiosis) and produces spores (7).

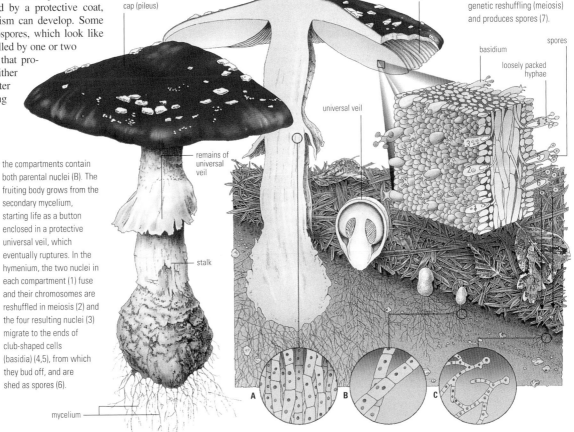

▶ **Fly agaric's fruiting** body consists of a stalk (stipe), made of closely packed hyphae (A), attached to a buried mycelium and crowned with a broad cap (pileus), which protects the delicate spore-bearing layer (hymenium) on the gills. The life cycle of this toadstool begins with the germination of spores to form a mycelium, the compartments of which contain one nucleus each (C). Hyphae of different "sex" fuse, and a secondary mycelium develops, in which the compartments contain both parental nuclei (B). The fruiting body grows from the secondary mycelium, starting life as a button enclosed in a protective universal veil, which eventually ruptures. In the hymenium, the two nuclei in each compartment (1) fuse and their chromosomes are reshuffled in meiosis (2) and the four resulting nuclei (3) migrate to the ends of club-shaped cells (basidia) (4,5), from which they bud off, and are shed as spores (6).

cap (pileus)

gills

remains of universal veil

universal veil

basidium

spores

loosely packed hyphae

stalk

mycelium

F

fumarole

Vent in the ground that emits gases and vapours, usually found in volcanic areas. The term also refers to a hot spring or geyser that emits steam. A fumarole is sometimes defined in terms of the composition of its gases, such as a chlorine fumarole.

fumitory

Any of more than 40 species of herb. They have divided, fern-like leaves and irregular flowers, which are often white with red petal tips. Family Fumariaceae; species include *Fumaria capreolata* (ramping fumitory), *Fumaria officinalis* (common fumitory) and *Adlumia fungosa* (climbing fumitory, Allegheny vine or mountain fringe).

fungus

See feature article, page 155

fungus bug

See FLATBUG

fungus gnat

Mosquito-like fly with a humped thorax and long legs. Its hind-legs are modified for jumping, and its thorax and tibiae have bristle-like hairs. The fungus gnat is commonly found in moist, wooded areas but also occurs in houses. Most species attack wild fungi, although some species are pests of roots of wheat seedlings, cucumbers and pot plants. Adult body length: *c.*7mm (*c.*0.3in). Order Diptera; family Mycetophilidae; genera include *Exechia*, *Mycetophila* and *Phronia*.

funnel cap

Fungus with a funnel-shaped cap and decurrent gills that run down the stem. Many funnel caps have a strong and distinctive smell of meal or aniseed. Common funnel cap (*Clitocybe infundibuliformis*) has pinkish-buff to pale yellow-brown caps and inhabits deciduous woodlands or heaths. Phylum Basidiomycota; genus *Clitocybe*.

fur

Soft, dense hair covering the skin of certain mammals. Such mammals include MINK, FOX, STOAT, MUSKRAT, WOLF, BEAR, SQUIRREL and RABBIT. Some of the animals are hunted and killed for their pelts, which, when manufactured into clothing, may command high prices. Some fur-bearing animals are now protected by law because overhunting has made extinction likely.

furniture beetle (woodworm beetle)

Small, hairy, light brown to black BEETLE. It is found in all types of dry wood, both indoors and outdoors. The larvae, known as woodworms, are soft and white and burrow into wood, making small circular tunnels. The adult beetles emerge through distinctive circular holes. Adult body length: 1–8mm (0.04–0.3in). Order Coleoptera; family Anobiidae; species include *Anobium punctatum*.

fur-seal

Any of a group of 14 species of SEAL. They have ear flaps and can tuck their rear flippers in under the body as they move about on land. Order Pinnipedia; family Otariidae.

fur-seal, Antarctic

Fur-seal native to the Antarctic region. It comes ashore to breed on South Georgia, and there are small populations on other ice-free islands around Antarctica. Black pups moult to reveal a silvery or ginger coat; adult males are darker. They feed mostly on krill. Length: male *c.*183cm (*c.*72in); female *c.*129cm (*c.*51in). Family Otariidae; species *Arctocephalus gazella*.

fur-seal, Australian

Subspecies of fur-seal; it breeds on islands off Australia and Tasmania. It is one of two subspecies, the other being the Cape fur-seal. Its prey includes fish, cephalopods and crustaceans. Australian fur-seals have been known to dive to more than 200m (660ft). Length: male 180–230cm (71–91in); female 120–170cm (47–67in). Family Otariidae; species *Arctocephalus pusillus doriferus*.

fur-seal, Cape

Subspecies of fur-seal found, during the breeding season, on the coast and rocky inshore islands off Namibia and South Africa. It feeds on schooling fish, cephalopods and penguins. Length: male 230–235cm (91–93in); female *c.*180cm (*c.*71in). Family Otariidae; species *Arctocephalus pusillus pusillus*.

fur-seal, Galápagos

Relatively small species of fur-seal; it is found on rocky beaches of the Galápagos Islands during the breeding season. Pups may be nursed for two or three years. Length: male *c.*154cm (*c.*61in); female *c.*120cm (*c.*47in). Family Otariidae; species *Arctocephalus galapagoensis*.

fur-seal, New Zealand

Dark grey fur-seal that comes ashore to breed on rocky coasts from s Australia to New Zealand. It feeds on surface fish, cephalopods and sometimes penguins. Length: males 145–250cm (57–98in); females 125–150cm (49–59in). Family Otariidae; species *Arctocephalus forsteri*.

fur-seal, Northern

Fur-seal found in subarctic waters of the N Pacific Ocean, from the Bering Sea to Japan and s California, coming ashore for only a few months a year. Between October and November, adult females migrate south, spending up to eight months at sea. Length: male *c.*210cm (*c.*83in); female *c.*40cm (*c.*16in). Family Otariidae; species *Callorhinus ursinus*.

fur-seal, South American

Fur-seal that comes ashore to breed on rocky beaches around the coast of South America from s Peru to s Brazil. South American fur-seals are grey and their size varies widely according to geographic position. They feed mainly on fish and krill. Length: male *c.*200cm (*c.*80in); female *c.*150cm (*c.*59in). Family Otariidae; species *Arctocephalus australis*.

fur-seal, Subantarctic

Grey seal that breeds on temperate islands in the s Atlantic and Indian oceans, north of the Antarctic polar front. They are distinguished by a creamy or yellow face mask and chest. Males have a dark crest on the top of the head. Length: males *c.*180cm (*c.*71in); females 145–150cm (57–59in). Family Otariidae; species *Arctocephalus tropicalis*.

furze

See GORSE

FRUIT

Seed-containing mature OVARY of an ANGIOSPERM (flowering plant), in which the seeds are surrounded by the PERICARP (fruit wall). Fruits serve to disperse seeds and are an important food source (they provide vitamins, acids, salts, calcium, iron and phosphates). They can be classified as simple, aggregate or multiple. **Simple fruits**, dry or fleshy, are produced by one ripened ovary of a single PISTIL (a unit comprising a STIGMA, STYLE and OVARY); they include LEGUMES (PEAS and BEANS) and NUTS. **Aggregate fruits** develop from several simple pistils; examples are RASPBERRY and BLACKBERRY. **Multiple fruits** develop from a flower cluster; each flower produces a fruit which merges into a single mass at maturity; examples are PINEAPPLES and FIGS. Although considered fruits in culinary terms, APPLES and PEARS are regarded botanically as "false" fruits (PSEUDOCARPS), because the edible parts are created by the RECEPTACLE and not by the carpel walls. Some fruits spontaneously disperse their seeds (*see* DEHISCENT), others keep their seeds and the fruit is dispersed as a whole (*see* INDEHISCENT).

▶ **A fruit is** the ripened ovary of a flowering plant, enclosed by the fruit wall, which is known as the pericarp. Most fruits, such as blackcurrants (1), cherries (2), strawberries (3), oranges (4) and peppers (5), contain more than one seed. The avocado (6), however, contains only one seed, about the size of a golf ball. The largest fruit, the double coconut (7), is also single-seeded.

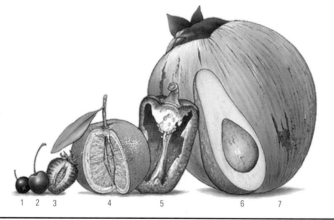

1   2   3   4   5   6   7

gabbro
Coarse-grained, basic IGNEOUS ROCK. It can be regarded as the PLUTONIC equivalent of BASALT, being much coarser because of its slow crystallization. The constituents are sodium and calcium FELDSPAR and the dark minerals OLIVINE and PYROXENE.

gadfly
See DEER-FLY

Gaia hypothesis
Scientific theory that relates the Earth's many and varied processes – chemical, physical and biological. Popular in the 1970s, when it was proposed by British scientist James Lovelock (1919–), the Gaia hypotheses showed the Earth as one single living organism, with its components made up of all living things. It was popular with ecological groups because it explained the delicate interrelationship between people and the environment.

gaillardia
Any member of the *Gaillardia* genus, which comprises *c.*30 species of annual, biennial and perennial plants. They are found in sunny open habitats of North and South America. The long, hairy leaves can be entire, toothed or divided. Gaillardias are grown in gardens for their large, daisy-like flowerheads, which are red, orange or yellow with darker centres. Family Asteraceae/Compositae; species include *Gaillardia pulchella*.

galago
See BUSH BABY

galah
Familiar and abundant COCKATOO from Australia and Tasmania. It is pale grey above and rose pink to deep rose-red below, with a pink or reddish cap-like crest. It has an unmistakable, high-pitched *"chill, chill"* call. Galahs form noisy flocks that fly wildly about and can become pests on grain and fruit farms. Length: 34–38cm (13–15in). Family Psittacidae; species *Cacatua roseicapilla*.

Galápagos Islands (Sp. *Archipiélago de Colón*)
Pacific archipelago on the Equator; a province of Ecuador, *c.*1050km (650mi) w of mainland South America. The capital is Baquerizo Moreno, on San Cristóbal. Other main islands include Santa Cruz, San Salvador and Isabela. The islands are volcanic with sparse vegetation, except for dense forests on the high lava craters. Mangrove swamps and lagoons teem with wildlife. The islands were visited in the 1830s by Charles DARWIN aboard HMS BEAGLE. The distinctive fauna of the islands (resulting from their geographical isolation) formed the basis of Darwin's theory of EVOLUTION as presented in his book *The Origin of Species* (1859). The islands are now a nature reserve and world heritage site. Their unique fauna, which includes Darwin's FINCHES, giant TORTOISES, IGUANAS and flightless CORMORANTS, is under threat from introduced species. Area: 7845sq km (3029sq mi) Pop. (1990) 9785.

galena
Grey, brittle, metallic mineral, lead sulphide (PbS). It is the major ore of lead. It occurs as granular masses, and commonly as cubic or octahedral crystals with a lead-grey streak. It is widely found in hydrothermal veins and as a replacement in limestone and dolomite rocks. Hardness 2.5–2.7; r.d. 7.5.

gall bladder
Muscular sac, found in most VERTEBRATES, which stores BILE. In humans it lies beneath the right lobe of the LIVER and releases bile into the duodenum by way of the bile duct. The release of bile is signalled by a hormone that is secreted when food is present in the duodenum.

galliform
Member of the bird order Galliformes. It comprises six families of game birds, including TURKEYS (Meleagrididae), GUINEAFOWL (Numididae) and PHEASANTS (Phasianidae).

galliwasp
Any of *c.*40 species of smooth-scaled, SKINK-like LIZARDS that inhabit moist habitats in Central and South America and the West Indies. Most galliwasps have short limbs and are terrestrial, although some species climb well. They have diverse diets, with various species feeding on fruits, carrion and insects. Length: 13–69cm (5–27in). Family Anguidae.

gall midge
Very small, slender, long-legged fly. Its wings have reduced venation, which is characteristic of the family. Many gall midges cause galls to form on plants as a result of larval feeding, and many species are pests. Adult body length: 1–8mm (0.04–0.1in). Order Diptera; family Cecidomyiidae; genera include *Rhabdophaga*, *Dasineura* and *Contarinia*.

gamete
Reproductive (sex) CELL that during FERTILIZATION fuses with another reproductive cell of the opposite sex to form a ZYGOTE, the start of a new individual. Female gametes (*see* OVUM) are usually motionless; in many organisms, the male gametes (in this example SPERM) have a tail (FLAGELLUM), which enables them to swim to the ova. All gametes are HAPLOID – they contain only a single set of CHROMOSOMES due to MEIOSIS. On fusion, the resulting zygote is DIPLOID. *See also* SEXUAL REPRODUCTION

gametogenesis
Formation of GAMETES. In the male it is called SPERMATOGENESIS and in the female OOGENESIS. Both types involve a multiplication phase, a growth phase and a maturation phase. *See also* EGG; SPERM

gametophyte
Generation of PLANTS and ALGAE that bears the female and male GAMETES (reproductive cells). In flowering plants (ANGIOSPERMS) these are the germinated pollen grains (male) and the embryo sac (female) inside the OVULE. *See also* ALTERNATION OF GENERATIONS; FERN; MOSS

ganglion
Cluster of nervous tissue containing cell bodies and SYNAPSES, usually enclosed in a fibrous sheath. In a VERTEBRATE, most ganglia occur outside the CENTRAL NERVOUS SYSTEM.

gangue
Waste material in an ORE or deposit, as opposed to metal-containing or other useful minerals.

gannet
Any of three species of large sea bird found worldwide. It has a cigar-shaped body, stout, conical bill, long wings and a long, wedge-shaped tail. Adults are white, with yellow-tinged heads and contrasting black and white wings. Gannets nest in huge island colonies and catch fish by plunging headlong into the sea. Length: 84–92cm (33–36in); wingspan 173cm (68in). Family Sulidae; genus *Sula*. *See also* BOOBY

gar
Any of several species of fish found in North and Central America; most species are found in fresh water, although some are found in brackish or salt water. They are commonly found in slow-moving rivers or lakes, basking near the surface. Gars have long, narrow bodies and are noted for their armour of diamond-shaped scales. Most species, like the ALLIGATOR GAR, have long, usually pointed, sharp-toothed beaks, which make them efficient predators. Length: 3.7m (12ft). Family Lepisosteridae; genus *Lepisosteus*.

garden chafer
Small BEETLE with clubbed, fan-like antennae. Its wing cases are brown and its thorax is iridescent green or blue. The garden CHAFER prefers dry habitats and sometimes swarms in sunshine. It can be a pest, with the adults feeding on various trees and shrubs, and the larvae feeding on the roots of cereals and grasses. Adult body length: 14mm (0.6in). Order Coleoptera; family Scarabaeidae; species *Phyllopertha horticola*.

gardenia
Any member of the *Gardenia* genus, comprising evergreen shrubs and small trees. Gardenias are native to tropical and subtropical Asia and Africa. They have white or yellow, fragrant, waxy flowers. Height: to 5.5m (18ft). Family Rubiaceae.

garlic
Bulbous herb native to s Europe and central Asia. It has onion-like foliage and a bulb made up of cloves, which are used for flavouring. It is also claimed to have medicinal properties. Family Liliaceae; species *Allium sativum*.

garnet
Two series of common orthosilicate minerals: the **pyralspite series** and the **ugradite series**. Garnet is found in METAMORPHIC ROCKS and PEGMATITES as cubic system crystals, rounded grains and granular

▲ **gannet** The Atlantic gannet (*Sula bassana*) is found in some coastal regions of N Europe and E North America. Gannets spot their prey of surface-swimming fish from the air, before dropping in a near-vertical dive to catch the fish. They snatch and swallow the prey before re-emerging.

157

masses. It is brittle, glassy and occurs in many hues; some varieties (particularly the red form) are important as gemstones. Hardness 6.5–7.5; r.d. 4.

garnierite
Ore of nickel. It is a lustrous green SERPENTINE, also containing magnesium and silicon. Garnierite occurs in ultrabasic rocks as a decomposition product of OLIVINE.

garpike (garfish)
Marine NEEDLEFISH found in all tropical and temperate waters, and also in bays and coastal rivers. Its long silvery body has a dark green or blue-black stripe; the jaws are elongated and pointed, with sharp teeth. Length: to 1.2m (4ft). Family Belonidae.

gas, natural
See NATURAL GAS

gas exchange
See feature article

gastropod
Member of the class Gastropoda, a class of molluscs, which includes the SNAIL, SLUG, WHELK, LIMPET, ABALONE and SEA SLUG. Many gastropods possess a single spiral shell, produced by chemical precipitation from the MANTLE. Many species live immersed in seawater, breathing through gills. Some freshwater snails, however, breathe through lungs and need to surface periodically for air. Like slugs, sea slugs are entirely without shells and are often brilliantly coloured.

gastrotrich
See HAIRY-BACK

gastrula
Early stage in the development of the EMBRYO in animals; it follows the BLASTULA stage. The gastrula is a hollow sac with two layers (*see* GERM LAYER) of cells – the inner ENDODERM and the outer ECTODERM. The sac cavity is called the **archenteron** and its mouth the **blastopore**.

gaur
Large, wild ox found in tropical forests in India and Southeast Asia. It is distinguished by a dark coat with white stockings, a hump and large horns (in both sexes). Gaurs live in small herds. Head-body length: 250–330cm (100–130in); tail: 70–100cm (28–40in). Family Bovidae; subfamily Bovinae; species *Bos gaurus*.

gavial
See GHARIAL

gazelle
Any of several species of graceful, small to medium ANTELOPES native to Africa and Asia, often inhabiting plains. Most species are light brown with a white rump and horns. Family Bovidae; genus *Gazella*.

gazelle, Cuvier's
See EDMI

gazelle, dama
White gazelle with a reddish-brown back. It has long,

▲ **gaur** Found in mountain forests – up to 3500m (11,482ft) above sea level – the gaur (*Bos gaurus*) is the largest species of wild ox. It has distinctive curved horns with a covering of white hair at the bass and black tips.

thin legs and a slender neck; both sexes have strongly ribbed, s-shaped horns. Very rare, the dama gazelle lives in the Sahara region of Africa. Head-body length: 140–165cm (55–65in); tail: 23–35cm (9–14in); horn: 23–43cm (9–17in). Family Bovidae; subfamily Antilopinae; species *Gazella dama*.

gazelle, dorcas
Pale brown or reddish gazelle, with white underparts, dark and white face-markings and a reddish side band. Both sexes have gently curving, ribbed horns. Well adapted to living in desert and semidesert conditions across North Africa and w Arabia, the dorcas gazelle does not need to drink, obtaining water from leaves and grasses. Head-body length: 90–110cm (35–43in); tail: 15–20cm (6–8in); horn: up to 38cm (15in). Family Bovidae; subfamily Antilopinae; species *Gazella dorcas*.

gazelle, goitered (Persian gazelle)
Gazelle that is found in semidesert conditions across s and central Asia. It is pale brown in colour, darkening towards the belly, which is white. Only the males generally have horns, which diverge at the base and curve gently towards the tips; they also have a swollen throat during the breeding season. The goitered gazelle's legs are relatively short. Head-body length: 90–115cm (35–45in); tail: 15–20cm (6–8in); horn: 32–45cm (13–18in). Family Bovidae; subfamily Antilopinae; species *Gazella subgutturosa*.

gazelle, Grant's
Large gazelle found on open savannas in E Africa. It is brown with a white belly and eye stripes. Both sexes have long, slightly curving, black horns. They live in herds numbering up to thirty individuals. Head-body length: 140–166cm (55–65in); tail: 20–28cm (8–11in); horn: 45–81cm (18–32in). Family Bovidae; subfamily Antilopinae; species *Gazella granti*.

gazelle, Mongolian
Gazelle that lives on the E steppes of Mongolia, China and s Siberia. Thousands of these migratory gazelles move northwards in the spring. Their coats are pale brown, fading to white underneath. Only the males have horns, which are slightly ridged and curving, and a swollen throat during the breeding season. Mongolian gazelles are good swimmers. Head-body length: 100–150cm (40–60in); tail: 8–12cm (3–5in); horn: 25–40cm (10–16in). Family Bovidae; subfamily Antilopinae; species *Procapra gutturosa*.

gazelle, mountain
Small, brown gazelle with short, black horns, large

GAS EXCHANGE

Uptake and output of gases, especially OXYGEN and CARBON DIOXIDE, by living organisms. In animals and other organisms that obtain their energy by the breakdown of food in the chemical reactions of AEROBIC RESPIRATION, gas exchange involves the uptake of oxygen and the output of carbon dioxide. In plants, algae and photosynthetic bacteria, which carry out PHOTOSYNTHESIS, the opposite may occur when photosynthesis is active, with a net carbon dioxide uptake and net oxygen output. At the cellular level, gas exchange takes place by DIFFUSION across cell MEMBRANES in solution.

In multicellular animals there may be a specialized transport system for transporting these gases between the cells and the outside environment. By using up one or other of these gases and generating the other, respiration and photosynthesis maintain their own concentration gradients for diffusion. Where transport systems are involved, the gradient may be enhanced by other means. For example, in vertebrate ERYTHROCYTES (red blood cells), the affinity of the pigment HAEMOGLOBIN for oxygen changes as the local oxygen concentration varies, enabling it to take up oxygen in the lungs and release it to respiring cells. *See also* BREATHING; CIRCULATORY SYSTEM; RESPIRATORY SYSTEM; VENTILATION

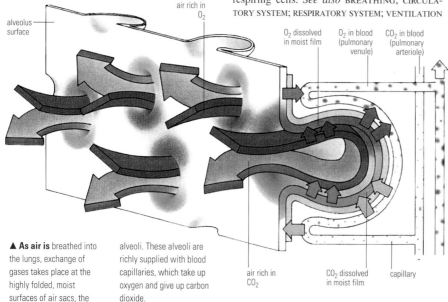

▲ **As air is** breathed into the lungs, exchange of gases takes place at the highly folded, moist surfaces of air sacs, the alveoli. These alveoli are richly supplied with blood capillaries, which take up oxygen and give up carbon dioxide.

air rich in O₂

alveolus surface

O₂ dissolved in moist film

O₂ in blood (pulmonary venule)

CO₂ in blood (pulmonary arteriole)

air rich in CO₂

CO₂ dissolved in moist film

capillary

ears and distinct white belly and eye stripes. The mountain gazelle can be found in areas of mountainous desert scrub in Palestine and the Arabian Peninsula. Family Bovidae; subfamily Antilopinae; species *Gazella gazella*.

gazelle, Przewalski's
Gazelle that is native to the semidesert steppe of China. It has ridged horns with curved tips. Head-body length: 91–105cm (36–41in); tail: 2–10cm (1–4in). Family Bovidae; subfamily Antilopinae; species *Procapra przewalskii.*

gazelle, Thomson's
Gazelle that is brown with a white belly and a prominent, dark side stripe and facial markings. Males have long, ridged horns, which curve only slightly; the horns of females are much shorter. Large, single-sex herds of this abundant gazelle live on the open grassy plains of Tanzania and Kenya. Height: 60–65cm (24–26in). Family Bovidae; subfamily Antilopinae; species *Gazella thomsoni.*

gazelle, Tibetan
Gazelle that is pale brown without prominent facial markings. It is native to Tibet, where it selectively grazes on forbs on the plateau grasslands. Males have s-shaped, ridged horns. Head-body length: 91–105cm (36–41in); tail: 2–10cm (1–4in); horn: 28–40cm (11–16in). Family Bovidae; subfamily Antilopinae; species *Procapra picticaudata.*

gecko
Any of *c*.650 species of LIZARDS, native to warm regions of the world. Most of the species are nocturnal and nearly all are drab in colour. They owe their remarkable climbing ability to minute hooks on their feet. Length: 3–15cm (1–6in). Family Gekkonidae.

gem
Any of *c*.100 minerals, either opaque, transparent or translucent, valued for their beauty, rarity and durability. Transparent stones, such as DIAMOND, RUBY, EMERALD and SAPPHIRE, are the most highly valued. PEARL, AMBER and CORAL are gems of organic origin. During the Middle Ages, many gems were thought to have magical powers. The art of cutting and polishing gemstones to bring out their colour and brilliance was developed in the 15th century, particularly in Italy. Stones with a design cut into them are **intaglios**; with a design in relief, **cameos**. The study of gems is known as GEMMOLOGY.

gemma
In botany and zoology, a BUD that will give rise to a new individual. The term also refers to a multicellular reproductive structure found in ALGAE, LIVERWORTS and MOSSES.

gemmology
Scientific study of precious and semi-precious gemstones, including their origin, identification, properties and valuation.

gemsbok
See ORYX, BEISA

gene
Unit by which hereditary characteristics or traits are passed on from one generation to another in plants and animals. A gene is a length of DNA that codes (*see* GENETIC CODE) for a particular protein or peptide. Genes are found along the CHROMOSOMES of the CELLS of plants, animals, fungi and protoctists (in bacteria the DNA is not contained in chromo-somes). In most cell nuclei genes occur in pairs, one located on each of a chromosome pair. In cases where different forms of a gene (ALLELES) are present in a population, some forms may be RECESSIVE to others (DOMINANT allele) and will not be expressed unless present on both members of a chromosome pair. *See also* GENETICS; GENETIC ENGINEERING; HEREDITY

gene bank
Collection of genetic material kept for possible future use. Material stored includes cultures of bacteria and moulds; seeds, spores and tubers; frozen sperm, eggs and embryos; and even live plants and animals. The material can be used in plant and animal BREEDING, GENETIC ENGINEERING and in medicine. Live species are used for restocking natural habitats in which species are extinct or in danger of EXTINCTION.

gene pool
All of the GENES, and their various ALLELES, that occur in all the members of a particular species or population of species at any given moment. For a species to be vigorous and survive, the gene pool must be large enough for natural variation to take place through CROSS-FERTILIZATION. A large population, however, does not necessarily imply a large gene pool. For example, there is concern about the viability of some sizeable populations of cheetahs that, despite their numbers, have insufficient variation in the gene pool.

genet
Cat-like carnivore of the CIVET family, native to W Europe and S and E Africa. Solitary and nocturnal, genets have slender bodies, grey to brown spotted fur, and banded tails. Head-body length: 40–50cm (16–20in); tail: 37–46cm (15–18in). Family Viverridae; genus *Genetta.*

genet, common
Arboreal carnivore found in wooded areas of Africa, the Iberian Peninsula, France and Palestine. It has pale grey fur with rows of dark spots, white eye patches and a long, bushy tail ringed in black. It hunts small mammals and birds on the ground. Family Viverridae; species *Genetta genetta.*

genet, feline
Genet that is similar in appearance to the common genet. It is found in wooded areas south of the Sahara and on the Arabian Peninsula. Family Viverridae; species *Genetta felina.*

genet, forest
African genet that is found in densely forested areas of central and S Africa. It is more heavily spotted than the common genet; its black tail has a few lighter rings and a pale tip. Family Viverridae; species *Genetta maculata.*

▲ **gecko** The banded gecko (*Coleonyx variegatus*) is one of a great many species of gecko inhabiting desert regions. It is nocturnal, hiding under rocks during the day and foraging for insects at night. It grows to a length of *c*.15cm (*c*.6in).

▲ **genet** There are six species of genet, but only one lives in Europe. The rest inhabit forest and dense brush in Africa, spending the day sheltering in rock crevices or hollow trees. They feed on the ground, mainly eating rodents and birds.

G

genetically modified organism (GMO)
Organism whose genetic material has been deliberately manipulated by biochemical techniques, such as RECOMBINANT DNA technology. The process is often carried out to breed organisms that are functionally specific, such as tomatoes that do not easily soften, herbicide-resistant soya beans and insect-resistant maize. Such techniques can improve yields, but there are environmental concerns about the possible natural transfer of transplanted genes into other organisms where they may have undesirable effects.

genetic code
Arrangement of information stored in GENES. It is the ultimate basis of HEREDITY and forms a blueprint for the entire organism. The genetic code is based on the genes that are present, which in molecular terms depends on the arrangement of nucleotides in the long molecules of DNA in the cell CHROMOSOMES. Each group of three nucleotides specifies, or codes, for an AMINO ACID or for an action such as "start" or "stop". By specifying which PROTEINS to make and in what quantities, the genetic code not only directly controls production of structural materials, but also, by coding for ENZYMES, indirectly codes for the production of other cell materials.

genetic drift
Chance alteration in the GENE POOL of a small, usually isolated, population – the smaller and more isolated the population, the greater the chance of genetic drift. Genetic drift may greatly affect the genetic characteristics of the population. For example a specific gene may either randomly disappear or become widespread depending on the specific genetic traits of individuals and the reproduction habits of the population.

genetic engineering
Construction of a DNA (deoxyribonucleic acid) molecule containing a desired GENE, which is then introduced into a bacterial, fungal, plant or mammalian cell, so that this cell then produces the desired protein. The technique has been used successfully to alter bacterial genetic material to produce substances such as human growth hormone, insulin and enzymes for biological washing powder. Many people are concerned about the ethics of genetic engineering, given the possibility that scientists may one day be able to alter the genetic structure of humans, or accidentally release genetically engineered, disease-causing bacteria into the environment.

genetics
Study of HEREDITY. Geneticists study how the characteristics of an individual organism depend on its GENES, how the characteristics are passed down to

G

the next generation, and how changes may occur through MUTATION. A person's behaviour, learning ability and physiology may be explained partly by genetics, although the environment in which an individual grows up may also have a considerable influence. The deliberate modification of GENETIC CODES by scientists is called genetic manipulation or GENETIC ENGINEERING. Scientists can modify the genes of livestock and crops in order to improve the quality or quantity of the produce. Genetics was founded by Gregor MENDEL, following experiments with successive generations of peas.

genome

Entire complement of genetic material carried within the CHROMOSOMES of a single cell. In effect, a genome carries all the genetic information about an individual coded in sequence by the DNA that makes up the chromosomes. The term genome has also been applied to the whole range of GENES in a particular species. *See also* GENETICS; HUMAN GENOME PROJECT

genotype

Genetic composition of an organism. It sets limits within which individual characteristics may vary as a result of environmental influences. For example, the genotype may be for light-coloured skin, but the colour of any part of the skin depends upon the extent to which it is exposed to sunlight. *See also* PHENOTYPE

gentian

Perennial herb native to temperate regions, although many species are alpines. It has heart-shaped leaves and usually blue tubular flowers. Among the *c*.500 species are the dark blue *Gentiana clusii*, the Chinese *Gentiana sino-ornata* and yellow *Gentiana lutea*, the bitter root of which is used as a tonic. Family Gentianaceae; genus *Gentiana*.

genus

Part of the CLASSIFICATION of living organisms, ranking below FAMILY and above SPECIES. A genus is a group of closely related biological species with common characteristics. Genus names are printed in *italic* with a capital initial letter; for example the domestic cat belongs to the genus *Felis*.

geochemistry

Study of the chemical composition of the Earth, particularly the abundance and distribution of the chemical elements and their isotopes, and the changes that have resulted in it from chemical and physical processes.

geochronology

Dating of rocks or of Earth processes. Absolute dating techniques (radiometric dating) involve the measurement of radioactive decay to determine the actual date in years for a given rock. Relative dating involves the use of fossils, sediments or relationships between structures to place rock sequences and geological events in order. *See also* CARBON DATING

geode

Hollow rock nodule with inner walls lined with crystals, generally quartz or calcite. A geode is formed by gelatinous silica and mineral-bearing water within a cavity.

geodesy

Determination of the size and shape of the Earth, its gravitational field, and the location of fixed points.

geography

Science that studies the spatial relationships between the surface of the Earth and humankind. It includes the size and distribution of land masses, seas, resources, climatic zones, and plant and animal life. Because it seeks to relate all the Earth's features to human existence, geography differs from other Earth sciences such as GEOLOGY, METEOROLOGY and OCEANOGRAPHY, which study this planet's features as specific phenomena.

geological time

Timescale of the history of the EARTH, divided into periods of time millions of years long. Various methods of relative dating are possible. These methods include the worldwide study, comparison and correlation of sequences of rock formations and the FOSSILS they contain. The information thus gathered is used to distinguish earlier from later deposits, to estimate periods of passed time, and to reconstruct geologic and climatic events by assuming that geological processes in the past were the same as today. Geological time is divided into four eras: PRECAMBRIAN, PALAEOZOIC, MESOZOIC and CENOZOIC, which are further divided into periods. Periods, in turn, are subdivided into series or epochs. Epochs are subdivided into stages and then zones.

geology

Study of the materials of the Earth, their origin, arrangement, classification, change and history. Geology is divided into several categories, the major ones being MINERALOGY (arrangement of minerals), PETROLOGY (rocks and their combination of minerals), STRATIGRAPHY (arrangement and succession of rocks in layers), PALAEONTOLOGY (study of fossilized plant and animal remains), GEOMORPHOLOGY (study of landforms), structural geology (classification of rocks and the forces that produced them) and environmental geology (geological study applied to the best use of the environment by humans).

GEOTHERMAL ENERGY

Heat contained in the Earth's rocks. It is produced by radioactivity and by the movement of tectonic plates (*see* PLATE TECTONICS). It is released naturally in GEYSERS and VOLCANOES. It is used as a power source for generating electricity in several countries, including the United States, Iceland, Italy and New Zealand.

▼ **An artificial hot** spring can be used as a source of heat energy. A borehole is drilled several hundred metres into a natural cavity in the Earth, in which the temperature may be as high as 300°C (570°F). Water pumped down the bore is heated, turns to steam and is forced up a second borehole. At the surface the steam drives turbines to produce electricity.

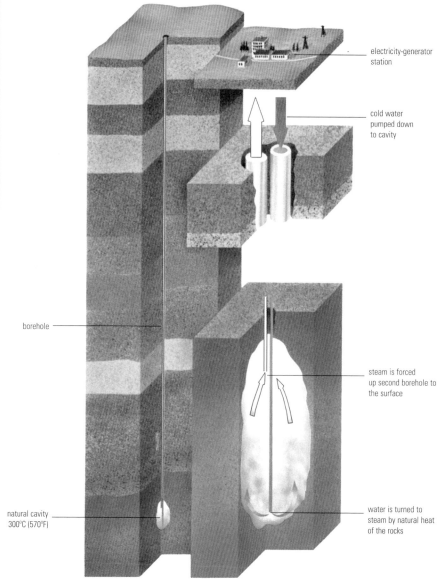

electricity-generator station

cold water pumped down to cavity

borehole

steam is forced up second borehole to the surface

natural cavity 300°C (570°F)

water is turned to steam by natural heat of the rocks

geomagnetism

Physical properties of the Earth's magnetic field. Geomagnetism is thought to be caused by the metallic composition of the Earth's CORE. The gradual movements of magnetic north result from currents within the MANTLE.

geometrid moth

See MOTH, GEOMETRID

geomorphology

Scientific study of features of the Earth's surface and the processes that have formed them.

geophone

Seismic detection device placed on or in the ground to measure the echoes produced by volcanic or seismic (earthquake) activity.

geophysics

Study of the characteristic physical properties of the Earth as a whole system. It uses parts of chemistry, GEOLOGY, astronomy, SEISMOLOGY, METEOROLOGY, and many other disciplines. From the study of seismic waves, geophysicists have worked out the structure of the Earth's interior.

geosyncline

Great basin or trough in which deposits of SEDIMENTS and volcanic rock, thousands of metres thick, have accumulated during slow subsidence over long geological periods. *See also* SYNCLINE

geothermal

Referring to heat from the interior of the Earth. Geothermal activity is responsible for many geological phenomena, including hot springs, GEYSERS and VOLCANOES. Some of this natural geothermal heat is being harnessed and used in the form of GEOTHERMAL ENERGY.

geothermal energy

See feature article

geotropism

In plant growth, the response to the stimulus of GRAVITY. Plant stems are generally negatively geotropic and grow upwards; roots are positively geotropic and thus grow downwards. Growth curvature in a negatively geotropic plant is caused by the accumulation of the plant hormone AUXIN in the tissue on the lower side of the stem; growth increases on that side and the stem bends upwards. *See also* TROPISM

geranium

Any member of the *Geranium* genus, comprising *c*.300 species of perennial herbs. Geranium species are found throughout the world in all but the very wettest of habitats. The leaves are often aromatic, with interesting coloured patterns or textures. The flat, five-petalled flowers can be white, pink, purple or blue. The garden bedding plants popularly known as geraniums actually belong to the related genus *Pelargonium*. Family Geraniaceae; species include *Geranium phaeum* (mourning widow or dusky CRANESBILL) and *Geranium sylvaticum* (wood cranesbill).

gerbil

Nocturnal RODENT native to arid areas of Asia and Africa; it is a popular pet. It has long hind legs and tail, and its fur may be fawn, grey, brown or red. The gerbil is a subterranean herbivore and often hoards food. Family Cricetidae.

▶ **gerbil** Like other desert rodents, the naked-soled gerbil (*Tatera indica*) has powerful hind legs with which it can make long, swift leaps to escape from predators. Using its tail as a rudder, the gerbil can alter course in mid-air. It is also protected by its sensitive hearing.

gerenuk

ANTELOPE that is found in dry savanna regions of E Africa. It has a very long neck, small head and huge ears. It has a reddish coat, darker on the back, with white eye patches and underparts. Only the males have horns, which are short and ribbed. Head-body length: 140–160cm (55–63in); tail: 22–35cm (9–14in). Family Bovidae; subfamily Antilopinae; species *Litocranius walleri*.

germ

Popular term for any infectious agent. Germs can be pathogenic BACTERIA, FUNGI or VIRUSES. The word "germ" is used in biology to denote a rudimentary stage in plant growth, such as an embryo in a seed, or a bud.

germination

Growth of the embryo in a SEED to produce a new plant following FERTILIZATION. It may occur immediately after fertilization or after a period of DORMANCY. In order to germinate, a seed or spore needs favourable conditions of temperature, light, moisture and oxygen. The process begins after the seed has taken up water. Germination is complete when a root appears outside the seed coat.

germ layer

Any one of three layers of cells found in a developing EMBRYO. The three layers are the ECTODERM, MESODERM and ENDODERM, each one giving rise to particular tissues and organs.

gerygone (dusky warbler)

Australian warbler that is plain brown above and whitish below, with a whitish line from its bill to its eye. It moves quickly through dense mangrove and creek-side scrub, making it difficult to see. The gerygone makes a domed nest of bark fibre bound with spiders' webs. Length: 11cm (4in). Family Acanthizidae; species *Gerygone tenebrosa*.

gesneria

Any member of the *Gesneria* genus, which comprises *c*.50 species of usually tuberous, evergreen perennials and shrubs from tropical America and the West Indies. Many species are epiphytes; others grow on rocks. They bear bell-shaped, white, red, orange, yellow or green, five-lobed flowers. Family Gesneriaceae; species include *Gesneria cuneifolia*.

gestation (pregnancy)

Period of time from CONCEPTION until BIRTH; in humans and many apes, it is normally about 40 weeks (280 days). In humans, it is generally divided into three 3-month periods called trimesters. In the first trimester, the EMBRYO grows from a small ball of cells to a FETUS about 7.6cm (3in) in length, during which time the skeleton, brain and such vital organs as the heart and lungs develop. At the beginning of the second trimester, movements are first felt and the fetus grows to about 36cm (14in). In the third trimester, the fetus attains its full

G

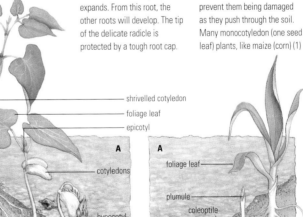

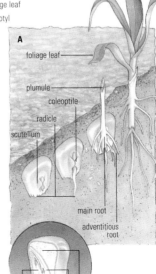

▼ **germination** Germination of the seed (**A**) is the beginning of all new plants. The *radicle* (young root) is the first part of the young plant to break through the seed case, as it absorbs water and rapidly expands. From this root, the other roots will develop. The tip of the delicate radicle is protected by a tough root cap.

The *plumules* (young shoots), however, do not have the same protection, and different strategies are employed to prevent them being damaged as they push through the soil. Many monocotyledon (one seed leaf) plants, like maize (corn) (1)

and other grasses, first send up a protective sheath (coleoptile) within which the plumule grows. In maize, the single cotyledon stays underground within the seed, absorbing food from the *endosperm* (food store), and is known as the *scutellum*. The endosperm provides enough food for the plumules to enlarge and develop into the plant's first green leaves, at which point it can start to photosynthesize for itself. Within the maize seed (**B**), food is stored outside the plant embryo as dry, powdery *endosperm* (1). When environmental conditions trigger the process of germination, the single cotyledon (2) absorbs food from the endosperm and delivers it to the developing plumule (3) and radicle (4). Inside a bean (**C**), the radicle (1) is positioned to burst through the seed case (*testa*) at the start of germination. Food stored within the swollen cotyledons (2) will nourish the plant as the plumules (3) grow and develop into young leaves. As the nutrients are used up they will shrivel and wither.

shrivelled cotyledon
foliage leaf
epicotyl

A

cotyledons

hypocotyl
seed coat

main root
lateral root
hook

A

foliage leaf

plumule
coleoptile
radicle
scutellum

main root
adventitious root

C   1 2   3

B   3 4   2 1

G

body weight. The gestation period for mammals varies greatly. For instance, a female elephant (cow) gives birth to its calf after 18 to 22 months' gestation, whereas the Virginia opossum gives birth after 12 days.

geum
Any member of the *Geum* genus, comprising *c*.50 perennial plants from Arctic and temperate regions of Europe, Asia, New Zealand, Africa and the Americas. Geums have wrinkled leaves, which are divided, toothed and saucer-shaped, and five-petalled flowers in cream, yellow, orange, pink or red. Their elongated hooked fruits are borne on a spherical head. Family Rosaceae; species include *Geum rivale* (water avens) and *Geum urbanum* (wood avens).

geyser
Hot spring that erupts intermittently, throwing up jets of superheated water and steam to a height of about 60m (200ft), followed by a thunderous roar. Geysers occur in the United States, where the best known is Yellowstone Park's Old Faithful, Iceland and New Zealand.

gharial (gavial)
Reptile native to N India; it is related to the CROCODILE. It has a long, narrow snout, an olive or brownish back and a lighter belly. Length: to 5m (16.4ft). Family Gavialidae; there is only one species, *Gavialis gangeticus*.

gherkin
Type of CUCUMBER. The gherkin is a small, green, sausage-shaped fruit, which is usually pickled in vinegar. The vine-like plants are originally from India; they are now grown worldwide, under glass where the climate is too cold. Family Cucurbitaceae; species *Cucumis sativus*.

ghost crab
See CRAB, GHOST

giant bellflower
Tall perennial plant that consists of a clump of unbranched stems growing from a single taproot. Native to stony slopes of Uzebekistan and Tajikistan,

A

B

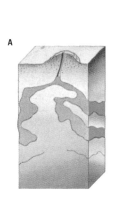

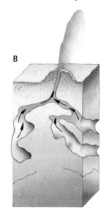

C

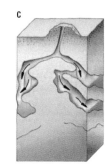

▲ **geyser** A plume of hot water and steam, a geyser is the result of the boiling of water at depth in a series of interconnecting chambers by volcanic heat (A). The expansion of steam produced drives the water and steam above it out at the surface (B), and this is followed by a period of refilling and heating making it a periodic phenomenon (C).

▲ **giant water bug** Using its front legs to grasp its prey, the giant water bug injects it with a powerful toxin. It also injects a digestive juice, which breaks down the animal's insides, so that they can be sucked out. The water bug's hind legs help to propel it through the water.

the giant bellflower is now grown in gardens for its large, pale blue or purple, bell-shaped flowers. Height: to *c*.1.5m (*c*.5ft). Family Campanulaceae; species *Ostrowskia magnifica*.

giant earthworm
Any of several species of Australian and South African EARTHWORM. Some individuals of these species can reach lengths of more than 1m (3.3ft). Phylum Annelida; class Oligochaeata; order Haplotaxida; family Lumbricidae; genera *Megascolides* and *Microchaetus*.

giant hogweed (cartwheel flower)
Biennial herb with thick, hollow, purple-blotched stems. Its flowerheads can be up to 60cm (24in) wide. Originally from the Caucasus, the giant hogweed has become a common weed across Europe. It contains a substance that can cause severe blistering of the skin, especially in sunlight. Height: to 4m (13ft). Family Umbelliferae; species *Heracleum mantegazzianum*.

giant protea
Evergreen shrub from the rocky hillsides of s Africa. It has leathery leaves and large, showy, cone- or thistle-like flowerheads, which are surrounded by red, yellow or white petal-like bracts. Family Proteaceae; species *Protea magnifica* and *Protea cynaroides* (king protea).

giant spider crab
See CRAB, GIANT SPIDER

giant tortoise
See TORTOISE, GIANT

giant water bug
Aquatic BUG found worldwide. It preys on other insects, tadpoles, snails and small fish. A strong flier, it is attracted to lights. Length: to100mm (4in). Order Hemiptera; family Belostomatidae.

gibberbird (desert chat)
Small Australian perching bird of arid, wind-blasted scrub and grassland. It is uncommon, nomadic and difficult to locate. The gibberbird has mottled, sandy coloured plumage, with a yellowish face and breast and a dark tail. It walks and runs with a swagger in a very upright manner. Length: 12cm (5in). Family Ephthianuridae; species *Ashbyia lovensis*.

gibberellin
Any of a group of organic compounds (HORMONES) found in plants; they stimulate cell division, stem elongation, the breaking of DORMANCY (by triggering the production of enzymes essential for germination) and response to light and temperature.

Gibberellins interact with some AUXINS to promote cell enlargement and have been used to increase crop yields substantially.

gibbon
Agile, tailless PRIMATE with very long arms and legs. It lives in tropical and subtropical rainforests of Southeast Asia. Gibbons move rapidly through trees, swinging by their arms; they are also capable of upright locomotion. Most species are similar in size. They communicate using loud, complex calls, which are often duets between monogamous pairs. All species are frugivores, preferring ripe fruit, but they also take young leaves and sometimes invertebrates. Head-body length: 45–65cm (18–26in). Family Hylobatidae.

gibbon, agile
Widely distributed gibbon, found mostly on Sumatra and the Malay Peninsula. It has variable colouring, from golden to red, brown or black. Family Hylobatidae; species *Hylobates agilis*.

gibbon, hoolock (white-browed gibbon)
Gibbon found in India, Bangladesh and s China. Female hoolock gibbons are golden in colour; males are black. Family Hylobatidae; species *Hylobates hoolock*.

gibbon, kloss (Mentawai gibbon, beeloh)
Gibbon that is unusual in that both males and females are completely black. Family Hylobatidae; species *Hylobates klossi*.

gibbon, lar (white-handed gibbon)
Gibbon found in Thailand, Sumatra and the Malay Peninsula. It is variable in colour, from red or brown to black. Family Hylobatidae; species *Hylobates lar*.

gibbon, moloch (silvery gibbon, Javan gibbon)
Gibbon found on Java. Both males and females are grey in colour. Family Hylobatidae; species *Hylobates moloch*.

gila monster
Large, blunt-headed, short-tailed LIZARD. It has beaded scales and a contrasting pattern of black and pink or yellow markings. Gila monsters and their relatives, the Mexican beaded lizards, are the only venomous lizards in the world. They are native to sw United States and N Mexico. They feed on eggs and small

▶ **gibbon, lar** Found in the tropical rainforests of s and Southeast Asia, the lar gibbon has distinctive facial markings and white extremities. It eats a very selective diet consisting of ripe fruit, new leaves and buds. It uses its long arms to swing from branch to branch high up in the forest canopy when searching for food. Gibbons are largely monogamous creatures and the lar gibbon is one of the few animal species to sing in couples; its song is highly unusual. The lar gibbon population has declined severely due to deforestation in its native countries and live capture for the pet trade.

vertebrates. Length: 40–60cm (16–24in). Family Helodermatidae; species *Heloderma suspectum*.

Gilbert, Walter (1932–)

US molecular biologist who determined the sequence of NUCLEOTIDES in DNA. In 1966 Gilbert identified a repressor substance, a protein that regulates gene activity. He then experimented with enzymes that split the DNA molecule at known places; he was gradually able to discover the sequence of nucleotides along the molecule. For devising this technique he shared the 1980 Nobel Prize for chemistry with fellow US biochemist Paul Berg (1926–) and Frederick SANGER.

gills

Organs through which most FISH, some larval AMPHIBIANS, such as TADPOLES, and many aquatic invertebrates obtain oxygen from water. When a fish breathes it opens its mouth, draws in water and shuts its mouth again. Water is forced over the gills, through the gill slits and out into the surrounding water. Oxygen is absorbed into small capillary blood vessels, and, at the same time, waste carbon dioxide carried by the blood diffuses into the water through the gills. The gills of young tadpoles, AXOLOTLS (a kind of SALAMANDER) and many invertebrates are on the outside of their bodies.

ginger

Herbaceous perennial plant native to tropical E Asia and Indonesia and grown commercially in Jamaica and elsewhere. It has fat tuberous roots and yellow-green flowers. The kitchen spice is made from the tubers of *Zingiber officinale*. Family Zingiberaceae.

ginger lily (garland lily)

Perennial plant that grows from thick RHIZOMES; it is found in damp wooded regions of Asia. Its wide, lance-shaped leaves are borne in two parallel rows on unbranched stems. It produces dense spikes of fragrant, two-lipped, white, yellow or orange, tubular flowers at the ends of the stems. Family Zingiberaceae; species include *Hedychium gardnerianum* (Kahili ginger lily) and *Hedychium coccineum* (scarlet ginger lily).

ginkgo (maidenhair tree)

Tree that dates from the late Permian period. The ginkgo is native to temperate regions of China but occurs only rarely in the wild. It has fan-shaped leaves, small, foul-smelling fruits and edible, nut-like seeds. Height: to 30m (100ft). Phylum Ginkgophyta; species *Ginkgo biloba*.

ginseng

Either of two perennial plants, one native to the United States (*Panax quinquefolius*) and one native to E Asia (*Panax ginseng*). Ginseng has yellow-green flowers and compound leaves. The dried tuberous roots are used in Chinese traditional medicine. Height: to 50cm (20in). Family Araliaceae.

giraffe

Any of nine subspecies of herbivorous, hoofed mammals, native to Africa. The tallest land animals, giraffes have very long necks, short, tufted manes and two to four skin-covered horns. The coat is pale brown with red-brown blotches. Giraffes can gallop at speeds of up to 50km/h (30mph). Height: to 5.5m (18ft). Family Giraffidae; species *Giraffa camelopardalis*. *See also* HERBIVORE

glacial groove

Deep, wide, usually straight furrow cut in bedrock.

It is caused by the abrasive action of large rock fragments dragged along the base of a moving GLACIER. The grooves are larger and deeper than glacial striations, ranging in size from a deep scratch to a glacial valley.

glaciation

Covering of a large region or a landscape by ice. The term is also used to refer to an ICE AGE.

glacier

Large mass of ice, mainly recrystallized snow, that moves slowly by CREEP downslope or outwards in all directions due to the stress of its own weight. The flow terminates where the rate of melting is equal to the advance of the glacier. There are three main types: the mountain (or valley) glacier, originating above the snow line in mountain regions; the PIEDMONT, which develops when valley glaciers spread out over lowland; and the ICE SHEET and ICE CAP. *See* illustration, page 164

glaciology

Study of ice. No longer restricted to the study of glaciers, this science deals with ice and the action of ice in all its natural forms. Glaciology, therefore, draws upon the knowledge of many other related subjects, notably physics, chemistry, geology and meteorology.

gladiolus

Any member of the *Gladiolus* genus, comprising *c.*250 species of perennial plants native to Europe and Africa but cultivated widely. Gladioli pass the dry season as CORMS, which sprout in spring to pro-

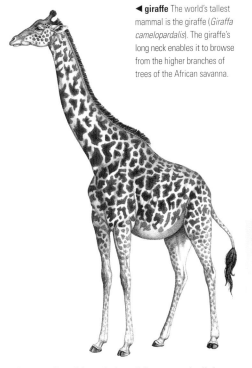

◄ **giraffe** The world's tallest mammal is the giraffe (*Giraffa camelopardalis*). The giraffe's long neck enables it to browse from the higher branches of trees of the African savanna.

G

duce a spike of funnel-shaped flowers and tall, lance-shaped leaves. Height: to 1m (3ft). Family Iridaceae.

gland

Cell or tissue that manufactures and secretes special substances. The glands of animals are of two basic types. EXOCRINE GLANDS make such substances as

◄ **gila monster** Found in the deserts of the sw United States, the gila monster (*Heloderma suspectum*) spends most of its life sheltering underground. Its ability to eat a large amount in one session and to store fat in its tail means that frequent hunting trips are unnecessary. The gila monster's teeth have grooves along which its venom passes into its prey. Except during the breeding season, it is a solitary animal.

hydrochloric acid, mucus, sweat, sebaceous fluids and ENZYMES, and secrete these usually through ducts to an external (such as the SKIN) or internal body surface. Endocrine glands (*see* ENDOCRINE SYSTEM) contain cells that secrete HORMONES directly into the bloodstream.

glass fish

Small, perch-like fish of fresh and brackish waters in the Indo-Pacific region. Many species lack scales and have a semi-transparent body. Glass fish are popular aquarium fish. Length: to 5cm (2in). Family Ambassidae.

glasswort (samphire, marsh samphire)

Small annual plant that is adapted to grow on salt marshes and pebbly beaches in Europe. Its fleshy jointed stems lack leaves, giving it a cactus-like appearance. Glasswort is eaten as a fresh vegetable or pickled. It was once used to make glass by fusing its ash, which has a high soda content, with sand. Family Chenopodiaceae; species include *Salicornia perennis* (perennial glasswort).

glauconite

Complex silicate mineral of iron, magnesium and aluminium, a member of the MICA family. It forms very small lath-shaped crystals (monoclinic), which occur as rounded grains in SEDIMENTARY ROCKS. It is bluish or dark green with a dull lustre; in sufficient quantity, it can colour the entire rock green, in which case it is known as greensand. Hardness 2.0–2.5; r.d. 2.7–2.9.

glider

POSSUM that has a thin membrane stretched between its fore and hind limbs to enable it to glide. Three families have evolved gliders – the Petauridae (gliders), the Burramyidae (pygmy possums) and the Pseudocheiridae (ringtail possums). Some species can glide more than 100m (330ft). Most species feed on nectar and tree gum.

glider, feathertail (pygmy glider, flying mouse)

Smallest flying possum, native to E Australia. It feeds mainly on nectar and sugary sap. Its back is uniform brown and its underparts are white; it has feathery extensions of stiff hairs along its tail. Its gliding membrane stretches from elbow to knee. Head-body length: 6–8cm (2–3in); tail: 7–8cm (c.3in). Family Burramyidae; species *Acrobates pygmaeus*.

glider, sugar

Flying possum of which there are several subspecies; they inhabit forests in Australia and Tasmania. Sugar gliders are grey with a black stripe along the back. They have dark facial markings, a long bushy tail and a gliding membrane stretching from wrist to ankle. They feed mainly on insects. Head-body length: 12–32cm (5–13in); tail: 15–48cm (6–19in). Family Petauridae; species *Petaurus breviceps.*

global warming

See feature article

globe artichoke

Tall, thistle-like, perennial plant from the Mediterranean region, NW Africa and the Canary Islands. Globe artichoke has deeply lobed, sharply pointed, grey-green leaves, which are covered with grey hairs. The buds of the late-summer, purple, cone-like flowerheads, which can be up to 15cm (6in) across, are eaten as a vegetable. Height: to 2m (6.6ft). Family Asteraceae/Compositae; species *Cynara scolymus.*

globeflower

Any member of the genus *Trollius*, comprising *c.*24 species of clump-forming, herbaceous, perennial plants. Globeflowers grow in cool, damp meadows of Europe, Asia and North America. They have deeply divided leaves. In spring or summer they produce buttercup-like, bowl-shaped, cream or bright yellow flowers. Family Ranunculaceae; species include *Trollius europaeus* (common European globeflower).

globe thistle

Any of *c.*120 species of annual, biennial and perennial plants belonging to the genus *Echinops*. They are found in dry regions of central and s Europe, central Asia, India and tropical Africa. They have spiny, silver-grey, woolly foliage and produce white, grey or blue spherical flowerheads at the ends of the stems. Family Asteraceae/Compositae; species include *Echinops bannaticus.*

globigerina

Any member of the *Globigerina* genus of one-celled marine PROTOZOA. The empty shells of globigerinas are an important component of ocean floor ooze. The shell is spiralled into a lumpy sphere with needle-like extensions. One species is an indicator of sea temperature, and therefore of ocean palaeoclimatology. Shells coiling to the left indicate that the animals lived in cold water; shells coiling to the right were of animals that lived in warm water.

glomerulus

Mass of capillary blood vessels within a BOWMAN'S CAPSULE, the funnel-shaped end of a NEPHRON in a KIDNEY. Fluid passes from the BLOOD in the capillaries into the capsule and then down the tubule of the nephron. It eventually passes out of the kidney along the ureter as urine as part of the process of EXCRETION.

glossopterid

Member of an extinct group of plants that evolved and became common during Permian and Triassic times within the supercontinent of GONDWANALAND only to die out in Jurassic times. The distribution of their characteristic strap-shaped fossil leaves in India, South Africa, Australia, Antarctica and South America is evidence that these continents were once joined together.

glow-worm

Any of a number of wingless female BEETLES or beetle larvae that possess light-emitting organs. The name glow-worm is used especially for the European beetle *Lampyris noctiluca*. A winged male is known as a FIREFLY. Family Lampyridae; genus *Lampyris* .

gloxinia

Any member of the *Gloxinia* genus, a group of perennial plants found in the forests of Central and South America. The plant's erect stems, which grow from fleshy rhizomes, bear opposite pairs of oval leaves. The five-petalled, blue or pink, funnel-shaped flowers are covered outside with fine hairs. Family Gesneriaceae. The plant known as **florist's gloxinia** belongs to the similar and closely related genus *Sinningia*. Family Gesneriaceae; species *Sinningia speciosa.*

glucagon

Hormone secreted by cells in the ISLETS OF LANGERHANS in the PANCREAS. It helps to regulate blood sugar levels by activating the ENZYMES in the LIVER that form GLUCOSE from GLYCOGEN and AMINO ACIDS. *See also* INSULIN

glucose (dextrose, $C_6H_{12}O_6$)

Colourless, crystalline SUGAR that occurs in fruit and honey. It requires no digestion before being absorbed into the bloodstream. In the bodies of animals, the storage carbohydrate GLYCOGEN is converted to glucose before being utilized as an energy source in cellular RESPIRATION. Glucose is a MONOSACCHARIDE sugar (having a single sugar unit). It is prepared commercially by the HYDROLYSIS of starch using hydrochloric acid. It is used in foods, especially confectionery, as a sweetener, and in tanning and pharmaceuticals.

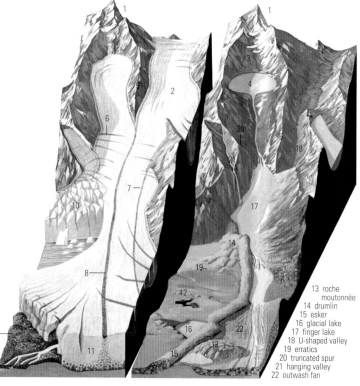

▶ **glacier** In spite of a return to warmer conditions, some regions of the world (namely those nearer the poles) are still covered by ice, and are being greatly altered by its action. Glaciated regions have been subjected to erosion and deposition, the erosion mainly taking place in the highland areas, leaving features such as pyramidal peaks, cirques, roches moutonnées, truncated spurs and hanging valleys. Most deposition has occurred on lowlands, where, after the retreat of the ice, moraines, drumlins, eskers, erratic boulders and alluvial fans remain.

KEY
1 pyramidal peak
2 firn (granular snow)
3 cirque
4 tarn (corrie lake)
5 arête
6 marginal crevasse
7 lateral moraine
8 medial moraine
9 terminal moraine
10 sérac
11 subglacial moraine
12 glacial table
13 roche moutonnée
14 drumlin
15 esker
16 glacial lake
17 finger lake
18 U-shaped valley
19 erratics
20 truncated spur
21 hanging valley
22 outwash fan

Global warming is an overall increase in the Earth's temperature. The world has always undergone periodic fluctuations in temperature, but many scientists believe that GREENHOUSE GASES, which produce a GREENHOUSE EFFECT, are responsible for a further rise in temperature over the Earth. Many of the gases are the result of human activities.

CARBON DIOXIDE is produced naturally, and the amount used by plants in photosynthesis is normally balanced by that produced in organisms during respiration. However, the burning of forests and fossil fuels has increased overall levels in the past 200 years. Carbon dioxide accounts for approximately 50% of the greenhouse effect. METHANE is produced by anaerobic bacteria that live in such diverse habitats as waterlogged land, rubbish tips and the intestines of animals, notably cattle. An increase in cattle and sheep farming has led to an increase in methane production. OZONE forms an important layer between 15 and 50km (9–30mi) above the Earth. Its most important function, however, is to absorb ultraviolet light and so prevent it reaching the Earth's surface. WATER VAPOUR in the form of clouds can keep the Earth's surface cooler by blocking the sun's rays and can help keep it warmer by acting as an insulating blanket retaining the heat that does penetrate. CHLOROFLUOROCARBONS (CFCs) are used commercially in refrigerators, aerosols and foam plastics. They are very inert, lasting for 60 years or more. In addition to being greenhouse gases, they also deplete the ozone layer through a series of chemical reactions. This allows additional ultraviolet radiation to reach the Earth. To prevent this harmful effect, the use of CFCs is being phased out through an international agreement called the Montreal Protocol, signed in 1987.

The greenhouse effect is caused by short-wavelength radiation striking the Earth's surface and being converted to heat, which has a longer wavelength. The greenhouse gases absorb this longer wavelength radiation, preventing it being reflected back into space. The gases therefore act in the same way as the glass of a greenhouse, accumulating heat beneath.

Global warming causes expansion of the oceans and melting of the ice caps, both resulting in a rise in sea level with the consequent risk of flooding low-lying land. Other effects are changes in the distribution of vegetation and unusual weather patterns.

The greenhouse effect is neither new, nor all bad. Indeed it is the greenhouse gases that maintain the Earth's surface temperature at an average of 15°C (59°F) rather than the −18°C (0°F) it would be without them. Nevertheless the problem of global warming is of such concern that there is now international action to reduce the emission of greenhouse gases. The first Earth Summit, in Rio de Janeiro (1992), was followed by a second in New York (1997), in which the European Union (EU) proposed a target of reducing carbon dioxide emissions in developed countries to 15% below their 1990 level by the year 2010. Complete agreement is still far from being achieved, with many developed countries not anxious to make the changes to their patterns of living that a significant reduction in greenhouse gas emissions would require.

G

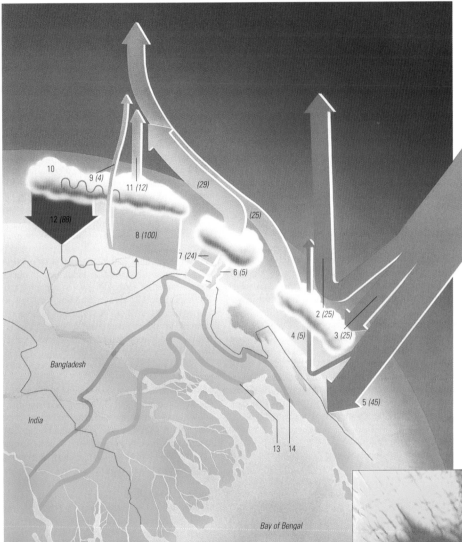

(figures in brackets are approximate percentages of the total incoming solar radiation)

▲ Greenhouse gases are fairly transparent to the short-wavelength, visible and ultraviolet light that brings most of the Sun's energy (1), though c.25% is reflected by the atmosphere (2), and 25% is absorbed by it (3). About 5% is reflected from the Earth (4), which absorbs the rest (5). Some of this absorbed energy rises again in thermals (6) or in the heat of evaporated moisture (7). The rest is reradiat-ed (8) as long-wavelength infrared rays. The infrared radiation emitted by the Earth (8) is partially transmitted straight back into space (9). A much greater amount is absorbed by the greenhouse gases (10), which are very efficient absorbers of the long infrared wavelengths. Some of the absorbed heat is reradiated into space (11), but a lot is radiated downwards (12) to fuel global warming.

Half the world's population lives in low-lying coastal areas, such as the Bay of Bengal (shown), which is particularly vulnerable to flooding. Global warming could cause the sea level to rise. A 2m (6ft) rise in sea level (13) would inundate close to 20% of Bangladesh and require tens of millions to be evacuated. A larger rise (14) of 5m (16ft) would drown close to half the country.

▲ Antarctic ozone depletion can be seen in this coloured image made using satellite mapping spectrometer data. The ozone hole (blue, centre) can be seen with the outline of Antarctica and South America. The hole reached a record size in September 1998. Ozone concentrations run from red (highest), through yellow and green to blue (lowest).

▶ **gnu** The migration of gnu herds in Africa follows the movement of the equatorial rainbelt and the grass growth it sustains. Gnus spend November to April in the Serengeti Plain and, after mating, migrate to the W Serengeti just before May. August and September are spent in the N Serengeti.

G

glucoside
Carbohydrate-containing compound that yields a GLUCOSE and a nonsugar component (either an alcohol or phenol) when decomposed by the process of HYDROLYSIS. Natural glucosides are important in plant metabolism, and many POLYSACCHARIDES, such as CELLULOSE, STARCH and GLYCOGEN, are regarded chemically as glucosides. They may be used as drugs, colouring agents and aromatics.

glycerol (glycerine)
Syrupy, sweet liquid (1,2,3–trihydroxypropane, HOCH₂CH(OH)CH₂OH) obtained from animal and vegetable fats and oils or from propene (propylene). It is used in the manufacture of various products, including plastics, explosives, cosmetics, foods, antifreeze and paper coatings.

glycogen
CARBOHYDRATE stored in the animal body, principally by the liver and muscles. Glycogen is sometimes known as animal starch, and, like starch and cellulose, it is a POLYMER of GLUCOSE. When the body needs energy, glycogen is broken down to glucose, which is further metabolized to carbon dioxide and water, providing ADENOSINE TRIPHOSPHATE (ATP), a source of chemical energy, in the process. *See also* METABOLISM; RESPIRATION

glycol (ethylene glycol, ethane-1,2-diol, (CH₂OH)₂)
Colourless, odourless liquid containing two HYDROXYL groups. It is a viscous liquid used in plastics, solvents, antifreeze and artificial fibres.

glycolipid
Substance made up of both LIPID and CARBOHYDRATE. Glycolipids occur on CELL MEMBRANES, where they act as recognition sites. For example, the ABO blood system is the result of different glycolipids on the cell membrane of erythrocytes (red blood cells). Glycolipids also help to make the cell membrane more stable. *See also* GLYCOPROTEIN

glycolysis
Series of biochemical reactions in which glucose is converted to PYRUVATE. It takes place during RESPIRATION in CELLS. The nine stages of glycolysis are accompanied by the net release of two molecules of the energy-containing substance ADENOSINE TRIPHOSPHATE (ATP) per glucose molecule. During AEROBIC respiration, the pyruvate enters the KREBS CYCLE, with the ultimate yield of 12 more molecules of ATP. During ANAEROBIC respiration, the pyruvate is converted to lactic acid. *See also* ELECTRON TRANSPORT SYSTEM; PHOSPHORYLATION

glycoprotein
Substance made of both PROTEIN and CARBOHYDRATE. Glycoproteins are found on CELL MEMBRANES, where they act as recognition sites for NEUROTRANSMITTERS and HORMONES. Mucin, a major component of MUCUS, is an example of a glycoprotein. *See also* GLYCOLIPID

glycosidic bond
Bond that is formed when MONOSACCHARIDES unite by CONDENSATION reactions to form DISACCHARIDES or POLYSACCHARIDES.

gnat
Common name for several small FLIES, mainly of the family Culicidae. The female gnat bites human beings. *See also* MOSQUITO.

gneiss
METAMORPHIC ROCK with a distinctive layering or banding formed by high pressure or high temperature conditions of regional metamorphism. The darker minerals are likely to be hornblende, augite, mica or dark feldspar.

gnu (wildebeest)
Large, ox-like African ANTELOPE. The **white-tailed gnu** (*Connochaetes gnou*) is almost extinct. The **brindled gnu** (*Connochaetes taurinus*) lives in E and S Africa, where large herds migrate annually. It has a massive, buffalo-like head and a slender body. Both sexes are horned. Length: up to 2.4m (7.8ft); height: 1.3m (4.3ft); weight: up to 275kg (600lb). Family Bovidae.

goanna
Australian term for a MONITOR lizard.

goat
Horned RUMINANT raised for its milk, meat, leather and hair. Goats are closely related to sheep. They are brown or grey in colour. The male is a ram or billy, the female a doe or nanny, and the young a kid. Wild species are nomadic, living in rugged mountain areas. Family Bovidae; true goats belong to the genus *Capra*.

goat, mountain
Massive animal found in steep, rocky areas of North America. Its coat is white in summer and long, thick and yellowish in winter. Both sexes have sharp, black horns 20–30cm (8–12in) in length. It feeds on grass, lichen and moss. Head-body length: 125–178cm (49–70in); tail: 8–20cm (3–8in). Family Bovidae; subfamily Caprinae; species *Oreamus americanus*.

goat, wild (bezoar goat)
Ancestor of the domestic goat; it is found on rocky

▲ **goat** Bred mainly in countries where the pasture is too poor for sheep, goats are an important source of milk and meat in many desert and mountain regions worldwide. Angora goats (A) originated in Turkey, near Ankara. They have now spread to other parts of the world, and are bred for their fleece, known as mohair. The quality of mohair is important and animals are carefully bred to produce long, fine-haired fleece. The Granada (B) is a black, hornless Spanish breed, kept for its milk. Although still popular in Spain, it has not spread further afield. The Toggenburg (C) is a hardy, hornless breed. It originated in Switzerland, but is now used in many countries for cross-breeding.

slopes of some Mediterranean islands, the Middle East and Asia, from Turkey to Pakistan. It is brown with darker stripes along its back and face, and long, gently curving horns. Height: 70–100cm (28–40in). Family Bovidae; subfamily Caprinae; species *Capra aegagrus*.

goat-antelope
Member of a group of even-toad ungulates related to cattle. There are 26 species, including CHAMOIS, IBEX, MARKHOR, SAIGA and MUSK OX, as well as SHEEP and GOATS. Most are stockily built and many have heavy horns, often curved or twisted. They inhabit steep, rocky terrain and can clamber about quite nimbly. Family Bovidae; subfamily Caprinae.

goatfish
Perch-like marine fish found worldwide in tropical and temperate shallow waters. It is characterized by a pair of chin barbels that it uses to probe the sea bed in search of food. Family Mullidae.

go-away bird
Bird of central and s Africa; its plumage is grey, with black wing bars and a long grey tail. A poor flyer, it likes to stay deep within forest cover. The go-away bird's uniquely shaped feet have the fourth toe set at right angles, allowing it to climb backwards and forwards through vegetation. Length: 35–75cm (14–30in). Family Musophagidae; species *Corythiaxoides leucogaster*.

goby
Any of more than 800 species of small, colourful, marine and freshwater fish belonging to the very diverse suborder Goboidei (which comprises some 2000 species). Gobies are common on coral reefs. Some species live in association with snapping shrimps or other invertebrates; some change sex from female to male; others demonstrate cryptic coloration. Many belong to the family Gobiidae.

godwit
Medium-sized, long-legged wading bird with a long, slightly up-curved bill. In spring and summer, the godwit has handsome reddish-brown or chestnut plumage. It breeds on wet grasslands and marshy tundra and winters in flocks on coastal estuaries. Length: 37–44cm (15–17in). Family Scolopacidae; genus *Limosa*; there are three species worldwide.

godwit, bar-tailed
Godwit with a slightly up-curved bill. Its tail is white, with fine, brown bars. In flight it has no white on the upper wing. The bar-tailed godwit breeds on marshy Scandinavian and Siberian tundra and winters in large flocks on the coasts; it is rare inland. Length: 37–39cm (15in). Family Scolopacidae; species *Limosa lapponica*.

godwit, black-tailed
Largest species of godwit. In flight it has a conspicuous white wing bar and a white tail with a black terminal band. The black-tailed godwit breeds further south than the bar-tailed godwit, on inland marshes and wet grasslands of Europe and Eurasia. Length: 40–44cm (16–17in). Family Scolopacidae; species *Limosa limosa*.

godwit, Hudsonian
Godwit that is similar in shape to the bar-tailed godwit but that has the wing and tail patterns of the black-tailed godwit. In flight its black underwing is distinctive. In spring the Hudsonian godwit migrates through the Great Plains of North America to N

Canada; in autumn it migrates along E North America to South America. Length: 39cm (15in). Family Scolopacidae; species *Limosa haemastica*.

goldcrest
Smallest bird to breed in Europe. It resembles a tiny green warbler, with a black-bordered orange or yellow crest, which is raised only in display. The goldcrest breeds mostly in conifers in woods, parks and gardens; it winters in broad-leaved woods, often in loose flocks with tits. Length: 9cm (4in). Family Sylviidae; species *Regulus regulus*.

golden bells
See FORSYTHIA

goldeneye
Diving DUCK found in Europe and North America. The male goldeneye is distinguished by its black or purple glossed, strikingly peaked head, with a distinctive white mark in front of the eye. It nests in holes in trees or in nestboxes by forest lakes. Length: 42–53cm (17–21in). Family Anatidae; genus *Bucephala*.

goldeneye, common
Most common species of goldeneye in Europe, Asia and North America. The male has a black head, glossed green, with a large, round, white spot in front of its yellow eyes. In flight both sexes have broad, white wing bars. Length: 42–50cm (17–20in). Family Anatidae; species *Bucephala clangula*.

goldeneye, Barrow's
Goldeneye found in North America and Iceland. The male differs from the common goldeneye in its purple glossed head and the bold white crescent, rather than spot, in front of the eye. It often nests in caves and ruined buildings. Length: 42–53cm (17–21in). Family Anatidae; species *Bucephala islandica*.

golden-green alga
See CHRYSOPHYTE

goldenrod (Aaron's rod)
Any member of the *Solidago* genus, which comprises *c*.100 woody perennials from roadsides and riverbanks, mainly of North America. They are popular garden plants despite their invasive habits. Their tall stems bear alternate lance-shaped leaves and branch at the top to produce one-sided, dense spikes of tiny yellow flowers, all facing upwards. Height: to 2m (6.6ft). Family Asteraceae/Compositae; species include *Solidago canadensis* (Canadian goldenrod) and *Solidago caesia* (wreath goldenrod).

golden wattle
Australian WATTLE tree that has tough, flattened, silvery leaf stalks (phyllodes) rather than the typical feathery leaflets. The golden wattle of Victoria is widely cultivated for its tan-coloured bark and pretty, fragrant, yellow, pompom flowers. Family Mimosaceae; species *Acacia pycnantha*.

goldfinch
Small, gregarious songbird that has strikingly yellow-gold plumage. It has a characteristic bounding or dancing flight and a sweet tinkling song. Goldfinches are often kept as cagebirds. Length:. 12–13cm (*c*.5in). Family Carduelidae; genus *Carduelis*.

goldfinch, American
Goldfinch that is common throughout North America. The breeding adult male is bright canary

▲ **goby** The striped or Japanese goby (*Tridentiger trigonocephalus*) was discovered as recently as the 1960s. It is native to Japan and China and is found in shallow water, usually on sandy, mud tidal flats. A bottom dweller, it spends most of its time resting under rocks or in crevices.

yellow; it has a black cap and wings, which show white bars in flight. The female is a dull olive green. Length: 12–13cm (*c*.5in). Family Carduelidae; species *Carduelis tristis*.

goldfinch, Eurasian
Goldfinch of Europe and Asia. It has a unique combination of red face, with white and black crescents, yellow wing bars and a white rump. It has a notably dancing flight. In winter the Eurasian goldfinch often feeds in large flocks on the seedheads of thistles. Length: 12–13cm (*c*.5in). Family Carduelidae; species *Carduelis carduelis*.

goldfish
Freshwater CARP originally found in China. It is the most popular aquarium fish. The goldfish was domesticated in China *c*.1000 years ago. The wild form is plain and brownish, but selective breeding has produced a variety of colours. Family Cyprinidae; species *Carassius auratus*.

Golgi, Camillo (1843–1926)
Italian histologist (specialist in the structure of CELLS). In 1873 he developed a method of staining tissue with silver nitrate for microscopic study. With this he discovered the GOLGI BODY within the CELL. Golgi shared the 1906 Nobel Prize for physiology or medicine with the Spanish histologist Santiago Ramón y Cajal (1852–1934) for his work on the structure of the NERVOUS SYSTEM.

Golgi body
Collection of microscopic vesicles or packets observed near the nucleus of many living CELLS. The Golgi body is a part of a cell's inner membrane structure, or ENDOPLASMIC RETICULUM, specialized for the purpose of packaging and dispatching proteins made by the cell.

gonad
Primary reproductive organ of male and female animals, in which develop the GAMETES or sex cells. Thus, the gonad in the male is a TESTIS and in the female an OVARY. Hermaphrodite animals possess both types.

Gondwanaland
Southern supercontinent. It began to break away from the single land mass, PANGAEA, *c*.200 million years ago. It became South America, Africa, India, Australia and Antarctica. The northern supercontinent, which eventually became North America and Eurasia without India, was LAURASIA.

goniatite
Any CEPHALOPOD mollusc belonging to the order Goniatitida. Goniatites have coiled shells divided into chambers by zigzag partitions. They first appeared in the upper Devonian period, *c*.350 million years ago. The group became extinct at the end of the Permian period. They are useful as zone fossils. Goniatites and AMMONITES belonged to the same subclass, Ammonoidea.

Goodall, Jane (1934–)
British zoologist famous for her studies of chimpanzees in the wild. She began observing the primates in the African bush in 1960, and her work became a model of how to study animal behaviour. Among her many discoveries was that chimpanzees use primitive tools, such as grass stems, to extract termites from their mounds. She also noted that the animals are carnivorous and that they engage in cannibalistic warfare among themselves.

goosander
See MERGANSER, COMMON

goose
Large, thickset, long-necked and web-footed water bird. The downy young leave the nest soon after hatching and follow the parents to water. Geese form large noisy flocks, which fly in a "V" formation. Most species nest on marshy northern tundra and spend the winter on farmland, estuaries and marshes. Family Anatidae.

goose, Canada
Common and familiar North American goose; it is now well established in Europe. A large, grey-brown goose, it has a black neck and head and a bold white patch on its cheeks and throat. There are several races, those that inhabit the more northerly regions being smaller. Length: 64–114cm (25–45in). Family Anatidae; species *Branta canadensis*.

goose, Egyptian
African goose; it has been introduced in other areas, including Britain. It appears grey-brown at a distance, with a darker brown patch around each eye. In flight the Egyptian goose has conspicuous white shoulder patches. Length: 63–73cm (25–29in). Family Anatidae; species *Alopochen aegyptiacus*.

goose, greylag
Heavily built grey goose. It has a thick, orange bill and orange legs. In flight it has conspicuous, pale-grey forewings and a loud, honking call. The greylag goose is the wild ancestor of the farmyard

G

▲ **goose** Unlike most species of birds, geese mate for life. Found in freshwater habitats all over the world, geese have been domesticated for their eggs and down. The species shown here are the Roman (A), the Egyptian (B), the Chinese (C), the greylag (D), the embden (E) and the Toulouse (F).

G

▶ **gooseberry** The bitter fruit of the gooseberry plant is used to make jams, jellies and pies. The European species (*Ribes uva-crispi*) is larger than the principal North American one (*Ribes hirtellum*). Due to the spread of white-pine blister rust, however, gooseberry cultivation has been restricted in many parts of the United States.

goose. Length: 75–90cm (30–35in). Family Anatidae; species *Anser anser*.

goose, Hawaiian
Goose that is found wild only on Hawaii; it is widely kept in wildfowl collections. Its plumage is mostly brown, with a black face and neck, bright buff cheeks and black streaks on its buff neck. In 1947 there were fewer than 50 birds, but intense recovery programmes have brought it back from the brink of extinction. Length: 65cm (26in). Family Anatidae; species *Branta sandvicensis*.

goose, Magellan
South American goose found in the Falkland Islands, Chile and s Argentina. It has a white head and breast, which can be heavily barred with black, and a black barred back. Length: 65cm (26in). Family Anatidae; species *Chloephaga picta*.

goose, magpie
Long-legged, boldly black-and-white goose found only in tropical Australia. It has a strange knobbed head. Its feet are partially webbed and strongly clawed, and its long bill is hooked at the tip. Once widespread, the magpie goose has now become rare due to shooting and loss of habitat. Length: 75–86cm (30–34in). Family Anatidae; species *Anseranus semipalmata*.

goose, pygmy
Small, duck-like goose found worldwide. It is often seen perching on logs, and it nests in hollow trees. Male pygmy geese are beautifully coloured in glossy green, white or bronze; they have brilliant white flashes, visible in flight, on the wings. They feed in deep vegetated lagoons. Length: 30–38cm (12–15in). Family Anatidae; genus *Nettapus*; there are four species.

goose, red-breasted
Strikingly coloured goose. Its breast, neck and cheek patches are chestnut-red; they are separated from the black upper- and underparts by white lines and a broad white patch on the flanks. The red-breasted goose nests on Siberian tundra; the majority of the world's population winters on the Danube delta. Length: 53–56cm (21–22in). Family Anatidae; species *Branta ruficollis*.

goose, snow
Goose that breeds on high arctic tundra in North America and winters on coastal wetlands farther south. The two distinct types of snow goose were once thought to be separate species: one is all white with black wing tips; the other ("blue" phase) has a bluish grey-brown back and wings, white head and blue-grey or white underparts. Length: 71cm (28in). Family Anatidae; species *Chen caerulescens*.

gooseberry
Hardy, deciduous, spiny shrub of the Northern Hemisphere. Its edible fruit, which are also known as gooseberries, are generally green, hairy and fairly acidic. Family Grossulariaceae; genus *Ribes*.

goosefoot
Any of *c*.18 species of annual or perennial herbs that colonize waste sites in Europe. They have branched stems and large, triangular leaves, which can be divided or spearhead-shaped and white beneath. The flowerhead spikes are covered with tiny, white, red or green, petalless flowers. Height: *c*.1m (*c*.3.3ft). Family Chenopodiaceae; species include *Chenopodium bonus-henricus* (good King Henry) and *Chenopodium album* (white goosefoot or pigweed).

gopher
Any of numerous species of small, stout, burrowing RODENTS of North and Central America. The gopher has fur-lined external cheek pouches and long incisor teeth outside the lips. It lives underground for shelter and food storage, digging tunnels to find roots and tubers. Length: 13–46cm (5–18in). Family Geomyidae.

goral
Small, long-haired member of the GOAT-ANTELOPE subfamily. It inhabits steep, rocky slopes in Asia, from India to Siberia and Thailand. Both males and females have short, ribbed horns. Gorals are red to dark grey in colour. Head-body length: 106–117cm (42–46in); tail: 69–78cm (27–31in). Family Bovidae; subfamily Caprinae; species *Nemorhaedus goral*.

gorge
Narrow, deep-sided valley. Gorges form only in hard rock, such as carboniferous limestone, otherwise erosion would soon break down the steep sides. A very large gorge is known as a CANYON.

gorilla
Powerfully built great APE native to the forests of equatorial Africa. The largest PRIMATE, it is brown or black, with long arms and short legs. It walks on all fours and is herbivorous. Height: to 175cm (70in); weight: 140–180kg (300–400lb). Family Pongidae; species *Gorilla gorilla*.

▲ **gorilla** Although capable of aggressive displays if attacked, gorillas are naturally peaceable creatures. Destruction of their natural habitat and trophy hunting has led to their becoming an endangered species. It is estimated that the mountain gorilla population stands at less than 1000.

gorse (furze)
Any of several dense thorny shrubs (genus *Ulex*) found mainly in Europe. The common European species, *Ulex europaeus*, bears yellow flowers and thrives in open hilly regions. Family Fabaceae/Leguminosae.

goshawk
Name given to certain large HAWKS. Goshawks are recognised by their long tails, broad, rounded wings, barred underparts and fast, dashing flight. The females are usually larger than the males. They build their own nests, unlike the falcons, and hunt in woodlands and scrub. Length: 28–62cm (11–24in), wingspan: 55–165cm (22–65in). Family Accipitridae; main genus *Accipiter*.

goshawk, gabar
Goshawk found in sub-Saharan Africa. It occurs in two colour forms: a very pale grey phase, with brown barred tail and wing tips; and a dark chocolate brown type. Both forms have a red base to the bill, black eyes and red legs. Length: 35cm (14in). Family Accipitridae; species *Micronisus gabar*.

goshawk, northern
Large, deep-chested, powerful hawk. Its plumage is mostly grey, with finely barred underparts and underwings. It hunts in dense woodlands for mammals and large birds. The northern goshawk is widely distributed in North America, Europe and Asia. Length: 48–62cm (19–24in). Family Accipitridae; species *Accipiter gentilis*.

Gould, Stephen Jay (1941–)
US palaeontologist. He proposed that EVOLUTION could occur in sudden spurts rather than gradually. Gould's theory of PUNCTUATED EQUILIBRIUM suggested that sudden accelerations in the evolutionary process could produce rapid changes in species over the comparatively short time of a few hundred thousand years. He has written many popular science books, including *Hen's Teeth and Horses' Toes* (1983) and *Bully for Brontosaurus* (1992).

gourami
Freshwater fish of Africa and Southeast Asia. Gouramis are characterized by their ability to breathe air, using an accessory respiratory organ located above each gill chamber. Most species brood eggs in their mouths or in floating bubble nests. They are popular aquarium fish. Length: from the licorice gourami at 2.5cm (1in) to the giant gourami at 1m (39in). Suborder Anabantoidei.

gourd
Annual VINE and its ornamental, hard-shelled fruit. These range from almost spherical, as in *Cucurbita pepo*, to irregular or bottle-shaped, as in *Lagenaria siceraria*. The rind may be smooth or warty. Family Cucurbitaceae. *See also* PUMPKIN

goutweed
See GROUND ELDER

Graafian follicle (ovarian follicle)
Fluid-filled, cyst-like cavity found in the OVARIES of MAMMALS. It surrounds and protects the developing OVUM. Once the ovum is released into a FALLOPIAN TUBE, the follicle develops a yellowish mass of tissue called the CORPUS LUTEUM.

graben
Elongated, trench-like, down-dropped block of the Earth's crust bordered by two or more similarly

▲ **goshawk** The black-mantled goshawk (*Accipiter melanochlamys*) is one of eight species of goshawk found in New Guinea. It ambushes smaller birds at water holes, flying in to seize its prey on the wing.

trending normal FAULTS. The Basin and Range province in Utah and Nevada, United States, consists of grabens and HORSTS, forming sedimentary basins and mountain ranges. A long graben found at the Earth's surface can also be called a RIFT VALLEY, such as the Great Rift Valley in E Africa.

grackle
Any of several different species of starling-like songbirds. The **North American grackle** (species of the genus *Quiscalus*) is glossy purple-black; it is a common bird of marshes, parks and gardens. Length: 32cm (13in). The **grackle** or **common mynah** (*Acridotheres tristis*) is found from Afghanistan to Southeast Asia; it was introduced to Australia, where it is now locally abundant. Length: 24cm (9in). **Tristram's grackle** (*Onychognathus tristrami*) occurs mainly in Saudi Arabia and the Yemen. Length: 25cm (10in). Family Icteridae.

grain weevil
Small brown or black WEEVIL with shiny wing cases (elytra) and a prominent snout (rostrum). It spends all year in granaries and breeds in stored grain of all kinds. Adult body length: 3mm (0.1in). Order Coleoptera; family Curculionidae; species *Sitophilus granarius*. See also BEETLE

gram-negative bacterium
BACTERIUM that reacts negatively to the GRAM'S STAIN, owing to its particular cell-wall composition. Staining with crystal violet, followed by iodine and treatment with alcohol leaves a colourless cell wall. A negative reaction to the Gram's stain correlates with a large number of physiological and biochemical characteristics. Examples of gram-negative bacteria include *Pseudomonas*, *Agrobacterium* and *Xanthomonas*.

gram-positive bacterium
Bacterium that reacts positively to the GRAM'S STAIN, owing to its cell-wall composition. Staining with crystal violet, followed by iodine, turns all bacterial cell walls blue; a final treatment with alcohol leaves the cell wall blue, a reaction that correlates with a number of other physiological and biochemical traits. Examples of gram-positive bacteria include *Streptomyces* and *Corynebacterium*.

Gram's stain
Differential staining method named after the Danish physician Hans Christian Gram (1853–1938). It aids in the categorizing and identification of BACTERIA, which are said to be GRAM-POSITIVE or GRAM-NEGA-

TIVE, depending on whether or not they retain the original violet stain at the end of the process.

granite
Coarse-grained, acid IGNEOUS ROCK from deep within the Earth, composed chiefly of FELDSPAR and QUARTZ, with some MICA or HORNBLENDE. Its colour is usually light grey, although feldspar may redden it. Its durability makes it a valuable construction material. Granite is thought to have solidified from magma (molten rock), but the occurrence of some granite with features normally associated with rocks of metamorphic origin suggests that not all granites are igneous. It crystallizes at great depths where the pressure is high; it becomes exposed at the Earth's surface only by erosion of surface rocks or by movements in the Earth's crust.

granulite (leptites)
Granular METAMORPHIC ROCK that derives largely from QUARTZ and FELDSPAR. Granulites often have a banded appearance.

grape (grapevine)
VINE that grows in temperate and subtropical climates, producing fruit that is eaten raw, dried or used for making wine. The classical European vine (*Vitis vinifera*) had its origins in Asia. The climate, soil, topography and methods of cultivation all determine the quality of the crop. Family Vitaceae.

grapefruit
CITRUS tree that is thought to have developed from a natural mutation of the pomelo tree in the West Indies. It is now grown worldwide wherever there is a Mediterranean-like climate. The grapefruit is a small evergreen tree with dark green, oval leaves and white, sweetly scented flowers. The fruits are large and spherical, with sharply sweet juicy flesh. Height: to 10m (33ft). Family Rutaceae; species *Citrus x paradisi*.

grape hyacinth
Any of c.30 species of perennial plants belonging to the genus *Muscari*. They grow from bulbs mainly in woodland areas of the Mediterranean and sw Asia. Grape hyacinths have long, fleshy, spoon or lance-shaped leaves and produce spikes of tubular or spherical flowers in spring or autumn. Height: to 60cm (24in). Family Hyacinthaceae/Liliaceae; species include *Muscari neglectum* (common grape hyacinth) and *Muscari comosum* (tassel hyacinth).

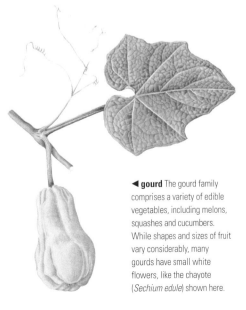

◀ **gourd** The gourd family comprises a variety of edible vegetables, including melons, squashes and cucumbers. While shapes and sizes of fruit vary considerably, many gourds have small white flowers, like the chayote (*Sechium edule*) shown here.

▲ **grape** There are more than 5000 varieties of the European wine grape (*Vitis vinifera*). The three standard grape wine colorations are white, red and rosé, depending on the grape used and whether, and for how long, the grape skins are left on. For white wine, the grapes are fermented without the skin; for red wine, the whole grape is used; for rosé wine, the skins are removed after fermentation has begun. Dry wines are fermented until all the sugar has turned to alcohol; sweet wines are fermented for less time so that some sugar remains. Champagne is bottled while it is still fermenting.

grape ivy
Vigorous, evergreen, climbing plant, which originates from the forest edges of tropical America. It is often grown as a houseplant. Its leaves, which consist of three diamond-shaped leaflets, are glossy green above, with red hairs beneath; forked tendrils grow from the branching stems. In summer it produces hairy green flowers, which are followed by blue-black berries. Height: to 3m (10ft). Family Vitaceae; species *Cissus rhombifolia*.

graphite (plumbago)
Dark grey, soft crystalline form of CARBON; it occurs naturally in deposits of varying purity and is made synthetically by heating petroleum coke. It is used in pencils (a mixture of graphite and clay is the "lead"), lubricants, electrodes, brushes of electrical machines, rocket nozzles and as a moderator to slow down neutrons in nuclear reactors. Graphite is a good conductor of heat and electricity. It owes its lubricating properties to overlapping scale-like crystals, which tend to slide, giving it a smooth, slippery feel. Properties: r.d. 2–2.25.

graptolite
Any of an extinct group of colonial, marine, drifting organisms. Graptolites are sometimes considered to belong to a separate phylum but they are also thought to be related to the CHORDATES. They are found most frequently as flattened fibres of carbon, resembling pencil marks, in black shales of the ORDOVICIAN and SILURIAN ages. Their uncompressed skeletons etched out of limestone show that graptolites were composed of many small tubes regularly arranged along branches, which are presumed to have been attached to a common bladder-like float. Graptolites first appeared in the Middle Cambrian and the last are known from the Lower Carboniferous. They are important zone fossils, used for correlating and dating rocks of the Lower Palaeozoic.

grass
Any one of about 8000 species of the class Monocotyledonae (see MONOCOTYLEDON). They are

G

G

nonwoody plants, with fibrous roots and long, narrow leaves enclosing hollow, jointed stems. The stems may be upright or bent, lie on the ground, or grow underground. The flowers are small, without PETALS and SEPALS. The leaves grow from the base, and so removal of the tips does not inhibit growth, making grass suitable for lawns and pastures. Cereal grasses, such as RICE, MILLET, MAIZE and WHEAT, are cultivated for their edible seeds. Others are grown as food for animals and for erosion control and ornament. Family Poaceae/Gramineae.

grasshopper

Plant-eating ORTHOPTERAN insect. Its enlarged hind legs make it a powerful jumper. The forewings are leathery, and the hind wings are membranous and fan-shaped; when the insect is at rest, the wings are folded over its back. Length: 8–11cm (3–4in). Order Orthoptera; families Acrididae and Tettingoniidae. *See also* LOCUST

grasshopper, short-horned

Grasshopper with short, heavy antennae. Several species are serious crop pests. The female lays eggs in the soil with her short OVIPOSITOR. The eggs usually overwinter and hatch in the following year. Family Acrididae; largest genus *Melanophus*.

grassland

Region of the world where the natural vegetation is dominated by plant species from the family Gramineae (GRASSES). While the rainfall in such areas is insufficient to permit forest growth, it is nevertheless heavy enough to prevent the development of deserts. There are two main types of grassland: the tropical grasslands or SAVANNA; and the temperate grasslands, which include the STEPPES, prairies and pampas.

grass of Parnassus (bog star)

Any member of a genus of *c.*15 species of herbaceous perennial plants found in boggy places of the Northern Hemisphere. These plants grow as rosettes of pale green, heart-shaped leaves. Each white, star-like flower is borne on a stem *c.*20cm (*c.*8in) tall in early summer. Family Parnassiaceae/Saxifragaceae; species include *Parnassia palustris*.

grass-pink

ORCHID that grows in boggy places of E North America. It consists of a single, lance-shaped leaf and flowering stalk, which appear from a rounded

▶ **grass** Meadow grass (*Poa pratensis*) is an important hay and green pasture grass in North America and Europe, and as such it is an economically valuable member of the large and widespread grass family. The flower of the grass is a minute spikelet, usually arranged in open branching clusters known as panicles. The flowers are cross-fertilized by the wind and the single ovule then develops into a seed or grain. Grassland will evolve readily wherever forest or scrub cover is sparse and where there are sufficient moisture and nutrients in the soil. Vast areas of the world are natural grasslands, such as the steppes of Asia and the North American prairies.

▲ **grasshopper** Because they have problems visually attracting mates in long grass, grasshoppers (order Orthoptera) seek partners using sound signals. By scraping a row of protruding pegs on the inside of each back leg against hardened ridges on their forewings, they make high-frequency mating calls. The calls, known as stridulation, vary from species to species depending on the number of pegs on each leg.

CORM in early summer. All the petals and sepals are pink to rose-purple, and the lip has a yellow beard. Family Orchidaceae; species *Calopogon pulchellus*.

grassquit

Small, gregarious BUNTING found in the Caribbean region and South America. The male black-faced grassquit (*Tiaris bicolor*) is all black; the females are olive-brown. It is an occasional stray to Florida from the West Indies in winter. Length: 11cm (4in). Family Emberizidae; genus *Tiaris*.

grass snake

See SNAKE, GRASS

grass tree

Any of 12 species of woody Australian plants belonging to the genus *Xanthorrhoea*. They are characterized by trunks that are thickened by old leaf bases. Grass trees are topped by tufts of long, narrow, strap-like leaves. The white flowers are borne in dense spikes above the leaves. The plants produce resins, which are used for varnishes and sizing paper. Height: to 4.5m (15ft). Family Liliaceae; species include *Xanthorrhoea australis*.

grasswren

Distinctive, very secretive and little-known Australian wren. It is mostly reddish-brown to cinnamon, or grey with long, white streaks; it often has black whisker marks and a long, erect tail. Five of the eight species of grasswren are endangered. Grasswrens are very difficult to see and scuttle off when disturbed. Length: 14–23cm (6–9in). Family Maluridae; genus *Amytornis*.

gravel

Mixed pebbles and rock fragments, 2mm to 60mm (0.1–3in) in diameter. Gravel beds are generally the remains of ancient seashores or river beds.

gravimetric analysis

See feature article

gravitational field

Region around an object that has mass in which there is an attractive force on any other object. The force divided by the mass of the second object is the gravitational field strength. A massive object has a powerful gravitational field. The attractive force around the Earth is called the force of gravity. Weak gravitational forces exist between even very small particles.

gravity

Gravitational force of attraction at the surface of a

planet or other celestial body. The Earth's gravity produces an acceleration of $9.8ms^{-2}$ ($32fts^{-2}$) for any unsupported body. If the mass M and radius R of a planet are known, the acceleration due to its gravity (g) at its surface can be determined from the equation $g = GM/R^2$, where G is the universal constant of gravitation. The weight of a body is a measure of the force with which the Earth's gravity attracts it. Unlike mass, which remains constant at normal speeds, weight (or the force of gravity) varies with altitude.

gravity anomaly

Deviation in GRAVITY from the expected value. Gravity measurements over deep ocean trenches are lower than average; those in mountainous regions are higher than average. Higher values are also found over deposits of dense minerals.

Gray, Asa (1810–88)

US botanist. He made many contributions to plant CLASSIFICATION. His donation of a valuable collection of books and plants to Harvard University in 1865 led to the establishment of its department of botany. His *Manual of Botany for the Northern United States* (1848) is considered a classic.

grayling

Freshwater food and sport fish of the SALMON family. It is found in N North America and Eurasia. The grayling is characterized by an unusually long and tall dorsal fin and a small mouth. Length: to 60cm (24in). Family Salmonidae; species include *Thymallus thymallus*.

grebe

Water bird that dives for fish. It uses its lobed toes to propel itself through the water. Some species of grebe are long-necked, others are small and dumpy. In flight they appear humpbacked. Grebes breed mostly on fresh water, sometimes in colonies, and often winter at sea. Length: 25–64cm (10–26in). Family Podicipedidae.

grebe, Atitlán

Large grebe. Its head and neck are almost black, and its heavy bill is white with a contrasting black band. It is an endangered species found only on Lake Atitlán, Guatemala. Length: 35–40cm (14–16in). Family Podicipedidae; species *Podilymbus gigas*.

grebe, great crested

Large grebe, the most common species in Europe and Asia. It has a dagger-like pink bill. Breeding adults have a double-horned crest and a neck ruff with chestnut tips. The feathers were once used to adorn hats, causing a dramatic decline in numbers. Length: 46–51cm (18–20in). Family Podicipedidae; species *Podiceps cristatus*.

grebe, little (dabchick)

One of the smallest species of grebe. In summer it has distinctive chestnut cheeks, with a white patch at the base of the bill. Its dumpy shape and blunt rear-end is characteristic. The little grebe's song is a whinnying trill. It is found on rivers, lakes and small ponds. Length: 25–29cm (10–11in). Family Podicipedidae; species *Tachybaptus ruficollis*.

grebe, pied-billed

Small grebe from North and Central America. The breeding adult is mostly brown, with a black chin and throat and a black ring round its stout, whitish bill. It hides from intruders by sinking into the water until only its head shows. The pied-billed grebe occasion-

ally strays across the Atlantic Ocean to W Europe. Length: 34cm (13in). Family Podicipedidae; species *Podilymbus podiceps*.

grebe, Slavonian (horned grebe)
Grebe that is distinctive for its chestnut golden "horns". It has a short, straight bill, red neck and black ruffed throat. In winter it is mostly black and white. The Slavonian grebe breeds on sheltered lakes and ponds and winters along coasts. Length: 34cm (13in). Family Podicipedidae; species *Podiceps auritus*.

grebe, western
Large grebe that is found in North America. It is strikingly black and white, with a swan-like neck and a long, thin, dagger-shaped, yellow-green bill. It has a black cap, which extends below the eye, and a white throat and neck. Its spectacular courtship display involves scampering across the water to exchange nest material with its partner. Length: 64cm (25in). Family Podicipedidae; species *Aechmophorus occidentalis*.

grebe, red-necked
Large, solitary grebe, with a heavy, tapered bill. Its summer plumage is white cheeks and throat and a reddish-chestnut neck. It breeds mainly in E Europe, parts of Asia and N North America. Length: 40–50cm (16–20in). Family Podicipedidae; species *Podiceps grisegena*.

green alga
See CHLOROPHYTE

green belt
Area of open land maintained as a barrier between adjoining built-up areas. Green belts provide insulation from factories and intensive commercial areas. They are a source of recreational space and aid in the replenishment of atmospheric oxygen.

greenbottle
True FLY, a member of the BLUEBOTTLE family. The larvae live in carrion and dung; they sometimes live in wounds on sheep and other animals, and can be a veterinary pest. The fly's thorax and abdomen are a bluish-green to emerald colour. Adult body length: 8–10mm (0.3–0.4in). Order Diptera; family Calliphoridae; species *Lucilia ceasar*.

greenbrier
Any of *c*.200 species of tropical, woody or herbaceous, vine-like plants belonging to the genus *Smilax*. Its thorny stem, with string-like tendrils, grows from fleshy tuberous roots. The greenbrier is DIOECIOUS, meaning that male flowers are borne on one plant and female on another. On female plants, berries follow the clusters of flowers. Greenbriers are the source of sarsaparilla, which is used in medicine and as a flavouring. Family Liliaceae; species include *Smilax rotundifolia*.

greenfinch
Any of several species of songbird of the genus *Carduelis*. The European Greenfinch is Europe's largest songbird. It is yellow-green, with bright yellow wing patches. Length: 14cm (6in). Family Carduelidae; species *Carduelis chloris*. Other greenfinches occur in China and central Asia, including the grey-capped (Oriental) greenfinch, which is mainly dark grey, with yellow wing-patches. It strays to the Alaskan mainland. Length: 15cm (6in). Family Carduelidae; species *Carduelis sinica*.

▲ **grayling** Male graylings are more colourful than females and during spawning the dorsal, caudal and anal fins become deep purple in colour. Shown here is the common European grayling (*Thymallus thymallus*).

greenfly
See APHID

greengage
Variety of PLUM tree and its spherical, green fruit. A small tree, it has pointed, oval leaves and flat, white, five-petalled flowers. The fruit has sweet flesh and a large stone. Greengages, plums and DAMSONS originated in antiquity in the Middle East from crosses between the BLACKTHORN and the CHERRY plum. Height: to 7m (23ft). Family Rosaceae; species *Prunus x domestica*.

greenhouse effect
Raised temperature at a planet's surface as a result of heat energy being trapped by gases in the atmosphere. Certain gases cause the atmosphere to act like the glass in a greenhouse. As a result, the temperature of a planet's surface may be higher than it otherwise would be – on Earth about 33°C (59°F) higher. The main gases that produce the greenhouse effect on Earth are water vapour and CARBON DIOXIDE. Scientists suspect that increased discharge of carbon dioxide from human activity (notably gasoline-powered car engines and industry) is contributing to GLOBAL WARMING.

greenhouse gases
Gases that enhance the GREENHOUSE EFFECT; they include CARBON DIOXIDE, METHANE, nitrous oxide, OZONE, WATER VAPOUR and CHLOROFLUOROCARBONS (CFCs). Carbon dioxide is the most important single greenhouse gas and much of it is produced by human activity. Methane is 30 times more powerful and CFCs are 10,000 times more powerful than carbon dioxide in contributing to the greenhouse effect, but they are present in much smaller volumes in the atmosphere. *See also* GLOBAL WARMING

greenleaf worm
Predacious marine POLYCHAETE that lives on rocky shores. It is often sighted among seaweed near to barnacle beds. Length: *c*.100mm (*c*.14in). Phylum Annelida; class Polychaeta; order Phyllodocida; family Phyllodocidae; species *Eulalia viridis*.

greenlet
Very small, warbler-like songbird of the VIREO family. It lacks any distinctive plumage features. It is mainly olive-brown or olive-green, with a longer, more curved bill than most warblers. The greenlet is found in humid rainforests from S Mexico to the Amazon basin. Length: 9–11cm (4in). Family Vireonidae; genus *Hylophilus*.

grenadier (rattail)
Marine fish related to the cod, belonging to the order Gadiformes. The grenadier is characterized by an elongate, tapered tail. It is found near the bottom in virtually all oceans; it is most abundant between 200 and 2000 metres. A few species are the basis for a small deepwater fishery in the Bering Sea, N Pacific and N Atlantic oceans. Family Macrouridae.

GRAVIMETRIC ANALYSIS

In geology, study of the magnitude of the Earth's GRAVITATIONAL FIELD in a particular area. Small variations in the gravitational field can be caused by the density of the rocks beneath the surface and can provide information about structures that are otherwise inaccessible. The instrument used for such a survey is known as a gravimeter. In chemistry, gravimetric analysis is a method of determining the composition of a substance by making weighings.

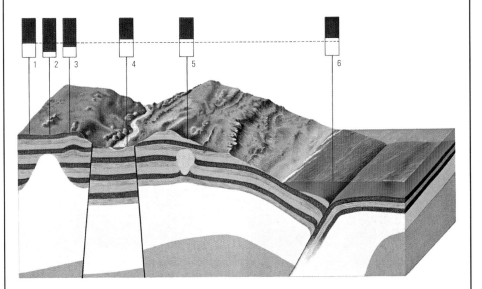

▲ **Underground rock formations** can be detected by measuring the local variations in the pull of gravity on a delicate balance called a gravimeter. The lighter the

material the weaker the pull.
KEY
1) Normal gravity reading
2) Heavy igneous material near surface gives high reading

3) Anticline gives gravity high
4) Rift valley where lighter surface material continues to a greater depth gives gravity low

5) Salt dome or upward emplacement of light material giving gravity low
6) Oceanic trough where lighter crustal material deep in mantle gives gravity low

G

greylag goose
See GOOSE, GREYLAG

grey matter
Darker-coloured nerve tissue that forms the cerebral cortex of the BRAIN and is also present in the spinal cord. It is distinct from the so-called white matter, which contains more nerve fibres and larger quantities of the whitish insulating material called MYELIN.

greywacke
Any variety of SANDSTONE that consist of a mixture of rock fragments, FELDSPAR and QUARTZ, strongly bonded together in a mud matrix. They are characterized by poor sorting of angular or sub-angular particles. They are often interpreted as indicating short-distance, rapid-sediment deposition.

gribble
Any member of the genus *Limnoria*, comprising marine, ISOPOD crustaceans related to the WOODLOUSE. Gribbles bore into the wood of piers and jetties, causing considerable damage. Family Limnoriidae; genus *Limnoria*; there are *c*.20 species

grike (gryke)
In an area of bare LIMESTONE, enlarged vertical crack formed by solution along JOINTS. The resulting limestone blocks are called CLINTS and the two features together form a limestone pavement.

grit
Coarse SANDSTONE. It is usually formed in a river delta where material eroded from a landmass has been deposited rapidly before the fragments have been rounded or sorted. The Upper Carboniferous deltas left thick beds of grit in many areas of the British Isles.

gritstone
Medium- to coarse-grained SEDIMENTARY ROCK with angular grains that may rub off easily. Most gritstones are formed in water. The chief mineral components are QUARTZ, FELDSPAR and MICA. Those with more than 75% quartz are called **quartz gritstone**, whereas more than 25% feldspar gives rise to **feldspathic gritstone**; the former has an orange colour and the latter is brown, sometimes tinged with pink.

grizzly bear
See BEAR, GRIZZLY

grooming
Behaviour pattern of self-cleaning of the body surface, usually stereotyped, practised by many animals. Mutual grooming, such as fur grooming among monkeys and apes, serves to cement pair-bonding and social bonds in groups.

grosbeak
Any of several large, stocky, boldly coloured finches. Their heavy triangular bills are adapted to eating fruits and nuts and to cracking seeds. The evening grosbeak (*Coccothraustes vespertinus*) is strikingly black and yellow, with white wing bars. The pine grosbeak (*Pinicola enucleator*) is greenish; the males are tinged pink in spring. Length: 20cm (8in) Family Fringillidae.

ground bug
Ground-dwelling BUG that feeds mainly on seeds; it has a distinctly triangular scutellum (part of the thorax). Mainly dull-coloured, the ground bug's body is elongated and tough. Some species are ant mimics. A few species are plant feeders; the chinch bug (*Blissus leucopterus*) is a serious pest of grain crops in the United States. Adult body length: 2–18mm (0.08–0.7in). Order Hemiptera; family Lygaeidae; genera include *Nysius*, *Drymus* and *Heterogaster*.

ground elder (goutweed, bishop's-weed)
Invasive perennial plant that grows from very deep roots throughout the woodlands of Europe, Siberia and w Asia; it has been naturalized in North America. Its leaves have three oval leaflets, and it has umbrella-like flowerheads (umbels) of tiny white flowers. It has been used as a medicinal and edible herb. Family Apiaceae/Umbelliferae; species *Aegopodium podagraria*.

groundhog
See WOODCHUCK

groundhopper
Drab-coloured insect that resembles a locust but has a pronotum (cover of the prothorax) that covers its abdomen. Its forewings are reduced and its hind-wings well developed. The groundhopper is found in moist woodlands and lake margins. Some species are semiaquatic. Groundhoppers are active all year round in the sunshine. They eat moss and small plants. Adult body length: 6–18mm (0.2–0.7in). Order Orthoptera; family Tetrigidae; genus *Tetrix*.

ground ivy
Any of *c*.12 species of creeping perennial plants, belonging to the genus *Glechoma*. Ground ivy grows from RHIZOMES or STOLONS in the woodlands of Europe. Pairs of toothed leaves grow along the stems, which root at intervals. The tiny flowers, which are two-lipped and violet-blue, appear in the summer. Variegated forms of ground ivy are often grown in gardens for ground cover. Family Labiatae/Lamiaceae; species include *Glechoma hederacea*.

groundnut
See PEANUT

ground-roller
Any of four species of forest birds found in Madagascar. Ground-rollers are rather slow-moving birds, which hunt on the forest floor for lizards and invertebrates. They are secretive and rather hard to observe. Length: *c*.30cm (*c*.12in). Family Coraciidae; genera *Atelornis* and *Brachypteracias*.

groundwater
Water that lies beneath the surface of the Earth. The water comes chiefly from rain, although some is of volcanic or sedimentary origin. Groundwater moves through porous rocks and soil and can be collected in wells. Groundwater can dissolve minerals from the rocks and leave deposits in other places, creating such structures as CAVES, STALAGMITES, STALACTITES, and cavities called SINK HOLES. *See also* WATER TABLE

ground pine
Small, hairy, annual plant that grows in stony ground of Europe and Asia. It resembles, in appearance and smell, a pine seedling, with its dense leaves divided into needle-like lobes. It produces yellow flowers with red spots. Family Labiatae; species *Ajuga chamaepitys*.

groundsel
Annual plant that is a common weed of gardens and waste ground. It has reddish stems and long, lobed, stemless leaves, which are bright green above and paler beneath. The yellow flowers resemble daisies without the outer ray florets, and the seeds are attached to feathery "parachutes". Groundsel is used in herbal medicine. Height: *c*.30cm (*c*.12in). Family Compositae; species *Senecio vulgaris*.

grouper
Tropical marine fish found from the coast of Florida, United States, to South America, and in the Indian and Pacific oceans. It has a large mouth, sharp teeth, a mottled body and the ability to change colour. Length: to 3.7m (12ft); weight: to 450kg (1000lb). Family Serranidae; species include *Epinephelus itajara* (giant grouper) and *Epinephelus lanceolatus* (Australian grouper).

◄ **grooming** A family of pygmy chimpanzees (*Pan paniscus*) indulges in mutual grooming in the lowland forests of central Democratic Republic of Congo. The chimpanzees groom each other more often than is necessary simply for the removal of dirt. Grooming is a vital means of confirming the social relationships and hierarchies within a group.

grouse
Game bird with a short, thick bill, short wings and direct, whirring flight. It differs from PARTRIDGES and PHEASANTS in its feathered legs and nostrils. Some species are specialized for life in Arctic prairies and tundra; others are adapted to live in heathland or the dense scrub layer beneath woodlands. Family Phasianidae.

grouse, red
Grouse that is found on heather moors of Britain and Ireland. It was once thought to be a separate species but is now considered an all-dark race of the willow grouse. It never turns white in winter. A much prized game bird, the red grouse is raised on upland estates for hunting. Length: 37–42cm (15–17in). Family Phasianidae; species *Lagopus lagopus;* subspecies *scotica.*

grouse, black
Grouse that is found on moors and woodland edges. The male, known as a blackcock, is a large, black bird, with a lyre-shaped tail and white wing bars. The female, or greyhen, is much smaller, with a forked tail. Displaying males congregate at "leks" to attract a mate. Length: 40–55cm (16–22in). Family Phasianidae; species *Tetrao tetrix.*

grouse, ruffed
Common North American grouse found in woodland areas. The male has a black ruff on the side of its neck and a many-banded tail with a wide brown band near the tip. Males attract females by raising their ruffs and fanning their tails. Length: 42cm (17in). Family Phasianidae; species *Bonasa umbellus.*

grouse, spruce
North American grouse. The male has a dark throat and a white-edged breast; the red combs on the top of its head are raised in display. Females may be reddish or grey and are heavily barred and spotted. Spruce grouse are often seen perching in trees. Length: 40cm (16in). Family Phasianidae; species *Dendragapus canadensis.*

growth
Process by which an organism increases in size and mass. It involves CELL DIVISION or enlargement, or both.

growth curve
Line produced when any parameter of GROWTH (such as mass, height, volume) is measured against set intervals of time. For many populations, organisms or organs, the growth curve is S-shaped and is called a sigmoid curve. It represents an initial slow growth rate, followed by a rapid growth phase that then slows; it culminates in an equilibrium, where new cells/numbers exactly balance those being lost/dying and there is, therefore, no net growth. This basic sigmoid curve is modified in certain organisms. In humans, for example, there are two rapid phases – one for the first eighteen months of life, the second in adolescence. Many perennial plants never reach a maximum size but grow continually throughout their lives.

growth ring
See ANNUAL RING

groyne
Artificial dam of rocks or wooden pilings that juts out from a beach face, built in an attempt to combat LONGSHORE DRIFT. Groynes are now considered a less effective and more expensive way of maintaining beaches than a beach-nourishment programme, in which material swept along the beach is replaced by new material.

grunion
Small marine fish found on the Pacific coast of the United States, mainly off California. It is known for its habit of swimming onto sandy beaches at night during spring tides to spawn. The grunion is the basis for a small recreational fishery. Family Atherinidae; species *Leuresthes tenuis.*

grunt
Fish that is commonly found in shoals on coral reefs. It makes sounds by grinding its throat teeth, with an air bladder acting as a resonator. There are marine and brackish species, and they are found in the Atlantic, Indian and Pacific oceans. Many of the species are striped. They mostly feed on bottom-dwelling invertebrates. Family Haemulidae.

gryke
See GRIKE

grysbuck
Shy, nocturnal, dwarf ANTELOPE found in dense thicket in Africa. There are two species, both of which are red-brown with white guard hairs that give a grizzled appearance. Males have short, vertical horns. Head-body length: 61–75cm (24–30in); tail: 5–7cm (2–3in). Family Bovidae; subfamily Antilopinae; genus *Raphicerus.*

guan
Medium-sized bird found in Central and South American tropical forests. It is green, brown or greyish, with brownish-red or coppery markings. It feeds mainly on fruit. Family Cracidae.

guanaco
Large species of LLAMA. It is native to the Andean foothills and the pampas of South America. A New World relative of the CAMEL, the guanaco is used as a beast of burden. It has a brown, soft, woolly coat and grey head. Height: up to 110cm (43in) at the shoulder. Family Camelidae; species *Lama guanicoe.*

guanine
One of the nitrogen-containing bases in DNA and RNA. Guanine is a derivative of PURINE and in DNA

◄ **guava** The fruit of the tropical American tree (*Psidium guajava*) is high in vitamin C. It is most commonly made into guava jelly, but it can also be stewed and canned.

is always paired with the pyrimidine derivative CYTOSINE. *See* BASE PAIR

guano
Dried excrement of seabirds and bats. Containing phosphorous, nitrogen and potassium, it is a natural fertilizer. Guano is found mainly on certain coastal islands off South America and Africa, and on some Pacific islands.

guarana
Climbing, fruit-bearing plant native to the Amazon basin. Locally, the fruit is prized for its single seed, which is roasted, ground and dissolved in water. Guarana's stimulant properties have become well-known in the West, where it is marketed in the form of soft drinks, tablets and chewing gum. Family Sapindaceae; species *Paullinia cupana.*

guard cell
Crescent-shaped, specialized epidermal cell. Guard cells occur in pairs on aerial parts of plants. They surround an opening called the stomatal aperture. Unlike other epidermal cells, guard cells possess CHLOROPLASTS and have denser CYTOPLASM, with a more prominent NUCLEUS. The inner walls of the cells are thicker and less elastic than the outer ones. The osmotic uptake of water causes the volume of the guard cells to increase and bend, due to the uneven thickening of their walls, making the stomatal aperture increase in size. Alterations in the turgidity of the guard cells, therefore, open and close the stomatal aperture thus controlling the uptake of carbon dioxide and the loss of water by the plant.

guava
Fruit of a tender evergreen shrub from Brazil. Guavas are large, oval or pear-shaped berries with yellow skin. The pinkish, sharply sweet flesh is full of seeds. The trees have been cultivated for *c.*1000 years and are

G

► **guanaco** Commonly found on mountain slopes, guanacos (*Lama guanicoe*) live in small herds of four to ten females led by a male. Females bear young every other year. Like its close relation the camel, the guanaco has a three-chambered stomach. It can also lift two legs on the same side of the body simultaneously. It spits when angry. As a result of adaptation to a high-altitude environment, the guanaco has more red corpuscles than other mammals.

grown throughout tropical America and parts of Europe. Family Myrtaceae; species *Psidium guajava*.

guayule
Sunflower-like herb from sw United States and N Mexico. In the early 20th century it was cultivated for rubber production. Modern research is trying to improve the yields for commercial use. Height: *c*.1m (*c*.3.3ft) Family Compositae; species *Parthenium argentatum*.

gudgeon
Freshwater CARP found in rivers from Britain to China. It has an elongated body and a small mouth with barbels. Gudgeons can be various colours. Length: 20cm (8in). Family Cyprinidae; species *Gobio gobio*.

guillemot
Short-necked, black-and-white, diving seabird, belonging to the AUK family. Its legs are set well back, giving it a shuffling gait on land. Its wings are short and narrow, and its flight is whirring, direct and low over the water. Guillemots are sometimes called the "penguins" of the Northern Hemisphere. Family Alcidae.

guillemot, black
Seabird that is all black in summer, with large, white upper wing patches and bright red legs. In winter it is the only seabird with barred black and white upper parts. The black guillemot is the least sociable of the auks, nesting in solitary pairs or loose colonies. Length: 30cm (12in). Family Alcidae; species *Cepphus grylle*.

guillemot, common (murre guillemot)
Most common species of auk. It has a dagger-like bill. Its head, neck and upper breast are dark brown and its lower breast and belly are white. It nests in huge colonies on narrow cliff ledges. The common auk lays a single, pear-shaped egg. Length: 40cm (16in). Family Alcidae; species *Uria aalge*.

guineafowl
Very large, plump, short-tailed, gregarious game bird. It is found in dry scrub and forest edges in Africa. It has short wings, which produce the whirring direct flight that is typical of game birds. Family Numididae.

guineafowl, helmeted
Ancestor of the domesticated guineafowl. Its plumage is grey, mottled with white spots; the sides of its head are featherless and bluish, with red wattles at the base of the bill and an erect brown horny crest. Length: 60–65cm (24–26in). Family Numididae; species *Numida meleagris*.

guineafowl, vulturine
Long-legged guineafowl. Its grey body has white streaks, with long, white-streaked feathers on its neck and upper breast. The face is featherless and blue, with red wattles at the back of the head. Length: 60cm (24in). Family Numididae; species *Acryllium vulturinum*.

guinea pig
Type of CAVY found in South America. The domestic *Cavia porcellus* is a popular pet. It has a large head, soft fur, short legs and no tail. It eats grass and other green plants. *Cavia aperea* is a wild species. Family Caviidae.

Guinea worm
NEMATODE worm that is transmitted by an aquatic COPEPOD which may be inadvertently drunk in India, Pakistan and parts of Africa. Infection by the Guinea worm results in the formation of nodules, which may cause severe pain, on the lower legs. Phylum Nematoda; species *Dracunculiasis medinensis*

guitarfish
Marine, and sometimes estuarine, elasmobranch (SHARK relative) of the Atlantic, Indian and Pacific oceans. It has a flattened body form, intermediate between a shark and a skate, and two large dorsal fins. It feeds on bottom-dwelling invertebrates and small fish. Length: 1.5–2m (5–6.6ft). Family Rhinobatidae.

Gulf Stream
Relatively fast-moving current of the N Atlantic Ocean. It flows from the straits of Florida, along the E coast of North America, then E across the Atlantic Ocean (at which point it is known as the **North Atlantic Drift**) to the NW European coast. It was long considered to be one wide mass of water, but research now indicates that it is made up of many thin streams that cause local variations in the water temperature. The current has a warming effect on the coastal climates along its course.

▶ **gull, herring** This abundant species of gull (*Larus argentatus*) is often seen following fishing boats, but it never flies far away from the coast. It is a scavenger bird and will eat almost any organic matter, so is also found near rubbish dumps. The herring gull nests in large colonies, usually on cliffs.

gull (seagull)
Any member of a family of seabirds found worldwide. They are mainly found in coastal regions, but some species breed far inland. Most gulls have white bodies, grey to blackish backs, and wings with black wing tips. Some species have a dark brown hood in breeding plumage. They nest in noisy colonies. Family Laridae.

gull, common (mew gull)
Gull that, despite its name, is not the most common gull in America and Europe. It has a white body and a dark grey back. Its wings have white spots ("mirrors") on the black wing tips. Its bill and legs are yellow-green. The gull's usual call is a weak, cat-like "*mew*". Length: 42cm (17in). Family Laridae; species *Larus canus*.

gull, great black-backed
One of the largest species of gull. Its huge size, massive bill and black back and wings are distinctive. Its flight is heavy and ponderous. It takes from three to four years to become adult. The great black-backed gull is found in Europe and E North America. It is more solitary than other gulls and predates other gull colonies. Length: 64–78cm (25–31in). Family Laridae; species *Larus marinus*.

gull, herring
Large gull, the most common species in North America and Europe. It is variable in colour and size, with the males larger than the females. Typically, it has a white body, slate grey back and wings with white-spotted black tips. Its legs are pink and its bill yellow with a red spot. The herring gull breeds in colonies. Length: 52–60cm (20–24in). Family Laridae; species *Larus argentatus*.

gull, ivory
Pure white gull. It has a plump body and rather short wings. Young birds are white with small black spots. It often flies with its black feet hanging down. The ivory gull breeds in the Arctic and winters near the edge of pack ice. Length: 42cm (17in). Family Laridae; species *Pagophila eburnea*.

gull, silver
Common and familiar gull of Australia and New Zealand. It is white with a pale silver-grey back; its wings have white-spotted black tips. The bill, eye-ring and legs are scarlet. The silver gull has adapted to urban areas and scavenges on rubbish tips and at fishing ports. Length: 38–43cm (15–17in). Family Laridae; species *Larus novaehollandiae*.

gull, laughing
Gull that breeds in central North America and winters south along the coasts from Panama to Chile. It regularly strays across the Atlantic Ocean to Europe. The breeding adult has a black hood and white underparts; it has slate grey wings, with a white bar and black-and-white tips. Length: 38cm (15in). Family Laridae; species *Larus atricilla*.

gull, little
Smallest species of gull. In summer it has a black hood, white body and pale grey back and wings. Its under wing is strikingly dark grey. Young birds have a diagonal dark wing bar. It is a summer visitor to central Eurasia, breeding on freshwater marshes; it winters at sea. Length: 26cm (10in). Family Laridae; species *Larus minimus*.

gull, ring-billed
Gull that is similar to the common gull, but with

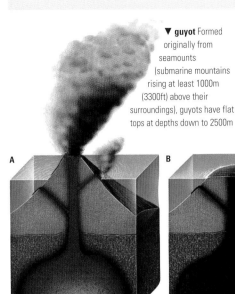

▼ **guyot** Formed originally from seamounts (submarine mountains rising at least 1000m (3300ft) above their surroundings), guyots have flat tops at depths down to 2500m (8200ft). These tops are often much too large to be explained as ancient craters filled to the rim by sediment and other material. It has been proposed that guyots were originally volcanoes above sea level (A),, which after extinction were,

over many years, worn flat by the action of waves (B) and which then sunk as the sea level rose or as the sea bed subsided (C). This theory has subsequently been confirmed by the presence of beach pebbles.

darker grey back and wings and yellow legs and bill. In adults, the bill has a black ring near the tip. It is common throughout North America and is now regularly recorded in w Europe. Length: 42cm (17in). Family Laridae; species *Larus delawarensis*.

gull, California

Common gull of w North America. It winters south to the Pacific coast of Guatemala. The California gull is midway in size between the herring gull and the ring-billed gull. It is dark grey with greenish-yellow legs. As with other large gulls, it takes four years to become adult. Length: 53cm (21in). Family Laridae; species *Larus californicus*.

gull, glaucous

Large, heavy-bodied gull. It has a pale grey back and translucent white wing tips. The glaucous gull takes four years to reach maturity, and during the second and third years its plumage is uniformly ghostly white. It has a heavy predatory bill. The glaucous gull breeds along Arctic coasts and winters south to the coasts of N North America and Europe. Length: 62–68cm (24–27in). Family Laridae; species *Larus hyperboreus*.

gum

Secretions of some plants. Some gums are soluble in water; others absorb water and swell. Gums are chemically complex, consisting mainly of various saccharides bound to organic acids. Common examples are GUM ARABIC, agar and tragacanth. Many substances of similar appearance, such as some RESINS, are classed as gums.

gum arabic

Gum obtained from some species of ACACIA tree, especially the gum arabic tree (*Acaci senegal*) found in North Africa. It is used in making adhesives, in confectionery and medicine.

gumtree

Any of more than 500 species belonging to the *Eucalyptus* genus, native to Australia. However, only those species with smooth bark are correctly termed gumtrees. They shed their old bark in long, narrow strips every season; the smooth new bark beneath can be ghostly white, coloured or richly patterned. The resin that some gumtrees exude from damaged bark is used in medicine and in the leather industry. Family Myrtaceae; genus *Eucalyptus*.

gundi

Any member of four genera of small rodents that live in desert regions of North Africa. They have short legs, blunt heads, large eyes and small, rounded ears. Diurnal or crepuscular in habit, they feed on all parts of desert plants. Head-body length: *c*.17cm (*c*.7in); tail: 3–6cm (1–2in). Family Ctenodactylidae.

guppy

Small, freshwater fish native to NE South America and the West Indies. It is a a popular aquarium fish. The male is smaller and brighter in colour than the female. The females breed live young at monthly intervals. They feed on mosquito larvae and algae. Length: up to 6cm (2.5in). Family Poeciliidae; species *Lebistes reticulatis*.

gurnard (gurnet)

Tropical, marine, bottom-dwelling fish. It has a large spiny head and enlarged pectoral fins. It is related to the SEA ROBIN. Length: to 50cm (20in). Family Triglidae.

gurnet

See GURNARD

gutta-percha

Deciduous tree native to the woodlands of China. It is grown in gardens for its rounded shape and glossy green leaves, which, when torn, exude a rubbery LATEX (gutta-percha) in strands. The spring flowers are green and inconspicuous. Height: to 12m (40ft). Family Eucommiaceae; species *Eucommia ulmoides*.

guyot (tablemount)

Flat-topped, submarine mountains. Guyots rise 1000m (3300ft), with tops about 2.5km (1.5mi) below sea level. Before becoming submerged, they are believed to have been volcanic islands with peaks flattened by wave erosion. If so, this is evidence for the subsiding of the SEAFLOOR.

gymnosperm

See CONIFEROPHYTE

gynoecium

Collective name for the female elements of a FLOWER. The gynoecium is composed of a flower's CARPELS, consisting of the STIGMA, STYLE and OVARY. *See also* ANDROECIUM

gypsophila

Any of more than 100 species belonging to the *Gypsophila* genus of herbaceous or evergreen perennials. They grow on dry stony slopes from the Mediterranean region across Asia to NW China. Gypsophilas bear large numbers of small, five-petalled, star-shaped, white or pink flowers. They are grown as border plants or for cut flowers. Family Caryophyllaceae; species include *Gypsophila paniculata* (baby's breath).

gypsum

Most common sulphate mineral, hydrated calcium sulphate ($CaSO_4.2H_2O$). It is formed by precipitation from evaporating seawater. Huge beds of gypsum occur in SEDIMENTARY ROCKS, where it is associated with HALITE. It can be clear, white or tinted. It crystallizes in the monoclinic system as prismatic or bladed CRYSTALS. Varieties are alabaster (massive), selenite (transparent and foliated) and satinspar (silky and fibrous). Gypsum is a source of plaster of Paris. Hardness 2; r.d. 2.3.

gyres

Large scale and permanent circulation of surface water in the three major oceans; it is controlled by prevailing winds and the CORIOLIS EFFECT. Gyres circulate clockwise in the Northern Hemisphere and anticlockwise in the Southern Hemisphere.

gyrfalcon

See FALCON, GYR

H

habitat
Place in which an organism normally lives. A habitat is defined by characteristic physical conditions and the presence of other organisms.

hackberry
North American tree found from Nova Scotia south to Florida and west to Texas; it is related to the ELM. Tolerant of city conditions, the hackberry is often planted as a shade or ornamental tree. Its timber is used for fences and furniture. Height: to 36m (120ft). Family Ulmaceae; species *Celtis occidentalis.*

haddock
Marine fish found in cold and temperate waters, mainly in the Northern Hemisphere. It is dark grey and silver, with a dark blotch near the pectoral fins. Length: to *c.*90cm (*c.*36in); weight: to 11kg (24lb). Family Gadidae; species *Melanogrammus aeglefinus.*

Hadley cell
Atmospheric circulation cell, named after the British meteorologist George Hadley (1685–1768). Hadley proposed it (1735) to explain the TRADE WINDS, in which winds rise and flow polewards from the Equator and then descend and flow back towards the Equator, transferring heat by CONVECTION. *See also* FERREL CELL

hadrosaurid
Any member of a group of large two- or four-legged, plant-eating, ORNITHOPOD dinosaurs such as *Hadrosaurus.* They evolved in mid-Cretaceous times and died out at the end of the period along with the other remaining DINOSAURS. Hadrosaurids were characterized by horny beaks for browsing vegetation and batteries of cheek teeth for chewing it prior to digestion.

haematite (hematite)
One of the most important iron ores, containing mainly ferric oxide (Fe_2O_3). Containing 70% iron by weight, it occurs in several forms, frequently in small dome-shaped masses called **kidney-ore**. Haematite varies in colour from steel-grey to black, but sometimes red. Deposits are found on all continents. Hardness 5–6; r.d. 4.9–5.3.

haemoglobin
Protein present in ERYTHROCYTES (red blood cells) of

▲ **haddock** One of the mainstay species of the world's commercial fish catch, the haddock is found in cold and temperate waters of the Northern Hemisphere. One of the best fishing areas for this member of the cod family lies off the coast of New England, United States.

vertebrates. Haemoglobin carries oxygen to all cells in the body. It is scarlet when combined with oxygen to form OXYHAEMOGLOBIN and bluish-red when deoxygenated. Oxygen attaches to the haem– part of the protein, which contains iron; the –globin part is a globular PROTEIN. Worn-out erythrocytes are destroyed by the liver, and the iron is used again to make more haemoglobin. *See also* BLOOD

hagfish (slime eel)
Eel-like, primitive, jawless fish found in temperate to cold marine waters. It has under-developed eyes and four to six fleshy whiskers around its sucking mouth. A scavenger, it feeds on dead or dying fish. It secretes a slimy mucus from pores along its sides. Length: to 80cm (31in). Family Myxinidae.

hail
PRECIPITATION from clouds in the form of balls of ice. Hailstorms are associated with atmospheric turbulence extending to great heights together with warm, moist air nearer the ground. Hailstones are usually less than 1cm (0.4in) across but some have exceeded 13cm (5in).

hair
Outgrowth of mammalian SKIN; it has insulating, protective and sensory functions. In MAMMALS, a thick coating of hair is usually called FUR. Hair grows in a FOLLICLE, a tubular structure extending down through the EPIDERMIS to the upper DERMIS. New cells are continually added to the base of the hair; older hair cells become impregnated with KERATIN and die. A muscle attached to the base of the hair allows it to become erect in response to nerve signals sent to the follicle. Erecting the hairs traps a thicker layer of air close to the skin. There are about one million hairs on the head of an average person. Each hair grows about 5–10mm (0.2–0.4in) a month; it grows for about three years before falling out and being replaced. *See also* CILIA

hairy-back (gastrotrich)
Any of *c* 450 species of small, unsegmented, worm-like animals that swim by virtue of the CILIA on their epidermis. They are so named because the CUTICLE is often covered in bristles. Hairy-backs lack circulatory and respiratory systems. Phylum Gastrotricha.

hake
Relative of the COD found in temperate waters of the Atlantic and Pacific oceans. The hake is silver and brown and is an economically important food fish. Length: to 1m (3.3ft); weight: to 14kg (30lb). Family Gadidae or Merluccidae; species include *Merluccius bilinearis* (Atlantic hake) and *Merluccius productus* (Pacific hake).

Haldane, John Burdon Sanderson (1892–1964)
British scientist whose work formed the basis of the mathematical study of population genetics. His book *The Causes of Evolution* (1933) examined the theory of NATURAL SELECTION in the light of modern genetic research. In 1932 he was the first to estimate the mutation rate of a human gene. His *Daedalus, or*

Science and the Future (1924) was an early attempt to popularize science.

halfbeak
Any of *c.*70 species of marine and freshwater fish belonging to the family Hemiramphidae. Marine species are found in the Atlantic, Indian and Pacific oceans. Freshwater species are found in Neotropical (that is, North and South America south of the Tropic of Cancer) and Indo-Australian regions. Halfbeaks are silver, slender fish, characterized by an upper jaw that is much shorter than the lower jaw. They are related to FLYING FISH. Family Hemiramphidae.

halibut
FLATFISH found worldwide in deep, cold to temperate seas. It is brownish on the eye side and white below. Family Pleuronectidae; species include *Hippoglossus hippoglossus* (Atlantic halibut) and *Hippoglossus stenolepis* (giant Pacific halibut).

halite
Mineral form of sodium chloride (NaCl), or common (rock) salt. It is found in evaporite SEDIMENTARY ROCKS, in association with gypsum and in salt domes and dried lakes. It is colourless, white, orange or grey, with a glassy lustre. It has a cubic system of interlocking cubic crystals, granules and masses. It is important as table salt and as a source of CHLORINE. Hardness 2.5; r.d. 2.2.

halobacterium
BACTERIUM that is adapted to live under high salt conditions. It has a rhodopsin pigment system, which causes reddening of salted foods and explains the red colour of water during the manufacture of salt from sea water. They are found in salt lakes such as the Dead Sea and Great Salt Lake. Examples include *Halobacterium* and *Halococcus.*

halophyte
Any plant, usually an ANGIOSPERM (flowering plant), able to live in a salty environment. Typical examples include MANGROVE trees and SEA LAVENDER.

Hamilton, William D. (1936–)
New Zealand geneticist. Hamilton developed a theory that sought to explain the evolution of ALTRUISM in animals in terms of Darwinian NATURAL SELECTION. He theorized that if an organism sacrificed itself to save its relatives, it was doing so to ensure that at least some of its own GENE variants, or ALLELES, were passed on to the following generation. The success with which an individual's alleles are passed on is called **inclusive fitness**. His theories were taken up by Richard DAWKINS.

hammerkop
Small HERON with all-brown plumage. It is unusual in appearance, with a large, hammer-shaped head, a heavy bill and a blunt crest on the back of its head. The hammerkop is often seen hunched, standing still or running with jabbing movements in shallow water to catch small fish. It breeds mostly in Africa. Length: 60cm (24in). Family Scopidae; species *Scopus umbretta.*

hamster
Almost tailless, rather squat RODENT that belongs to the MOUSE family. The hamster is found mainly in Asia and E Europe. Tending to live in areas with cold winters, it spends a lot of time gathering and storing food to see it through times of hardship. Family Muridae; subfamily Cricetinae.

hamster, common (black-bellied hamster)
Small, mainly herbivorous rodent that is native to Europe and Russia; it is declining in numbers in W Europe. The common hamster sometimes hunts insects and small vertebrates, such as mice or young birds. It has a short body, short legs, no tail, large ears and long whiskers. Head-body length: 20–28cm (8–11in). Family Muridae; subfamily Cricetinae; species *Cricetus cricetus*.

hamster, golden
Hamster, originally from Syria, that is now a common pet. In the wild it has a golden-brown back and white underparts. It inhabits dry rocky steppes. The golden hamster is usually solitary and nocturnal, constructing burrow systems in which it lives. It is omnivorous. Head-body length: *c*.17cm (*c*.7in); tail: *c*.1cm (*c*.0.4in). Family Muridae; subfamily Cricetinae; species *Mesocricetus auratus*.

hamster, Siberian
Dwarf hamster found in Siberia, Mongolia and N China. It has a grey to pinkish back and whitish underparts. The Siberian hamster prefers arid grasslands, eating seeds and other plant material. Head-body length: 5–10cm (2–4in); tail: *c*.1cm (*c*.0.4in). Family Muridae; subfamily Cricetinae; species *Phodopus sungorus*.

handkerchief tree (dove tree)
Deciduous tree native to China and grown elsewhere as an ornamental. Its flowerheads are surrounded by two or three large, white or cream bracts. It gets its Latin name from the French Jesuit Abbé David, who discovered it in 1869. Height: to 18m (60ft). Family Nyssaceae; species *Davidia involucrata*.

hanging valley
Tributary valley that ends high up the face of a larger main valley, possibly with a stream running through it and ending in a waterfall. Most hanging valleys result from glacial deepening of the main valley. *See also* GLACIER

haploid
Term describing a CELL that has only one member of each CHROMOSOME pair. All human cells except GAMETES are DIPLOID, having 46 chromosomes. A gamete (OVUM and SPERM) is haploid, having 23 chromosomes. The body cells of many lower organisms, including many ALGAE, single-celled organisms and some MOSS plants, are haploid. *See also* ALTERNATION OF GENERATIONS; CELL DIVISION; MEIOSIS

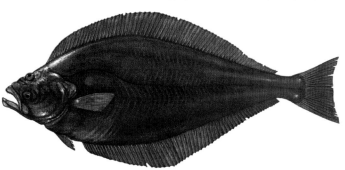
► **halibut** The Atlantic halibut (*Hippoglossus hippoglossus*) is the largest species of flatfish, growing up to 2m (7ft) in length.

haptophyte
Any member of the algal phylum Haptophyta. Haptophytes are pigmented with CHLOROPHYLL a and c, as well as fucoxanthin. All haptophytes have flagella and a haptonema, which is a threadlike process, structurally distinct from a FLAGELLUM, with various functions. Haptophytes are important in marine food webs. Some species produce toxins.

hardhead
See CROAKER

hardness
Resistance of a material to abrasion, cutting or indentation. The MOHS SCALE is a means of expressing the comparative hardness of materials.

hardpan
Hardened or compacted layer of soil lying below the surface. It is impervious to water, which cannot therefore drain away.

hard parts
Those parts of an organism that remain after death and decay and have a high FOSSILIZATION potential. Hard parts include shells and bones.

Hardy-Weinberg principle
Mathematical law that forms the basis for the study of gene frequencies in a population. The principle is expressed as:
$$p^2 + 2pq = q + 1.0$$
(where p and q represent the respective frequencies of the dominant and recessive alleles of any particular gene)
As HOMOLOGOUS RECESSIVE individuals will be recognisable in a population, the value of q can be measured. From this the values of p^2 and $2pq$ can then be calculated. To be accurate, the calculation depends on the population having no MUTATIONS, no NATURAL SELECTION, being isolated, being large, and mating being random. While these conditions are probably never met in a natural population, the principle is nevertheless useful in estimating the number of HETEROZYGOUS (carrier) individuals with a particular recessive allele, for example one causing a genetic disorder such as cystic fibrosis.

hare
Long-legged relative of the RABBIT. Hares live mainly in open habitats and rely on their sudden bursts of speed to avoid their predators. Typically hares have longer ears than rabbits, and some species turn white in the winter. Order Lagomorpha; family Leporidae (part).

hare, Arctic (mountain hare, blue hare)
Hare found in tundra regions around the Arctic and Scandinavia, and in the moorlands of Scotland and Ireland. In northern regions, it remains white with black ear tips all year around, but more southerly animals have a grey summer coat. Only the young (lev-

▲ **hare** The brown hare (*Lepus capensis*) is widespread in Europe, Scandinavia and Eurasia and is often found on agricultural land, usually near woodland. Its diet consists of cereals, berries and vegetation and it will redigest its own droppings as a means of gaining extra nourishment.

erets) spend any time in burrows, which may be taken over from other animals. Head-body length: 43–61cm (17–24in); tail: 4–7cm (2–3in). Family Leporidae; species *Lepus timidus*.

hare, bushman
Rare nocturnal animal. Its riverside habitats in central S Africa are being lost to cultivation. It is grizzled grey or reddish in colour, with a bushy tail and long ears. Head-tail length: 38–48cm (15–19in); tail: 7–11cm (3–4in). Family Leporidae; species *Bunolagus monticularis*.

hare, European (brown hare)
Hare that is widespread across much of central and W Europe. It has a larger body and longer limbs than a rabbit. European hares have been introduced to Australia, New Zealand and Argentina. Preferring an open habitat, they can be found in grassland and on arable farms, resting in woodland and hedgerows. Head-body length: 50–76cm (20–30in); tail: 7–12cm (3–5in). Family Leporidae; species *Lepus europaeus*.

hare, red rock-
Any of three species of hare native to Africa. They are all nocturnal grazers, preferring rocky grassland. They have thick, woolly, grey to reddish coats. Head-body length: 35–50cm (14–20in); tail: 5–10cm (2–4in). Family Leporidae; genus *Pronolagus*.

hare, snowshoe
Hare found in N United States and most of Canada. In the summer it is a grizzled red-grey colour, paler underneath, but in winter it is completely white except for black eyelids and ear tips. Nocturnal, the snowshoe hare is also active at dawn and dusk, feeding on a wide variety of plant material. It is known to swim to avoid predators. Head-body length: 40–50cm (16–20in); tail: *c*.4cm (*c*.2in). Family Leporidae; species *Lepus americanus*.

harebell
Slender, herbaceous, perennial plant, native to Europe, Asia and North America. It has blue or blue-violet, bell-shaped flowers, which hang along the uppermost parts of slender stems. The harebell is found growing in small patches in grassy places, fixed dunes and rock ledges. Family Campanulaceae; species *Campanula rotundifolia*.

haricot bean
One of a number of cultivated beans that have been developed from *Phaseolus vulgaris*, which originated in South America. Haricot beans are an important

H

source of protein and carbohydrate in the human diet. The plant has medium-sized, creamy coloured seeds, which are favoured in French cuisine and also used to make baked beans. Family Fabaceae; species *Phaseolus vulgaris.*

harlequin bug (fire bug, calico bug, collard bug)

Brightly coloured orange and black PENTATOMID BUG belonging to the STINKBUG family of the order Hemiptera. It is a pest on vegetable crops in North America, sucking juices from the plants. Eggs are laid on the undersides of leaves; the larvae resemble the adults, but are wingless. Length: *c.*9mm (*c.*0.4in). Family Pentatomidae; species *Murgantia histrionica.*

harp shell

Predatory GASTROPOD mollusc that feeds mainly on crustaceans. The harp shell's raised axial ribs give it the appearance of a harp. It is found in tropical seas. Family Harpidae.

H

harrier

Graceful, medium-sized BIRD OF PREY. It has long, narrow wings, long legs and a long tail. The harrier hunts by gliding low over the ground and pouncing on prey with its wings held in a shallow, upwards-tilted v-shape; it can also accelerate rapidly to catch small birds in flight. Harriers nest on the ground. Family Accipitridae; genus *Circus*; there are nine species worldwide

harrier, hen (northern harrier)

Most widespread harrier of North America and Europe. Males are uniformly pale grey above and whitish below, with black wing tips. The females are brown above and whitish below. Both sexes have a prominent white rump. The hen harrier breeds on northern moors and winters further south on marshes and coastal salt flats. Length: 44–52cm (17–20in). Family Accipitridae; species *Circus cyaneus.*

harrier, marsh

Largest species of harrier. It is characterized by broad wings and heavy flight. Males are mainly brown, with grey only on the wings and tail. Females are uniformly dark brown with a cream-coloured face patch. During display, the march harrier has a cat-like

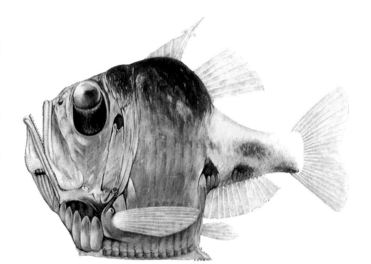

mewing call. It breeds on wetlands. Length: 48–56cm (19–22in). Family Accipitridae; species *Circus aeruginosus.*

harrier, Montagu's

Slender, narrow-winged harrier. It is mainly grey, with dark-barred, black-tipped wings. In summer it migrates to Europe and Asia from its winter quarters in Africa, Pakistan and India. Montagu's harrier is a sociable harrier; it nests in small colonies and winters communally in large roosts. Length: 43–47cm (17–19in). Family Accipitridae; species *Circus pygargus.*

harrier, pied

Asiatic harrier. The male is distinctive, with a black head, neck, back and wing tips and white underparts; its grey wings have a black lateral band. Female pied harriers are mainly grey-brown above and whitish below, with a white rump. The pied harrier inhabits open grasslands and plains. Length: 41–46cm (16–18in). Family Accipitridae; species *Circus melanoleucos.*

hartebeest

Large ANTELOPE native to African grasslands s of the Sahara Desert. It has a reddish or yellowish-brown

coat and short, sharply rising horns united at the base. Length: up to 200cm (80in); height: to 150cm (60in); weight: up to 180kg (400lb). Family Bovidae.

harvestman (daddy-longlegs)

ARACHNID with legs that may be several times its body length. The harvestman feeds on insects and plant juices. Body length: 2.5–13mm (0.1–0.5in). Family Phalangidae.

harvest mouse

See MOUSE, HARVEST

hatchetfish

Carnivorous hatchet-shaped fish with light-emitting organs on the underside of its muscular abdomen. There are two groups: deep-sea hatchetfish (family Sternoptychidae) related to salamander; and flying hatchetfish (family Gasteropelecidae) of South America, which "fly" by beating their pectoral fins. Length: to 10cm (4in).

hatchling

Organism that has just emerged from the EGG. The term is almost exclusively reserved for vertebrates, especially birds and fish.

hausa potato

Herbaceous perennial plant native to tropical w Africa. It is cultivated for its edible TUBERS, which are used as a substitute for potatoes. The plant is covered with fine, whitish hairs. It has erect stems and long, yellow flowers. Family Lamiaceae; species *Plectranthus esculentus.*

haustorium

Specialized, invasive, sucker-like or tube-like structure in a parasitic plant or FUNGUS. It is used to penetrate the outer tissues of a HOST plant in order to absorb nourishment. *See also* PARASITE

hawfinch

Europe's largest species of FINCH; it has a huge triangular bill, which it uses to crack nuts and fruit stones. Its plumage is mostly chestnut, with black throat and wing tips and white wing patches. The hawfinch is an uncommon and shy bird of broad-

◄ hartebeest These hartebeest (*Alcelaphus buselaphus*) are in the Kalahari Game Reserve, s Africa. Hartebeest live in large herds, usually of several hundred individuals, but sometimes of several thousand. The herd is well organized, and it is thought that the dominance of the various females defines the social structure. Very alert animals, hartebeest snort to warn one another of danger.

leaved woodlands; it has a distinct preference for hornbeam. It often feeds in the topmost branches. Length: 18cm (7in). Family Fringillidae; species *Coccothraustes coccothraustes.*

hawk

BIRD OF PREY. True hawks (accipiters) belong to the genus *Accipiter*. Hawks are recognised by their long tails, broad, rounded wings, barred underparts and fast, dashing flight. The females are usually larger than the males. Family Accipitridae; genus *Accipiter*. Some species of BUZZARDS are sometimes referred to as hawks. These birds of prey have broad, banded tails and rounded wings. They typically soar over open country. Family Accipitridae; main genus *Buteo*.

hawk, common black

Rare, stocky, black hawk. It has very broad wings, long, yellow, chicken-like legs and a short, broad tail with a white band. It is found from N Mexico south to Venezuela. It hunts from a low perch for crayfish, frogs and reptiles. Length: 53cm (21in). Family Accipitridae; species *Buteogallus anthracinus.*

hawk, Cooper's

Hawk with a long, rounded tail. In flight it appears short-winged, with heavily barred under wings. The Cooper's hawk is a widely distributed summer visitor to North America; it winters in Central America and South America. It preys on songbirds and is often seen perched on telephone poles. Length: 36–51cm (14–20in). Family Accipitridae; species *Accipiter cooperis.*

hawk, grey

Buteo hawk with grey upper parts, grey barred underparts and grey under wings. Its wings are rounded, and it flies with several fast wing beats followed by a glide. It swoops on frogs, lizards and snakes. The grey hawk is found from Mexico to Argentina. Length: 43cm (17in). Family Accipitridae; species *Buteo nitidus.*

hawk, Harris' (bay-winged hawk)

Hawk that is chocolate brown with conspicuous chestnut shoulder patches, thighs and under wings; it has a white base and white tip to its black tail. Harris' hawk breeds in semideserts and savannas from sw United States to Chile and Argentina. Easily trained, it is a favourite of falconers. Length: 53cm (21in). Family Accipitridae; species *Parabuteo unicinctus.*

hawk, red-tailed

Most common North American buteo hawk. It has broad, rounded wings and a distinctively reddish-brown upper tail. It hunts, mainly for rodents, over open country, plains and prairie. The red-tailed hawk breeds from the tree line in Canada to as far south as Panama. Length: 56cm (22in). Family Accipitridae; species *Buteo jamaicensis.*

► **hawthorn** An ideal tree for hedge-planting because of its hardiness and its display of thorns, the hawthorn (family Rosaceae) can grow to 11.5m (35ft) if left untrimmed. Its heavily scented blossom is conspicuous in late spring and early summer in the hedgerows of Europe.

hawk, sharp-shinned

Most common North American accipiter. It resembles the Cooper's hawk, but has proportionally longer wings, a shorter tail and a smaller head. It breeds as far north as Alaska and migrates to South America. Length: 25–36cm (10–14in). Family Accipitridae; species *Accipiter striatus.*

hawk, zone-tailed

Slate black buteo with a long tail that is banded with pale grey. It hunts rodents, lizards and small birds in mountain country, often near watercourses, by swooping on them from a low glide. It is uncommon throughout its range, which is from sw United States to Brazil. Length: 51cm (20in). Family Accipitridae; species *Buteo albonatus.*

hawk-eagle

Medium-sized BIRD OF PREY with a conspicuous crest. The black-and-white hawk-eagle (*Spizastur melanoleucus*) has a black back and crest and a pure white face and body. The black hawk-eagle (*Spizastur tyrannus*) is blackish-brown with a black-and-white crest. Hawk-eagles are found in the humid lowland forests of Central America. Length: 55–70cm (22–28in). Family Accipitridae.

hawkmoth (sphinx moth)

Medium to large MOTH characterized by narrow wings, a spindle-shaped body and a long sucking-tube coiled beneath its head. Hawkmoths are strong fliers. They usually feed at dusk, hovering over flowers and sucking nectar through the extended tube. Their larvae – large, smooth-skinned caterpillars – are called hornworms because of a horn-like protrusion on the posterior segment. Order Lepidoptera; family Sphingidae.

hawkmoth, bee

Any of several species of hawkmoth belonging to the genus *Hemaris*. They are called bee hawkmoths because of their resemblance to bees. They bear yellow and brown hairs, have scales on their thoraxes and wings, and have the distinctive stout shape of a bee. Adult body length: 30–60mm (1.2–2.4in). Family Sphingidae.

hawkmoth, death's-head (death's-head moth)

Large hawkmoth found in Europe and Africa. It is named after the skull-like markings on the back of its thorax. It has a short proboscis and often feeds on

► **hawkmoth** Found worldwide, the hawkmoth is named after its ability to hover while sucking nectar from a flower. It is a powerful flier and some species, especially those found in tropical regions, grow to 10cm (4in) in length. Shown here is the convolvulus hawkmoth (*Herse convolvuli*). The larva is sometimes called a hornworm because of the prominent horn on the end of its abdomen, which it raises up to deter predators.

H

honey from beehives. It makes a squeaking sound that can be detected by the human ear. Family Sphingidae; species *Acherontia atropos.*

hawkmoth, hummingbird

Hawkmoth that can hover in one spot by moving its wings at very high speed. It feeds on nectar by extending its proboscis into flowers, resembling a hummingbird. It migrates over large distances and can be found even in polar regions and at high mountain elevations. Adult wingspan: 40–50mm (1.6–2in). Family Sphingidae; species *Macroglossum stellatarum.*

hawksbill

See SEA TURTLE, HAWKSBILL

hawkweed

Any member of the genus *Hieracium*, a group of perennial plants native to Europe and South America. Some hawkweed species are grown as ornamentals. The plants are often hairy, with a basal rosette of leaves. The yellow or deep orange flowers grow in clusters. Family Asteraceae; genus *Hieracium.*

hawthorn

Any of more than 200 species of thorny deciduous shrubs and trees of the genus *Crataegus*. They grow in temperate parts of the Northern Hemisphere. Their flowers are white or pink, and small berries are borne in clusters. Hawthorns are widely used in hedgerows. Family Rosaceae; genus *Crataegus.*

hazel

Any of about 15 species of bushes or small trees of the genus *Corylus*, native to temperate regions of the Northern Hemisphere. There are separate male and

◄ **hazel** Ripe, fresh hazel nuts are partially covered with leafy husks. These nuts grow wild but cobnuts and filberts are two varieties of hazelnut that are commonly cultivated in the Northern Hemisphere.

H

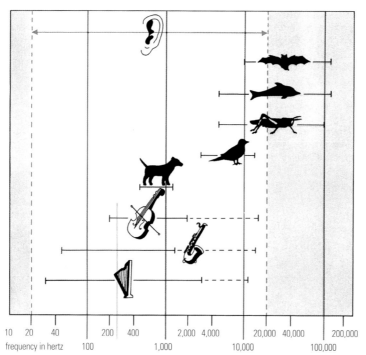

► **hearing** Human hearing extends from a frequency of about 20 cycles per second (Hertz, Hz) to 20,000 cycles. Some animals are able to generate sounds far beyond this range: the chart shows the frequencies generated by bats, porpoises and grasshoppers, and for comparison the frequency-production ranges of birds and dogs. Musical instruments have two kinds of frequency-range: the range of notes that can be played (shown as a solid line) and the range of overtones that go to make up the characteristic sound of the instrument (broken line). The ranges shown are those of the violin, the saxophone family (from bass to soprano) and the harp. For reference, the note middle-C is marked in yellow.

female flowers. The fruit is a hazelnut, known in some species as a COBNUT or filbert. Family Betulaceae; genus *Corylus*.

hearing
Process by which sound waves are experienced. Humans and many other mammals hear when sound waves enter the EAR canal and vibrate the eardrum. The vibrations are transmitted by three small bones (ossicles) to the COCHLEA. In the cochlea, receptors generate nerve impulses that pass via the auditory nerve to the brain to be interpreted as sound.

heart
See feature article

heat balance (heat budget)
Balance between the Sun's heat received by the Earth's atmosphere and that returned back into space. About two-thirds of solar radiation is absorbed by clouds, the atmosphere and the Earth, and about one-third is reflected back, mainly by clouds. The heat absorbed powers the circulation of the atmosphere, oceans and hydrological cycle. Eventually the heat is reradiated into space, maintaining the Earth's heat equilibrium. *See also* CIRCULATION, ATMOSPHERIC; GREENHOUSE EFFECT

heath
See ERICA

heather (ling)
Evergreen shrub native to moors and bogs of Europe and Asia Minor. It has been naturalized in North America, and many varieties are cultivated as ornamentals. Its small, bell-shaped flowers are white or various shades of pink. The plant has numerous uses, from fuel and bedding to medicinal. Family Ericaceae; species *Calluna vulgaris*.

heat transfer (heat exchange)
Flow of heat energy from one object to another. This flow of energy occurs at all times when two or more bodies at different temperatures are in thermal contact. Three methods of heat transfer may be distinguished: conduction, convection and radiation. In **conduction**, heat is transferred from molecule to molecule within a body, as in an iron rod stuck in a

fire. In **convection**, heat is transferred by circulation of fluid, as in boiling. In **radiation**, heat is transferred in the form of electromagnetic waves, as in sunlight.

Heaviside-Kennelly layer (E-layer)
Region that lies within the IONOSPHERE of the Earth's ATMOSPHERE.

hebe
Any member of the genus *Hebe*, a group of evergreen shrubs, most of which are native to New

Zealand. Hebes are grown as ornamentals in temperate climates but are not fully hardy. Their somewhat leathery leaves are arranged in opposite pairs; white, pink or blue showy flowers are produced in axillary racemes (*see* INFLORESCENCE) or small heads. Many varieties have been developed for ornamental use. Family Scrophulariaceae; genus *Hebe*.

hedgehog
Any of 12 species of small, nocturnal mammals found in Africa, Europe and Asia. Spiny insectivores, they protect themselves by curling into a tight ball, such that the spines cross over and present a sharp barrier to attack. Order Insectivora; family Erinaceidae; subfamily Erinaceinae.

hedgehog, desert
Insectivore with spines that cover its whole body except the face, legs and underside. Its preferred habitat is desert in Asia and North Africa. Desert hedgehogs often have a dark face mask with a white forehead. They dig and live in burrows, which usually house a single adult. Head-body length: 14–27cm (6–11in); tail: 1–4cm (0.4–1.6in). Family Erinaceidae; genus *Paraechinus*.

hedgehog, European
Spiny, omnivorous hedgehog, widespread across Europe and Asia. It has a long, pointed snout, and its preferred food is invertebrates such as earthworms. Size, shape and colour varies across its range, and there may be several subspecies. Head-body length: 13–30cm (5–12in); tail: 1–5cm (0.4–2in). Family Erinaceidae; species *Erinaceus europaeus*.

hedgehog cactus
CACTUS native to SW United States, found from S Utah to Mexico. It grows in large clumps and has strongly ribbed projections (tubercules). It has yel-

HEART

M uscular organ that pumps BLOOD through the body by means of the CIRCULATORY SYSTEM. In humans, the heart is located behind the breastbone between the lower parts of the lungs. Divided longitudinally by a muscular wall, the right side contains only deoxygenated blood, the left side contains only oxygenated blood. Each side of the heart is divided into two chambers, an atrium and a ventricle, both separated by valves. The average heartbeat rate for an adult human at rest is 70–80 beats per minute. *See also* BLOOD VESSEL

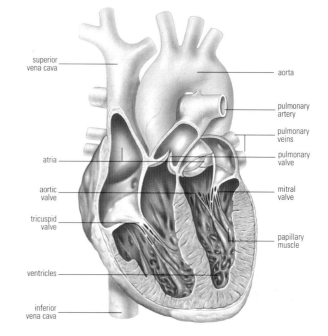

◄ **The human heart** contains four chambers – two atria and two ventricles – and four sets of valves. Blood from the body passes into the right atrium, via the vena cavae. Flow of blood into the right ventricle is controlled by the tricuspid valve. Pulmonary arteries carry blood from the right ventricle to the lungs, while the pulmonary veins carry oxygenated blood back from the lungs to the left atrium. In a similar way, the mitral valve controls the flow of blood between the left atrium and the left ventricle. The aorta conducts the oxygenated blood from the left ventricle to all parts of the body.

▲ **hedgehog** The long-eared hedgehog (*Hemiechinus auritus aegyptiacus*) is found in arid deserts and steppes across Asia. Its ears are much longer than other hedgehogs and it uses its acute senses of hearing and smell to find food and to protect itself from predators.

lowish-brown spines and purple flowers. Family Cactaceae; species *Echinocereus engelmannii*.

heliotrope (cherry pie)
Herbaceous perennial plant native to Peru. Grown in gardens for its fragrant flowers, it is used in scent-making. Its leaves are oblong or oval with prominent veins. The flowers, which are violet or white to purple, are produced in a tight cluster, with tubular corollas. Family Boraginaceae; species *Heliotropium arborescens*.

heliotropism
See PHOTOTROPISM

helium (symbol He)
Gaseous, nonmetallic element discovered in 1868. It was first obtained in 1895 from the mineral clevite; the chief source today is from natural gas. It is also found in some radioactive minerals and in the Earth's ATMOSPHERE (0.0005% by volume). Helium is the second-most common element in the Universe and the second-lightest element (after HYDROGEN). It has the lowest melting and boiling points of any element. A colourless, odourless, nonflammable gas, it is used in meteorological balloons, to make artificial "air" (mixed with oxygen) for deep-sea divers, and in welding, semiconductors, lasers, metallurgy, and other applications requiring an inert atmosphere. Liquid helium is used in cryogenics (physics dealing with low temperatures). The element forms no chemical compounds. Properties: at.no. 2; r.a.m. 4.0026; r.d. 0.178; m.p. −272.2°C (−458°F); b.p. −268.9°C (−452.02°F); single isotope ^{4}He.

helix, double
See DOUBLE HELIX

hellbender
Large, aquatic SALAMANDER with a broad, flat head, small eyes, gill slits and loose folds of skin along the flanks. Hellbenders are native to upland areas of the E United States. They live in fast-flowing streams, sheltering beneath large submerged boulders by day. Length: to 75cm (30in). Family Cryptobranchidae; genus *Cryptobranchus*.

hellebore
Any of *c.*20 species of poisonous, herbaceous plants of the genus *Helleborus*, native to Eurasia. The best-known species is the Christmas rose, *Helleborus niger*, which bears white flowers from mid-winter to early spring. Family Ranunculaceae.

helmetcrest, bearded
Sparrow-sized, dark brown HUMMINGBIRD. It has a

white throat and chest and a "beard" comprising six downwards-pointing white feathers. It lives in the mountains of Venezuela and Colombia. It has a short bill, with which it catches insects or sips nectar from flowers. Length: 15cm (6in). Family Trochilidae; species *Oxypogon guerinii*.

hemipteran
Any member of the order Hemiptera of the class Insecta (*see* INSECT). Hemipterans have two pairs of wings. Their symmetrical mouthparts are adapted for piercing and sucking.

hemlock
Poisonous herbaceous plant that is native to Eurasia. Hemlock has a long taproot and flat clusters of white flowers. The leaf stalks have purple spots. Family Apiaceae/Umbelliferae; species *Conium maculatum*.

hemp
Herb that is native to Asia and cultivated in Eurasia, North America and parts of South America. It has hollow stems with fibrous inner bark, also called hemp, which is used to make ropes and cloth. Oil from the seeds is used in soap and paint. Some strains of the plant, generally known as CANNABIS, are used to produce marijuana and hashish. Height: to 5m (16ft). Family Cannabaceae; species *Cannabis sativa*.

henbane
See BLACK HENBANE

heparin
ANTICOAGULANT substance that is produced by many animals; it inhibits the production of thrombin, an ENZYME involved in blood clotting. A purified extract of heparin is used after surgery to minimize the risk of thrombosis and to prevent the formation of further clots in anyone who has had a pulmonary embolism.

herb
Seed-bearing plant (SPERMATOPHYTE), usually with a soft stem that withers away after one growing season. Most herbs are ANGIOSPERMS (flowering plants).

herbaceous
Term for any nonwoody plant. Herbaceous plants can be either ANNUAL (they die completely after one season), BIENNIAL (they take two seasons to

complete the lifecycle) or PERENNIAL (they live for three or more seasons).

herbivore
Animal that feeds solely on plants. Although strictly most herbivores are insects, the term is closely associated with mammals, especially UNGULATES (hoofed mammals). Mammalian herbivores are characterized by broad molars and blunt-edged teeth, which they use to pull, cut and grind their food. Their digestive systems are adapted to the breakdown of CELLULOSE, using mutualistic microorganisms, and subsequent ASSIMILATION of the products. In a standard FOOD CHAIN, herbivores are PRIMARY CONSUMERS. *See also* DIGESTION

herb Robert
Annual or biennial plant native to Europe and temperate regions of Asia and North Africa; it has been naturalized in North and South America. Herb Robert grows in moist, shady places and has an unpleasant smell. Its deeply divided leaves are often tinged with red, and it produces small, pinkish-red flowers. It has been used medicinally as a lotion or mouthwash. Family Geraniaceae; species *Geranium robertianum*.

heredity
See feature article, page 182

hermaphrodite
Organism that has both male and female sexual organs. Most hermaphroditic animals are INVERTEBRATES, such as the EARTHWORM and the SNAIL. They reproduce by the mating of two individuals, each of which receives SPERM from the other. Sometimes, in both plant and animal hermaphrodites, self-FERTILIZATION takes place.

hermit
Any of *c.*28 species of HUMMINGBIRDS. The long-tailed hermit (*Phaethornis superciliosus*) has a long, curved bill and long central tail feathers. Length: 15cm (6in). The little hermit (*Phaethornis longuemareus*) is much smaller, with a shorter bill. Length: 8cm (3in). Both species are found in lowland forests from Panama to the Amazon region. Family Trochilidae; genera *Phaethornis*, *Ramphodon* and *Glaucis*.

hermit crab
See CRAB, HERMIT

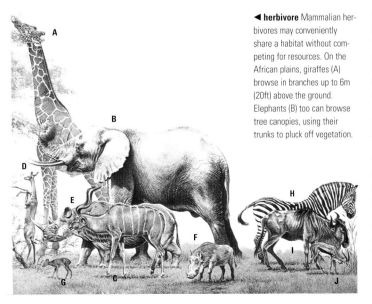

◄ **herbivore** Mammalian herbivores may conveniently share a habitat without competing for resources. On the African plains, giraffes (A) browse in branches up to 6m (20ft) above the ground. Elephants (B) too can browse tree canopies, using their trunks to pluck off vegetation. Eland (C) attack the middle branches with their horns, twisting twigs to break them off, while gerenuk (D) stand on their hind legs to reach higher branches. The black rhino (E) uses its hook-like upper lip to feed on bark, twigs and leaves (white rhinos have lengthened skulls and broad lips for grazing the short grasses that they favour). The wart hog (F) and dik-dik (G) eat buds and flowers and will also dig up roots and tubers. Such sharing of resources also occurs among grazers. Migrating zebra (H) crop the taller, coarse grasses; wildebeest (I) feed on the leafy centre layer, allowing small gazelles (J) to reach the tender new shoots.

Heredity is the transmission of physical and other characteristics from one generation of plants or animals to another. Characteristics such as blue eyes and red hair may be specific to the individuals involved; other features, such as erect posture and the possession of external ears, may be typical of the type of organism. The combination of characteristics that makes up an organism and makes it different from others is set out in the organism's GENETIC CODE, passed on from parent(s) to offspring. It had always been recognised that children resembled their parents without being identical to them, but it was the rediscovery of Gregor MENDEL's theory of inheritance (Mendelism) that provided an explanation of heredity.

In human body cells there are 23 pairs of CHROMOSOMES, which carry all the genetic material. Chromosomes are made up of DNA and proteins. A section of DNA is called a GENE, which may exist in two or more different forms called ALLELES; for example, the gene for eye colour has two forms – one for brown colour and one for blue.

In sexual reproduction both parents provide alleles within SPERM or OVA. The offspring, therefore, have two sets of genetic information for each character they possess. For any character, however, the individual will normally only show the feature of one parent. For example, if one parent has brown eyes and the other blue ones, the offspring will either have brown or blue eyes rather than an intermediate colour. Occasionally an intermediate form

does arise: a cross between a snapdragon with red flowers and one with white flowers leads to offspring with pink blooms.

Mendel realised that if both parents contributed alleles (he called them factors) for each characteristic, then every organism must possess a pair for each character. Where these alleles are the same they are said to be homozygous (*see* HOMOZYGOTE), where different they are called heterozygous (*see* HETEROZYGOTE). The allele that expresses itself in the heterozygous state is said to be DOMINANT, the other is RECESSIVE. During MEIOSIS only one of each pair of alleles enters each sperm or egg.

All the alleles that an organism inherits from its parents are known as its GENOTYPE and this sets the limits within which characteristics may vary. What an organism actually looks like is called its PHENOTYPE and depends on the extent to which the genotype is affected by the environment. For example, the alleles may determine that an individual will be 1.8m tall, but the actual height will depend upon factors such as the diet during development. Changes in the phenotype due to the environment are not passed on to the next generation.

Variation of the genotype may arise due to changes in the structure or amount of DNA making up the alleles. These changes are called MUTATIONS and may be inherited by the offspring. Most mutations are harmful and result in genetic disor-

ders of body parts, such as polydactyly (fingers), cystic fibrosis (cell membranes), Huntington's disease (nervous system) and sickle cell anaemia (erythrocytes).

The understanding of the principles of heredity has made it possible for humans selectively to breed varieties of plants and animals to give increased yields. SELECTIVE BREEDING is achieved in animals by choosing individuals with the desired characteristics and interbreeding them. This interbreeding, however, leads to a reduction in the variety of alleles in a population and hence to genetic disorders. In plants, desired characteristics can be passed on by taking cuttings – an asexual process that ensures the offspring produced are identical to the parent.

Cloning is another asexual process that ensures identical offspring (CLONES). In plants, groups of cells are separated and each grown into a new individual, a process called tissue culture. In animals, embryo cells can be separated and transplanted into host mothers. With the Human Genome Project having identified and recorded all human genes, the ability now exists for humans to control their own heredity through the manipulation of genes, a process called GENETIC ENGINEERING. Many moral and ethical issues arise, concerning the problem of balancing the advantage of eradicating most genetic disorders against the consequences of accidentally releasing new genes into the environment, or the use of the process for political ends.

MENDELISM

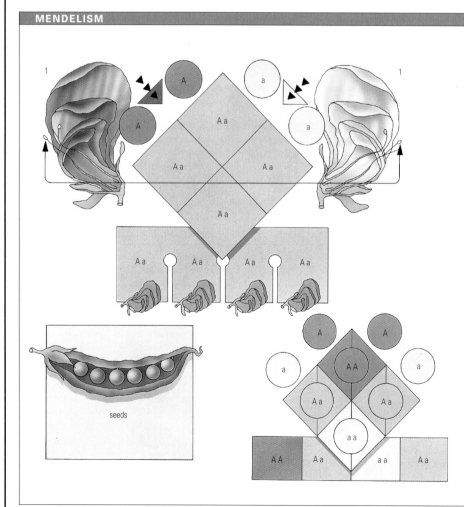

Gregor Mendel is widely accepted as making the initial discoveries of the laws of heredity and hence genetics. His discoveries were primarily based on the crossbreeding of plants. The genetic characteristics of plants and animals can be studied by crossbreeding under controlled conditions. Mendel discovered that some characteristics are determined by genes that contain a dominant allele (A) over others that contain a recessive allele (a). Flowering plant cells usually contain two alleles, but pollen or eggs (ova) contain only one. The pure-bred pea plants (1) are either purple or white. The F1 crosses produced by crossbreeding them are all purple, but carry one dominant and one recessive allele. The F2 generation will produce flowers in the ratio three purple to one white flower, as any flower with an A allele will be dominant.

seeds

heron
Large, long-necked, long-legged and long-billed water bird. It wades in shallow water, hunting for its prey of small fish, frogs and crayfish. Some species have elongated head feathers or plumes when breeding. The wings are broad and rounded. Herons fly with ponderous wing beats and with their necks drawn in and their legs outstretched. Most species nest colonially, usually in trees. Family Ardeidae.

heron, night (black-crowned night heron)
Small stocky heron found worldwide. The night heron is mainly grey, with a black crown and back. It roosts in trees during the day and hunts at night in densely vegetated fresh or saltwater swamps. Length: 44–47cm (18–19in). Family Ardeidae; species *Nycticorax nycticorax*.

heron, goliath
Huge, shy, solitary heron found in Asia and E Africa. It has a chestnut crown. The goliath heron hunts in shallow water in mangrove swamps and tidal creeks. Its long legs enable it to wade well out from the shore. Length: 135–150cm (53–59in). Family Ardeidae; species *Ardea goliath*.

heron, great blue
Common large heron found throughout North America, from Alaska to Mexico. It has a tawny-brown neck and reddish-brown thighs and leading edge of the wings. Length: 117cm (46in). Family Ardeidae; species *Ardea herodias*.

heron, green-backed
Small, chunky heron. It has short legs, green or blue-grey upper parts and a chestnut neck and side of face. Its legs are yellow but in males become bright orange when breeding. Solitary, the green-backed heron is found in marshes with woodland cover, from Canada to Panama. Length: 46cm (18in). Family Ardeidae; species *Butorides striatus*.

heron, grey
Most common large heron of Europe and Asia. It is mainly grey, with a white head and neck, a black crest and a long, yellow, dagger-like bill. It feeds in shallow, fresh or coastal water, sometimes visiting garden ponds. The grey heron nests in trees and reedbeds. Length: 90–98cm (35–39in). Family Ardeidae; species *Ardea cinerea*.

heron, purple
Shy and secretive, large, dark grey heron found in Europe, Africa and Asia. It has a black crown and a long, snake-like neck that is striped reddish brown. The change to adult plumage can take up to five years. The purple heron breeds in reedbeds. Length: 78–90cm (31–36in). Family Ardeidae; species *Ardea purpurea*.

heron, squacco
Small, skulking, brownish heron; it appears white in flight. When breeding, its crown and long plume feathers are streaked black and its legs change from yellow-green to bright red. The squacco heron feeds in marshy riversides and nests colonially with other herons. It is found in Europe, Asia and Africa. Length: 45cm (18in). Family Ardeidae; species *Ardeola ralloides*.

herring
Marine fish found worldwide. It is one of the most important food fish, and various species are canned as pilchard or sardine or sold fresh, pickled (rollmops) or smoked (as kippers or bloaters). Herrings

▲ **heron, purple** One of the smaller heron species, the purple heron is difficult to see in the wild as it spends most of its time in long grass or reeds. Purple herons are monogamous birds and the male and female build a nest of reeds within a small colony. Like most herons, its diet consists mainly of fish.

have a laterally compressed body and a deeply forked tail fin. They feed on plankton. Length: 8–46cm (3–18in). Family Clupeidae; the 190 species include *Clupea harengus*.

herring gull
See GULL, HERRING

Hershey, Alfred Day (1908–97)
US biologist who shared the 1969 Nobel Prize for physiology or medicine with Max DELBRÜCK and Salvador LURÍA for his part in discovering the way VIRUSES reproduce. Through his study of bacteriophages, Hershey confirmed that the NUCLEIC ACID RNA is solely responsible for infection and subsequent viral development.

hesperidin
VITAMIN P. Hesperidin affects the permeability of blood capillaries.

hessian fly
Brown to black FLY of the GALL MIDGE family. It is found in temperate parts of the Northern Hemisphere and in New Zealand. It is a serious pest of wheat and other grains. The eggs are laid on young plants; the larvae emerge soon afterwards and feed on the plant sap. Length: 4–6mm (0.16–0.24in). Family Cecidomyidae, species *Mayetiola destructor*.

heteropteran
Any member of the Heteroptera, which in some classification systems is defined as a suborder of HEMIPTERANS and in other systems is an alternative term for Hemiptera.

heterosexuality
Emotional or sexual attraction to individuals of the opposite sex; being involved in sexual relationships with members of the opposite sex. See also HOMOSEXUALITY

heterosis
Increased strength and vitality, especially in the growth and fertility of an organism, as a result of a cross between two genetically different lines. Also known as HYBRID VIGOUR, such crosses are carried out to improve existing varieties by combining one or more beneficial features from each of the parents. A racehorse breeder might, for example, cross a strong stallion with a fast mare in expectation of a strong, fast foal. The process is particularly effective where there have been many generations of inbreeding of the two parental lines.

heterosomes
Non-typical pair of CHROMOSOMES, such as the sex chromosomes. In humans, for example, each of 22 pairs of chromosomes are identical in appearance, but the 23rd pair (the sex chromosomes) differ in that females have a pair that are both X in shape, while males have one X- and one Y-shaped chromosome. See also AUTOSOMES

heterostyly
Condition found in some ANGIOSPERMS (flowering plants) in which the STYLES are of different lengths. The classic example of heterostyly is the primrose *Primula vulgaris*, in which there are two distinct flower forms, each occurring on different plants. Each form has a different-sized style and STAMEN from the other so that pollen collected by insects from the ANTHER of one type is dropped on the STIGMA of the other. Heterostyly increases the likelihood of CROSS-POLLINATION because pollen cannot be passed between plants with sex organs of the same size.

heterotroph
Organism that obtains its energy from the digestion of organic matter (usually plant or animal tissue) through a process known as **heterotrophic nutrition**. All animals and fungi are heterotrophs. The digestive process breaks down the tissue to provide material with which the organism can synthesize essential nutrients, such as, in the case of humans, carbohydrates, protein, fat, vitamins and minerals.

heterozygote
Organism possessing two contrasting forms (ALLELES) of a GENE in a CHROMOSOME pair. In cases where one of the forms is DOMINANT and one RECESSIVE only the dominant form will be expressed in the PHENOTYPE. See also HOMOZYGOTE

heterozygous allele
See HETEROZYGOTE

hexapod
Organism with six legs. See INSECT

▲ **herring** Found in large numbers in the North Atlantic, the Atlantic herring (*Clupea harengus*) is an important food fish. Blue or green above with a silvery underside, it grows to 30cm (12in). It feeds on plankton and fish eggs and is an important source of food for larger fish and birds.

H

H

▲ **hippopotamus** The common hippopotamus (*Hippopotamus amphibius*) has the largest mouth of any mammal. Its canine teeth can reach 60cm (24in) in length. The female produces a single calf. Hippos usually travel in herds of between 10 and 15 animals.

hibernation
Dormant (sleep-like) condition adopted by some animals in order to survive the harsh conditions of winter. Adaptive mechanisms to avoid starvation and extreme temperatures include reduced body temperature, a slower heartbeat, slower breathing rate and slower rate of METABOLISM. *See also* AESTIVATION; DIAPAUSE

hibiscus
Any member of the genus *Hibiscus*, which comprises plants, shrubs and small trees native to tropical and temperate regions. They are cultivated worldwide. Hibiscus plants produce large, white, pink, yellow, blue or red, bell-shaped flowers with darker centres. Family Malvaceae.

hickory
Deciduous tree of the WALNUT family native to E North America. Hickories are grown for ornament, timber and for their nuts. Height: 25m (80ft). Family Juglandaceae; genus *Carya*. *See also* PECAN

Hill, John (1716–75)
English botanist and writer whose book on British flora was the first to be based on the Linnaean system of nomenclature. His *Vegetable System*, in 26 folio volumes, was published between 1759 and 1775.

hindbrain
One of the three primary parts of the BRAIN. In the embryo, the hindbrain develops into the CEREBELLUM, the part of the brain concerned with unconscious muscle coordination, and also into the pons and the medulla oblongata. The **pons** contains the nerve fibres connecting the two halves of the cerebellum. The **medulla oblongata** controls respiration and heartbeat – the functions necessary to maintain life. *See also* FOREBRAIN; MIDBRAIN

hippopotamus (Gr. river horse)
Either of two species of bulky, herbivorous mammals, native to Africa. *Hippopotamus amphibius* has a massive grey or brown body, a large head and bulbous snout, short legs and tail. It has the largest mouth of any mammal: it gapes open to reveal very long incisor and canine teeth. The hippopotamus' skin dehydrates easily and it spends the day in water, emerging at night to graze on pastures. Males can weigh up to 3200kg (7050lb). **Pygmy hippopotamuses** (*Choeropsis liberiensis*) are much smaller animals. They spend more time on land. Pygmy hippopotamuses weigh *c*.180kg (*c*.400lb). Family Hippopotamidae.

histamine
Substance derived from the AMINO ACID HISTIDINE. It occurs naturally in many plants and in animal tissues and is released on tissue injury. Histamine's several functions in the body include dilation of the capillaries. It is implicated in allergic reactions (such as hay fever), which can be treated with ANTIHISTAMINE drugs.

histology
Biological, especially microscopic, study of TISSUES and structures in living organisms.

histone
Basic protein found associated with DNA in CHROMOSOMES. Histones function during CELL DIVISION to condense CHROMATIN and coil the chromosomes. There are five kinds, each containing large amounts of the AMINO ACIDS arginine, histidine and lysine. Histones are soluble in water.

hoarhound (horehound)
Aromatic perennial plant native to the Mediterranean region and central Asia; it has been naturalized in North and South America. Hoarhound grows in pastures and along roadsides. It has hairy stems and felty, wrinkled, rounded leaves; its small white flowers are clustered in leaf axils. Since Egyptian times, hoarhound has been used medicinally to treat numerous ailments. Family Lamiaceae; species *Marrubium vulgare*.

hoatzin
Shaggy-crested bird belonging to the CUCKOO family. It resembles a long, slender crow, with the brownish adult having rounded wings and a long tail.It has a large crop (a distensible part of the oesophagus) for storing vegetable matter. The hatchlings have claws on their wings and are able to climb trees. The hoatzin is found in river valleys of N South America. Family Cuculidae; species *Opisthocomus hoazin*.

hobby
Streamlined FALCON with scythe-shaped wings and a slender tail. Its plumage is dark slate-grey above, with a white face and black "moustache". Its flight is very fast and agile, enabling it to catch small birds on the wing and large flying insects, such as dragonflies. Length: 25–30cm (10–12in). Family Falconidae; species *Falco subbuteo* (Eurasian

▲ **hoatzin** Living in communities of up to 50 birds, hoatzins lay their eggs on platforms made of sticks up to 6m (20ft) above the water. On hatching, the chicks creep in a manner characteristic of reptiles, and are capable of swimming should they fall in the water.

hobby), *Falco cuvieri* (African hobby), *Falco severus* (Oriental hobby) and *Falco longipennis* (Australian hobby or little falcon).

hog
Any member of the PIG family Suidae. Hogs are generally short-legged omnivores with a thick skin.

hog, giant forest
Largest member of the pig family. A grazer, it inhabits tropical forest and adjacent grassland in central Africa. It has grey skin, with brown or black bristles, small, pointed ears and, on the the face of the male, warts. It has sharp, upwardly curved canine teeth. Head-body length: 130–210cm (51–83in); tail: 30–45cm (12–18in). Family Suidae; species *Hylochoerus meinertzhageni*.

hog, pygmy
Smallest member of the pig family. Endangered due to habitat loss, the pygmy hog is now found only in NW Assam, India. It is omnivorous, feeding mainly on roots, but it will also take eggs, small vertebrates and insects. It is grey brown with dark bristles, a sharply tapered head and short legs. It prefers areas with tall grasses. Head-body length: 58–66cm (23–26in); tail: 3cm (1.2in). Family Suidae; species *Sus salvanius*.

hogfish
Large WRASSE found on coral reefs of the Atlantic and Pacific oceans. Several species are known as hogfish. They feed on bottom-dwelling invertebrates. Family Labridae; species include *Lachnolaimus maximus*.

hog plum
See AMERICAN HOG PLUM

hogweed
Herbaceous biennial or monocarpic (having one carpel per flower) perennial native to the Northern Hemisphere; it is found in rough ground and along roadsides. Hogweed is tall and hairy, with large, coarse leaves. Its flowerheads of white or pinkish flowers are produced in flattened umbels. Height: 2–3m (6.6–10ft) Family Apiaceae; species *Heracleum sphondylium*.

Holley, Robert William (1922–93)
US biochemist. He shared with Har KHORANA and Marshall NIRENBERG the 1968 Nobel Prize for physiology or medicine for his work on the way GENES determine the function of CELLS. Holley described the first full sequence of subunits in nucleic acid, the genetic material of a cell. This was an important step toward the understanding of gene action.

holly
See ILEX

hollyhock
Herbaceous biennial or perennial thought to be native to China; it was introduced into Europe in the 16th century and is now widely grown in gardens as an ornamental. It has a stout, hairy stem and produces rounded, lobed leaves and large, saucershaped, white to yellow, red, pink or purple flowers. Height: to 3m (10ft). Family Malvaceae; species *Alcea rosea*.

Holmes, Arthur (1890–1965)
British geologist and geophysicist who studied the age of rocks by measuring their radioactivity. He devised the first quantitative GEOLOGICAL TIMESCALE

in 1913 and estimated the Earth's age by means of temperature measurement.

Holocene (Recent or Post-Glacial Epoch)
Division of GEOLOGICAL TIME extending from roughly 10,000 years ago to the present. It includes the emergence of human beings as settled members of communities. The first known villages dating from *c*.8000 years ago.

homeostasis
Processes that maintain constant conditions within a cell or an organism in response to either internal or external changes.

homeothermic
See ENDOTHERMIC

hominid
Any member of the family Homonidae. Members include modern humans and our earliest ancestors. *See also* HOMO

Homo
Genus to which humans belong. Modern humans are classified *Homo sapiens sapiens. See also* HOMO ERECTUS; HOMO HABILIS; HUMAN EVOLUTION; NEANDERTHAL

Homo erectus
Species of early human dating from *c*.1.5 million to 0.2 million years ago. The "Ape Man of Java" was the first early human fossil to be found, late in the 19th century. Both it and Peking man, another early discovery, represent more advanced forms of *Homo erectus* than older fossils found more recently in Africa. *See also* HUMAN EVOLUTION

Homo habilis
Species of early human. It was discovered by Kenyan palaeoanthropologist Louis Leakey (1903–72) in 1964 in the Olduvai Gorge, E Africa. Its fossil remains have been estimated to be between 1.8 and 1.2 million years old, being contemporary with those of AUSTRALOPITHECINES. The development of hand and skull is much more like that of modern human. *See also* HUMAN EVOLUTION

homologous
Term that describes similarity in essential structure of organisms based on a common genetic heritage. It often refers to organs that now have a different superficial appearance and function in different organisms. For example, despite appearances, a human arm and a seal's flipper are homologous, having evolved from a common origin. *See also* EVOLUTION

homologous chromosome
One of a pair of CHROMOSOMES that share the same genetic structure but not always the same ALLELES for a given characteristic. Found in DIPLOID cells, pairs of homologous chromosomes are composed of one chromosome from the female parent, the other from the male. During MEIOSIS, when GAMETES (sex cells) are formed, homologous chromosomes undergo a complex process known as CROSSING OVER, when strands of the chromosomes (CHROMATIDS)

▶ **hog, pygmy** The world's smallest pig, the pygmy hog (*Sus salvanius*) is now a critically endangered species due mainly to habitat destruction. Pygmy hogs are found in small family groups, which usually contain one or more adult females, several young and occasionally an adult male (males are usually solitary). The entire group lives in a nest made of vegetation.

break from the original chromosome and exchange places with the other member of the pair. This "reshuffling" gives rise to genetic variation, which, together with random MUTATION, is an essential part of EVOLUTION.

homology
See HOMOLOGOUS

Homo neanderthalensis
See NEANDERTHAL

homopteran
Any member of the INSECT order Homoptera, found worldwide. Among the many thousands of homopterans are SCALE INSECTS, LANTERN FLIES, APHIDS, CICADAS and LEAFHOPPERS. Most are terrestial plant feeders, with sucking mouthparts on the back of the head, although some adults lack mouthparts. Homopterans may be winged or wingless. They have three life stages – egg, nymph and adult. Length: to 150mm (6in).

Homo sapiens
Our own species. Genetic analysis has shown that all people living on Earth today belong to the human species *Homo sapiens*, which first evolved in Africa *c*.150,000 years ago. There are also what are known as archaic *Homo sapiens* fossils, which date back to 250,000 years ago in Africa; no continuous record exists between the two. Our ancestors spread northwards out of Africa, reaching the Middle East by 90,000 years ago, and moved on to dominate the world. Game hunters to begin with, modern humans had displaced the NEANDERTHAL people in Europe by 28,000 years ago and finally occupied the Americas *c*.20,000 years ago. By 10,000 years ago agriculture and the domestication of animals began fundamentally to change the human way of life. Modern humans evolved from an earlier human species in Africa, possibly *Homo heidelbergensis*.

homosexuality
Emotional or sexual attraction to individuals of the same sex; being involved in sexual relationships with members of the same sex. *See also* HETEROSEXUALITY

homozygote
Organism possessing identical forms (ALLELES) of a GENE on a CHROMOSOME pair. It is a purebred organism and always produces the same kind of GAMETE (sex cell). *See also* HETEROZYGOTE

homunculus
Miniature of the human fetus once thought to be contained in each human sperm. It was believed that once introduced into the uterus this miniature simply grew into a full-sized fetus before being born. The term is also used to describe a normally proportioned human dwarf.

honesty
Herbaceous biennial native to Europe and Asia and naturalized elsewhere. It is grown as an ornamental for its clusters of showy purple or white flowers and its rounded, flattened seed pods, the valves of which fall away to leave a thin, papery, silvery septum used in decoration. Family Brassicaceae; species *Lunaria annua*.

honeybee
Any of several species of BEE belonging to the family Apidae. The most common species is *Apis mellifera*, found worldwide, which has long been domesticated for the production of honey. It is yellow and black. It constructs combs of six-sided cells using wax produced by glands on its abdomen. Honey is stored in the cells. The honeybee lives in colonies with a social structure. A colony may have up to 60,000 individuals, consisting mainly of infertile female workers, with a few male drones and one egg-laying queen. Length: 12mm (0.5in). Family Apidae.

honeycomb worm
Any of several species of colonial POLYCHAETE worms. They are found on exposed coasts. The colony inhabits a series of densely aggregated tubes, which are constructed from sand. These tube clusters resemble a honeycomb. Phylum Annelida; class Polychaeta; order Terebellida; family Sabellariidae; genus *Sabellaria*.

honeycreeper
Any of a group of small, slender-billed birds related to the tanagers. They are found in tropical South

H

H

liiwi

blue/red-legged honeycreeper

crested honeycreeper

Apapane

▲ **honeycreeper** The iiwi (*Vestaria coccinea*), apapane (*Himatione sanguinea*) and crested honeyeater (*Palmeria dolei*) belong to the Hawaiian honeycreeper family, Drepanididae. The evolution of Hawaiian honeycreeper species is similar to that of the finches studied by Charles Darwin on the Galápagos Islands. In both cases, one species diversified into several in response to environmental variations. Over time, groups of honeycreepers adapted to different diets which eventually resulted in their having different shaped bills. The red-legged, or blue, honeycreeper (*Cyanerpes cyaneus*) is native to South America and belongs to the Emberizidae family.

America, where they feed on nectar and berries. The red-legged honeycreeper (*Cyanerpes cyaneus*) and the shining honeycreeper (*Cyanerpes lucidus*) have down-curved bills and iridescent, violet-blue male plumage. Family Emberizidae (part). **Honeycreeper** is also the name given to several species belonging to the family Drepanididae, found only on the Hawaiian Islands.

honeyeater
Any of *c.*170 species of nectar-feeding birds belonging to the family Meliphagidae. They have long, brush-tipped tongues with which they sip nectar from the base of tubular flowers at the rate of up to 10 licks per second. Their beaks are thin, curved and sharply pointed. Honeyeaters are found mainly in New Guinea, Australasia or nearby regions. Family Meliphagidae.

honeyeater, blue-faced (banana bird)
Familiar large honeyeater, widely distributed in Australia and New Guinea. It is golden-olive above, with a patch of bright blue skin on its face, and white below. The honeyeater is bold around human habitations, raiding poultry yards and rubbish for sweet food. Length: 30cm (12in). Family Meliphagidae; species *Entomyzon cyanotis*.

honey fungus (boot-lace fungus)
FUNGUS with long, black, cord-like rhizomorphs (root-like HYPHAE) that enable it to spread long distances. It is a dangerous parasite of trees. The fruiting bodies have honey-coloured caps and can be found in dense clusters on or around trunks or stumps of deciduous and coniferous trees. Phylum Basidiomycota; species *Armillaria mellea*.

honeyguide
Small, dull-coloured bird that inhabit forests in India and Southeast Asia. Honeyguides eat insects and wax, usually as bee combs; the males vigorously defend the bees' nests on which they feed. They are used by local forest people to locate bees' nests. Family Indicatoridae; species *Indicator xanthonotus*.

honey locust
Deciduous tree with stout, branched thorns. It is native to central North America, where it grows on the rich soil of river bottoms. It is planted as an ornamental in the United States and Europe. The foliage turns yellow in autumn and the inconspicuous flowers give rise to long, bean-like pods. Height: to 42m (140ft). Family Caesalpiniaceae; species *Gleditsia triacanthos*.

honey mesquite
Deciduous thorny shrub or small tree native to South America. It has long, flexible branches. The tiny, pale yellow flowers, produced in long cylindrical spikes, are used as a source of a honey. The pods contain seeds embedded in a sweet, gummy pulp; they are used for fodder. Family Mimosaceae; species *Prosopis pallida*.

honeysuckle
Any of a large group of deciduous or evergreen shrubs or climbers found throughout the Northern Hemisphere. The leaves are paired and the tubular, sometimes two-lipped flowers range in colour from white to yellow or red. Many species and varieties are grown as ornamentals for their often sweetly scented flowers and climbing habit. Family Caprifoliaceae; genus *Lonicera*; species include *Lonicera periclymenum* (woodbine).

hookworm
Any of several species of NEMATODE worms. Two species, which are found in tropical and subtropical climates, are PARASITES of humans. Hookworm larvae usually enter the host through the skin of the feet and legs. They travel to the lungs, from where, via the mouth, they reach the small intestine. The larvae

▲ **hoopoe** The hoopoe's striking black and white wing patterns are visible in flight and, when calling, it puffs out its neck feathers and colourful head crest. It uses its long bill to comb the ground for insects and worms. Shown here is the Eurasian hoopoe (*Upupa epops*).

attach themselves to the lining of the small intestine, where they mature. Adult females can lay thousands of eggs a day, which pass out in the faeces. Symptoms of hookworm infestation include anaemia and constipation. Phylum Nematoda; species *Necator americanus* (the New World species) and *Ancyclostoma duodenale* (the Old World species).

hoopoe
Bird that has pinkish-cinnamon-coloured head and shoulders, a black-tipped crest and strongly barred black-and-white wings and tail. In flight the hoopoe looks like a huge, round-winged, black-and-white moth or butterfly. It feeds on grubs in grassy areas and is found in Europe, Asia and Africa. Length: 28cm (11in). Family Upupidae; species include *Upupa epops*.

hop
Twining vine native to Eurasia and the Americas. It has heart-shaped leaves and small male and female flowers on separate plants. The female flowers of *Humulus lupulus* are used to flavour beer. Family Cannabaceae.

hop-hornbeam
Any of a small group of deciduous trees native to North and Central America, Europe and Asia. The flowers are produced in male and female catkins, and the characteristic fruits consist of a cluster of nutlets, each enclosed in a bladder-like, thin papery husk, resembling hops. The hard timber is used for making mallets. Family Betulaceae; genus *Ostrya*.

horehound
See HOARHOUND

horizon
Geological term used in three ways: 1) a continuous horizontal surface or time-plane between two STRATA that has no thickness; 2) a horizontal layer generally less than 1m (3ft) in thickness that is characterized either by a distinct fossilized FLORA or FAUNA or by a distinctive rock type; 3) a distinct layer in soil. *See also* SOIL HORIZON

hormone
Chemical substance secreted by living CELLS that affects the METABOLISM of cells in other parts of the body. In MAMMALS, hormones are secreted by glands of the ENDOCRINE SYSTEM and are released directly into the bloodstream. They exercise chemical control of physiological functions, regulating growth, development, sexual maturity and functioning, metabolism, and (in part) emotional balance. Hormones circulate in the body in minute quantities and usually exert their effects at considerable distances from their sites of origin. Most are slow to take effect, exert widespread action, and are also slow to disappear from the system. The secretion and activity of the various hormones are closely interdependent; one can stimulate or inhibit the secretion of another, or two or more can act together to produce a certain effect. In general they maintain a delicate equilibrium that is vital to health. The HYPOTHALAMUS, which lies at the base of the brain and is adjacent to the PITUITARY GLAND, is responsible for overall coordination of the secretion of many hormones. Familiar hormones include thyroxine, ADRENALINE, INSULIN, OESTROGEN, PROGESTERONE, TESTOSTERONE and antidiuretic hormone (ADH). In plants, hormones control many aspects of metabolism, including cell elongation, direction of growth, cell division, initiation of flowering, development of fruits, leaf fall, and responses to environmental fac-

▲ **hop** Members of the hemp family Cannabaceae, hops are relatively hardy plants and are grown on inclined strings and wires. After harvesting, by hand or machine, they are dried in preparation for brewing.

tors such as light, water and gravity. The most important plant hormones include AUXIN, GIBBERELLIN, CYTOKININ and abscisic acid, a growth inhibitor that prevents buds from opening too soon in spring and keeps seeds DORMANT through adverse seasons. *See also* HOMEOSTASIS

horn
Defensive or offensive structure that grows from the head of some mammals. A typical horn is made up of a central bony core covered by a layer of the skin protein KERATIN; in the RHINOCEROS, the entire horn is made of keratin. Horns are generally retained for life, although DEER shed their antlers annually.

hornbeam
Any of a number of small, hardy trees of the genus *Carpinus*, found throughout the Northern Hemisphere. They have smooth bark, a short trunk, spreading branches and clusters of green nuts. Family Betulaceae.

hornbill
Medium to very large bird with a massive bill. It feeds on wild figs, fruits, small mammals and insects. The hornbill uses natural tree holes as nests. The female seals herself in for protection with mud, and, whilst incubating, she is fed by the male through a small slit. Family Bucerotidae.

hornbill, great Indian
Very large, Asiatic, pied hornbill; it is black and white with a large yellow casque on top of its huge, down-curved bill. It keeps to a regular schedule of feeding circuits, flying low over subtropical forests and jungle. Its flight is characterized by slow, powerful flaps that are interspersed with glides. Length: 95–105cm (37–41in). Family Bucerotidae; species *Buceros bicornis*.

hornbill, Malabar grey
Small, grey hornbill. It is found in s India, in forests where figs grow. It makes loud, cackling noises. Length: 45cm (18in). Family Bucerotidae; species *Tockus griseus*.

hornblende
Black or green mineral found in IGNEOUS and META-MORPHIC ROCKS. The commonest form of AMPHIBOLE, hornblende contains iron and silicates of calcium, aluminium and magnesium. Hardness 5.5; r.d. 3.2.

hornero
Any of about seven species of small songbirds belonging to the ovenbird family. They are found in South America. The rufous (reddish-brown) hornero (*Furnarius rufus*) builds a domed mud nest, which is shaped like a traditional baker's oven. Family Furnariidae; genus *Furnarius*.

hornet
Large, orange-and-brown WASP native to Europe, or a yellow-and-black wasp found in the United States. Hornets build egg-shaped paper nests, with one queen and many nectar-gathering workers. They have a powerful sting but are less aggressive than the common wasp. Family Vespidae.

hornfels
Any of a group of hard, fine-grained METAMORPHIC ROCKS formed originally in a high-temperature area in near contact with an IGNEOUS INTRUSION. They all contain QUARTZ and MICA, with a third component that gives them their individual names: **chiastolite** hornfels, **cordierite** hornfels, **garnet** hornfels and **pyroxine** hornfels. All are dark grey or black, although garnet hornfels has reddish patches.

horn of plenty
FUNGUS with a thin, somewhat leathery fruiting body, which is trumpet-shaped with a flared mouth. The horn of plenty is dark brown to black, with an ash-grey outer surface where the spores are released. It grows in clusters amongst leaf litter of deciduous woods. It is edible. Phylum Basidiomycota; species *Craterellus cornucopioides*.

horse
Hoofed mammal. It evolved in North America but became extinct there during the late Pleistocene epoch. Early horse forms crossed the land bridge across the Bering Strait, dispersed throughout Asia, Europe and Africa, and produced the modern horse family. The only surviving true wild horse is Przewalski's horse. The horse was first domesticated *c*.5000 years ago in central Asia. Horses returned to the New World with the Spanish conquistadores in the 1500s. Horses are characterized by one large

▲ **hornbill** The world population of the Narcondam hornbill (*Rhyticeros* *narcondami*) is confined to Adaman island in the Bay of Bengal.

functional toe, molars with crowns joined by ridges for grazing, an elongated skull and a simple stomach. Fast runners, they usually live in herds. Family Equideae; species *Equus caballus*.

horse, Przewalski's (Mongolian wild horse)
Only surviving species of the original wild horse. It is found only in Mongolia and Sinkiang, NW China. Przewalski's horse is small and stocky with an erect black mane. Its red-brown coat is marked with a darker line on the back and shoulders, and by leg stripes. Height: to 1.5m (4.9ft) at the shoulder. Family Equidae; species *Equus caballus przewalskii*.

horse chestnut
Any of *c*.25 species of deciduous trees that grow in temperate regions, especially the common horse

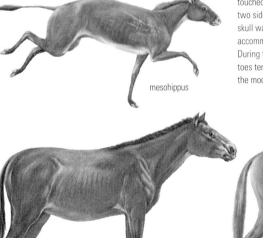

▼ **horse** *Mesohippus* was a typical Oligocene horse. It was about the size of a large dog. It had three toes on each of its feet. By the Miocene, the horse had evolved into a form

mesohippus

merychippus

typified by *Merychippus*. This was a much large animal than *Mesohippus*, with longer legs. Only one toe on each foot touched the ground, although two side toes still existed. The skull was larger to accommodate longer teeth. During the Pliocene, the side toes tended to disappear and the modern horse evolved. By the beginning of the Ice Age, horses of the modern genus *Equus* were present on every continent except Australia. They had strong hooves rather than toes, and their limbs were adapted for powerful locomotion. Today Przewalski's horse found on the Asian steppes is the only living species of wild horse.

equus

H

chestnut, *Aesculus hippocastanum*. It has large leaves, long flower spikes and round prickly fruits containing one or two inedible nuts. Height: to 30m (100ft). Family Hippocastanaceae.

horsefly
Any of several species of flies belonging to the family Tabanidae, especially *Tabanus lineola*. It is a pest to livestock and human beings. The female horsefly inflicts a painful bite and sucks blood. Length: to 30mm (1.2in).

horsehair worm (nematomorph, hair worm, thread worm)
Any member of the phylum Nematomorpha. They are long, thin, usually black or brown worms, with featureless bodies. The young are parasitic in arthropods, and the adults are free-living in soil or fresh water. Length: to *c*.800mm (*c*.30in). Phylum Nematomorpha.

horse latitudes
Either of two areas of high pressure found near 25°N and 25°s of the Equator. The air rises at or near the Equator because of low pressure and then circles in the atmosphere, with much falling near the tropics of Cancer and Capricorn. The falling air gives rise to fairly permanent regions of high pressure, known as the horse latitudes. Both the TRADE WINDS, which blow from the horse latitudes toward the Equator, and the WESTERLIES, which blow from the horse latitudes toward the poles, are caused by the high pressure.

horseradish
Perennial plant that is native to E Europe. Horseradish is cultivated for its pungent, fleshy root, which is a useful seasoning. It has lance-shaped, toothed leaves, and white flower clusters. Height: *c*.1.2m (*c*.4ft). Family Brassicaceae/Cruciferae; species *Armoracia rusticana*.

horseshoe crab
Marine ARTHROPOD that is common to the NW Atlantic coast and the Gulf of Mexico. Horseshoe crabs are dark brown and have five pairs of walking legs. The body is divided into a cephalothorax and an abdomen, with a long, triangular, spike-like tail. Horseshoe crabs are scavengers, feeding on molluscs, worms and other organisms. They are one of only five living species that represent an ancient group stretching back to the Ordovician period (505–438 million years ago). Length: to 60cm (24in). Class Merostomata; species *Limulus polyphemus*.

▲ **horseshoe crab** The horseshoe, or king, crab is not a true crab, but a primitive arthropod closely related to fossil forms and allied to spiders and scorpions. It is commonly found in estuaries and mud flats. It burrows into the sand or mud to find food. The horseshoe crab's diet consists of worms and small invertebrates, which it crushes with the pincer-like chelicera surrounding its mouth.

horseshoe worm (phoronid)
Any member of the phylum Phoronida, comprising *c*.15 species of marine invertebrates. They have worm-like, non-segmented bodies. Adult horseshoe worms are sedentary. They live in membranous tubes, sometimes covered with sand or shell particles, into which they retreat when disturbed. Length: 5–250mm (0.2–10in).

horsetail
Any of *c*.30 species of flowerless, rush-like plants of the phylum Sphenophyta. They grow in all continents except Australasia. The hollow, jointed stems have a whorl of tiny leaves at each joint. Spores are produced in a cone-like structure at the top of a stem. Horsetails date from the Carboniferous period. Phylum Sphenophyta, genus *Equisetum*.

horst
In geology, an elongated upthrust block that is bounded by parallel normal FAULTS on its long sides. *See also* GRABEN

host
Organism infected by a PARASITE, either **definitive**, in which the parasite reaches sexual maturity, or **intermediate**, in which it does not.

hosta (plantain-lily)
Any member of the genus *Hosta*, a group of herbaceous perennials native to China and Japan. Hostas are grown for their ornamental foliage. Broad leaves, with several prominent ribs, form a basal tuft, and the white or blue tubular flowers are held aloft on tall stems. The genus is named after the Austrian botanist N.T. Host (1761–1834). Family Liliaceae; genus *Hosta*.

hot spot
Area of high volcanic activity. Some hot spots are located on CONSTRUCTIVE MARGINS (boundaries between plates), for example Iceland. Other hot spots, for example Hawaii, occur within plates where the crust is thin rather than at an edge. Hot spots are thought to be caused by upwelling of MAGMA in the MANTLE beneath (mantle plumes). *See also* PLATE TECTONICS

Hottentot bread
See ELEPHANT'S FOOT

Hottentot fig
Perennial plant that grows on rocks, cliffs and sands near the sea; it is native to s Africa and has been naturalized elsewhere. Its woody stems grow along the ground, and its leaves are fleshy and triangular in outline. The large, solitary flowers are yellow or pinkish-purple. It produces fleshy, edible fruits, which can be eaten fresh, dried or in jam. Family Aizoaceae; species *Carpobrotus edulis*.

Hottentot tea
Straggling, somewhat shrubby plant that is native to s Africa. It has simple leaves. Its flowers, which grow in daisy-like heads, have distinct rays. It is used as a substitute for tea, hence its common name. Height: to 1.5m (5ft). Family Asteraceae; species *Helichrysum serpyllifolium*.

house-fly
Common FLY found worldwide. It is black and grey with large compound eyes. It lays its eggs in animal waste and decaying vegetable matter. It commonly feeds on the food of human beings and can transmit, on its feet, disease-causing microorganisms.

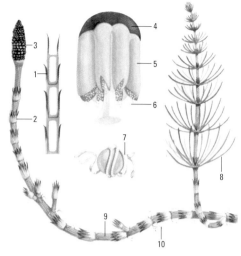

▲ **horsetail** The field horsetail (*Equisetum arvense*) has a stem that in longitudinal section (1) is seen to be hollow; it is useful as a scouring material. The leaves (2) are reduced to scales. The cone (3) is a reproductive structure; it consists of a short axis bearing clusters of whorled sporangiphores (4), which have sac-like sporangia (5) bearing spores (6) attached to their inner surfaces. Changes in air humidity cause coiled elators (7) round the spores to uncoil and eject them. The rhizome (8) anchored in the soil by adventitious roots (9) can also produce a vegetative shoot (10).

Length: 5–7mm (0.2–0.3in). Order Diptera; family Muscidae; species *Musca domestica*.

houseleek
Perennial SUCCULENT plant, native to Europe and Asia and naturalized in North America. Its fleshy, oblong leaves are produced in basal rosettes, from which arises the flowering stem, bearing a cluster of pinkish flowers at the apex. The houseleek is grown on wall tops and on cottage roofs to keep the slates in position. Family Crassulaceae; species *Sempervivum tectorum*.

house martin
See MARTIN, HOUSE

hoverfly
Two-winged INSECT of the large family Syrphidae. The hoverfly is easily recognizable from its habit of hovering then darting forwards. Many species are banded with yellow and black like wasps; others resemble bees. Their coloration is a form of protective MIMICRY, because none of the species has a sting. Order Diptera.

Howard, Leland Ossian (1857–1950)
US entomologist. His work helped to achieve control over parasitic insects, especially the house-fly and the mosquito, and crop destroyers such as the boll weevil. Howard's many books include *The Insect Book* (1901) and *The House Fly – Disease Carrier* (1911).

howler monkey
See MONKEY, HOWLER

huckleberry
Deciduous, low-growing, ericaceous shrub. It is found on acid soil throughout E North America. Its leaves are elliptic to oblong, and it produces reddish, bell-like flowers in drooping racemes; the branches are somewhat sticky when young. The edible fruit is a blueberry- or blackberry-like drupe composed of ten one-seeded nutlets. Family Ericaceae; main species *Gaylussacia baccata*.

Physical structure of a human. It is composed of water, protein and other organic compounds, and some inorganic material (minerals). It has a bony framework, the SKELETON, consisting of more than 200 bones, sheathed in SKELETAL MUSCLE to enable movement. A protective bony case, the SKULL, surrounds the large BRAIN. The body is fuelled by nutrients absorbed from the DIGESTIVE SYSTEM and oxygen from the LUNGS, which are pumped around the body by the CIRCULATORY SYSTEM. Metabolic wastes are eliminated by the process of EXCRETION. Continuation of the species is enabled by the REPRODUCTIVE SYSTEM. Overall control is exerted by the NERVOUS SYSTEM, working closely with the ENDOCRINE SYSTEM. The body surface is covered by a protective layer of SKIN.

The body as a whole is a compromise between mobility and rigidity. The internal organs, such as the HEART, LIVER, STOMACH and the INTESTINES, are closely packed together and yet can work freely and easily. The surrounding framework of bone and muscles applies support and protection. The skeleton gives upright strength to the body and in some places, such as the skull and THORAX, acts as a protective layer. The joints give the bones mobility and the muscles strength and suppleness. The contents of the chest and ABDOMEN are constantly moving – the beating of the heart, inhalation and exhalation of the lungs during BREATHING, and PERISTALSIS of the bowel. These structures move without difficulty as they are surrounded by smooth pericardium, PLEURA and peritoneum.

The body's largest organ is the skin. It not only envelops the whole body in a protective water-proof layer but is also part of the heat-regulating system. The liver is the most complicated organ and has the greatest number of functions – transforming digested food into usable materials and disposing of waste substances.

The circulation is constantly restoring and revitalizing as well as removing waste products from the basic unit of the body – the CELL. Each of the billions of cells that build up the body carries out its own particular function. All the structures and organs are held together by connective tissue, made up of cells that act as a packing to protect and support the internal mechanisms.

H

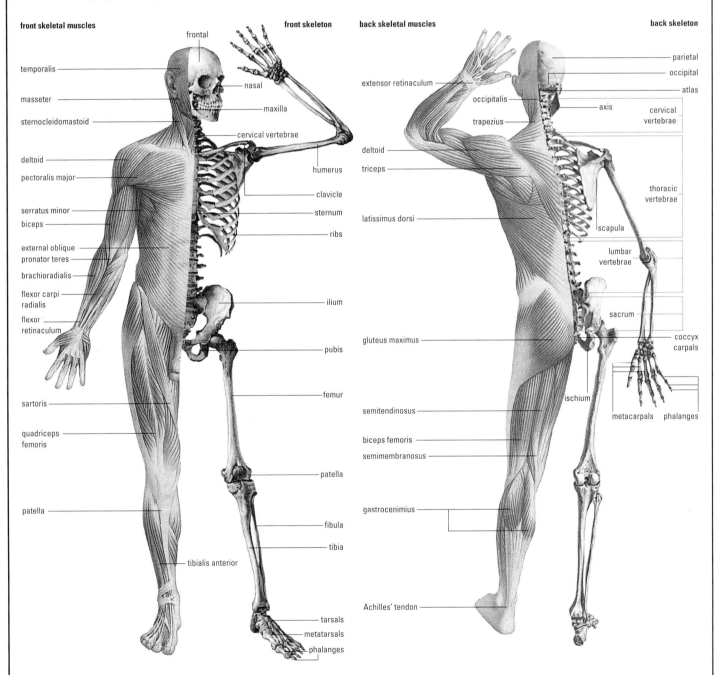

▲ **The human skeleton** consists of about 206 bones, divided into two groups, the appendicular and axial skeletons. The skeleton has three functions; it provides support, protects the internal organs, and with some muscles, it provides movement. The axial skeleton (the skull, spine and rib cage) supplies the structure on which the limbs, the appendicular skeleton, are joined via the shoulder and pelvic girdles. Muscles are made up of contractile tissue and are involved in movement. Muscles comprise 35–40% of total body weight, and there are more than 650 skeletal muscles controlled by the nervous system. Three kinds of muscle exist; smooth, cardiac and skeletal. Skeletal muscle is under voluntary control, cardiac muscle occurs only in the heart, and smooth, or involuntary, muscle controls organs such as the digestive tract.

► **human evolution** Although the fossil record is not complete, we know that humans evolved from ape-like creatures. Our earliest ancestor, *Australopithecus afarensis* (A), lived in NE Africa some 5 million years ago. Over the next 3–4 million years *Australopithecus africanus* (B) evolved. *Homo Habilis* (C), who used primitive stone tools, appeared *c*.500,000 years later. *Homo erectus* (D) is believed to have spread from Africa to regions all over the world 750,000 years ago. Records indicate that from *Homo erectus* evolved two species, Neanderthal man (E), who died out 40,000 years ago, and who could have been made extinct by the other species, the earliest modern man *Homo sapiens sapiens* (F).

huemul
Either of two species of DEER found high in the Andes of South America. The huemul's coat is generally brown, paler in the winter, and it has large ears and a black, y-shaped face-marking. Males have branching antlers. Head-body length: 150–170cm (59–67cm); tail: 11–13cm (4–5in). Family Cervidae; subfamily Odocoilinae; genus *Hippocamelus*.

human body
See feature article, page 189

human evolution
Process by which humans developed from pre-human ancestors. The FOSSIL record of human ancestors is patchy and unclear. Some scientists believe that our ancestry can be traced back to one or more species of AUSTRALOPITHECINES, which flourished in S and E Africa between four and one million years ago. Other scientists believe that we are descended from some as yet undiscovered ancestor. The earliest fossils that can be identified as human are those of *Homo habilis* (handy people), which date from two million years ago. The next evolutionary stage was *Homo erectus* (upright people), who first appeared *c*.1.5 million years ago. The earliest fossils of our own species, *Homo sapiens* (wise people), date from *c*.250,000 years ago. An apparent side-branch, the NEANDERTHALS (*Homo sapiens neanderthalensis*), existed in Europe and W Asia *c*.130,000–30,000 years ago. Fully modern humans, *Homo sapiens sapiens*, first appeared *c*.100,000 years ago. All human species apart from *Homo sapiens sapiens* are now extinct.

Humboldt, Baron Friedrich Heinrich Alexander von (1769–1859)
German scientist and explorer. His special subject was mineralogy, but on his scientific trips in Europe and Central and South America he studied volcanoes, the origins of tropical storms, and the increase in magnetic intensity from the Equator towards the poles. His principal, five-volume work, *Kosmos* (1845–62), is a comprehensive description of the physical universe.

Humboldt current (Peru current)
Current in the SE Pacific Ocean. An extension of the West Wind Drift, the Humboldt current flows north along the W coast of South America. A cold current, it lowers temperature along its course until it joins the warm Pacific South Equatorial current. It is named after Baron HUMBOLDT, who studied it in the early 19th century.

humidity (relative humidity)
Measure of the amount of water vapour in air. It is the ratio of the actual vapour pressure to the saturation vapour pressure at which water normally condenses; it is usually expressed as a percentage. Humidity is measured by a hygrometer.

hummingbird
Brightly coloured bird that hovers to sip nectar with its long, needle-like bill. The male hummingbird has iridescent throat feathers, called a gorget. Hummingbirds are found mainly in South and Central America. Despite their size, some species undertake long distance migrations, with the males migrating before the females and immatures. Family Trochilidae; there are *c*.335 species.

hummingbird, bee
Smallest of all birds. The male is iridescent green above with a full red gorget; the female is similar, but lacks the red head and throat. It is found in Cuba. The bee hummingbird my be mistaken for an insect as it feeds. Its wings beat at up to 80 times per second. Length: 6cm (2in). Family Trochilidae; species *Calypte helenae*.

hummingbird, calliope
Smallest North American bird. Its plumage is green above and whitish below; the male has purple-red streaks on its gorget. Calliope hummingbirds are common along streams in W United States; they winter as far south as Mexico. Length: 8cm (3in). Family Trochilidae; species *Stellula calliope*.

hummingbird, ruby-throated
Familiar North American hummingbird. It breeds in S Canada and E United States and winters in Mexico and Panama. The male has a brilliant red throat and a black, forked tail. It is found in woodland edges and gardens. Length: 10cm (4in). Family Trochilidae; species *Archilochus colubris*.

humus
Dark brown organic substance, resulting from partial decay of plant and animal matter. It improves soil by retaining moisture, aerating, and increasing mineral nutrient content and bacterial activity. Humus can be made in a compost heap or obtained naturally. Types of humus include PEAT MOSS, leaf mould and soil from woods.

hurricane
Wind of force 12 or greater on the BEAUFORT WIND SCALE. A hurricane is an intense and devastating tropical CYCLONE, with winds ranging upward from 118km/h (73mph); it is known also as a **typhoon** in the Pacific. Originating over oceans 10° to 20° from the Equator, hurricanes have a calm central hole, called the **eye**, surrounded by inward spiralling winds and cumulonimbus CLOUDS. Weather satellites often

sword-billed hummingbird

streamer-tailed hummingbird

▲ **hummingbird** The sword-billed hummingbird (*Ensifera ensifera*) is one of the *c*.300 species of hummingbird found in the Americas. It has the longest bill. The streamer-tailed hummingbird (*Trochilus polytmus*) is one of three species native to Jamaica. Its long tail feathers making a distinctive whirring noise when in flight.

give adequate warning of their approach, but the wind and rain of hurricanes take many lives and cause extensive damage, particularly in the West Indies and the SE and E coasts of the United States.

hutia
Rodent that is found only in the West Indies. It is a strong tree-climber and prefers woodland habitats. Hutias resemble short-legged rats. Their tails range from practically non-existent to long and prehensile. Their diet includes a variety of plant material and small vertebrates. Head-body length: 20–60cm (8–24in). Family *Capromyidae*.

Hutton, James (1726–97)
Scottish geologist. Hutton sought to formulate theories of the origin of the Earth and of atmospheric changes. He concluded that the Earth's history could be explained only by observing current forces at work within it, thereby laying the foundations of modern geological science.

Huxley, Sir Julian Sorell (1887–1975)
British biologist, grandson of Thomas HUXLEY. His researches were chiefly on the behaviour of birds and other animals in relation to EVOLUTION. His writings greatly promoted public interest in the subject. He served as secretary of the Zoological Society of London (1935–48) and as the director general of the United Nations Educational, Scientific and Cultural Organization (UNESCO) (1946–48). His books include *The Individual in the Animal Kingdom* (1911) and *Evolutionary Ethics* (1943).

Huxley, Thomas Henry (1825–95)
British biologist. Huxley was a champion of Charles DARWIN's theory of EVOLUTION and of the scientific method in research. His works include *Zoological Evidences as to Man's Place in Nature* (1863), *Manual of Comparative Anatomy of Vertebrated Animals* (1871) and *Evolution and Ethics* (1893).

hyacinth
Any member of the genus *Hyacinthus*, a group of bulbous plants that are native to the Mediterranean region and Africa. Hyacinths have long, thin leaves and spikes of bell-shaped flowers, which may be white, yellow, red, blue or purple. Family Liliaceae; genus *Hyacinthus*.

hybrid
See feature article

hybridization
CrossBREEDING of plants or animals between different species in order to produce offspring that differ in genetically determined traits; it is commonly the result of human intervention. Changes in climate or in the environment of an organism may give rise to natural hybridization, but often humans use specialized techniques to produce hybrids that may be hardier or more resistant to disease than the original forms, or more economical.

hybrid vigour
Inordinate strength demonstrated in some HYBRID offspring that is not characteristic of the parents. *See also* HETEROSIS

hydra
Any member of the *Hydra* genus of HYDROZOANS. It spends its entire life as a POLYP, usually attached to a surface, feeding on small floating organisms, which it catches with its tentacles. It reproduces by small budding growths that form on its body. It is

◄ **hyacinth** Most cultivated hyacinth varieties originate from the Dutch hyacinth (*Hyacinthus orientalis*), shown here. One smaller variety commonly seen in ornamental displays is the Roman hyacinth (variety *albulus*), which has blue or white flowers and is produced in S France and Italy.

capable of regenerating much of its body. Phylum Cnidaria; class Hydrozoa; order Hydroida; family Hydridae. *See also* HYDROID

hydrangea
Any member of the *Hydrangea* genus, comprising c.80 species of deciduous woody shrubs, small trees and vines, native to the Western Hemisphere and Asia. Hydrangeas are grown for their showy clusters of flowers, which may be white, pink or blue. Family Hydrangeaceae.

hydraulic action
Erosive effect of water. The force of moving water can be an effective agent of EROSION. It is important both in rivers and on coastlines. In rivers the move-

ment of currents causes hydraulic action, though if a load of silt or sand were added the process would be called CORRASION. Along the coast, breaking waves batter cliffs and may open out JOINTS in the rock, forming caves or undermining the cliff and leading to collapse.

hydrogen (symbol H)
Gaseous, nonmetallic element; it was first identified as a separate element in 1766 by English chemist Henry Cavendish, who called it "inflammable air". Colourless and odourless, hydrogen is usually classified with the alkali metals in group I of the periodic table. Isotopes include DEUTERIUM and the radioactive tritium. Hydrogen is the lightest and most abundant element in the Universe (76% by mass), mostly found on Earth combined with oxygen in water. It is used to manufacture ammonia, to harden fats and oils, and in rocket fuels. The hydrogen bomb is produced by the nuclear fusion of hydrogen isotopes. Properties: at.no. 1; r.a.m. 1.00797; r.d. 0.0899; m.p. −259.1°C (−434.4°F); b.p. −252.9°C (−423.2°F); most common isotope ^1H (99.985%).

hydrogen bond
Chemical bond formed between certain hydrogen-containing molecules. The hydrogen atom must be bound to an electronegative (electron-withdrawing) atom; the bond is formed between the positive charge on hydrogen and the negative charge on an atom in an adjacent molecule. Hydrogen bonding occurs in water and in many biological systems.

hydroid
Any member of the order Hydroida of the class Hydrozoa. They are aquatic, marine organisms, and some have chitinous exoskeletons. Hydroids spend

HYBRID

Offspring of two parents of different GENE composition. It often refers to the offspring of different varieties of a species or of the cross between two separate species. Most interspecies hybrids, plant or animal, are unable to produce fertile offspring. *See also* BACKCROSS

◄ **It is occasionally** possible to interbreed two closely related species to produce a hybrid. Male donkeys (1) mated with female horses (2) produce mules (3), which are sterile because their chromosomes cannot pair properly during meiosis, the form of cell division required to produce sperm or eggs. Modern bread wheat (8) is a product of many years of selective breeding during which many varieties have been developed (7, 9). They have their origins in the hybridization of wild wheat and grass species to increase the number of chromosomes in the wheat cells from pairs of seven chromosomes, to four sets of seven (4) and then to six sets of seven (5, 6), which could divide properly during meiosis and breed normally.

H

▶ **hyena** The spotted, or laughing, hyena (*Crocuta crocuta*) is the largest and boldest species. Spotted hyenas are often seen hunting in packs and will enter villages looking for food or livestock. They are noted for their wailing call, which sometimes resembles manic laughter, and their powerful jaws, which can crush heavy bones. Both the striped hyena (*Hyaena hyaena*) and the brown hyena (*Hyaena brunnes*) are more solitary and predominantly nocturnal hyenas. The coarse manes along their necks and backs become erect when the animal is threatened. The striped hyena differs from its relatives, however, as it rarely attacks livestock. Hyenas live in territorial clans dominated by females. Female hyenas are larger than the males; they decide on their breeding partners and often lead the pack when hunting. The young are raised in communal dens.

striped hyena

spotted or laughing hyena

brown hyena

much of their lives as POLYPS (cylinder-like bodies, usually attached to a substrate), which are usually colonial. Some species produce medusae, which float and swim freely. Hydroids feed via oral tentacles. Phylum Cnidaria. *See also* HYDROZOAN

hydrological cycle
See feature article

hydrology
Study of the Earth's waters, their sources, circulation, distribution, uses, and chemical and physical composition. The HYDROLOGICAL CYCLE is the Earth's natural water circulation system. Hydrologists are scientists and engineers involved in various aspects of hydrology, including the provision of fresh water, building dams and irrigation systems, and controlling floods and water pollution.

hydrolysis
Chemical reaction in which molecules of a substance are split into smaller molecules by reaction with water, often assisted by a CATALYST. In DIGESTION, for example, ENZYMES catalyze the hydrolysis of CARBOHYDRATES, PROTEINS and FATS into smaller, soluble molecules that the body can assimilate.

hydrophily
POLLINATION of a FLOWER through the agency of water. It is a rare type of pollination employed by aquatic plants and can occur in one of two ways. Either the pollen grains themselves are carried on or under the surface of the water, or the male flowers break off and float along until they come into contact with a female flower.

hydrophone
Specialized microphone designed to detect sounds and ultrasonic waves underwater. Initially used to detect submarines, hydrophones have, more recently, been used in oceanography, for example, for listening to whale song.

hydrophyte (aquatic plant)
Plant that grows only in water or in damp places. Examples include water lilies, water ferns, water milfoil, water hyacinth, duckweed and various pondweeds.

hydrosphere
Water on the surface of the Earth, including oceans, lakes, streams and groundwater.

hydrothermal process
Geological activity produced by the action of very hot subterranean water, at temperatures between 300 and 500°C (570–930°F). Superheated water can dissolve many minerals, such as those of copper, lead and zinc, depositing them as veins in rock crevices. It can also trigger chemical changes, for example turning the mineral OLIVINE into SERPENTINE. Much of this hydrothermal activity takes place in the deep ocean seabeds. Hot water welling from the floor of oceanic trenches is responsible for colonies of life 2.5km (1.5mi) below the surface, where tube worms, crustaceans and fish thrive without the benefit of the Sun's warmth.

hydrothermal vent (smoker)
Fissure in the SEAFLOOR through which mineral-rich water escapes. Hydrothermal vents form in areas of volcanic activity. Seawater seeps down through the bottom sediments into the hot rocks beneath and dissolves various minerals. When the water erupts through a vent, it cools rapidly and the dissolved minerals are precipitated out of solution as a "smoke". Unique species of bacteria and animals have been found living in the mineral-rich water around such vents. *See also* VOLCANO

hydrotropism
Plant growth in response to water stimulus. Almost all plant roots bend towards moisture (that is, they are positively hydrotropic) whereas stems and leaves show no response. It is not a strong TROPISM.

hydrozoan
Any member of the class Hydrozoa. They typically alternate between a POLYP state (a sessile state in which the animals' cylinder-like bodies are secured to the substratum) and a MEDUSA state (a free-living state in which movement is usually facilitated by a bell-like structure similar to that of the jellyfish). Polyps are usually colonial; they are specialized into digestive, feeding, reproductive and defensive forms. The class Hydrozoa contains more than 2500 species in seven orders.

hyena
Any of four species of carnivore, mostly native to Africa, although the striped hyena also lives in the Middle East and s Asia. Hyenas are efficient carnivores: they cooperate to kill animals as large as zebras and forage at carcasses. They also eat a wide range of other food. Order Carnivora; family Hyaenidae.

hyena, brown
Hyena that is found in dry, rocky areas of s Africa. It has a dark brown, long-haired coat, with a whitish collar and horizontal, dark stripes on the legs. It is dog-like in appearance. The brown hyena mainly scavenges for food, but it will also eat fruit and hunt small vertebrates. Head-body length: 110–130cm (43–51in); tail: 20–25cm (8–10in). Family Hyaenidae; species *Hyaena brunnea*.

hyena, spotted (laughing hyena)
Largest species of hyena. It is known for its distinctive vocalizations. The spotted hyena is robustly built, yellow-brown in colour with darker, irregular spots. It can be found in central and s Africa, preferring flat, open grassland. Its prey includes mammals larger than itself. Head-body length: 120–140cm (47–55in); tail: 70–90cm (28–35in). Family Hyaenidae; species *Crocuta crocuta*.

hyena, striped
Generally solitary animal that inhabits dry, rocky

desert in E and North Africa, as well as the Middle East and India. It has similar feeding habits to the brown hyena. Its yellow-grey coat is striped on the back, legs and cheeks, and the front legs are noticeably longer than the back ones. Head-body length: 100–120cm (40–47in); tail: 25–35cm (10–14in). Family Hyaenidae; species *Hyaena hyaena*.

hymenopteran

Any member of the insect order Hymenoptera. It contains SAWFLIES, ANTS, WASPS, HORNETS and BEES. All hymenopterans have a complete life cycle – egg, larva, pupa and adult – and two pairs of membranous wings, which move together in flight. They are found worldwide, living solitarily or in social groups. The larvae (grubs or caterpillars) feed on plants or are parasitic or predacious.

hypertonic solution

Solution that has a higher SOLUTE concentration when compared to another solution. When the two solutions are separated from one another by a partially permeable membrane, the SOLVENT (usually water) will move into the hypertonic solution from the less concentrated (**hypotonic**) solution. A hypertonic solution has a lower water potential than a hypotonic one and so draws water into it. *See also* ISOTONIC SOLUTIONS

hypha (pl. hyphae)

Very fine, thread-like projection found in FUNGI.

Collectively a number will form the MYCELIUM, which is responsible for the reproduction and feeding of the fungus.

hypocolius, grey

Long-tailed, short-winged perching bird belonging to the WAXWING family. Mainly grey, the male has a black mask and conspicuous black flight feathers with white tips. It has a strong, swooping flight and feeds on berries. An uncommon bird, the hypocolius breeds in the Middle East and winters in India and Pakistan. Length: 23cm (9in). Family Bombycillidae; species *Hypocolius ampelinus*.

hypolimnion

Lower, colder layers of water in a lake, beneath the EPILIMNION. There is not enough light for PHOTOSYNTHESIS to occur and levels of dissolved oxygen are low.

hypothalamus

Region at the base of the vertebrate BRAIN, adjoining the PITUITARY GLAND. It contains centres that regulate body temperature, fluid balance, hunger, thirst and sexual activity. It is also involved in emotional activity, sleep and the integration of hormonal and nervous activity.

hypotonic solution

See HYPERTONIC SOLUTION

▲ **hyrax** The ground-dwelling rock hyrax (*Procavia capensis*) is active during the day. It is commonly found in deserts or in rocky environments. It feeds on grasses and leaves, which provide a large part of its water intake. Rock hyraxes live in large colonies dominated by a single male.

hypsilophodont

Any member of a group of small, bipedal, ORNITHOPOD dinosaurs, such as *Hypsilophodon*. They evolved in late Jurassic times and died out in the end Cretaceous EXTINCTION event. Hypsilophodonts were fast moving and, apart from their long stiff tails, were ostrich-like in appearance. They used their horny beaks and cheek teeth to browse plants.

hyrax

Small, herbivorous, hoofed mammal of Africa and SW Asia. Rock hyraxes (genus *Procavia*), which live in deserts and hills, are larger than the solitary, nocturnal, tree-dwelling hyraxes (genus *Dendrohyrax*). Length: to 50cm (20in). Family Procaviidae.

H

HYDROLOGICAL CYCLE

Circulation of water around the Earth. Water is evaporated from the sea; most falls back into the oceans, but some is carried over land. There it falls as PRECIPITATION (for example, rain or snow) and, either by EVAPORATION, EVAPOTRANSPIRATION or TRANSPIRATION by plants, is returned to the ATMOSPHERE. Alternatively, it gradually finds its way back to the sea, by surface runoff, infiltration or seepage. Less than 1% of the world's water is involved in this cycle; 97% of all water is in the oceans, and much of the remainder is held as snow or ice.

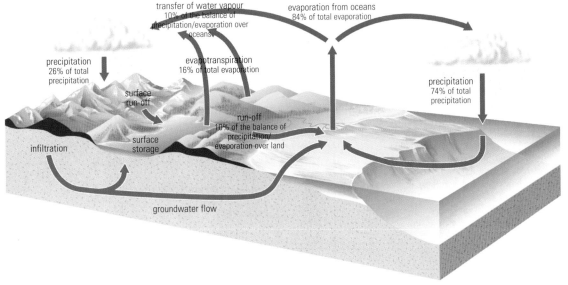

► **The Earth's water** balance is regulated by the constant recycling of water between the oceans, the atmosphere and the land. The movement of water between these three "reservoirs" is called the hydrological cycle. The oceans play a vital role in this cycle: 74% of the total precipitation falls over the oceans and 84% of the total evaporation comes from the oceans. Water vapour in the atmosphere circulates around the planet, transporting energy as well as water itself. When the vapour cools it falls as rain or other precipitation.

transfer of water vapour 10% of the balance of precipitation/evaporation over oceans

evaporation from oceans 84% of total evaporation

precipitation 26% of total precipitation

evapotranspiration 16% of total evaporation

precipitation 74% of total precipitation

surface run-off

run-off 10% of the balance of precipitation/evaporation over land

infiltration

surface storage

groundwater flow

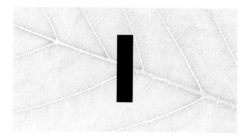

ibex

Mountain GOAT. It is distinctive for its massive, ribbed horns, up to 100cm (40in) long, possessed by both sexes. The classification of ibexes is still unresolved, and there may be four separate species. They inhabit mountainous regions of Europe, central Asia, North Africa and Arabia. More uniform in colour than wild goats, they are usually shades of brown, with darker legs and sometimes a dark back stripe. Head-body length: 75–170cm (30–67in); tail: 15–30cm (6–12in). Family Bovidae; subfamily Caprinae; genus *Capra*.

ibex, Spanish (Spanish goat)

Ibex that inhabits mountainous regions of the Iberian Peninsula. There are several subspecies. Their horns are shorter than those of other ibexes and have a slight twist. Family Bovidae; subfamily Caprinae; species *Capra pyrenaica*.

ibis

Any of *c*.26 species of medium to large birds found in tropical or subtropical regions of the world. Most species are found near water. In appearance, ibises vary in colour, but most species have long necks, long legs and long, usually down-curved bills. They feed on a variety of aquatic animals. Most species breed in colonies in trees. Family Threskiornithidae.

ibis, glossy

Medium to large, gregarious ibis found in marshland in parts of E Europe, Asia, Indonesia, Australia, Madagascar and Central America. It has dark, copper-coloured, glossy plumage, long legs, a long neck and a down-curved bill. It feeds mainly on aquatic invertebrates. Length: 55–62cm (22–24in). Family Threskiornithidae; species *Plegadis falcinellus*.

ibis, hermit (waldrapp, northern bald ibis)

Medium to large ibis found in dry country in Southeast Asia and NE Africa. It has metallic bronze plumage, a bald face and a ruff of feathers on its neck. The hermit ibis nests on rocky cliffs and in caves. It feeds mostly on beetles. It is now rare. Length: 70–80cm (28–31in). Family Threskiornithidae; species *Geronticus eremita*.

ibis, sacred

Medium-sized ibis found in the wetlands of Africa,

▶ **ibis, scarlet** The scarlet ibis is born with a dull brown plumage and white underparts, which develop into a brilliant red colour. As with flamingos, the coloration comes from pigments in the bodies of the crustaceans on which the ibis feeds. Unless scarlet ibises are fed a special diet, the plumage of birds in captivity fades to pink.

ICEBERG

Large, drifting piece of ice, broken off from a GLACIER or polar ICE CAP. As the ice moves slowly outwards from a snow-cap, some reaches the sea. It floats and is gradually broken off by the movement of tides and waves. Some icebergs may be several hundred metres across, but they gradually melt and shrink as they float across the oceans. Icebergs from Greenland are quite tall, whereas those from the Antarctic region are generally flat and tabular in shape. As much as 80% or 90% of an iceberg is below the surface of the water. As they melt, icebergs sometimes turn over, which readjusts the balance. One of the major areas for icebergs is on the route of the cold Labrador Current, which brings them south along the coast of Greenland towards Newfoundland, where they can be a hazard to shipping.

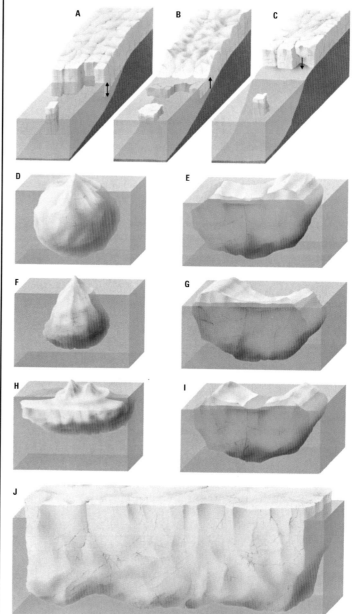

◀ **Icebergs form in** several ways. When a glacier reaches the sea it floats away from the bed. The movement of waves and tides exerts pressures on this floating ice causing lumps to break away (A). If the glacier is moving rapidly when it reaches the sea, a projecting shelf of ice forms under the water. The buoyancy of this shelf exerts an upward pressure causing pieces to break off (B). The snout of the glacier may be above the level of the sea and hence lumps may break off under the force of gravity and fall into the water (C). The forming of new icebergs is known as "calving". D–I show typical shapes of icebergs. Northern icebergs come from the Greenland ice sheet, but the largest ones originate in Antarctica (J). The largest iceberg ever seen was 336km (208mi) long and 97km (60mi) wide.

Madagascar and Arabia. It has white plumage and a black head and tail. It feeds on insects (including locusts), reptiles, small fish, crustaceans and worms. The sacred ibis nests colonially. Length: 38–40cm (15–16in). Family Threskiornithidae; species *Threskionis aethiopica*.

ibis, scarlet

Medium to large ibis with entirely scarlet plumage. It is found in the tropical wetlands of South America, where it feeds on crustaceans, molluscs, fish and insects. It nests in large colonies in trees. Length: 57–59cm (22–23in). Family Threskiornithidae; species *Eudocemus ruber*.

ibisbill

Medium-sized wading bird found along shingle rivers in the high plateaux of central Asia; it winters in the foothills of the Himalayas. The ibisbill is grey above and white below, with a red, down-curved bill. It is classified in its own family. It feeds on aquatic animals. Length: 40cm (16in). Family Ibidorhynchidae; species *Ibidorhyncha struthersii*.

ice

Water frozen to 0°C (32°F) or below, when it forms complex six-sided crystals. Ice is less dense than water and floats. When water vapour condenses below freezing point, ice crystals are formed. This occurs mainly in high, cirrus CLOUDS, but also in the grey portions of other clouds. Clusters of these ice crystals form snowflakes. The formation of ice crystals also occurs near the ground and gives rise to FROST.

ice ages

Prolonged period of colder climatic conditions, during which snow and ice covered large areas of the Earth. There is evidence of about 20 ice ages having occurred throughout Earth's history, the earliest dating back to 2300 million years ago. The most recent began about 2 million years ago and is often referred to as the "Ice Age". During this period, ice advanced for several thousand years, and then retreated for about the same period. An advance of ice is called a **glacial phase**, and the retreat is an **interglacial**. The Earth is experiencing an interglacial at present, although there are still ice-age conditions over Greenland and Antarctica. During the glacial phases, ice covered Britain as far south as the Bristol Channel and the Thames estuary. Areas farther south experienced PERMAFROST and TUNDRA conditions. When the ice melted, finally disappearing about 12,000 years ago, the climate warmed up, enabling different types of vegetation to colonize s England, and eventually spread farther north. The last ice age produced many of the landforms seen in the Northern Hemisphere continents and affected sea level on a global scale. *See also* GLACIER

iceberg

See feature article

ice cap

Small ICE SHEET, often in the shape of a flattened dome, which spreads over the mountains and valleys of polar islands. The floating ice fields surrounding the North Pole are sometimes incorrectly called an ice cap.

ice fish

Any member of the family Salangidae, comprising small food fish related to cod. Native to E Asia, they inhabit coastal regions of the cold N Pacific Ocean. **Ice fish** also refers to the members of six families of marine, perch-like fish of the suborder Notothenioidei. Found in Antarctic and sub-Antarctic waters, they are characterized by the presence of "antifreeze" protein molecules in their blood, which prevents the blood freezing in near-freezing seawater temperatures.

Iceland poppy

Perennial POPPY found in arctic regions. It is grown as an ornamental, and many garden varieties have been developed. The Iceland poppy is somewhat blue-green, with lobed leaves. Its tall, slender stems bear large, fragrant, showy flowers. Family Papaveraceae; species *Papaver nudicaule*.

Iceland spar (calcium carbonate, CaCO₃)

Transparent form of CALCITE that has the property of birefringerence (or double refraction) – that is it bends light two ways so that an image seen through it appears double. It is used for polarizing prisms and in polarizing microscopes and other optical instruments.

ice plant

Annual or biennial ground-covering plant, native to the Mediterranean region. It is grown as a bedding plant for its brilliantly coloured flowers. It has flat, fleshy leaves. The ice plant is so called because it is densely covered in crystal-like vesicles, which give it a crystalline appearance. Family Aizoaceae; species *Mesembryanthemum crystallinum*.

ice sheet (continental GLACIER)

Large expanse of snow and ice covering a land mass. Ice sheets can cover entire mountain ranges

---

IGNEOUS ROCK

Term denoting rocks of volcanic origin that were formed from MAGMA. If the magma solidified beneath the Earth's surface, cooling would have been slow; if it solidified at the surface, cooling would have been more rapid. The faster the cooling process, the smaller are the crystals that make up the rock. All igneous rocks are crystalline. In addition to grain size, the other important differences found in igneous rocks are related to the chemical content of the minerals in the rock. Acidic minerals, including QUARTZ, some FELDSPARS and some MICAS, are generally light in colour. Conversely, basic minerals are generally dark in colour; they include some feldspars, biotite mica, HORNBLENDE and AUGITE. Igneous rocks formed at depth are called **plutonic**, those formed at the surface are called **volcanic**, and those formed between are **hypabyssal**. Volcanic rocks are EXTRUSIVE, and the commonest variety is BASALT. Hypabyssal rocks are found in SILLS and DYKES, and they are INTRUSIVE ROCKS. Plutonic rocks form in large bodies of magma called BATHOLITHS, stocks and "bosses" (circular intrusions, lying at a steep angle to the surface). The commonest plutonic rock is GRANITE, which is acidic in mineral content; the basic equivalent is called GABBRO. Igneous rocks do not have BEDDING PLANES, and they do not contain fossils. They are mostly quite resistant to erosion, and often form high ground; examples in Britain include Dartmoor, Bodmin Moor, the Malvern Hills, parts of the Lake District and the Cairngorms. *See also* ACID ROCK; BASIC ROCK

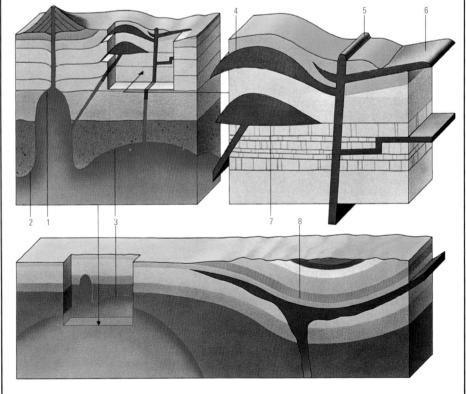

▲ **Many different shapes** of igneous rocks can be found. Among the most common are the neck (1), which is a circular vertical feed channel of a volcano. A stock (2) is a large mass of rock that solidified at great depth. A batholith (3) is a large body of granite that has no detectable bottom. A laccolith (4, 7) is a dome-shaped mass that has forced the rock above it to arch. A dyke (or dike) (5) is a vertical, sheet-like mass of rock. A sill (6) is a horizontal, sheet-shaped body of rock. A lopolith (8) is a saucer-shaped mass of rock.

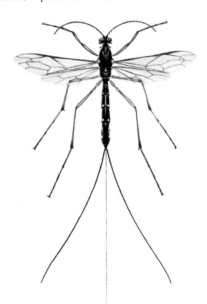

▲ **ichneumon** The female ichneumon wasp, such as the species shown above, is characterized by an extremely long ovipositor. It is used to lay eggs under the skins of the insects and larvae that the wasp parasitizes.

and can spread across lowlands and oceans. The ice may become very thick: in Greenland and Antarctica there are places where the ice measures 3000m (9800ft) in depth. An ICEBERG formed when ice breaks from the margins of such a sheet may be many square kilometres in area.

ice wedge

Sliver of wedge-shaped ice that penetrates the surface layers of landscapes in PERIGLACIAL regions of PERMAFROST.

ichneumon

Any member of a family of WASPS that consume other insects and spiders. Found worldwide, the females are characterized by an ovipositor (often longer than the body) that is used to inject eggs into hosts. Length: *c*.1cm (*c*.0.4in). Family Ichneumonidae. *See also* PARASITE; illustration, page 195

ichthyology

Zoological study of FISH, including their classification, structure, distribution and ecology. The ancient Greeks, particularly Aristotle, are regarded as the pioneers of this science in the West.

ichthyosaur

Member of an extinct group of fast-swimming, predatory marine reptiles with dolphin-shaped bodies, for example *Ichthyosaurus*. They evolved in early Triassic times and died out in late Cretaceous times, before the terminal EXTINCTION event.

idocrase (vesuvianite)

Orthosilicate mineral, consisting of hydrous calcium, iron, magnesium, aluminium silicate. Found in impure limestone, it forms tetragonal system crystals and is glassy green, brown, yellow or blue. Hardness 6.5; r.d. 3.4. Its transparent green or brown crystals are cut as gems.

igneous rock

See feature article, page 195

ignimbrite

Rock formed from the consolidation of the PYROCLASTIC FLOW from a volcano. It comprises poorly sorted fragments of TUFF, PUMICE, crystals, rock and volcanic glass.

iguana

Any of numerous species of terrestrial, arboreal (tree-dwelling), burrowing or aquatic LIZARDS that live in tropical America and the Galápagos Islands. The common iguana (*Iguana iguana*) is greenish-brown

▲ **ichthyosaur** A highly specialized representative of the ichthyosaurs, *Ichthyosaurus* (family Ichthyosauridae) was *c*.3m (*c*.9ft) long and probably fed on fish and other marine life. A fast swimmer, *Ichthyosaurus* used its paddle-like limbs to steer itself. It had no gills and breathed air through nostrils at the top of its snout. It was entirely adapted to marine habitation and gave birth to live young.

◀ **iguanodont** The largest iguanodont was the *Iguanodon*, which measured up to 9m (29.5ft). It had a distinctive conical thumb spike protruding from each forelimb and hoof-like claws on its hind feet.

with a serrated dewlap and a crest along its back. Length: to 2m (6.5ft). Family Iguanidae.

iguana, marine

Large LIZARD from the Galápagos Islands. It has a short, blunt head and a prominent dorsal crest on its head and body. It is black with conspicuous red patches in the breeding season. Marine iguanas are the only lizards to spend long periods in the ocean, where they feed on marine algae. Nasal glands help to eliminate the salt they ingest in their diet. Length: to 1.7m (5.6ft). Family Iguanidae; species *Amblyrhynchus cristatus*.

iguanodont

Member of a group of medium-sized, plant-eating ORNITHOPOD dinosaurs. The iguanodonts walked on two legs. The group included forms such as *Iguanodon*. Iguanodonts evolved in late Jurassic times and died out slightly before the Cretaceous/Tertiary (K/T) boundary EXTINCTION event. It was one of the first groups of dinosaurs to be recognised as fossils, by the British palaeontologist Gideon Mantell (1790–1852).

iiwi

Small finch-like bird found exclusively on the Hawaiian Islands. Its plumage is scarlet and black. It has a long down-curved bill and feeds on nectar and insects. It is often known as a Hawaiian HONEYCREEPER. Length: 15–16cm (6in). Family Drepanididae; species *Vestiaria coccinea*.

ileum

Major part of the small INTESTINE, *c*.6m (*c*.20ft) long. Its inner wall is lined with finger-like projections (villi), which increase the surface area available for the absorption of nutrients. *See also* DIGESTION

ilex

Any member of the genus *Ilex*, a large group of species that includes English and American holly. Ilex are evergreen trees or shrubs, with glossy leaves that bear spines around the margins. The small male and female flowers usually grow on separate trees. In winter the female flowers develop into red berries. They are widely grown as hedging. Many ornamental varieties with variegated foliage have been developed. The wood may be used for inlay work. Family Aquifoliaceae; genus *Ilex*; species include *Ilex aquifolium* (English holly).

ilium

Broad flat bone on either side of the PELVIS. Joined by the SACRUM, it is fused with the ISCHIUM and PUBIS in a triangular suture at the hip socket. The ilia form the back of the "basin" of the pelvic girdle and anchor the muscles that form the frontal wall of the abdomen. *See also* HUMAN BODY

ilmenite (iron titanate, FeTiO₃)

Black oxide mineral, a major ore of the metal titani-

um. It is found in basic IGNEOUS ROCKS and beach sands as tabular to fine, scaly crystals in the rhombohedral system, and as compact masses or granules. It has a metallic lustre and is magnetic. Hardness 5–6; r.d. 4.7.

imago

Adult, reproductive stage of an INSECT that has undergone full METAMORPHOSIS. Imagos are the winged insects, such as BUTTERFLIES and DRAGONFLIES, that emerge from the PUPAS or develop from the NYMPHS.

immigration

Process by which individuals join a POPULATION from neighbouring ones. *See also* EMIGRATION

immortelle

Any member of the genus *Erythrina*, a group of plants from tropical and subtropical regions. Their large, showy, brightly coloured, usually red flowers grow in dense flower heads and appear before the leaves. Trees of this genus are often grown in coffee and cocoa plantations to provide shade. Family Fabaceae; genus *Erythrina*.

immune system

System by which the body defends itself against disease. It involves many kinds of LEUCOCYTES (white blood cells) in the blood, lymph and bone marrow. Some of the cells (B-cells) make ANTIBODIES against invading microbes and other foreign substances (ANTIGENS), or neutralize TOXINS produced by PATHOGENS; other antibodies encourage PHAGOCYTES and MACROPHAGES to attack and digest invaders. Another type of cell, the T-CELL, provides a variety of functions in the immune system.

immunoglobulin

PROTEIN found in the bloodstream that plays a role in the body's IMMUNE SYSTEM. Immunoglobulins act as ANTIBODIES for specific ANTIGENS. They can be obtained from donor plasma and injected into patients most at risk of particular diseases.

▲ **iguana** The common, or green, iguana is a strong swimmer and is usually found near streams and rivers in the rainforest. A cold-blooded animal, it spends most of its time in the forest canopy basking in the sun.

▲ **iiwi** Named after the squeaky sound of its call, the iiwi makes a whirring sound during flight. Iiwis are susceptible to avian malaria, which has been partially responsible for a decline in their numbers.

impala (pala)
Long-legged, medium-sized African ANTELOPE. It has sleek, glossy, brown fur with black markings on the rump. The male has long, lyre-shaped horns. Length: to 1.5m (5ft); height: to 1m (3.3ft) at the shoulder. Family Bovidae; species *Aepyceros melampus*.

impatiens (jewel weed)
Any of *c*.450 species of herbaceous annuals and perennials belonging to the genus *Impatiens*. They are found in tropical and temperate regions. They have succulent stems and simple toothed leaves. The brightly coloured flowers have a long spur. Their seedpods, when ripe, pop and scatter the seeds. Some species are known as touch-me-not. Family Balsaminaceae; genus *Impatiens*; species include the BUSY LIZZIE. *See also* BALSAM

impermeable
Term that describes rock that does not allow water to pass through it. Slate is one example. *See also* IMPERVIOUS; PERMEABILITY

impervious
Term that describes rocks that contain no cracks or fissures for water to flow through, although the rock itself may absorb water. Clay is one example. *See also* IMPERMEABLE

imprinting
Form of learning that occurs within a critical period in very young animals. A complex relationship develops between the newborn infant and the first animate object it encounters; this is usually a parent. The future emotional development of the infant depends upon this relationship. Imprinting in birds has been studied by Konrad LORENZ, who believed that it is an irreversible process.

inbreeding
Mating of two closely blood-related organisms. It is the opposite of OUTBREEDING and over successive generations causes much less variation in GENOTYPE and PHENOTYPE than is normal in a wild population. A form of GENETIC ENGINEERING, inbreeding can be used to improve breeds in domestic plants and animals. In humans, it can have harmful results, such as the persistence of haemophilia in some European royal families. *See also* HETEROSIS

inca
Any of four species of HUMMINGBIRD found in the forests of South America. The collared inca (*Coeligena torquata*) is one of the more common species. It has a white collar and a white base to its tail. Length: 15cm (6in). Family Trochilidae; genus *Coeligena* (part).

incense cedar
Tree native to w United States and planted as an ornamental in Europe and elsewhere in North America. It is often columnar in shape, with cinnamon-red bark, flattened branchlets and cones of five or six woody scales. The timber is used for shingles. Height: 30–60m (100–200ft). Family Cupressaceae; species *Calocedrus decurrens*.

incisor
Any of the chisel-shaped cutting TEETH between the CANINES in the front of the mouths of mammals. There are eight in humans, four in the centre front of each jaw. *See also* DENTITION

inclination, magnetic (magnetic dip)
Angle between the direction of the Earth's magnetic field and the horizontal, measured by a free-floating magnet. At the north magnetic pole the inclination is zero; at the magnetic equator it is 90°. *See also* DECLINATION, MAGNETIC

incomplete dominance
In GENETICS, a situation in which neither GENE for a particular characteristic is DOMINANT. As a result, the organism shows the influence of both genes. For example, a plant with genes for both red flowers and white flowers may have pink flowers.

incubation
Process of maintaining stable, warm conditions to ensure that eggs develop and hatch. Incubation is carried out by birds and by some reptiles. It is accomplished by sitting on the eggs, by making use of volcanic or solar heat or the warmth of decaying vegetation, or by covering the eggs with an insulating layer of soil or sand.

incubation period
Time lag between becoming infected with a disease and the appearance of the first symptoms. In many infectious diseases, the incubation period is quite short – anything from a few hours to a few days – although it may be more variable. In leprosy, for example, incubation periods range from a few months to as much as 20 years.

indehiscent
Describing a FRUIT or seed pod that does not open spontaneously to release its seeds when ripe. Release of the seeds takes place when the fruit rots or is eaten by an animal. Fungi that do not release their spores are also termed indehiscent. *See also* DEHISCENT

independent assortment
Separation of the ALLELES of a GENE into the GAMETES (sex cells) with no regard to the way in which the alleles of other genes have separated. It takes place during MEIOSIS – the type of CELL DIVISION that gives rise to gametes. Theoretically, as a result, all possible combinations of alleles should occur with equal frequency, giving rise to maximum genetic variation. It does not always happen in practice because alleles on the same CHROMOSOME are usually inherited together. *See also* CROSSING OVER; LINKAGE

index mineral
Mineral that crystallizes under specific conditions of pressure and temperature; its existence in a rock thus reflects those conditions of formation such as the METAMORPHIC GRADE of a METAMORPHIC ROCK.

Indian almond
Tall tree that is native from India to New Guinea; it is also widely grown in parts of tropical Africa and the Americas. It has wide, spreading branches, smooth, greyish bark and slender spikes of greenish-white flowers. The edible kernel of the fruit yields a valuable oil similar to almond oil. Family Combretaceae; species *Terminalia catappa*.

Indian corn
See MAIZE

Indian millet (Indian ricegrass)
GRASS species native to the arid and semi-arid deserts of w United States. It grows in dense tufts of narrow leaf blades. The flowers are produced in open heads. The seed has been used for food by Native American tribes. Height: 60cm (24in). Family Poaceae; species *Oryzopsis hymenoides*.

Indian pipe
Parasitic plant that has no CHLOROPHYLL. The Indian pipe plant grows in deep shaded woods of North and Central America, Japan and the Himalayas. A waxy white plant, it blackens with age. A bell-like flower hangs at the end of each stem. The Indian pipe plant is connected to its green host plant via a fungus. Family Monotropaceae; species *Monotropa uniflora*.

indicator species
Organism whose sensitivity to a particular ABIOTIC FACTOR enables it to be used to detect the presence or absence of that factor. An example is LICHENS, which are sensitive to the sulphur dioxide concentration in the atmosphere. By investigating which species of lichen are present in an area it is possible to determine the level of sulphur dioxide in the surrounding atmosphere.

indri
Large, black-and-white, almost tailless LEMUR that is found in the rainforest of Madagascar. It is active in the daytime, feeding mainly on fruit and leaves. Identified by loud vocalizations, the indri leaps vertically from branch to branch, spending most of its time in trees. Head-body length: 57–70cm (22–28in); tail: 5cm (2in). Family Indriidae; species *Indri indri*.

▲ **impala** Commonly found at the edges of forests and near water sources, impalas are capable of huge leaps, up to 3m (10ft) in the air. They form large herds of up to several hundred animals which, if attacked, will scatter in all directions.

inflorescence

FLOWER or flower cluster. Inflorescences are classified into two main types according to their branching characteristics. A **racemose inflorescence** has a main axis and lateral flowering branches, with flowers opening from the bottom up or from the outer edge in; types of racemose inflorescence include panicle, raceme, spike and umbel. A **cymose inflorescence** has a composite axis with the main stem ending in a flower and lateral branches bearing additional, later-flowering branches.

inlier

Area of old rocks surrounded by younger ones. The old rocks may have resisted EROSION and stand as hills above the surrounding eroded area. Alternatively, the upper and outer rocks of an ANTI-CLINE may have been eroded, leaving the older, once lower, rocks surrounded by younger ones. *See also* OUTLIER

inner ear

See EAR

insect

See feature article, pages 200–201

insecticide

Substance used to destroy or control insect pests. Insecticides may be stomach poisons, such as lead arsenate and sodium fluoride; contact poisons, such as DDT and organophosphates; or systematic poisons, such as octamethylpyrophosphoramide, which are toxic to insects that eat plants into which the poisons have been absorbed. Organophosphates are preferred to chlorinated hydrocarbons (such as DDT) because they break down into nontoxic substances. They are, however, hazardous to humans and must be handled with care.

insectivorous plant (carnivorous plant)

See feature article, page 203

inselberg

Steep-sided, round-topped hill rising abruptly from a plain, found in semi-arid, tropical and subtropical regions. Inselbergs are probably formed by EXFOLIA-TION and EROSION of old mountains.

inspiration (inhalation)

Process by which air (or water in the case of many aquatic organisms) is taken into the LUNGS (or GILLS). In mammals it involves an increase in the volume of the thoracic cavity, which is achieved by contraction of the muscles that flatten the diaphragm, together with contraction of the external intercostal muscles between the ribs in order to move the rib-cage outwards. The increase in volume reduces the pressure of the thoracic cavity. With atmospheric pressure now greater than the thoracic pressure, air enters the lungs until both pressures are again equal. Together with the opposite process, EXPIRATION, inspiration is fundamental to GAS EXCHANGE, which forms part of the overall process of RESPIRATION.

instinct

Behaviour that is genetically determined and, therefore, shows itself from birth. As instincts can be modified through experience it is often difficult to say how much of an animal's behaviour is the result of instinct and how much is due to learning. A basic TAXIS or kinesis is innate. Much instinctive behaviour is highly complex and consists of a chain of actions, the completion of each stage in the chain acting as the stimulus for the commencement of the next stage. *See also* INTELLIGENT BEHAVIOUR; LEARNED BEHAVIOUR

insulin

HORMONE that is secreted by the ISLETS OF LANGHERHANS in the PANCREAS, important in the maintenance of blood-glucose levels. Insulin has the effect of lowering the blood-glucose level by helping the uptake of glucose into cells, where it is used up, and by causing the liver to convert glucose to GLYCOGEN, which is then stored in the liver. Glucose, unmetabolized because of lack of insulin, accumulates in excess amounts in the blood and urine, resulting in diabetes.

◄ **iris** Grown mainly in temperate regions for displays, the many plants of the genus *Iris* usually feature narrow, pointed leaves. The flowers can be either purple, white or yellow.

intelligent behaviour

Highest form of learning. It involves the recall of previous experiences and their adaptation to help solve a new problem. The speed with which a solution is achieved excludes the possibility of trial and error. An example of intelligent behaviour occurs when chimpanzees pile up boxes to reach bananas that would otherwise be out of reach. *See also* INSTINCT; LEARNED BEHAVIOUR

interglacial

Interval between ICE AGES; the period of glacial retreat. *See also* GLACIER

interoceptor

Type of nervous RECEPTOR that responds to stimuli from within the organism, as opposed to **exteroceptors**, which respond to external stimuli. Interoceptors provide information on such things as, in mammals, the temperature and carbon dioxide concentration of the blood. **Proprioceptors**, which are special forms of interoceptors, give information on the position of muscles and are, therefore, important in coordinating movement in animals.

interphase

Stage following cell division (MEIOSIS or MITOSIS) in which the nucleus "rests". The nucleus is not dividing and adopts its final form in each of the daughter cells.

interrupted fern

FERN native to the Northern Hemisphere and cultivated as an ornamental. It produces clusters of arching fronds, with spore-bearing regions near the middle of some fronds. Height: 1.5m (5ft). Family Osmundaceae; species *Osmunda claytoniana*.

interstitial cells

Cells that form the connective tissue between other tissues or organized groups of cells. In CNIDARIANS (such as JELLYFISH), for example, interstitial cells take the form of embryonic cells in the spaces between the columnar cells forming the body structure. In the TESTES of vertebrates, interstitial cells between the seminiferous tubules secrete androgen male sex HORMONES.

intervertebral disc

Ring of CARTILAGE that separates the VERTEBRAE – the bones of the SPINE. Intervertebral discs allow, with the exception of the axial skeleton (skull, spine and ribcage) and atlas bone (topmost vertebra), small amounts of movement, thus providing the spine with a degree of flexibility. A second function is to absorb shock, particularly for the skull and brain. The discs consist of a fibrous ring containing a soft, pulpy substance. Strain or injury to the spine may rupture or herniate a disc so that the pulpy interior protrudes and presses on a spinal nerve. This condition, commonly called a slipped disc, causes pain and immobility.

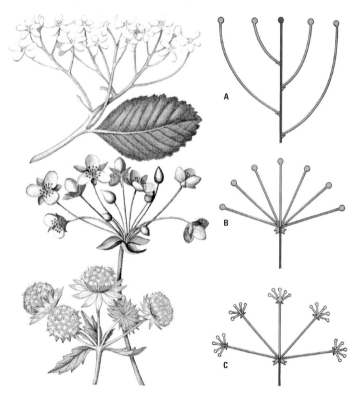

► **inflorescence** An inflorescence is a group of individual flowers borne on the same main stalk. Examples (A), (B) and (C) are inflorescences in which the main axis (red) increases in length by growth at its tip, giving rise to lateral branches (blue) which bear flowers. The flowers of *Sorbus aria*, whitebeam, form an inflorescence (A) called a corymb in which all the lateral branches are of different lengths, with the lowermost of the greater length so that all the flowers are brought to the same level. The flowers of *Bubomus umbellatus*, the water gladiolus, form an umbel (B) where all flower stalks arise from the same point. The inflorescence of *Astrantia major*, the masterwort, is a compound umbel (C) in which the lateral branches are themselves subdivided (yellow).

intestine

Lower part of the ALIMENTARY CANAL, situated beyond the STOMACH; it is part of the DIGESTIVE SYSTEM. Food is moved through the intestine by the wave-like action known as PERISTALSIS. Food undergoes the final stages of DIGESTION and is absorbed into the bloodstream in the **small intestine**, which is a coiled tube that extends from the stomach to the large intestine. In the **large intestine** (divided into three sections known as the caecum, colon and rectum) water is absorbed from undigested material, which is then passed out of the body through the anus.

intrusion

Emplacement of rock material that was either forced or flowed into spaces among other rocks. An igneous intrusion, sometimes called a **pluton**, consists of MAGMA that never reached the Earth's surface but instead filled cracks and FAULTS, before cooling and hardening.

intrusive rock

Any IGNEOUS ROCK that forms by slow cooling under the Earth's surface (INTRUSION). In general, they are coarser grained than volcanic rocks that cooled on the surface.

inversion

Atmospheric condition in which a property of the air, such as moisture content or temperature, increases with altitude. In a **temperature inversion**, the air temperature rises with altitude and a cap of hot air encloses the cooler air below. With little wind or turbulence to break up the condition, pollution can build up, often to a dangerous extent. *See also* FOG

invertebrate

Term for an animal without a backbone. There are more than a million species of invertebrates, which are divided into 30 major groups. One of these groups is Arthropoda (ARTHROPODS), which is the largest animal PHYLUM in terms of number of species. Most invertebrates are INSECTS, but the term also covers, among others, CRUSTACEANS and ARACHNIDS. MOLLUSCS make up the second-largest group of invertebrates.

involuntary muscle

One of three types of MUSCLE in VERTEBRATES, so called because, unlike SKELETAL MUSCLE, it is not under the conscious control of the brain. Instead, it is stimulated by the AUTONOMIC NERVOUS SYSTEM and by HORMONES in the bloodstream. Involuntary muscle is of two kinds: **smooth muscle** is the muscle of the ALIMENTARY CANAL, blood vessels and bladder; **cardiac muscle** powers the HEART. *See also* HUMAN BODY

ion

ATOM or group of atoms with an electric (positive or negative) charge resulting from the loss or gain of one or more ELECTRONS. Positive ions are called **cations** and move toward the cathode in electrolysis; negative ions are called **anions** and move toward the anode. Many crystalline inorganic solids are composed of arrays of ions of opposite charge. The process of forming ions is called ionization.

ionic bond (electrovalent bond)

Type of chemical bond in which IONS of opposite charge are held together by electrostatic attraction.

ionosphere

See feature article

iora

Any of four species of LEAFBIRD found in arboreal habitats and gardens in tropical Asia and Indonesia. Most species feed on insects, fruit and berries. Family Chloropseidae (part); genus *Aegithina*.

ipecacuanha

Drug extracted from the dried rhizome and roots of a small shrub from the forests of Brazil and Colombia. The plant contains the ALKALOIDS emetine and cephaeline. The drug is used mainly as an emetic and expectorant. Family Rubiaceae; species include *Psychotria ipecacuanha*.

iris

Coloured part of the EYE. It controls the amount of light that enters the PUPIL in the centre of the eye by increasing or decreasing the size of the pupil. The changes are brought about by muscles in the iris contracting or relaxing.

iris (flag)

Any of the *c.*300 species belonging to the *Iris* genus, native to the Northern Hemisphere. Perennial plants, they grow from bulbs or rhizomes and have long, lance-shaped, pointed leaves. The yellow or blue flowers are formed from three large flat petals alter-

IONOSPHERE

Region around a planet in which there are free ELECTRONS and IONS produced by ultraviolet radiation and X-rays from the Sun. The degree of ionization is greatly affected by solar activity. The Earth's ionosphere extends from 80km (50mi) to 1000km (625mi) above the surface (that is, to the limits of the ATMOSPHERE in the VAN ALLEN RADIATION BELTS). It is divided into distinct layers distinguished by the concentration of electrons. The lowest layers, D and E or Kennelly-Heaviside layers, undergo molecular ionization, while the upper layer, the F, or Appleton layer, undergoes atomic ionization. These layers reflect radio waves of long wavelengths while shorter wavelengths can pass through undisturbed. The reflecting power of these layers makes long-range radio broadcasting possible up to frequencies of about 30MHz.

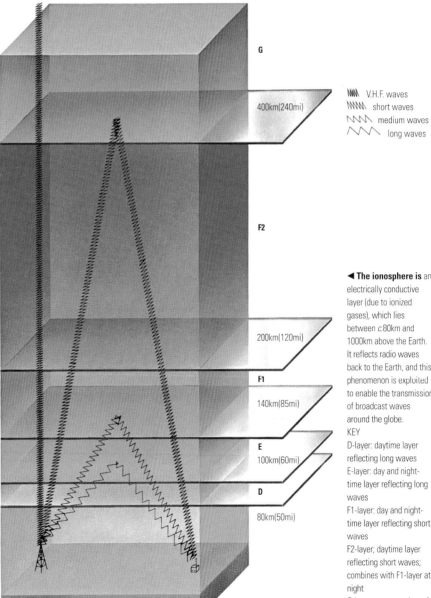

WWWW V.H.F. waves
WWWW short waves
NANA medium waves
NANA long waves

◄ **The ionosphere is** an electrically conductive layer (due to ionized gases), which lies between *c.*80km and 1000km above the Earth. It reflects radio waves back to the Earth, and this phenomenon is exploited to enable the transmission of broadcast waves around the globe.
KEY
D-layer: daytime layer reflecting long waves
E-layer: day and night-time layer reflecting long waves
F1-layer: day and night-time layer reflecting short waves
F2-layer: daytime layer reflecting short waves; combines with F1-layer at night
G-layer: upper reaches of ionosphere

G

400km(240mi)

F2

200km(120mi)

F1

140km(85mi)

E
100km(60mi)

D

80km(50mi)

Insects are INVERTEBRATE animals comprising the order Insecta. They are the most numerous of all living creatures, representing *c*.80% of all animal species. There are more than one million known species and probably as many again are still to be discovered.

Adult insects have three pairs of jointed legs, usually two pairs of wings, and a three-segmented body (**head**, **thorax** and **abdomen**), with a horny outer covering or EXOSKELETON. The head has three pairs of mouthparts, a pair of COMPOUND EYES, three pairs of simple eyes and a pair of antennae. Most insects can detect a wide range of sounds through ultrasensitive hairs on various parts of their bodies. Some can "sing" or make sounds by rubbing together parts of their bodies. Most insects are herbivores; many are farm and garden pests. Some prey on small animals, especially other insects, and a few are scavengers. There are two main kinds of mouthparts – chewing and sucking.

Insect reproduction is usually sexual. Of all insects, those that have a four-stage life cycle – OVUM (egg), LARVA (caterpillar or grub), PUPA (chrysalis) and IMAGO (adult) – are the ones that are both most advanced and most successful. They account for more than two-thirds of all insect species and include such familiar groups as the MOTHS and BUTTERFLIES, BEETLES, BEES, WASPS, ANTS and true FLIES. Young GRASSHOPPERS and some other insects, called NYMPHS, resemble wingless miniatures of their parents. The nymphs develop during a series of moults (incomplete METAMORPHOSIS). SILVERFISH and a few other primitive, wingless insects do not undergo metamorphosis.

There are enough insect fossils and primitive living forms to serve as a guide to the evolution of the 29 orders into which all insects are classified. Most of the evidence dates from the advent of the Carboniferous period, when a number of winged insects inhabited the coal-forming swamps. Insects are thought to have evolved from a centipede-like ancestor. The most primitive of modern insects are possibly the wingless species, such as the North American SPRINGTAIL.

Because of their numbers and worldwide distribution, insects are of great biological importance, both beneficial and damaging to the human health and economy. For example, pollination by insects, particularly bees, is essential for many crops, including most fruits. Other insects provide us with silk and biological pest control. However, insects also cause untold damage. Insect pests, such as LOCUSTS and the COLORADO BEETLE, damage crops and stored products, and some, such as the TSETSE FLY and MOSQUITOES, carry diseases potentially fatal to people and livestock.

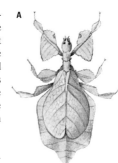

A

◀ **Leaf insects such** as *Phyllium crurufolium* (A) have legs and wings adapted to resemble leaves. In their tropical Asian habitats their predators find them difficult to spot. Some species have taken this adaptation a stage further, by laying eggs that resemble the seeds of various plants.

B

◀ **Highly modified for** the purposes of camouflage, stick insects, such as *Euryacantha horrida* (B), mimic the plants on which they live. Because they look like twigs, they are protected from predators. Their legs are barely noticeable at rest. Some stick insects may remain motionless for hours; other species sway backwards and forwards as if moving with a breeze.

▶ **The greenbottle fly** has highly adapted mouthparts. When it finds food, the greenbottle secretes enzymes from its salivary gland (1), via the salivary channel (2) in the proboscis (3), on to the food. The saliva is squirted over the food through grooves (4) in the labella (5), situated on the end of the proboscis. The grooves keep their shape because of rings of chitin (6). Once the food has been partly broken down to a liquid form by the enzymes, the greenbottle sucks up the liquid (7) through the grooves of the labella, via the food channel (8) and into the midgut (9), where digestion is completed.

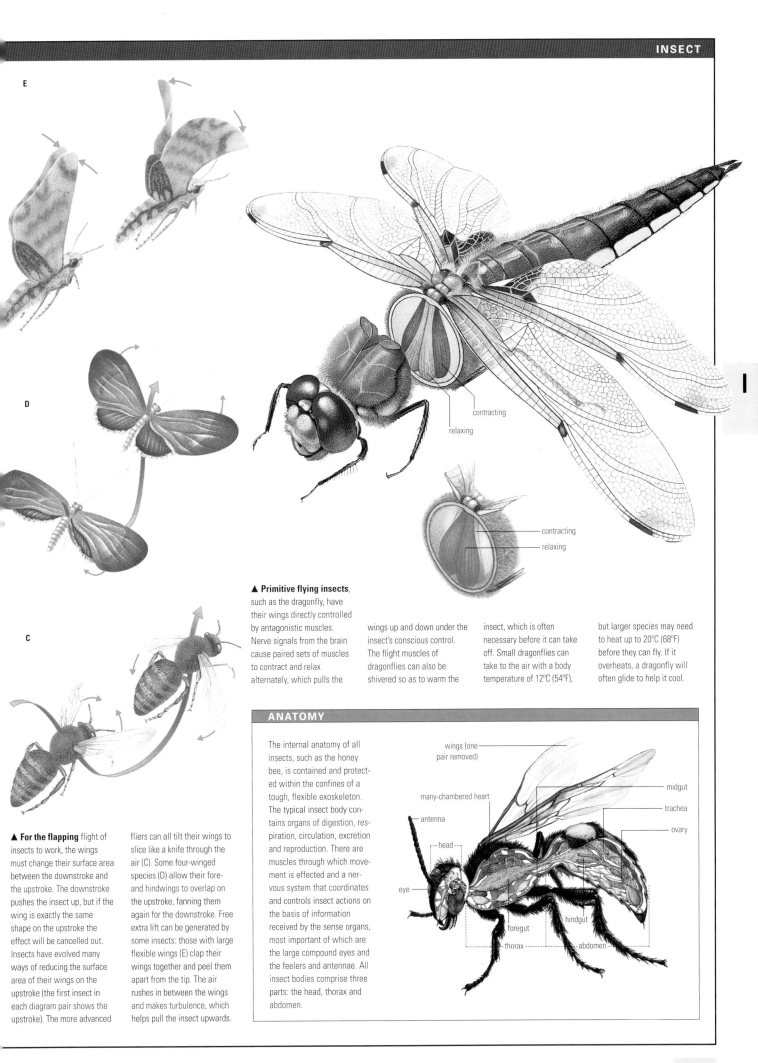

E

D

C

contracting
relaxing

contracting
relaxing

▲ **Primitive flying insects**, such as the dragonfly, have their wings directly controlled by antagonistic muscles. Nerve signals from the brain cause paired sets of muscles to contract and relax alternately, which pulls the wings up and down under the insect's conscious control. The flight muscles of dragonflies can also be shivered so as to warm the insect, which is often necessary before it can take off. Small dragonflies can take to the air with a body temperature of 12°C (54°F), but larger species may need to heat up to 20°C (68°F) before they can fly. If it overheats, a dragonfly will often glide to help it cool.

▲ **For the flapping** flight of insects to work, the wings must change their surface area between the downstroke and the upstroke. The downstroke pushes the insect up, but if the wing is exactly the same shape on the upstroke the effect will be cancelled out. Insects have evolved many ways of reducing the surface area of their wings on the upstroke (the first insect in each diagram pair shows the upstroke). The more advanced fliers can all tilt their wings to slice like a knife through the air (C). Some four-winged species (D) allow their fore- and hindwings to overlap on the upstroke, fanning them again for the downstroke. Free extra lift can be generated by some insects: those with large flexible wings (E) clap their wings together and peel them apart from the tip. The air rushes in between the wings and makes turbulence, which helps pull the insect upwards.

ANATOMY

The internal anatomy of all insects, such as the honey bee, is contained and protected within the confines of a tough, flexible exoskeleton. The typical insect body contains organs of digestion, respiration, circulation, excretion and reproduction. There are muscles through which movement is effected and a nervous system that coordinates and controls insect actions on the basis of information received by the sense organs, most important of which are the large compound eyes and the feelers and antennae. All insect bodies comprise three parts: the head, thorax and abdomen.

wings (one pair removed)
many-chambered heart
antenna
head
eye
foregut
thorax
midgut
trachea
ovary
hindgut
abdomen

I

nating with three smaller erect petals and three flap-like stigmas. Their seeds are borne in large green capsules. Height: to *c*.1m (*c*.3.3ft). Family Iridaceae; species include *Iris versicolor* (blue flag) and *Iris pseudacorus* (yellow flag).

iroko-wood (African teak)

Valuable hardwood from a tree once common in w Africa. It compares favourably with teak in terms of durability but is less decorative. It is used for ship building, joinery, counter and bench tops, and parquet flooring. Height: to 50m (160ft). Family Moraceae; species *Milicia excelsa*.

ironbark

Any of several species of Australian EUCALYPTUS trees with hard, rough-fissured bark, which often turns black with age. Family Myrtaceae; genus Eucalyptus; species include *Eucalyptus crebra* (red ironbark) and *Eucalyptus paniculata* (grey ironbark).

iron meteorite (siderite)

METEORITE consisting mainly of iron (90–95%) and some nickel, with traces of other metals. Iron meteorites are classified into a number of groups according to the proportions of these other metals that they contain; each group is thought to correspond to a different parent asteroid.

iron pyrites

See PYRITE

ironstone

Ancient medium- to fine-grained SEDIMENTARY ROCK containing iron-rich minerals such as HAEMATITE and SIDERITE; MAGNETITE and PYRITE may also be present. Ironstones were formed 2000–3000 million years ago in the Precambrian era. In **banded ironstone**, the basic rock is CHERT interspersed with layers of ferruginous minerals. **Oolitic ironstone**, formed in sediments at the bottom of ancient seas, consists of small rounded grains

(OOLITHS) in which ferruginous minerals have replaced lime-rich ones. In both types, the iron-containing minerals result in a deep red colour.

iron tree

Alternative name for AFRICAN OAK

ischium

U-shaped bone at the base and on either side of the PELVIS. It is fused with the ILIUM and the PUBIS in the hip socket; its lower edge meets the pubis. In primates the ischium takes most of the body's weight when sitting. *See also* HUMAN BODY

island arc

Chain of VOLCANOES that occurs along one side of a deep ocean TRENCH. The volcanoes rest on the plate of LITHOSPHERE that is not moving down into the Earth. Their andesitic (*see* ANDESITE) lavas may be formed from the partially melted material of the descending plate. Northern Japan and the Aleutian Islands are examples.

islets of Langerhans

Clusters of cells in the PANCREAS that produce two hormones: INSULIN to raise the level of GLUCOSE in the blood and GLUCAGON to counteract the effect of insulin when necessary.

isobar

Line on a weather map connecting points of equal pressure, either at the Earth's surface or at a constant height above it. The patterns of isobars depict the variation in ATMOSPHERIC PRESSURE, showing areas of high and low pressure on the map.

isoelectric point

During ELECTROPHORESIS, the pH at which the total positive charge on a MOLECULE is exactly equal to the total negative charge, thus it is electrically neutral and has no tendency to move to either the anode or the cathode of an electrical field.

► **island arc** The Hawaiian island chain is shown in this photograph taken from the space shuttle Discovery in 1988. North is at the bottom of the image. The islands are, from bottom right, Niihau, Kauai, Ouahu, Molokai, Lanai, Maui, Kahoolawe and Hawaii. These islands are the tops of a chain of volcanoes, most of which are now dormant. There are an additional 124 much smaller islands in this island arc.

isogamy

State of having male and female reproductive cells that act like GAMETES (sex cells) but that are similar to each other in size and structure. Isogamy is found in algae, some protozoans and primitive plants. It is distinct from **anisogamy,** where male and female sex cells differ in appearance.

isohyet

Line on a weather map connecting points with equal rainfall. Isohyets are usually drawn for a particular period of time, to show the distribution of rainfall over a few months in the summer or winter, or perhaps for a whole year.

isolation mechanism

Reproductive separation from other members of the same species, leading to the formation of separate breeding sub-units called DEMES. Continued isolation of these demes prevents the flow of GENES between them, allowing each to evolve along its own lines until interbreeding is impossible. Each group is then considered a separate SPECIES. Isolation may be geographical, behavioural, physiological or anatomical. It is important to EVOLUTION.

isomers

Chemical compounds having the same molecular formula but different properties due to the different arrangement of atoms within the molecules. **Structural isomers** have atoms connected in different ways. **Geometric isomers**, also known as cis-transisomers, differ in their symmetry about a double bond. **Optical isomers** are mirror images of each other.

isomorphism

Similarity of shape observed in unrelated groups due to CONVERGENT EVOLUTION.

isopod

Any of *c*.4000 species of CRUSTACEAN, including seven aquatic and one terrestrial suborder. Isopods are characterized by flattened, oval bodies, with several hard-plated segments of similar appearance. Land forms include the familiar WOODLOUSE; marine species include GRIBBLES and specialized fish parasites.

isostasy

Theory describing the maintenance of an equilibrium in the total mass of the Earth's CRUST despite its crustal movement. There exists a balance between the land masses and the MANTLE of the Earth on which the continental plates float, so that the plates rise and sink on the semi-molten surface of the mantle in such a fashion that the relative mass weighing upon the Earth's crust is constant. The spread of the continental plates by the upwelling of material from deep within the Earth's crust is balanced by the submergence of the opposite edges of the plates. *See also* CONTINENTAL DRIFT; PLATE TECTONICS

isotonic solutions

Describes solutions that have the same SOLUTE concentration. When separated from one another by a partially permeable membrane there is no net movement of the SOLVENT (usually water) between the two solutions. The water potential of the two solutions is the same. *See also* HYPERTONIC SOLUTION

isotope

Variety of a chemical element that differs from other varieties of the same element in the number of particles in the nuclei of its ATOMS. Atoms of different iso-

Insectivorous plants, also known as carnivorous plants, are plants that obtain missing nutrients by trapping, "digesting" and absorbing insects. All plants need a range of basic nutrients, including carbon, oxygen, nitrogen, phosphorus, potassium and other minerals as well as trace elements, which keep the plants alive and help them to build new tissues. Oxygen comes from the atmosphere, and all plants except parasitic plants also get their carbon from the air as carbon dioxide. Most plants take in the other nutrients, such as nitrogen, potassium and phosphorus, from the soil. Insectivorous plants, however, live in soils that are poor in nitrates and other minerals; they have overcome this problem by becoming carnivorous. They supplement their nitrogen by digesting the protein in the bodies of insects and other small animals which they catch in a variety of traps.

Insectivorous plants have evolved several different strategies for trapping their prey. The leaves of SUNDEWS (*Drosera* spp.) are covered with sticky tentacles. An insect alighting on the edge of the leaf is trapped by the tentacles, which are also triggered by touch to bend inwards, thus moving the captured insect to the centre of the leaf. Powerful digestive enzymes in the fluid released by glands at the tips of the tentacles rapidly liquefy the contents of the insect's body, which are then absorbed by the leaf. Other insectivorous plants bear modified leaves in the shape of hollow pitchers, which trap hapless insects. In some species of PITCHER PLANTS the mass of decaying bodies also provides food for the maggots of certain species of fly, which are resistant to the digestive enzymes. Some species of birds slit the sides of the pitcher in order to get at the maggots on which they feed.

The size of pitcher plants varies considerably according to the species. The vine-like tropical pitcher plants found in the forests of Malaysia and Borneo are the largest. After heavy rains the pitchers fill with water; in some cases the pitchers are large enough for birds and even small mammals to drown. At the other end of the size scale is the aquatic BLADDERWORT (*Utricularia* spp.). Bladderworts float just under the surface of the water, where there is little nitrogen available. The bladderwort's stem carries tiny, translucent, air-filled, bladder-like traps. The mouth of each bladder is shut by a "door" carrying a few stiff bristles on the lower free edge, called the trigger hairs. When a tiny creature, such as a water flea or a mosquito larva, brushes against the trigger hairs the door springs open and the victim is swept into the bladder as it fills with water. The door then snaps shut and the animal is trapped.

▼ **The hollow, jug-shaped** traps of the *Nepenthes* pitcher plant hang at the end of its long leaves (A). Each one has a lid at the top to keep out the heavy tropical rains (1). Insects are attracted to the pitcher by its bright colours and by a sugary nectar produced by glands around the rim (2). The surface of this rim is waxy and very slippery, and most visiting insects rapidly lose their footing and fall in. Once inside, it is very difficult for them to escape: the upper areas of the inner surface are waxy; the lower regions are glassy smooth and covered with digestive glands; neither offer any foothold to an insect attempting to escape. They quickly tire of struggling and drown in the pool of water and digestive juices in the base of the trap (3). The digestion and absorption of the insects' bodies is very efficient in *Nepenthes*, taking about two days for an average fly, but only two hours for a small midge. The sticky leaves of the common European butterwort act like flypaper (B). A sticky mucilage is produced by stalked glands scattered over the leaf surface (1). When insects land on a leaf, they pull the mucilage out into strands, which set and hold them fast (2). As they struggle, more glands are touched and they are held even firmer. The insects' movements also stimulate the leaf to start rolling up (3). This

forms a temporary "stomach" into which digestive enzymes are released by stalkless glands (4). The enzymes are stored at the tip of the gland, in large vacuoles (5), and in the cell walls (6) of special secretory cells. Capture of prey stimulates a rush of water from the vascular system (7) through the gland, flushing out the enzymes onto the leaf surface (8) to form a pool around the insect. The products are absorbed by the leaf (9) and distributed around the plant (10). The Venus fly trap (C) is found in the bogs of North Carolina in the E United States of America. Ants, spiders and flies are its usual prey, though it may also capture other small animals

such as snails and slugs. The leaf tips of the Venus fly trap are modified into two kidney-shaped lobes (1) hinged at the mid-rib (2). Covering the inner surface of the lobes are two kinds of glands. The alluring glands, on the green outer margins of the trap, secrete a sugary nectar that attracts insects (3). Farther in towards the midrib are the digestive absorptive glands (4), which give the lobes their red colour. Also on the inner surface of each lobe is a triangle of three tiny hairs, which act as triggers. If two or more of these hairs are

touched in quick succession by an insect, they produce a tiny electrical current. This causes a change in the water retention of the membranes of the motor cells in the midrib region. These cells

quickly lose pressure and become limp, and the pressure from the cells in the outer epidermis forces the two lobes together. Within

two-fifths of a second, the trap has closed sufficiently to prevent the escape of larger insects. As the prey struggles to escape it further

stimulates the trap to close completely. The insect's soft parts are slowly broken down by acids and enzymes released from the digestive glands and then absorbed. After the insect's soft parts have been digested, the leaves open again, releasing the indigestible skeleton.

◄ **ivory** During the 20th
century the elephant
population declined
drastically, partly due to the
trade in their tusks. Elephants
are now listed by CITES
(Convention on International
Trade in Endangered Species),
which means that the sale of
elephant products is strictly
controlled. Illegal poaching,
however, has continued.
Shown here are large
amounts of ivory and rhino
horns seized from poachers.
The seizure is burned to
prevent any further profit
being made.

ivory

Hard, yellowish-white dentine of some mammals.
The most highly prized variety is obtained from ELE-
PHANT tusks. The term also refers to the teeth of HIP-
POPOTAMUSES, WALRUSES, sperm WHALES and sever-
al other mammals.

ivory nut palm

Low-growing PALM tree that is found along river
banks in Central America. The fruits contain
between six and nine bony seeds with a thin brown
layer on the outside. The seeds, also known as vegetable ivory, can be carved and have been used
extensively to make such things as buttons, chess-
men, knobs and inlays. Family Arecaceae; species
Phytelephas macrocarpa.

ivy

Woody, evergreen VINE that is native to Europe and
Asia. It has leathery leaves and long, climbing
stems, which cling to upright surfaces, such as trees
or walls, by aerial roots. The common English ivy
(*Hedera helix*) is propagated by cuttings and grows
outdoors in moist shady or sunny areas. Family
Araliaceae; most common genus *Hedera*; a large
number of varieties are cultivated.

topes have the same number of electrons or protons
(same atomic number) but a different number of neutrons, so that both the mass number and the mass of
the nucleus are different for different isotopes. The
relative atomic mass (r.a.m.) of an element is an average of the relative atomic masses of the element's
naturally occurring isotopes. Isotopes are distinguished by writing the mass number by the name or
symbol of the element, for example, ^{14}C or carbon-
14. The isotopes of an element all have similar chemical properties, but physical properties vary slightly.
Most elements have two or more naturally occurring
isotopes, some of which are radioactive (radioisotopes). Many radioisotopes can be produced artificially by bombarding elements with high-energy particles such as alpha particles. Radioisotopes are used
in medicine, research and industry. Isotopes are also
used in radioactive dating.

jabiru
Large STORK found in muddy wetlands from Mexico south to Argentina. It has white plumage but a bare upper neck and head. It has a heavy, slightly upturned bill. The jabiru feeds on aquatic animals, reptiles and insects. Length: 147cm (58in). Family Ciconiidae; species *Jabiru mycteria*.

jaborandi
Name given to a drug obtained from the dried aromatic leaves of various plant species belonging to the genus *Pilocarpus*, found in South America. The drug increases saliva flow and contains the alkaloid pilocarpine. Family Rutaceae; species *Pilocarpus jaborandi* and *Pilocarpus microphyllus*.

jacamar
Any member of a small group of *c*.17 species of brightly coloured birds that make up the family Galbulidae. Jacamars are found in damp forests from Mexico to Paraguay and s Brazil, where they nest in holes dug in sloping river banks. They feed on insects. Family Galbulidae.

jacamar, great
Largest jacamar. Its plumage is golden and green, and it has a red breast, long tail and a longish, slightly curved, black bill. The great jacamar is found in Central and South America, from Costa Rica to the Amazon basin. It feeds on insects. Length: 30cm (12in). Family Galbulidae; species *Jacamerops aurea*.

jacamar, paradise
Slender, long-billed jacamar. It has dark, bluish-green plumage and a white throat. Its narrow tail is longer than its body. The paradise jacamar lives close to water in tropical forests of South America. It feeds mainly on insects. Length: 30cm (12in). Family Galbulidae; species *Galbula dea*.

jacana (lilytrotter)
Long-legged tropical marsh bird with long toes and claws. It gets its alternative name from its habit of striding along floating leaves. The jacana is mostly brown or black, with colourful patches on its head. Its food is taken from the water, and its nest is made of floating plants. The male bird incubates the eggs. The jacana is found in Asia, Africa, South America and Australia. Family Jacanidae.

jacana, pheasant-tailed
Medium-sized jacana that is found in open water from India to s China. It is mainly brown and black, with a white head and wing flash and a yellow nape. It is distinguished by its long, plumed tail. The pheasant-tailed jacana feeds on aquatic plants and animals. Length: 35cm (14in). Family Jacanidae; species *Hydrophasianus chirurgus*.

jacana, wattled
Jacana that lives in damp meadows and wetlands in much of tropical South America. The red wattles at the base of the bill give it its common name. Length: 22cm (9in). Family Jacanidae; species *Jacana jacana*.

jacaranda
Any member of the *Jacaranda* genus, a group of trees native to tropical America. The ornamental *Jacaranda mimosifolia* and *Jacaranda cuspidifolia* have ornate blue flowers and fern-like leaves. Family Bignoniaceae; there are *c*.50 species.

jack
Any of a group of large, silvery, laterally compressed marine fish of the Atlantic, Indian and Pacific oceans. They are important food fish and are related to scads and POMPANOS. Family Carangidae; species include *Seriola dumerli* (AMBERFISH or amberjack).

jackal
COYOTE-like omnivore with long legs and a bushy tail. It belongs to the DOG family. The various species are of similar size. Family Canidae.

jackal, golden (common jackal)
Most widespread species of jackal. It is found in arid grasslands of North Africa, SE Europe and s Asia. Its coat is yellow to pale gold. It lives and hunts in pairs or family groups, feeding on fruit, invertebrates and small vertebrates, sometimes as large as young antelope. A small part of the golden jackal's diet consists of prey scavenged from larger animals. Head-body length: 65–106cm (26–42in); tail: 20–41cm (8–16in). Family Canidae; species *Canis aureus*.

jackal, sidestriped
Nocturnal jackal that lives in woodland or savanna in tropical Africa. It is grey-brown with a distinctive white side stripe; it has shorter legs and ears than other jackals. Its tail is dark with a white tip. Family Canidae; species *Canis adustus*.

jackal, silverbacked (blackbacked jackal)
Jackal found in dry brush or woodland of E and s Africa. It is reddish-brown, with a grizzled, black-and-white back. Away from human settlements it tends to be diurnal; near human settlements it is active at night. A social animal, the silverbacked jackal hunts in packs for larger animals. Family Canidae; species *Canis mesomelas*.

jackal, Simien (Ethiopian wolf)
Jackal that inhabits mountainous grasslands in Ethiopia. It is reddish, with white underparts. The Simien jackal's diet consists largely of rodents, which it often digs out of their burrows. Family Canidae; species *Canis simensis*.

jackal-fly (insect jackal)
Fly that is so called because the adult attaches itself to and feeds on predatory insects and spiders. Jackal-flies breed in dung. They are sometimes found indoors. Adult body length: *c*.10mm (*c*.0.4in). Order Diptera; family Milichiidae; species *Madiza glabra*.

jack bean
LEGUME native to West Indies; it is grown in many tropical countries for green manure, stock feed and beans. The plants are bushy annuals; their long, sword-like pods contain several large beans. Unripe pods are used for human consumption, and the whole plant can be used for green forage. Family Fabaceae; species *Canavalia ensiformis*.

jackdaw
Medium-sized bird, the smallest member of the CROW family. It is mostly black, with a grey nape and breast and grey eyes. It is found in open country and woodland across Europe and w Asia, often in flocks. The jackaw feeds mostly on invertebrates, but it also eats corn and seeds. It nests in holes in trees or in old buildings. Length: 33cm (13in). Family Corvidae; species *Corvus monedula*.

Jack Dempsey
Freshwater fish native to the central Amazon region of South America. It has a laterally compressed body. Its colour varies from pale brownish to blue-

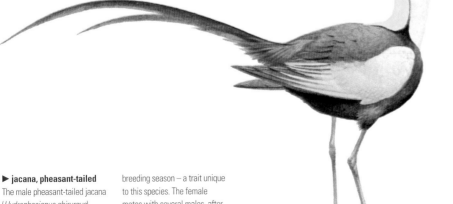

► jacana, pheasant-tailed The male pheasant-tailed jacana (*Hydrophasianus chirurgus*) grows long tail feathers, up to 15cm (6in) in length, during the breeding season – a trait unique to this species. The female mates with several males, after which the male incubates the eggs and raises the brood.

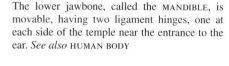

◄ **jaguar** Most commonly found in the Amazonian rainforest, the jaguar (*Panthera onca*) is a highly adaptable creature. It is usually found near swampy areas but during the wet season, when the jungle floor is flooded, it can live for long periods in the forest canopy. While demand for jaguar pelts has declined since the 1970s, jaguars are still at risk from being shot by farmers attempting to protect their cattle herds.

► **jaguarundi** Sometimes called an otter cat, the jaguarundi (*Felis yagouaroundi*) is an unusual feline in its preference for living near water and its willingness to swim. It is an adept hunter.

jade
Semi-precious silicate mineral of which there are two major types: **jadeite,** which is often translucent, and **nephrite,** which has a waxy quality. Both types are extremely hard and durable. Jade is found mainly in Burma and comes in many colours, most commonly green and white. Hardness 5–6; r.d. 3–3.4.

jade plant
Succulent shrubby plant native to s Africa; it is grown as an ornamental. The jade plant has a thick stem, which supports fleshy, oval, shiny leaves, often tinged with red. Mature plants, under appropriate conditions, produce tiny, pinkish-white flowers. Family Crassulaceae; species *Crassula argentea*.

jaguar
Largest member of the CAT family found in the Americas. It inhabits woodland or grassland from sw United States south to Argentina. It has a chunky body and a spotted, yellowish coat with black rosettes. The black rings distinguish it from the LEOPARD. It eats large mammals, turtles and fish. Length: up to 2.5m (8.2ft), including tail; weight up to 140kg (300lb). Family Felidae; species *Panthera onca*.

jaguarundi
Small, ground-dwelling CAT found in Central and South America. It is black, brown, grey or fox red. It

black, with blue-green spots. The Jack Dempsey is an aggressive fish. It is related to DISCUS FISH and TILAPIA and is a popular aquarium fish. Length: to 23cm (9in). Family Cichlidae; species *Cichlasoma biocellatum*.

jack fruit
Tree native to s India; it is grown in the tropics for the large fruits borne on its trunk or main branches. These fruits can be up to 0.6m (2ft) long and weigh as much as 18kg (40lb). The seeds are embedded in a fleshy, swollen receptacle, which is edible raw or cooked. Height: to 21m (70ft). Family Moraceae; species *Artocarpus heterophyllus*.

jack-rabbit
See RABBIT, JACK-

jacky winter (Australian brown flycatcher)
Small FLYCATCHER found in dry forest, woodlands, mallee and farmland across Australia. It has an olive-brown back, a light grey breast and white outer tail feathers. It feeds on insects. Length: 13cm (5in). Family Muscicapidae; species *Microeca leucophaea*.

Jacob, François (1920–)
French biologist. With Jacques MONOD he discovered that a substance that they named MESSENGER RNA (mRNA) carried hereditary information from the CELL nucleus to the sites of PROTEIN SYNTHESIS and that certain GENES, called **operator genes,** control the activity of others. Jacob and Monod shared the 1965 Nobel Prize for physiology or medicine with another French biologist, André LWOFF. *See also* HEREDITY

Jacob's ladder
Any of *c*.30 species of wild and cultivated plants belonging to the genus *Polemonium*; they are found in temperate areas. They produce clusters of delicate blue, violet or white flowers and alternate compound leaves. The species *Polemonium caeruleum* is known as Greek valerian. Height: up to 90cm (3ft). Family Polemoniaceae.

JAW

Either of two bony structures that hold the TEETH and frame the mouth in humans and most other vertebrates. The upper jawbone, known as the MAXILLA, is fused to the SKULL.

The lower jawbone, called the MANDIBLE, is movable, having two ligament hinges, one at each side of the temple near the entrance to the ear. *See also* HUMAN BODY

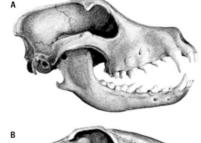

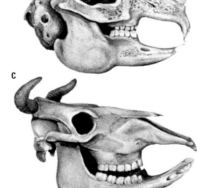

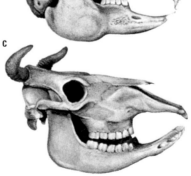

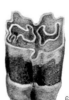

▲ **The jaws of** mammals such as the dog (A), rabbit (B) and cow (C), have become adapted to the type of food that the animal usually eats. The dog is a flesh eater, with sharp canines (1) for killing its prey. It has specialized molar teeth (2), with sharp cutting edges for slicing the meat. The rabbit is a herbivore and has chisel-shaped incisors (3) for gnawing. Its molars (4) slide over each other sideways to grind up vegetation. The cow is a ruminant, tearing up grass with its incisors (5). The cow chews its tough food with broad, flat molars (6). The enamel (shown here in green) is harder than the dentine (yellow) and forms a series of ridges when the crown is flattened due to wear and tear.

preys on small mammals and birds. Length: to 67cm (26in), excluding tail; weight: to 9kg (20lb). Family Felidae; species *Felis yagouaroundi*.

Japanese cherry
Tree native to Japan and China; it was introduced into Europe in *c*.1870. It is often planted in gardens and parks for its ornate flowers. It has smooth, chestnut-brown bark. Several varieties exist, which have rose, pink or white, single or double flowers; the rounded black fruits form only rarely. Height: to 12m (40ft). Family Rosaceae; species *Prunus serrulata*.

Japanese quince
See FLOWERING QUINCE

japonica (Chinese quince)
Spiny, herbaceous shrub native to China; it is widely grown as an ornamental. The white to deep pink or red, cup-shaped flowers are produced early in the year. The japonica's yellowish-green, apple-like fruits are used in preserves. Family Rosaceae; species *Chaenomeles speciosa*.

jarrah
Large EUCALYPTUS tree native to w Australia. It has red-grey bark, which develops vertical fissures. The hardwood timber is the principal timber of w Australia, and large quantities of it are exported. It has been used extensively for paving blocks, sleepers and cabinet woods. Height: to 45m (150ft). Family Myrtaceae; species *Eucalyptus marginata*.

jasmine
Any evergreen or deciduous shrub or vine of the genus *Jasminum*, common in the Mediterranean region. It has fragrant yellow, pink or white flowers. Jasmine oil is used in perfumes. Height: to 6.5m (20ft). Family Oleaceae; species include *Jasminum officinale* (common jasmine) and *Jasminum nudiflorum* (winter jasmine).

jaw
See feature article

jay
Any of several species in the CROW family. Their plumage is usually colourful, often with purple or blue hues. Jays are omnivorous, noisy and aggressive. They are widespread, mostly found in woodland or scrub of temperate regions of the Northern Hemisphere. Family Corvidae (part).

jay, blue
Jay that is found in woodland of North America, from Newfoundland to Texas. Its plumage is bright blue above and light grey below, with a black collar and a slight crest. The wings and tail are blue with black bars. It feeds on fruit, seeds, small mammals, amphibians and insects. Length: 27–29cm (*c*.11in). Family Corvidae; species *Cyanocitta cristata*.

jay, Eurasian
Jay that is found in woodland and parkland throughout Europe and in some parts of w Asia and North Africa. It is mostly pinkish-brown, with a white rump and undertail, and white and blue flashes on its wings. It is omnivorous, feeding particularly on acorns (which it often hoards), berries, corn and insects. Length: 34cm (13in). Family Corvidae; species *Garrulus glandarius*.

jay, scrub
Jay that is found in North American oak scrub; it ranges from NW United States to the Florida penin-

▲ **jay** The green jay (*Cyanocorax yncas*) is found in Central and South America and measures up to 33cm (13in) in length. Found in tropical forest as well as lowland and mountainous areas, the green jay eats a variety of invertebrates, fruit and seeds.

sula and Mexico. The scrub jay has blue upperparts, except for a brown patch on its back, and light grey underparts. It has no crest. It often hoards food. Length: 30cm (12in). Family Corvidae; species *Aphelocoma coerulescens*.

jay, grey (Canada jay)
Jay found in the coniferous forests of North America, from New England north to the limit of pine forest in Canada, and south along the Rockies. It is mostly grey, with a white forehead. It is omnivorous, feeding particularly on seeds and insects. Length: 28–33cm (11–13in). Family Corvidae; species *Perisoreus canadensis*.

jay, pinyon
Rather thickset and gregarious jay. It has mainly blue-grey plumage. It is found in scattered pines and sagebrush in mountainous parts of the w United States. It feeds on pinyon pine nuts, seeds and insects. Length: 22–27cm (9–11in). Family Corvidae; species *Gymnorhinus cyanocephalus*.

jay, Steller's
Medium-sized jay found in conifer forests in w America, from Alaska to Nicaragua and east to the Rocky Mountains. It is mostly dark grey, with a black head and crest; its wings and tail are blue barred black. Steller's jay feeds on insects and spiders and often forages at camp sites. Length: 31–33cm (12–13in). Family Corvidae; species *Cyanocitta stelleri*.

jellyfish
Marine animal, which, for most of its life cycle, takes the form of a MEDUSA (a bell-shaped, soft-bodied organism). The bell proper is able to contract to produce limited movement and oral arms surround the mouth. The tentacles are used both in

defence and in capturing prey. Phylum Coelenterata/Cnidaria; class Scyphozoa.

jellyfish, lion's mane
Any member of the *Cyanea* genus of jellyfish. They are thought to be the largest members of the jellyfish group: bell diameters of more than 2m (6.6ft) have been recorded. The jellyfish's name is derived from the appearance of the many golden tentacles. The stinging cells borne by these tentacles can be extremely harmful to humans. Class Scyphozoa; genus *Cyanea*.

jellyfish, moon
Any member of the *Aurelia* genus of jellyfish. They are small, with bell diameters of less than 0.2m (8in). Moon jellyfish possess stinging tentacles, but they are harmless to humans. They are common off coasts worldwide. Class Scyphozoa; genus *Aurelia*.

jellyfish, stalked
Sessile jellyfish. They are often seen in rock pools, being attached to the substrate by a stalk arising from the convex side of the bell. Class Scyphozoa; order Stauromedusae.

jerboa (desert rat)
Nocturnal, herbivorous, burrowing RODENT of Eurasian and African deserts. It has a satiny, sand-coloured body, long hind legs and a long tail. Length: to 15cm (6in), excluding tail. Family Dipodidae; genera include *Alactagulus*, *Allactaga*, *Dipus*, *Jaculus*, *Paradipus* and *Salpingotulus*.

Jerusalem artichoke
Erect, roughly hairy, herbaceous, perennial plant; it is native to North America. It has large, golden-yellow, daisy-like flowers. It is grown for its irregularly shaped TUBERS, which are produced on underground stems. The Jerusalem artichoke was originally cultivated by Native North Americans for these edible tubers, which are highly nutritious and can be eaten boiled or roasted. Family Asteraceae; species *Helianthus tuberosus*.

jet
Dense variety of LIGNITE coal formed from wood buried on the seafloor. Jet is often polished and used in jewellery.

jet stream
Strong current of air blowing through the atmosphere at a high altitude. The main jet streams are in the middle and subtropical latitudes. The temperate jet stream flows from west to east, though along a wave-like route going north and south as it travels all around the world. It can blow at speeds of up to 370km/h (230mph) and so is an important factor for aircraft. If planes can fly with the jet stream, which often blows at a height of between 10,000m and 13,000m (33,000–42,600ft) above the Earth's sur-

J

◄ **jerboa** The desert jerboa (*Jaculus jaculus*) is found in North Africa and central Asia. It moves around on its hind legs, making leaps of up to 3m (9.5ft). It uses its tail as a prop when stationary. Like many desert-dwelling animals, the jerboa aestivates in order to survive the extreme heat. It digs itself a burrow and blocks the entrance to protect itself from predators such as the fennec fox.

J

▲ **John Dory** An important food fish, the John Dory (*Zeus faber*) is usually found in shallow to moderate waters amongst rocks and weeds. It is a predominantly solitary fish. It feeds on smaller fish, which it catches by drifting into shoals of fish then engulfing one with its large protrusile mouth.

face, it can increase the speed of the journey and save fuel costs. Jet streams influence the weather systems in the lower layers of the atmosphere, as depressions tend to follow their route.

jewel weed
See IMPATIENS

jew's ear fungus
FUNGUS with an ear-shaped fruiting body that is rubbery tan-brown and covered with minute downy hairs when fresh. The undersurface is grey-brown. Jew's ear fungus is most commonly found on branches of trees, particularly elder, and is edible. Phylum Basidiomycota; species *Auricularia auricula-judae*.

jimson weed
Poisonous annual plant that has been naturalized worldwide; it grows on waste and cultivated ground. The white to purplish, trumpet-shaped flowers produce green seed capsules covered in spines. Jimson weed contains the powerful alkaloids hyoscyamine and hyoscine; it has been used as a narcotic and pain-reliever. Family Solanaceae; species *Datura stramonium*.

jird
Rodent that belongs to the GERBIL family; it inhabits arid regions of Africa and Asia. It can be diurnal or nocturnal, depending on local temperatures. It digs burrows, which are often deep and extensive. The jird's fur is usually camouflaged to match the ground where it feeds, but its long tail is tipped with a contrasting colour. Head-body length: 10–18cm (4–7in); tail: 10–19cm (4–7in). Family Muridae; subfamily Gerbillinae; genus *Meriones*.

Job's tears
Annual GRASS from Southeast Asia. It has large, sword-shaped leaves. It is grown for its fruits, which have a hard, shiny, grey or white shell when mature. The fruits resemble beads and are used in rosaries and ornamentation. Thin-shelled types are grown as cereal food in parts of Asia. Height: to 1.8m (6ft). Family Poaceae; species *Coix lacryma-jobi*.

John Dory (dory)
Marine food fish found along the Atlantic coast of Europe. Its disc-shaped body is yellow to olive in colour, and there is a prominent black spot on each side. Length: to 70cm (28in). Family Zeidae; species *Zeus faber*.

joint
Upright or near-upright crack in a rock. Joints occur in SEDIMENTARY ROCKS, such as LIMESTONE, along lines of weakness caused by shrinking or WEATHERING. Their position influences the structure of CLIFFS and ESCARPMENTS. Joints form in IGNEOUS ROCKS, such as BASALT, as the magma solidifies and cooling and contraction take place.

jonquil
Slender, bulbous plant that is native to s Europe and Algeria; it is cultivated as an ornamental. Jonquil has flattened leaves. It bears between two and six yellow, very fragrant flowers, which have cup-shaped corollas. A sweet-smelling oil used in perfumery is obtained from the jonquil plant. Height: to 46cm (18in). Family Amaryllidaceae; species *Narcissus jonquilla*.

Joshua tree
Tree-like SUCCULENT belonging to the YUCCA genus; it is native to the w deserts of North America. Its stiff leaves are produced in rosettes at the ends of the trunk or branches. Cup-shaped, creamy, fragrant flowers, which open at night, are borne on erect clusters that overtop the leaves. Joshua trees often grow in clusters, forming "forests". Family Agavaceae; species *Yucca brevifolia*.

joule (symbol J)
SI unit of energy. One joule is the work done by a force of one newton acting over a distance of one metre. It was named after British physicist James Joule (1818–89) and replaced the erg.

Judas tree
Shrub or tree native to the Mediterranean region; it is often planted in gardens as an ornamental. It has rounded leaves. Clusters of between three and six purplish-rose or white, pea-like flowers are produced from joints on branches before the leaves appear. Height: to 12m (40ft). Family Caesalpiniaceae; species *Cercis siliquastrum*.

jujube
Either of two species of small, thorny trees belonging to the genus *Zizyphus*; jujube is also the name of their fruit. The common jujube, *Zizyphus jujuba*, native to China, has elliptical leaves. Its reddish-brown, plum-sized fruits have a crisp, white, sweet flesh. The Indian jujube, *Zizyphus mauritanica*, has smaller fruit. Family Rhamnaceae.

jumping bean plant
Any of several tropical plants, native to Mexico, belonging to the family Euphorbiaceae. The seeds become infested with insect larvae of the species *Cydia saltitans*. When the seeds are heated, the larvae make jerking movements, causing the seeds to "jump". Family Euphorbiaceae; species include *Sebastiania pavoniana* and *Sebastiania pringlei* and those belonging to the genus *Sapium*.

jumping plant louse
Small insect that looks like a leafhopper but has longer antennae. Jumping plant lice are often found in conjunction with particular plant species. They are important pests and are also vectors of plant viruses. The nymphs are gregarious and have noticeable wing pads. Adult body length: 1.5–5mm (0.06–0.2in). Order Hemiptera; family Psyllidae; species include *Psylla pyricola* (pear sucker) and *Psylla mali* (apple sucker).

junco
Any member of the genus *Junco*, a small group of drab-coloured birds related to SPARROWS and BUNTINGS. They are found in North America. Juncos are mostly open-country birds but are also found in suburbia. Their food is mainly seeds and insects. Family Emberizidae; genus *Junco*.

June beetle
See BEETLE, JUNE

◀ **Joshua tree** The Mojave Desert, California, w United States, provides the ideal growing conditions for Joshua trees (*Yucca brevifolia*) and the golden California poppies (*Eschscholzia californica*). The tallness of the Joshua tree is unusual for a member of the *Yucca* genus. Certain individuals have been known to reach heights of 15m (50ft); this is thought to be an important factor in the Joshua tree's ability to survive in desert conditions, because it keeps the leaves far away from the hot sand.

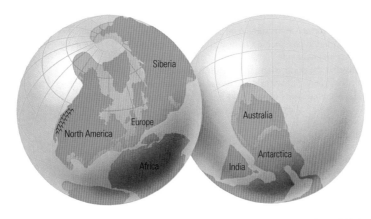

► **Jurassic** By the Jurassic period, the Gondwanaland landmass had begun to break into separate continents.

June bug
See BEETLE, MAY

junglefowl, red
Medium-sized bird, the ancestor of the domestic fowl or chicken. The male has pronounced wattles, a dark breast and a plumed tail with an orange "mane"; the female is rather dull brown. The junglefowl is found in thick rainforest and bamboo scrub in India, Southeast Asia and Indonesia. It feeds on fruit and seeds on the forest floor. Length: 43–60cm (17–24in). Family Phasianidae; species *Gallus gallus*.

jungle runner
Any of several species of terrestrial, diurnal, insectivorous lizards that occur from Mexico to South America. Jungle runners are larger relatives of whiptail LIZARDS and, like them, are very fast-moving. Their snouts are pointed and their heads are some-what laterally compressed. Length: to 50cm (20in). Family Teiidae; genus *Ameiva*.

juniper
Any evergreen shrub or tree of the genus *Juniperus*, native to temperate regions of the Northern Hemisphere. Junipers have needle-like or scale-like leaves. The aromatic timber is used for making pencils, and the berry-like cones of common juniper (*Juniperus communis*) for flavouring gin. Family Cupressaceae; genus *Juniperus*.

Jurassic
Central period of the MESOZOIC era; it lasted from 213 to 144 million years ago. In this period there were large saurischian DINOSAURS, such as *Atlantosaurus* and *Allosaurus*, and ornithischian dinosaurs, such as *Camptosaurus* and *Stegosaurus*. Archaeopteryx, plesiosaurs and pterosaurs also date from the Jurassic.

Primitive mammals began to evolve; they were the ancestors of later marsupial and placental species.

jute
Either of two plants, both native to India, grown for their fibre. They have thick stalks, pale green leaves and bear small, yellow flowers. The fibre is obtained from the bark by soaking (retting) and beating. It is used to make sacking, twine and rope. Height: to 4.6m (15ft). Family Tileaceae; species *Corchorus capsularis* and *Corchorus olitorius*.

juvenile hormone (neotenin)
HORMONE found in INSECTS that prevents the development of adult characteristics when larval insects moult. It is produced in the corpora allata glands behind the brain. These organs become inactive at the last moult, and METAMORPHOSIS then begins.

◄ **jute** Two very similar annual plant species are grown for jute production, *Corchorus capsularis* and *Corchorus olitorius*. The plants are harvested when mature and retted in water for several weeks, which causes the gum tissue surrounding the bast fibres to dissolve. The fibres are separated by beating and can then be processed into yarn. High quality woven yarn is known as hessian.

J

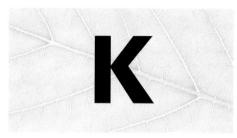

▲ **kagu** The introduction of cats, pigs, rats and dogs to New Caledonia, sw Pacific Ocean, which previously had no predatory mammals, pushed the kagu to the brink of extinction. Its numbers have increased in recent years, due to the culling of dogs and the establishment of reserves, but still remain critical.

Kaffir plum
Dioecious tree from s Africa. It has shiny, pinnate, leathery leaves clustered at the ends of branches. Its small white or greenish flowers grow in compact, axillary clusters. The edible fruit is dark red and is used to make jelly and local medications. Family Anacardiaceae; species *Harpephyllum caffrum*.

kagu
Medium-sized, virtually flightless bird found in the mountain forests of New Caledonia in the sw Pacific Ocean. It has grey plumage, a plumed crest, long legs and a red bill. The kagu is classified in its own family and is highly endangered. Its food includes snails, worms and insects. It is ground-nesting and largely nocturnal. Length: 56cm (22in). Family: Rhynochetidae; species *Rhynochetos jubatus*.

kakapo (owl parrot)
Medium-sized, ground-dwelling parrot with dull green plumage. It is nocturnal and virtually flightless. The kakapo is very rare, found only in one or two localities in New Zealand. It feeds mainly on vegetable matter but also on lizards and insects. Length: 56–63cm (22–25in). Family Psittacidae; species *Strigops habroptilus*.

kalanchoe
Any member of the genus *Kalanchoe*, a group of SUCCULENT PLANTS mostly native to Africa and Madagascar; they are also grown as house or greenhouse plants. Kalanchoe plants are usually erect and branched, with opposite, fleshy leaves and yellow, red or purple flowers in terminal clusters. Some types produce plantlets along the leaf margins. Family Crassulaceae; genus *Kalanchoe*.

kale
Hardy variety of CABBAGE. It is a short-stemmed plant, with large, bluish-green, curly-edged leaves. Height: to 61cm (24in). Family Brassicaceae; (sub)species *Brassica oleracea acephala*.

kame
Deposit formed by a subglacial stream near the terminal margin of a melting GLACIER. Streams flowing down mountainsides onto glaciers deposit sand and gravel at the point where the stream first reaches the ice, or where the water goes down into a crevasse. The accumulations of sand and gravel gradually fall down to the valley floor as the ice melts. Kames are generally small features, 20–30m (65–100ft) in length or breadth.

kangaroo
Any of *c*.60 species of marsupial mammals that belong to one of two families. Smaller species are often called WALLABIES. Size varies considerably between the species, but all kangaroos have shorter fore than hind limbs, and they all have a heavy tail used for balance and support. Families Macropodidae and Potoroidae.

kangaroo, grey
Either of two species of kangaroo native to Australia. The Eastern grey kangaroo is slightly larger than the Western grey kangaroo. Males can reach 240cm (94in) head-tail. Family Macropodidae; genus *Macropus*.

kangaroo, rat
Any member of the second of the two kangaroo families. Rat kangaroos include the BETTONGS. Head-body length: 24–52cm (9–20in); tail: 13–40cm (5–16in). Family Potoroidae.

kangaroo, red
Largest living marsupial. The red kangaroo inhabits the interior grasslands of Australia. The females are often blue-grey in colour. Length: up to 280cm (110in) head-tail. Family Macropodidae; species *Macropus rufus*.

▲ **kakapo** The largest species of parrot, the kakapo is one of the most critically endangered bird species. It is easy to catch for many predators and has lost much of its natural habitat. Its population today stands at around 50 birds and attempts to save the species include the relocation of some birds to islands where they will be less at risk.

kangaroo, tree
Any member of a genus of kangaroos with strong fore limbs and rough-soled feet. Most species of tree kangaroo live in New Guinea, but two are found in Australia. They stay in trees during the day, descending to the ground to feed at night. Head-body length: 52–81cm (20–32in); tail: 42–94cm (17–37in). Family Macropodidae; genus *Dendrolagus*; there are seven species.

kangaroo rat
See RAT, KANGAROO

grey kangaroo

red kangaroos

▲ **kangaroo** Male red kangaroos (*Macropus rufus*) sometimes fight each other to gain supremacy in their group; the forelegs are used to grasp the opponent, the hind legs to inflict wounds, and the tail is sometimes used as an additional support. Both red and grey kangaroos graze on vegetation in forests and savannas. The joey of the grey kangaroo lives in its mother's pouch for about 320 days. The reproductive cycle of the female kangaroo allows two or three young to develop simultaneously, so that shortly after one joey leaves the pouch, another is born and starts growing inside the pouch.

KARST

Limestone plateau characterized by irregular protuberant rocks, sinkholes, CAVES, disappearing streams and underground drainage. This type of landscape forms where solution WEATHERING wears away much of the limestone, and where rivers erode the rock. Most rivers are underground, and there are caves and large caverns. The largest caverns may collapse to form gorges, and gradually the entire area of limestone may be worn away. Such topography is named after its most typical site in the Karst region of former Yugoslavia; in Britain, the most spectacular example is above Malham, North Yorkshire.

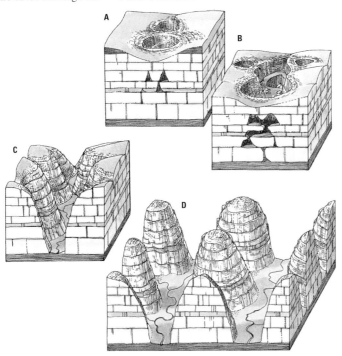

► The Karst landscapes of the Dinaric Alps, Appalachian Mountains and areas of s China occur because beds of limestone rock, composed primarily of the mineral calcite (calcium carbonate), up to 200m (650ft) thick are progressively eroded by water. Carbon dioxide from the atmosphere dissolves in rain to form weak carbonic acid, which dissolves the rock, particularly along joints and bedding planes, enlarging them to produce sink holes (A). Dolines (B) are produced by cave roofs falling in; they can be enlarged to produce gorges (C), finally leaving the characteristic uneroded limestone cores of the Karst landscape (D).

kaolang
Cultivated GRASS of Chinese origin; it is one of China's oldest crops. Kaolang plants are drought resistant and have been used to provide grain, sugar and forage. Their slender stalks have few leaves; they have loose or compact, erect flowering heads and small, brown or white seeds. Family Poaceae; species *Sorghum nervosum*.

kaolinite
Sheet silicate mineral, hydrous aluminium silicate ($Al_2Si_2O_5(OH)_4$). It is a product of the weathering of feldspar and has triclinic system tabular crystals. It is white with a dull lustre. Hardness 2–2.5; r.d. 2.6.

kapok
Tropical tree with compound leaves and white or pink flowers. Its seed pods burst to release silky fibres, commonly used for stuffing and insulation. Height: to 50m (165ft). Family Bombacaceae; species *Ceiba pentandra*.

Kariba weed
Floating aquatic plant from tropical America. Widely naturalized, it has become a pestilential weed of inland waterways. It has almost circular leaves, which form mats on the water. It gets its name from the population explosion in the 1980s in Lake Kariba, on the Zimbabwe–Zambia border, after construction of the Kariba Dam provided ideal growth conditions. Family Salviniaceae; species *Salvinia auriculata*.

karst
See feature article

karyotype
Arrangement, structure and number of CHROMOSOMES in the nucleus of a CELL. All the body cells of an organism have the same karyotype. The number of chromosomes varies widely with species, for example eight in fruit flies, 12 in kangaroos, 46 in humans, and 200 in crayfish.

katydid
See CRICKET, BUSH

kauri pine
Broad-leaved CONIFER native to New Zealand. It has flaky bark, bronze-green leaves and round cones. It was extensively milled by the early settlers of New Zealand. The trees made fine masts, and its fossilized gum (copal) is still used in the manufacture of lacquers and varnishes. Maoris regard the trees as forest gods. Height: to 45m (150ft). Family Araucariaceae; species *Agathis australis*.

kea
Medium-sized member of the PARROT family. It is has mostly dull green plumage, with a purple rump and a large, hooked bill. It is found in upland areas of New Zealand's South Island. It is omnivorous, feeding on fruit, buds, vegetable material and carrion. Length: 24cm (9in). Family Psittacidae; species *Nestor notabilis*.

keelworm
Small POLYCHAETE worm. It dwells inside tubes of calcium carbonate, which are laid down on the rocks of ocean shores. The keelworm feeds by means of a ring of feeding tentacles, which filter detritus from seawater. The tubes are triangular in cross-section and thus appear to have a distinct keel. Phylum Annelida; class Polychaeta; order Sabellida; family Serpulidae; genus *Pomatoceros*.

kelp
Any of several brown SEAWEEDS commonly found on Atlantic and Pacific coasts; it is a type of brown ALGAE. A source of iodine and potassium compounds, kelps are now used in a number of industrial processes. Giant kelp (*Macrocystis* sp.) exceeds 45m (150ft) in length. Phylum Phaeophyta.

kelp fish (kelp blenny)
Fish found in coastal waters of temperate regions north and south of the Equator; it is closely associated with KELP beds. The giant kelpfish (*Heterostichus rostratus*), 61cm (24in) in length, is cryptically coloured and sexually dimorphic. Suborder Blennoidei.

kelp-fly
Any member of a small family of flies, which breed in rotting seaweed on beaches. They are black, with very flat bodies. Kelp-flies swarm over the shore throughout the year and can be found on coastal flowers in the summer. Adult body length: *c*.7mm (*c*.0.3in). Order Diptera; family Coelopidae; species include *Coelopa frigida* and *Coelopa pilipes*.

kelvin (symbol K)
SI unit of TEMPERATURE. The Kelvin temperature scale has a zero point at absolute zero, and degree intervals (kelvins) that are the same size as degrees CELSIUS. The freezing point of water occurs at 273K (0°C or 32°F) and the boiling point occurs at 373K (100°C or 212°F). It is named after the British physicist and mathematician William Thomson, 1st Baron Kelvin (1824–1907).

Kennelly-Heaviside layer (E-layer)
Region that lies within the IONOSPHERE of the Earth's ATMOSPHERE.

keratin
Fibrous PROTEIN present in large amounts in the superficial cells of the SKIN, where it serves as a protective layer. Hair and fingernails are made up of modified epidermal cells filled with keratin, which is also the basis of claws, FEATHERS and the HORNS of some animals. *See also* EPIDERMIS

▲ **kea** Due to the scarcity of food in its habitat during the winter, the kea supplements its diet with carrion from dead sheep. Known to attack live sheep as well, aiming for the sheep's kidneys with its sharp beak, the kea is very unpopular with farmers and large numbers have been shot in the past.

K

211

kestrel

Any of *c*.20 species of small FALCON belonging to the genus *Falco*. Kestrels are mostly open country birds. They feed on small mammals and large insects, which are hunted from the wing, usually by hovering overhead. Family Falconidae (part). *See also* BIRD OF PREY

kestrel, common

Small- to medium-sized falcon found in open country across Europe, Asia and parts of Africa. It has a russet back with black blotches; the female has a brown breast, and the male has a light blue head and tail. The common kestrel breeds in the old nests of other birds. It feeds on mice, voles, worms and large insects. Length: 32–35cm (13–14in). Family Falconidae; species *Falco tinnunculus*.

kestrel, Australian

Kestrel found in open country across Australia. It is brown, with black patches and white underparts. It feeds on small mammals, lizards and large insects. Length: 30–35cm (12–14in). Family Falconidae; species *Falco cenchroides*.

kestrel, lesser

Rather dainty kestrel. Its plumage is similar to that of the common kestrel, but the male is brighter. It is found in open country around the Mediterranean basin and into Asia; it winters in India and Africa. The lesser kestrel is a sociable species, which nests in colonies. It feeds almost entirely on large insects. Length: 29–32cm (11–13in). Family Falconidae; species *Falco naumanni*.

kestrel, Mauritius

One of the rarest birds; there are probably fewer than 100 left, all of which are on the Indian Ocean island of Mauritius. It inhabits forested areas. The Mauritius kestrel was saved from extinction by captive breeding and release. Length: 28–33cm (11–13in). Family Falconidae; species *Falco punctatus*.

kestrel, fox

Largest kestrel; it is native to Africa, mainly found

in a belt of dry rocky country south of the Sahara. The male is rich brown with black markings and wingtips; the female is lighter brown and more heavily marked. It feeds on insects, small reptiles and small mammals. Length: 36cm (14in). Family Falconidae; species *Falco alopex*.

ketose

MONOSACCHARIDE that contains a ketone (C=O) group in its chemical structure. Examples include fructose and ribulose.

kettle hole

Steep-sided basin formed when a chunk of ice left behind by a receding glacier is covered by rocks and debris previously pushed forward by the glacier. The ice melts and the rocks fall through, creating a kettle pot-shaped depression.

khamsin

Hot southerly wind that blows across North Africa from the Sahara Desert during spring and summer. It is very dry, with relative humidity sometimes as low as 10%. The name means "fifty" in Arabic, the number of days during which the wind is supposed to blow.

khat tree

Evergreen shrub native from Ethiopia to South Africa; it is grown in terraced gardens in Ethiopia, Somalia and Yemen for its dark green leaves, which provide the beverage known as khat. Dried or fresh leaves and buds are also used as a stimulant and masticatory. Height: to 3m (10ft). Family Celastraceae; species *Catha edulis*.

Khorana, Har Gobind (1922–)

US biochemist who shared the 1968 Nobel Prize for physiology or medicine with Robert HOLLEY and Marshall NIRENBERG for discoveries about the way in which GENES determine cell function. They established that most CODONS, combinations of three of the four different bases found in DNA and RNA, eventually cause the inclusion of a specific AMINO ACID into the cell proteins.

kidney

In vertebrates, one of a pair of organs responsible for regulating blood composition and the EXCRETION of waste products. The kidneys are at the back of the abdomen, one on each side of the backbone. The human kidney consists of an outer cortex and an inner medulla with about one million tubules (NEPHRONS). Nephrons contain numerous CAPILLARIES, which filter the blood entering from the renal ARTERY. Some substances, including water, are reabsorbed into the blood. URINE remains, which is passed to the URETER and on to the BLADDER. *See also* HOMEOSTASIS

kidney bean

One of several cultivated beans developed from the FRENCH BEAN (*Phaseolus vulgaris*), originating from warm temperate regions of Central and South America. The name kidney bean usually refers to a specific type, which is kidney shaped and red, dark red or white in colour. Family Fabaceae; species *Phaseolus vulgaris*.

killdeer

Medium-sized PLOVER found on grassland and arable open country in North America. It has a brown back and cap, black markings on its white face, and white underparts with two black breastbands. The killdeer feeds mostly on invertebrates taken from the soil. Length: 25–26cm (10in). Family Charadriidae; species *Charadrius vociferus*.

killifish

Any member of a large group of elongated and often colourful fish, widely distributed in tropical and temperate, fresh, brackish and marine waters. The group includes the GUPPY, SWORDTAIL, FOUR-EYED FISH, Devil's Hole PUPFISH and mummichug (*Fundulus heteroclitus*). Killifish exhibit diverse reproductive strategies, including hermaphroditism. Length: to 15cm (6in). Order Cyprinodontiformes.

kilogram (symbol kg)

SI unit of mass defined as the mass of the international prototype cylinder of platinum-iridium kept at the International Bureau of Weights and Measures near Paris; 1 kilogram is equal to 1000g (2.2lb).

kimberlite

Ultrabasic rock found in diamond-bearing pipes, mainly in South Africa. It is a MICA PERIDOTITE, consisting chiefly of OLIVINE and PHLOGOPITE. Kimberlite weathers to the yellow and blue grounds of diamond mines.

kingbird

Any member of the genus *Tyrannus*, a small group of about a dozen insect-eating birds belonging to the tyrant flycatcher family. Most kingbirds have drab, brown or green plumage. They are found exclusively in the Americas. Kingbirds can be aggressive when defending their nests. Family Tyrannidae (part); genus *Tyrannus*.

kingdom

One system for CLASSIFICATION of living organisms is the Five Kingdoms system, in which the kingdom is the topmost level, or **taxon**. The five kingdoms

◄ **kestrel, Australian** This kestrel (*Falco cenchroides*) is found in New Guinea as well as Australia. It feeds mainly on insects but will sometimes take small mammals or birds. The female stays in or near the nest for the first two weeks after the young have hatched; the male does all the hunting during this period. The young leave the nest after about three weeks.

▶ **kingfisher** The common kingfisher (*Alcedo atthis*) is found throughout Europe, Asia, N Africa and eastward to the Solomon Islands. It lives on the banks of freshwater streams and lakes and feeds on small minnows and sometimes reptiles and crustaceans.

are Animalia (ANIMAL), Plantae (PLANT), Fungi (FUNGUS), PROKARYOTAE and PROTOCTISTA. Two subkingdoms, Archaebacteria and Eubacteria, are often recognized within Prokaryotae, but the bacteria are so diverse that many taxonomists think they comprise more than one kingdom. Some believe that the bacteria merit the status of a new, even higher category, DOMAIN. *See also* EUKARYOTE; Ready Reference, pages 462–63

kingfish
Name applied to several varieties of fish valued for food or sport. They include *Scomberomorus cavalla*, a type of large MACKEREL, and *Menticirrhus saxitalis*, a member of the CROAKER family, also known as WHITING.

kingfisher
Any member of a large family of gaudy-coloured, small- to medium-sized birds found worldwide. Most, though not all, species are associated with inland water and feed on fish. Some kingfishers, however, can also be found in woodland, where they feed on insects. They nest in holes. Family Alcedinidae; there are more than 90 species.

kingfisher, African pygmy
Very small kingfisher. It is found singly in wooded habitats and along roadsides in tropical Africa, south of the Sahara, usually away from water. It has a turquoise back, orange breast, a blue head and a stout, red bill. It feeds on insects on the ground, which it catches by pouncing from a branch lookout. Length: 12cm (5in). Family Alcedinidae; species *Ceyx picta*.

kingfisher, azure
Small kingfisher with violet-blue upperparts and orange-brown underparts. It is found along rivers and creeks and in mangrove swamps of N and E Australia. Its food includes fish, crabs and frogs. Length: 18cm (7in). Family Alcedinidae; species *Alcedo azurea*.

kingfisher, belted
Only species of kingfisher in most of North America, where it is common on inland waterways. It winters in the West Indies. It has a grey-blue back and head, white underparts and neck, and a black "belt" around its neck and upper breast. It feeds on fish, amphibians and small reptiles. Length: 28–36cm (11–14in). Family Alcedinidae; species *Megaceryle alcyon*.

kingfisher, green
Rather small kingfisher, found in S United States and South America. Its dark green back and head are flecked with white, and it has a white collar and a red chest. It feeds on fish. Length: 18cm (7in). Family Alcedinidae; species *Chloroceryle americana*.

kingfisher, malachite
Very small kingfisher found along streams, rivers and lakes in tropical Africa. It has a bright blue back, orange breast and a bright red bill. It feeds on fish and some large insects. Length: 14cm (6in). Family Alcedinidae; species *Alcedo cristata*.

kingfisher, paradise
Beautiful kingfisher found in Australasia. It is brilliant blue above and yellow-chestnut below, with two elongated white tail plumes. Its lower back and tail are white and its bill is red. The paradise kingfisher is shy and secretive, and it often stays hidden in the forest canopy. It nests near the ground in termite mounds. Length: 30–36cm (12–14in). Family Alcedinidae; species *Tanysiptera sylvia*.

kingfisher, pied
Medium-sized kingfisher found alongside lakes, streams and coastal waters in Africa, Middle East and S Asia, often in pairs or small groups. It is largely black, with white scalloping on its back, a black crest and white throat, ears and breast. It feeds by hovering over the water to take fish. Length: 26–29cm (10–11in). Family Alcedinidae; species *Ceryle rudis*.

kingfisher, river
Common kingfisher of Europe; it is also found in North Africa and parts of Asia and Indonesia. It is nearly always seen by water. It flies rapidly, close to the water surface, and dives for small fish and large invertebrates. Length: 16cm (6in). Family Alcedinidae; species *Alcedo atthis*.

kingfisher, sacred
Small- to medium-sized kingfisher. It is found throughout Australia in eucalyptus and paperbark forests and mangrove swamps. It is also found in Indonesia, New Guinea, New Zealand and the sw Pacific region. The sacred kingfisher has a green head and back, yellow underparts and a yellow neck. It has a black band through its eyes and a large bill. It feeds on large insects, lizards, crabs and some fish. Length: 19–23cm (7–9in). Family Alcedinidae; species *Halcyon sancta*.

kingfisher, shovel-billed
Medium-sized kingfisher found in mangrove forests and upland wooded areas of New Guinea. It has a brown back and head, a light blue rump and pale brown underparts. It has a deep, heavy bill. It feeds on beetles, snails, lizards and earthworms. Length: 30–33cm (12–13in). Family Alcedinidae; species *Clytoceyx rex*.

kingfisher, stork-billed
Large kingfisher found along rivers and streams in India and Southeast Asia. It has orange underparts, a blue back and a grey-brown head. It feeds on fish,

▲ **kinkajou** Despite being a member of the raccoon family, the kinkajou (*Potos flavus*) is more similar to the primates because it has a prehensile tail. It uses its tail to climb among the tree tops of the tropical forests of South and Central America in search of the soft fruit that is its main food.

lizards, frogs, crabs, insects and young birds. Length: 37cm (15in). Family Alcedinidae; species *Halcyon capensis*.

kingfisher, white-breasted
Kingfisher found in both wet and dry habitats from the Middle East to S Asia. It is mostly chocolate-brown, with a white chest and upper breast, turquoise flashes on its wings, and a blood-red bill. It feeds on frogs, lizards, snakes, large insects, crabs, shrimps, mice, birds and fish. Length: 25–28cm (10–11in). Family Alcedinidae; species *Halcyon smyrnensis*.

kinglet
Very small bird, closely related to the WARBLER. It is found mainly within conifer woods or plantations in temperate North America and N Europe. Most species are olive-brown, with golden or yellow crests. Kinglets feed mainly on small insects and seeds. They are partial migrants. The GOLDCREST is a type of kinglet. Family Silviidae (part); genus *Regulus*; there are five species.

kinkajou
Nocturnal, foraging mammal of the RACCOON family. It inhabits forests of Central and South America, where it lives almost entirely in trees. It is primarily a fruit and insect eater. Length: to 57cm (22in); weight: to 2.7kg (6lb). Family Procyonidae; species *Potos flavus*.

kinorhynch
Any member of the class Kinorhyncha, a group of microscopic, spiny, worm-like marine animals. Their tubular bodies consist of *c*.13 segments, with a mouth at one end and an anus at the other. They live mainly in the mud of the sea bed. Phylum Aschelminthes; class Kinorhyncha.

kiskadee
Either of two small- to medium-sized members of the tyrant flycatcher family; they are found in the Americas, from S United States to Argentina. Kiskadees are named after their calls. The great kiskadee (*Pitangus sulphuratus*) is *c*.24cm (*c*.9in) long and is found as far north as S Texas. The lesser kiskadee (*Philohydor lictor*) is *c*.16cm (*c*.6in) long and lives further south. Kiskadees feed on insects and fruit and also some fish, which they catch like kingfishers. Family Tyrannidae (part).

kissing bug
See ASSASSIN BUG

kite
Any member of a group of *c*.20 agile BIRDS OF PREY with a cosmopolitan distribution. Kites may be brown, black or pale grey, depending on the species, and they often have a forked or notched tail. Many kites are predominantly carrion feeders, but their prey items vary from species to species. Family Accipitridae (part).

kite, American swallow-tailed
Graceful kite found around river swamps in America, from S United States down to Argentina. It has black-and-white plumage and a long, forked tail. It is sometimes seen in flocks. It feeds mainly on insects, which it catches in the air, and also on small reptiles and amphibians, taken on the ground. It nests in tall trees. Length: 60cm (24in). Family Accipitridae; species *Elanoides forficatus*.

kite, black
Large bird of prey found in a wide variety of habitats

K

▲ **kiwi** The kiwi has poor eyesight and finds food mainly by scent, burrowing into the ground with its unusual bill, which has the nostrils at the tip. The bristles at the base of its bill are thought to aid its mobility when looking for food.

in central and s Europe, Africa, s Asia, Indonesia and Australia. It is dark brown, with a slightly forked tail. It feeds on carrion, offal, small animals, insects and reptiles. Length: 48–58cm (19–23in). Family Accipitridae; species *Milvus migrans*.

kite, black-shouldered (black-winged kite)
Small kite found in open country in Africa, s Europe and Southeast Asia. It is light grey above and white below, with a distinct black "shoulder" and a square tail. It feeds on insects, particularly locusts, as well as small birds and mammals. Length: 33cm (13in). Family Accipitridae; species *Elanus caeruleus*.

kite, brahminy
Kite found inland and on coastal wetlands in Asia, Indonesia and Australia. It has chestnut-brown plumage, with a white head, neck and breast. The brahminy kite feeds mainly on carrion, fish and amphibians. Length: 45–51cm (18–20in). Family Accipitridae; species *Haliastur indus*.

kite, hook-billed
Rare kite that is native to Central and South America; it is also found, very occasionally, in Texas, s United States. It is grey or brown, with barred underparts. Its upper mandible is deeply hooked. Length: 40cm (16in). Family Accipitridae; species *Chondrohierax uncinatus*.

kite, letter-winged
Small kite found in desert grassland and wooded watercourses of central Australia. It is mainly dove-grey, with white underparts, a black shoulder patch, and a distinctive, letter-like, black line on its underwing. It is nocturnal, preying mainly on rodents. It roosts communally during the day. Length: 35–38cm (14–15in). Family Accipitridae; species *Elanus scriptus*.

kite, red
Large bird of prey found in open country across Europe, NW Africa and w Asia. It is russet-brown with a distinctive forked tail. It feeds on carrion, offal, mice, reptiles, insects and worms, taken on the ground. Length: 61–72cm (24–28in). Family Accipitridae; species *Milvus milvus*.

kite, snail (Everglades kite)
Kite found in American wetlands, from Florida, United States, south to Argentina. The male is dark, except for a white undertail patch; it has a bright red face patch from eye to beak and red legs. The female is mostly streaky brown. Both sexes have a deeply hooked bill and feed mainly on snails. They are colonial nesters. Length: 43cm (17in). Family Accipitridae; species *Rostrhamus sociabilis*.

kittiwake
Either of two species of elegant gulls found around oceans of the Northern Hemisphere, mainly the Atlantic. They are almost totally white, with black tips to the end of their wings. They have either black or red legs, depending on the species. The kittiwakes' food consists of fish and crustaceans. Both species breed in large colonies on coastal cliffs. Length: 40–46cm (16–18in). Family Laridae; species *Rissa tridactyla* (black-legged kittiwake) and *Rissa brevirostris* (red-legged kittiwake).

kiwi
Any of three species of flightless birds found exclusively in New Zealand. They have compact, rounded bodies, hair-like feathers, vestigial wings and no tail. Kiwis have very powerful feet. They have nostrils on the tips of their long, down-turned bills. They are nocturnal, feeding on worms and insects. Length: 50–70cm (20–28in). Family Apterygidae; genus *Apteryx*.

klipspringer
Dwarf ANTELOPE that lives on rocky outcrops in s, central and E Africa. It is usually found in small family groups. The klipspringer's coat is yellowish and flecked with grey. Males and occasionally females have short, slender, vertical horns, which reach a maximum length of 15cm (6in). Head-body length: 75–115cm (30–45in); tail: 7–13cm (3–5in). Family Bovidae; subfamily Antilopinae; species *Oreotragus oreotragus*.

knapweed (black knapweed)
Herbaceous perennial plant native to Europe and naturalized in North America; it is found growing on grassland and cliffs. The plant is hairy with rigid, grooved and branched stems. Its rounded flowerheads have black, fringed bracts and purple florets. Knapweed was once highly regarded as a wound herb. Family Asteraceae; genus *Centaurea nigra*.

knifefish
Member of any of several families of elongate fish. The knifefish of Africa and Southeast Asia belong to the family Notopteridae; they inhabit fresh and brackish waters. Knifefish of the families Sternopygidae, Rhamphichthyidae, Apteronotidae, Gymnotidae and Electrophoridae are found in the neotropical waters of Central and South America. All knifefish are characterized by a long ventral fin and electrosensory organs capable of detecting electric fields. They have electric organs, which produce an electric discharge used for prey capture and/or communication. Length: to 90cm (35in).

knot
Either of two species of medium-sized, rather plump, migratory waders. Both species breed in the Arctic and winter in the Southern Hemisphere. They are found away from their breeding grounds in large flocks on coastal mudflats and estuaries, where they feed on marine invertebrates, particularly worms. Family Scolopacidae (part); genus *Calidris* (part); species *Calidris canuta* (red knot) and *Calidris tenuirostris* (great knot).

knotweed
Herbaceous annual or perennial with white, pink or red flowers. It is native to temperate regions of the Northern Hemisphere. Some species are grown as ornamentals; other species, for example Japanese knotweed (*Fallopia japonica*), are garden escapes that have naturalized to become aggressive weeds. Knotweed is so-called because its stems, and those of the related knotgrasses (*Polygonum* spp.), often have swollen nodes. Family Polygonaceae; genera include *Fallopia* and *Persicaria*.

koala
Grey and white marsupial that is found in E Australia. It is nocturnal and a specialized tree climber. The koala prefers to eat eucalyptus leaves, which provide a low-nutrition diet, resulting in a slow animal that sleeps a lot. Length: 60–85cm (24–33in). Family Phascolarctidae; species *Phascolarctos cinereus*.

▲ **knifefish** The bronze featherback (*Notopterus notopterus*) belongs to the Notopteridae family of knifefish and is found in s Asia. It inhabits the weedy regions of rivers and backwaters and is a carnivorous species, feeding on crustaceans, insects and the new roots of some aquatic plants. Like all knifefish, it uses its long ventral fin to swim forwards and backwards. It produces an electric field which enables it to navigate in the murky water.

▲ **koala** Previously hunted for its fur, and the victim of deforestation and disease, the koala is a protected species. It is a very sedentary animal and has a specific home range. Baby koalas remain in the pouch for six or seven months then travel around on the mother's back for several months.

kob
ANTELOPE that lives on lowland plains of central Africa, close to permanent water. It is reddish, with a white underside, eye rings and throat patch, and black markings on its legs and tail. Male kobs have s-shaped horns, which reach 40–69cm (16–27in) in length. Head-body length: 160–180cm (63–71in); tail: 10–15cm (4–6in). Family Bovidae; subfamily Hippotraginae; species *Kobus kob*.

Koch, Robert (1843–1910)
German bacteriologist. He first came to public notice with his discovery of the life cycle of the anthrax-causing organism. Koch devised methods of studying bacteria and isolated the bacterium that causes tuberculosis. For this work, he was awarded the 1905 Nobel Prize for physiology or medicine. His work laid the foundation for methods of determining the causative agent of a disease.

koel
Medium-sized member of the CUCKOO family. It is found in forest and tall trees in India, Southeast Asia, Indonesia, New Guinea and Australia. The male is mostly black; the female is brown, with white spots and bars. The koel is a brood parasite, often using the house crow as a host. It feeds on insects and fruit. Length: 39–46cm (15–18in). Family Cuculidae; species *Eudynamys scolopacea* (common koel). **Koel** is also the name given to two other birds: the white-crowned koel (*Caliechthrus leucolophus*) and the long-tailed koel (*Urodynamis taitensis*).

kohlrabi
Edible crop vegetable; it has lobed leaves and a greenish-white or purple, turnip-like stem. Kohlrabi is unusual in that both the stem and leaves may be eaten. Family Brassicaceae/Cruciferae; (sub)species *Brassica oleracea gongylodes*.

kolanut (colanut)
Fruit of the evergreen kola tree, native to tropical Africa. The nuts are high in caffeine and act as a powerful stimulant. Family Sterculiaceae; species *Cola acuminata*.

kolinsky (Siberian weasel)
Long-bodied mammal with round ears, short legs and a thick, bushy tail. Its coat is dark brown, paler under-neath, with a dark facial mask; it has white lips and chin and sometimes a white throat patch. Several sub-species can be found across N and E Asia, from Siberia to Japan. Male kolinskies are larger than females. Head-body length (male): 28–39cm (11–15in); tail: 15–21cm (6–8in). Family Mustelidae; species *Mustela sibirica*.

Kölliker, Rudolph Albert von (1817–1905)
Swiss physiologist and histologist. Kölliker studied the cellular nature of tissue and demonstrated that spermatoza are cellular in structure. He also developed theories on spontaneous evolutionary change. Kölliker's works include *Handbook of Human Histology* (1852) and *Embryology of Man and Higher Animals* (1861).

Kölreuter, Josef Gottlieb (1733–1806)
German botanist. As curator of the Botanical Gardens at Karlsruhe, Kölreuter experimented with the fertilization and development of plants and made significant developments in the study of the hybridization of plants. He also recognized the importance of insects and wind in the pollination process.

Komodo dragon
Very large MONITOR lizard. It is found only on three islands in Indonesia. Komodo dragons, which were not scientifically described until 1912, are the largest living LIZARDS in the world. As adults they feed on large mammals, such as deer and goats. The Komodo dragon is not venomous, but its saliva contains a large number of potentially pathogenic bacteria. Length: to 3m (10ft); weight: to 165kg (364lbs). Family Varanidae; species *Varanus komodoensis*.

kookaburra
Any member of the genus *Dacelo*, comprising four species of medium-sized woodland kingfishers found exclusively in Australia and New Guinea. Two species are normally known as kookaburras: the laughing kookaburra (*Dacelo novaeguineae*) and the blue-winged kookaburra (*Dacelo leachii*). They are brown and white, with a heavy bill. They feed mainly on lizards, snakes, crabs and rodents. Family Alcedinidae (part); genus *Dacelo*.

Köppen, Wladimir Peter (1846–1940)
German meteorologist who devised (1900) a mathematical system of climate classification. Köppen classified the climate of a country according to major vegetation types, ranges of temperature and levels of precipitation. From 1927 to his death, he collaborated with Rudolph Geiger on the *Handbook of Climatology*.

Kornberg, Arthur (1918–)
US biochemist. He was medical director of the US Public Health Service and chairman of the department of biochemistry at Stanford University. In 1959 he shared the Nobel Prize for physiology or medicine with Severo OCHOA for work on the synthesis of

▲ **kouprey** Close to extinction, fewer than 200 koupreys are known to exist in hilly forested areas of Cambodia, Vietnam, Laos and Thailand where it lives in herds of about 20 animals. It became known to Western science only in the 1930s when a specimen was brought to Europe from central Cambodia.

RNA and DNA, an important contribution to the study of GENETICS.

kouprey
Rare wild cattle that inhabits forest and wooded savanna in Indochina. Young koupreys and females are grey with a lighter underside, whereas older bulls are much darker and have a very long dewlap hanging below the neck. Horns are long and curved (up to 80cm/31in) in the male, about half that length in the female. Head-body length: 210–220cm (83–87in); tail: 100–110cm (39–43in). Family Bovidae; subfamily Bovinae; species *Bos sauveli*.

kowari (Byrne's marsupial mouse)
Marsupial mouse that inhabits the deserts and dry grasslands of central Australia. Aggressive, nocturnal and solitary, it feeds on insects, spiders and small vertebrates. Its tail is tipped with a black brush. Head-body length: 13–18cm (5–7in); tail: 11–14cm (4–5.5in). Family Dasyuridae; species *Dasyuroides byrnei*.

krait
Any of several species of banded, nocturnal, terrestrial snakes found in S and Southeast Asia. Kraits have small, blunt heads and in some species the body is rather triangular in cross-section. Kraits are highly venomous, and many human deaths are attributable to kraits; most species, however, are quite inoffensive. Length: to 2m (6.6ft). Family Elapidae; genus *Bungarus*.

Krebs, Sir Hans Adolf (1900–81)
British biochemist, b. Germany. While still in Germany, he discovered how ammonia is converted to urea in the bodies of mammals. He moved to England in 1933. Krebs is best known for his discovery of the KREBS CYCLE, the process that results in the production of energy in living organisms (RESPIRATION). For this work, he shared with Fritz LIPMANN the 1953 Nobel Prize for physiology or medicine.

K

◀ **Komodo dragon** Feeding mainly on large mammals and carrion, the Komodo dragon may also eat smaller members of its own species. A solitary reptile, it hunts over a wide area and can move swiftly in pursuit of prey. With only *c*.3000 Komodo dragons distributed on several Indonesian islands, it is listed as an endangered species.

KREBS CYCLE

Biochemical pathway by which most EUKARYOTE organisms obtain much of their energy by oxidizing foodstuffs. Occurring in the MITOCHONDRIA of CELLS, the Krebs cycle comprises a number of complex chemical reactions, many of which, in association with a process called the ELECTRON TRANSPORT SYSTEM, convert ADENOSINE DIPHOSPHATE (ADP) into ADENOSINE TRIPHOSPHATE (ATP). ATP provides chemical energy for metabolic reactions. The Krebs cycle is an essential part of the process of cell RESPIRATION and METABOLISM. The cycle is named after the British biochemist Sir Hans KREBS. *See also* GLYCOLYSIS

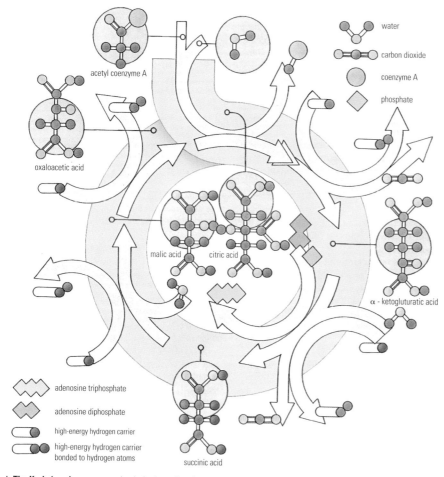

water
carbon dioxide
coenzyme A
phosphate

acetyl coenzyme A

oxaloacetic acid

malic acid   citric acid

α - ketogluturatic acid

adenosine triphosphate

adenosine diphosphate

high-energy hydrogen carrier

high-energy hydrogen carrier bonded to hydrogen atoms

succinic acid

▲ **The Krebs' cycle** or citric acid cycle is fundamental to the reactions that oxidize food to provide energy in the mitochondria of living cells. Energy is extracted from glucose by glycolysis, the end product being pyruvate, which is converted to acetyl coenzyme A, which in turn is converted to citric acid. A series of reactions catalysed by enzymes reduce the pyruvate to carbon dioxide and water, and energy is produced as adenosine triphosphate (ATP), which is converted to adenoside diphosphate (ADP). At the same time, during a series of oxidation reactions known as the electron transport system, more energy is stored in the form of adenosine triphosphate (ATP) molecules.

Krebs cycle (citric acid or tricarboxylic acid cycle)
See feature article

krill
Collective term for the large variety of marine CRUSTACEANS found in all the world's oceans. They are strained and used as food by various species of baleen WHALE.

kudu
Spiral-horned ANTELOPE found in S, central and E Africa. Family Bovidae; subfamily Bovinae.

kudu, greater
Kudu that has a reddish to blue-grey coat, with a series of thin, vertical, white stripes on its back, and various white face-markings. Only the males have horns, which may be up to 140cm (55in) in length with three full twists, and a fringe of hair beneath the chin. Both sexes have large, rounded ears and a crest along the neck and shoulders. Head-body length: 185–245cm (73–96in); tail: 30–55cm (12–22in). Family Bovidae; subfamily Bovinae; species *Tragelaphus strepsiceros*.

kudu, lesser
Kudu that is smaller than the greater kudu but similar in appearance. It has a reddish coat, which becomes blue-grey in older males, and prominent, vertical, white stripes on its side. Males have horns that can reach 90cm (35in) in length. The lesser kudu can be found in dry forests in E Africa. Head-body length: 110–140cm (43–55in); tail: 25–40cm (10–16in). Family Bovidae; subfamily Bovinae; species *Tragelaphus imberbis*.

kultarr
Marsupial mouse from central Australia. It has large ears and a long tail, with dark patches present around the eyes, in the middle of the forehead and at the tip of the tail. Kultarrs inhabit dry desert and grassland regions, nesting in logs and vegetation. Head-body length: 8–11cm (3–4in); tail: 10–14cm (4–5.5in). Family Dasyuridae; species *Antechinomys laniger*.

kumquat
Any of several species of small CITRUS trees native to E Asia; also their edible fruit. Many varieties have been developed, which are widely cultivated. The aromatic rind of the fruit can be eaten with the flesh, and fruits are often preserved or candied. The genus is named after Robert Fortune, an English traveller, who introduced the kumquat into Europe in 1846. Family Rutaceae; species include *Fortunella japonica* and *Fortunella margarita*.

kyanite (disthene)
Mineral form of aluminium silicate (Al_2SiO_5). It occurs in SCHISTS and other METAMORPHIC ROCKS, generally as elongated, blue-bladed crystals (triclinic) or aggregates, although it may also be white, green or grey. Colour may vary within a single crystal, which is usually transparent with a vitreous lustre. Kyanite is used in making high-grade porcelain for electrical insulators; good clear crystals are used as gemstones. Hardness: 4–5 along the crystal, 6–7 across; r.d. 3.5–3.7.

▲ **krill** The shrimp-like krill are about 5cm (2in) long when fully grown. They belong to a group of crustaceans characterized by luminescent organs along their sides, on their undersides and heads. The Antarctic krill (*Euphausia superba*), shown here, is a very important species because it supports much of the warm-blooded life in the Antarctic seas.

L

labium
Term meaning a lip or lip-shaped organ. In arthropods it refers to the lower lip, which may be modified in insects to form sucking mouthparts. In human anatomy, it denotes the labia majora and labia minora, skin folds of the female genitals. In botany, it refers to the lower lip of plants of the Labiatae family.

lablab (hyacinth bean)
Leguminous plant that probably originated in the Old World tropics; it is widely cultivated in tropical areas worldwide. Lablab is grown as a food crop for its green pods or seeds. Its foliage provides hay, silage and green manure. Some lablab cultivars have elaborate purple flowers and are grown as ornamentals. Family Fabaceae/Leguminosae; species *Lablab purpureus*.

labour
See BIRTH

laburnum
Any of several species of Eurasian shrubs and small trees belonging to the genus *Laburnum*. The common Laburnum (*Laburnum anagyroides*) has drooping clusters of bright yellow flowers. It bears pods that contain poisonous seeds. Family Fabaceae/Leguminosae.

lac
Type of SCALE INSECT; also the name of the sticky substance it secretes onto twigs. The sticky deposit is harvested in Asia for use in shellac and red lac dye. Order Homoptera; species *Laccifer lacca*.

laccolith
Dome of INTRUSIVE ROCK formed over the STRATA it has penetrated. The base is typically horizontal while the upper surface is convex. They are generally less than 16km (10mi) in diameter with thicknesses of 30–900m (100–3000ft). Laccoliths are formed of MAGMA; they are smaller than BATHOLITHS.

lace bark (gauze-tree)
Small tree native to Jamaica. Its inner bark can be removed in sheets and stretched into a lace-like material, which can be used for a variety of textile and ornamental articles. Family Thymeleaceae; species *Lagetta lintearia*.

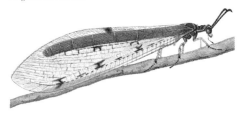

▲ **lacewing** There are more than 4000 species of lacewing; shown here is the European lacewing (*Eurolean europaeus*), which is also known as the ant lion. The larva of the lacewing is a fierce predator of certain small insects, particularly aphids.

lace plant
Aquatic plant native to Madagascar; it is grown in aquariums for its foliage, which resembles lace. The submerged leaves are reduced to a network of veins, due to patches of tissue between the veins dying away when leaves are immature; several strong veins run parallel to the midrib, with numerous cross veins. Family Aponogetonaceae; species *Aponogeton madagascariensis*.

lacewing
Any of numerous species of NEUROPTERAN insects, especially members of the families Chrysopidae and Hemerobiidae, which are found worldwide. Common green lacewings have a slender greenish body, long antennae and two pairs of delicate, lacy, veined wings. Length: to 2cm (0.8in).

lactation
Secretion of milk by female MAMMALS to feed their young. In pregnant women, HORMONES induce the breasts to enlarge, and prolactin (a hormone of the PITUITARY GLAND) stimulates breast cells to begin secreting milk. The milk "comes in" the breast immediately after the birth of the baby. Its flow is stimulated by suckling, which, in turn, triggers the release of the hormone oxytocin, which controls the propulsion of milk from the breast.

lactic acid (2-hydroxypropanoic acid, CH_3 CHOHCOOH)
Colourless organic acid that is formed from LACTOSE in milk by the action of LACTOBACTERIA. Lactic acid is also produced in muscles when ANAEROBIC respiration occurs, due to insufficient oxygen, and causes muscle fatigue. Lactic acid is used in foods and beverages, in tanning, dyeing and adhesive manufacture. Properties: r.d. 1.206; m.p. 18°C (64.4°F); b.p. 122°C (251.6°F).

lactobacterium
BACTERIUM that has a fermentative metabolism, resulting in the production of LACTIC ACID; other compounds produced may include acetate, ethanol and carbon dioxide. Lactobacteria, such as *Lactobacillus*, are commonly found in dairy products, grain products, beer and fruit juices. They form part of the normal flora of the mouths and intestines of animals. *See also* FERMENTATION

lactose (milk sugar)
DISACCHARIDE present in milk, made up of a molecule of GLUCOSE linked to a molecule of galactose. It is important in cheese making, when LACTOBACTERIA turn it into LACTIC ACID, thus souring the milk in the production of cheese curd.

ladybird (ladybug)
Any of a large number of small, brightly coloured BEETLES. The most common species are red with conspicuous black spots and a black-and-white head. Ladybirds and their larvae are regarded as useful by farmers because their diet consists primarily of aphids. Family Coccinellidae.

ladyfern
FERN that is found in moist woods, shady hedgebanks and rocky places of w North America, Europe, Africa and Asia. It is popular as an ornamental. The ladyfern has tall, bright-green fronds; the blades are almost three-pinnate and taper towards the base and tip. Family Woodsiaceae; species *Athyrium filix-femina*.

ladyfish (tenpounder)
Large silvery, marine fish of tropical and subtropical

◄ **ladybird** Found throughout Europe, the seven-spot ladybird (*Coccinealla septempunctata*) is the largest of the European ladybirds, up to 8mm (0.4in) in length. Both the adults and larvae feed on aphids, making them popular with gardeners. During the winter, large numbers hibernate together.

oceans. Ladyfish are related to TARPONS and BONEFISH and are important game fish. Length: to 1m (3.3ft). Family Elopidae; species *Elops saurus*.

lady's mantle
Perennial herb native to temperate regions of the Northern Hemisphere and high mountain ranges in southern latitudes. The plant is downy, with large, kidney-shaped leaves arranged in rosettes. It produces tiny, yellowish-green flowers. Lady's mantle has been used since ancient times to stop wounds bleeding. Family Rosaceae; species *Alchemilla vulgaris*.

lady's slipper
Any member of the genus *Cypripedium*, a small group of hardy terrestrial ORCHIDS found in temperate regions of the Northern Hemisphere. They are sometimes grown as ornamentals in moist borders and rock gardens. The characteristic flowers, produced one to a few at the tops of stems, have a large, inflated, slipper-like lower lip with inrolled margins; they are of various colours. Family Orchidaceae; genus *Cypripedium*.

lady's smock (cuckooflower)
Perennial flowering plant of North American and Eurasia, where it is common in moist meadows. It has a stout stem, fine leaves and clusters of pink or purplish flowers. Family Brassicaceae/Cruciferae; species *Cardamine pratensis*.

lagoon
Stretch of shallow water partially or completely cut off from the sea. If it is completely cut off, there will be some percolation of water through the ridge or spit separating the lagoon from the sea. Lagoons are often found behind spits, bars and CORAL REEFS.

lake
See feature article, page 218

Lamarck, Jean Baptiste Pierre Antoine de Monet, Chevalier de (1744–1829)
French biologist. His theories of EVOLUTION (Lamarckism), according to which ACQUIRED CHARACTERISTICS are inheritable, influenced evolutionary thought throughout most of the 19th century. They were subsequently disproved by Charles DARWIN. In *Philosophie zoologique* (1809) Lamarck proposed that new biological needs of an organism promote a change in habits from which develop new physical structures. These are then transmitted to offspring as permanent characteristics. For example, he erroneously believed giraffes' long necks evolved because they reached for leaves.

lamb's lettuce (corn salad)
Small, branched, annual herb that is native to Europe

L

and naturalized in North America; it is used as a potherb. Lamb's lettuce is found on cultivated land. It has a tuft of basal leaves and very small, whitish to light blue flowers, which are produced in dense heads at the ends of forked branches. Family Valerianaceae; species *Valerianella locusta*.

laminarian

Marine SEAWEED that usually has one long, flattened, ribbon-like blade fixed to its SUBSTRATE by a holdfast. Laminarians are widespread; they are the dominant plant of subtidal zones of many cold-water shores. Mostly perennial, many laminarian species are grown for food, especially in China. Family Laminariaceae; genus *Laminaria*.

lammergeier

See VULTURE, BEARDED

lamprey

Eel-like, jawless fish that is found in marine and freshwater environments on both sides of the Atlantic Ocean and in the Great Lakes of North America. The lamprey feeds by attaching its mouth to fish and sucking their blood. Length: to 91cm (36in). Family Petromyzondiae.

lamprophyre

Member of a group of medium-grained IGNEOUS ROCKS that occur in DYKES and SILLS. Their composition is rich in augite, biotite and other coloured silicates, which form relatively large crystals, with little or no feldspar.

lamp shell

See BRACHIOPOD

lancelet

See AMPHIOXUS

land bridge

Temporary, natural connection between continents that can allow animal migration. A land bridge existed across the Bering Strait until comparatively recently, and a modern example is the isthmus of Panama. Before the theory of CONTINENTAL DRIFT, such bridges were proposed as a possible major influence on fossil distribution.

landslide

Relatively rapid displacement of rock or soil slipping over a definite surface. It may be caused by an EARTHQUAKE, but it is generally the result of rain

▲ **lamprey** To enhance the flow of blood from its victim, the blood-sucking adult lamprey injects an anticoagulant. The lamprey's skeleton is made of cartilage, rather than bone, and it has no jaws, just a circular mouth containing horny teeth.

soaking the ground; the effects are exaggerated if there is an impervious layer beneath the surface. In colder climatic areas, the saturated rock may be affected by freezing and thawing of the water, and this increases the likelihood of landslides.

langur (leaf monkey)

Any of *c*.15 species of medium to large MONKEYS of Southeast and s Asia. They are slender, with long hands and tails. Tree dwellers, langurs are found from sea level to snowy Himalayan slopes up to an elevation of 4000m (13,000ft). The langurs of Indonesia are know as SURELI. Length: 43–78cm (17–31in). Family Cercopithecidae; genus *Presbytis*. *See also* MONKEY, LEAF

La Niña

Periodic disruption of the ocean-atmosphere system in the tropical zone of the Pacific Ocean. A La Niña system is characterized by unusually cold ocean temperatures in the central and E Pacific Ocean. As with the EL NIÑO system, La Niña affects global weather patterns. Its effects are generally the opposite of those of La Niña, and the impact is usually less devastating.

lanner falcon

See FALCON, LANNER

lantern fish

Any of numerous species of fish found in Atlantic and Mediterranean waters. Lantern fish have light organs along their heads, sides and tails; the distribution and pattern depends on the species. Length: 7.5cm (3in). Family Myctophidae; species include *Diaphus rafinesquiei*.

lantern fly (fulgorid bug)

Large, brightly coloured PLANTHOPPER. It lives on trees. The lantern fly is distinguished by an inflated prolongation of the head, which contains an extension of the digestive tract. This structure can appear luminous. Lantern flies secrete a white wax. They are relatively uncommon. Adult body length: *c*.8cm (3in). Order Homoptera; family Fulgoridae; species include *Lanternaria phosphorea*.

lapis lazuli (lazurite)

Glassy, blue, semi-precious gemstone, a silicate mineral found in metamorphosed limestones (*see* META-MORPHIC ROCK). It can occur as crystals in the cubic system, but more often as granular masses. Hardness 5–5.5; r.d. 2.4.

lapwing

One of a group of *c*.10 species of large, long-legged PLOVERS. Most species have striking plumage and often have a coloured facial wattle. Lapwings are

LAKE

Inland body of water, occupying a hollow in the Earth's surface. Lakes are generally of considerable size and too deep to have rooted vegetation completely covering the surface. Usually freshwater, lakes may have an in- or outflowing river and are not always permanent features on the landscape. The expanded part of a river and a reservoir behind a dam are also termed "lakes". A particularly large lake that is natural and saline may be called a "sea", for example, the Dead Sea.

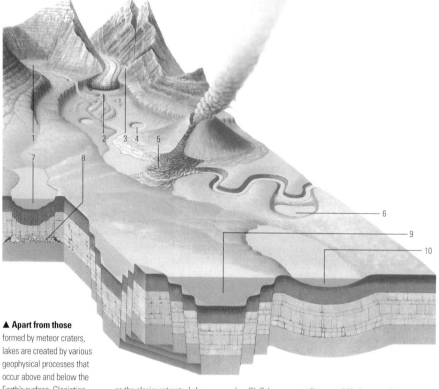

▲ **Apart from those** formed by meteor craters, lakes are created by various geophysical processes that occur above and below the Earth's surface. Glaciation during the last ice age accounts for most lakes. A *cirque* lake (1) forms as water collects in the hollow left at a glacier head. At the snout of a glacier, a lake may form as meltwater is trapped by the *terminal moraine* (2), a bank of rock and debris left behind as the glacier retreats. Lakes may also form behind *lateral moraines* (3) at the glacier's sides. Blocks of ice buried in glacial debris eventually melt, leaving hollows that become *kettle* lakes (4). Lakes may also be created by volcanic activity, as when larva flows into a river and solidifies into a dam (5). Subsequent cooling of the volcanic cone may permit a crater lake to form in the caldera. An *oxbow* lake (6) forms when accumulated sediment cuts off an exaggerated loop of a river. In regions where the underlying rock is limestone, a surface lake (7) may form in the sinkhole created by the collapse of an underground cave system (8). Large-scale earth movements may form a lake by creating surface depressions in which water can accumulate. Faulting of the rock strata (9) tends to produce deeper lakes than folded rock strata (10).

L

noisy and gregarious, with slow, deliberate wing beats. The common lapwing (*Vanellus vanellus*) has black and white plumage and a distinctive black crest. It is found around farmland in Europe and Asia. Length: 25–31cm (10–12in). Family Charadriidae; genus *Vanellus*.

larch
Any CONIFER tree of the genus *Larix*; they are native to cool and temperate regions of the Northern Hemisphere. Larches bear cones and needle-like leaves, which, unusually for a conifer, are shed annually. Family Pinaceae.

lark
Small, ground-living songbird, usually with brown or buff plumage. Its flight is strong and undulating. Many species have a melodious song, which is delivered in aerial display. Larks live mostly in open country, including grasslands, desert and farmland. Family Alaudidae. The MEADOWLARKS of North America are members of the American ORIOLE family.

lark, shore (horned lark)
Lark found in North America, Eurasia and North Africa. It inhabits dry open country, arctic shores and alpine zones; it breeds on tundra. An adult shore lark is pale brown, with a distinctive yellow face. It has a black throat, a black mark under its eyes and small black "horns". Length: 14–17cm (6–7in). Family Alaudidae; species *Eremophila alpestris*.

lark, sky (skylark)
Plump brown lark. It has a slight crest and a sustained aerial song. The common lark of Europe and w Asia, it was introduced by settlers to w Canada, Australia and New Zealand. The sky lark is found in open treeless country and farmland. In Britain, its numbers have declined due to intensive farming. Length: 18cm (7in). Family Alaudidae; species *Alauda arvensis*.

larkspur
See DELPHINIUM

larva
Developmental stage in the life cycle of many INVERTEBRATES and some other animals. A common LIFE CYCLE, typified by the BUTTERFLY, is egg, larva, PUPA, IMAGO (adult). The larva fends for itself and is

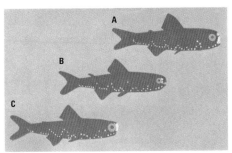

▲ **lantern fish** Common inhabitants of the deep sea at depths of around 2000m (6600ft), lantern fish have light organs concentrated on the lower parts of their bodies. Shown here are the light organ patterns of *Diaphus macrophus* (A), *Diaphus splendidus* (B) and *Diaphus effulgens* (C).

▲ **lantern fly** The Brazilian lantern fly (*Laternaria phosphorea*) is the largest species of lantern fly. It has black "eyes" on its wings which it displays when threatened.

mobile, but it is distinctly different in form from the sexually mature adult. It has a well-developed alimentary system and often stores food until it metamorphoses (or pupates) to become an adult. Names for the larval stage in different organisms include MAGGOT, CATERPILLAR and TADPOLE. *See also* INSECT; METAMORPHOSIS

larvacean
Any member of a class of marine, free-swimming, solitary, planktonic animals; they are found in seas worldwide. They belong to a group known as tunicates. Larvaceans resemble a bent tadpole, with gill slits and a dorsal nerve chord. They secrete a gelatinous structure, called a "house", which is used in filter-feeding. Phylum Chordata; subphylum Urochordata; class Larvacea. *See also* NEOTENY

larynx (voice box)
In tetrapods, a triangular cavity located between the TRACHEA and the root of the tongue. In most mammals, the larynx contains thin bands of elastic tissue known as vocal cords. These cords vibrate when outgoing air passes over them, setting up resonant waves that are changed into sound by the action of throat muscles, the shape of the mouth and the tongue.

laterite
Reddish, hard-baked soil found in tropical parts of the world. It results when hot, wet conditions wash away most of the nutrient content of the soil, leaving behind hydrated oxides of iron and aluminum. The top is baked hard by the Sun, and this factor, together with the leached nature of the soil, means that it is poor for agriculture. Some laterites, however, contain sufficient iron to be of commercial value. *See also* LEACHING

latex
Milky fluid produced by certain species of plant, the most important being that produced by the RUBBER TREE. Rubber latex is a combination of gum resins and fats in a watery medium. It is used in paints, special papers and adhesives, and to make sponge rubbers. Synthetic rubber latexes are also produced.

laughing-thrush
Long-tailed Asiatic perching bird often found in

noisy mixed groups. It feeds on the ground, rummaging amongst leaf litter and moving with long, springy hops. When disturbed, laughing-thrushes make a chorus of laughing and chattering calls and fly off clumsily in a follow-my-leader fashion. They breed in groups. Length: 23–29cm (9–11in). Family Timaliidae; genus *Garrulax*.

Laurasia
Ancient northern continent, containing North America and Eurasia, that formed when a rift, the Tethyan trench, split PANGAEA (the Earth's single original land mass) from east to west along a line slightly north of the Equator. The name is a combination of Laurentian, a geological period in North America, and Eurasia. CONTINENTAL DRIFT and PLATE TECTONICS caused Laurasia to split up into the separate continents that exist today.

laurel
Any of several species of evergreen shrubs and trees belonging to the genus *Laurus*. Laurels are native to s Europe and are cultivated in the United States. Included in this group is the noble, or bay, laurel (*Laurus nobilis*), which has leathery, oval leaves, tiny, yellowish flowers and purple berries. Height: 18–21m (60–70ft). Family Lauraceae.

lava
Molten rock or MAGMA that reaches the Earth's surface and flows out through a volcanic vent in streams or sheets. There are three main types of lava: **vesicular**, like pumice; **glassy**, like obsidian; and **even-grained**. Chemically, lavas range from acidic to ultrabasic. If it is acidic it is viscous and slow-flowing, but if it is basic it is more fluid. Basic lavas form lava flows and often erupt out of fissures, as well as from volcanic craters. Basic lavas are commonest at

sky lark

crested lark

woodlark

▲ **lark** The sky lark (*Alauda arvensis*) is found throughout temperate Eurasia and in N Africa. The crested lark (*Galerida cristata*) has a sandy coloration for camouflage in the dry, dusty grassland habitats in which it is found. The woodlark (*Lullula arborea*) is found on the edges of forests and heaths of Europe, sw Asia and nw Africa.

L

L

► **lavender** Although native to the Mediterranean region, the main commercial production of lavender takes place in France and England. The principal species used to produce perfume oil are English lavender (*Lavandula officinalis*) and French lavender (*Lavandula stoechas*). A less fragrant oil, used for perfumery and varnishes, is produced from spike lavender (*Lavandula latifolia*).

points where plate margins are moving apart. Acidic lavas occur at colliding plate margins and are often associated with very explosive VOLCANOES. Once they reach the surface, lavas cool and solidify. If the lava is very gaseous, a rough, jagged surface will result, which is described as "scoriaceous".

lavender

Aromatic shrub native to mountainous regions of the w Mediterranean. It is cultivated for lavender oil and perfume. Cultivated varieties, with many different flower colours, are grown as ornamentals. Lavender has been used since ancient times for its antiseptic and disinfectant qualities. Family Lamiaceae; species include *Lavandula angustifolia*.

lazurite

See LAPIS LAZULI

laws of inheritance

Fundamental rules of INHERITANCE as discovered by the Austrian naturalist Gregor MENDEL. His law of segregation concerned MONOHYBRID inheritance and stated that "the characteristics of an organism are determined by internal factors which occur in pairs. Only one of a pair of such factors can be represented in a single gamete". His law of independent assortment concerned DIHYBRID inheritance and stated that "each of a pair of contrasting characters may be combined with either of another pair". *See also* HEREDITY

leaching

Process by which chemicals and nutrients are removed from a soil. Rainwater, especially in warm climatic regions, will dissolve anything soluble and wash it away. Once removed, these solubles can only be replaced very slowly. As a result, leached soils become coarse and are infertile. Saline soils can, however, be reclaimed for agriculture by deliberately leaching out salts. The term is also used to describe the industrial process of extracting a soluble material from a solid by washing the solid with solvents.

leaf

Part of a plant, an organ that contains the green pigment CHLOROPHYLL; it is involved in PHOTOSYNTHESIS and TRANSPIRATION. A leaf usually consists of a blade and a stalk (**petiole**), which attaches it to a stem or twig. Most leaves are simple; some are compound and divided into leaflets. Modifications include: suc-

culent types with fleshy tissue for water storage; tendrils that coil around supports; and needles, which are common in conifers.

leafbird

Any of *c*.12 species of mainly green perching birds found in Southeast Asia. Some species have glistening violet-blue or red throats and crown patches. Leafbirds have long, slender, down-curved bills, with which they feed on insects, berries and nectar in dense forest canopy. Length: 19–25cm (7–10in). Family Chloropseidae.

leaffish

Any of several species of freshwater fish, occasionally found in brackish waters, that are named after their resemblance to a dead leaf. Leaffish are found in NE South America, w Africa and s Asia. Length: 7cm (2.8in). Families Nandidae, Badidae or Pristolepidae; species include *Monocirrhus polyacanthus*.

leafhopper

Any of numerous species of small, slender insects of the family Cicadellidae. Leafhoppers feed by sucking the sap of plants and may, in large numbers, do a great deal of damage. Many species are brightly coloured. Order Homoptera.

leaf insect

Any of several species of flat, green INSECTS that resemble leaves. They are found throughout tropical Asia. The female has large leathery forewings with markings like leaf veins. Order Phasmida; family Phylliidae. *See also* STICK INSECT

leaflove

Member of the BULBUL family found in forests of w Africa. Its green and yellow plumage makes it hard to spot. The leaflove utters a loud, bubbling call. Length: 18cm (7in). Family Pycnonotidae; species *Chlorocichla flavicollis*.

leaf roller

Insect larva that nests in a rolled leaf. Leaf rollers include some CATERPILLARS of the MOTH family Tortricidae. The caterpillars of some SKIPPERS, notably the bean skipper (*Urbanus proteus*) and canna skipper (*Calpodes ethlius*), are also leaf rollers.

learned behaviour

Behaviour that is acquired rather than inherited and that can be modified in response to experience. As it takes time to refine, learned behaviour is of greatest benefit to animals with relatively long life spans. There are many forms, including habituation and

conditioning, all of which have the advantage of being adaptable thus allowing the behaviour to be modified to suit changing circumstances. *See also* INSTINCT; INTELLIGENT BEHAVIOUR

leatherback

See SEA TURTLE, LEATHERBACK

leatherjacket

Larva of the CRANE-FLY.

lechwe

ANTELOPE that grazes on the floodplains and wetlands of s Africa. Its long coat is red-brown to black with white underparts. Male lechwes have thin, s-shaped horns, up to 90cm (35in) in length. There are three subspecies, all of which have long, narrow hooves. Head-body length: 135–165cm (53–65in); tail: 45–50cm (18–20in). Family Bovidae; subfamily Hippotraginae; species *Kobus leche*.

lechwe, Nile (Mrs Gray's lechwe)

Antelope found in swampy areas close to rivers in central Africa. Both sexes are red-brown in colour, with a short beard. Males have horns reaching 87cm (34in) in length. Old males are much darker, with a white shoulder patch. The Nile lechwe's diet consists of water plants, for which it will often wade or swim. Head-body length: 135–165cm (53–65in); tail: 45–50cm (18–20in). Family Bovidae; subfamily Hippotraginae; species *Kobus megaceros*.

Lederberg, Joshua (1925–)

US geneticist. In 1958 he shared, with George BEADLE and Edward TATUM, the Nobel Prize for physiology or medicine for work that initiated the study of bacterial genetics. Lederberg discovered that sexual recombination of genetic materials occurs in bacteria and that genetic materials are linked in groups in bacteria as well as in other organisms.

ledum

Any member of the genus *Ledum*, a group of evergreen shrubs found in damp and cold areas of the Northern Hemisphere. They produce small white flowers in terminal clusters. Labrador Tea (*Ledum palustre*), native to North America and naturalized elsewhere, is grown as an ornamental and also used as tea by Native Americans. Its leaves have dense, rusty-coloured, woolly undersides. Family Ericaceae; genus *Ledum*.

leech

Any member of the class Hirudinea of the phylum ANNELIDA. There are more than 300 species of leech,

► **lechwe** This herd of lechwe were photographed in the Okavango Delta of Botswana, s Africa. Lechwe are well adapted to their habitat of wetlands and swamp areas, being strong swimmers and having spread hooves that help them to balance in water. They feed on water plants and are never far from permanent water. Gregarious animals, they are always found in herds, each with a dominant male.

▲ **leaf** Leaves exhibit a wide variety of shapes. The pendunculate oak (*Quercus rober*) (A) and the Scots pine (*Pinus sylvestris*) (B) have simple leaves, with a single leaf blade, whereas the horse chestnut (*Aesculus hippocastrum*) (C) and ferns, such as Polypodium (D) have compound leaves. The leaflets of compound leaves either radiate from one point (palmate), as is the case with the horse chestnut, or are arranged in opposite pairs down the main stalk (pinnate) as is the case with ferns. The primary function of leaves is photosynthesis but, in addition, leaflets may be modified into climbing tendrils (E), or protective spines, as in the cactus *Mammillaria zeilmannia* (F).

living in marine, freshwater and terrestrial environments. They range in size from 1cm (0.4in) to 20cm (8in) in length, the longest being the medicinal leeches (*Hirudo medicinalis*); most are in the range 2–5cm (0.8–2in). Leeches are often striking colours, with black, brown, olive-green and red being common, sometimes with striped and spotted patterns. Parasitic leeches have end segments modified to form suckers, with which they attach themselves to the host while feeding. Although popularly known as blood suckers, a large number of leeches are not actually parasitic.

leek
Biennial plant related to the ONION. It originated in the Mediterranean region and is cultivated widely for culinary purposes. Family Liliaceae, species *Allium porrum*.

Leeuwenhoek, Anton van (1632–1723)
Dutch scientist. Leeuwenhoek was a scientific amateur who built simple microscopes with a single lens; they were made so accurately that they had better magnifying powers than the compound microscopes of his day. He investigated many microorganisms and their life histories and described various microscopic structures, such as spermatozoa.

legume
Member of the PEA family (Leguminosae) of ANGIOSPERMS. The roots of legumes bear nodules that contain NITROGEN-FIXING BACTERIA. The family includes many trees, shrubs, vines and herbs. The fruit is typically a pod (legume) containing a row of seeds. Important food species include the pea, SOYA BEAN, LENTIL, BROAD BEAN, KIDNEY BEAN and HARICOT BEAN. *See also* NITROGEN CYCLE; NITROGEN FIXATION; ROOT NODULE

leiothrix
Either of two species that make up the genus *Leiothrix*. They are strikingly coloured, stocky perching birds, belonging to the BABBLER family.

They are silver-grey above and orange below. The silver-eared mesia (*Leiothrix argentauris*) has a black cap; the red-billed Leiothrix (*Leiothrix lutea*) has a bright crimson bill. They are found in open woodland, especially tea plantations in India and Southeast Asia. Length: 13–15cm (5–6in). Family Timaliidae; genus *Leiothrix*.

lemming
Any of several species of RODENT; they are native to arctic regions. Lemmings have brown fur, small ears and a short tail. They occasionally migrate in large numbers, and some species in Norway have suffered great losses by drowning while doing so. Family Cricetidae.

lemon
Evergreen tree and its sour, yellow CITRUS fruit. Grown primarily in the United States and subtropical regions, it is mostly used in cooking and in drinks. Height of tree: to 6m (20ft). Family Rutaceae; species *Citrus limon*.

lemon grass
Perennial aromatic GRASS known only in cultivation; it originated in India and is now cultivated elsewhere. The plant is strongly lemon-scented owing to the high proportion of citral in its oil. Aromatic oil distilled from lemon grass is used in the manufacture of artificial violet perfume. Lemon grass is also prized as a culinary herb in oriental cooking. Family Poaceae; species *Cymbopogon citratus*.

lemon verbena
Aromatic deciduous shrub; it is native to Argentina and Chile and cultivated elsewhere as an ornamental. The yellow-green, lance-shaped leaves are densely dotted with glands that give off a lemon scent when crushed. The leaves are used in South America for a fragrant sedative tea; the essence is used for liqueurs and perfume. Family Verbenaceae; species *Aloysia citrodora*.

lemonwood
Any of various unrelated species of tree. The bark of the **lemonwood** tree of Brazil is used in tanning. Family Apocynaceae; species *Aspidosperma tomentosum*. The **lemonwood** tree of tropical Central and South America has straight-grained, dense and even-textured timber, which was once used for wheel spokes, carriage shafts, fishing rods, billiard cues, archery bows and tool handles. Family Rubiaceae; species *Calycophyllum candidissimum*. The **lemonwood** tree from tropical and South Africa

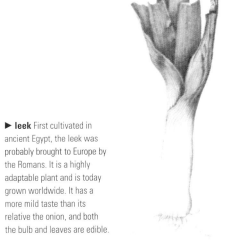

► **leek** First cultivated in ancient Egypt, the leek was probably brought to Europe by the Romans. It is a highly adaptable plant and is today grown worldwide. It has a more mild taste than its relative the onion, and both the bulb and leaves are edible.

▲ **lemming** The Norway lemming (*Lemmus lemmus*) has a four-year cycle of abundance. A small population can, under favourable conditions, build up to great numbers. These attract predators, but lemmings continue to multiply and deplete their food source. Popularly supposed to commit mass suicide, many lemmings die through attempts to migrate. A few remain to restart the cycle.

also produces useful timber. Family Monimiaceae; species *Xymalos monospora*. The **lemonwood** tree native to the lowland and lower montane forests of New Zealand is used locally for timber. It is also grown for its flowers and attractive foliage. Height: to 12m (40ft). Family Pittosporaceae; species *Pittosporum eugenioides*.

lemur
Any of several small, primitive, mainly arboreal (tree-dwelling) PRIMATES that live in Madagascar. They have large eyes and are mostly nocturnal, foraging for fruits, seeds, flowers and insects. Many species are now endangered by the destruction of their forest homes. Order Primates; suborder Prosimii; families Lemuridae, Cheirogaleidae, Indriidae and Daubentoniidae. *See also* INDRI; SIFAKA

lemur, black
Primarily arboreal primate found in the rainforest of NW Madagascar. Both sexes are of similar size, but the male is all black, and the female is reddish to brown with a darker face and white ear tufts. They feed mostly on leaves, but supplement their diet with fruit, flowers and insects. Head-body length: 38–45cm (15–18in); tail: 51–64cm (20–25in). Family Lemuridae; subfamily Lemurinae; species *Lemur macaco*.

lemur, brown
Lemur that has been introduced to the Comoros Islands but can still be found on its native Madagascar. Both sexes are similar in appearance, grey-brown with dark faces and pale beards. They live in groups, feeding on leaves, fruit, flowers and bark. Head-body length: 43–50cm (17–20in); tail: 50–55cm (20–22in). Family Lemuridae; subfamily Lemurinae; species *Lemur fulvus fulvus*.

lemur, crowned
Lemur that is found in dry forests of N Madagascar. It is mainly diurnal but will feed and travel during the night. Males are dark brown with dark tails and a grey face; females are paler with light cheeks and throat. Both sexes have an orange marking on the forehead, which sometimes extends around the face. Crowned lemurs feed mostly on fruit, but also eat leaves, flowers and insects. Head-body length: 23–36cm (9–14in); tail: 42–51cm (17–20in). Family Lemuridae; subfamily Lemurinae; species *Lemur coronatus*.

lemur, dwarf
Any of four species of small, nocturnal lemurs found in forests across Madagascar. In general, dwarf lemurs have grey-brown backs and are whitish underneath. During the day they sleep in nests of twigs and leaves. Most dwarf lemurs become dormant for some part of the year. They feed largely on fruit. Head-body length: 14–24cm (6–9in); tail: 16–36cm (6–14in). Family Cheirogaleidae; genera *Cheirogaleus*, *Allocebus* and *Phaner*.

L

lemur, flying
See COLUGO

lemur, gentle
Either of two species of lemur that inhabit forest and reedbeds in coastal Madagascar. They are grey brown in colour and are specialized in eating bamboo shoots and leaves. Their hind limbs are longer than their fore limbs. Gentle lemurs live in small social groups but are close to extinction. Head-body length: 27–40cm (11–16in); tail: 32–45cm (13–18in). Family Lemuridae; subfamily Hapalemurinae; genus *Hapalemur*.

lemur, mongoose
Lemur that is found in moist, deciduous forest on the Comoros Islands and NW Madagascar. It feeds on nectar, with flowers, fruit and leaves. Males are grey with red cheeks; females are browner with darker faces and white cheeks. Mongoose lemurs live in small groups and may be active during the day or night. Head-body length: 32–37cm (13–15in); tail: 47–51cm (19–20in). Family Lemuridae; subfamily Lemurinae; species *Lemur mongoz*.

lemur, mouse
Any of several species of small primate from Madagascar. Mouse lemurs are nocturnal. They spend most of their time in trees, but sometimes hunt beetles on the ground. Their diet consists of plants and insects. Head-body length: 13–21cm (5–8in); tail: 14–33cm (6–13in). Family Cheirogaleidae; genus *Microcebus*.

lemur, red-bellied
Lemur that is found in the rainforests of Madagascar. It is brown with a black tail and dark face. Males have brown underparts, whereas females are much paler. They live in small groups. The red-bellied lemur emits loud calls. Head-body length: 36–42cm (14–17in); tail: 46–54cm (18–21in). Family Lemuridae; subfamily Lemurinae; species *Lemur rubriventer*.

lemur, ring-tailed
Lemur that is found in deciduous forests in Madagascar, where it lives in large mixed groups. The ring-tailed lemur is grey backed, with white underparts and distinctive black marks on the top of its head, around its eyes and on its nose. Its tail, which is often held in the air, is banded in black and white. Unusually for a lemur, this species habitually travels on the ground, as well as being agile in trees. Head-body length: 39–46cm (15–18in); tail:

56–63cm (22–25in). Family Lemuridae; subfamily Lemurinae; species *Lemur catta*.

lemur, ruffed
Either of two similarly sized subspecies of lemur occurring in the rainforest of Madagascar. The red ruffed lemur is mainly deep red-brown in colour, with a white patch on its neck and a black face. In contrast, the other subspecies is black and white; it is known to leave its young in nests whilst foraging. Both types of ruffed lemur live in small groups, feeding on fruit, leaves and seeds. Head-body length: 51–60cm (20–24in); tail: 56–65cm (22–26in). Family Lemuridae; subfamily Lemurinae; species *Varecia variegata*.

lemur, sportive
Any of several subspecies of lemur that inhabit a variety of wooded habitats on Madagascar. They are all nocturnal, generally grey-brown in colour, and feed on leaves, with some flowers and fruit. Head-body length: 24–30cm (9–12in); tail: 22–29cm (9–11in). Family Lemuridae; subfamily Lepilemurinae; species *Lepilemur mustelinus*.

lemur, woolly
Either of two subspecies of lemur that inhabit rainforest on Madagascar. The eastern subspecies has a black face, the western subspecies a beige face. Both are generally grey, with reddish hands and feet. Relatively long legs enable the woolly lemur to leap from branch to branch. Head-body length: 27–35cm (11–14in); tail: 28–39cm (11–15in). Family Indriidae; species *Avahi laniger*.

lenten lily
See DAFFODIL

lenticel
Small raised area of bark in woody stems, occurring where the EPIDERMIS is replaced by loosely packed CORK cells. Lenticels allow gaseous exchange to occur between the inside of the stem and the atmosphere.

lentil
Annual plant of the PEA family. It grows in the Mediterranean region, SW Asia and North Africa. It is cultivated for its nutritious seeds. Height: to 51cm (20in). Family Fabaceae/Leguminosae; species *Lens culinaris*.

leopard (panther)
Powerful big CAT. Various subspecies are found in African and S Asia. Typically, a leopard has a pale brown coat with black spots, although melanic black leopards occur (often called black panthers). Leopards feed mainly on small mammals and birds, but they can catch larger prey. They often drag their meal into a tree to feed. Family Felidae; species *Panthera pardus*.

leopard, clouded (mint leopard)
Big cat with distinctive patterns of dark stripes, spots and patches on a coat that varies from dark brown to yellow. It inhabits dense, high-altitude forests in India and Southeast Asia. An excellent climber, the clouded leopard hunts pigs and deer on the ground and squirrels and monkeys in the trees. It is heavily built with short stocky legs. Head-body length: 60–110cm (24–43in); tail: 60–90cm (24–35in). Family Felidae; species *Neofelis nebulosa*.

leopard, snow (ounce)
Big cat that lives high on the slopes of the Altai, Hindu Kush and Himalayan mountains. Shy and soli-

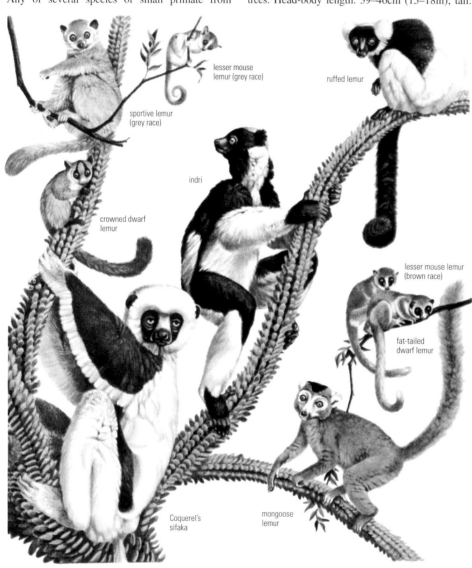

lesser mouse lemur (grey race)

sportive lemur (grey race)

ruffed lemur

crowned dwarf lemur

indri

lesser mouse lemur (brown race)

fat-tailed dwarf lemur

Coquerel's sifaka

mongoose lemur

▲ **lemur** There are c.40 species of lemur on Madagascar. They vary considerably in size, appearance and habit. It is thought that lemurs arrived on Madagascar from mainland Africa c.50 million years ago, and thrived and diversified due to there being few predators. The arrival of humans, c.2000 years ago, led to the extinction of some species, but the lemur population has been most threatened over the last few centuries, most notably by deforestation.

L

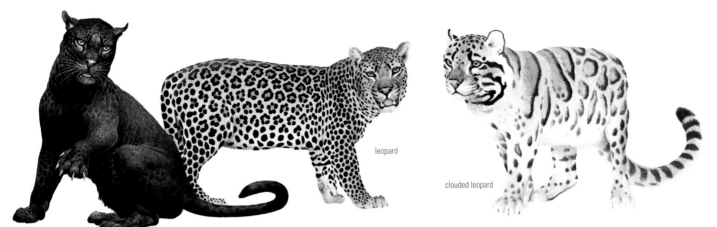

black panther

leopard

clouded leopard

snow leopard

▲ **leopard** The leopard and the black panther (*Panthera pardus*) are actually members of the same species but with different coloration. Relatives of the true leopard include the clouded leopard (*Neofelis nebulosa*) and snow leopard (*Panthera uncia*), which are both endangered. The clouded leopard is smaller, but it has large teeth and a long tail in proportion to its body. The snow leopard has long fur with grey rosettes and a dark stripe along its spine.

tary, it follows the seasonal migrations of the ibex, wild sheep, marmots and ground-dwelling birds on which it preys. Once hunted for its beautiful, darkly ringed, silver-grey coat, it is now endangered. The pads of its feet are thickly furred to act as insulated "snow shoes". Females usually give birth to two cubs after a gestation of *c*.100 days. Head-body length: 120–150cm (47–59in); tail: 90cm (35in). Family Felidae; species *Panthera uncia*.

lepidopteran
Any member of the order Lepidoptera; it includes BUTTERFLIES and MOTHS. Their soft bodies are covered with pigmented scales, as are their wings and appendages. Adult mouthparts are modified into a coiled proboscis, which is used to suck nectar from flowers; they have large compound eyes. Their development is holometabolous (complete METAMORPHOSIS). The larval caterpillars feed on vegetation, and some are serious crop pests. *See also* INSECT

lettuce
Important salad plant. It is thought to have derived from *Lactuca serriola*, which is native to the E Mediterranean region and has been grown since ancient times. The main salad types are crisphead, butterhead, cos or romaine and leaf; stem lettuce is used in Chinese cookery. Numerous varieties are available for home and horticultural production. Family Asteraceae; species *Lactuca sativa*.

leucite
Grey or white FELDSPAR mineral, a potassium aluminium silicate (KAl(SiO$_3$)$_2$). Unstable at high pressures, it has a restricted occurrence. It can be found in potassium-rich lava flows and volcanic plugs. Hardness 5.5–6; r.d. 2.5.

leucocyte
White blood cell, a colourless structure containing a NUCLEUS and CYTOPLASM. There are two types of leucocytes – LYMPHOCYTES and PHAGOCYTES. Lymphocytes produce ANTIBODIES, and phagocytes destroy harmful organisms (by engulfing them) when the body is infected. Normal blood contains 5000–10,000 leucocytes per mm^3 of blood. Excessive numbers of leucocytes are seen in such diseases as leukaemia. *See also* IMMUNE SYSTEM

levee
Natural embankment that is formed alongside a RIVER by the deposition of SILT when the river is in flood. Silt is deposited all over the FLOODPLAIN, but most is deposited near to the river banks, and so a slightly higher area is created alongside the river. Levees can help to prevent flooding and are sometimes built up and strengthened artificially. Some levees grow so large that flood water cannot return to the main channel. When this happens, the river may change course. Levees may be only a few centimetres in height, but on some larger rivers, such as the Mississippi River, they may reach heights of 15m (50ft).

liana
Any ground-rooting, woody VINE that twines and creeps extensively over other plants for support; it is common in tropical forests. Some liana species may reach a diameter of 60cm (24in) and a length of 100m (330ft).

lichen
Plant consisting of a FUNGUS in which microscopic (usually single-celled) ALGAE are embedded. The fungus and its algae form a symbiotic association in which the fungus contributes support, water and minerals, while the algae contribute food produced by photosynthesis. *See also* SYMBIOSIS

life
Widely accepted as the ability of organisms to obtain energy from the Sun or from food and to use this for growth and reproduction. All living organisms interact with their environment: they take in energy and materials from their environment and respond to changes in that environment. When they reproduce, they pass on instructions for their characteristics to the next generation in the form of DNA or RNA. Debate continues over the status of VIRUSES, which do not grow, and, although they do contain DNA or RNA, use the host cell's machinery to reproduce themselves. The current theory on life's origin is that giant molecules, similar to proteins and nucleic acids, reacted together in the watery surface environment of the young Earth that is now commonly called the **primordial soup**. In this environment the giant molecules multiplied by consuming smaller molecules. Despite much research, the EVOLUTION and development of cellular life out of this molecular prelife remains a controversial subject and has yet to be explained fully.

L

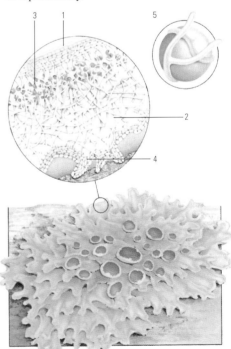

▲ **lichen** The lichen *Xanthoria* is found on coastline rocks. Lichens are the product of an intimate symbiosis between fungi and algae. The algae provide energy-rich sugars from photosynthesis; the fungi provide protection, water and minerals. The lichen's protective upper layer (1) is made up of matted fungal strands (*hyphae*) (2). Below this is a layer of algal cells (3) closely associated with hyphae. The lichen clings on with root-like structures at its base (4). Vegetative asexual reproduction is achieved by *soredia* (5): small clumps of algae and hyphae which disperse to form new colonies.

life cycle

Sequence of stages in the development of an organism from its formation to the creation of its offspring, followed by death. In organisms that reproduce sexually, formation corresponds to the fusion of sex cells (GAMETES) from the parents. The resulting ZYGOTE develops into an organism similar to the parents, which goes on to mature and produce new gametes that create the next generation. In organisms that reproduce asexually, formation occurs through FISSION (simple division), BUDDING or VEGETATIVE REPRODUCTION. In plants, there is an ALTERNATION OF GENERATIONS in which the plants (GAMETOPHYTE generation) differ from the spore-forming (SPORO-PHYTE) generation.

light-dependent reaction (light reaction)

One of the two distinct phases of PHOTOSYNTHESIS; the other being the DARK REACTION. During the light-dependent reaction, the green pigment CHLOROPHYLL absorbs sunlight and uses its energy to break down water into electrons, protons (hydrogen ions) and oxygen. The energy of the electrons is used to convert ADENOSINE DIPHOSPHATE (ADP) to ADENOSINE TRIPHOSPHATE (ATP) and NADPH (the hydrogenated form of nicotinamide adenine dinucleotide phosphate). The process can be summarized as: $2H_2O \rightarrow 4H + 4e + O_2$. Together ATP and NADPH ensure the dark reaction can take place.

light-independent reaction

See DARK REACTION

lightning

See feature article

lightwood

Timber from a tall tree native to New South Wales, Australia. The wood is light brown to pinkish brown and is used in carpentry and cabinet-making; it is also used for flooring, panelling, skirting, and for plywood veneer and aircraft veneer. Family Cunoniaceae; species *Ceratopetalum apetalum*. The name **lightwood** may also refer to a member of the WATTLE family. Family Mimosaceae; species *Acacia implexa*.

lignin

Complex, non-carbohydrate substance that occurs in the woody tissues (especially XYLEM) of plants, often in combination with CELLULOSE. It makes the CELL walls stronger, helping them to resist compression and tension. It is lignin that gives WOOD its strength. To obtain pure cellulose for the paper and rayon industries, the lignin has to be removed from wood. Lignin is also a major source of vanillin, a white, crystalline aldehyde used as a flavouring and in perfumes and pharmaceuticals.

lignite

Soft COAL, brown-black in colour, with a carbon con-

LIGHTNING

Visible flash of light that accompanies an electrical discharge between clouds or between clouds and the ground. Lightning is most commonly produced in a THUNDERSTORM.

A typical discharge consists of several lightning strokes, which are initiated by leaders that follow an irregular path of least resistance; this path is known as the **lightning channel**. Intense heating by the discharge expands the channel rapidly up to a diameter of 13–25cm (5–10in), creating the sound waves that are heard as thunder. *See also* ST ELMO'S FIRE; STORM

▼ Once an electrical potential of a million volts/m (300,000 volts/ft) has been created in a thunder cloud, the lightning process begins (**A**). A stream of electrons flows down, colliding with air molecules and freeing more electrons, and in the process giving the air molecules a positive charge (ionizing the air). This intermittent low-current discharge forms a highly branched pathway and is called the stepped leader (1). As the leading branches of the stepped leader, carrying large negative charges, near the ground they induce short upward streamers of positive electrical charges from good conducting points on the ground (2). When a branch of the stepped leader contacts an upward positive streamer, a complete channel of ionized air has been created. This allows a huge positive current called the return stroke to flow upward in to the cloud in the form of a bright lightning stroke (3). The different strokes have been given different colours to distinguish between them. In nature, all lightning is colourless. The return stroke causes the first of the shock waves we hear as thunder (**B**). The flash effectively reaches the eye instantaneously, whereas the sound of thunder travels at approximately 330m/s (1100ft/s). Therefore, the number of seconds between the flash and the thunder multiplied by 330 tells us how far away the lightning stroke is in metres. A fraction of a millisecond after the return stroke (3), a negatively charged dart leader passes down the ionized channel (4) and triggers another upward return stroke. The process is repeated several times within fractions of a second until the charge in the cloud is completely neutralized.

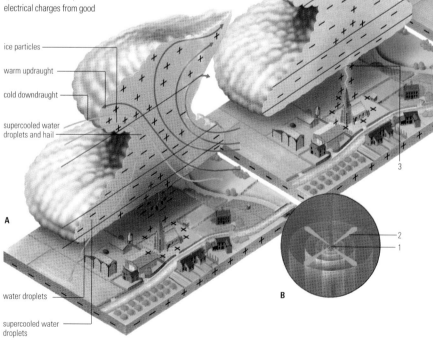

ice particles

warm updraught

cold downdraught

supercooled water droplets and hail

A

water droplets

supercooled water droplets

B

-70°C 11km
-60°C 10
-50°C 9
-40°C 8
-30°C 7
-20°C 6
-10°C 5
4
0°C 3
2
10°C 1

▲ Lightning conductors (5) generate a strong positive streamer which encourages electrical contact with an approaching stepped leader. Consequently, potential lightning strikes within 50–100m (170–330ft) of a building are attracted to a lightning conductor. Return strokes and dart leaders are safely routed to the Earth along a wide copper strip with one end buried in the ground.

▲ Thunder (B) is caused by the narrow lightning stroke heating the column of air (1) surrounding it to around 30,000°C (54,000°F), expanding it explosively (2) at supersonic speeds under a force of 10–100 times normal atmospheric pressure. The immense shock wave becomes a sound wave within about a metre, producing the sound of thunder.

L

▲ **lilac** There are several hundred varieties of common lilac (*Syringa vulgaris*), but the most common ones have dense purple or white flowers, which appear in spring. Lilac is native to SE Europe and is widely cultivated elsewhere as an ornamental in temperate regions.

tent higher than that of PEAT but lower than that of other coals. Sometimes the shape of its original woody structures is visible.

lignum vitae
Any of several trees of the genus *Guaiacum*, a group of evergreen trees native to Mexico, Central America and the West Indies. The wood is dark brown, tough and strong, the hardest of commercial woods. It is used for making bowling balls, pulley blocks and furniture. It also produces the gum resin guiacum, which is used in medicine. Family Zygophyllaceae; species include *Guaiacum officinale* and *Guaiacum sanctum*.

lilac
Any of *c*.20 species of evergreen ornamental shrubs and small trees belonging to the genus *Syringa*. They bear pointed clusters of tiny, fragrant, white to purple flowers. Height: to 6m (20ft). Family Oleaceae.

Lillie, Frank Rattray (1870–1947)
US zoologist and embryologist, b. Canada. Lillie was noted for his discoveries in the field of fertilization and the role of HORMONES in SEX DETERMINATION. He helped to develop the Marine Biological Laboratory and the Oceanographic Institution at Woods Hole, Massachusetts. His book *The Development of the Chick* (1908) is a leading work in EMBRYOLOGY.

lily
Any member of the genus *Lilium*, a large group of leafy-stemmed perennials found in temperate

▶ **lily** Grown mainly in temperate and tropical regions, the showy displays of colour make lilies a common sight in gardens in many regions of the world. In addition, many species are valued for their attractive fragrance. Most species thrive in well-drained, moist soil and a sunny location.

regions of the Northern Hemisphere. Many species and varieties are grown as ornamentals. Lilies grow from scaly bulbs. The large, ornate, single or clustered, often fragrant flowers are composed of six separate segments, which are rolled back in some forms, for example in the Turk's cap lily. Family Liliaceae; genus *Lilium*.

lily of the valley
Perennial woodland plant native to Europe, Asia and E United States. It has broad, elongated leaves and bears stalks of tiny, white, bell-shaped, fragrant flowers. Family Liliaceae; species *Convallaria majalis*.

lilytrotter
See JACANA

lima bean (butter bean)
Large-seeded climbing perennial from South America; it is known to have been cultivated for *c*.6500 years. It is grown in the tropics and subtropics for food. The large, flat, thin seeds are kidney shaped in outline; they are used as a vegetable or pulse. Family Fabaceae; species *Phaseolus lunatus*.

limb
Jointed extension of the VERTEBRATE body, used for locomotion and manipulation of the physical environment. The human forelimb (arm) is particularly specialized in the latter function. The form of the limbs is regarded as a criterion of evolutionary development. *See also* PENTADACTYL LIMB; HUMAN BODY

lime
Small tropical tree of the RUE family; it yields small, green, CITRUS fruits. In the 18th and 19th centuries, lime juice was used on long voyages by English sailors because its vitamin C helped to ward off scurvy. Height: 2.4–4.6m (8–15ft). Family Rutaceae; species *Citrus aurantifolia*. **Lime** is also the name for any of the deciduous linden trees of the genus *Tilia* that grow in temperate regions of the Northern Hemisphere. They have serrated, heart-shaped leaves and small, fragrant, yellowish flowers. The common British linden, *Tilia vulgaris*, is one of three British species. The American lime, *Tilia americana*, is also known as basswood. Family Tiliaceae.

limestone
SEDIMENTARY ROCK formed on the bed of a warm sea by an accumulation of dead sea creatures. At least 50% of a limestone consists of CALCITE ($CaCO_3$). There are many different types, including CARBONIFEROUS limestone, CHALK, dolomitic limestone and oolitic limestone. They all contain FOSSILS or fragments of fossils. Because of the calcium carbonate content, limestones are soluble and permeable, and generally give rise to dry landscapes. Chalk is pure limestone and forms rounded hills and vertical cliffs. Carboniferous limestone is hard and forms high ground; oolitic hills are generally more gentle. Carboniferous limestone, like chalk and oolitic limestone, has numerous dry valleys, but also contains CAVES with STALACTITES and STALAGMITES. Limestone is used to make cement, as a source of lime and as a building material.

limestone pavement
Bare surface of LIMESTONE strata, mostly devoid of soil, produced by WEATHERING and EROSION of the calcium carbonate rock substrate. Dissolution by slightly acidic groundwater produces a distinctive dissected topography of deep angular fissures (GRIKES) separated by slabs of rock (CLINTS), which may be further reduced to sharp ridges.

◀ **lime** The American lime or linden (*Tilia americana*), also known as American basswood, has some of the largest leaves of any deciduous tree, with some reaching 30cm (12in) in length. In the past, the wood was commonly used in carving, as it has both pliability and strength.

limiting factor
Any variable that limits the rate of a specific reaction or process. At any given moment, the rate of a process is limited by the one factor that is in shortest supply, and by that factor alone. This is called the limiting factor and any change in its level will affect the rate of the reaction. To take an example, PHOTOSYNTHESIS cannot proceed in the dark, because the absence of light limits the process. If light is supplied, photosynthesis will occur, and the more light there is the faster the process will be. Adding carbon dioxide or increasing the temperature to a plant in the dark will not affect the rate of photosynthesis. Light is therefore the limiting factor because it alone can alter the rate of the process.

limnology
Science of freshwater LAKES, ponds and streams. These bodies of water are explored in terms of chemistry, physics and biology. The plants, animals and environment are quantitatively examined in light of FOOD CHAINS, HABITATS and ZONATION of organisms. Freshwater bodies are subject to greater extremes of temperature and are therefore more fragile and more specialized ECOSYSTEMS than those in marine environments. *See also* HYDROLOGY

limonite (brown iron or bog ore, FeO(OH).nH_2O)
One of the most important sources of iron. Limonite may appear lustrous black, brown to yellow and is streaky, porous and often mixed with sand or clay.

limpet
Primitive gastropod MOLLUSC commonly found fixed to rocks along marine shores. It has a cap-like shell and a large muscular foot. Length: to 13cm (5in). Families Patellacea, Acmaeidae and Fissurellidae.

limpkin
Large, long-necked wading bird, related to the RAIL and CRANE; it is found in swamps from Florida, s

▲ **limpet** The conical shell of limpets (*Patella* species shown) differs from most other gastropods, which have coiled shells. Found in rocky, coastal regions of the Pacific and Atlantic oceans, limpets remain attached to the rock by a muscular "foot", occasionally moving to feed on seaweed.

L

► **lion** Prides of lions are commonly seen lazing in the shade of a tree. Prides vary in size but usually include one or two male lions and several generations of lionesses and their cubs; they live within a well defended territory. Lions themselves have no natural predators except humans.

L

United States, to Argentina. It is named after its limping walk. The limpkin is chocolate brown in colour, with dense white streaks. It has a long, down-curved bill. Length: 66cm (26in). Family Aramidae; species *Aramus guarauna*.

Lindley, John (1799–1865)
British botanist, who is known for his CLASSIFICATION of plants in a natural system in which all characteristics of a plant are considered. Among Lindley's best-known books are *Theory and Practice of Horticulture* (1842) and *The Vegetable Kingdom* (1846), which included his new classification of plants.

ling
Food fish related to the COD, found in the Atlantic Ocean. It is brown and silver and has long dorsal and ventral fins. Length: to 2m (6.6ft). Family Gadidae; species *Molva molva*.

ling
See HEATHER

linkage group
Group of inherited characteristics or GENES that occur on the same CHROMOSOME and that remain connected in such a way that they are usually inherited together through successive generations.

Linnaeus, Carolus (1707–78) (Carl von Linné)
Swedish botanist and taxonomist. His *Systema Naturae* (1735) laid the foundation of the modern science of TAXONOMY by including all known organisms in a single CLASSIFICATION system. Linnaeus was one of the first scientists clearly to define the differences between species; he devised the system of BINOMIAL NOMENCLATURE, which gave standardized Latin names to every organism.

linsang
Any of three species of small carnivores belonging to the MONGOOSE family; they are closely related to GENETS and CIVETS. One species is found in Africa, and the other two in Asia and Southeast Asia. Linsangs are small and secretive animals. They hunt amongst forest trees at night. Like genets and most

cats, linsangs have retractile claws. Family Viverridae; subfamily Viverrinae; genera include *Poiana* and *Prionodon*.

linsang, African
Arboreal linsang that inhabits dense forest in w Africa, where it hunts small vertebrates and builds nests in trees. The African linsang is yellow-brown with dark spots on its body, and there are stripes on its neck and tail. Head-body length: 33cm (13in); tail: 38cm (15in). Family Viverridae; species *Poiana richardsoni*.

linsang, spotted
Linsang that is found in Indochina. It is similar in colour to the African linsang. It is a secretive, arboreal carnivore, with large eyes and ears. Head-body length: 39cm (15in); tail: 34cm (13in). Family Viverridae; species *Prionodon pardicolor*.

linseed
See FLAX

lion
Large CAT that lives on African savannas south of the Sahara and on reserves in sw Asia. It is golden yellow with light spots under its eyes. The male has a deep neck mane. The smaller female does most of the hunting and preys on antelopes, zebras and bush pigs. Lions live in prides of between four and 30 individuals. They travel and hunt mainly at twilight and can cover 48km (30mi) in a single night. Lionesses can reach speeds of 48km/h (30mph). Length of male: to 2.5m (8.2ft) including tail. Family Felidae; species *Panthera leo*.

lionfish
Ornate and conspicuous marine fish found in Indo-Pacific waters. It is boldly striped and has poisonous dorsal spines. The lionfish is related to the SCORPION FISH. Family Scorpaenidae; species include *Pterosis volitans*.

lipase
ENZYME that breaks down LIPIDS (fats) into FATTY ACIDS and monoglycerides (GLYCEROL and one fatty acid) by HYDROLYSIS. In the mammalian gut enzymes are produced by the pancreas. They are also commercially produced for use in washing powders and in the food industry, where they are involved in cheese and chocolate manufacture.

lipid
One of a large group of organic compounds in living organisms that are insoluble in water but soluble in alcohol. They include animal fats, vegetable oils and natural waxes. Lipids form an important food store and energy source in plant and animal cells. Storage fat is composed chiefly of triglycerides, which consist of three molecules of FATTY ACID linked to GLYCEROL.

Lipmann, Fritz Albert (1899–1986)
US biochemist b. Germany. He isolated and partially explained the molecular structure of COENZYME A,

► **lionfish** The spectacular lionfish (*Pterosis volitans*) is found in tropical waters of the Indo-Pacific region. This specimen was photographed in the Red Sea. Its distinctive coloration serves as a warning to predators, enabling the lionfish to swim in open water without much fear of attack. If threatened, the lionfish erects its poisonous dorsal spines and can inflict a nasty wound. It is a fiercely predatory fish.

derived from the B vitamin pantothenic acid. For this and other work on METABOLISM, he shared the 1953 Nobel Prize for physiology or medicine with Hans KREBS. In 1950 Lipmann demonstrated the formation of citric acid from oxalo-acetate and acetate, and found that this process required coenzyme A.

liquorice (licorice)
Perennial plant of the PEA family; it is native to the Mediterranean region and cultivated in temperate and subtropical areas. It bears spikes of blue flowers. The dried roots are used to flavour confectionery, tobacco and medicines. Height: to 90cm (35in). Family Fabaceae/Leguminosae; species *Glycyrrhiza glabra*.

lithification
Process by which SEDIMENTS and FOSSIL remains are turned into rock, primarily through compaction and recrystallization of some mineral components.

lithosphere
Upper layer of the solid EARTH; it includes the CRUST and the uppermost MANTLE. It is of variable thickness, from 60km (40mi) extending down to approximately 200km (125mi). Rigid, solid and brittle, the lithosphere is made up of a number of tectonic plates that move independently and give rise to PLATE TECTONICS.

littoral zone
Beach area between high and low tides. It also refers to the benthic division – between high tide and a depth of 200m (656ft). The larger zone is divided into the **eulittoral**, from high tide to a 50m (164ft) depth, and the **sublittoral**, from 50–200m (164–656ft). The lower edge of the eulittoral is the lowest limit at which abundant attached plants can grow.

live oak
Evergreen OAK native to SE United States. It has a spreading shape and almost horizontal branches. Live oaks are noted for their picturesque appearance in the landscape of the S United States, often draped with Spanish moss. The trees were formerly an important source of ship-building timber. Height: to 18m (60ft). Family Fagaceae; species *Quercus virginiana*.

liver
Large organ located in the upper right abdomen of vertebrates. It can weigh up to 2kg (4.5lbs) in an adult human. The liver is divided into four lobes and has many functions. It is extremely important in the control of the body's internal environment (HOMEOSTASIS). It receives nutrients from the intestine and is a site of METABOLISM of proteins, carbohydrates and fats. It synthesizes BILE and some vitamins, regulates the blood-glucose level, produces blood-clotting factors, breaks down worn-out ERYTHROCYTES (red blood cells) and removes toxins from the blood. The many metabolic reactions that go on in the liver are the body's main source of heat, which is distributed around the body by the blood. ENDOTHERMIC (warm-blooded) animals maintain a constant body temperature by producing too much heat, then controlling its dissipation. The liver has phenomenal powers of regeneration: if part of it is removed, it regrows within weeks. *See also* INSULIN

liverwort
Any of *c*.9000 species of tiny, non-flowering green plants that, like the related MOSSES, lack specialized tissues to transport water, food and minerals. Liverworts belong to the plant phylum Bryophyta. *See also* BRYOPHYTE

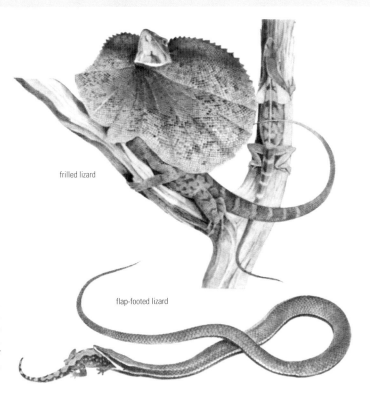

frilled lizard

flap-footed lizard

◀ **lizard** Lizards form a diverse group of reptiles. Two of the most unusual species are the frilled lizard (*Chlamydosaurus kingii*) and the flap-footed lizard (*Lialis burtoni*). The frilled lizard erects its frill and hisses when alarmed. The frill is *c*.30cm (*c*.12in) in diameter and is supported by cartilaginous rods connecting it to the facial muscles. Frilled lizards vary in colour depending on their habitat. They can run very quickly, holding their forelegs and tail clear of the ground. The snake-like flap-footed lizard of Australia relies on geckos as its main source of food. Flap-footed lizards are distinguished from snakes by their ear openings, moveable eyelids and less flexible jaws. They are limbless, but some species have small vestigial flaps of skin instead. Many flap-footed lizards make a chirping sound.

living stone
Any member of the genus *Lithops*, a small group of SUCCULENTS from S Africa, many of which, including hybrids, are cultivated as ornamentals. The plants produce cylindrical growths of two flat-topped, fleshy leaves, some of which have transparent, stone-coloured "windows" that camouflage the plant in its stony habitat. Family Aizoaceae; genus *Lithops*.

lizard
REPTILE found on every continent; there are 20 families and *c*.4300 species. Most species have a scaly cylindrical body with four legs, a long tail and moveable eyelids. Some species, such as glass lizards, SLOW-WORMS and some SKINKS, have reduced or absent limbs. Most lizards are terrestrial, and many live in deserts. There are also semi-aquatic and arboreal forms. Many lizards have an autotomic defence mechanism – they shed their tail when attacked. Most lay eggs rather than bear live young. They feed mainly on insects and vegetation. They range in size from the *c*.5cm (*c*.2in) GECKO to the *c*.3m (*c*.10ft) KOMODO DRAGON. Order Squamata; suborder Sauria. *See also* CHAMELEON; IGUANA; MONITOR

lizard, alligator
Secretive lizard of North and Central America. It has a large head, plate-like scales and a distinctive fold along each side of its body. Alligator lizards may be terrestrial or arboreal, and their tails can be prehensile. Some species give birth to live young. Length: 10–40cm (4–16in). Family Anguidae.

lizard, armadillo
Heavy-bodied, viviparous lizard found in S Africa. It has very large body plates and a very spiny tail. When threatened, it curls into a ball and holds its tail in its mouth, presenting a spiny defence to would-be predators. Armadillo lizards live in family groups in rock crevices. Length: to 20cm (8in). Family Cordylidae; species *Cordylus cataphractus*.

lizard, beaded
Lizard that is found in arid areas and deciduous woodlands of Mexico and N Central America. It is closely related to the GILA MONSTER and, like that

species, is venomous. Beaded lizards are larger and more slender-bodied than gila monsters. They often climb trees in search of bird eggs and other prey. Length: to 100cm (39in). Family Helodermatidae; species *Heloderma horridum*.

lizard, blind
Any member of several groups of limbless, burrowing lizards that have eyes covered by scales and thus reduced vision. Blind lizards include several groups of SKINKS, as well as the dibamid lizards of Asia and Mexico. Many blind lizards feed on termites and ants. Length: to 40cm (16in). Families Scincidae and Dibamidae.

lizard, flap-footed
Any of *c*.30 species of elongate lizards that have no forelimbs and only small, flap-like remnants of hindlimbs. Flap-footed lizards are found in mainland Australia and New Guinea. Like their relatives the GECKOS, they lack eyelids. Some species are burrowers, but others are nocturnal and surface active. Length: to 59cm (23in). Family Pygopodidae. *See also* LIZARD, SNAKE

lizard, flat
Any member of the genus *Platysaurus*, a group of flattened, long-legged, rock-living lizards native to S Africa. They are diurnal. Flat lizards run rapidly across boulder faces and use narrow rock crevices as retreat sites and to protect their elongate eggs. Males are usually brightly coloured and engage in complex social interactions. Length: to 35cm (14in). Family Cordylidae; genus *Platysaurus*.

lizard, frilled
Large lizard found in N Australia and S New Guinea. It has a long tail, long hind legs and a frill around its neck. When the lizard is alarmed, it can erect its frill by opening its mouth. Frilled lizards are capable of running on their hindlegs. Length: 44–55cm (17–22in). Family Agamidae; species *Chlamydosaurus kingii*.

lizard, glass (glass snake)
Any member of the genus *Ophisaurus*, a group of

L

▲ **llama** Found in semidesert habitat, the llama is used primarily as a pack animal in S and W South America, from sea level to elevations of 5000m (16,500ft). It grows to 1.2m (4ft) long, and to a height at the shoulder of 1.2m (4ft).

legless lizards that are so called because their tails are frequently broken off. They resemble snakes but can be distinguished by the possession of small ears and moveable eyelids. Several species are found in North America; others are found in SE Europe, S Asia, the Middle East and North Africa. They feed mainly on insects but some larger individuals will take small mammals. Family Anguidae; species include *Ophisaurus attenuatus*.

lizard, green
Large, fairly heavy-bodied, egg-laying lizard. It inhabits forest edges and many relatively open habitats across Europe, from France to Russia and Turkey; it is also found on the Channel Islands. Males are green above, speckled with black, and usually have a blue throat. Length: to 40cm (16in). Family Lacertidae; species *Lacerta viridis*.

lizard, night
Any of 19 species of nocturnal lizards; they are found from California, United States, to Panama, with a single species on Cuba. Night lizards have granular or tuberculate scales on their backs and smooth, rectangular scales on their bellies. They lack eyelids; instead their eyes are covered by a transparent spectacle. All species give live birth to a small number of young. Some species live in rock crevices, but *Xantusia vigilis* of California lives among fallen debris from Joshua trees. Length: 7–20cm (3–8in). Family Xantusiidae.

lizard, plated
Any of c.40 species of mostly terrestrial African and Madagascan lizards. Their bodies are covered by rectangular, bony, plate-like scales. Savanna-dwelling species have small but well-formed limbs; the grass-swimming *Tetradactylus* species have reduced limbs; *Angolosaurus* species have limbs modified for movement in sand dunes. All plated lizards lay eggs and many have an omnivorous diet. Length: 20–70cm (8–28in). Family Gerrhosauridae.

lizard, sand
Relatively heavy-bodied, diurnal, egg-laying lizard. It has a distinctive pattern of brown blotches, each with a small central white spot. In males the flanks and side of the head are green. Sand lizards range from Britain, Spain and Scandinavia to central Asia. Length: to 25cm (10in). Family Lacertidae; species *Lacerta agilis*.

lizard, sleepy
See SKINK, PINE CONE

lizard, snake
Large, terrestrial, flap-footed LIZARD that is found in all types of habitat throughout Australia and New Guinea. It has a characteristically elongate snout. The snake lizard's teeth and skull are modified to feed on small skinks. Length: to 59cm (23in). Family Pygopodidae; genus *Lialis*.

lizard, viviparous
Small, day-active lizard that lives in a wide range of habitats. The viviparous lizard has the largest range of any lizard, stretching from Ireland, Britain and Scandinavia to Sakhalin Island in the Russian Far East. The eggs are retained internally, and females give birth to between five and 15 young during the summer months. Length: to 18cm (7in). Family Lacertidae; species *Zootoca* (or *Lacerta*) *vivipara*.

lizard, wall
Slender, somewhat flattened lizard found from France and Spain to Greece and Turkey; it has been introduced in England. It has a long tail, which is about twice the length of its head and body. The wall lizard favours dry, sunny habitats, including cliffs, clearings, and man-made structures such as vineyard walls and buildings. Length: to 23cm (9in). Family Lacertidae; species *Podarcis muralis*.

lizard, whiptail (racerunner)
Any of c.45 species of long-limbed, narrow-snouted, diurnal lizards of North, Central and South America. They have granular dorsal scales and large, rectangular ventral scales. Whiptails are among the fastest of all lizards. Some species are unisexual, consisting only of females that reproduce parthenogenetically. Length: to 30cm (12in). Family Teiidae; genus *Cnemidophorus*.

llama
Domesticated, even-toed, ruminant mammal found in South America. It has been used as a beast of burden by Native Americans for more than 1000 years. The llama has a long woolly coat and slender limbs and neck. The smaller and closely related alpaca (*Lama pacos*) is bred for its wool. Family Camelidae; species *Lama glama*.

load
SEDIMENT carried along by ice, a river or the sea. Ice sheets and large GLACIERS can carry a greater load than a thin glacier, so that they dump larger amounts of TILL when the ice melts. The load carried by a river depends on the type and amount of material available and the speed of the current. It may be in solution or in suspension, or be rolled along the river bed. A stream or slow-moving river can normally transport only mud and sand, whereas a fast-moving torrent can shift large boulders.

lobefinned fish
One of the two major groups of bony FISH. Lobefinned fish include LUNGFISH, COELACANTHS and the ancestors of AMPHIBIANS and other vertebrates. Members of the group are characterized by fins with an internal structure that resembles the forelimbs and hindlimbs of terrestrial vertebrates.

lobelia
Any of c.365 species belonging to the genus *Lobelia*, a group of flowering plants found worldwide. They are mainly trailing or bedding plants. The flowers can be blue, red or white and irregularly shaped; the leaves are simple. Family Lobeliaceae.

lobster
Large DECAPOD, with a tough CARAPACE, large pincers and well-developed walking legs. Unlike CRABS, to which they are related, lobsters have elongated bodies. Most are scavengers. Many species are harvested for food. Adult body length: to 1m (39in). Order Decapoda; family Nephropidae; species include *Homarus gammarus* (common lobster).

lobster, spiny
See CRAWFISH

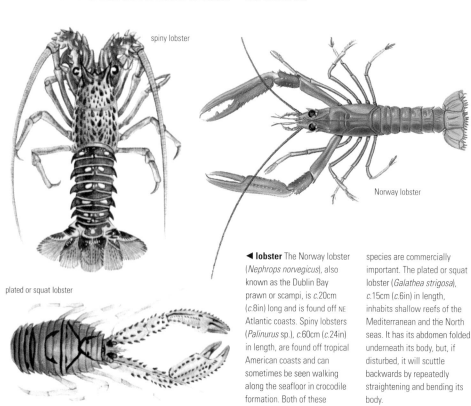

plated or squat lobster

◀ **lobster** The Norway lobster (*Nephrops norvegicus*), also known as the Dublin Bay prawn or scampi, is c.20cm (c.8in) long and is found off NE Atlantic coasts. Spiny lobsters (*Palinurus* sp.), c.60cm (c.24in) in length, are found off tropical American coasts and can sometimes be seen walking along the seafloor in crocodile formation. Both of these species are commercially important. The plated or squat lobster (*Galathea strigosa*), c.15cm (c.6in) in length, inhabits shallow reefs of the Mediterranean and the North seas. It has its abdomen folded underneath its body, but, if disturbed, it will scuttle backwards by repeatedly straightening and bending its body.

locoweed

Any of several plants, native to North America, belonging to the PEA family. They are poisonous to livestock, particularly horses in the grasslands of the United States and Canada. They get their name from the Spanish *loco*, meaning crazy, because of their poisonous effect. Family Fabaceae; genera *Atragalus* and *Oxytropis*; species include *Atragalus mollissimus* and *Oxytropis lambertii*.

locust

Type of GRASSHOPPER that migrates in huge swarms. Locust swarms may contain as many as 40 billion insects and can cover an area of *c*.1000sq km (*c*.385sq mi). Length: 12.5–100mm (0.5–4in). Order Orthoptera; family Acrididae; species include *Schistocerca gregaria*.

locust tree

Any of *c*.20 species of the genus *Robinia*, a group of deciduous trees from North America. They are grown as ornamentals. They have pinnate leaves and white, rose or purple pea flowers, which hang in elongated clusters. The timber has been used for construction and fuel. It gets its Latin name from Jean and Vespasien Robin, who were herbalists to the king of France in the 16th and 17th centuries. Family Fabaceae; genus *Robinia*.

lode

ORE formation consisting of a closely spaced series of veins, usually in stratified layers. Often several different minerals occur along the same lode. Lodes were probably formed as a result of liquids or gases, heated by volcanic activity, forcing their way through existing rocks and then cooling and solidifying.

lodestone

See MAGNETITE

Loeb, Jacques (1859–1924)

US biologist, b. Germany, who studied the chemical processes of living organisms. He stressed the importance of physical and chemical laws in understanding life phenomena in both animals and plants. He achieved popular notoriety for experiments on artificial PARTHENOGENESIS in animals.

loess

Fine-grained clay, a sedimentary material made up of rock fragments. Loess is earthy, porous and crumbly; it is usually yellowish or brown in colour. Loess consists of very small angular particles of mainly quartz and calcite from glaciated areas; the particles are blown by the wind and often built up into thick layers. The largest expanse of loess is in the valley of the River Huang He, N China, where dust from the Gobi Desert has accumulated. The Huang is sometimes called the Yellow River because of all the loess it transports.

Loewi, Otto (1873–1961)

German pharmacologist and medical researcher. He shared the 1936 Nobel Prize for physiology or medicine with Henry DALE for discovering that a chemical substance (later shown by Dale to be acetylcholine) mediated the transmission of NERVE IMPULSES from one NEURONE to another.

loganberry

Biennial, hybrid, red-berried BRAMBLE. A cross between the BLACKBERRY and RASPBERRY, the loganberry is disease-prone and is grown only in sheltered areas. Family Rosaceae; subspecies *Rubus ursinus loganobaccus*.

solitary form

gregarious form

▲ **locust** Locusts respond to overcrowding by migrating in huge swarms, which involves a transition from a solitary form to a gregarious form. The solitary form is relatively inactive and is the same colour as the environment in which it lives. The active gregarious form (bottom) has a black and orange pattern; it has larger wings and hindlegs for flying. Migrating swarms of locusts are capable of devastating very large areas of vegetation or crops.

loggerhead

See SEA TURTLE, LOGGERHEAD

logrunner

Australian songbird with strong legs and a tail of stiff spines. The northern logrunner (*Orthonyx spaldingii*) is blackish-brown above and white below. The southern logrunner (*Orthonyx temminckii*) is smaller; it is mottled black, white and reddish-brown above. When feeding, the logunner rummages in leaf litter, propping itself up on its stiff tail. Length: 20–28cm (8–11in). Family Orthonychidae; genus *Orthonyx*.

logwood

Small thorny tree from Mexico and the West Indies; it is grown as an ornamental and as hedging. The dark red heartwood is used as a source of haematoxylin for microscopy preparations and as a mainly blue or black dye in stains and inks. The timber is used for furniture. Family Caesalpiniaceae; species *Haematoxylum campechianum*.

Lombardy poplar

Male mutant form of the Asiatic black POPLAR, propagated by cuttings from a tree in Lombardy in the early 18th century. Lombardy poplars have a tall, narrow growth habit with erect branches. They have been planted as ornamentals for centuries. Height: to 36m (120ft). Family Salicaceae; species *Populus nigra* 'Italica'.

longclaw

Large, colourful PIPIT that inhabits the grasslands of Africa. Longclaws are found both singly and in pairs, often standing upright on a grass tuft or anthill. They are brown and streaked above, often with a red throat bordered by black, and a red or yellow breast and belly. Length: 20cm (8in). Family Motacillidae; genus *Macronyx*.

longshore drift

Movement of sand and pebbles along a seacoast. The material is carried along the beach by the waves hitting the coast obliquely (swash) but is swept back at right angles to the beach by the backwash. If the carrying power of the waves decreases, the material may be deposited to form a SPIT. To combat the effect of longshore drift, GROYNES are constructed. Another increasingly used method to combat the effect is to replace the material in a process known as "beach nourishment".

Lonicera

See HONEYSUCKLE

loofah

Old World tropical VINE of the GOURD family. It has lobed leaves and bright yellow or whitish flowers. Its cylindrical fruits can reach 0.6m (2ft) in length. The inner fibrous mesh formed by the vascular system of the mature fruit is used as a sponge or loofah. Family Cucurbitaceae; species *Luffa aegyptiaca*.

loon

See DIVER

loop of Henle

Portion of the NEPHRON of the KIDNEY. It has two regions: the descending limb, which has narrow walls readily permeable to water; and a wider ascending limb, with thick walls that are far less permeable to water. The loop of Henle is associated with the reabsorption of water by the kidney. Desert living mammals have longer loops of Henle than mammals living in regions where water is plentiful so that they can conserve water more effectively by producing small amounts of highly concentrated urine.

loosejaw

Any of several species of marine fish, related to VIPERFISH and DRAGONFISH. They have elongate jaws and bioluminescent light organs. Loosejaws are found in moderately deep waters. Family Stomiidae; species include *Aristostomias scintillans* (shiny loosejaw).

loosestrife

Any member of the genus *Lysimachia*, a large group of herbaceous perennials widely distributed in temperate and subtropical regions. Yellow loosestrife (*Lysimachia vulgaris*) is native to Europe and naturalized in the United States. It is densely covered in fine hairs and produces yellow flowers. Family Primulaceae; genus *Lysimachia*. The unrelated purple-loosestrifes belong to the genus *Lythrum* of the family Lythraceae.

loquat (Japanese medlar)

Small, evergreen, round-headed tree from China; it

L

▲ **lorikeet** The colourful purple-crowned lorikeet (*Glossopsitta prophyrocephala*) is found in dry woodland areas along only two stretches of coast in w Australia. Their diet consists of fruit, nectar and pollen and they play an important role in the pollination of flowers.

is widely cultivated in the tropics as a shade and ornamental tree. It is drought-resistant. Its yellow, woolly fruits have pleasant, acid-flavoured, white or yellow flesh and large brown seeds; the fruits are eaten fresh or preserved. Family Rosaceae; species *Eriobotrya japonica*.

L

lords-and-ladies
See CUCKOOPINT

Lorenz, Konrad (1903–89)
Austrian pioneer ethologist. Unlike psychologists, who studied animal behaviour in laboratories, Lorenz studied animals in their natural habitats. He observed that instinct played a major role in animal behaviour – for example in IMPRINTING, by which an animal may learn to identify its parents. Some of his views are expressed in his book *On Aggression* (1966). In 1973 he shared, with Nikolaas TINBERGEN and Karl Von FRISCH, the Nobel Prize for physiology or medicine. *See also* ETHOLOGY

lorikeet
Any of seven species of small green PARROT; they are found only in Australia. Lorikeets have brush-tipped tongues for feeding on nectar and pollen. They fly in noisy hurtling flocks looking for blossoms. The rainbow lorikeet (*Trichoglossus haematodus*) is the most common; it has a scarlet bill, streaked blue head and yellow nape. The purple-crowned lorikeet (*Glossopsitta porphyrocephala*) has crimson wing linings visible in flight. Length: 15–32cm (6–13in). Family Psittacidae; genera *Glossopsitta* and *Trichoglossus*.

loris
Either of two species of lower primate found in India and Southeast Asia. They are slow-moving and clamber amongst the tree branches using a strong grip aided by an opposable thumb. Order Primates; suborder Prosimii; family Lorisidae; subfamily Lorisinae (part).

loris, slender
Prosimian primate found in tropical forests of India and Sri Lanka. It is a slow-moving, nocturnal, arboreal mammal, which feeds mainly on insects and small vertebrates. It is grey or reddish, with large, dark eye patches and no tail. There are several sub-

species. Head-body length: 25cm (10in). Family Lorisidae; species *Loris tardigradus*.

loris, slow
Primate found in the rainforest of Southeast Asia. There are various subspecies of slow loris, all of which are similar to the slender loris. Its short, woolly fur can be light grey-brown to deep red-brown. It has dark eye rings and a stripe along its back. It feeds on insects and small vertebrates, with some fruit. Head-body length: 30–38cm (12–15in); tail: 5cm (2in). Family Lorisidae; species *Nysticebus coucang*.

lory
Any of various species of medium-sized PARROTS with rounded tails. They include the black lory (*Chalcopsitta atra*), found in New Guinea, and the red lory (*Eos bornea*), found in the Moluccas. Family Psittacidae.

lotus
Common name for any WATER LILY of the genus *Nelumbo* and several tropical species belonging to the genus *Nymphaea*. The circular leaves and flowers of some species can be 60cm (24in) wide. Family Nymphaeaceae. The genus *Lotus* is made up of the TREFOILS of the unrelated family Fabaceae/Leguminosae.

louse
Common name for various small, wingless insects that are parasitic on birds and mammals. There are two main groups, in different sub-orders of Phthiraptera: the biting lice (Mallophaga) and the sucking lice (Anoplura).

louse, biting
Any louse belonging to the Mallophaga order. Biting lice are small, flattened, wingless insects. They are parasitic mostly on birds. The females cement their eggs (known as nits) to feathers and hair. The newly hatched nymphs as well as the adults feed on scurf, hair and feathers. Among the many species of biting lice are the chicken louse (*Meriopori gallinae*), which parasitizes many types of fowl, and the pigeon louse (*Columbicola columbae*), whose hosts are doves and pigeons. Both species are less than 2.5mm (0.1in) long.

louse, sucking
Any louse belonging to the Anoplura order. Sucking lice ingest the blood of mammals. There are two main subspecies: *corporis*, found mainly on the body; and *capitis*, found mainly on the head. Both subspecies can breed very speedily. Eggs cemented to the hair or clothing of hosts hatch within 14 days; emerging larvae are immediately able to suck blood. Individuals are sexually mature between eight and 16 days later.

▲ **loris, slow** The slow loris (*Nysticebus coucang*) is found in the tropical forests of Southeast Asia. It is solitary, nocturnal and an excellent tree-climber capable of hanging by its feet and using its hands to feed. If threatened, it can exude a foul-smelling odour to deter predators.

▲ **lovebird** The black-masked lovebird (*Agapornis personata*) is native to Tanzania, E Africa, where it inhabits woody savanna. Lovebirds are named after their tendency to remain with a mate for life. They are often seen sitting and preening in pairs, which contributes to their popularity as cage birds.

The human louse (*Pediculus humanus*) usually attacks no other species. It is *c*.3mm (*c*.0.1in) long.

lousewort
Any member of the genus *Pedicularis*, a large group of herbaceous annuals and perennials from the Northern Hemisphere. They bear tubular, two-lipped, yellowish to purplish flowers in terminal spikes. The genus name comes from the Latin for louse: it refers to the superstition that livestock would suffer from lice if they fed on the plants. Family Scrophulariaceae; genus *Pedicularis*.

lovage
Herbaceous perennial that is native to Europe and has been introduced into North America. It smells of celery when crushed. Lovage was grown in medieval times for culinary and medicinal uses; the root and seeds have diuretic and carminative properties. An essence distilled from lovage is used in perfumery. Family Apiaceae; species *Levisticum officinale*.

lovebird
Small, green, African PARROT. It has a large head, a short neck and a very short tail. It typically has a pink face and a pink or yellow bill. The lovebird feeds on fruit and seeds, often on the ground, and flocks to water late in the afternoons. Length: 13–18cm (5–7in). Family Psittacidae; genus *Agapornis*.

love-in-a-mist
Herbaceous annual from s Europe; it is grown as a garden ornamental. Love-in-a-mist has finely divided leaves and ornate blue, white or pink flowers. Each flower sits above a profuse collar of finely dissected leaves. The fruit is a globular seed capsule. Family Ranunculaceae; species *Nigella damascena*.

love-lies-bleeding
Cultivated herbaceous annual, possibly originating in South America; it is grown as an ornamental. Its distinctive, long, trailing flower tassels are branched to varying degrees. They are usually deep red to maroon, although different varieties may have white, yellow or green flowers. Family Amaranthaceae; species *Amaranthus caudatus*.

lucerne
See ALFALFA

luciferin

Protein found in animal tissue that produces light when oxidized in the presence of the ENZYME luciferase. Luciferin is found in the light-generating organs of GLOW-WORMS and FIREFLIES. *See also* BIOLUMINESCENCE

lugworm

Marine ANNELID worm that lives in the sand of the seabed. With the aid of bristles, it burrows a u-shaped tunnel in sand or mud from which it rarely emerges. Length: up to 30cm (12in). Class Polychaeta; phylum Annelida; genus *Arenicola*.

lumpsucker (lumpfish or sea hen)

Marine fish of the North Atlantic coasts. The lumpsucker's pectoral fins are joined to form a sucker with which it attaches itself to rocks. Length: to 61cm (2ft). Family Cyclopteridae.

lungfish

Elongate fish from which the first AMPHIBIANS developed. It is found in shallow fresh water and swamps in Africa, South America and Australia. The lungfish has primitive lungs; during a dry season the various species can breath air or survive total dehydration by burrowing into the mud. Order Dipnoi.

lungs

Organs of the RESPIRATORY SYSTEM of vertebrates, in which the exchange of gases between air and blood takes place. They are located in a cavity (the **pleural cavity**) within the rib cage. This cavity is lined by two sheets of tissue (the PLEURA), one coating the lungs and the other lining the walls of the thorax. Between the pleura is a fluid that cushions the lungs and prevents friction. Light and spongy, lung tissue is composed of tiny air sacs, called alveoli, which are served by networks of fine CAPILLARIES. *See also* GAS EXCHANGE; VENTILATION

lupin

Any annual or perennial plants of the genus *Lupinus*, in the PEA family. They have star-shaped compound leaves and tall showy spikes of flowers. Height: to 2.4m (8ft). Family Fabaceae/Leguminosae.

Luría, Salvador Edward (1912–91)

US biologist, b. Italy. He shared the 1969 Nobel Prize for physiology or medicine with Max DELBRÜCK and Alfred HERSHEY for contributing to the knowledge of the growth, reproduction and mutation of viruses.

Lwoff, André Michel (1902–94)

French microbiologist. He shared the 1965 Nobel Prize for physiology or medicine with François

▲ **lungfish** The modern African lungfish (*Protopterus* sp.) is descended from the now extinct Dipterus (shown in outline), which evolved nearly 300 million years ago when inland waters gradually subsided as the land rose. African lungfish can survive dry periods for several years by burying themselves in mud and taking in air through a breathing hole.

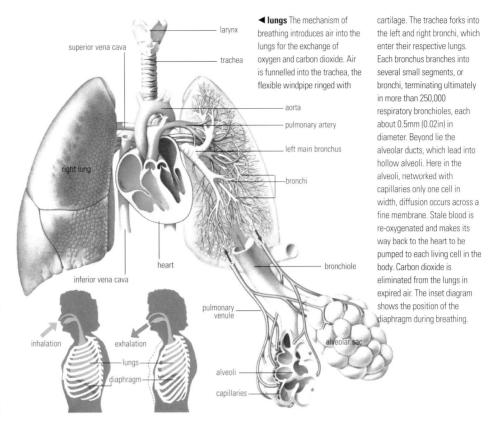

superior vena cava
larynx
trachea
aorta
pulmonary artery
left main bronchus
bronchi
right lung
heart
inferior vena cava
bronchiole
pulmonary venule
inhalation   exhalation
lungs
diaphragm
alveoli
capillaries
alveolar sac

◄ **lungs** The mechanism of breathing introduces air into the lungs for the exchange of oxygen and carbon dioxide. Air is funnelled into the trachea, the flexible windpipe ringed with cartilage. The trachea forks into the left and right bronchi, which enter their respective lungs. Each bronchus branches into several small segments, or bronchi, terminating ultimately in more than 250,000 respiratory bronchioles, each about 0.5mm (0.02in) in diameter. Beyond lie the alveolar ducts, which lead into hollow alveoli. Here in the alveoli, networked with capillaries only one cell in width, diffusion occurs across a fine membrane. Stale blood is re-oxygenated and makes its way back to the heart to be pumped to each living cell in the body. Carbon dioxide is eliminated from the lungs in expired air. The inset diagram shows the position of the diaphragm during breathing.

JACOB and Jacques MONOD for work on the genetics of VIRUSES. Lwoff studied the means by which these destroy the bacteria they infect.

lychee

Round-topped tree from China; it is widely grown in tropical regions. Its round fruits, which are bright red when ripe, have a hard, brittle, rough outer shell; the edible, white, translucent and juicy flesh separates readily from the seed and has a sweet-acid flavour. Height: 12m (39ft). Family Sapindaceae; species *Litchi chinensis*.

lycopodophyte

Any member of the phylum Lycopodophyta, which comprises c.1000 species of VASCULAR PLANTS, including the CLUB MOSSES, spike mosses and QUILLWORTS. Related to FERNS, lycopodophytes have branching underground stems (RHIZOMES) and upright shoots supported by roots. Some lycopodophyte species are EPIPHYTES.

Lyell, Sir Charles (1797–1875)

British geologist who was influential in shaping 19th-century ideas about science. He wrote the popular books *Principles of Geology* (1830–33), *Elements of Geology* (1838) and *The Geological Evidence of the Antiquity of Man* (1863).

lygus bug

Brightly coloured true BUG that feeds primarily on plant sap. Lygus bugs damage fruit and field crops and are considered pests. They become most injurious between the fourth and fifth moults. Areas containing permanent crop cover, for example orchards, are favoured by lygus bugs. Order Heteroptera; family Miridae.

lymph

Clear, slightly yellowish fluid derived from BLOOD and similar in composition to PLASMA. Circulating in the LYMPHATIC SYSTEM, it conveys LEUCOCYTES (white blood cells) and some nutrients to the tissues.

lymphatic system

See feature article, page 232

lymphocyte

Type of LEUCOCYTE (white blood cell) found in vertebrates. Produced in the bone MARROW, it is mostly found in the LYMPH and blood and around infected sites. In humans lymphocytes form about 25% of leucocytes and play an important role in combating disease. There are two main kinds: B-lymphocytes, responsible for producing antibodies, and T-lymphocytes, which have various roles in the IMMUNE SYSTEM.

lynx

Medium-sized CAT distributed from W Europe to Siberia, Canada and N United States. It hunts small mammals, birds and fish in a variety of habitats, often

L

▲ **lynx** The endangered south European lynx (*Felis pardina*) is found only in inaccessible mountain sierras in S Spain and Portugal. Closely related to the common lynx (*Felix lynx*), it is usually classed as a separate species, and it has more clearly defined markings.

LYMPHATIC SYSTEM

System of connecting vessels and organs in vertebrates that transports LYMPH through the body. Lymph flows into tiny and delicate lymph capillaries and from these into lymph vessels, or lymphatics. Lymphatics extend throughout the body, joining to form larger vessels, which lead to lymph nodes. The nodes collect lymph and store some of the LEUCOCYTES (white blood cells). Lymph nodes empty into large vessels, linking up into lymph ducts that empty back into the CIRCULATORY SYSTEM. The lymphatic system plays a major role in the body's IMMUNE SYSTEM. At the lymph nodes, MACROPHAGES (large leucocytes) trapped in a network of fibres remove foreign particles, including bacteria, from the lymph. The lymph

nodes also supply LYMPHOCYTES to the blood. The lymph vessels provide a route for certain nutrients to enter the bloodstream. Fat droplets that are too large to enter the capillaries of the VILLI in the small intestine pass into the lymph vessels for transport to the circulatory system.

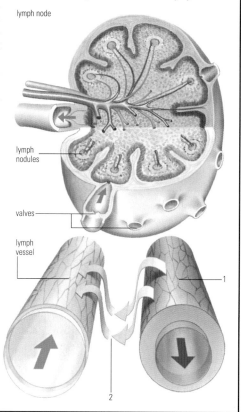

lymph node

lymph nodules

valves

lymph vessel

1

2

► **The lymphatic system** is a network of lymphatic vessels that collect tissue fluid (the lymph) and conduct it back to the bloodstream. The lymph is formed when high arterial pressure forces fluid out of the capillaries (1) into the tissue spaces (2), from where it is taken up into the lymphatic vessels. In the process it transports nutrients from blood to cells, and cell wastes back into capillaries. Lymph drains through the system, but the lymphatics possess valves to prevent backflow. Lymphatic nodes are scattered along the lymph vessels, but particularly in the neck, armpits and groin. In the tissue around the nodes micro-organisms are destroyed by macrophage cells, while anti-body-synthesizing white blood cells, the lymphocytes, are produced by the lymph nodules.

feeder. Length: male, including tail, 100cm (39in); females: 86cm (34in). Family Menuridae; species *Menura novaehollandiae*.

Lysenko, Trofim Denisovich (1898–1976)
Russian agronomist and geneticist. He expanded the theory of LAMARCK to include his own ideas of plant genetics (**Lysenkoism**). Lysenko promised the Soviet government vast increases in crop yields through the application of his theories. He enjoyed official sanction under Stalin, but in the late 1950s his influence waned.

lysis
Destruction of a CELL. A living cell may be destroyed when its outer cell wall is dissolved by LYSOSOMES or when it is digested in phagocytosis by PHAGOCYTES – a normal reaction against invading bacterial cells.

lysosome
Small membranous sac that occurs within the cytoplasm of an animal CELL. The lysosome contains enzymes that control the breakdown of foreign substances entering the cell, the digestion of the contents of food VACUOLES and the breakdown of the cell itself after it dies.

L

in forest or dense vegetation. Its coat colour varies from grey-brown to reddish, sometimes with dark spots. The lynx is distinguished by its short tail and by its ear tufts tipped with black. Head-body length: 67–110cm (26–43in); tail: 5–17cm (2–7in). Family Felidae; species *Felis lynx*.

lyrebird, superb
Songbird of Australian rainforests. The male lyrebird is rich-brown above, with a long lyre-shaped tail. It displays to the female on small raked earth mounds, raising and spreading its tail whilst delivering a spectacular song. It is a specialized ground-

▲ **lyrebird, superb** A secretive bird, the superb lyrebird is rarely seen as it hides in densely vegetated gullies in inaccessible parts of temperate forests. The male bird uses his impressive tail feathers in a spectacular courtship display. The female is remarkably fastidious – she carries all the droppings from the nest and puts them in a nearby stream.

M

◄ **mackerel** The common
mackerel (*Scomber scombrus*),
*c.*30cm (*c.*12in) in length, is
found in huge shoals along the
coasts of the N Atlantic Ocean.
Like all species of mackerel,
they spawn in the spring;
females can produce up to
200,000 eggs in one season.

maar
Coneless volcanic crater formed by a single explosive eruption that is not accompanied by a flow of LAVA. A crater ring surrounds the hole. *See also* VOLCANO

macadamia
Any member of the *Macadamia* genus, a group of trees found in Australia. Most species have stiff, oblong, lance-like leaves. The edible seeds are round, hard-shelled nuts (also known as Queensland nuts), covered by thick husks that split when ripe. Height: to 18m (59ft). Family Proteaceae.

macaque
Any of 15 species of heavily built MONKEYS belonging to the genus *Macaca*. Most species eat fruit, leaves, crops and small animals in both terrestrial and arboreal habitats. The often naked skin on the face and rump of some species is usually bright red. Family Cercopithecidae.

macaque, Barbary (Barbary ape, rock ape)
Macaque that is native to mountainous regions of N Algeria and Morocco. The Barbary macaque has been introduced to Gibraltar. Head-body length: 50–60cm (20–24in); no tail. Family Cercopithecidae; species *Macaca sylvanus*.

macaque, bonnet
Macaque that inhabits forest edges and outskirts of human habitations in s India. It is distinguished by a noticeable whorl of hair growing on the top of its head. Head-body length: 35–60cm (14–24in); tail: 48–69cm (19–27in). Family Cercopithecidae; species *Macaca radiata*.

macaque, crab-eating (long-tailed macaque)
Macaque that lives along the forest edges and watercourses of Indonesia and the Philippines. Head-body length: 38–65cm (15–26in); tail: 40–66cm (16–26in). Family Cercopithecidae; species *Macaca fasciularis*.

macaque, Japanese
Macaque that is native to the forests of Japan. Head-body length: 47–60cm (19–24in); tail: 7–12cm (3–5in). Family Cercopithecidae; species *Macaca fuscata*.

macaque, pig-tailed
Macaque that inhabits wet forests from E India to Indonesia. Head-body length: 47–60cm (19–24in); tail: 13–24cm (5–9in). Family Cercopithecidae; species *Macaca nemestrina*.

macaque, rhesus (rhesus monkey)
Macaque that lives along forest edges and outskirts of human habitations from India and Afghanistan to China and Vietnam. Head-body length: 47–64cm (19–25in); tail: 19–30cm (7–12in). Family Cercopithecidae; species *Macaca mulatta*.

macaw
Very large South American PARROT with a long, slender tail. The scarlet macaw is bright red with a wing pattern of red, yellow and blue. The military macaw is green all over with bright yellow under its wings and tail. Length: 27–38cm (11–15in). Family Psittacidae; genus *Ara*.

McClung, Clarence Erwin (1870–1946)
US zoologist who discovered the mechanism of chromosomal SEX DETERMINATION. He postulated that CHROMOSOMES determine sex and that the X-chromosome is the crucial element. His work stimulated further research, and by 1905 Edmund WILSON had developed the theory, now generally accepted, that both X- and Y-chromosomes form the basis of sex determination.

mace
Spice obtained from the network of bright red tissue (aril) that covers the seed of the NUTMEG. Mace has a delicate flavour and is used in cooking, particularly for fish, and also in baking. Family Myristicaceae; species *Myristica fragrans*.

mackerel
Fast-swimming, agile, marine food fish related to the TUNA. It is found in shoals in the N Atlantic, N Pacific and Indian oceans. The mackerel has a streamlined body and powerful tail. Its body is silvery blue with dark side bars. It has a voracious appetite and feeds on smaller fish and plankton. Length: 61cm (24in). Family Scombridae.

macromolecule
MOLECULE that is composed of a very large number of ATOMS. Examples of macromolecules include PROTEINS and NUCLEIC ACIDS.

macronutrient
Element needed in relatively large amounts by growing plants. Macronutrients include carbon, hydrogen, oxygen and nitrogen, as well as calcium, magnesium, phosphorus, potassium and sulphur. *See also* MICRONUTRIENT

macrophage
Large LEUCOCYTE (white blood cell) found mainly in the liver, spleen and lymph nodes. It engulfs foreign particles and microorganisms by PHAGOCYTOSIS. Working together with other LYMPHOCYTES, it forms part of the body's IMMUNE SYSTEM.

madder
Perennial VINE native to s Europe and Asia. It bears greenish-yellow flowers. A red dye was once produced from the roots. Height: to 1.2m (3.9ft). Family Rubiaceae; species *Rubia tinctorium*.

Madeira vine
Fast-growing, ornamental, climbing VINE. Native to tropical America, it has long been cultivated in Madeira and is grown as a decorative cover for porches and arbours. The plant has been known as a weed in sugar cane. Family Basellaceae; species *Anredera cordifolia*.

madroña (laurelwood)
Broadleafed, evergreen tree native to British Columbia, Canada, and N United States. It has small, white flowers and orange-red fruit. Height: 15–30m (49–98ft). Family Ericaceae; species *Arbutus menziesii*.

maggot
Name commonly given to the legless LARVA of a FLY. It is primarily used to describe those larvae that infest food and waste material; others are generally called grubs or CATERPILLARS. *See also* METAMORPHOSIS

magma
Molten rock beneath the surface of the Earth; it forms IGNEOUS ROCKS when it solidifies. Below the surface, cooling is slow and large crystals form as the rock solidifies. Large masses of magma are in BATHOLITHS, and thin seams of magma create SILLS and DYKES. If magma reaches the surface, it flows out as LAVA. The different igneous rocks formed by magma vary according to their chemical content as well as according to the depth of formation. *See also* EXTRUSIVE ROCK

magma chamber
Reservoir of molten rock several kilometres below

M

blue and
yellow macaw

hyacinth
macaw

▲ **macaw** Blue and yellow macaws (*Ara arauna*) are usually seen in pairs. They inhabit forested areas along rivers and swamps. The hyacinth macaw (*Anodorhynchus hyacinthinus*) is the largest species of parrot, reaching up to 1m (39in) in length. It is more commonly found in grassland or wetlands than in rainforest.

MAGNETOSPHERE

Region of space surrounding a planet in which the planet's magnetic field predominates over the SOLAR WIND and controls the behaviour of plasma (charged particles) trapped within it. The boundary of the magnetosphere is called the **magnetopause**, outside which is a turbulent mag-netic region called the **magnetosheath**. Downwind from the planet, the solar wind draws the magnetosphere out into a long, tapering **magnetotail**. Mercury, Earth and the giant planets have magnetospheres. The Earth's contains the VAN ALLEN RADIATION BELTS of charged particles.

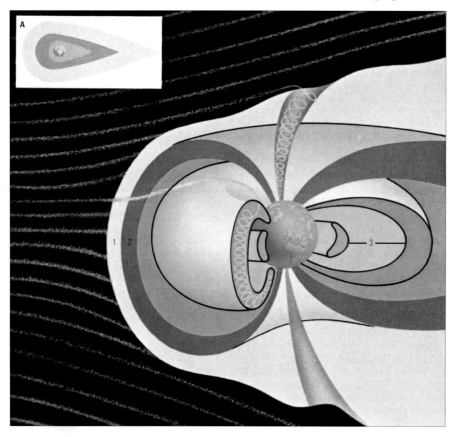

▲ **The magnetosphere is** the region in which the Earth's magnetic field can be detected. It would be symmetrical were it not for electrically charged particles streaming from the Sun (A), which distort it to a teardrop shape. The particles meet the Earth's magnetic field at the shock front (1). Behind this is a region of turbulence, and inside the turbulent region is the magnetopause (2), the boundary of the magnetic field. The Van Allen belts (3) are two zones of high radiation in the magnetopause. The inner belt consists of high-energy particles produced by cosmic rays and the outer belt of solar electrons.

the surface of the Earth's CRUST. Processes of differentiation may significantly change the composition of the magmatic product, for example producing lava from the parent MAGMA.

magnet

Object that produces a MAGNETIC FIELD, an area around the magnet in which other magnetizable objects experience a force. Lodestones, which are naturally magnetic, were used as early magnets; strong magnetic materials were later recognized as containing IRON, COBALT or NICKEL. A typical permanent magnet is a straight or horseshoe-shaped magnetized iron bar with the ends called the north and south magnetic poles. The EARTH is a giant magnet, its magnetic lines of force being detectable at all latitudes.

magnetic anomaly

Small variations in the Earth's MAGNETIC FIELD caused by large iron objects or deposits.

magnetic field

Region surrounding a MAGNET, or a conductor through which a current is flowing, in which magnet-ic effects, such as the deflection of a compass needle, can be detected. A magnetic field can be represented by a set of lines of force (flux lines) spreading out from the poles of a magnet or running around a current-carrying conductor. These lines of force can be seen if iron filings are sprinkled on to a sheet of paper below which a magnet is placed. The filings line up along the lines of force, the density of the lines being greatest where the field is strongest. The direction of a magnetic field is the direction a tiny magnet takes when placed in the field. **Magnetic poles** are the field regions in which MAGNETISM appears to be concentrated. If a bar magnet is suspended to swing freely in the horizontal plane, one pole will point north; this is called the north-seeking or **north pole**. The other pole, the south-seeking or **south pole**, will point south. Unlike poles attract each other; like poles repel each other. **Earth's magnetic poles** are the ends of the huge "magnet" that is Earth.

magnetic field reversal

Reversal of polarity whereby the Earth's north magnetic pole becomes the south and vice versa. Analyses of the magnetic direction of land and ocean basaltic lavas and seafloor sediments have shown that the Earth's main MAGNETIC FIELD has undergone frequent and rapid reversals. The field has changed many times in the past four million years. *See also* PALAEOMAGNETISM

magnetic storm (geomagnetic storm)

Disturbance in the Earth's MAGNETIC FIELD. Since the field encompasses all the Earth, the effects of such a storm are global: AURORAS are seen, both in areas where such displays are normal and in others as well; and radio signals are disturbed.

magnetism

Properties of matter and of electric currents associated with a field of force (MAGNETIC FIELD) and with a north–south polarity (magnetic poles). All substances possess these properties to some degree because orbiting ELECTRONS in their atoms produce a magnetic field in the same way as an electric current produces a magnetic field; similarly, an external magnetic field will affect the electron orbits. All substances possess weak magnetic properties and will tend to align themselves with the field, but in some cases this diamagnetism is masked by the stronger forms of magnetism: paramagnetism and ferromagnetism. **Paramagnetism** is caused by electron spin and occurs in substances having unpaired electrons in their atoms or molecules. The most important form of magnetism, **ferromagnetism,** is shown by substances such as IRON and NICKEL, which can be magnetized by even a weak field due to the formation of tiny regions, called domains, that behave like miniature magnets and align themselves with an external field. These domains are formed as a result of strong, interatomic forces caused by the spin of electrons in unfilled, inner electron shells of the atoms. **Permanent magnets**, which retain their magnetization after the magnetizing field has been removed, are ferromagnetic. Electromagnets have a ferromagnetic core around which a conducting coil is wound. The passage of a current through the coil magnetizes the core.

magnetite (ferrosoferric oxide, Fe_3O_4)

Oxide mineral, iron(II)-iron(III) oxide. The most magnetic mineral, it is a valuable iron ore found in IGNEOUS and METAMORPHIC ROCKS. It displays cubic system, octahedral and dodecahedral crystals, and granular masses are also common. It is black, metallic and brittle. Permanently magnetized deposits are called **lodestone**. Hardness 6; r.d. 5.2.

magnetosphere

See feature article

magnolia

Any of *c*.40 species of trees and shrubs of the genus *Magnolia*, native to North and Central America and E Asia. Magnolias are valued for their white, yellow, purple or pink flowers. Height: to 30m (98ft). Family Magnoliaceae.

magpie

Name given to a variety of birds, most of them

◄ **magnolia** The flowers of the magnolia tree or shrub reveal it to be a relatively primitive plant. As with the earliest known flowering plants, its sepals resemble its petals. Shown here is the star magnolia (*Magnolia stellata*) native to Japan.

M

▲ **magpie** The common magpie (*Pica pica*) of Europe and North America, which grows to c.46cm (c.18in), has gained an unfavourable reputation primarily due to its aggressive behaviour towards other birds, and its tendency to kill distressed lambs or sickly calves.

belonging to the CROW family. Some species, such as the Eurasian magpie (*Pica pica*), have bold, black-and-white plumage and long tails; other species, such as the green magpie (*Cissa chinensis*) found in Asia, are bright green. The Australian magpie (*Gymnorthina tibicen*) is unrelated to the crows, but it shares the black-and-white plumage. The azure-winged magpie (*Cyanopica cyana*) has a jet black cap and bright blue wings and tail; it is found in China, with an isolated population in Spain and Portugal thought to have been introduced by 17th-century sailors. Length: to 45cm (18in). Family Corvidae.

magpie-lark
Bold, aggressive, medium-sized ground bird. It is found in Australasia. It has conspicuous, black-and-white plumage. The magpie-lark has a distinctive flight on rounded pulsating wings. It is most closely related to the torrent lark of New Guinea. Length: 26–30cm (10–12in). Family Grallinidae; species *Grallina cyanoleuca*.

magpie-robin
Medium-sized songbird found in s Asia; it belongs to the THRUSH family. It is blackish all over with white wing patches and a long cocked tail with white sides. It frequents gardens and woodlands. Length: 23cm (9in). Family Turdidae; species *Copsychus saularis*.

mahogany
Any of numerous species of tropical American deciduous trees and their hard, reddish wood, valued for furniture making. Mahogany trees have composite leaves, large clusters of flowers and winged seeds. Height: to 18m (59ft). Family Meliaceae.

maidenhair fern
Any member of the genus *Adiantum*, a group of dainty FERNS found in limestone areas in Europe and North America. The wedge-shaped leaves are borne on slender, shiny, black stalks. Leaves of most species are pink as they unfold, then turn pea-green. Height: 25–50cm (10–20in). Family Adiantaceae; species include *Adiantum capillus-veneris*.

maidenhair tree
See GINKGO

maiden's hair
Olive or yellowish-brown SEAWEED common in colder seas of the Northern Hemisphere and found from NW Europe to the Mediterranean. It has limp, irregularly divided fronds up to 30cm (12in) long, which are made up of plaited, branching, fine filaments. Maiden's hair grows from a creeping holdfast attached to stones, rocks or larger seaweeds. Family Ectocarpaceae; genus *Ectocarpus*.

maize (corn or sweet corn)
CEREAL plant of the GRASS family. Originally from Central America, it is now the key cereal in most subtropical zones. Edible seeds grow in rows upon a cob, protected by a leafy sheath. Height: to 5m (16ft). Family Graminae; species *Zea mays*.

malachite ($Cu_2CO_3(OH)_2$)
Carbonate mineral, basic copper carbonate, found in

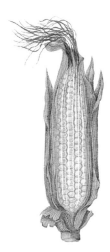

◄ **maize** One of the most important grain crops, maize is cultivated worldwide for human and animal consumption, although it is less nutritious than other cereals. It is a good source of carbohydrates but contains poor quality protein. Corn oil, flour and popcorn are among the most common uses for corn seeds. They are also used in various manufacturing processes, paint and linoleum for example, and as a source of furfural, which is used as a solvent and in the manufacture of resins.

weathered copper ore deposits. Malachite has a monoclinic system, and is green in colour. It is sometimes used as a gemstone. Hardness 3.5–4; r.d. 4.

malimbe
Small, seed-eating, African finch; it is related to the WEAVERBIRD. The malimbe's plumage is black and red, usually having a black back, red body, red crested head and red throat. The malimbe is found in forest canopies and along streams in dense undergrowth. Length: 15–20cm (6–8in). Family Ploceidae; genus *Malimbus*.

mallard
Large dabbling DUCK found throughout North America and Europe; it has been introduced into Australia and New Zealand. The mallard is the ancestor of the farmyard duck. The male mallard, or drake, has a green head, narrow white collar and purple-brown breast; the female is mottled brown. Both sexes have a purple wing patch. Length: 51–62cm (20–24in). Family Anatidae; species *Anas platyrhynchos*.

mallee
Type of scrub consisting mainly of trees and shrubs

M

▶ **mahogany** The tropical forest in the Amazon basin in Peru is full of valuable hardwood trees. Roads have been built by logging companies in order to access this strong timber. Settlers from the overpopulated highlands of Peru also travel along these roads in order to find land. Forest destruction in this region is caused by the practice of slash-and-burn farming by these settlers as well as by the commercial loggers.

► **mammoth** The mammoth was a hairy, elephant-like mammal that inhabited the steppes and tundra of North America, Europe and Asia during the Ice Ages of the Pleistocene period. The mammoth was a herbivore, with a body that was of a similar size to that of a modern elephant but with a larger head and tusks.

of the genus *Eucalyptus*. Mallee is found mainly in Australia, especially in areas with a semi-arid or dry climate. EUCALYPTUS plants have leathery leaves, which conserve moisture during dry periods.

mallee fowl

Large Australian fowl. It is barred grey, black and white, with a bold, black breast mark. The male has a far carrying, three-noted, booming voice. The mallee fowl is found in sandy-soiled scrubland, but it is now becoming rare, unable to compete with land clearance and food competition from rabbits and sheep. It hatches its large clutch inside a specially constructed mound of sand and rotting leaves. Length: 55–60cm (22–24in). Family Megapodiidae; species *Leipoa ocellata*.

mallow

Any member of the family Malvaceae, a group of annual, biennial and perennial plants found in tropical and temperate regions. The flowers are pink and white. The family includes more than 900 species of plants, of which COTTON, OKRA and HIBISCUS are among the best known. Family Malvaceae; main genus *Malva*.

Malpighi, Marcello (1628–94)

Italian physiologist. He was a founder of microscopic anatomy, demonstrating how blood reaches the tissues through tiny vessels (CAPILLARIES). Malpighi explained the network of capillaries on the surface of the lung. The Malpighian tubules of the kidney and the MALPIGHIAN LAYER are among the structures named after him.

Malpighian layer

Innermost layer of the EPIDERMIS of the skin. A fibrous basement membrane separates the Malpighian layer from the DERMIS beneath. The layer

contains polygonal cells, which continually divide by MITOSIS. As the cells grow older, they move slowly through the epidermis to replace dead surface skin cells that have been worn away. The layer is named after Marcello MALPIGHI.

maltose (malt sugar, $C_{12}H_{22}O_{11}$)

Disaccharide that contains two molecules of the simple sugar GLUCOSE. Maltose is produced by the HYDROLYSIS of STARCH by the enzyme AMYLASE and by the breakdown of starches and GLYCOGEN during DIGESTION.

mamba

Any of several large, poisonous African tree snakes of the COBRA family. The **black mamba** (*Dendroaspis polylepsis*) is the largest species. It is grey, greenish-brown or black and is notoriously aggressive; its bite is almost always fatal. Length: to 4.3m (14ft). Family Elapidae.

mammal

See feature article, pages 238–39

mammary gland (breast)

Organ of a female MAMMAL that secretes milk to nourish newborn young. In males the glands are rudimentary and nonfunctional. The human female breast, which develops during puberty, is made up of between 15 and 20 irregularly shaped lobes separated by connective and fat tissue. Lactiferous ducts lead from each lobe to the nipple.

mammoth

Any member of a group of extinct elephant relatives, such as *Mammuthus primigenius*, which developed adaptations to life in cold climates during early Pleistocene times. They survived until 3700 years ago on Wrangel island in the Arctic. Mammoths developed a covering of thick, woolly hair and fat reserves; they had small ears and tails and long curved tusks. Their FROZEN BODIES have been found in permafrost. Images of mammoths were painted by early modern humans.

man

See HOMO

manakin

Any member of a family of small, large-headed forest birds that are found in South America. The males

▲ **mandrill** The extraordinary colours of the mandrill's face intensify if the animal becomes annoyed or excited. Zoologists believe that this visual display has replaced the baring of teeth to express anger common to most other baboons.

usually have bright plumage, whereas the females are mostly a dull green. Family Pipridae; there are c.50 species.

manatee

Any of three species of large, plant-eating, subungulate, aquatic mammals found primarily in shallow coastal waters of the Atlantic Ocean. The manatee's tapered body ends in a large rounded flipper; there are no hindlimbs. Length: to 4.5m (14.7ft); weight: 680kg (1500lb). Family Trichechidae; genus *Trichechus*. See also DUGONG

mancineel tree

Coastal tree native to Mexico and the West Indies; it is grown as a wind-break. The latex of the mancineel tree is poisonous and if the eyes are exposed to it, temporary blindness may result. Family Euphorbiaceae; species *Hippomane mancinella*.

mandarin (mandarine)

Type of ORANGE popular for its sweet flavour. The **tangerine** is a flattish, loose-skinned variety of mandarin orange. Family Rutaceae; species *Citrus reticulata*.

mandible

In vertebrates, the lower JAW. In insects and CRUSTACEANS, one of a pair of mouthparts used for crushing and eating.

mandrake

Plant of the POTATO family, native to the Mediterranean region and used since ancient times as a medicine. It contains the ALKALOIDS hyoscyamine, scopolamin and mandragorine. Its leaves are borne at the base of the stem, and the large greenish-yellow or purple flowers produce a many-seeded berry. Height: 40cm (16in). Family Solanaceae; species *Mandragora officinarum*.

mandrill

Large BABOON that lives in dense rainforests of central W Africa. Mandrills roam in small troops and forage for their food on the forest floor. The male has a red-tipped, pale blue nose, yellow-bearded cheeks and a reddish rump. Height: 75cm (30in) at the shoulder; weight: to 54kg (119lb). Family Cercopithecidae; species *Mandrillus sphinx*.

mangabey

Any of four species of Old World MONKEY belong-

► **manatee** Found in warm shallow waters, manatees are marine mammals that feed exclusively on vegetation. The fleshy lobes on their upper lips are sufficiently mobile to seize food and pass it to the mouth. They have no natural enemies but are sometimes hunted for meat, blubber and hides.

M

ing to the genus *Cerocebus*. Mangabeys resemble light-weight, long-tailed BABOONS, to which they are closely related. They are very vocal and live in large noisy groups containing both sexes and all ages. Mangabeys inhabit closed-canopy forests of tropical Africa, two species living high in the branches, and two species nearer the ground to reduce competition. Their strong teeth enable them to eat very hard seeds. Head-body length: 45–70cm (18–27in) tail: 70–100cm (28–39in). Family Cercopithecidae; species include *Cerocebus aterrimus* (black mangabey).

manganese nodules
Concretions with diameters averaging 4cm (2in) that occur in red clay and ooze on the floor of the Pacific Ocean, with the major concentrations around the Samoan Islands. They contain high concentrations of manganese. They are thought to have formed as agglomerates from colloidal solution in the ocean's waters. The commercial mining of the nodules is being delayed by legal controversy over international rights to this valuable mineral resource.

manganite (MnO[OH])
Hydroxide mineral of the diaspore group, manganese oxyhydroxide. It occurs as low-temperature veins and secondary deposits. It has monoclinic system, striated prisms, which are often crusts of small crystals. Its colour is black or grey with a submetallic lustre. Hardness 4; r.d. 4.3.

mangel-wurzel (fodder beet)
Cultivated variety of BEET, originating in Europe. It is a biennial. It has a whorl of leaves and a swollen tap root, which contains reserves of sugar. Mangel-wurzel is cultivated for its heavy yielding roots, which are used for feeding livestock. Family Chenopodiaceae; species *Beta vulgaris*.

mango
Evergreen tree native to Southeast Asia and grown widely in the tropics for its fruit. It has lance-shaped leaves and pinkish-white, clustered flowers. Its yellow-red fruit is eaten ripe or preserved when green. Height: to 18m (59ft). Family Anacardiaceae; species *Mangifera indica*.

mangosteen
Small tropical fruit tree, native to Southeast Asia. The roundish fruit has thick, hard purple rind, which surrounds the white, edible flesh. Family Guttiferae; species *Garcinia mangostana*.

mangrove
Common name for any of *c*.120 species of tropical trees or shrubs found in marine swampy areas. Their stilt-like aerial roots, which arise from the branches and hang down into the water, produce a thick undergrowth, which is useful in the reclaiming of land along tropical coasts. Some mangrove species

▶ **mango** The fruit of the mango tree has a delicate fragrance. Its juicy flesh surrounds a single flat seed. The tree itself is grown as a garden plant throughout the tropical region.

▲ **mantis** When lying in wait for insects, the praying mantis (*Sphodromantis lineata*) sits motionless, holding its forelegs in a pose reminiscent of a person praying, hence its name. Its diet consists solely of live prey, which it grasps tightly between its spiny forelegs. The mantis is the only species of insect able to turn its head in any direction.

also have roots that rise up out of the water. Height: to 20m (70ft). The main family is Rhizophoraceae.

manila hemp
See ABACA

manioc
See CASSAVA

manna ash
See FLOWERING ASH

mantis (praying mantis)
Any of several species of mantids, insects found throughout the world. They have powerful front legs, which they use to catch and hold their insect prey. Colours range from brown and green to bright pinks. Length: 25–150mm (1–6in). Family Mantidae.

mantispid (mantis fly)
Insect that is related to the LACEWING but resembles the praying mantis. It has a long prothorax (first segment of the THORAX), with front legs modified to catch its prey, mainly other insects. The larvae predate spiders and wasps. Adult body size: *c*.7mm (*c*.0.3in). Order Neuroptera; family Mantisipidae; genus *Mantispa*.

mantle
Layer of the EARTH between the CRUST and the CORE, down to 2900km (1800mi). Its boundaries are determined by major changes in seismic velocity. The mantle forms the greatest bulk of the Earth – 82% of its volume and 68% of its mass. Several distinct parts of the mantle have been recognized. The uppermost part is rigid, solid and brittle and together with the Earth's crust forms the LITHOSPHERE. The upper mantle also has a soft zone, which is called the ASTHENOSPHERE. Temperature and pressure are in delicate balance, so that much of the mantle material is near melting point, or partially melted and capable of flowing. Recent studies have suggested this layer is responsible for the production of basaltic MAGMAS. The remainder of the mantle is thought to be more solid, but still capable of creeping flow. In the lower mantle, several changes in seismic velocity can be detected, interpreted as mineral phase changes, in which the atomic packing is rearranged into denser and more compact units. The chemical constitution of the mantle is uncertain, but it is thought to be made up of iron-magnesium silicates.

mantle plume
Persistent upwelling of hot MANTLE material beneath the CRUST. It is thought to be responsible for HOT SPOTS, such as those that lie beneath the volcanic islands of Hawaii

manucode
Any of five species of glossy, blue-black, medium-sized songbirds found in Australasian rainforests; they belong to the BIRD OF PARADISE family. Manucodes are shy birds of the forest canopy. The males produce loud, often trumpet-like calls. Length: 32cm (13in). Family Paradisaeidae; genus *Manucodia*.

maple (acer)
Any member of the genus *Acer*, a group of deciduous trees native to temperate and cool regions of Europe, Asia and North America. They have yellowish or greenish flowers and winged seeds. They are grown for ornament, shade or timber, depending on the species; the sugar maple is also tapped for maple syrup. Height: 4.6–36m (15–118ft). Family Aceraceae; genus *Acer*.

mara (Patagonian cavy, Patagonian hare)
Long-legged relative of the GUINEA PIG, native to dry scrubland in Argentina. Maras are among the very few mammals to live in life-time monogamous pairs. Twice a year they produce litters of between one and three young, which, despite being unsociable animals, they leave in communal burrows. Maras feed during the day on grasses and herbs. Head-body length 50–75cm (20–30in); tail: 5cm (2in). Family Caviidae; species *Dolichotis patagonum*.

marble
METAMORPHIC ROCK composed largely of recrystallized LIMESTONES and DOLOMITES. The term is more loosely used to refer to any crystalline CALCIUM CARBONATE (CaCO₃) rock that has a good pattern and colour when cut and polished. The colour is normally white, but when tinted by serpentine, iron oxide or carbon it can vary to shades of yellow, green, red, brown or black. Marble has been a favourite building and sculpting material of many ancient and modern civilizations.

march-fly
Any member of the family Bibionidae found worldwide. The larvae feed on plant roots and decaying vegetable matter. Adults employ a variety of predacious techniques in capturing and eating other insects. Species include the assassin-fly and the fever-fly. Adult body size: *c*.7mm (*c*.0.3in). Order Diptera; family Bibionidae; there are *c*.700 species.

mare's tail
Aquatic perennial plant found throughout temperate and cold regions of the Northern Hemisphere. The creeping stem produces erect leafy shoots, which

▲ **mara** An inhabitant of open arid grassland in Patagonia, the mara is well adapted to running swiftly, having longer legs than other species of cavy. It has sharp claws on each foot, which help it to dig large burrows.

M

ammals make up the class Mammalia. They
are vertebrate animals characterized by MAM-
MARY GLANDS in the female and full, partial or vestigial hair covering. As a group, mammals are
active, alert and intelligent. There is a wide range of
features, shapes and sizes among mammals. The
class Mammalia includes 17 orders of PLACENTALS,
one MARSUPIAL order – all live-bearing – and an
order of egg-laying MONOTREMES. Mammals probably evolved about 180 million years ago from a
group of warm-blooded reptiles.

Mammals are the largest land animals to rise to
prominence since the dinosaurs and are one of the
most successful groups in the animal kingdom.
From 4-cm (1.6-in) pygmy SHREWS to 100-ton
WHALES, the 4500 species of mammal have
explored and adapted to most of the planet's different habitats, evolving a wide range of shapes,
sizes and lifestyles on the way.

Mammals owe their success to two essential factors:
they are ENDOTHERMIC (warm-blooded), which
means that they can function regardless of the temperature; and they suckle and look after their young.

The evolution of endothermy gave early mammals an essential competitive edge over reptiles,
because it enabled mammals to be more active at
lower temperature, and so able to exploit more ecological niches. The suckling of the young on the
female's milk and the investment of parental care
are also highly important. Protected and fed, the
young can grow rapidly and learn skills from adults:
chimpanzees, for example, learn to use sticks as
tools, and many carnivorous mammals learn hunting techniques.

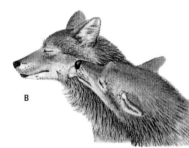

M

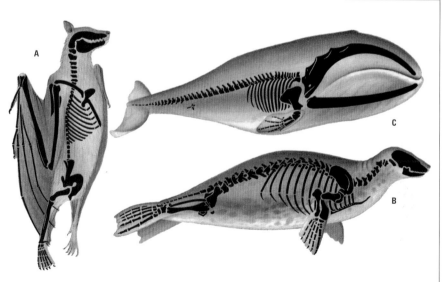

mammary duct

nipple

A

B

C

◀ ▲ **The feeding of** offspring
(A) on the female's milk is one
of the distinctive features of
mammals. In most mammals,
the milk is exuded from nipples
situated on the belly. The
number of nipples roughly
matches the largest number of

young commonly produced at
one time by that species.
Hence pigs have many more
nipples with which to feed
their young than do humans.
Milk production is stimulated
by hormones released toward
the end of pregnancy. Once the
young are weaned, milk
production ceases, thus saving
the adult energy. Milk provides
a complete meal for the young
mammal: fats for energy;
proteins for tissue
development; calcium and iron
for bones and the blood. Many
young mammals, especially
predatory species, spend a
long time in the care of their
parents. This allows them to
build up adult skills. Play (C) is
an important part of growth,
improving coordination and
developing the responses
important for defence (and in
some species also for
predation). Fur is another
special characteristic of
mammals, providing insulation,
important in the maintenance
of temperature. Mutual
grooming (B) has an important
social function, strengthening
the bonds within family groups.

MAMMALIAN SKELETONS

Mammalian skeletons have
become modified in many different ways as animals have
adapted to different habitats
and lifestyles. In primitive
mammals, limbs tended to be
relatively short, as for
instance in the opossum. But
adaptations, such as running
faster, led to changes, like the
elongation of limbs. In bats
(A), the forelimbs have
become wings, while in seals
(B) the limbs form paddle-like
flippers. Whales' limbs have a
minimal steering function; in
baleen whales (C), the jawbones are greatly enlarged
and curved to accommodate
the animal's huge, sieve-like
plates of baleen (whalebone).

A

B

C

A wide range of mammalian feeding habits has evolved to make full use of the Earth's food resources. Nocturnal and diurnal species coexist in the same ecosystem, allowing greater exploitation of the habitat. Migrants, such as CARIBOU and the vast herds of African ANTELOPES and ZEBRA, move around to exploit seasonal food sources. Other mammals, such as whales and FUR SEALS, migrate to sheltered bays to breed, living on fat until they are free to return to more food-rich waters. Many small RODENTS and even a few larger animals, such as the black BEAR of North America, are able to survive severe winter conditions by hibernating. Others escape environmental fluctuations by retreating underground to burrows or to the depths of caves.

Some mammals with terrestrial ancestors have evolved to exploit the air and the sea. BATS are the only vertebrates other than birds capable of sustained flight. Whales and DOLPHINS have become so well adapted to the marine environment that they never come ashore. The baleen whales have evolved huge filters of baleen (whalebone) with which they sieve the vast shoals of krill that abound in the oceans, particularly in the Antarctic region.

In areas with little prey, predatory mammals tend to be solitary, like the polar bear, whereas where food is more plentiful, cooperative hunting techniques have evolved, where groups of predators, such as hunting DOGS or LIONS, cooperate to bring down prey that may be larger than themselves. Many herbivorous mammals have evolved symbiotic relationships with cellulose-digesting bacteria so that they can take advantage of relatively indigestible plant food for which there is less competition. Bears and many PRIMATES are omnivorous, feeding on fruits, leaves and berries, but hunting other creatures when they get the opportunity. Other mammals, such as RACCOONS and HYENAS, are mainly scavengers.

Despite geographical isolation, many mammals have adapted in corresponding ways to similar lifestyles in different continents; examples are the ANTEATERS and ARMADILLOS of South America, the AARDVARK of Africa, the PANGOLIN of Asia, and the ECHIDNAS of Australia and New Guinea – these creatures are all anteaters with long, tough snouts, long tongues and powerful claws for breaking into nests of ants and termites.

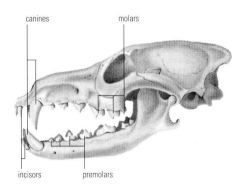

▲ **Having specialized teeth** of different kinds is a unique mammalian adaptation. Variety is greatest in the carnivores (meat-eaters), which have biting incisors, tearing canine teeth, and sharp molars and premolars for crushing bones. Herbivores have more uniform teeth designed for grinding vegetation such as grass.

▲ **Tracing the origins** of mammals depends on the availability of a good fossil record and DNA data. Unfortunately, for many of the 18 orders of mammals the record is incomplete. However, possible lines of descent have been suggested. It seems increasingly likely that mammals are all descended from lizard-like reptiles known as synapsida. The synapsida evolved many millions of years before splitting into two subclasses – the prototheria (the monotreme egg layers) and the theria (which give birth to live young). The theria themselves are divided into two further groups – the eutheria, or placental mammals, and the metatheria, the marsupials.

KEY

- proposed-linkage
- fossil record
- prototheria
- metatheria
- eutheria

1 Cetacea (whales)
2 Insectivora (insectivores)
3 Tubulidentata (aardvarks)
4 Chiroptera (bats)
5 Artiodactyla (even-toed ungulates)
6 Dermoptera (flying lemurs)
7 Perissodactyla (odd-toed ungulates)
8 Primates (primates)
9 Hydracoidea (hyraxes)
10 Rodentia (rodents)
11 Proboscidea (elephants)
12 Lagomorpha (rabbits)
13 Sirenia (sea cows)
14 Pholidota (pangolins)
15 Monotremata (monotremes)
16 Edentata (anteaters)
17 Carnivora (carnivores)
18 Marsupialia (marsupials)

MAMMALIAN HEART

In the mammalian heart, the right and left sides are completely separate. The left side of the heart receives oxygenated blood from the lungs via the pulmonary veins (1). This is pumped to the body's organs at high pressure via the aorta (2) and its branches. Deoxygenated blood returns to the heart via the inferior and superior venae cavae (3 and 4), and is pumped back to the lungs via the pulmonary arteries (5). This is done by the right side of the heart at a lower pressure, which is important to avoid damaging the lungs. The left side of the heart is frequently larger since it pumps at higher pressure.

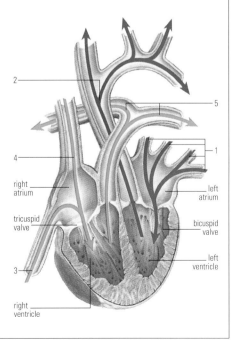

right atrium
tricuspid valve
right ventricle
left atrium
bicuspid valve
left ventricle

M

bear small, inconspicuous flowers above the water level. The Inuit gather young shoots to eat, and submerged shoots are important food sources for animals in winter. Family Hippuridaceae; species *Hippuris vulgaris*.

margay
See CAT, MARGAY

marguerite
Perennial herb of the DAISY family. It is native to the Canary Islands. Marguerite has white-rayed, yellow-centred flower heads. Height: to 91cm (36in). Family Asteraceae/Compositae; species *Argyranthemum frutescens*.

marigold
Any of several mostly golden-flowered plants, mainly belonging to the genera *Chrysanthemum*, *Tagetes* and *Calendula*, all of the DAISY family. Those most commonly cultivated are the French marigold (*Tagetes patula*) and the African marigold (*Tagetes erecta*). Family Asteraceae/Compositae. *See also* CHRYSANTHEMUM

marine biology
Science and study of life in the sea. It covers organisms that live in the ocean waters, on the seabed and along shores. Marine biologists explore the ways in which these organisms fit into their environments, as well as their interactions with the human environment.

maritime climate
CLIMATE that is strongly influenced by proximity to the sea. Oceans warm up more slowly than land, because the heat of the Sun is spread out through a great depth of water and because ocean currents allow the heat to move vertically as well as horizontally. However, oceans also retain heat for much longer than land. For this reason, climatic conditions near an ocean tend to be much warmer in winter and slightly cooler in summer than in inland areas at the same latitudes. In addition to the effects on temperature, the sea also influences precipitation, which is greater on the coast than in inland locations.

marjoram
Perennial herb belonging to the MINT family. It has purplish flowers. Marjoram is native to the Mediterranean region and w Asia. It is cultivated as an annual in northern climates. Height: *c*.60cm (*c*.24in). Family Lamiaceae/Labiatae; species include *Origanum vulgare*.

markhor
Largest species of GOAT-ANTELOPE. It inhabits low mountain woodlands of Afghanistan, N India, N Pakistan, Kashmir and s Uzbekistan. Markhors have twisted horns, which, in the males, continue to grow through life. Males also have long display hairs,

which form neck manes and leg "pantaloons". They are gregarious animals, the males indulging in head-to head battles to establish a strict hierarchy. Head-tail length: 140–168cm (55–66in), the females being smaller than the males. Family Bovidae; species *Capra falconeri*.

marl (mudrock)
Extremely fine-grained, SEDIMENTARY ROCK that is an intermediate between a CLAY and a LIMESTONE. It contains up to 60% of calcareous minerals such as CALCITE, with some QUARTZ and particles of SILT. Red marl owes its colour to the presence of iron oxide, whereas green marl contains chlorite or glauconite. They formed from deposits at the bottoms of lakes or the sea. Marls of marine origin may occur in beds with gypsum and halite.

marlin
Any of several species of large marine fish found in warm waters of the Atlantic and Pacific oceans, especially the blue marlin (*Makaira mitsukurii*). The marlin is blue with a coppery tint and violet side markings. Its fins and long snout are sharply pointed. It is often fished for sport. Length: to 8m (26ft). Family Istiophoridae.

marmoset
Any of eight species, in two genera, of small MONKEY found in tropical forests of Bolivia, Paraguay and Brazil. Marmosets have long tails and silky, often colourful coats with tassels and fringes. Their long, chisel-like incisor teeth are adapted to gouging holes in tree bark to allow the gum on which they feed to ooze out; they also eat flowers, insects and small animals. Head-body length: 19–21cm (7–8in); tail: 25–29cm (10–11in). Family Callitrichidae.

marmoset, bare-ear
Any of three subspecies of marmoset, none of which has ear-tufts. The silvery marmoset, *Callithrix argentata argentata*, is white with a pink face and ears and a black tail. *Callithrix argentata leucippe* is pale all over with an orange-gold tip.

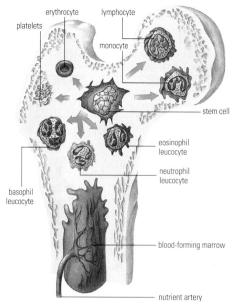

▲ **marrow** Most bones have hollow cavities that are filled with spongy bone marrow. Some of this (not, however, in the long bones) forms new erythrocytes and leucocytes. Little more than 250g (0.5lb) of bone marrow is sufficient to provide the 5000 million erythrocytes a day needed to replace old cells that have worn out after their 120-day lifetime. Some leucocytes are also formed in the lymph nodes.

The black-tailed marmoset, *Callithrix argentata melanura*, is dark brown or black all over except for pale hip and thigh patches. Family Callitrichidae; species *Callithrix argentata*.

marmoset, black tufted
Either of two subspecies of black tufted-ear or black-eared marmoset from central Brazil. *Callithrix pencillata pencillata* has a mottled grey coat, ringed tail and black face. *Callithrix pencillata kuhlii* has brown flanks, thighs and crown and pale cheek patches. Family Callitrichidae; species *Callithrix pencillata*.

marmoset, common
Marmoset that is native to NE Brazil. It has long, white ear-tufts, a mottled grey-brown body and a ringed tail. The top of its head is black and there is a white blaze on its forehead. Family Callitrichidae; species *Callithrix jacchus*.

marmoset, pygmy
Smallest living monkey. It has a head-body length of only 17cm (7in) and a tail length of 19cm (7.5in). It is found in the Amazon forest of Colombia, Peru, Ecuador, Bolivia and Brazil. The pygmy marmoset's coat is tawny-grey, with long hairs on its head and dark rings on its tail. Family Callitrichidae; species *Cebuella pygmaea*.

marmot
Any of *c*.14 species of heavy, ground-dwelling rodents from Europe, Asia and North America; they belong to the SQUIRREL family. Marmots feed on green herbage and dig extensive burrows in open areas. They hibernate for up to nine months of each year, during which time their metabolism, breathing, heart-rate and body temperature can drop dramatically for up to a month at a time. Family Sciuridae. *See also* WOODCHUCK

marmot, alpine
Marmot that lives in sociable colonies in the alpine meadows of the mountains of Europe. It has a pale brown coat, with black markings on its head, back and tail; it has grey hairs on its face. Head-body length: 53–73cm (21–29in); tail: 13–16cm (5–6in). Family Sciuridae; species *Marmota marmota*.

marmot, Himalayan (bobak, steppe marmot)
Marmot that is similar to the alpine marmot in size and habits. It lives on open grasslands of Himalayan slopes although it has become extinct over much of its former range. It is golden-brown with a black tail tip. Family Sciuridae; species *Marmota himalayana*.

marram grass
See BEACH GRASS

marrow
Soft tissue containing blood vessels, found in the hollow cavities of BONE. The marrow found in many adult bones, including the shafts of long bones, is somewhat yellowish and functions as a store of fat. The marrow in the flattish bones, including the ribs, breastbone, skull, spinal column and the ends of the long bones, is reddish; it contains cells that give rise eventually to ERYTHROCYTES (red blood cells) as well as to most of the LEUCOCYTES (white blood cells), but not LYMPHOCYTES or PLATELETS.

marrow
Climbing or trailing annual VINE, probably native to tropical America but now grown worldwide. Marrows produce elongated fruits (SQUASHES) that are popular vegetables. Varieties of marrow include

▶ **marsupial** Both the marsupial cat and the marsupial mouse are nocturnal hunters found in rocky forested areas in Australia. Marsupial cats are aggressive predators, which prey on small mammals, reptiles and birds. They are mainly terrestrial, but are adept at climbing rocks and trees. The marsupial mouse is distinguished by its long snout and large ears. Unlike true mice, it is a carnivore, preying on small vertebrates and insects.

marsupial cat

marsupial mouse

the ZUCCHINI. Family Cucurbitaceae; species *Cucurbita pepo*. *See also* GOURD; PUMPKIN

marsh
Flat, grassland area, devoid of peat, that is saturated by moisture during one or more seasons. Typical vegetation includes GRASSES, SEDGES, REEDS and RUSHES. Marshes are sometimes the breeding sites of mosquitoes and other disease carriers, but they are valuable WETLANDS and maintain water tables in adjacent ECOSYSTEMS.

marshbird
Small, inconspicuous WARBLER found in swamps and marshes of Australia. It is a reluctant flier, preferring to keep low, creeping amongst vegetation. Length: 13cm (5in). Family Sylviidae; species *Megalurus gramineus*.

marshbuck
See SITATUNGA

marsh gas
See METHANE

marsh marigold
Perennial plant of the BUTTERCUP family; it is native to cold and temperate swamps of the Northern Hemisphere. Marsh marigold has hollow stems, kidney-shaped leaves and large, pink, white or yellow flowers. Family Ranunculaceae; genus *Caltha*; there are *c*.20 species.

Marsigli, Count Luigi Ferdinando
(1658–1730)
Italian soldier, naturalist and oceanographer. After long service in the Austrian army, during which he was captured, he was demoted in 1704. Thereafter, Marsigli engaged in scientific study, founding the Accademia delle Scienze in Bologna (1712) and becoming a member of the Royal Society (1722), to which he was presented by Isaac Newton.

marsupial
MAMMAL of which the female usually has a pouch, known as a marsupium, within which the young are suckled and protected. At birth, the young are in a very early stage of development. Most marsupials are found in Australasia; they include such varied types as the KANGAROO, KOALA, WOMBAT, TASMANIAN DEVIL, BANDICOOT and MARSUPIAL MOLE. The only marsupials to live outside Australasia are the OPOSSUMS and similar species found in the Americas. *See also* MONOTREME

marsupial cat (quoll, native cat, tiger cat)
Any member of the genus *Dasyurus*, a group of small- to medium-sized carnivores native to Australia, Tasmania and New Guinea. The marsupial cat is a nocturnal hunter. The various species include the New Guinea marsupial cat (*Dasyurus albopunctatus*), the cluditch (*Dasyurus geoffroi*) and the

satenellus (*Dasyurus hallucatus*). Various species are known as quolls. Head-body length: 24–76cm (9–30in); tail: 21–56cm (8–22in). Family Dasyuridae; genus *Dasyurus*.

marsupial mole
Pale yellow, burrowing mammal; it has a reinforced head and hands modified for digging. It inhabits dry, sandy areas, tunnelling below the surface in search of earthworms and insects. Its excavations are not permanent, and they collapse immediately. Marsupial moles are found in s central and NW Australia. Head-body length: 12–15cm (5–6in). Family Notoryctidae; species *Notoryctes typhlops*.

marsupial mouse
Common name for many small mouse-like MARSUPIALS belonging to the family Dasyuridae, including the NINGAUIS, DUNNARTS and ANTECHINUS. Found in Australia, Tasmania and New Guinea, many marsupial mice are rare or endangered. *See also* DASYURID

marten
Nocturnal, solitary and rarely seen member of the BADGER family. Martens have long, lithe bodies, short legs and pointed faces. There are several species from Europe, Asia and North America. They are efficient hunters of squirrels and other small animals and will also eat insects, slugs, eggs, honey and fruit. Family Mustelidae.

marten, pine
Marten that inhabits forests from the British Isles across Europe to Siberia. It has a bushy tail and a broad triangular head. Its fine coat is a rich brown, with grey underparts and a cream patch under its chin. Head-body length: 45–58cm (18–23in); tail: 16–28cm (6–11in). Family Mustelidae; species *Martes martes*.

marten, stone (beech marten)
Marten that inhabits open rocky areas from the Baltic to the Mediterranean regions and across to the Himalayas and Mongolia. Its coarse hairs are greyish brown and it has a cream throat patch. Head-body length: 40–54cm (16–21in); tail: 22–30cm (9–12in). Family Mustelidae; species *Martes foina*.

martin
Any of several members of the SWALLOW family. They have slender bodies, long wings, short, forked tails and short bills. They have a wide gape for catching insects on the wing. Most species nest socially and may gather in communal roosts. Their flight is graceful and fast. Most species are strongly migratory. Family Hirundinidae.

M

house martin

crag martin

sand martin

◀ **martin** Highly adaptable birds, martins are found in a variety of environments. The crag martin (*Hirundo rupestris*) inhabits mountains and rocky sea cliffs in warmer climates. The house martin (*Delichon urbica*) originally nested in caves, but it is today commonly seen in urban areas. It constructs its nest in spring with sticky mud collected from puddles, which it mixes with its own saliva. The sand martin (*Riparia riparia*) breeds in large colonies in sandy riverbanks or cliff faces. It excavates a tunnel, up to 30cm (1ft) long, with its claws and builds a nest of hay and feathers at the end.

martin, crag

Martin that is found singly or in pairs, mainly on cliffs. It is brown above and buff below, with small, white spots on its tail and blackish wing linings. Its flight is slower and more gliding than that of most martin species. The crag martin's distinctive call sounds like stones hitting each other. Length: 15cm (6in). Family Hirundinidae; species *Ptyonoprogne rupestris*.

martin, house

Familiar martin of N Europe, where it is a summer visitor from Africa. It is blue-black above and pure white below, with a white rump and a short, forked tail. It nests in a cup-shaped, mud nest under the eaves of buildings. Length: 13cm (5in). Family Hirundinidae; species *Delichon urbica*.

martin, purple

Martin that is widespread in North America during the summer; it migrates in large flocks to South America in winter. It has glossy purple plumage and a forked tail. The purple martin nests mainly in old woodpecker holes. Numbers are declining in some areas because of competition with starlings for nest sites. Length: 20cm (8in). Family Hirundinidae; species *Progne subis*.

martin, sand

Smallest European swallow. The sand martin is one of the earliest spring migrants to arrive. It is earthy brown above and white below, with a brown breast band. It has a fluttering flight, which is less gliding than that of most swallow species. It nests in holes in sandy or gravel banks near water. Length: 12cm (5in). Family Hirundinidae; species *Riparia riparia*.

marvel of Peru (four-o'clock)

Fast-growing herb that is native to tropical America. It has highly branched stems. The trumpet-shaped flowers, which can be white, red or yellow, open in the evening. Dwarf, compact and variegated forms are found in cultivation. Family Nyctaginaceae; species *Mirabilis jalapa*.

massasauga (pygmy rattlesnake)

RATTLESNAKE found in central and sw United States. It has large black blotches down its back and spots along its sides. Length: to 76cm (30in). Family Viperidae; species *Sistrurus catenatus*.

mass flow

Bulk movement of materials from one part of an organism to another. Such movements may be the result of pressure differences between one part of the system and another, as in the flow of BLOOD in animals, or the result of concentration differences, as in the TRANSLOCATION of sugars in the PHLOEM of plants.

mass movement

Gravity-controlled downslope movement of material at the Earth's surface. It may be manifested in many different environments, from mountain sides to subaqueous slopes, and on a variety of scales, from rock falls to the collapse of mountain sides. Mass movement can involve materials ranging from avalanching snow to consolidated rock. Movement may be initiated by a number of processes, including rapid temperature change, rainfall and earthquakes. *See also* AVALANCHE; LANDSLIDE

matamata

Side-necked TURTLE found in tropical regions of South America. It has a long neck, flattened head and long, pointed snout. The matamata has a rough, three-keeled CARAPACE, which is usually covered in algae.

It has fringes of skin along its neck. Such features provide good camouflage. It feeds by ambushing fish and invertebrates, which it rapidly sucks into its mouth. Length: to 45cm (18in). Family Chelidae; species *Chelus fimbriatus*.

maté (yerba maté)

South American evergreen shrub or tree. In the wild, it is a tree; in cultivation, it is pruned as a small shrub. The dried leaves are infused to make a stimulating beverage known as Paraguayan tea, which is a staple drink of the gauchos of the pampas. Height: to 6m (20ft). Family Aquifoliaceae; species *Ilex paraguariensis*.

mathematical biology

Modern branch of applied mathematics and theoretical BIOLOGY dealing with the growth of organisms, the development of patterns and the spread of populations and disease. Also, recent advances have been made in medicine where mathematics has been used to describe wound healing, the events leading to heart attacks and the growth of tumours within the body.

Maury, Matthew Fontaine (1806–73)

US naval officer, a proponent of oceanography. As superintendent of the US Naval Observatory and Hydrographic Office (1842–61), he produced charts showing winds and currents for the Atlantic, Pacific and Indian oceans. Maury proved the feasibility of laying a transatlantic cable. His books include *The Physical Geography of the Sea* (1855).

maxilla

Upper jawbone of a vertebrate, or one of a pair of mouthparts in various arthropods. Centipedes, crustaceans, insects and millipedes have maxillae that move sideways to manipulate food. They lie close to the mouth, behind the MANDIBLES. In insects, a second pair of maxillae are united to form the LABIUM; in crustaceans, the two pairs of maxillae are separate. *See also* JAW

May beetle

See BEETLE, MAY

mayfly

Soft-bodied insect found worldwide. The adult does not eat and lives only a few days, but the aquatic larvae (NYMPH) may live several years. Adults have triangular front wings, characteristic thread-like tails, and vestigial mouthparts; they often emerge from streams and rivers in swarms. The flying dun

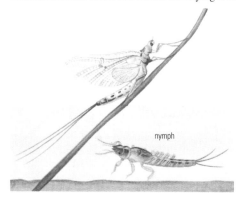

nymph

▲ **mayfly** As nymphs, mayflies pass through between 10 and 20 moults; they are the only insects to moult with functional wings. Mayflies take three years to reach maturity but as adults they only live long enough to mate, after which the male dies, followed shortly by the female once she has deposited her eggs in water.

is used in fly-fishing. Length: 10–25mm (0.4–1in). Order Ephemeroptera.

meadowlark

Either of two species belonging to the American ORIOLE family; they are not true larks. Meadowlarks have a distinctive, V-shaped breast-band, yellow underparts, and black crown stripes and eye lines. They are common in open country and prairie in North America. The clear song of the eastern meadowlark is a distinctive "*see you see-yeer*". Length: 24cm (9in). Family Icteridae; genus *Sturnella*.

meadowsweet (queen of the meadow)

European plant that thrives in damp areas, especially beside streams. It has fern-like leaves and fragrant white flower clusters. Height: 120cm (47in). Family Rosaceae; species *Filipendula ulmaria*.

mealybug

Any member of the family Pseudococcidae, comprising SCALE INSECTS found worldwide. Their bodies are covered in a waxy powder. Mealybugs suck sap from trees and other plants. Length: *c*.5mm (*c*.0.2in). Order Homoptera; family Pseudococcidae.

meander

Naturally occurring, loop-like bend in the course of a RIVER. A river will wind round an obstacle such as hard rock. Once a meander has been created, it will become accentuated by the erosive action of the river. On the outside of a bend there will be lateral CORRASION, which will gradually work out sideways. On the inside of the bend there is likely to be some deposition, which will build up a flat flood plain. Meanders gradually move downstream. Sometimes meanders make complete loops, which, when cut off, form OXBOW LAKES. The name comes from the winding River Maeander in Turkey.

mecopteran

Any member of the order Mecoptera. *See also* SCORPION FLY

Medawar, Sir Peter Brian (1915–87)

British biologist. He shared the 1960 Nobel Prize for physiology or medicine with Sir Frank Macfarlane Burnet (1899–1985) for the discovery of acquired immune tolerance. Medawar confirmed Burnet's theory that an organism can acquire the ability to recognize foreign tissue during embryonic development, and if that tissue is introduced in the embryonic stage it may be reintroduced later without inducing an immune reaction. *See also* IMMUNE SYSTEM

medick

Any member of a large group of mostly herbaceous annuals or perennials from Europe, Asia and Africa, some of which are grown for forage. The leaves have three leaflets. The small, yellow or purple pea-flowers are produced in small axillary heads, which give rise to curved or spiralled, often spiny pods. Family Fabaceae; genus *Medicago*.

mediterranean climate

Type of CLIMATE associated with the countries surrounding the Mediterranean Sea, but also found in s California, United States, central Chile and parts of Australia. Summers are hot and sunny, averaging 25°C (77°F) or more; winters are mild, ranging from 5°C to 15°C (41–59°F). Summers are very dry, but winters can be quite wet, with up to 600mm (24in) of rainfall, some of which comes as thunderstorms at the end of the summer.

▼ **mitosis** Mitosis (**A**) ensures that a cell divides to produce two "daughters", each of which contains the same number and type of chromosomes as the "parent" cell. A typical animal cell might contain between 10 and 50 pairs of chromosomes, but for the sake of simplicity only two paired chromosomes are shown here (1). Before mitosis begins, the chromosomes are duplicated in the cell nucleus (2) by special replicating enzymes. They then coil up and condense, a process that prevents them becoming tangled. Each chromosome now consists of two identical units – or sister *chromatids* (3) – joined together by special regions known as *centromeres* (4). The nuclear membrane then breaks down and a network of *microtubules* begins to develop in the cell (5): the microtubules radiate from structures called *centrioles* (6), one of which is located at each end of the cell. Each chromatid becomes attached to one or several microtubules at its centromere (7). The microtubules are involved in the movement of the chromatids to opposite ends of the cell. The sister chromatids first become aligned along the cell's central axis (7). They then separate at their centromeres and one chromatid from each pair is drawn towards one end of the cell, while the other moves to the other end. Each end of the parent cell now possesses a full set of chromosomes. The parent cell constricts along its central axis (8), "pinching off" two daughter cells (9). The cell membrane regrows around each daughter and a nuclear membrane re-forms, enclosing the chromosomes.

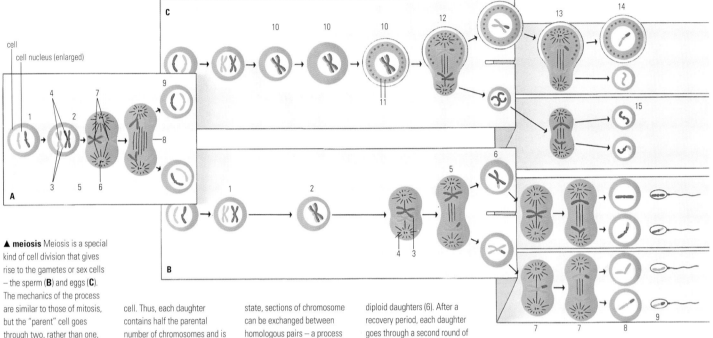

▲ **meiosis** Meiosis is a special kind of cell division that gives rise to the gametes or sex cells – the sperm (**B**) and eggs (**C**). The mechanics of the process are similar to those of mitosis, but the "parent" cell goes through two, rather than one, round of cell division to form four, rather than two, "daughters". The parent cell is diploid, which means it contains two versions – or *homologues* – of each chromosome; one inherited from its mother and one from its father. Meiosis allocates one homologue to each daughter cell. Thus, each daughter contains half the parental number of chromosomes and is said to be haploid. As in mitosis, the chromosomes are first duplicated in the nucleus to form pairs of sister chromatids joined at their centromeres (1). Homologous chromosomes then become closely associated into *tetrads* (2), with each tetrad composed of two pairs of sister chromatids. In this tightly paired state, sections of chromosome can be exchanged between homologous pairs – a process known as *recombination* (3). This brings together different versions of genes in new combinations. This genetic reassortment is followed by spindle formation (4) and movement of the two, paired sister chromatids to opposite ends of the cell (5). The parent cell then splits, producing two diploid daughters (6). After a recovery period, each daughter goes through a second round of cell division (7). This creates a total of four haploid daughter cells (8). After meiosis, the mature spermatozoa form by a complex process of cell differentiation (9). Egg formation (**C**) differs from sperm formation (**B**) not in the mechanics of meiosis, but in the importance of the other cell contents. A mature egg cell must contain adequate food reserves: for this reason meiosis is temporarily arrested at the tetrad stage to allow time for growth (10). At this stage the *cortical granules* develop (11). These will ensure that fertilization by only one sperm goes ahead normally. In addition, cell divisions in egg formation are unequal, with one of the daughters getting more than its fair share of cytoplasm (12, 13). This one daughter develops into the egg itself (14); the other three smaller cells, known as *polar bodies* (15), eventually degenerate.

medlar
Fruit-bearing shrub or small tree; it is native to s Europe and the Middle East and naturalized in central Europe and Britain. It has oblong leaves and is often gnarled in appearance. Its brown, apple-like fruit are edible only at the onset of decay. Height: 4.5–7.6m (15–25ft). Family Rosaceae; species *Mespilus germanica*.

medusa
Free-swimming stage in the lifecycle of a CNIDARI-AN. There are many types of medusa. Some medusae are small creatures, which are transient stages in the life cycle of the Cnidaria; they soon change into the dominant, POLYP stage. Other medusae are larger and live longer, the polyp stage being the briefer of the two stages. Yet other medusae, including many JELLYFISH, have no polyp stage; when they reproduce they give rise directly to medusa offspring.

meerkat (suricate)
Any of a number of small, carnivorous mammals closely related to the MONGOOSE, native to the bush country of s Africa. The meerkat is similar in appearance to the mongoose but without the bushy tail. Length: 47cm (19in). Family Herpestidae; species include *Suricata suricatta*.

megalopteran
Any member of the order Megaloptera. *See* ALDERFLY

meiosis
Process of CELL DIVISION that reduces the CHROMO-SOME number from DIPLOID to HAPLOID. Meiosis involves two nuclear divisions. The first meiotic division halves the chromosome number in the two resulting cells; the second division then forms four haploid cells. In most organisms, the resulting haploid cells are the GAMETES, or sex cells, the OVA and SPERM. However, in other organisms, notably those that show ALTERNATION OF GENERATIONS, these haploid cells may give rise to a new generation of plants or algae, the haploid "gametophyte" generation. The "gameto-phyte" generation will later produce gametes by MITO-SIS, which is the normal cell division that does not involve halving of the chromosome number. *See also* ANAPHASE; CROSSING OVER; METAPHASE

melidectes
Any member of the genus *Melidectes*, a group of ten species of long-billed birds belonging to the HON-EYEATER family. They are found mainly in New Guinea. Length: 27cm (11in). Family Meliphagidae.

meliphaga
Any member of the genus *Meliphaga*, which com-prises six similar species of HONEYEATER. They are found in forests of the New Guinea region, some-times visiting gardens. Length: 16cm (6in). Meliphagidae; species include *Meliphaga leucotis*.

melon
Annual vine and its large, fleshy, edible fruit. Melons grow in warm temperate and subtropical

▲ **melon** Many different types of melon have been cultivated. Cantaloupe melons (*Cucumis melo*) (right) are true melons, whereas watermelons (*Citrullus lanatus*) (left) belong to the same family but to a different genus. Melons grow well in warm climates or under glass in cooler temperatures.

M

climates. The cantaloupe melon, with its rough skin, probably originated in Armenia. The honeydew, with smooth, yellow rind, originated in Southeast Asia. The large, dark-green watermelon, with its red, watery flesh, is believed to have come from Africa. Family Cucurbitaceae.

melon aphid
See COTTON APHID

meltwater
Water that originates from melted ice or snow. When temperatures rise, snow produces meltwater, which swells rivers and may contribute to flooding. Meltwater from glaciers may add to the water in an existing river or supply streams that form a new river.

membrane
Boundary layer inside or around a living CELL or TISSUE. Cell membranes include the plasma membrane surrounding the cell, the network of membranes inside the cell (ENDOPLASMIC RETICULUM), and the double membrane surrounding the NUCLEUS. The multicellular membranes of the body comprise mucous membranes of the respiratory, digestive and urogenital passages, synovial membranes of the joints, and the membranes that coat the inner walls of the abdomen, thorax and the surfaces of organs. *See also* EPITHELIUM

Mendel, Gregor Johann (1822–84)
Austrian naturalist and monk who discovered the laws of HEREDITY and in so doing laid the foundation for the modern science of GENETICS. Mendel grew pea plants and observed how various characteristics, such as tallness, flower colour and seed shape, appeared in the plants' offspring. He proposed that the characteristics were inherited, carried by "factors" (now known to be GENES) contributed by each parent. His study was published in *Experiments with Plant Hybrids* (1866), which was rediscovered in 1900.

Mendelism
Theory of inheritance originally proposed by Gregor MENDEL. This theory established the science of classical GENETICS.

menhaden
Any of several species of marine fish belonging to the genus *Brevoortia*. Schools of menhaden are found in coastal waters of the Atlantic Ocean, from Canada to South America. They are obligate filter feeders, straining plant-like plankton from the water. Menhaden are related to HERRING. Length:

38cm (15in). Family Clupeidae; species include *Brevoortia tyrannus*.

menstrual cycle
Cycle in female humans and some higher primates of reproductive age, during which the body is prepared for pregnancy. In women, the average cycle is 28 days. At the beginning of the cycle, HORMONES from the PITUITARY GLAND stimulate the growth of an OVUM (egg cell) contained in a follicle in one of the two OVARIES. At approximately mid-cycle, the follicle bursts, the egg is released (ovulation) and travels down the FALLOPIAN TUBE to the UTERUS. The follicle (now called the CORPUS LUTEUM) secretes two hormones, PROGESTERONE and OESTROGEN, during this secretory phase of the cycle, and the endometrium thickens, ready to receive the fertilized egg. Should fertilization (conception) not occur, the corpus luteum degenerates, hormone secretion ceases, the endometrium breaks down and menstruation occurs; the unfertilized egg is discharged in the blood flow from the VAGINA. In the event of conception, the corpus luteum remains and maintains the endometrium with hormones until the PLACENTA is formed. Menstruation, therefore, marks the end of the cycle. The onset of the menstrual cycle (menarche) is called puberty (age 10–15 years); it ceases with the menopause (around 50 years).

Mercalli scale
Scale of 12 points used for measuring EARTHQUAKE intensity. Named after the Italian seismologist Giuseppe Mercalli (1850–1914), it is based on damage done at any point and so varies from place to place. Earthquake magnitude, on the other hand, is a function of the total energy released. *See also* RICHTER SCALE

mercury (quicksilver, symbol Hg)
Liquid, metallic element, known from earliest times. The chief ore is CINNABAR (a sulphide), from which it is extracted by roasting. The silvery element is the only metal that is liquid at normal temperatures. It is a dangerous cumulative poison. Mercury is used in barometers, thermometers, laboratory apparatus, mercury-vapour lamps and mercury cells. It forms two series of salts, termed mercury(I), or mercurous, and mercury(II), or mercuric. Mercury's toxic effects have always plagued workers in industries using its compounds. The industrial dumping of mercury wastes into the sea allows it to enter the human food cycle, because fish and birds ingest the mercury and these are eaten, passing on the poison to the next level in the food chain. Symptoms of mercury poisoning include loss of coordination, balance and peripheral

vision, sensory disturbance and deformed offspring. Properties: at.no. 80; r.a.m. 200.59; r.d. 13.6; m.p. −38.87°C; (−37.97°F); b.p. 356.58°C (673.84°F); most common isotope ^{202}Hg (29.8%).

merganser
Boldly coloured diving DUCK with a saw-edged bill and a crested head. The small hooded merganser (*Mergus cucullatus*) of North America has fan-shaped, white head patches that are raised to a crest. The red-breasted merganser (*Mergus serrator*) has a green head with a shaggy double crest. Length: 38–66cm (15–26in). Family Anatidae; genus *Mergus*.

merganser, common (goosander)
DUCK that is found throughout Britain, continental Europe and N North America. It is similar to the red-breasted merganser, but with different markings on its head and neck. The common merganser is a low flier. It favours lakes, rivers and wooded areas. Length: 67cm (26in). Family Anatidae; species *Mergus merganser*.

meristem
In plants, a layer of cells that divides repeatedly to generate new tissues. It is present at the growing tips of shoots and roots, and at certain sites in leaves. In MONOCOTYLEDONS, the leaf meristem is at the base, which explains why grasses continue to grow when the leaf tips are removed by grazing or mowing. *See also* CAMBIUM

merlin
Small FALCON found in hills and open moorland of Europe and the United States. It is streaked blue-grey above, with a barred tail. Its underparts are cream with darker streaks. The merlin preys on small birds. Length: to 33cm (13in). Family Falconidae; species *Falco columbarius*.

mermaid's tresses
Brown-pigmented SEAWEED composed of narrow, slimy cords filled with gas. The cords can be up to 6m (20ft) long and grow from a tiny holdfast. It is found in shallow water in sheltered bays and estuaries of the Northern Hemisphere. It often grows in dense populations and is tolerant of brackish water. Family Chordaceae; species *Chorda filum*.

mesa (Sp. *mesa*, table)
Flat area of upland that resembles a table. Mesas often have horizontal strata of SEDIMENTARY ROCK. They are found primarily in SW United States; well-known examples are the Mesa Verde in Colorado and the Enchanted Mesa in New Mexico.

mesembryanthemum
Any member of the genus *Mesembryanthemum*, numerous species of which grow in dry regions. They are erect or creeping shrubs, with succulent leaves. The ice plant, *Mesembryanthemum crystallinum*, is commonly grown as an ornamental. Family Aizoaceae.

mesite
Any of three species of medium-sized, ground-dwelling birds found only on Madagascar. They are drab pale brown, with a thick, down-curved bill.

◄ **merganser, common** A group of female mergansers are seen here in their typical habitat, a wooded lake or river, in Alaska, United States. They will migrate south in winter. They feed by diving for fish and also take molluscs and crustaceans. They are fast fliers, although take off is rather clumsy as their wings are relatively small compared to their body size.

M

Mesites run through their habitat like a rail or large thrush, but they are actually related to the cranes and coots. Habitat loss means that the species are now considered endangered. Length: 25cm (10in). Family Mesitornithidae; genus *Mesitornis*.

mesoderm
One of the three so-called GERM LAYERS of tissue formed in the early development of a fertilized OVUM (egg) of higher animals. It is the middle layer, and in later development of the embryo, the mesoderm gives rise to muscles, blood and connective tissues. The other germ layers are the ECTODERM and the ENDODERM.

mesophyll
Soft tissue located between the two layers of EPIDERMIS in a plant leaf. In most plants, mesophyll cells contain chlorophyll-producing structures called CHLOROPLASTS, which are essential to the processes of PHOTOSYNTHESIS.

mesophyte
Plant that grows under average moisture conditions, thriving where there is a good balance of water and evaporation. Such plants have well-developed root and leaf systems. *See also* HYDROPHYTE; XEROPHYTE

mesosphere
Middle shell of gases in the Earth's ATMOSPHERE between the STRATOSPHERE and the THERMOSPHERE.

Mesozoic
Third era of GEOLOGICAL TIME, extending from about 248 million to 65 million years ago. It is divided into three periods: the TRIASSIC, JURASSIC and CRETACEOUS. For most of the era, the continents are believed to have been conjoined into one huge land mass called PANGAEA. There was much volcanic activity and mountain building throughout the period, which was also characterized by the variety and size of its reptiles. For this reason the Mesozoic is sometimes called the "Age of Reptiles".

mesquite (honey mesquite)
Deciduous tree common in sw United States and Mexico. Its roots can extend to depths of more than 15m (50ft), allowing it to grow in desert regions. It has small leaflets and spines. Bees make honey from the nectar of the flowers, and the pods are used as fodder. Height: to 6m (20ft). Family Mimosaceae; species *Prosopis juliflora*.

messenger RNA (mRNA)
Type of RNA (ribonucleic acid) that carries the GENETIC CODE for PROTEIN SYNTHESIS. The mRNA transcribes the code from DNA and carries it to RIBOSOMES within the cell, where AMINO ACIDS are assembled to make polypeptides and proteins.

metabolic pathway
Sequence of ENZYME-controlled chemical reactions in organisms whereby a specific substrate is converted into one or more products. With many hundreds of reactions taking place in a cell it is essential that each metabolic pathway is carefully controlled. Enzymes for any pathway are bound to the membranes of cell ORGANELLES such as MITOCHONDRIA in an ordered sequence.

metabolism
Chemical and physical processes and changes continuously occurring in a living organism. They include the breakdown of organic matter (CATABOLISM), resulting in energy release, and the

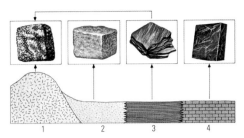

▲ **metamorphic rock**
Common metamorphic rocks are shown above: igneous rock (1) may become gneiss or schist; sandstone (2) may become quartzite; shale (3) may become slate, and if the metamorphism is more pronounced, gneiss; limestone (4) may become marble.

synthesis of organic components (ANABOLISM) to store energy and build and repair TISSUES. *See also* BASAL METABOLIC RATE (BMR)

metacarpals
In humans and other primates, bones of the palm of the hand. The metacarpals articulate with the CARPALS (wrist bones) and PHALANGES (finger bones). In four-footed animals, metacarpals are the bones of the forefoot.

metamorphic grade
Measure of the intensity of the temperature and pressure conditions under which a METAMORPHIC ROCK formed. It is gauged by the difference between the parent rock and its metamorphosed equivalent.

metamorphic rock
Broad class of rocks that have been changed by heat or pressure, or both heat and pressure, from their original nature – SEDIMENTARY, IGNEOUS, or older metamorphic. Heat is the result of volcanic activity, and pressure is the result of earth movements. Metamorphic rocks are generally hard and resistant to erosion; they are likely to form high ground. In metamorphic rocks, minerals may re-crystallize or be compressed, and the new rock may look completely different from the original sedimentary or igneous rock. Thus, the metamorphic rock SLATE is made from sedimentary SHALE, the metamorphic GNEISS from igneous GRANITE.

metamorphism
Processes of temperature and pressure change within the Earth's CRUST that alter the structure and mineralogy of rocks. Metamorphism is a solid state change that involves recrystallization and the growth of new crystals; it involves little change in composition. **Dynamic** metamorphism involves mainly pressure change; it produces mylonites along fault zones and compresses mudrocks into slates. **Thermal** (or contact) metamorphism results from temperature increase, generally emanating from an IGNEOUS ROCK. **Regional** metamorphism incorporates both temperature and pressure change throughout a large volume of rock and involves significant restructuring of pre-existing rocks.

metamorphosis
Change of form or structure during the development of various organisms, such as the changing of a CATERPILLAR into a MOTH, or a TADPOLE into a FROG. Sometimes the change is gradual, as with a GRASSHOPPER, and is known as incomplete metamorphosis (hemimetabolous). Complete metamorphosis (holometabolous) involves a change in habit or environment and usually involves the more distinct stages of LARVA, PUPA and IMAGO (adult stages). *See also* AMPHIBIAN

metaphase
Stage in cell division that occurs during MITOSIS and MEIOSIS. During metaphase, the nuclear membrane breaks down, the SPINDLE forms, and CHROMOSOMES become attached to the centre of the spindle. In the first metaphase of meiosis, paired chromosomes attach to the spindle. In the second metaphase of meiosis and in mitosis, individual chromosomes attach to the spindle. The division then proceeds to ANAPHASE.

metasomatism
Production of mineral deposits by the movement of hot fluids from an igneous body through cracks or pores in the surrounding rock. Veins of lead and tin ores surrounding the Cornish granites were formed in this way.

metatarsals
Bones of the feet (hind feet in quadrupeds). They articulate at one end with the TARSALS (ankle bones) and at the other with the PHALANGES (toe bones).

metazoan
Any member of the group Metazoa. Metazoans are animals whose bodies are made up of many cells, in contrast to the PROTOZOA, which consist of single cells. SPONGES differ so much from other multicellular animals that they are not normally included in the Metazoa.

meteor (shooting star)
Brief streak of light in the night sky caused by a **meteoroid** (a solid particle, usually the size of a grain of dust) entering the Earth's upper atmosphere at high speed from space. They occur at altitudes of about 100km (60mi). The typical meteor lasts for a few tenths of a second to a second or two, depending on the meteoroid's impact speed, which can vary from about 11–70km s^{-1} (7–45mi s^{-1}). A few meteors per hour may be seen on any clear, moonless night at any time of year. But at certain times of the year there are METEOR SHOWERS, which occur when the Earth passes through a meteor stream – dust particles spread around the orbit of a comet. Most of the meteors appearing during the year are sporadic meteors, not associated with cometary orbits.

meteorite
That part of a large **meteoroid** (a solid particle moving in interplanetary space) that survives passage through the Earth's atmosphere and reaches the ground. Most of a meteoroid burns up in the atmosphere to produce a METEOR, but about 10% reaches the surface in the form of meteorites or micrometeorites. Meteorites generally have a pitted surface and a fused charred crust. There are three main types: IRON METEORITES (siderites); STONY METEORITES (aerolites); and STONY-IRON METEORITES. Some are tiny particles; others weigh up to 200 tonnes. Meteoroids weighing more than 100 tonnes that do not break up are not decelerated as much as lighter bodies, and produce impact craters, known as meteoric craters.

meteorology
Study of weather conditions, a branch of the study of CLIMATOLOGY. Meteorologists study and analyse data from a network of weather ships, aircraft and satellites in order to compile maps showing the state of the high- and low-pressure regions in the Earth's atmosphere. They also anticipate changes in the distribution of the regions and forecast the future weather. Wind strength and direction can be predicted accurately by measuring the differences in air pressure over the surface of the Earth.

M

245

meteor shower

Appearance of METEORS from the same point in the sky, the **radiant**, at around the same time each year. Nearly all showers are named after the constellation in which their radiant lies. There are a dozen or so major showers and many minor ones. During major showers there is a build-up of activity to a maximum, when between 10 and 100 shower meteors may be visible each hour from any one location. A shower occurs when the Earth passes through a meteor stream. In an **annual** shower, the meteor rates vary little from one year to the next because the meteoroids in the stream are spread evenly around the orbit. With streams in which the meteoroids are bunched together in a swarm, meteor numbers are low except when the Earth intersects the swarm. Such **periodic** showers may produce a meteor storm.

methane (CH$_4$)

Colourless, odourless hydrocarbon, the simplest alkane (paraffin). It is the chief constituent of NATURAL GAS, from which it is obtained, and of firedamp. Methane explodes when mixed with oxygen and ignited. It is produced naturally by decomposing organic matter, such as in marshes, which led to its original name, marsh gas. In the air, it contributes to the GREENHOUSE EFFECT and to increases in global temperature. Methane is used in the form of natural gas as a fuel and, in its pure form, as a starting material for the manufacture of many chemicals. Properties: m.p. $-182.5°C$ ($-296.5°F$); b.p. $-164°C$ ($-263.2°F$).

methanogenic bacterium

BACTERIUM that is an obligate methane producer; it requires methane synthesis for growth and exposure to oxygen is lethal. The methanogenic bacteria comprise a major group of the ARCHAEA and are found in anaerobic habitats such as sediment, sludge digestors, insect guts and the large bowel of mammals. Examples include *Methanobacterium*, *Methanococcus* and *Methanospirillum*.

metre (symbol m)

SI unit of length. Conceived as being one ten-millionth of the surface distance between the North Pole and the Equator, it used to be defined by two marks on a platinum bar kept in Paris. It is now defined as the length of the path travelled by light in a vacuum during 1/299,792,458 of a second. One metre equals 39.3701 inches.

mica

Group of common rock-forming minerals of the sheet silicate (SiO$_4$) type, characterized by a platy or flaky appearance. All contain aluminium, potassium and water in the form of OH$^-$ ions; other metals such as iron and magnesium may be present. Micas have perfect basal cleavage; common members are MUSCOVITE and the BIOTITE group, which includes a number of varieties.

mica schist

One of a number of METAMORPHIC ROCKS that have QUARTZ and MICA as their main constituents. Like all SCHISTS, mica schists have the bulk of their mineral components arranged in parallel, giving them a characteristic striped appearance. They often contain other metamorphic minerals such as garnet. Mica schists are found worldwide.

micelle

Roughly spherical group of large molecules that come together in a COLLOID. For example, a molecule of detergent or soap has a hydrophilic ("water-loving") polar head and a long hydrophobic ("water-hating") nonpolar tail. When detergents or soaps dissolve in water, the molecules clump together to form micelles with the nonpolar tails at the centre, surrounded by a sphere of polar heads linked to water molecules. Bile salts in the intestine make the products of fat digestion form micelles, which are thereby more easily absorbed.

Michaelmas daisy

Any of a large group of perennial plants belonging to the genus *Aster*. They are found in temperate zones and are particularly abundant in North America. They have leafy stems and conspicuous daisy flowers. The flowers, which often grow in clusters, are white to blue, pink or purple, with yellow centres. A number of species and their hybrids are grown as garden ornamentals. Family Asteraceae; genus *Aster*.

Michurin, Ivan Vladimirovich (1855–1935)

Russian plant breeder. His unorthodox theories of HEREDITY (Michurinism), which included belief in the theory of ACQUIRED CHARACTERISTICS, were for a time accepted as the official science of GENETICS by the Soviet Union. Through GRAFTING he managed to produce new strains of fruit, but his belief that grafting produces heritable changes has since been discredited.

microbe

Microscopic organism. The term is generally applied to VIRUSES and BACTERIA. *See also* MICROORGANISM

microbiology

Study of microorganisms, their structure, function and significance. Mainly concerned with single-cell forms, such as VIRUSES, BACTERIA, PROTOZOA and FUNGI, it has immense applications in medicine and the food industry. Microbiology began in the 17th century with the invention of the microscope, which enabled scholars to view microorganisms for the first time.

microclimate

See CLIMATE

M

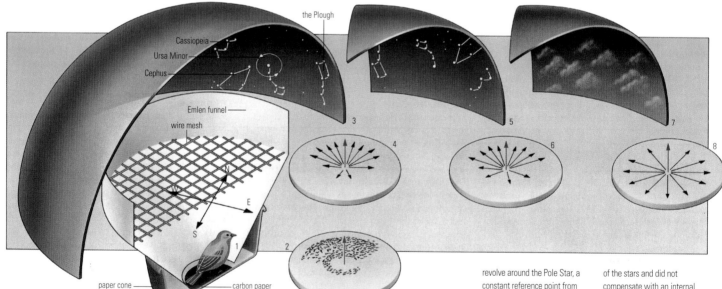

▲ **migration** Experiments with homing pigeons have shown that birds that migrate during the day have an internal body clock, which they use while referring to the position of the Sun to navigate. A night-migrating bird, however, does not use the Sun to navigate during the migrating season. A caged, night-migrating bird that can see the stars moves fretfully, orientating itself in the same direction to its normal flight – north in the spring and south in the autumn. This observation led to experiments to see how indigo buntings (1) were able to migrate using the stars (Moon and planet motions were ruled out as too complex) to navigate by and to investigate whether they too, like homing pigeons, had an internal body clock. When caged in an Emlen funnel placed under stars projected in a planetarium, the bunting could see the sky and tried to escape, leaving carbon paper footprints on the paper funnel (2), which could then be interpreted to show the direction of orientation. The projected stars could be repositioned to change the apparent time and alter the bunting's clock. As the Earth revolves every 24 hours and its axis of revolution points north to the Pole Star, the stars appear to revolve around the Pole Star, a constant reference point from which to orientate. Under stars set at normal time (3), the bird orientated successfully north (4) (in all diagrams red arrows show the correct migratory direction and black arrows show the scatter of actual observed orientations). When the stars were shifted 12 hours forward (5), the bird still orientated in the correct direction (6), showing that the bunting made direct use of the stars and did not compensate with an internal clock. But if the stars were eliminated and the planetarium diffusely lit to simulate stars obscured by clouds (7), the bunting's orientation attempts were entirely random (8). Further experiments confirmed that the birds navigate by observing the rotation of the stars closest to the Pole Star, which could be eliminated from the sky yet not impede correct orientation.

microfilament

Very thin strands, around 6nm in diameter, found in MUSCLE. They are usually made of the protein ACTIN, but some may be composed of myosin. It seems probable that microfilaments play a role in movement within cells, and possibly of whole cells in some cases.

microfossil

General name for the large variety of small FOSSILS (less than a millimetre or so in size), the remains of which are not clearly visible to the unaided eye. Microfossils include fossil pollen, spores, single-celled animals and the tiny teeth of CONODONTS. Many are very abundant in sedimentary rocks and are of considerable stratigraphic use for dating strata.

micronutrient

Element needed in relatively small amounts by growing plants. Micronutrients include iron, boron, zinc, copper, molybdenum and chlorine. *See also* MACRONUTRIENT

microorganism (microbe)

Organism that can be seen only with the help of a microscope. Microorganisms include BACTERIA, PROTOZOA, RICKETTSIAE, VIRUSES and some microscopic ALGAE and FUNGI. Disease-causing microorganisms are called PATHOGENS.

micropyle

In botany, the opening at the apex of the OVULE through which the pollen tube grows; also the minute pore in the covering of a seed through which water enters at the start of GERMINATION. In zoology, the micropyle is the aperture in the membrane of an ovum, especially in insects, through which a sperm reaches and fertilizes the ovum.

microsporan

Member of a group of intracellular, single-celled, parasitic protozoans; they are among the smallest and most primitive of eukaryotic cells. Microsporans live inside the cells of almost all groups of animals, but are particularly common in arthropods. Some are of economic importance as parasites of bees and silkworms. Phylum Microspora; genus *Microspora*.

microtubule

Thin, protein filament in the CYTOPLASM of a CELL, which may form pairs or bundles; it helps to maintain the shape of the cell. During cell division (MEIOSIS and MITOSIS), the microtubules from the SPINDLE are responsible for the movement of the chromosomes. Microtubules also occur in CENTRIOLES, CILIA and FLAGELLA.

microvilli

Tiny, finger-like projections found on the membranes of certain cells, such as the intestinal EPITHELIUM and the kidney tubules. Grouped together, they have a microscopic appearance similar to the bristles of a brush and are hence termed a brush border. ACTIN filaments within the microvilli allow them to contract, which, along with their large surface area, facilitates absorption. *See also* VILLI

micro whip-scorpion

Any of *c.*60 species of tiny SCORPION relatives, with a whip-like tail. Most species are found in tropical regions. Length (excluding "whip"): up to 20mm (0.8in). Subclass Palpigradi.

Mid-Atlantic Ridge

Underwater mountain range along the margin

▶ millet An important food grain in many parts of Asia and Africa, millet exists in numerous varieties. It is a valuable crop in areas of poor soil quality because it ripens quickly and can be stored for long periods. It is also cultivated in Europe and the USA as livestock fodder. Shown here is Indian finger millet (*Eleusine coracana*), which is grown in India and parts of Africa.

between the American crustal plate on one side and the European and African plates on the other. It runs from Iceland to near the Antarctic Circle along the middle of the Atlantic Ocean. It is formed at a CONSTRUCTIVE MARGIN, where two plates are diverging and new magma is flowing upward and outward to form new ocean crust. Iceland is located on the ridge itself and was formed by the outpourings of volcanic lava. *See also* PLATE TECTONICS

midbrain (mesencephalon)

One of the three divisions of the embryonic BRAIN of vertebrates. In a fully formed human being, the midbrain has become overlaid by the greatly developed cerebral lobes. It is thick-walled and is concerned particularly with sight and hearing. *See also* FOREBRAIN; HINDBRAIN

midge

Small mosquito-like fly of the order Diptera. Some midge species have red aquatic larvae called BLOODWORMS, which are a favourite food of fish. The majority of midges are harmless, but some species suck human and animal blood. BITING MIDGES are species within the family Ceratopogonidae. GALL MIDGES belong to the family Cecidomyiidae. Some members of the family Chironomidae are called NON-BITING MIDGES. Order Diptera.

mid-ocean ridge

Great median ridge of the SEAFLOOR; it is the place where new LITHOSPHERE is being formed. The ridges are the spreading edges of the tectonic plates that cover the Earth. They form a world-encircling system that extends, with several side branches, along the MID-ATLANTIC RIDGE, up, around and down through the Indian Ocean (the Mid-Indian Ridge) and across the Pacific (the Pacific-Antarctic Ridge). *See also* OCEANIC BASIN; PLATE TECTONICS; SEAFLOOR SPREADING

migmatite

Coarse-grained METAMORPHIC ROCK, often found in the shield of an ancient continent. It is formed at high temperatures deep within the Earth's crust. It has a granular texture consisting of dark SCHIST or GNEISS, with lighter folded bands of granitic rock.

mignonette

Any member of the genus *Reseda*, comprising *c.*70 species of plants native to N Africa, Asia and Europe. They have small flowers, clustered in a terminal spike, thick stems and coarse, lance-shaped leaves. A common species is the annual *Reseda odorata*, which has strongly scented flowers. Height: to 45cm (18in). Family Resedaceae.

migration

Periodic movement of animals or humans, usually in groups, from one area to another, in order to find food, breeding areas or better conditions. Animal migration involves the eventual return of the migrant to its place of departure. Fish migrate between fresh water and saltwater or from one part of an ocean to another. Birds usually migrate along established routes. Mammals usually migrate in search of food. For thousands of years, the deserts of central Asia widened inexorably, and this phenomenon resulted in the human migration of prehistoric tribes to China, the Middle East and Europe. *See also* EMIGRATION; IMMIGRATION

mildew

External filaments and fruiting structures of numerous mould-like FUNGI. Mildews are parasites of plants and cause substantial damage to growing crops.

milfoil (yarrow)

Strongly scented perennial herb; it is native to temperate areas of Europe and W Asia and has been introduced elsewhere. It is commonly found in meadows and hedgerows. It has feathery, divided leaves. The numerous, small, white to pink flowers form a dense, flat-topped cluster. Milfoil has long been valued for its medicinal value. Family Asteraceae; species *Achillea millefolium*.

milk

Liquid food secreted from MAMMARY GLANDS by the females of nearly all mammals in order to feed their young. The milk of domesticated cattle, sheep, goats, horses, camels and reindeer has been used as food by humans since prehistoric times, both directly and to make butter, cheese and fermented milks such as yogurt. Milk is a suspension of fat and protein in water, sweetened with lactose sugar. The proportions of these constituents vary with each mammal, those of cows' milk being water 87.1%, protein 3.4%, fat 5.9%. In modern dairying, cows' milk is pasteurized at about 72°C (160°F) for 16 seconds in order to kill all harmful microbes; it is then bottled under aseptic conditions. Nevertheless, unrefrigerated milk sours after a day or so at usual environmental temperatures because of the action of LACTOBACTERIA.

milkfish

Silvery fish that lives in marine and brackish, tropical and subtropical waters of the Indian and Pacific oceans. It is related to the CATFISH and MINNOW. The milkfish is an important food fish in Southeast Asia, where the young are captured and reared in coastal ponds. In the Philippines it is known as bangos, bangus or sabalo. Adult fish feed on algae. Length: to 1.8m (5.9ft). Family Chanidae; species *Chanos chanos*.

milkweed

Any of numerous perennial plants belonging to the family Asclepiadaceae. They produce a milky sap. The family include shrubs, woody vines and some succulent desert plants. They grow in tropical or subtropical regions in Africa and the Americas. Height: to 1.8m (6ft). Family Asclepiadaceae.

miller's thumb

Freshwater fish found in fast-flowing streams of Europe. It is one of the SCULPINS. It is brown, with a large bony head and tapered body. Length: to 10cm (4in). Family Cottidae; species *Cottus gobio*.

millet

CEREAL grass that produces small, edible seeds. The stalks have flower spikes, and the hulled seeds are white. In Russia, W Africa and Asia, it is a staple

M

food. In w Europe it is used mainly for pasture or hay. Pearl millet (*Pennisetum glaucum*) grows in poor soils and is used as food in India and Africa. Height: 100cm (39in). Family Poaceae/Gramineae.

millipede (diplopod)
Any member of the class Diplopoda, comprising numerous species of elongated, invertebrate, ARTHROPOD animals with large numbers of legs. Found throughout the world, millipedes have a segmented body, one pair of antennae and two pairs of legs per segment; they can be orange, brown or black. All species avoid light. They feed on plant tissues. Length: 0.2–28cm (0.08in–11in).

Milne, John (1850–1913)
British geologist. His invention (1880) of the seismograph helped to found the science of SEISMOLOGY. He helped to establish many seismological stations, particularly those for recording earthquakes in Japan. His books include *Earthquakes* (1883) and *Seismology* (1898).

mimicry
See feature article

mimosa
Any member of the genus *Mimosa*, comprising *c*.400 species of plants, shrubs and small trees. They are native to tropical North and South America. Mimosas have showy, feather-like leaves and heads or spikes of white, pink or yellow flowers. Family Mimosaceae.

miner
Any member of the bird genus *Manorina*, which belongs to the HONEYEATER family. Miners are found in the temperate rainforests of Australasia. Some species can be aggressive and noisy, and some display mob predator behaviour. Length: 25–30cm (10–12in). Family Meliphagidae; genus *Manorina*; there are five species.

mineral
Natural, homogeneous and, with a few exceptions, solid and crystalline materials that form the Earth and make up its ROCKS. Most minerals are formed through inorganic processes, and more than 3000 minerals have been identified. They are classified on the basis of chemical makeup, crystal structure and physical properties such as hardness, specific gravity, cleavage, colour and lustre. Some minerals are economically important as ORES from which metals are extracted. Some minerals, such as calcium and zinc, are vital for good NUTRITION in humans and animals.

mineralization
FOSSIL-forming process whereby preserved parts of plants and animals are altered by the minerals in the soil. Circulating water dissolves certain constituents of bones and shells, which are replaced by silica, iron or other compounds. This replacement can be so exact as to preserve the finest structures. It is a type of PETRIFICATION.

▶ **millipede** The pill millipede (*Glomeris marginata*) has the peculiar ability to roll up when disturbed, tucking its head in. The shell-like cuticle covering the segments of a millipede's body provides excellent protection against prying predators.

▲ **minnow** The European minnow (*Phoxinus Phoxinus*) is found in freshwater lakes and streams and is *c*.7cm (*c*.3in) in length. During the spring breeding season, the underside of the male turns red. Minnows often swim in shoals to reduce the chance of individuals being preyed upon.

mineralogy
Investigation of MINERALS, naturally occurring inorganic substances found on Earth and elsewhere in the Solar System. Major subdivisions are: CRYSTALLOGRAPHY, which studies the composition and atomic arrangement of minerals; **paramagnetic** mineralogy, which deals with the associations and order of crystallization of minerals; **descriptive** mineralogy, concerned with the physical properties used in identification of minerals; and **taxonomic** mineralogy, the classification of minerals by chemical and crystal type. *See also* GEOCHEMISTRY; PETROLOGY

minivet
Any member of the genus *Pericrocotus*, a group of medium-sized, brightly coloured perching birds. Minivets can be black above and red below or contrasting grey and black. They flit about in treetops, making aerial sallies for insects and occasionally hovering to glean prey from buds and leaves. They make constant contact calls. Minivets are found mainly in Southeast Asia. Length: 15–22cm (6–9in). Family Campephagidae; genus *Pericrocotus*.

mink
Small, semi-aquatic mammal of the WEASEL family; it has soft, durable, water-repellent hair of high commercial value. It has a slender body, short legs and a bushy tail. Wild mink have dark brown fur with long black outer hair. Ranch mink have been bred to produce fur of various colours. They eat fish, rodents and birds. Escaped ranch mink can be a serious threat to indigenous wildlife. Length to: 73cm (29in) including the tail; weight: 1.6kg (3.5lb). Family Mustelidae.

minla
Any of four species of small, strikingly coloured, long-tailed perching birds belonging to the BABBLER family. Most are green or brown above and yellow below, with chestnut wing panels. They have a white eye stripe, which contrasts with the black crown and eye patch. Minlas are restless insect feeders found in damp forests in Asia. Length: *c*.15cm (*c*.6in). Family Timaliidae; genus *Minla*.

minnow
Any member of a family of freshwater fish of temperate and tropical regions. It includes SHINERS, DACE, TENCH and BREAM. Specifically, the term minnow indicates fish of the genera *Phoxinus* and *Leuciscus*. Length: 4–46cm (2–18in). Family Cyprinidae.

mint
Any member of the genus *Mentha*, a group of aromatic herbs with a characteristic flavour. Mint is commonly used as a flavouring in cooking, confectionery and medicines. Most species have oval leaves and spikes of purple or pink flowers. Family Lamiaceae/Labiatae. *See also* PEPPERMINT

Miocene
Geological epoch beginning about 25 million and ending about 5 million years ago. It falls in the mid-

dle of the TERTIARY period and is marked by an increase in grasslands over the globe at the expense of forests, and the development of most of the modern mammal groups. No British Miocene deposits are known, although some folding took place caused by the rising of the Alps to the south.

mirage
Type of optical illusion sometimes seen near the Earth's surface when light is refracted as it passes between cool, dense air to warmer, less dense air. Mirages are most commonly seen shimmering on desert sands or hot, dry roads; the shimmer is a refracted image of the sky.

mirid bug (jumping plant bug)
Any of various member of the BUG family Miridae. The feeding habits of mirid bugs vary depending on the genus. Some species are predatory on insects infesting plants; they are economically important as a natural pest killer. Adult body size: 1–2mm (0.04–0.08in). Order Heteroptera; family Miridae.

mist
Water droplets in the atmosphere at ground level that decrease visibility. By standard definition, visibility in a mist is between 2000–1000m (6560–3280ft). When visibility drops below 1000m (3280ft), the mist is referred to as FOG. *See also* SMOG

mistletoe
Any of numerous species of evergreen plants that are semi-parasitic on tree branches. Mistletoe has small, spatula-shaped, yellowish-green leaves and generally forms a large, dense ball of foliage. The mistletoe taps into the branch of its host to sap its food supply, avoiding the necessity of growing roots itself. It also carries out photosynthesis, so is not entirely parasitic. Families Loranthaceae/Viscaceae.

mistletoebird
Small songbird of the FLOWERPECKER family. Its fine bill and tongue are adapted to eating nectar. Its staple diet is the fruit of mistletoe, and its stomach is specially adapted for digesting the soft mistletoe berries. The seeds are excreted in a viable state, thus spreading the parasitic plant. Length: 10cm (4in). Family Dicaeidae; species *Dicaeum hirundinaceum*.

mistral
Cold, winter, N wind that sweeps down the Rhône valley from the Massif Central of France. It is caused by cold air from Europe blowing southwards into a low-pressure area over the Mediterranean. When the mistral blows, temperatures sometimes fall as low as freezing point and strong gusts of up to 60 km/h (37mph) make conditions very unpleasant. Most farmhouses have rows of trees on their N side as protection from the wind, and many fields of fruits and vegetables shelter behind rows of cypress trees.

◀ **mint** Long used as a food flavouring, many species of mint are known, and they show subtle differences in the aroma they discharge. Crosses between water mint (*Mentha aquatica*) and spearmint (*Mentha spicata*) are the basis of cultivated peppermint (*Mentha x piperita*), which is commercially grown on a wide scale in the USA. It is used to flavour gums, toothpaste and a variety of drugs.

M

Mimicry is a form of animal protection through deception. The mimic, generally a harmless, edible species, imitates the warning shape or coloration of a "model", a poisonous or dangerous species. When coloration increases an animal's chances of survival, it is commonly referred to as protective coloration. **Batesian mimicry**, named after the British naturalist Henry BATES, is exemplified by HOVERFLIES, which mimic inedible WASPS. Similarly, the viceroy BUT-TERFLY imitates the inedible MONARCH BUTTER-FLY. The less-common **Müllerian mimicry**,

named after the German naturalist Fritz Müller, involves two or more unpalatable species that share a similar pattern, thus reinforcing it as one of the warnings to predators. A third form is **aggressive mimicry**, in which a predatory or parasitic species resembles a harmless one, thus allowing the former to remain undetected by its prey or host. A species of African jumping SPIDER both looks and moves like an ANT. This means that ants, which are often aggressive, mistake it for one of their own and relax their guard.

Animals have not just evolved structural and surface appearances to escape predation, behavioural strategies have also developed to rein-

force deception. When at rest, stick caterpillars hold their bodies away from the bark of trees, rigid and unmoving like a branching twig.

Animals are not the only mimics. Some plants mimic animals in order to attract pollinators. Carrion plant flowers – with their mottled red surface and foetid smell – lure flies that come to lay their eggs on the "food". Defensive mimicry also occurs in plants. The gaily coloured *Heliconia* butterflies of South and Central American rainforests lay their eggs on passion-flower vines, so their caterpillars can feed on the vine leaves. However, to ensure an ample supply of food for her offspring, the female butterfly will not lay her eggs on stems and leaves already occupied by eggs. The passion vine produces mock eggs on its leaves to deter this invasion.

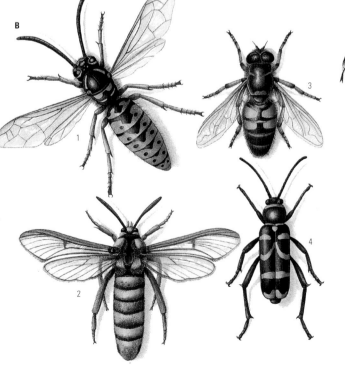

► **A stick insect** (A) shows the important defensive play of mimicking inedible objects such as dry sticks. Many insects use this disguise, including caterpillars, moths and praying mantises. A stick insect has spindly legs that are barely noticeable at rest. Its head is small and its body is smooth and textured like a twig, with slight ridges and markings mimicking twig nodes. Stick insects may remain motionless for hours. Some stick insects grow up to 30cm (12in) long, yet are almost invisible until they move; even then, they move each leg very slowly and respond to any disturbance by keeping still.

► **Many different insects** (B) mimic wasps or bees that deter predators with unpleasant stings. Key recognition points of the common wasp (1) are its size, a black and yellow body, transparent wings and a tiny waist. One "impostor" is the wasp-mimic moth (2), whose transparent wings are shaped like a hornet's; the moth even mimics its role model's flight patterns. The wasp beetle (3) convinces at a distance, and also imitates the jerkiness of a wasp's flight. A hoverfly (4) has a black thorax, which gives the impression that the abdomen ends abruptly in a narrow waist, even though this is only an optical illusion.

▲ **Many coral snakes** (C) of South America have black, red and yellow warning stripes. Some species have no poison, some like *Micrurus lemniscatus* (1), have lethal venom, and some, like *Oxyrhopus trigeminus* (2) are mildly poisonous: all inhabit the same areas. A mildly poisonous snake gives a predator an unpleasant taste that it remembers when it sees a similar snake. A harmless species has no poison, but it is protected by mimicking the poisonous species.

Lethal species also benefit – if attacked, their predators would not live to learn by experience. So both harmless and lethal species mimic moderately poisonous species, which must be the most numerous locally for a statistical probability that an attacker's experience will be unpleasant. Disputed by some scientists, Mertensian mimicry, as this is known, may be used by king snakes (3), which, although unrelated to coral snakes, have very similar colour banding but no venom.

M

◀ **mite** During the early part of its life, the mite species shown here (*Trombicula autumnalis*) is parasitic on vertebrate tissue. Its mouthparts are borne on a false head and its total body length is only 1mm (0.04in).

◀ **mole-rat** The African mole-rat (*Tachyoryctes splendens*) is a nocturnal rodent found in E and W Africa. It uses its large incisor teeth and sharp claws to dig burrows and tunnels underground. Although this species has reduced eyes, it is still able to see.

mite

ARACHNID found worldwide. All mites are small and lack external body segmentation; they have mouth parts on a discrete body region. Mites are widely distributed, from Oceanic trenches to the upper atmosphere. Due to their ubiquity, many mite species are pests. Beetle mites (Oribatei) are found in mosses. Gall mites (Eriophyidae) cause the plant host tissue to hypertrophy, providing the mites with shelter and food. The follicle mite (Demudicidae) is found in hair follicles. Adult body length: 0.1–30mm (0.004–1.2in). Class Arachnida; subclass Acari (part).

mite, harvest
See CHIGGER

mite, spider (red spider)
Red mite found throughout the world. A serious plant pest, it has been known to develop resistance to pesticides, making control difficult. Length: 0.3–0.8mm (0.01–0.03in). Subclass Acari; family Tetranychidae.

mite, water
Bright red to green aquatic mite found worldwide. The larva is parasitic on aquatic insects; most nymphs and adults are predators. Length: 6mm (0.25in). Subclass Acari; suborder Prostigmata.

mitochondrion
Structure (organelle) inside a CELL containing ENZYMES necessary for energy production. Mitochondria are found in the cytoplasm of most types of cell (but not in bacteria). *See also* RESPIRATION

mitosis
Nuclear division of a CELL resulting in two genetically identical daughter cells with the same number of chromosomes as the parent cell. Mitosis is the normal process of TISSUE growth; it is also involved in ASEXUAL REPRODUCTION. *See also* ANAPHASE; METAPHASE; MEIOSIS; illustration, page 243

mockingbird
Thrush-like North American songbird. It is noted for its rich loud song that imitates other species and often includes other sounds, such as dogs barking, pianos and squeaky gates. It has rather drab grey and black plumage. It feeds on insects, seeds and berries. Length: 22–25cm (9–10in). Family Mimidae; genus *Mimus*.

mock orange (Philadelphus or sweet syringa)
Any of various species belonging to the genus *Philadelphus*. They are ornamental, deciduous shrubs and are native to North America and Asia. They have solitary, white or yellowish, fragrant flowers. Family Hydrangeaceae; species include *Philadelphus coronarius*.

Mohl, Hugo von (1805–72)
German botanist who did pioneering research into the anatomy and physiology of plant CELLS. He formulated the idea that the cell nucleus is surrounded by a granular, colloidal substance, which in 1846 he called PROTOPLASM, although the term had been invented by Jan Purkinje (1787–1869). Mohl was the first to propose that new cells arise from CELL DIVISION. In 1851 he claimed that the secondary wall of a plant cell is fibrous, and this was subsequently confirmed. He also gave the first distinct account of the function of OSMOSIS.

Moho (Mohorovičić discontinuity)
Boundary between the Earth's LITHOSPHERE and MANTLE. It is identified by a change in the velocity of seismic waves passing through the Earth. It is named after the Croatian geophysicist Andrija Mohorovičić (1857–1936), who first recognized it in 1909. The velocity change is explained by a change to more dense rocks in the mantle; above the Moho the waves travel at about 6.4km s^{-1} (4mi s^{-1}), whereas below they travel at 8.2km s^{-1} (5.1mi s^{-1}). The depth of the Moho varies from about 5km (3mi) to 60km (37mi) below the Earth's surface; it is usually deeper beneath landmasses than beneath the sea. Initially interpreted as a sharp boundary, it is now known to be a wider zone in some locations, and its exact nature remains a matter of scientific debate. The **Gutenberg** discontinuity, discovered in 1912 by the American seismologist Beno Gutenberg (1889–1960), separates the mantle and the core; it is *c.*2900km (1800mi) deep. EARTHQUAKE and other shock waves are deflected at these boundaries.

Mohs scale
Range of HARDNESS used by geologists to express the comparative hardness of MINERALS by testing them against ten standard materials. It was devised in 1812 by the German mineralogist Friedrich Mohs (1773–1839). The hardest mineral, DIAMOND, has a hardness of 10 on the Mohs scale. It can scratch, or mark, any mineral with a lower Mohs number, including CORUNDUM (9), TOPAZ (8), QUARTZ (7), ORTHOCLASE (6), APATITE (5), FLUORITE (4), CALCITE (3), GYPSUM (2) and talc (1). A mineral hard enough to scratch material 3, but soft enough to be scratched by material 5, would be rated as having hardness 4 on the Mohs scale. Useful tools for determining hardness are the finger nail (about 2.5) and a penknife (about 5.5).

mojarra
Any member of the family Gerreidae, comprising marine, perch-like fish; there are also some freshwater representatives. Mojarras are silvery with protusile jaws (that is, the jaws can be thrust forwards). Length: to 35cm (14in). Family Gerreidae; there are 49 species.

molar
One of the large back TEETH of MAMMALS, adapted for grinding and chewing food. In most HERBIVORES the cusps (points or ridges on the top surface) are fused to form ridges for grinding plants. In adult humans there are 12 permanent molars, three on each side of each jaw, top and bottom.

mole (symbol mol)
SI unit of amount of substance. It is the amount of substance that contains as many elementary units, such as atoms and molecules, as there are atoms in 0.012kg of carbon-12. The mass of one mole of a compound is its relative molecular mass (molecular weight) in grams.

mole
Any of several species of small mammal in the family Talpidae (true moles); also 19 species of golden mole in the family Chrysochloridae. True moles are small, sausage-shaped mammals that burrow under grasslands of the Northern Hemisphere. They have short, smooth, velvet-like fur, which allows them to move easily through their tunnels. They dig with their short, powerful front limbs; their wide hands are turned outwards and have massive claws. As they tunnel the spoil is pushed up in "molehills". Moles are almost blind but are very sensitive to vibrations. They feed on underground invertebrates, especially worms.

mole, Californian
Any of three species of mole native to W United States. They have silky black fur, nostrils that open upwards and visible eyes. They live in forests and grasslands up to an altitude of 2700m (8900ft). Head-body length: 11–19cm (4–7in); tail: 2–5cm (1–2in). Family Talpidae; species include *Scapanus latimanus*.

▶ **mole** Relatives of the European mole (*Talpa europaea*) have evolved worldwide; all the species have similar shape of body and foot, but are not closely related. The marsupial mole (*Notoryctes typhlops*) of Australia has distinctive broad forefeet with five claws on each which it uses for digging and paddling through water. The large golden mole (*Chrysospalax villosus*) of central and S Africa is found in a variety of environments, ranging from forests and swamps to deserts. Grant's desert mole (*Eremitalpa granti*) is found on coastal dunes in S Africa.

marsupial mole

Grant's desert mole

large golden mole

European mole

mole, Eastern American
Mole that inhabits well-drained grasslands in s North America. It has black or copper-coloured fur. The Eastern American mole has nostrils that open upwards, and its eyes and ears are hidden. It has webbed fingers and toes but despite these adaptations only swims when necessary. Head-body length: 11–17cm (4–7in); tail: 2–4cm (1–2in). Family Talpidae; species *Scalopus aquaticus*.

mole, European
Mole that is found across Europe from the British Isles (except Ireland) to Russia. Across this range, it varies from black through brown and cream to almost white. Head-body length: 11–18cm (4–7in); tail: 1–5cm (0.5–2in). Family Talpidae; species *Talpa europaea*.

mole, golden
Any member of a family of small mammals; they are not true moles, and they resemble them only in that they lead a similar lifestyle. All golden moles live in Africa. They have a horny pad on the nose and only four, heavily clawed fingers on each hand. Their short fur has a metallic sheen and is gold, bronze, green or violet. Head-body length: 8–23cm (3–9in); no tail. Family Chrysochloridae.

mole, marsupial
See MARSUPIAL MOLE

mole, star-nosed
Mole found in North America; it is a colonial animal. It has black fur, and its hairless tail gets fatter before the breeding season. Its nose is surrounded by pink fleshy "rays", which are sensitive to a range of stimuli, including electrical fields. Head-body length: 10–13cm (4–5in); tail: 6–8cm (2–3in). Family Talpidae; species *Condylura cristata*.

molecular biology
Biological study of the makeup and function of molecules found in living organisms. Major areas of study include the chemical and physical properties of proteins and of NUCLEIC ACIDS such as DNA. *See also* BIOCHEMISTRY

molecule
Smallest particle of a substance (such as a compound) that exhibits the chemical properties of that substance. A molecule may consist of one ATOM, but

▲ **mollusc** Members of the *Neopilina* genus are the earliest molluscs still in existence, dating from the Paleaozoic era. *Neopilina* species are flattened limpets with a single shell, *c.*35mm (*c.*1.4in) wide. The reason for this mollusc's survival is probably that it retreated to the depths of the sea, where it had little competition from other mollusc species.

it generally consists of two or more atoms held together by CHEMICAL BONDS. For example, water molecules consist of two atoms of hydrogen bonded to one atom of oxygen (H_2O). A molecule (unlike an ION) has no electrical charge. *See also* MACROMOLECULE

mole-rat
Rodent that digs extensive burrow systems; for this reason it resembles a mole, although some species are more rat-like. Most mole-rats are from Africa, except for one species, which lives east of the Mediterranean. They have short, dumpy bodies and short but strong limbs with powerful claws. The mole-rat's tail may be long or absent. Their heads are large with tiny ears and eyes but very big incisor teeth. Family Bathyergidae.

mole-rat, common
Any of nine species of mole-rat; they range in colour from white, through yellow, fawn, grey or reddish to black. Common mole-rats live in a variety of habitats, from savanna to forest and from flood plains to mountain slopes. They have velvety fur and are very sensitive to vibrations and air movements. Head-body length: 9–27cm (4–11in); tail: 1–3cm (0.5–1in). Family Bathyergidae; species include *Cryptomys damarensis*.

mole-rat, naked (sand puppy)
Mole-rat native to arid areas of Ethiopia, Somalia and Kenya. It has almost hairless, wrinkled, pale skin. Naked mole-rats live entirely underground in large colonies. Only a single female "queen" and her three or four mates reproduce. All the offspring have non-breeding worker status, similar to bees in a hive. Head-body length: 8–9cm (3–4in); tail: 3–4cm (1–2in). Family Bathyergidae; species *Heterocephalus glaber*.

mollusc
Any of more than 80,000 species of INVERTEBRATE animals in the phylum Mollusca. They include the familiar SNAILS, SLUGS, CLAMS and SQUIDS, and a host of less well-known forms. Originally marine, members of the phylum Mollusca are now found in the oceans, in fresh water, and on land. Classes of mollusc include the primitive GASTROPODS, univalves (slugs and snails), BIVALVES, TUSK SHELLS and CEPHALOPODS. The mollusc body is divided into three: the head, the foot and the visceral mass. Associated with the body is a fold of skin called the mantle, which secretes the limy shell typical of most molluscs. The head is well developed only in snails and in the cephalopods, which have eyes, tentacles and a well-formed mouth. The visceral mass contains the internal organs of circulation (blood vessels and heart), respiration (gills), excretion (kidney), digestion (stomach and intestine) and reproduction (gonads). The sexes are usually separate but there are many hermaphroditic species. Cephalopods, bivalves and gastropods feature as important fossils in the geological past. *See also* HERMAPHRODITE

◀ **moloch** The spiny appendage on the back of a moloch's neck is an unusual defence mechanism. When threatened, the moloch tucks its head between its forelegs so that this appendage appears to be its real head. This makes it difficult for predators to catch or swallow the moloch.

moloch (thorny devil)
Flattened, wide-bodied LIZARD that is covered by large spines; it has particularly large spines over each eye and an enlarged spiny hump on its neck. The moloch is a desert-dwelling species native to central and w Australia. It feeds exclusively on ants. Channels in its skin help to funnel scarce water to its mouth. Length: to 18cm (7in). Family Agamidae; species *Moloch horridus*.

monarch
Any of several members of the monarch flycatcher family, found in Africa and Asia. Some species are blue, others black and white, and others drab with white spotted or reddish-brown fan-shaped tails; most species have crests. Family Monarchidae; genera *Hypothymis*, *Monarcha* and *Philentoma*.

monarch butterfly (milkweed butterfly)
Large, migratory BUTTERFLY found mainly in North, Central and South America. It has brownish-orange wings with black veins and borders. Its caterpillars feed on milkweed, which gives their bodies a taste disliked by birds. The unrelated viceroy butterfly mimics the coloration of the monarch in order also to be avoided by birds. Family Danaidae; species *Danaus plexippus*.

Monera
See PROKARYOTAE

mongoose
Active carnivore from Asia, Africa and Madagascar; it has also been introduced in parts of Europe. It has a long, slender body, short legs, a short tail and a pointed face. Mongooses are mostly diurnal and solitary but some live in sociable colonies. They feed on small mammals, birds, eggs, reptiles and invertebrates. Family Herpestidae.

mongoose, banded
Mongoose found from Gambia to Ethiopia and south to South Africa. It is brownish-grey with yellow or white stripes across its back. Head-body length: 30–45cm (12–18in); tail: 23–30cm (9–12in). Family Herpestidae; species *Mungos mungo*.

▲ **monarch butterfly** Every autumn the monarch butterflies of North America form huge swarms and migrate southwards towards the Equator. They fly en masse from the Rocky mountain region to central Mexico, a journey of several thousand miles, and return in the spring.

M

► **mongoose, banded** A gregarious creature, the banded mongoose lives in groups of up to 40 animals in communal burrows. It hunts and forages as a group, communicating by a constant twittering noise. If one member of the group is threatened by a predator, the others will often come to its defence.

mongoose, broad-striped
Either of two species of mongoose from Madagascar. It has a brown body with wide, black, longitudinal stripes along its flanks and back. Head-body length: 32–34cm (13in); tail: 28–30cm (11–12in). Family Herpestidae; species *Galidictis fasciata*.

mongoose, brown
Mongoose found in Madagascar. It has a reddish-brown coat and lives in pairs. Head-body length: 24cm (9in); tail: 16cm (6in). Family Herpestidae; species *Salanoia unicolor*.

mongoose, dwarf
Either of two species of mongoose that live in brush and scrubland of s Africa. They are speckled brown, with dark legs and tail. Head-body length: 18–26cm (7–10in); tail: 12–20cm (5–8in). Family Herpestidae; species *Helogale parvula*.

mongoose, Egyptian (African mongoose, ichneumon)
Mongoose native to N and s Africa; it has been introduced to Spain and Portugal. Head-body length: up to 65cm (26in); tail: 50cm (20in). Family Herpestidae; species *Herpestes ichneumon*.

mongoose, narrow-striped
Mongoose native to Madagascar. It is grey-beige with thin, dark stripes along its back and sides. Head-body length: 25–35cm (10–14in); tail: 23–27cm (9–11in). Family Herpestidae; species *Mungotictis decemlineata*.

mongoose, ring-tailed
Mongoose that inhabits humid forests in Madagascar. It is dark chestnut in colour and its tail is ringed with black. It climbs trees, swims and digs burrows for shelter. Head-body length: 40cm (16in); tail: 30cm (12in). Family Herpestidae; species *Galidia elegans*.

mongoose, ruddy
Nocturnal mongoose from India and Sri Lanka. It has a light-brown coat, speckled with white and red, and dark feet and tail-tip. Head-body length: 45cm (18in); tail: 40cm (16in). Family Herpestidae; species *Herpestes smithi*.

mongoose, small Indian (Indian grey mongoose)
Mongoose that is found from Arabia eastwards to Nepal, India and Sri Lanka. It has a black-speckled, light-brown coat. Head-body length: 43cm (17in); tail: 39cm (15in). Family Herpestidae; species *Herpestes edwardsi*.

mongoose, white-tailed
Mongoose that inhabits the savanna of the Arabian Peninsula, N and E Africa. Its body is greyish with black legs; its bushy tail is white. Head-body length: 47–71cm (18–28in); tail: 35–47cm (14–18in). Family Herpestidae; species *Ichneumia albicauda*.

monito del monte (colocolo)
Small, grey-brown, arboreal marsupial with a thick tail and round ears. It inhabits humid forests of central Chile, where it constructs spherical nests in which to hibernate. Head-body length: 8–13cm (3–5in); tail: 9–13cm (4–5in). Family Microbiotheriidae; species *Dromiciops australis*.

monitor (goanna)
Any of several species of moderate to very large lizards occurring throughout Africa, Asia and Australia. They have long necks and tails, and powerful, strongly clawed limbs. Most species are dull-coloured, with yellow markings. Most are terrestrial carnivores, but some species climb or spend much of their time in water; one species has a largely vegetarian diet. Length: 30–300cm (12–120in). Family Varanidae.

monitor, Komodo
See KOMODO DRAGON

monjita
Any of a group of about six species of tyrant flycatchers found in South America. Most species have bold white or black-and-white plumage. Family Tyrannidae; genera *Xolmis* and *Neoxolmis*.

monkey
Member of any of three families belonging to the PRIMATE order. The families are: Callitrichidae, which includes the MARMOSETS and TAMARINS; Cebidae, the capuchin-like monkeys; and Cercopithidae, which comprises the MACAQUES and

▲ **monito del monte** The only living member of the Microbiotheriidae family of marsupials, the monito del monte is a nocturnal hunter which eats insects and small invertebrates and usually hibernates during the winter. Females have between one and five offspring, which grow in the pouch before moving into the nest.

BABOONS. The Callitrichidae and Cebidae are often termed New World monkeys, because they come mainly from the Americas; they are also termed platyrrhines because they have flat noses. Many New World species have prehensile tails, with which they can cling to branches. The Cercopithidae are termed Old World monkeys and are found in Africa and Asia; they are also called catarrhines because their nostrils are narrow, close together and point downwards. Old World monkeys do not have prehensile tails but often have hard callosities on their buttocks. Monkeys are usually diurnal creatures, depending on sight rather than smell. Most species live in trees and are very agile, moving rapidly through the branches. Their varied diet includes flowers, leaves, seeds, nectar and sap, as well as eggs, invertebrates, small reptiles, birds and mammals. Monkeys have dextrous fingers, with which they manipulate their food. Most monkey species live in highly sociable family groups and communicate vocally.

monkey, blue
Any of three subspecies of blue monkey: the blue, which has a blue-grey coat; the silver, which has a grey coat; and the golden or Samango monkey, which has a yellowish coat. Blue monkeys are found in the rainforests of Angola, Ethiopia and s Africa. Head-body length: 49–66cm (19–26in); tail: 50–70cm (20–28in). Family Cercopithidae; species *Cercopithecus mitis*.

monkey, capuchin
Any of four species of monkey that live in polygamous groups in forests and swamps of Central and South America. Head-body length: 33–48cm (13–19in); tail: 40–50cm (16–20in). Family Cebidae; genus *Cebus*.

monkey, colobus
Member of either of two genera of slender, long-tailed monkeys. Colobus monkeys are found in forests and swamps of central and s Africa. Head-body length: 43–70cm (17–28in); tail: 40–80cm (16–31in). Family Cercopithidae; genera *Colobus* (black colobus) and *Procolobus* (red colobus).

monkey, Diana
Monkey that lives in forests from Sierra Leone to Ghana. It has a striking coat pattern of black with white throat, chest and arms and chestnut back and hind legs. Head-body length: 41–53cm (16–21in); tail: 50–75cm (20–30in). Family Cercopithidae; species *Cercopithecus diana*.

monkey, douc (red-shanked douc, cochin China monkey)
Monkey from forests of Vietnam and Laos. It is one of the most colourful of all mammals, with white areas on its face, throat, rump and tail, surrounded by orange bands on a black coat. Head-body length: 53–63cm (21–25in); tail: 57–67cm (22–26in). Family Cercopithidae; species *Pygathrix nemaeus*.

monkey, howler
Either of two species of monkey found in South American forests and mangroves. They are large, loudly vocal monkeys, with inflatable throat pouches. Head-body length: 40–72cm (16–28in); tail: 48–71cm (19–28in). Family Cebidae; species *Alouatta seniculus* (red howlers) and *Alouatta caraya* (black howlers).

monkey, leaf
See LANGUR; SURELI

M

monkey, mona
Monkey that lives in rainforests of Senegal and Uganda. It has a brownish back, white underparts, a blue face surrounded by a yellow band, and a pink muzzle. Head-body length: 46–56cm (18–22in). Family Cercopithidae; species *Cercopithecus mona*.

monkey, moustached
Monkey that inhabits the rainforests of Cameroon to Angola. It has a greyish-red coat with white underparts and a white moustache. Head-body length: 48–56cm (19–22in); tail: 60–70cm (24–28in). Family Cercopithidae; species *Cercopithecus cephus*.

monkey, night (owl monkey, douroucouli)
Monkey found in the savanna and forests of Panama to Paraguay. It has a grey coat with a white face and a chestnut chest. It has the large eyes of a nocturnal animal. An inflatable throat pouch amplifies its calls. Head-body length: 24–47cm (9–19in); tail: 31–40cm (12–16in). Family Cebidae; species *Aotus trivirgatus*.

monkey, owl-faced (Hamlyn's monkey)
Monkey found in forests from the Democratic Republic of Congo to Rwanda. It is olive-coloured, with dark extremities and a white stripe along its nose. Head-body length: 56cm (22in). Family Cercopithidae; species *Cercopithecus hamlyni*.

monkey, patas (military monkey, hussar monkey)
Terrestrial monkey from Senegal, Ethiopia, Kenya and Tanzania. It has a shaggy, reddish-brown coat with white extremities. Head-body length: 58–75cm (23–30in); tail: 62–74cm (24–29in). Family Cercopithidae; species *Erythrocebus patas*.

monkey, proboscis
Monkey found in the mangroves and lowland forests of Borneo. It has a reddish-orange coat. The adult male is twice the size of the female and has a pendulous, tongue-shaped nose. Head-body length: 54–76cm (21–30in); tail: 52–75cm (20–30in). Family Cercopithidae; species *Nasalis larvatus*.

monkey, red-bellied
Monkey that lives in the rainforest of Nigeria. It is brown with a black face and a white throat ruff. Head-body length: 46cm (18in). Family Cercopithidae; species *Cercopithecus erythrogaster*.

▲ **monkey, howler** One of the loudest animals in the world, the howler monkey has a call that can be heard up to two miles away. It spends most of its time in the highest branches of the forest and uses its prehensile tail to hang from branches while feeding on fruit and vegetation.

▲ **monkey, proboscis** A female proboscis monkey (*Nasalis larvatus*) and her young are shown here. The distinguishing feature of this species – the long nose – is most noticeable in the male, whose nose is so long that he has to move it out of the way in order to eat. The young monkey has a distinctive blue face, which soon becomes grey.

monkey, red-eared
Monkey that inhabits the rainforests of Nigeria and Cameroon, w Africa. It has a brown coat, with pale limbs and a red tail. Its face is blue with a red nose and ear-tips. Head-body length: 36–51cm (14–20in). Family Cercopithidae; species *Cercopithecus erythrotis*.

monkey, redtail (coppertail monkey, Schmidt's guenon)
Monkey that lives in the rainforests of central Africa. It has a speckled yellow-brown body with pale underparts and a chestnut tail. Head-body length: 41–48cm (16–19in). Family Cercopithidae; species *Cercopithecus ascanius*.

monkey, saki
Any of six species of monkey – four of the genus *Pithecia* and two of the genus *Chiropotes* (bearded sakis). They are native to the forests and savannas of the Amazon basin, South America. Head-body length: 33–46cm (13–18in); tail: 33–50cm (13–20in). Family Cebidae.

monkey, snub-nosed
Monkey that lives in the forests of s China, Tibet and e India. It is large and long-tailed with an upturned nose. It has greyish fur with a golden face and underparts. Head-body length: 50–83cm (20–33in); tail: 51–100cm (20–39in). Family Cercopithecidae; genus *Pygathrix*; there are six species, including *Pygathrix roxellana* (golden monkey).

monkey, spider
Five species of monkey – the rare woolly spider monkey or muriqui (*Brachyteles arachnoides*) and four of the genus *Ateles*. Spider monkeys swing through the canopies of the rainforests of n South America, holding on with their hands, feet and long prehensile tails. Head-body length: 34–82cm (13–32in); tail: 75–92cm (30–36in). Family Cebidae.

monkey, spot-nosed (greater white-nosed monkey, hocheur)
Monkey found from the rainforests of Sierra Leone to the Democratic Republic of Congo. It has a dark olive coat, with black belly, feet and tail and a white spot on its nose. Head-body length: 44–66cm (17–26in). Family Cercopithecidae; species *Cercopithecus nictitans*.

monkey, squirrel
Either of two species of monkey, *Saimiri sciureus* and the much rarer *Saimiri oerstedii*, from moist forests of Central and South America. Squirrel monkeys have yellow-green coats with white underparts and face; the tail tip, muzzle and top and sides of the head are black. Head-body length: 23–37cm (9–15in); tail: 37–47cm (15–19in). Family Cebidae; genus *Saimiri*.

monkey, titi
Red-brown monkey from the understorey of rainforests of South America. It lives in small monogamous family groups. There are three species: the dusky or red titi, *Callicebus moloch*; the yellow- or white-handed titi, also called the collared titi or widow monkey, *Callicebus torquatus*; and the masked titi, *Callicebus personatus*. Head-body length: 30–46cm (12–18in); tail: 29–55cm (11–22in). Family Cebidae; genus *Callicebus*.

monkey, uakari
Either of two species of monkey from the swampy Amazonian forest of Brazil. The red, white or bald uakari (*Cacajao rubicundus*) has a naked pink face and a white or reddish coat. The black uakari (*Cacajao melanocephalus*) has black fur and skin. Both have short tails and consequently prefer to walk on all fours rather than leap. Head-body length: 36–48cm (14–19in); tail: 15–16cm (6in). Family Cebidae; genus *Cacajao*.

monkey, vervet (grivet, savanna or green monkey)
Monkey that lives near the ground along the watercourses of Senegal to Somalia and s Africa. It has a grey or yellow-green coat with a black face. Head-body length: 46–80cm (18–31in); tail: 50–70cm (20–28in). Family Cercopithecidae; species *Cercopithecus aethiops*.

monkey, woolly
Either of two species of monkey from the rainforests of South America. They are: the common woolly

M

◄ **monkey, squirrel** The common squirrel monkey (*Saimiri sciureus*) spends most of its time in the treetops, feeding on fruit and nuts as well as insects, eggs and young birds. However, they are also known to feed on the ground and to make bold raids on areas of cultivated fruit. Lively and friendly, they commonly live in groups of up to 30 individuals and sleep huddled together on large tree branches.

▲ **monkey puzzle** The tangled branches of the monkey puzzle tree make it difficult for animals to climb. It has male and female cones for reproduction, which often develop on separate trees. The female cone (shown here) is rounded, whereas the male cone is long and thin.

monkey, also known as Humboldt's or smokey, *Lagothrix lagotricha*; and the yellow-tailed woolly monkey *Lagothrix flavicauda*. They both have very dense coats of fur. Head-body length: 39–58cm (15–23in); tail: 56–73cm (22–29in). Family Cebidae; genus *Lagothrix*.

monkey flower
Any of a number of annual or perennial plants belonging to the genus *Mimulus* of the FIGWORT family. Monkey flowers have two-lipped, tubular flowers, resembling those of the antirrhinum (snapdragon); they have a spotted pattern suggesting a monkey's face. Family Scrophulariaceae.

monkey puzzle (Chilean pine)
Evergreen tree native to the Andes mountains, South America. It has tangled branches, with spirally arranged, sharp, flat leaves. The seeds are edible. Height: to 45m (150ft). Family Araucariaceae; species *Araucaria araucana*.

monkfish (angelshark)
Cartilaginous fish, a type of SHARK. It has a flattened head with lateral gill openings, an elongated body with wing-like pectoral fins and a slender tail. The monkfish is found in warmer waters of the Atlantic and Pacific oceans. It is a popular food fish. Length: to 2.5m (8.2ft). Family Squatinidae.

monkshood
Poisonous perennial herb found wild or cultivated throughout temperate regions of the Northern Hemisphere. It grows on shady stream banks or in mountain meadows. The dark blue or purple flowers, borne on erect stems, resemble the shape of a monk's hood. Extracts, particularly of the fleshy roots, can be highly poisonous in large concentrations. Family Ranunculaceae; species *Aconitum napellus*.

monoamine oxidase (MAO, adrenaline oxidase, tryaminase)
ENZYME widely distributed in animals. Its function in the body is the breakdown of certain biologically active amines, three of the most important of which are the tryptamine derivatives, the catechol amines (such as ADRENALINE and DOPAMINE) and histamine. **Monoamine oxidase inhibitors** are used as antidepressants.

monocotyledon
Any member of the Monocotyledonae subclass of flowering plants (ANGIOSPERMS) characterized by one seed leaf (COTYLEDON) in the seed embryo; the leaves are usually parallel-veined. LILIES, ONIONS, ORCHIDS, PALMS and GRASSES are examples of monocotyledons. The larger subclass of plants is the Dicotyledonae (*see* DICOTYLEDON).

monocyte
Large LEUCOCYTE (white blood cell). A monocyte has a kidney-shaped nucleus and its protoplasm stains a blue-grey colour. It is a PHAGOCYTE, actively digesting foreign particles, such as bacteria and debris from dead cells. A millilitre of normal blood contains up to a million monocytes. *See also* IMMUNE SYSTEM

Monod, Jacques (1910–76)
French biochemist. With François JACOB, Monod developed the idea that MESSENGER RNA (mRNA) carries hereditary information from the nucleus of a CELL to the cellular sites during PROTEIN SYNTHESIS. He also introduced the concept of the operator GENE controlling the activity of other genes. Together with André LWOFF, they were awarded the 1965 Nobel Prize for physiology or medicine.

monoecious
Having both male and female FLOWERS on the same plant. The male flowers bear STAMENS, and the females bear one or more CARPELS. The MAIZE plant (*Zea mays*) is an example of a monoecious plant. *See also* DIOECIOUS

monohybrid cross
Inheritance of a single character. In a case where the parents are pure breeding for a different form of the character being studied, for example blue eyes and brown eyes, red fruit and yellow fruit, the offspring of the cross exhibit only the DOMINANT feature (brown eyes or red fruit). *See also* DIHYBRID CROSS

monomer
Chemical compound composed of single molecules, as opposed to a POLYMER, which is built up from repeated monomer units. For example, an AMINO ACID is a monomer of a protein, and propylene is the monomer from which polypropylene is made.

▲ **monocotyledon** The autumn crocus (*Colchicum autumnale*) is a typical example of a monocotyledon species. Monocotyledonous plants generally have long, narrow leaves with veins that run lengthways. The leaves usually grow from the base of the stem.

monosaccharide
Sweet-tasting CARBOHYDRATE that cannot be broken down into smaller units by HYDROLYSIS; it is a simple sugar. Monosaccharides are the basic respiratory SUBSTRATES in living organisms. Examples of monosaccharides include GLUCOSE, FRUCTOSE, galactose and RIBOSE. *See also* DISACCHARIDE; POLYSACCHARIDE

monotreme
Member of the Monotremata order, which comprises primitive MAMMALS that lay eggs. The only monotremes are the PLATYPUS and two species of ECHIDNA, all native to Australasia. The eggs are temporarily transferred to a pouch beneath the female's abdomen, where they eventually hatch and are nourished by rudimentary MAMMARY GLANDS. *See also* MARSUPIAL; PROTOTHERIAN

monsoon
Seasonal wind, especially in S Asia. In summer, which is the monsoon season, the winds normally blow from the sea to the land and bring RAIN, but in winter there is a complete change of direction and the winds blow out from the land, giving dry weather. Some monsoon regions are very wet; Cherrapunji in India, for example, receives over 11,000mm (433in) of rain each year. But others can be dry, such as the Thar Desert between India and Pakistan, where the rainfall is usually less than 250mm (10in). The major monsoon areas are in Asia, where the seasonal reversal of wind is greatest. This is because Asia, the largest continent, is adjacent to the largest ocean, the Pacific. In the smaller continents of South America, Africa, Australia and North America, the monsoonal effects are less marked. These smaller continents do not have such wet summers or such dry winters; they are sometimes referred to as "eastern marginal" rather than true monsoon.

monsoon forest
Type of tropical forest that is found in parts of Southeast Asia and the Indian subcontinent, where rainfall averages between *c*.100–200cm (40–80in) annually. It consists of sal and TEAK trees, both of which are valuable export commodities, with some evergreen undergrowth.

monstera
Any member of the *Monstera* genus, a group of climbing or trailing plants found in tropical America. Their large glossy leaves are commonly holed or deeply incised. *Monstera deliciosa*, often called a Swiss-cheese plant, is a popular houseplant. Family Araceae.

montbretia
Perennial plant with rhizome-producing corms; it is widely grown in gardens. Montbretia developed from a hybrid between two species native to South Africa; it first flowered in France in 1880. It has slender stems and sword-shaped leaves and bears yellow or orange, trumpet-shaped flowers. Family Iridaceae; hybrid *Crocosmia x crocosmiiflora*.

moonfish
Any of several fish of the order Perciformes, many of which live in the Atlantic and Pacific oceans. Species of moonfish include the thin silvery or golden *Vomer setapinnis*, up to 30cm (12in) in length, and the spotted silver *Mene maculata*, up to 20cm (8in) in length. Family Menidae or Monodactylidae.

moonrat
Small, rat-like mammal that is found only in

M

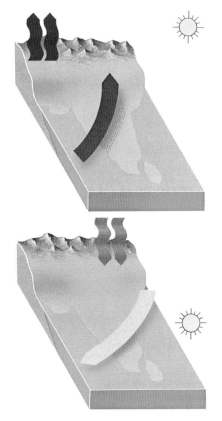

▲ **monsoon** Caused by low pressure areas over land masses in the summer, monsoons bring wet winds from the sea. In the winter high pressure areas cause dry winds to blow from the land. During the summer (top) large areas of mainland Asia are heated by the Sun. The air over these regions expands and rises forming regions of low pressure. Wet winds from the sea then blow into these areas giving the summer monsoons. In the winter (bottom), the situation is reversed and regions of high pressure are formed over the land. Dry winter monsoon winds the blow out to sea. The paths of these winds are deflected due to the Coriolis effect.

Southeast Asia. It is nocturnal and primarily insectivorous. The moonrat has bristly black fur and white markings on its head. Length: to 58cm (23in) overall. Family Erinaceidae; species *Echinosorex gymnurus*.

moorhen
Medium-sized waterbird of Europe, Asia and America; it is the commonest member of the RAIL family. The moorhen is often found around water margins or swimming in the open, using a constant flitting of its white under tail feathers. It flies weakly, with dangling legs. It is mainly blackish-brown, with a red forehead. Length: 34cm (13in). Family Rallidae; species *Gallinula chloropus*.

moorland
Tract of bleak open land, generally on a plateau or mountain. The vegetation is likely to be HEATHER or BRACKEN, with some coarse GRASSES. Many moorland areas, for example parts of the Pennines and Dartmoor in England, have extensive stretches of peat bog. Acid soils often develop, especially in areas of heavy precipitation.

moose
DEER found in North America and N Eurasia (when it is sometimes known as the European elk). It is the largest of all deer. Height at the shoulder: to 1.8m (6ft); weight: 820kg (1800lb). Family Cervidae; species *Alces alces*.

moraine
Accumulation of boulders and rock fragments that have been deposited by a GLACIER. Some of the rocks may have been eroded by the ice; some may be the result of freeze-thaw activity; and others are weathered blocks that have simply been transported by the ice. Morainic debris is carried by the ice and dumped at the sides or at the end, or at the bottom of the ice if it falls through crevasses. Accumulations at the side of a glacier are called **lateral moraines**; at the end of the glacier they are called **terminal moraines**. When two glaciers merge, two lateral moraines unite in the middle of the enlarged glacier to form a **medial moraine**. Beneath the ice there will be gradual accumulations of **ground moraine**, but much of it is reduced to small fragments and powder by the effect of the ice grinding it on the bedrock. Ground moraine can be an effective abrasive tool, if scraped along the valley floor by the movement of the ice.

Morgan, Thomas Hunt (1866–1945)
US biologist. He was awarded the 1933 Nobel Prize for physiology or medicine for the establishment of the CHROMOSOME theory of HEREDITY. His discovery of the function of chromosomes through experiments with the fruit-fly (*Drosophila*) is related in his book *The Theory of the Gene* (1926, rev. ed. 1928).

morning glory
Any of several species of twining and trailing vines that are native to warm climates. The blue, purple, pink or white flowers of morning glory plants are funnel-shaped with a flaring disc. Species include common morning glory, *Ipomoea purpurea*, with heartshaped leaves, and *Ipomoea violacea* of tropical America, which bears seeds that contain ALKALOIDS. Family Convolvulaceae.

morphology
Biological study of the form and structure of living things, especially the external form. It ranges from visible characteristics to microscopic structures, and often focuses on the relation between similar features in different organisms.

morula
Early stage in the development of the EMBRYO in animals when the cells are in the process of splitting before the BLASTULA stage. The morula consists of a number of blastomeres, the cells formed from the fertilized OVUM as a result of CELL DIVISION.

mosasaur
Any member of an extinct group of very large, powerful and ferocious marine predators, for example *Mosasaurus*. These lizard relatives were a short-lived group, evolving in mid-Cretaceous times and dying out in the late Cretaceous. Length: to 15m (49ft).

mosquito
See feature article

mosquitofish
Small, grey or grey-and-black, live-bearing fish. It is related to the GUPPY and the KILLIFISH. It lives in fresh, brackish and marine coastal waters. Mosquitofish feed on mosquito larvae and have been introduced into many parts of the world for mosquito control. Length: female to 6cm (2.4in); male to 4cm (1.6in). Family Poeciliidae; species *Gambusia affinis*.

moss
Any of *c*.14,000 species of small, simple, non-flowering green plants belonging to the Bryophyta phylum. They typically grow in colonies, often forming dense carpets. They do not have specialized tissues

MOSQUITO

Long-legged, slender-winged insect found throughout the world. The female sucks blood from warm-blooded animals. They have a characteristic elongated proboscis, containing the mouthparts. The larvae are aquatic. Some species carry the parasites of diseases, including malaria, yellow fever, dengue, viral encephalitis and filariasis. Members of the genera *Anopheles* spread malaria. Adult length: 3–9mm (0.1–0.4in) Order Diptera; family Culicidae; there are *c*.2500 species.

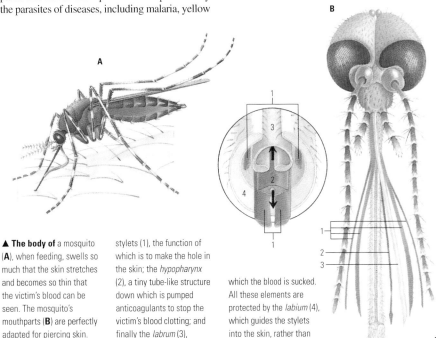

▲ **The body of** a mosquito (**A**), when feeding, swells so much that the skin stretches and becomes so thin that the victim's blood can be seen. The mosquito's mouthparts (**B**) are perfectly adapted for piercing skin. They consist of: four piercing stylets (1), the function of which is to make the hole in the skin; the *hypopharynx* (2), a tiny tube-like structure down which is pumped anticoagulants to stop the victim's blood clotting; and finally the *labrum* (3), another tube-like organ up which the blood is sucked. All these elements are protected by the *labium* (4), which guides the stylets into the skin, rather than piercing it.

for transporting water, food and minerals, although they do have parts resembling the stems, leaves and roots of the higher (flowering) plants. Mosses reproduce by means of SPORES produced in a capsule on a long stalk. The spores germinate into branching filaments, from which buds arise that grow into moss plants. Mosses grow on soil, rocks and tree trunks in a wide variety of land habitats, especially in shady, damp places. *See also* ALTERNATION OF GENERATIONS; BRYOPHYTE; SPHAGNUM

moss animal (bryozoan)
Any member of the phylum Ectoprocta (also known as Bryozoa). It comprises numerous species of small, invertebrate, mainly marine animals. Moss animals live in colonies attached to rocks, seaweed or large shells. Length: to *c*.1mm (*c*.0.04in).

moth
Insect of the order LEPIDOPTERA, found in almost all parts of the world. It is distinguished from a BUTTERFLY mainly by its non-clubbed antennae, although there are a few exceptions. Most moths are nocturnal. Like a butterfly, a moth undergoes METAMORPHOSIS. It has a long, coiled proboscis for sipping liquid food, particularly the nectar of flowers. There are *c*.800 species.

moth, alder
NOCTUID moth that is distributed across most of Europe and part of E Asia. It is named after one of its larval host plants, the alder (*Alnus* spp.); various other species of tree may also be hosts. Family Noctuidae; species *Acronicta alni*.

moth, antler
NOCTUID moth. The adult moth is greyish- or reddish-brown in colour, with antler-like markings on its wings. The caterpillars are herbivorous, sometimes feeding on grasses in plague proportions. Adult body length: 30–40mm (1.2–1.6in). Family Noctuidae; species *Cerapteryx graminis*.

moth, bagworm (bagmoth)
Any member of the moth family Psychidae, found worldwide. Bagworm moths are named after the bag within which the caterpillar partly conceals itself. The bag, made of silk strands and particles of leaves and twigs, is also used as a COCOON. The common bagworm (*Thyridopteryx ephemeraeformis*) attacks trees and shrubs, especially arborvitae and cedars. Family Psychidae.

moth, browntail
Species of tussock moth. The caterpillar is a serious pest of many fruit and deciduous shade trees, especially in the New England states, New Brunswick and Nova Scotia, United States. The caterpillar is dark brown and hairy, with tufts of white hairs along each side. Caterpillar length: *c*.38mm (*c*.1.5in). Family Lipanidae; species *Nygmia Phaeorrhoea*. *See also* MOTH, TUSSOCK

moth, burnet
Any member of the genus *Zygaena*, a group of day-flying moths. Adult burnet moths are mainly black-brown, with characteristic bright red spots on their forewings and bright red hindwings, which are edged with black. Adult body length: 20–40mm (0.8–1.6in). Family Zygaenidae.

moth, cactus
Small moth; it is yellow or white with dark markings. Its orange-red caterpillar destroys cactus plants. In the early 20th century the cactus moth was

introduced into Australia as a biological control against prickly pear. Family Pyralidae; species *Cactoblastis cactorum*.

moth, cinnabar
Day-active moth belonging to the family Arctiidae. The larvae are conspicuous because of their yellow and black stripes; they feed on ragwort (*Senecio* spp.). Adult cinnabar moths are mainly black, except for their red hindwings and the red stripes and spots on their forewings. They get their common name from the intense colour of this red, which is similar to that of the mineral cinnabar. Adult body length: *c*.20mm (*c*.0.8in). Family Arctiidae; species *Callimorpha jacobaeae*.

moth, clearwing (wasp moth)
Any member of the family Aegeriidae, a group of small, day-flying moths with transparent hindwings. Many species have dark bodies with bright red or yellow marks, resembling a wasp. Clearwing caterpillars bore into the roots and stems of trees and shrubs. Family Aegeriidae.

moth, clothes
Any of several species of small moth, the larvae of which attack woollen fabrics and furs. The most destructive is the caterpillar of the case-making clothes moth (*Tinea pellionella*). It lives and pupates in a small case, which it builds from silk and food particles. Adult wingspan: 12mm (0.5in). Family Tinidae; species include *Tineola bisselliella* (webbing clothes moth) and *Trichophaga tapetzella* (carpet moth).

moth, codling
Small, grey moth; it is native to Europe but is now found wherever apples are grown. The larvae, known as apple worms, are pale pink with brown head mark-

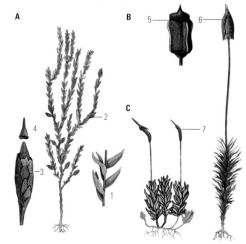

ings. They cause serious damage to crops by burrowing into the fruit to feed. Family Torticidae; species *Carpocapsa pomonella*.

moth, corn borer
See CORN BORER

moth, currant
See MOTH, MAGPIE

moth, death's-head
See HAWKMOTH, DEATH'S-HEAD

moth, emperor
Saturniid moth with a broad European and Asian distribution. It has a large body and striking wings, each with an eyespot near the centre. The larvae feed on a range of plants, including blackthorn, willows, birches and heather. Adult wingspan: 40–60mm (1.6–2.4in). Family Saturniidae; species *Saturnia pavonia*.

moth, geometrid (looper, inchworm)
Any member of the family Geometridae, which comprises *c*.18,000 moth species worldwide. The larvae move with a characteristic looping motion. They have only two pairs of abdominal prolegs and often freeze if disturbed, assuming a twig-like appearance. Many species are agricultural or horticultural pests. Adult wingspan: 11–60mm (0.4–2.4in). Family Geometridae; genera include *Scopula*, *Idaea*, *Eupithecia* and *Semiothisa*.

moth, gipsy
Small tussock moth. The adult female has black zigzag markings; the male is smaller in size and darker in colour. The caterpillars have tufts of brown and yellow hairs on their sides. Feeding on forest and fruit trees, they can be serious pests. Caterpillar length: 50mm (2in). Family Liparidae; species *Lymantria dispar*. *See also* MOTH, TUSSOCK

moth, goat
Large moth that is found in deciduous habitats throughout Europe, Asia and N Africa. The larvae, which live for two years before pupating, bore into the trunks of trees. Infestations of the larvae are recognisable by the smell of wood-vinegar and sawdust ejected from bored-out galleries. Adult wingspan: 65–80mm (2.6–3in). Family Cossidae; species *Cossus cossus*.

moth, grain
Moth that is so called because the larvae attack stored and growing grain. The whitish larvae hollow out the inside of the kernels; they can be a serious pest. The adult grain moth is grey with blackish spots. Adult wingspan: *c*.12mm (*c*.0.5in). Family Gelechiidae; species *Sitotroga cerealella*.

moth, gypsy
See MOTH, GIPSY

moth, hawk
See HAWKMOTH

moth, hooktip
Any of several species of NOCTUID moths found in woods and hedgerows. They are so-called because the larvae taper to a point at the rear and rest with both ends raised. Adult wingspan: 30–40mm (1.2–1.6in). Family Noctuidae; genera *Drepana*, *Falcaria* and *Sabre*.

moth, luna
Large moth found mainly in S North America. Its

▲ **moss** Mosses vary in growth and colour according to species. *Fontinalis anti pyretica* (A) is an aquatic moss, whose boat-shaped leaves have a sharp keel (1); the capsules are oblong or cylindrical (2, 3) and there is a pointed cap (4). *Polytrichum commune* (B) is extremely common; it has a capsule (5) that looks like a four-sided box. It bears a long, golden brown cap (6), which is released before the spores are dispersed. *Atrichum undulatum* (C) is common on heaths and in woods; it has a capsule (7) with a long, pointed cap. *Schistostega pennata* (D) has flattened, translucent leaves.

M

▲ **moth, cinnabar** Although native to Europe, the cinnabar moth (*Callimorpha jacobaeae*) has been introduced to many countries to control the spread of ragwort. The adult moth retains the alkaloid poisons it has absorbed from the ragwort plant, making it unpleasant to eat for predators.

wings are bright green, with a purplish-brown band on the leading edge of the front wings and a large dark spot near the centre of each hind wing. Adult wingspan: *c.*100mm (*c.*3.9in). Family Saturniidae; species *Actias luna.*

moth, magpie (currant moth)
Slow-flying, white, black and yellow, geometrid moth. Its larvae, which are yellow with black spots, feed on gooseberries, redcurrants, sloes, plums and cherries. Adult wingspan: 40mm (1.6in). Family Geometridae; species *Abraxes grossulariata. See also* MOTH, GEOMETRID

moth, peppered
Geometrid moth found mainly in wooded areas, where it rests on trees. Its morphology is highly dependent on the level of pollution: in the absence of pollution more than 90% of peppered moths are white with a few black specks; in areas of high pollution, the majority of peppered moths are black with a few white specks. It is believed that coloration equals CAMOUFLAGE, and the changes observed support the NATURAL SELECTION hypothesis. Adult body size: *c.*22mm (0.9in). Family Geometridae; species *Biston betularia. See also* EVOLUTION; MOTH, GEOMETRID

moth, plume
Any member of the genus *Pterophorus*, a group of nocturnal, weak-flying moths. The plume moth has a slender body and long, fragile legs. The deep divisions within each wing pair resemble plumes or lobes, giving the moth its common name. The larvae have varying habits, including rolling leaves and boring into stems. Adult body size: *c.*7mm (*c.*0.3in). Family Pterophoridae; genus *Pterophorus.*

moth, regal
Large American moth. Its olive-grey front wings are marked with reddish veins and yellow spots; its orange-red hind wings have yellow markings. The caterpillars are known as hickory horned devils because of prominent horn-like appendages. Adult wingspan: up to 150mm (6in). Family Citheroniidae; species *Citheronia regalise.*

moth, silk (silkworm)
Any member of the genus *Bombyx*, native to China but introduced worldwide. The caterpillar feeds chiefly on mulberry leaves. The common domesticated silk moth (*Bombyx mori*) is raised commercially for its silk COCOON. Adult wingspan: 40–50mm (1.6–2in); silkworm length: *c.*75mm (*c.*3in). Family Bombycidae.

moth, sphinx
See HAWKMOTH

moth, swift
Any member of the superfamily Hepialoidea, a group of moths mainly found in Australia and South Africa. Members of the family Hepialidae are the only swiftmoths to be found outside these areas; five species are found in the British Isles. As their common name suggests, these moths are strong, fast fliers. The larvae feed on plant roots. The pupae are active and move to the soil surface for adult emergence. Superfamily Hepialoidea; families include Hepialidae; species include *Hepialus lupulina.*

moth, tiger
Any of numerous species of stout-bodied, nocturnal moths. They have bright orange, white and black wings. The caterpillars of most tiger moth species are covered with long hairs; they are commonly called WOOLLY BEARS. Family Arctiidae.

moth, tussock
Any of several species of moth, the larvae of which are typically covered with tussocks or tufts of long hairs; many species have stinging hairs. The larvae of most species feed on the leaves of trees and shrubs, often causing much damage. Adult females are commonly white and brown. The white marked tussock moth (*Hemero-campa leucostigma*) has no wings. Family Lipanidae. *See also* MOTH, BROWN-TAIL; MOTH, GIPSY

moth, underwing
NOCTUID moth. It has brightly banded underwings and grey or brown front wings with wavy markings. Family Noctuidae; genus *Catocalla.*

moth, wax
Moth species of the family Pyralidae. It is a pest of bee hives, where the larvae feed on the combs and cover them with silken tunnels. The larvae are sometime sold as reptile food. Family Pyralidae; species *Galleria mellonella.*

moth, winter
Species of geometrid moth. Its larvae are a serious commercial pest, causing damage to a range of fruit crops, including apple, apricot, blackcurrant, cherry, plum and redcurrant. The adults are a dull, grey-brown; the females have atrophied wings and are thus flightless. The winter moth's larvae are fairly stout; they have green heads and yellowish-green bodies, which have a brown dorsal median line, flanked by white strips. Adult body length: 8–10mm (0.3–0.4in). Family Geometridae; species *Operophtera brumata.*

moth, yucca
Any member of the genus *Tegeticula*, a group of small white moths that have a symbiotic relationship with the yucca plant. Yucca plant flowers are pollinated exclusively by yucca moths, and the moth larvae feed only on yucca plant seeds. Family Prodoxidae; genus *Tegeticula*; there are four species. *See also* SYMBIOSIS

moth-fly
See OWL-MIDGE

motmot
Any of about nine species of solitary birds found in humid forests of Central and South America. The motmot's plumage is iridescent green, blue-black and brown. It has a strongly down-curved bill. Its two long central tail feathers are stripped of webbing to form racket-shaped tips. Their third and fourth toes are partly fused. Length: 25–42cm (10–17in). Family Momotidae.

motor cell *See* MOTOR NEURONE

motor neurone (motor neuron)
Nerve that carries messages to an effector organ (usually a muscle) from the CENTRAL NERVOUS SYSTEM (CNS), thereby causing an appropriate response. The cell bodies of some motor neurones form part of the spinal cord. The AXONS (electro-chemically conductive extensions) of these nerves, which are sheathed with MYELIN (an insulating substance), pass from the spinal cord to connect with the muscles. These nerves are involved in spinal REFLEX ACTIONS. Motor neurones are, however, also linked to the BRAIN by the descending spinal tracts. The cell bodies of these tracts lie in the cerebral cortex, and their axons, which pass down the spinal cord, connect the nerves to the brain, so allowing voluntary muscular control. Some motor neurones act on glands of the ENDOCRINE SYSTEM to make them release their hormone secretions. *See also* NERVOUS SYSTEM; NEURONE; SENSORY NEURONE

mouflon
Wild sheep that lives on the cold, arid mountain slopes of Iran, Sardinia and Corsica; it has been introduced across Europe. Males are dark brown with a lighter "saddle patch" that disappears in summer; females have a lighter coat and no patch. In winter the thick, woolly under-fleece is covered by long, coarse, guard hairs. Both sexes have coiled horns, those of the female being much shorter than those of the male. Mouflons will eat almost any vegetation, even poisonous plants. Groups of females with young or all males live together, never straying far from their home range. In the rutting season, mature males fight to mate with females; one lamb is born after five months' gestation. Head-body length: 1.2m (4ft); tail: 7cm (3in). Family Bovidae; species *Ovis orientalis.*

mould
Mass composed of the spore-bearing mycelia (vegetative filaments) and fruiting bodies produced by numerous FUNGI. Many moulds live off fruits, vegetables, cheese, butter, jelly, silage and almost any dead organic material. Roquefort, camembert and stilton cheeses involve the use of mould. Although many species are pathogenic (disease-causing), penicillin and a few other ANTIBIOTICS are obtained from moulds. *See also* SLIME MOULD

moulting
Process involving the shedding of the outermost layers of an organism and their replacement. Mammals moult by shedding outer skin layers and hair, often at seasonal intervals; human beings do

M

M

not moult but lose dead, dry skin continuously as it is replaced from below. Birds moult their feathers, and amphibians and reptiles their skin. In all cases the process is controlled by HORMONES. It often serves, in growing animals, to replace worn out tissues that have become too small. The moulting of INSECTS and other ARTHROPODS is known as ECDYSIS. A more elaborate affair, ecdysis is fundamental to growth. *See also* METAMORPHOSIS

mountain

Part of the Earth's surface that rises conspicuously higher, at least 380m (1250ft) higher than the surrounding area. Mountains have a restricted summit area, comparatively steep sides and considerable bare rock surface. They are formed in three main ways. First, FOLD mountains, such as the Himalayas, are formed by a squeezing in of rock layers, caused by movements of the tectonic plates (*see* PLATE TECTONICS) of the Earth's CRUST. Second, BLOCK MOUNTAINS, such as the Sierra Nevada of North America, are formed by vertical movements between geological FAULTS, leading to the tilting of large blocks of STRATA. Third, a typical VOLCANO forms from the molten rock and ash that piles up around its original vent hole. The extent and speed of this process is illustrated by Parácutin, a Mexican volcano that rose out of a cornfield to a height of 450m (1475ft) from its base between 1943 and 1952. Mountains may occur as single isolated masses, as ranges, and in systems or chains. *See also* OROGENISIS

mountain ash

Any of several species of trees of the ROSE family. The European mountain ash, the rowan tree (*Sorbus aucuparia*), has white flowers and, later, orange-red berries. It grows to a height of about 13m (45ft). In Australia, several tall slender trees (for example, of the genera *Fraxinus* and *Eucalyptus*) are also known as mountain ash. Family Rosaceae.

mountain building

See OROGENISIS

mountain lion

See PUMA

mouse

Any member of a highly successful and diverse group of rodents, to which more than half of all species of mammal belong. Mice are small, agile, versatile and adaptable animals. They reproduce rapidly. Usually grey or brown, they have large ears and eyes, a long pointed face, long fingers and toes and a long tail. Most are nocturnal, terrestrial seed-eaters, but they can use their strong teeth and jaws to tackle a wide range of food. Suborder Myomorpha (mouse-like); family Muridae (RATS and mice); there are several subfamilies, including the Murinae from the Old World and the Hesperomyinae from the New World.

mouse, birch

Any of nine species of mouse-like rodents from the steppes and forests of E Europe and Asia. The upper parts of their bodies are brown, the underparts are paler. By day they sleep in nests made of dry vegetation deep in burrows. At night they jump through undergrowth and climb with ease, using their semi-prehensile tails to cling to stems. In winter they hibernate in their burrows. Birch mice are related to JERBOAS, but they do not have elongated hind legs. Head-body length: 5–9cm (2–4in); tail: 6–11cm (2–4in). Suborder Myomorpha; family Zapodidae; genus *Sicista*; species include *Sicista betulina*.

▲ **moulting** As with all land-living vertebrates, snakes produce keratin – a hard, water-resistant protein – in the outer skin layer cells. Keratinization causes many cell components to degenerate and eventually die, so the layer of keratinized cells is shed from time to time. This process allows snakes and other reptiles literally to crawl out of their skins.

mouse, deer (white-footed mouse)

Any member of the mouse genus *Peromyscus*. Several species are threatened or endangered. The deer mouse *Peromyscus maniculatus* is found in forest, grassland and scrub of North America. It lives in underground nests of dry leaves. It can run and hop through dense bush, finding seeds, fruit and insects to eat. Deer mice breed in summer, producing litters of up to nine young after a three- to four-week gestation period; most females only produce two litters in a lifetime. Head-body length: 12–22cm (5–9in); tail: 8–18cm (3–7in). Suborder Myomorpha; subfamily Hesperomyinae.

mouse, field (South American)

Any member of the genus *Akodon*, comprising 33 mouse species found throughout South America, often at high elevations. Field mice forage on the ground, both by day and night, for leaves, fruit, insects and seeds. Head-body length: 11–14cm (4–6in); tail: 4–6cm (2in). Suborder Myomorpha; family Muridae; subfamily Hesperomyinae; species include *Akodon arviculoides*.

mouse, field (Old World) (wood mouse)

Any member of the genus *Apodemus*, comprising 22 mouse species found in forests and cultivated land across Europe and Asia. Old World field mice have soft, grey-brown fur with white underparts. They climb, jump and swim well, feeding on roots, grains, berries, nuts and insects. They dig burrow systems amongst the tree roots where they live. Head-body length: 8–13cm (3–5in); tail: 7–10cm (3–4in). Suborder Myomorpha; family Muridae; subfamily Murinae; species include *Apodemus sylvaticus* (*see* MOUSE, WOOD).

mouse, grasshopper

Any of three species of mouse found in semi-arid scrub and deserts of North America. They hunt anything they can catch, including grasshoppers, scorpions and even their own kind. In spring or summer a pair will dig or take over a burrow and produce a litter of between two and six young, born after a 33-day gestation. Both sexes produce very high-pitched squeaks, which are thought to ensure even spacing of the burrows. Head-body length: 9–13cm (4–5in); tail: 3–6cm (1–2in). Suborder Myomorpha; family Muridae; subfamily Hesperomyinae; genus *Onychomys*; species include *Onychomys leucogaster*.

mouse, harvest (New World)

Any member of the genus *Reithrodontomys*, comprising 19 mouse species found in both North and Central America. They are nocturnal seed-eaters. New World harvest mice construct globular nests of leaves, fixed to grass stems *c*.24cm (*c*.9in) above the ground, where litters of up to four babies are born after 23 days' gestation. Head-body length: 6–14cm (2–6in); tail: 7–10cm (3–4in). Suborder Myomorpha; family

Muridae; subfamily Hesperomyinae; species include *Reithrodontomys megalotis* (western harvest mouse).

mouse, harvest (Old World)

Mouse that lives in hedgerows and reedbeds across Europe as far as the Urals. It feeds on both seeds and insects. Harvest mice build similar nests to their American cousins but litter sizes can reach 12. They are the only Old World mammals to have prehensile tails, with which they cling to grass stems. Head-body length: 5–8cm (2–3in); tail: 5–8cm (2–3in). Suborder Myomorpha; family Muridae; subfamily Murinae; species *Micromys minutus*.

mouse, house

Mouse that originated in India but is now found across the world wherever people live. In the wild, house mice are nocturnal, feeding on grass seeds, plant stems and a few insects. In buildings and food stores they actually consume little but do much damage by nibbling or contaminating food and other goods. They live in territorial colonies of a male and several females and their young. Each female produces between five and ten litters of about six pups per year after 20 days of gestation. House mice have been bred in a range of varieties to be kept as pets or as laboratory animals. Head-body length: 6–9cm (2–4in); tail: 6–10cm (2–4in). Suborder Myomorpha; family Muridae; subfamily Murinae; species *Mus musculus*.

mouse, pocket

Any member of the genus *Perognathus*, comprising mouse-like rodents related to the kangaroo RATS. The 25 species of pocket mouse live in arid areas of North America. They are nocturnal and dig complex burrow systems in which they live alone. They only come above ground to gather food, which includes seeds, leaves, shoots and insects. They store their food in fur-lined cheek pouches. Pocket mice rarely need to drink, but they may become torpid in their burrows if conditions become extreme. One or two litters of about four young each are produced every year. Some species are threatened with extinction due to habitat destruction. Head-body length: 6–9cm (2–4in); tail: 4–10cm (2–4in). Suborder Sciuromorpha; family Heteromyidae; species include *Perognathus alticola* (silky pocket mouse).

mouse, spiny

Any member of the genus *Acomys*, comprising 14 mouse species found in arid regions and human habitations of Europe and Africa. Spiny mice may be yellow, red or brown, with white underparts; the back and scaly tail, which is often lost, is covered with coarse spines. They have the large ears of nocturnal creatures. They are omnivorous: the Egyptian spiny mouse feeds on dates and the remains of mummified bodies. Spiny mice breed all year round, producing litters of between one and five young after a five- to six-week gestation period. Head-body length: 7–17cm (3–7in); tail: 4–12cm (2–5in). Suborder Myomorpha; family Murinae; species include *Acomys cahirinus* (Egyptian spiny mouse).

mouse, wood (common field mouse, long-tailed field mouse)

Mouse that is found in woods, moors, gardens and hedgerows across Europe. It is probably the commonest mammal of the British countryside. Wood mice are nocturnal, often going into torpor during cold weather. They feed on seeds, shoots, buds and small invertebrates. Each female produces four litters of five young each season; the gestation period is 23 days. Head-body length: 17–19cm (7in); tail: 15cm (6in). Suborder Myomorpha; family Murinae;

species *Apodemus sylvaticus*. *See also* MOUSE, FIELD (OLD WORLD)

mousebird
Any of about six species of crested birds found in s and E Africa. They have soft, grey, hair-like plumage and long stiff tails. They feed on fruit, which they gather by clambering about bushes, maintaining constant contact calls. Length: 30–35cm (12–14in). Family Coliidae; genera *Colius* and *Urocolius*.

mouse-deer
Smallest of the even-toed ungulates or hoofed animals. It lives in the tropical rainforests of Asia. Regarded as "living fossils", mouse-deer represent an intermediate stage between pigs and deer and have remained unchanged for 30 million years. They have continuously growing upper canines, which in males protrude outside the lower jaw like fangs. Mouse-deer have no horns or antlers. They have stocky bodies with short legs and they walk on all four toes of each foot. Feeding on fruit and foliage, mouse-deer are solitary and nocturnal. Only one young is born each year to each female. Family Tragulidae; genus *Tragulus*. *See also* CHEVROTAIN

mouse-deer, larger
Mouse-deer that has a reddish coat with white herringbone stripes. Head-body length: 50–60cm (20–24in); tail: 3–7cm (1–3in). Family Tragulidae; species *Tragulus napu*.

mouse-deer, lesser
Mouse-deer with a reddish coat. Head-body length: 44–48cm (17–19in); tail: 3–7cm (1–3in). Family Tragulidae; species *Tragulus javanicus*.

mouse-deer, spotted
Mouse-deer with a white-spotted reddish coat. Head-body length: 50–60cm (20–24in); tail: 3–7cm (1–3in). Family Tragulidae; species *Tragulus meminna*.

mouth
In animals, the anterior (front) end of the ALIMENTARY CANAL where it opens to the outside. In humans and other higher animals it is the cavity within the JAWS, containing the TEETH and TONGUE.

mouthbrooder
Male or female fish that gathers up eggs into its mouth after or before fertilization (which occurs when sperm are introduced into the mouth). Mouthbrooders retain the eggs in their mouths at least through hatching. The group includes many CICHLIDS.

mucous membrane
Sheet of TISSUE (or EPITHELIUM) lining all body channels that communicate with the air, such as the mouth and respiratory tract, the digestive and urogenital tracts and the various glands that secrete MUCUS. The "membrane" contains gland cells that secrete mucus, which serves for lubrication and protection.

mucus
Slippery, viscous fluid containing mucin, produced by MUCOUS MEMBRANES of the body. It serves for lubrication and protection. Nasal mucus traps airborne particles; mucus of the stomach protects the lining from irritation by hydrochloric acid secreted during DIGESTION.

mudfish
Any member of the genus *Neochanna*, a group of freshwater fish found in New Zealand. They inhabit swamps, where they aestivate (form mud cocoons

and become inactive) during dry seasons. Their transparent young, referred to as WHITEBAIT, travel down river to the sea. Family Galaxiidae.

mud minnow
Any member of three genera of freshwater fish found in the Northern Hemisphere. They often bury themselves in the mud at the bottom of rivers or lakes. Length: 7.5–15cm (3–6in). Family Umbridae.

mudpuppy
Large, spotted, aquatic SALAMANDER with external gills and four well-developed limbs. Mudpuppies (*Necturus maculosus*) and waterdogs, their smaller relatives, occupy streams and lakes in E North America, where they feed on invertebrates (especially crustaceans), fish and other small vertebrates. Length: to 49cm (19in). Family Proteidae.

mudrock
See MUDSTONE

mudskipper
Any member of several genera of amphibian-like fish found in tidal swamps in Africa, Asia and Australia. Mudskippers retain moisture in their gill cavities in order to survive out of water when the tide recedes. With their specialized pectoral fins, they can hop on mud and can even climb trees to cling with a sucker for several hours. Length: to 20cm (8in). Family Periophthalmidae.

mudstone
Rock made of consolidated mud. Although firmer than CLAY, it lacks the laminated structure and tendency to cleave to SHALE and sometimes decomposes into mud when exposed to the atmosphere.

mugger
Large CROCODILE found in the lakes, rivers and estuaries of s Asia, from Iran to India, Bangladesh and Sri Lanka. Young muggers feed on insects and other small prey, switching to larger and larger prey as they grow. Adults are capable of taking deer and buffalo. Eggs are laid in excavated nest holes. Length: to *c*.4m (*c*.13ft). Family Crocodylidae; species *Crocodylus palustris*.

leaf-eared mouse

house mouse

striped field mouse

▲ **mouse** The leaf-eared mouse (*Phyllotis darwinii*) is found in South America, usually in sparsely vegetated areas among rocks or in disused burrows of other rodents. Found worldwide, the house mouse (*Mus musculus*) is considered a pest due to the damage it can cause to food supplies. The striped field mouse (*Rhabdomys pumilio*) is chiefly herbivorous. It usually lives in a nest of moss, leaves and grass.

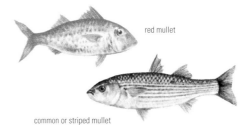

red mullet

common or striped mullet

▲ **mullet** The common or striped mullet (*Mugli cephalus*) is a popular food fish found worldwide. The red mullet (*Mullus barbatus*) is found in the Mediterranean Sea and is distinguished by the long barbels on its chin, which aid it in searching the sea bed for food.

Muir, John (1838–1914)
US naturalist, b. Scotland. An advocate of forest preservation, he was influential in the establishment of many national parks. Muir studied the glaciers and forests of the Sierra Nevada. He also explored Alaska, where he discovered Glacier Bay and Muir Glacier. By 1867 he was urging the US government to endorse a policy of forest conservation, and his writings and lobbying influenced conservation programmes of presidents Grover Cleveland and Theodore Roosevelt.

mulberry
Any member of the genus *Morus*, a group of trees and shrubs that grow in tropical and temperate regions. They have simple leaves. The male flowers are catkins, whereas the female flowers are borne in spikes. *Several* species are cultivated for their fleshy, edible fruits. Family Moraceae.

mulgara
Small MARSUPIAL that inhabits stony and spinifex deserts of central Australia. It has a thick tail with a black crest. The mulgara feeds on mice, spiders and insects. Head-body length: 12–22cm (5–9in); tail: 7–12cm (3–5in). Family Dasyuridae; species *Dasycercus cristicauda*.

mullein
Hardy biennial or perennial plant of the genus *Verbascum*, native to temperate regions of the Northern Hemisphere. The common mullein (*Verbascum thapsus*) has large leaves and long, dense, yellow flower spikes. Height: to 1.8m (6ft). Family Scrophulariaceae.

Muller, Hermann Joseph (1890–1967)
US geneticist. He found that he could artificially increase the rate of MUTATIONS in the FRUIT FLY by the use of X-rays. He thus highlighted the human risk in exposure to RADIOACTIVITY. For this work Muller was awarded the 1946 Nobel Prize for physiology or medicine.

Müller, Paul Hermann (1899–1965)
Swiss chemist who was awarded the 1948 Nobel Prize for physiology or medicine for his discovery of the use of DDT as an INSECTICIDE. In 1944 DDT was successfully employed against a typhus epidemic in Naples, and for more than 20 years it was the most widely used insecticide. In the 1970s, however, DDT was implicated as a hazard to animal life because it persists in FOOD CHAINS; its use has been banned in many countries.

mullet
Any member of the family Mugilidae, comprising *c*.80 species of fish. They are found in coastal waters, both salt and brackish, of tropical and tem-

M

perate seas. Mullets are filter feeders, with long gill rakers and a unique pharyngeal apparatus that enables them to concentrate planktonic prey. Their teeth are small or absent. Length: 30–90cm (12–35in). Family Mugilidae.

Mullis, Kary (1944–)
US biochemist who discovered how to copy minute quantities of DNA millions of times for research purposes. This technique, POLYMERASE CHAIN REACTION (PCR), has been used in a variety of ways, including tests for HIV and for DNA forensic-science investigations. For his research, Mullis shared the 1993 Nobel Prize for chemistry with Michael SMITH, who worked independently on altering the genetic code.

mummification
Relatively uncommon process of FOSSILIZATION in which some soft tissues are preserved through dehydration. Mummification occurs mainly in dry desert conditions but is also involved in freeze-drying FROZEN BODIES.

mung bean
Cultivated bean of ancient Indian origin, widely used as human food; it is not known in the wild. The slender pods produce small, oblong, usually green seeds, which are highly nutritious. Green pods may be eaten and seeds are sprouted and used in Chinese cooking. Family Fabaceae; species *Vigna radiata*.

munia
Small, slim, perching bird belonging to the WAXBILL family. It has a stout conical bill for feeding on seeds. Munias form large communal flocks of several species to feed and roost. They fly together in a close-knit pack, with whirring wingbeats. They are popular cage birds. Length: 10–12cm (4–5in). Family Estrildidae; genera include *Amandava* and *Lonchura*.

muntjac
Small, primitive, Asian DEER. It is brown with cream markings. It has tusk-like canine teeth and short, two-pronged antlers. There are two well-known species, the Indian muntjac or barking deer (*Muntiacus muntjak*) and the Chinese muntjac (*M. reevesi*). Height: to 60cm (24in) at the shoulder; weight: to 18kg (40lb). Family Cervidae.

Murchison, Sir Roderick Impey (1792–1871)
Scottish geologist. His work on the rocks underlying the Old Red Sandstone in s Wales led to the definition of the strata known as the SILURIAN system (corresponding to that period of geological time). He worked with Sir Charles LYELL on the Auvergne volcanics and with Adam SEDGWICK on the structure of the Alps. He later collaborated with Sedgwick on a study of the rocks that were to become known as the DEVONIAN system. He is also responsible for founding the PERMIAN system.

murrelet
Small AUK found off the Pacific coasts of North America. It nests in colonies on rocky islands and winters far out to sea. The ancient murrelet (*Synthliboramphus antiquus*) has white streaks on its neck in summer. The marbled murrelet (*Brachyramphus marmoratus*) is mottled brown. Length: 25cm (10in). Family Alcidae.

muscle
Tissue that has the ability to contract, enabling movement. There are three basic types: voluntary muscle (or skeletal muscle); involuntary muscle (or smooth muscle); and cardiac muscle. **Voluntary** muscle is the largest tissue component of the human body, comprising about 40% by weight. It is attached by TENDONS to the BONES of the SKELETON and is characterized by cross-markings known as striations; it typically contains many nuclei per cell. Most voluntary muscles require conscious effort for contraction (when they move the limbs and body). A muscle whose contraction causes a limb or a part of the body to straighten (extend) is called an EXTENSOR. A muscle whose contraction causes a limb or part of the body to bend (flex) is called a FLEXOR. **Involuntary** muscle lines the digestive tract, blood vessels and many other organs. It is not striated and typically has only one nucleus per cell. It is not under conscious control, and is therefore known as involuntary muscle. **Cardiac** muscle is found only in the HEART and differs from the other types of muscle in that it beats rhythmically and does not need stimulation by a nerve impulse to contract. Cardiac muscle has some striations (but not as many as in voluntary muscle) and has only one nucleus per cell.

muscovite
Sheet silicate mineral, hydrous potassium aluminium silicate ($KAl_2(Si_3Al) O_{10}(OH)_2$), the most common MICA. Found in many kinds of rocks, muscovite crystallizes in hexagonal, tabular forms in the monoclinic system. Its name derives from its use as a glass in Muscovy, Russia. It is tinted with varied lustres or clear. Hardness 2–2.5; r.d. 2.9.

mushroom
Any of numerous relatively large fleshy FUNGI, many of which are gathered for food. A typical mushroom consists of two parts: an extensive underground cobwebby network of fine filaments (HYPHAE), called the MYCELIUM, which is the main body of the fungus, and a short-lived fruiting body (the visible mushroom).

mushroom-fly
See SCUTTLE-FLY

musk
Perennial plant (*Mimulus moschatus*) that produces a scent from which it takes its name. Musk is also the name of the scent produced by the abdominal gland of the musk DEER, which is used both in perfumes and as a medicine.

musk deer
See DEER, MUSK

muskeg
Area of boggy ground found in the TUNDRA regions of the Northern Hemisphere. Most of the ground in such regions, such as the tundra of N Canada and Russia, is PERMAFROST. In summer, however, the top few centimetres of soil thaw, and the MELTWATER, unable to run away, forms muskegs. The bogs sup-

◄ **muskeg** In Svalbard, which is an archipelago in the Arctic Ocean, belonging to Norway, the ground is permanently frozen, often to great depths. The surface sometimes thaws in summer, forming a region of muskeg. Only moss and lichen can survive on such boggy ground. The wildlife on Svalbard includes reindeer, polar bears, seals and walruses.

M

▲ **muskrat** The scent of the muskrat (*Ondatra zebithicus*), from which it gets its name, comes from special glands. It was originally a native of North America but it has been introduced into other parts of the world for its fur.

port LICHENS and MOSSES, which are important food for herds of reindeer.

muskellunge

Freshwater fish found in the Great Lakes of North America. A type of PIKE, it has a shovel-like bill, sharp teeth and an elongated body. It eats fish, amphibians, birds and small mammals. Length: to 1.6m (5.2ft). Family Esocidae; species *Esox masquinongy*.

musk ox

Large, wild, shaggy RUMINANT, related to the OX and GOAT, native to N Canada and Greenland. Its brown fur reaches almost to the ground, and its down-pointing, recurved horns form a helmet over its forehead. When threatened, the herd forms a defensive circle round the calves. Length: to 2.3m (7.5ft); weight: to 410kg (900lb). Family Bovidae; species *Ovibos moschatus*.

muskrat

Large, aquatic RODENT (a type of VOLE) native to North America. It is a good swimmer, with partly webbed hind feet and a long, scaly tail. Its commercially valuable fur (musquash) is glossy brown and durable. Length, including tail: to 53cm (21in); weight: to 1.8kg (4lb). Family Cricetidae; species *Ondatra obscura* and *Ondatra zibethica*.

mussel

Any of several species of bivalve MOLLUSCS with thin oval shells. Marine species of the family Mytilidae are found worldwide in dense colonies on sea walls and rocky shores, where they attach themselves by means of strands called byssus threads. Freshwater mussels of the family Unionidae, found in the Northern Hemisphere only, produce PEARLS. Species include the edible mussel, *Mytilus edulis*.

mustard

Any of various species of annual and perennial plants native to temperate regions. They have pungent-flavoured leaves, cross-shaped, four-petalled flowers, and carry pods. The seeds of some species are ground to produce the condiment mustard. Family Brassicaceae/Cruciferae.

mutagen

Anything that causes an increase in the number of MUTATIONS in a population of organisms. Mutagens work by affecting the GENES, thus producing inherited defects. They may damage chromosomes, or change the DNA and affect the DNA code. Mutagens include chemicals (such as colchicine) and ionizing radiation (such as radioactivity and X rays). Some mutagens have been shown to cause cancer.

mutation

Sudden change in an inherited characteristic of an organism. This change occurs in the DNA of the GENES. Natural mutations during reproduction are rare, occur randomly and usually produce an organism unable to survive in its environment. Occasionally the change results in the organism being better adapted to its environment, and through NATURAL SELECTION the altered gene may pass on to the next generation. Natural mutation is therefore one of the key means by which organisms evolve. The mutation rate can be increased by exposing genetic material to ionizing radiation, such as X rays or ultraviolet radiation, or mutagenic chemicals. *See also* EVOLUTION

mutualism

Relationship with mutual benefits for the two or more organisms involved. For example, the microorganisms in the rumen of cattle obtain a constant supply of food while the cattle obtain fatty acids from the DIGESTION of cellulose by the microorganism. *See also* SYMBIOSIS

mycelium

Vegetative body of a FUNGUS, found underground. It is made up of a web of filaments (HYPHAE), sometimes massed like felt. The hyphae are of two types, those that feed and those responsible for reproduction.

mycology

Science and study of FUNGUS.

mycorrhiza (fungus root)

Association between certain fungi and the root cells of some VASCULAR PLANTS. The FUNGUS may penetrate the root cells or form a mesh around them. Water and minerals enter the roots via these threads.

◄ **mussel** The common mussel (*Mytilis edulis*) is edible and is cultivated on ropes hanging from stakes or similar structures driven into seabeds, or on ropes suspended from floating rafts. Both methods involve the collection by settlement of mussel "seed" or "spat". The seed may then be transferred to farming areas free from predators or pollution.

Sometimes the fungus digests organic material for the plant. *See also* SYMBIOSIS

myelin sheath

Protective layer around the AXONS of peripheral and some central nerve fibres. It insulates the fibre to prevent loss of electrical impulses and aids conduction. The myelin sheath is composed of specialized cells (SCHWANN CELLS) made up of proteins and fats.

mylonite

Any of several laminated, fine-grained rocks formed when layers of parent rock fault, granulate or flow. It is chemically stable but partly melted and is reduced to a powder by the movement of rock along a fault line. It generally contains fragments of the parent rock.

mynah

Robust, noisy, medium-sized, gregarious perching bird, belonging to the STARLING family. Most species have dark plumage; some, like the common mynah (*Acridotheres tristis*), have bold white wing patches, and others, such as the hill mynah (*Gracula religiosa*), have bright yellow facial wattles. Mynahs feed on the ground for insects and seeds. Length: 23–29cm (9–11in). Family Sturnidae.

myoglobin

Protein found in animals. In vertebrates it is the pigment producing the red colour of MUSCLE tissue. Like HAEMOGLOBIN, myoglobin combines readily with oxygen for use in rapidly contracting muscles. It has been used extensively in research into the structure of PROTEINS. In 1962 British biologist John Kendrew shared the Nobel Prize for chemistry for his construction of a three-dimensional crystalline model of sperm whale myoglobin. The prize was shared with Max Perutz, who used a similar process to discover the structure of haemoglobin.

myriapod

Member of the Myriapoda class of ARTHROPODS with bodies made up of many similar segments. Each segment has one or more pairs of legs. CENTIPEDES and MILLIPEDES are myriapods.

myrrh

Aromatic, resinous, oily gum obtained from thorny, flowering trees, such as *Commiphora myrrha*. Known and prized since ancient times, myrrh has commonly been used as an ingredient in incense, perfumes and medicines. Family Burseraceae.

myrtle

Any of numerous species of evergreen shrubs and trees that grow in tropical and subtropical regions, especially the aromatic shrub, *Myrtus communis*, of the Mediterranean region. Its leaves are simple and glossy; the purple-black berries that follow the white flowers were once dried and used like pepper. Family Myrtaceae.

N

nappe

In geology, large-scale FOLD thrown up by mountain-building (OROGENESIS) processes and transported over large distances. The Alps are a system of several such nappes.

narcissus

Any member of the genus *Narcissus*, comprising Old World, bulb-forming garden flowers, including DAFFODILS and JONQUILS. The long, pointed leaves surround yellow, orange or white trumpet-like flowers. Family Amaryllidaceae; genus *Narcissus*.

narwhal

Small, toothed Arctic WHALE. The male has a twisted horn, half as long as its body, which develops from a tooth and protrudes horizontally through one side of the upper lip. Length: up to 5m (16.4ft). Family Monodontidae; species *Monodon monoceros*.

nasturtium

Annual trailing plant native to Central and South America. It is cultivated as a garden ornamental. The nasturtium has round leaves and spurred, trumpet-shaped flowers of yellow, salmon or scarlet. Family Tropaeolaceae; there are *c*.80 species, including *Tropaeolum majus* (common nasturtium).

N

national parks

Areas of land, the landscape, species and ecosystems of which are of scientific, educational or aesthetic value. This land is permanently set aside to be managed by the state for CONSERVATION purposes. Examples include Yellowstone National Park in the United States, which was the first so designated in 1872. The first in the United Kingdom was the Peak District National Park, established in 1949.

natrolite

Hydrated silicate mineral, hydrous sodium aluminium silicate ($Na_2Al_2Si_3O_{10}.2H_2O$). It has orthorhombic system, needle-like crystals, with radiating nodules or compact fibrous masses. It is colourless or white, glassy and brittle. Hardness 5–5.5; r.d. 2.2. *See also* ZEOLITE

natural gas

Naturally occurring, combustible, gaseous mixture of hydrocarbons trapped in pore spaces in sedimentary rocks. It is used as a fuel and in the production of plastics, drugs, antifreeze and dyes. Natural gas is the gaseous component of PETROLEUM and is extracted from OIL wells. Certain wells, however, yield only natural gas. Before natural gas can be used as a fuel, the heavier hydrocarbons of butane and propane are extracted; in liquid form these hydrocarbons are

forced into containers as bottled gas. The remaining gas, called "dry gas", is piped to consumers for use as fuel. Dry gas is composed of the light hydrocarbons methane and ethane.

naturalization

ADAPTATION of an organism to a different climate or different conditions of life.

natural selection

In EVOLUTION, theory that advantageous changes in an organism will tend to be passed on to successive generations. Changes arise out of natural genetic VARIATION, especially MUTATION. Those changes that give an individual organism a greater capacity for survival and reproduction in a particular environment will help it to produce more offspring bearing the same beneficial characteristic or trait. Thus the proportion of individuals in the population bearing that trait will increase through successive generations. This theory was put forward by Charles DARWIN in his book *The Origin of Species* (1859). It is still regarded as the key mechanism of evolution.

nature reserve

Area of land, sometimes including inland waters and estuaries, set aside for the study and CONSERVATION of wildlife, HABITAT or geological features. Reserves are usually looked after by a warden or a conservation officer. The style of management on a reserve varies according to its main interest and purpose; some may allow permission to enter only for a serious study whereas others may encourage people to visit through a nature trail. *See also* NATIONAL PARKS

nautilus (chambered nautilus)

Any member of the genus *Nautilus*, a group of CEPHALOPOD MOLLUSCS found in W Pacific and E Indian oceans at depths down to 200m (660ft). The large coiled shell of the nautilus is divided into numerous, gas-filled chambers, which give it buoyancy. The body is located in the foremost chamber. Its head has between 60 and 90 retractable, thin, sucker-less tentacles, which are used to catch prey. The nautilus moves by squirting water from a funnel. Shell size: *c*.25cm (*c*.10in). Class Cephalopoda; family Nautilidae; genus *Nautilus*.

nautilus, paper (argonaut)

Any member of the genus *Argonauta*, a group of ocean-dwelling CEPHALOPOD MOLLUSCS found in many parts of the world. The paper nautilus has eight arms with suckers and is related to the OCTOPUS. Two of the female's arms are modified to secrete a coiled, paper-thin, ridged shell used an egg-case. Length: to 40cm (16in). Class Cephalopoda; family Argonautidae; genus *Argonauta*.

Neanderthal

Middle PALAEOLITHIC variety of human, known from fossils in Europe and Asia. Neanderthals were discovered in 1856 when a skeleton was unearthed in the Neander Valley in W Germany. The bones were thick and powerfully built and the skull had a pronounced brow ridge. Neanderthals are now considered to be a separate species of human, possibly a local adaptation during the ice ages; they are not

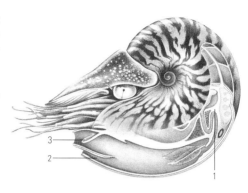

▲ **nautilus** The nautilus' body (1) occupies the largest of its shell's many chambers. In order to move, the nautilus utilizes the movement of water into the mantle (2) and around its whole edge. Propulsion is created by the expulsion of the water from the funnel (3) by the funnel muscles themselves and by the animal expanding its body in the shell. Unlike its relatives, squids, octopuses and cuttlefish, the nautilus cannot contract its mantle, which is attached to its shell.

thought to be ancestral to modern humans. Neanderthals predated modern humans in Europe, but were superseded by them about 35,000 years ago. *See also* HUMAN EVOLUTION

necklace shell

Small marine SNAIL. It is predatory on bivalve molluscs. Necklace shells are so called because their highly polished, red-spotted, yellow and brown shells are popular in necklace manufacture. Length: up to 20mm (0.8in). Phylum Mollusca; class Gastropoda; order Mesogastropoda; family Naticidae; genus *Natica*. *See also* GASTROPOD

nectar

Sweet liquid secreted by most flowering plants (ANGIOSPERMS). It consists mainly of a solution of GLUCOSE, FRUCTOSE and SUCROSE in water. The glands (nectaries) that produce nectar usually lie at the base of the flower petals, but they may also be found in parts of the stem or at the leaf bases. Nectar attracts insects, which help with cross-POLLINATION. BEES turn nectar into honey.

nectarine

Variety of PEACH tree; also its sweet, smooth-skinned, fleshy fruit. The tree and stone are identical to those of the peach. Family Rosaceae; species *Prunus persica nectarina*.

needlefish

Any member of the family Belonidae, comprising up to 30 species of marine and freshwater fish of South America, Pakistan, India and Southeast Asia. They are long, thin and silver coloured, with green or blue backs. Their upper and lower jaws are elongate with numerous needle-like teeth, although some species have a shorter upper jaw similar to halfbeaks. Length: to 1.2m (4ft). Family Belonidae.

nekton

Active swimming organisms that are found at the sea's surface, as opposed to the floating PLANKTON. Nekton includes the large migrating marine ani-

► **narwhal** Generally found only in the male, the distinctive tusk of the narwhal (*Monodon monoceros*) develops from the left tooth of a pair in the upper jaw. The function of the tusk remains unknown. Narwhals feed on fish and squid. They are social animals, often travelling in small family groups. They use a wide range of sounds to communicate. Narwhals are found in the Arctic region.

mals, such as adult SQUIDS, FISH and WHALES. *See also* BENTHOS; PELAGIC

nematocyst
In CNIDARIANS such as JELLYFISH, a tiny, fluid-filled sac containing a coiled, hollow thread that can be shot out at prey. It forms part of a thread cell (**nematoblast**) in the ECTODERM of the animal. When a "trigger" (**cnidocil**) on the thread cell is touched, the thread is rapidly projected to coil around the prey or to inject poison. The poisonous stings on the tentacles of jellyfish derive from thread cells and their nematocycts.

nematode (roundworm, threadworm)
Any member of the phylum NEMATODA. There is a huge number of species, only a small proportion (*c*.10,000) of which have been described. Nematode worms are characterized by unsegmented, cylindrical bodies covered in a thick cuticle. Parasitic forms have been known for thousands of years, and there are also many free-living species. They are some of the most widespread and numerous of all multicellular animals; they are found from polar regions to deserts and hot springs, and from high mountains to deep oceans. Most species have males and females and reproduction is sexual. The life cycles of nematodes is complex; it often includes free-living and parasitic stages, as well as stages in which the nematodes are dormant or carried by a secondary host or vector. Parasitic nematodes are found in most groups of plants and animals and can cause damage and disease. A hectare of good farm soil contains billions of nematodes and a single decomposing apple was found to contain 90,000 roundworms of a number of different species. Phylum Nematoda; classes Adenophorea (mainly free-living) and Secernentea (terrestrial or parasitic). *See also* AFRICAN EYE WORM; FILARIAL WORM; GUINEA WORM; ROUNDWORM, PIG

neo-Darwinism
Theory of EVOLUTION that incorporates the modern ideas of genetic HEREDITY (notably Gregor MENDEL's) with Charles DARWIN's ideas of evolution through NATURAL SELECTION. It uses research into GENETICS to explain the origin of VARIATION within a species.

Neolithic (New Stone Age)
Stage in human cultural development following the PALAEOLITHIC. The Neolithic began *c*.8000 BC in W Asia and *c*.4000 BC in Britain. It was during this period that people first lived in settled villages, domesticated and bred animals, cultivated cereal crops and practised stone-grinding and flint-mining.

neoteny
Persistence in an adult animal of larval characteristics. It includes the retention of GILLS, as in some SALAMANDERS, the best example of which is the AXOLOTL of W United States and Mexico. An entire order of tunicates, the LARVACEANS, is permanently larval, never reaching a typical adult form.

nephron
Basic functional unit of the mammalian KIDNEY, involved in the formation of URINE. There are more than a million nephrons in a human kidney. Each consists of a GLOMERULUS (a cluster of tiny blood capillaries) cupped in a structure called a BOWMAN'S CAPSULE, with an attached long, narrow tubule. Blood enters the kidney under pressure, and water and wastes are forced into the tubule by a process known as ultrafiltration. Some water and

essential molecules are reabsorbed into the bloodstream; the remaining filtrate, urine, is passed to the BLADDER for voiding.

Neptune grass
Aquatic plant, a marine relative of PONDWEED. Neptune grass is found growing on the seabed in shallow coastal waters. One species, *Posidonia oceanica*, is especially common in the Mediterranean Sea; several species grow in Australian waters. Neptune grass sheds fibres, which often appear on beaches, rolled into small balls by tidal action. These fibres are sometimes gathered for use as a natural fertilizer. Family Posidoniaceae.

nerve impulse
Electrical signal that travels along the AXON of a NEURONE. Nerve impulses carry information throughout the NERVOUS SYSTEM. As an impulse passes, sodium and potassium ions flow into and out of the axon's membrane, creating a voltage reduction called the ACTION POTENTIAL. Nerve impulses can travel at up to 150m (500ft) per second.

nervous system
See feature article, pages 264–65

nest
Structure built by a living organism to house itself, its eggs or its young. Nest-builders include some invertebrates, particularly social insects, and members of all the larger groups of vertebrates. The nests of ANTS, BEES, WASPS and TERMITES may be highly elaborate, involving tunnels, passages and chambers. The nests of fish may be simple gravel scoops or enclosed structures, sometimes made of bubbles. BIRDS' nests vary enormously from simple, cup-shaped arrangements of twigs and other organic materials, to woven or knotted grass or leaves; some birds scrape a hollow in the ground to make a nest, others make nestholes in cliffs, earth banks or trees. The most highly evolved animal to make a form of a nest is probably the GORILLA, which builds a new sleeping platform of leafy branches every night.

▲ **nettle** The stinging nettle (*Urtica dioica*) has bristle-like stinging hairs, which are long, hollow cells. The tips of these are toughened with silica, and they are easily broken off.

When the plant is touched, the hairs penetrate the skin like surgical needles, the tips are lost, and the formic acid contained in the cells is released.

nettle
Any of numerous species of flowering plants of the genus *Urtica*. The stinging nettle (*Urtica dioica*) is typical of the genus in that it has stinging hairs along the leaves and stem. It has heart-shaped serrated leaves, small green flowers and is sometimes used for medicinal or culinary purposes. The stinging agent is formic acid. Family Urticaceae.

neuromuscular junction (end plate)
Point where an effector NEURONE meets a skeletal MUSCLE. When a nerve impulse reaches a neuromuscular junction, ACETYLCHOLINE is released, which diffuses across the membrane of the muscle (sarcolemma). The membrane then becomes permeable to sodium ions, which rush in producing the electrical activity that makes muscle fibres contract. To

N

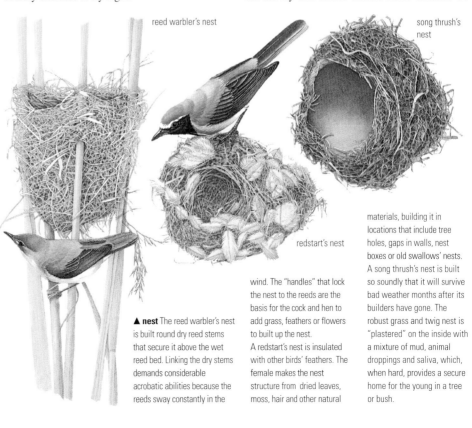

reed warbler's nest

song thrush's nest

redstart's nest

▲ **nest** The reed warbler's nest is built round dry reed stems that secure it above the wet reed bed. Linking the dry stems demands considerable acrobatic abilities because the reeds sway constantly in the wind. The "handles" that lock the nest to the reeds are the basis for the cock and hen to add grass, feathers or flowers to built up the nest. A redstart's nest is insulated with other birds' feathers. The female makes the nest structure from dried leaves, moss, hair and other natural materials, building it in locations that include tree holes, gaps in walls, nest boxes or old swallows' nests. A song thrush's nest is built so soundly that it will survive bad weather months after its builders have gone. The robust grass and twig nest is "plastered" on the inside with a mixture of mud, animal droppings and saliva, which, when hard, provides a secure home for the young in a tree or bush.

A nervous system is a communications system consisting of interconnecting nerve cells or NEURONES, which coordinate all life, growth and physical and mental activity. In simple animals, such as jellyfish and sea anemones, it consists of a **nerve-net** without a centre, or brain. The vertebrate nervous system consists of the CENTRAL NERVOUS SYSTEM (CNS), comprising the BRAIN and SPINAL CORD, and the PERIPHERAL NERVOUS SYSTEM, which serves all parts of the body outside the CNS.

An animal's nervous system, like a computer, employs electronics as the means of transmitting information. Also like a computer, it has memory banks, information processors and output devices that deliver the nerve signals to their destinations. Without a nervous system an animal cannot function: it cannot move, digest its food or breathe, since all these activities are triggered and controlled by the nerve network.

Nerve cells, or neurones, are some of the most specialized of cells. They carry information through the animal's body to coordinate its actions. A typical neurone resembles a tiny tree, with branches, roots and a thick stem. The roots of one neurone connect with the branches of others to form extensive chains and networks, allowing a signal generated within any one neurone to be passed on through the system. Each neurone has a very weak electrical charge. Normally the inside of the neurone is negative while the outside is positive, but if part of the cell is stimulated – by a sensory mechanism or by another nerve signal – the inside of the cell in the immediate vicinity becomes briefly positive. This effect ripples along the neurone like a wave. The impulse travels the length of the cell's stem - known as the AXON - and along the roots and branches, or DENDRITES. It carries on until it reaches the very tip of each dendrite, where it jumps a tiny gap, a SYNAPSE, over to the next neurone.

The nervous system of an extremely simple animal, such as a sea anemone, consists of a network of very similar neurones that extend throughout its body. In more sophisticated creatures the nervous system is based on a central core, and the neurones are of three basic types. SENSORY NEURONES collect information that has been gathered by the senses, while MOTOR NEURONES deliver messages to the animal's muscles. The sensory and motor neurones are linked by the interneurones of the central nervous system, which process the sensory information and coordinate the motor neurones to produce an appropriate response.

Most bodily functions, such as the beating of the heart, digestion and heat regulation, are performed without conscious thought. Such functions are governed by the AUTONOMIC NERVOUS SYSTEM (ANS), itself composed of two systems – the sympathetic and the parasympathetic. The sympathetic nerves, when stimulated, prepare the body for emergency action, such as fight or flight, by increasing heart and respiration rates and slowing down less immediately vital activities such as digestion. The parasympathetic nerves are most active during periods of rest. They slow the heart and breathing, but increase rates of activities such as digestion.

Sending signals is fairly straightforward, but analysing those signals is complex. As a result the central nervous system of an advanced animal, such as a mammal, has become highly sophisticated, with millions of interneurones linked together in complex electronic circuits, creating a central information processor, or brain. In many animals the potential of the neurone has been exploited still further, and their brains have the capacity to store information, recall it and use it: the basis of intelligence.

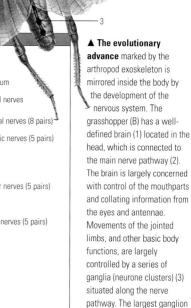

◄ **The hydra** (A), a close relative of the sea anemone, has an extremely primitive nervous system that is often called a nerve-net. Individual neurones, some of which act as receptors, are distributed throughout the animal's body and are linked into a non-directional network. A stimulus, such as physical contact, detected at a particular place on the body triggers a nerve impulse, which diffuses through the nerve-net to all parts of the animal. As the impulse spreads, it triggers a generalized contraction of all the hydra's muscular cells. This results in the animal shrinking into itself away from potential danger.

N

NERVOUS SYSTEM

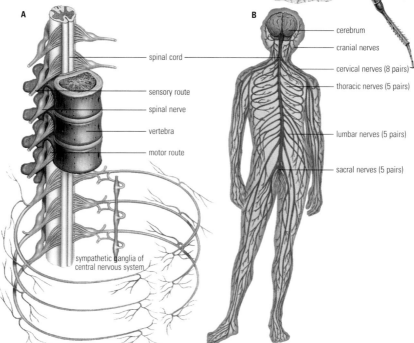

► **The nervous system** is divided into two parts: central and peripheral. The central nervous system (CNS) (A) includes the brain and spinal cord. It receives information, makes decisions and transmits instructions. The peripheral nervous system (B) consists chiefly of nerve fibres leading to and from the CNS. It cannot make "decisions" and acts only as a message transmitter.

A

spinal cord
sensory route
spinal nerve
vertebra
motor route

sympathetic ganglia of central nervous system

B

cerebrum
cranial nerves
cervical nerves (8 pairs)
thoracic nerves (5 pairs)
lumbar nerves (5 pairs)
sacral nerves (5 pairs)

▲ **The evolutionary advance** marked by the arthropod exoskeleton is mirrored inside the body by the development of the nervous system. The grasshopper (B) has a well-defined brain (1) located in the head, which is connected to the main nerve pathway (2). The brain is largely concerned with control of the mouthparts and collating information from the eyes and antennae. Movements of the jointed limbs, and other basic body functions, are largely controlled by a series of ganglia (neurone clusters) (3) situated along the nerve pathway. The largest ganglion is that corresponding with the grasshopper's hind limbs.

▼ **The cat** (C), a vertebrate, has a central nervous system consisting of a brain and spinal cord connected to a branching network of sensory and motor nerves. Sensory nerves pass information to the brain; and motor nerves convey instruction to muscles. Although all nerves are ultimately interconnected with the brain, a considerable amount of processing is carried out within the spinal cord, as in the case of the reflex action shown. When receptors are stimulated, a pulse passes along sensory neurones (1) into the spinal column (2) via a bundle of nerve fibres (3). Inside the grey matter (4) of the spinal cord, the impulse triggers an immediate motor response, via the motor neurone (5), to the relevant muscles (6).

Nerve impulses are passed along motor neurones (D) by an electro-chemical process. A ripple of potential travels down an axon until it reaches the tangle of dendrites (1) at the synapse (2) with another neurone. Each dendrite ends in synaptic knobs (E). Within each synaptic knob are small presynaptic vesicles (3) that contain chemicals known as neurotransmitters. The electrical impulse causes the vesicles to move to the surface of the synaptic knob (4), releasing neurotransmitters, which travel across the synaptic gap (5) and are absorbed at specialized sites (6) on the receiving cell (7).

Inside a motor neurone, the neurotransmitters provoke a change in potential in the cell body (8) around the nucleus (9) and an impulse is "fired" down the axon (10). The axon is insulated by a fatty myelin sheath (11) secreted by a series of individual Schwann cells (12). An axon connects to muscle fibres through an end-plate structure (13). The terminal synapses (14) can only make contact through synaptic clefts (15), which extend into the muscle (16). Specialized neurotransmitters contained in synaptic vesicles (17) are released across these clefts.

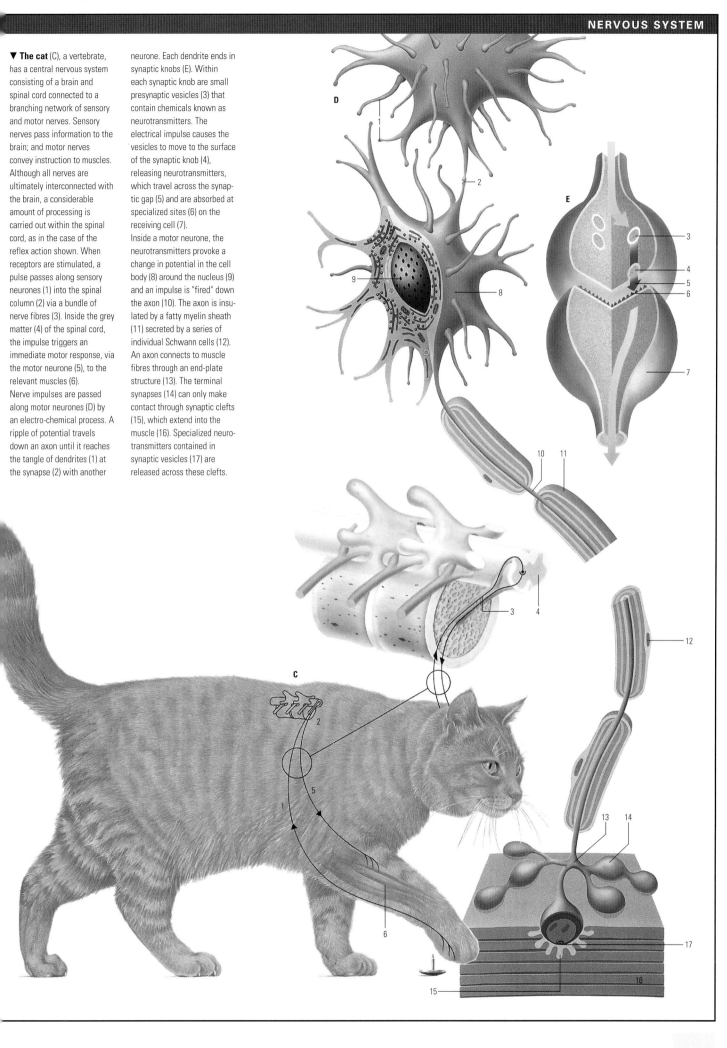

N

▲ **newt** An amphibian found in mountainous regions of central Europe, as well as many lowland areas, the alpine newt (*Triturus alpestris*) feeds on worms and insects. It is normally dull brown or black, but during the breeding season the male develops bright colours.

ensure the simultaneous contraction of all fibres in a muscle there are many neuromuscular junctions at intervals along a muscle.

neurone (neuron, nerve cell)
Basic structural unit of the NERVOUS SYSTEM; it enables rapid transmission of NERVE IMPULSES between different parts of the body. It is composed of a cell body, containing a nucleus, and a number of trailing, finger-like processes. The largest of these processes is the AXON, which carries outgoing impulses, causing the release of NEUROTRANSMITTERS across a junction (SYNAPSE) resulting in the stimulation of another neurone. The rest of the finger-like processes are DENDRITES, which receive incoming impulses. *See also* MOTOR NEURONE; SENSORY NEURONE

neuropteran
Any member of the order Neuroptera, comprising carnivorous INSECTS found worldwide. It includes LACEWINGS and ANT LIONS. Neuropterans undergo complete METAMORPHOSIS, from an egg through larval and pupal stages to the adult form. The adult has two pairs of membranous wings, which, at rest, are folded over the body. Length: to 7cm (3in).

neurotransmitter
Any one of several dozen chemicals involved in communication between NEURONES (nerve cells) or between a nerve and muscle cells. When an electrical impulse arrives at a nerve ending, a neurotransmitter is released to carry the signal across the specialized junction (SYNAPSE) between the nerve cell and its neighbour. Fast-acting neurotransmitters either prompt nerves to fire or inhibit them from firing; slow acting ones seem to be involved in modifying the activity of whole groups of nerve cells. ACETYLCHOLINE, the neurotransmitter that causes muscle to contract, is the target of nerve gases. Some drugs work by disrupting neurotransmission. *See also* ADRENALINE; NERVOUS SYSTEM; NORADRENALINE; SEROTONIN

neutron (symbol n)
Uncharged elementary particle that occurs in the atomic nuclei of all chemical elements, except the lightest isotope of HYDROGEN. It was first identified (1932) by British physicist James Chadwick (1891–1974). Outside the nucleus, it is unstable, decaying with a half-life of 11.6 minutes into a PROTON, ELECTRON and antineutrino. Its neutrality allows it to penetrate and be absorbed in nuclei and thus to induce nuclear transmutation and fission. It is a baryon with spin $\frac{1}{2}$ and a mass slightly greater than that of the proton.

neutrophil
Form of LEUCOCYTE (white blood cell) that carries out PHAGOCYTOSIS. It has granular cytoplasm and an irregular, multi-lobed nucleus. Neutrophils make up 60% of all leucocytes. They migrate from blood capillaries to help fight infections arising in the tissues.

névé
See FIRN

newt
Any member of a family of 60 species of SALAMANDER occurring in North America, Europe and temperate and subtropical Asia. Adults have well-developed limbs. They lack gills and often have both terrestrial and aquatic life stages. Many newt species have poisonous skin secretions and are brightly coloured. Family Salamandridae.

newt, alpine
Granular-skinned newt with a dark, mottled back and a bright orange or red belly. Males have a light blue marking between their front and hind legs and when in breeding condition have a low, black-and-white crest down the middle of the back. Alpine newts are found at both low and high elevations throughout much of Europe. Length: to 10cm (4in). Family Salamandridae; species *Triturus alpestris*.

newt, red-spotted
Common newt of E North America. Adults are olive with many small dark marks and several larger red spots on the sides. The juvenile EFT stage is red with markings similar to the adult. Red-spotted newts occur in all types of still or slow-flowing waters. Length: 6–11cm (2–4in). Family Salamandridae; species *Notophthalmus viridescens*.

newt, smooth
Widespread and common newt found in much of Europe, including Great Britain and Ireland. The smooth newt's olive skin lacks the granulations common in other newts. Males have large black spots and in the breeding season develop a large fleshy crest on the back that is used in complex courtship rituals. Length: to 10cm (4in). Family Salamandridae; species *Triturus vulgaris*.

New Zealand flax
Plant of the AGAVE family, native to swampy regions in New Zealand. It is grown throughout the tropics as an ornamental or as a source of fibre. It has rosettes of tough, sword-shaped, fibrous leaves, which can be up to 2.7m (9ft) long. The leaves are used to produce a fibre that is softer and more flexible than ABACA with a high lustre. It is used for matting, tow lines and cordage. Family Agavaceae; species *Phormium tenax*.

New Zealand spinach
Annual plant native to Australia, New Zealand and Asia; it is related to the ICE PLANT. New Zealand spinach is a coarse, ground-covering plant. It is grown for its edible leaves, which are used in cooking. Family Aizoaceae; species *Tetragonia expansa*.

nicator
Any member of the genus *Nicator*, a small group of African birds in the BULBUL family. They are brownish above and are characterized by a heavy bill and yellow-spotted wing feathers. They are usually found singly in bush country and riverside thickets. But for their mellow calls, they would be easily overlooked. Length: 14–23cm (6–9in). Family Pycnonotidae; genus *Nicator*.

niccolite (kupfernickel)
One of the chief ores of nickel, consisting of nickel arsenide (NiAs), often also with some cobalt, iron and sulphur. It has hexagonal system of crystals generally in columnar masses, rarely as tabular crystals. It is found in vein deposits and is copper coloured, with an easily tarnished metallic lustre. Hardness 5–5.5; r.d. 7.8.

Nicolle, Charles Jules Henri (1866–1936)
French bacteriologist. Nicolle was awarded the 1928 Nobel Prize for physiology or medicine for his discovery (1909) that typhus is transmitted by the body louse. He later distinguished between classical typhus and murine typhus, which is passed on to humans by the rat flea. Nicolle was head of the Pasteur Institute in Tunis (1902–32), which under his direction became a distinguished centre for bacteriological research.

nicotiana
Any of more than 100 species belonging to the genus *Nicotiana*. *Nicotiana tabacum*, originally a tropical species, is the source of commercial tobacco, although *Nicotiana rustica*, a shrubby plant native to E United States, has a higher nicotine content and was used by Native Americans. Other species include jasmine tobacco, *Nicotiana alata*, which has tubular flowers that open at dusk and emit a jasmine-ike odour. Family Solanaceae.

nicotinamide adenine dinucleotide (NAD)
Organic chemical important in respiration as a carrier of hydrogens in the ELECTRON TRANSPORT SYSTEM. It helps to synthesise ADENOSINE TRIPHOSPHATE (ATP) from the hydrogen ions produced during the KREBS CYCLE. *See also* FLAVINE ADENINE DINUCLEOTIDE

niger seed
Erect annual plant native to Ethiopia. It has lance-shaped leaves and yellow flowers. Niger seed is cultivated in warm climates, particularly India, as an oilseed for feeding to caged birds; the oil is used for cooking and paint. It is found as an escape on wasteground near oil-mills and as an introduction from birdseed. Height: to 2m (6.6ft) Family Asteraceae; species *Guizotia abyssinica*.

nighthawk
Nightjar-like bird, with a long, slightly forked tail and camouflaged, intricate brown plumage. It is active

◄ **nighthawk** The common nighthawk (*Chordeiles minor*) feeds entirely on flying insects, which it catches with its large, bristle-fringed mouth. The male's display flight is spectacular: it dives at great speed towards the ground, before braking suddenly, which produces a strange booming sound. The nighthawk makes no nest, preferring to lay its eggs on the ground in clearings or on flat roofs in urban areas.

N

▲ nightjar The standard-winged nightjar (*Macrodipteryx longipennis*) is one of the most spectacular of nightjar species. Its streamer feathers are about three times longer that its body. These extraordinary feathers function as a courting display during the breeding season.

and agile, hunting insects in twilight. The common nighthawk (*Chordeiles minor*) is a widespread summer visitor to North America; it winters south to Argentina. Length: 20–24cm (8–9in). Family Caprimulgidae; genus *Chordeiles*.

nightingale
Any of several species of songbird belonging to the THRUSH family. Nightingales are brown, with long legs and a reddish-brown tail. They live in damp thickets, where they feed on insects. The nightingale is considered the finest European songster, with an outstandingly rich, loud and varied voice. Its song is the subject of much praise in European literature and verse. Length: 16cm (6in). Family Turdidae; genus *Luscinia*; species include *Luscinia megarhynchos* and *Luscinia luscinia*.

nightjar
Member of a group of nocturnal birds with long tails and large eyes. Their tiny bills have a huge gape with sensitive bristles for catching night-flying insects. By day, the nightjar rests horizontally on branches or the ground, camouflaged by its delicate, "dead leaf" patterned plumage. Many species are most easily identified by their voices. Length: 25–35cm (10–14in). Family Caprimulgidae; main genus *Caprimulgus*; there are c.65 species.

nightshade
Name given to various species of poisonous flowering plants, but mainly to those of the family Solanaceae, especially those of the genus *Solanum*. Woody nightshade (*Solanum dulcamara*) has poisonous foliage and poisonous red berries. Another member of the family is DEADLY NIGHTSHADE (*Atropa belladonna*).

Nile perch
Large, predatory fish found from w Africa to the Nile River. It is green or brown, with a silvery underside. The Nile perch is a major predator on cichlids in the African Rift Valley lakes, as for example in Lake Victoria, where it threatens the survival of the endemic cichlid. The Nile perch is an important food fish. Length: to 1.8m (6ft). Family Latidae; species *Lates niloticus*.

nilgai
Large ANTELOPE that ranges in wooded areas of the Indian subcontinent. The male is blue-grey and the female red-brown. Both sexes have a short mane and white markings on the belly and throat. The male bears short, curved horns and a tuft of black hair at the throat. Height: to 1.4m (4.6ft). Family Bovidae; species *Boselaphus tragocamelus*.

niltava
Any member of the bird genus *Niltava*, a group of FLYCATCHERS found mainly in mountain forests of Southeast Asia. The male of many species has beautiful iridescent colours. Niltavas usually sit quietly on a low branch deep in the forest, then dart out to catch

a passing insect. Length: 11–20cm (4–8in). Family Muscicapidae; genus *Niltava*; there are c.24 species.

nimbostratus
See CLOUD

ningaui
Any member of the genus *Ningaui*, a group of mouse-like DASYURIDS, which are amongst the smallest of Australia's marsupials. The ningaui is primarily nocturnal and feeds in grassland areas on insects and small vertebrates. Three species are known from distinct arid and semi-arid regions: the Pilbara ningaui, Wongai ningaui and Southern ningaui. Head-body length: 5–6cm (2in); tail: 6–8cm (2–3in). Family Dasyuridae; genus *Ningaui*.

Nirenberg, Marshall Warren (1927–)
US biochemist who found the key to the amino acid GENETIC CODE by deciphering different combinations of three nucleotide bases (called "codons") within long nucleotide chains in DNA and RNA. Each combination is coded to convert a different AMINO ACID to PROTEIN, a key process in transferring inherited characteristics. Nirenberg found he could decipher the unknown configurations by synthesizing a nucleic acid with a known base combination, and then recording the amino acid that it changed to protein. He was awarded the 1968 Nobel Prize for physiology or medicine, together with Robert W. HOLLEY and Har Gobind KHORANA, for his part in discovering how GENES determine cell function.

nitrate
Salt of nitric acid (HNO_3). Nitrate salts contain the nitrate ion (NO_3^-) and some are important naturally occurring compounds, such as saltpeter (potassium nitrate, KNO_3) and Chile saltpeter (sodium nitrate, $NaNO_3$). Nitrates are used as food preservers, fertilizers, explosives and as a source of nitric acid.

nitrification
Conversion of ammonium compounds to nitrites and nitrates. The process typically takes place in soil

NITROGEN CYCLE

Circulation of nitrogen through plants and animals in the BIOSPHERE. NITROGEN-FIXING BACTERIA in the soil or in plant root nodules take free nitrogen from the soil and air to form the nitrogen compounds (NITRATES) used by plants in ASSIMILATION. HERBIVORES obtain their nitrogen from the plants, and in turn CARNIVORES obtain nitrogen by eating herbivores. SAPROPHYTES decompose the tissue of all the organisms concerned and the nitrogen is released back into the cycle. *See also* FOOD CHAIN; NITROGEN FIXATION

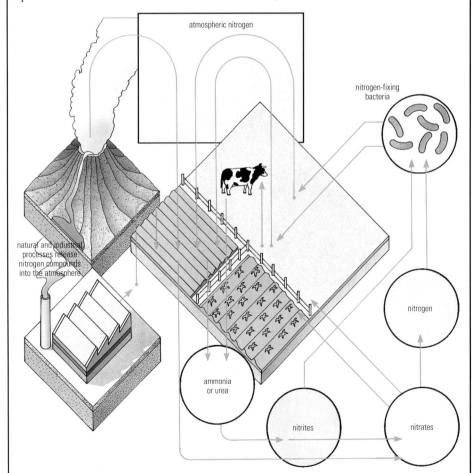

▲ Free nitrogen (N_2) in the atmosphere cannot be absorbed directly by plants or animals. Soil-dwelling bacteria known as nitrogen-fixing bacteria convert the nitrogen into nitrates, in which form it can then be absorbed by plants. The plants are eaten by herbivores, the "primary consumers" of the standard food chain. Some of the excess nitrogen in the animals' bodies is converted to ammonia or urea and then returned to the soil. In addition, when the animals die, saprophytes decompose the tissue and release any remaining nitrogen to the soil. The nitrogen cycle can then begin again.

BACTERIA such as *Nitrosomonas* and *Nitrobacter*. The bacteria thereby provide green plants with nitrogen that would otherwise be unavailable. *See also* NITROGEN CYCLE

nitrogen (symbol N)
Common gaseous, nonmetallic element of group V of the periodic table, discovered in 1772. Colourless and odourless, it is the major component of Earth's ATMOSPHERE (78% by volume), from which it is extracted by fractional distillation of liquid air. The NITROGEN CYCLE is an essential process for the existence of life on Earth. The main industrial use is in the Haber process, which produces ammonia for fertilizers and making nitric acid. Nitrogen compounds are used in fertilizers, explosives, dyes, foods and drugs. The element is chemically inert. Properties: at.no. 7; r.a.m. 14.0067; r.d. 1.2506; m.p. −209.86°C (−345.75°F); b.p. −195.8°C (−320.4°F); most common isotope ^{14}N (99.76%).

nitrogen cycle
See feature article, page 267

nitrogen fixation
Incorporation of atmospheric NITROGEN into chemicals for use by organisms. Nitrogen-fixing microorganisms (mainly BACTERIA and CYANOBACTERIA) absorb nitrogen gas from the air, from air spaces in the soil, or from water, and build it up into compounds of ammonia. Other bacteria then change these compounds into NITRATES, which can be taken up by plants. Some NITROGEN-FIXING BACTERIA live in symbiotic association with other organisms. Bacteria in the root nodules of plants, especially members of the PEA family (LEGUMES), exchange nitrogen compounds for carbohydrates. If the remains of these plants are ploughed back into the soil, they enrich it with nitrates. Cyanobacteria are important nitrogen fixers in the sea, in fresh water, and in soil, and are particularly important in rice fields. *See also* NITROGEN CYCLE; SYMBIOSIS

nitrogen-fixing bacterium
BACTERIUM that is able to reduce NITROGEN to ammonia. This ANAEROBIC process is widespread among physiologically distinct microbial groups and is readily inactivated by the presence of oxygen. Some examples of nitrogen-fixing bacteria are *Clostridium*, *Klebsiella* and *Azotobacter*. *Rhizobium* is able to nodulate and establish a nitrogen-fixing SYMBIOSIS with roots of various leguminous plants. *See also* LEGUME; NITROGEN CYCLE; NITROGEN FIXATION

noctuid (owlet)
Any member of the MOTH family Noctuidae; it contains more than 6000 species worldwide. Immature noctuid caterpillars are a common pest to plant crops in Australia. Adult moths fly mainly at night and are able to respond to the echolocation clicks of bats, their major predators. Adult body size: 10–25mm (0.4–1in). Order Lepidoptera; family Noctuidae. *See also* MOTH, ALDER; MOTH, ANTLER; MOTH, HOOKTIP; MOTH, UNDERWING

nocturnal animal
Animal that is active at night rather than during the day (diurnal animal). Nocturnal animals include BADGERS and OWLS. Those active at twilight are termed crepuscular. *See also* DIURNAL RHYTHM

node
In botany, a node is the position on the stem of a plant from which a leaf or leaves grow. In anatomy, a node is a thickening or enlargement of an organ or tissue, such as a lymph node (gland) or the sinoatrial node of nervous tissue in the heart, which controls the heartbeat.

node of Ranvier
Point along a NEURONE where the MYELIN SHEATH is absent. The nodes are important in the propagation of a nerve impulse along the neurone because they enable the impulse to jump from one node to the next. This speeds the rate of transmission along a neurone, which is therefore considerably faster in a myelinated nerve than it is in an unmyelinated one. *See also* SCHWANN CELLS

non-biting midge (gnat)
Any member of the MIDGE genus *Chironomus*. They are always found close to still water. After mating in male swarms, the females oviposit their eggs at the water surface. The aquatic larvae possess a large amount of haemoglobin and are commonly known as red bloodworms. Adult body size: *c*.5mm (*c*.0.2in). Order Diptera; family Chironomidae; genus *Chironomus*.

non-sulphur bacterium
BACTERIUM that does not oxidize hydrogen sulphide and consequently does not deposit sulphur either externally or internally in its cells. The group includes photosynthetic red, purple and brown non-sulphur bacteria, such as *Rhodopseudomonas* and *Rhodospirillum*, which have bacteriochlorophyll and carotenoid pigments. The group also includes the green non-sulphur bacterium *Chloroflexus*, which uses chlorophyll to capture light.

noradrenaline
Hormone secreted by nerves in the autonomic NERVOUS SYSTEM and by the ADRENAL GLANDS. Chemically, it is closely related to ADRENALINE and has similar effects on the cardiovascular system. It slows the heart rate and constricts small arteries, thus raising the blood pressure. It is used therapeutically to combat the fall in blood pressure that accompanies shock. *See also* NEUROTRANSMITTER

▲ **nutcracker** The spotted nutcracker (*Nucifraga caryocatactes*) can store pine nuts in a sack in its beak. It then hides the nuts among moss and tree roots so that it has a food store to last it through the often harsh winters of N Eurasia.

Norfolk Island Pine
Evergreen tree native to Norfolk Island in the s Pacific Ocean. Its branches grow in tiers, with between four and seven branches at each layer. It bears bright green needles. The tree is propagated by seeds or cuttings of tip growth. It is widely grown as a house plant in its sapling stage. Height: to 60m (200ft). Family Araucariaceae; species *Araucaria excelsia*.

notochord
In CHORDATES and the early embryonic stages of vertebrates, the flexible, primitive backbone; in mature vertebrates, it is replaced by the SPINE.

nucellus
Tissue that forms most of the OVULE in a FLOWER. It consists of nutrient tissue and an embryo sac, enclosed by a skin that has a small hole in it called the MICROPYLE.

nucleic acid
Giant chemical molecules present in all living cells and in viruses. There are two types: DNA (deoxyribonucleic acid) stores the GENETIC CODE that functions as the basis of heredity; and RNA (ribonucleic acid) delivers these coded instructions to the cell's PROTEIN manufacturing sites. Chemically, nucleic acids are polymers of NUCLEOTIDES. *See also* CHROMOSOME; DNA; ENZYME; GENE; MESSENGER RNA (mRNA); RNA

nucleolus
Darkly staining spherical body that occurs in the NUCLEUS of a CELL. It is not a distinct ORGANELLE because it is not bound by a membrane. It contains DNA (deoxyribonucleic acid), which codes for RNA (ribonucleic acid), which the nucleolus manufactures and stores. It also carries out the initial phases of RIBOSOME formation.

nucleoside
Subunit of NUCLEIC ACID, consisting of a sugar linked to a nitrogenous base (purine or pyrimidine).

nucleotide
Complex naturally occurring chemical group that contains a nitrogen base linked to a sugar and an acid phosphate. Nucleotides are the building blocks of NUCLEIC ACIDS (such as DNA and RNA). In the molecules of nucleic acids, nucleotides are linked together by bonds between the sugar and the phosphate groups. Nucleotides also occur freely in a CELL as various COENZYMES, such as ADENOSINE TRIPHOSPHATE (ATP), the principal carrier of chemical energy in the metabolic pathways of the body.

► **numbat** This marsupial is an endangered species, found only in open eucalyptus forests of sw Australia. It feeds almost exclusively on termites, using its sticky tongue, which can be as much as half the length of its body. This marsupial is unusual in that it is pouchless. The blind and hairless young cling to their mother's fur for the first six months while suckling.

N

nucleus
In biology, membrane-bound structure that, in most CELLS, contains the CHROMOSOMES. As well as holding the genetic material, the nucleus is essential for the maintenance of cell processes. It manufactures the RNA used to build RIBOSOMES. Other RNA molecules carry the genetic code from the DNA through pores in the nuclear membrane into the CYTOPLASM, where it is used as a template for PROTEIN SYNTHESIS by the ribosomes. CELL DIVISION involves the splitting of the nucleus and CYTOPLASM. Cells without nuclei include BACTERIA and mature mammalian ERYTHROCYTES (red blood cells). Instead of chromosomes, bacteria have a naked, circular molecule of DNA in the cytoplasm.

nucleus
In physics, central core of an ATOM. Made up of nucleons (PROTONS and NEUTRONS), the nucleus accounts for almost all of an atom's mass. Because protons are positively charged and neutrons have no charge, a nucleus has an overall positive charge; this is cancelled out, however, by the negatively charged ELECTRONS that orbit the nucleus. The number of protons in a nucleus is called its atomic number; the number of nucleons is the mass number.

nudibranch
See SEA SLUG

nuée ardente
See PYROCLASTIC FLOW

numbat (banded or marsupial anteater)
Marsupial mammal native to sw Australia. It has distinctive white bars across its back, a long bushy tail and a black stripe through the eyes. A daytime feeder, it uses its long tongue to collect termites from rotting logs in open woodland. Length: 35–45cm (14–18in). Family Myrmecobiidae; species *Myrmecobius fasciatus.*

nunbird
Any of about five small species of the PUFFBIRD family, often with dark plumage. Found in the tropical forests of South America, the nunbird is an active bird which feeds like a FLYCATCHER. Length: 30cm (12in). Family Bucconidae; genera *Hapaloptila* and *Monasa.*

nunlet
Any of five small species of the PUFFBIRD family, found in the tropical forests of South America. The nunlet has an upright stance and feeds mainly on insects. Length: 15cm (6in). Family Bucconidae; genus *Nonnula.*

nurse hound (larger spotted dogfish)
Relatively unspecialized SHARK species. It lays eggs. It is related to catsharks and the ROUGH HOUND. The nurse hound is pale or dark brown in colour and is covered in darker spots. Length: to 1.5m (4.9ft). Family Scyliorhinidae; species *Scyliorhinus stellaris.*

nut
Dry, one-seeded FRUIT with a hard woody or stony wall. It develops from a flower that has petals attached above the ovary (inferior ovary). Examples include acorns and hazelnuts.

nutcracker
Either of two grey-brown birds belonging to the CROW family. The spotted nutcracker (*Nucifraga caryocatactes*) is found in N European and Asian forests. It has distinctive bold white spots and a noticeable white undertail. Clark's nutcraker (*Nucifraga columbiana*), found in North America, is greyish-white with black wings and a black tail. Both species feed exclusively on pine seeds or hazel nuts. If these crops fail, nutcrackers fly south on extremely long-distance migrations in search of food. Length: 32cm (13in). Family Corvidae; genus *Nucifraga.*

nuthatch
Any member of the genus *Sitta*, a group of small, compact, short-tailed, woodpecker-like woodland birds. The nuthatch is unusual in its ability to descend tree trunks and branches head downwards. It feeds on insects, grubs, nuts and seeds, consuming any tough seeds by wedging them in crevices and hammering them open. Family Sittidae; genus *Sitta*; there are *c.*22 species.

nuthatch, Eurasian
Nuthatch common in Europe and Asia. It is slaty blue above and whitish to reddish-brown below, with a black stripe through the eyes. It is found in woodlands and parks. In winter it often feeds with tits in loose flocks. Length: 14cm (6in). Family Sittidae; species *Sitta europaea.*

nuthatch, red-breasted
Small nuthatch that is widespread in North America, where it is found in conifer forests; strays have been known to reach mainland Europe. The red-breasted nuthatch is bluish above and rich reddish-brown below, with a black cap, white stripe above the eyes and a black stripe through the eyes. Its call resembles a toy tin horn. Length: 12cm (5in). Family Sittidae; species *Sitta canadensis.*

nuthatch, rock
Large nuthatch; its plumage is similar to but more drab than that of the Eurasian nuthatch. It is found only on rocky hillsides, gorges and inland cliffs in s Europe. It is noisy and boldly aggressive. Length: 15cm (6in). Family Sittidae; species *Sitta neumayer.*

nuthatch, pygmy
Small nuthatch. It is found in pine forests of North America, as far south as Mexico. It has a grey-brown cap, bluish-grey back and creamy-buff underparts. In winter, it roams in loose flocks with chickadees. Length: 11cm (4in). Family Sittidae; species *Sitta pygmaea.*

nutmeg
Evergreen tree native to tropical Asia, Africa and America. Its seeds yield the spice nutmeg; the spice MACE comes from the seed covering. Height: up to 18m (60ft). Family Myristicaceae; species *Myristica fragrans.*

nutria (coypu)
Large rodent native to South America; it has been introduced to North America, Europe and Asia, where it has been farmed for the fur-trade. Semi-aquatic, the nutria lives in marshes, lakes and streams. It resembles a beaver, with dense fur and webbed feet but a rat-like tail. An excellent swimmer, it feeds mainly on water vegetation. Its trail-making and tunnelling activities are very destructive to agricultural land, and it is considered a pest. Two or three litters of up to 10 babies are produced every year after a gestation of 132 days. Head-body length: 43–63cm (17–25in); tail: 25–42cm (10–17in). Family Capromyidae; species *Myogastor coypus.*

nutrition
All the processes by which plants and animals take in and make use of food. The science of nutrition involves identifying the kinds and amounts of nutrients necessary for growth and health. Nutrients are generally divided into PROTEINS, CARBOHYDRATES, FATS, MINERALS and VITAMINS.

nymph
Young INSECT of primitive orders that do not undergo complete METAMORPHOSIS. The term is used to designate all immature stages after the OVUM. The nymph resembles the adult (IMAGO) and does so more closely with each successive MOULTING. Some examples are the aquatic nymphs of DRAGONFLIES, MAYFLIES and DAMSELFLIES.

N

▲ **nutria** This semi-aquatic, nocturnal rodent lives in burrows near water, usually along river banks. Its predators include wild cats, wolves and large snakes. It enters water to escape danger, being a very strong swimmer.

O

oak

Common name for *c*.600 species belonging to the genus *Quercus*, which are found in temperate areas of the Northern Hemisphere and at high elevations in the tropics. Most species are hardwood trees, reaching heights of between 18m and 30m (60–100ft). Leaves are simple, often lobed and sometimes serrated. The flowers are greenish and inconspicuous; male flowers hang in catkins. The fruit is an acorn surrounded by a cup. Family Fagaceae; genus *Quercus*.

oarfish

Any of several deepwater, ribbon-shaped fish found in tropical and suptropical marine waters. Its long, thin, silvery body has a dorsal fin extending along its entire length. Two long, oar-like, pelvic fins protrude from beneath its head. Length: to 6m (20ft). Family Regalecidae; genus *Regalecus*.

oarweed

Type of SEAWEED. It has a long, smooth, oval stem and a broad blade that splits into several strap-like fingers as it matures. Oarweed reaches 2m (6ft) or more in length and is found on coasts around the Northern Hemisphere. It stores sodium glutamate and can therefore be tasty when dried. Family Laminariaceae; species *Laminaria digitata*.

oasis

Fertile location that has water in an arid landscape. Usually GROUNDWATER is brought to the surface in a well, but an oasis may occur at the point where a river flowing from a wetter region crosses the desert on its way to the sea, such as the Nile in North Africa or the Indus in s Asia. Most Saharan oases contain large numbers of date palms, and there are also many fields of grains, vegetables and fruits. There is often a settlement at the oasis, sometimes with as many as 30,000 inhabitants.

oat

CEREAL plant native to w Europe and cultivated worldwide. The flower comprises numerous florets, which produce one-seeded fruits. Mainly fed to livestock, oats are also eaten by humans. Family Poaceae/Gramineae; species *Avena sativa*.

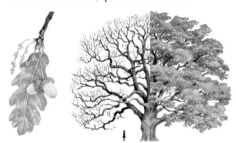

▲ **oak** The common or English oak (*Quercus robur*) is found throughout the British Isles, w Europe and into Asia. It can live up to 1000 years. The oak is monoecious, that is, having both male and female flowers on the same tree. The fruits are acorns, which are borne singly or in clusters of up to five.

oarfish

► **oarfish** The longest of the bony fish, the oarfish is thought to have given rise to legends of sea serpents. It is found at depths of up to 900m (3000ft) and only rarely comes to the surface. It feeds on krill, which it strains through its gill rakers.

obelia

See feature article

obsidian

Rare, grey to black, glassy, volcanic rock. High in silica, obsidian is the uncrystallized equivalent of RHYOLITE and GRANITE. It polishes well and makes an attractive semi-precious stone. Hardness 5.5; r.d. 2.4.

ocean

Continuous body of salt water that surrounds the continents and fills the Earth's great depressions. Oceans cover about 71% of the Earth's surface (more than 80% of the Southern Hemisphere) and represent about 98% of all the water on the face of the Earth. There are five main oceans: Atlantic, Pacific, Indian, Arctic and Antarctic. They may be described by distinct region (LITTORAL, BENTHOS, PELAGIC and ABYSSAL) or by depth (CONTINENTAL MARGIN, deep sea plain and deep TRENCHES). The SEAFLOOR has a varied topography. SEAWATER contains salt and other mineral deposits; the salt content, between 3.3% and 3.7%, is the result of washout from the land and interchange with the ATMOSPHERE over the ages. Light penetrates seawater to a maximum depth of about 300m (1000ft), below which plant life cannot grow. The oceans are constantly moving in CURRENTS, TIDES and WAVES. They form an integral part of the Earth's HYDROLOGICAL CYCLE and CLIMATE. Oceans are a rich source of FOSSILS, providing invaluable evidence of the evolution of life on Earth. They also provide minerals, such as MANGANESE NODULES, OIL and NATURAL GAS. The CONTINENTAL SHELF yields sand and gravel. Marine fauna, such as FISH and PLANKTON, are a vital part of the food chain.

Through volcanic activity the oceans have been forming over the last 200 million years. The theory of CONTINENTAL DRIFT (and associated SEAFLOOR SPREADING) has revealed that PANGAEA was surrounded by one vast ocean, Panthallasia. As

OBELIA

Any member of the *Obelia* genus, a group of small, marine HYDROZOAN animals. The obelia is best known in its MEDUSA form, which resembles the true JELLYFISH. The "bell" of the medusa state is usually less than 10mm (0.4in) in diameter. Phylum Coelenterata/Cnidaria; class Hydrozoa; order Hydroida; family Campanulariidae; genus *Obelia*.

▲ **Like some other** marine invertebrates, *Obelia* species can alternate between asexual and sexual reproduction, often synchronized with particular seasons. Obelia consists of a colony of sub-individuals called polyps, some of which are specialized for feeding (1, also shown in section) and others for reproduction. Asexual reproduction occurs when a new polyp buds off from the parent (2), staying attached to the stem. The sexual phase occurs between free-swimming jellyfish-like medusae, which escape from the medusae buds (3) at the polyp top. Male medusae have testes, and females have ovaries, both of which positioned under the bell.

They swim by pulsating their bells. A male medusa releases sperm (4) to fertilize the female's eggs (5). The fertilized egg develops into a larva (6) that swims until it finds a surface on which it can settle (7), grow and eventually commence to reproduce as mature obelia (8 and 9).

Pangaea began to split, a smaller and shallower ocean, the Tethys Sea, formed between the continents. By about 65 million years ago, the Atlantic and Indian oceans appeared. The Pacific was separated from the Atlantic and Indian oceans when the North and South American continents joined. The separation of Greenland from North America, and the widening of the North Atlantic, completed the encirclement of the Arctic Ocean. Total area: 360 million sq km (138 million sq mi). Total volume: c.1.4 billion cu km (322 million cu mi). Average depth: 3500m (12,000ft). Average temperature: 3.9°C (39°F).

oceanic crust
See CRUST

ocean floor
See SEAFLOOR

ocean formation
See SEAFLOOR SPREADING

oceanic basin
One of two major provinces of the deep ocean floor, lying at more than 2km (1.2mi) in depth. The MID-OCEAN RIDGES form the other province. Together they constitute 56% of the Earth's surface. The deep ocean basin is underlain by a basaltic crust, about 7km (4.3mi) thick, and is covered in sediment and dotted by low ABYSSAL hills. *See also* TRENCH

oceanography
Study of the OCEANS. The major subdisciplines of oceanography include marine geology (*see* PLATE TECTONICS), MARINE BIOLOGY, marine METEOROLOGY and physical and chemical oceanography. The science of oceanography dates from the Challenger Expedition (1872–76).

ocean perch
See ROSEFISH

ocelot
Small CAT that lives in the s United States, Central and South America. Its valuable fur is yellowish with elongated dark spots. It feeds on small birds, mammals and reptiles. Length (including the tail): to 1.5m (4.9ft). Family Felidae; species *Felis pardalis*.

Ochoa, Severo (1905–93)
US biochemist, b. Spain. Ochoa shared the 1959 Nobel Prize for physiology or medicine with Arthur KORNBERG for their work on the synthesis of RNA, which helped greatly in the study and development of GENETICS.

octopus
Any of c.150 species of predatory CEPHALOPOD MOLLUSCS lacking an external shell. The octopus has a sac-like body, with eight powerful, suckered tentacles. It feeds mostly on crabs and other shellfish, paralysing its prey with poison. Many of the species are small, but the common octopus (*Octopus vulgaris*) grows to c.9m (c.30ft). Phylum Mollusca; class Cephalopoda; family Octopodidae.

odonatan
Any member of the order Odonata, a group of primitive winged insects found worldwide. The DAMSELFLY, in the suborder Zygoptera, has a thin body, with wings that are held vertically along the body when at rest. The long, slender, aquatic nymphs have three, leaflike gills on the abdomen.

▲ **ocelot** The ocelot is primarily a terrestrial cat, but it will sometimes hunt in trees. It is nocturnal, resting in dense scrub during the day. The ocelot is found in a variety of habitats, from brushland to tropical rainforests. It is very rare in the north of its range, due to habitat destruction.

The DRAGONFLY, in the suborder Anisoptera, has a heavy body with wings held horizontally when at rest. The stout nymphs have gills at the anal end. All odonatans prey on insects; none attack humans. Length: 18–193mm (0.7–8in).

oesophagus (gullet)
Muscular tube, part of the ALIMENTARY CANAL (or gut), that carries swallowed food to the STOMACH. Food is moved down the lubricated channel by a wave-like movement known as PERISTALSIS. *See also* DIGESTION

oestrogen
Female SEX HORMONE. First produced by a girl at puberty, oestrogen leads to the development of the SECONDARY SEXUAL CHARACTERISTICS that turn her body into a woman's: breasts, body hair and redistributed fat. It regulates the MENSTRUAL CYCLE and prepares the UTERUS for pregnancy. Oestrogen is also a constituent of the contraceptive pill.

oestrous cycle
Physiological changes occurring during the female reproductive cycle of most placental MAMMALS. Controlled by HORMONES, it is evident among animals other than humans. Cycles of different animals vary in frequency and length. Typically, ovulation is associated with the oestrous (heat) period. *See also* MENSTRUAL CYCLE

oil
General term to describe a variety of substances, the chief shared properties of which are viscosity at ordinary temperatures, a density less than that of water, flammability, insolubility in water and solubility in ether and alcohol. There are three main types. **Mineral oils** are hydrocarbon mixtures occurring, most notably, in crude or PETROLEUM oil. They are extracted by refining to be used primarily as fuels. **Animal oils** are glycerides of FATTY ACIDS; they are used as food, lubricants and as a major ingredient of soap, paints and varnishes. There are two kinds of **vegetable oil** (fixed oil): drying, such as linseed or poppyseed oil, and non-drying, such as olive and castor oil. All vegetable oils are esters or mixtures of substances called terpenes. Essential oils are obtained from plants; unlike other vegetable oils, they are volatile. Such oils are found in perfumes and food flavourings.

oilbird
Nocturnal bird that inhabits deep caves in Trinidad and N South America; it is the sole member of the Steatornithidae family. Owl-like in appearance, the oilbird flies using bat-like sonar. It feeds on fruit, using its powerful hooked beak. The oilbird is so called because its young were once caught and used as a source of oil. Length: 33cm (13in); wingspan: 91cm (36in). Family Steatornithidae; species *Steatornis caripensis*.

O

◄ **octopus** The common octopus (*Octopus vulgaris*) is a solitary and nocturnal animal. It uses a hole or rock crevice as a home, often concealing and protecting it with stones or shells. It leaves this den to hunt at night. The common octopus inhabits coastal waters or those of the upper continental shelf worldwide. It is notable for its ability to change colour according to its surroundings, a skill brought about by its sophisticated pigment-bearing cells. The octopus is considered to be among the most intelligent of invertebrates: its nervous system is as complex as that of many birds and fish.

▶ **okra** Originating in Africa and now widely cultivated throughout the tropics, the okra plant (*Hibiscus esculentus*) is related to the cotton plant. Its sticky green pods, which are hairy at the base, contain numerous oval seeds. If picked ten weeks after planting, when still immature, the pods can be eaten as a vegetable.

oil palm
PALM tree grown in tropical regions of Africa and Madagascar. It is a source of oil for margarine and soap. The long, feather-shaped fronds rise from a short trunk. Height: 9–15m (30–49ft). Family Arecaceae/Palmae.

oilseed rape
See RAPE

oil shale
Dark, soft rock containing hydrocarbon compounds that can be distilled off as SHALE oil. Oil shales yielding more than a small percentage of oil can be valuable as fuels and as sources of organic chemicals. They are found in many countries, sometimes in vast deposits; that of the Green River shales in the United States alone has been estimated to contain approximately 960,000 million barrels of oil.

okapi
Even-toed, hoofed RUMINANT of African equatorial rainforests. It is the closest living relative of the GIRAFFE. The okapi is a purplish colour, with striped legs. Family Giraffidae; species *Okapia johnstoni*.

okra (gumbo)
Annual tropical plant. Its yellow flowers have red centres. The green fruit pods are eaten as a vegetable. Height: 0.6–1.8m (2–6ft). Family Malvaceae; species *Hibiscus esculentus*.

old-man's beard
See CLEMATIS

Oldowan
Type of stone tool dating from the early PLEISTOCENE epoch (*c*.2 million years ago). The name comes from the Olduvai Gorge in Tanzania, where archaeologists found the first tools of this kind. Made from quartz or basalt stones, the edges were chipped away to form tools capable of chopping, scraping or cutting. Oldowan tools were made for about 1.5 million years.

Olduvai Gorge
Site in N Tanzania where remains of primitive humans have been found. Kenyan archaeologist Louis Leakey (1903–72) uncovered four layers of remains dating from about 2 million years ago to about 15,000 years ago. In 1964 he announced the discovery of *Homo habilis*, whom he believed to have been a direct ancestor of modern humans. The gorge, which is 40km (25mi) long and 100m (320ft) deep, runs through the Serengeti Plain.

oleander
Any member of the genus *Nerium*, a group of evergreen shrubs native to the Mediterranean region. Oleanders have milky, poisonous sap, clusters of white, pink or purple flowers and smooth leaves. The best-known species is the rosebay (*Nerium oleander*). Family Apocynaceae; genus *Nerium*. *See also* FRANGIPANI; PERIWINKLE

oleaster
Small, spiny-branched, deciduous tree, native to Eurasia. Its narrow leaves have hairy, silver undersides. The small, fragrant, silver-scaled flowers yield yellow, olive-shaped fruits. Height: to 6m (20ft). Family Elaeagnaceae; species *Elaeagnus angustifolia*.

Oligocene
Extent of GEOLOGICAL TIME from about 38 to 25 million years ago. It is the third of five epochs of the TERTIARY period in the CENOZOIC era. During the Oligocene epoch, the climate cooled. Many modern mammals evolved, including early ELEPHANTS and *Mesohippus*, an ancestor of the modern horse. Only a few archaic mammals, such as titanotheres, survived into the epoch, and they became extinct before it ended.

oligochaete
Any member of the class Oligochaeta. Oligochaetes are ANNELID (segmented) worms, characterized by long, naked bodies that bear a few bristles (chaetae) on each segment. EARTHWORMS are the best-known oligochaetes, but many species are freshwater worms as small as 1mm (0.025in) in length. Giant Australian earthworms grow up to several metres long. Phylum Annelida; class Oligochaeta.

olingo
Member of the genus *Bassaricyon* of the RACCOON family, found in the forests of Central America. It has a long body and short legs. It has long, grey-brown fur on its back and sides, yellow-white fur on its underparts and cheeks, and black rings on its tail. It is a nocturnal tree-dweller. Olingoes live alone or in pairs but join with others and with kinkajous at feeding sites. They eat fruit as well as invertebrates and small vertebrates. Breeding takes place at any time of the year and one young is produced after a 74-day gestation; the female rears her baby alone. Head-body length: 35–47cm (14–19in); tail: 40–48cm (16–19in). Family Procyonidae; genus *Bassaricyon*; species include *Bassaricyon gabbi*.

olive
Tree, shrub or vine and its fruit, especially the common olive tree (*Olea europaea*), native to the Mediterranean region. It has leathery, lance-shaped leaves and a gnarled, twisted trunk. Olive trees can live for more than 1000 years. The fruit is bitter and inedible before processing. Height: to 9m (30ft). Family Oleaceae.

olivine
Ferromagnesian mineral, $(Mg,Fe)_2SiO_4$, found in

◀ **Olduvai Gorge** Running through the Serengeti Plain in Tanzania, E Africa, the Olduvai Gorge is one of the world's most important archaeological sites and is now a World Heritage Site.

O

basic and ultrabasic igneous rocks. Olivine has orthorhombic system crystals of usually granular masses. Its colour is commonly olive-green but can be brown or grey. It is glassy and brittle with no cleavage. Hardness 6.5–7; r.d. 3.3.

olm
Elongate, aquatic SALAMANDER. It has a flattened head, external gills, slender limbs with a reduced number of toes, and small eyes covered by skin. It inhabits caves in Slovenia and NE Italy. Most olms are pale pink because they are unpigmented, but a black form also exists. Length: to 33cm (13in). Family Proteidae; species *Proteus anguinus*.

onager
See ASS, ASIATIC

onion (allium)
Hardy, bulb-forming, biennial plant of the LILY family. It is native to central Asia and cultivated worldwide for its strong-smelling, edible bulb. The onion plant has hollow leaves and white or lilac flowers. Height: to 130cm (51in). Family Liliaceae; species *Allium cepa*.

ontogeny
Total biological development of an organism. It

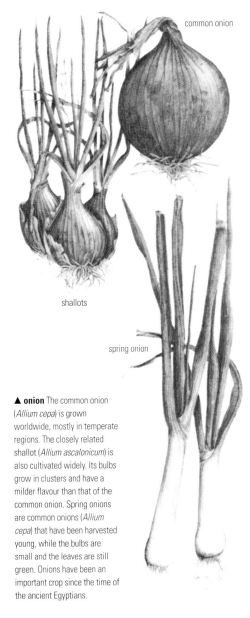

common onion

shallots

spring onion

▲ **onion** The common onion (*Allium cepa*) is grown worldwide, mostly in temperate regions. The closely related shallot (*Allium ascalonicum*) is also cultivated widely. Its bulbs grow in clusters and have a milder flavour than that of the common onion. Spring onions are common onions (*Allium cepa*) that have been harvested young, while the bulbs are small and the leaves are still green. Onions have been an important crop since the time of the ancient Egyptians.

includes the embryonic stage, birth, growth, body changes and death. *See also* BIOGENETIC LAW; PHYLOGENETICS

onyx
Variety of the mineral CHALCEDONY with straight parallel bands. Black and white onyx is often used for making cameos; white and red forms are called **carnelian** onyx; white and brown, **sardonyx**. It is widely distributed but found mostly in India and South America. Onyx is a form of AGATE.

oocyte
Female gametocyte, an animal OVUM before the first polar body is formed. *See also* OOGENESIS

oogenesis
Process by which a female reproductive cell develops, ready for fertilization. DIPLOID primary egg cells (**oogonia**) divide by MITOSIS to produce many prospective eggs cells (**oocytes**). Each of these oocytes divides by MEIOSIS to produce a HAPLOID secondary oocyte and a **polar body**. The secondary oocyte then divides again to produce an OVUM and a second polar body.

o-o, Kauai
HONEYEATER found only on the island of Kauai in Hawaii. It is critically endangered due to habitat loss. The Kauai o-o feeds on nectar from the ohia tree and grubs found on mossy branches. It is blackish-brown, with a long, curved bill and bright yellow, feathered thighs. Length: 20cm (8in). Family Meliphagidae; species *Moho braccatus*.

oolite
SEDIMENTARY ROCK composed of OOLITHS.

oolith
Small, spherical concretion that occurs in SEDIMENTARY ROCKS. Oolitic grains, up to 2mm (0.1in) in diameter, usually consist of CALCIUM CARBONATE, DOLOMITE (magnesium calcium carbonate) or chamosite (an iron silicate mineral). They have a radiating, fibrous structure, or one consisting of concentric layers. The centre of an oolith may be a grain of shell or quartz, which suggests to geologists that they grow in oceans or streams by accreting layers of calcium carbonate as they roll about in the turbulent water. Ooliths give the rounded grainy structure to oolitic LIMESTONE.

ooze
Fine-grained, deep-ocean deposit containing materials of more than 30% organic origin. Oozes are divided into two main types: **calcareous** ooze at depths of 2000–3900m (6600–12,800ft) contains the skeletons of animals such as FORAMINIFERA and pteropods; **siliceous** ooze, at depths of more than 3900m (12,800ft), contains skeletons of radiolarians and DIATOMS.

opal
Non-crystalline variety of QUARTZ. It is found in recent volcanoes, deposits from hot springs and sediments. Usually colourless or white with a rainbow play of colour in gem forms, it is the most valuable of quartz gems. Hardness 5.5–6.5; r.d. 2.0.

opalinan
One of a group of PROTOZOA; they have numerous CILIA and often have multiple nuclei. Opalinans are parasites in the intestines of amphibians. The individual cells are often oval or elongated, flat and leaf-like; their multiplication coincides with the

◄ **opossum** The Virginia opossum (*Didelphis virginiana*) has a pointed white face, black ears and a stout body covered in grey fur. It has a long, scaly, prehensile tail. One toe on each hindfoot is opposable in order to help grip branches. It only rarely hangs by its tail. The Virginia opossum is familiar for its defensive habit of feigning death when surprised. It can "play possum" for as much as several hours, during which it is in a catatonic state. The opossum has broad eating habits, feeding on insects, small mammals, eggs, fruit and berries. It is largely arboreal and nocturnal.

breeding season of the amphibian host. Opalina species are rectal parasites of the frog. Phylum Protozoa; genera include *Cepedea* and *Zelleriella*.

operon
Any of a group of GENES on a CHROMOSOME comprising structural genes and an operator gene. **Structural genes** direct the synthesis of ENZYMES involved in the formation of a cell constituent or the utilization of a nutrient. The **operator gene** responds to a **repressor** molecule and can exist open or closed. When the operator gene is open, the genes it controls are functional, producing PROTEINS. When interacting with the repressor, the operator gene is closed. REGULATORY GENES control the operons.

opium poppy
See POPPY

opossum
Common name given to members of a MARSUPIAL family found throughout most of South and Central America, and E North America. Opossums are characterized by a long, pointed nose and a long, scaly, usually prehensile tail. Family Didelphidae.

opossum, mouse (murine opossum)
Any member of the genus *Marmosa*, which includes the smallest opossums. The mouse opossum is found in a range of habitats throughout South America. Head-body length: 8–18cm (3–7in); tail: 9–28cm (4–11in). Family Didelphidae; genus *Marmosa*.

opossum, shrew (rat opossum)
Any member of several genera of opossums belonging to the family Caenolestidae. They feed on insects and small invertebrates in the Andean regions of South America. Head-body length: 9–14cm (4–6in); tail: 10–14cm (4–6in). Family Caenolestidae; genera *Caenolestes*, *Lestoros* and *Rhyncholestes*.

opossum, southern
Opossum that inhabits forests, open land and urban areas of Mexico and Argentina. Head-body length: 32–50cm (13–20in); tail: 25–53cm (10–21in). Family Didelphidae; species *Didelphis marsupialis*.

opossum, Virginia (common opossum)
Largest species of opossum and the only one to be found in the United States. Head-body length: 33–55cm (13–22in); tail: 25–54cm (10–21in). Family Didelphidae; species *Didelphis virginiana*.

O

opossum, water
See YAPOK

opossum, woolly
Any of three species of opossum of the *Caluromys* genus, found in Central and South America. Highly specialized tree dwellers, woolly opossums feed on fruit and nectar. Head-body length: 18–29cm (7–11in); tail: 27–49cm (11–19in). Family Didelphidae; genus *Caluromys*.

optic nerve
Second cranial nerve. It carries the visual stimuli from the RETINA of the EYE to the visual centre in the CORTEX of the BRAIN. That part of the retina where the optic nerve enters the eye is known as the blind spot. Approximately one million optic nerve fibres comprise the optic nerve, and these fibres are arranged in such a way that impulses from the left side of the visual field travel to the right side of the brain, and vice versa. *See also* NERVOUS SYSTEM; SIGHT

opuntia
See PRICKLY PEAR

orange
Evergreen CITRUS tree and its fruit. There are two basic types. The sweet orange (*Citrus sinensis*) is native to Asia and widely grown in the United States and Israel. The fruit develops without flower pollination and is often seedless. The sour orange (*Citrus aurantium*) is widely grown in Spain for the manufacture of marmalade. Related fruits include the MANDARIN, tangerine and satsuma, all varieties of *Citrus reticulata*. Height: to 9m (30ft). Family Rutaceae; genus *Citrus*.

orang-utan
Great APE native to forests of Sumatra and Borneo. It has a bulging belly and a shaggy, reddish-brown coat. It swings by its arms when travelling through trees but proceeds on all fours on the ground. Height: 1.5m (4.9ft); weight: to 100kg (220lb). Family Pongidae; species *Pongo pygmaeus*. *See also* PRIMATES

orca
See WHALE, KILLER

orchid
Any plant of the family Orchidaceae, common in the tropics. There are *c*.35,000 species. All species are perennials. They grow in soil or as EPIPHYTES on other plants; parasitic and saprophytic species are also known. The flowers of many species are adapted to allow pollination only by a particular species of insect, bat or even frog. All orchids have bilaterally symmetrical flower structures, each with three sepals. They range in diameter from *c*.2mm (*c*.0.1in) to 38cm (15in). Family Orchidaceae. *See also* VANILLA

▶ **orchid** The bee orchid (*Ophrys apifera*) of Europe tempts its pollinators with sex rather than nectar. Its elaborate flowers imitate the colour, shape, texture and scent of female bees of the genus *Eucera*. Male bees, which emerge before the females, alight on the flower's broad labellum and attempt to mate with it. Structures containing pollen grains adhere to the bee's body and are transferred to other flowers. Cross-fertilization is followed by the formation of thousands of tiny seeds.

order
CLASSIFICATION of living organisms ranking below CLASS and above FAMILY. Order names are printed in Roman (ordinary) letters and begin with a capital letter. Among animals, the names of most orders end in -a, such as Anura (FROGS and TOADS) and Chiroptera (BATS), although bird orders end in -iformes, such as Columbiformes (PIGEONS) and Strigiformes (OWLS). In plants, order names generally end in -ales, such as Rosales (ROSES).

Ordovician
Second-oldest period of the PALAEOZOIC era, from 505 to 438 million years ago. All animal life was restricted to the sea. Numerous invertebrates flourished, including TRILOBITES, BRACHIOPODS, CORALS, GRAPTOLITES, MOLLUSCS and ECHINODERMS. Remains of jawless FISH in coastal deposits mark the first record of the vertebrates.

ore
MINERAL or combination of minerals from which metals and nonmetals can be extracted. Ores occur in veins, beds or seams parallel to the enclosing rock or in irregular masses. Industrial rock deposits in beds, such as GYPSUM and LIMESTONE, are not called ores.

oregano (marjoram)
Dried leaves and flowers of several perennial herbs of the genus *Origanum*, native to the Mediterranean region and w Asia. It is a popular culinary herb. Family Lamiaceae/Labiatae; genus *Origanum*. *See also* MARJORAM

Oregon grape (Mahonia)
Any of several species belonging to the genus *Mahonia*, a group of evergreen shrubs native to North and Central America and E and Southeast Asia. Oregon grape is grown for its attractive, glossy, pinnate leaves and its small, yellow, cup-shaped flowers. The flowers, borne in dense clusters, may be highly scented. It gets its Latin name from Bernard M'Mahon (1775–1816), an American horticulturalist. Family Berberidaceae; species include *Mahonia aquifolium*.

Oregon pine
See DOUGLAS FIR

organ
Group of TISSUES that form a functional and structural unit in a living organism. The major organs of the body include the BRAIN, HEART, LUNGS, SKIN, LIVER and KIDNEYS. LEAVES, FLOWERS and ROOTS are examples of plant organs.

organic compounds
Compounds that contain the element CARBON; they are about a hundred times more numerous than inorganic compounds. Examples include hydrocarbons (compounds containing only carbon and hydrogen), basic structures that, when combined with atoms of other elements (such as oxygen and nitrogen), form a vast range of compounds, including those essential to life.

organ of Corti
Complex structure within the inner EAR of mammals, birds, and reptiles. It is concerned with the final reception of inner ear movements resulting from sound waves striking the eardrum. It rests on a platform of membrane and bone extending along the COCHLEA. It contains sensory hair cells, which detect movements caused by sound waves; these cells connect with nerve fibres that carry messages to the brain.

oribi
Dwarf ANTELOPE from the grassy plains of s Africa. It is a small, graceful animal, with a long neck and long hind legs. Its sleek coat is sand-coloured, with white underparts and a black tip to its tail. The female is larger than the male but only the male has short, sharp horns. Oribis live in territorial pairs or small family groups, feeding on grass and never straying far from water. Territorial boundaries are marked with scent from conspicuous glands beneath each ear, in front of each eye and on the feet. Head-body length: 92–110cm (36–43in); tail: 6–10cm (2–4in). Family Bovidae; subfamily Antilopinae; species *Ourebia ourebi*.

Origin of Species by Means of Natural Selection
Book by Charles DARWIN published in 1859. Its full title was *On the Origin of Species by Means of Natural Selection or the Preservation of Favoured Races in the Struggle for Life*. In the book Darwin put forward his theory of EVOLUTION, which aroused much controversy because it disagreed with the established religious view that humans arose as stated in the biblical Book of Genesis. Instead, Darwin suggested that humans arose from ape-like animals by gradual progression. *See also* NATURAL SELECTION

origma (rock warbler)
Australian warbler found only in rocky limestone and sandstone outcrops in NE Australia. It is olive-brown above, with rich reddish-brown underparts. It hops, flicks its tail and creeps mouse-like into crevices. It is a restless feeder. Length: 13cm (5in). Family Acanthizidae; species *Origma solitaria*.

oriole
Medium-sized, woodland bird; it has a stout bill and strong, direct flight. The golden oriole (*Oriolus oriolus*) of Europe and Asia is strikingly black and yellow.

◀ **Ordovician** The most significant movement of the plates during the Ordovician period was the movement of North America towards N Europe, thus compressing the sea area between the two land masses.

Australia
Antarctica
India
North America
N Europe
South America
Africa

O

The black oriole (*Oriolus husii*) lives in the mountain forests of Borneo and Sulawesi. The northern oriole (*Icterus galbula*) of North and Central America is black and orange; it belongs to the American blackbird/oriole family. Despite their bold plumage, orioles are often difficult to see in the treetops and are best located by their fluty, whistling calls. Length: to 25cm (10in). Family Oriolidae or Icteridae.

ornithine cycle

Biochemical process by which ammonia and carbon dioxide are combined in the excretory product UREA. The breakdown of PROTEINS produces the highly toxic molecule ammonia, which combines with ornithine to make urea, which is much less toxic and so can be temporarily stored before being periodically removed from the body.

ornithischian

Member of one of the two main groups of DINOSAURS (the other being the SAURISCHIANS). Ornithischians evolved in late Triassic times. They had a bird-like pelvis and were entirely plant eating. They include groups such as the ORNITHOPODS, STEGOSAURS and CERATOPSIANS.

ornithology

Study of BIRDS. Included in general ornithological studies are classification, structure, function, evolution, distribution, migration, reproduction, ecology and behaviour.

ornithopod

Member of a group of ORNITHISCHIAN dinosaurs that walked mainly on their hind legs and had three-toed, bird-like feet. The group includes IGUANODONTS and HADROSAURIDS.

orogeny

See OROGENESIS

orogenesis (mountain building)

Process of crustal shortening and thickening resulting from collision of CRUSTAL PLATES, whereby the land surface is elevated several kilometres to form MOUNTAINS. Deep root zones, tens of kilometres thick, consisting of folded and faulted rocks, which may also be metamorphosed and intruded by igneous rocks, continue to support the mountains over long periods of time through ISOSTASY.

oropendola

Any member of the genus *Psarocolius*, a group of medium to large ORIOLES native to Central America. They have large, conical bills, which are often yellow- or orange-tipped. Their plumage is glossy black or bronze, with a yellow and black tail. Oropendola colonies are made up of stocking-like nests, where the male displays with deep, upside down bows and gurgling calls. Length: 24–50cm (9–20in). Family Icteridae; genus *Psarocolius*; there are 12 species.

orrisroot

Rootstock or RHIZOME of several species of IRIS from s Europe, especially the pale-blue Mediterranean species, also known as the "fleur-de-lys". When dug up and dried, orrisroot acquires the distinct scent of violets. It is used in medicine and in perfumery.

orthoclase

Essential mineral found in igneous and metamorphic rocks that contain potassium FELDSPAR. It is a potassium aluminium silicate ($KAlSi_3O_8$), with monoclinic system crystals. Its colour is generally white, but there are pink varieties. Hardness 6–6.5; r.d. 2.5–2.6.

orthopteran

Any member of the order Orthoptera, an order of insects represented by 20,000 species found worldwide, especially in tropical regions. Orthopterans include CRICKETS, GRASSHOPPERS and LOCUSTS in the suborders Ensifera and Caelifera. The term was formerly used to group together the orders Dictyoptera (MANTIDS and COCKROACHES), Phasmida (LEAF INSECTS and STICK INSECTS) and Grylloblattidae (grylloblattids). Most of the species feed on plants, have chewing mouthparts and undergo incomplete METAMORPHOSIS from egg to nymph and adult. Length: to 10cm (4in).

oryx

Any of three species of grazing, horse-like ANTELOPES found in the deserts of Africa and Arabia. They have short manes, large hooves and a hump on the shoulder; both males and females have long, ridged horns. Oryxes live in small, well-organized sociable groups, seeking shade during the hottest parts of the day, grazing and trekking to new pastures at cooler times. They need very little water. Family Bovidae; subfamily Hippotraginae.

oryx, Arabian

Smallest and rarest oryx, the only species to live outside Africa. It was declared extinct in its homeland, the Arabian desert, in 1972. Since then efforts have been made to reintroduce captive bred animals. The Arabian oryx is white with black markings on its face, belly, tail and legs. Head-body length: 1–1.2m (3–4ft); tail: 40cm (16in). Family Bovidae; subfamily Hippotraginae; species *Oryx leucoryx*.

oryx, Beisa (gemsbok)

Oryx that lives in arid places of s Africa. It is grey with black markings on its face, belly, tail and legs. Head-body length: 1.5–1.7m (5–5.6ft); tail: 50cm (20in). Family Bovidae; subfamily Hippotraginae; species *Oryx gazella*.

oryx, scimitar (white oryx)

Endangered species of oryx; it is confined to a tiny area of North Africa near the Red Sea. Its coat is pale, with brown markings on its chest and face; it has scimitar-shaped horns. Head-body length: 1.5–1.7m (5–5.6ft); tail: 50cm (20in). Family Bovidae; subfamily Hippotraginae; species *Oryx dammah*.

osier

Any of various species of WILLOW, especially *Salix viminalis* and *Salix purpurea*, the flexible branches and stems of which are used for wickerwork. Family Salicaceae; genus *Salix*.

osmoregulation

Process by which the amount of water and concentration of salts are regulated in the bodies of animals and protozoans. In saltwater environments, water tends to pass from an animal's body through the action of OSMOSIS. This effect is counteracted by the KIDNEYS. Similarly, in freshwater environments the kidneys of higher animals, and the contractile VACUOLES of protozoans, prevent water from passing into the body.

osmosis

Diffusion of a SOLVENT (such as water) through a natural or artificial partially permeable membrane (one that allows only the passage of certain dissolved substances) into a more concentrated solution. Because the more concentrated solution contains a lower concentration of solvent molecules, the solvent flows by DIFFUSION to dilute it until concentrations of solvent are equal on both sides of the membrane. Osmosis is a vital cellular process. Plant roots absorb water by osmosis, and plant cells are kept firm as a result of the uptake of water by osmosis (turgor); membranes of all living cells use it to control the passage of required substances. *See also* PRESSURE POTENTIAL

osmotic pressure (symbol Π)

Pressure exerted by a dissolved substance by virtue of the motion of its molecules. In dilute solutions, it varies with the concentration and temperature as if the solute were a gas occupying the same volume. Osmotic pressure can be measured by the pressure that must be applied to counterbalance the process of OSMOSIS into the solution. Osmotic pressure is given by $\Pi V = nRT$, where n = moles in solution, V = volume, T = temperature, and R = gas constant.

osprey

Large BIRD OF PREY with a worldwide distribution. It is found near water, including inland lakes and coasts, where it plunges into water to catch fish. The osprey is brown above, with a white head and white underparts. Length: 58cm (23in); wingspan: 145–170cm (57–67in). Family Pandionidae; species *Pandion haliaetus*.

ossicle

Any one of the small bones found in the middle EAR of most mammals. The ossicles are the **malleus** (hammer), **incus** (anvil) and **stapes** (stirrup). Vibrations of the eardrum (tympanum) are picked up by the malleus, amplified by the movement of the incus and passed on to the stapes, which connects with the oval window in the COCHLEA of the inner ear.

Osteichthyes (bony fish)

Class of FISH found in almost every environment. Their characteristics include a bony skeleton, a single flap (operculum) covering the gill openings, and erythrocytes (red blood cells) with nuclei. Most members of this class have scales. Osteichthyes first appeared during the DEVONIAN period, when they were heavily armoured and lived in fresh water.

ostrich

Enormous and unmistakable flightless bird. It is found in semi-deserts, but not sand dunes, of sub-Saharan Africa. The ostrich has a long, pink or bluish neck and long, powerful, flesh- or grey-coloured legs, which allow it to run very fast for long distances. Length: 1.8–2.4m (5.9–7.9ft). Family Struthionidae; species *Struthio camelus*.

0

◄ **ostrich** Africa is the home of the ostrich, the largest living bird. It is the only member of the order Struthioniformes. Several large ground-dwelling birds, the ostrich, rhea, emu and cassowary, all resemble each other quite closely, but are thought to have arisen independently, and as such are examples of a phenomenon called convergent evolution. The ostrich runs to escape its predators and can reach speeds of up to 65 km/hour (40mph).

▶ **otter** The giant otter (*Pteroneura brasiliensis*) inhabits the lakes and rivers of the Brazilian rainforests, where it is now an endangered species due to hunting and habitat destruction. It lives in sociable groups, known as holts, which have their own particular territory. The sea otter (*Enhydra lutris*) rarely leaves the sea, usually living about one kilometre from the shore. During the day it floats on its back, cracking open shellfish with its strong teeth or placing a stone on its chest on which to smash the shells.

giant otter

sea otter

otter
Any of 12 species of WEASEL-like animals with long, supple bodies and short legs. Otters are equally at home on land as in the water, although the sea-otter rarely comes ashore. The otter's dark coat is dense, insulating and water-repellent; the paws are webbed in most species and the tail is flattened. The otter's ears and nose close under water, where they use their sensitive whiskers and keen eyesight to hunt fish and shellfish. Most species of otter are under threat of extinction due to persecution by people or habitat destruction. Most otter species are sociable, and they communicate vocally and by scent marking. Adults and young appear to spend time "playing". Family Mustelidae; subfamily Lutrinae.

otter, Eurasian (Eurasian river otter)
Otter found in Europe, Africa and Asia. Its numbers have been badly affected by pollution and by competition from introduced mink. It has brown fur, with paler underparts and white face patches. Head-body length: 50cm (20in). Family Mustelidae; subfamily Lutrinae; species *Lutra lutra*.

otter, giant
Large otter that is found in the slow-flowing waters of South America. Its numbers have been affected by hunting. The giant otter has brown fur and a pale patch on its chest. Head-body length: to 1.5m (4.9ft). Family Mustelidae; subfamily Lutrinae; species *Pteronura brasiliensis*.

otter, Cape clawless
Otter usually found in slow-flowing waters in s Africa. The Cape clawless otter is brown, with pale face patches. Family Mustelidae; subfamily Lutrinae; species *Aonyx capensis*.

otter, North American river (Canadian otter)
Otter that is widespread in Canada and the United States. It is usually solitary, only pairing in the breeding season. It has dark, sometimes almost black fur above, with a silvery belly and chin. Head-body length: 70cm (28in). Family Mustelidae; subfamily Lutrinae; species *Lutra canadensis*.

otter, sea
Otter that lives off the w coast of North America, often near kelp forests. It has thick, reddish-brown fur. Family Mustelidae; subfamily Lutrinae; species *Enhydra lutris*.

otter shrew
Any of three species of aquatic mammals that live in equatorial Africa. They have long, pointed shrew-like faces, long bodies and flattened tails for paddling. They feed mainly on insects. The largest species can be up to 64cm (25in) long. Family Tenrecidae; genera *Potamogale* and *Micropotamogale*.

ounce
See LEOPARD, SNOW

outbreeding
REPRODUCTION by the mating of individuals who are not closely genetically related. It frequently produces tougher individuals with a better chance of survival, especially where many generations of INBREEDING have taken place. Extreme examples of outbreeding include the mating of different species. Only rarely is this successful and when it is the offspring are usually sterile. One example is a cross between a horse and a donkey, which produces a mule, an animal with strength and endurance. *See also* HETEROSIS

outcrop
Exposure at the surface of the Earth of an edge of rock stratum. This phenomenon may be caused by the EROSION of soil by water, wind, ice (especially glaciers) or gravity.

outlier
Mass of newer rocks surrounded by older rocks. The newer rocks may have become detached from a larger formation by EROSION. *See also* INLIER

ovary
See feature article

ovenbird
Thrush-like WARBLER found in North America. It has a russet crown and spotted underparts. The ovenbird walks on the ground with its tail cocked. Length: 15cm (6in). Family Parulidae; species *Seiurus aurocapillus*. The name also applies to birds of the family Furnariidae of Central and South America.

overfishing
Situation in which more fish are taken from a population than the numbers being hatched or immigrating into the population. The result is a depletion in the population with resulting lower yields

OVARY

Part of a multicellular animal or a seed-bearing plant that produces egg cells (ova), the female reproductive cells. In vertebrates, it also produces female SEX HORMONES. In human females, there is an ovary on each side of the UTERUS. Controlled by the PITUITARY GLAND, each ovary, as well as the ova, produces two major female sex hormones, OESTROGEN and PROGESTERONE, which in turn control development and functioning of the female reproductive system. In seed-bearing plants, the female sex cells are contained within structures called OVULES inside the ovary. After FERTILIZATION, the ovules develop into seeds and the ovary develops into one or more FRUITS. *See also* HORMONE; MENSTRUAL CYCLE; OVUM

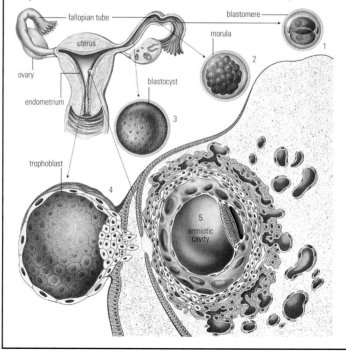

◀ **In humans it** takes about one week for a fertilized ovum to pass down the Fallopian tube and implant itself in the uterine lining. The endometrium. Within hours of conception, mitosis begins with the development of a sphere of an increasing number of cells. The sphere starts as the blastomere (1) and develops into the morula (2) of about 64 cells. At this stage, it changes into a hollow, fluid-containing ball – the blastocyst (3) – with the inner cell mass at one end. It can now begin implantation (4). By the ninth day after conception, the blastocyst has sunk deep into the endometrium (5) and is already receiving nutrition from the mother.

► **owl** The ferruginous pygmy owl (*Glaucidium brasilianum*) is found from SW United States to S South America. It rarely exceeds 17cm (7in) in length. The collared or Indian scops owl (*Otus bakkamoena*) inhabits forests from India and Nepal to China and Thailand. The saw-whet owl (*Aegolius acadicus*) is found from Alaska to N Mexico. It is small, rarely exceeding 21cm (8in) in length. It gets its name from its call, which sounds like a saw being whetted (sharpened). The tiny elf owl (*Micrathene whitneyi*) feeds almost entirely on insects but will occasionally take mice or lizards. It nests in saguaro cacti. The burrowing owl (*Athene cunicularia*) is so called from its habit of nesting in abandoned burrows. In certain conditions it will dig its own burrow; the owl often returns to the same burrow each year.

pygmy owl

burrowing owl

elf owl

scops owl

saw-whet owl

for fishermen. The stocks of herring in the North Sea, for example, had declined from 2 million tonnes in 1967 to only 100,000 tonnes by 1977.

oviparity (ovipary)
Type of REPRODUCTION in which fertilization of the female ova (eggs) occurs inside the body, but once achieved the eggs are laid and subsequently hatch outside her body. Unlike VIVIPARITY, the developing EMBRYO receives all its nutrition from the egg. It is the most common form of reproduction and occurs in all animals except MARSUPIALS and PLACENTAL MAMMALS. *See also* OVOVIPARITY

ovoviparity (ovoviviparity)
Type of REPRODUCTION in which a female's fertilized ova (eggs) develop and then hatch inside her OVIDUCTS. Unlike VIVIPARITY, during ovoviparity development the ZYGOTES receive no nutrition from the mother because no PLACENTA is present. Ovoviparity is common in many invertebrate animals and some FISH and SNAKES. When the young emerge, the mother appears to be giving birth to live young, although they have only just hatched. *See also* OVIPARITY

ovulation
Release of a mature OVUM (egg) from the OVARY ready for FERTILIZATION. In women, one egg (ovum) is released into the oviduct midway through the MENSTRUAL CYCLE, stimulated by luteinizing hormone from the PITUITARY GLAND.

ovule
In seed-bearing plants (SPERMATOPHYTES), the part of the female reproductive organ that contains an egg cell or OVUM and develops into a seed after FERTILIZATION. In ANGIOSPERMS (flowering plants), ovules develop inside an OVARY. In CONIFEROPHYTES (conifers), ovules are borne on the inner surface of the female cone without any covering.

ovum
Female GAMETE (reproductive cell) produced in an OVARY (in animals) or an OVULE (in plants). After FERTILIZATION by the male gamete (SPERM in animals, POLLEN in plants), it becomes a ZYGOTE that is capable of developing into a new individual.

owl
Any of *c.*120 species of BIRDS OF PREY, many of which hunt at night. Most species have brown, "dead-leaf" plumage, short tails and often feathered legs and feet. Their long, rounded wings have specially adapted feathers for noiseless flight. The head is big, with large, forward-looking eyes set in a flattened facial disk. An owl's eyes contain many more rods (cells that enable night vision) than do the eyes of other birds but no cones (cells that enable colour vision). They feed mainly on rodents. Families Strigidae and Tytonidae.

owl, barn
Medium-sized owl found in farmland and open, often arid, country worldwide. Golden buff above and white below, it can appear to be ghostly white at night. The barn owl breeds in derelict buildings, barns and churches. Its common call is a blood-curdling scream. Length: 34cm (13in). Family Tytonidae; species *Tyto alba*.

owl, burrowing
Small owl, often active by day, found in the deserts and grasslands of North, Central and South America. It has long legs and bobs up and down when disturbed. Burrowing owls usually nest in an abandoned burrow. They feed on insects and small mammals. Length: 20cm (8in). Family Strigidae; species *Athene cunicularia*.

owl, eagle
Enormous owl the size of a medium-sized eagle. It hunts animals up to the size of small deer. It has brown plumage, with prominent, feathery ear-tufts and large, orange eyes. The eagle owl is widely distributed in Europe and Asia, from dense coniferous forests in the north to semi deserts in the south. Length: 60–75cm (24–30in). Family Strigidae; species *Bubo bubo*.

owl, elf
Tiny, sparrow-sized owl. It has yellow eyes and a very short tail. The elf owl is active at night, hunting in desert lowlands and canyons. It roosts during the day in a rock crevice or tree cavity. Although now rare in S United States, it is still common in Central America. Length: 15cm (6in). Family Strigidae; species *Micrathene whitneyi*.

owl, horned
Any of 11 owl species that have feathery tufts resembling horns on their heads. Fierce and strong, horned owls feed on rodents and other small mammals. The eagle owl (*Bubo bubo*) is the largest European species, but the most common is the long-eared owl (*Asio otus*). Length: to 60cm (24in). Family Strigidae.

owl, scops
Any of several species of small owl. It has feathery ear-tufts, unfeathered toes and streaky, grey-brown plumage. It roosts during the day, often against a tree trunk in an elongated posture that makes it very difficult to see. The scops owl can be located by its nocturnal, monotonous "piu" call. Length: 20cm (8in). Family Strigidae; genus *Otus*; species include *Otus scops* (common scops owl).

owl, snowy
Large, nearly all-white species of owl. It has a rounded head and yellow eyes. The female is larger than the male and has more brown spots and stripes. The snowy owl breeds on the ground in the Arctic tundra. It feeds mainly on lemmings. Length: 56–66cm (22–26in). Family Strigidae; species *Nyctea scandiaca*.

O

▲ **ox** The various cattle of Southeast Asia occupy different environments, an example of adaptive radiation. The gaur (*Bos gaurus*) is found in hilly forests. The wild buffalo (*Bubalus bubalis*) in upland swampy areas. The banteng (*Bos banteng*) in Java. The yak (*Bos grunniens*) is adapted to withstand the cold of Tibet and central Asia. The small anoa (*Anoa depressicornis*) lives in wet, hilly regions of Sulawesi.

owl, tawny

Most common European owl. It is found in woodlands, parks and large gardens, nesting in tree holes. It hunts in the evenings and at night, mainly for rodents but occasionally for earthworms. The tawny owl has brown plumage and can be identified by its hooting "*toowit toowoo*" call. Length: 38cm (15in). Family Strigidae; species *Strix aluco*.

owlet

Any of a group of *c*.20 species of small owls. They are heavily barred and spotted and inhabit dense forests and jungle. Owlets do not quarter the ground hunting for prey but sit in wait to pounce. Most species are very shy and secretive. Length: 17–23cm (7–9in) Family Strigidae; main genus *Glaucidium*.

owlet-nightjar

Any member of the genus *Aegotheles*, a group of small, nocturnal birds of Australasia. They resemble miniature owls and are similar to nightjars. The owlet-nightjar has camouflaged, brown and buff plumage. It has a tiny but broad bill with prominent bristles, large, forward-facing eyes and tiny feet. It can revolve its head like an owl. Length: 16–22cm (6–9in). Family Aegothelidae; genus *Aegotheles*; there are eight species.

owl-midge (moth-fly)

Any member of the family Psychodidae. The owl-midge is a small, hairy FLY that breeds in decaying matter; it is abundant at sewage works. It often flies to lit windows in the evening. The larvae feed on decaying matter and are commonly found in drainpipes. Adult body size: *c*.7mm (*c*.0.3in). Order Diptera; family Psychodidae.

ox

Any of five species of cattle, all of which are large and powerful, with a long, tufted tail. Oxen can be a variety of colours. Both males and females have widely set, curved, pointed horns and no external scent glands. Domestic cattle are probably the most numerous of all large mammals except humans. All other species of cattle are threatened with extinction due to hunting and habitat destruction. Head-body length: 1–3m (39–118in); tail: 50–70cm (20–28in). Family Bovidae; main genus *Bos*. *See also* GAUR; KOUPREY; YAK

ox (domestic cattle)

Ox descended from the now extinct wild auroch. It was domesticated *c*.8000 years ago. There are now many breeds all over the world. Family Bovidae; species *Bos taurus*.

ox (Bali cattle, banteng, tsaine tembadau)

Ox of the Indonesian islands; it has been introduced to N Australia. Most frequently known as Bali cattle, they are dark chestnut brown with white face-markings, stockings and rump patch. Family Bovidae; species *Bos javanicus*.

ox (Vu Quang or sao la)

Ox that inhabits dense forest of Vietnam and Laos; it was only discovered in 1992 and is endangered. It has similar horns to the oryx. It has a red-brown coat, with a black dorsal stripe and white markings on its face and feet. There is a large scent gland beneath each eye. Head-body length: 1.5–2m (4.9ft–6.6ft); tail: 13cm (5in). Family Bovidae; species *Pseudoryx nghetinhensis*.

oxalis (wood-sorrel)

Any member of the genus *Oxalis*, a large group of annuals or perennials often with underground BULBILS. They produce digitate leaves of between three and 20 leaflets and small, white, pink, red or yellow flowers. Some species have edible TUBERS. Several species are cultivated as garden plants; others have become noxious weeds because their bulbils allow them to spread with ease. Family Oxalidaceae; genus *Oxalis*.

oxbow lake

Crescent-shaped section of a RIVER channel that no longer carries the main discharge of water. An oxbow lake forms from a MEANDER. As sediment is deposited, the meander becomes cut off from the river to create a lake. Once formed, the lake gradually shrinks because sediment fills it in; vegetation grows on the new muddy area, and the land can soon be reclaimed. The name oxbow lake derives from the shape of the lake, which is said to resemble an ox's collar.

ox-eye daisy

Perennial DAISY native to Europe and Asia and naturalized in North America. It is found in grassy places and is often regarded as a weed. Its erect stems bear basal leaves and terminal flowers, which have white rays and yellow centres. Family Asteraceae; species *Leucanthemum vulgare*.

oxidation

Chemical reaction that involves a loss of one or more ELECTRONS by an atom or molecule. Oxidation is always part of an OXIDATION-REDUCTION reaction in which those electrons lost are gained by another atom or molecule. Previously the term oxidation was more strictly applied to a reaction in which oxygen combines with another element or compound to form an oxide.

oxidation-reduction (redox)

Chemical reaction involving simultaneous OXIDATION (a loss of one or more electrons by an atom or molecule) and REDUCTION (a gain of those electrons by another atom or molecule). In general, oxidation and reduction reactions occur together and in the same quantities. For example, in the reaction between iron oxide and carbon, iron (the electron acceptor) is **reduced** by carbon (the reducing agent), and the carbon (the electron donor) is **oxidized** by iron oxide (the oxidizing agent). Oxidation-reduction reactions are important in many biochemical systems.

oxpecker

Either of two species of specialized African birds – the red-billed oxpecker (*Buphagus erythrorhynchus*) and the yellow-billed oxpecker (*Buphagus africanus*). They are related to STARLINGS. Oxpeckers use their brightly coloured bills to comb animals for ticks and flies, clinging on with their sharp claws and using their tails as a prop. Length: 20–22cm (8–9in). Family Sturnidae.

oxygen (symbol O)

Common gaseous element that is necessary for the RESPIRATION of plants and animals and for combustion. It was discovered in 1774 by Joseph PRIESTLEY and independently (*c*.1772) by Swedish chemist Karl Scheele (1742–86). Oxygen, which is colourless and odourless, is the most abundant element in the Earth's crust (49.2% by weight) and is a constituent of water and many rocks. It is also present in the atmosphere (28% by volume), being extracted by fractional distillation of liquid air. It can also be obtained by the electrolysis of water. Oxygen is used in steelmaking (Bessemer process), welding, the manufacture of industrial chemicals, and in apparatus for breathing (oxygen masks) and resuscitation (oxygen tents); liquid oxygen is used in rocket fuels. It is chemically reactive, forming compounds with nearly all other elements (especially by OXIDATION). Properties: at.no. 8; r.a.m. 15.9994; r.d. 1.429; m.p. −218.4°C (−361.1°F); b.p. −182.96°C (−297.3°F); most common isotope ^{16}O (99.759%). *See also* OXIDATION-REDUCTION; OZONE

oxygen cycle

Interchange of OXYGEN among agencies such as the ATMOSPHERE, the oceans, animal and plant processes and chemical combustion. The main renewable source of the Earth's oxygen is the plant process of PHOTOSYNTHESIS, wherein oxygen is liberated. Oxygen is utilized by life-forms through RESPIRATION, which is a process essential to most living forms except ANAEROBIC bacteria. *See also* CARBON CYCLE

◄ **oxbow lake** Small variations in the speed of water flow can alter the course of a river. Water flowing at the outside of a bend (1) moves more quickly and cuts away the bank as it picks up sediment. On the inside of the bend the water moves more slowly and deposits sediment. Over time a meander (2) forms. The river soon cuts an alternative course across the neck of the meander (3). Sediment builds up at the ends of the loop, which eventually becomes separated, forming an oxbow lake.

oxyhaemoglobin

Combination of HAEMOGLOBIN in ERYTHROCYTES (red blood cells) with OXYGEN from the lungs, in which form oxygen is transported in the BLOOD to all cells of the body. When oxyhaemoglobin gives up its oxygen to cells, a chemical reaction is promoted that makes CARBON DIOXIDE (CO_2) from the tissues more soluble in the blood for transport back to the lungs and elimination from the body.

oyster

Edible BIVALVE MOLLUSC found worldwide in temperate and warm seas. The European flat, or edible, oyster (*Ostrea edulis*) occurs throughout coastal waters. The pearl oyster (*Pinctada fucats*) is used to produce cultured pearls. Phylum Mollusca; class Bivalvia; families Ostreidae and Aviculidae.

oystercatcher

Chunky, black-and-white shorebird. Its heavy, long, orange, flattened bill can pry open bivalve shells and probe sand for crabs and worms. The oystercatcher is noisy and excitable, often feeding in large flocks. There are six species worldwide, although two are now believed to be extinct. Length: 40–45cm (16–18in). Family Haematopodidae; genus *Haematopus*.

oyster nut

Climbing member of the GOURD family; it is native to tropical E Africa. It produces large fruits, which can weigh up to 27kg (60lbs) and contain as many as 500 large, flat seeds. The edible kernel of the seeds is a source of oil used in soap and candle-making. Height: to 30m (100ft). Family Cucurbitaceae; species *Telfairia pedata*.

ozone (O_3)

Unstable, pale blue, gaseous allotrope of OXYGEN. It has a characteristic pungent odour and decomposes into molecular oxygen. It is present in the atmosphere, mainly in the OZONE LAYER, where it is formed by the action of ultraviolet radiation on oxygen. It acts as a filter, preventing much harmful ultraviolet radiation from reaching the Earth's surface. Ozone, prepared commercially by passing a high-voltage discharge through oxygen, is used as an oxidizing agent in bleaching, air-conditioning and purifying water.

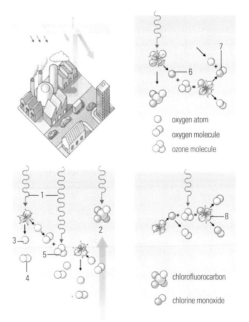

oxygen atom
oxygen molecule
ozone molecule

chlorofluorocarbon
chlorine monoxide

ozone depletion (ODP)

Measure of a substance's potential for reducing the protective OZONE shield around the Earth. Most CHLOROFLUOROCARBONS (CFCs) have an ODP value of one, but halogenated fluorocarbons (halons) are much more destructive, having ODPs ranging from three to 10.

ozone layer

Region of the Earth's atmosphere in which the gas OZONE (O_3) is concentrated. Ozone is densest at altitudes of between 21km and 26km (13–16mi). Produced by incoming sunlight, the ozone layer absorbs much of the solar ultraviolet radiation, thereby shielding the Earth's surface. Aircraft, nuclear weapons and some aerosol sprays and refrigerants all yield chemical agents that can break down high-altitude ozone, which could lead to an increase in the amount of harmful ultraviolet radiation reaching the surface of the Earth. *See also* CHLOROFLUOROCARBON

0

◀ **ozone** A naturally occurring substance, ozone acts as a sunscreen for the Earth because its molecules absorb the Sun's ultraviolet radiation (1). The presence of chlorofluorocarbon pollution (2) causes the ozone layer to break down allowing ultraviolet rays through. Ozone is created when ultraviolet rays split oxygen molecules. The lone oxygen atoms (3) bond with oxygen molecules (4) to make ozone (5). When, however, chlorofluorocarbons are present, they are split by the ultraviolet rays. The released chlorine atom (6) in turn splits ozone molecules to form a chlorine monoxide molecule (7) and oxygen. The process is continued as the chlorine monoxide absorbs the lone oxygen atoms that previously formed ozone. This frees the chlorine atom, which splits another ozone molecule (8) creating another chlorine monoxide molecule and oxygen.

P

▲ **paca** The preferred habitat of the paca is forested areas near water. It is a good swimmer and will take to the water if threatened. It usually takes the same route from burrow to feeding ground each night, creating a well-worn track.

paca (spotted cavy)

Shy, nocturnal, tailless rodent of South America. It is brown with rows of white spots and has a relatively large head. A burrow dweller, it feeds mainly on leaves, roots and fruit. Length: to 76cm (30in). Family Dasyproctidae; species *Cuniculus paca*.

pacarana

Heavyweight, shuffling rodent with short, sturdy limbs and long claws. It is found in South America. The pacarana resembles a porcupine but has coarse hair instead of spines. It is black-brown, with white stripes and spots along each side. The pacarana sits on its haunches to manipulate its plant food in its hands. Its habits are little known, but it is probably nocturnal. Head-body length: 73–79cm (29–31in); tail: 20cm (8in). Family Dinomyidae; species *Dinomys branicki*.

paddlefish

Either of two species of primitive bony fish related to the STURGEON. The paddlefish is found in the basins of the Mississippi and Yangtze rivers. It is blue, green, grey or brown, with a long, paddle-like snout. Length: 1.8m (6ft). Family Polyodontidae.

paddleworm

Any member of the genus *Phyllodoce*, a group of free-living POLYCHAETE species. Paddleworms bear extremely well-formed, leg-like appendages (parapodia) on most of their body segments. These parapodia are used in locomotion and are paddle shaped. Phylum Annelida; class Polychaeta; order Phyllodocida; family Phyllodocidae; genus *Phyllodoce*.

painted lady butterfly

See BUTTERFLY, PAINTED LADY

painted-snipe

Either of two species of unusual wading birds – the greater painted-snipe (*Rostratula benghalensis*), of Africa and s Asia, and the South American painted-snipe (*Nycticryphes semicollaris*). Painted-snipes creep about in marshes and fly on rounded, owl-like wings. Their plumage is black, chestnut and white, although the female is brighter than the male. Length: 23–28cm (9–11in). Family Rostratulidae.

Palade, George Emil (1912–)

US cell biologist, b. Romania. He shared the 1974 Nobel Prize for physiology or medicine with Albert CLAUDE and Christian de DUVE. Using sophisticated electron microscopic techniques and other methods, Palade discovered RIBOSOMES, which are the sites of PROTEIN SYNTHESIS in the cell.

palaeobiology

Study of FOSSIL plants and animals. *See also* PALAEOBOTANY; PALAEOZOOLOGY

palaeobotany

Study of ancient plants that have been preserved by carbonization, waterlogging or freezing. Some plants have been preserved almost intact in frozen soils and in AMBER. Pollen is also very resistant and has characteristic patterns for identification. The earliest land plants grew in the CAMBRIAN period, but some water plants flourished earlier. Such plants provide important evidence of prehistoric climates and ECOSYSTEMS.

Palaeocene

Geological epoch that extended from about 65 to 55 million years ago. It is the first epoch of the TERTIARY period in the CENOZOIC era, when the majority of the DINOSAURS had died out and small herbivores and ungulates were flourishing. Primates and rodents evolved towards the end of the Palaeocene epoch.

palaeoclimatology

Study of prehistoric CLIMATES. Records of past climates are found in SEDIMENTARY ROCKS, in cores taken through deep layers of ice, and in FOSSIL-bearing cores from the beds of seas and lakes. From such evidence, climatologists have discovered that the Earth is subject to alternate periods of cold, called glacials or ICE AGES, and warmth, called INTERGLACIALS. During the last two million years there have been 17 ice ages.

Palaeolithic (Old Stone Age)

Earliest stage of human history, from *c*.2 million years ago until between 40,000 and 8000 years ago. It was marked by the use of stone tools. It covers the period of HUMAN EVOLUTION from *Homo habilis* to *Homo sapiens*. The Palaeolithic was followed by the NEOLITHIC.

palaeomagnetism

Study of changes in the direction and intensity of the Earth's MAGNETIC FIELD in GEOLOGICAL TIME. It is important to the theory of CONTINENTAL DRIFT. Since the "magnetic memory" of rocks is measurable, this determines their orientation in relation to magnetic north at the time of their solidification. The Earth's polarity has reversed at least

▲ **paddlefish** Both species of paddlefish, the American and the Chinese, are distinguished by their long, paddle-shaped bills, which can account for as much as one third of their body length. Paddlefish swim with their large mouths open, straining plankton or tiny fish from the water.

20 times in the past four to five million years; earlier changes cannot at present be determined. The gross displacement of large rock formations as measured by their magnetic qualities can be explained by SEAFLOOR SPREADING. *See also* MAGNETIC FIELD REVERSAL

palaeontology

Study of the FOSSIL remains of plants and animals. Evidence from fossils is used in the reconstruction of ancient environments and in tracing the EVOLUTION of life on Earth.

Palaeozoic

Second era of GEOLOGICAL TIME, after the PRECAMBRIAN era, lasting from 590 million to 248 million years ago. It is sub-divided into six periods: CAMBRIAN, ORDOVICIAN, SILURIAN, DEVONIAN, CARBONIFEROUS and PERMIAN. Invertebrate animals evolved hard skeletons capable of being preserved as fossils in the Cambrian; fish-like vertebrates appeared in the Ordovician; amphibians emerged in the Devonian; and reptiles appeared in the Carboniferous.

palaeozoology

Study of ancient animals that have been preserved by FOSSILIZATION, formation of CASTS AND MOULDS or in natural preservatives such as AMBER, tar or asphalt. Other forms of preservation include freezing and waterlogging. *See also* FOSSILS; PALAEOBOTANY

palate

In vertebrates, roof of the MOUTH. It comprises the bony front part known as the hard palate and the softer fleshy part at the back known as the soft palate.

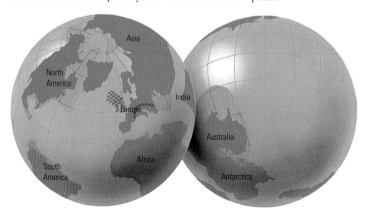

◄ **Palaeocene** The drifting apart of continents continued during the Palaeocene epoch. The movement between Africa and Europe raised the Alps. A great area of volcanic activity reached from the British Isles towards the position of Iceland.

banana

bread fruit

areca palm

coconut palm

nipa palm

papaya

▲ **palm** Members of the palm family are found in tropical and subtropical regions worldwide. Many species are important economically, particularly the coconut palm (*Cocos nucifera*), with its clusters of green or reddish-orange fruits. The nipa palm (*Nipa fruticans*) grows best in muddy coastal parts of Sumatra and Borneo. Its large fruit is edible, as is juice from the flower stalk. The areca palm (*Areca catechu*) is cultivated in Asia for its fruits (betel nuts), the seeds of which are crushed and chewed for their stimulant properties. The papaya (*Carica papaya*), which is not a true palm, banana plant (*Musa sapientum*) and bread fruit (*Artocarpus incisa*) grow in lowland tropical forests and are cultivated for their edible fruits.

palila
Small, finch-like bird found only on the slopes of Mauna Kea in Hawaii. It has a golden-yellow head and a stubby, black bill. The palila feeds mainly on the unhardened seeds of trees found only on Hawaii. It is an endangered species due to livestock grazing its habitat. Length: 15cm (6in). Family Drepanididae; species *Loxiodes bailleui*.

palm
Any member of a family of monocotyledonous trees found in tropical and subtropical regions. It has a woody, unbranched trunk covered with fibres and a crown of large, stiff leaves. Its leaves may be palmate (fan-like) or pinnate (feather-like). All palms produce DRUPES, such as dates or coconuts.

Palms are the source of wax, oil, fibre and sugar. Height: 60m (200ft). Family Arecacae/Palmae. *See also* BETEL NUT; DATE PALM; COCONUT PALM; LIANA; PALMETTO

palmchat
Unusual bird that is classified in a family of its own. It is found in open woodlands in the West Indian islands of Hispaniola and Gonâve. The palmchat is a noisy and aggressive bird. It builds large, communal nests, with a separate entrance to each nest. Length: 18cm (7in). Family Dulidae; species *Dulus dominicus*.

palmetto
Any of 25 species of fan-leaved PALM trees found from s United States to Central America. The trunk is often covered with dead leaf bases. Species include: *Sabal palmetto*, the 27m (90ft) cabbage palm of SE United States; *Sabal bermudiana*, the 12m (40ft) Bermuda palmetto, which has a crooked trunk; *Sabal umbraculifera* native to the West Indies, which has a massive trunk; and *Sabal texana*, the 50ft (15m) Texas palmetto, which has a bright red-brown trunk. Family Palmaceae.

palolo worm
POLYCHAETE that lives in holes among coral reefs of the s Pacific Ocean. It is a nocturnal swimmer at breeding time. The palolo worm's rear portion is filled with eggs or sperm; this part develops an eyespot, separates from the rest of the body and then swims to the surface to mate. Phylum Annelida; class Polychaeta; family Eunicidae; species *Eunice viridis*.

palynology
Study of SPORES, SEEDS and POLLENS; it is a part of such disciplines as archaeology, PALAEOBOTANY, palaeogeography and PALAEONTOLOGY. Studies of pollen in lake sediments have provided much information about the vegetation, climate and environmental conditions in past ages. Palynology has also helped to deduce the patterns of land use and settlement of primitive humans.

pampas grass
Tall, reed-like GRASS native to South America; it is widely cultivated as a lawn ornamental. Female plants bear flower clusters, 90cm (35in) tall, which are silvery and plume-like. Family Poaceae/Gramineae; species *Cortaderia selloana*.

pancreas
Elongated gland lying behind the STOMACH to the left of the midline. It secretes pancreatic juice into the small INTESTINE to aid digestion. Pancreatic juice contains the enzymes AMYLASE, TRYPSIN and LIPASE. The pancreas also contains a group of cells known as the ISLETS OF LANGERHANS, which secrete the hormones INSULIN and GLUCAGON concerned in the regulation of blood-sugar level.

panda
Either of two mainly nocturnal mammals of the family Ailuropodidae, related to RACCOONS and BEARS. The lesser or **red panda** (*Ailurus fulgens*) ranges from the Himalayas to w China. It has soft, thick, reddish brown fur, a white face and a bushy tail. It feeds mainly on fruit and leaves but is also a carnivore. Length: 115cm (45in) overall. The rare **giant panda** (*Ailuropoda melanoleuca*) inhabits bamboo forests in China (mainly Tibet). It has a short tail and a dense white coat with characteristic black fur on its shoulders, limbs, ears and around the eyes. It eats mainly plant material, particularly bamboo shoots. Length: 150cm (59in); weight: 160kg (350lb).

Pangaea
Name for the single supercontinent that formed about 240 million years ago and that began to break up at the end of the TRIASSIC period. It was surrounded by Pantalassa, the ancestral Pacific Ocean. Using calculations based on computer data, present land masses plus their continental shelves can be fitted together into this one continent. Pangaea was first written about by Alfred WEGENER in his theory of CONTINENTAL DRIFT. *See also* GONDWANALAND; LAURASIA

P

pangolin (scaly anteater)
Any of several species of toothless, insectivorous mammals that live in Asia and Africa. The pangolin is covered with horny overlapping plates. It has short, powerful forelegs with which it climbs trees and tears open the nests of the tree ants on which it feeds. Length: to 175cm (70in). Family Manidae; genus *Manis*.

▲ **panda** The giant panda (*Ailuropoda melanoleuca*) is found in mountain forests in Sichuan, central China, and on the slopes of the Tibetan plateau. A rare, solitary animal, it usually lives on the ground but will climb trees if pursued. Giant pandas spend about 12 hours a day feeding, mainly on bamboo stems and shoots. It is an endangered species; pairs have been encouraged to breed in captivity.

◀ **pangolin** The African tree pangolin (*Manis tricuspis*) inhabits the rainforests of w and central Africa. It uses smell to locate its prey, mainly tree ants. Its short, powerful forelegs are armed with sharp claws, which help it to climb and to tear open the nests of the ants. Its tail also helps its progress through the trees, by holding on to branches. If threatened, the pangolin will curl up into a ball, presenting its hard scales to the enemy. Another means of defence is the emission of an unpleasant-smelling anal secretion.

P

pansy

Common name for a cultivated hybrid VIOLET. An annual or short-lived perennial, the pansy has velvety flowers, usually in combinations of blue, yellow and white, with five petals. Height: 15–30cm (6–12in). Family Violaceae; species *Viola tricolor.*

panther

See LEOPARD

papaya (pawpaw)

Palm-like tree widely cultivated in tropical America for its fleshy, melon-like, edible fruit. It also produces the enzyme papain, which breaks down proteins. Height: to 6m (20ft). Family Caricaceae; species *Carica papaya.*

papilla

Small, conical protuberance found in mammals and plants. In mammals papillae project into the EPIDERMIS from the DERMIS; they are found in many parts of the body, including the mammalian inner ear and on the surface of the TONGUE.

paprika

Red powder ground from the fruit of a sweet PEPPER (capsicum) native to central Europe. It is a popular, spicy condiment. Family Solanaceae.

papyrus

Stout, perennial, water plant, native to s Europe, North Africa and the Middle East. It was used by the ancient Egyptians to make writing material. Strips of papyrus stem were arranged in layers, crushed and hammered to form a loosely textured, porous kind of paper. Height: to 4.5m (15ft). Family Cyperaceae; species *Cyperus papyrus.*

paradise fish

Small, hardy, freshwater fish, marked with red and blue bands. Native to s China, the paradise fish was the first tropical aquarium fish to be introduced to Europe (1869). Family Anabartidae; species *Macropodus opercularis.*

paradise kingfisher

See KINGFISHER, PARADISE

paradise nut (monkey pot)

Any member of the genus *Lecythis*, a group of trees native to South America. Their edible nuts resemble Brazil nuts. The fruits of the paradise tree are woody capsules, which resemble a pot with a lid; empty pots are used to trap wild monkeys, which grab for sugar inside the capsule and then cannot withdraw their extended fist. Family Lecythidaceae; species include *Lecythis zabucajo.*

parakeet

Any of numerous species of long-tailed PARROT. It feeds on fruits and seeds, which it holds with one foot whilst perching with the other, using its short, stout, hooked bill to dehusk them. It climbs about fruit trees, grasping branches in a "hand-over-hand" fashion. The parakeet's plumage is mostly bright blue-green or green with bold facial patterns. It is noisy and sociable. Family Psittacidae; species include *Melopsittacus undulatus* (BUDGERIGAR).

parasite

Organism that lives on or in another organism (the HOST) upon which it depends for survival; this arrangement may be harmful to the host. Parasites occur in many groups of plants and in virtually all major animal groups. A parasite that lives in the host

▶ **papaya** The skin of the papaya, or pawpaw, ripens from green to yellow or orange. Its succulent pulp encloses small, blackish-brown seeds in its centre. The fruit can be eaten raw when ripe or cooked when unripe.

is called an **endoparasite**; a parasite that survives on the host's exterior is an **ectoparasite**. Many parasites, such as PROTOZOA, FLEAS and WORMS, carry disease or cause sores or lesions, which may become infected. The European CUCKOO and COWBIRD rely on other birds to rear their young, and are therefore considered "brood parasites". In **parasitoidism**, the relationship results in the death of the host. For example, various flying insects, such as the ICHNEUMON flies, lay their eggs on or in a host that becomes food for the insect LARVAE. A **hyperparasite** is one that parasitizes another parasite. *See also* COMMENSALISM; MUTUALISM; SYMBIOSIS

parasol

Any member of the Lepiotaceae family of common terrestrial FUNGI. They have shaggy, umbrella-shaped caps. *Lepiota procera* is considered one of the best edible species. Some parasol species are poisonous and many species resemble AMANITAS. Phylum Basidiomycota.

parasympathetic nervous system

One of two parts of the AUTONOMIC NERVOUS SYSTEM, the other being the SYMPATHETIC NERVOUS SYSTEM. Both systems are involved with the action of INVOLUNTARY MUSCLES. The parasympathetic nervous system controls muscles that prepare the body for a relaxed state, for example by decreasing heart rate and aiding digestion by encouraging PERISTALSIS. The sympathetic nervous system does the reverse. *See also* NERVOUS SYSTEM

pardalote

Any of four species of small, rather dumpy birds found in Australia. Pardalotes feed partly on the sweet secretions exuded by insect larvae. Length: 10cm (4in). Family Dicaeidae.

parenchyma

Soft tissue made up of non-specialized, thin-walled CELLS, which are either spherical or blunt-edged in shape, often with spaces between the cells. Parenchyma is one of the chief tissues of plant stems, leaves and fruit pulp. It stores nutrients and water, and helps to support the plant. In animals, parenchyma is similar loose, connective, indeterminate tissue. It packs the spaces between the organs of simple animals such as worms.

parr

Newly hatched form of SALMON (genera *Salmo* and *Onchorhynchus*). They are typically banded with red spots. Parrs remain in fresh water for up to five years, depending on the species, before migrating downstream into the ocean.

parrot

Any of several hundred species belonging to the bird family Psittacidae. Parrots are similar to PARAKEETS but with short, square tails. They are fruit eaters

found in dense forest and jungle. Parrots are prized as cage birds due to their spectacular plumage; many species are now seriously endangered because of loss of habit and capture. Family Psittacidae.

parrot, Australian king

Long-tailed Australian parrot. It forms flocks dominated by young, all-green birds. The male has a bright scarlet head and body; the female has a scarlet belly. The Australian king parrot sometimes feeds on ripening crops, even potatoes. It can become tame. Length: 42cm (17in). Family Psittacidae; species *Alisterus scapularis.*

parrot, Bourke's

Small parrot that resembles a BUDGERIGAR in shape. It is brown with a whitish eye-ring and a pale pink breast. When disturbed, Bourke's parrot freezes or darts into a dead tree, where its plumages matches the colour of the wood. Length: 18–22cm (7–9in). Family Psittacidae; species *Neophema bourkii.*

parrot, eclectus

Stocky, short-tailed parrot with unusual colour reversal in the sexes. The male is all green with a red breast patch; the female is all red with a blue breast patch. In flight, scarlet wing linings contrast with the black flight feathers. The eclectus parrot is found in tropical forests in Australia. Length: 42cm (17in). Family Psittacidae; species *Eclectus roratus.*

parrot, mugla

Small, slender, Australian parrot. It is a brilliant emerald green, with scarlet and yellow crown, belly and rump patches. The mugla parrot feeds in small family parties on the ground near trees; it flies to cover with quick, undulating wing beats. Length: 25–30cm (10–12in). Family Psittacidae; species *Psephotus varius.*

parrot, swift

Streamlined Australian parrot. It is green with a red spike-shaped tail, forehead and crown. It flies in flocks at great speed, weaving through the trees. The swift parrot feeds on the blossoms and foliage of eucalyptus; it occasionally attacks soft fruits and cultivated berries. It is often tame and approachable. Length: 24cm (9in). Family Psittacidae; species *Lathamus discolor.*

parrotbill

Medium-sized, stocky perching bird. It has reddish-brown plumage, with a long tail and a stout, yellow bill. Some species, for example the spot-breasted parrotbill (*Paradoxornis guttaticollis*), have bold black facial markings. Parrotbills are specialized feeders, often found only in bamboo forest or dense reed beds. Length: 15–28cm (6–11in). Family Panuridae; genera include *Paradoxornis.*

parrot-finch

Any member of the genus *Erythrura*, a group of 11 species of small birds belonging to the WAXBILL family. They are found in the Australasian region. Parrot-finches are sparrow-like in shape and bill size. Most species are brightly coloured. They feed in flocks in rainforest habitats. Family Estrildidae; genus *Erythrura.*

parrotfish

Any of *c*.83 species of colourful, tropical, marine fish, common on coral reefs. Its jaw teeth are usually fused into a parrot-like beak, which it uses to graze on the algae on the coral rock. Some parrotfish species secrete a mucous cocoon in which they rest at night. Sex change is common in parrotfish. Family Scaridae.

parrotlet
Any member of the genus *Forpus*, a group of seven species of small PARROT. They are found in Central and South America. Parrotlets are sociable birds, which call to each other with finch-like twitters as they forage for fruits and seeds. The male is brightly coloured, often green and blue. Length: *c*.12cm (*c*.5in). Family Psittacidae; genus *Forpus*.

parsley
Branching, biennial herb, native to the Mediterranean region. It is cultivated widely for its aromatic leaves, which are used for flavouring and as a garnish. It has heads of small, greenish-yellow flowers. Height: to 90cm (35in). Family Apiaceae/Umbelliferae; species *Petroselinum crispum*.

parsnip
Biennial plant native to Eurasia and widely cultivated for its edible white taproot. The plant has many leaves. The roots develop slowly until cool weather sets in, when they mature quickly. Family Apiaceae/Umbelliferae; species *Pastinaca sativa*.

parthenogenesis
In biological reproduction, development of a female sex cell or GAMETE without FERTILIZATION. Since there is no involvement of a male gamete, it leads to the production of offspring that are genetically identical to the mother. This process produces little VARIATION and occurs naturally among some invertebrate animals, such as APHIDS and BEES. The same process occurs in a few plants, for example DANDELIONS, and is termed **parthenocarpy**.

partial dominance
See CODOMINANCE

partially permeable membrane
Thin, sheet-like material that permits the passage of a SOLVENT (such as water) but not larger dissolved SOLUTES (such as salt and sugar). The property of permeability depends on the molecular diameter of the dissolved substance and the nature of the membrane. Common membranes include thin palladium foil, pig's bladder, copper ferrocyanide (cyanofer-

▲ **parsnip** Cultivated since ancient times, the parsnip is thought to have been used for food by the Romans. It was introduced to the Americas by colonizers in the 17th century. It grows best in cool climates and can survive in frozen soil.

rate) and the walls of plant and animal cells. *See also* OSMOSIS; SEMIPERMEABLE MEMBRANE

partridge
Stoutly built, medium-sized gamebird. It has mainly brown plumage, with a reddish-brown tail. The grey partridge (*Perdix perdix*) has an inverted brown horseshoe-shaped mark on its lower breast; the red-legged partridge (*Alectoris rufa*) and similar species have bold black bars on their flanks and a red bill and legs. Partridges are found in open country, from farmland to semideserts. Length: 29–35cm (11–14in). Family Phasianidae; genera *Perdix* and *Alectoris*.

parula
Small, short-tailed WARBLER of North and Central America; it winters in South America. It is bluish-grey above and bright lemon yellow below; some species have an orange breast band and two white wing bars. The parula breeds in coniferous woodlands near water. Length: 11cm (4.5in). Family Parulidae; genus *Parula*.

passeriform
Member of the bird order Passeriformes, comprising the perching birds. It is the largest order of birds, containing about half of all known bird species, in 57 families. It includes: the true songbirds, such as ROBINS, BLACKBIRDS and THRUSHES; the CROW family; SWALLOWS and MARTINS; BIRDS OF PARADISE; and many more. Perching birds have grasping feet on which one toe points backwards and the other three point forwards, thus enabling the birds to grip and remain on their perches.

passion flower
Any plant of the genus *Passiflora*, a group of climbing tropical plants that probably originated in tropical America. The best-known species is the widely cultivated blue passion flower (*Passiflora caerulea*). Flowers are red, yellow, green or purple; the outer petals ring a fringed centre. The leaves are lobed. Some species produce edible fruits, such as granadilla. Family Passifloraceae.

passive margin
Crustal plate boundary that is free from relative movement or activity, such as volcanicity and earthquakes. Passive margins are often the sites of significant deposition of sediment, for example the boundaries between oceanic and continental CRUST on either side of the Atlantic Ocean.

Pasteur, Louis (1822–95)
French chemist, one of the founders of MICROBIOLOGY. He made important contributions to chemistry, bacteriology and medicine. He discovered that microorganisms can be destroyed by heat, a technique now known as PASTEURIZATION. Pasteur also discovered that he could weaken certain disease-causing microorganisms – specifically those causing anthrax in animals and rabies in man – and then use the weakened culture to vaccinate individuals against the disease.

pasteurization
Controlled heat treatment of food to kill bacteria and other microorganisms, discovered by Louis PASTEUR in the 1860s. Milk is pasteurized by heating it to 72°C (161.6°F) and holding it at that temperature for 16 seconds. Ultrapasteurization is now used to produce UHT (ultra-heat-treated) milk; the milk is heated to 132°C (270°F) for one second to provide a shelf-life of several months.

▲ **passion flower** The giant granadilla (*Passiflora quadrankgularis*) is unusual among passion flowers in that its fruit, shown left, is large and gourd-like. The flesh, which is delicately perfumed, is edible. The flowers are strongly scented and large, sometimes up to 13cm (5in) in diameter.

patchouli
Shrub of the mint family, native to Southeast Asia. It yields a fragrant, brownish yellow essential oil. The leaves yield a heavy perfume, also called patchouli, used in the manufacture of soaps. Family Lamiaceae/Labiatae; species *Pogostemon patchouli*.

patella (knee-cap)
Large, flattened, roughly triangular bone just in front of the joint where the FEMUR and TIBIA are linked. It is present in most mammals, birds and reptiles. The patella is surrounded by bursae (sacs of fluid), which cushion the joint.

pathogen
MICROORGANISM that causes disease in plants or animals. Animal pathogens are most commonly BACTERIA and VIRUSES; common plant pathogens include FUNGI.

Pavlov, Ivan Petrovich (1849–1936)
Russian neurophysiologist. His early work centred on the physiology and neurology of digestion. In 1904 Pavlov received the Nobel Prize for physiology or medicine. He is best known for his classical (Pavlovian) conditioning of behaviour in dogs. His major works are *Conditioned Reflexes* (1927) and *Lectures on Conditioned Reflexes* (1928).

pea
Climbing annual plant, probably native to w Asia. It has small oval leaves and white flowers. The flowers give rise to pods containing wrinkled or smooth seeds, which are a popular vegetable. The family to which the pea plant belongs is often referred to as the pea family. Height: to 1.8m (6ft). Family Fabaceae/Leguminosae; species *Pisum sativum*. *See also* ACACIA; BEAN; LEGUME; PEANUT; VETCH

peach
Small fruit tree native to China and grown throughout temperate areas. The lance-shaped leaves appear after the pink flowers in spring. The fruit has a thin, downy skin and white or yellow flesh, with a hard "stone" in the middle. It is eaten fresh or preserved. Height: to 6.5m (21ft). Family Rosaceae; species *Prunus persica*.

peacock
See PEAFOWL

peacock butterfly
Any of several species of BUTTERFLY, the wings of which have a pattern of eyespots, resembling those on the tails of peacocks. Family Nymphalidae.

P

peacock's tail

SEAWEED composed of a flat, fan-shaped frond that curls and becomes funnel-like when mature. It is found in rock pools and stones of the lower seashore in SW Britain, the Atlantic Ocean and the Mediterranean Sea. The outside is brown with green bands and the inside is green with a light calcareous deposit. Height: *c*.10cm (*c*.4in). Family Dictyotaceae; species *Padina pavonia*.

peacock worm

Any member of the genus *Sabella*, a group of sedentary, marine FANWORMS that live in tubes *c*.40cm (*c*.16in) long. The peacock worm feeds and breathes via numerous tentacles, which extend from the openings of its tubes. The tentacles can be retracted quickly when the animal is disturbed. It is these long, colourful tentacles that give the peacock worm its name. Phylum Annelida; class Polychaeta; order Sabellida; family Sabellidae; genus *Sabella*.

peafowl

Any of several species of unmistakable, pheasant-like ground birds found in Asia. The male (peacock) has a fan-like crest and a spectacular train of upper tail feathers, comprising numerous elongated feathers with blue-centred bronze, blue, green and copper "eyes". During display, the male erects its tail into a huge quivering fan. Length: male 1.8–2.3m (5.9–7.5ft), females 0.9–1m (2.6–3.3ft). Family Phasianidae; species include *Pavo cristatus* and *Pavo muticus*.

peanut (groundnut)

Annual leguminous plant of the PEA family. Native to South America, it is now grown in temperate regions of the world; the major producers are China and India. The 19th-century US scientist George Washington Carver researched more than 300 uses for the peanut plant. The seeds (peanuts) are a valuable source of protein and yield an oil used both in food (margarine) and in industry. Family Fabaceae/Leguminosae; species *Arachis hypogaea*

peanut worm (sipunculan)

Any member of the phylum Sipuncula, a group of unsegmented marine worms. Peanut worms burrow in the substratum. They feed by filtering suspended detritus and microorganisms from the water with a mass of tentacles. Length: 2–500mm (0.08–20in). Phylum Sipuncula.

pear

Tree and its edible fruit, native to N Asia and S Europe and grown worldwide in temperate regions. The tree has white flowers and glossy, green leaves. The greenish-yellow, brownish or reddish fruit, picked unripe and allowed to mature, is eaten fresh or preserved. Height: 15–23m (49–75ft). Family Rosaceae; species *Pyrus communis*.

► **peanut** The peanut (*Arachis hypogaea*) is unusual in that its fruits, which are not true nuts, develop underground. After the flower has died, a shoot grows from the base of the flower towards the ground. It penetrates the soil and a pod develops, as seen in the diagram. The pods absorb nutrients from the soil for the developing seeds (peanuts).

◄ **pear** The pear tree is a member of the rose family. It thrives in warm temperate regions and is one of the world's most important fruit trees. The flesh of the fruit is soft, sweet and sometimes slightly gritty. Many different varieties are cultivated.

pearl

Hard, smooth, iridescent concretion of CALCIUM CARBONATE produced by certain marine and freshwater bivalve MOLLUSCS. It is composed almost entirely of nacre, or mother-of-pearl, which forms the inner layer of mollusc shells. A pearl, the only GEM of animal origin, results from an abnormal growth of nacre around minute particles of foreign matter, such as a grain of sand.

pearlfish

Any member of the family Carapidae, a group of small, elongate fish found in tropical and temperate marine waters of the Southern Hemisphere. Some species of pearlfish live as parasites in the digestive tract of SEA CUCUMBERS and eat their internal organs. Other species are commensal, living in a variety of invertebrates. Pearlfish have planktonic larvae with elongated fin rays. Length: 15cm (6in). Family Carapidae.

peat

SOIL that is composed of dead and decaying remains of vegetation. It is generally dark brown or black in colour. It is thought to be similar to the first stage in the formation of COAL. Peat forms in areas of high rainfall or very poor drainage, and it contains a high proportion of water. In very wet conditions, plants do not decay when they die because the conditions are nearly ANAEROBIC, which means that the vegetation is not broken down by BACTERIA. Waterlogged and airless conditions create a very acidic and infertile landscape, which can become very boggy. Only specialized plants, notably SPHAGNUM MOSS, can survive in such areas. Peat is used sometimes as a fuel.

pecan

North American tree that bears a nut resembling a small, smooth-shelled WALNUT, to which it is related. Valued for its flavour, the pecan nut consists of 70% fat and is used in many desserts. Family Juglandaceae; species *Carya illinoiensis*.

peccary

Omnivorous, pig-like mammal native to the SW United States and Central and South America. It has coarse, bristly hair. Collared peccaries, or javelinas (*Tayassu taja*), have dark-grey hair with a whitish collar. White-lipped peccaries (*Tayassu pecari*) have brown hair. Weight: 23–30kg (50–66lb). Family Tayassuidae.

pectin

Water-soluble POLYSACCHARIDE found in the cell walls and intercellular tissue of certain ripe fruits or vegetables. When fruit is cooked, pectin yields a gel that is the thickening agent of jellies and jams.

pectinase

ENZYME that breaks down PECTIN. It is responsible for the softening of fruit during the ripening process. In industry, manufactured pectinases are used to digest the pectin in fruit juices and wines to give a good quality, clear product.

pedicel

In botany, term for a flower stalk. The pedicel attaches an individual flower to the **peduncle** (the main floral axis), often growing out of the AXIL of a BRACT. In zoology, a pedicel is the second joint of an insect's ANTENNA or any other stalk-like appendage.

pedology

Scientific study of SOILS. Pedologists divide soils according to their physical and chemical composition. These SOIL HORIZONS are determined by factors such as the presence of organic matter and the extent of drainage. Soil types are classified by such names as PODZOL and CHERNOZEM, reflecting the pioneering work of Russian pedologists.

pegmatite

Very coarse-grained IGNEOUS ROCK, generally light in colour and often of GRANITIC composition. Pegmatites are the chief sources of GEMS, MICA and FELDSPAR.

pelagic

Zone of an OCEAN and the marine organisms that inhabit it. Pelagic organisms live anywhere in oceans, seas or lakes, except on the bottom (*see* BENTHOS). They are divided into NEKTON (large fish and whales) and PLANKTON (small plants and animals) on which the nekton feed.

pelargonium

Any member of the genus *Pelargonium*, native to South Africa; they are often known as GERANIUMS, to which they are closely related. The circular or lobed, often aromatic leaves alternate on the stalk. The five-petalled flowers are red, pink, purple or white. Family Geraniaceae; genus *Pelargonium*.

pelican

Any member of the family Pelecanidae, a group of large, mainly white, long-necked water birds. The pelican has a massive bill and a throat pouch and flies with its neck retracted. It feeds mostly on freshwater fish, although the brown pelican (*Pelecanus occidentalis*) is coastal. Numbers of European white pelican (*Pelecanus onocrotalus*) are decreasing as wetlands are drained; however, the North American white pelican (*Pelecanus erythrorhynchos*) is becoming more common. Length: 1.2–1.6m (3.9–5.2ft); wingspan: 200–280cm (80–110in). Family Pelecanidae.

pelvis (pelvic girdle)

Dish-shaped bony structure that supports the internal organs of the lower abdomen in vertebrates. It serves as a point of attachment for muscles that

◄ **pecan** The pecan tree is a large tree, up to 45m (150ft) tall, native to temperate regions of North America. Its compound leaves can be up to 50cm (20in) long. The fruits are arranged in clusters of between three and seven. When mature the green husk splits to reveal the nut. The mottled brown shells later burst apart to release the ripe nut. Pecan nuts have a mild but distinctive flavour.

P

▲ **pelican** The brown pelican (*Pelecanus occidentalis*) lives on the coasts of tropical America. It is the only pelican species to dive for its prey. The great white pelican (*Pelecanus onocrotalus*), of sw Europe, Africa and Asia, hunts cooperatively in groups. Pelicans use their throat pouches as scoops with which to catch fish.

move the limbs or fins. In women, the pelvis is broader than in men, to facilitate childbirth. *See also* ILIUM; ISCHIUM; PUBIS

pelycosaur
Member of a group of extinct, reptile-like, SYNAPSID tetrapods that evolved in late Carboniferous times. They showed some mammalian features, such as different tooth shapes. Some types of pelycosaur, such as *Dimetrodon*, had webbed, sail-like structures on their backs, which were internally supported by bony extensions of the backbones. The "sails" may have helped the animals to warm up and cool down. Pelycosaurs died out in late Permian times.

peneplain
Fairly flat area of land formed over millions of years by the wearing down of ancient mountains by EROSION. Such long-term erosion, called **denudation**, often results from the action of rivers. It may leave areas of more resistant rock, which stand up as monadnocks or residual hills.

penguin
Flightless, fish-eating bird found only in the Southern Hemisphere. Apart from breeding and moulting at its rookery, it spends most of its time at sea. It travels at great speed underwater, using flippers to propel itself, and often leaps clear of the water to land feet first. Length: 40–120cm (16–47in). Family Spheniscidae.

penguin, emperor
Largest species of penguin. It has a black back, white front and orange-yellow neckband. It is unique amongst penguins in incubating its one egg during the Antarctic winter darkness. The egg is held by the male between the feet and brood pouch. Length: 120cm (47in). Family Spheniscidae; species *Aptenodytes forsteri*.

penguin, jackass
Only species of penguin to be found on the coasts of South Africa. It has a broad, white band above its eyes and a narrow, black, horseshoe band across its breast and down the flanks. Length: 63–68cm (25–27in). Family Spheniscidae; species *Spheniscus demersus*.

penguin, rockhopper
Medium-sized penguin. It has red eyes, an orange-red bill and yellow plumes on each side of its head. It breeds on islands off the southern tip of South America and in the subantarctic. Length: 63cm (25in). Family Spheniscidae; species *Eudyptes chrysocome*.

penis
Male reproductive organ in mammals, some reptiles and a few bird species. In mammals, it contains the URETHRA, the channel through which URINE and SEMEN pass to the exterior, and erectile tissue that, when engorged with blood, causes the penis to become erect during arousal. *See also* SEXUAL REPRODUCTION

penny bun
FUNGUS that has a fruiting body with a rounded, domed, brown cap, a much-thickened, pale brown to whitish stem, and whitish flesh. It grows in coniferous or broad-leaved woodland. It is one of the most important edible fungi. Commercially it is dried and used for flavouring soups. Phylum Basidiomycota; species *Boletus edulis*.

pennyroyal
Common name for a number of plants, including the European *Mentha pulegium*, which is a sweet herb of the MINT family. It has purple flowers and its leaves are said to discourage mosquitoes.

penstemon
Any member of the genus *Penstemon*, a group of perennial herbs or shrubs native to North America and Mexico. Many species are grown ornamentally. The flowers, which range in colour from white through yellow to deep pink, red, blue or purple, are massed in terminal inflorescences. Penstemon plants thrive in the sun and are mostly only half-hardy. Family Scrophulariaceae; genus *Penstemon*. *See also* BEARDTONGUE

pentadactyl limb
Limb with five digits (fingers or toes); it is characteristic of four-legged vertebrates. It is generally used for locomotion. It is found in amphibians, reptiles, birds and mammals but may be greatly modified (as in the flippers of seals and whales or the wings of bats). It probably evolved from the fins of

▲ **penguin** These flightless birds are adapted to a life of swimming and diving. Their streamlined bodies are insulated by close-set feathers and fatty blubber. All penguin species spend most of their lives at sea, coming ashore to breed and moult. Several species inhabit true Antarctica, others live in subantarctic and temperate regions, some as far north as the Galápagos Islands. The largest and best insulated species, the emperor penguin, occupies the most southerly regions.

primitive fish, which are the only modern vertebrates not to retain it.

pentastomid
See TONGUE WORM

pentatomid bug
Any member of a large order of bugs, all of which have shield-shaped bodies and five segments on their antennae. The pentatomid bug is a garden pest, which feeds on plant roots, stems and seeds; it is not host plant specific. It has a relatively low fecundity, producing only one generation per year. Adult body size: *c*.10mm (*c*.0.4in). Order Hemiptera.

pentose sugar
MONOSACCHARIDE that comprises five carbon atoms. Biologically important pentose sugars include ribose and deoxyribose, both of which are major components of the NUCLEIC ACIDS ribonucleic acid (RNA) and deoxyribonucleic acid (DNA). Ribulose is the pentose sugar found in RIBULOSE BISPHOSPHATE, the molecule that acts as the carbon dioxide acceptor in the DARK REACTION stage of PHOTOSYNTHESIS.

peony
Any member of the genus *Paeonia*, a group of perennial plants native to North America and Eurasia. The herbaceous peonies have glossy, divided leaves and large, white, pink or red flowers. They are frequently cultivated in gardens. Height: to 0.9m (3ft). Tree peonies grow in hot, dry areas and have brilliant blossoms of many colours. Height: to 1.8m (6ft). Family Paeoniaceae; genus *Paeonia*.

pepo
Many seeded pulpy FRUIT of the Cucurbitaceae family; the CUCUMBER is an example.

pepper (capsicum)
Any of several species of perennial woody shrubs belonging to the NIGHTSHADE family, native to tropical America. Its fruit is a many-seeded, pungent berry, the size of which depends on the species. Included are bell, red, cayenne and CHILLI peppers. Family Solanaceae; genus *Capsicum*.

pepper (sweet pepper)
Shrubby perennial plant of the NIGHTSHADE family, native to the Americas; it is sometimes cultivated as an annual. It has simple, oval- or lance-shaped leaves and white or greenish-white flowers, sometimes tinged with violet. The fruits, green, red or yellow, are cooked or used raw in salads. An extract of the plant is used in ointments as a heat producer and counter-irritant for rheumatic pains. Height: 91–120cm (36–47in). Family Solanaceae; species *Capsicum frutescens* and *Capsicum annuum*.

peppermint
Perennial herb of the MINT family. It is cultivated for

▶ **pepper** The bell pepper, a type of *Capsicum annum*, is a tropical, heat-loving plant. It is thought to have been first domesticated in Mexico. Most peppers turn from green to red as the fruit ripens, but other colours are also common. The pepper's strong flavour is due to the presence of capsaicin in the walls of the fruit.

its ESSENTIAL OIL, which is distilled and used in medicine and as a flavouring. Family Lamiaceae/Labiatae; species *Mentha piperita*

peppershrike
Chunky perching bird, related to the VIREO, found in open woods, bushy clearings and forest edges in Central and South America. It is olive-black above and yellowish below. The rufous-browed peppershrike (*Cyclarhis gujanensis*) has a reddish stripe across its forehead over the eyes. Length: 15cm (6in). Family Vireonidae; species include *Cyclarhis gujanensis* and *Cyclarhis nigrirostris*.

pepper tree (Peruvian mastic)
Evergreen tree native to tropical America. Grown as an ornamental, it has feather-like leaves, yellow flowers and reddish berries. Height: to 15m (50ft). Family Anacardiaceae; species *Schinus molle*.

pepsin
Digestive ENZYME that is secreted by GLANDS of the STOMACH wall as part of the gastric juice. In the presence of hydrochloric acid, pepsin, an ENDOPEPTIDASE, catalyzes the splitting of PROTEINS in food into POLYPEPTIDES.

peptidase
ENZYME that breaks down PROTEINS and POLYPEPTIDES into smaller units by hydrolysis of the PEPTIDE bond between adjacent AMINO ACIDS. There are two groups of peptidases – ENDOPEPTIDASES, which act on peptide bonds in the central region of a protein molecule, and EXOPEPTIDASES, which act on the terminal peptide bonds of polypeptides.

peptide
Molecule consisting of two or more AMINO ACID molecules linked by bonds between the amino group of one acid and the carboxyl group of another. This type of linkage is called a **peptide bond**. Peptides containing several amino acids are called POLYPEPTIDES. PROTEINS consist of polypeptide chains having up to several hundred amino acids cross-linked to each other in various ways.

perception
Ability of the SENSES to recognise aspects of the environment, in particular any variation that may occur. *See also* RECEPTOR

perch
Either of two species of freshwater food fish. The European perch (*Perca fluviatilis*) is deep-bodied and greenish in colour with dark vertical banding. The North American yellow perch (*Perca flavescens*) is gold-coloured with black side-bars. Length: to 40cm (16in). Family Percidae.

peregrine falcon
See FALCON, PEREGRINE

perennial
In plants, condition whereby growth continues from year to year. In herbaceous perennials, such as DAHLIAS and RHUBARB, the aerial parts die away in autumn leaving underground structures to survive the winter and give rise to new growth in spring. In woody perennials, such as OAKS and CONIFERS, permanent structures remain above ground throughout the winter, thus allowing the plant to acquire a very large size over a number of years. *See also* ANNUAL; BIENNIAL

perentie
Very large MONITOR lizard. It has dark-edged light

▲ **perch** The European perch (*Perca fluviatilis*) inhabits quiet lakes and rivers throughout Europe. Young and medium-sized perch tend to live in shoals and feed on plankton. Older and larger perch feed on other fish and become more solitary. Perch are distinguished from other species by the presence of two dorsal fins, the first of which has several sharp spines.

spots on its brown body and dark reticulations on its head and neck. Perenties are chiefly terrestrial but can also climb. They use crevices and burrows as retreat sites. They occur in arid central and w Australia, where they feed on small vertebrates, insects and carrion. Length: to *c*.2m (*c*.6.6ft). Family Varanidae; species *Varanus giganteus*.

perianth
Outer region of a FLOWER. The perianth includes all the structures surrounding the reproductive organs and usually consists of an outer whorl of SEPALS (CALYX) and an inner whorl of PETALS (COROLLA).

pericarp
In SPERMATOPHYTES (seed-bearing plants), the wall of a ripened FRUIT; it is derived from the ovary wall. The tissues of the pericarp vary from fibrous to stony or fleshy.

perichondrium
In a developing EMBRYO, membrane surrounding the CARTILAGE that eventually becomes BONE. The perichondrium is well supplied with BLOOD VESSELS and is the source of the osteoblasts (bone-building cells) that invade the embryonic cartilage and lay down the hard bone matrix.

pericycle
Cylinder of PARENCHYMA cells between the ENDODERMIS and the vascular tissue in the roots of ANGIOSPERMS.

peridotite
Coarse-grained, heavy IGNEOUS ROCK that is composed of OLIVINE and PYROXENE with small flecks of MICA or HORNBLENDE. It alters readily into SERPENTINE. Rocks that consist mainly of olivine are called DUNITES.

periglacial
Associated with or marginal to GLACIATION. It is used to describe processes, environments or organisms that are found adjacent to glacial ones.

periodical cicada
See CICADA, PERIODICAL

peripheral nervous system
All parts of the NERVOUS SYSTEM that lie outside the CENTRAL NERVOUS SYSTEM (CNS). The peripheral nervous system comprises the 12 pairs of cranial nerves, which principally serve the head and neck region, and 31 pairs of spinal nerves, the fibres of which extend to the furthermost parts of the body. The peripheral nervous system carries impulses from receptors to the CNS, and carries back responses from the CNS to effectors. *See also* AUTONOMIC NERVOUS SYSTEM (ANS)

P

perissodactyl
Member of the mammal order Perissodactyla. They are characterized by hoofs with an odd number of toes. All perissodactyls are HERBIVORES. The only living members of the order are HORSES, TAPIRS and RHINOCEROSES; there are more than 200 extinct forms known from fossils. *See also* ARTIODACTYL

peristalsis
Series of wave-like movements that propel food through the digestive tract. It is caused by contractions of the smooth INVOLUNTARY MUSCLE of the gut wall. The reverse process, antiperistalsis, produces vomiting.

periwinkle
See WINKLE

periwinkle
Any of several species of trailing or erect evergreen plants that are cultivated as ground cover and for hanging baskets. Family Apocynaceae.

permafrost
Land that is permanently frozen, often to a considerable depth. The top few centimetres generally thaw in summer, but the MELTWATER is not able to sink into the ground because of the frozen subsoil. If the landscape is fairly flat, surface water lies on the ground throughout the summer. Construction work is very difficult, and many methods have been employed in Russia, Canada and Alaska to overcome the problems. *See also* MUSKEG; TUNDRA

permeability
Ability of rock to transmit water; it is not directly related to POROSITY. Limestone, for example, is a permeable but non-porous rock; water percolates only through the joints and fissures.

Permian
Last geological period of the PALAEOZOIC era, lasting from 286 to 248 million years ago. There was widespread geologic uplift, resulting in the formation of PANGAEA. The major climatic characteristics of the period were aridity and glaciation. Many groups of marine invertebrate animals became extinct in the Permian period, but reptiles flourished.

persimmon
Any of several trees of the genus *Diospyros*. They produce reddish-orange fruits, which are sour and astringent until ripe. Family Ebenaceae; species include *Diospyros virginiana* (North American persimmon) and *Diospyros kaki* (Japanese persimmon).

perspiration
See SWEATING

Perutz, Max Ferdinand (1914–)
British biochemist, b. Austria, who studied the X-ray diffraction of proteins. In 1953 Perutz discovered that adding a heavy atom, such as gold or mercury, to each molecule of HAEMOGLOBIN produces a slightly different diffraction pattern. By this means he demonstrated the structure of haemoglobin. For this work Perutz shared the 1962 Nobel Prize for chemistry with the British biologist John C. Kendrew (1917–97), who, by a similar method, discovered the structure of MYOGLOBIN.

pesticide
Chemical substance that is used to kill insects, rodents, weeds and other pests. Among pesticides, a herbicide is used for weeds, an INSECTICIDE for insects and a fungicide for fungal pests. Pesticides are usually harmful chemicals and an important factor in their manufacture is that they should decompose after they have performed their function. Some previously common pesticides, such as DDT, have been shown to be too toxic and long-lasting, so their use is now restricted.

petal
Part of a FLOWER. The petals of a flower are known collectively as the COROLLA. Surrounded by SEPALS, flower petals are usually brightly coloured and often secrete NECTAR and scent to attract the insects and birds necessary for CROSS-POLLINATION. Once fertilization occurs, the petals usually drop off. The petals of wind-pollinated flowers are often small and inconspicuous, allowing the STAMENS and STIGMA to be exposed for POLLINATION.

petrel
See feature article, page 288

petrification
Fossilizing process in which organic material changes into stone. Petrification is caused by mineral-rich water seeping into the empty spaces of dead buried trees or animals, which eventually become stone. Although petrified remains can be up to 300 million years old, the stone often reproduces the original living material so clearly that the cell structure is identifiable. The Petrified Forest National Park in Arizona, United States, has many examples of petrified wood. *See also* FOSSIL; FOSSILIZATION; MINERALIZATION

petroleum (crude oil)
FOSSIL FUEL that is chemically a complex mixture of hydrocarbons. It accumulates in underground deposits. The chemical composition of petroleum strongly suggests that it originated from the bodies of long-dead organisms, particularly marine plankton. After death these organisms sank to the ocean

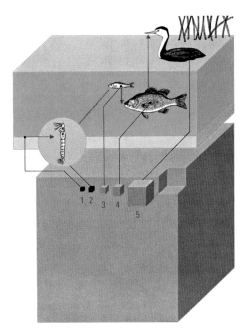

▲ **pesticide** Applied to the land, pesticides, even in small doses, are poisonous to many animals. The concentration of some pesticide poisons increases along the food chain, finally becoming lethal to animals at the end of the chain. A pesticide (1), such as DDT, is applied to water at 0.015 parts per million (ppm) to control midge larvae, but the plankton (2) accumulates it at 5ppm. The fish population (3,4) builds up still higher concentrations, and finally a grebe (5), which feeds on the fish, accumulates as much as 1600ppm of the pesticide in its body fat – enough to kill the bird.

floor, to be broken down by bacteria in oxygen-poor conditions into simpler organic materials, including hydrocarbons. Petroleum is rarely found at the original site of formation: it migrates laterally and vertically until it is trapped. Most petroleum is extracted via oil wells from reservoirs in the Earth's crust sealed by upfolds of impermeable rock or by salt domes which form traps. During petroleum refining, the heavier hydrocarbons, which usually have higher boiling points than lighter ones, are distilled (separated from the original crude substance) as the first stage of refining. The next stage is cracking, which breaks the heavy hydrocarbons down into more economically useful products, such as petrol and paraffin. Purification of the various products to remove impurities, such as sulphur and nitrogen compounds, completes the refining process. The most versatile end products are ethene and propene, which are widely used in the plastics and chemical industries.

petrology
Study of rocks, including their origin, chemical composition and where they are found. Formation of the three classes of rocks – IGNEOUS (of volcanic origin), SEDIMENTARY (deposited by water) and METAMORPHIC (either of the other two changed by temperature and pressure) – are studied.

petunia
Any member of the genus *Petunia*, a group of flowering plants of the NIGHTSHADE family. They originated in Argentina. Petunia is the common name for any of the varieties that are popular as bedding plants. Most varieties derive from the white flowered *Petunia axillaris* and the violet-red *Petunia integrifolia*. The plants may be erect, shrubby or pendant. The bell-shaped flowers have five petals of almost any colour. Family Solanaceae.

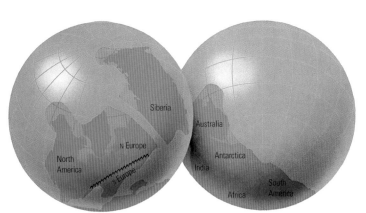

◄ **Permian** During the Permian period N Europe collided with S Europe, pushing up the Variscan-type fold mountains. This combined block began to move towards the Siberian plate.

P

PETREL

Oceanic seabird related to the SHEARWATER. Its bill has two nostrils that open together at the end of a double tube, hence the group name "tubenoses". Petrel species vary in size and plumage. The pintado petrel (*Daption capensis*) is chequered black and white. The storm petrels (family Hydrobatidae) and Leach's petrel (*Oceanodroma leucorhoa*) are small and sooty-black, with a conspicuous white rump. The giant petrel (*Macronectes giganteus*) is large and grey-brown. Families Procellariidae, Hydrobatidae and Pelecanoididae. *See also* DIVING-PETREL

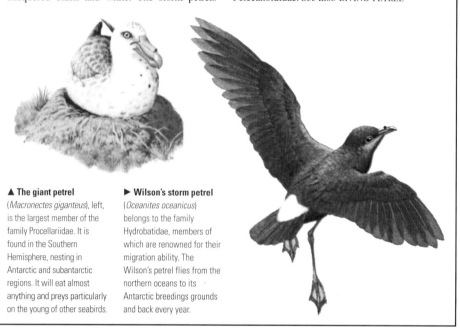

▲ The giant petrel (*Macronectes giganteus*), left, is the largest member of the family Procellariidae. It is found in the Southern Hemisphere, nesting in Antarctic and subantarctic regions. It will eat almost anything and preys particularly on the young of other seabirds.

▶ Wilson's storm petrel (*Oceanites oceanicus*) belongs to the family Hydrobatidae, members of which are renowned for their migration ability. The Wilson's petrel flies from the northern oceans to its Antarctic breedings grounds and back every year.

peyote (mescal)
Either of two species of cactus belonging to the genus *Lophophora*; they are native to the United States. The soft-stemmed *Lophophora williamsii* has pink or white flowers in summer and a blue-green stem. *Lophophora diffusa* has white or yellow flowers. Peyote contains many ALKALOIDS, the principal one being mescaline, a hallucinogenic drug. Family Cactaceae.

Pfeffer, Wilhelm Friedrich Philipp (1845–1920)
German botanist. He developed a method for measuring OSMOTIC PRESSURE and showed that such pressure is caused by the accumulation of molecules on one side of a semi-permeable membrane because they are too large to pass through it.

pH (abbreviation of potential of hydrogen)
Indication of the acidity or alkalinity of a SOLUTION. The **pH scale** expresses a range of pH values based on a logarithmic measure of the concentration or, more properly, activity of hydrogen ions. The scale runs from 0 to 14, and a neutral solution, such as pure water, has a pH of 7. A solution is acidic if the pH is less than 7 and alkaline if greater than 7. The pH may be measured with an indicator or meter. The scale was introduced in 1909 by S.P. Sørensen (1868–1939).

phaeophyte (brown alga)
Any member of the phylum Phaeophyta, which consists of the brown ALGAE. Phaeophytes are part of the kingdom PROTOCTISTA, which until recently was known as Protista. Classified by some biolo-gists as plants, the simple organisms belonging to this group are mostly marine, found mainly in the intertidal zone of rocky shores. They include familiar seaweeds such as *Fucus* (WRACKS), *Ascophyllum* (bladder wrack) and the KELPS. The largest, *Macrocystis*, grows to more than 100m (320ft) at up to 0.5m (18in) per day. *Sargassum* forms vast floating masses in the Sargasso Sea in the mid-Atlantic, with their own distinctive communities of animals and microorganisms.

phagocyte
Type of LEUCOCYTE (white blood cell) that is able to engulf other CELLS, such as bacteria. The phagocyte digests what it engulfs (in a process known as **phagocytosis**) in the defence of the body against INFECTION. Phagocytes also act as scavengers by clearing the bloodstream of the remains of the cells that die as part of the body's natural processes. *See also* IMMUNE SYSTEM; LYMPHOCYTE; MACROPHAGE; MONOCYTE

phainopepla
Slim bird of the WAXWING family. It has glossy black plumage, with a slender crest and conspicuous white wing patches. It is found in s United States and Mexico. The phainopepla nests early in spring in dry bush then moves to cooler, wetter habitats to raise a second brood. Length: 20cm (8in). Family Bombycillidae; species *Phainopepla nitens*.

phalanges
Bones in the toes and fingers of vertebrates. In humans there are 14 phalanges in each hand and foot, two in each thumb and big toe and three in the remaining digits. They are connected to the METACARPALS in the hand and to the METATARSALS in the foot.

phalarope
Any of three species of small, sandpiper-like wading birds with webbed toes. The phalarope breeds in arctic tundra and winters in the Southern Hemisphere, often far out to sea, where it feeds on plankton. When the phalarope swims it spins like a top on the water. The female is more colourful than the male. Family Scolopacidae (part); species *Phalaropus lobatus* (red-necked phalarope), *Phalaropus tricolor* (Wilson's phalarope) and *Phalaropus fulicarius* (red/grey phalarope).

phanerogam
Early botanical term for seed-bearing flowering plants, now called SPERMATOPHYTES. *See also* CRYPTOGAM

Phanerozoic
Geological timescale describing the whole of time that has elapsed since the end of the PRECAMBRIAN period. It has lasted for about 570 million years since life first evolved and thus includes the PALAEOZOIC, MESOZOIC and CENOZOIC eras.

phantom midge
Any insect of the genus *Chaoborus*. The phantom midge gets its name from its almost transparent larvae, which float horizontally in the water. The antennae of adults are modified into grasping organs, possibly to facilitate mating. Adult body size: *c*.7mm (*c*.0.3in). Order Diptera; family Chaoboridae; genus *Chaoborus*.

pharynx
In mammals, cavity at the back of the nose and mouth that extends down towards the OESOPHAGUS and TRACHEA. Inflammation of the pharynx, usually caused by viral or bacterial infection, is known as pharyngitis.

▶ **peyote** Well known for its hallucinogenic effects, peyote played an important role in the rituals of the Native North Americans. It has also been used for medicinal purposes. The peyote cactus is found mainly in sw North America, particularly in Arizona and Mexico. The most common species, *Lophophora Williamsii*, is shown here.

phascogale (wambenger, brush-tailed marsupial mouse, tuan)
Any member of the genus *Phascogale*, a group of small, carnivorous MARSUPIALS found in Australia. The phascogale hunts insects and small vertebrates. It is characterized by long hairs at the end of its tail and large ears. Head-body length: 12–22cm (5–9in); tail: 15–23cm (6–9in). Family Dasyuridae; species include *Phascogale tapoatafa*.

phasmid
Any member of the Phasmoptera order of insects. It includes LEAF INSECTS and STICK INSECTS. Some phasmid species are wingless; others have tegmina (leathery forewings) shorter than wings, or modified and enlarged hindwings. All phasmids have legs developed for walking and mouthparts for chewing. They are found mainly in tropical regions. There are c.2500 species.

pheasant
Gamebird usually found in open country. Many species are now endangered due to habitat loss. Their bills are short and thick. Their legs are unfeathered and strong for foraging; pheasants often prefer to escape by running rather than flying. The male pheasant often has spectacular plumage used in impressive courtship displays. Family Phasianidae.

pheasant, common
Gamebird native to SE Europe; it has been widely introduced for shooting. The metallic green head and red facial wattle of the male is distinctive. The male's body is rich reddish-brown and heavily barred, with a long tail. The female is dull mottled brown. The common pheasant flies straight and fast for short distances on whirring wings. Length: 53–89cm (21–35in). Family Phasianidae; species *Phasianus colchicus*.

pheasant, golden
Slim, brightly coloured gamebird. The male has a golden plumed crown and back, a gold and black barred neck ruff, green mantle and crimson underparts. The female is brown with fine black bars. The golden pheasant is native to central China, where it is becoming endangered, but it has been widely introduced, partly through escaping from collections. Length: 60–115cm (24–45in). Family Phasianidae; species *Crysolophus pictus*.

▶ **pheasant** The various species of pheasant shown here illustrate the contrast between the striking plumage of the males and the inconspicuous coloration of the females. The koklass pheasant (*Pucrasia macrolopha*) is a medium-sized pheasant found on steep, wooded slopes throughout the Himalayas, from Afghanistan to central China. The Chinese monal (*Lophophorus lhuysii*) is the largest of the monal pheasants. It is limited to the mountains of Sichuan, w China, inhabiting open meadows above the forest zone. It roosts in scrub rhododendron but is now an endangered species. Lady Amherst's pheasant (*Chrysolophus amherstiae*) is, along with the golden pheasant, one of only two species of ruffed pheasant. Its gorgeous plumage has led to it being kept as an ornamental species for centuries. It is now more common in captivity than in the wild.

pheasant, Himalayan monal
Pheasant that is found in the Himalayas, where it summers on high pastures and winters in forests. The male is iridescent green, copper and purple with a white lower back; the female is mottled brown with a white throat. Length: 63–70cm (25–28in). Family Phasianidae; species *Lophophorus impejanus*.

pheasant, Mikado
Endangered species of pheasant found only in the mountains of central Taiwan. It is an elegant bird, with blackish plumage that is delicately scalloped white. In flight it has a conspicuous white wing bar and wing tips. Shy and secretive, the Mikado pheasant keeps to dense forests and bamboo thickets. Length: 86cm (34in). Family Phasianidae; species *Syrmaticus mikado*.

phenacite (beryllium silicate, Be$_2$SiO$_4$)
Orthosilicate mineral that is found in PEGMATITES and high-temperature veins. It has hexagonal system, rhombohedral crystals. Phenacite is either colourless or glassy white, yellow, red or brown in colour. It is sometimes used as a gemstone. Hardness 7.5–8; r.d. 3.

phenotype
Physical characteristics of an organism that result from HEREDITY. Phenotype is distinct from GENOTYPE, since not all aspects of the GENETIC makeup manifest themselves.

pheromone
Substance secreted externally by certain animals that influences the behaviour of members of the same species. Common in mammals and insects, these substances are often sexual attractants. They may be a component of body products such as URINE, or they may be secreted by specific GLANDS.

phillipsite (KCa(Al$_2$Si$_6$O$_{16}$).6H$_2$O)
White or reddish ZEOLITE mineral. Phillipsite occurs in vein formations as monoclinic crystals. Hardness 4.5–5; r.d. 2.2.

philodendron
Any member of the genus *Philodendron*, a group of shrubs native to tropical America. Many species are climbing plants, some of which become epiphytes once they have reached a certain height. Philodendrons have shiny, heart-shaped leaves that are sometimes split. They are popular house plants. Height: 10–180cm (4–71in). Family Araceae; species include *Philodendron domesticum*.

phloem
Vascular tissue for distributing dissolved food materials in plants. Phloem tissue contains several types of CELLS. The most important are long, hollow cells called SIEVE TUBE CELLS. Columns of sieve tube cells are joined end to end, allowing passage of materials from cell to cell. The sieve tubes are closely associated with COMPANION CELLS, which have dense CYTOPLASM and many MITOCHONDRIA and are thought to produce the energy needed to transport the food substances (*see* ACTIVE TRANSPORT).

koklass pheasant

Chinese monal

Lady Amherst's pheasant

P

Phloem may also contain PLANT FIBRES that help to support the tissue. *See also* XYLEM

phlogopite $(KMg_3Fe_3AlSi_3O_{10}(OH)_2)$
White or brown MICA mineral. Phlogopite is found in LIMESTONES as monoclinic crystals. Hardness 2.5–3; r.d. 2.8.

phlox
Any member of the genus *Phlox*, a group of mostly perennial plants native to North America. The flowers are of various colours and are often cultivated as garden plants. Height: to 1.5m (5ft). Family Polemoniaceae; species include *Phlox divaricata* (blue phlox).

phoebe
One of a group of rather drab-looking, black-billed FLYCATCHERS found in North America and Mexico. It sits quietly on an exposed branch and sallies forth to catch passing insects. The black phoebe (*Sayornis nigricans*) is all black with a white belly. The eastern phoebe (*Sayornis phoebe*) and Say's phoebe (*Sayornis saya*) are greyish to brown above and yellowish to buff below. Length: 18cm (7in). Family Tyrannidae.

phoronid
See HORSESHOE WORM

phosphate
Chemical compounds derived from phosphoric(V) acid (H_3PO_4) and other phosphorus(V) oxyacids, for example salts with the phosphate ion $(PO_4)^{3-}$.

phospholipid
Type of LIPID that contains a phosphoric acid group or groups and an alcohol base. Phospholipids are found in egg yolk and brain tissue. They are also important constituents of all membranes, where their inwardly directed hydrophobic tails and outwardly directed water soluble heads affect the fluidity and permeability of membranes.

phosphorescence
Form of luminescence in which a substance emits light of one wavelength without associated heat. Phosphorescence may persist for some time after the initial excitation. It is a natural as well as artificial phenomenon; in warm climates, for example, the sea often appears phosphorescent at night as a result of the activities of millions of microscopic ALGAE, which phosphoresce when disturbed by the movements of the water.

phosphorylation
Biochemical reaction in which a PHOSPHATE group is introduced into a MOLECULE. Controlled by the ENZYME phosphorylase, it is the initial stage in many natural biochemical processes, such as the conversion of ADENOSINE DIPHOSPHATE (ADP) to energy-rich ADENOSINE TRIPHOSPHATE (ATP). Phosphorylation is also an important reaction in the activation or deactivation of enzymes, often under hormone control.

photolysis
See LIGHT-DEPENDENT REACTION

photoperiodism
Biological mechanism that governs the timing of certain activities in an organism by reacting to the duration of its daily exposure to light and dark. For example, the start of flowering in plants and the beginning of the breeding season in animals are determined by day length. *See also* BIOLOGICAL CLOCK; CIRCADIAN RHYTHM

photoreceptor
In animals, a sensory cell (RECEPTOR) or collection of CELLS that react to the presence of light. Most photoreceptors contain a pigment that undergoes a chemical change when it absorbs light, producing a NERVE IMPULSE. The rods and cones in the retina of the EYE are examples of photoreceptors. In plants, photoreceptors are light detectors containing the blue-green pigment PHYTOCHROME. They are involved in many plant processes, such as seed germination, flowering and leaf fall.

photosynthesis
See feature article

phototaxis
Movement of a freely motile organism, or a freely motile part of an organism, in response to the directional stimulus of light. Most unicellular algae, such as *Chlamydomonas*, move towards light (positive phototaxis), whereas an EARTHWORM will move away from light (negative phototaxis). *See also* PHOTOTROPISM

phototropism (heliotropism)
Growth of a plant in response to the stimulus of light, which increases CELL growth on the shaded side of the plant, resulting in curvature towards the source of light. AUXIN hormones are involved in this process. These hormones are produced in the tip of the shoot, and when light shines on the shoot, auxin travels preferentially down the shaded side of the shoot, where it promotes cell elongation, causing the shoot to bend towards the light. Leaves and stems respond positively to light and roots respond negatively or not at all. Indoor plants lean toward windows; leaves usually grow at right angles to light and are positioned to ensure that overlapping occurs as little as possible. *See also* PHOTOTAXIS

phyllite
Medium-grained METAMORPHIC ROCK formed from SEDIMENTS at low temperatures and only moderate pressure. It is composed of QUARTZ, FELDSPAR and MICA, with chlorite, which imparts a green or grey colour to the shiny foliated structure. It may also contain small crystals of GARNET.

phyllotaxis (phyllotaxy)
Arrangement of leaves on the STEM of a plant. In nearly all LEAF-bearing plants, each leaf grows out from the stem according to a regular pattern that is characteristic of the species. Most leaves grow either in a spiral arrangement up the stem or an alternate arrangement, with one leaf on one side of the stem and the next leaf on the other side. In an opposite arrangement, two leaves originate from the same leaf NODE. In a whorled arrangement, three or more leaves grow from the same node.

phylloxera
Small, yellowish insect of the order Homoptera. It is a pest on grape plants in Europe and the w United States. It attaches itself to the leaves and roots and sucks the plant's fluids, resulting in the rotting of the plant. It destroyed all of France's native root stock of *vitis vinifera* grapes. Family Phylloxeridae; species *Phylloxera vitifoliae*.

phylogenetics
Study of the evolutionary relationships between organisms. In molecular phylogeny, the evolutionary distances between organisms are analyzed by comparing the DNA sequences of specific GENES. These analyses confirm, for example, that seals are more closely related to dogs than they are to whales. At the most fundamental level, molecular phylogeny has revealed that all known organisms evolved from a common ancestor and can be grouped into five KINGDOMS, the members of which are more closely related to each other than to members of other kingdoms.

phylum
Part of the CLASSIFICATION of living organisms, ranking above CLASS and below KINGDOM. Phylum names are written in Roman (ordinary) letters and begin with an initial capital letter; for example all animals with backbones (VERTEBRATES) are members of the phylum Chordata. Some phyla are further subdivided into subphyla (**subphylum**). In PLANT CLASSIFICATION, the analogous category is sometimes called division. *See also* TAXONOMY

physiology
Branch of biology concerned with the functions of living organisms, as opposed to anatomy, which is concerned with their structure. Vast in scope, physiology includes the study of single cells as well as multicellular organisms.

phytochrome
PLANT PIGMENT that is sensitive to light. It exists in two interconvertible forms: phytochrome 660 (P_R), which absorbs red light (peak absorption is at a wavelength of 660nm); and photochrome 730 (P_{FR}), which absorbs far-red light (peak absorption is at a wavelength of 730nm). Even a short exposure to the appropriate light wavelength causes the conversion of one form of phytochrome to the other. During daylight P_R is converted to P_{FR}; in the dark, a rather slower conversion of P_{FR} to P_R occurs. Phytochrome is involved in the flowering of plants. *See also* PHOTOPERIODISM

phytohormone
See PLANT HORMONE

phytoplankton
Free-floating oceanic plant life, as opposed to ZOOPLANKTON, which is the animal life. Most of the organisms are microscopic, for example DIATOMS. *See also* PLANKTON

piapiac
Medium-sized bird belonging to the CROW family. It is native to Africa. It is widespread in lightly wooded grasslands with palms, where it associates with cattle and wild game. The piapiac is sooty black with a long, brown tail and a short, crow-like bill. Length: 35cm (14in). Family Corvidae; species *Ptilostomus afer*.

piciform
Member of the bird order Piciformes. They are characterized by their backwards-pointing first and fourth toes. The order includes WOODPECKERS, TOUCANS, BARBETS and HONEYGUIDES. Most species nest in holes in trees and eat insects and fruit. Length: to 61cm (24in).

pickerel
Predatory freshwater fish of the Northern Hemisphere, related to the MUSKELLUNGE and PIKE. It has an elongated snout and a forked tail; its dorsal and anal fins are placed far back on the body. Family Esocidae; genus *Esox*.

P

Photosynthesis is the chemical process occurring in green plants, algae and many bacteria by which water and carbon dioxide are converted into food and oxygen using energy absorbed from sunlight. There are two distinct stages of photosynthe-

sis: LIGHT-DEPENDENT REACTION and DARK REACTION (light-independent reaction). In green plants and algae, photosynthesis takes place in the CHLOROPLASTS, which are miniature solar converters inside the plant's cells. Chloroplasts contain the green pigment CHLOROPHYLL, which, during the first part of the process, absorbs light and splits water into hydrogen and oxygen. The hydrogen attaches to a carrier molecule and the oxygen is set free. The hydrogen and light energy build a supply of cellular chemical energy, ADENOSINE TRIPHOSPHATE (ATP). In the dark reaction, hydrogen and ATP, by a process called the

CALVIN CYCLE, convert the carbon dioxide into sugars, including glucose and starch.

Sugars are used by the plant as fuel for RESPIRATION, which generates chemical energy in MITOCHONDRIA to power biochemical reactions essential for survival and growth. Respiration also produces carbon dioxide (CO_2) as a waste product, which can then be used again for photosynthesis. The products of photosynthesis also represent the starting point for the formation of other simple organic molecules. These can then be combined into larger molecules, such as proteins, nucleic acids, polysaccharides and lipids, from which all living material is made. Plants generally store food in the form of sucrose, a compound of the sugars glucose and fructose, together with starch. See also AUTOTROPH

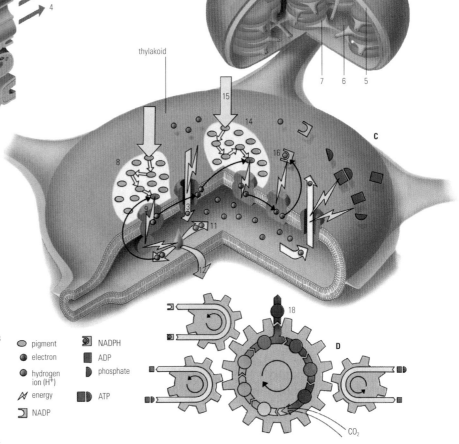

waxy cuticle
epidermal cells
chloroplasts
A
2
nucleus
thylakoid
B
7 6 5
C
3
3
4
4
15
14
8
16
9
10
11
12
13
17
18
D
CO_2

pigment
electron
hydrogen ion (H^+)
energy
NADP
NADPH
ADP
phosphate
ATP

▲▶ **Carbon dioxide (CO_2)** and water are the inorganic raw materials of photosynthesis. They arrive at a leaf's photosynthesizing cells by different routes (A): CO_2 gas simply diffuses in via pores in the leaf stomata (1) and through the air spaces between the loosely packed cells of the leaf mesophyll (2); water is drawn up from the roots through a system of woody xylem vessels (3). The products of photosynthesis – simple water-soluble sugars – are loaded into phloem sieve tubes and distributed throughout the plant (4). Photosynthesis in a plant cell takes place within structures (organelles) called chloroplasts (B). Each chloroplast is bounded by a double membrane (5) that encloses a dense fluid known as the stroma (6). A third system of membranes within the chloroplast forms an interconnected set of flat, disc-shaped sacs called thylakoids (7), which are frequently stacked on top of one another to form struc-

tures called grana. The chloroplasts contain photosynthetic pigments, the most important of which is chlorophyll. This pigment absorbs light primarily in the blue, violet and red parts of the spectrum. Green light is not absorbed: it is because this light is reflected that leaves appear green. Photosynthesis involves a complex series of chemical reactions: for the sake of convenience, these are usually divided into the light-dependent reactions, which occur on the thylakoid membrane, and light-independent reactions (dark reactions), which take place in the stroma.
In the light-dependent reaction of photosynthesis (C), sunlight energy is trapped by chlorophyll and converted first into electrical, then into chemical energy, which is temporarily "stored" in the compounds ATP and NADPH. These compounds are later used as "fuel" to power the light-independent fixation of CO_2 into sugars. All the chemical equipment needed for the light-dependent reac-

tion is located on the thylakoid membrane.
Light-trapping pigments, including chlorophyll, are grouped together on the outer wall of the thylakoid sac into units called photosystems (8). When light strikes a pigment molecule, one of its electrons becomes "energized" and is passed through the photosystem to an electron carrier in the membrane (9). Having lost an electron, the photosystem is left with a net positive

charge: it is resupplied with electrons by the splitting of water (H_2O) (10), which also releases hydrogen ions (H^+) into the thylakoid sac (11), and liberates gaseous oxygen (O_2) (12). The energized electron is passed to another carrier in the thylakoid membrane: in this process, some of its energy is used to "pump" more H^+ into the thylakoid sac (13). The electron passes through a second photosystem (14): this absorbs more light (15),

boosting the electron's energy level. The re-energized electron is now passed through other electron carriers, giving up some of its energy on the way to fuel the formation of NADPH from NADP and hydrogen ions (16). The result is that the H^+ concentration within the thylakoid sac rises to more than 1000 times that in the stroma, generating a chemical pressure. H^+ can only "leak" back into the stroma through special membrane-spanning

turbines – ATP synthetase enzymes (17). As H^+ passes through these it drives the synthesis of ATP from ADP and phosphate, as in cell mitochondria.
The "energy-rich" compounds ATP and NADPH are then used to power the formation of sugar in the light-independent reactions in the stroma (D). CO_2 is bound to a series of intermediate compounds, using energy along the way, before being released as a sugar (18).

P

piculet

Tiny WOODPECKER found in South America. It clings to and moves along the thinnest of branches. The piculet often feeds on the ground, with its stumpy tail cocked like a wren. Despite its size, it can drum loudly. Length: 10cm (4in). Family Picidae; genera *Picumnus*, *Sasia* and *Nesoctites*.

piddock

Any member of the family Pholadidae, a group of marine, bivalve MOLLUSCS found worldwide. Most species are found in the intertidal zone. The piddock is distinguished by its ability to bore into rock. It does this by moving its serrated shells back and forth, wearing a hole that enlarges to a comma-shape as the animal grows. Family Pholadidae; species include *Pholas dactylus*.

piedmont

Describing the foot of a mountain or a place where GLACIERS merge. The term is used of areas near mountains, such as the Piedmont (It. *Piemonte*) region in N Italy or the Piedmont Plateau to the east of the Appalachian Mountains in the United States. A piedmont glacier is formed when two or more glaciers flow from their valleys onto a plain and merge with their neighbours.

pig

Stocky animal with short legs, a bristly coat and a long face; it is found in forested areas of the Old World. There are eight species. Pigs have a flattened, mobile snout, with which they grub in the soil for food. They will eat almost anything they can find, including roots, fruit, fungi and small animals. The upper canine teeth grow outwards and upwards to form tusks. There are four hoofed toes on each foot, but only the middle two touch the ground. Family Suidae.

pig, bush- (red river hog)

Pig from s Africa. It is reddish with a white dorsal stripe and a black top-knot. Head-body length: 100–150cm (40–60in); tail: 40cm (16in). Family Suidae; species *Potamochoerus porcus*.

pig, Celebes (wild pig)

Small pig found in tropical forest of Sulawesi. It has well-developed facial warts. Family Suidae; species *Sus celebensis*.

pig, Javan (warty pig)

Species of pig found in Indonesia. As its alternative name suggests, it has wart-like growths all over its face. Head-body length: 90–160cm (35–63in). Family Suidae; species *Sus verrucosus*.

pigeon

Any member of the family Columbidae, a group of medium-sized land birds. The smaller species are called DOVES and the larger ones pigeons, but there is no real distinction. Pigeons are often soberly coloured grey, and some have iridescent green or purple neck patches. They are powerful flyers. Pigeons have small bills and a crooning or cooing voice. Family Columbidae.

pigeon, band-tailed

Pigeon common in pine and oak highlands of South America. It is greyish with claret-coloured underparts and a broad, pale band at the end of its tail. It has a white crescent on its neck above an iridescent green patch. Length: 32cm (13in). Family Columbidae; species *Columba fasciata*.

pigeon, feral (domestic pigeon)

Familiar pigeon found in towns and cities worldwide, often in huge flocks. Its plumage is varied, but it is usually a mixture of white, grey, brown, cinnamon or black. It probably originated from the rock dove, but, owing to interbreeding, pure colonies of its ancestor are now rare. Family Columbidae; species *Columba livia*.

pigeon, green imperial

Large pigeon found in moist tropical forests in Southeast Asia. It has metallic green upperparts, a maroon under tail and a stone-grey head, neck and belly. It is rather solitary and keeps to the tops of trees. Length: 43–47cm (17–19in). Subfamily Treroninae; species *Ducula aenea*.

pigeon, rock

African pigeon with white-spotted, russet upperparts and a red facial mask. It is not the same species as the rock dove. Flocks of rock pigeons inhabit cliffs, mineshafts, road bridges and caves, often making lengthy daily flights to water and to feed. Length: 33cm (13in). Family Columbidae; species *Columba guinea*.

pigeon, white-crowned

Large, blackish, square-tailed pigeon found in s

domestic homing pigeon

Victoria crowned pigeon

▲ **pigeon** The Victoria crowned pigeon (*Goura victoria*) is native to the island of New Guinea. A large bird, the size of a turkey, it is strikingly different in appearance from other pigeon species. It is found in forested areas, where it feeds on fruits and insects. The domestic homing pigeon (*Columba livia*) can successfully navigate its way home from hundreds of kilometres away, and from sites never previously visited. It is thought to use the stars to navigate at night, while during the day it relies on the position of the Sun. Experiments have also shown that homing pigeons have a navigational back-up, using the Earth's magnetic fields.

P

▲ **pika** Usually found in rocky areas, pikas occupy cavities in the rocks or, if necessary, dig burrow systems. They have much shorter ears than their relatives, the hares and rabbits, and as a result their hearing is less acute. They prefer to stay close to their burrows so that they can hide from predators.

United States and Central America, from the Florida Everglades to Honduras. It has a white crown and a small, iridescent green collar, which is barely visible. Flocks of white-crowned pigeons commute from nests in coastal mangroves to feed inland on fruit. Length: 34cm (13in). Family Columbidae; species *Columba leucocephala*.

pigfish
Marine fish of the Southern Hemisphere. It tends to be a bottom-dweller, living in depths of up to 500m (1640ft). The pigfish has a prominent dorsal fin. Family Congiopodidae.

pigmentation
Natural chemical that gives colour to animal TISSUE. In humans, the skin, hair and the IRIS of the eye are coloured by the pigment melanin. HAEMOGLOBIN in erythrocytes (red blood cells) also acts as a pigment.

pig-nut (earth-nut, hog-nut)
Slender, perennial European plant of the CARROT family; its name derives from its edible TUBER. It has small white flowers and complex divided leaves. Height: to 1m (39in). Family Umbelliferae; species *Conopodium majus*.

pigweed
See GOOSEFOOT

piha
Any of a small group of tropical perching birds belonging to the COTINGA family. They are found in Central and South America. Most species are dark reddish-brown above and paler brown below, especially on the throat and belly. Their loud whistling call is a familiar sound in humid rainforests. Length: 18–24cm (7–9in). Family Cotingidae; genera *Lipaugus* and *Chirocylla*.

pika
Small mammal with rounded ears and short legs; they are almost tailless. Pikas look like cavies but are actually relatives of the RABBIT. They live near mountain screes or in desert burrows. Agile, diurnal creatures, they feed on plant material and, like rabbits, they eat their own faeces (a habit known as refection) to increase the efficiency of their digestion. There are *c*.12 species in Eurasia and two in North America. Head-body length: 18–20cm (7–8in). Family Ochotonidae.

pika, large-eared
Pika that lives high in the Nepalese Himalayas. It has the largest ears of all pikas. Family Ochotonidae; species *Ochotona macrotis*.

pika, North American
Pika that is distinguished by the long calls it utters to advertise its territory and the short calls it makes to warn of danger. It gathers grass in autumn and makes haystacks for winter fodder. Family Ochotonidae; species *Ochotona princeps*.

pike
Predatory freshwater fish found in temperate regions of Europe, Asia and North America. It is related to the PICKEREL and the MUSKELLUNGE. The pike has a shovel-shaped mouth, with huge teeth in the lower jaw. It has a mottled, elongated body. The pike is a voracious predator. Length: to 137cm (54in). Family Esocidae; genus *Esox*.

pike perch
Any of several species of predatory freshwater fish found in the Northern Hemisphere. The pike perch is more elongated than the PERCH, to which it is related. Pike perch are usually green or grey in colour. The European pike perch is known as the ZANDER. Length: to 90cm (35in). Family Percidae; genus *Stizostedion*.

pilchard
Marine food fish belonging to the HERRING family. It is found in shoals along most coasts except those of Asia. Pilchards support a huge canning industry. They are a type of SARDINE. Length: to 46cm (18in). Family Clupeidae; species *Sardina pilchardus*.

pillow lava
LAVA that has occurred when MAGMA is expelled under water, or when it flows into water before solidifying. It commonly takes the form of a distorted globular mass that resembles the shape of a pillow. Pillow lava apparently results from the rapid chilling of the outer skin, thus making a more or less spherical "balloon" that grows and flattens under its own weight.

pilotbird
Plump, tame ground bird. It has brown plumage with a scaled pattern. It constantly flicks its tail, which is held high. The pilotbird's name comes from its habit of accompanying the superb LYREBIRD, snapping-up some of the insects and grubs it uncovers. (PILOT FISH behave in the same way with sharks.) Length:

▲ **pike** The elongated body of the pike is camouflaged by the dense colonies of plants among which it lives. It darts out to attack and devour fish, waterfowl and even small mammals. Its large mouth bears backward-curving, sharp teeth from which no prey can escape once caught.

17cm (7in). Family Acanthizidae; species *Pycnoptilus floccosus*.

pilot fish
Marine fish that lives in warm seas. It is often found swimming close to sharks, ships and other large objects, probably in order to feed on discarded food. Pilot fish are blue, with between five and seven dark bar markings on the sides and a white tail. They feed on smaller fish. Length: to 60cm (24in). Family Carangidae; species *Naucrates ductor*.

pimento
See ALLSPICE

pimpernel
Any member of the genus *Anagallis*, a group of small, trailing annual plants, native to Britain and the United States. The single, small, five-petalled flowers are scarlet, white or blue. *Lysimachia nemorum*, a creeping European plant of shady areas, is inaccurately known as the yellow pimpernel; it is actually a LOOSESTRIFE. Family Primulaceae.

▼ **pillow lava** When a lava flow enters the sea it breaks up into a number of globular structures. These structures may come to rest piled on top of one another. The same formation occurs if magma is expelled directly into the sea

► **pine** The lodgepole pine (*Pinus contorta*) grows in w North America, reaching a height of 18m (60ft). It is a small, vigorous mountain tree, hardy to an altitude of 3500m (11,000ft).

pine

Any member of the genus *Pinus*, a large and economically important group of evergreen, resinous and cone-bearing trees widely distributed in the Northern Hemisphere. *Pinus sylvestris* (SCOTS PINE), *Pinus resinosa* (red pine) and *Pinus ponderosa* (Ponderosa pine) are sources of commercial timber. *Pinus pinaster* (Maritime pine) is a source of turpentine. Edible nuts are obtained from *Pinus cembroides* (PIÑON PINE). Pinus mugo (mountain pine) is of value as an ornamental. *Pinus radiata* (Monterey pine) and *Pinus nigra* (Austrian pine) are planted as windbreaks. There are many other uses. Family Pinaceae.

pineapple

Tropical, herbaceous, perennial plant that is commonly cultivated in the United States, South America, Asia, Africa and Australia; it is also the name for the fruit of the plant. The pineapple fruit is formed from the flowers and bracts; it grows on top of a short, stout stem, which bears stiff, fleshy leaves. Height: to 1.2cm (4ft). Family Bromeliaceae; species *Ananas comosus*.

pine chafer

Any member of the genus *Polyphylla*, a group of BEETLES that chew on pine needles. The female pine chafer lays eggs in light sandy soil; the larvae then feed on the roots of grasses. After emergence, adults communicate by rubbing the tips of their wing-cases on their abdomens, producing loud screeching sounds. Adult body size: *c.*20mm (*c.*0.8in). Order Coleoptera; family Scarabidae; genus *Polyphylla*.

pinecone fish

Any of four species of small, deepwater marine fish. It is characterized by heavy, plate-like scales covering its oval body. It has bioluminescent light organs on its lower jaw. Family Monocentridae.

pine marten

See MARTEN, PINE

pingo

Cone-shaped mound that stands alone and has a core of ice. It is formed when freezing water expands and is forced upwards. Pingos are generally found in areas of PERMAFROST, where water cannot reach the surface and therefore pushes up the ground as it freezes. Pingos may be up to 90m (330ft) high and 800m (2600ft) across.

pink

Common name for several genera of the family Caryophyllaceae, especially those of the genus *Dianthus*. Most pinks are short, herbaceous perennials; many species are hardy evergreens with showy, fragrant flowers. The leaves are simple and usually opposite; the symmetrical flowers are usually bisexual. Family Caryophyllaceae. *See also* CARNATION; DIANTHUS

pinna (auricle)

In mammals, flap of skin and cartilage that comprises the visible, external part of the EAR. The pinna helps to collect sound waves and direct them into the ear canal.

pinocytosis

Intake and transport of fluid by living CELLS. Rather than entering and passing through the cell membrane as individual molecules, a droplet becomes bound to the membrane. A pocket then forms, which pinches off to form a vesicle in the CYTOPLASM. The vesicle may then pass across to the far side of the cell, where reverse pinocytosis occurs. It is a type of ENDOCYTOSIS.

piñon pine (Mexican stone pine)

Evergreen PINE tree found in Mexico and sw United States. Its large, edible seeds are commonly called pine nuts. Height: to 7.6m (25ft). Family Pinaceae; species *Pinus cembroides*.

pintail

Elegant DUCK with a long neck and elongated central tail feathers. The male has a grey body, with a distinctive, chocolate-brown head and a white breast and neck stripe. It breeds on tundra and moorlands and in coniferous forests of North America and Asia; it winters farther south. Length: 51–66cm (20–26in). Family Anatidae; species *Anas acuta*.

pipefish

Any of numerous species of marine fish found in the shallow, warm and temperate waters of the Atlantic and Pacific oceans. Related to the SEAHORSE, it has a pencil-like body. Its mouth is at the end of a long snout. Length: to 58cm (23in). Family Syngnathidae.

pipi (Goolwa cockle)

Bivalve MOLLUSC that burrows just below the surface of marine and estuarine sediments. It is highly sought after as a food resource. Its alternative name,

▲ **pineapple** Native to tropical and subtropical areas, the pineapple is now an important cash crop in many parts of the world. When the plant is about 15 months old an inflorescence develops. Violet flowers then appear, each blooming for only one day. The flowers then develop into small fruits, which combine with the stalk to form the pineapple.

◄ **pink** Deptford pink (*Dianthus armeria*) was once abundant in Deptford, s England, but it is now a threatened species in Britain due to habitat loss. It prefers dry grasslands, field borders and hedgerows. It has been introduced from Europe to North America, where it is quite widespread. Deptford pink reaches a height of 20–50cm (8–20in), with flowers *c.*1cm (*c.*0.5in) in diameter.

the Goolwa cockle, comes from the fact that it is widely harvested in the s Australian port town of Goolwa. Length: *c.*100mm (*c.*4in) Order Veneroida; family Donacidae; species *Donax deltoides*.

pipit

Any member of the genus *Anthus*, a group of brown, streaked, restless ground birds. Pipits are often difficult to identify apart from their calls and song. The meadow pipit (*Anthus pratensis*) is common throughout Europe. The tree pipit (*Anthus trivialis*) has a distinctive song delivered from a tree. The rock pipit (*Anthus petrosus*) is dark, lacking any white on its tail, and has a strident call. Family Motacillidae; genus *Anthus*.

piranha (piraya)

Tropical, bony, freshwater fish. It lives in rivers in South America. It is a voracious predator, with razor-sharp teeth and an aggressive temperament. Piranhas usually travel and attack in shoals and can pose a serious threat to creatures much larger than themselves. Length: to 61cm (24in). Family Characidae; genus *Serrasalmus*.

pirarucu

See ARAPAIMA

Pirie, Norman Wingate (1907–97)

British biochemist. In 1936, together with fellow British biochemist Frederick Bawden, he became the first scientist to crystallize a virus. This achievement had important repercussions on later research into the nucleic acids DNA and RNA. Pirie went on to study the subtle differences between living and non-living macromolecules. He wrote about the problems of population and food resources.

pistachio

Deciduous tree native to the Mediterranean region and E Asia. It is grown commercially for the edible greenish seed (the pistachio nut) of its wrinkled red fruit. Height: to 6m (20ft). Family Anacardiaceae; species *Pistacia vera*.

pistil

Female organ located in the centre of a FLOWER. It consists of an OVARY, a slender STYLE, and a STIGMA, which receives POLLEN.

pitchblende

See URANINITE

pitcher plant

Any of several species of INSECTIVOROUS PLANTS of

P

the tropics and subtropics. Insects are trapped in the vase-shaped, bristle-lined leaves. Trapped insects decompose and are absorbed as nutrients by plant cells. The flower is usually red. Height: 20–61cm (8–24in). Family Sarraceniacea; genera *Sarracenia* and *Nepenthes*.

pith

Central strand of parenchymatous tissue that occurs in the STEMS of most VASCULAR PLANTS. It is usually surrounded by vascular tissue and is believed to function chiefly for storage. The term is also used for the soft core at the centre of the heartwood of logs, consisting of the dried remains of the pith. *See also* PARENCHYMA

Pithecanthropus erectus

Old name for a FOSSIL of an early form of human found in Java in the 1930s. It is now generally recognized to be *Homo erectus*. *See also* HOMO

pitohui

Any member of the genus *Pitohui*, a group of birds found in the New Guinea region. They feed mainly on insects. Pitohuis make loud, whistling calls and long, trilling songs. Family Pachycephalidae; genus *Pitohui*; there are seven species.

pitta

Any member of the genus *Pitta*, a group of brilliantly coloured, medium-sized, ground-loving forest birds. They are stocky, with long legs and a short tail. The pitta forages for insects, flicking over leaf litter and damp earth. It is found in Africa, Asia and Australia. Several species, such as Gurney's pitta (*Pitta gurneyi*), are now seriously endangered as forests are felled. Family Pittidae; genus *Pitta*.

pituitary gland

Major gland of the ENDOCRINE SYSTEM located at the base of the BRAIN. In human beings it is about the size of a pea and is connected to the hypothalamus by a stalk. It produces many HORMONES, some of which regulate the activity of other endocrine glands, while others control growth.

placenta

Organ in PLACENTAL MAMMALS that connects the FETUS to the wall of its mother's UTERUS, providing a means of NUTRITION, GAS EXCHANGE and EXCRETION for the fetus. Part of the placenta contains tiny blood vessel branches through which oxygen and food are carried from the mother to the embryo, via the umbilical cord, and wastes are carried from the

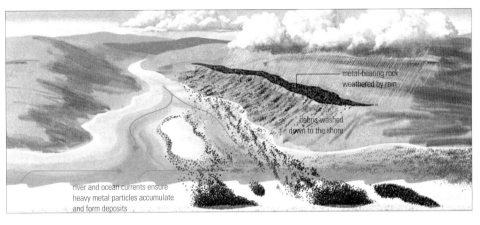
metal-bearing rock weathered by rain
debris washed down to the shore
river and ocean currents ensure heavy metal particles accumulate and form deposits

▲ placer deposits Most offshore minerals, with the exception of oil and gas, do not occur in sufficiently high-ore grades to warrant their economic production. Nevertheless significant amounts of tin, diamonds, gold and titanium are recovered from beach and offshore placer deposits all over the world. Sulphur is extracted commercially in a number of areas, including the Gulf of Mexico. The most important mineral resources after oil and gas are sand and gravel dredged from offshore deposits for use in the construction industry. Placer deposits occur where metal-bearing rock on land is weathered and the debris produced is washed down to the sea by rivers. There it is sorted by the currents, waves and tides so that the heavy metal particles accumulate to form deposits of mineral sand. These typically take the form of beach deposits, but where the sea level has changed they can be found well out on the continental shelf. The sands are lifted by dredgers and sifted for their metal content.

embryo to the mother's bloodstream to be excreted. The placenta secretes HORMONES that maintain pregnancy. It is discharged from the mother's body as the afterbirth, immediately after delivery.

placental mammals

MAMMALS whose young develop to an advanced stage attached to the PLACENTA – a life-support organ inside the mother's UTERUS. All mammals except the MONOTREMES and most MARSUPIALS are placentals. *See also* VIVIPARITY

placer deposits

Concentrations of heavy minerals formed by the action of gravity, usually found in streams. Minerals that occur as placer deposits include gold, copper, rutile, cassiterite and magnetite.

placoderm

Any member of an extinct group of primitive jawed fish that existed in the DEVONIAN period. They were characterized by armoured plates on the front part of the body. Most placoderms were quite small, but some grew to lengths of 9m (30ft).

plagioclase

Type of FELDSPAR (the most abundant group of minerals on Earth). Plagioclase minerals are widely distributed and occur in many IGNEOUS ROCKS and METAMORPHIC ROCKS. Off-white, or sometimes pink, green or brown in colour, they are composed of varying proportions of the silicates of sodium and calcium with aluminium. They show an oblique cleavage and have triclinic system crystals. Hardness 6–6.5; r.d. 2.6.

plaice

Marine FLATFISH found along the w European coast. An important food fish, it is brown or grey with orange spots. Length: to 90cm (35in). Family Pleuronectidae; species *Pleuronectes platessa*.

plain

Large area of flat or slightly undulating, low-lying land. Some plains, such as a PENEPLAIN, result from the wearing away of higher terrain. Most plains result from deposition of SEDIMENTS, as by rivers and lakes, which leave flat plains when the water dries up. FLOODPLAINS are formed in river valleys (*see* ALLUVIAL FAN). Glacial plains are large, level areas of TILL, which is left by retreating GLACIERS.

plains-wanderer

Upright, long-legged, quail-like, Australian bird. It has an oddly angular head. The plains-wanderer is mottled brown, with a black spotted neck and chestnut breast band. It runs through grass like a rat, stands tiptoe for a better view and then crouches motionless. The female is larger than the male. Length: 13–18cm (5–7in). Family Pedionomidae; species *Pedionomus torquatus*.

planarian

FLATWORM found in marine and fresh water. It is characterized by a triangular head with two light-sensitive eyespots. Planarians have flat, tail-like bodies, with extendable pharynxes for sucking in food. Reproduction is hermaphroditic or by asexual splitting or regeneration. Length: 2–16mm (0.08–0.6in). Phylum Platyhelminthes; class Turbellaria; genera include *Dugesia* and *Polycelis*.

plane

Deciduous tree found from SE Europe to India and North America. It has palmately lobed leaves. The flowers grow in dense, spherical clusters, two or more together on a hanging stalk. The bark peels away in large flakes. The London plane, believed to be of hybrid origin, is widely used for street and park plantings. Family Platanaceae; genus *Platanus*.

planigale (flat-skulled marsupial mouse)

Any of five species of MARSUPIAL MOUSE found in Australia and New Guinea. Planigales inhabit both woodland and grassland, where they hunt insects and small vertebrates. Head-body length: 5–10cm (2–4in); tail: 5–9cm (2–4in). Family Dasyuridae; genus *Planigale*.

plankton

All the floating or drifting life of open waters, especially that near the surface. The organisms are very small or microscopic and move with the currents. There are two main kinds: PHYTOPLANKTON, which comprises the floating plants such as DIATOMS and DINOFLAGELLATES; and ZOOPLANKTON, floating ani-

▲ piranha The red piranha (*Serrasalmus natterei*) is notorious for its ferocity. Its powerful jaws have sharp teeth, and it makes up for its relatively small size – 35cm (14in) – by swimming in shoals that are large enough to represent a threat to larger fish, land animals, and even humans. They feed in bouts, rather than continuously, and use their sense of smell to locate their prey.

P

mals such as radiolarians, plus the larvae and eggs of larger marine animals.

plant

Any member of the KINGDOM Plantae, a large kingdom of multicellular organisms, the cells of which have CELLULOSE cell walls and contain CHLOROPLASTS or similar structures (PLASTIDS). Plants develop from DIPLOID embryos and have a regular alternation of HAPLOID and diploid generations in their life cycles. Most plants are green, contain chloroplasts and make their own food by PHOTOSYNTHESIS. A few are colourless PARASITES or SAPROPHYTES. Simple plants reproduce by means of SPORES, whereas more advanced plants produce SEEDS and FRUITS. Plants show a wide range of biochemistry; some produce chemicals such as ALKALOIDS, narcotics and even poisons such as cyanide; others secrete substances into the soil to prevent other plants growing near them. Many of these chemicals form the bases for the development of drugs. Plants are classified on the basis of their MORPHOLOGY (shape and structure). The most important phyla are the Bryophyta (BRYOPHYTES), which include the MOSSES and LIVERWORTS; Lycopodophyta (LYCOPODOPHYTES); Sphenophyta (HORSETAILS); Filicinophyta (FERNS); Cycadophyta (CYCADS); Ginkgophyta (GINKGO); Coniferophyta (CONIFERS); and Angiospermophyta (ANGIOSPERMS). *See also* ALTERNATION OF GENERATIONS

plantain

Any plant of the genus *Plantago*, characterized by a rosette of basal leaves and spikes of tiny, greenish-white flowers. It grows in temperate regions and has been used for medicinal purposes. Family Plantaginaceae. The name **plantain** is also given to a species of tropical BANANA plant believed to be native to SE Asia and now cultivated throughout the tropics. It produces green fruits, which are larger and starchier than bananas. It is eaten cooked. Height: to 10m (33ft). Family Musaceae; species *Musa paradisiaca*.

plantain-lily

See HOSTA

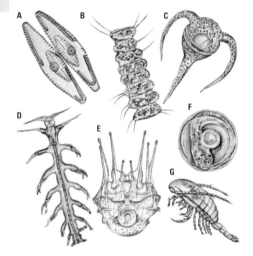

▲ **plankton** The upper levels of fresh and marine waters contain plankton. Phytoplankton includes diatoms (A), green algae (B) and dinoflagellates (C). These single cells often cling together in chains. Using minerals from the water and the Sun's energy, plants act as primary producers of food. Zooplankton includes fish eggs (F) and small animals such as worms (D), copepods (G) and larvae (E). Plankton is eaten by many other creatures and is the base of marine and freshwater ecosystems.

plant classification

System devised to group PLANTS according to relationships among them. The currently accepted system of plant classification includes the following phyla: Bryophyta, Lycopodophyta, Sphenophyta, Filicinophyta, Cycadophyta, Ginkgophyta, Coniferophyta and Angiospermophyta. An older system split plants into four divisions: Thallophyta (ALGAE and LICHENS), Pteridophyta (CLUB MOSSES and FERNS), Spermotophyta (which included the gymnosperms and ANGIOSPERMS) and Bryophyta (LIVERWORTS and MOSSES). *See also* TAXONOMY

plantcutter

Any of three species belonging to the family Phytotomidae, a group of South American, scrub-dwelling birds. The plantcutter has a long tail and a serrated beak, which it uses to cut off pieces of plant. Length: 20cm (8in). Family Phytotomidae; genus *Phytotoma*.

plant fibres

In general usage, any of the structural tissues of a plant. Specifically, the elongated SCLERENCHYMA cells used to provide mechanical strength in mature stems of plants. *See also* COLLENCHYMA; PARENCHYMA; PHLOEM; XYLEM

plant genetics

Science of HEREDITY and VARIATION in plants. Research in GENETICS since 1900 has supplied the principles of plant breeding, especially HYBRIDIZATION – the controlled crossing of plant varieties in order to reproduce new and improved plants. Breeders can select for specific characteristics, such as resistance to disease, or size and quality of yield. The development of consistently reliable and healthy first-generation crosses (**F1 hybrids**) has revolutionized the growing of food crops, ornamental annuals and bedding plants. Genetic engineers grow CELL and TISSUE CULTURES by the replication or cloning of sterile plant types. They also concentrate on isolating individual GENES with the aim of producing new colour varieties for traditional flowers, improving the flavour of food crops, breeding resistance to pests and HERBICIDES, and lengthening the shelf life of harvested crops. *See also* CLONE; GENETIC ENGINEERING

planthopper

Insect that eats plant juice and excretes honeydew, which is a food source for many other insects. Adult planthoppers are easily identified by the presence of hollow, enlarged head extensions, which, in some species, for example the LANTERN FLY, are luminous. Adult body size: 10–50mm (0.4–2in), depending on the ambient temperature. Order Homoptera; family Fulgoroidae.

plant hormone (phytohormone)

Organic chemical produced in plant cells and functioning at various sites to affect plant growth, leaf and fruit drop, healing, cambial growth and, possibly, flowering. HORMONES are transported away from the STEM tip. They include abscisic acid (leaf fall), AUXINS (growth), CYTOKININS (leaf and bud growth and development) and GIBBERELLINS (growth). *See also* ABSCISSION

plant louse

Any member of the APHID family Aphididae. Plant lice are winged or wingless, soft-bodied insects found throughout the world. They transmit viral diseases of plants when sucking plant juices. Females reproduce with or without mating, producing one to

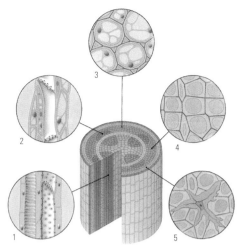

▲ **plant fibres** Wide, elongated xylem cells (1) have thickened, rigid cell walls. Aligned end to end they form hollow vessels to carry water and minerals from the roots to the growing shoots. Unlike xylem, phloem (2) cells are alive when mature. These highly specialized cells form structures known as sieve tubes, which together with small companion cells actively transport dissolved sugars to wherever they are needed. Much plant tissue is composed of polygonal, thin-walled parenchyma cells (3), which can take on a variety of functions, including photosynthesis, sugar storage and support, depending on their location in the plant body. Collenchyma (4) and sclerenchyma (5) are simple tissues, the cells of which have thick walls and thus help to support the plant.

several generations annually. Common species are also known as blackfly (*see* APHID, BEAN) and greenfly. Length: to 5mm (0.2in). Order Hemiptera; family Aphididae.

plant morphology

Study of form and structure of PLANTS, especially external shape.

plant physiology

Study of the functions and activities of PLANTS. It covers a wide range of processes including PHOTOSYNTHESIS, TRANSPIRATION and RESPIRATION.

plant pigment

Organic compound that is present in plant CELLS and tissues that colours the plant. The most common plant pigment is green CHLOROPHYLL, which exists in all higher plants. Carotenoids colour plants yellow to tomato red. Located in CHLOROPLASTS and chromoplasts are more than 150 varieties of these durable pigments. Many are essential to PHOTOSYNTHESIS and are a source of vitamin A. Anthocyanins, responsible for pink, red, blue and purple, are found in the cell SAP. The shorter days and lower temperatures of autumn cause these plant pigments to combine with other substances to produce the brilliant foliage colours of deciduous trees. *See also* PHYTOCHROME

plant response

Ability of plants to react to certain stimuli. Although plants do not possess any contractile tissue such as muscle, their survival can still depend on their ability to move toward certain stimuli, such as light and water. These movements are usually gradual and are the result of growth. *See also* TROPISM

plasma

Liquid portion of the BLOOD in which the CELLS are suspended. It contains an immense number of ions, inorganic and organic molecules such as

P

IMMUNOGLOBULINS, and HORMONES and their carriers. It clots on standing.

plasmid
Strand or loop of NUCLEIC ACID, containing GENETIC information. It can be introduced to a host CELL, where it will replicate independently of the host's CHROMOSOMES. Plasmids are used in RECOMBINANT DNA RESEARCH.

plasmodesmata
Extremely thin cytoplasmic threads that pass through the CELLULOSE cell walls of living plant CELLS. They form a link between the CYTOPLASM of adjacent cells, allowing substances to be exchanged between cells. Water and mineral ions can move throughout the plant in this way.

plasmodium
Any member of the genus *Plasmodium*, a group of parasitic PROTOZOA that cause malaria. Various plasmodium species infect the ERYTHROCYTES (red blood cells) of mammals, birds and reptiles worldwide. They are transmitted by the bite of a female *Anopheles* MOSQUITO.

plasmolysis
In plants, shrinkage of the cell PROTOPLAST away from the CELL wall due to the osmotic withdrawal of water from the central VACUOLE of the cell. This shrinkage occurs when a plant cell is surrounded by a solution that has a higher concentration of SOLUTES than the cell vacuole (that is, it is HYPERTONIC). When a plant cell is surrounded by a less concentrated solution (hypotonic), water enters by OSMOSIS and creates a PRESSURE POTENTIAL on the cell wall. The cell is said to be turgid. The point at which the protoplast just begins to separate from the cell wall is called **incipient plasmolysis**. *See also* WATER POTENTIAL

plastid
Type of ORGANELLE found in the CELLS of plants and green algae. Plastids have a double membrane and contain DNA. CHLOROPLASTS and leucoplasts are examples of plastids.

plate
See LITHOSPHERE

plateau
Fairly flat, raised area of land. Mountains may stand up above the general level of a plateau, or it may be carved by deep river valleys or canyons to form a **dissected plateau**. An **intermontane plateau** is completely surrounded by mountains.

plate collision
Process in PLATE TECTONICS whereby crustal plates are pushed together. Where oceanic CRUST meets continental crust the denser oceanic crust is SUBDUCTED. Where two continental plates collide there is crustal shortening and thickening, which results in mountain building (OROGENESIS).

platelet
Colourless, usually spherical structures found in mammalian BLOOD. Chemical compounds in platelets, known as factors and cofactors, are essential to the mechanism of blood clotting. The normal platelet count is about 300,000 per cu mm of blood.

plate tectonics
See feature article

platyhelminth
See FLATWORM

platypus
See feature article, page 298

▲ **plesiosaur** These marine reptiles occupied the seas at the time when dinosaurs, to which they were only distantly related, were dominant on land. Fossil remains of plesiosaurs indicate that they were very widely distributed.

Pleistocene
Sixth epoch of the CENOZOIC era of GEOLOGICAL TIME; it began about 2 million years ago. During the Pleistocene epoch, humans and most forms of familiar mammalian life evolved. Episodes of climatic cooling in this epoch led to widespread GLACIATION in the Northern Hemisphere; the Pleistocene is the best-known glacial period or ICE AGE in the Earth's history. The present HOLOCENE epoch succeeded the Pleistocene around 8000 BC.

plesiosaur
Member of an extinct group of large, marine reptiles (3–12m/10–39ft in length) that evolved in late Triassic times and died out in the late Cretaceous. They were mainly medium- to long-necked, fish-eating predators, such as *Plesiosaurus*, but there were also short-necked forms called pliosaurs, for example *Kronosaurus*, which was more than 12m (39ft) long with a 2.7m (8.9ft) skull.

PLATE TECTONICS

Theory or model to explain the distribution, evolution and causes of the EARTH's crustal features. It proposes that the Earth's CRUST and part of the upper MANTLE (the LITHOSPHERE) are made up of several separate rigid slabs, termed **plates**, which move independently and form part of a cycle in the creation and destruction of crust. The plates collide or move apart at the CONTINENTAL MARGINS, and these produce zones of EARTHQUAKE and volcanic activity. Three types of plate boundary can be identified. At a CONSTRUCTIVE MARGIN (or divergent margin), new basaltic MAGMA originating in the mantle is injected into the plate, which forces the crust to separate, and an oceanic ridge is formed. At a DESTRUCTIVE MARGIN (or convergent margin), plates collide and one plate moves into the mantle at the site of an oceanic TRENCH. The recycling of crust by SUBDUCTION results in the melting of some crustal material and volcanic island arcs (such as the islands of Japan) are produced. Material that cannot be subducted is scraped up and fused onto the edge of plates. This can form a new CONTINENT or add to existing continents. Mountain chains are explained as the sites of former subduction or continental collision. At a conservative margin, plates move past each other along a transform fault. Plate movement is thought to be driven by convection currents in the mantle. *See also* SEAFLOOR SPREADING

P

▶ **The discovery that** the continents are carried along on the top of slowly moving crustal plates provided the mechanism for continental drift theories to work. The plates converge and diverge along margins marked by seismic and volcanic activity. Plates diverge from mid-ocean ridges, where molten lava pushes up and forces the plates apart at a rate of up to 3.75cm (1.5in) a year. Converging plates form either a trench, where the oceanic plates sink below the lighter continental rock, or mountain ranges, where two continents collide.

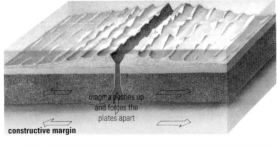

magma pushes up and forces the plates apart

constructive margin

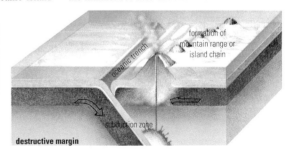

formation of mountain range or island chain

oceanic trench

subduction zone

destructive margin

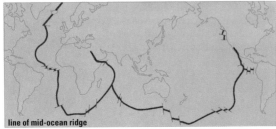

line of mid-ocean ridge

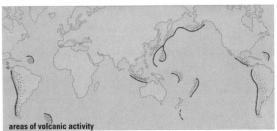

areas of volcanic activity

PLATYPUS

MONOTREME that inhabits freshwater streams and lakes in E Australia and Tasmania. Its extraordinary snout, which is shaped like a duck's bill, is covered with moist, sensitive skin. Adult platypuses are toothless, but they have horny plates with which they grind invertebrates and small fish. They construct burrows both for shelter and for nesting. Platy-

puses are capable of injecting venom by means of a horny spur on the back of the ankle. Length: 45–60cm (18–24in). The platypus is the sole member of the family Ornithorhynchidae. Species *Ornithorhynchus anatinus*.

▲ **The female playtpus** builds a winding tunnel system a short distance above the water level. There are often several side branches, designed to outwit predators. The nesting chamber is lined with gum leaves and kept moist and warm by the mother's fur. Usually two eggs are laid, which have soft, typically reptilian shells. Incubation last two weeks, during which the mother never leaves the nest. For defence, the male platypus has backward-facing hollow spines on each of its hind feet (shown far right).

pleura
Double membrane that lines the space between the LUNGS and the walls of the THORAX.

pleural cavity
Narrow space between the PLEURA of the lungs and the THORAX wall. It is filled with a fluid that acts as a lubricant, preventing friction when the lungs expand and contract during INSPIRATION and EXPIRATION.

Pliocene
Last epoch of the TERTIARY period. It lasted from 5 to 2 million years ago and preceded the PLEISTOCENE. Animal and plant life was similar to that of today.

plover
Any of numerous species of small- to medium-sized wading birds. When feeding, the plover runs for a short distance then stops to bob down and pick up food. Many species, such as the mountain plover (*Charadrius montanus*) and DOTTEREL, breed on short grasslands or tundra; other species, such as the ringed plovers (genus *Charadrius*), breed on seashores. When not breeding, plovers often form large flocks. Length: 15–30cm (6–12in). Family Charadriidae.

plover, blacksmith
Plover that is common along the shores of inland lakes and the margins of marshes in S Africa. It has striking black-and-white plumage, with grey wings and a grey back. Like many plovers, the blacksmith plover is noisy and conspicuous when disturbed. Length: 30cm (12in). Family Charadriidae; species *Vanellus armatus*.

plover, golden
Any member of the genus *Pluvialis*, a group of three very similar species distinguished by call, size and shape. In summer all are spangled golden above, with a black face, breast and belly and contrasting

white sides to the neck. Golden plovers breed on arctic heaths and moorland; they winter in flocks on fields. Length: 23–29cm (9–11in). Family Charadriidae; genus *Pluvialis*.

plover, grey
Large, plump plover. In summer, it is spangled grey above, with a black face and breast and contrasting white sides to its neck. In winter, it loses its black markings and in flight its black "armpits" become characteristic. The grey plover breeds on tundra and winters along shores, singly or in small groups. Length: 27–30cm (11–12in). Family Charadriidae; species *Pluvialis squatarola*.

plover, ringed
One of the most common shorebirds of the Northern Hemisphere. Its plumage is sandy-brown above, with a distinctive black-and-white head and breast pattern. Adults lure predators away from the nest by feigning a broken wing. It also nests inland along rivers and on marshes. Length: 20cm (8in). Family Charadriidae; genus *Charadrius*; species include *Charadrius hiaticula*.

plum
Any member of the genus *Prunus*, a group of fruit trees mostly native to Asia and naturalized in Europe and North America. Plum trees are widely cultivated for their fleshy, edible fruits, which have a hard "stone" at the centre. The most common cultivated plum of Europe and Asia is *Prunus domestica*; in North America, the Japanese plum (*Prunus salicina*) is crossed with European varieties to give several cultivated strains. Family Rosaceae.

plumbago
See GRAPHITE

plumule
In plants, embryonic shoot that develops during GERMINATION of a SEED.

plutonic
Describing a rock that has formed beneath the surface of the Earth. Plutonic rocks are coarse-grained IGNEOUS ROCKS consisting of solidified MAGMA, which has cooled slowly, allowing large crystals to form in the rock. The most common plutonic rock is GRANITE, which is light in colour because its mineral content is acidic. The most common of the basic plutonic rocks is GABBRO. Most plutonic rocks form in BATHOLITHS beneath the surface, but because of the EROSION of overlying rocks, they are now commonly found on the surface.

pochard
Any of several species of diving DUCK. The male is grey with a rounded, chestnut head and black breast; the female is grey-brown. In winter, pochards form large mixed flocks with other diving ducks on reservoirs and freshwater lakes. The red-crested pochard (*Netta rufina*) has a crested chestnut head, black breast and a red bill; it is widely kept in wildfowl collections. Family Anatidae; species include *Aythya ferina*.

pocket mouse
See MOUSE, POCKET

pod
Fruit of any leguminous plant, such as a PEA or BEAN. A pod is an elongated case-like structure filled with SEEDS. It develops from a single CARPEL, and when ripe it splits down both sides to release the seeds. In some plants, the pods burst explosively, scattering the seeds widely. See also LEGUME

podzol
Light-coloured, infertile SOIL, poor in lime and iron. The name comes from the Russian word for "ash soil". It forms under cool, humid conditions and is typical of the taiga forests of North America and Eurasia. The upper layer is light grey. The lower layer is darker and contains HUMUS and minerals, such as alumina, iron and lime, that have been leached out of the upper layer by rainfall. The minerals form a hard layer that is impervious to water and prevents good drainage. See also LEACHING

pogonophoran (beardworm)
Any member of the phylum Pogonophora, which comprises *c*.80 known species of sedentary, worm-like, marine invertebrates. Pogonophorans inhabit chitinous tubes on the seafloor. Their bodies are divided into three regions: the protosome, bearing tentacles; a short mesosome; and a long trunk or metasome. Length: to 50cm (20in). Phylum Pogonophora.

poikilothermic
See ECTOTHERMIC

poinsettia
Ornamental shrub, native to Mexico. It has tapering

◀ **plum** The common European plum tree (*Prunus domestica*) is a hardy tree that thrives in temperate regions of Europe and Asia. The species is thought to be at least 2000 years old and might be an ancient natural hybrid between two other fruits – the cherry plum and the sloe. Numerous varieties of *Prunus domestica* are cultivated worldwide for their edible fruits.

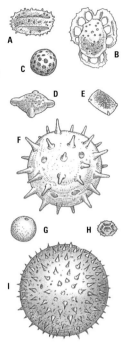

▶ **pollen** Pollen grains are found in flowers' pollen sacs, which are themselves located in the anthers (part of the stamens). Pollen grains are safe and effective stores of the male gametes (sex cells). They come in all shapes and sizes depending on the species of plant. The selection shows mistletoe (A), Venus flytrap (B), spinach (C), honeysuckle (D), touch-me-not (E), cotton (F), rice (G), dandelion (H) and hollyhock (I).

leaves and tiny, yellow flowers centred in leaf-like, red, white or pink bracts. It is a popular house plant. In its natural environment, the tree grows to *c*.5m (*c*.16ft). Height: to 60cm (24in) when potted. Family Euphorbiaceae; species *Euphorbia pulcherrima*.

poison ivy
Either of two species of North American shrubs that cause a severe itchy rash on contact with human skin. They have greenish flowers and white berries. Family Anarcardiacea; species *Rhus radicans* and *Rhus toxicodendron*.

pokeweed
Any member of the family Phytolaccaceae, comprising *c*.150 species of plants, most of which are native to tropical America. Included in the family are herbs, shrubs, trees and vines. They all have toothed, alternate leaves, stalked clusters of petal-less flowers, and either dry or fleshy fruit. The most common species, *Phytolacca americana*, has white flowers, reddish berries and red-veined leaves. Its poisonous root resembles a horseradish. It is found in wet or sandy parts of E North America. The berries are used to colour wine, candy and cloth. Family Phytolaccaceae.

polar bear
See BEAR, POLAR

pole
Generally either of the two points of intersection of the surface of a sphere and its axis of rotation. The Earth has four poles: the North and South geographic poles, where the Earth's imaginary axis meets its surface; and the north and south magnetic poles, where the Earth's MAGNETIC FIELD is most concentrated. A bar magnet has a north pole, where the magnetic flux leaves the magnet, and a south pole, where it enters. A pole is also one of the terminals (positive or negative) of a battery, electric machine, generator or circuit. *See also* GEOMAGNETISM; MAGNETISM

polecat
Any of several species of small, carnivorous, nocturnal mammals found in wooded areas of Eurasia and N Africa; especially *Mustela putorius*, the common polecat. It has a slender body, long bushy tail and

brown to black fur (known as fitch). The polecat eats small animals, birds and eggs. Length: 45cm (18in). Family Mustelidae.

pollack (pollock, saithe)
Marine food fish of the COD family. It is found in large shoals on both sides of the N Atlantic Ocean. The pollack's body is green with yellow or grey. It has a jutting lower jaw. Length: to 100cm (40in). Family Gadidae; species include *Pollachius pollachius* and *Pollachius virens.*

pollen
Powder-like SPORES, usually yellow in colour, that give rise to the male GAMETES (sex cells) in plants. In ANGIOSPERMS (flowering plants), pollen grains are produced in the ANTHERS on the STAMEN, whereas in CONIFEROPHYTES (cone-bearing plants), they are produced by the male cones. Pollen has thick resistant walls with a characteristic pattern of spines, plates or ridges, according to species. During POLLINATION, the pollen lands on the STIGMA of a flower, or a female cone, of a compatible plant. It germinates, sending a long pollen tube down through the STYLE to the OVARY. During this process, one of its nuclei divides, giving rise to two male nuclei, one of which will fuse with a female sex cell (actually a HAPLOID nucleus in the embryo sac inside the OVULE) in FERTILIZATION. The other male sex cell fuses with two more of the female nuclei to form a special tissue, the ENDOSPERM, the cells of which contain three sets of CHROMOSOMES (triploid). In many species, this tissue develops into a food store for the EMBRYO in the seed.

pollination
Transfer of POLLEN (containing male GAMETES) from the ANTHER to the STIGMA in ANGIOSPERMS (flowering plants), or from the male cone to the female cone in CONIFEROPHYTES (cone-bearing plants), resulting in FERTILIZATION. Pollination occurs mainly by wind (ANEMOPHILY) in the cases of most trees and coniferophytes, and by flying insects (ENTOMOPHILY) for angiosperms. Other agents of pollination include grazing mammals, birds, bats and non-flying insects. **Self-pollination** occurs when the pollen of one flower (or male cone) pollinates the same flower or another flower (female cone) of the same plant. However, plants have developed intricate incompatibility mechanisms to ensure self-pollination occurs as infrequently as possible, such as chemicals that make the pollen and eggs of the same plant sterile. CROSS-POLLINATION occurs between two flowers (or male and female cones) on different plants. It results in a great variety of genetic combinations, thereby improving the chances of survival. *See also* SEXUAL REPRODUCTION

polyanthus
Any of a group of spring-flowering, perennial PRIMROSES of the genus *Primula*. They are found mainly in temperate zones of the Northern Hemisphere. They have basal leaves and disc-shaped flowers, which may be almost any colour, branching from a stalk to form a ball-like cluster. Height: to 15cm (6in). Family Primulaceae.

polychaete
Any member of the class Polychaeta, comprising marine ANNELID worms characterized by distinctive segmentation of the body. The class includes RAGWORMS and BRISTLEWORMS. Polychaetes have a distinct head with sensory projections; most segments have outgrowths or bristles.

polymer
Substance formed by the union of from two to several thousand simple molecules (MONOMERS) to form a large molecular structure. Some polymers, such as CELLULOSE, occur in nature; others form the basis of the plastics and synthetic resin industry.

polymerase chain reaction (PCR)
Chemical reaction that is used to make large numbers of copies of a specific sequence of DNA, or part of a GENE, starting from only one or few DNA molecules. It is speeded up by the ENZYME DNA polymerase. The reaction enables scientists to make large enough quantities of DNA to be able to analyze it or manipulate it. The starting piece of DNA may be extracted from an organism, it may have been "designed" and synthesized in the laboratory, or it may be a forensic sample taken from the scene of a crime. PCR is extremely important in GENETIC ENGINEERING and genetic fingerprinting.

polymorphism
In mineralogy, the existence of a substance in two (dimorphic) or more crystal forms. Polymorphism is caused by different temperatures or pressures or both. The separate forms are called **polymorphs**; for example, DIAMOND and GRAPHITE are polymorphs of CARBON. Polymorphism of the elements is also known as allotropy. In biology and botany, polymorphism is the existence of two or more types of individual within a single SPECIES. For example, some social insects, such as the ANT and BEE, have several polymorphic types of worker adapted structurally to perform different tasks within their colony. Flowers can also assume more than one form.

polyp
Body type of various species of animals within the phylum Cnidaria. It has a mouth surrounded by extensible tentacles and a lower end that is adapted for attachment to a surface. It may be solitary, as in the sea ANEMONE, but it is more often an individual of a colonial organism such as CORAL.

P

polypeptide
Chemical that consists of a long chain of AMINO ACIDS linked by PEPTIDE bonds. PROTEINS are polypeptides.

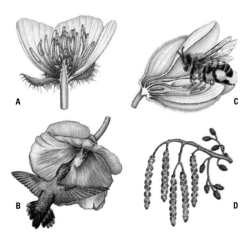

▲ **pollination** Flowers are adapted to different pollination methods. Non-specialized simple flowers, such as the buttercup (A), can be pollinated by a variety of means. Other flowers can only be pollinated by one method. There are bird-pollinated flowers, such as the hummingbird-pollinated hibiscus (B); bee-specialized flowers, including the gorse (C); and wind-pollinated flowers, such as the catkins found on the hazel (D).

polyploidy

State of a cell or nucleus that has more than two sets of CHROMOSOMES. More likely to occur in plants than in animals, polyploidy is found in many CEREALS. Polyploidy can be introduced artificially using chemicals to produce HYBRID plants with desirable characteristics, such as increased size and hardiness. *See also* DIPLOID; HAPLOID

polypore

Any member of a group of FUNGI that have fruiting bodies with a porous undersurface from which the spores are released. The fruiting body may consist of a definite cap and stem, or a flattened fan-like or rounded and convoluted cap with a small stem. Only some polypores are edible. Phylum Basidiomycota; genera *Polyporus* and *Coriolus*.

polysaccharide

Any of a group of complex CARBOHYDRATES made up of long chains of MONOSACCHARIDE (simple-sugar) molecules, often thousands of them. GLUCOSE is a MONOSACCHARIDE, and the polysaccharides STARCH and CELLULOSE are both POLYMERS of glucose. Higher carbohydrates are all polysaccharides and decompose by HYDROLYSIS into a large number of monosaccharide units. Polysaccharides function as both food stores (starch in plants and GLYCOGEN in animals) and as structural materials (cellulose and PECTIN in the cell walls of plants, and CHITIN in the protective skeleton of insects).

pomace fly

See FRUIT FLY

pome

Fleshy FRUIT formed from the flower RECEPTACLE or base. It is not developed from the CARPEL, and is therefore a PSEUDOCARP (false fruit). Familiar examples are the APPLE, PEAR and QUINCE.

pomegranate

Deciduous shrub or small tree native to W Asia and cultivated in warm regions worldwide. It has shiny, oval leaves and orange-red flowers. The round fruit has a red, leathery rind and numerous seeds that are coated with an edible pulp. Family Punicaceae; species *Punica granatum.*

pompano

Laterally compressed, deep-bodied, silvery marine fish; it is related to the JACK. The pompano is an important food fish of subtropical and tropical waters. Length: *c.*45cm (*c.*18in). Family Carangidae.

pond skater

See WATER STRIDER

pondweed

Any member of the genus *Potamogeton*, a group of aquatic, perennial flowering plants, native to temperate regions. They are found mostly in freshwater lakes, but also in brackish and salt water. Most pondweed species have spike-like flowers that stick

▶ **pomegranate** The flesh of the pomegranate (*Punica granatum*), a fruit about the size of an apple, is densely packed with seeds that scatter when the fruit is burst. The pale yellow seeds are surrounded by a bright red, fleshy coating, which has a refreshing, astringent flavour.

▶ **poppy** Cultivated since the Middle Ages, the opium poppy (*Papaver somniferum*) is the natural source of the drug opium and its derivatives, morphine and heroin. These are extracted from the latex of the seed pods. The seeds themselves are used as cattle food and as a source of oil. The dramatic flower makes the plant a popular ornamental.

out of the water; leaves can be submerged or floating. Family Potamogetonaceae; species include *Potamogeton crispus*.

poorwill

Any of several species belonging to the NIGHTJAR family, found in North and South America. The poorwill is named after its loud "*whip-poor-will*" song. It is smaller than most nightjars but has the same camouflaged plumage and nocturnal habits. Length: 25cm (10in). Family Caprimulgidae; genus *Caprimulgus*; species include *Caprimulgus vociferus* (WHIP-POOR-WILL).

poplar

Any of a number of deciduous, softwood trees of the genus *Populus*, native to cool and temperate regions. The oval leaves grow on stalks, and flowers take the form of catkins. Some species are called cottonwoods because of the cotton-like fluff on their seeds. Three species are called ASPEN. Height: to 60m (200ft). Family Salicaceae.

poppy

Any member of the genus *Papaver*, a large group of annuals and perennials, most of which are native to the Old World. Most poppy species contain a milky juice. They have lobed or dissected leaves and large red, orange, pink or white flowers, making them popular garden plants. Latex obtained from fruit capsules of the opium poppy, *Papaver somniferum*, is used as a source of ALKALOIDS for pharmaceutical preparations. Family Papaveraceae; genus *Papaver*.

porbeagle

Atlantic mackerel SHARK. The porbeagle is a large, predatory, oceanic shark. It has a symmetrical tail fin. It occupies the surface waters. The porbeagle is related to the mako shark. Family Lamnidae; species *Lamna nasus*.

porcupine

Stocky rodent with sharp spines. When threatened, the porcupine raises its spines, rattles its quills and grunts. Then it may turn away from its attacker and run backwards into it. The spines easily detach and remain embedded in the skin of the attacker, where they can cause fatal infections. Porcupines may damage crops. Families Hystricidae and Erethizontidae.

porcupine, African

Stocky animal that has a crest of long, upright, grey hairs on the top of its head and neck. Its back is covered with long, black-and-white spines and quills which can be rattled. Head-body length: 60–93cm (24–37in); tail: 8–17cm (3–7in). Family Hystricidae; species *Hystrix cristata*.

porcupine, brush-tailed

Either of two species of porcupine, one from central Africa and one from Asia. Both species have long

tails that end in a tuft of stiff, hollow hairs, which rustle as the animal moves. Long, slender, forest-dwelling animals, brush-tailed porcupines are covered with short, brown bristles with only a few long spines. They feed on a variety of fruits. Head-body length: 36–57cm (14–22in); tail: 10–26cm (4–10in). Family Hystricidae; genus *Atherurus*; species include *Atherurus macrourus* (Asiatic brush-tailed porcupine).

porcupine, Indian

Porcupine found from India and Kazakstan to the Arabian Peninsula. It has a long, erect mane, sharp spines, rattling quills and a short tail. It shelters in small groups in crevices or burrows by day and feeds alone on plant parts, insects and some carrion by night. Indian porcupines move with a shuffling gait but can cover 15km (9m) in one night. Head-body length: 60–93cm (24–37in); tail: 8–17cm (3–7in). Family Hystricidae; species *Hystrix indica*.

porcupine, tree

Any member of several genera of porcupines from North and South America, all of which are good tree climbers. They have spiny coats and long, often prehensile tails. Though short sighted, they have large brains and keen senses of hearing, smell and touch. Leaves form their basic diet, but they also eat shoots, roots, fruits and bark. Although the single, well-developed young can climb trees and feed on leaves just days after birth, they are suckled for about two months. Head-body length: 30–80cm (12–31in); tail: 7–45cm (3–18in). Family Erethizontidae; genera *Coendou* and *Sphiggurus*; species include *Sphiggurus spinosus* (South American tree-porcupine).

porcupinefish (burrfish)

Any member of the family Diodontidae, a group of fish found in subtropical and tropical marine waters. It is related to the PUFFERFISH and the FILEFISH. Its dark-spotted, brownish, inflatable body is covered by sharp spines. Its jaw has fused teeth. Length: to 90cm (35in). Family Diodontidae.

porgy

Deep-bodied fish found in temperate and tropical marine waters. The porgy is found especially in shallow waters where its shellfish prey are common. It has incisor-like front teeth and molar-like rear teeth. It is an important food and sport fish and is related to the pinfish, SEA BREAM and SHEEPSHEAD. Length: 30–120cm (12–47in). Family Sparidae.

poriferan

Any member of the phylum Porifera – the SPONGES.

▲ **porcupine** The Indian porcupine (*Hystrix indica*), as with all porcupines, is protected by its coat of spines, which it can erect when danger threatens. The spines are loosely attached and may become embedded in predators. Porcupines thrive in a wide variety of habitats, from semideserts, grasslands and scrub to woodlands.

Poriferans are many-celled, stationary animals; they remain permanently fixed to rocks. They feed by filtering food particles from the water.

porosity
Degree to which rock is capable of holding GROUNDWATER. The porosity depends on the numbers of AQUIFERS, cracks, fissures and holes present. Porosity is measured and expressed as a percentage of the rock's total volume. *See also* HYDROLOGY; PERMEABILITY

porphyry
Rock that contains large crystals (phenocrysts) in a fine-textured igneous matrix. They are found in both INTRUSIVE and EXTRUSIVE rocks. Different varieties are named after the phenocrysts.

porpoise
Any of a group of six species of small, toothed WHALE. Porpoises have rounded snouts, without a beak, and rather few teeth. They are sometimes seen breaking the surface of inshore waters, in small groups. Suborder Odontoceti (toothed whales); family Phocoenidae.

porpoise, common (harbour porpoise)
Porpoise that lives in shallow coastal waters of the N Pacific and N Atlantic oceans, and the Bering, Baltic, Mediterranean and Black seas. It is dark grey, with paler grey on the flanks and white beneath; there is a grey line from the flipper to the corner of the mouth. The dorsal fin is low with a concave trailing edge. Gregarious, sociable creatures, porpoises communicate vocally and come to each other's aid when in difficulty. They use echolocation to find herring and mackerel. Gestation is 11 months and calves are suckled for eight months; individuals live for 12–13 years. Head–tail length: 1.5–1.8m (5–6ft). Family Phocoenidae; species *Phocoena phocoena*.

porpoise, Dall's
Porpoise found in coastal and deep waters of the N Pacific Ocean and Bering Sea. Dall's porpoises are larger and heavier than other porpoises, with a small head and protruding lower jaw. They are black with white patches on the flanks, belly, fins and flukes. The tall dorsal fin often has a characteristic hooked tip. They feed on squid and fish. Gestation is 11.4 months and calves are suckled for two years; individuals live for more than 17 years. Head-body length: 1.7–2.2m (5.6–7.2ft). Family Phocoenidae; species *Phocoenoides dalli*.

porpoise, Gulf of California (cochito, "little pig")
Porpoise that lives in the Gulf of California. Its colouring is similar to that of the common porpoise, but it is a darker grey. It feeds on croakers and grunts. It is rare and classed as a vulnerable species. Head-body length: 1.2–1.5m (4–5ft). Family Phocoenidae; species *Phocoena sinus*.

porpoise, harbour
See PORPOISE, COMMON

porpoise, spectacled
Sleekest species of porpoise. It lives off the E coasts of South America. It is black above, with a white belly and flippers, and a grey stripe from its flippers to the corner of its mouth. The spectacled porpoise feeds on mullet, anchovies and squid. Head-body length: 1.5–2.1m (5–7ft). Family Phocoenidae; species *Phocoena dioptrica*.

▲ **possum** Leadbeater's possum (*Gymnobelideus leadbeateri*) is completely arboreal and its paws are adapted to its lifestyle, being very wide at the tips, with strong, short claws. This possum displays great agility in pursuit of its insect prey, which it catches by night.

Portuguese man-of-war
Colonial HYDROZOAN animal that is widely distributed in subtropical and tropical marine waters. It has a bright blue gas float and long, trailing tentacles, which have highly poisonous stinging cells. The Portuguese man-of-war is not a true JELLYFISH because the tentacles are actually clusters of several kinds of modified MEDUSAE and POLYPS. Length: to 18m (59ft). Phylum Cnidaria; class Hydrozoa; genus *Physalia*; species include *Physalia utriculus* (bluebottle).

possum
Any member of five MARSUPIAL families found in Australia, Tasmania, New Guinea and nearby islands. Most possum species are nocturnal tree climbers, with grasping, hand-like feet and prehensile tails. They usually feed on leaves, fruit and flowers, but some species also eat insects and small vertebrates. Head-body length: 6–65cm (2–26in); tail: 7–61cm (3–24in).

possum, brushtail
Any of three species of nocturnal, arboreal possums found in Australia. One of these species is able to live in treeless regions in central Australia and is well adapted to living in urban areas. Head-body length: 32–58cm (13–23in); tail: 24–35cm (9–14in). Family Phalangeridae; genus *Trichosurus*.

possum, feathertail
Small, brown possum found in New Guinea. It has dark eye stripes and a long tail fringed with stiff hairs. Head-body length: 10–12cm (4–5in); tail: 12–16cm (5–6in). Family Burramyidae; species *Distoechurus pennatus*.

possum, honey
Marsupial found in SW Australia; it is not a true possum. It feeds only on nectar and pollen, with its long snout. The honey possum is grey-brown with dark stripes along its back. Head-body length: 6–8cm (2–3in); tail: 7–10cm (3–4in). Family Tarsipedidae; species *Tarsipes rostratus*.

possum, Leadbeater's
Possum that is found in the mountainous forests of SW Australia. It is grey-brown, paler underneath, with a dark stripe along its back. The Leadbeater's possum has a long, furry tail. Small colonies nest in hollow trees. Head-body length: 15–17cm (6–7in); tail: 19–20cm (7–8in). Family Petauridae; species *Gymnobelideus leadbeateri*.

possum, pygmy
Small, nectar-feeding possum from Australia and New Zealand. Pygmy possums are insectivorous, nocturnal and good tree climbers. They have long prehensile tails. One species, the feathertail glider, has a gliding membrane. Head-body length: 6–12cm (2–5in); tail: 6–17cm (2–7in). Family Burramyidae.

possum, ringtail
Highly specialized, tree-climbing, leaf-eating possum found in Australia, Tasmania and New Guinea. It has a long, prehensile tail. One species, the greater glider, has a gliding membrane. Head-body length: 16–46cm (6–18in); tail: 17–40cm (7–16in). Family Pseudocheiridae.

possum, scaly-tailed
Rare possum. It has a limited distribution, found only in NW Australia, where it inhabits rocky areas with trees. It is grey, paler underneath, sometimes with a dark stripe along its back; it has a naked prehensile tail. Unusually for a possum, it seems to be monogamous. Head-body length: 34–40cm (13–16in); tail: 27–28cm (11in). Family Phalangeridae; species *Wyulda squamicaudata*.

potato
Plant native to Central and South America and introduced into Europe by the Spaniards in the 16th century. Best grown in a moist, cool climate, it has oval leaves and violet, pink or white flowers. The potato itself is an edible TUBER. The leaves and green potatoes contain the alkaloid solanine and are poisonous if eaten raw. Family Solanaceae; species *Solanum tuberosum*. *See also* SWEET POTATO

pothole
In geology, various formations that are pot-shaped. Most commonly it denotes a circular, bowl-shaped hollow formed in a rocky stream-bed by CORRASION, which is the grinding action of sand and stones whirled around by eddies or by the force of the stream. Such potholes are usually found in rapids or at the foot of a waterfall. It is also used to describe

P

◄ **potato** The growth of the potato (*Solanum tuberosum*) takes three to seven months depending on variety. The tuber is covered with earth in fertile ground; it shoots its stems through "eyes" in the skin surface (A). At six weeks, a large canopy of leaf growth develops and tubers grow (B) on underground shoots, or stolons. Leaf growth is dried chemically (C) to aid lifting.

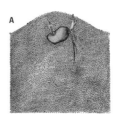

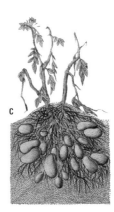

A

B

C

the vertical pits worn in LIMESTONE rocks by the action of water, occurring where a JOINT has been enlarged by SOLUTION; they often provide the entrances to CAVE systems.

potoo
Any member of the genus *Nyctibius*, a group of solitary, nocturnal birds found in Central and South America. Similar to the NIGHTJAR and the WHIP-POOR-WILL, the potoo perches during the day in an upright position resembling a broken tree stub. It has brown, camouflaged plumage and a small bill with a huge gape for catching insects. The potoo's legs are short, and it has long, curved claws. Length: 35–45cm (14–18in). Family Nyctibiidaeenus; genus *Nyctibius*.

potoroo
Any of several species of small rat KANGAROO found in Australia and Tasmania. Potoroos live in grassland or thick scrub, where they dig for roots, fungi and insects. Head-body length: 30–41cm (12–16in); tail: 15–32cm (6–13in). Family Potoroidae; genus *Potorous*.

potter wasp
See WASP, POTTER

potto
Slow-moving African PRIMATE with large eyes and a pointed face; it is nocturnal and arboreal. The common potto (*Perodicticus potto*) has sturdy limbs, a short tail and a small spine. Its woolly fur is grey-red. Length: 37cm (15in), excluding the tail. Family Lorisidae.

prairie chicken
Either of two species of partridge-like gamebirds of the North American prairies. Both species, the greater (*Tympanuchus cupido*) and lesser (*Tympanuchus pallidicinctus*) prairie chickens, are becoming rare. They are heavily barred with dark brown, cinnamon and buff below. During display, the male inflates its golden neck sacks and erects its elongated hind neck feathers. Length: 40–43cm (16–17in). Family Tetraonidae; genus *Tympanuchus*.

prairie dog
Any of several species of rodents native to W North America; they are closely related to ground SQUIRRELS. The prairie dog is so called because of its barking cry. It has a short tail, and its fur is grizzled brown to buff. Active by day, the prairie dog feeds on plants and insects. It lives in communal burrows that are interconnected to form colonies. Length: 30cm (12in). Family Sciuridae; genus *Cynomys*.

pratincole
Any of several species of short-legged, plover-like birds that hawk insects over marshes and dry grasslands. The pratincole has long, pointed wings, a forked tail and a short bill. It often appears to stand on tiptoe, stretching its neck. It is noisy and sociable, often feeding at a great height before swooping down in family groups to rest. Length: 19–25cm (7–10in). Family Glareolidae; genus *Glareola*.

prawn
Any of numerous species of edible, marine DECAPOD CRUSTACEANS. A prawn is generally larger than a SHRIMP; large prawns are sometimes known as scampi. Order Decapoda; suborder Natantia; families include Palaemonidae, Alpheidae, Hippolytidae and Processidae; genera include *Penaeus*, *Pandalus*, *Crangon* and *Nephrops*.

prawn, Aesop (pink shrimp)
Large prawn that is common off the coasts of N Europe. It is one of the main commercially fished species. Length: to 16cm (6in). Family Pandalidae; species *Pandalus montagui*.

prawn, burrowing
Prawn that burrows into the sediment on the seafloor. It has a long, narrow body and usually one large pincer. Family Callianassidae; genera include *Callianassa*.

prawn, chameleon
Brown, red or greenish prawn; it belongs to the family known as the humpback prawns. It is a common prawn, found from Norway south to the Mediterranean Sea. Length: to 32mm (1.3in). Family Hippolytidae; species *Hippolyte varians*.

prawn, Dublin Bay (Norway lobster, langoustine)
Commercially valuable LOBSTER widely found in the Mediterranean Sea and NE Atlantic Ocean. It lives in burrows on the seafloor. It is often sold as scampi. Length: to 20cm (8in). Family Nephropidae; species *Nephrops norvegicus*.

praying mantis
See MANTIS

Precambrian
Oldest and longest era of Earth's history, lasting from the formation of the Earth about 4600 million years ago to the beginning of a good FOSSIL record about 590 million years ago. It is often split into the subdivisions ARCHAEAN and PROTEROZOIC. Precambrian fossils are extremely rare because the earliest life forms are presumed not to have had HARD PARTS suitable for preservation. Also, Precambrian rocks have been greatly changed and deformed by metamorphism. Nonetheless, primitive bacteria have been identified in deposits more than 3000 million years old.

precipitation
See feature article

predator
Animal that gets its food by hunting and killing its PREY. Many, but not all, CARNIVORES are predators (some, such as VULTURES and HYENAS, are scavengers). Predators are SECONDARY CONSUMERS,

▲ **prawn** The luminous prawn (*Notostomus longirostris*) is one of many crustaceans capable of producing light - some can even produce a luminous secretion. This large species can be up 18cm (7in) in length.

occupying the top position in a FOOD CHAIN or web. Most predator-prey relationships naturally regulate one another's population. *See also* ECOSYSTEM

pregnancy
See GESTATION

premolar
In the DENTITION of adult human beings and other mammals, the two crushing or cutting TEETH between the CANINES and MOLARS on both sides of the upper and lower jaws; there are usually eight in all.

pressure
Force on an object's surface divided by the area of the surface. The SI unit is the pascal (symbol Pa), which is $1Nm^{-2}$ (newton per sq m). In meteorology, the millibar (symbol mb), which equals 100 pascals, is commonly used.

pressure potential
Hydrostatic pressure created on a plant CELL wall as a result of the cell contents pushing on it. The pressure is the result of water entering the cell by OSMOSIS and causing it to swell. In most instances the pressure potential has a positive value, but in XYLEM vessels, where the TRANSPIRATION stream is pulling water up the plant, the value is negative.

prey
See feature article, page 304

priapulid worm
Any of *c.*20 species of marine worm that are considered sufficiently unique to make up an entire phylum. Priapulid worms are found mainly in the colder ocean regions, where they burrow in the substratum. Most species feed by capturing soft-bodied invertebrates with their reversible pharynx; other species are detritivores. Phylum Priapula.

prickly pear (opuntia)
Any member of the genus *Opuntia*, a large group of cacti native to the United States, Central and South America. Prickly pear plants have flattened, jointed, often spiny stems and vary widely in size and habit. One species is grown for its edible fruit, which is red and pulpy; others are used for hedges or livestock forage. Family Cactaceae; genus *Opuntia*.

Priestley, Joseph (1733–1804)
British chemist and clergyman who discovered (1774) OXYGEN, which he called "dephlogisticated air". He also discovered a number of other gases, including ammonia and the oxides of NITROGEN. Priestley studied the properties of CARBON DIOXIDE (then called "fixed air") and invented carbonated drinks. He was an advocate of the later discredited phlogiston theory.

▲ **potto** The common potto (*Perodicticus potto*) is found in the forests of W Africa. It is omnivorous, eating seeds, fruit, insects and insect larvae, as well as the gum from certain species of tree. It has several hard raised bumps on its upper back, which are thought to act as a shield against predators.

primary consumer

Any HETEROTROPH that feeds on PRIMARY PRODUCERS in the FOOD CHAIN but does not occupy the top position. Most HERBIVORES are primary consumers, feeding on plants (below them in the food chain) but themselves providing food for SECONDARY CONSUMERS (above them in the food chain). *See also* ECOSYSTEM

primary producer

Any organism at the lowest level of a FOOD CHAIN. Primary producers are AUTOTROPHS. They ultimately feed all the consumers (HETEROTROPHS) above them. Most primary producers are ALGAE or PLANTS. *See also* ECOSYSTEM

primate

Any member of the Primates order of MAMMALS. It includes MONKEYS, APES and human beings (HOMO SAPIENS). Primates, native to most tropical and subtropical regions, are mostly herbivorous, diurnal (day-active), arboreal (tree-dwelling) animals. Their hands and feet, usually with flat nails instead of claws, are adapted for grasping. Most species have opposable thumbs, and all but humans have opposable big toes. They have a poor sense of smell, good hearing and acute binocular vision. The outstanding feature of primates is a large complex brain and high intelligence. Primate characteristics are less pronounced in the relatively primitive prosimians (including the TREE SHREW, BUSH BABY, LORIS and TARSIER) and are most pronounced in the more numerous and advanced Anthropoidea (monkeys, apes and human beings).

primrose

Any of numerous species of herbaceous, generally perennial plants of the genus *Primula*. Primroses grow in the cooler climates of Europe, Asia, Ethiopia, Java and North America. They have tufts of leaves rising from the rootstock and clustered flowers of pale yellow to deep crimson. In Britain the name primrose refers to *Primula vulgaris*. Family Primulaceae.

primula

Any member of the genus *Primula*; they are often known as PRIMROSES. Species include the common primrose (*Primula vulgaris*), oxlip (*Primula elatior*) and cowslip (*Primula veris*). In common usage the term primula usually refers to a cultivated variety of the group.

Pringsheim, Nathanael (1823–94)

German botanist who investigated the reproductive systems of lower plants. Pringsheim discovered the occurrence of SEXUAL REPRODUCTION in ALGAE and, after further studies, concluded that NATURAL SELECTION plays only a minor part in EVOLUTION. He believed that VARIATIONS are spontaneous and

PRECIPITATION

In meteorology, all forms of water particles, whether liquid or solid, that fall from the ATMOSPHERE to the ground. Precipitation is distinguished from CLOUD, FOG, DEW and FROST, in that it must fall and reach the ground. It includes RAIN, drizzle, SNOW (ice pellets and crystals) and HAIL. Measured by rain and snow gauges, the amount of precipitation is expressed in millimetres or inches of liquid water depth. Precipitation occurs with the CONDENSATION of WATER VAPOUR in clouds into water droplets that coalesce into drops as large as 7mm (0.25in) in diameter. It also forms from melting ice crystals in the clouds. **Drizzle** consists of fine droplets, and snow of masses of many-sided ice crystals. **Sleet** is formed when raindrops freeze into small ice pellets, and hail when concentric layers of ice in cumulonimbus clouds freeze, forming lumps measuring from 0.5–10cm (0.2–4in) in diameter.

► **precipitation** Shallow clouds and those in the tropics do not reach freezing level, so ice crystals do not form (A). Instead, a larger-than-average cloud droplet may coalesce with several million other cloud droplets to reach raindrop size. Electrical charges may encourage coalescence if droplets have opposite charges. Some raindrops then break apart to produce other droplets in a chain reaction that produces an avalanche of raindrops. Most rainfall in the mid-latitudes is the result of snowflakes melting as they fall (B). It takes many millions of moisture droplets and ice crystals to make a single raindrop or snowflake heavy enough to fall from a cloud.

Yet a snowflake can be grown from ice crystals in only 20 minutes. Large hailstones need strong upcurrents of air in order to form (C). A 30-mm (1.2-in) diameter hailstone probably needs an updraught of 100km/h (60mph). The turbulent air currents in a thunderstorm turn a frozen water droplet into an embryonic hailstone. The abundant supercooled moisture droplets in a storm will readily freeze on to its surface. It is swept up and down by the currents and accumulates numerous layers of thick ice, which are alternately clear and milky. The opaque layer is made when air bubbles and sometimes ice crystals are trapped during rapid freezing in the cloud's cold upper levels. The clear layers form in the cloud's warmer, lower levels, where water freezes slowly. There can be as many as 25 layers in a hailstone (D) and the last – a clear layer of ice, which is often the thickest – develops as the hailstone falls through the wet, warm cloud base.

P

Aprey animal is one that is hunted and killed for food by a PREDATOR. Prey animals generally occupy the last place but one in a FOOD CHAIN or web.

When some species of SEA CUCUMBER are being chased by a predator, they expel their entrails through the mouth and anus. This has the effect of distracting the attacker so that the sea cucumber can escape to safety. The entrails grow back in a few weeks. Other animals may use startling or distracting tactics to avoid capture, although few methods are as drastic as that of the sea cucumber.

Startle displays usually rely on using warning colours generally recognized throughout the animal world – reds, oranges and yellows. There are three main kinds of startle display. There is the sudden revelation of large false eyes, which are intended to deceive the predator into thinking that it is attacking a much larger animal. Alternatively, flash colours (generally red, orange or yellow), unexpectedly displayed in underwing, throats or other parts of the body, will scare most predators. A sudden increase in size is also a very effective deterrent – as in the case of great horned OWLS, which fluff their feathers and spread their wings when in danger, or TOADS that puff themselves up and stand on tiptoe. Sudden noises – like the hissing of geese – are also deterrents, and can be particularly effective when combined with flashing warning colours. Animals that do not have natural armour or warning colours with which to deter their attackers usually run away or hide. These are popular defence strategies because, in the long run, they use up less energy than developing survival weapons.

◄ **The Australian frilled** lizard (A), when threatened, hisses violently, lashes its tail and fans out its black and red frill to startle predators away. Many butterflies, such as the peacock butterfly (B), use eyespots to trick predators into thinking that they have disturbed a large animal. Persistent hunters will attack the spots, not the vulnerable body. The hognosed snake (C) feigns death if threatened. It rolls onto its back, hangs open its mouth and emits a smell similar to decaying flesh. The five-lined skink (D) wiggles its tail to distract predators. The vertebrae of the tail have special fracture points so that, if pulled, the tail breaks off, allowing the skink to escape. The tail eventually grows back. The fire-bellied toad (E) warns off predators by rolling onto its back and revealing its black and red underside, demonstrating that it is poisonous. The porcupine fish (F) can inflate its body so that the spines in its skin stick out and deter larger fish from biting.

▶ **Some animals resort** to flight to escape their enemies, but for some, additional physical adaptations can greatly improve the chance of survival, not just for the individual but for the whole group. Impala (G) are just one of many species of grazing antelope that have conspicuous black and white "flash" markings on their rumps. When one member of the group senses danger and runs away, its flash markings are quickly spotted by other members of the group grazing nearby, which are then also alerted. Other species of animals, such as rabbits, have a similar survival technique.

P

tend towards greater complexity. Pringsheim was the first to demonstrate **apospory**, the production of a sexual generation from an asexual generation without the intervention of SPORES.

prinia
Any member of the genus *Prinia*, a large group of tiny, long-tailed perching birds. The prinia's plumage is usually shades of brown, buff and tawny; some species are streaked. It is found in grassy habitats. Its aerial display includes a repetitive clicking song. Length: 10–17cm (4–7in). Family Sylviidae; genus *Prinia*.

prion (whale-bird)
Small seabird belonging to the PETREL family. It is found in oceans of the Southern Hemisphere. Its upperparts are a delicate blue-grey, with a distinctive, black "W" wing pattern visible in flight. There are six species, several of which can only be told apart by details of their bills. Length: 25–28cm (10–11in). Family Procellariidae; genus *Pachyptila*.

prion
Infective agent that appears to consist simply of a PROTEIN. Prions are thought to cause diseases such as Creutzfeldt-Jakob disease (CJD) in humans, bovine spongiform encephalopathy (BSE) in cattle and scrapie in sheep. It is not understood how prions work, or how they persist in nature: unlike VIRUSES and BACTERIA, they do not contain DNA or RNA. Infection with a prion appears to cause a change in shape of the prion protein to a form that has a harmful effect.

privet
Any of several species of deciduous shrubs belonging to the genus *Ligustrum*. The privet is native to Australia, Asia, Europe and North Africa; it is frequently planted to form a hedge. It has smooth, lance-shaped leaves and loose clusters of tiny white flowers that appear in summer; it bears small, black berries. Species include the common, or European, privet (*Ligustrum vulgare*) and the hardier California privet (*Ligustrum ovalifolium*), which is native to Japan. Height: to 4.6m (15ft). Family Oleaceae.

proboscidean
Member of the Proboscidea order of MAMMALS. Members of the order have lived on Earth from the EOCENE to the present day, but it is now represented only by ELEPHANTS (genera *Elephas* and *Loxodon*). They have primitive limbs but specialized trunks and teeth. Family Elephantidae.

procellariiform
Member of the bird order Procellariiformes. It includes the ALBATROSS, SHEARWATER, storm PETREL and DIVING-PETREL.

progesterone
Steroid HORMONE secreted mainly by the corpus luteum of the mammalian OVARY and by the PLACENTA during pregnancy. Its principal function is to prepare and maintain the inner lining (endometrium) of the UTERUS for pregnancy. Synthetic progesterone is one of the main components of the contraceptive pill.

Prokaryotae (formerly Monera)
In one system of CLASSIFICATION, a KINGDOM that includes BACTERIA and CYANOBACTERIA. *See also* PROKARYOTE

prokaryote
In the five KINGDOM system of CLASSIFICATION, a member of the kingdom Prokaryotae, which includes BACTERIA and CYANOBACTERIA. Prokaryotes have more simple CELLS than other organisms. DNA is not contained in CHROMOSOMES in the NUCLEUS, but lies in a distinct part of the CYTOPLASM, called the nucleoid. They have no distinct membrane-surrounded structures (ORGANELLES). Cell division is simple and in the rare cases where SEXUAL REPRODUCTION occurs, genetic material is simply transferred from one partner to another; there are no separate sex cells. In photosynthetic prokaryotes, PHOTOSYNTHESIS takes place on the cell membrane. *See also* ASEXUAL REPRODUCTION; EUKARYOTE

pronghorn
Only extant member of the family Antilocapridae, related to the ANTELOPE. It is a horned, hoofed, herbivorous animal native to the plains and deserts of the W United States and N Mexico. The swiftest North American mammal, it is capable of speeds of up to 80km/h (50mph) over short distances. Height: 90cm (35in). Family Antilocapridae; species *Antilocapra americana*.

propagation
In botany, method of producing several individual plants from one original plant. Propagation may be in the form of SEXUAL REPRODUCTION, in which the plant is pollinated and the seed produced in the normal way, or VEGETATIVE REPRODUCTION (vegetative propagation), in which plants reproduce asexually by means of CORMS, BULBS, TUBERS or RUNNERS. Vegetative reproduction can be performed artificially by taking cuttings or by grafting. In zoology, ASEXUAL REPRODUCTION, for example the BUDDING of new individuals in hydra, is also called vegetative propagation. In other areas of science, the term propagation describes a spreading out, for example of waves from a central source or of nerve impulses along the AXON of a NEURONE. *See also* POLLINATION

prophase
Stage in cell division, the first stage of MITOSIS or MEIOSIS. During prophase, CHROMOSOMES become visible, shrink and split along their length to form CHROMATIDS.

prop root (stilt root)
Type of ROOT that grows from the STEMS of a plant and gives it extra support. Prop roots continue to be produced as the thin, main stem grows taller. They are often necessary to prevent the plant from falling over. Prop roots occur in herbaceous plants, such as maize, and in some trees, such as mangroves. In other tropical trees, wide, flat-topped prop roots called **buttress roots** grow from the base of the trunk and help to support the shallow-rooted trees.

protease
ENZYME that hydrolyses the PEPTIDE bonds between AMINO ACIDS. Some proteases will hydrolyse the peptide bond wherever it arises whereas others are more specific and only operate on peptide bonds between particular amino acids. Examples of peptidases include dipeptidase, which hydrolyses dipeptides into amino acids, and the EXOPEPTIDASE called aminopeptidase. Industrial uses of proteases include the tenderization of meat, biological washing powders and contact lens cleaning solutions. *See also* HYDROLYSIS

protective coloration
Natural CAMOUFLAGE or warning colours of organisms that serve to blend it in with the surrounding environment or to ward off PREDATORS. Tigers and some moths have permanent protective colouring. Chameleons and some flatfish can change colour to match the background. Warning colours of an animal usually mean it is poisonous, aggressive or distasteful to most predators. Predators learn to recognize and avoid these colorations, which may be mimicked by harmless species. *See also* MIMICRY; PIGMENTATION; PREY

protein
Organic compound containing many AMINO ACIDS linked together by covalent, PEPTIDE bonds. Protein molecules consist of POLYPEPTIDE chains. Living CELLS use about 20 different amino acids; because proteins have thousands of amino acids in each

P

▶ **pronghorn** This group of females and young pronghorns (*Antilocapra americana*) were photographed in the Badlands National Park, South Dakota, N United States. Pronghorns are unusual in having horns rather than antlers. The females' horns grow to *c.*13cm (*c.*4in) in length. The males' horns are much longer, with a forwards facing prong. Unlike any other animal, the pronghorns shed their horns every year.

MOLECULE, the number of possible proteins is very large. The order of amino acids in proteins is controlled by the GENES in the cell's DNA. The most important proteins are ENZYMES, which determine all the chemical reactions in the cell, and ANTIBODIES, which combat infection. **Structural proteins** include KERATIN and COLLAGEN. **Gas transport proteins** include HAEMOGLOBIN. **Nutrient proteins** include casein. METABOLISM is regulated by protein HORMONES. Actin and myosin are contractile **muscle proteins**. *See also* NUCLEIC ACID

protein synthesis
Production within CELLS of PROTEINS from their component AMINO ACIDS. The GENETIC CODE, carried by the DNA of the CHROMOSOMES, determines which amino acids (of the 20 available) are used and in which order they are combined. The code is, in turn, encoded in MESSENGER RNA (mRNA) transcribed from the DNA in the cell's NUCLEUS. The mRNA carries the information to the RIBOSOMES, where protein synthesis actually takes place. *See also* NUCLEIC ACID

proteobacteria
Very diverse group of BACTERIA; it includes purple bacteria and NITROGEN-FIXING BACTERIA found in the root nodules of legumes, as well as bacteria that inhabit the intestines of animals. An example of the latter group is *Escherichia coli.*

Proterozoic
Period of GEOLOGICAL TIME, the second of the two subdivisions of the PRECAMBRIAN era. Dating from about 2.5 billion years ago to about 590 million years ago, it saw the emergence of the very earliest life forms such as BACTERIA and ALGAE.

prothallus
In some primitive plants, part that carries the sex organs. The prothallus is a flattened green structure found in FERNS, CLUB MOSSES and HORSETAILS. It is the independent GAMETOPHYTE generation (*see* ALTERNATION OF GENERATIONS). It is anchored to damp soil by hair-like RHIZOIDS. A single prothallus may bear a male sex organ (ANTHERIDIUM) or a female sex organ (ARCHEGONIUM), or both types. The prothallus initially provides nourishment for

the EMBRYO and young SPOROPHYTE after it forms in the archegonium.

protist
See PROTOCTIST

protoceratops
Ornithischian dinosaur of the CRETACEOUS period; it lived in central Asia. It had beak-like jaws and a frill of bone on the back of its skull. Although hornless, unlike later forms, it had two bony bumps in the place of horns. Length: 1.8m (6ft). Suborder Ceratopsia; genus *Protoceratops.*

protoctist
Any member of the kingdom Protoctisa (formerly Protista). It includes such widely differing groups as ALGAE (including large seaweeds), AMOEBAS and other PROTOZOA, SLIME MOULDS and downy MILDEWS.

proton (symbol p)
Stable fundamental particle with a positive charge equal in magnitude to the negative charge of an ELECTRON. Protons are one of the three primary constituents of the ATOM. A proton forms the NUCLEUS of the lightest element, HYDROGEN. Together with the NEUTRON, protons are constituents of the nuclei of all other elements.

protonema
Early stage in the development of the GAMETOPHYTE of a MOSS or LIVERWORT. Most protonemata consist of green branched threads that grow on the soil surface. They carry buds that eventually develop into the adult form of the plant. *See also* ALTERNATION OF GENERATIONS

◄ **protoceratops** This dinosaur was an ancestor of the horned ceratopsians. It lived in the Gobi Desert during the Cretaceous period. Fossil evidence – the finding of groups of bones of the same species in the same area – indicates that the protoceratops might have lived in herds.

proton pump
Mechanism in some living cells whereby hydrogen ions (PROTONS) are actively pumped out of cells and/or organelles using energy provided by ADENOSINE TRIPHOSPHATE (ATP). The protons may return to the cell along a concentration gradient with the assistance of a carrier molecule. The process occurs in MITOCHONDRIA, where it contributes to oxidative phosphorylation, and in GUARD CELLS, where it helps to control the opening and closing of stomata.

protoplasm
Term referring to all the discrete structures within a plant or animal CELL, including the cell membrane. It includes both the NUCLEUS and the CYTOPLASM of cells.

protoplast (energid)
Term that describes the living unit of a plant CELL. The protoplast includes the cell NUCLEUS and the CYTOPLASM with its various ORGANELLES, but excludes the cell wall. *See also* PROTOPLASM

prototherian
Any member of the Mammalia subclass Prototheria. Prototherians are represented in living fauna only by the MONOTREMES – ECHIDNAS and PLATYPUSES.

protozoan
Any member of the phylum Protozoa, which comprises unicellular organisms found worldwide in oceans or fresh water, free-living and as PARASITES. These microscopic organisms have the ability to move (by CILIA or PSEUDOPODIA) and have a NUCLEUS, CYTOPLASM and cell wall; some contain CHLOROPHYLL. Reproduction is by FISSION or encystment. Length: 0.3mm (0.1in). The 30,000 species are

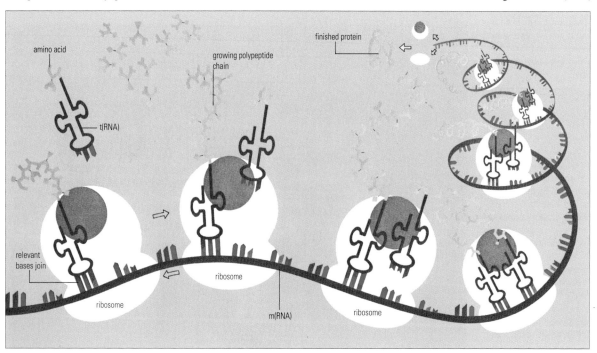

◄ **protein synthesis** The production of proteins occurs in ribosomes, the sites where amino acids become linked together to form protein chains. They attach to the messenger RNA (mRNA) template, which moves relative to them. Amino acids join up in sequence because the bases of the transfer RNA (tRNA) molecules, on which they are carried, must combine with the relevant bases on mRNA as it passes the ribosome. Adenine (blue) always pairs with uracil (green), and cytosine (red) pairs with guanine (orange). One mRNA molecule may carry many ribosomes, with protein chains growing on each (this is called a polysome).

divided into four classes – Flagellata, Cnidospora, Ciliophora and Sporozoa. One of the better know genera is AMOEBA.

protura

Any of *c*.50 species belonging to the class Protura, which is represented worldwide. It comprises primitive, pale, wingless, blind insects. Proturas are the most primitive of the hexapods. Most species live in damp soil, feeding on decaying organic matter. Length: to 2mm (0.08in). Class Protura.

prunus

Any member of the genus *Prunus*, containing *c*.430 species of flowering trees and shrubs. It includes the APRICOT, PLUM, CHERRY, ALMOND, NECTARINE and PEACH. Many species are cultivated and are highly important as fruit crops. Family Rosaceae.

Przewalski's horse

See HORSE, PRZEWALSKI'S

pseudocarp (false fruit)

Fruit that is formed from other parts of a FLOWER as well as the OVARY wall. A pseudocarp may incorporate tissue from the CALYX or RECEPTACLE. In a STRAWBERRY, for example, the receptacle becomes the fleshy part while the true fruits are the "seeds" embedded in it. Other examples include apples, figs and pears.

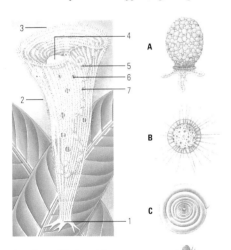

▲ **protozoan** Members of the genus *Stentor*, a species of which is shown above, are among the largest protozoa known, reaching lengths of up to 2mm (0.08in). The *Stentor* can attach itself to a rock or large alga by means of a holdfast at its base (1), but it may also swim free, propelled by its many cilia (2). At the broad end of its body, the cilia are arranged in a spiral (3); when these cilia beat, they create a vortex that draws particles in the water towards the oral pouch (4). Here, suitable food – bacteria and small algae – is selected and passes into the buccal funnel or "gullet" (5). Once packaged into vacuoles (6), the food particles pass through the protozoan's body and are broken down. Undigested material is expelled through the cell wall. Like other ciliated protozoa, *Stentor* has a

large string-of-beads shaped nucleus (7).
In appearance, the protozoa are highly variable. *Difflugia* (A) makes a "shell" out of sand grains cemented together with organic matter. *Actinophrys* (B), like amoeba, has pseudopodia, but they are long, slender and spine-like. *Ammodiscus* (C) lives in marine environments; it produces a hard, inorganic case with many chambers. *Cementella* (D) builds a composite "shell" from the skeletons of other protozoa. Much of the deep ocean floor is covered by the hard shells of organisms like *Cementella*; over time they may become compacted into limestone.

pseudopodia

Temporary extensions of a cell as a result of the flow of CYTOPLASM. They arise in certain PROTOZOA, such as AMOEBA, where the pseudopodia engulf particles of food, which are then ingested. Mammalian leucocytes (white blood cells) carry out PHAGOCYTOSIS in a similar way, engulfing harmful particles and organisms, so protecting the host from infection. *See also* ENDOCYTOSIS

pseudoscorpion

Any of numerous species of small ARACHNIDS found throughout the world. The pseudoscorpion has paired, pincer-like appendages known as pedipalps; it resembles a true scorpion but without the tail. Length: to 7.5mm (0.3in). Family Arachnida.

psittaciform

Member of the bird order Psittaciformes. It includes strong-flying birds, such as the COCKATOO, LOVEBIRD, BUDGERIGAR, MACAW, PARAKEET and PARROT. The order has been represented since the Miocene epoch. Many species are brightly coloured, with stout, hooked bills. They eat seeds, fruit or nectar. Length: to 9cm (4in).

psocid

Any member of the family Psocidae, a group of widely distributed soft-bodied insects; it includes the well-known BOOKLOUSE. Psocids are usually found out of doors, infesting conifers and fruit trees, and are occasionally found in swarms. The eggs are hidden under debris and will only survive the winter if laid in mid-July. Adult body size: *c*.2–3mm (0.08–0.12in). Order Psocoptera; family Psocidae.

psychobiology

Field, closely related to physiological psychology, that studies anatomical and biochemical structures and processes as they affect behaviour.

ptarmigan

Any of three species of northern or alpine GROUSE, all of which have feathered legs. The wings and breast are white in colder months, but in the spring they become a mottled grey-brown. The ptarmigan inhabits high barren regions, feeding on leaves and lichens. Length: to 36cm (14in). Family Phasianidae; genus *Lagopus*; species include *Lagopus mutus* (Eurasian ptarmigan).

pteridophyte

Commonly used, but now obsolete, name for any of a group of SPORE-bearing VASCULAR PLANTS. At one time, pteridophytes were taken to include CLUB MOSSES, HORSETAILS and FERNS. These plants have similar life cycles but in other respects are quite distinct and are now classified as separate phyla. *See also* FILICINOPHYTE; LYCOPODOPHYTE; SPHENOPHYTE

pterodactyl

Any of several species of small PTEROSAURS. Almost tailless, the pterodactyl had a large, toothed beak and flimsy, membranous wings. Fossil remains show a lack of muscular development and the absence of a breast keel. It is, therefore, believed that pterodactyls were gliders, incapable of sustained flapping flight.

pterosaur

Member of a large group of extinct flying reptiles that evolved in late Triassic times and died out in the late Cretaceous, for example *Rhamphorhynchus*. Pterosaurs' wings were bat-like with a thin membrane of skin stretched over elon-

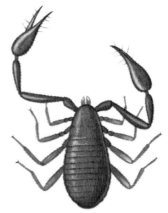

▲ **pseudoscorpion** The species shown here, *Chelifer cancroides*, is one of the larger pseudoscorpions, reaching lengths of up to 7.5mm (0.3in).

It has small chelicerae (1), which contain silk-producing glands. Its large pedipalps (2) have pincers and poison glands.

gate hollow bones. Unlike the bats, however, the skin stretched from the body over the forelimbs and along the fourth finger. *Quetzalcoatlus*, one of the last of the pterosaurs, was also one of the largest, having a wingspan of 12m (39ft).

pubis

In the PELVIS (pelvic girdle), either of a pair of small bones at the front of the hip bones. They are almost U-shaped and meet at the pubic symphysis, which is closed by a pad of cartilage. Each pubis joins an ILIUM and an ISCHIUM at a triangular suture in the hip socket.

pudu

Tiny, shy, lightly built DEER that inhabits the thickly forested lower slopes of the Andes in South America. Family Cervidae (deer).

pudu, southern

Endangered species of pudu, found in Chile and Argentina. Its coat is reddish, with paler sides, legs and feet. Its antlers are short, sharp spikes. Single, spotted fawns are born in winter after a 210-day gestation. Pudus are thought to live in small groups feeding on any vegetation. Height: *c*.16cm (*c*.6in). Family Cervidae; species *Pudu pudu*.

P

▲ **pterodactyl** Living during the late Jurassic and early Cretaceous periods, the flying reptiles known as pterodactyls varied in size. The smallest specimen was the size of a

sparrow (1), while the largest was the size of a hawk (2). Like the bats of today, it had a wing membrane (3) attached to an elongated fourth finger, and hind limbs and tail.

pudu, northern

Pudu found in Ecuador, Colombia and Peru; it is unclear whether or not it is endangered. It has a reddish coat, with a black head and feet. It is slightly larger than the southern pudu. Head-body length: 65cm (26in); tail: 3cm (1in). Family Cervidae; species *Pudu mephistophiles*.

puff adder

Widely distributed African VIPER. Its skin usually has yellow markings on brown. The puff adder hunts large rodents, and its poisonous bite can be fatal to humans. Up to 80 young are born at one time. Length: to 1.2m (4ft). Family Viperidae; species *Bitis arietans*.

puffback

Common songbird of s Africa. It has black-and-white plumage and crimson eyes. When excited, the male raises his back feathers to form a white puff. The puffback's flight is rather heavy and its wings make a distinctive purring sound. Length: 18cm (7in). Family Laniidae; genus *Dryoscopus*.

puff-ball

Any of a large order of MUSHROOMS (Lycoperdiales), the spore masses of which become powdery at maturity and are expelled in "puffs" when the case is pressed. Puffballs are stemless, and some species, but not all, are edible. Phylum Basidiomycota.

puffbird

Any of *c*.30 species of large-headed, large-billed FLYCATCHERS found in forests of Central and South America. The puffbird sits quietly on a branch in humid forests and undergrowth, darting out occasionally to catch passing insects. Length: 20–28cm (8–11in). Family Bucconidae.

pufferfish (blowfish or swellfish)

Any of *c*.100 species of fish found in warm and temperate seas. When threatened, the pufferfish inflates itself to nearly twice its body size by a special adaptation of its gullet. Pufferfish species vary widely in colour. Smaller, sharp-nosed varieties are often kept in home aquariums. Length: to 91cm (36in). Family Tetraodontidae.

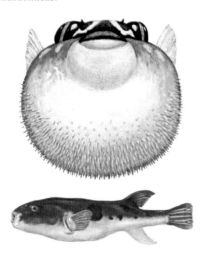

▲ **pufferfish** The (inflated) pufferfish shown above, *Spheroides spengleri*, like all pufferfish, protects itself by puffing itself up in order to appear twice its real size and perhaps to deter attempts by other species to swallow it. The

(uninflated) Japanese pufferfish below (*Fugu rubripes rubripes*) is regarded as a delicacy in Japan. Like other puffer species, it contains tetraodontoxin, which is highly poisonous, but if certain organs are removed it can be eaten.

puffin

Seabird belonging of the AUK family. It has a parrot-like, white face and a large, red-and-yellow, conical bill. The common puffin (*Fratercula arctica*) and horned puffin (*Fratercula corniculata*) have black backs and white fronts. The tufted puffin (*Fratercula cirrhata*) is all black except for a white face; it has long, yellow, drooping headplumes in spring. Family Alcidae; genera *Fratercula* and *Lunda*.

puffleg

Any of *c*.12 species of HUMMINGBIRD found in South America. The puffleg has cottony soft feathers on its legs. It has bright, iridescent plumage. Family Trochilidae; genus *Eriocnemis*.

pulse

Regular wave of raised pressure in ARTERIES that results from the flow of BLOOD pumped into them at each beat of the HEART. The pulse is usually taken at the wrist, although it may be observed at any point where an artery runs close to the body surface. The average pulse rate is about 70 per minute in a resting adult.

pulse

Any leguminous plant of the PEA family with edible seeds, such as the BEAN, LENTIL, pea, PEANUT and SOYA BEAN. The term may also refer to the seed alone. Pulses are also used for oil production. Family Fabaceae/Leguminosae. *See also* LEGUME

puma (mountain lion, cougar)

Large CAT found in mountains, forests, swamps and jungles of the Americas. It has a small, round head, erect ears and a heavy tail. Its coat is tawny with dark brown on the ears, nose and tail; the underparts are white. It preys mainly on deer and small animals. Length: to 2.3m (7.5ft), including the tail; height: to 75cm (30in) at the shoulder. Family Felidae; species *Felis concolor*.

pumice

Rhyolitic LAVA blown when it is molten to a low density rock froth by the sudden discharge of gases during a volcanic action. It tends to be very acidic in chemical content. When ground to a powder and pressed into cakes it can be used as a light abrasive.

pumpkin

Edible garden fruit of a trailing annual VINE found in warm regions of the Old World and the United States; it is a variety of *Cucurbita pepo*. The fruit is large and orange with hard rind. In the United States the pumpkin is also called a squash, especially the winter pumpkin (*Cucurbita maxima*). Family Cucurbitaceae.

pumpkinseed (common sunfish)

Freshwater fish found in e North America. A colourful, iridescent fish, it is distinguished by a bright red spot on the rear of the gill cover. The male pumpkinseed builds a nest in sand and guards the eggs and young. Length: to 23cm (9in). Family Centrarchidae; species *Lepomis gibbosus*.

punctuated equilibrium

Theory expounded by US palaeontologists Stephen Jay GOULD and Niles Eldredge in 1972, strongly sceptical of the notion of "gradual" change in the EVOLUTION of the natural world, as advocated by such theorists as Charles DARWIN. FOSSIL records rarely document the gradual development of a new SPECIES, rather its seemingly sudden appearance. Darwin reasons that this is due to gaps in the fossil

◄ **puffin** Feeding entirely on prey that they find under water, puffins (*Fratercula artica*, shown here) can catch small or slow-moving fish for themselves or for their unfledged chicks. They can carry as many as ten small fish at a time in their colourful beaks. They nest in large colonies on cliffs by the sea.

records. Punctuated equilibrium explains these "missing links" by rejecting a notion of gradual change and by invoking a different model of evolution. Each species is predominantly in a steady state (equilibrium), but this state is punctuated by brief, intense periods of sudden change, giving rise to new species in relatively short periods of time.

punkie

See BITING MIDGE

pupa

Non-feeding, developmental stage during which an INSECT undergoes complete METAMORPHOSIS. It generally occurs as part of a four-stage life cycle from the OVUM, through LARVA to pupa, then IMAGO (the adult). Most pupae consist of a tough protective outer casing, inside which the tissues of the insect affect a drastic reorganization to form the adult body. Insects that undergo pupation include the many species of BUTTERFLY, MOTH, BEETLE and many kinds of FLY. The pupa is frequently called a CHRYSALIS in butterflies and moths. It often acts as a resting or dormant stage, providing a resistant form within which the insect can survive severe weather or drought.

pupfish

Several species of KILLIFISH found in small, relic populations that are adapted to isolated and harsh environments. The entire population of the Devil's Hole pupfish (*Cyprinodon diabolis*) is found in a limestone shelf (measuring 3m by 5.5m/10ft by 18ft) in Death Valley National Monument, United States. Length (Devil's hole pupfish): to 2.5cm (1in). Family Cyprinodontidae.

pupil

In the structure of the EYE, circular aperture through which light falls onto the lens; it is located in the centre of the IRIS. Its diameter changes by reflex action of the iris to control the amount of light entering the eye.

purine

White, crystalline, organic compound ($C_5H_4N_4$) related to URIC ACID. ADENINE and GUANINE are both purines and are two of the four bases that comprise DNA. Another derivative of purine is ADENOSINE TRIPHOSPHATE (ATP), a NUCLEOTIDE essential to the transfer of energy within living cells.

purslane

Any of several species of small annual plants which have red stems, oval leaves and small red, brown, white or yellow flowers. Common European purslane, *Portulaca oleracea*, is typical in that it grows well in dry soil and can still bloom and produce seeds if uprooted. Family Portulacaceae; genus *Portulaca*.

pussy willow

Deciduous shrub or small tree native to e North

P

America. Its long, oval leaves have bluish green undersides. The large, silvery, fuzzy female catkins appear before the leaves in late winter or early spring. Height: to 6m (20ft). Family Salicaceae; species *Salix discolor*.

putrefaction

DECOMPOSITION of organic matter, especially PROTEINS, by FUNGI, BACTERIA and OXIDATION. It results in foul-smelling products. Putrefaction of meat, for example, yields hydrogen sulphide, amines and thiols.

pyracantha (fire thorn)

Any member of the genus *Pyracantha*, a group of thorny evergreen shrubs found from SE Europe to China. They have toothed, leathery leaves, white flowers, and red, orange or yellow berries. Easily grown in subtropical and temperate regions, they are popular garden shrubs. Family Rosaceae.

pyrethrum

Popular name for the painted daisy (*Chrysanthemum coccineum*) and for several other species of the genus *Chrysanthemum*. Pyrethrum is also the name for the insecticide made from the dried flower heads of the Dalmatian CHRYSANTHEMUM (*Chrysanthemum cinerariaefolium*). Family Asteraceae/Compositae.

pyrimidine

Colourless liquid ($C_4H_4N_2$) characterized by a heterocyclic ring structure composed of four CARBON atoms and two NITROGEN atoms. It may be prepared from URACIL (a dihydroxy pyrimidine compound) by chemical reactions that remove two OXYGEN atoms. CYTOSINE and THYMINE are both pyrimidines and are two of the bases that comprise DNA. In RNA uracil replaces thymine. It is used in the manufacture of various sulphonamide drugs and barbiturates.

▲ **puma** The puma (*Felis concolor* and subspecies) is now only found in remote and thinly populated areas. It is a territorial and solitary animal, apart from during its brief breeding period. The female puma gives birth to between one and six cubs once every two to three years.

pyrite (iron pyrites)

Most common and widespread sulphide mineral, iron sulphide (FeS_2), occurring in all types of rocks and veins. It is a brass-yellow colour and, because of this, is often called "fool's gold". It was formerly used widely to produce sulphuric acid. It crystallizes as cubes and octahedra, and also as granules and globular masses. It is opaque, metallic and brittle. Hardness 6.5; r.d. 5.0.

pyroclastic

Term that describes any rock fragments thrown out in the PYROCLASTIC FLOW by volcanic activity, generally in association with some violent explosive action. Pyroclasts normally include solidified LAVA left behind by a previous eruption of the VOLCANO, as well as rocks from the crust, smaller pieces of cinders, ash and dust. The largest pyroclastic fragments, known as "volcanic bombs", weigh several metric tons. Smaller pieces are known as "lapilli". When the pyroclastic activity ceases, outpourings of lava often follow. Rocks formed by consolidation of these pyroclastic fragments, such as IGNIMBRITE, volcanic BRECCIA and TUFF, are also termed pyroplastic.

pyroclastic flow (nuée ardente, Fr. fiery cloud)

Discharge of material from a VOLCANO as the result of a violent explosion. It involves the rapid release of hot gases and fragmentary PYROCLASTIC material. Some pyroclastic eruptions are very large, releasing up to 1000km³ (240 cubic miles) of rock material. This material can rise up to 40km (25mi) through the atmosphere or burst out laterally and flow great distances (tens of kilometres) at speeds of up to 200km per hour (120mph). Pyroclastic flows are very destructive and dangerous; they destroyed the Roman cities of Herculaneum and Pompeii in AD 79.

pyrolusite

Mineral form of manganese dioxide (MnO_2), an ore of manganese. It is formed as a precipitate in lakes and bogs at low temperatures, often in veins of QUARTZ. It also occurs as MANGANESE NODULES on the floor of the Pacific Ocean. Pyrolusite is black or dark grey, usually occurring in masses that have an earthy lustre, although it may form prismatic crystals (tetragonal) and fern-like aggregates in the joints of sedimentary rocks. Hardness: massive form 2–6, crystals 6–7; r.d. 4.5–5.

pyrope ($Mg_3Al_2(SiO_4)_3$)

Magnesium aluminium GARNET, the most common form of garnet. It may be purplish or brownish red. It is found mainly in South Africa and the United States. Often used in jewellery, pyrope has been given such misleading names as Bohemian garnet and is often mistaken for a RUBY.

pyroxene

Any of an important group of rock-forming minerals. They are single-chain SILICATES. Their colours are variable, but they are usually dark greens,

◀ **pumpkin** Related to the cucumber, the pumpkin has soft flesh with a high water content. As food, the rind is removed and the flesh is pulped. As well as serving as food for humans, pumpkins are also cultivated as livestock feed.

browns and blacks. Crystals are usually short prisms with good cleavages. Hardness 2.3–4; r.d. 5.5–6.

pyrrhotite

Magnetic mineral form of iron sulphide, FeS (but variable), containing more sulphur than PYRITE. Its colour is a metallic bronze and it forms massive aggregates or hexagonal, flat crystals (monoclinic). It may contain nickel and in such cases is mined as a nickel ore. Hardness: 3.5–4.5; r.d. 4.6.

python

Any of more than 20 species of non-poisonous SNAKES belonging to the BOA family. They are found in tropical regions. Like boas, pythons kill their prey (birds and mammals) by squeezing them in their coils. Unlike boas, pythons lay eggs. The reticulated python (*Python reticulatus*) of Southeast Asia vies with the ANACONDA to be the world's largest snake, reaching up to *c*.9m (*c*.30ft) in length. Family Boidae; subfamily Pythoninae.

python, ball

Small, stout-bodied python of w Africa. It twists itself into a ball when frightened or handled. It is pale yellow, with slate grey markings. It kills its prey by constriction. Length: to 1.5m (4.9ft). Family Boidae; species *Python regius*.

python, reticulated

Largest species of PYTHON. Reticulated pythons are boldly patterned, heavy-bodied snakes, with wide heads. They occupy forests and agricultural lands in tropical Asia, from Burma to the Philippines and Indonesia. They generally feed on small to mid-sized vertebrates, but can take larger prey, including (very rarely) human children. Length: to 10m (33ft), usually less than 7m (23ft). Family Pythonidae; species *Python reticulatus*.

pytilia

Any member of the genus *Pytilia*, comprising four species of WAXBILL found in Africa. They have red bills and red face patches. Their plumage is green or grey above, strikingly barred with green on the breast and belly. Pytilias are very sociable and flock with small finches, especially near drinking ponds. Length: 11cm (4in). Family Estrildidae; genus *Pytilia*.

P

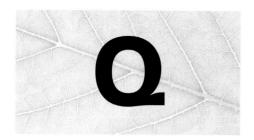

quadrat

Square frame used to mark out an area of ground for quantifying and studying the plants it encloses. The area is typically 1m^2 or 0.5m^2 (11sq ft or 5.5sq ft). Botanists and ecologists can count the numbers of species within a quadrat and estimate their abundance. Repeated measurements at several locations provide information about overall species distribution.

quail

Any member of a large group of small gamebirds. Quails are usually streaked brown; some species have black and white face patterns. The California quail (*Callipepla californica*) is boldly patterned; it has black and brown scales and a teardrop-shaped head plume. The common quail (*Coturnix coturnix*) of

Europe and Asia is a long distance migrant, despite its normal reluctance to fly. Quails scrape for fruits and seeds and nest on the ground. Length: *c*.18cm (7in). Family Phasianidae.

quartz (silica, SiO$_2$)

Rock-forming mineral, the natural form of silicon dioxide. It occurs in IGNEOUS and METAMORPHIC ROCKS (notably GRANITE and GNEISS), and in clastic sediments. It is also a common gangue mineral in mineral veins. Pure quartz is clear and colourless, but the mineral is often opaque or translucent; it may be coloured by impurities. Quartz forms six-sided crystals. The most common varieties are colourless quartz (known as rock crystal), rose, yellow, milky and smoky. The most usual cryptocrystalline varieties, the crystals of which can be seen only under a microscope, are CHALCEDONY and FLINT. Quartz crystals exhibit the piezoelectric effect and are used in electronic clocks and watches to keep accurate time. Hardness 7; r.d. 2.65.

quartzite

METAMORPHIC ROCK usually produced from sandstone, in which the quartz grains have recrystallized. Fracturing through these grains rather than between them, quartzite is a hard and massive rock. Its colour is usually white, light grey, yellow or buff, but it can be coloured green, blue, purple or black by minerals.

Quaternary

Most recent period of the CENOZOIC era, beginning about 2 million years ago and extending to the present. It is divided into the PLEISTOCENE epoch, characterized by a periodic succession of great ice ages, and the HOLOCENE epoch, which started some 10,000 years ago.

Queensland nut

See MACADAMIA

quelea

Small finch-like bird belonging to the WEAVER family. It is mainly brown, with a red bill and a black and red face. It occurs in enormous flocks that resemble columns of smoke. The quelea nests in huge colonies consisting of tens of thousands of birds and covering many acres of bush. It is possibly the world's most abundant bird. Length: 11–13cm (4–5in). Family Ploceidae; genus *Quelea*.

quetzal

Any of five species of brightly coloured forest birds of the TROGON family. The quetzal has a short neck, a short stubby bill and long, streaming tail feathers. The resplendent quetzal (*Pharomachrus mocinno*), often described as the most spectacular bird of the Americas, is intense emerald and golden green above and crimson below, with an extremely long green tail. Length: *c*.38cm (*c*.15in) plus 60cm (24in) tail plumes. Family Trogonidae; genus *Pharomachrus*.

quillwort

SPORE-bearing plant that is native to cool swamps

▲ **quetzal** The resplendent quetzal (*Pharomachrus mocinno*) is a rare perching bird found in tropical rainforests from s Mexico to Costa Rica. It was highly revered by the Aztec and Maya peoples. It is the national bird of Guatemala.

▲ **quokka** A large proportion of the quokka population lives on Rottnest island off the west coast of Australia. The environment on this island is arid and, due to the lack of fresh water, the quokka has adapted to drinking brackish water to help it make up its mineral and water needs.

of Eurasia and North America. Most quillwort species grow in water, but a few species are terrestrial. Their grassy, quill-like, hollow leaves are spirally arranged. A large spore capsule is embedded in each leaf base. Height: 15–50cm (6–20in). Phylum Lycopodophyta; genus *Isoetes*; there are 60 species. *See also* LYCOPODOPHYTE

quince

Shrub that is native to the Middle East and central Asia. Its greenish-yellow fruit is used in preserves. Height: to 6m (20ft). Family Rosaceae; species *Cydonia oblonga*.

quinine

White, crystalline alkaloid that was isolated in 1820 from the bark of the CINCHONA tree. It was once widely used to treat malaria, but it has been largely replaced by drugs that are less toxic and more effective.

quinine bush

Erect shrub or small tree native to Australia. It produces bitter, round, yellow or orange fruits, which are up to 2.5cm (1in) in diameter. The fruits are eaten by emus; following excretion, the endocarp (inner layer of the PERICARP) explodes in the sun to expose the seeds, which are then dispersed by ants. Height: to 6m (20ft). Family Euphorbiaceae; species *Petalostigma pubescens*.

quokka

Small KANGAROO that is found in sw Australia and nearby islands. It is a nocturnal herbivore, with a rounded body and thick shaggy fur. Its preferred habitat is dense vegetation near swamps or streams. Head-body length: 48–60cm (19–24in); tail: 25–35cm (10–14in). Family Macropodidae; species *Setonix brachyurus*.

quoll (native cat, tiger cat)

See MARSUPIAL CAT

Q

► **rabbit** The volcano rabbit (*Romerolagus diazi*) is mainly found in pine forests on the slopes of several volcanos in central Mexico. It feeds on young shoots of the native zacotan grasses.

rabbit

Small, herbivorous animal with cryptic brown coloration and lighter underparts. It lives in forests and grasslands worldwide. Its elongated hind legs provide propulsion for fast running and leaping: the jack-rabbit can reach speeds of 56km/hour (35mph). Rabbits have long ears and a short tail, often used for visual communication. Their long, chisel-like incisor teeth continue to grow through life and are ideal for gnawing vegetation. They eat their own faeces, a process called refection, which ensures maximum digestive efficiency. Order Lagomorpha; family Leporidae.

rabbit, eastern cottontail

Rabbit that is very common in North and Central America. It is so called because of its tail, which is brown above and white beneath. The eastern cottontail rabbit is less colonial than many other rabbits and does not dig its own burrows. Family Leporidae; species *Sylvilagus floridanus*.

rabbit, European (common rabbit)

Ancestor of the domestic rabbit. It originated in Europe but has been introduced worldwide. It has become a serious pest of arable crops in places such

as Australia. European rabbits dig underground burrow systems called warrens, where they live in large colonies. Famous for their reproductive success, each female may produce several litters of up to nine babies each year. Head-body length: 30cm (12in); tail: 7cm (3in). Family Leporidae; species *Oryctolagus cuniculus*.

rabbit, jack-

Any of six species of rabbit from North America. More correctly called HARES, they are bigger and have longer legs and larger ears than rabbits. Head-body length: 50cm (20in). Family Leporidae; species include *Lepus californicus* (the black-tailed jack-rabbit).

raccoon (racoon)

Stout-bodied, omnivorous, mostly nocturnal mammal. It is found in wooded areas of North and Central America. The raccoon has a black, mask-like marking across its eyes and a long, black-banded tail. It has agile and sensitive front paws, and it typically dips for food in water. Length: 40–61cm (16–24in); weight: 10–22kg (22–48lb). Family Procyonidae; there are seven species, including the North American *Procyon lotor*.

racemose inflorescence

Type of FLOWER cluster that has a main axis with stalked flowers arising from it. These flowers ripen and open in sequence from the bottom up towards the apex.

racer

Any of c.20 species of slender, fast-moving SNAKES that are native to the Americas, ranging from S Canada to Central America. Racers are broad-headed and large-eyed. They vary in colour according to species. Length: to 1.8m (6ft). Family Colubridae; species include *Coluber constrictor*.

racerunner

See LIZARD, WHIPTAIL

radiation

See ADAPTIVE RADIATION

radicle

Part of a plant embryo that develops into the ROOT. When the radicle emerges from a germinating seed, its tip is protected by a root cap (**calyptra**), which enables it to break through the seed case (**testa**) and penetrate the soil. In most plants, the radicle originates the whole root system. *See also* GERMINATION

radioisotope

ISOTOPE that undergoes radioactive decay. Radioisotopes occur in nature along with the stable isotopes of an element, but they can also be made artificially by bombarding other isotopes with high-energy elementary particles in a nuclear reactor or a particle accelerator. Radioisotopes are formed naturally in the atmosphere as the result of collisions between ATOMS in the air and cosmic radiation. Among the elements with radioactive isotopes of economic importance are cobalt, hydrogen, plutonium, radium, strontium and uranium.

radish

Annual garden vegetable developed from a wild plant native to cooler regions of Asia. Its leaves are long and deeply lobed. The fleshy root, which may be red, white or black, is eaten raw. Family Brassicaceae; species *Raphanus sativus*.

▲ **raccoon** An agile climber, the raccoon often makes its den in a hollow tree. It is commonly found near water in forested areas and hunts at night for small mammals, birds' eggs and insects. Adult males are solitary, whereas females and their young form close attachments and live in family groups.

radula

Structure found in the mouths of some MOLLUSCS; they use it to rasp their food. A radula consists of a tongue-like strip of horny material (modified EPITHELIUM), which bears many rows of chitinous or horny teeth. In SLUGS and SNAILS, the radula is used to rasp off pieces of leafy food. In some marine molluscs, it is modified for boring or scraping.

raffia

African PALM tree. Its large, pinnate leaves yield a fibre commonly used for matting and baskets. Family Arecacae/Palmae; species *Raphia ruffia*.

rafflesia

Parasitic plant native to Sumatra and Java. It grows as a PARASITE on the roots of jungle vines and has no stem or leaves. It produces foul-smelling, reddish-brown flowers, up to 1m (3.3ft) in diameter, which are the world's largest flowers. Family Rafflesiaceae; species include *Rafflesia arnoldii*.

ragged robin

Flowering plant found in Europe, Asia, Canada and NE United States. Its pink petals are divided into four narrow and unequal lobes. Family Caryophyllaceae; species *Lychnis floscuculi*.

▲ **rabbit, jack-**The fastest species of hare or rabbit, the jack-rabbit can run at up to 56km/h (35mph) and make huge leaps. It is often found in arid environments and gains most its water intake from plant material. Unlike true rabbits, it does not dig a burrow but squats in a scrape in the ground.

▲ **rafflesia** The largest species of rafflesia is the monster flower (*Rafflesia arnoldi*). Its germinating seeds produce strands of cells that penetrate the water- and food-conducting channels of the host plant to absorb water and nutrients. The bloom lives for less than a week.

ragworm

Any member of a group of free-living, marine, POLY-CHAETE worms. The ragworm is predacious on smaller marine invertebrates such as SHRIMPS. It moves by means of leg-like appendages called parapodia, which are found on most of the body segments. Phylum Annelida; class Polychaeta; order Phyllodocida; family Nereidae; genus *Nereis*.

ragwort

Any of several plants that bear daisy-like flowers. The common ragwort (*Senecio jacobaea*) has flat-topped clusters of yellow flower heads. Height: to 1.2m (4ft). Family Asteraceae/Compositae.

rail

Any member of the family Rallidae, a group of small-to medium-sized, ground-living birds. The rail has short wings, a short tail, and long legs and toes. It often flies with dangling legs. Most species, such as the clapper rail (*Rallus longirostris*) and water rail (*Rallus aquaticus*), inhabit dense wetlands and are very shy and secretive. The flightless rail (*Gallirallus australis*), unique to New Zealand, has vestigial wings. Length: 10–45cm (4–18in). Family Rallidae.

rail-babbler

Any of three species of long-tailed birds belonging to the LOGRUNNER family. They are found in the forests of the New Guinea region, where they forage on the forest floor. Rail-babblers have pleasant songs with bell-like notes. Length: 23cm (9in). Family Orthonychidae; genus *Ptilorrhoa*.

R

railroad worm

See APPLE MAGGOT

rain

Water drops that fall from the Earth's atmosphere to its surface, as opposed to FOG or DEW, which drift as suspensions, and SNOW or HAIL, which fall in the form of ice particles. CLOUDS are aggregates of minute droplets of moisture, and raindrops are formed when these enlarge by further CONDENSATION and by coalescence with other drops as they fall. Warm air passing over the sea absorbs water vapour; the air rises in thermal currents or on reaching a mountain range. The water vapour condenses and forms clouds, which account for the usually heavier annual rainfall on windward, compared to leeward, mountain slopes. Rainfall is measured by a rain gauge. *See also* PRECIPITATION; RAINSHADOW

rainbow

See feature article

rainbowfish

Any member of the family Melanotaeniidae, which comprises small, colourful, freshwater fish. Rainbow fish are found at elevations below 1500m (4900ft) in tropical and subtropical regions of New Guinea and Australia. They have compressed bodies with slightly pointed heads. Rainbow fish are popular aquarium fish. Length: to 12cm (4.7ft). Family Melanotaeniidae.

rainforest

Dense forest of tall trees that grows in hot, wet regions near the Equator. The main rainforests are in Africa, Central and South America, and Southeast Asia. They comprise 50% of the timber growing on Earth and house 40% of the world's animal and plant species. They also, through PHOTOSYNTHESIS, supply most of the world's oxygen. This is why the present rapid destruction of the rainforests (up to 20 million hectares are destroyed annually to provide timber and land for agriculture) is a cause of great concern. Also, clearing rainforests contributes to the GREENHOUSE EFFECT and may lead to GLOBAL WARMING. There are many species of broad-leaved evergreen trees in rainforests, which grow up to 60m (200ft) tall. The crowns of other trees, up to 45m (150ft) tall, form the upper canopy of the forest. Smaller trees form the lower canopy. Climbing vines interconnect the various levels, providing habitats for many kinds of birds, mammals and reptiles. Very little light penetrates to the forest floor, which consequently has few plants. Rainforest trees provide many kinds of food and other useful materials, such as BRAZIL NUTS, FIGS and MANGOSTEENS, as well as fibrous KAPOK and the drugs QUININE and curare.

rainshadow

Leeward area of high ground that experiences low rainfall. The uplift of moist air on the windward side

▲ **rail** Native to marshes worldwide, rails are poor fliers that rely on their dull coloration for protective camouflage. Their strong legs allow them to run through dense undergrowth. The Ypecaha wood rail (*Aramides ypecaha*), shown here, is found in Paraguay Uruguay, Brazil and Argentina.

of mountains leads to cooling and PRECIPITATION; the descending air on the leeward side is depleted in moisture and thus has less capacity to produce RAIN.

rain tree (saman)

Tree native to the West Indies and Central America. It gets its popular name from the fact that cicadas regularly eject juice on it, thus giving the impression that it is always raining under its branches. Height: to 30m (100ft). Family Leguminosae; species *Samanea saman*.

rainwash

Process in which drops of rainwater hit rock and soil,

RAINBOW

Bright, multicoloured band, usually seen as a circular or partial arc formed opposite to the Sun or other light source. The **primary bow** is the one usually seen; in it the colours are arranged from red at the top to violet beneath. A **secondary bow**, in which the order of the colours is reversed, is some-times seen beyond the primary bow. The colours are caused by reflection of light within spherical drops of falling RAIN, which disperses white light into its constituent wavelengths. The colours usually seen are those of the visible spectrum: red, orange, yellow, green, blue, indigo and violet.

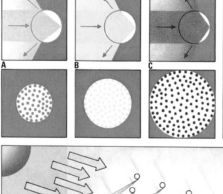

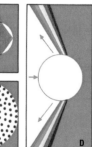

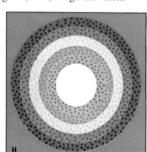

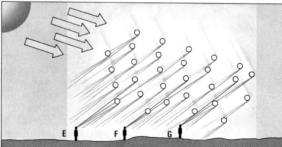

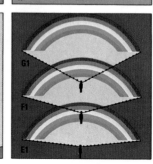

▲ **A rainbow is** a natural demonstration of the mixture of wavelengths that makes up white light. Drops of moisture in the atmosphere act as prisms, dispersing the light into its component colours. Violet (A) is always refracted, diffracted and finally reflected at an angle of *c.*40° parallel to the Sun's rays, yellow (B) at *c.*41° and red at *c.*42°. In this way the complete spectrum is formed (D). As each colour is formed by rays that reach the observer at a certain angle, no matter what the position of the observer (E, F and G) in relation to the Sun and the raindrops, the same spectrum is seen as E1, F1 and G1. From an aircraft, however, an observer might see the complete circle (H).

washing away tiny particles. It contributes significantly to the EROSION of the sides of VALLEYS, especially if they have no covering vegetation, and helps to form V-shaped valleys in areas of significant rainfall. In the absence of rainwash, as in deserts, the sides of valleys carved out by rivers remain very steep and form WADIS, GORGES or CANYONS.

raised beach
Elevated beach that is above sea level because of an uplift of the land or a retreat of the sea. A raised beach is often bounded on its inland edge by old cliffs, sometimes with caves. The uplift of land may have been the result of tectonic movements or the isostatic readjustment of the land after ice has melted. When the weight of ice has been removed by melting, the land gradually rises, relative to the sea. The same effect can be produced by the retreat of the sea; this occurred when snow and ice increased during the glacial phases: as water becomes locked in ice and snow there is less water in the sea and it retreats from the beach.

Ramapithecus
Fossil found in India in 1934; it was once thought to be an early hominoid ancestor of present humans. Most anthropologists now believe it to be the same as, or closely related to, *Sivapithecus* – a non-hominoid Miocene ape.

rambutan
Tall tree native to Malaysia; it is also cultivated in the Philippines, Australia and Central America. It produces a pinkish or deep red rounded fruit, which has many small, soft protruberances, hence its nickname of "hairy lychee". The acid pulp of the fruit is much-prized in the Old World tropics. Family Sapindaceae; species *Nephelium lappaceum*.

ramie (ramee)
Perennial plant that grows in warm climates. The strong bast fibre of its rod-like stems is used to make fine cloth. Family Urticaceae; species *Boehmeria nivea*.

rape
Annual or biennial plant that originated as a hybrid, possibly in the Mediterranean region. It has erect, blue-green stems and elongated, lobed leaves. Its yellow flowers are clustered into branched terminal heads. Rape is extensively cultivated for its oil-bearing seeds (oilseed rape). It is also used as a seedling-salad plant and is occasionally grown for fodder or green manure (forage rape). Height: to 1.5m (5ft). Family Brassicaceae; species *Brassica napus*.

rasbora
Any member of the genus *Rasbora*, comprising small, freshwater MINNOWS from Asia and Africa. They are colourful, with protruding lower jaws. The genus includes the harlequin fish (*Rasbora heteromorpha*), a popular aquarium fish. Length: to 5cm (2in). Family Cyprinidae.

▶ rape Widely cultivated throughout China, India and Europe, rape produces seeds that have an oil content of 40–50%. Once it is extracted, the oil is used for cooking, lubrication, fuel and the manufacture of soap and rubber. The seed residue is used for animal feed and fertilizer.

▶ raspberry Popular as a wild fruit from ancient times, raspberries have been cultivated since the early 17th century. The fruits grow on usually thorny bushes, although thornless varieties also exist. There are more than 200 varieties of raspberry in Asia, where the fruit is thought to have originated.

raspberry
Fruit bush grown in temperate regions of Europe, North America and Asia. The black, purple or red fruit is eaten fresh or preserved. Canes, rising from perennial roots, bear fruit the second year. Family Rosaceae; species *Rubus idaeus*.

rat
Any of a large number of mostly medium or quite large members of the MOUSE family. Rats are opportunistic animals, some species of which have adapted to changing environments and become associated with human habitations. Order Rodentia; family Muridae (part); subfamilies containing rat species include Murinae, Hesperomyinae, Cricetomyinae, Otomyinae, Lophiomyinae, Rhizomyinae, Nesomyinae and Hydromyinae.

rat, bamboo
Any of three species of heavily built, gopher-like rats that are native to China and Southeast Asia. They have short, strong legs and long claws for digging large burrow systems under bamboo plants. They feed on bamboo roots and stems, and also crop plants, which they take back to the burrows to eat. Their large incisor teeth are not covered by the lips. Slow, waddling creatures, bamboo rats bite viciously if disturbed. They are sometimes caught for meat. Litters of about four babies are born in spring and again in autumn. Head-body length: 23–48cm (9–19in); tail: 5–20cm (2–8in). Family Muridae; subfamily Rhizomyinae; species include *Rhyzomys pruinosus*.

rat, black (ship rat, roof rat)
Rat that lives in tropical climates in association with people. It is a carrier of the plague virus, which it transmits to people via a flea. It is omnivorous, eating any human food and many other things as well, such as soap, paper and beeswax. It gnaws through electricity cables, lead pipes and concrete. Together with the brown rat, the black rat causes perhaps a billion dollars worth of damage every year. Head-body length: 25–30cm (10–12in); tail 25–30cm (10–12in). Family Muridae; species *Rattus rattus*.

rat, brown (Norway rat, common rat)
Rat that originated in Asia but is now found worldwide; it is very common in association with people. It is brown, with pink ears, feet and tail and a white underside. Brown rats have a high reproductive rate and breed throughout the year. They are adaptable and will feed on a wide variety of food. Brown rats are pests, destroying human food stores and spreading serious human diseases, such as plague, typhus and food poisoning. Together with black rats, brown rats are thought to have taken more human lives than all human conflicts. Where they have been introduced into new habitats, they have caused the extinction of many other species. Head-body length: 25–30cm (10–12in); tail: 25–30cm

(10–12in). Family Muridae; subfamily Murinae; species *Rattus norvegicus*.

rat, cane
Either of two species of large, beaver-like rodents from sub-Saharan Africa; they are serious pests of sugar cane. The cane rat's coat is brown-grey above with a lighter underside. It constructs sleeping platforms of chopped up vegetation, but sometimes shelters in empty burrows or rock piles. Mating takes place in early summer and two to four well-developed young are born two months later. Head-body length: 35–60cm (14–24in); tail: 7–25cm (3–10in). Suborder Caviomorpha; family Thryonomyidae; species include *Thryonomys swinderianus*.

rat, fish-eating
Rat that is highly adapted to a fish-eating way of life; several species are found in South America. It is a strong swimmer, having webbed feet, and its upper incisors are sharp spikes, rather than the usual rodent chisel-shape, for catching slippery fish. The fish-eating rat digs burrows in river banks where it breeds, producing up to two litters every year. Head-body length: 15–21cm (6–8in); tail: 15–19cm (6–7in). Family Muridae; subfamily Hesperomyinae; genera *Daptomys*, *Neusticomys* and *Ichthyomys*; species include *Ichthyomys stolzmanni*.

rat, kangaroo
Rat that inhabits the arid grasslands of North America, where it digs burrows in the loose soil. It only comes out of its burrow at night, when it travels widely in search of seeds and small invertebrates. Kangaroo rats carry any food they find back to their burrows in cheek pouches. They never need to drink water: the efficiency of their kidneys means that they get all the moisture they need from their food. They breed all through the year, producing litters of up to five young after a gestation of 30 days. Head-body length: 30–38cm (12–15in); tail: 18–21cm (7–8in). Family Heteromyidae; genus *Dipodomys*; species include *Dipodomys deserti*. *See also* MOUSE, POCKET

rat, spiny
Any of more than 70 species of South American rodents. They look like rats but belong to the CAVY group. They have spines amongst the brownish-grey hairs on their backs; their underparts are pale. The tail is thinly haired and breaks off easily. Spiny rats live in forests close to water and feed on seeds, shoots and leaves. Breeding is continuous; well-developed babies are born after a two-month gestation. The young are themselves able to breed within two months. Head-body length: 10–50cm (4–20in); tail: 5–40cm (2–16in). Suborder Caviomorpha; family Echimyidae; species include *Proechimys guairae* (spiny rat casiragua).

R

▲ rat, black Widespread in the Mediterranean and North and Central America, the black rat prefers warm conditions and often inhabits buildings, especially attic floors. It breeds all year round, and female black rats usually give birth in the summer to litters of up to 10 young.

313

rat, tree-

Either of two rare rat species found in Australian woodland. Tree-rats have yellowish fur with black guard hairs and feet; the underparts are cream and there is a white tail tuft. They are nocturnal and arboreal, hiding in leafy nests in hollow trees by day and searching for seeds, nuts and small insects by night. They make loud whirring noises and bite savagely if disturbed. Breeding takes place throughout the year. Head-body length: 24–35cm (9–14in); tail: 27–39cm (11–15in). Family Muridae; species include *Mesembriomys gouldii*.

rat, water-

Thickset rat that lives in marshland of South America. It is an excellent swimmer and climber. It has grey-black upper parts, pale grey lower parts and a long tail. It eats insects and seeds. The water-rat makes its nest amongst the roots and stems of waterside plants, taking refuge in the water if disturbed. It has good hearing and communicates vocally. Litters of about four babies are produced throughout the year. Head-body length: 15–19cm (6–7in); tail: 13–16cm (5–6in). Family Muridae; species *Scapteromys tumidus*.

ratel

See BADGER, HONEY

ratite

Any of a group (Ratitae) of large, usually flightless birds with flat breastbones instead of the keel-like prominences found in most flying birds. Ratites include the OSTRICH, RHEA, CASSOWARY, EMU, KIWI and the unusual flying TINAMOU.

rat-tailed maggot

Larva of HOVERFLIES in the genus *Eristalis*. The rat-tailed maggot lives in drains and polluted water where there is a limited oxygen supply. Its "rat-tail" is in fact a telescopic breathing tube, which it uses to access the air above its aquatic habitat. Adult body size: *c*.7mm (*c*.0.3in). Order Diptera; family Syriphidae; genus *Eristalis*.

rattan

Any of several species of climbing PALM native to Southeast Asia and Africa. Rattan is noted for its very long stems, which can grow to 150m (500ft). The stems are used for making ropes and furniture. Family Arecacae/Palmae; genus *Calamus*.

rattlesnake

Any of *c*.30 species of venomous pit VIPERS characterized by a tail rattle of loosely connected segments of unshed skin. Rattlesnakes range from Canada to South America and are usually found in arid regions. Most species are blotched with dark diamonds, hexagons or spots on a lighter background. They feed mostly on rodents. Length: 0.3–2.5m (1–8ft). Family Viperidae. *See also* SNAKE

rattlesnake, diamondback

Largest rattlesnake in the United States. It is identified by dark, diamond-shaped patterns on its back and a broad triangular head. As with other members of the pit VIPER family, the diamondback rattlesnake has deep infrared sensory pits on its head, which it uses to locate prey. The diamondback rattlesnake inhabits dry, shrub terrain, where it feeds on small mammals, birds and sometimes other reptiles. The western diamondback (*Crotalus atrox*), found in W United States, can grow up to 2.1m (6.9ft). The eastern diamondback (*Crotalus adamanteus*), found in E United States, can grow to 2.4m (7.9ft). Family Viperidae; genus *Crotalus*.

rattlesnake, pygmy

See MASSASAUGA

raven

Any of several species of very large CROWS. The raven has a massive bill and a "shaggy" throat. Most species, such as the common (*Corvus corax*) and Australian (*Corvus coronoides*) ravens, are glossy black all over, but the white-necked raven (*Corvus albicollis*) has a striking white nape patch. The raven is a great scavenger. Despite its ungainly appearance,

▲ **rattlesnake** Not normally aggressive, rattlesnakes try to avoid confrontation by warning of their presence. Their unmistakable and menacing rattle is produced by "bells" of hard skin on the end of the tail. The amount of venom they produce far exceeds that needed to kill the rodents that form their usual prey. They can also use the venom to protect themselves against large predators.

it can perform remarkable aerobatics. Length: to 65cm (26in). Family Corvidae; genus *Corvus*.

Ray, John (1627–1705)

English naturalist. His work on plant and animal classification later influenced Carolus LINNAEUS and Georges CUVIER. Ray was the first to distinguish the two main types of flowering plants: MONOCOTYLEDONS and DICOTYLEDONS.

ray

Any of *c*.350 species of cartilaginous, mostly marine fish, related to the SKATE, SHARK and CHIMAERA. Order Batoidei.

ray, devil (manta ray)

Any member of the family Mobulidae, comprising rays that are some of the largest cartilaginous fish. The devil ray can weigh up to 1360 kg (3000lb). Its expanded fins form a pair of "wings", which are used to propel it through the water. It feeds by straining small planktonic animals out of the water. Length: 1–7m (3–23ft). Family Mobulidae.

ray, electric

Cartilaginous, flattened, bottom-dwelling, marine fish of the Atlantic, Indian and Pacific Oceans. Electric organs located behind its eyes can produce high voltage discharges, which are used to stun prey. Length: 0.3–2m (1–6.6ft). Family Torpedinidae; genera include *Torpedo* and *Narcine*.

ray, manta

See RAY, DEVIL

razorfish (shrimpfish)

Any of several species of tropical marine fish. It has a long, sharply pointed dorsal covering that looks like a shrimp's rostrum. It gets its common name from its sharp, razor-like belly, which is formed by bony plates. Length: 14–30cm (6–12in). Family Centriscidae. The name **razorfish** also refers to tropical marine WRASSES of the genus *Hemipterontus* (family Labridae); they occur in the Atlantic Ocean.

razor shell

Marine bivalve MOLLUSC with a long, thin, narrow, hinged shell. It is common in the intertidal zone of temperate seas of the Northern Hemisphere. Length: to 20cm (8in). Family Solenidae.

Réaumur, René Antoine Ferchault de (1683–1757)

French physicist. Réaumur is chiefly remembered for

▼ **rattan** A worker harvests rattan palm (*Calamus* sp.) in Sumatra, Indonesia. The slender, flexible stems are used to make baskets, mats and even furniture. The cultivation of rattan is very labour intensive and is an important source of work for the poorest members of the communities.

R

his thermometer scale, which designates 0° as the freezing point of water and 80° as its boiling point. He wrote widely on natural history and conducted research in mining, metallurgy, fossils and insects.

recapitulation theory
See BIOGENETIC LAW

receptacle
Biological structure that serves as a container for reproductive cells or organs in plants. In ANGIOSPERMS (flowering plants), the receptacle is the enlarged end of a stalk to which the FLOWER is attached. In FERNS, it is the mass of tissue that forms the sporangium (the SPORE-bearing organ). In some SEAWEEDS, the receptacle is the part that seasonally becomes swollen and carries the reproductive organs.

receptor
In higher organisms, tiny organs found on both NEURONES (nerve cells) and ENDOCRINE cells. They detect physical stimuli, such as light, sound, touch and taste, and chemical changes occurring inside the body and on or near its surface. The receptors then transform the physical or chemical signals into electrical energy or the secretion of HORMONES. For example, the RODS AND CONES of the retina of the eye are receptors that transform light energy into the nerve impulses sent via SENSORY NEURONES to the brain. Other receptors, such as those in muscles, the ear and visceral organs, tell the brain how the body is positioned and how it moves.

recessive
In genetics, describes a form of GENE (ALLELE) that does not express itself when paired with a DOMINANT allele. Although it is part of the GENOTYPE (genetic make-up) of a HETEROZYGOTE (an organism containing both dominant and recessive alleles for a particular gene), it does not contribute to the PHENOTYPE (physical characteristics) of the organism. It becomes expressed only when the same recessive allele form appears on both CHROMOSOMES of a HOMOZYGOTE. Recessive alleles were discovered by Gregor MENDEL, who found that a cross between purebred red- and white-flowering garden peas always produced red flowers in the offspring. The allele for red coloration is dominant; the allele for white is recessive. In humans, the alleles for blue eyes are recessive to those of brown eyes.

reclamation of land
Making safer, and more aesthetically pleasing, land that has been left derelict and that is often polluted. It includes land that has been occupied by factories, mines and soil heaps. The establishment of vegetation is vital to the process. Reclamation involves determining the factors that are preventing plant growth and remedying them. Reclamation may require drainage, incorporation of organic material, levelling the ground, ploughing, adding fertilizers and sowing the seeds of species able to tolerate pollutants in the soil.

recombinant DNA research
Branch of GENETIC ENGINEERING involving the transfer of a segment of DNA from a source organism into a host organism (typically a microbe). It is also known as GENE splicing because the transferred segment is spliced into the overall DNA structure of the host, thus altering the information contained in its GENETIC CODE. When the host undergoes asexual CELL DIVISION, each product cell carries a replica of the new DNA. In this way, numerous CLONES of the new cell can be made. Gene splicing can be used to design cells to produce medicines, to digest spilled oil or waste products, and for numerous other purposes.

recombination
Process that rearranges GENES to increase genetic VARIATION in sexually produced offspring. Recombination takes place during MEIOSIS, the type of CELL DIVISION that leads to the formation of sex cells (GAMETES). It is achieved by CROSSING OVER of paired CHROMATIDS. Its effect is to "shuffle" genes derived from both parents and thereby create genetic variation. Some GENETIC ENGINEERING techniques can induce recombination artificially.

rectum
In humans and many other vertebrates, last part of the large INTESTINE, where the faeces accumulate prior to voiding.

recycling
Natural and synthetic processes by which substances are broken down and reconstituted. In nature, elemental cycles include the CARBON CYCLE, NITROGEN CYCLE and HYDROLOGICAL CYCLE. Natural cyclic chemical processes include the metabolic cycles, such as the KREBS CYCLE, in the bodies of living organisms. Synthetic recycling includes using bacteria to break down excreta and many kitchen and factory organic wastes to harmless, or even beneficial, substances. Large quantities of inorganic waste, such as metal scrap, glass bottles and building refuse, are recycled. Polymer wastes are often burned rather than recycled, with consequent atmospheric pollution and loss of material resources. Controlled burning (pyrolysis) recovers useful substances from plastics.

red alga
See RHODOPHYTE

red blood cell
Common name for an ERYTHROCYTE

red bud
Spreading shrub or small tree found in woodlands of the United States. It is closely related to the JUDAS TREE. The red bud has rounded, heart-shaped leaves and small, rosy-pink, pea-like flowers. The clusters

▲ **ray, electric** Found in all oceans, the various species of electric ray use the electric charge they can generate both for stunning prey and for warding off predators – the shock of between 35 and 60 volts may be strong enough to stun humans. They feed on smaller animals and have specially adapted teeth for crushing shells.

of flowers are produced on old wood, including the trunk, and appear before the leaves. A white-flowered form also exists. Height to 12m (39ft). Family Caesalpiniaceae; species *Cercis canadensis*.

redbush
Shrub that is native to mountainous areas of South Africa; it is a member of the LEGUME family. Redbush turns from dark-green to red-brown as it matures. It has been used as a tea by the Hottentots for centuries. It has been cultivated since 1930 for its leaves, which are used as a caffeine-free, low-tannin red tea. Family Fabaceae; species *Aspalathus linearis*.

redcurrant
Widely cultivated shrub and its small, round, red, edible fruit; it is closely related to the BLACKCURRANT. Family Grossulariaceae; species *Ribes silvestre*.

red deer
See DEER, RED

redgum
Red-wooded EUCALYPTUS tree from Australia. It has smooth, grey bark and narrowly lance-shaped leaves. It is commonly grown for ornamental and commercial purposes because it is drought resistant and can endure extremes of temperature. Redgum is favoured as a shade tree and windbreak. Height: to 60m (200ft). Family Myrtaceae; species *Eucalyptus rostrata*. **Redgum** is also the name for a tall pyramidal tree native to E and central United States. It has star-shaped leaves, which turn crimson and yellow in the autumn, and spherical, spiky fruits. The redgum tree provides heavy, close-grained heartwood, used for furniture, and a fragrant gum, used in perfumery and as a fumigant. Height: to 40m (130ft). Family Hamamelidaceae; species *Liquidambar styraciflua*.

red-hot poker
Perennial plant that originated in South Africa. It is commonly cultivated as a garden plant. Red-hot poker has an underground rhizome and narrow, tubular, red or yellow flowers. Height: 1m (3.3ft). Family Liliaceae; species *Kniphofia uvaria*.

redox
See OXIDATION-REDUCTION

redpoll
Any of several species of delicate FINCHES found in the Northern Hemisphere. Most species have a small red crown patch, a black chin and a pink blush on the breast. Redpolls breed in coniferous and birch forests. They fly with an undulating, twittering flight. In win-

▲ **raven** A hardy and adaptable bird, the raven makes its nest in cliffs or trees. It is distinguished from other crows by its wedge-shaped tail and noisy guttural call. Ravens are sociable and intelligent creatures and can be tamed and taught to mimic human speech.

R

▲ red snapper Young red snappers can be found on sandy and muddy seafloors, but adults prefer cooler, deeper waters. The red snapper has a large mouth and pointed teeth and feeds on crustaceans and small fish. Although the red snapper is abundant in areas like the Gulf of Mexico, in recent years measures have been taken to counteract over- fishing.

ter, they form mixed flocks with other finches and sometimes visit gardens. Length: 13–15cm (5–6in). Family Carduelidae; genus *Carduelis* (part).

red snapper
Tropical marine fish found from the West Indies to Florida, s United States. It is bright scarlet, with sharp teeth and a flattened snout. The red snapper is a popular food fish. Length: 60–90cm (24–35in). Family Lutjanidae; species *Lutjanus campechanus*.

red spider
See MITE, SPIDER

redstart
Any of several species of small birds from two families. The common redstart (*Phoenicurus phoenicurus*) belongs to the THRUSH family (Turdidae). The male is boldly patterned red and slaty blue. The redstart makes fly-catching sallies and constantly quivers its reddish-brown tail. The American redstart (*Setophaga ruticilla*) belongs to the American wood warbler family (Parulidae). It is glossy black with bright orange patches on its wings, tail and belly. Length: 13–18cm (5–7in).

reduction
Chemical reaction in which an ELECTRON is added to an ATOM or an ION. It is always part of an OXIDATION-REDUCTION reaction.

R

redwood
See SEQUOIA

reed
Any of several species of aquatic GRASS found in wetlands worldwide. The common reed (*Phragmites communis*) has broad leaves and feathery flower clusters. Its stiff, smooth stems are used for thatching, construction and musical pipes. Height: to 3m (10ft). Family Poaceae/Gramineae.

reedbuck
Light, graceful ANTELOPE native to Africa s of the Sahara; it is usually found near water. Its body is brown to grey, and when disturbed it erects its bushy tail. The male has short horns, curved forwards at the tips. Length: to 1.4m (4.6ft). Family Bovidae; genus *Redunca*.

reedmace
See BULRUSH

reef
Rocky outcrop lying in shallow water, especially one built up by CORALS or other organisms. *See also* CORAL REEF

reflex action
Rapid, involuntary response to a particular stimulus – for example, the "knee-jerk" reflex that occurs when the bent knee is tapped. A reflex action is controlled by a reflex arc found in the CENTRAL NERVOUS SYSTEM. A reflex arc consists of a sensory receptor (which detects the stimulus), an afferent (or sensory) nerve, which conveys the impulse to the grey matter of the SPINAL CORD, and an efferent (or motor) nerve, which carries the response impulse to the EFFECTOR, in this case the muscles in the knee, causing the leg to jerk. This type of response is only detected by the brain once the reflex has taken place. This reflex is sometimes called a **spinal reflex**. A **cranial reflex** involves the brain, whereby the initial reflex can be overridden by the brain and either stopped or altered.

reflexor
Any MUSCLE that when contracted causes an appendage or limb to bend (flex) about a joint. The biceps muscle in the arm is an example of a flexor.

reforestation
Planting of trees in a region where DEFORESTATION has occurred. Throughout the world, trees have been cut down for fuel or wood pulp, or to clear land for agriculture. On sloping land with no trees, soil EROSION soon takes place as rain washes away the soil. Replanting trees prevents erosion and provides a renewable resource of timber and fuel.

regeneration
Biological term for the ability of an organism to replace one of its parts if it is lost. Regeneration also refers to a form of ASEXUAL REPRODUCTION in which a new individual grows from a detached portion of a parent organism.

regolith
Loose fragments of rock between the layers of SOIL and the BEDROCK beneath. The fragments are usually thin and have broken away from the bedrock. Eventually they break down and become mineral particles in the soil. *See also* SOIL HORIZON

regulatory gene
Any GENE that controls the way in which another gene is produced. Regulatory genes activate or deactivate a group of neighbouring genes called an OPERON, which functions as a unit. Usually found in BACTERIA, operons are responsible for the formation of ENZYMES that control various processes in a metabolic pathway.

▲ reindeer Always found in large herds, reindeer migrate vast distances between summer and winter feeding grounds. They are adapted to two different environments – tundra and woodland. Their large hoofs spread out when they walk on snow or soft ground.

reindeer (caribou)
Large DEER of northern latitudes; it ranges from Scandinavia across Siberia to North America. It has thick fur and broad hoofs, which help to spread the animal's weight on snow. It feeds on grasses and saplings in the summer and lichens it finds beneath the snow in the winter. The reindeer is domesticated for meat and as a pack animal by the Lapps. It is the only deer in which both sexes have antlers. Height: up to 1.4m (4.6ft) at the shoulder. Family Cervidae; species *Rangifer tarandus*.

relative density (r.d.) (formerly specific gravity)
Ratio of the density of a substance to the density of water. Thus, the relative density of gold is 19.3: it is 19.3 times denser than water.

releasing hormone
HORMONE secreted by the HYPOTHALAMUS in the brain; it travels to the nearby PITUITARY GLAND, where it stimulates the release of another hormone. Each of the pituitary hormones has a specific releasing hormone (also called a releasing factor). For example, the production of thyrotrophin (thyroid-stimulating hormone, TSH) by the pituitary gland is triggered by thyrotrophin-releasing hormone from the hypothalamus.

Remak, Robert (1815–65)
German physician and physiologist who laid the foundation of modern EMBRYOLOGY. In 1842 he simplified Karl BAER's four germ layers to three, which he named ectoderm, mesoderm and endoderm, and showed their significance in embryological development. He later identified the sympathetic ganglia in the heart – Remak's ganglia. Remak was also a pioneer in the use of electrotherapy for treating nervous disorders.

remora (suckerfish)
Any of several species of marine fish found worldwide in tropical and temperate seas. The various species are grey, reddish or brown. The remora has a ridged sucking disc on top of its head, with which it clings to sharks, turtles, rays, whales and sometimes even boats. Length: 18–9lcm (7–36in). Family Echeneidae.

renal
Relating to the KIDNEY. The renal ARTERY for example is the blood vessel that carries blood to the kidney; the renal VEIN carries blood from the kidney towards the heart.

Rennell, James (1742–1830)
English cartographer, geographer and oceanographer. He was an expert on the geography of w Asia and N Africa, constructing the most accurate map of India of his time (1783). Rennell pioneered the scientific study of winds and ocean currents.

reproduction
Process by which living organisms create new organisms similar to themselves. Reproduction may be **sexual** or **asexual**, the first being the fusion of two special reproductive CELLS from different parents, and the second being the generation of new organisms from a single organism. ASEXUAL REPRODUCTION is the more limited, found mainly in PROTOZOA, some INVERTEBRATES, and in many plants. By contrast, almost all living organisms have the capacity for SEXUAL REPRODUCTION. In the majority of cases, the species has two kinds of individuals – male and female – with different sex functions. Male and female sex cells (in animals, SPERM and OVA) fuse to

▶ **rhea** The flightless rhea roams the pampas of South America in flocks of up to 30. Its height enables it to detect danger even in high grass, and it can run faster than a horse. The male rhea is responsible for incubation of eggs.

produce a new cell, the ZYGOTE, which contains genetic information from both parents, and from which a new individual develops. Alternatively, organisms may be HERMAPHRODITE (like the earthworm), each individual of the species having male and female functions, so that when two of them mate each individual fertilizes the other's eggs. Usually, animals that can reproduce asexually have alternating (not always regularly) generations of asexual and sexual individuals. Examples are the aphid, jellyfish and some parasitic worms. Some plants have alternating life cycles. Sexually reproducing plants (or generations) are called GAMETOPHYTE; ones which reproduce asexually, SPOROPHYTE. *See also* ALTERNATION OF GENERATIONS; PARTHENOGENESIS

reproductive system
Organs of a plant or animal necessary for SEXUAL REPRODUCTION. In plants, the reproductive system comprises the STAMENS and CARPALS. In mammals, the male system comprises the TESTES, the epididymis, prostate and associated glands, and the PENIS; the female system consists of the OVARIES, VAGINA, the UTERUS and the FALLOPIAN TUBES.

reptile
See feature article, pages 318–19

reservoir rocks
Rocks that are porous and permeable enough to hold and store fluids such as gas, oil and water. Some SANDSTONES are reservoir rocks. *See also* PERMEABILITY; POROSITY

resin (rosin)
Artificial or natural POLYMER that is generally viscous and sticky. **Artificial resins**, such as polyesters and epoxy resins, are used as adhesives and binders. **Natural resins** are secreted by various plants. Resin is impermeable to water; when present in large amounts, such as in PINE, resin makes wood resistant to rot and weather. Oleoresin, secreted by CONIFERS, is distilled to produce turpentine; rosin (a yellow, brown or black material) remains after the oil of turpentine has been distilled off. AMBER is fossilized resin.

respiration
See feature article, page 321

respiratory quotient (RQ)
Measure of the ratio of CARBON DIOXIDE evolved by an organism to the OXYGEN consumed over a fixed period. The figure varies for different respiratory substrates. Hexose sugars, for example, have an RQ equal to 1.0, whereas fats have a value of 0.7. Organisms rarely, if ever, respire a single food substance, nor is a substance always completely oxi-

dized. Experimental RQ values therefore do not give an accurate indication of the material being respired.

respiratory system
System of the body concerned with GAS EXCHANGE. The respiratory tract of an air-breathing animal begins with the nose and mouth, through which air enters the body. The air then passes through the LARYNX and into the TRACHEA. At its lower end, the trachea branches into two bronchi and each BRONCHUS leads to a lung. Inside the LUNGS, the bronchi divide into many tiny bronchioles that lead in turn to bunches of tiny air sacs (ALVEOLUS), where the exchange of gases between air and blood takes place. Exhaled air leaves along the same pathway.

restio
Any member of the genus *Restio*, a small group of perennial plants endemic to tropical and s Africa, including Madagascar. The plants are xeromorphic (adapted to prevent excessive loss of moisture), having leaves that are reduced to sheaths. The stems are photosynthetic, a typical characteristic of plants that grow in nutrient-poor soils. The small flowers are usually wind-pollinated; a persistent perianth helps with wind dispersal of seeds. Family Restionaceae; genus *Restio*.

restriction enzyme
ENZYME used in GENETIC ENGINEERING to cut a molecule of DNA at specific points in order to insert or remove a piece of DNA. There are many different restriction enzymes. Each cuts the DNA at a specific sequence of BASES, allowing great precision in genetic engineering. A piece of DNA may be cut out and removed for insertion into another organism. Or the geneticist may wish to insert a different piece of DNA at that point. Pieces of DNA are joined together again with enzymes called ligases. These enzymes are also used when analysing DNA to find out its sequence of bases.

resurrection plant (rose of Jericho)
Plant of the MUSTARD family found in w Asia. The resurrection plant survives dessication by curling up its leaves tightly when dry and unfolding them when moistened. Family Brassicaceae; species *Anastatica hieronochuntica*.

retina
Inner layer of the EYE, composed mainly of different kinds of NEURONES (nerve cells), some of which are the visual receptors of the eye. Receptor cells (RODS AND CONES) are sensitive to light. **Cones** respond primarily to the spectrum of visible colours; **rods** respond mainly to shades of grey and to movement. The rods and cones connect with SENSORY NEURONES, which in turn connect with the OPTIC NERVE, which carries the visual stimuli to the brain.

retrovirus
Any of a large family of VIRUSES (Retroviridae) that, unlike other living organisms, contain the genetic material RNA (ribonucleic acid) rather than the customary DNA (deoxyribonucleic acid). In order to multiply, retroviruses make use of a special ENZYME to convert their RNA into DNA, which then becomes integrated with the DNA in the CELLS of their hosts. Diseases caused by retroviruses include acquired immune deficiency syndrome (AIDS) and some forms of leukaemia.

reverse transcription
Method of producing a double-stranded DNA copy of RNA from a VIRUS. The technique is used often in GENETIC ENGINEERING to make DNA copies of MESSENGER RNA (mRNA). It is achieved using an ENZYME called **reverse transcriptase**, which occurs in RETROVIRUSES.

rhea
Either of two species of large flightless birds found in South America; they are similar to the OSTRICHES of Africa. The male rhea attracts females to his nest and encourages them to lay up to 30 eggs. He alone incubates the eggs and rears the young. The young from each nest often remain together until they are two to three years of age. Family Rheidae; genus *Pterocnemia*.

rhebok
Small, graceful ANTELOPE found on the upland grasslands of s Africa. The rhebok has a woolly, yellow-grey coat. Males (rams) have short, straight horns; they keenly defend their territories by clicking and urinating displays. They will attack, and sometimes kill, any animal that does not back off. Female rheboks live in groups with their young and one ram. When disturbed, rheboks run off, flicking up their rear ends as they go. During the rutting season, fighting between males is ritualized and little harm is done. One or two lambs are born after a gestation of nine and a half months. Head-body length: 1–1.2m (3.3–4ft); tail: 10–20cm (4–8in). Family Bovidae; species *Pelea capreolus*.

rhesus macaque
See MACAQUE, RHESUS

rhinoceros
Any of five species of large, odd-toed ungulates. The rhinoceros (or rhino) has thick, armour-like hide, a bulky body and a heavy head. The "horns" are composed of very tightly packed hair. Order Perrisodactyla, family Rhinocerotidae.

rhinoceros, black (hooked-lipped rhinoceros)
Rhinoceros that lives in bush land of Africa, from Chad and Sudan to South Africa; it is classified as a

R

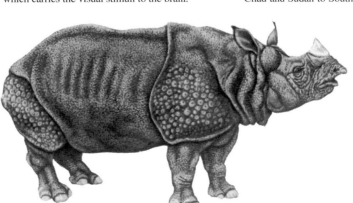

◀ **rhinoceros, Indian** The largest of the three species of Asian rhinoceros, the Indian rhinoceros is distinguished from other rhinos by the tubercles on its skin. It also has large folds of skin around its joints and neck and a prehensile upper lip. It spends long durations wallowing in bathing pools in order to escape the heat and avoid flies. Although it is the most numerous of the Asian species, its population stands at c.1700.

Reptiles make up the class Reptilia. Most reptiles were wiped out 65 million years ago by the natural disaster that ended the Cretaceous period. There remain about 6000 different reptile species - few in numbers and small in size compared with past ages, but still great in diversity. They range from small, legless, eyeless creatures, easily mistaken for worms, to predatory CROCODILES, which can grow to lengths of more than 6m (20ft), and massive TORTOISES and TURTLES that may weigh upwards of a tonne. Most reptile species have dry skin that is covered with scales or embedded with bony plates. Their limbs are poorly developed or non-existent.

It was about 300 million years ago that reptiles began to dominate the world of their predecessors, the AMPHIBIANS. Over the millennia, many reptiles grew to huge size, notably the DINOSAURS. Today, except for the crocodiles and ALLIGATORS, most are relatively small. There are four major reptilian orders: the Chelonia, which include tortoises, turtles and TERRAPINS; the Crocodilia, which include crocodiles, alligators, CAYMANS and the GAVIAL; the Squamata, which include SNAKES and LIZARDS; and the Rhynchocephalia, the lone member of which is the TUATARA.

Reptiles are ENTOTHERMIC, which does not mean that they are "cold-blooded", rather their blood can be "hot" or "cold" according to the temperature of their surroundings. Reptiles have optimum temperature ranges for bodily processes: a snake, for example, needs heat to digest food; if too cold the snake dies because food rots in its stomach. Reptiles have developed various behavioural means to control their temperature, typically basking in the morning sun to warm up or absorbing heat from the ground below them, using shade to cool down, and modifying posture for "fine-tuning" body temperatures. Few reptiles can survive cold for long, but one reason they have survived strong mammalian competition is that they need less food than mammals to maintain their metabolism and can thus exist on a meagre diet.

Many reptiles engage in complex behavioural patterns before and during mating. Around this time secondary sexual characteristics distinguishing males and females may also become apparent. Most lizards lay eggs, although a small number, including a few species of SKINKS and GECKOS, give birth to live young. For most of those lizards it is usually a matter of the mother retaining the eggs inside her until they have hatched, before "giving birth" (known as OVOVIVIPARITY). Most lizard species, however, bury their eggs – protected by a leathery shell – for the Sun to incubate through the soil. Similarly, most snakes simply lay their eggs and abandon them. A minority of snakes, however, give birth to live young, either by hatching eggs inside the mother or – much more rarely – after direct nourishment of the growing young from the mother's bloodstream via the oviduct, which functions similarly to the placenta of the higher mammals (known as VIVIPARITY). There are also some snake species that show some signs of parental care for their eggs by, for example, coiling their bodies around them. Both tortoises and turtles lay their eggs in sunny places on land, buried in large numbers in a nest that is then concealed. The mothers then display no further interest in either their eggs or their hatchlings.

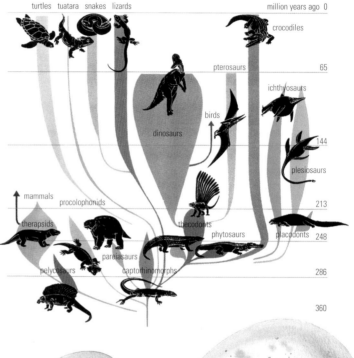

◄ A reptile evolutionary tree indicates how few species survived from the reptiles' heyday. Crocodiles and alligators are the closest living relatives to dinosaurs and also have the most advanced brains and hearts. Turtles and tortoises have changed very little over millions of years; like many areas of reptilian evolution, their origins are obscure. Therapsids, though all species are now extinct, are a vital branch of evolution, for it is from them that the synapsids evolved, which in turn led to the mammals. All, however, evolved from the earliest group of reptiles, the captorhinomorphs, otherwise known as the "stem reptiles".

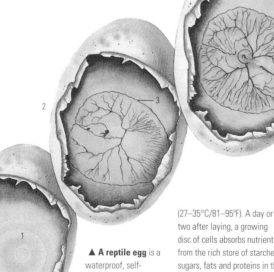

▲ A reptile egg is a waterproof, self-sufficient entity that lacks nothing apart from an external heat source to keep it at the correct temperature for hatching (27–35°C/81–95°F). A day or two after laying, a growing disc of cells absorbs nutrient from the rich store of starches, sugars, fats and proteins in the yolk (1). As the early embryo develops (2), blood vessels (3) begin to cover the yolk surface; these extract nutrient from the yolk to feed the embryo. By the time an extensive blood vessel network develops, the embryo's internal organs are taking form (4). When the embryo is half-developed (5), the various "life- support" systems of the egg are clearly differentiated. Between the shell and the embryo are three membranes. The innermost is the amniotic sac (6), a fluid-filled shock-absorbing sac surrounding the embryo, which connects to the yolk via the umbilical cord (7). The yolk sac and amnion are enclosed in the allantois (8), which collects waste products and separates them from the embryo. It also acts as the lung of the egg, transferring oxygen from the chorion (9), just under the shell, which has blood vessels filled with haemoglobin molecules to absorb oxygen.

R

▶ **Heat is essential** for reptiles to survive, but the blisteringly hot, loose sand of desert dunes can get too hot for one of its inhabitants, the Namib dune lizard. The ideal sand surface temperature for the lizard is 30–40°C (86–104°F), when the reptile can gather food or find a mate. However, since for much of the day the sand surface is so hot that it would quickly kill the lizard, the animal has little time to move around normally and conduct its activities. To increase its "socializing" and feeding time, the lizard speeds up its morning basking – when it warms up – by pressing its underbody against the sand and holding its legs and tail up in the air (A). When sufficiently warm, the lizard is agile enough to move about normally. Later in the day, however, the sand temperature reaches 40°C (104°F) and the lizard avoids overheating by "stilt-walking" on the hot sand with outstretched legs (B). Occasionally its lifts two legs at opposite corners of its body (C) and, using its tail as an extra support, raises its feet off the otherwise intolerably hot sand. By noon, surface temperatures reach 45°C (113°F) and the lizard seeks protective cooler sand by flicking its tail to burrow down into the dune (D).

A

B

C

D

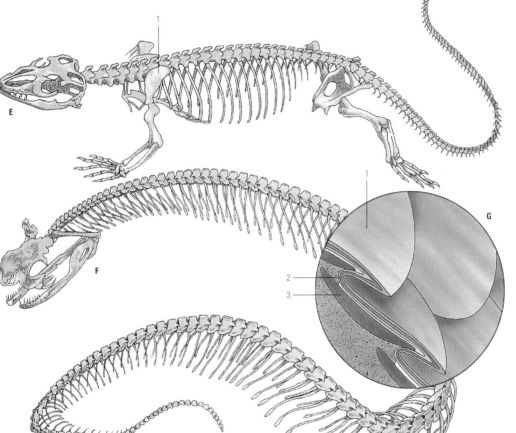
E

F

G

H

◀ **Lizard skeletons** (E, right-hand limbs omitted for clarity) have a pivoting shoulder girdle (1) to permit the typical side-to-side body locomotion. Most reptiles lack bony epiphyses (cartilage at bone ends, which in mature mammals fuse to the bone to restrict further growth). Snake skeletons (F) have no limbs. The spine, however, has an unusually high number of vertebrae, up to 400 in some pythons. A complex ball and socket joint links each vertebra, allowing horizontal movement up to 25°, making a strong but highly flexible sup-port for the ribs, to which join powerful locomotive muscles. A section through reptile scales (G) shows layers of thick, horny keratin (1) hinged at thinner layers (2) to allow movement. Pigment cells below (3) include black ones that can darken the skin and increase heat absorption when basking.

Turtle (H) shells consist of a carapace, made of an outer keratin layer and an inner bone structure (1) fused to the ribs and vertebrae, and a plastron (2), evolved from some of the shoulder girdle bones and ribs.

R

▲ **rhinoceros, Javan** The extremely rare Javan rhinoceros lives in lowland rainforests, preferring areas with plentiful water hollows for wallowing in mud. Despite having smaller ears than other rhinoceros species, it is known for its keen sense of hearing. Its eyesight is poor.

vulnerable species. It is grey, with a large head, two horns (sometimes even a small third) and no hump. It uses its mobile, pointed upper lip to grab the leaves and buds of the small trees on which it feeds. Unsociable, solitary animals, they occupy overlapping ranges, the boundaries of which are marked by dung heaps. Males and females only come together for a few days to mate. The calf is born after 15 months and stays with its mother for up to three years. Head-body length: 3–3.6m (10–12ft); tail: 60–70cm (24–28in). Family Rhinocerotidae; species *Diceros bicornis*.

rhinoceros, Indian (greater one-horned rhinoceros) Endangered species of rhinoceros that once lived in the swampy grassland of Nepal and NE India. Its numbers have been severely reduced by hunting and poaching, its horns being valued as a traditional medicine, and by habitat destruction. It has thick, dark-grey, knobbly and deeply folded skin. The male has a larger horn than the female. Solitary animals, they feed on grass and twigs early and late in the day and rest at other times. A single calf is born after a 16-month gestation; it suckles for up to two years. Head-body length: 4.2m (14ft); tail: 75cm (30in). Family Rhinocerotidae; species *Rhinoceros unicornis*. *See* illustration, page 317

rhinoceros, Javan (lesser one-horned rhinoceros) Endangered species of rhinoceros, perhaps the rarest wild animal in the world. It lived in dense rainforests across Southeast Asia, but there may now only be *c*.50 individuals living in a reserve in Java. Males have a single horn but the larger females are often hornless. They are smaller and have fewer skin folds than the Indian rhino. Javan rhinos have a pointed, prehensile upper lip, which is used to browse on leaves, shoots and fruit. They live alone, except for mothers and calves, which stay together for up to two years. Head-body length: 3–3.2m (10–10.5ft); tail: 70cm (28in). Family Rhinocerotidae; species *Rhinoceros sondaicus*.

rhinoceros, Sumatran (Asian two-horned rhinoceros) Endangered species of rhinoceros. It inhabits dense forests of Sumatra, Borneo, Burma, Thailand and Malaysia; it is the smallest rhino. The male's two horns are larger than those of other rhino species, and he has more bristly hairs, which cover the folded hide and fringe the ears. Sumatran rhinos live alone or in male-female pairs, feeding on leaves, fruit and bamboo shoots, often trampling down trees. Like other rhinos they have good hearing and smell but poor sight. A single calf is born after a gestation period of seven to eight months. Head-body length: 2.4–2.7m (8–9ft); tail: 60cm (24in). Family Rhinocerotidae; species *Dicerorhinus sumatrensis*.

rhinoceros, white (square-lipped rhinoceros) Huge rhinoceros that lives on the savanna of Uganda and Zimbabwe. Its long head is held low and it has a pronounced hump on its neck. It gets its names from its wide, square lip and its light grey skin, although it is usually the colour of the mud in which it last wallowed. A placid, shy animal, the white rhinoceros is more sociable than other rhino species and lives in loose same-sex groups, grazing throughout the day. Single calves are born after 16 months' gestation and suckle for about three years. Head-body length: 3.6–5m (12–16.4ft); tail: 90–100cm (35–39in). Family Rhinocerotidae; species *Ceratotherium simum*.

rhizoid
Fine, hair-like growth used for attachment to a solid surface by some simple organisms, such as certain FUNGI and MOSSES. The rhizoid lacks the conducting TISSUES of a ROOT.

rhizome
Creeping, root-like underground stem of certain plants. It usually grows horizontally, is rich in accumulated starch, and can produce new roots and stems asexually. Examples include the IRIS and WATER LILY. Rhizomes differ from roots in having nodes, buds and scale-like leaves. *See also* ASEXUAL REPRODUCTION; TUBER

rhododendron
Any member of the genus *Rhododendron*, a large group of shrubs and small trees that grow in the acid soils of cool temperate regions of North America, Europe and Asia. Most of the species are evergreen, with leathery leaves and bell-shaped white, pink or purple flowers. Certain species are known as AZALEAS. Family Ericaceae; genus *Rhododendron*.

rhodophyte (red alga)
Any member of the ALGAE phylum Rhodophyta. They are numerous in tropical and subtropical seas. Most rhodophytes are slender, branching SEAWEEDS that form shrub-like masses. Some become encrusted with CALCIUM CARBONATE and are important in REEF formation. Rhodophytes have red and purplish pigments, which help to absorb light for PHOTOSYNTHESIS. They also have CHLOROPHYLL. They have complex life cycles with two or three distinct stages, involving ALTERNATION OF GENERATIONS.

rhodopsin (visual purple)
Visual pigment present in the RODS in the eye's RETI-

▲ **rhinoceros, white** The yellow-billed oxpecker (*Buphagus africanus*) and the African white rhinoceros (*Cerato therium simum*) have a symbiotic relationship. The oxpecker, a type of African starling, feeds by pulling ticks from the animal's hide and sipping the blood that oozes from the wounds. The rhino benefits by the removal of the parasites.

◄ **rhizome** This swollen underground stem produces both roots and leafy shoots. Unlike other plant storage organs, rhizomes grow continually, branching as they do so. Each tip produces aerial shoots and the oldest parts slowly die off.

NA. It absorbs light, producing a NERVE IMPULSE that is perceived as SIGHT.

rhodophyte (red algae)
Any member of the ALGAE phylum Rhodophyta. They are numerous in tropical and subtropical seas. Most rhodophytes are slender, branching SEAWEEDS that form shrub-like masses. Some become encrusted with CALCIUM CARBONATE and are important in REEF formation. Rhodophytes have red and purplish pigments, which help to absorb light for PHOTOSYNTHESIS. They also have CHLOROPHYLL. They have complex life cycles with two or three distinct stages, involving ALTERNATION OF GENERATIONS.

rhubarb
Any of several species of perennial herbaceous plants native to Asia. Rhubarb is cultivated in cool climates worldwide for its edible leaf stalks. It has large, poisonous leaves and small, white or red flowers. Height: to 1.2m (4ft). Family Polygonaceae; genus *Rheum*.

rhyolite
Fine-grained, extrusive IGNEOUS ROCK with a similar composition to GRANITE. It is an uncommon, light-coloured rock made up of alkali feldspars, quartz and sometimes mica. It forms by the rapid cooling of viscous LAVA explosively ejected from a VOLCANO and as a result is made up of tiny crystals, too small to be seen with the naked eye. It may contain small cavities (vesicles) caused by gas bubbles and areas of glassy material.

ribbon fish (scythe or deal fish)
Any member of the family Trachipteridae, comprising marine fish found in cold, deep waters worldwide. The ribbon fish is identified by its long, thin body and plume-like dorsal fin, which extends along the entire length of its body. Length: 2.4m (8ft). Family Trachipteridae.

ribbon worm
See BOOTLACE WORM

ribonucleic acid
See RNA

ribose ($C_5H_{10}O_5$)
PENTOSE SUGAR (five-carbon sugar) occurring in the structure of RNA. It is an isomeric form of arabinose. Ribose, which can be obtained by the hydrolysis of RNA, is composed of a large string of NUCLEOTIDES derived from NUCLEIC ACIDS.

ribosome
Tiny structure in the CYTOPLASM of cells; it is involved in PROTEIN SYNTHESIS. Each protein is made up of a specific sequence of AMINO ACIDS. The genetic material DNA is made up of a long string of organic BASES of four different kinds. The order of these bases is like a code (the GENETIC CODE) for all the instructions needed to make a living organism. The code specifies the sequence of amino acids for all the proteins the cell needs to make. Segments of

R

Respiration is the process by which living organisms release energy by breaking down complex molecules in a series of enzyme-controlled reactions. Respiration is an essential part of metabolism. These are two forms: aerobic respiration, which occurs when oxygen is involved, and anaerobic respiration, where oxygen is absent.

AEROBIC RESPIRATION

Aerobic respiration is divided into three stages. The food produced in plants or eaten by animals is first converted to GLUCOSE, which is then split into two molecules of pyruvate in a process called GLYCOLYSIS. This process occurs in the cytoplasm of all living cells. In the second stage, known as the KREBS CYCLE, the pyruvate enters cell organelles called MITOCHONDRIA and is broken down into carbon dioxide and hydrogen ions. In the final stage, the ELECTRON TRANSPORT SYSTEM, the hydrogen ions are used to form energy rich ADENOSINE TRIPHOSPHATE (ATP). The process is summarized as:

$$C_6H_{12}O_6 + 6O_2 \rightarrow 6CO_2 + 6H_2O + ATP \text{ (energy)}$$

ANAEROBIC RESPIRATION

Life on Earth probably originated in an atmosphere without oxygen; early life was, therefore, anaerobic. Many organisms today are also anaerobic; indeed some find oxygen toxic. Without the presence of oxygen, neither the Krebs cycle nor the electron transport system can take place. The pyruvate produced in glycolysis must therefore be converted into another substance to release the energy it possesses. In some organisms, such as yeast, the pyruvate is converted to ethanol and carbon dioxide, as follows:

$$C_6H_{12}O_6 \rightarrow 2C_2H_5OH + 2CO_2 + \text{energy}$$

This process is the basis of both the brewing industry, where the ethanol (alcohol) is the desired product, and the baking industry, where carbon dioxide is used to make bread rise. Under anaerobic conditions, for example when roots are the waterlogged, plant cells also carry out this process.

In animals, the pyruvate is converted to lactate, as shown below:

$$C_6H_{12}O_6 \rightarrow 2C_3H_6O_3 + \text{energy}$$

This process typically occurs in muscle when the blood is unable to deliver oxygen fast enough to meet the demands of aerobic respiration. Too great a build up of lactate in muscle leads to cramp. Some animals that live in anaerobic conditions, for example worms burrowing in mud or parasites living in animal intestines, use the process as the main means of obtaining their energy.

Of the two forms of respiration, aerobic is by far the most efficient, with around 40% of the available energy in glucose being released; anaerobic respiration yields only 2%. By comparison the efficiency of a car engine is about 25%.

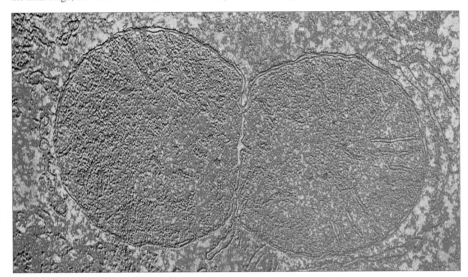

▲ **A mitochondrion from** a rat liver cell in is shown in this false-colour transmission electron micrograph; the mitochondrion is in the process of division. Mitochondria are the sites of chemical energy synthesis during respiration. Adenosine triphosphate (ATP) is synthesized, which is involved in the transfer of metabolic energy. Each mitochondrion is bounded by a double membrane, the inner one being folded inwards to form projections (cristae), which partially compartmentalize the mitochondrion. In this image, the organelle appears pinched at the top and bottom; when both advancing edges of the outer membrane meet and fuse, the detachment of the daughter mitochondrion will be complete.

▼ **A colony of** yeast cells, *Saccharomyces cerevixiae*, also known as baker's or brewer's yeast, is shown in this coloured scanning electron micrograph. Some cells can be seen dividing by budding off new cells: a small bump appears, which enlarges and then detaches once mature. *Saccharomyces cerevixiae* respires anaerobically, breaking down sugar to produce ethanol (alcohol) and carbon dioxide. It has long been used in the brewing of beer, the production of wine and in baking leavened bread.

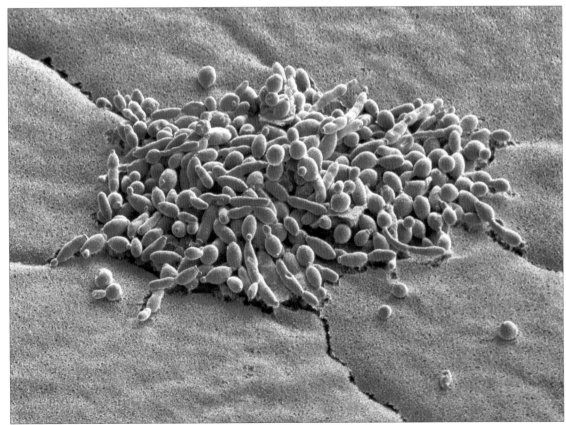

R

DNA, called GENES, contain the instructions for individual proteins. The DNA molecule is too large to escape from the nucleus into the cytoplasm, but a "working copy" is made in the form of a molecule of MESSENGER RNA (mRNA), and this travels to the ribosomes in the cytoplasm. Ribosomes attach themselves to the messenger RNA, then assemble the amino acids in the correct sequence to form a particular protein. Each ribosome is itself made up of proteins and a special kind of RNA.

ribulose bisphosphate (RuBP) (ribulose disphosphate)

PENTOSE SUGAR (RIBULOSE) linked to two phosphate groups. Involved in the CALVIN CYCLE, it combines with CARBON DIOXIDE in the first stage of the DARK REACTION of PHOTOSYNTHESIS. The reaction is mediated by an ENZYME called ribulose bisphosphate carboxylase, which, because of its presence in every green plant, is reputed to be the most abundant PROTEIN on Earth.

rice

Plant native to Southeast Asia and cultivated in many warm humid regions worldwide. The main grain food for Middle and Far East countries, it provides a staple diet for half the world's population. Rice is an annual GRASS. The seed and husk are the edible portion. It is usually grown in flooded, terraced paddies, with hard subsoil to prevent seepage. Family Poaceae/Gramineae; species *Oryza sativa*.

ricefish

Small fish found in fresh and brackish waters of s and E Asia. The ricefish is related to KILLIFISH. Species belonging to the most common ricefish genus (*Oryzias*) have been used extensively in genetic and developmental investigations. The ricefish is often found in Japanese rice paddies and is characterized by a highly modified jaw. Family Adrianichthyidae.

Richter scale

Classification of EARTHQUAKE magnitude set up in 1935 by the US geologist Charles Richter (1900–85). The scale is logarithmic – each point on the scale increases by a factor of ten. It is based on the total energy released by an earthquake as opposed to a

▲ **rice** Once harvested, rice kernels are processed in a mill to remove the husks and fibrous bran layer, producing white rice. For brown rice the bran layer is not removed, which means it has greater nutritional value, as this part contains protein, minerals, vitamins and oil. White rice can be stored for longer periods of time, however. By-products of rice are used in livestock fodder and to produce oil and starch.

▲ **ricinuleid** These little-known arachnids are found in leaf mould and caves in tropical America and Africa. They have a hood-like structure on the carapace which can be raised and lowered, and inside which the female stores her eggs. Shown here is an African species (*Ricinoides afzeli*).

scale of intensity, which measures the damage done at a particular place.

ricinuleid

Any member of the subclass Ricinulei, a group of ARACHNIDS. Ricinuleids resemble TICKS in movement and appearance. They are found in tropical regions of Africa and the Americas. Two anterior appendages are chelate; in the male, the terminal segments of the third legs are used in mating. Ricinuleids are well represented in fossil records, but only *c*.35 species are extant. Adult body length: to 25mm (1in). Subclass Ricinulei.

rickettsiae

Group of tiny, rod-shaped BACTERIA that are PARASITES of the FLEA, LOUSE and TICK. They cause many diseases of vertebrates, including typhus, Rocky Mountain spotted fever and Q fever, all of which can be transmitted to humans.

riflebird

Australasian forest bird belonging to the BIRD OF PARADISE family. It has a long, curved bill and spectacular, glossy black plumage, with iridescent green patches on its throat, head and tail. During its spectacular displays, the riflebird raises its neck feathers to form a fan. It inhabits tropical rainforests, where it feeds on insects in dead wood. Length: 24–33cm (9–13in). Family Paradisaeidae; genus *Ptiloris*.

rifleman

Small, insectivorous bird found in New Zealand. It has brown and yellow plumage. The rifleman feeds by climbing, treecreeper-like, in spirals up tree trunks. Length: 8cm (3in). Family Xenicidae; species *Acanthisitta chloris*.

rifting

Process whereby crustal rocks fail upon being stretched; the lines of failure are marked by normal dip-slip FAULTS, which are often paired with an intervening topographical valley-like depression (RIFT VALLEY or GRABEN).

rift valley

DEPRESSION formed by the subsidence of land between two parallel FAULTS. Rift valleys are believed to be formed by thermal currents within the Earth's MANTLE that break up the CRUST into large slabs or blocks of rock, which then become fractured. The best example on land is the Great Rift Valley in E Africa. Rift valleys are also characteristic of MID-OCEAN RIDGES. *See also* GRABEN

ringtail (civet cat, miner's cat, ring-tailed cat)

Solitary and nocturnal member of the RACCOON

family; it lives in dry rocky habitats of w North America. The ringtail has a grey or brown coat with white spots on its face. It has a long, bushy, black-and-white, banded tail. It is a graceful animal, with a dog-like head and semi-retractable claws. Ringtails are fierce hunters of small animals, but they are easily tamed as pets or to catch vermin. The ringtail's fur is known as California mink or civet cat. Head-body length: 31–38cm (12–15in); tail: 31–44cm (12–17in). Family Procyonidae; species *Bassariscus astutus*.

rip current

Narrow, swift, short-lived surface CURRENT that flows seawards at right angles to the shoreline. It occurs at the mouth of a bay or along a coast where wind and incoming waves pile up the water until the excess rushes quickly and forcefully back into the sea.

river

See feature article, page 324

river oak

CASUARINA tree from Australia and Tasmania. It has long, drooping, green, wiry, scale-like structures in the place of leaves, which give its plumage a feathery appearance. The river tree is cultivated for its valuable and extremely hard timber, which is used for furniture manufacture. Family Casuarinaceae; species *Casuarina cunninghamiana*.

RNA (ribonucleic acid)

Chemical (NUCLEIC ACID) that controls the synthesis of PROTEIN in a CELL; it is the genetic material in some VIRUSES. The molecules of RNA in a cell are copied from DNA and consist of a single strand of NUCLEOTIDES, each containing the sugar RIBOSE, phosphoric acid and one of four BASES: ADENINE, GUANINE, CYTOSINE or URACIL. MESSENGER RNA (mRNA) carries the information for PROTEIN SYNTHESIS from DNA in the cell NUCLEUS to the RIBOSOMES in the CYTOPLASM. During a process known as TRANSLATION, TRANSFER RNA (tRNA) brings AMINO ACIDS to their correct position on the mRNA to form POLYPEPTIDE chains.

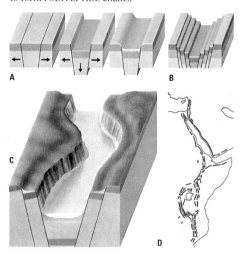

▲ **rift valley** Rift valleys are formed by tension between two roughly parallel faults (A), causing downward earth movement resulting in the formation of a *graben* (trough of land between two faults). Sometimes a number of parallel faults result in land sinking in steps (B). A typical example of a step-faulted rift valley is shown (C). A series of block faults can occur on either side of a graben, sometimes tilting in the process of creating the block-faulted rift valley. The East African Rift Valley (D) is perhaps the world's best example of this type of geological formation.

R

▲ **roach** Found in slow-moving, and often poorly oxygenated, lakes and rivers, the roach is one of the most common fish in Europe. It is a bottom-feeder, eating midge larvae, freshwater shrimps, crustaceans and insects.

roach

European freshwater CARP found in muddy and, occasionally, brackish waters. The roach's body can be silver, white or green, with reddish fins. Length: to 40cm (16in). Family Cyprinidae; species *Rutilus rutilus*.

roadrunner

Large, strange-looking, ground-dwelling CUCKOO. It has streaked brown and white plumage and is often seen speeding across the desert on its long, strong legs. It has a long bill and tail. Two roadrunner species (*Geococcyx californianus* and *Geococcyx velox*) are widespread in desert scrub of s United States and Central America. Length: 42–57cm (17–22in). Family Cuculidae; genus *Geococcyx*.

robber-fly

Any member of the family Asilidae, which comprises numerous species of large, dull-coloured flies found worldwide. The robber-fly preys on other insects, catching them in flight. Adult body length: to 8cm (3in). Order Diptera; family Asilidae.

robber crab

See CRAB, ROBBER

robin

Any of several species of birds, not all related, most of which have a red breast. Robins are often familiar birds in local and national folklore. It is claimed that the European robin (*Erithacus rubecula*), for example, got its red breast from pricking itself on the crown of thorns placed around the head of Jesus Christ as he was led to his crucifixion. Most robin species feed on insects and berries. They make nests, from moss, leaves and feathers, in trees or nooks of buildings.

robin, American

Familiar woodland and garden bird of North and Central America; it belongs to the THRUSH family. The male is grey-brown above, with a brick-red chest and white throat. The female has an orange breast. The American robin is often seen on lawns, head cocked, as it searches for earthworms. Length: 25cm (10in). Family Turdidae; species *Turdus migratorius*.

robin, European

One of the most familiar of European birds, and the only one to have a red face and breast. Closely related to the CHAT, it is common in open woodlands and gardens. It can become very tame, but it is often aggressive to other robins. The European robin has a pleasant, short, warbling song, which is heard throughout the year. Length: 14cm (6in). Family Turdidae; species *Erithacus rubecula*.

robin, flame

Australian FLYCATCHER with a flame-red breast and throat. It has a dark blue head and back, and the male has a white forehead. The flame robin is familiar in autumn and winter, when it congregates on golf courses, paddocks and grasslands in flocks of mostly brown and immature birds with a few adult males. Length: 14cm (6in). Family Muscicapidae; species *Petroica phoenicea*.

robin, white-throated

Robin found from Turkey to Afghanistan; it winters in Africa. The male is slate blue above, with a deep orange breast. Both sexes have a white throat. The robin's preferred habitat is stony ground and scrub. Length: 18cm (7in). Family Turdidae; species *Irania gutturalis*.

robin, Siberian blue

Small songbird found in dense forests of NE Asia; it belongs to the same genus as the NIGHTINGALE. The male is strikingly blue above and white below; the female is olive-brown suffused with blue. The Siberian robin stays on or near the ground. Length: 14cm (6in). Family Turdidae; species *Luscinia cyane*.

Robinson, Sir Robert (1886–1975)

British chemist who was awarded the 1947 Nobel Prize for chemistry for research into alkaloids and other plant chemicals. Robinson synthesized the alkaloid tropinone using three simple compounds found in plants. This led to his theory of organic molecular structure based on electronic processes occurring during the formation and disruption of chemical bonds. The theory proved important for the understanding of all biosynthetic mechanisms. His other research concerned plant pigments and the genetics of variations in flower colours.

roche moutonnée (Fr. sheep rock)

Rock that has been scraped smooth by ice on one side, but that has been plucked into a jagged shape on the other, downhill side. They are found in glacial valleys. Roches moutonnées can be only a few metres in height, but some are much bigger, reaching 30–40m (100–130ft). It is said that roches moutonnées were so named because they resemble sheep lying down.

rock

Solid material that comprises the Earth's CRUST.

▲ **roadrunner** This desert bird is noted for its expertise in killing snakes and lizards, which it does by a series of quick stabs with its long, pointed beak. It rarely flies but is a very fast agile runner.

Pairs of roadrunners build twig-nests in a cactus or small tree, in which the female lays up to 10 eggs which are then incubated by the male. It is often seen basking in the sun to absorb warmth.

Although solid, it is not necessarily hard – CLAY and volcanic ASH are also considered to be rocks. Rocks are classified by origin into three major groups. IGNEOUS ROCK is any rock formed by the cooling and solidification of molten material from the Earth's interior; volcanic LAVA and GRANITE are igneous rocks. Igneous rocks can also be classified as INTRUSIVE and EXTRUSIVE ROCK. SEDIMENTARY ROCK is formed from older rock that has been transported from its original position by water, glaciers or the atmosphere, and consolidated again into rock; LIMESTONE and SANDSTONE are examples. METAMORPHIC ROCK originates from igneous or sedimentary rocks, but has been changed in texture or mineral content or both by extreme pressure and heat deep within the Earth; MARBLE, derived from limestone, is a metamorphic rock.

▼ **roche moutonnée** The ice-scraped schist shown here is in the form of a roche moutonnée. It is near to the Franz Josef Glacier in the Westland National Park, New Zealand. A roche moutonnée is formed when a glacier rides over a lump of bedrock in a mountainous region.

R

rock cod (coral trout)
Medium-sized marine fish found in tropical waters of the Red Sea and Indo-Pacific region. It is related to the GROUPER. The rock cod is bright red with blue flecks. Length: to 40cm (16in). Family Serranidae; species *Cephalopholis miniatus*.

rocket (salad or garden rocket)
Strong-smelling annual or overwintering herb native to the Mediterranean and E Asia; it has been naturalized in North America. Rocket has an erect hairy stem and creamy-yellow flowers. The young leaves are eaten as salad greens and are reputedly a good tonic. Family Brassicaceae; species *Eruca vesicaria* ssp. *sativa*. **Rocket** (sweet rocket or dame's violet) is also the name of a biennial or perennial herb native to Italy and naturalized in North America. Its erect, leafy stems produce heads of white, purple or variegated scented flowers. The somewhat bitter-tasting leaves are favoured in salads in some countries. Family Brassicaceae; species *Hesperis matronalis*.

rockfish
See SCORPION FISH

rockfowl
Secretive bird that inhabits central African jungles. It has long legs and a long tail. It is grey above and white below, with black wing tips and a bare red hind neck. It feeds on the forest floor but nests and roosts in thick mud nests stuck to the walls of caves. Length: 57cm (22in). Family Timaliidae; subfamily Picathartinae; genus *Picathartes*.

rockling
Any of several species of small marine fish belonging to the COD family. The rockling inhabits coastal waters of the Atlantic Ocean. Family Gadidae; genus *Gaidropsarus*.

rockrose
Any member of a family of bushy plants or shrubs native mainly to the Mediterranean region. The rockrose has small, scale-like leaves and five-petalled flowers. Among the 170 species is the common yellow-flowered *Helianthemum chamaecistus*, which is found in grasslands of Europe and w Asia. Family Cistaceae.

rodent
Any member of the mammalian order Rodentia. Examples include RATS, MICE and SQUIRRELS. They gnaw their food using a pair of large chisel-like incisors in the upper and lower jaw; these incisors grow continuously as they would otherwise wear away. The food is ground up using flattened molars. Rodentia is the most widespread and numerous of all the mammalian orders, to some extent as a result of their close association with man.

rods and cones
Cells in the RETINA of the EYE that are sensitive to light. Located in the pigmented layer, the rod-shaped RHODOPSIN-secreting cells are the RECEPTORS for low-intensity light, and the cone-shaped iodopsin-secreting cells are adapted to distinguish colour. Rods detect only shades of black and white, but they are particularly sensitive to movement.

roe deer
See DEER, ROE

roller
Large, brightly coloured, crow-like bird. It is named after its somersaulting courtship displays. Its plumage is often vivid blues and pink, and its bill is stout and slightly hooked. The roller sits on a tree or telegraph pole, waiting for the ground-living insects on which it feeds. Length: 30–34cm (12–13in). Family Coraciidae; genus *Coracias*; species include *Coracias garrulus*.

root
Underground portion of a VASCULAR PLANT that serves as an anchor and absorbs water and minerals from the soil. Some plants, such as the DANDELION, have TAPROOTS with smaller lateral branches. Some of these plants, such as CARROTS and PARSNIPS, have large taproots that store nutrients; they are grown as food for humans and farm animals. Other plants, such as the GRASSES (including cereal crops), develop fibrous roots with lateral branches.

RIVER

Large natural channel containing water, which flows downhill under gravity. The water in a river is supplied by tributary streams, by direct runoff over the land, by seepage from valley side slopes, by water emerging from underground sources in springs, by water falling on the river surface, and by the melting of snow and glacier ice. A river system is a network of connecting channels. It can be divided into tributaries, which collect water and SEDIMENT, the main trunk river, and the dispersing system at the river's mouth where much of the sediment is deposited. The DISCHARGE of a river is the volume of water flowing past a point in a given time. It is usually expressed as cubic metres per second (cumecs) and is calculated by multiplying the cross-sectional area of the river by the velocity (speed) of the water. The velocity of a river is controlled by the slope of the river, the depth of the river and the roughness of the river bed. Rivers transport sediment as they flow, by the processes of trac-tion (rolling), saltation (jumping), suspension (carrying) and solution. A greater discharge increases the amount of sediment that can be transported. Most river sediment is transported during flood conditions, but as a river returns to normal flow it deposits sediment. A river adjusts its channel shape to be able to transport sediment most efficiently. This can result in the EROSION of a river channel or in the building up of FLOOD-PLAINS, sand and gravel banks. All rivers tend to flow in a twisting pattern, even if the slope is relatively steep, because water flow is naturally turbulent. The force of the water striking the river bank causes erosion and undercutting, which starts a small bend in the river channel. Over time the bend grows into a large MEANDER. The current flows faster on the outside of the bend, eroding the bank, while sedimentation occurs on the inside of the bend where the current is slowest. Eventually, the river channel cuts across the loop and follows a more direct course downstream and the loop is abandoned as an OXBOW LAKE. Rivers flood when their channels cannot contain the discharge. Flood risk can be reduced by straightening the channel, dredging sediment or making the channel deeper by raising the banks. *See also* DELTA; LEVEE

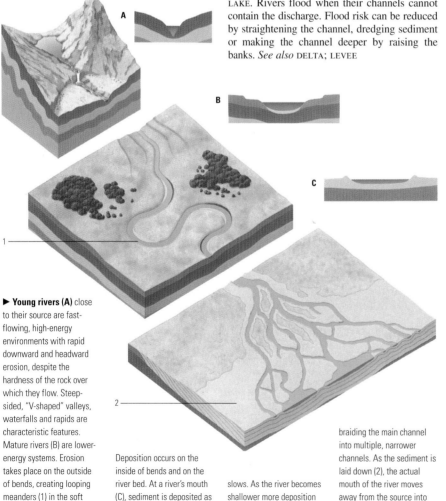

▶ **Young rivers (A)** close to their source are fast-flowing, high-energy environments with rapid downward and headward erosion, despite the hardness of the rock over which they flow. Steep-sided, "V-shaped" valleys, waterfalls and rapids are characteristic features. Mature rivers (B) are lower-energy systems. Erosion takes place on the outside of bends, creating looping meanders (1) in the soft alluvium of the river plain. Deposition occurs on the inside of bends and on the river bed. At a river's mouth (C), sediment is deposited as the velocity of the river slows. As the river becomes shallower more deposition occurs, forming islands and braiding the main channel into multiple, narrower channels. As the sediment is laid down (2), the actual mouth of the river moves away from the source into the sea or lake.

▶ **roller** Widespread throughout most of Africa, the broad-billed roller (*Eurystomus glaucurus*) is found on the edges of forests or on solitary trees near water. Rollers congregate in flocks and often forage for insects in the evening.

root hair
Unicellular, tubular outgrowth of a plant ROOT epidermis. Its thin walls are in close contact with the soil solution. Formed in large numbers behind the growing tip of the root, the root hair provides a large surface area for the absorption of water and mineral salts. Collectively they form the **piliferous layer**.

root nodule
Small swelling in the ROOTS of various plants, such as LEGUMES, that contains NITROGEN-FIXING BACTERIA. *See also* NITROGEN CYCLE; NITROGEN FIXATION

root pressure
Means by which water travels from the soil through the ROOTS of a plant and up its STEM. The XYLEM conducts the water, while the pressure is produced by a combination of OSMOSIS, which forces water from the soil into the CELLS of the root, and an active pumping mechanism that creates a concentration gradient of salt IONS in the xylem. Excessive root pressure may cause "bleeding" of SAP from a wound in the plant or the collection of drops of water from undamaged leaf margins. *See also* TRANSPIRATION

rose
Any wild or cultivated flowering shrub of the genus *Rosa*. Most roses are native to Asia, several to America, and a few to Europe and NW Africa. The stems are usually thorny. The flowers range in colour from white to yellow, pink, crimson and maroon; many are fragrant. The flowers are followed by false fruits called hips. Family Rosaceae; there are *c*.250 species.

rosebay willowherb
See WILLOW HERB

rosefinch
Any member of the genus *Carpodacus*, a group of medium-sized to large, stout-billed, seed-eating birds. The males are mainly red or pink, occasionally streaked with white; the females are brownish and streaked. The rosefinch's flight is undulating. Some species are found near the snow line in mountains, where they feed on wind-blown seeds stuck in snow patches. Length: 14–23cm (6–9in). Family Fringillidae; genus *Carpodacus*.

rosefish (ocean perch, redfish)
Marine food fish found in the N Atlantic Ocean. It is perch-like in appearance. The rosefish is usually fished by trawlers at depths of between 100 and 200m. (300–700ft). It is bright red or rose in colour. Family Scorpaenidae; species *Sebastes marinus*.

rosella
Any of several species of beautiful, long-tailed PARROTS found in Australia. It has crimson, blue, green and yellow plumage. The rosella feeds on fruit and eucalyptus blossoms in rainforests and wet wooded country. It can be quite tame, sometimes coming to garden feeders. Its flight is fast and swooping. Length: 29–37cm (11–15in). Family Psittacidae; genus *Platycercus*.

rosemary
Perennial evergreen herb of the MINT family. It has small, needle-like leaf clusters of small, pale-blue flowers. Sprigs of rosemary are commonly used as a flavouring. Family Lamiaceae/Labiatae; species *Rosmarinus officinalis*.

rose of Sharon
Any of several species of hardy shrubs native to E Asia. It usually refers to *Hibiscus syriacus*, which can be grown farther north than many other HIBISCUS plants. The showy flowers are red, purple, rose or white. Height: to 3.6m (12ft). Family Malvaceae.

rose pink (American centaury)
Plant of the S and mid-western United States; it is cultivated elsewhere as an ornamental and used as a cut flower. It has a four-angled stem and numerous opposite flowering branches. It gets its scientific name from the Italian botanist Liberato Sabbati (b.*c*.1714), who was the curator of Rome Botanic Garden. Family Gentianaceae; species *Sabatia angularis*.

rosewood
Any of several kinds of ornamental hardwoods derived from various tropical trees. The most important are Honduras rosewood (*Dalbergia stevensoni*) and Brazilian rosewood (*Dalbergia nigra*). Rosewood varies from a deep, ruddy brown to a purplish colour; it has a black grain. Family Fabiaceae/Leguminose.

Ross, Sir Ronald (1857–1932)
British bacteriologist, b. India. In 1898 he discovered the PARASITE (*Plasmodium*) that carries malaria in the stomach of the *Anopheles* MOSQUITO. Ross was awarded the 1902 Nobel Prize for physiology or medicine for his work.

rotifer
See WHEEL ANIMALCULE

rough hound (lesser spotted dogfish)
Small SHARK. It is related to the NURSE HOUND. The rough hound has a brown spotted body. It is a food fish. Length: to 90cm (35in). Family Scyliorhinidae; species *Scyliorhinus caniculus*.

roundworm
See NEMATODE

roundworm, pig
NEMATODE worm that is a PARASITE of pigs. It is closely related to and has a similar pathology to the human roundworm (*Ascaris lumbricoides*). Eggs survive in the soil until they are ingested by the pig. Nematode larvae migrate from the small intestine into the blood and collect in the liver, where they may cause a localized inflammatory reaction. The nematodes then move to the lungs, where they may cause irritation before ascending to the mouth to be swallowed once more. The life-cycle in completed when adult worms sexually reproduce in the small intestine and the eggs are shed along with the faeces. Phylum Nematoda; species *Ascaris suum*.

rowan
See MOUNTAIN ASH

royal fern (flowering fern)
Common, widely distributed FERN of wetlands. Cylindrical leaflets on the ends of its fronds are densely covered with SPORANGIA (sacs in which SPORES are produced). Height: to 1.8m (6ft). Family Osmundaceae; species *Osmunda regalis*.

royal jelly
In HONEYBEE colonies, the food given to female bee LARVAE destined to become queens. It is a glandular secretion of young worker bees, who themselves are females but who have been fed on honey and POLLEN and so have not developed into queens.

royal palm
Ornamental PALM tree native to the Caribbean islands and Central America. It has a tall, light-coloured trunk and feather-shaped leaves. Height: to 30m (100ft). Family Palmaceae; species *Roystonea regia*.

rubber plant
Evergreen plant of the FIG genus; it is native to India and Malaysia. The rubber plant reaches tree size in the tropics; in temperate regions juvenile specimens are popular house plants. It used to be cultivated for its white LATEX, which was used to make India rubber. The rubber plant has large, glossy, leathery leaves and a stout, buttressed trunk. Height: to 30m (100ft). Family Moraceae; species *Ficus elastica*.

rubber tree
See feature article, page 326

ruby
Gem variety of the mineral CORUNDUM (aluminium oxide); its characteristic red colour is due to impurities of chromium and iron oxides. The traditional source of rubies is Burma. Today, synthetic rubies are widely used in industry, especially in laser technology.

rudaceous
Describing a coarse-grained SEDIMENTARY ROCK. Examples of rudaceous rocks include BRECCIA, CONGLOMERATE and GRAVEL, as well as types of stony boulder clay. The particles in the rock range in size from large grains of sand to fragments of gravel.

R

rudd (red eye)
Freshwater fish that is related to the MINNOW and the ROACH. It belongs to the CARP family. It is found in Europe, N and W Asia and in the United States, where it is known as the pearl roach. The rudd is a large, full-bodied fish with reddish fins. Length: to 41cm (16in). Family Cyprinidae; species *Scardinius erythrophthalmus*.

◀ **rosemary** A strongly flavoured culinary herb, rosemary leaves are used as a seasoning for meat and fish. Its aromatic oil is used in perfumes and medicines. It is widely cultivated throughout Europe and the Americas.

rue

Any member of the genus *Ruta*, a group of *c*.40 species of evergreen plants or shrubs. Rue species grow in warm regions of s Europe and sw Asia. They have aromatic leaves used in medicine or as flavouring. Family Rutaceae; species include *Ruta graveolens* (common rue).

ruff

Medium-sized wading bird found on marshland in Europe. The male, known as a ruff, is larger than the female, known as a reeve. In spring the male develops a neck ruff and ear tufts of any combination of black, white, reddish-brown and buff feathers. Males gather, or "lek", at traditional display grounds for mock display battles. Length: 20–30cm (8–12in). Family Scolopacidae; species *Philomachus pugnax*.

ruffe

Small freshwater PERCH native to Eurasia. It has a greenish brown body with sharp rays on its dorsal fin. It was accidentally introduced into the Great Lakes of North America. Family Percidae; species *Gymnocephalus cerruus*.

ruminant

Cud-chewing, even-toed, hoofed mammal. Ruminants include the OKAPI, CHEVROTAIN, DEER, GIRAFFE, ANTELOPE, cattle, SHEEP and GOAT. All ruminants except the chevrotain have four-chambered STOMACHS. They rechew food that has previously been swallowed (cud) and stored in one of the stomach chambers.

runner

In botany, a long, thin STEM (STOLON) that extends along the surface of the soil from the AXIL of a plant's LEAF. It serves to propagate the plant. At points (NODES) along its length, a runner produces small leaves and buds that develop shoots and roots and turn into small independent plants as the runner dies. Runners are produced by such plants as STRAWBERRIES and creeping BUTTERCUPS. *See also* ASEXUAL REPRODUCTION

rush

Any of *c*.700 species of perennial tufted bog plants found in temperate regions. Most rush species have long, narrow leaves and small flowers, which are crowded into dense clusters. The most familiar rush

◀ **rush** A decorative aquatic plant, the flowering rush (*Butomus umbellatus*) has an attractive, three-petalled flower that grows above the surface of the water. The long leaves have parallel veins without a central vein or midrib.

is *Juncus effusus*, found in Europe, Asia, North America, Australia and New Zealand. It has brown flowers and ridged stems. Height: 30–152cm (12–60in). Family Juncaceae.

rust fungus

Any of a group of fungi (Urediniomycetes) that live as PARASITES on many kinds of higher plants. Rust fungi damage cereal crops, such as wheat and barley, and several fruits and vegetables. Their complex life cycles involve growth on more than one host plant.

rutile (titanium dioxide, TiO$_2$)

Black to red-brown oxide mineral; it is found in IGNEOUS and METAMORPHIC rocks and QUARTZ veins. Rutile occurs as long prismatic and needle-like crystals in the tetragonal system and as granular masses. It has a metallic lustre, is brittle and is used as a gemstone. Hardness 6–6.5; r.d. 4.2.

rye

Hardy CEREAL grass originating in sw Asia and naturalized throughout the world. It grows in poorer soils and colder climates than most other cereals can stand. Its flower spikelets develop one-seeded grains. Rye is used for flour, as a forage crop and for making alcoholic drinks. Height: to 90cm (35in). Family Poaceae/Gramineae; species *Secale cereale*.

rye grass

Any member of the genus *Lolium*, a group of annual and perennial grasses native to temperate Eurasia. Rye grass is cultivated as pasture and meadow grass. The inflorescence is typically a spike with flattened spikelets arranged alternately, the edge of the spikelet towards the main stem. Perennial ryegrass (*Lolium perenne*) and Italian ryegrass (*Lolium multiflorum*) are valuable grazing crops. Family Poaceae/Gramineae; genus *Lolium*.

R

RUBBER TREE

Any of several species of trees native to South America, the exudations of which can be made into rubber. The most common species is *Hevea brasiliensis*, a tall softwood tree of the family Euphorbiaceae. Native to Brazil, it has been introduced to Malaysia. The milky exudate, called LATEX, is obtained from the inner bark by tapping. It is then coagulated by smoking.

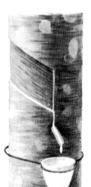

◀ The *Hevea* genus of rubber tree was once the primary source of natural rubber. It is still cultivated in Southeast Asia and w Africa, but today the majority of rubber is produced synthetically from unsaturated hydrocarbons. In order to extract the latex from the trunk, a cut is made in the bark and the milky liquid is drained into a container. It is then strained and diluted with water before being treated with formic acid, which coagulates the latex particles. Following this process, it is rolled into sheets and put through a vulcanization process in preparation for manufacturing objects.

sable

MARTEN native to Siberia, Russia. It has been hunted almost to extinction for its soft, dark-brown fur, which is sometimes flecked with white. Length: to 60cm (24in). Family Mustelidae; species *Martes zibellina*.

sablefish

Any member of a group of large fish found in cold waters of the Pacific Ocean. Sablefish are usually found at depths of between 300 and 1800m (980–5900ft). They are fished commercially. Sablefish are closely related to skilfish. Family Anoplopomatidae; species include *Anoplopoma fimbria*.

sabre-tooth cat

Member of either of two extinct groups of predatory CATS. Some of the primitive nimravid cats of Tertiary times, such as *Nimravus*, evolved long upper "sabre-toothed" canines. However, the true sabre-tooths, such as *Smilodon*, were members of the felid family. Both groups initially overlapped in time, but the latter survived until *c*.14,000 years ago. Their sabre-teeth were used either to inflict deep wounds, which resulted in the prey bleeding to death, or to break the neck of their prey.

sabrewing

Any of several species of South American HUMMINGBIRD. Its plumage is mostly shimmering green above, with vivid blue on the throat or breast. It has a down-curved bill. The sabrewing perches conspicuously in the open in humid woodland, either singly or in loose groups of between two and four males. Length: 11–13cm (4–5in). Family Trochilidae; genus *Campylopterus*.

Sachs, Julius von (1832–97)

German botanist known for his studies of the metabolism of plants, notably the role of chlorophyll. He wrote *Textbook of Botany* (1868).

sacrum (sacral bone)

Triangular segment of the lower backbone formed by

▲ **sabre-tooth cat** A fierce, carnivorous mammal, the sabre-toothed tiger (*Smilodon* sp.) lived in North and South America during the Pleistocene period. It possessed two long fangs and a wide-opening jaw structure that enabled it to kill its prey by stabbing and slashing at its throat. *Smilodon* was more powerfully built than a modern tiger, but it is not thought to have been a fast runner; it probably ambushed its prey at waterholes.

▶ **sage** Common sage (*Salvia officinalis*) is cultivated worldwide for its leaves and is used as a flavouring in many foods, especially meat and poultry. The oil extracted from its leaves is valued for its medicinal properties and used in perfumery.

the fusion of five VERTEBRAE. It articulates above with the last lumbar vertebra, below with the coccyx and, to either side, with the hip bones.

sacred bamboo

Small evergreen shrub that resembles bamboo. It is distributed from India to Japan, where it is used in temples. Sacred bamboo is grown for its bright red berries. The young pinnately compound leaves are often tinged with red and turn red in winter. It bears clusters of cream-coloured flowers. Family Berberidaceae; species *Nandina domestica*.

sacred lotus

Perennial WATER LILY distributed from s Asia to tropical Australia; it is regarded as a sacred plant in India, Tibet and China. The sacred lotus has a creeping rootstock. Its large, round, blue-green leaves grow up to 2m (6.6ft) above the water level. The fragrant, white to pink or dark red flowers are produced on tall stems. Family Nymphaceae; species *Nelumbo nucifera*.

saddleback

Rare songbird found only in the woodlands of New Zealand. The male has glossy black plumage with a chestnut saddle and pendulous red wattles at the base of its bill. The female is chocolate brown. The saddleback feeds on the forest floor and bounds from branch to branch rather than flying. Length: 25cm (10in). Family Callaeidae; species *Philesturnus carunculatus*.

safflower

Annual plant found from s Asia to North Africa. Its large, red, orange or white flower heads are used in making dyestuffs. The seeds yield an oil that is used in cooking and in the manufacture of margarine. Family Asteraceae/Compositae; species *Carthamus tinctorius*.

saffron (autumn crocus)

Perennial CROCUS native to Asia Minor. It produces purple or white flowers, the golden stigmas of which are dried and used as a flavouring or dye. Family Iridaceae; species *Crocus sativus*.

sage

Common name for a number of plants of the MINT family, native to the Mediterranean region. The best-known species is *Salvia officinalis*, an aromatic herb used for seasoning. Height: 15–38cm (6–15in). Family Lamiaceae/Labiatae.

sagebrush

Aromatic shrub common in arid areas of w North America. The common sagebrush (*Artemisia tridentata*) has small, silvery green leaves. It bears clusters of tiny, white flower heads. Height: to 2m (6.6ft). Family Asteraceae/Compositae.

sago palm (fern palm)

Feather-leaved PALM tree native to swampy areas of Malaysia and Polynesia. Its thick trunk contains sago, a starch used in foodstuffs. Height: 1–9m (3.3–30ft). Family Arecaceae/Palmae; species *Metroxylon sagu*.

saguaro

Large CACTUS native to sw North America. When the plant is between 50 and 70 years old, it produces white, night-blooming flowers. Its red fruit is edible. Height: to 12m (39ft). Family Cactaceae; species *Carnegiea gigantea*.

saiga

ANTELOPE found only in s Russia and central Asia. It is a sheep-like animal, with a "swollen" nose that ends in a pig-like snout. Its coat is brown in summer and white in winter. Males have short, ridged, slightly curved horns. Height: to 80cm (31in) at the shoulder. Family Bovidae; species *Saiga tatarica*.

sailfish

Marine fish found throughout the world in tropical seas. It is identified by a large, sail-like dorsal fin and a sword-shaped upper jaw. It is deep blue above and silvery below. The sailfish is a popular sport fish. Length: to 3.5m (11ft). Family Istiophoridae; genus *Istiophorus*.

St Anthony's fire

See ERGOT

St Elmo's fire (corposant)

Electrical discharge illuminating the tops of tall

◀ **sago palm** Flourishing in Southeast Asian freshwater swamps, the sago palm is a primary source of carbohydrate in tropical regions. Each palm flowers once in its lifetime. Just before flowering, the palm is cut, and the pith of the trunk is ground down to make sago flour.

S

▶ **salamander** The dusky salamander (*Desmognathus* sp.) is a member of the family of lungless salamanders. Respiration is carried out entirely through surface gas exchange. The moisture of its respiring surface, the skin is maintained by secretions from mucous glands.

objects. It usually occurs during a storm, when the atmosphere becomes charged strongly enough to create a discharge between the air and an object. Early sailors named this phenomenon after their patron saint.

St John's wort

Perennial herb native to Europe, w Asia and North Africa. Its oval leaves are covered with translucent dots that contain an ESSENTIAL OIL. It produces small, star-like, golden-yellow flowers. St John's wort is highly regarded for the soothing and healing properties of the oil obtained from its flowers and leaves. Family Clusiaceae; species include *Hypericum perforatum*.

St Mark's-fly

Fly that it is often seen around St Mark's Day (25 April), hence its common name. It has a characteristic flight, with its legs hanging down loosely as it dances up and down over vegetation. Order Diptera; suborder Nematocera; family Bibionidae; species *Bibio marci*.

Saintpaulia

See AFRICAN VIOLET

saithe

See POLLACK

salamander

Any of *c*.450 species of aquatic and/or terrestrial, tailed amphibians, with fully developed or partly reduced limbs. Salamanders are distributed throughout temperate regions of the Northern Hemisphere and in tropical America. Most have internal fertilization and lay eggs. Some species have aquatic larvae with external gills; in other species development is direct. Many species retain larval features as adults. In some groups the skin produces noxious secretions. Length: 2–180cm (1–71in). Order Caudata.

salamander, fire

Large, stout, terrestrial salamander of Europe, North Africa and the Middle East. Fire salamanders are conspicuously marked with yellow and black and have extensive poison glands in their skin. They give birth to well-developed larvae or metamorphosed young, rather than laying eggs. Length: 15–30cm (6–12in). Family Salamandridae; species *Salamandra salamandra*.

salamander, giant

Very large, aquatic salamander with a flattened head and lateral skin folds. Giant salamanders undergo incomplete metamorphosis and retain gill slits as adults. They are native to China and Japan, where they feed chiefly on crustaceans. The Chinese species *Andrias davidianus* is the largest living amphibian, at up to 1.8m (6ft) in length. Family Cryptobranchidae.

salamander, lungless

Any of a large family of salamanders that as adults lack both lungs and gills. Lungless salamanders respire through their skin and are usually slender and elongate. They are represented by many species in temperate and tropical America, including the slimy salamander, and by a few species in Europe. Length: 2–32cm (1–13in). Family Plethodontidae; there are *c*.275 species.

salamander, marbled

Stout-bodied salamander found in the E United States. It is black, with a pattern of white or grey bands, and has prominent eyes. Marbled salamanders lay their eggs in dry pond beds; hatching occurs when the eggs are covered by rising waters. Length: to 12cm (5in). Family Ambystomatidae; species *Ambystoma opacum*.

salamander, mole

Small, stout, brown, grey or black salamander with a large head and short tail. It lives in burrows in forests of the SE United States and is surface active during its autumn-winter breeding period. Mole salamander larvae are important predators of zooplankton in spring ponds. Length: 8–12cm (3–5in). Family Ambystomatidae; species *Ambystoma talpoideum*.

salamander, slimy

Elongate, terrestrial, lungless salamander. It has a dark back speckled with white. The slimy salamander inhabits woodlands in the E United States, where

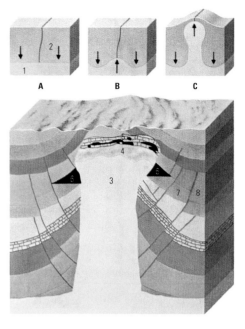

▲ **salt dome** A salt dome, or diapis, is caused by a massive plug of salt that has been forced upwards through a fault in overlying sedimentary strata by subterranean pressure. Oil and gas are often trapped in rock strata associated with salt domes.

Key
1) halite beds (salt)
2) sedimentary overburden
3) salt plug
4) gypsum and anhydrite
5) porous limestone caprock
6) oil trap
7) sand
8) shale
A) sedimentary beds overlying halite beds
B) pressure of denser overlying beds causing peripheral sinking and salt to rise up fissure
C) formation of salt plug and dome

it is often found under rocks and logs. Length: 12–20cm (5–8in). Family Plethodontidae; species *Plethodon glutinosus*.

salamander, tiger

Large, robust, terrestrial salamander. It is black with yellowish spots, bands or reticulations. Most adult tiger salamanders spend much time in burrows underground. The adults of some species, such as the AXOLOTL, retain larval features, including gills. Certain larvae are cannibalistic. Length: to 35cm (14in). Family Ambystomatidae.

salamander, torrent

Small, stout-bodied salamander. It has a short tail, prominent eyes, a dark back, and a bright yellow or orange belly. Torrent salamanders live in and near cold streams and waterfalls in the American Pacific Northwest. Length: to 12cm (5in). Family Rhyacotritonidae; genus *Rhyacotriton*.

salina (playa lake)

Dried lake bed that is found in desert or semiarid areas. Salinas form where a stream has flowed into an area of inland drainage and then evaporated, leaving behind tiny deposits of salt. The deposits can accumulate for hundreds of years to form large salty areas.

salinity

Degree of saltiness, as of the OCEANS. The average proportion of salt in the sea is about 35 parts per 1000 (3.5%). In the Red Sea, because of high evaporation rates, the figure is over 40, but in the northern parts of the Baltic Sea it is less than 10, and in the Dead Sea the figure is about 250. The salts found in the oceans

▲ **salmon** The sockeye salmon (*Oncorhynchus nerka*) is found in the N Pacific Ocean. It is also known as the red salmon due its vibrant colour. Unlike other species of salmon, the sockeye salmon has no black spots on its skin. The male atlantic salmon (*Salmo salar*) develops a distinctive hook on the lower jaw during the spawning season which it uses to fight off other males. The Atlantic salmon's numbers in the wild have declined significantly due to overfishing.

sockeye salmon

Atlantic salmon

S

include sodium chloride (common salt), which accounts for about 75%, magnesium chloride, magnesium sulphate and calcium sulphate.

saliva
Fluid released into the mouth by the salivary glands. In vertebrates, saliva is composed of about 99% water, with dissolved traces of sodium, potassium, calcium and the enzyme AMYLASE. Saliva softens and lubricates food to aid swallowing; amylase starts the DIGESTION of starches.

sallow (goat willow)
Species of WILLOW tree found in Europe and North Africa. Its large catkins appear in early spring before the unfolding of the leaves. Family Salicaceae; species *Salix caprea*.

salmon
Marine and freshwater fish of the Northern Hemisphere. The Pacific salmon (*Oncorhynchus* spp.) hatches, spawns and dies in fresh water but spends its adult life in the ocean. The Atlantic salmon (*Salmo salar*) is a marine trout that spawns in rivers on each side of the Atlantic Ocean and then returns to the sea. Length: to 1.5m (5ft). Family Salmonidae.

salmonella
Any member of the *Salmonella* genus of rod-shaped BACTERIA; they cause intestinal infections in human beings and animals. *Salmonella typhi* causes typhoid, but other species may cause only mild gastroenteritis. The bacteria are transmitted by carriers, particularly flies, and in food and water.

salmon fly
See STONEFLY

salp
Any member of a small group of pelagic tunicates that are especially abundant in warm seas. Salps are small, transparent, invertebrate animals; their bodies are ringed with bands of muscle used in propulsion, respiration and feeding. Phylum Chordata; subphylum Urochordata; class Thaliacea; order Salpida.

salsify (oyster plant, vegetable oyster)
Hardy biennial plant with a taproot. It is grown as a vegetable and prized for its oyster-like flavour. Height: to 1.2m (4ft). Family Asteraceae/Compositae; species *Tragopogon porrifolius*.

salt
Ionic compound formed, along with water, when an acid is neutralized by a base. The hydrogen of the acid is replaced by a metal or ammonium ion (NH_4^+). The most familiar salt is sodium chloride (NaCl). Salts are typically crystalline compounds with high melting points; they tend to be soluble in water. They are formed of ions held together by electrostatic forces; in SOLUTION they conduct electricity.

salt dome
Body of salt that has intruded into a SEDIMENTARY ROCK overlay. The flow of the relatively plastic salt

▶ sandgrouse The ground-feeding Pallas sandgrouse (*Syrrhaptes paradoxus*) inhabits s Russia and the central Asian steppes. Like several species of desert birds, the Pallas sandgrouse has been known to make mass migrations to areas that it does not normally occupy. In the 19th and early 20th century, it was found as far afield as w Europe but did not survive long.

into a dome may be the result of a difference in density between the salt and the overlying rock, but the process is not completely understood.

salt lake
Saline lake in a desert region. The lake originates in an area of inland drainage. The salinity increases as the water evaporates, and layers of salt may crystallize out along the lake's shores. Prolonged rain may redissolve the salt and wash most of it away. The largest salt lakes are Lake Eyre in Australia and the Great Salt Lake in Utah, United States.

salt marsh
Low-lying, vegetation-covered mudflat, especially one in a coastal environment, that is saturated or frequently inundated by saline water. The plants have to be able to tolerate the saline conditions and to maintain growth through periodic coverings by sediment. The plants trap fine-grained sediment and help build up the marsh surface; they also, however, gradually sink as older, buried deposits become compacted.

saltwort (grasswort)
Annual, weedy herb of temperate seashores in Eurasia and the United States. It has greyish leaves and was once a source of crude soda ash. Height: to 60cm (24in). Family Chenopodiaceae; species *Salsola kali*.

salvia
Any member of the *Salvia* genus, which comprises c.700 species of flowering plants. It includes common SAGE (*Salvia officinalis*), which is used as a culinary herb. The genus is represented throughout the world. Family Lamiaceae/Labiatae.

samara
Form of ACHENE in which the FRUIT wall dries out to form a wing-like structure. Common examples include ASH and ELM. The SYCAMORE samara, which has two wings, is called a schizocarp.

samphire
Small perennial herb native to Europe. It grows on rocks and shingle areas by the sea. Samphire has fleshy leaves, which are used in salads and pickles. Family Apiaceae; species *Crithmum maritimum*.

samphire
See GLASSWORT

sand
Mineral particles worn away from rocks by EROSION, individually large enough to be distinguished with the naked eye. Sand is composed mostly of QUARTZ, but black sand (containing volcanic rock) and coral sand also occur. It is usually classified according to grain size. *See also* DUNE; SANDSTONE

sandalwood
Any of several species of Asian trees of the genus *Santalum*, many of which are PARASITES on the roots of other plants. The fragrant wood is used in carving and joss sticks. The distilled oil is used in perfumes and medicines. Height: to 10m (33ft). Family Santalaceae.

sand dollar
Marine ECHINODERM that resembles the STARFISH. It has a round, flattened body, a fused skeleton and five radiating double rows of respiratory feet on both sides. Phylum Echinodermata; class Echinoidea; order Clypeastroida; species *Echinarachnius parma*.

sand dune
See DUNE

sandeel
Elongate, scaleless marine fish found in coastal waters of the Northern Hemisphere. It resembles an eel in shape and movement but is not related. Family Hypoptychidae and Ammodytidae; species include *Hypoptychus dybowskii*.

sandfish
Any member of the LIZARD genus *Scincus*, a group of thick-bodied, short-tailed, sand-living SKINKS. They are found in deserts of the Middle East and North Africa. Sandfish have fringed toes, smooth scales and valved nostrils. Their countersunk lower jaw helps them move through the sand. Length: to 22cm (9in). Family Scincidae; genus *Scincus*.

sand-fly
Any of several species of two-winged flies, not all of which are closely related. Included in the sand-fly group are species of the *Phlebotomus* genus, which, when biting human beings, transmit pappataci fever. Other serious diseases spread in this manner by sand-flies include leishmaniasis and dengue. Order Diptera.

sandgrouse
Any member of the family Pteroclididae, a group of sandy coloured birds found in semideserts of Asia and Africa. The sandgrouse has a plump body, short legs and, in most species, a long tail. It flies in close flocks, with fast, whirring wing beats. The adult can fly up to 40mi (65km) and back in search of water, soaking it up in its belly feathers for its young. Length: 27–40cm (11–16in). Family Pteroclididae.

S

▲ sandeel The greater sandeel (*Ammodytes lanceolatus*) is found in large shoals on sandy banks in British and Nordic waters. It measures up to 35cm (14in) in length and sometimes uses its snout to bury itself in the sand when the tide is out. It feeds on crustaceans, molluscs and fish fry. Sandeels form an important link in the marine food chain because they are eaten by many species of fish, including cod, bass, herrings and flatfish.

sand hopper (sand flea)
Any of several species of semi-terrestrial, amphipod CRUSTACEANS. The nocturnal European sand hopper (*Talitrus saltator*) hides in burrows in wet sand near the high tide mark during the day, emerging at night to feed on organic debris. Its legs are modified for hopping. Length: to 1.5cm (0.6in). Order Amphipoda; family Talitridae.

sand martin
See MARTIN, SAND

sand mason
Small marine POLYCHAETE that burrows in coastal sediments. It binds sand and other particles with mucous to create small cylinders that protrude upwards from the surface of the substratum. Phylum Annelida; class Polychaeta; order Terebellida; family Terebellidae; genus *Lanice*.

sandpiper
Any of numerous species of migratory wading birds, most of which nest on Arctic tundra. The smallest species are known as peep or stint. Sandpipers belong to two main genera – *Calidris* and *Tringa*. *Calidris* species have short or medium-sized bills, short legs and short necks. They have white wingbars, reddish-brown breeding plumage and drab winter colouring. They are often distinguished by their calls. *Tringa* species are larger and longer billed. They are darker in colour, with spangled summer plumage. Family Scolopacidae.

sandpiper, common
Small, short-legged, solitary sandpiper. It has grey-brown plumage and a grey smudge on its breast. It breeds in Europe and Asia along freshwater streams. The common sandpiper flies low over the water, with flickering wing beats. It has a shrill call and often perches on stones. Length: 20cm (8in). Family Scolopacidae; species *Actitis hypoleucos*.

sandpiper, curlew
Small sandpiper. It has a white rump and down-curved bill; in summer plumage the underparts are brick-red. The curlew sandpiper breeds on Siberian tundra and winters south, mostly in small flocks along freshwater margins. Length: 9cm (4in). Family Scolopacidae; species *Calidris canutus*.

sandpiper, green
Medium-sized sandpiper. It is dark above with a conspicuous white rump; in flight it has contrasting dark under wings and white belly. When flushed, the green sandpiper often dashes upwards with a shrill and fluty call. It breeds in swampy woodlands in N Europe and Asia, using the old nests of other birds. Length: 23cm (9in). Family Scolopacidae; species *Tringa ochropus*.

sandpiper, pectoral
Medium-sized sandpiper. It is best distinguished by the sharp division between its streaked neck and breast and its white belly. It breeds in Arctic Siberia and Canada and winters farther south. It is a frequent stray across the Atlantic Ocean to w Europe. Length: 19–23cm (7–9in). Family Scolopacidae; species *Calidris melanotos*.

sandpiper, purple
Small, round-shouldered wading bird found along rocky shores, reefs, breakwaters and patches of stones. It is dark above, with an inconspicuous purple gloss on its back. It has yellow legs and a yellow base to its bill. Length: 20cm (8in). Family Scolopacidae; species *Calidris maritima*.

sandpiper, spotted
Sandpiper found in temperate and sub-Arctic regions of North America. It is very similar in plumage, habits and habitat to the common sandpiper (*Actitis hypoleucos*) of Europe and Asia, but in summer it has striking black-spotted underparts and yellow legs. Length: 20cm (8in). Family Scolopacidae; species *Actitis macularia*.

sandpiper, terek
Small wader that breeds by fresh water in Siberian forests and scrub; it winters on estuaries farther south. The terek sandpiper has a distinctly upturned bill and short, yellow legs. In summer it has two black lines that form a "V" on its back. It often bobs its head. Length: 23cm (9in). Family Scolopacidae; species *Xenus cinereus*.

sandstone
SEDIMENTARY ROCK composed of SAND grains cemented in such materials as SILICA or iron oxide. Sandstones are ARENACEOUS rocks. They are very variable in character as a result of differences in grain size, chemical content and cementing materials. Most sand grains contain QUARTZ, which is hard and resistant. Other minerals in sandstones include FELDSPARS and MICAS, and iron also occurs, which tends to give sandstones a reddish or brownish colour. Most sandstones are formed by the accumulation of river sediments on the seabed. They are then compressed and uplifted to form new land. There are also a few sandstones that have been formed of wind-blown materials, especially in desert regions.

sandstorm
See DUST STORM

Sanger, Frederick (1918–)
English biochemist who became the first person to win two Nobel Prizes for chemistry. Sanger was awarded his first prize in 1958 for finding the structure of insulin. His second came in 1980 after work on the chemical structure of NUCLEIC ACID. Sanger and his colleagues found the entire sequence of the more than 5400 bases in the DNA of a VIRUS and some 17,000 bases of another DNA. His work was instrumental in the breakthrough, in 1999, by an international team of scientists who successfully mapped chromosome 22.

San Jose scale
SCALE INSECT native to E Asia. It was introduced into California (*c*.1880) and has now spread across the United States. It sucks the juices from trees and shrubs, often destroying the plants. Length: 2.5mm (0.1in). Family Diaspididae; species *Quadraspidiotus perniciosus*.

sansevieria (snake plant)
Any member of the genus *Sansevieria*, a group of plants native to tropical Africa. They are primarily used as ornamental house plants. Their erect, sword-shaped leaves are green with various markings. Shorter species grow in spreading rosettes. Height: 46–76cm (18–30in). Family Agavaceae; species include *Sansevieria thyrsiflora*.

sap
Fluid that circulates water and nutrients through plants. Water is absorbed by the ROOTS and carried, along with minerals, through the XYLEM to the leaves. Sap from the leaves is distributed throughout the plant. It travels upwards by OSMOSIS, ROOT PRESSURE and pressure differences created by TRANSPIRATION.

sapphire
Transparent to translucent gemstone variety of CORUNDUM. It has various colours produced by impurities of iron and titanium, the most valuable being deep blue. Sapphires are brilliant when cut and polished. *See also* RUBY

saprophyte
Plant or fungus that obtains its food from dead or decaying plant or animal tissue. Most saprophytic species have no CHLOROPHYLL. Saprophytes include fungi, such as MUSHROOMS and MOULDS, and some flowering plants. *See also* COMMENSALISM; MUTUALISM; PARASITE

sapsucker
WOODPECKER found in North and Central America. It is so called because it drills evenly spaced rows of holes in trees; it then visits these "wells" for sap and for the insects it attracts. The sapsucker's plumage is mostly black and white; males have bright red head patches. The most common species, the yellow-bellied sapsucker (*Sphyrapicus varius*), has a yellow breast. Length: to 23cm (9in). Family Picidae; genus *Sphyrapicus*.

sardine
Small, marine fish found worldwide; it belongs to the

◀ **sandpiper** The common sandpiper (*Actitis hypoleucos*) is a medium-sized wading bird. Like most other sandpiper species, it nests on the ground, concealed amongst vegetation. Common sandpipers migrate from their breeding grounds in Eurasia to Africa or Australia during the winter months.

S

▲ **sawfly** Sawflies are mainly found on oak, birch and willow trees and rose bushes. In order to lay her eggs, the female sawfly carves a small incision in the stem or leaves of the host plant with her ovipositor. Once hatched, the larvae are capable of causing much damage by stripping off the leaves. Shown here is the gooseberry sawfly and larva (*Nematus ribesi*).

HERRING family. It has a laterally compressed body, a large, toothless mouth and oily flesh. It is an important food fish. Length: to 30cm (12in). Family Clupeidae; species include *Sardinops caerulea* (Californian sardine), *Sardinops sagax* (South American sardine) and *Sardina pilchardus* (the European sardine or PILCHARD).

sargassum fish
See FROGFISH

sarsaparilla
Any of several species of tropical, perennial vines native to Central and South America. The roots of certain species, notably *Smilax aristolochiaefolia*, *Smilax regelii* and *Smilax febrifuga*, are used to impart an aromatic flavour to medicines and drinks. Family Liliaceae; genus *Smilax*.

sassafras
Small tree with furrowed bark, green twigs, yellow flowers and blue berries. It is found in E North America. Oil from the roots is used to flavour root beer. Family Lauraceae; species *Sassafras albidum*.

satellite-fly
Grey fly with unusually large feet. It lays larvae rather than eggs. The female follows a solitary, prey-carrying wasp and attempts to deposit her larvae on the prey. Adult body size: *c*.2mm (*c*.0.08in). Order Diptera; family Sarcophagidae; genus *Senotainia*.

satinwood
Tree that grows in Southeast Asia and India. Its smooth, hard wood is valued for furniture and veneer. Height to 15m (49ft). Family Rutaceae; species *Chloroxylon swietana*.

satsuma
Evergreen tree native to Southeast Asia. It has slender, spiny branches and glossy green, lance-shaped leaves. It bears orange or reddish-orange fruits, which have a very loose, smooth, shiny skin and segments that separate easily. The well-known MANDARINS and tangerines are part of the same group. Family Rutaceae; species *Citrus reticulata*.

saucer bug
Any member of the genus *Ilyocoris*, a group of bugs that are well adapted for living in or on the water. The saucer bug is a predacious muddy pond dweller. It swims actively along pond floors, searching for water lice and other small aquatic animals. Adult body size: *c*.18mm (*c*.0.7in). Order Hemiptera; family Naucoridae; genus *Ilyocoris*.

saurischian
Member of one of the two major groups of DINOSAURS (the other group being the ORNITHISCHIANS). Saurischians evolved in late Triassic times and were distinguished by a reptile-like pelvis. They included the large, plant-eating, quadrupedal SAUROPODS and the usually smaller, bipedal, carnivorous THEROPODS.

sauropod
Plant-eating, SAURISCHIAN dinosaur that evolved in late Triassic times and died out in late Cretaceous times. It had a small head, long neck and tail, a massive body and elephant-like legs. Sauropods included the largest land-living animals known, such as the brachiosaurs *Brachiosaurus*, *Supersaurus* and *Seismosaurus*, some of which may have been more than 30m (98ft) long and have weighed as much as 80 tonnes.

sausage tree
Tree that is native to tropical Africa; it is grown elsewhere in the tropics as an ornamental. It has compound leaves and bat-pollinated, claret-coloured flowers. Its gourd-like fruits, which resemble large sausages, hang on cord-like stalks that may be several feet long. The fruits are used medicinally as a purgative. Height: 15m (49ft). Family Bignoniaceae; species *Kigelia pinnata*.

Saussure, Horace Benedict de (1740–99)
Swiss geologist. He studied the region of the Alps, publishing his study of its weather, geology and botany in *Voyages dans les Alpes* (4 vols., 1779–96). Saussure also developed the first electrometer (1766) and the first hygrometer (1783).

savanna
Area of tropical grassland found between the Earth's major DESERT regions and the tropical forests. Savannas occur mainly between 5° and 20° north and south of the Equator, except in E Africa, where, because the land is elevated, savanna regions are situated on the Equator. The savanna climate is hot and wet in summer, when the Sun is overhead; temperatures average *c*.25°C (*c*.77°F) and the rainfall is 250mm to 1250mm (10–50in). In winter, the tropical high-pressure system controls the climate, and so the conditions are warm but very dry. Temperatures 15°C to 25°C (59°–77°F), and rainfall totals are less than 250mm (10in). In such a climate, grass grows very well in summer – up to 2m (6ft) in height – but shrivels in winter. Trees do not grow well, although BAOBABS and BOTTLE TREES survive by storing water in their trunks. Pastoral farming is the main activity on the savanna grasslands.

savory
Any of several hardy aromatic herbs of the MINT family. Its long, thin leaves are used, green or dried, for flavouring. Summer savory (*Satureja hortensis*) is an annual; winter savory (*Satureja montana*) is a perennial. Family Lamiaceae/Labiatae.

sawfish
Any member of the genus *Pristis*, comprising several species of shark-like, flat-bodied RAYS found in tropical marine and brackish waters. The sawfish has a grey or black-brown body. Its elongated, saw-toothed snout resembles a flat blade. Length: to 5m (16ft). Family Pristidae; genus *Pristis*.

sawfly
Any of *c*.400 species of primitive, plant-feeding WASPS. They lack a narrow waist between thorax and abdomen. Most sawfly species are in the family Tenthredinidae. Length: to 20mm (0.8in). Order Hymenoptera.

saw grass (prickly sedge)
Large member of the SEDGE family; it is common in marshes of tropical and subtropical America. Saw grass forms dense masses of vegetation. Its long leaves are wide, with spiny, serrated margins. The stems are used as a source of cheap paper. Family Cyperaceae; species *Cladium effusum*.

saw-wing
Any of several species of non-migratory SWALLOWS found in North Africa. The saw-wing has a swift-like, sooty brown, cigar-shaped body and a long, brown, forked tail. Like a typical swallow, it catches insects on the wing and is often found near human settlements and in forest glades and wooded grasslands. Length: 20cm (8in). Family Hirundinidae; genus *Psalidoprocne*.

saxifrage
Any member of the genus *Saxifraga*, a group of perennial plants native to temperate and mountainous regions of Europe and North America. The leaves are massed at the base, and the branched clusters of small flowers are white, pink, purple or yellow. Height: to 60cm (24in). Family Saxifragaceae; species include *Saxifraga callosa*.

scab disease
Any of various plant diseases, the symptoms of which include scabby, scaly spots on fruits and twigs or velvety spots on leaves. Scabby fruit is often stunted or deformed. Scab diseases are serious pests of apples, pears, pecans, peaches, cucumbers and potatoes.

scabious
Any plant of the genus *Scabiosa*, belonging to the TEASEL family. They are native to temperate parts of Europe and Asia, and the mountains of E Africa. The flowers grow in dense clusters and can be any of a variety of colours, according to the species. Family Dipsacaceae; species include *Scabiosa atropurpurea*.

scale
Small hard plate that forms part of the external SKIN of an animal. It is usually a development of the skin layers. In most fish, scales are composed of bone in the dermal skin layer. The scales of reptiles and those on the legs of birds are horny growths of the epidermal skin layer; they are comprised mostly of the fibrous protein KERATIN.

 S

◄ **saxifrage** The rue-leaved saxifrage (*Saxifrage tridactylites*) thrives in dry conditions and is capable of growing on rocks and walls. It is a member of the widespread family Saxifragaceae, whose name in Latin means "breaker of rocks".

▶ **scallop** There are *c*.360 species of scallop, found on sandy and muddy seabeds worldwide. The shell is opened and closed by a single muscle, which is the only edible part of the animal.

scale insect
Any of several species of small insects found worldwide. All species are covered by a waxy, scale-like covering secreted by the insect. The scale insect feeds by sucking plant juices. Length: to 25mm (1in). Order Homoptera.

scaleworm
Free-living POLYCHAETE worm. Its dorsal surface is covered in flattened, overlapping scales. It has four tentacles, which are used in feeding and respiration, and four jaws, which are used in prey capture and maceration. Phylum Annelida; class Polychaeta; order Aphroditamorpha.

scallop
Any member of the family Pectinidae, a group of edible BIVALVE MOLLUSCS. One shell, or valve, is usually convex and the other almost flat. The shell's surface is ribbed (scalloped). Most scallops have a row of eyes that fringe the fleshy mantle. Width: 2.5–20cm (1–8in). Family Pectinidae.

scaphopod
See TUSK SHELL

scapolite (wernerite)
Group of SILICATE minerals that are related to the FELDSPARS; they are of variable chemical composition. Scapolites are common in metamorphosed limestones. They are grey and glassy in appearance. Hardness 5–6; r.d. 2.7.

scapula (shoulder blade)
In vertebrates, either of two large, roughly triangular, flat bones found one on either side of the upper back. They form part of the PECTORAL girdle and provide for the attachment of muscles that move the forelimbs.

scarab beetle
Any member of the BEETLE family Scarabaeidae, comprising numerous species of broad beetles distributed worldwide. Most species, including the June beetle (*Cotinus nitida*), Japanese beetle (*Popillia japonica*) and Hercules beetles (*Dynastes hercules*), are leaf chafers. A smaller group, including the DUNG BEETLE, are scavengers. Family Scarabaeidae.

scarp
See ESCARPMENT

scaup
Any of several species of diving DUCK. Scaups breed mainly on tundra and in coniferous forests of Eurasia and North America; they winter farther south in flocks at sea. The male has a grey back, dark glossy-green or purple head and black breast. The female is brown with a white base to the bill. The New Zealand scaup (*Aythya novaeseelandiae*) is all black. Length: 42–51cm (17–20in). Family Anatidae; genus *Aythya*.

Scheele, Karl Wilhelm (1742–86)
Swedish chemist who discovered OXYGEN. He was an apothecary and his interest in chemistry led to an investigation of combustion and the discovery of oxygen in 1771. Publication of his discovery was delayed, however, and the credit went to Joseph PRIESTLEY. Scheele made other important discoveries, including chlorine, glycerol and a number of organic acids.

scheelite (Ca[WO₄MoO₄])
Mineral, calcium tungstatemolybdate, an important ore of TUNGSTEN. It is found in metamorphic deposits and in pegmatites. Scheelite has tetragonal system and bipyramidal crystals; it also occurs as massive and granular aggregates. It is brittle and reveals various tints with adamantine lustre. It fluoresces under ultraviolet light. Hardness 4.5–5; r.d. 6.

scheltopusik
Limbless LIZARD native to SE Europe and W and central Asia. It has a conspicuous fold running along the length of its body. It has bony, rectangular scales and a long tail, which is 1.5 times the body length. The scheltopusik prefers dry habitats. It is chiefly active during the day. Length: to 120cm (47in). Family Anguidae; species *Ophisaurus apodus*.

schist
Large group of METAMORPHIC ROCKS that have become cleavable, causing the rocks to split into thin plates leaving a wavy, uneven surface. Almost any type of rock will become a schist if subjected to sufficient metamorphism. Schists are named after their predominant mineral; a common example is MICA SCHIST.

schizomid
Any member of a group of *c*.130 species of small ARACHNIDS. Schizomids vary in colour from white to tan, due to the cryptic nature of their habitat. Prone to desiccation, they inhabit moist places, such as leaf litter, caves and soil, in tropical to warm temperate regions. Schizomids are carnivorous and fast-running. The female makes a brood chamber in the soil and remains with the young until the first moult. Adult body length: 3–11mm (0.1–0.4in). Cass Arachnida; subclass Schizomida.

schizophyte
Plant that reproduces solely by FISSION. Schizophytes include BACTERIA, YEAST and CYANOBACTERIA.

larva

▲ **scorpion fly** The head of the scorpion fly is shaped like a snout and has biting jaws at the lower end. The fly feeds on dead animals, which it sometimes scavenges from spider-webs, and ripe fruit. The larvae develop in soil, feeding on dead animals and plants.

Schultze, Max Johann Sigismund (1825–74)
German biologist. He studied the nervous system of vertebrates, the electric organs of fish and the anatomy of worms and molluscs. Schultze's most important work was the identification of a cell as an organism containing both nucleus and protoplasm and his recognition that protoplasm is a basic substance of plant and animal cells.

Schwann, Theodor (1810–82)
German biologist who laid the foundation of modern HISTOLOGY by establishing the cell theory. In 1836 he isolated and named PEPSIN, becoming the first person to prepare an enzyme from animal tissue.

Schwann cells
Cells that wrap around the AXONS of NEURONES to form a fatty, protective MYELIN SHEATH. Between sections of myelin sheath are small gaps called NODES OF RANVIER. The sheath serves to insulate the nerve electrically and to allow the more rapid passage of nerve impulses. The cells were named after their discoverer, Theodor SCHWANN. *See also* NERVOUS SYSTEM

sclerenchyma
In botany, plant support tissue, the cells of which have become rigid due to the formation of LIGNIN. Sclerenchyma occurs in veins, stems and midribs of leaves. Sclerenchyma cells die as they mature because the lignin in the thickened cell wall does not

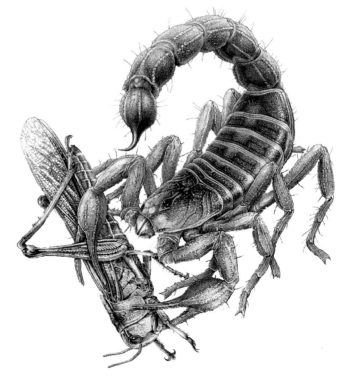

◀ **scorpion** Scorpions of the family Buthidae, such as the species shown here, are among the few whose sting is potentially lethal to humans. Most scorpions are active at night and hunt mainly insects, although some of the larger species, which grow up to 19cm (7.5in) long, will attack rodents and small lizards. Most scorpions kill by holding their prey with their pincers and injecting poison via the sting. The sting of the scorpion is worked by opposing muscles fixed to the base of the sting, which contract and relax, forcing the sharp tip into its prey's tissue. The poison, stored in the poison gland, is forced down and out of the tip of the sting by muscles located around the gland.

▶ scorpion fish The large-scaled scorpion fish (*Scorpaena scrofa*) is found on rocky seabeds and reefs in the shallow waters of the E Atlantic Ocean and the Mediterranean Sea. It has *c*.45 dorsal spines, some of which contain poison glands for defence, and is up to 50cm (20in) long. Like all scorpion fish, it is carnivorous, feeding on molluscs, crustaceans and small fish, swallowing them whole with its large mouth. Its reddish-brown coloration and textured skin camouflage it well amongst the rocky reefs it inhabits.

allow the passage of gases and water; however shallow pits (PLASMODESMATA) in the wall are free from lignin and permit some exchange of substances between adjacent cells. In zoology, the hard skeletal tissue of corals is also called sclerenchyma.

scorpion

Any of more than a thousand species of ARACHNIDS characterized by large claws and a sting at the end of the tail. They have both lateral and median eyes. The scorpion's body is split into a cephalothorax (prosoma), covered by an unsegmented carapace, and a segmented abdomen (opisthosoma). Scorpions are well distributed in the tropics and in warm temperate regions. Only a minority of species have stings that can be lethal. Subclass Scorpiones.

scorpion fish (rockfish, sea scorpion)

Any of numerous species of perch-like marine fish found in temperate waters. There are colourful and camouflaged species; many species are bottom-dwelling. Scorpion fish can be identified by their venomous fin spines, which are capable of inflicting painful and sometimes fatal injury. Length: to 1m (3.3ft). Family Scorpaenidae. *See also* LIONFISH

scorpion fly

Any of several species of brown to grey insects found throughout the Northern Hemisphere. Its chewing mouthparts are at the end of a long, beak-like structure. Males of some species have an abdomen that resembles a scorpion's tail. Length: to 40mm (1.6in). Order Mecoptera.

scoter

Any of three species of diving DUCK. The scoter has black plumage and a red and yellow bill. It breeds on tundra or in pine forests and winters at sea. The male common scoter (*Melanitta nigra*) is all black; the male velvet scoter (*Melanitta deglandi*) has white wing patches; the male surf scoter (*Melanitta perspicillata*) has white head patches. The females are mainly brown. Length: 44–58cm (17–23in). Family Anatidae; genus *Melanitta*.

Scots pine

Common PINE tree found in Europe and Asia, from Spain to Siberia. It is widely planted for timber and as a feature in parks and large gardens. The upper trunk becomes reddish with age. Height: to 35m (115ft). Family Pinaceae; species *Pinus sylvestris*.

screamer

Goose-like water bird found in South America, where it inhabits marshes. It has a crest or horny spike on the top of its head and sharp spurs at the bend of its wing. Its voice is among the loudest of all birds. Length: 76–94cm (30–37in). Family Anhimidae; genera *Chauna* and *Anhima*.

scree (talus)

Loose fragments of rock that have accumulated on a hillside. Scree is made up of particles ranging in size from sand grains to boulders. It mainly results from WEATHERING processes, such as freeze-thaw activity. Scree forms more frequently on certain rock types, such as LIMESTONE.

screw pine

Woody plant distributed throughout tropical Asia, the islands of Polynesia and the Indian Ocean; a few species are found in Africa. It is not a true pine. Its long, tough, narrow leaves rise from a rosette in a spiral, like the thread of a screw. It bears cone-like fruit. Height: to 12m (39ft). Family Pandanaceae; genus *Pandanus*.

screwworm

Larva of several species of bluegreen BLUEBOTTLES (blow-flies). It is a parasite of warm-blooded animals. The screwworm enters through wounds in the skin. It is a serious pest of domestic animals in the United States and South America. Family Calliphoridae; genus *Callitroga*.

scrub-bird

Either of two species of small, rare, brown birds found in Australia. They run swiftly and rarely fly. Their calls are loud and on various notes. The reddish-hued scrub-bird (*Atrichornis rufescens*) was discovered in the wet forests of New South Wales, SE Australia, in the 1860s. Length: to 18cm (7in). The noisy, or western, scrub-bird (*Atrichornis clamosus*) is found in Western Australia. Believed to have become extinct after 1889, it was rediscovered in 1961. It inhabits dense coastal scrub and bushlands. Length: 22cm (9in). Family Atrichornithidae; genus *Atrichornis*.

scrub-robin

Ground-living, inquisitive, thrush-like songbird found in Australasia. It has reddish-brown or grey plumage, with black face markings and black-tipped wing bars. It rummages in leaf litter in varied habitats from rainforests to scrub. When feeding, the scrub-robin constantly raises and lowers its tails. Length: 20–23cm (8–9in). Family Petroicidae; genus *Drymodes*.

scrubwren

Small, undergrowth-dwelling bird found only in Australia. Its plumage is mostly sombre brown and buff, with black facial markings. The nine species can be distinguished by their large domed nests, which vary from species to species. They are fine songsters. Length: 11–17cm (4–7in). Family Acanthizidae; genus *Sericornis*.

sculpin

Any member of the family Cottidae, comprising *c*.300 species of bottom-dwelling, usually marine fish. Most sculpin species are found in the temperate and cold waters of the N Atlantic Ocean, although some species are found in the Pacific Ocean and some in fresh water. Sculpins are greyish and are often mottled with yellow. Their large bony heads are covered with prickles. Length: to 60cm (24in). Family Cottidae.

scurvy grass

Plant of the MUSTARD family, native to N Europe and Arctic regions. It produces white flowers. Its stems and leaves have an unpleasant taste; they were used on early polar expeditions to treat scurvy, hence its common name. Family Brassicaceae/Cruciferae; species *Cochlearia officinalis*.

scuttle-fly

Any member of the family Phoridae, a group of small, hump-backed flies. Its common name comes from its rather agitated scurrying behaviour on plants.

S

◀ screw pine Common near sandy beaches on the Pacific Ocean, the screw pine takes its name from the growth of its leaves in a spiral-like pattern. It has distinctive stilt-like roots, which grow above ground. The tough, pliable leaves are used to make mats and baskets.

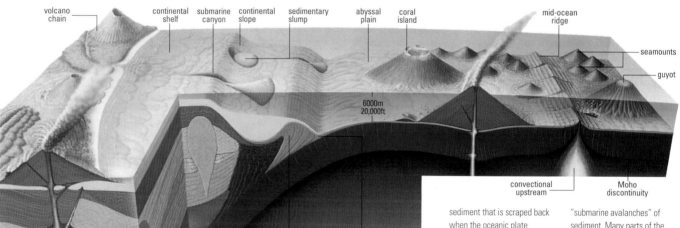

▲ **sea cucumber** There are hundreds of species of sea cucumber, ranging between 2cm (0.8in) and 2m (6.6ft) in length. It moves along the seabed by means of the hundreds of suctioned tube feet on its body.

Most species feed and reproduce on decaying matter. The coffin-fly (*Conicera tibialis*) regularly breeds on freshly buried corpses; the mushroom fly (*Megaselia halterata*) feeds on fungi. Adult body size: *c*.4mm (*c*.0.2in). Order Diptera; family Phoridae.

scythebill

Any of several species of brown, medium-sized forest birds that are related to the WOODPECKER. They are found in South America. Scythebills have very long, slender, down-curved, sickle-shaped bills. Shy and wary birds, scythebills climb trunks and limbs, probing for insects in moss, fronds and epiphytes. Length: 20–25cm (8–10in), of which 5–6cm (*c*.2in) is the bill. Family Dendrocolaptidae; genus *Campylorhamphus*.

sea

See OCEAN

sea anemone

See ANEMONE

sea bream

Any of numerous species of marine, spiny finned fish. They have deep bodies and massive jaws with heavy crushing teeth. Length: to 50cm (20in). Most species belong to the family Sparidae.

sea buckthorn

Deciduous, thorny, spreading shrub, native to w and central Europe and temperate Asia. It forms thickets on sand dunes by the sea, where its suckering habit helps to bind loose sand. It has silvery green leaves and small green flowers, which are followed by edible, orange, globular fruits. Family Elaeagnaceae; species *Hippophae rhamnoides*.

sea cucumber (*bêche de mer*, Fr. "spade of the ocean")

Marine ECHINODERM that occurs both on and within marine sediments; it is closely related to the STARFISH and SEA URCHIN. Some sea cucumber species move very little, filtering detritus and planktonic organisms from the water with their tentacles. Others move actively along the sea bottom, using their tentacles to ingest organic material and sediment. Other species are predominantly burrowers; they move through the sediment by peristaltic movements, ingesting much of it as they proceed. Phylum Echinodermata; class Holothuroidea. *See also* COTTON SPINNER

sea dragon

Marine fish found in coastal waters of Australia. It is a PIPEFISH, closely related to the SEAHORSE. Its reddish-brown body is covered with leafy and spine-like projections, making it resemble floating seaweed. Family Syngnathidae.

sea fan (gorgonian)

Colonial CNIDARIAN animal found in CORAL REEFS of tropical marine waters. Sea fans form branching, flat colonies. The eight-tentacled POLYPS live in tiny pits along the horny branches. Phylum Coelenterata/Cnidaria; class Anthozoa; species *Eunicella verrucosa*.

sea fern

Small aquatic animal, a marine HYDROID named after its superficial resemblance to the terrestrial ferns. It is often harvested and dyed for use in floral arrangements and aquaria. Phylum Coelenterata/Cnidaria; class Hydrozoa; order Hydroida.

sea fir

Sedentary marine animal. A HYDROID, it has a fine branching structure reminiscent of the needles of terrestrial fir trees. It is often seen in shallow waters and rock pools. Phylum Coelenterata/Cnidaria; class Hydrozoa; order Hydroida.

seafloor

See feature article

seafloor spreading

Theory suggested (1960) by the US geologist Harry Hess to explain how CONTINENTAL DRIFT occurs. It is now a key part of PLATE TECTONICS. It proposes that the SEAFLOOR is moved laterally as new rock is injected along MID-OCEAN RIDGES. Submarine volcanic eruptions and intrusions along these ridges generate the new seafloor rocks, which spread laterally, a few centimetres per year. Thus, the seafloor spreads symmetrically, becoming older with increasing distance from the ridge. As the Earth is not

S

SEAFLOOR

Floor of the OCEANS. The major features of the seafloor are the CONTINENTAL SHELF, the CONTINENTAL RISE, the ABYSSAL floor, seamounts, oceanic TRENCHES, and MID-OCEAN RIDGES. The **abyssal** or deep ocean floor is *c*.3km (1.8mi) deep and is mostly made of basaltic rock

covered with fine-grained (PELAGIC) sediment consisting of dust and the shells of marine organisms. **Oceanic trenches** are up to 11km (7mi) deep, typically 50–100km (30–60mi) wide and may be thousands of kilometres long. The slopes are usually asymmetrical, with the steeper slope

on the landward side and a more gentle slope on the side of the ocean basin. They are regarded as the site of plate SUBDUCTION. **Oceanic ridges** are long, linear volcanic structures that tend to occupy the middle of seafloors; they are the sites of crustal spreading. *See also* SEAFLOOR SPREADING

volcano chain · continental shelf · submarine canyon · continental slope · sedimentary slump · abyssal plain · coral island · mid-ocean ridge · seamounts · guyot

6000m 20,000ft

convectional upstream · Moho discontinuity

asthenosphere · accretionary ridge · ocean trench 10,000m (33,000ft) deep

▲ **The lithosphere "floats"** in the Earth's mantle, and this defines where the surface of the crust – oceanic or continental – will be. Thus, thicker, less dense continents "float" higher than the thinner,

denser oceanic lithosphere. The continental shelves are the transition. Chains of volcanoes or volcanic islands are often found at active margins, as shown in the – vertically exaggerated – diagram. The

sediment that is scraped back when the oceanic plate subducts beneath the continental plate forms the accretionary wedge. Submarine canyons are more common on passive margins, but can be found here too. They were probably caused by surface erosion during periods of low sea level, and were subsequently widened by turbidity currents, or

"submarine avalanches" of sediment. Many parts of the seafloor are highly fractured, especially around the mid-ocean ridge. There are many volcanoes; those that never emerge are seamounts. Guyots are volcanoes with their tops cut off flat, probably by wave erosion when the sea level was lower. Their great weight has sunk them down into the ocean crust.

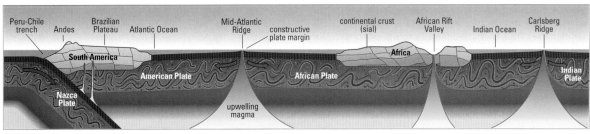

► **seafloor spreading** The vast ridges that divide the Earth's crust beneath each of the world's oceans mark the boundaries between tectonic plates that are gradually moving in opposite directions. As the plates shift apart, molten magma rises from the mantle to seal the rift and the seafloor slowly spreads toward the continental landmasses. The rate of spreading has been calculated by magnetic analysis of the rock at *c*.3.75cm (*c*.1.5in) a year in the N Atlantic Ocean. Underwater volcanoes mark the line where the continental rise begins. As the plates meet, much of the denser ocean crust dips beneath the continental plate and melts into the magma.

Seafloor spreading in the Atlantic Ocean

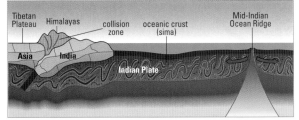

Seafloor spreading in the Indian Ocean and continental plate collision

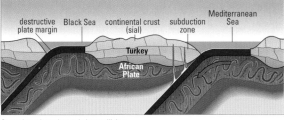

Oceanic and continental plate collision

expanding, however, the seafloor must be lost as well as generated. Seafloor rocks are dragged down into the MANTLE at specific sites, known as SUBDUCTION zones, which are marked topographically by submarine TRENCHES. Thus seafloor rocks are constantly being recycled, and none are older than around 180 million years. In 1963 British geophysicists F.J. Vine and D.H. Matthews uncovered supporting evidence for the theory of seafloor spreading. They tested the patterns of FOSSIL magnetism in the rocks of the seafloor and discovered a symmetrical pattern of stripes centred on mid-ocean ridges. By matching the stripes with known dates it became possible to calculate the rate of spreading.

sea gooseberry
See COMB JELLY

sea-grass
Aquatic plant that grows submerged in water; it is found in tropical and subtropical seas. The linear leaves are arranged in two vertical rows. Male and female flowers are borne on separate plants; pollination by thread-like pollen grains takes place in water. Beds of sea-grasses are useful as food and spawning grounds for fish. Family Cymodoceaceae; genera *Amphibolis*, *Cymodocea*, *Halodule*, *Syringodium* and *Thalassodendron*.

seagull
See GULL

sea hair
Widely distributed CHLOROPHYTE (green alga) found in all of the world's major oceans. It is the food of

▲ **seahorse** Related to the pipe fishes (back), the sea horse is the only fish with a prehensile tail, which it uses to cling to seaweed. The sea horse swims weakly with an upright stance; it is carried along by ocean currents.

many marine herbivores. Its name is derived from the short, hair-like covering that it gives to the substrate on which it grows. Class Ulvophyceae; order Ulvales; family Ulvaceae; genus *Enteromorpha*.

sea hare
Marine GASTROPOD found on shore or in shallow offshore waters. It has no shell and in some species no mantle cavity. Its gills are visible externally. The sea hare secretes a purple mucus for defence. Class Gastropoda; order Anaspidea; genus *Tethys*.

sea holly
Perennial plant native to Europe and naturalized in North America. It grows on sand or shingle by the sea. Sea holly has bluish foliage, and its leaves have lobes that terminate in sharp prickles. Clusters of stalkless, blue flowers are produced in whorls of the uppermost leaves. The roots have been regarded since ancient times as an excellent flavouring, vegetable and medicine. Family Apiaceae; species *Eryngium maritimum*.

seahorse
Any of several species of PIPEFISH found in warm seas. The seahorse is characterized by a horse-like head, which is oriented at right angles to the body. It has an elongated, prehensile tail and bony plates covering its body. The male broods fertilized eggs in a pouch on the abdomen. Length: 4–30cm (2–12in). Family Syngnathidae; genus *Hippocampus*.

sea kale
Any of several species of fleshy, cabbage-like plants that grow in coastal regions of Eurasia. Common sea kale (*Crambe Maritina*) has bluish leaves and small clusters of white flowers. Its young leaves can be cooked and eaten, and have a bitter taste. Family Brassicaceae.

sea krait
Any of several species of venomous marine SNAKES. They mate and lay their eggs on land. Although dangerously poisonous, sea kraits are typically docile and rarely bite. Most species feed on eels. They are widespread in the W Pacific and Indian oceans. One species is found in a freshwater lake in the Solomon Islands. Length: to 1.4m (4.6ft). Family Elapidae; genus *Laticauda*.

seal
Streamlined marine mammal. The 19 species belong-

ing to the family Phocidae are known as true seals. Seals' limbs are highly modified as flippers. Unlike FUR-SEALS and SEA-LIONS, true seals are almost helpless on land (or ice): they can only hump along, rather than using their limbs. Once swimming, however, seals are fast and graceful. Order Pinnipedia; family Phocidae.

seal, Baikal
Seal that lives in the deeper waters of Lake Baikal, Russia. Baikal seals are silver grey, darker above and paler below. They have large eyes and foreshortened faces. They use their heavily clawed forefeet to keep holes open in the freshwater ice so that they can dive to feed on deep-water fish. Solitary females make snow lairs on the ice, where they give birth to pure white pups, which they feed for about two months. There are only *c*.70,000 Baikal seals. Head-body length: 1.2m (4ft). Family Phocidae; species *Phoca sibirica*.

seal, crabeater
Extremely numerous species of seal. It lives along the edges of the Antarctic pack ice, where its only natural enemy is the killer whale. It is dark grey above and slightly paler grey beneath. The crabeater seal can move across the ice with a "galloping" motion at speeds of up to 25km/h (15mph). It feeds mainly by straining krill from the water with its specially adapted three-pronged teeth. Females give birth between October and December, and the pups are suckled for five weeks. Head-body length: 2–2.4m (6.6–8ft). Family Phocidae; species *Lobodon carcinophagus*.

seal, elephant
Largest species of seal. It is found off the Pacific

S

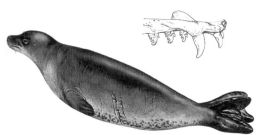

▲ **seal, crabeater** This seal (*Lobodon carcinophagus*) has specially adapted teeth (upper jaw shown above) which fit closely together so that it can strain krill from the water. These seals often bear scars from attacks by killer whales.

coast of North America. Male elephant seals can weigh 2700kg (6000lb), whereas females are only half this size. Their bodies are thickly covered with blubber, which keeps them warm when they dive deeply to feed on squid. Numbers of elephant seals were severely reduced by commercial sealers 100 years ago, but strict protection has allowed them to recover to a healthy population. Breeding takes place on offshore islands. The males snort loudly at each other through their enlarged noses and fight fiercely over the females. The females suckle the pups for a month, and the pups take to the sea a month later. Head-body length: 6m (20ft). Family Phocidae; species *Mirounga angustirostris*.

seal, grey

Huge seal that lives in the N Atlantic Ocean. Its massive shoulders are covered with thickly folded and wrinkled skin. It feeds on fish and shellfish in coastal waters. Females arrive first at the breeding grounds, rocky coasts of N Europe and North America, where they give birth and suckle their single pups for three weeks. When the males arrive, the more experienced ones move to the centres of groups of females and drive off other males. Head-body length: 1.6–2.3m (5.2–7.5ft); weight (males) 300kg (660lb). Family Phocidae; species *Halichoerus grypus*.

seal, harbour (common seal)

Seal that lives in temperate and subarctic waters of the N Atlantic and Pacific oceans. It has a large head, a short body and a blotchy dark grey coat. As with most seals, the male is larger than the female. The harbour seal is non-migratory and often hauls out onto rocky shores or travels up rivers. It can dive for up to 30 minutes to feed on fish and shellfish. The single pup is suckled and guarded by its mother for about six weeks, though it can swim from birth and dive when only two days old. Mating takes place in the water as soon as the pups are weaned. Head-body length: 1.4–1.8m (4.6–6ft). Family Phocidae; species *Phoca vitulina*.

seal, harp

Fast-swimming seal that spends most of its life at sea. It makes long north–south migrations across

► **seal** Harp seals (*Pagophilus groenlandicus*) migrate up to 2500km from their winter breeding grounds on the pack ice of the N Atlantic and Arctic oceans to their summer feeding grounds. There are three distinct populations: the NW Atlantic, the E Greenland and the Barents Sea. The male hooded seal (*Cystophora cristata*) inflates its nasal sack during the breeding season to intimidate his rivals. The Hawaiian monk seal (*Monachus schauinslandi*) is one of the most endangered of seal species. Its population is threatened by human disturbance, habitat loss and the decrease of available food. The Weddell seal (*Leptonychotes weddelli*) is one of the most vocal of seal species, producing a variety of sounds that can be heard from quite a distance.

subarctic and arctic waters of the N Atlantic and Arctic oceans. Its coat is white or pale grey, with a black head and a black band along its flanks. It lives in sociable groups and can move quickly over ice. The harp seal feeds on fish and crustaceans caught during long, deep dives. Females give birth to their young on ice floes in February and suckle them for four weeks. Head-body length: 1.6–2m (5.2–6.6ft). Family Phocidae; species *Pagophilus groenlandicus*.

seal, hooded

Seal that spends most of its life at sea, along the edges of the pack ice of arctic and subarctic waters of the N Atlantic Ocean, where it dives deeply for fish and squid. It migrates to E Greenland, where it hauls out onto the ice to moult. Pups are born in the spring and suckled for just over one week. During this time the female is attended by a male who drives off other males by making threatening noises with his inflatable nasal sac. Mating takes place two weeks after the birth. Head-body length: 2–2.6m (6.6–8.5ft). Family Phocidae; species *Cystophora cristata*.

seal, leopard

Slender seal that is found on pack ice and in coastal waters of the Antarctic Ocean. It is a fast-swimming predator of penguins and other seals. Penguins are caught by leopard seals as they enter the water from the ice and are efficiently skinned before being

◄ **seal, leopard** The hunter of the southern oceans is the leopard seal (*Hydrurga leptonyx*). A solitary animal, it hunts along the edge of the pack ice in search of its favourite prey – the Adélie penguin. This continual persecution has led Adélies to become reluctant to be the first of their group to enter the water, which is the time at which they are most vulnerable to attack.

swallowed. Leopard seals also catch fish, squid and other shellfish. The coat is dark grey above, pale grey below and covered with small dark spots. Little is known about the breeding cycle, but pups are thought to be born early in the year. Head-body length: 3–3.5m (9.8–11.5ft). Family Phocidae; species *Hydrurga leptonyx*.

seal, monk

Any of three species of seal found in the Atlantic or Pacific oceans. Monk seals are very rare because their breeding grounds, on islets and isolated cliffs, have become accessible to people. They are shy, nervous creatures; pregnant and nursing mothers often abort or desert their young if disturbed. Family Phocidae; genus *Monachus*. The **Mediterranean monk seal** lives in the Atlantic Ocean, from the Canary Islands to the Mediterranean and Black Sea. There are *c.*500 individuals. Head-body length 2.3–2.7m (7.5–8.9ft). Species *Monachus monachus*. The **Caribbean monk seal** once lived off SE North America but is now thought to be extinct. Head-body length: 2.1m (7ft). Species *Monachus tropicalis*. The **Hawaiian monk seal** lives off Hawaiian islands. There are thought to be *c.*1000 individuals. Head-body length: 2.1m (7ft). Species *Monachus schauinslandi*.

seal, ringed

Seal that can be found in arctic and subarctic waters of the N Atlantic Ocean. It is dark grey above and silvery beneath, with dark rings on its sides and back. Ringed seals feed on cod and planktonic crustaceans. The males defend underwater territories. In March and April, white pups are born in snow lairs over breathing holes in the ice; they are suckled for up to 10 weeks. Ringed seals do not start to breed until they are six or seven years old, and they may live for more than forty years. Head-body length: 1.2–1.5m (3.9–4.9ft). Family Phocidae; species *Phoca hispida*.

seal, Weddell

Seal found at the edge of the pack ice in the Antarctic Ocean. It has a small head, large eyes and a short muzzle. Its large body is dark grey above and pale beneath, covered with pale grey spots. Weddell seals feed on deep water cod, for which they dive deeper and longer than any other seal. Dives of up to 600m (2000ft), lasting more than 70 minutes, during which the heart rate is reduced by 75%, have been recorded. In the breeding season, male Weddell seals set up underwater territories that females visit. Birth takes place on land, and the female does not leave the pup for 12 days. Suckling continues for another four weeks, when the adults mate and return to the sea. The pups can dive for food at seven weeks old. Head-body length: 2.9m (9.5ft). Family Phocidae; species *Leptonychotes weddelli*.

hooded seal

harp seal

Hawaiian monk seal

Weddell seal

sea lavender

Plant that is widespread in coastal areas, particularly in the Middle East and Europe. It is a stiff, branching plant, with broad, basal leaves. It produces sprays of tiny white, pink, yellow or lavender flowers. Height: 30–61cm (12–24in). Family Plumbaginaceae; species include *Limonium vulgare*.

sea level

Level from which topographic heights are measured. It is usually the mean sea level and is reckoned on being the average of regular sea levels taken over a long period of time. It may also be referred to as the Ordnance Datum (OD).

sea level rise

Increase in SEA LEVEL. Geological history shows that sea levels have changed throughout much of GEO-LOGICAL TIME. Global changes in sea level mainly result from the growth and decay of the polar ice caps, with water being withdrawn from the oceans or released back into them. Cooling and warming of ocean water results in expansion and contraction of ocean volume, which promotes sea level change. The net effect can change sea levels by as much as 100 metres. Apparent regional or local changes in sea level may be the result of the vertical movement of the continental crust.

sea lily

CRINOID ECHINODERM found in deep marine waters. It has many branched arms, with ciliated grooves for collecting food, radiating from a tiny body disc. Spineless, it attaches itself to the ocean bottom with a stalk. Class Crinoidea.

sea lion

Any of several members of the family Otariidae, comprising the eared SEALS. Unlike true seals, sea lions have conspicuous ear flaps. They use their fore flippers to swim, and on land they can tuck their hind flippers underneath the rear end of the body to help them move about. Males are larger than females, often with lion-like manes. Mating takes place around the time the young are born and there is delayed implantation. Pups are suckled for up to a year. Order Pinnipedia; family Otariidae.

sea lion, Australian

Sea lion that lives around the islands and reefs of W and S Australia. Females are silver-grey above and creamy yellow below; males are black-brown. They feed on fish and shellfish. Births occur from October to December. Head-body length: 1.5–2m (4.9–6.6ft). Family Otariidae; species *Neophoca cinerea*.

sea lion, California (Galápagos sea lion)

Sea lion found on the west coast of North America. It has a dark brown coat and feeds on fish and shellfish. The young are born in May and June. Head-body length: 1.8–2.2m (5.9–7.2ft). Family Otariidae; species *Zalophus californianus*.

sea lion, New Zealand

Sea lion that inhabits the Australasian region. Females are silver-grey above and creamy yellow below; males are black-brown. They feed on fish and shellfish, squid and penguins. Dark brown pups are born on sandy beaches in December and January. Head-body length: 1.8–2.2m (5.9–7.2ft). Family Otariidae; species *Phocarctos hookeri*.

sea lion, South American

Golden to dark brown sea lion found on the coast of South America. It feeds on fish, crustaceans and molluscs. Black pups are born in January. Head-body length: 2–2.5m (6.6–8.2ft). Family Otariidae; species *Otaria flavescens*.

sea lion, Steller's

Large, reddish-brown sea lion found in the N Pacific region. It feeds on fish and shellfish and sometimes seal pups. The young are born in May and June. Head-body length: 2.4–2.9m (7.9–9.5ft). Family Otariidae; species *Eumetopias jubatus*.

sea-mat

See MOSS ANIMAL

sea mouse

Any member of the genus *Aphrodita*, a group of large marine ANNELID worms. The sea mouse has matted bristles on the sides and top of its body. The common sea mouse (*Aphrodita aculeata*) lives in sandy mud on both sides of the N Atlantic Ocean. Length: 15cm (6in). Class Polychaeta; phylum Annelida; genus *Aphrodita*.

sea pen

Any of several species of marine animals that are related to sea ANEMONES and CORALS. Sea pens live in feather-shaped colonies, which resembles a quill pen. Order Pennatulaceae; genera include *Stylatula* and *Funiculina*.

sea pink (thrift)

Small, perennial herb that is native to Eurasia and North America. It forms spreading, grassy mounds of evergreen, narrow leaves The pink, papery flowers are borne in dense globular heads; varieties with white and dark pink flowers are cultivated in rock gardens and borders. Family Plumbaginaceae; species *Armeria maritima*.

sea potato

SEA URCHIN that spends most of its life buried in the sediment of shallow waters. It is so called because of

its potato-like appearance: it is light brown in colour and does not have the distinctive, long spines of many other sea urchins. Diameter: *c*.10cm (*c*.4in). Phylum Echinodermata; class Echinoidea; order Spatangoida; family Loveniidae; species *Echinocardium cordatum*.

sea robin

Marine, bottom-dwelling fish of tropical and temperate waters. It is found primarily on the sandy or muddy sediments of continental shelves, at depths of up to 200m (660ft). It is brightly coloured and elongated, and its head is encased in bone. Some species of sea robin are capable of producing sounds with their swim bladders. It is related to the GURNARD. Length: to 70cm (28in). Family Triglidae.

sea scorpion

See SCORPION FISH

sea slater

Any member of a group of widely distributed and relatively abundant ISOPODS. The sea slater lives in the middle and upper shore on the coast, feeding mainly on fucus (wrack seaweed). It is active at night and hides in cracks, crevices and under seaweed during the day. The sea slater has a greyish-green, roughly oval body. Adult body length: 28mm (1.1in). Order Isopoda; family Ligiidae; species include *Ligia oceanica*.

▶ **sea lion** The South American sea lion (*Otaria flavescens*) is found in large herds on both the Atlantic and Pacific coasts of South America. Males arrive at the breeding grounds in December, before the females, in order to claim territory. The rare Australian sea lion (*Neophoca cinerea*) is found on sandy beaches and smooth rock. It is the only seal species to have a non-annual breeding cycle.

Australian sea lion

South American sea lion

S

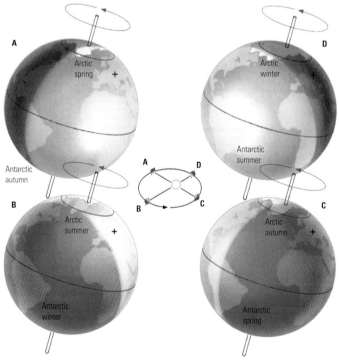

▲ sea snake The olive sea snake (*Aipysurus laevis*) is found in tropical waters of the Indo-Pacific region. It is typical of sea snakes in that it has a flattened tail, which aids swimming. It is aggressive and grows up to 1.8m (6ft) long.

sea slug (nudibranch)

Any member of the order Nudibranchia, comprising numerous species of marine GASTROPOD MOLLUSCS. The sea slug frequents shallow water worldwide, feeding primarily on sea anemones. It has no shell, quills or mantle cavities. Order Nudibranchia.

sea snake

Any of *c*.55 species of venomous marine SNAKE. The sea snake is characterized by a laterally compressed tail, nasal salt excretion glands, and weak ventral body musculature. Sea snakes never come to land; they mate and give birth to live young in the ocean. Most species live in shallow coastal waters and are specialist feeders on fish or their eggs. Length: 0.5–2.75m (1.6–9ft). Family Elapidae; subfamily Hydrophiinae.

seasons

See feature article

sea spider (pycnogonid)

Any of numerous species of small, bottom-dwelling, marine ARTHROPOD. The sea spider has between four and seven pairs of long, slender legs. Most species feed on juices, which they suck from small invertebrates. Body length: 0.3–50cm (0.1–20in). Class Pycnogonida.

sea squirt

See ASCIDIAN

sea turtle

Large marine TURTLE. It has a short neck and modified limbs, which serve as broad, paddle-like flippers. Sea turtles come to land only to lay eggs, which are deposited in nests dug in the sand by the females. They range widely in temperate and tropical oceans. Length: 0.6–2.4m (2–7.9ft). Families Cheloniidae and Dermochelyidae.

sea turtle, green

Large sea turtle. Its broad, flat carapace is serrated

▲ sea spider Members of the class Pycnogonida, sea spiders are so called because of their resemblance to spiders. Unlike spiders, however, they can have up to seven pairs of legs. As with some other species, the sea spider shown here (*Nymphon rubrum*) has such a small body that some of its digestive and reproductive tracts are in its legs.

posteriorly. Juveniles are omnivorous, but adults eat mostly algae and plants. Several nests of more than 100 eggs are laid each breeding season, but females may only breed every second or third year. Eggs are vulnerable to predators, including humans. Length: to 1.5m (4.9ft); weight: to 375kg (827lbs). Family Cheloniidae; species *Chelonia mydas*.

sea turtle, hawksbill

Small sea turtle. It has a small head and a distinctive narrow snout. In younger animals, the scutes (horny plates) on the carapace are overlapping. Hawksbill sea turtles favour coral reefs and shallow coastal waters. Adults feed mostly on invertebrates. They are exploited for their tortoiseshell, meat and eggs. Length: to 91cm (36in); weight: 12–45kg (26–99lbs). Family Cheloniidae; species *Eretmochelys imbricata*.

sea turtle, leatherback

Large sea turtle found in open oceans. It has a smooth, tapering carapace of ridged skin and extremely long foreflippers. Leatherback sea turtles can maintain high body temperatures, allowing them to exploit colder waters than other sea turtles. Jellyfish are their preferred prey. Length: to 2.4m (7.9ft); weight: to 867kg (1910lbs). Family Dermochelyidae; species *Dermochelys coriacea*.

sea turtle, loggerhead

Large sea turtle. It has a low keel down the middle of its reddish-brown carapace and a very large head. Loggerhead sea turtles are omnivorous. They nest at night, laying up to 200 eggs at a time. Length: to 2.1m (6.9ft); weight: to 450kg (990lbs). Family Cheloniidae; species *Caretta caretta*.

sea turtle, Ridley

Either of two species that are the smallest of the sea turtles. It has a nearly circular, smooth carapace and a prominent, parrot-like beak. The grey Kemp's (Atlantic) Ridley (*Lepidochelys kempii*) is restricted to the Atlantic Ocean; it breeds in the Gulf of Mexico. The larger green Pacific Ridley (*Lepidochelys olivacea*) inhabits the Indo-Pacific region. Females come ashore in large numbers during daylight to nest. Length: 55–75cm (22–30in); weight: to 50kg (110lbs). Family Cheloniidae; genus *Lepidochelys*.

S

SEASONS

Four astronomical and climatic periods of the year based on differential solar heating of the Earth as it makes its annual revolution of the Sun. Due to the parallelism of the Earth's axis of rotation, pointed near the North Star throughout the year, the Northern Hemisphere receives more solar radiation when its pole is aimed towards the Sun in summer and less in winter when it is aimed away, whereas the opposite holds for the Southern Hemisphere. The seasons are conventionally initiated at the vernal (spring) and autumnal EQUINOXES and the winter and summer SOLSTICES.

► Each of the four seasons begins and ends at one of the two solstices (the shortest and longest days of the year), which are separated by six months, or one of the equinoxes (when day and night are equal), also separated by six months. The solstices mark the days when one pole is at its closest position to the Sun and the other is farthest away from it. Equinoxes mark the days when each pole is the same distance from the Sun. For example, spring in the Northern Hemisphere at the spot marked by a cross on the globe commences on the equinox of 20 March (A), when day and night are equal length, and is followed by the summer solstice on 20 or 21 June (B) (the dates vary because of leap years), when the North Pole is at its closest to the Sun and the day is the longest of the year. Autumn equinox commences on 22 or 23 September (C), when day and night are once again equal in length. Winter in the Northern Hemisphere beings on 21 or 22 December (D), when the day is shortest in the year. This seasonal sequence is reversed in the Southern Hemisphere, where, for example, winter starts on 20 or 21 June when the South Pole is farthest away from the Sun but the North Pole is closest and the Northern Hemisphere's summer begins. The start and finish of each season can thus be defined in very precise astronomical terms by the Earth's position relative to the Sun.

▶ **sea urchin** The sharp, often poisonous, spines of the sea urchin are used for protection, for burrowing into rocks and, in conjunction with five columns of tube-feet, for locomotion. Pincer-like stalks between the spines prevent anything settling on the sea urchin.

sea urchin
Spiny ECHINODERM animal found in marine tidal pools along rocky shores. Urchins may be predators, scavengers, detritivores or herbivores. Many species graze on the algae coating submerged rocks; others filter living and dead material from the water, using specialized structures located around their mouths. Sea urchins are roughly spherical in shape; they usually bear long, sharp, often poisonous, moveable spines on much of their bodies. These spines, along with podia, may be used in movement, and the skeletal plates fuse to form a perforated shell. The eggs of some sea urchin species are considered a delicacy, and the adults are often fished in order for the eggs to be harvested. Phylum Echinodermata; class Echinoidea.

seawater
Solution of several minerals in the OCEAN. Seawater has a high concentration of microscopic life and tastes salty. The dissolved salt content varies between 3.3% and 3.7%, most of which is common salt (sodium chloride, NaCl). Nearly all elements are found in seawater, including vast reserves of magnesium, potassium and calcium. Large amounts of nitrogen, oxygen and carbon dioxide are present as dissolved gases. The freezing point of seawater of salt content 3.5% is −1.9°C (28.6°F). *See also* SALINITY

seaweed
Any of many species of brown, green or red ALGAE, found in greatest profusion in shallow waters on rocky coasts. KELP is the largest form of seaweed. Many species are important for the manufacture of fertilizers or food, or as a valuable source of chemicals such as iodine. Kingdom PROTOCTISTA. *See also* CHLOROPHYTE; PHAEOPHYTE; RHODOPHYTE

seaweed-fly (kelp-fly)
Largest species of the Coelopidae family. It is abundant on wet and rotten wrack seaweed during autumn and winter. Eggs are laid in the wrack, and the emerging larvae help to decompose the seaweed. Attracted to trichlorethylene, seaweed-flies are a nuisance in seaside garages and in drycleaners.

Adult body size: *c*.8mm (*c*.0.3in). Order Diptera; family Coelopidae; genus *Coelopa*.

sea whip
Any of several species of CORAL. Groups of sea whip POLYPS form long, often branching, brightly coloured structures that are attached to the substratum. Phylum Coelenterata/Cnidaria; class Anthozoa.

sebaceous gland
Gland in the SKIN of mammals that produces the oily substance sebum; it opens into a hair follicle. Sebum acts as a skin lubricant and also contains some antibacterial substances.

second (symbol s)
SI unit of time defined as the time taken for 9,192,631,770 periods of vibration of the electromagnetic radiation emitted by a caesium-133 atom.

secondary consumer
In a FOOD CHAIN, an organism that feeds on the PRIMARY CONSUMERS. The primary consumers, which themselves feed on PRIMARY PRODUCERS, are predominantly herbivores. Secondary consumers are, therefore, mainly CARNIVORES that feed on the herbivores. If a secondary consumer has no PREDATORS (that is, there are no **tertiary consumers**), it is known as the **top carnivore**. *See also* ECOSYSTEM

secondary sexual characteristics
External features that identify a sexually mature animal and distinguish the sexes. Such characteristics play a part in reproductive behaviour, although they are not essential for mating. Their development is brought about by the first production of SEX HORMONES in a maturing juvenile. For example, ANDROGENS in male deer stimulate the growth of antlers (except in reindeer, in which the females also bear antlers). *See also* SEX

secondary thickening (secondary growth)
Increase in the girth of STEMS and ROOTS, especially in shrubs and trees, as a result of the generation of new cells in the CAMBIUM. The cambium cells differentiate to produce additional XYLEM on the inside and PHLOEM on the outside. A further cylinder of cambium near the surface of the stem or root may produce a tough outer layer of CORK cells or BARK. *See also* VASCULAR BUNDLE

secretary bird
Unmistakable, very tall, extremely long-legged bird found in dry open bush of Africa. It has a large, strongly hooked bill. It has pale-grey plumage, with a

▲ **secretary bird** Found in sub-Saharan Africa, the secretary bird (*Sagittarius serpentarius*) gets its name from the feathers that protrude behind its head, resembling quill pens. It runs after its snake prey on foot. The snake is killed by a blow from the foot, followed by battering from the wings.

long crest, red face patch, black edge to the wings, black thighs and long, black-tipped tail feathers. The secretary bird feeds on snakes, which it catches with its long legs. Length: 1.2m (3.9ft). Family Sagittaridae; species *Sagittarius serpentarius*.

secretion
Production and discharge of a substance, usually a fluid, by a cell or a GLAND. It usually performs a specific function in an organism. The substance so discharged is also known as a secretion. Secretions include ENZYMES, HORMONES, SALIVA and sweat.

sedge
Any of numerous species of grass-like perennial plants, especially those of the genus *Carex*. Sedges are widely distributed in temperate, cold and tropical mountain regions, usually in wet conditions. Cultivated as ornamentals, they have narrow leaves and spikes of brown, green or greenish-yellow flowers. Family Cyperaceae.

sedge fly
Member of an unspecific, unrelated group of CADDIS FLIES. Most species are nocturnal and fly readily towards artificial light. Order Trichoptera.

sedge fly, grannom
CADDIS FLY that is on the wing from March to May. The female is larger than the male and and can often be seen carrying a bright green ball of eggs beneath her body. Larvae live in fast-flowing water, where they anchor their cases to weeds in order to avoid being swept away. Order Trichoptera; species *Brachyantris subnubilus*.

sedge fly, great red
Large CADDIS FLY. The larvae build spiral-shaped cases out of plant material. They are omnivorous and will attack small fish. Length: to 65mm (2.6in). Order Trichoptera; species *Phryganea grandis*.

sedge fly, silver horns
CADDIS FLY named after its large black and white antennae. It flies close to the water surface throughout summer. The aquatic larvae construct tubular cases out of stone fragments. Length: 9mm (0.4in). Order Trichoptera; species *Mystacides azurea*.

S

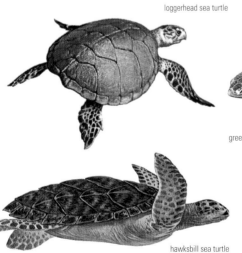

loggerhead sea turtle

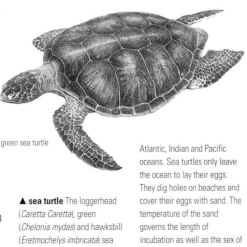

green sea turtle

hawksbill sea turtle

▲ **sea turtle** The loggerhead (*Caretta Caretta*), green (*Chelonia mydas*) and hawksbill (*Eretmochelys imbricata*) sea turtles range through the Atlantic, Indian and Pacific oceans. Sea turtles only leave the ocean to lay their eggs. They dig holes on beaches and cover their eggs with sand. The temperature of the sand governs the length of incubation as well as the sex of the hatchlings.

Sedgwick, Adam (1785–1873)
British geologist. He was appointed professor of geology at the University of Cambridge in 1818. He is famed for his work, much of it done jointly with Roderick MURCHISON, on the Lower Palaeozoic rocks and the Cambrian period rocks. His books include *A Synopsis of the Classification of the British Palaeozoic Rocks* (1855).

sediment
General term used to describe any material (such as gravel, sand and clay) that is transported and deposited by water, ice, wind or gravity. Most sediment is eventually deposited in the sea. The term includes material such as lime that is transported in solution and later precipitated, as well as organic deposits such as coal and coral reefs.

sedimentary basin
Large topographical depression that acts as a longterm trap for SEDIMENTS. Accumulations of sediment and organic remains may reach considerable thickness over millions of years and consequently persist in the STRATIGRAPHIC record.

sedimentary rock
Type of rock that has been formed by the deposition of SEDIMENT derived from pre-existing rocks, which may have been sedimentary, IGNEOUS or METAMORPHIC. Most sediment accumulates on the bed of the sea, having been dumped there by RIVERS, or having accumulated there as dead sea creatures fell to the seafloor. This accumulated sediment is consolidated and compressed. Earth movements uplift the sediments, and they may be tilted, folded or faulted. The resulting rocks are sedimentary, and their type depends on their composition. The layers in sedimentary rocks, known as strata, may be a few centimetres or many metres in thickness. Sedimentaries consisting of land sediment are clastic rocks, and are GRAVELS, SANDS, SILTS or CLAYS, according to the size of the particles. Other types of sedimentary rock include: LIMESTONE, which consists of fragments of dead sea creatures, sometimes mixed with land sediment; EVAPORITE, which comprises saline deposits; COAL, which is accumulated vegetation; coralline, which contains large quantities of CORAL; and CHALK, which is a pure form of limestone, with very little land sediment. *See also* FAULT; FOLD; STRATUM

seed
Part of a flowering plant (ANGIOSPERM) that contains the EMBRYO and food store. It is formed in the OVARY by FERTILIZATION of the female GAMETE. Food may be stored in a special tissue called the ENDOSPERM, or it may be concentrated in the swollen seed leaves (COTYLEDONS). Seeds are often capable of surviving quite harsh conditions and provide a means of survival for many plants in extreme environments. They are also the unit of dispersal of flowering plants (angiosperms) and CONIFERS. *See also* GERMINATION

seedeater
Any member of the genus *Sporophila*, a varied group of small FINCHES found in Central and South America. All seedeaters have thick bills. The males are variously plumaged, from black with bold white wing bars to indigo and red. Most species are ground feeders and are found in mountain pastures above 2500m (8200ft). Length: to 13cm (5in). Family Fringillidae; genus *Sporophila*.

seed plant
Member of a large grouping of plants that includes the seed plants (CONIFEROPHYTES, formerly gymnosperms) and flowering plants (ANGIOSPERMS). The coniferophytes evolved first, in late Devonian times, and have naked seeds; the angiosperms evolved in late Jurassic/early Cretaceous times and have seeds enclosed in an ovary. The angiosperms became dominant, but the others still survive in the form of the common CONIFERS and the rarer CYCADS and GINKGOS.

seedsnipe
Any of several species of small, seed-eating birds of the South American grasslands. The seedsnipe resembles a cross between a partridge and a short-tailed sandgrouse. It has mottled brown plumage and a very stout, triangular bill. It has long, pointed wings and dashing, wader-like flight. Length: 20cm (8in). Family Thinocoridae; genus *Thinocorus*.

segmented worm
Any member of the phylum ANNELIDA. They are characterized by having the body divided into rings or segments called metameres. The group includes BRISTLEWORMS, EARTHWORMS and LEECHES.

seif
Elongated sand DUNE. Seifs may be several kilometres long and often occur in groups. The narrow ridge of the dune runs parallel to the direction of the prevailing wind, and its height and width can be increased by the action of cross-winds. Seifs are found mainly in the sand deserts of North Africa.

seismic profile
Continuous record of sound waves bounced off sediments on the SEAFLOOR. The sounds become seismic waves and as such are used to determine the thickness and structure of bottom sediments.

seismic wave
Shock wave produced by EARTHQUAKES and man-made explosions. The velocity (speed and direction) of seismic waves varies according to the material (type of rock, molten core or oil) through which they pass. Primary (P) and secondary (S) waves are transmitted by the solid Earth. **P waves** vibrate in the direction that they are advancing; **S waves** vibrate at right angles to the direction in which they are advancing. Only P waves are transmitted through fluid (liquid or gas) zones. *See also* SEISMOLOGY

seismograph (seismometer)
Instrument for measuring and recording SEISMIC WAVES caused by movement (EARTHQUAKE or explosion) in the Earth's crust. The vibrations are recorded by a pen on a revolving drum. Some seismographs are sensitive enough to pick up seismic activity thousands of kilometres away. *See also* RICHTER SCALE

seismology
Study of EARTHQUAKES and the SEISMIC WAVES they produce. The movement of seismic waves is detected and recorded by SEISMOGRAPHS. The detection involves the separation of events from the ever-present background of seismic noise. Pinpointing sites of events has become very accurate since the development of precise instrumentation and the establishment of the World Wide Standard Seismograph Network (WWSSN). Seismology is very important in the exploration of the Earth's internal structure.

selaginella (spike moss)
Any member of the genus *Selaginella*, comprising small-leaved, moss-like plants found worldwide. They bear two kinds of spores in cones at the branch tips. Some species grow on trees, others on the ground. Height: 8cm (3in). Family Selaginellaceae; there are more than 700 species. *See also* CLUB MOSS

selection
In GENETICS, probability that one ALLELE will be passed on in favour of another. There are three main types of selection, DIRECTIONAL SELECTION, STABILIZING SELECTION and DISRUPTIVE SELECTION. *See also* DOMINANT; NATURAL SELECTION; RECESSIVE

selective breeding
Process by which stockbreeders and agriculturalists improve the strains of domesticated animals and cultivated plants; it involves selection and pairing of individuals with desirable qualities in the PHENOTYPE. Today a growing knowledge of GENETICS ensures more predictable results.

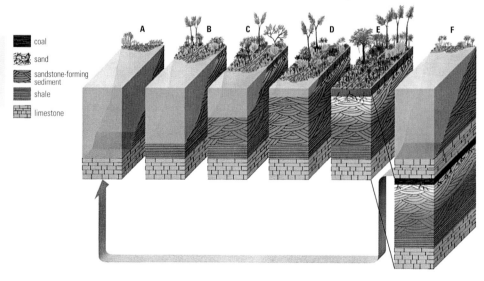

▲ **sediment** A delta's sediments are laid down in a specific order that may be endlessly repeated if the region where deposition takes place is sinking. Limestone deposits cover the seabed when the delta is too distant to be influential (A). As the delta encroaches (B), fine-grained muds that will become shale are deposited, followed by coarser, sandstone-forming sediments as the advance continues (C). As the water shallows, current bedding (D) indicates that sand is being deposited. Once the delta builds above water level (E) it can support swamp vegetation, which will eventually form coal. When the region sinks (F) the cycle restarts.

coal
sand
sandstone-forming sediment
shale
limestone

S

semicircular canals
Three parts of the inner EAR that function as balance organs. The semicircular canals are tubular ducts that project in different planes and can detect, by the movement of a liquid within them, movement in any direction in space.

semipermeable membrane
See PARTIALLY PERMEABLE MEMBRANE

senna
Any member of the plant genus *Senna*, a group of shrubs and trees native to warm and tropical regions; some species grow in temperate areas. They have rectangular, feathery leaves and yellow flowers. Family Fabaceae/Leguminosae.

sensation
Any effect on the SENSES; the ability to perceive stimuli such as sound and temperature.

senses
Means by which animals gain information about their environment and physiological condition. The five senses (SIGHT, HEARING, TASTE, SMELL and TOUCH) all rely on specialized RECEPTORS on or near the external surface of the body. SENSORY NEURONES carry information from the sense organs to the brain. Additionally, receptors within the body detect internal physical and chemical changes.

sensitive plant
Shrubby perennial plant native to tropical America. It is widely naturalized in warm countries elsewhere, where it is grown as an ornamental curiosity and as a sand-binder. It has branching, hairy, spiny stems. The long-petioled leaves are sensitive to touch and fold down when disturbed. The small purple flowers are produced in globular heads. Family Mimosaceae; species *Mimosa pudica*.

sensory adaptation
Ability of a sensory receptor gradually to cease to respond to a continuous stimulus. Some receptors adapt very quickly while others never do so. The process is important in preventing over-stimulation of sensory nerves. While we would rightly respond to something touching our face for example, we do not respond to the clothing that constantly touches most

parts of our body, except for the first few seconds after getting dressed.

sensory neurone
NEURONE that carries information from a RECEPTOR organ in any part of the body to the CENTRAL NERVOUS SYSTEM (CNS). Their nerve endings are in the sense organs. *See also* MOTOR NEURONE; NERVOUS SYSTEM; SENSES

sepal
Modified LEAF that makes up the outermost portion of a FLOWER bud. Although usually green and inconspicuous once the flower is open, in some species, such as ORCHIDS, the sepals look like the PETALS. In other species, such as ANEMONES, the sepals are absent.

sequoia
Either of two species of giant evergreen CONIFER trees native to California and s Oregon, United States. They are the giant sequoia (*Sequoiadendron giganteum*) and the CALIFORNIAN REDWOOD (*Sequoia sempervirens*). Height: to 100m (330ft). Family Taxodiaceae.

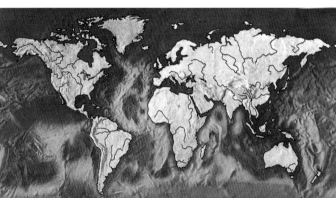

- terrigeneous deposits
- red clay
- globigerina ooze
- pteropod ooze
- diatom ooze
- radiolarian ooze

▶ **sedimentation** The seafloor is covered by unconsolidated sediments that are classified according to the nature of their main constituent. This constituent is determined by the distance from the landmasses, the nature of the winds and currents, the surface water temperature and the depth. The major types are: the terrigeneous deposits, which are debris derived from the weathering of the continents; the red (or brown) clays that form the inorganic sediments; and the globigerina, radiolaria and diatomaceous oozes, which are formed by the accumulation of the shells of dead planktonic animals.

◀ **selaginella** Spike moss species of the genus *Selaginella* grow mainly in tropical areas. The species shown here is on the island of Martinique in the Caribbean. It is a mossy perennial, with a rather fern-like appearance.

séracs
Very irregular ice surface on a GLACIER. It may include an impenetrable system of pillars and pinnacles several metres tall. A séracs usually forms at the foot of an icefall. It is caused by compression of a crevassed section of the glacier. This, in turn, results from an increase in the gradient of the moving ice or because its speed is somehow reduced.

sere
SUCCESSION of plant communities that eventually produces the CLIMAX COMMUNITY. Any one sere has a series of seral communities that change with time. There are various recognized types of seres: a **hydrosere**, occurring in shallow fresh water; a **lithosere**, on rocky ground; a **plagiosere**, on cleared ground; and a **xerosere**, on dry ground.

seriema
Unusual, primitive-looking ground bird found in South America. It is descended from giant, predatory Pleistocene birds. The seriema has extremely long legs, grey plumage and a stiff crest on its neck. It roams grasslands, scratching for grasshoppers, rodents and snakes. It is one of the few birds to have eyelashes. Length: 90cm (35in). Family Cariamidae; genus *Cariama*.

serotonin
Chemical found in cells of the gastro-intestinal tract, blood platelets and brain tissue, concentrated in the midbrain and HYPOTHALAMUS. It is a vasoconstrictor (a substance that causes constriction of blood vessels). Serotonin has an important role in the functioning of the NERVOUS SYSTEM and in the stimulation of smooth muscles.

serow
Sure-footed animal that lives on forested mountain slopes of India, China and Southeast Asia. It feeds on grass early and late in the day, sheltering under overhangs in between. Its coat is grey, with a black stripe along its back and a black or white mane. Both males and females have short, sharp horns, which they use to defend themselves. Some parts of the serows' bodies are believed by local people to have

S

healing properties. One or two young are born after an eight-month gestation. Head-body length: 1.4–1.5m (4.6–4.9ft); tail: 8–21cm (3–8in). Family Bovidae; species *Capricornis sumatraensis*.

serpent-eagle (snake-eagle)

Any member of the genus *Spilornis*, comprising several species of small to medium-sized EAGLES native to Asia. The serpent-eagle hunts over forests for snakes, lizards, small rodents and birds. It spends hours perched watching for prey. Some species raise their crest if alarmed. In flight the serpent-eagle has distinctive black and white bars on the under wing. Length: 46–74cm (18–29in). Family Accipitridae; genus *Spilornis*.

serpentine

Group of sheet silicate minerals, hydrated magnesium silicate ($Mg_3Si_2O_5(OH)_4$). Serpentine minerals come in various colours, usually green, although sometimes brownish, with a pattern of green mottling. They have monoclinic system crystals. Serpentines are secondary minerals, formed from minerals such as OLIVINE and orthopyroxene, and they occur in IGNEOUS ROCKS containing these minerals. They are commonly used in decorative carving; fibrous varieties are used in asbestos cloth. Hardness 2.5–4; r.d. 2.5–2.6.

serpentinite

Rock comprised of SERPENTINE minerals, altered by HYDROTHERMAL PROCESSES and derived from BASIC ROCKS such as volcanic BASALTS and GABBROS.

serpent star

See BRITTLE STAR

serval (bush cat)

CAT found in grassy areas of sub-Saharan Africa. Its coat is orange above, with many black spots. It has a narrow head and long legs, neck and ears. It is a nocturnal hunter of birds and small mammals. Length: body 70–100cm (28–39in); tail 35–40cm (14–16in). Family Felidae; species *Felis serval*.

service tree

Tree of the ROSE family. It is native to the Mediterranean region, where it is cultivated for its acid-flavoured fruit. It resembles the MOUNTAIN ASH. Height: 9–15m (30–49ft). Family Rosaceae; species *Sorbus domestica*.

sesame

Tropical plant cultivated for its oil and seeds. It is native to Asia and Africa. It has oval leaves, pink or white flowers, and seed capsules along its stem. Height: 60cm (24in). Family Pedaliaceae; species *Sesamum indicum*.

sessile

In zoology, describing an animal that remains fixed in one place. Such sedentary animals are usually permanently attached to a surface, such as sea ANEMONES, BARNACLES, LIMPETS and MUSSELS. The term sessile is also used to describe in CRUSTACEANS the eyes that lack stalks and sit directly on the animal's head. In botany, sessile describes any structure that has no stalk (in cases where one might be expected) and grows directly from a stem. Examples include the acorns and leaves of some oak trees.

Seville orange

Medium-sized evergreen tree native to Asia and naturalized in s United States. It has long spines and fragrant white flowers. Its fruits, which have an acidic

▲ **shag** The blue-eyed shag (*Phalacrocorax atriceps*) breeds in large colonies on islands off s South America, including parts of Antarctica. It feeds on fish and invertebrates, sometimes diving to depths of up to 100m (330ft) to catch its prey.

pulp and bitter membranes, are used for marmalade making. The flower petals yield neroli oil, which is used in perfumery and is the chief ingredient of eau-de-cologne. Height: 6–9m (20–30ft). Family Rutaceae; species *Citrus aurantium*.

sewellel

See BEAVER, MOUNTAIN

sex

Classification of an organism denoting the reproductive function of the individual. There are two divisions of the classification – male and female. In mammals, the presence of sex organs (OVARIES in the female, TESTES in the male) are primary sexual characteristics. SECONDARY SEXUAL CHARACTERISTICS, such as size, coloration, and, in human beings, the development of the breasts and the growth of facial and body hair, are governed by the secretion of SEX HORMONES. In flowering plants, the female sex organs are the CARPEL (including the OVARY, STYLE and STIGMA), and the male organs the STAMENS. Male and female organs may occur in the same flower or on separate flowers or plants. In lower organisms, such as fungi, where the differences are biochemical rather than morphological, the term "mating strains" is used instead of male and female. *See also* SEXUAL REPRODUCTION

sex determination

Genetic basis for the gender of an organism. Gender depends on the combination of sex CHROMOSOMES. In mammals, which have a pair of sex chromosomes, there are two types, the X-CHROMOSOME and the Y-CHROMOSOME. All ova have one X-chromosome, whereas sperm have either an X- or a Y-. If the sperm that fertilizes the OVUM has an X-chromosome, the resulting ZYGOTE and the organism that develops from it will be XX, or female. If the egg is fertilized with a Y-carrying sperm, the zygote will be XY, or male.

sex hormones

Chemical "messengers" secreted by the gonads (TESTES and OVARIES). They regulate sexual development and reproductive activity and influence sexual behaviour. In males, they include the androgen TESTOSTERONE, made by the testes; in females, the sex hormones OESTROGEN and PROGESTERONE are produced by the ovaries.

sex linkage

Carrying of GENES on the sex CHROMOSOMES. These genes determine body features. The X-CHROMOSOME carries many genes, the Y-CHROMOSOME very few. Features linked on the Y-chromosome will normally only arise in the heterogametic (XY) sex (males in mammals, females in birds). Features linked on the X-chromosome may arise in either sex, but are far more prevalent in the heterogametic

sex (a recessive trait is more likely to be expressed in this case because the Y-chromosome does not bear a corresponding allele to mask the recessive one). It is for this reason that human sex-linked features such as red/green colour blindness and haemophilia occur almost exclusively in males. *See also* LINKAGE GROUP

sexual reproduction

Biological process of REPRODUCTION involving the combination of genetic material from two parents. It occurs in different forms throughout the plant and animal kingdoms. This process gives rise to variations of the GENOTYPE and PHENOTYPE within a species. GAMETES, which are HAPLOID sex cells produced by MEIOSIS, contain only half the number of CHROMOSOMES of their DIPLOID parent cells. At FERTILIZATION, the gametes, generally one from each parent, fuse to form a ZYGOTE with the diploid number of chromosomes. The zygote divides repeatedly, and the cells differentiate to give rise to an EMBRYO and, finally, a fully formed organism. In mammalian reproduction, the male's erect PENIS is inserted into the female's VAGINA. Rhythmic, thrusting movements of the penis cause the male to ejaculate and so introduce SEMEN (containing SPERM) into the vagina in order for fertilization of the OVUM to take place.

sexual selection

Process among animals that derives from the successful finding of a mate and the production of young. It is similar to NATURAL SELECTION but involves mainly the SECONDARY SEXUAL CHARACTERISTICS. For example, if a female chooses to mate with the male that has the brightest coloration and best courtship display, these features (being genetically controlled) will tend to be inherited by the male offspring. In succeeding generations the same features will be exaggerated. By the same mechanism, males may develop longer horns or louder roars to better compete with other rival males.

shad

Any of several species in the HERRING family that swim upriver to spawn. Shads are marine food fish and are particularly prized for their roe. Many shad species are deep-bodied, with a notch in the upper jaw for the tip of the lower jaw. Length: to 75cm (30in). Family Clupeidae; genera include *Alosa*.

shag

Large sea bird in the CORMORANT family. It is found along the coasts of N Europe, North Africa and the Mediterranean. It has glossy green plumage. In summer, the shag has a noticeable crest on its forehead and yellow naked skin patches near the bill. It nests in colonies on rocky coasts and is rare inland. Length: 66–76cm (26–30in). Family Phalacrocoracidae; species *Phalacrocorax aristotelis*. The blue-eyed cormorant (*Phalacrocorax atriceps*) is also known as the blue-eyed shag.

shale

Common SEDIMENTARY ROCK similar to clay. It is fine grained and consists of thin layers or sheets, with each layer probably representing a period of DEPOSITION. Shales may contain various materials such as fossils, carbonaceous matter and oil.

shallot

Perennial plant native to w Asia and widely cultivated in temperate climates. It has thin, small leaves and clustered bulbs, which have a mild, onion-like flavour. Family Liliaceae; species *Allium cepa*.

shamrock

Any of several plant species with three-part leaves. It usually refers to *Trifolium repens* or *Trifolium dubium*. Shamrock is the national emblem of Ireland: legend tells that Saint Patrick used it to symbolize the Trinity. Family Leguminosae.

shark

Torpedo-shaped, cartilaginous fish found in subpolar to tropical marine waters. It has well-developed jaws, bony teeth, usually five gill slits on each side of its head and a characteristic lobe-shaped tail with a longer top lobe. Sharks are carnivorous and at least 10 species are known to attack humans. There are *c*.250 living species. Order Selachii. *See also* CHONDRICHTHYES

shark, hammerhead

Any member of the family Sphyrnidae, a group of large, predatory sharks. Its head has flat, shovel or blade-like extensions, on which the eyes and nasal openings are located. It is found in tropical marine waters and warmer temperate zones; some species inhabit estuaries. Length: to 6m (20ft); weight: to 900kg (2000lb). Family Sphyrnidae.

shark, mako (sharp-nosed mackerel shark)

Either of two species of shark found in temperate and tropical waters worldwide. The mako shark is blue-grey above and white below. It has a sharp snout, a slender body and a crescent-shaped tail, with a distinctive horizontally flattened keel. It has very long teeth. It is related to the PORBEAGLE. Length: to 4m (13ft). Family Isuridae; species *Isurus glaucus* and *Isurus oxyrinchus*.

shark, nurse

Shark found in shallow tropical and subtropical waters of the Atlantic and E Pacific oceans, particularly in inshore areas. It is yellow to grey-brown above and lighter below. It is recognized by the thick, fleshy whiskers near its mouth. Length: 2.5m (8.2ft); weight: 150–170kg (330–370lb). Family Orectolobidae; species *Ginglymostoma cirratum*.

shark, tiger

Large shark found in inshore and offshore tropical

waters worldwide. It is grey, with dark vertical bars along its sides. It has a long, upper lobe on its tail. A noted scavenger, it preys on sea turtles, carrion and other sharks; it is regarded as a man-eater. Length: to 6m (20ft). Family Carcharhinidae; species *Galeocerdo cuvieri*.

shark, whale

Largest species of shark. It inhabits tropical waters worldwide. It is brown to dark grey, with white or yellow spots and stripes. It is a docile, egg-laying fish, which often travels near the surface. Length: 9m (30ft). Family Rhincodontidae; species *Rhincodon typus*.

shark, white (great white shark)

Shark that is found in tropical and sub-tropical waters; it is considered to be the most aggressive shark species. It is grey, blue or brown, with a white belly and a crescent-shaped tail. It has saw-edged triangular teeth. Length: to 11m (36ft); weight: to 3000kg (6600lb). Family Isuridae; species *Carcharodon carcharias*.

sharksucker

See REMORA

sharpbill

Small forest bird found in Central and South America. It has a sharp bill for catching insects and eating soft fruits and often hangs upside down while feeding. Its plumage is olive-green above, with yellowish-white underparts thickly spotted black. Length: 15cm (6in). Family Oxyruncidae; species *Oxyruncus cristatus*.

shearing force (shearing stress)

Force tending to cause deformation of a material by slipping along a plane parallel to the imposed STRESS. In nature, the resulting shear is related to the downslope of Earth materials as well as to earthquakes.

shearwater

Oceanic seabird that is related to the PETREL. It has a slightly hooked bill and a "tube-nose". Except when breeding, the shearwater spends its whole life at sea. It is constantly on the wing, making use of

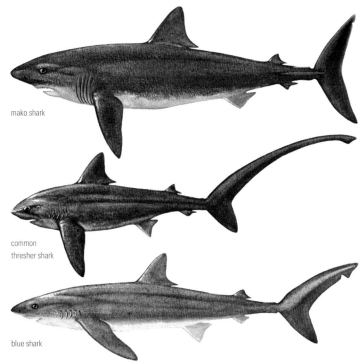

▶ **shark** The mako shark (*Isurus oxyrhyncus*) is a ferocious predator. Its streamlined body enables it to swim at speeds of more than 65km/h (40mph). Mako sharks are found in the Atlantic, Pacific and Indian oceans. Like the white sharks, to which they are related, makos have been known to attack humans. The common thresher shark (*Alopias vulpinus*) is found in tropical and temperate parts of the Atlantic and Pacific oceans. It is distinctive for its long tail fin, which can account for more than half its total body length. It uses its tail to frighten and round up its prey. The blue shark (*Prionace glauca*) is one of the most widely distributed shark species, being found in all tropical and temperate seas, usually away from the shore. Its prey includes schooling fish and, less frequently, squid.

mako shark

common thresher shark

blue shark

◀ **shearwater** The Manx shearwater (*Puffinus puffinus*) is a bird of the open sea, except during the breeding season. It nests in large and noisy colonies around the coasts of w Britain and the Mediterranean. Like other shearwaters, the Manx shearwater glides just above the water, diving to catch fish. It is renowned for its navigational abilities.

up-currents in the troughs of the sea swell. It feeds on plankton, squid, fish and scraps from boats. Family Procellariidae.

shearwater, Cory's

Large shearwater that breeds on islands in the N and s Atlantic Ocean and in the Mediterranean region. It is pale brown above and white below, with a large yellow bill. It soars, on bowed wings, more than most shearwaters. Length: 46–56cm (18–22in); wingspan: 112cm (44in). Family Procellariidae; species *Calonectris diomedea*.

shearwater, great

Shearwater that breeds in the s Atlantic Ocean and migrates into the N Atlantic during the southern winter. It is similar to Cory's shearwater but has a dark crown that contrasts with its white cheeks; it has a white base to its dark-tipped tail. Length: 46–53cm (18–21in); wingspan: 112cm (44in). Family Procellariidae; species *Puffinus gravis*.

shearwater, little

Small shearwater. It has slaty black upperparts, white underparts and white underwing feathers. It flies with rapid wing beats and glides on short, stiff wings. The little shearwater is found mainly in the oceans of the Southern Hemisphere but also breeds on Madeira, the Azores and the Canary Islands. Length: 26–30cm (10–12in); wingspan: 53cm (21in). Family Procellariidae; species *Puffinus assimilis*.

shearwater, Manx

Medium-sized shearwater with a worldwide distribution. It is dark above and white below. It glides on rigid wings close to the sea, often in huge flocks. There are several regional races and some are now considered separate species. Length: 31–38cm (12–15in); wingspan: 80cm (31in). Family Procellariidae; species *Puffinus puffinus*.

sheathbill

Unusual pigeon-like bird that is found in Antarctica and nearby islands. It is a link between the wader and the gull. The sheathbill has mainly dirty-white plumage. It scavenges for offal along shores and in the breeding colonies of other birds. There are two species, the snowy sheathbill (*Chionis alba*) and the lesser sheathbill (*Chionis minor)*, which are distinguished by bill and leg colour. Length: 41cm (16in). Family Chionididae.

S

sheep

▶ sheep There are several hundred breeds of domestic sheep (*Ovis aries*), including the Clun Forest sheep shown here. Most have been bred for the type of wool or the quality of meat. Particular breeds are usually found in specific regions.

sheep

Any member of the genus *Ovis*, which comprises seven species of ruminant mammals; these species are known as true sheep. Many GOAT-ANTELOPES, not in the genus *Ovis*, bear the common name of sheep. Sheep have scent glands in front of their eyes, on their feet and in the groin. Male sheep (rams) are usually much larger than females and have larger, curved horns, which are used in fierce rutting fights. Sheep are grazing animals, usually living in gregarious groups. They were domesticated for meat and wool c.10,000 years ago. There are now one billion sheep in the world. Order Artiodactyla; family Bovidae; genus *Ovis*; species include the domestic sheep *Ovis aries*.

sheep, American bighorn (mountain sheep)

True sheep that inhabits upland deserts of North America. The dominant males have massive coiled horns more than 1m (3.3ft) long. Bighorn sheep are on the CITES list of threatened animals. Head-body length: 1.2–1.8m (4–6ft); tail: 15cm (6in). Family Bovidae; species *Ovis canadensis*.

sheep, Barbary (aoudad)

GOAT-ANTELOPE that inhabits the arid mountain slopes of North Africa. Its coat is short on the body but long along the throat and front legs. It relies on camouflage alone for defence and is thus an easy target for hunters. Barbary sheep are on the CITES list of threatened animals. Head-body length: 1.3–1.9m (4.3–6.2ft); tail: 25cm (10in). Family Bovidae; species *Ammotragus lervia*.

sheep, blue (bharal)

GOAT-ANTELOPE from the Himalayas. It has a short-haired, bluish coat marked with white and black. Head-tail length: 1–1.6m (3.3–5.2ft). Family Bovidae; species *Pseudois nayaur*.

sheep, snow (Siberian bighorn)

Dark brown sheep that is found in mountainous areas of Siberia, NE Russia. Head-tail length (male): 1.6–1.8m (5.2–5.9ft). Family Bovidae; species *Ovis nivicola*.

sheep, thinhorn (Stone's sheep, white sheep, Dall's sheep)

Sheep found in arctic regions of North America. Head-tail length (male) 1.3–1.5m (4.3–4.9ft). Family Bovidae; species *Ovis dalli*.

sheep ked

External PARASITE on sheep. It has large claws, wings that are often reduced or absent, and a head that is sunken back into the thorax. One species (*Melophagus ovinus*), also known as the sheep tick, is wingless and does not cause much direct harm to its host. It does irritate the skin, however, causing the sheep to scratch itself, which may lead to infection. Order Diptera; suborder Cyclorrhapha; family Hippoboscidae; species include *Melophagus ovinus*.

sheep nostril-fly (sheep bot)

BOT-FLY that is a PARASITE on sheep. It belongs to a family of rather hairy flies, although this species is less hairy than other members. It has a warty texture on the top of its head and thorax. The larvae are internal parasites of mammals. The adult female places larvae into the nostrils of sheep and goats. Larval development is completed in the nasal cavities and sinuses, resulting in giddiness of the host. When the host sneezes, the fully grown larvae are expelled and pupate on the ground. Order Diptera; suborder Cyclorrhapha; family Oestridae; species *Oestrus ovis*.

sheepshead

Marine food and game fish found in tropical and temperate waters. It is a deep-bodied fish. It is greenish yellow with seven dark bars on each side. Length: 76cm (30in). Family Sparidae; species *Archosargus probatocephalus*.

shelduck

Large, boldly patterned, goose-like DUCK found in both the Northern and the Southern Hemispheres. It associates mainly in pairs, but some species congregate in large flocks to moult. There are eight species worldwide, although the crested shelduck (*Tadorna cristata*) is known only from three specimens and illustrations in ancient Japanese prints. Length: 58–71cm (23–28in). Family Anatidae; genus *Tadorna*.

shelf fungus

See BRACKET FUNGUS

shell

In biology, hard protective covering. In MOLLUSCS the shell is secreted by the EPIDERMIS and consists of a protein matrix strengthened by calcium carbonate. Other examples include the shell of a TORTOISE, shells of the eggs of birds, and in plants the protective layer around certain nut fruits.

she oak

Tall CASUARINA tree native to Australia. It has a characteristic weeping habit, owing to its jointed branches with short internodes. The she oak bears highly reduced leaves in the form of many-toothed sheaths. The fruit is produced in small woody cones. The wood is regarded as a valuable timber for furniture. Family Casuarinaceae; species *Casuarina stricta*.

shepherd's purse

Wild flower found worldwide. It has deeply lobed, basal leaves and tiny, white flower clusters. The pouch-like seedpods have a peppery flavour. Height: 20–45cm (8–18in). Family Cruciferae; species *Capsella bursa-pastoris*.

▶ shieldbug The red cabbage bug (*Eurydema ornatum*) is a member of the shieldbug family Pentatomidae. It is a pest on cabbage plants and, less frequently, on potato plants. It feeds on the leaves, causing much damage.

Sherrington, Sir Charles Scott (1857–1952)

British physiologist, pioneer in the study of how the NERVOUS SYSTEM works. His book *The Integrative Action of the Nervous System* (1906) helped to establish physiological psychology. Sherrington shared with fellow British physiologist Edgar Adrian (1889–1977) the 1932 Nobel Prize for physiology or medicine.

shieldbug (stink-bug)

Small bug that is a shield-like in shape. Some species produce a foul smell. The Pentatomidae family is the largest shieldbug family. Most species are sap feeders, although several, including *Picromerus bidens*, are largely or entirely carnivorous. Order Hemiptera; suborder Heteroptera; super family Pentatomoidea; species include *Picromerus bidens*.

shiner

Small freshwater fish of the MINNOW family; it is often used for bait. Among the 100 species of shiner are the spottail (*Notropis hudsonius*), the golden (*Notemigonus crysoleucas*) and the sailfin (*Notropis hypselopterus*). Family Cyprinidae.

shipworm (teredo)

Any of c.15 species of small, bivalve MOLLUSCS that bore into wood. The shipworm has a worm-like body, with the halves of its shell greatly reduced and modified to act as a drill. It spends its life in submerged wood, doing considerable damage to ships' hulls and wooden pilings. Length: to 30cm (12in). Family Teredidae; genus *Teredo*.

shoebill stork (whale-headed stork)

Tall wading bird found in papyrus marshes of tropical NE Africa. It has a shoe-shaped bill, with a sharp hook, darkish plumage and long legs. It feeds on small animals. Height: to 1.4m (4.6ft). Family Balaenicipitidae; species *Balaeniceps rex*.

shore-fly

Small fly, mostly found by the seashore or at lake and pond edges. The adults of most shore-fly species feed on decaying matter, but some species are predators. The larvae include leaf miners, predators and detritus feeders, on land and water. Order Diptera; family Ephydridae; species include *Psilopa nigritella*.

shore-weed

Perennial aquatic plant native to Europe. It has creeping runners that form tufts of erect, linear, spongy-centred leaves. It is found in shallow water at lake edges, sometimes submerged to 4m (13ft) or on exposed shore when the water-level subsides. Family Plantaginaceae; species *Littorella uniflora*.

short-horned grasshopper

See GRASSHOPPER, SHORT-HORNED

shortwing

Small, chat-like THRUSH found in Southeast Asia. It has short, rounded wings, a square tail and strong legs. It rummages for insects on the ground in dense forests, rhododendron and bamboo thickets. Its habits and distribution are poorly known. Length: 13–15cm (5–6in). Family Turdidae; genus *Brachypteryx*.

shoveler

Medium-size dabbling DUCK. It has a large, shovel-shaped bill, which gives it a characteristic head-down attitude when swimming. It grazes on vegetation in shallow muddy pools. There are four species worldwide. Length: 49–52cm (19–20in). Family Anatidae; genus *Anas*.

S

▶ **shoebill stork** Although it displays some behavioural similarities to pelicans and herons, the silent and solitary shoebill stork (*Balaeniceps rex*) is the sole member of a separate family. It uses its distinctive, shovel-like bill to dig in the mud to find the fish and aquatic animals on which it feeds. Despite its large size and clumsy appearance on land, it is a graceful flyer with broad wings. Its unwebbed feet are specially adapted to walking on marshy land.

shrew
Any of c.200 species of mouse-like mammals found worldwide, except in Australia and South America. Tiny but very active creatures, they have high metabolic rates and need to consume large amounts of food, mainly insects. They eat their own faeces to improve digestive efficiency. Some species have venomous bites and are unpalatable to most predators. They have keen hearing and smell, but their sight is poor. Order Insectivora; family Soricidae.

shrew, American short-tailed
Shrew found in E North America, where it climbs trees in the forests and grasslands. Head-body length: 7–10cm (3–4in); tail: 1.5–3cm (0.6–1in). Family Soricidae; species *Blarina brevicauda*.

shrew, African forest (mouse shrew)
Primitive member of the shrew family. It is characterized by the possession of two extra teeth. Head-body length: 6–11cm (2–4in); tail: 3–5cm (1–2in). Family Soricidae; species *Crocidura odorata*.

shrew, elephant-
See ELEPHANT-SHREW

shrew, Etruscan (pygmy white-toothed shrew)
Smallest living species of vertebrate land animal. The Etruscan shrew is native to the arid grasslands of Europe, Asia and Africa. Head-body length: 3.5–5cm (1.4–2in); tail: 2.5–3cm (c.1in). Family Soricidae; species *Suncus etruscus*.

shrew, pygmy
Any of several species of shrew found in heaths and grasslands of Europe and Asia. Pygmy shrews are good swimmers and climbers. Head-body length: 4–6cm (c.2in); tail: 3–5cm (1–2in). Family Soricidae; species include *Sorex minutus*.

shrew, water
Any of many shrew species found in both the New and Old Worlds. They feed on underwater prey and have special adaptations for swimming, such as fringes of long, stiff hairs on their hands and feet or webbed toes. Family Soricidae; species include *Neomys fodiens* (European water shrew), *Nectogale elegans* (web-footed water shrew) and *Chimarrogale himalayica* (Asiatic water shrew).

shrike (butcher bird)
Aggressive, hook-billed songbird. It perches on a prominent lookout before swooping on large insects, rodents or small birds. It sometimes impales its prey on thorns as a "larder" to eat later. Its habitat is mainly woodland edges, open scrub and hedgerows with scattered bushes. Length: c.24cm (c.9in). Family Laniidae.

shrike, fiscal
Common shrike of central and s Africa. It is heavy bodied, with a large bill. Its plumage is black above, with a white wing bar that extends to the shoulder, and white below. It is found singly or in pairs in lightly wooded country and suburbia. Length: 23cm (9in). Family Laniidae; species *Lanius collaris*.

shrike, great grey
Shrike that is similar to but slightly larger than the loggerhead shrike. Its black mask does not extend above the eye and its bill is longer and more hooked. It is widespread in Europe, Asia, North Africa and North America. In Africa, the birds are much paler grey in the south of the range. Length: 25cm (10in). Family Laniidae; species *Lanius excubitor*.

shrike, loggerhead
Shrike that is widespread in central North America; it winters south to Mexico. It is grey, with a black mask, black wings with a white wing bar, and a black tail with white tips. It hunts in areas of brush, diving from a low perch then rising swiftly to the next lookout. Length: 23cm (9in). Family Laniidae; species *Lanius ludovicianus*.

shrike, woodchat
Conspicuous shrike that is a widespread summer visitor from Africa to s Europe and the Middle East. It has a chestnut head and nape, bold white shoulder patches and a black forehead and mask. In flight it has a white rump and wing bars. Length: 17cm (7in). Family Laniidae; species *Lanius senator*.

shrike-tanager
Shrike-like perching bird found in forests of South America. It sits on an open perch waiting for passing insects; it sallies like a flycatcher to catch them in mid-air. Some species sit below the forest canopy and wait for prey to be dislodged from above. Length: 16cm (6in). Family Laniidae; genus *Lanio*.

shrike-tit
Either of two bird species that make up the genus *Falcunculus*; they are found in Australasia. The shrike-tit has strong face patterns and yellow underparts. It has a strong notched bill for removing bark, opening seeds and eating large insects. It is similar to the true tits and chickadees of the Northern Hemisphere. Length: 15–19cm (6–7in). Family Pachycephalidae; genus *Falcunculus*.

shrike-vireo
Any of several species of South American birds belonging to the VIREO family. Unlike typical vireos, the shrike-vireo has bright blue-green and yellow plumage. It is a small, tree-living songbird. It has a heavy, hooked bill for dealing with the large insects and caterpillars on which it feeds. The shrike-vireo can be difficult to see despite constant-

▲ **shrew** The American pygmy shrew (*Microsorex hoyi*) is one of the smallest mammalian species. It is slightly larger than the European pygmy shrew (*Sorex minutus*). Very active, the shrew has a high metabolic rate and has to eat large amounts of food, sometimes more than its body weight daily.

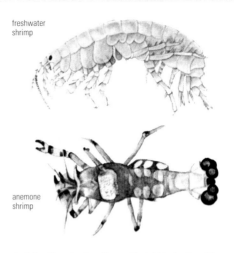

freshwater shrimp

anemone shrimp

▲ **shrimp** The coloration of the freshwater shrimp (*Gammarus* sp.) depends on its diet because its digestive tract is visible through its semi-transparent shell. It feeds mainly on plants, which give it a greenish hue.

The bright coloration of the anemone shrimp (*Periclimenes brevicarpalis*) camouflages it on the coral reefs and sea anemones that are its usual habitat. It is found in the s Pacific Ocean.

ly calling and singing. Length: 14–15cm (c.6in). Family Vireonidae; genus *Vireolanius*.

shrimp
Mostly marine, decapod CRUSTACEAN; it is related to CRABS and LOBSTERS but is generally smaller and swims in the open water. Its compressed body has long antennae, stalked eyes, a beak-like prolongation, a segmented abdomen with five pairs of swimming legs and a terminal spine. Large edible shrimps are often called PRAWNS. Length: 5–7cm (2–3in). Order Decapoda; family Crangonidae.

shrimp, banded coral
One of many species of brightly coloured, tropical shrimps. It inhabits CORAL REEFS, where it clambers about on its long, thin legs feeding on morsels gleaned from the rocks and corals. Its abdomen and claws are banded in bright red. Order Decapoda; species *Stenopus hispidus*.

shrimp, brine
Small, branchiopod CRUSTACEAN found in salt lakes worldwide; it is related to the fairy shrimp. The brine shrimp can live in high concentrations of brine. It swims belly-up. It has no carapace and has stalked, compound eyes and a long tail. Length: 13mm (0.5in). Order Anostraca; genus *Artemia*.

shrimp, brown
Common shrimp of the Atlantic Ocean. It has a translucent, brownish body. It is found on muddy and sandy shores at the intertidal level. The brown shrimp is fished commercially in many places. Length: to 90mm (3.5in). Order Decapoda; species *Crangon crangon*.

shrimp, fairy
Any of several species of branchiopod CRUSTACEANS found in temporary pools and small ponds. The fairy shrimp has an elongated trunk, comprising 20 or more segments, and anterior paddle-like limbs. It has gills for feeding and respiration. It has no carapace and its eyes are on stalks. Length: 10–130mm (0.4–5.1in). Order Anostraca; species include *Chirocephalus diaphanus*.

shrimp, freshwater
Marine CRUSTACEAN; it is an AMPHIPOD, related to the

S

SAND HOPPER, rather than a true shrimp. The freshwater shrimp's body is flattened sideways. It scurries and swims amongst weeds in brackish and fresh water. Order Amphipoda; genera include *Gammarus*.

shrimp, mantis

Large shrimp that is found in CORAL REEFS of the tropics and warm temperate regions. It is easily recognized by its bright colours, with striped or mottled patterns. The mantis shrimp captures prey by a grabbing action of the second thoracic appendages. It has a dorso-ventrally flattened body, a shield-like carapace and abdominal gills. The entire dorsal surface is armed with ridges and spines. Its head has stalked compound eyes and a median eye. Adult body length: 5–36cm (2–14in). Order Stomatopoda; there are *c*.300 species, including *Squilla mantis* and *Odontodactylus scyllarus*.

shrimp, opossum

Any member of the order Mysidacea, a group of CRUSTACEANS found in coastal waters and freshwater lakes. The opossum shrimp's eyes are stalked, and there are ten pairs of appendages in the thoracic region. Adult body length: 24mm (0.9in). Order Mysidacea; species include *Praunus flexuosus* (chameleon shrimp).

shrimp, ostracod (mussel or seed shrimp)

Any member of a subclass of small CRUSTACEANS common in salt and fresh water. It has a rounded or elliptical carapace, resembling two halves of a clam

▲ **sicklebill** The white-tipped sicklebill (*Eutoxeres aquila*) feeds from a *Heliconia* plant in the forest of NW Ecuador. It has adapted to feed from this species, the flowers of which bend at the same angle as its bill. Thus, the plant has a good pollinator, and the bird has food inaccessible to others.

shell. The African species *Mesocypris terrestis* is terrestrial, living in damp humus. Length: 15–20mm (0.6–0.8in). Subclass Ostracoda.

shrimp, skeleton

Any of certain species of AMPHIPOD CRUSTACEANS. The skeleton shrimp is not a true shrimp, but resembles it in general shape, although it is much smaller and extremely thin. Length: to *c*.25mm (*c*.1in). Order Amphipoda; suborder Caprellidea.

shrimpfish

See RAZORFISH

shrub (bush)

Woody, perennial plant that is smaller than a TREE. Instead of having a main STEM, it branches at or slightly above ground level into several stems. Its hard stem distinguishes it from a HERB. RHODODENDRONS and AZALEAS are popular ornamental shrubs.

sial

In geology, uppermost of the two main rock classes in the Earth's CRUST. Sial rocks are so called because their main constituents are **si**licon and **al**uminum. They make up the material of the CONTINENTS and overlay the SIMA. The sial is less dense than the sima and is generally not carried beneath the surface when subduction occurs.

Siamese fighting fish

Colourful, large-finned, freshwater fish of Southeast Asia. It is named after its characteristically aggressive displays. It makes bubble nests in which eggs are laid. It is related to the GOURAMI and is a popular aquarium fish. Length: 6cm (2.4in). Family Belontiidae; species *Betta splendens*.

sicklebill

Any of several species of South American HUMMINGBIRDS. It has a distinctive, sickle-shaped bill, which is bent at a near 90-degree angle. Its plumage is dark shining green above, and its underparts are usually heavily streaked sooty black or brown. The sicklebill is shy and retiring; it is found in deep shade and dense thickets in humid forests. Length: 11cm (4in). Family Trochilidae; genus *Eutoxeres*.

siderite

Green, brown or white mineral, iron(II) carbonate ($FeCO_3$), found in sedimentary iron ores and as vein deposits with other ores. Its crystals are rhombohedral in the hexagonal system and it occurs as massive deposits or in granular form. Hardness 4; r.d. 3.8. IRON METEORITES are sometimes known as siderites.

sidewinder (horned rattlesnake)

Nocturnal RATTLESNAKE found in deserts of SW United States and Mexico. It has horn-like scales

▲ **sifaka** Verreaux's sifaka (*Propithecus verreauxi*) is a critically endangered species. It is found only in certain forests on Madagascar, where it feeds mainly on leaves, flowers and bark. It is active during the day and often sits on a sunny branch with its arms outstretched. It lives in small groups, which usually have an equal number of males and females.

over its eyes and is usually tan with a light pattern. It loops obliquely across the sand, leaving a J-shaped trail. Length: to 75cm (30in). Family Viperidae; species *Crotalus cerastes*. Sidewinder is also the name for several species of Old World desert-dwelling snakes.

sieve tube cell

Elongated cell that is part of the PHLOEM tissue of a plant. It has small pores in its end walls, which are called sieve plates because of their characteristic appearance. The sieve tube cell has a well-defined plasma membrane and its cytoplasm contains numerous PLASTIDS and MITOCHONDRIA. Strands of CYTOPLASM run continuously from cell to cell through the pores in the sieve plate. Sieve tube cells function to translocate organic material through the plant. Mature sieve tube cells lack a nucleus and are therefore often called sieve tube elements. *See also* COMPANION CELL

sifaka

Arboreal PRIMATE found only on Madagascar. The sifaka lives in small, territorial, family groups, feeding on leaves, buds and shoots, high up in rainforest trees. Its coat can be any shade from white through brown and maroon to black, but all species have black, hairless faces. Newborn babies are also black and hairless and cling to their mother's stomach, transferring to her back when about four weeks old. Head-body length: 39–48cm (15–19in); tail: 50–60cm (20–24in). Suborder Prosimii; family Indriidae; genus *Propithecus*; species include *Propithecus verreauxi*.

sight

See feature article

Silent Spring

Title of a book written by the American naturalist Rachel CARSON. Published in 1962, the book attacked the indiscriminate use of pesticides and had a major impact in making the public aware of the potential dangers from pollution.

silica (SiO_2)

Silicon dioxide, a compound of SILICON and OXYGEN. It occurs naturally as QUARTZ and CHERT (which includes flint). Silica and SILICATE minerals (silica combined with other elements) are the main constituents of 95% of all rocks and account for 59% of the Earth's crust. Silica is used in the manufacture of glass, ceramics and silicone.

Sight is the SENSE by which form, colour, size, movement and distance of objects are perceived. Essentially, it is the detection of light by the EYE, enabling the formation of visual images.

▶ **Light entering the** eye (A) is focused by the action of a lens (1) under the control of the ciliary muscles (2), which act on the suspensory ligaments (3). The image (4) formed by an object (5) on the retina is actually upside down, but the brain is able to correct this. The eyeball (A) is held in place in the orbit by muscles (6), which also allow it to move. It is covered in three layers of tissue: the sclera (7), a tough, fibrous coat; the choroid (8), which supplies nutrients, and is pigmented to reduce internal reflection; and the retina (9), where the light-sensitive cells are located. The front of the eye is protected by the transparent cornea (10) and conjunctiva (11). The aqueous (12) (behind the cornea) and vitreous humours (13) help to keep the shape of the eye and also contain blood vessels (14). The iris (15) can be dilated or contracted by muscles to control the amount of light entering the eye through the pupil (16). The optic nerve (17) carries the visual information into the brain. Where it exits the retina there are no receptors, and there is a blind spot (18). Most of the time, however, the brain can compensate. The light-sensing cells in the vertebrate retina (B) are the rods (1) and cones (2), highly specialized nerve cells. The outer segment is comprised of membranous discs (3) containing a light-sensitive pigment. The inner segment has a branched base (4) that links to nerve fibres. If sufficient light (5) is absorbed by the pigments an electrical signal is produced by the adjacent nerve fibre.

▼ **Before reaching the** brain via the optic nerve (6), messages pass through a series of neurones in the retina — horizontal cells (7), bipolar cells (8), amacrine cells (9), ganglion cells (10) - which organize the sensory information. Rods are found throughout the retina, except at the fovea, and are sensitive to different wavelengths of light. The degree to which different cones are stimulated gives the brain information about colour. Cones are highly concentrated at the fovea, giving great detail here where most images are focused. Each cone has its own connection to the brain so that very detailed information is received.

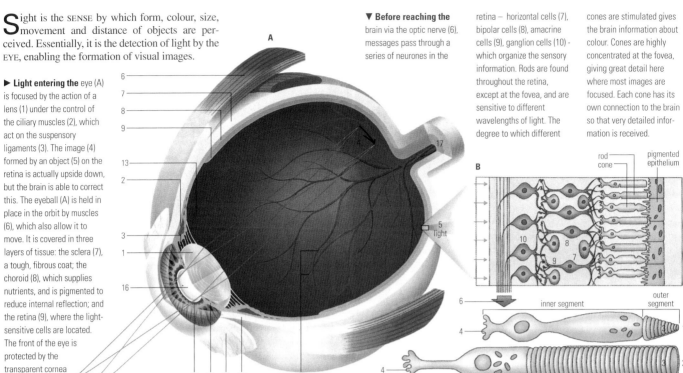

EYE DESIGNS

The simplest eyes, like those of flatworms (1), are just cups lined with a light-sensitive retina. In tubeworm eyes (2) each light receptor lies at the bottom of a pigmented tube. It receives only light from a particular angle and functions as a basic compound eye. The mirror eyes of scallops (3) form an image by reflection of incident light, in a similar way to a reflecting telescope. Shrimp and lobsters have a superimposition eye (4) in which mirrors channel light to form a single particularly bright image.

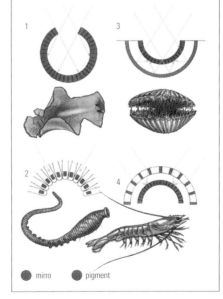

● mirror   ● pigment

▲ **Insect compound eyes** (D and E) are made up of many individual units (from one up to 28,000) called ommatidia, which are arranged in hemispherical fashion. Each ommatidium (1) has its own cornea (2) and lens (3). A light-sensitive region called the rhabdom (4) contains the visual pigment. This is surrounded by retinal cells (5) that transmit the electrical stimulus from the excited visual pigment to the brain. Cells containing screening pigment (6) prevent light entering one ommatidium from infiltrating its neighbour. In the apposition eye of daytime insects (D), this means each ommatidium can only receive light from a small part of the whole field of view. Thus the whole image formed in the brain consists of the overlap of many adjacent spots of light. Nocturnal insects have a superposition eye (E), which is constructed in a very similar way to the apposition eye and acts in the same way during the day (F). In dim light, however, the pigment withdraws towards the outer surface of the eye (G), thus allowing diffracted light to reach the rhabdom from adjacent ommatidia as well. This produces an image that is brighter than it otherwise would be, though it may be less distinct.

▶ **The visible spectrum** (C) of deep-sea fish is limited to a little blue light. Other fish have a broad range. Many snakes can see far-red, using special pit organs, as well as ultraviolet. Birds and insects may also see into the ultraviolet. The primate range, including human beings, lies between red and blue.

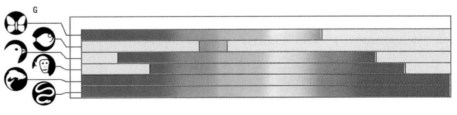

S

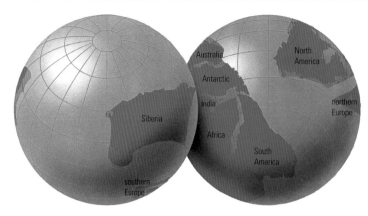

silicate

Any of a large group of rock-forming minerals made up of silicon and oxygen in SiO_4 units bonded to various metals. The SiO_4 units may form single or double chains (as in PYROXENE and AMPHIBOLE), sheets (as in MICA), rings (as in BERYL) or ionic bonds to a metal (as in OLIVINE). Silicate minerals, such as FELDSPAR, GARNET and mica, form 95% of the material of the Earth's crust. Glass is a mixture of silicates with small amounts of other substances. Sodium silicates are used as adhesives and in the production of detergents. QUARTZ (SiO) is also usually regarded as a silicate mineral.

silicula

Dry, cylindrical FRUIT. It has a similar structure to a SILIQUA but is shorter and broader in shape. It is found in HONESTY and SHEPHERD'S PURSE.

siliqua

Long, dry, cylindrical FRUIT formed from an OVARY made up of two CARPELS that are divided by a false septum into two compartments called locules. The seeds are dispersed by the carpel walls separating from below. It is found in CABBAGES and other species of the family Cruciferae. *See also* SILICULA

silk

Natural FIBRE produced by many creatures, notably the silkworm. Some other insects and spiders produce silk, but it is most economic to take it from the silkworm. Silk is a strong, high-quality material used to make fabric. The fibre consists mainly of fibroin (tough, elastic protein) covered with sericin (gelatinous protein). Almost all silk is obtained from silkworms reared commercially. Silkworms feed on mulberry leaves and a single COCOON can provide 600–900m (2000–3000ft) of filament (thread). Fibre is formed from a liquid that the caterpillar produces from its spinning glands. It spins a silk cocoon around its body in preparation for its change into a silk MOTH. When the cocoons have been spun, the silk farmer heats them to kill the insects inside. The cocoons are then soaked to unstick the fibres, and the strands from several cocoons are unwound together to form a single thread of yarn. The yarn may be dyed before or after weaving into fabric. The Chinese were the first to use silk, and its production was a closely guarded secret, since it could fetch its own weight in gold. Sicily was one of the first European production centres and the industry spread to Italy, Spain and France. Silk manufacturing developed in England in the 17th century. China is still the largest producer of raw silk in the world.

silk cotton tree

Tree found in the American and African tropics. It has immense spreading branches and leaves with between six and nine leaflets. The white or pink flowers give rise to leathery, capsular fruits. The fruits contain seeds embedded in a cotton-like fibre, which is known and used in commerce as "kapok". Family Bombacaceae; species *Ceiba pentandra*. **Silk cotton tree** also refers to a related tree found in tropical Asia. It has edible red flowers and produces a fibre of inferior quality to commercial kapok. The timber of both silk cotton trees may be used for matches and canoes. Height: to 30m (100ft). Family Bombacaceae; species *Bombax ceiba*. **Silk cotton tree** is also the name for an unrelated xeromorphic tree from Burma and India. It is cultivated for its ornate yellow flowers, which are produced at the top of an unbranched, pole-like trunk. The silk cotton tree yields an insoluble gum, which is used as a substitute for tragacanth. Hairs from the fruits are used for pillow stuffing. Family Bixaceae; species *Cochlospermum religiosum*.

silk oak

Tree that is native to Queensland and New South Wales, Australia; it is also grown in glasshouses as an ornamental shrub. It has pinnate leaves, which have a silky undersurface, and orange flowers. The timber is used for cabinet work. The tree gets its scientific name from Charles F. Greville, a patron of botany in the early 19th century. Height: to 45m (148ft). Family Proteaceae; species *Grevillea robusta*.

sill

Sheet-like intrusion of IGNEOUS ROCK that is parallel to the bedding or other structure of the surrounding rock. Sill rock is normally medium-grained; basic sills (DOLERITES) are the commonest.

sillimanite (fibrolite)

Mineral, aluminium silicate (Al_2SiO_5), found in mica SCHISTS and GNEISS. Its crystals are of the orthorhombic system, usually fibrous masses, and are satin-like or glossy white, brown, green or blue. A pale blue gem variety occurs in Sri Lanka. Hardness 6–7.5; r.d. 3.2.

silt

Mineral particles, produced by the WEATHERING of rock. These particles, varying in size between grains of SAND and CLAY, are carried along in streams and RIVERS, to be deposited in the gently flowing lower reaches of rivers. When the river changes course or overflows its bank, the silt deposit forms very fertile land. Siltstone (flagstone) is a hard, durable stone formed from hardened silt. *See also* ALLUVIUM

Silurian

Third oldest period of the PALAEOZOIC era, lasting from 438 to 408 million years ago. Marine invertebrates resembled those of ORDOVICIAN times, and fragmentary remains show that jawless fishes (agnathans) began to evolve. The earliest land plants (psilopsids) and first land animals (archaic mites and millipedes) developed. Mountains formed in NW Europe and Greenland.

silvereye (white-eye)

Any member of a family of small, mainly tropical songbirds found worldwide. The plumage ranges from grey to olive green to bright yellow. Silvereyes are characterized by a slightly down-curved bill, surrounded by a conspicuous ring of fine white feathers. Length: *c*.10cm (*c*.4in). Family Zosteropidae; main genus *Zosterops*; there are 89 species.

silverfish (bristletail)

Primitive, grey, wingless insect found worldwide. It lives in cool, damp places, feeding on starchy materials such as food scraps and paper. It gets its name from the silvery scales that cover its body. Length: 13mm (0.5in). Family Lepismatidae; species *Lepisma saccharina*.

silver gar

Marine NEEDLEFISH found in all tropical and temperate waters; it is also found in bays and coastal rivers. Its long, silvery body has a dark green or blue-black stripe. Its jaws are elongated and pointed, with sharp teeth. The flesh is edible. Length: to 1.2m (4ft). Family Belonidae.

silverside (spearing, smelt)

Any of several species of small marine fish found in temperate and tropical seas. The silverside is characterized by broad silvery side bands. The GRUNION is a species of silverside. Length: 8–51cm (3–20in). Family Atherinidae.

sima

In geology, undermost of the two main rock-classes that make up the Earth's CRUST, so called because its main constituents are **si**licon and **ma**gnesium. It underlies the SIAL of the CONTINENTS.

Simpson, George Gaylord (1902–84)

US palaeontologist whose studies gave support for neo-Darwinism and the role of genetics in evolution. He worked at the American Museum of Natural History in New York City (1927–59), before going to teach at Harvard. His early work was on taxonomy and mammal classification, and he did not turn to genetic studies until after World War 2.

sinkhole

Hollow or hole in LIMESTONE formations that extends from the surface all or part of the way down to underground channels and caverns. Such holes are formed by water dissolving the limestone.

siphonapteran

Any member of the order Siphonaptera, comprising the FLEAS.

◄ **silverfish** Belonging to the order Thysanura, one of only two orders of flightless insects, silverfish (*Lepisma saccharina*) are found in temperate climates worldwide, usually indoors. They have long antennae and three long thin appendages extending from the end of the abdomen. They avoid light.

S

▶ **skate** The little skate (*Raia erinacea*) is found in the W Atlantic Ocean, along the coasts of Canada and United States, as far south as North Carolina. It is active at night, usually remaining near the sandy seafloor, against which it is camouflaged. As with other members of the skate and ray family, it has an electric organ near the base of its tail. It also has a row of small spines along its back.

siphonophore
Marine organism that is notable for being made up of a colony of HYDROZOAN individuals in many different forms. The two major forms of the cnidarian life-cycle, the MEDUSA and the POLYP, are represented concomitantly in siphonophore species. The PORTUGUESE MAN-OF-WAR is a type of siphonophore. Phylum Coelenterata/Cnidaria; class Hydrozoa; order Siphonophora.

sipunculan
See PEANUT WORM

siren
Aquatic SALAMANDER with an elongate body and external gills; it possesses only one pair of limbs, the hindlimbs being completely absent. Sirens inhabit ponds, swamps and other water bodies in the SE United States and NE Mexico. They can survive dry periods by encasing themselves in a mucus cocoon. Length: 25–95cm (10–37in). Family Sirenidae; genera *Siren* and *Pseudobranchus*.

sisal (sisal hemp)
Plant that is native to Central America; it is cultivated in Mexico, Java, E Africa and the Bahamas. Fibres from the leaves are used for rope, matting and twine. Family Agavaceae; species *Agave sisalana*. *See also* AGAVE

siskin
Any of several species of small, green, seed-eating, finch-like birds. The siskins of Europe and Asia, for example the common siskin (*Carduelis spinus*), are arboreal birds found in pine and alder forests. Their plumage is streaked yellow-green. The Andean siskin (*Carduelis spinescens*), found at altitude in the South American Andes, is also a tree bird. It is brightly coloured black and yellow. The African siskin (*Carduelis notata*) has a black head. Length: *c*.12cm (*c*.5in). Family Carduelidae.

sitatunga (marshbuck)
Medium-sized antelope found in central and W Africa; it is closely related to the BUSHBUCK. Its long hoofs are an adaptation for life in marshes. Height: 82–106cm (32–42in). Family Bovidae; species *Tragelaphus spekii*.

sittella
Small, climbing bird of Australasia. It has a slightly upturned bill, strong feet and large wings. It feeds in flocks. Like the closely related NUTHATCHES, the sittella feeds by descending tree branches head downwards. Its plumage is grey, streaked black, with orange wing patches. Length: to 12cm (5n). Family Sittidae; genus *Noesitta*.

SI units (*Système International d'Unités*)
Internationally agreed system of units, derived from the mks system (metre, kilogram and second). SI units are now used for many scientific purposes and have replaced the fps system (foot, pound and second) and cgs system (centimetre, gram and second). The seven basic units are: the metre (m), kilogram (kg), second (s), ampere (A), kelvin (K), mole (mol) and candela (cd).

skate
Any of numerous species of flattened food fish belonging to the RAY family. The skate lives mainly in shallow temperate and tropical waters. The pectoral fins are greatly expanded to form wing-like flaps. Length: to *c*.2.5m (*c*.8ft). Family Rajidae.

skeletal muscle
Alternative name for VOLUNTARY MUSCLE

skeleton
Bony framework of the body of a VERTEBRATE. It supports and protects the internal organs, provides sites of attachment for MUSCLES and a system of levers to aid locomotion. In the HUMAN BODY the skeleton consists of 206 BONES and is divided into two parts. The **axial skeleton**, or main axis of the body, includes the SKULL, the SPINE, the STERNUM (breastbone) and the RIBS. The **appendicular skeleton**, serving for the attachment of limbs, includes the shoulder girdle and arm bones and the pelvic, or hip, girdle and leg bones. The external skeleton of some insects is called an EXOSKELETON. *See also* ENDOSKELETON

skimmer
Any of several species of large tern-like birds. The skimmer flies very close to the water, with very shallow wing beats; its lower mandible cuts the water surface. When a fish is located its bill snaps shut. The skimmer is black or brown above and white below. Length: 36–48cm (14–19in); wingspan: 107–114cm (42–45in). Family Rynchopidae; genus *Rynchops*.

skin
Tough, elastic outer covering of the body, serving many functions. It is sometimes regarded as the largest organ of the body. The skin protects the body from injury and from the entry of some microorganisms and prevents dehydration. Nerve endings in the skin provide the sensations of touch, warmth, cold and pain, each perceived at discrete points on the surface. It helps to regulate body temperature through sweating, regulates moisture loss, and keeps itself smooth and pliable with an oily secretion from the SEBACEOUS GLANDS. Structurally, the skin consists of two main layers: an outer layer, called the EPIDERMIS; and an inner layer, known as the DERMIS. The top layer of epidermis is made of closely packed dead cells constantly shed as microscopic scales. Below this is a layer of living cells that contain pigment and nerve fibres, and which divide to replace outer, shed layers. The dermis contains dense networks of connective tissue, blood vessels, nerves, glands and hair follicles.

skink
Any of *c*.1600 species of small to moderate-sized LIZARDS, most of which are active in the day. Most species are covered by shiny, overlapping scales. Many lineages of skinks exhibit limb reduction or loss. Skinks occur in most temperate and tropical areas of the world; they are especially numerous in Australia and are relatively poorly represented in the Americas and Europe. Most species eat insects, but some larger species eat plant material. Length: 5–50cm (2–20in). Family Scincidae.

skink, blue-tongued
Large, heavy-bodied skink. It has small legs, a short tail and a series of dark cross bands on its back. Its broad tongue is a distinctive blue colour. Blue-tongued skinks occupy the less arid regions of Australia, where they feed on insects, snails, flowers and fruits. They give birth to large litters of live young. Length: to 50cm (20in). Family Scincidae; genus *Tiliqua*.

skink, pine cone
Large, heavy-bodied skink. It has short, stubby legs and a very short, fat tail. The pine cone skink is covered by very large, wrinkled scales, after which it is named. It is widely distributed and particularly common in S Australia. Pine cone skinks eat both plant and animal matter. They produce litters of between one and three very large young. Length: to 37cm (15in). Family Scincidae; species *Trachydosaurus rugosus*.

skink, sand
Small skink that is found in sandy soils only in central Florida, United States. It has tiny legs, and its ears have no external openings. There are only two toes on the skink's hind feet and one on the forefeet. Sand skinks "swim" a few centimetres beneath the surface, hunting for termites and insect larvae. Length: to 13cm (5in). Family Scincidae; species *Neoseps reynoldsi*.

skipjack
Any of several species of fish, not closely related, that swim near or on the surface. The best known is the skipjack tuna (*Katsuwonus pelamis*). Length: 1m (3.3ft).

skipper
Any of numerous species of day-active insects char-

S

▼ **skink** The sand skink (*Scincus scincus*) is found in the deserts of North Africa and S Asia. It is mainly active at night. It is often known as a sandfish because of the way it slithers across the sand in a swimming-like motion. It burrows beneath the hot sand during the day. It feeds on insects.

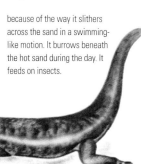

▲ **skipper** There are as many as three thousand species of skipper butterflies. Shown here is the large European skipper (*Ochlodes venata*), which has a wing span of up to 3.5cm (1.4in). It is found in England and Wales and across Europe and Asia to China. Skippers are so called because of their erratic flight.

acterized by darting or skipping flight. They are related to the BUTTERFLY and the MOTH. The skipper has a stouter body than a butterfly but is more slender than a moth. It usually has a hook-like extension at the end of each knobbed antenna. Order Lepidoptera; superfamily Hesperioidea.

skua
Any of several species of dark, predatory, gull-like seabirds. The skua chases terns and gulls, forcing them to regurgitate their food, which it catches before it falls into the water. The great skua (*Catharacta skua*) is heavily built and resembles a brown gull. The arctic skua or jaeger (*Stercorarius parasiticus*) is slimmer and more hawk-like. Both have white wing flashes. Length: 48–58cm (19–23in); wingspan: 105–140cm (41–55in). Family Stercorariidae; genera *Catharacta* and *Stercorarius*.

skull
SKELETON of the head. In mammals, it comprises the cranium casing of the BRAIN and the facial and upper jawbones (the lower jawbone, or MANDIBLE, attaches to the skull). There are 14 facial bones, mostly in symmetrical pairs. These are the zygomatic arches (cheekbones), the lacrimals around the eye socket, the nasals, nasal conchae and vomer (nasal septum) of the nose, the palatines (palate) of the mouth and the maxillae (upper jaw). The adult human cranium is formed of fused skull bones with immovable joints: the frontal, occipital, temporals, parietals, ethmoid and splenoid. The occipital bone at the base of the skull forms a joint with the first (atlas) VERTEBRA of the neck.

skunk
Nocturnal, omnivorous mammal that is found in the United States and Central and South America. It has powerful anal scent glands, which eject a foul-smelling liquid, used in defence. It has a small head and a slender, thickly furred body, with short legs and a large, bushy tail. The coat is black with bold white warning markings along the back. The most common species is the striped skunk, *Mephitis mephitis*. Length: to 38cm (15in); weight: 4.5kg (10lb). Family Mustelidae.

skylark
See LARK, SKY-

slate
Grey to blue, fine-grained, homogeneous METAMOR-

PHIC ROCK, which splits into smooth, thin layers. It is formed by the metamorphosis of SHALE. It is valuable as a roofing material.

slider, red-eared
Common aquatic TURTLE of E North America. It is characterized by a red stripe behind its eye. Its carapace is greenish, with yellow and black markings, but its colour fades with age. The red-eared slider's feet are strongly webbed. Males have long claws on the front feet, which are used in courtship. Red-eared sliders have been introduced in waters worldwide and can be detrimental to native species. Length: 12–28cm (5–11in). Family Emydidae; species *Trachemys scripta*.

slime eel
See HAGFISH

slime mould
Any of a small group of strange, basically single-celled organisms that are intermediate between the animal and plant kingdoms. During their complex life cycle, slime moulds pass through several stages. These include a flagellated swimming stage, an amoeba-like stage, a stage consisting of a slimy mass of protoplasm with many nuclei, and a flowering sporangium stage.

slipper flower
See CALCEOLARIA

slipper limpet
Marine GASTROPOD mollusc found in shallow waters around the world. Its shell contains a platform-like internal partition, which gives the empty shell the appearance of a slipper from the underside. Phylum Mollusca; class Gastropoda; order Mesogastropoda; family Calyptraeidae; genus *Crepidula*; species include *Crepidula fornicata* (Atlantic slipper limpet).

▲ **skua** The pomarine skua (*Stercorarius pomarinus*) is primarily a bird of the open seas. It is a powerful flier and will pursue other birds in order to steal their prey (fish). The pomarine skua breeds in the Arctic region and travels great distances during the rest of the year.

▲ **skunk** The striped or common skunk (*Mephitis mephitis*) is found in much of North America. If threatened it stamps on the ground, stands on its hind legs and spits. If the intruder remains, the skunk will spray it with a foul-smelling, yellow liquid, which it can eject a considerable distance.

slippery elm
ELM tree native to North America; it is found along streams, commonly in limestone areas. It has a flat-topped head and rough, hairy, red-orange twigs. The wood has been used for fence posts and railroad ties. Its inner bark, when steeped in water, has medicinal uses. Height: 18m (59ft). Family Ulmaceae; species *Ulmus rubra*.

slippery jack
Edible FUNGUS that has a mushroom-like fruiting body with a large, domed, chestnut-coloured cap. The brown, glutinous covering becomes shiny on drying. The thickened stem is pale straw-coloured at the top, becoming darker brown below. Slippery jack is found growing in association with conifers. Phylum Basidiomycota; species *Suillus luteus*.

sloe
See BLACKTHORN

sloth
Any of five species of mammal that are so specialized for hanging upside down from branches by their hooked claws that they find it difficult to move on the ground. At night sloths move about very slowly, feeding exclusively on leaves; they sleep during the day. Their hair grows from the belly towards the back, so that rain runs off while the animal is upside down. Sloths often have green algae growing on them for camouflage. Order Edentata; family Bradypodidae.

sloth, three-toed
Sloth found in South America. It comes down to the ground about once a week to defecate. Head-body length: 50–60cm (20–24in); tail: 6–7cm (2–3in). Family Bradypodidae; species *Bradypus tridactylus*.

sloth, two-toed
Tailless sloth found in Central America. It has two digits with strong, hooked claws on each forefoot. Head-body length: 60–64cm (24–25in). Family Bradypodidae; species *Choloepus didactylus*.

sloth bear
See BEAR, SLOTH

slow-worm (blind-worm)
Snake-like, legless LIZARD found in grassy areas and woodlands of Europe. It is generally brownish; the female has a black underside. The slow-worm has pointed teeth and feeds primarily on slugs and snails. Length: to 30cm (12in). Family Anguidae; species *Anguis fragilis*.

sludge worm (bloodworm)

OLIGOCHAETE worm that lives in freshwater ponds and slow-flowing streams. It feeds on detritus. Many species are bright red in colour, hence their alternative name. The susceptibility of sludge worms to environmental change and their narrow ecological niches make them ideal indicators in pollution monitoring. Phylum Annelida; class Oligochaeta; order Haplotaxida; family Tubificidae; genus *Tubifex*.

slug

Mostly terrestrial, GASTROPOD MOLLUSC. It is identified by its lack of shell and uncoiled viscera. It secretes a protective slime, which is also used to aid locomotion. Length: to 20cm (8in). Class Gastropoda; subclass Pulmonata; genera include *Arion* and *Limax. See also* SEA SLUG

slump

Downslope movement under the influence of gravity of a coherent mass along a basal glide plane with low friction. Slumps may occur both subaqueously or subaerially, from metre to kilometre-scale, and may be triggered by a variety of processes, from earthquakes to heavy rainfall.

smell (olfaction)

SENSE that responds to airborne molecules. The olfactory RECEPTORS can detect even a few molecules per million parts of air. There are different receptors for different chemical groups.

smelt

Any of several species of small, silvery-coloured food fish related to SALMON and TROUT. Smelts are found in the cold waters of the N Atlantic and Pacific oceans and in some North American inland waters. Family Osmeridae.

Smith, Michael (1932–2000)

Canadian biochemist, b. Britain. He discovered site-specific mutagenesis, a method of altering the GENETIC CODE through specific MUTATIONS instead of the previous random ones. This method has enabled the production of new proteins with a variety of functions. For this work, Smith shared the 1993 Nobel Prize for chemistry with Kary MULLIS.

Smith, William (1769–1839)

British geologist. A founder of STRATIGRAPHY, he

▲ **sloth** The two-toed sloth (*Choloepus didactylus*) is an unusual herbivore in that it can survive on a particularly poor diet of tough leaves by means of a lifestyle that involves very little expenditure of energy. It sleeps a lot and moves extremely slowly. In fact, the two-toed sloth has only half the musculature of most mammals, and its food may take a whole week to pass through the digestive system.

▲ **slug** The many species of slug are distinguished from other gastropods by their lack of shell. To conserve moisture slugs usually only emerge on damp evenings. They have eyes on the ends of their tentacles. *Limax* species, such as the slug here, are common garden pests, causing much damage to plants.

studied the geological strata of England and Wales, relating his findings to identified fossils and thus estimating the age of geological formations.

Smithson, James (1765–1829)

British chemist and mineralogist; the mineral SMITHSONITE is named after him. Angered at the Royal Society's rejection of a paper by him in 1826, Smithson left £105,000 to found an institution, the Smithsonian Institution in Washington, D.C., for the "increase and diffusion of knowledge among men". Today, it is one of the leading American scientific research and education centres.

smithsonite

Carbonate mineral, zinc carbonate ($ZnCO_3$). It is found in ore deposits of zinc minerals, commonly associated with sphalerite, hemimorphite, galena and calcite. Its crystals, which are rare, are rhomobohedral in the trigonal system; it usually occurs as masses. Smithsonite is generally white, but it may be other colours; blue specimens from New Mexico have been used as gemstones. Hardness 4–4.5; r.d. 4.4.

smog

Dense, atmospheric mixture of smoke and FOG or chemical fumes, commonly occurring in urban or industrial areas. Smog generally occurs when there is radiation fog. If the air remains calm, the fog gets worse; more industrial grime accumulates because it is unable to escape into the atmosphere. The water droplets condense around the pollutants, forming thick smog. One of the worst areas for smog is Los Angeles, W United States. This is a result of the exhaust emissions of the city's vast number of automobiles. The air pollution is exacerbated by Los Angeles' topography: it lies in a large basin, noted for inversions of temperature, which create ideal conditions for the formation of fog and smog.

smoke tree (wig tree)

Dense, spreading shrub distributed from s Europe to China. It has oval leaves and tiny flowers in purplish, feathery clusters. It is commonly grown in parks and gardens as an ornamental. Among the several varieties are plants with dark purple foliage or drooping branches. The smoke tree's leaves are used for tanning, and the wood gives a yellow dye. Family Anacardiaceae; species *Cotinus coggygria*.

smut fungus (smuts)

Any of a group of plant diseases caused by parasitic fungi. They attack many cereals. The diseases are named after the sooty black masses of reproductive spores produced by the fungi.

snaggletooth

Predatory, elongate marine fish. It is found at depths of up to 3000m (9800ft). The snaggletooth resembles a DRAGONFISH. It has bioluminescent light organs along the length of its belly, a luminescent barbel on its lower jaw and prominent jaw teeth. Family Stomiidae; genus *Astronesthes*.

snail

Any of numerous species of marine, aquatic or terrestrial GASTROPODS. Although a snail requires moisture for active life, it can survive in dry environments thanks to structures that work in conjunction with its shell to prevent water loss. Snails and SLUGS belong to the same class, a snail being distinguished by the possession of a shell that houses its internal organs and muscular foot (when retracted). Most species have eyes as well as tentacles and are herbivorous, feeding with rasping, strap-like mouthparts. Phylum Mollusca; class Gastropoda.

snail, African giant

Largest species of land snail; it is found in E Africa. Its ability to survive on a wide variety of host plants means that it can become a crop pest. Severe quarantine restrictions are enforced by most countries. The African giant snail is considered a culinary delicacy. Length: to 20cm (8in). Family Achatinidae; species *Achatina fulica*.

snail, common garden

Abundant snail found on all continents except Antarctica. It is most active at night. It is usually considered a pest because of its habits of feeding on garden plants and leaving unsightly trails of mucous. Subclass Pulmonata; species *Helix aspersa*.

snail, ramshorn

Any of a great number of species of aquatic snails, including several freshwater species. Ramshorn snails are distinguished by their spiral, flattened shells. Their name is due to the fact that, viewed laterally, their shells resemble the spiral made by a ram's horn. Class Gastropoda; family Planorbidae; genera include *Planorbis*.

snail darter

Rare and endangered species of freshwater, bottom-dwelling fish. It is native to the Little Tennessee River, Tennessee, United States. It was feared that the building of the Tellico Dam (completed 1980) on the river would threaten the snail darter's existence, but it has since been found in a different stream. Length to 7.5cm (3in). Family Percidae; species *Percina tanasi*.

snake

Any of *c*.2700 species of legless, elongate reptiles forming the sub-order Serpentes of the order Squamata (which also includes LIZARDS). There are 11 families. Snake species range in length from *c*.10cm (*c*.4in) to more than 9m (30ft). There are terrestrial, arboreal, semi-aquatic and aquatic species; one group is entirely marine; many are poisonous. They have no external ear openings, eardrums or middle ears; instead sound vibrations are detected

S

▲ **snail** Remarkably adept at exploring new habitats, snails originated in the sea, but gradually the *c*.22,000 species adapted to life on dry land, losing their gills and evolving air-breathing lungs. Most species of land snail, such as *Helix pomatia*, shown here, live on the ground and are dull in coloration. A few species are arboreal: these tend to be brightly coloured. Others have returned to aquatic environments and must surface periodically to breathe.

▲ **snake, bull** Found in the prairies of North America, the bull snake (*Pituophis melanoleucus*) preys on rodents. It is non-poisonous, instead suffocating its prey with its strong, constricting coils. Its camouflaging coloration allows it to lie unnoticed among the rocks or in vegetation.

through the ground. Their eyelids are immovable and their eyes are covered by a transparent protective cover. The long, forked, protractile tongue is used to detect odours. Their bodies are covered with scales. Poisonous snakes have hollow or grooved fangs through which they inject venom into their prey.

snake, blind
Burrowing, almost sightless, legless reptile; it has the vestiges of a pelvic girdle. There are two families of blind snakes: the Typhlopidae family (blind snakes) and the Leptotyphlopidae family (slender blind snakes). They are found throughout the world in tropical and temperate areas. Length: to 30cm (12in). Genera include *Typhlops* and *Leptotyphlops*.

snake, brown
Dangerously venomous snake distributed throughout mainland Australia and into New Guinea. The various species can be uniformly coloured, banded or with markings only on the head and neck. They lay clutches of up to 35 eggs. Brown snakes feed on small mammals and reptiles. Length: to 150cm (59in). Family Elapidae; genus *Pseudonaja*.

snake, bull
Nonpoisonous snake found in central and w United States and Mexico. Its powerful body is yellow marked with dark splotches. It kills by constriction. Length: to 150cm (59in). Family Colubridae; species *Pituophis melanoleucus*.

snake, cat-eyed
Slender, arboreal or terrestrial snake found in tropical America. It has a broad, flat head and large eyes. The cat-eyed snake has enlarged fangs in the back of its mouth, but it is not dangerous to humans. It specializes in eating frogs and, in some species, the egg masses of frogs. Length: *c*.1m (*c*.40in). Family Colubridae; genus *Leptodeira*.

snake, coachwhip (whipsnake)
Slender, agile snake that is found from the United States to n South America. The species vary in colour but are frequently brown and striped or cross-barred. Unrelated species in Asia and Australia are also called whipsnakes. Length: to 150cm (59in). Family Colubridae; genus *Masticophis*.

snake, colubrid
Any member of the family Colubridae, a group of more than 1600 species of snakes occurring worldwide. Most colubrids are not dangerously venomous, although human fatalities have been associated with the BOOMSLANG (*Dispholidus typus*) and the twig snake (*Thelotornis kirtlandi*). Colubrids are the most numerous snakes on all continents except Australia. Family Colubridae.

snake, coral
Poisonous burrowing snake found in the Americas and Southeast Asia. It is shy and docile, but its venom is fatal. Most species are brightly coloured, ringed with red, yellow and black. The coral snake feeds on lizards, frogs and other snakes. Family Elapidae; genera include *Micrurus*.

snake, egg-eating
Any of several species of snake that feed exclusively on bird eggs. The most well-known are members of the African genus *Dasypeltis*. These snakes can extend the jaws and throat to accommodate eggs much wider than their own bodies; the processes of the vertebrae are used to break the eggshell, which is then regurgitated. Length: to 100cm (39in). Family Colubridae.

snake, false coral
Any of several harmless or mildly venomous snakes of tropical America. They closely mimic the coloration of the highly venomous elapid coral snake, having red and black or red, yellow and black banded patterns. Some species have fragile tails that easily break when grasped. Most species live in forest leaf litter. Length: 70–100cm (28–39in). Family Colubridae; genera include *Erythrolamprus*. *See also* MIMICRY

snake, flying
Slender, arboreal snake native to Southeast Asia. It has a green belly and a blackish back with red and white markings. The flying snake is able to spread its ribs in order to increase its surface area and can parachute from higher to lower surfaces in a controlled descent. Length: to 150cm (59in). Family Colubridae; species *Chrysolpelea paradisi*.

snake, garter (ribbon snake)
Common, medium-sized snake found in North America and Central America. It is characterized by keeled scales and often a striped pattern. Many species live near water. Garter snakes bear live young. They feed on fish, crustaceans, frogs and other small prey. Length: 45–145cm (18–57in). Family Colubridae; genus *Thamnophis*. The name **garter snake** is also applied to a group of venomous, banded snakes that are found in Africa. They burrow by day and feed on small vertebrates on the surface at night. Length: to 93cm (37in). Family Elapidae; genus *Elapsoidea*.

snake, glass
See LIZARD, GLASS

snake, grass (European water snake)
Non-poisonous snake found in Europe, North Africa and central Asia. It swims readily but is generally found in long grass and undergrowth. It is greenish-brown with a yellow collar. In Britain it is sometimes mistaken for the ADDER. Length: to 100cm (39in). Family Colubridae; species *Natrix natrix*.

snake, green (grass snake)
Slender snake found in North America and Asia. The rough species (*Opheodrys aestivus*) of North America has keeled scales; the smaller, smooth species (*Opheodrys vernalis*) is unkeeled. Both species are solid green in colour with pale bellies. Length: to 76cm (30in). Family Colubridae.

snake, hognose
Medium-sized colubrid snake found in North America. It has a strongly upturned snout. It has enlarged teeth at the rear of its mouth, which it uses to inject mild venom into toads, its preferred prey. The hognose snake spreads its neck if alarmed; it also "plays dead", turning on to its back with its tongue extended, in order to avoid being preyed upon. Length: 36–115cm (14–45in). Family Colubridae; genus *Heterodon*.

snake, hoop
See SNAKE, MUD

snake, indigo
Harmless, dark blue, colubrid snake that ranges from SE United States to Argentina. It hisses and vibrates its tail when disturbed. Length: to 280cm (110in). Family Colubridae; species *Drymarchon corais*.

◄ **snake, flying** The flying snake (*Chrysolpelea paradisi*) is one of the most remarkable of present-day gliding reptiles. It has a long, slender body and grooved fangs. It is well adapted to its habitat, moving quickly through the branches to catch its agile prey of geckos. It is likely that the flying snake evolved its gliding adaptation to help it to hunt. When gliding, the snake launches itself from an appropriate branch into the air, where it makes a rapid series of S-shapes, while at the same time flattening its body to increase its surface area, thereby creating as much lift as possible.

S

► **snake, grass** The European grass snake (*Natrix natrix*) hunts for food in the water and on land. It preys on toads, frogs, newts and sometimes fish. On land it takes small birds and mammals. It usually swims with its head above water but can remain submerged when hunting (or being hunted). Across the grass snake's wide range there are several subspecies, which differ slightly in coloration but retain the yellow collar. The female is usually larger than the male.

snake, king
Any member of the genus *Lampropeltis*, a group of several species of nonpoisonous colubrid snakes found in the United States. The king snake is generally black, with white or yellow markings. It kills by constriction, preying on other snakes, mammals, amphibians and birds. Length: to 130cm (51in). Family Colubridae, species include *Lampropeltis getulus* (common king snake).

snake, milk
Species of king snake found from Canada to Ecuador. It is usually shiny and patterned with brown or red, black and yellowish transverse rings or saddles. It was once believed to suck milk from cows. Length: 92cm (36in). Family Colubridae; species *Lampropeltis triangulum*.

snake, mud (hoop snake)
Large, smooth-scaled water snake that is found in the SE United States. It feeds mostly on amphiumas but also takes frogs and eels. The mud snake has a black back and a red or pink belly. Mud snakes often lie in a loose, circular coil and have a pointy tail tip. They have become associated with the myth of the hoop snake, which was believed to take its own tail into its mouth in order to form a hoop so as to escape predators; the hoop snake was said to kill with a sting from a venomous spine at the end of its tail. Length: to 200cm (79in). Family Colubridae; species *Farancia abacura*.

snake, pilot (black rat snake)
Common, non-venomous, colubrid snake of E and central North America. It is found in farmlands and forests, where it feeds on small mammals. Pilot snakes are excellent climbers and can scale vertical tree trunks. Length: to 250cm (98in). Family Colubridae; species *Elaphe obsoleta*.

snake, pine
Subspecies of bull SNAKE. It is a common, harmless snake found in pine barrens and dry areas of the United States. It is black and white or brown with a faded pattern. Length: to 170cm (67in). Family Colubridae; species *Pituophis melanoleucus*.

snake, pipe
Any of several species of elongate, burrowing snakes. They have small, blunt heads and small eyes. Asian pipe snakes (genera *Cylindrophis* and *Anomochilus*) are dark, often with brighter spots or irregular markings. The South American pipe snake (*Anilius scytale*) has a bright red and black banded pattern, which may mimic the coral snake. Length: 35–100cm (14–39in). Families Aniliidae, Anomochelidae and Cylindrophidae.

snake, rat
Any member of the genus *Elaphe*, a group of *c*.50 species of terrestrial and arboreal colubrid snakes. Rat snakes are distributed widely in North America and Europe. Common species in North America are the black rat snake (*Elaphe obsoleta obsoleta*), the yellow rat snake (*Elaphe obsoleta*), the fox snake (*Elaphe vulpina*) and the corn snake (*Elaphe guttata*). In Europe are found the four-lined (*Elaphe quatuorlineata*) and Aesculapian (*Elaphe longissima*) rat snakes. Length: to 180cm (71in). Family Colubridae.

snake, red-bellied
Small, secretive snake that inhabits open woods and bogs of E and central United States. It is usually brown or grey, with four narrow dark stripes. It has a plain red belly and three pale spots on its neck. Length: to 25cm (10in). Family Colubridae; species *Storeria occipitomaculata*.

snake, ribbon
See SNAKE, GARTER

snake, snail-eating
Any of several species of snake adapted to feed largely or exclusively on snails. These species include the South American snail-eaters (genus *Dipsas*) and Asian snail-suckers (genus *Pareas*). Snails are bitten with long, needle-like teeth; the coils of the body push against the shell to remove the mollusc from its shell. Length: *c*.50–110cm (*c*.20–43in). Family Colubridae.

snake, sunbeam
Terrestrial snake found in India and Southeast Asia. It has glossy, iridescent scales. It retains some primitive features, such as vestiges of a pelvis and hindlimbs. The sunbeam snake is a generalist feeder on many small vertebrates. Length: to 100cm (39in). Family Xenopeltidae; species *Xenopeltis unicolor*.

snake, thread
Any of *c*.90 species of small, slender, burrowing snakes. They lack teeth in the upper jaw, and their eyes are small and covered by scales. Most species feed on ants, termites and their eggs. Pheromones released by the snakes are thought to protect them from attack by their colonial insect prey. Thread snakes occur in Africa, W Asia and the Americas. Length: to 35cm (14in). Family Leptotyphlopidae.

snake, vine
Any member of several groups of tropical arboreal snakes; they have elongate, slender bodies and prominent, forward-directed eyes. Vine snakes remain motionless in the foliage waiting to ambush small prey animals. Their head shape allows them to use binocular vision, giving them excellent depth perception. Most vine snakes are green or brown to blend in with their surroundings. Length: *c*.60–200cm (*c*.24–79in). Family Colubridae.

snake, whipsnake
Any of several species of large, slender, fast-moving, diurnal snakes of North America. Whipsnakes have large eyes and often hunt with their heads raised well above the ground to help them find prey and escape potential predators. Length: 110–260cm (43–102in). Family Colubridae; genus *Masticophis*.

snake-eagle
Any of several species of medium-sized EAGLES found in S Europe and Africa. The snake-eagle spends most of the day soaring and hovering over dry open country in search of snakes, lizards and rodents; it plummets vertically to seize them. Most species have pale underparts and a large owl-like head. Length: 60–67cm (24–26in); wingspan: to 200cm (79in). Family Accipitridae; genus *Circaetus*.

snake fly
Any of *c*.20 species of NEUROPTERAN insects found in Europe. The snake fly has a long prothorax, which raises its head above the rest of its body. Snake flies of the family Raphidiidae are terrestrial. The larvae live under bark, feeding on other insects. The female uses her long ovipositor to place her eggs in crevices. Order Neuroptera; suborder Megaloptera; family Raphidiidae.

snakehead
Any of several species of elongate, predatory freshwater fish found in tropical Africa and S Asia. They have a suprabranchial chamber, which enables them to breathe air and thus to survive for periods outside water. Length: to 1.2m (3.9ft). Family Channidae.

snake root (Texas or Virginian snakeroot)
Perennial plant with deep green foliage; it is native to the United States. It has few leaves, erect, zigzag stems and S-shaped, purplish flowers. The rhizome, which is snake-like in appearance, is regarded as having medicinal properties. It is effective in the treatment of snake bites. Family Aristolochiaceae; species *Endotheca serpentaria*.

snake root (black cohosh)
Plant that has feathery plumes of creamy white flowers and shiny green leaves. It is native to E North America. The dried rhizome has medicinal uses. Cultivated plants with this name are usually a related species, *Cimicifuga simplex*, found in E Asia. Family Ranunculaceae; species *Cimicifuga racemosa*.

snapdragon
Any of several species of perennial plants of the

S

larva

▲ **snake fly** The European snake fly (*Raphidia notata*) has the long neck typical of members of the snake fly family. It is a large, predacious insect, feeding mainly on aphids. The female lays eggs, by means of a long ovipositor, in slits in the bark of coniferous trees. The larvae prey on other insects.

genus *Antirrhinum*. They have sac-like, two-lipped, purple, red, yellow or white flowers. The common snapdragon (*Antirrhinum majus*) is a popular ornamental garden plant. Height: 15–91cm (6–36in). Family Scrophulariaceae.

snapper
Any member of the family Lutjanidae, which comprises *c.*250 species of marine food fish. Shoals of snappers are found in tropical waters of the Indo-Pacific and Atlantic oceans. They have elongated bodies and sharp teeth. Most species are food fish. Length: to 90cm (35in). Family Lutjanidae; species include *Lutjanus campechanus* (red snapper).

snipe
Medium-sized wading bird. It has rich brown mottled plumage, short legs and a very long bill. It breeds in freshwater marshes, bogs and fens. The giant snipe (*Gallinago undulata*) of South America is the largest species. The jack snipe (*Lymnocryptes minimus*) is the smallest species and has the shortest bill; like a crake, the jack snipe prefers to run for cover rather than fly. Length: 17–37cm (7–15in). Family Scolopacidae; genera *Gallinago* and *Lymnocryptes.*

snipe-fly
Any member of a family of slender, long-legged flies. Most species are brown and yellow, with three pads on their feet. Snipe-fly larvae live in rotting wood, leaf litter and soil, feeding on other insects. Order Diptera; suborder Brachycera; family Rhagionidae.

snook (robalo)
Any of several species of marine and freshwater fish found in tropical waters. Large snooks, such as the Atlantic snook (*Centropomus undecimalis*) and freshwater Nile perch (*Lates niloticus*), are commercial and sport fish. Small snooks are popular aquarium fish. Family Centropomidae.

snow
Type of PRECIPITATION consisting of WATER VAPOUR that has frozen into ICE crystals. Several ice CRYSTALS join together to form a **snowflake**, which will gradually fall to Earth. Snowflakes, which are symmetrical (usually hexagonal) crystalline structures, often melt as they fall, especially if the temperature is near freezing point. In such conditions, **sleet** occurs and CLOUDS yield snowfall on mountains, while producing rainfall on adjacent lowland areas. Snow is dry and powdery if it has come from a dryish area, and wetter if its source is over the sea. Interior regions, such as prairies, generally have dry snow, which is blown by powerful winds in blizzards. *See also* RAIN

snowball tree
Cultivated variety of a deciduous shrub native to Europe, North Africa and N Asia. It has smooth grey branches and lobed leaves. The snowball tree is grown as an ornamental for its inflorescences, which are composed of white, sterile flowers clustered into large globose heads. Family Caprifoliaceae; species *Viburnum opulus* var. *Roseum.*

snowberry
Shrubby plant native to North America and China. It has pink or white bell-shaped flowers and soft berries. The various wild species include coralberry, wolfberry and snow- or waxberry. The latter has large, pulpy, white berries. Family Caprifoliaceae; genus *Symphoricarpos*; there are 18 species.

snowcock
Large, PARTRIDGE-like gamebird that lives close to the snow line in the mountains of central Asia. It is mottled grey and buff with reddish-brown streaks. It has a loud, far-carrying, fluty call. The snowcock uproots plants by scraping in the ground with its stout bill. Length: 54–62cm (21–24in). Family Phasianidae; genus *Tetraogallus.*

snowdrop
Low-growing perennial plant of the Mediterranean region; it is widely cultivated as a garden ornamental. The drooping, green and white, fragrant flowers appear early in spring. The common snowdrop (*Galanthus nivalis*) has narrow leaves. Height: to 15cm (6in). Family Amaryllidaceae.

snowflake
Any member of the genus *Leucojum*, a group of hardy, bulbous plants found in the Mediterranean region. The snowflake is cultivated in gardens for its spring or autumn flowers. The few fleshy, strap-shaped leaves appear either with the flowers (spring and summer snowflake) or afterwards (autumn snowflake). The white flowers, tinged with green or red, are produced in a cluster. Family Liliaceae; genus *Leucojum.*

snow flea
Insect that is found in autumn and winter, when it feeds on mosses. It is not a true flea, but it is commonly referred to as the snow flea because of its jumping ability and its presence when snow is on the ground. Length: to 3mm (0.1in). Order Mecoptera; family Boreidae; species *Boreus hyemalis.*

snow leopard
See LEOPARD, SNOW

snowshoe hare
See HARE, SNOWSHOE

soapstone (steatite)
Rock with a soft soapy or greasy texture. There are many types of soapstone, all of which contain a large proportion of magnesium silicate. Soapstones are often associated with various amounts of serpentine and carbonates. Food vessels and carvings made from soapstone have been found among the remains of prehistoric human cultures.

soapwort
Perennial herb that is native to Europe and w Asia; it has been introduced into North America. It is found by streams and roadsides and is also grown in gar-

S

◄ **snipe** The great snipe (*Gallinago media*) breeds in mountainous areas of N Europe, notably Sweden, Norway and Poland. Shown here are two male great snipes at a gathering place known as a lek. During the breeding season, the snipes gather at a lek and the males display to the females as a prelude to mating. The display involves wing flapping, neck stretching, tail spreading and jumping.

▶ **soil profile** The composition and colour of a soil identifies it to a pedologist. This tundra soil (A) has a dark, peaty surface. Light-coloured, desert soil (B) is coarse and poor in organic matter. Chestnut-brown soil (C) and chernozem (D) – Russian for "black earth" – are humus-rich grassland soils typical of the steppes and the prairies of North America. The reddish, leached latosol (E) of tropical savannas has a very thin but rich humus layer. Podzolic soils are typical of northerly climates, where rainfall is heavy but evaporation is slow. They include the organically rich brown forest podzol (F), the grey-brown podzol (H) and the grey-stony podzol (I) that supports mixed growths of conifers and hardwoods. All are relatively acidic. The red-yellow podzol (G) of pine forests is quite highly leached.

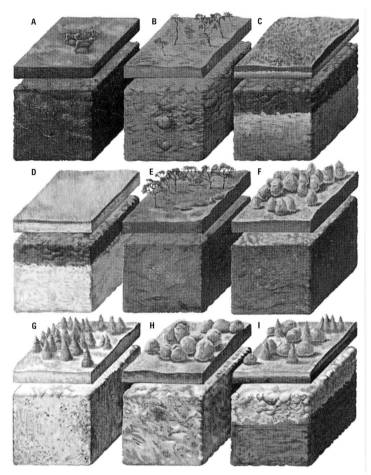

dens. Owing to its high saponin content, soapwort has traditionally been used for washing and cleaning. The pink or white flowers are produced in terminal clusters. Family Caryophyllaceae; species *Saponaria officinalis*.

sodalite

Glassy silicate mineral, sodium aluminium silicate with some chloride, found in alkaline IGNEOUS ROCKS. It occurs as small, dodecahedral crystals in the cubic system and also as masses. It may be colourless, white, blue or pink; it is sometimes used as a gemstone. Hardness 5–6; r.d. 2.2.

sodium-potassium pump

Process that exists in most cell MEMBRANES whereby sodium ions are actively removed from CELLS while potassium ions are actively absorbed from the surroundings.

soil

Surface layer of loose material resting on top of the rock that makes up the surface of the Earth. Soil consists of undissolved minerals, produced by the WEATHERING and breakdown of surface rocks, organic matter, water and gases. The organic remains provide the HUMUS and the inorganic particles provide the vital minerals. The inorganic fraction of the soil includes CLAY, SILT, SAND, GRAVEL and stone. Soils are according to their structure and texture. The structure is determined by the aggregation of particles. The four main textures of soil are sand, silt, clay and loam. Loam soils are the best for cultivation, since they are able to retain more water and nutrients. Erosion and mismanagement are the most common causes of soil infertility. Fertility can be restored with the correct use of FERTILIZERS. A SOIL PROFILE reveals a number of distinct SOIL HORIZONS (layers).

soil erosion

Process whereby SOIL is removed by a variety of agents, such as wind and rain, from the landsurface thus rendering the ground less fertile and open to degradation into BADLANDS. *See also* LEACHING

soil horizon

Layer of SOIL that shows in a SOIL PROFILE – a cross-section of the soil. Usually soil is divided into three horizons, designated A, B and C. A is the topsoil, B the subsoil and C the BEDROCK. Fine particles and organic HUMUS make up the **A horizon**, much more inorganic material and larger particles occur in the **B horizon**, and the **C horizon** is ROCK. There may be a layer of REGOLITH between the B and C horizons. *See also* CHERNOZEM; PODZOL

soil profile

Vertical view of layers of SOIL from the surface down to the unaltered parent material. It is used in classifying soils. A layer of soil in a soil profile is known as a SOIL HORIZON.

solar cell

Device that converts sunlight directly to electricity. It normally consists of a ***p*-type** silicon crystal coated with an ***n*-type**. Light radiation causes electrons to be released and creates a potential difference so current can flow between electrodes connected to the two crystals. All wavelengths shorter than one micrometre can create electrical energy. Cells convert about 10% of sunlight into useful energy. Solar cells are often used to power small electronic devices such as pocket calculators. Several thousand cells may be used in panels to provide power of a few hundred watts. *See also* SOLAR ENERGY

solar energy

Heat and light from the SUN consisting of electro-

magnetic radiation, including heat (infrared rays), light and radio waves. About 35% of the energy reaching the Earth is absorbed: most is spent evaporating moisture into CLOUDS, and some is converted into organic chemical energy by PHOTOSYNTHESIS in plants. All forms of energy (except nuclear energy) come ultimately from the Sun. SOLAR CELLS are used to power instruments on spacecraft, and experiments are being done to store solar energy in liquids from which electricity can be generated. The effective use of solar energy is hampered by the diurnal cycle, and by seasonal and climatic variations.

solar flare

Sudden and violent release of matter and energy from the Sun's surface, usually from the region of an active group of sunspots. In the **flash stage**, a flare builds to a maximum in a few minutes, after which it gradually fades and disappears within an hour or so. Flares emit radiation right across the electromagnetic spectrum. Charged particles are emitted, mostly ELECTRONS and PROTONS, and smaller numbers of neutrons and atomic nuclei. A flare can cause material to be ejected in bulk, most spectacularly in the form of prominences. When energetic particles from flares reach the Earth they may cause radio interference, magnetic storms and more intense AURORAE. Although not well understood, the origin of flares is believed to be connected with local discontinuities in the Sun's magnetic field.

solar wind

Steady flow of charged particles (mainly protons and electrons) accelerated by the high temperatures of the solar corona to velocities great enough to allow them to escape from the SUN's gravity. The solar wind deflects the tail of the Earth's MAGNETO-SPHERE and the tails of comets away from the Sun. Some solar wind particles get trapped in planetary magnetic fields. Closer to the Earth, some are trapped in the outer VAN ALLEN RADIATION BELTS; others reach the Earth's upper ATMOSPHERE in the region of the magnetic poles and cause AURORAE. The solar wind carries away about 10^{-13} of the Sun's mass per year. Its intensity increases during periods of solar activity.

soldier-fly

Any member of the family Stratiomyidae, a group of brightly coloured flies, some of which are aquatic. Some species have carnivorous larvae, but usually they are scavengers in leaves and other rotting matter. Adult soldier-flies have flattened bodies. They habitually bask in the sun, on the ground or plants, with their wings folded over their bodies. Order Diptera; suborder Brachycera; family Stratiomyidae; species include *Oxycera rara*.

sole

Any member of the family Soleidae, comprising *c*.100 species of marine flatfish found in the Atlantic Ocean from NW Africa to Norway. Perhaps the most

▲ **sole** The Dover sole (*Solea solea*) is a thick-bodied flatfish found in shallow waters from the Mediterranean to the North Sea. As with other members of the sole family, it has its eyes on the right-hand side. It often burrows in the sand of the seafloor. It feeds on small crustaceans and worms.

S

well-known species is *Solea solea* (the Dover sole). A food fish, it is green-grey or black-brown with dark spots. Length: to 60cm (24in). Family Soleidae.

solenodon

Either of two species of nocturnal insectivores that resemble large shrews. One species occurs in Cuba, the other in Hispaniola; both are endangered. They have long, scaly tails. Both species are thought to have poisonous saliva. Length: 30cm (12in). Family Solenodontidae; genus *Solenodon*.

solfatara

Small CRATER or vent in the Earth's surface through which steam and gases escape. Solfataras occur mostly in volcanic regions and many of the gases contain sulphur. They probably indicate an area of declining volcanic activity. *See also* VOLCANO

solitaire

Shy, thrush-like, woodland songbird. It is only seen occasionally but is notable for its beautiful, flute-like song. Its plumage is mostly sombre browns or greys, with buff wing patches. The solitaire is found in the Americas, where it feeds mainly on berries in wooded valleys and canyons. Length: 18–23cm (7–9in). Family Turdidae; genus *Myadestes*.

Solomon's seal (David's harp)

Any plant of the genus *Polygonatum*, a group of perennial plants native to cool, temperate regions of Europe and Asia. They have broad, waxy leaves and white, dangling flowers. Height: to 90cm (35in). Family Liliaceae.

solstice

Either of the two days each year when the Sun is at its greatest angular distance from the CELESTIAL EQUATOR, leading to the longest day and shortest night (**summer solstice**) in one hemisphere of the Earth, and the shortest day and longest night (**winter solstice**) in the other hemisphere. In the Northern Hemisphere, the summer solstice occurs on about 21 June, and the winter solstice on about 22 December. *See also* SEASONS

solute

Gaseous, liquid or solid substance that is dissolved in a SOLVENT to form a SOLUTION. Ionic solids, such as common salt, and sugars and starch dissolve in water. Liquids can dissolve in liquids; for example, ethanol and water are miscible – capable of mixing – in all proportions at room temperature. Some gases, for example hydrogen chloride (HCl), are soluble in water.

solute potential

Pressure that is created by the presence of SOLUTE molecules in a SOLUTION. The presence of solute molecules in a solution makes it more HYPERTONIC and so lowers its WATER POTENTIAL. As the solute molecules always lower the water potential the value of the solute potential is always negative. The relationship between the solute potential, PRESSURE POTENTIAL and water potential is shown in the equation:
water potential = solute potential + pressure potential

solution

Liquid (the SOLVENT) into which another substance (the SOLUTE) has dissolved. It is a liquid consisting of two or more chemically distinct compounds that are inseparable by filtering. The amount of a solute dissolved in a given volume of solvent is called the concentration of a solution. The ability of one substance

to dissolve another depends on the type of chemical bonding and the temperature. Heat can be released (an exothermic solution) or absorbed (an endothermic solution) during the formation of the solution.

solution

In geology, a form of chemical WEATHERING. It is particularly active in LIMESTONE areas where the JOINTS can be enlarged to form CAVES, GRIKES and POTHOLES. Solution can also be active in chalk areas and anywhere with rocks containing salts.

solvent

Liquid that dissolves a substance (the SOLUTE) without changing its composition to form a SOLUTION. Water is the most universal solvent, and many inorganic compounds dissolve in it. Ethanol (ethyl alcohol), ether, acetone (propanone) and tetrachloromethane (carbon tetrachloride) are common solvents for organic substances.

songlark

Slender, pipit-like WARBLER found in Australasia; it is so called because of its conspicuous lark-like flight song. Its plumage is reddish brown, streaked with brown above and white or sooty brown below. It is found in open grassy woodlands and scrub. Length: 16–25cm (6–10in). Family Sylviidae; genus *Cinclorhamphus*.

sorghum

Tropical cereal grass native to Africa and cultivated worldwide. Types raised for grain are varieties of *Sorghum vulgare,* which have leaves coated with white waxy blooms and flower heads that bear up to 3000 seeds. Sorghum yields meal, oil, starch and dextrose (a sugar). Height: 50–250cm (20–98in). Family Poaceae/Gramineae.

sorrel (dock)

Herbaceous perennial plant native to temperate regions. It has large leaves that can be cooked as a vegetable and small, green or brown flowers. Height: to 2m (6.6ft). Family Polygonaceae; genus *Rumex*; main species *Rumex acetosa.*

souslik

Any of several species of ground SQUIRREL found in alpine meadows of central Europe. The souslik has a mottled or marbled black coat, almost no external ears and a short tail. It feeds on seeds, shoots, roots, flowers and insects during the day. The souslik's complex burrow system contains individual dens. It hibernates through the winter, mates in March and the females give birth to between six and seven young in April and May. Head-body length: 19–22cm (7–9in); tail: 5–7cm (2–3in). Family

▲ **solenodon** The Cuban solenodon (*Solenodon cubanus*) is found only in a limited area of E Cuba. It feeds on beetles, crickets, termites and other invertebrates, which it locates by smell, using its long snout. Both species of solenodon are thought to use poisonous saliva to immobilize their prey.

◄ **sorghum** The most widely cultivated grain in Africa, sorghum is also commonly grown in Asia and the United States. It is more tolerant of a hot climate than corn and many other grains and is extremely resistant to drought. High in carbohydrates, sorghum is usually eaten after being ground into a paste and made into bread, cakes or porridge. It is also used extensively in the manufacture of beer.

Sciuridae; genus *Spermophilus*; species include the European souslik *Spermophilus citellus.*

soya bean

Annual plant native to China and Japan. It has oval, three-part leaves and small, usually lilac flowers. It is grown worldwide for food, forage and oil; its seeds are an important source of PROTEIN. Height 60cm (24in). Family Fabaceae/Leguminosae; species *Glycine max.*

spadebill

Any of several species of tiny, insect-eating perching birds found in the forests of South America. It has a stubby, broad, flat bill. It is mainly brown above and buff below, with strong face patterns. The spadebill is difficult to see and sits quietly for long periods before darting out to catch a passing insect. Length: 9–11cm (*c*.4in). Family Tyrannidae; genus *Platyrinchus.*

spadefoot toad

See TOAD, SPADEFOOT

spadix

In some flowering plants, a spike of small flowers, generally enclosed in a sheath called a SPATHE. A familiar plant with an inflorescence of this kind is the CUCKOOPINT (*Arum maculatum*).

Spanish fly

See BEETLE, OIL

Spanish moss

Epiphytic plant that grows in tropical and subtropical American forests; it is not a true moss. It is especially familiar on the oak of SE United States, where the loose grey clumps of Spanish moss hang from tree branches. Family Bromeliaceae; species *Tillandsia usneoides. See also* EPIPHYTE

sparrow

Any member of a large group of small, reddish-brown-streaked birds with stout bills for insect and seed eating. The sparrows of Europe, Asia and Africa (mainly of the genus *Passer*) are often gregarious and nest in large colonies. The sparrows of the Americas are more solitary and are classified in several different genera, including *Spizella*, *Passerculus* and *Zonotrichia*. Family Fringillidae, Ploceidae and Passeridae.

sparrow, chipping

Common sparrow of North and Central America; it is

readily identified by its bright chestnut crown and fairly long, notched tail. The male has white eyebrows. The chipping sparrow is common in gardens, grassy fields and woodland edges. Length: 14cm (6in). Family Fringillidae; species *Spizella passerina*.

sparrow, house
Small brown bird that is familiar worldwide, usually associated with human habitation. It is the common brown bird of Europe, Asia and North Africa. It has been introduced to and has colonized most other parts of the world where humans have settled. Length: 14cm (6in). Family Passeridae; species *Passer domesticus*.

sparrow, tree
Eurasian sparrow. It is similar to the house sparrow, having a chestnut crown and brown plumage streaked black, but it has a distinctive black ear patch. The males and females have the same plumage. In Europe populations have recently declined dramatically due to intensive agriculture. Length: 14cm (6in). Family Fringillidae; species *Passer montanus*.

sparrow, Java
Striking bird found in Southeast Asia. It has a grey back, a black tail, a thick red bill, a black crown, a black throat and contrasting white cheeks. It is a popular cage bird, and escapees have established colonies in Asia and Africa, especially where rice is cultivated. Length: 13cm (5in). Family Estrildidae; species *Lonchura oryzivora*.

sparrow, song
Common North American sparrow. Its upperparts are mostly brown streaked with black; its underparts are white with black streaks on the breast. It has a long rounded tail, which is pumped in flight. The song sparrow is common in bushy areas, especially dense streamside thickets. Length: 16cm (6in). Family Fringillidae; species *Melospiza melodia*.

sparrowhawk
Any of several species that belong to the world's largest group of BIRDS OF PREY. The sparrowhawk is recognized by its combination of long tail and rather short, broad, rounded wings. Its flight is fast and dashing, interspersed with short glides. The female is larger than the male. The sparrowhawk hunts birds along hedgerows and in woodlands and scrub. Family Accipitridae; genus *Accipiter*.

sparrowhawk, northern (Eurasian sparrowhawk)
Common HAWK of Europe and N Asia. The male is slate-grey above, whereas the larger female is brown; both sexes have barred underparts. In the 1960s the northern sparrowhawk's European population crashed due to pesticide poisoning; it is now recovering. Length: 28–38cm (11–15in); wingspan: 55–70cm (22–28in). Family Accipitridae; species *Accipiter nisus*.

sparrowhawk, tiny
Secretive African sparrowhawk. It is dark slaty grey above, with a distinctive white rump; its dark tail has two white spots on the upperside. The undersides and under wings are barred with a reddish-brown blush, and its legs are yellow. Length: 25–30cm (10–12in). Family Accipitridae; species *Accipiter minullus*.

sparrowhawk, collared
Sparrowhawk of Australasia; it is distinguished by its slightly forked tail and pale, reddish-brown collar. It often soars until it is nearly invisible and

throws itself about in dives, loops and twists. It usually flies straight before stooping on prey at an astonishing speed. Length: 30–40cm (12–16in); wingspan: to 76cm (30in). Family Accipitridae; species *Accipiter cirrhocephalus*.

sparrow-weaver
Any of several species of thick-billed birds found in central and S Africa. The white-browed sparrow-weaver (*Plocepasser mahali*) is brown above and pale below, with a black crown, white eyebrow, a white rump and white wing bars. The sparrow-weaver is a conspicuous and active bird of thorn bush country, where it feeds on seeds and insects. It nests all year round. Length: 18cm (7in). Family Ploceidae; genus *Plocepasser*.

spathe
Broad, leaf-like organ that spreads from the base of, or enfolds, the SPADIX of certain plants, such as the CUCKOOPINT (*Arum maculatum*).

spearfish
Any of several species of marine fish belonging to the genus *Tetrapturus*. The spearfish is silvery blue, with a long bill. Its smaller dorsal fin distinguishes it from the related SAILFISH. It is a popular sport fish. Length: 1.8m (6ft). Family Istiophoridae; species include *Tetrapturus angustirostris* (Pacific shortbill) and *Tetrapturus pfleugeri* (W Atlantic spearfish).

spearmint
Hardy perennial herb of the MINT family. Its leaves are used for flavouring, especially in sweets. Oil distilled from spearmint is used as a medicine. The plant has pink or lilac flowers that grow in spikes. Family Lamiaceae/Labiatae; species *Mentha spicata*.

spearwort
Perennial, semi-aquatic herb, typically found in marshes or along pond sides. Greater spearwort (*Ranunculus lingua*) is a vigorous, strongly stoloniferous plant, with oval leaves and large yellow buttercup flowers. It is native from Europe to Siberia and is often grown as an ornamental. Lesser spearwort (*Ranunculus flammula*) is found from Europe to temperate Asia. It is less robust and has smaller flowers. Family Ranunculaceae.

speciation
Emergence of new species in EVOLUTION. It results from the separation of parts of a homogeneous population. Over many generations, NATURAL SELECTION operates within the separated groups to produce gradually increasing differences. New species

◀ **soya bean** Now grown extensively throughout the world, soya beans are native to China, where they were first cultivated some 4000 years ago. They were introduced into North America in 1880. Their flowers vary from pure white to light purple. The beans themselves are yellow, brown or black, depending on the variety. Cultivation has spread in response to the increasing world demand for protein. The main areas of cultivation are the United States, with more than half of world production, and the Far East, notably China, Japan and Korea.

can be said to have evolved when individuals of the separated groups are no longer capable of interbreeding. *See also* SELECTION

species
Part of the CLASSIFICATION of living organisms. Species are groups of physically and genetically similar individuals that can interbreed to produce fertile offspring under natural conditions. Each species has a unique two-part Latin name (BINOMIAL NOMENCLATURE), the first part being the GENUS name. This name is written in italics. For example, the tiger's species name is *Panthera tigris*, *Panthera* being the genus of big cats. So far, more than 1.5 million plant and animal species have been identified, but estimates of the total number on land and in the oceans run as high as 100 million.

species diversity
Number and range of different SPECIES found in an ECOSYSTEM. A measure of species diversity is helpful when considering the factors that influence an ecosystem. In general, a stable ecosystem has a wide range of different species, each with a similar POPULATION size, and is dominated by BIOTIC factors. A less stable ecosystem, such as one under stress due to POLLUTION or extreme climatic conditions, has just a few species with very large populations and is dominated by ABIOTIC factors.

spectacled bear
See BEAR, SPECTACLED

speedwell (veronica)
Any member of the widely distributed genus *Veronica*, comprising *c*.250 species of annual and perennial, herbaceous plants of the FIGWORT family. The small flowers are white, blue or pink. Height: 7–153cm (3–60in). Family Scrophulariaceae; species include *Veronica officinalis* (common speedwell).

speleology
Scientific study of CAVES and cave systems. Also included are the hydrological and geological studies concerned with the rate of formation of STALAGMITES and STALACTITES, and the influence of GROUNDWATER conditions on cave formation. A special aspect is the study of the animals that live in caves.

sperm (spermatozoon)
Male sex cell (GAMETE) in sexually reproducing organisms. It corresponds to the female OVUM. The head of the sperm contains the genetic material of the male parent. The tail or other motile structure provides the means of moving the sperm to the ovum to carry out FERTILIZATION. *See also* SEXUAL REPRODUCTION

spermatogenesis
See feature article, page 358

spermatophyte
Traditionally a member of the division of seed-bearing plants (Spermatophyta), including most trees, shrubs and herbaceous plants. A spermatophyte has a stem, leaves, roots and a well-developed vascular system. The dominant generation is the SPOROPHYTE. The widely accepted Five Kingdoms classification now classifies seed plants as several distinct phyla: the Angiospermophyta (ANGIOSPERMS or flowering plants), Coniferophyta (CONIFERS), Ginkgophyta (GINKGO or maidenhair tree), Cycadophyta (CYCADS) and Gnetophyta (a group of cone-bearing desert plants).

S

SPERMATOGENESIS

Process by which SPERM are formed. Sperm (spermatozoa) are produced by a series of cell divisions that takes place in the seminiferous tubules of a male animal's TESTES. Initially, germ cells divide to produce **spermatogonia**, which further divide to form **spermatocytes**. These finally divide yet again to produce **spermatids**, which develop into spermatazoa.

▼ **Immature sex cells** in the testes divide by mitosis to become primary spermatocytes. Each one then divides by meiosis, a type of cell division peculiar to the reproductive organs, to form two secondary spermatocytes, each containing half the full number of chromosomes. A second meiotic division splits each of the spermatocytes into two spermatids, which then mature into sperm.

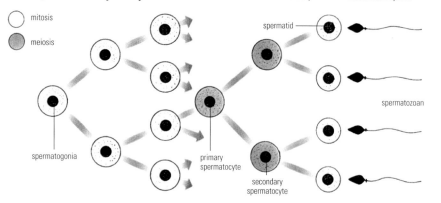

mitosis

meiosis

spermatogonia

primary spermatocyte

secondary spermatocyte

spermatid

spermatozoan

sphagnum
Any member of the genus *Sphagnum*, a group of MOSSES that grow on boggy soils. When decomposed under boggy conditions, sphagnum moss forms PEAT MOSS, which is much used in horticulture. Family Sphagnaceae.

spider
Active predatory ARACHNID with sharp, fang-like mouthparts and an unsegmented abdomen. It produces silk from special glands and uses this for many purposes, including web-making. Worldwide there are *c*.30,000 known species. Class Arachnida; subclass Araneae.

spider, bird-eating
Any of 400 species of tropical and subtropical, large, hairy spiders. It is sometimes erroneously called a tarantula. The bird-eating spider is a nocturnal, ground-based hunter, which preys on arthropods and vertebrates. Its enlarged chelicerae (paired prehensile appendages) are used to crush the prey. Following a powerful, vertical bite, the spider pours digestive juices over the prey. The liquidized prey is then sucked up. Many species can live for 10–30 years and are kept as pets. Adult body length: 12cm (5in). Family Theraphosidae; species include *Poecilitheria regalis*.

spider, black widow
Any member of the genus *Latrodectus*, a group of small spiders found in many warm regions of the world. The black widow spider is black, with red, hour-glass-shaped marks on its underside. Its bite is poisonous, though rarely fatal to humans. Length: 25mm (1in); the male is smaller. Family Theridae; species include *Latrodectus mactans*.

spider, bolas (angling or fishing spider)
Squat spider found in Australasia, Africa and North and South America. It is highly adapted to capturing moths, being camouflaged with horns and "warts" and able to remain motionless, hidden on twigs, for days at a time. When the time is right, the spider produces a silken line laced with one or more blobs of a sticky substance. It then whirls this line about and waits for a moth to be attracted to the female moth pheromones in the "glue". Within minutes a male

moth is trapped by the bolas. The spider's bite is potentially toxic to humans. Adult body length: 45mm (2in). Family Araneidae; species include *Dichrostichus magnificus. See also* SPIDER, ORB-WEB

spider, crab
Any member of the family Thomisidae, a group of webless spiders found worldwide. The crab spider walks sideways like a crab. It imitates the colours of the flowers on which it hides; it then grab its prey as it comes to feed. The spider injects venom into its victim's nervous system or blood or both. Length: 20mm (0.8in). Family Thomisidae.

spider, fishing
Any of several species of spider that can walk over water. The fishing spider feeds on aquatic insects but is large enough also to prey on small fish and tadpoles. Some species have sensitive legs that "hear" when the surface of the water has been broken and can pinpoint the location of the prey. Some species court fish by dabbling their front legs, thus mimicking a fly. The fishing spider's hairs can trap air, permitting 30 minutes of submerged hunting. Fishing spiders resemble wolf spiders (family Lycosidae) but have a different eye pattern. Adult leg span: 12mm (0.5in). Family Pisauridae; genera include *Dolomedes*.

spider, house
Any member of a family of funnel-weaving spiders; it is typified by the large spider often found in domestic bath tubs. The narrow front of the cephalothorax bears eight eyes. After mating, the pair remain together until the male dies. Parental care is high in the family, with the young being fed regurgitated food. More than 700 species are known throughout the world, all of which are carnivorous. Adult body length: 20mm (0.8in). Family Agelenidae; species include *Tegenaria domestica*.

spider, huntsman
Any member of the family Heteropodidae, comprising more than 1000 species of carnivorous spiders found worldwide. At night, the huntsman spider rushes onto prey from its hiding places under stones, bark and vegetation. Due to this mode of prey capture, the spider is drab with few distinctive markings. Its legs are often long and slender, affording great agility. There is evidence that many of the species display complex courtship. Spiderlings are released from an egg sac that is guarded by the female. Adult body length: 10–30mm (0.4–1.2in). Family Heteropodidae; genera include *Heteropoda*.

◄ **spider, bird-eating** The bird-eating spider *Sericopelma communis* of Panama is a fiercely predatory spider. It is shown here with its hummingbird prey. It is relatively harmless to larger creatures, however, having venom about as potent as that of a bee.

S

spider, jumping

Spider that leaps onto its prey. It trails a strand of silk, which it uses to return to its place of rest. Most jumping spiders are brightly coloured and active during the day. Length: to 18mm (0.7in). Family Salticidae.

spider, money

Small spider with large chelicerae and sharp teeth. The species range widely in colour. The money spider's legs often have strong bristles. It is so called because of a superstition that if a money spider lands on someone and is twirled around the head three times, good fortune will result. There are more than 4200 species worldwide. They can travel great distances by ballooning on silken threads. Adult body length: 1–10mm (0.04–0.4in). Family Linyphiidae; genera include *Gonatium*.

spider, nursery web

Any of *c*.550 species of spider named after the protective web spun by the female for her young. The nursery web spider is similar in appearance to the wolf spider, but has smaller eyes. Its colour ranges from brown to grey, with lighter coloured legs. The egg sac is carried by the female in her chelicerae. As soon as the brood hatches, a web is spun in vegetation and the female stands guard. Nursery web spiders are found worldwide. Adult body length: 10–26mm (0.4–1in). Family Pisauridae.

spider, ogre-faced (gladiator spider)

Any of many species of spider found in the tropics, as well as in Australia and North America. The ogre-faced spider is characterized by its huge eyes. It inhabits dense scrub, where it remains motionless for the daytime, cryptically protected to look like twigs. At night, it spins an extremely elastic net across its first two pairs of legs. The spider then lowers itself down below the bush and waits for prey to come in range. If this occurs, it drops the net onto the prey, rolls it up and then eats it. If no prey is caught that evening, the net is eaten and a new net spun the following evening. Families include Dinopidae; genera include *Dinopis*.

spider, orb-web

Any member of the spider family Araneidae. The abdomens of orb-web spiders vary greatly in terms of size, shape and colour. The legs have three claws and can be very spiny. The male is often smaller than the female. The webs consist of a central hub, which is then followed by radiating lines and spirals. In some species, for example bolas spiders, moths are caught on a single line. Orb-web spiders are found worldwide, and some webs are extremely strong, for example those of spiders in the *Nephilia* genus. Adult body length: 2–46mm (0.08–1.8in). Family Araneidae; genera include *Araneus*, *Argiope*, *Celaenia*, *Nephila* and *Micrathena*.

spider, spitting

Any of more than 180 spider species found mainly under rocks and on sunny buildings. It is an unusual spider, having only six eyes and having a first pair of legs that is longer than the others. Its carapace is domed towards the rear, where the glue-producing glands are situated. The spider captures its prey by moving its chelicerae rapidly from side to side; this action "spits" two streams of glue at the prey from close range and can affix it to the substrate. Spitting spiders are found worldwide, especially in warm regions, apart from Australia and New Zealand. Adult body length: 4–12mm (0.2–0.5in). Family Scytodidae; genus *Scytodes*.

▲ **spider, tarantula**
Tarantulas of the genus *Aphonopelma*, such as the species shown here, are found in sw United States. They usually dig burrows in which they hide during the day, becoming active in the late afternoon. They feed on small insects and other spiders.

spider, tarantula

Large, hairy wolf SPIDER native to s Europe. It was once thought to inflict a deadly bite that would cause madness. The tarantula spider spins no web; instead it chases and pounces on its prey. Adult body length: to 25mm (1in). Family Lycosidae; species *Lycosa tarantula*. The name **tarantula** is also applied to the sluggish, dark, hairy spiders of sw United States, Mexico and South America. Many species burrow and feed on insects. Adult body length: to 75mm (3in). Family Theraphosidae; genera *Aphonopelma* and *Eurypelma*.

spider, trap-door

Any of numerous species of brown and black spiders found worldwide. The trap-door spider digs a tube-like, silk-lined burrow with a hinged lid covering the entrance. When the spider feels vibrations from passing prey, it rushes out and retreats with its captive. Length: to 30mm (1.2in). Families include Ctenizidae and Actinopodidae (part); genera include *Actinopus*.

spider, tube-web

Any of more than 250 species of spider found worldwide. The tube-web spider has a distinctive appearance, with six eyes, enlarged chelicerae with long fangs, and a pinkish-grey abdomen. Many species are nocturnal and hunt on the ground or make tubular silk webs in cavities in bark, wood or small stones. Adult body length: 6–24mm (0.2–0.9in). Family Dysderidae; species include *Dysdera crocata* (woodlouse-eating spider).

spider, wandering

Any of more than 600 species of spider found on low-growing plants in many tropical and subtropical areas.

The wandering spider is a nocturnal, nomadic and aggressive hunter; some species are dangerous to humans. It is recognisable by a groove that runs lengthways down the rear portion of its carapace. Due to their nomadic habit, the female lays eggs in a sac that she carries with her. Adult body length: 15–50mm (0.6–2in). Family Ctenidae; genera include *Ctenus*.

spider, water

Sole member of the Argyronetidae family to be found in Europe. It lives almost permanently under water, using a bell-shaped tent of air that it traps by virtue of a sheet of silk placed in vegetation underwater. The spider adds more air to this diving-bell using its specially adapted hairy abdomen and third and fourth pairs of legs. It stalks small fish and tadpoles and takes them back to the bell to be consumed. After mating, eggs are wrapped in silk and left at the top of the bell to hatch. Adult body length: 7–15mm (0.3–0.6in). Family Argyronetidae; species *Argyroneta aquatica*.

spider, wolf

Any member of a family of spiders that are found in many different habitats; some species are even found in the Arctic. The wolf spider's colouring varies from brown to grey, with many variations of stripes and dots. Its head is narrow, and its front two pairs of legs have many strong spines. It has four large eyes and four smaller ones, arranged such that the best hunting view is afforded. Wolf spiders hunt at night by simple ambush capture. Many species show a high degree of parental care, the female carrying the egg sac on her spinnerets. Adult body length: 4–40mm (0.2–1.6in). Family Lycosidae; genera include *Pardosa*; there are more than 3000 species.

spider crab

See CRAB, SPIDER

spiderhunter

Forest bird of Southeast Asia. Despite its name, it is a blossom feeder, especially on the flowers of the wild banana. The spiderhunter's plumage is dull or streaked green, and it has a long, down-curved bill. It is an active feeder and often hangs upside down while probing for nectar. Length: 16–19cm (6–7in). Family Nectariniidae; genus *Arachnothera*.

spider monkey

See MONKEY, SPIDER

spider plant

Plant, native to s Africa, with green or green and white, arching, grass-like leaves. Plantlets and tiny flowers grow on long stems from the plant base. It is a popular house plant, well-suited to bright indirect

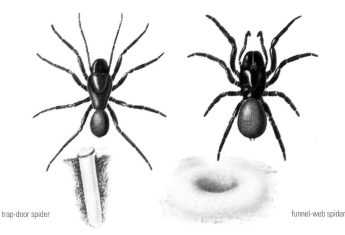

trap-door spider

funnel-web spider

◄ **spider** The trap-door spider (*Actinopus* sp.) and the Australian funnel-web spider (*Atrax robustus*) are among the many species that show great ingenuity in the ways in which they trap prey. The funnel-web spider has a silken burrow with a funnel-shaped entrance. Its prey slips down the funnel to be ensnared below and killed by the spider's venomous bite. The trap-door spider makes a burrow. Over the entrance is a hinged "door", which the spider can open quickly in order to grab passing insects.

S

light and moist soil. Propagation is by plantlets or root division. Height: to 46cm (18in). Family Liliaceae; species *Chlorophytum comosum*.

spiderwort

Any member of the genus *Tradescantia*, comprising several species of perennial plants native to North and South America. The spiderwort has long, keeled, grass-like leaves and flat-topped clusters of blue, rosy purple or white flowers. Family Commelinaceae; genus *Tradescantia*.

spike cap (pine spike cap)

FUNGUS that produces red-brick-coloured fruiting bodies that dry to a shiny surface; it has wine-coloured flesh in the cap and stem. The taste and smell are somewhat astringent, and, although edible, eating it is not recommended. The fungus is usually found with pine trees. Phylum Basidiomycota; species *Chroogomphus rutilus*.

spikenard

Plant that is native to the Himalayan region. It has fragrant rhizomes, which yield an oil esteemed as a perfume. It was formerly prized for salves in Roman society. Family Valerianaceae; species *Nardostachys grandiflora*. **Spikenard**, or American spikenard, also refers to a perennial plant native to rich woodlands of E North America. It has a large, thick, aromatic rootstock, which was pounded by some of the Native North American tribes to form a poultice to reduce swellings. Family Araliaceae; species *Aralia racemosa*.

spilite

Fine-grained, extrusive IGNEOUS ROCK found near VOLCANOES. The dark-coloured rock occurs as PILLOW LAVA, which is formed where LAVA from a volcanic eruption flows into the sea; it often contains cavities formed by gas bubbles. It is a basic rock containing up to 40% silica, and more sodium than basalt, the common volcanic rock.

spinach

Herbaceous annual plant cultivated in areas with cool summers. Spinach is used as a culinary herb and as a vegetable. Family Chenopodiaceae; species *Spinacia oleracea*.

spinal column

See SPINE

spinal cord

In vertebrates, tubular, central nerve cord, lying within the SPINE (vertebral column or backbone) and bathed in cerebrospinal fluid. It connects the PERIPHERAL NERVOUS SYSTEM to the BRAIN, with which it makes up the CENTRAL NERVOUS SYSTEM (CNS). It gives rise to the 31 pairs of spinal nerves, each of which has sensory and motor fibres. *See also* NERVOUS SYSTEM

spindle

Rod-shaped structure formed from MICROTUBULES in the CYTOPLASM of cells during MITOSIS or MEIOSIS. CHROMOSOMES are attached at the bulge of the spindle, which is known as the equator. The spindle draws the chromosomes apart, causing a cell to divide. *See also* ANAPHASE; METAPHASE

spindle tree

Deciduous shrub or small tree native to Europe and W Asia. It is distinguished by having many branches. Its inconspicuous, yellowish-green flowers produce red or pink, deeply four-lobed capsules with white seeds

bearing an orange aril. The spindle tree's wood, which is tough and close-grained, was used for spindles in home spinning. Family Celastraceae; species *Euonymus europaeus*.

spine

Backbone of VERTEBRATES, extending from the base of the SKULL to the tip of the tail and enclosing the SPINAL CORD. The human spine consists of 26 small vertebrae interspersed with INTERVERTEBRAL DISCS of CARTILAGE. It comprises seven cervical, 12 thoracic and five lumbar vertebrae. The five sacral and four vertebrae of the coccyx fuse together to make two solid bones. The spine articulates with the bones of the skull, ribs and hip bones and provides points of attachment for the back muscles. *See also* SKELETON

spinebill

Either of two species of small, blossom-feeding birds found in Australia. They are distinguished by their very long, fine, curved bills. Spinebills are very active. They hover at blossoms, rather like hummingbirds. Their flight is fast and erratic, with their tails displayed to show prominent white outer feathers. Length: 15–16cm (*c*.6in). Family Meliphagidae; genus *Acanthorhynchus*.

spinel

Oxide mineral, magnesium aluminium oxide (MgAl$_2$O$_4$), found in IGNEOUS and METAMORPHIC ROCKS. It has cubic system, frequently twinned, octahedral crystals. It is either glassy black, red, blue, brown or white in colour. Ruby spinel from Sri Lanka is a valuable gemstone. Hardness 7.5–8; r.d. 3.8.

spinetail (wiretail)

Any member of a large group of small, insect-eating birds native to South America. Spinetails prefer deep shade, making them hard to see as they skulk in forest thickets. They are mainly rich reddish-brown in colour, with a long double-pointed tail, which has two spiky central feathers. Length: 13–17cm (5–7in). Family Furnariidae; species include *Sylviorthorhynchus desmursii*.

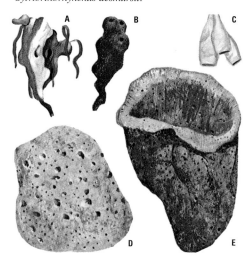

▲ **sponge** Classified according to the composition of the supporting skeleton, sponges include the breadcrumb sponge *Halichondria panica* (A), with a skeleton (B) made up of spicules of silicon, and the purse sponge *Grantia compressa* (C), which has a skeleton of calcium carbonate spicules. Two commercial sponges, *Hippospongia equina* (D) and *Euspongia officinalis* (E), have skeletons of a horny, elastic substance called spongin. After harvesting from the seabed, sponges are dried, beaten and washed to remove hard debris so that the only part remaining is the skeleton.

spinifex

Any member of the genus *Spinifex*, a group of sharp, tufted grasses found in coastal sandy or desert areas of Australia. Family Poaceae/Gramineae.

spinifexbird (desert bird)

Small, uncommon WARBLER species found in Australia; it is named after its grassland habitat. The spinifexbird is brown above and buff below, with a buff eyebrow. Its tail is as long as its body and is cocked as it dashes between tall clumps of grass. Length 14–16cm (*c*.6in). Family Sylviidae; species *Eremiornis carteri*.

spiny-headed worm (acanthocephalan)

Any member of the phylum Acanthocephala, comprising worms that parasitize the digestive tracts of vertebrates. The larvae develop in the intestines of crustaceans. The spiny-headed worm is named after its retractible proboscide, which bears a number of spines that facilitate firm attachment to the host's intestines. Human infection is rare. Phylum Acanthocephala.

spiracle

External opening used for RESPIRATION in various animals. In insects and spiders, the spiracle is the opening to a TRACHEA. In sharks, rays and some bony fish, water passes through a pair of spiracles during GILL respiration. In whales, the nasal opening is called a spiracle.

spiraea

Any member of the genus *Spiraea*, a group of flowering perennial shrubs native to the Northern Hemisphere. They have small, flat leaves and produce clusters of small, white, pink or red flowers. Many of the 100 species are grown as ornamentals. Height: 1.5m (4.9ft). Family Rosaceae.

spire shell

Type of SHELL that is characteristic of many species of marine SNAIL. It has an enlarged conical spire, which contains little or none of the snail's soft body parts. The body whorl, which is distinctly separated from the spire, contains the soft parts and, in most species, also accommodates the muscular foot. Phylum Mollusca; class Gastropoda; order Mesogastropoda. *See also* GASTROPOD

spirochaete

General name applied to a group of protozoa-like BACTERIA that are spiral-rod shaped and capable of flexing and wriggling their bodies. Syphilis is the best-known disease caused by a spirochete (*Treponema pallidum*).

spit

On a coastline, ridge of sand or shingle that has been built up as a result of LONGSHORE DRIFT. A spit is attached to the land at one end; it may consist of sand, mud, shingle or any combination of these. Most spits protrude across an ESTUARY, which they may eventually block to form a DELTA.

spittlebug

See FROGHOPPER

spleen

Dark-red organ found in most vertebrate species; it is located on the left side of the abdomen, behind and slightly below the stomach. It is important in both the BLOOD and LYMPHATIC SYSTEMS, helping to process LYMPHOCYTES, destroying worn out or damaged ERYTHROCYTES (red blood cells) and storing iron.

S

spleenwort
See ASPLENIUM

spodumene
Silicate mineral, lithium aluminium silicate ($LiAlSi_2O_6$). It is the chief source of lithium. Spodumene displays monoclinic system prismatic crystals or masses. It is opaque or transparent in many hues, and the transparent lilac and green varieties are used as gems. Hardness 6.5–7; r.d. 3.2.

sponge
Multicellular animal that must live in water to survive; it is found in both aquatic and marine environments. Sponges can be divided into three classes. **Calcarea** contains the calcareous sponges, such as the purse sponge (genus *Grantia*), which have a rigid mineral skeleton composed of calcium carbonate. The **Hexactinellida** class contains the glass sponges, which are usually found in the deep ocean. They have skeletons that are partially composed of silaceous particles called spicules. The **Demospongiae** class contains sponges with skeletons composed of either spicules or of a soft protein called spongin. Examples include the bath sponge (genus *Spongia*), the brain sponge (genera include *Guitara* and *Tethya*) and the breadcrumb sponge (genus *Halichondria*). Bath sponges continue to be harvested from the ocean for use in human bathing, but cleaning sponges are manufactured from cellulose or plastic. Phylum Porifera. *See also* PORIFERAN

spontaneous generation
Belief, now discredited, that living organisms arise from non-living matter. It supposedly explained the sudden appearance of maggots on decaying meat. *See also* EVOLUTION

spoonbill
Any of several species of heron-sized wading birds that, unlike the heron, fly with their necks outstretched. The spoonbill's long bill is spoon-shaped at the tip. Most species are all white, but some, such as the roseate spoonbill (*Ajaia ajaja*), are pink. Other species are distinguished by their bill colour, for example the yellow-billed spoonbill (*Platalea flavipes*) and the African spoonbill (*Platalea alba*), which has a pink bill and legs. Length: 60–80cm (24–31in). Family Threskiornithidae; genus *Platalea*.

spoon worm (echiuran)
Any member of the phylum Echiura, comprising worms that are closely related to ANNELIDS but that have a different segmentation. Spoon worms are found in marine and estuarine environments, where they burrow in the sediment. Most spoon worm species feed on sedimentary detritus, using their extensible proboscides, but some species filter planktonic organisms from the water with mucous nets. Phylum Echiura.

sporangium
Walled structure that produces SPORES in plants and some protozoa. It is found in groups on fern FRONDS.

spore
Small reproductive body that detaches from the parent organism to produce new offspring without having to fuse with another reproductive cell. Mostly microscopic, spores may consist of one or several cells (but do not contain an embryo) and are produced in large numbers. Some germinate rapidly, others "rest", surviving unfavourable environmental conditions. Spores are formed by FERNS, HORSETAILS, MOSSES, FUNGI, BACTERIA and some PROTOZOA.

◀ **spruce** The white spruce (*Picea glauca*) grows in Canada and Alaska and survives at very northerly latitudes. It is found in a wide variety of habitats within its range. Like other spruces, it is a prized timber tree. It reaches a height of 23m (75ft). Its cones are slender and elongated and it has light grey to brown bark.

Spores are formed during the SPOROPHYTE stage in the life cycle of such organisms. *See also* GAMETE

sporophyte
DIPLOID (having two sets of chromosomes) stage in the life cycle of plants or algae. In most plants and algae, the sporophyte gives rise to HAPLOID (having only one set of chromosomes) spores, which germinate to produce a haploid generation (the GAMETO-PHYTE stage). The haploid generation produces the GAMETES. In FERNS, HORSETAILS, CONIFERS and ANGIOSPERMS, the diploid sporophyte is the dominant phase of the life cycle – it is the plant body usually seen. In MOSSES and LIVERWORTS, the main plant body is the gametophyte. *See also* ALTERNATION OF GENERATIONS

sprat (brisling)
Small, herring-like, commercial fish that is found in the N Atlantic Ocean. It is slender and silvery. Length: to 13cm (5in). Family Clupeidae; species *Clupea sprattus*.

Sprengel, Christian (1750–1816)
German botanist and teacher. His studies of sex in plants and theories of fertilization form a basis for much knowledge in this field. He discovered that nectaries, organs that produce NECTAR in flowers, have specific colours to attract insects. Insects, he determined, convey POLLEN to the PISTILS of certain flowers from the STAMENS of others.

spring
Point on the Earth's surface at which underground water emerges. Springs may emerge at points on dry land or in the beds of streams or ponds. They are generally located where there is a change of rock type, and the water flows out at the top of an impervious layer, such as slate, shale or clay. Springs are an important part of the water cycle. The mineral content of spring water varies with the surrounding soil or rocks.

springbuck (springbok)
Small, horned ANTELOPE native to S Africa; it is the national emblem of South Africa. The reddish-brown colour on its back shades into a dark horizontal band just above the white underside. Height: to 90cm (35in) at the shoulder. Family Bovidae; species *Antidorcas marsupialis*.

springhare (springhaas)
Rodent found in central, E and S Africa. Its long, silky fur is buff- or reddish-brown above and white beneath. Its long tail has a thick, black brush at the end. The springhare has short front limbs; it has long, sharp fingers with curved claws for digging. Its hind limbs are long and kangaroo-like for hopping. The springhare lives in burrows in arid, sandy areas, coming out at night to search for bulbs, roots and grains. Head-body length: 35–43cm (14–17in); tail: 37–47cm (15–19in). Family Pedetidae; species *Pedetes capensis*.

spring peeper
Tree FROG native to E and S United States and S Canada. It is found on low tree branches or on the ground. The spring peeper is brown with a dark, cross-shaped mark on its back. Its high, peeping mating call is a characteristic sign of spring. Length: 40mm (1.6in). Family Hylidae; species *Hyla crucifer*.

springtail (collembolan)
Any member of the phylum Collembola, comprising *c*.2000 species of tiny, wingless insects found worldwide. They live in damp places, such as rotting vegetation and under stones and fallen logs. Springtail species vary in colour. They can jump up to *c*.10cm (*c*.4in) by forcing downwards and backwards using a lever-like, forked tail under the abdomen. Length: 3–10mm (0.1–0.4in). Order Collembola.

spruce
Any member of the genus *Picea*, a group of evergreen trees, related to FIRS, that are native to mountainous or cooler temperate regions of the Northern Hemisphere. The spruce tree is pyramid-shaped and dense, with angular rather than flattened needles and pendulous cones. The timber is used in cabinet-making. Some species yield turpentine. Height: to 50m (160ft). Family Pinaceae; genus *Picea*.

spurfowl
Stocky, grey-brown gamebird of central Africa. It is named after a conspicuous spur on its hind legs. It has a patch of bare red facial skin around its eyes. The spurfowl is found in grassy areas with scattered trees and in dense undergrowth along streams. Length 25–35cm (10–14in). Family Phasianidae; genus *Francolinus*.

spurge
See EUPHORBIA

squash
Any of several species of vine fruits of various shapes, for example the PUMPKIN, all of which belong to the genus *Cucurbita*. Squashes are native to the Americas and are cultivated as vegetables. Family Cucurbitaceae.

squash bug
Brown to grey bug found only in the Western Hemisphere. It sucks juices from the leaves of pumpkin, squash and related plants. There is one generation per year. Length: 13mm (0.5in). Family Coreidae; species *Anasa tristis*.

squat lobster
Any of a group of rather small, dumpy, lobster-like CRUSTACEANS. They are related to hermit and porce-

S

◀ **squash** The many types of edible squash include the winter squash (*Cucurbita maxima*) shown here. Squash grow in a range of colours and shapes. There are also several varieties of inedible squash, which are sometimes dried and used as, for example, bowls or cups.

S

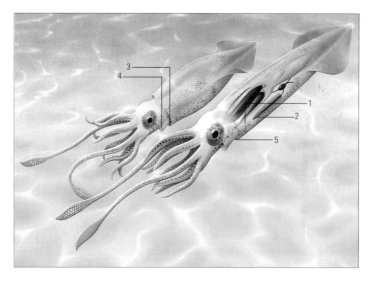

► **squid** Squids use jet-propulsion to propel themselves through the water. The highly muscular mantle cavity (1) completely encloses its gills (2). To generate a jet of water, muscles in the mantle enlarge the mantle cavity and water is sucked in through a wide slit at the front end of the body (3). Water is prevented from flowing up the funnel (4) by a one-way valve. The mantle muscles then contract the mantle, forcing the water out through the funnel. The overlapping edges of the slit (5) prevent any outflow, and ensure that all the water is expelled from the funnel in a narrow jet for maximum thrust.

lain CRABS. The abdomen is flexed underneath the thorax. Squat lobsters are more elongated than crabs, with long front limbs armed with sharp pincers. Order Decapoda; family Galatheidae; genera include *Galathea*.

squid

Any of numerous species of marine, cephalopod MOLLUSCS that have a cylindrical body with an internal horny plate (the pen) that serves as a skeleton. The squid has eight short, suckered tentacles surrounding its mouth, in addition to which there are two longer, arm-like tentacles that can be shot out to seize moving prey. Several species of giant squid (genus *Architeuthis*) can reach up to 20m (65ft) in length. Class Cephalopoda; order Teuthoidea.

squill

Perennial plant from the Mediterranean region. Its large bulbs are used medicinally as a cardiac stimulant. A red form from North Africa is a source of rat poison. Since 1946 squill has been grown commercially in the United States. The action of squill resembles that of DIGITALIS but is less potent. Family Liliaceae; species *Drimia maritima*.

squirrel

Any of many species of mainly tree-living rodents.

Squirrels have rat-like bodies and long, usually fluffy tails. They spend much of their lives climbing in trees and feeding on seeds and fruit. Squirrels can leap surprisingly far between branches or adjacent trees. Many species build nests of twigs and leaves, high in a tree or bush. Family Sciuridae (part). *See also* MARMOT

squirrel, bush

Any of 11 species of bushy-tailed squirrels native to Africa. The various species have striking colour patterns of yellow, black and red stripes and patches. Bush squirrels live wherever there are trees. They are active at any time, only resting during the midday heat. They feed on seeds and fruit, roots and insects. Sociable animals, bush squirrels live in small groups in holes in trees, communicating by smell and vocalizations. One or two babies are born in a nest after 57 days of gestation; they are weaned by six weeks. Head-body length: 9–12cm (4–5in); tail: 11–14cm (4–6in). Family Sciuridae; genus *Paraxerus*; species include *Paraxerus alexandri*.

squirrel, flying

Any of several squirrel species that are capable of gliding between the branches of trees; they spread out a flap of furred skin between the front and hind limbs and balance themselves with their tails. Flying squirrels are found in forests of North America and Eurasia. They are nocturnal, with large eyes and ears. They feed on buds, shoots, fruit, nuts and occasionally birds' eggs or nestlings. Head-

body length: 13–60cm (5–24in); tail: 9–63cm (4–25in). Family Sciuridae; genera include *Glaucomys*, *Aeromys* and *Pteromys*; species include *Pteromys volans*.

squirrel, giant

Any of four species of squirrel found in the forests of Asia. True giant squirrels can weigh up to 3kg (6.6lb), but they remain agile, able to leap 6m (20ft) or more between branches, using their long bushy tails for balance. Giant squirrels feed on fruit, nuts, bark and small animals. They live alone or in pairs in tree hole nests. During the breeding season they make much larger nests, where the female gives birth to one or two young after a four-week gestation. Head-body length: 30–45cm (12–18in); tail: 30–50cm (12–20in). Family Sciuridae; genus *Ratufa*; species include *Ratufa bicolor* (black giant squirrel).

squirrel, grey

Squirrel that is native to North America; it has been introduced to Britain, where it is replacing the native red squirrel. It thrives in deciduous forests, parks and gardens. The grey squirrel feeds on nuts and seeds, eggs and nestling birds; it will strip bark to feed on sap. Its grey coat is tinged with red, and its underside is white. The female gives birth to between one and eight young, after a gestation of 43 days, in a large nest or drey built high in the branches. Head-body length: 23–30cm (9–12in); tail: 21–23cm (8–9in). Family Sciuridae; species *Sciurus carolinensis*.

squirrel, ground

Any of *c*.38 species of squirrel found in Europe, Asia and North America. Most species are grey or yellowish-grey with pale underparts; the thirteen-lined ground squirrel has a pattern of lines and spots. Ground squirrels have short, furry tails and short legs. Sociable animals, they live in communities on treeless prairies and steppes, where they dig burrow systems. They feed on plant material and are active during the day. Those that live in hostile climates hibernate. Several species native to Europe are known as SOUSLIK. Head-body length: 13–40cm (5–16in); tail: 4–25cm (2–10in). Family Sciuridae; genus *Spermophilus*; species include *Spermophilus tridecemlineatus* (thirteen-lined ground squirrel).

squirrel, red

Squirrel that lives in conifer and mixed forests across Europe and Asia. It feeds on pine seeds, acorns, berries, nuts and fungi. It has a bright chestnut-red coat with white underparts; brown, grey and black forms also occur. Its tail is bushy and its ears have long tufts. About three young are born in a nest or drey and there can be two litters per year. Red squirrels in Britain have mainly been replaced by

▲ **squirrel, flying** By making adjustments to the positions of its four limbs, the flying squirrel can accurately control the shape and angle of its skin membrane, giving it great control in flight and the ability to make sudden manoeuvres.

The long, feathery tail is used as a rudder to stabilize the squirrel. Like other gliding animals, the flying squirrel has large, sharp claws with which to grasp the "target" tree. As it nears its landing point, the flying squirrel changes course

by raising its tail. This causes the squirrel to travel upwards and stall, thereby slowing the animal down.

▲ **stag beetle** During the mating season, male common stag beetles (*Lucanus cervus*) engage in ritualized duels, using their enlarged mandibles. The beetles are rarely injured; instead one will concede defeat. The winner becomes the dominant male of that territory.

introduced grey squirrels. Head-body length: 20–24cm (8–9in); tail: 15–20cm (6–8in). Family Sciuridae; species *Sciurus vulgaris*.

squirrelfish

Any of several species of fish found in tropical seas worldwide. The squirrelfish is bright red, often with white streaks or spots. It has large eyes and sharp spines on its gill covers and fins. Length: to 61cm (24in). Family Holocentridae.

squirrel monkey

See MONKEY, SQUIRREL

stabilizing selection

Evolutionary selection that tends to eliminate the extremes within a group, thus reducing the variability of a population and hence the opportunity for evolutionary change. *See also* DIRECTIONAL SELECTION; DISRUPTIVE SELECTION; EVOLUTION

stable-fly

Bloodsucking fly. It uses horses and cattle as its hosts, but it will also bite humans. The stable-fly pierces the skin using its labium, which is a non-retractile, rigid proboscis, and imbibes blood. Both males and females are blood feeders. The larvae feed in dung and stable litter. Order Diptera; family Muscidae; species *Stomoxys calcitrans*.

stack

Pillar of rock that forms an islet at the end of a headland. A stack is the result of a series of events caused by EROSION. Sea waves striking a headland first carve a CAVE by opening up JOINTS in the rock. The cave gradually penetrates the headland until an arch is formed. Finally, the top of the arch collapses and leaves a stack separated from the rest of the headland. The process may be repeated several times, giving a series of stacks.

stag beetle

Any member of the family Lucanidae. Male stag BEETLES have characteristically enlarged jaws. Most species inhabit tropical regions and are nocturnal. The common stag beetle (*Lucanus cervus*) is a large, brown or black beetle found in Eurasian oak forests. The male bears large antler-like mandibles. The larvae feed on rotten wood. Family Lucanidae; species include *Lucanus cervus* and *Cladognathus giraffa* (giraffe stag beetle).

stag's horn (candle-snuff fungus)

Inedible FUNGUS that is common on dead wood. It has small, elongated, flattened fruiting bodies, which are branched into antler-shapes, the upper branches powdery white and the stalks black and hairy. Phylum Ascomycota; species *Xylaria hypoxylon*.

stalactite

Icicle-shaped deposit of tiny CALCIUM CARBONATE crystals found hanging down from the roof of CAVES in Carboniferous limestone areas. Stalactites are formed by water slowly percolating through the rocks; as the water droplets are about to fall from the cave roof, a tiny layer of calcium precipitates out of the water and solidifies. Gradually, the deposits build up to form a column of calcium carbonate crystals known as CALCITE.

stalagmite

Column of CALCIUM CARBONATE crystals that grows upwards from the floor of CAVES in Carboniferous limestone areas. Stalagmites are formed as a result of water dripping from the ceiling of the cave and leaving tiny deposits of calcium carbonate on the floor. The deposits gradually build up into CALCITE crystals, and can sometimes extend upwards to meet the STALACTITE above, forming a column or pillar. Stalagmites tend to be fatter than stalactites, possibly because the water splashes out when it drops to the floor, causing a wider spread of calcium carbonate.

stalk-eyed-fly

Any of many species of FLY characterized by having their eyes on long stalks. Some species are pests of maize and other grains. Stalk-eyed flies are about the size of a HOUSE-FLY but are more slender and dark brown. They inhabit tropical rainforests, where they are usually found in damp undergrowth. Order Diptera; family Diopsidae; subfamilies Diopsinae (genera *Cyrtodiopsis*, *Eurydiopsis* and *Teleopsis*) and Sphyracephalinae (genus *Pseudodiopsis*); species include *Cyrtodiopsis dalmanni*.

stamen

POLLEN-producing element of a FLOWER. It consists of an ANTHER, in which pollen is produced, on the end of a stalk-like filament. The arrangement and number of stamens is important in the classification of ANGIOSPERMS (flowering plants).

Stanley, Wendell Meredith (1904–71)

US biochemist who shared the 1946 Nobel Prize for chemistry with John Northrop (1891–1987) and James SUMNER for his research into VIRUSES. In 1935 Stanley crystallized tobacco mosaic virus and showed that it consists of PROTEIN and NUCLEIC ACID molecules in a rod-shaped form. This enabled the exact molecular structure and means of proliferation of this and other viruses to be determined. Stanley also studied influenza viruses and developed a vaccine against the disease.

star, basket

Any of several species of BRITTLE STAR. It is a marine ECHINODERM. It has a basket-like appearance when filtering food from the water with its many long, branching, coiled arms. Class Ophiuroidea; species include *Astrophyton muricatum*.

starch

CARBOHYDRATE, stored in many plants, that provides about 70% of humankind's food in such forms as rice, potatoes and cereals. Animals and plants convert it to GLUCOSE for energy (RESPIRATION). Consisting of linked glucose units, starch exists in two forms: **amylose**, in which the glucose chains are unbranched, and **amylopectin**, in which they are branched. It is made commercially from cereals, corn, potatoes and other plants. Starch is used in the manufacture of adhesives and foods (as a thickening agent) and to stiffen laundered clothes and other fabrics.

starfish

ECHINODERM that is commonly seen in rockpools and the shallows of seas worldwide. It is radially symmetrical, usually with an odd number of arms. Most species are opportunistic detritivores and predators, feeding with a mouth located on the underside of the junction of the arms. Phylum Echinodermata; class Asteroidea.

starfish, blue star

Starfish with a bright blue upperside. It is found mainly in the s Pacific Ocean. Length: *c*.100mm

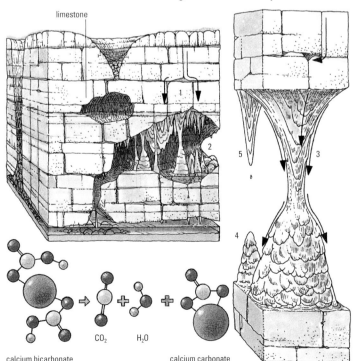

limestone

CO₂   H₂O

calcium bicarbonate   calcium carbonate

S

◀ **stalactite/stalagmite** Weak carbonic acid, which is formed when rain absorbs carbon dioxide from the atmosphere, dissolves tiny amounts of calcium carbonate from limestone rock as it percolates down through the rock (1). If the water enters a previously eroded cave (2), it forms drips (3). Some of the dissolved carbon dioxide escapes from the water, and the calcium bicarbonate in the water is precipitated as a calcite known as travertine, consisting of calcium carbonate. The travertine forms rising columns called stalagmites (4) and descending pillars from which water drips, called stalactites (5).

(*c*.4in). Class Asteroidea; genus *Linckia*; species include *Linckia laevigata*.

starfish, common
Sandy brown starfish found in the w Atlantic Ocean. It preys on clams and oysters. Length: 200mm (8in). Class Asteroidea; species *Asterias forbesi*.

starfish, crown-of-thorns
Starfish renowned for the long, sharp spines on its dorsal surface. It is found in the s Pacific Ocean, especially on the Great Barrier Reef. Its populations can multiply rapidly and large tracts of corals reefs can be destroyed as the starfish feed. Class Asteroidea; species *Acanthaster planci*.

starfish, cushion star
Yellow and brown starfish; it has a distinctive pattern radiating from its centre. It is called cushion star because of its shortened arms and plump appearance. Class Asteroidea; species *Pteraster tesselatus*.

starfish, sand star
Any member of the genus *Astropecten*, comprising starfish often found foraging on the surface of sand in shallow water. Most sand star species have spines along the margins of their arms. Length: to 300mm (12in). Class Asteroidea; genus *Astropecten*.

starfish, sun star
Any member of the genus *Crossaster*. The sun star is so called because of its coloration, which is red towards the junction of the arms, becoming orange to yellow toward the arms' tips. Length: to 300mm (12in). Class Asteroidea; genus *Crossaster*.

stargazer
Any of several species of bottom-dwelling, marine fish, whose eyes are located on top of a large, flat head. The electric stargazer (family Uranoscopidae) lives in warm and temperate seas worldwide. Some species have shoulder spines or electric organs. Length: to 55cm (22in). The sand stargazer (family Dactyloscopidae), a much smaller fish, is found in tropical waters. Length: to 10cm (4in).

starling
Any of numerous species of robust, medium-sized perching birds with strong legs and bills. Most species are insect- and fruit-eaters. Many form large flocks, especially when roosting. Their calls are many and varied; some species are excellent mimics, including others birds' calls in their own repertoire. Several species have adapted to town life. Family Sturnidae.

▲ **starling** The superb starling (*Spreo superbus*) of E Africa has the brightest plumage of its family. Like other starlings, it is noisy and bold and lives in large colonies, often near villages and towns. In general, the starling family is highly adaptable – the common starling had spread throughout North America within 80 years of its arrival (1890).

starling, European
European bird that has been widely introduced; in many places it has ousted native species in its aggressive search for nest sites. The adult has blackish plumage, with a green sheen and spangled pale spots. It has a bustling gait and flies fast and straight on its triangular wings. Length: 21cm (8in). Family Sturnidae; species *Sturnus vulgaris*.

starling, glossy
Any member of the genus *Lamprotornis*, a group of mainly African species. The adults have beautiful glossy azure blue and green plumage, with violet neck patches. They are found in flocks in bush forests and on heavily grazed areas following game. Glossy starlings are also common around safari camps in the game parks. Family Sturnidae; genus *Lamprotornis*.

starling, rose-coloured
Starling that inhabits dry grassy steppes and low rocky hills in central Asia. It has a pink back and body, black crested head, black wings and a black tail. It often follows locust swarms. The starling migrates westwards at irregular intervals. It forms large flocks and can be a pest of cereal crops. Length: 21cm (8in). Family Sturnidae; species *Sturnus roseus*.

starling, superb
Beautiful starling found in grassy bush country, often around towns and settlements, in E Africa. It has a white eye, black face, irridescent red crown, blue back and breast, white breast band, orange belly and glossy green wings. Length: 20cm (8in). Family Sturnidae; species *Spreo superbus*.

Star of Bethlehem
Bulbous plant native to s Africa. Its fragrant, star-shaped, white flowers grow on a central spike, which rises from slender, arching leaves. It is a popular house plant and ornamental garden plant. Height: to 46cm (18in). Family Liliaceae; species *Ornithogalum umbellatum*.

steenbuck (steenbok)
Small, slender-legged ANTELOPE native to the grasslands of E and s Africa. Its coat is shades of reddish-brown stippled with white. The male has short spiked horns. Length: to 85cm (33in); weight: to 14kg (31lb). Family Bovidae; genera *Raphicerus* and *Nototragus*.

stegosaur
Member of a group of quadrupedal, ORNITHISCHIAN dinosaurs, for example *Stegosaurus*. They evolved in mid-Jurassic times and died out in late Cretaceous times, before the major EXTINCTION event. They were medium-sized plant eaters. The rows of bony plates or spikes along the stegosaurs' backs were not attached to the skeleton and were probably used for sexual display or perhaps for heat regulation. Their heavy muscular tails were armed with pairs of long, sharp, bony spikes; these were probably used for protection.

Stein, William Howard (1911–80)
US biochemist. He shared the 1972 Nobel Prize for chemistry for research into the molecular structure of PROTEINS. Stein developed techniques for the analysis of PEPTIDES and AMINO ACIDS obtained from proteins and applied these methods to determining the molecular structure of the ENZYME ribonuclease. His work contributed greatly to the understanding of processes involved in protein synthesis within CELLS.

stem
Main, upward-growing part of a plant; it bears leaves, buds and flowers or other reproductive structures. In VASCULAR PLANTS, the stem contains conducting tissues (XYLEM and PHLOEM). In flowering plants, this vascular tissue is arranged in a ring (in DICOTYLEDONS) or scattered (in MONOCOTYLEDONS). Stems are usually erect but may be climbing (VINE) or prostrate (STOLON). They may also be SUCCULENT (CACTUS) or modified into underground structures (RHIZOMES, TUBERS, CORMS, BULBS). Stems vary in size from the thread-like stalks of aquatic plants to tree trunks. Woody stems have an outer layer of corky cells, called BARK. They increase in girth every year as specialized layers of CAMBIUM cells produce extra tissues in the cortex, and sometimes also just below the EPIDERMIS.

stephanotis
Any member of the genus *Stephanotis*, comprising climbing shrubs native to Madagascar; they are commonly grown as greenhouse plants elsewhere. The most well-known species is Madagascar Jasmine (*Stephanotis floribunda*). Its branches may reach sev-

◄ **steppe** Approximately three-quarters of Mongolia's land area is dry steppe, such as that seen here near the Hangai Mountains. Nomadic pastoralists form a significant proportion of Mongolia's population, travelling with their herds through the wide expanses of grassland.

S

eral metres in length and are thickly covered with large, white, strongly scented flowers and thick oval leaves. Family Asclepidaceae; genus *Stephanotis*.

steppe
Area of temperate grassland found in Mongolia, Kazakstan, Russia, Ukraine and neighbouring parts of s Europe. The landscape is often very flat and open and the climate is too dry to support much vegetation. When it is ploughed, the steppe can become very rich farmland, especially for growing cereals. Steppes are very similar to **prairies** and have a similar CONTINENTAL CLIMATE. Winters are very cold, but summers are quite warm. Rainfall is quite light, and falls mainly in the summer months.

sternum (breastbone)
Flat, narrow bone extending from the base of the neck to just below the diaphragm in the centre of the chest. It consists of three sections: the **manubrium**, or upper part; the **body** or gladiolus; and the **xiphoid process**, the lower and more flexible cartilaginous part. The top of the manubrium is attached by ligaments to the collarbones and the body is joined to the ribs by seven pairs of costal cartilages.

steroid
Class of organic compounds characterized by a basic molecular structure of 17 carbon atoms arranged in four rings and bounded by up to 28 hydrogen atoms. Steroids are widely distributed in animals and plants, the most abundant being the sterols (steroid alcohols) such as CHOLESTEROL. Another important group are the steroid HORMONES, including the corticosteroids, secreted by the adrenal cortex, and the sex hormones (OESTROGEN, PROGESTERONE and TESTOSTERONE).

stick insect
Any of numerous species of herbivorous insects belonging to the order Phasmida. They resemble the shape and colour of the twigs upon which they rest. Some lay eggs that resemble seeds. Length: to 32cm (13in). Order Phasmida. *See also* LEAF INSECT

▲ **stegosaur** The *stegosaurus* was the most distinctive stegosaur genus. The animal's front legs were much shorter than its hind legs, and its proportions were such that it would not have been capable of moving quickly. The *Stegosaurus* had an extremely small brain and a small mouth.

stickleback
Any of several species of small fish found in fresh, brackish and salt water. The stickleback is usually brown and green and may be identified by the number of spines along its sides and back. The male builds a nest of water plants and drives the female into it. He then watches the eggs and cares for the young. Length: 8–11cm (3–4in). Family Gasterosteidae; species include *Gasterosteus aculeatus* (three-spined stickleback).

stigma
Free upper part of the STYLE of the female organs of a FLOWER. It is the part to which a pollen grain adheres before FERTILIZATION.

stilt
Any of several species of wading bird. The stilt has a long neck, a long, finely pointed bill, black and white plumage and extremely long, pink or red legs. The black-winged stilt (*Himantopus himantopus*) of Europe and Asia is mainly white with a black back and wings. The banded stilt (*Cladorhynchus leucocephalus*) of Australasia has a chestnut breast band.

Length: 35–40cm (14–16in); leg length: 12–16cm (5–6in). Family Recurvirostridae.

stilt bug
Any member of the insect family Berytidae. Most species have very long, slender legs. They are generally found on legumes. The family also contains the genus *Cymus*, species of which have short legs. Order Hemiptera; family Berytidae; species include *Berytinus minor*.

stilt-legged-fly
Slender fly with long legs. It preys on insects in damp, shady places. The larvae live in decaying matter. Order Diptera; family Micropezidae; species include *Calobata petronella*.

stinging nettle
See NETTLE

stingray
Any of several species of bottom-dwelling, cartilaginous fish that live in marine waters and in some rivers in South America. It has a flattened body, with wing-like fins around the head. It has a long, slender tail. Its venomous sting is used to stun prey and can cause injury to humans. Width: to 2m (6.6ft). Family Dasyatidae.

stinkbug
Shield-shaped, brown, PENTATOMID BUG noted for its disagreeable odour; it is found worldwide. It lays barrel-shaped eggs in clusters on leaves. Members of the subfamilies Acanthosomatinae and Asopinae suck insect juices, whereas those belonging to Pentatominae suck plant juices. The HARLEQUIN BUG is a stinkbug. Length: 5–12mm (0.2–0.5in). Family Pentatomidae.

stinkhorn
Any of several species of foul-smelling fungi. At first the stinkhorn resembles a small, whitish "egg", which contains the unripe fruiting body (receptacle).

S

▲ **stickleback** The three-spined stickleback displays complex courtship and nesting behaviour. During the breeding season the male develops a distinctive coloration of vividly blue eyes, red underparts and silvery scales on the back. He excavates a hollow in the sand or mud and erects a dome-shaped structure made from weed fragments stuck together with mucus. He waits for a passing female. When a female is ready to mate, her belly appears swollen with eggs. The sight of the female stimulates the male into action. He zigzags towards her, turning away at the last instant (1). The female eventually signals her readiness to spawn by assuming a tilted-up position (2) near the surface of the water as she watches the male's display. The male then turns and leads the female down to the nest (3), indicating the entrance with his snout. In this manoeuvre, he turns on his side to display his red belly (4). Sometimes a female will not spawn, but remains in the area to be courted. Then the male may become frustrated and attack her, nipping her flanks (5). Eventually the female swims away, or returns to inspect the nest while the male nudges her belly to stimulate egg laying. The female enters the nest and sheds up to 100 eggs, provoked by the male quivering violently, while striking his snout against her tail (6). The female leaves the nest and the male enters to discharge his sperm (7). After the female has served her purpose, the male may chase her away from the nest site in anticipation of another female visitor. Should another male encroach upon his territory, the male stickleback puts on an aggressive display, darting towards the intruder with his dorsal fin erect and mouth agape. After several rounds of fertilization, the male shifts his attention to the care of the eggs. He guards the nest closely, chasing away hungry females, and constantly fans a current of fresh, oxygen-rich water over the eggs with his pectoral fins (8).

When ripe, the receptacle elongates to 10–20cm (4–8in) in height, rupturing the egg. It carries with it a glutinous brownish spore mass to attract the flies that disperse the spores. Phylum Basidiomycota; genus *Phallus*.

stinkpot

Small aquatic TURTLE from E North America. It has a relatively high and narrow shell. Its plastron is reduced, giving the limbs great mobility for swimming and even climbing. A pungent musk is released by glands situated on the underside of its body, accounting for both its common and scientific names. The name stinkpot is sometimes also applied to other turtles that produce noxious odours. Length: 5–13cm (2–5in). Family Kinosternidae; species *Sternotherus odoratus*.

stinkwood

Tree of the LAUREL family found in s Africa. It has an unpleasant odour but valuable timber. Family Lauraceae; species *Ocotea bullata*.

stitchbird

Small and very rare perching bird found only on a few predator-free islands in New Zealand. The male has a velvety black head, back and upper breast and a white tuft of feathers behind its eyes. The female is greyish brown and often cocks its tail. Length: 18cm (7in), Family Meliphagidae; species *Notiomystis cincta*.

stoat (ermine)

Carnivorous mammal of the WEASEL family. Short-legged and slim, it moves sinuously. It preys upon small animals in many temperate parts of the world. In northern regions its fur turns from red-brown and white to white in winter, when it is known as ermine. Length (including tail): *c*.30cm (*c*.12in). Family Mustelidae; species *Mustela ermina*.

stock (gilliflower)

Annual plant native to s Europe, s Africa and parts of Asia; it is widely cultivated as a garden flower. Stock has oblong leaves and pink, purple or white flower clusters. Height: to 80cm (31in). Family Brassicaceae/Cruciferae; species *Matthiola bicornis*.

stockfish (South African hake)

HAKE found in cold and temperate marine waters of the s Atlantic Ocean. It has an elongated body and a large head. It is a commercial food fish. Length: to 1.2m (3.9ft). Family Merluccidae or Gadidae; species *Merluccius capensis*.

▲ **stonechat** The stonechat (*Saxicola torquata*) is so called because of its harsh call. It is a restless bird and a fast flier. It is found from Europe and Africa to w and central Asia. Some of the more northerly populations migrate south for winter.

◀ **stonecrop** Creeping sedum (*Sedum acre*), like many other stonecrop species, lives on rocky ground. Also known as wall pepper, golden moss or biting stonecrop, it is found in central and E Europe. The juice from its fleshy leaves has been used medicinally.

stolon

Modified, horizontal, underground or aerial STEM, growing from the basal node of a plant. Aerial stolons, or RUNNERS, may be slender, as in STRAWBERRY plants, or stiff and arching, as in BRAMBLES. The stolon produces a new plant at its tip, which puts out ADVENTITIOUS ROOTS (roots that arise from nodes on the stem) to anchor itself. Underground stolons are characteristic of white POTATO plants. *See also* TUBER; VEGETATIVE REPRODUCTION

stoma

Pore, found mostly on the undersides of leaves, through which atmospheric gases pass in and out for RESPIRATION and PHOTOSYNTHESIS. Surrounding each stoma are TWO GUARD CELLS, which can swell and close the stoma in order to prevent excessive loss of water vapour. *See also* GAS EXCHANGE; TRANSPIRATION

stomach

One of the organs of the DIGESTIVE SYSTEM. It is J-shaped and lies to the left and slightly below the diaphragm in human beings. It is connected at its upper end to the gullet (OESOPHAGUS) and at the lower end to the small intestine. The stomach itself is lined by three layers of muscle (longitudinal, circular and oblique) and a folded mucous layer that contains gastric GLANDS. These glands secrete hydrochloric acid, which destroys some food bacteria and makes possible the action of PEPSIN, the ENZYME secreted by the glands, which digests PROTEINS. Gastric gland secretion is controlled by the sight, smell and taste of food, and by hormonal stimuli, chiefly the HORMONE gastrin. As the food is digested, it is churned by muscular action into a thick liquid state called chyme; then it passes into the small intestine.

stonechat

Small perching bird of the THRUSH family. The male is black above, with a bold white neck patch and chestnut underparts. The stonechat has a habit of perching upright on a prominent lookout, watching for passing insects and flicking its tail jerkily. Its call sounds like stones hitting each other. Length: 12–13cm (*c*.5in). Family Turdidae; genus *Saxicola*.

stonecrop

Any plant of the genus *Sedum*, especially creeping sedum (*Sedum acre*), which is a succulent, low-growing plant. Creeping sedum is of European origin and is found in rocky areas. It has pungent, fleshy leaves and yellow flowers. Family Crassulaceae.

stone-curlew (thick-knee)

Any of several species of large wading birds belonging to the genera *Burhinus* and *Esacus*. Most species are found away from water on stony semideserts and heaths. The stone-curlew has sandy brown plumage, a stout bill and long yellow legs with swollen knee joints (hence its alternative name). It has large eyes and feeds mainly at night. Most species have an eerie wailing call. The great thick-knee (*Burhinus recurvirostris*) is a large, distinctive bird found along the sandy riverbanks of the great Indo-Pakistan rivers, the Indus, Ganges and Brahamaputra. Length: 32–55cm (13–22in). Family Burhinidae; genera *Burhinus* and *Esacus*.

stonefish

Bottom-dwelling marine fish found in tropical waters of the Indo-Pacific Ocean. It has a warty, slime-covered body. Its sharp dorsal spines can inflict a painful, sometimes deadly, sting to humans. Length: to 33cm (13in). Family Synancejidae; species *Synanceja verrucosa*.

stonefly (salmon fly)

Any of numerous species of soft-bodied insects found worldwide. The adults are brown to black, with long, narrow front wings and chewing mouthparts. The aquatic nymphs have branched gills. Length: 5–60mm (0.2–2.4in). Order Plecoptera.

stony-iron meteorite

METEORITE consisting of approximately equal proportions of SILICATES (stony material) and metals, mostly nickel-iron. There are two main subtypes. **Pallasites**, which consist of olivine (a magnesium-iron silicate) mixed with nickel-iron, may have originated near the core/mantle interface of a planetary body. **Mesosiderites** are a much coarser combination of chunks of various silicates and nickel-iron; they could have been produced by impacts on a planetary surface.

stony meteorite (aerolite)

METEORITE that consists mostly of SILICATES (stony material, mainly olivine, pyroxene and feldspar), with only a small amount of chemically uncombined metals (typically 5% nickel-iron). There are two subtypes: chondrites and achondrites. In **chondrites**, the rocky minerals take the form of small spherical grains (chondrules), and there is some nickel and iron. **Achondrites** are coarser-grained and have no chondrules or metal. Both types are about 4600 million years old, dating from the formation of the Solar System.

strontianite

Carbonate mineral, strontium carbonate ($SrCO_3$). It has orthorhombic system, hexagonal twinned crystals, and it also occurs as massive or columnar aggregates. It can be pale green, white, grey, yellow or brown. Strontianite is found in low-temperature hydrothermal veins, often in limestone. Hardness 3.5–4; r.d. 3.7.

stork

Any member of the family Ciconiidae, comprising very large, long-legged, long-necked, heron-like birds with long, stout bills. The most common

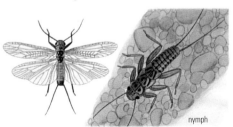

nymph

▲ **stonefly** An important source of food for freshwater fish, stoneflies (*Plecoptera* sp.) hatch in the water and spend most of their lives there. The aquatic nymph stage lasts from one to four years, whereas the adult phase, after they have left the water, lasts only a few weeks. As adults, they do not fly well and hover over the surface of streams, lakes and rivers.

S

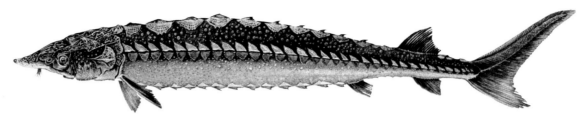

► **sturgeon** The freshwater sturgeon (*Acipenser sturio*), or beluga, is one of the largest freshwater fish. It swims at the bottom of the water, snuffling out invertebrates with its long, sensitive snout, from which hang several sensory barbels.

species, the white stork (*Ciconia ciconia*), is boldly black and white with a red bill and legs. The largest species, the marabou stork (*Leptoptilos crumeniferus*), has a bare reddish head and neck with a swollen neck pouch. Storks nest in trees and on cliffs. They migrate in flocks. Length: 95–152cm (37–60in); wingspan: 145–255cm (57–100in). Family Ciconiidae.

storksbill

Any of several species of annual or perennial herbs and shrubs belonging to the genus *Erodium*. Storksbill is found in temperate and semi-tropical regions; some species are grown in rock gardens and borders for their ornamental flowers. The storksbill has pinnately lobed or divided leaves and single or clustered flowers. The fruits resemble the head and bill of a stork, hence its common name. Family Geraniaceae; genus *Erodium*.

storm

Meteorological disturbance of the ATMOSPHERE involving pressure change and high winds, often with PRECIPITATION. A storm can move rapidly over many hundreds of kilometres. It can be locally extensive, covering hundreds of square kilometres. *See also* CYCLONE; HURRICANE; TYPHOON

stratification

Layering in ROCKS. It occurs in SEDIMENTARY ROCKS and in IGNEOUS ROCKS that formed from LAVA flows and volcanic fragmental deposits. Separations between individual layers are called stratification planes. They parallel the strata they bound, being horizontal near flat layers and exhibiting inclination on a sloping surface. *See also* STRATIGRAPHY; STRATUM

stratigraphy

Branch of geology concerned with stratified or layered ROCKS. It deals with the correlation of rocks from different localities using FOSSILS and distinct rock types. *See also* STRATUM

stratocumulus

See CLOUD

stratosphere

Section of the Earth's ATMOSPHERE between the TROPOSPHERE and the higher MESOSPHERE. It is about 40km (25mi) thick and for half this distance the temperature remains fairly constant. The stratosphere contains most of the atmosphere's OZONE LAYER.

stratum

Single layer or bed of SEDIMENTARY ROCK, usually one of a series of layers that have been deposited one on top of another. Each stratum indicates the conditions that prevailed at the time of its deposition. The study of the strata is called STRATIGRAPHY. The stratigraphical or geological column contains all the periods of geological time. Rock strata may be very thin, of just a few centimetres, or they can be several metres in extent. Initially, they are usually horizontal, but they are likely to be affected by folding and faulting.

stratus

See CLOUD

strawberry

Any of several species of low-growing, fruit-bearing plants of the ROSE family. The strawberry plant is common in Europe, Asia and the Americas. It has three-lobed leaves and clusters of white or reddish flowers. The large fleshy fruit is dotted with seeds (pips). Family Rosaceae; genus *Fragaria*.

strawflower

Annual plant native to Australia; it is widely cultivated for its white, yellow, orange or red flower heads, which keep their bright colour when dried. Height: to 91cm (36in). Family Compositae; species *Helchrysum bracteatum*.

streamertail

Any of several species of HUMMINGBIRD found in Central America. Two species are only found on the island of Jamaica: the red-billed streamertail (*Trochilus polytmus*) is the Jamaican national bird. The streamertail has iridescent, shimmering green plumage and a long, green, forked tail. Length: 20cm (8in). Family Trochilidae; genus *Trochilus*.

strelitzia

Any member of the genus *Strelitzia*, a small group of woody perennial plants native to s Africa. It may or may not have a main trunk, depending on the species. It has banana-like leaves and irregularly shaped, often brightly coloured flowers, which are produced in a rigid, boat-shaped bract. The genus includes the well-known BIRD OF PARADISE FLOWER (*Strelitzia reginae*), which is widely grown as a greenhouse ornamental. Family Musaceae; genus *Strelitzia*.

strepsipteran

Any member of the order Strepsiptera, comprising *c*.400 species of parasitic insects. Strepsipterans are parasitic on leafhoppers, planthoppers, bees and other insects. Species of the genus *Stylops* parasitize the bee. The female is wingless and never leaves its host, living first within the larva and then within the adult bee. The male has back wings and emerges from the bee as an adult. Order Strepsiptera.

stress

Force per unit area applied to an object. Tensile stress stretches an object, compressive stress squeezes it and shearing stress deforms it sideways. In a fluid, no shearing stress is possible because the fluid slips sideways, so all fluid stresses are PRESSURES (positive or negative).

◄ **strawberry** Intensively cultivated since the 15th century, the strawberry was brought to Europe by early explorers of the New World. The fruiting season is short and the fruit is easily perishable once picked.

strigiform

Any member of the bird order Strigiformes. It comprises the OWLS.

stromatolite

Layered mound structure up to a metre (about three feet) or so high, built up over many years in shallow and warm tropical seas by films of bacteria growing over the seabed and trapping fine sediment. Stromatolites first formed in Precambrian seas *c*.3.5 billion years ago. They are still to be found off the coast of w Australia.

sturgeon

Any of several species of large, primitive, bony fish that are found in temperate, fresh and marine waters of the Northern Hemisphere. The ovaries of the female sturgeon are the source of caviar. The sturgeon has five series of sharp-pointed scales along its sides, fleshy whiskers and a tapering, snout-like head. The Eurasian freshwater sturgeon (*Acipenser huso*) is also known as the beluga. Length: to 3m (10ft). Family Acipenseridae; species include *Acipenser sturio*.

style

Slender tube of a FLOWER that connects the pollen-receiving STIGMA at its tip to the OVARY at its base.

stylopid

Any of *c*.400 species of insects that are PARASITES of other insects. Adult male stylopids are free-living; their forewings are highly reduced to club-shaped structures. Adult female stylopids are grub-like and usually remain inside the host. Hosts include planthoppers, wasps and some bees. Many hosts, especially females, become sterile after attack by stylopids. Order Strepsiptera; families Stylopidae, Halictophagidae and Elenchidae; genera include *Stylops* and *Elenchus*.

subclass

Part of the CLASSIFICATION of living organisms, ranking above ORDER and below CLASS. Subclass names are printed in Roman (ordinary) letters, with an initial capital.

S

subduction

In PLATE TECTONICS, descent of rocky material from the edge of one of the Earth's tectonic plates into the semi-molten ASTHENOSPHERE below. It occurs where two plates collide, and one rides over the other (**subduction zone**); the lower one is subducted. Often the upper plate is a continental plate and the lower one is an oceanic plate, and subduction leads to the formation of an ocean TRENCH. This type of subduction is associated with volcanic eruptions, EARTHQUAKES and other seismic activity. *See also* CONTINENT

submarine canyon

Steep-sided, valley-shaped topographical depression in the CONTINENTAL SLOPE. It is initiated by rivers during periods of lowered sealevel. The submarine canyon is excavated and maintained by the passage of turbidity currents. *See also* TURBIDITE

► **succulent** Cacti have their stomata sunk down into pits (A), which helps cut down transpiration – the evaporation of water – because the air in the pit is protected from air movements above the surface of the leaf and becomes humid. Cacti have tough outer skins, which are often waxy to cut down water loss. Inside, they are fleshy and capable of storing a lot of moisture. Cacti flower rarely and briefly, after the often violent desert rains. The spherical shape of many cacti maximizes their volume while minimizing their surface area, so that they are ideal water barrels. The ridged body structure of a cactus also plays a role. It may help reduce tissue damage during the inevitable shrinkage that accompanies water loss.

Cactus spines are actually greatly reduced leaves. Along with the plant's hairs they hinder air flow and help reflect heat. They also increase the heat-losing surface area of the plant without increasing its water-losing area. In addition, they discourage grazing animals from eating its succulent flesh.

The roots of some xerophytes penetrate to a depth of 6m (20ft) in their search for water. Other xerophytes have root systems of swollen, water-retaining tubers. Most cacti, however, have a wide-ranging system of fine roots, which are equipped with microscopic hairs (B). The roots may only penetrate a short way underground, but they often cover a huge area (C) so that the cactus can quickly replenish its water supplies when water is available. Many cacti, such as the *Echinocereus pulchellus* (D), hide underground in the dry season. Only when conditions are favourable do they extend their green tops above the surface (E). In this way, they combine drought resistance with effective drought evasion.

subphylum
Part of the CLASSIFICATION of living organisms ranking above CLASS and below PHYLUM. Subphylum names are printed in Roman (ordinary) letters with an initial capital.

substrate
In biochemistry, a reactant that is acted on by an ENZYME or other catalyst. In biology, a substrate is a nutrient medium used to grow MICROORGANISMS. A substrate is also the surface on which a SESSILE organism (such as a LIMPET) lives and grows.

succession
In ecology, orderly change in plant and animal life in a biotic COMMUNITY over a long time period. It is the result of modifications in the community ENVIRONMENT. The process ends in establishment of a stable ECOSYSTEM, known as a CLIMAX COMMUNITY.

succulent
Plant that stores water in its tissues in order to resist periods of drought. It is usually perennial and evergreen. Most of the succulent plant body is made up of water-storage cells, which give it a fleshy appearance. A well-developed CUTICLE and low rate of daytime TRANSPIRATION also conserve water. Swollen leaves and stems have a smaller surface area to volume ratio than thin ones, thus further reducing water loss. Succulent plants include the CACTUS and STONECROP.

sucker
In botany, an upward-growing shoot that forms at the base of the plant stem or from an ADVENTITIOUS ROOT. In zoology, a disc-like structure found on the tentacles of CEPHALOPODS; it is used for grasping objects.

sucker
Any member of the family Catostomidae, a group of freshwater species found in the waters of North America, China and Siberia. Suckers are characterized by downward-directed, thick, fleshy lips and a benthic feeding habit. Length: to 90cm (35in). Family Catostomidae; there are *c*.68 species.

sucrose
Common, white, crystalline SUGAR ($C_{12}H_{22}O_{11}$). It is a DISACCHARIDE, consisting of linked GLUCOSE and FRUCTOSE molecules. It occurs in many plants, but its principal commercial sources are SUGAR CANE and SUGAR BEET. It is also obtained from MAPLE trees, DATE PALMS and SORGHUM. Sucrose is widely used for food sweetening and in the manufacture of confectionery and preserves.

sugar
Sweet-tasting, soluble, crystalline, MONOSACCHARIDE OR DISACCHARIDE CARBOHYDRATE. The common sugar used in food and beverages is the disaccharide SUCROSE, which is also the main sugar transported in plant tissues. The main sugar transported around the bodies of animals to provide energy in RESPIRATION is the monosaccharide GLUCOSE.

sugar beet
Variety of BEET grown commercially for its high

◄ **sugar** Sugar beet (left) and sugar cane (right) produce the same sugar – sucrose – but require completely different climatic conditions. Sugar cane is grown as a single crop in tropical regions, whereas sugar beet forms part of regular crop rotation in Europe, North America and South America. Although sugar is extracted by the same method from both sources, the yield of sugar cane is higher.

SUGAR content, which is stored in its thick, white roots. Family Chenopodiaceae; species *Beta vulgaris*.

sugarbird
Small, brown perching bird found in s Africa. It has a very long graduated tail, under which there is a yellow patch. It has a curved bill, with which it feeds on insects and nectar. The sugarbird is commonly found where proteas and aloes are flowering on coastal mountains. Length: 24–29cm (9–11in). Family Meliphagidae; genus *Promerops*.

sugar cane
Perennial GRASS cultivated in tropical and subtropical regions worldwide. After harvesting, the stems are processed in factories and are the main source of SUGAR. Cultivated canes are mainly of the species *Saccharum officinarum*. Height: to 4.5m (15ft). Family Poaceae/Gramineae.

sugar grass
Drought-resistant, tufted, perennial GRASS distributed from Southeast Asia to central and tropical Australia. Its slender stems arise from short rhizomes. It produces flower heads with finger-like branches, the spikelets clothed in brown hairs. The leaves are palatable to stock, especially horses. Family Poaceae; species *Eulalia fulva*.

sulphur bacterium
Bacterium that generates energy by metabolizing sulphur, either reducing it anaerobically or oxidizing it aerobically. The BACTERIA form a branch of the ARCHAEA. They are found in sulphur-rich hot springs, water- and mud-holes and seafloors; some can withstand temperatures up to 100ºC (212ºF). Examples of sulphur bacteria include *Sulpholobus* and *Thermococcus*.

sulphur tuft
Inedible FUNGUS that has mushroom-shaped fruiting bodies with bright sulphur-yellow caps tinged orange in the centre. Its slender, yellow to brownish stems are often curved. The fruiting bodies form dense clusters on stumps of coniferous and deciduous trees. Sulphur tuft is very common. Phylum Basidiomycota; species *Hypholoma fasciculare*.

sumac
Any of the shrubs and trees belonging to the genus *Rhus*. They are widely distributed in temperate regions. Sumacs have long, feather-like leaves and red, hairy fruit clusters. Some species, for example POISON IVY, are poisonous to touch. Height: to 9m (30ft). Family Anacardiaceae.

Sumner, James Batcheller (1887–1955)
US biochemist who shared the 1946 Nobel Prize for chemistry with John Northrop (1891–1987) and Wendell STANLEY for his discovery that ENZYMES could be crystallized. In 1926 Sumner isolated and crystallized the enzyme urease; it was the first enzyme to be crystallized and this achievement finally proved the PROTEIN nature of enzymes.

sun bear
See BEAR, SUN

sunbird
Any of several species of very small, beautifully coloured, nectar-feeding perching birds. The sunbird is found in Africa, s Asia and Australasia. When feeding it hovers momentarily but prefers to perch. Most species have down-curved bills. The male has iridescent plumage; the female is dullish green.

▶ **sunbird** The metallic sheen of the green plumage of the male malachite sunbird (*Nectarinia johnstonii*) contrasts with the duller-coloured, shorter-tailed female. The malachite sunbird and the purple-breasted sunbird (*Nectarinia purpureiventris*) are found at high altitudes in the mountain ranges of Africa, where they primarily feed on lobelia. Sunbirds are the Old World counterparts of the hummingbirds. They use their long beaks to reach nectar, sometimes piercing holes in the bases of large flowers if the nectar is otherwise out of reach. Also pictured is a cape **sugarbird** (*Promerops cafer*), which is found only in s Africa. It feeds mainly on the nectar of proteas. Its sharp claws enable it to grip onto the flowerheads.

male malachite sunbird

female malachite sunbird

cape sugarbird

purple-breasted sunbird

Length: 8–22cm (3–9in). Family Nectariniidae; species include *Nectarinia purpureiventris* (purple-breasted sunbird).

sunbittern

Elegant, sedate and solitary heron-like bird found in shady Central and South American forest streams. It has a long, slender neck, long legs and a long tail. Its sombre colours belie a "sunburst" of colour on its flight feathers, which can be seen during its spectacular mating displays. Length: 48cm (19in). Family Eurypygidae; species *Eurypyga helias*.

sundew

Any member of the genus *Drosera*, a group of INSECTIVOROUS plants native to temperate swamps and bogs. The sundew's hairy basal leaves glisten with a sticky dew-like substance that attracts and traps insects. The leaves then fold over the insect and secrete enzymes to digest it. Family Droseraceae.

sun dog (parhelion or mock sun)

Either of two bright coloured spots observed at 22° on each side of the Sun. The sun dogs are caused by refraction of sunlight by ice crystals in the Earth's ATMOSPHERE.

sunfish

Any of numerous species of freshwater fish found in North America. It is similar in appearance to the perch, with a continuous dorsal fin containing spiny and soft rays. The 30 species range in size from the

▶ **sunflower** Widely cultivated throughout Europe and North America, the common sunflower (*Helianthus annus*) produces seeds from which a light, high-quality oil is yielded. This oil is used in cooking, margarine, shortening and confectionery. The nutritious seeds can also be eaten whole or used in breads and cereals for human consumption, or in poultry feed.

blue spotted *Enneacanthus gloriosus* (length: 9cm/4in) to the large-mouth bass *Micropterus salmoides* (length: 81cm/32in). The sunfish is a popular angler's fish. Family Centrarchidae.

sunflower

Any of several annual and perennial plants of the genus *Helianthus*, native to North and South America. The flower heads resemble huge daisies, with yellow ray flowers and a central disc of yellow, brown or purple. The seeds yield a useful oil. The common sunflower (*Helianthus annuus*) has very long leaves and flower heads that are more than 30cm (12in) across. Height: to 3.5m (11.5ft). Family Asteraceae/Compositae.

sungazer

Large, diurnal LIZARD native to South Africa. It belongs to a group of lizards known as girdle-tailed lizards after the rings of scales that encircle their tails. The sungazer is found on the open savanna, where it excavates burrows up to 2m (6.6ft) in depth. It often basks in the sun outside its burrow but remains inactive during the cold winter months. Females give birth to one or two large young. Adult body length: to 40cm (16in). Family Cordylidae; species *Cordylus giganteus*.

sungrebe (finfoot)

Strange, duck-like water bird that is related to the RAIL. It is found in overgrown freshwater ponds of South America. It is mainly brown, with black and white head stripes. Of the two other species (both known as finfoots) in the family, one is found in Africa and the other in Asia. Length: 30cm (12in). Family Heliornithidae; species *Heliornis fulica*.

suni

Dwarf ANTELOPE that inhabits dense forests of Africa. It browses on leaves, buds, fruit and grass. The suni has a dark brown, freckled coat with pale underparts. Its ears are large and almost transparent. Males have short, straight horns; females are hornless but slightly larger. Sunis live in small groups of females and young led by a territorial male, who rubs his horns on tree trunks to mark the boundaries.

Breeding occurs throughout the year. Head-body length: 58–62cm (23–24in); tail: 11–13cm (4–5in). Family Bovidae; subfamily Antilopinae; species *Neotragus moschatus*.

sun spider (wind scorpion/scorpion)

Agile, fast-moving ARACHNID characterized by large, non-venomous jaws. It is native to the deserts of SE United States. The sun spider uses its adapted chelicerae (first pair of appendages) to hold and crush its prey. The second pair of appendages are tactile and end in an unusual adhesive structure. There are 12 families of sun spiders, containing more than 1000 species. Adult body length: 10mm (0.4in). Subclass Solifugae; families include Ammotrechidae; species include *Ammotrechella stimpsoni*.

sureli (leaf monkey)

Any of eight species of LANGUR monkey from tropical forests of Indonesia. They have extremely efficient digestive systems to cope with a poor quality leafy diet. Most species are brown, black or grey with pale underparts; some species have light markings on the head or thighs. Surelis are diurnal and live in small territorial groups of one male and two or more females and their young. Several species are endangered because of habitat destruction. Head-body length: 42–61cm (17–24in); tail: 50–85cm (20–33in). Family Cercopithecidae; subfamily Colobinae; genus *Presbytis*; species include *Presbytis femoralis* (banded sureli).

surfperch (seaperch)

Any of several species of live-bearing fish. Most species of surfperch are found off the Pacific coast of North America. Some are of commercial importance. Length: to 45cm (18in). Family Embiotocidae; species include *Amphistichus rhodoterus* (redtail surfperch).

surgeonfish (tang)

Any of c.70 species of colourful, laterally compressed fish found in subtropical and tropical marine waters. They are characterized by one or more blade-like processes just in front of the caudal fin. Length: to 50cm (20in). Family Acanthuridae; species include *Paracanthurus hepatus* (purple tang).

suricate

See MEERKAT

survival of the fittest

Term associated with Charles DARWIN and his theory of EVOLUTION. Among the offspring of any SPECIES there will be some who, by virtue of their genetic composition, are better adapted ("fitter") to survive in the struggle for existence. These types are more likely to survive long enough to bred and so perpetuate the favoured genes. *See also* SELECTION

S

▲ **surgeonfish** The sail-finned surgeon (*Zebrasoma veliferum*), also known as the sail-finned tang, is found in the tropical E Pacific Ocean, often on shallow reefs or in lagoons. It feeds primarily on algae. As with other surgeons it has a scalpel-like spine on each side of its body in front of the tail fin.

▲ **swallow** The barn swallow (*Hirundo rustica*) and the tree swallow (*Iridoprocne bicolor*) are native to temperate areas of North America. As with other members of the family, they migrate long distances: the barn swallow spends the summer in Canada and the winter in South America. Extremely agile, swallows spend most of their time in the air.

barn swallow

tree swallow

sustainable yield
Where the amount of a renewable resource removed is equal to, or less than, the rate of production. If the trees in a forest take 100 years to mature, one hundredth of the forest may be felled each year without the forest becoming smaller. A sustainable yield can be taken indefinitely.

swallow
Any member of the family Hirundinidae, a group of small, slender-bodied birds with long, pointed wings. They catch insects in flight. The most common species, the barn swallow (*Hirundo rustica*), is familiar in the Americas, Europe and Africa. It is deep blue above and has a deeply forked tail. The cliff swallow (*Hirundo pyrrhonota*) has a square tail with a buff coloured rump. The red-rumped swallow (*Hirundo daurica*) has a forked tail with a buff rump. Length: 13–17cm (5–7in). Family Hirundinidae.

swallow hole
See SINK HOLE

swallowtail butterfly
Any of numerous species of brightly coloured BUTTERFLIES that are found worldwide. They have characteristic tail-like extensions on their hind wings. Most swallowtail species are large and black, with bright yellow, blue, green and red markings. The yellow and black giant swallowtail (*Papilio cresphontes*) has a wingspan of up to 14cm (6in). Family Papilionidae.

Swammerdam, Jan (1637–80)
Dutch naturalist. His researches and his book *General History of Insects* provided a system for classifying insects and laid the foundations of ENTOMOLOGY, the scientific study of insects. Swammerdam also discovered (1658) the existence of red blood corpuscles.

swamp
Low-lying wetland area found near large bodies of open water. Swamps are characterized by numerous plants and animals, including RUSHES and SEDGE in northern areas, and species of trees, such as the swamp CYPRESS, in warmer areas. Swamps can prevent flooding by absorbing flood waters from rivers and coastal regions. *See also* BOG; MARSH

swamp-hen, purple (gallinule)
Large, uniformly dark blue, grey-blue or dark green swamp bird; its back colour varies according to the location. It belongs to the RAIL family. The purple swamp-hen has long, red legs and a heavy, red, triangular bill. It often climbs reed stems clumsily and noisily eats young reed shoots. The swamp-hen is becoming uncommon because of marshland drainage. Length: 50cm (20in). Family Rallidae; species *Porphyrio porphyrio*.

swan
Any member of the genus *Cygnus*, a group of large waterfowl. The swan has a long neck, black, webbed feet and a large, triangular bill. Most species are all white. The young (cygnets) are grey-brown, whitening in their first year and becoming mature adults in between two and three years. Some species migrate long distances in family groups. The adults remain faithfully together for life. Family Anatidae; genus *Cygnus*.

swan, black
Swan that is all black apart from its white wing feathers, which are conspicuous in flight. The bill is bright red with a white band near the tip. It is found wild only in Australia. It is widely kept in wildfowl collections, from which it frequently escapes to establish feral populations. Length: 1.2–1.4m (3.9–4.6ft); wingspan: 1.6–2m (5.2–6.6ft). Family Anatidae; species *Cygnus atratus*.

swan, mute
Heaviest flying bird in the world. The familiar, resident, all-white swan of Europe, it has been widely introduced elsewhere. The male has an orange bill with a black knob. In flight the wings make a loud throbbing noise. In the United Kingdom it is protected by royal decree. Length: 1.5–1.6m (4.9–5.2ft); wingspan: 208–238cm (82–94in). Family Anatidae; species *Cygnus olor*.

swan, trumpeter
All-white swan of North America; it is named after its sonorous single or double "honk". It has a black bill and a small patch of black facial skin that tapers to the eye. The forehead slopes evenly to the bill. It was once rare but is now being reintroduced to its former breeding grounds. Length: 1.5m (4.9ft). Family Anatidae; species *Cygnus buccinator*.

swan, whooper
Swan that is closely related to the trumpeter swan; it is found in Eurasia. It has a large, yellow, triangular face and bill patch that tapers to the eye; its bill has a black tip. The forehead slopes evenly to the bill. The whooper swan swims with its long neck held very straight. Length: 1.5m (4.9ft). Family Anatidae; species *Cygnus cygnus*.

swarm
Throng of insects or other small animals, for example a gathering of many HONEYBEES around a queen bee, when she flies off from a hive to found another colony. This happens when a young queen supplants the old queen, and it is the latter who leads off her retinue in a swarm.

sweat gland
One of many small GLANDS that open on the SKIN surface through pores and release sweat, composed mainly of water and some salt, to regulate body temperature. In humans, they are found all over the body, especially in places such as the armpits. In some mammals they are found only on the soles of the feet. The glands extract water, salts and urea from the blood capillaries that supply them and excrete them as sweat. SWEATING is under the control of the AUTONOMIC NERVOUS SYSTEM. It forms

Troides brookiana

Papilio thoas

Papilio zalmoxis

Eurytides protesilaus

▲ **swallowtail butterfly** *Papilio zalmoxis* is found in w Africa; *Eurytides protesilaus* is found in Central and South America; *Papilio thoas* is found in sw United States, Central and South America; *Troides brookiana* is found in Malaysia, Borneo and nearby islands. Swallowtail butterflies are named after the tail-like extensions on their hindwings, although, as can been seen above, many species do not have these extensions. Coloration and shape varies widely among swallowtails: even within a particular species the colour may vary according to the sex or the season. Swallowtails are day-active insects. Their caterpillars are distinguished by their ability to emit a pungent smell.

S

▲ **swede** The swede (*Brassica napobrassica*), also known as rutabaga, is a root vegetable that grows best in cooler climates. It is a biennial. It is closely related to the turnip but can be distinguished from it by its thick, smooth, blue-green leaves (those of the turnip and thin, hairy and green). Turnips and swedes are among the most commonly grown root crops.

an important part of the body's temperature control mechanism. *See also* HOMEOSTASIS

sweating
Loss of water, salts and urea from the body surface of many mammals as a result of the action of SWEAT GLANDS. The evaporation of sweat cools both the skin and the blood passing through capillaries close to the skin surface. Sweat evaporates most rapidly when the outside air is warm and dry, and when it is windy. Excessive sweating must be compensated for by increased intake of water and salt. Sweating may also increase in response to stress or anxiety.

swede
Root vegetable belonging to the MUSTARD family. The large, swollen taproot may be eaten cooked as a vegetable or fed raw to animals. It is closely related to the TURNIP. Height: *c*.30cm (*c*.12in). Family Brassicaceae/Cruciferae; species *Brassica napobrassica*.

sweetbriar (sweet-briar)
Small, dense hedgerow shrub native to Europe, North Africa and w Asia; it has been naturalized in North America. It has hooked prickles. The foliage, which is scented when damp, is composed of between five and nine leafleted leaves. The single, five-petalled flowers are pink and give rise to orange or red, rounded to oval fruits. Height: to 2m (6.6ft). Family Rosaceae; species *Rosa rubiginosa* or, in the United States, *Rosa eglanteria*.

sweet chestnut
Tree that is native to s Europe, North Africa and w Asia. It is grown for its edible nuts or as an ornamental in parks and gardens. The large nuts are encased in a green, burry fruitcase, which has long, branching spines. The bark is used in tanning and the timber for fencing and gates. Height: to 35m (115ft). Family Fagaceae; species *Castanea sativa*.

sweet gum
Deciduous tree that is native to E North America. In autumn, its maple-like leaves turn brilliant yellow, orange or red. Its spiny brown seedpods are often used for indoor decorations. Height: up to 37m (120ft). Family Hamamelidaceae; species *Liquidambar styraciflua*.

sweet pea
Climbing annual plant; it is native to s Europe and

widely cultivated as an ornamental. It has fragrant, butterfly-shaped flowers of white, pink, rose, lavender, purple, red or orange. Height: to 1.8m (6ft). Family Fabaceae/Leguminosae; species *Lathyrus odoratus*.

sweet pepper
See PEPPER

sweet potato
Trailing plant native to South America and cultivated as a vegetable in Japan, Russia and the Pacific region. It is a member of the MORNING GLORY family. The sweet potato is not related to the potato. Its funnel-shaped flowers are pink or violet. The orange or yellow flesh of the tuber-like root is edible. It is sometimes known as a yam. Family Convolvulaceae; species *Ipomoea batatas*.

sweet william
Flowering plant native to Europe. Introduced as a garden plant, it is now a wildflower in the United States. Its flower heads are pink, red or white. Height: to 60cm (24in). Family Caryophyllaceae; species *Dianthus barbatus*.

swift
Bird that is renowned for its fast flight and agility in the air. It has a brown, cigar-shaped body, long, narrow, curved wings and a short, forked tail. It feeds on flying insects. It resembles the swallow but is a much faster flier. Swifts often feed in large noisy parties over towns and cities. It can sleep in flight. Family Apodidae.

swift, African palm
Slender-winged, long-tailed, grey-brown swift. It is common in Africa. It flies in flocks rapidly around date palms, where it roosts and nests. Length: 17cm (7in). Family Apodidae; species *Cypsiurus parvus*.

swift, alpine
Largest species of swift. It is easily distinguished by its brown plumage, with a white throat and white underparts crossed by a brown breast band. Its flight is strong and powerful, resembling that of a small falcon. It is found around cliffs, where it breeds, and also in cities. It is strongly migratory. Length: 22cm (9in). Family Apodidae; species *Apus melba*.

▲ **sweet potato** The sweet potato (*Ipomoea batatas*) is one of the world's most important food crops. Various varieties are cultivated in warm temperate and tropical regions. It is a useful crop as it will grow in poor tropical soils. The sweet potato produces large, irregular tubers, which are edible when cooked. The leaves can also be eaten.

swift, chimney
Small, pale brown swift found in the Americas. It has a cigar-shaped body and a square tail. Its flight is more fluttering than that of other swifts; in its display flight it raises its wings while the body rocks from side to side. It nests in chimneys, barns and hollow trees. Length: 13cm (5in). Family Apodidae; species *Chaetura pelagica*.

swift, Eurasian
Swift that is a common visitor from Africa to Europe and Asia. It has long, curved wings, a forked tail and brown plumage with a whitish throat. Its flight is vigorous and dashing, wheeling and gliding in excitable parties that chase each other squealing around houses in towns and villages. Length: 17cm (7in). Family Apodidae; species *Apus apus*.

swift, needle-tailed
Either of two similar species of large swifts native to E Asia. The needle-tailed swift has broad wings and a very short, minutely spine-tipped, square tail. Its plumage is brown, glossed green or purple. It has a conspicuous white horseshoe-shaped patch on its underparts. Length: 20cm (8in). Family Apodidae; genus *Hirundapus*.

swiftlet
Any of numerous species of SWIFT-like birds belonging to the genus *Collocalia*. The swiftlet is smaller than the swift and has bat-like wing beats. Its tail is square ended or notched rather than forked. It is found mostly in Asia and Australasia. The nests

▲ **swift, African palm**
The palm swift (*Cypsiurus parvus*) is found in Southeast Asia and Indonesia as well as Africa. It builds a tiny nest of feathers on a palm leaf and sticks its eggs to the nest with saliva. Its salivary glands enlarge during the breeding season.

▲ **swift, alpine** Spending its summers in hilly areas of s Europe and North Africa, the alpine swift (*Apus melba*) nests in rocky crevices. As with other swifts, it has tiny feet and can barely walk.

S

▶ **swordfish** An extremely large and powerful fish, the swordfish (*Xiphias gladius*) can swim at speeds of up to 70km/h (40mph). Its only predators are sharks and humans. Primarily a solitary animal, it is only found in groups if there is an unusually good supply of food.

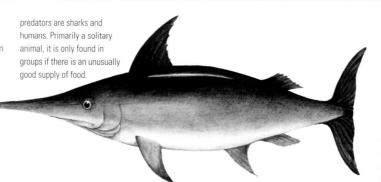

of edible swiftlets are made entirely of saliva; they are collected commercially to make bird's-nest soup. Length: 10–15cm (4–6in). Family Apodidae; genus *Collocalia*.

swim bladder (air bladder)
Air-filled sac that controls the buoyancy of bony FISH. The swim bladder is located above the gut. A connection from the bladder to the gut allows air to enter and leave the bladder. Air may also travel to the bladder along capillary blood vessels. The amount of air in the bladder can be changed so that the fish's specific gravity matches that of the surrounding water. In LUNGFISH the swim bladder also acts as a rudimentary lung.

Swiss chard (spinach beet)
Cultivated form of BEET that is popular as a vegetable. The leaves are eaten, fresh in salads or cooked. Family Chenopodiaceae; species *Beta vulgaris* (subspecies *vulgaris*).

swordfish (broadbill)
Marine fish found in temperate and tropical seas worldwide. It is silvery black, dark purple or blue. Its long flattened upper jaw, in the shape of a sword, is one-third of its body length; it is used to strike at prey. It is a food fish. Length: to 4.5m (15ft). Family Xiphiidae; species *Xiphias gladius*.

swordtail
Freshwater, live-bearing fish found in tropical waters from s Mexico to Guatemala. The male of this popular aquarium fish can be identified by a long extension of its tail fin. The many varieties include red-eyed, red wagtail and berlin swordtails. Length: to 13cm (5in). Family Poeciliidae; species *Xiphophorus helleri*.

sycamore (great maple, false plane)
Deciduous tree of the MAPLE family; it is native to central Europe and w Asia but is widely naturalized. The sycamore has deeply toothed, five-lobed leaves, greenish-yellow flowers and winged brown fruit. Height: to 33m (108ft). Family Aceraceae; species *Acer pseudoplatanus*.

sylph
Any member of the genus *Aglaiocercus*, comprising several species of short-billed, South American HUMMINGBIRDS. The male has a very long, notched tail, brilliant, glittering, metallic blue-green back feathers and bright cinnamon underparts. The sylph is found in humid forests, where it hovers and clings to flowers for nectar and flies from open perches. Length: male 18cm (7in); female 9cm (4in). Family Trochilidae; genus *Aglaiocercus*.

symbiosis
Relationship between two or more different organisms living in close contact with each other. Such relationships may be MUTUALISTIC, PARASITIC or COMMENSALISTIC. They include that of the CLEANER FISH that pick food from the teeth of larger fish, thus obtaining a meal while providing a service; or the presence of NITROGEN-FIXING BACTERIA in the roots of many plants, whereby the plant gains nitrogen compounds and the bacteria are supplied with food materials such as carbohydrates.

symmetry
Anatomical description of body form or geometrical pattern of a plant or animal. It can be used in the classification of living things (TAXONOMY).

sympathetic nervous system
One of the two parts of the AUTONOMIC NERVOUS SYSTEM, the other being the PARASYMPATHETIC NERVOUS SYSTEM. Both are involved with the action of INVOLUNTARY MUSCLES. The sympathetic NERVOUS SYSTEM controls the muscles that prepare the body for action, by, for example, increasing heart rate and slowing digestion. The parasympathetic nervous system does the reverse.

sympatric speciation
Situation that arises when organisms inhabiting the same area become reproductively isolated into two groups for reasons other than geographical isolation. Such reasons might include: incompatibility of the genitalia; incompatibility of the GAMETES; HYBRID inviability; hybrid sterility; or behavioural isolation. *See also* ISOLATION MECHANISM

synapse
Connection between the nerve ending of one NEU-RONE and the next or between a nerve cell and a muscle. It is the site at which NERVE IMPULSES are transmitted, using chemicals (NEUROTRANSMITTERS), such as ACETYLCHOLINE, secreted by structures in the nerve endings.

synapsid
Member of a group of extinct tetrapods, often classified with the reptiles, which evolved in late Carboniferous times and show some primitive mammalian characteristics. Synapsids include the PELYCOSAURS and THERAPSIDS. They have a single pair of openings low down in the skull behind the eyes. They died out in mid-Jurassic times.

syncline
Downward FOLD in rocks. When rock layers fold down into a trough-like form, it is known as a syncline. (An upward arch-shaped fold is called an ANTICLINE.) The sides of the syncline are called **limbs**, and the median line between the limbs along the trough is known as the axis of the fold.

synovial fluid
Viscous, colourless fluid that lubricates the movable joints between the bones. It is secreted by the synovial membrane, which links the bones at a freely movable joint. Synovial fluid is also found in the bursae, which are membranous sacs that help to reduce friction in major joints such as the shoulder, hip and knee.

syringa
Any member of the genus *Syringa*, comprising the LILAC species.

syrinx
Vocal organ of a BIRD. It consists of thin, vibrating muscles at the base of the windpipe.

Szent-Györgyi, Albert von (1893–1986)
US biochemist, b. Hungary. He was awarded the 1937 Nobel Prize for physiology or medicine for his work on biological oxidation processes and the isolation of vitamin C. Szent-Györgyi also studied the biochemistry of MUSCLES, discovering the muscle protein actin, which is responsible for muscular contraction when combined with the muscle protein myosin.

▶ **symbiosis** *Iridomyrmex* ants and the *Myrmecodia* (ant plant) benefit from a symbiotic relationship. The ants feed on the sugary nectar of the plant. This is produced in nectaries (1), which develop at the base of the flower (2) after the petals and sepals have fallen off. The plant benefits from the vital minerals contained in the ants' defecation and waste materials (3), which it absorbs through the inner surface of the chambers (4). The ant plant is epiphytic, growing suspended from trees in upland rainforests. In these areas the soils are often lacking in nutrients, so the mineral nutrients provided by the ants are an important supplement to the plant's poor diet. As the plant grows, its stem enlarges and develops cavities, which are invaded by the ants (5). These chambers do not interconnect, but have separate passages to the outside (6). A complete colony of ants soon becomes established within the plant.

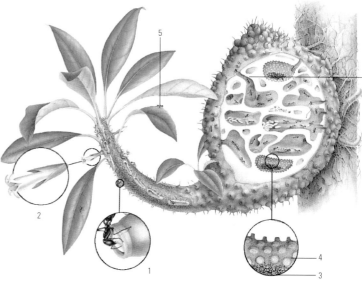

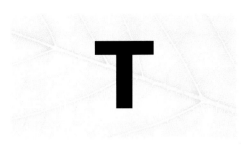

T

tachinid fly

Any member of the FLY family Tachinidae. It comprises insects, the large larvae of which are internal PARASITES of other insects, including the GYPSY MOTH, ARMYWORM and CUTWORM. Many tachinid fly species resemble the HOUSE-FLY. Order Diptera; family Tachinidae.

tadpole

Aquatic larva of a TOAD or FROG. It has a finned tail and gills; it lacks lungs and legs. Tadpoles of most species are herbivores, feeding on algae and other aquatic plants. During METAMORPHOSIS, legs are grown, the tail is reabsorbed, and internal lungs take the place of gills.

tadpole shrimp

Any of 15 species of large CRUSTACEAN found in freshwater pools. It is recognisable by its shield-like carapace. The abdomen contains more than 70 paired appendages. Vision is by close-set, sessile, compound eyes. All the species inhabit temporary pools, mainly in warm regions. The eggs can survive long periods of drought, sometimes for more than 15 years. Feeding is both predacious (by a powerful bite) and by filtering. The tadpole shrimp often reproduces asexually. Adult body length: 15–90mm (0.6–3.5in). Class Branchiopoda; order Notostraca; family Triopsidae; species include *Triops cancriformis*.

tahr

Sure-footed GOAT-ANTELOPE. It lives on steep cliff faces in large herds. The tahr feeds on any vegetation it can find. Males are bigger and have heavier horns than females. The young are born in winter after about seven months' gestation. Family Bovidae; genus *Hemitragus*.

tahr, Arabian

Smallest member of the genus *Hemitragus*. The Arabian tahr is found in Oman. It has a brownish

▲ **takahe** The rare takahe (*Porphyrio mantelli*), sometimes known as the giant rail, was thought to have become extinct in the 19th century. In 1948, however, it was rediscovered in the Murchison Mountains of New Zealand's South Island. Flightless, the takahe use its wings for display purposes only.

coat, with a black dorsal stripe and white underparts. It is an endangered species. Family Bovidae; species *Hemitragus jayakari*.

tahr, Himalayan

Tahr that is found in the Indian Himalayas. Its long coat varies from copper to black; the male has a ruff of long hair around the neck. Head-body length: 1.3–1.7m (4.3–5.6ft); tail: 9cm (4in). Family Bovidae; species *Hemitragus jemlahicus*.

tahr, Nilgiri

Tahr found in s India. The male has a short black coat with a silver saddle patch; the female is grey-brown with white underparts. The Nilgiri tahr is vulnerable to extinction. Head-body length: 1.3–1.7m (4.3–5.6ft). Family Bovidae; species *Hemitragus hylocrius*.

taiga

Coniferous forest that extends over thousands of square kilometres in Siberia, Russia, Finland, Sweden, Norway and Canada. Climatic conditions are unsuitable for deciduous woodland, but coniferous trees can survive. Summer temperatures are around 15°C (59°F), and January averages −10°C to −20°C (14°F to −4°F). There are several months with temperatures below freezing point, and the subsoil is frozen for much of the year. The roots of the coniferous trees spread out horizontally because they cannot penetrate vertically into the ground. The main types of CONIFER tree are SPRUCE, LARCH, FIR and PINE. In the southern parts of the taiga, the trees grow to 15m (50ft) in height, but further north the trees become smaller until they are little more than bushes, and TUNDRA vegetation can be seen. Wherever coniferous forests occur, the needles fall to the ground to produce the type of soil known as PODZOL, which is acid and ashy grey in colour. *See also* EVERGREEN

tailorbird

Any member of the genus *Orthotomus*, a group of small, green perching birds related to the WARBLER. The tailorbird has a long, curved bill, short wings and a graduated tail that is held cocked. It is found mostly in s Asia. It is so called because of its habit of sowing leaves together to build a nest. Length: 13cm (5in). Family Sylviidae; genus *Orthotomus*.

taipan

Large, brownish SNAKE that usually has a pale head or snout. The scales on its neck and the middle of its back are often keeled. Taipans live in forests and savannas of NE and N Australia, feeding mostly on small mammals. Their venom is highly toxic. The taipan is Australia's most dangerous snake. Length: *c*.2m (*c*.6.6ft). Family Elapidae; species *Oxyuranus scutellatus*.

takahe

Large, flightless bird, closely related to the SWAMP-HEN. It is found only in New Zealand and has become very rare due to predation from feral cats and rats. It is found in tussock grasslands, where it indicates its presence by leaving behind chewed stems. Length: 63cm (25in). Weight: to 3kg (7lbs). Family Rallidae; species *Porphyrio mantelli*.

takin

Heavy, goat-like mammal found in the forests of the Himalayan foothills and the mountains of central Asia. It has a thick, shaggy, brownish coat and backwards-pointing horns. It feeds primarily on bamboo shoots and other plants. Height: to 100cm (39in) at shoulder. Family Bovidae; species *Budorcas taxicolor*.

► **tamandua** Also known as the lesser anteater, the southern tamandua shown here (*Tamandua tetradactyla*) is found in tropical forests from Mexico to Brazil. It is one of the larger tamandua species, reaching lengths of up to 58cm (23in). It does not completely destroy the nest of the termites or ants on which it feeds, but leaves it fairly intact so that it can return to eat more insects on another occasion.

talus

See SCREE

tamandua (tree anteater, collared anteater)

Nocturnal EDENTATE animal that lives in savanna, scrub and forests of s North America, Central America and N South America. It hangs onto branches with its powerful, curved claws and prehensile tail. Its foreclaws are also used for striking out at attackers and for breaking open the nests of ants and termites, which it licks up with its long, sticky tongue. Head-body length: 54–58cm (21–23in); tail: 54–55 (21–22in). Family Myrmecophagidae; genus *Tamandua*.

tamandua, northern

Tamandua that has a fawn coat with a black "vest" pattern. Family Myrmecophagidae; species *Tamandua mexicana*.

tamandua, southern

Tamandua that can be gold, brown or black, either unpatterned or with a "vest". Family Myrmecophagidae; species *Tamandua tetradactyla*.

tamarin

Tiny MONKEY that lives in the Amazon rainforest. It has soft, silky fur in a variety of colours and patterns, often with tufts, ruffs or moustaches. It "gallops" along the branches of trees, rather than swinging. Tamarins live in sociable family groups and feed by day on plant and animal material. Head-body length: 19–21cm (7–8in); tail: 25–29 (10–11in). Family Callitrichidae; genera *Saguinus* and *Leontopithecus*; there are *c*.12 species.

T

◄ **tamarin** The cotton-top tamarin (*Saguinus oedipus*) is found in forests of Colombia but is now an endangered species. It feeds on insects, fruits and nectar. Cotton-top tamarins live in small groups, with one mated pair being dominant. They define their territory using scent.

tamarin, black-mantled (black and red tamarin)
Tamarin that has a dark brown back and green, buff or red underparts. Family Callitrichidae; species *Saguinus nigricollis*.

tamarin, cotton-top
Tamarin that is distinguished by the long white hairs over its head and shoulders. Family Callitrichidae; species *Saguinus oedipus*.

tamarin, lion (golden lion tamarin)
Largest species of tamarin; it is endangered. It has a mane of hair around its head and may be golden or black and gold. Head-body length: 34–40cm (13–16in); tail: 26–38 (10–15in). Family Callitrichidae; species *Leontopithecus rosalia*.

tamarin, moustached (black-chested moustached tamarin)
Tamarin that is black or rusty red. Family Callitrichidae; species *Saguinus mystax*.

tamarind
Tropical tree native to Asia and Africa. It has divided, feather-like leaves and pale yellow flowers streaked with red. The fruit pulp is used in beverages, food and medicines. Height: 12–24m (39–79ft). Family Fabaceae/Leguminosae; species *Tamarindus indica*.

tamarisk
Any of a group of deciduous shrubs usually found in semi-arid areas. They have slender branches covered with blue-green, scale-like leaves and clusters of small, white or pink flowers. Height: to 9m (30ft). Family Tamaricaceae; genus *Tamarix*.

tanager
Any member of a very large group of perching birds found in the Americas. Most are tropical species, some are warbler-like, whereas others are finch-like. Many species have beautiful multi-coloured plumage. Most species feed on fruit; some feed exclusively on one type of fruit and their droppings act as the means of seed dispersal. Length: 13–23cm (5–9in). Family Thraupidae.

tanaid
Any of many species of small CRUSTACEANS, most of which are marine. They resemble ISOPODS. Tanaids are found from shore to abyssal depths and are both free-swimming and burrowing in habit. The body is linear and either cylindrical or flattened, depending on the species. Adult body length: *c*.10mm (*c*.0.4in). Order Tanaidacea; genera include *Apseudes* and *Tanais*.

T

◄ **taro** The starchy tuberous root, shown here, of the taro plant is eaten cooked as a vegetable. It is poisonous if eaten raw. Taro is known by a variety of names, including "eddo" or "dasheen" in the West Indies and "old cocoyam" in w Africa.

tangerine (mandarin orange)
See SATSUMA

tansy
Any of several species of mostly perennial plants characterized by fern-like, aromatic leaves and clusters of yellow, button-like flower heads. *Tanacetum vulgare*, native to temperate regions of the Northern Hemisphere, is a common weed in North America. Height: to 90cm (35in). Family Asteraceae/Compositae.

tapaculo
Any member of a little-known group of solitary South American birds of the forest floor. They are mostly dark, small and wren-like, with a narrow, laterally compressed bill. Their name comes from Spanish, meaning "to cover your posterior", which is a reference to the habit of cocking their tail. Length: 13–19cm (5–7cm). Family Rhinocryptidae.

tapeworm
Any member of the class Cestoda, a group of several thousand parasitic worms. The name tapeworm usually refers to a PARASITE of the genus *Taenia*, which colonizes the intestines of vertebrates, including human beings. Caught from eating raw or undercooked meat, it can cause serious disease. Class Cestoda.

tapioca
See CASSAVA

tapir
Primitive relative of the HORSE. There are four species of tapir, all of which are stocky hoofed mammals with short legs and short, trunk-like noses. Nocturnal forest-dwellers, they feed on any vegetation. Tapirs have four toes on the front feet and three on the hind. Head-body length: 1.8–2.5m (5.9–8.2ft); tail: 5–10cm (2–4in). Family Tapiridae; genus *Tapirus*.

tapir, Baird's
Tapir that inhabits forests in Central America. It has a sparse reddish coat, a thick mane and white ear fringes. It is a vulnerable species. Family Tapiridae; species *Tapirus bairdi*.

tapir, Brazilian
Tapir found in South American forests. It is dark brown with a short mane. Family Tapiridae; species *Tapirus terrestris*.

tapir, Malayan (Asian tapir)
Endangered species of tapir from Southeast Asia. It is black, with a wide, white band around its body. Family Tapiridae; species *Tapirus indicus*.

tapir, mountain (woolly tapir, Andean tapir)
Tapir that inhabits mountainous forests of South America. It has a thick red coat, a white chin and ear fringes. It is a vulnerable species. Family Tapiridae; species *Tapirus pinchaque*.

taproot
First ROOT that develops from the RADICLE. The taproot grows directly downwards and remains the main root of the plant, sending off lateral side roots to extend the root system. In BIENNIAL plants, the leaves of which usually die down in the first winter, the root is the part of the plant that remains alive underground ready to grow new leaves the following year. In some plants (such as BEETS, CARROTS and PARSNIPS) the taproot develops into a fleshy organ for storing STARCH. In root vegetables, it forms the edible part of the plant.

tardigrade
See WATER-BEAR

taro
Large, tropical plant native to the Pacific Islands and Southeast Asia. It is cultivated in other parts of the world for its edible, tuberous root. Family Araceae; species *Colocasia esculenta*.

tarpon
Any of several species of tropical, marine fish. It is blue and bright silver, with a long, forked tail. It is a game fish. Length: to 1.8m (5.9ft). Family Megalopidae; species include *Megalops cyprinoides* (small Pacific tarpon) and *Megalops atlanticus* (large Atlantic tarpon).

tarragon
Perennial plant with liquorice-flavoured leaves used as a culinary HERB. Family Asteraceae/Compositae; species *Artemisia dracunculus*.

tarsals
In terrestrial vertebrates, the seven bones that make up the ankle and adjoining part of the foot. Strong, compact bones, they are arranged so that the foot can be rotated (to a limited extent) in any direction. The tarsals articulate with the lower leg bones above and with the METATARSALS of the foot below.

tar sands
Porous, often black, rocks such as LIMESTONES, SANDS and SANDSTONES found on the surface. They contain deposits of BITUMEN (asphalt) in the spaces between the grains and commonly have a distinct odour of tar. Extensive deposits are found in North America, primarily in Alberta and Texas. Estimates of the amount of bitumen contained in these deposits

▲ **tarsier** These small primates are so called because of their enlongated tarsals (foot bones), which enable them to leap great distances between trees. As with other tarsiers, the Philippine tarsier (*Tarsius syrichta*) has adapted neck vertebrae, which allow it to turn its head through 180 degrees.

▲ **Tasmanian devil** Once found on the Australian mainland, the Tasmanian devil (*Sarcophilus harrisii*) is now confined to remote parts of Tasmania. It preys by night on a variety of animals as well as scavenging. Very strong for its size, its prey is sometimes much larger than itself.

are extremely high, but its high viscosity makes extraction difficult.

tarsier
Any of three species of small, agile prosimians found in Southeast Asian forests. Tarsiers have long hind legs for leaping through the branches. They live in pairs or small family groups. They are nocturnal and have large eyes and ears with which to find their insect prey. Head-body length: 11–14cm (4–6in); tail: 20–26cm (8–10in). Suborder Prosimii; family Tarsiidae; genus *Tarsius*.

tarsier, Philippine
Endangered species of tarsier. It is grey or grey-buff with an ochre face. Family Tarsiidae; species *Tarsius syrichta*.

tarsier, spectral (Celebes or Sulawesi tarsier)
Tarsier found on the island of Sulawesia. It has a dark grey coat. Family Tarsiidae; species *Tarsius spectrum*.

tarsier, western
Tarsier that is buff-coloured with brown tips. Family Tarsiidae; species *Tarsius bancanus*.

Tasmanian devil
Large marsupial carnivore that is now found only in Tasmania. Its fur is dark, with occasional white patches. Apparently aggressive with strong vocalizations, Tasmanian devils are not, however, very effective hunters. They often feed on carrion, finishing off the whole carcass including the bones. Head-body length: 52–80cm (20–31in); tail: 23–30cm (9–12in). Family Dasyuridae; species *Sarcophilus harrisii*.

Tasmanian wolf (Tasmanian tiger, thylacine)
Large marsupial carnivore that has been considered extinct since the 1930s when the last known specimen died in captivity. Superficially similar to a dog

▶ **Tasmanian wolf** Now thought to be extinct, the Tasmanian wolf (*Thylacinus cynocephalus*) inhabited most recently the rainforests of sw Tasmania, but fossil remains have also been found in Australia and New Guinea. It closely resembled, in appearance and behaviour, members of the dog family – an example of convergent evolution.

or wolf, it was distinguished by dark black or brown stripes across a light grey or sandy brown back; it had a long, stiff tail. Head-body length: 85–130cm (33–51in); tail: 38–65cm (15–26in). Family Thylacinidae; genus *Thylacinus cynocephalus*.

taste
One of the five SENSES. It responds to the chemical constituents of food. In human beings, the taste buds of the tongue differentiate four qualities: sweetness, saltiness, bitterness and sourness. The sense of taste is supplemented by the sense of SMELL.

tattler
Any member of a small genus of uniformly grey, sandpiper-like wading birds. The tattler is found around rocky Pacific coasts in winter and breeds along freshwater streams. In breeding plumage its underparts become heavily barred grey. As the tattler feeds, its body teeters and bobs nervously. Length: 26cm (10in). Family Scolopacidae; genus *Heteroscelus*.

Tatum, Edward Lawrie (1900–75)
US geneticist and biochemist. He shared the 1958 Nobel Prize for physiology or medicine with George BEADLE and Joshua LEDERBERG for his part in the discovery that GENES act by regulating specific chemical processes, a basic principle explaining how genes determine hereditary characteristics. *See also* HEREDITY

taxis
Movement of a whole organism or a freely motile part of an organism, such as a GAMETE, in response to an external stimulus. Movement towards the stimulus is **positive taxis** and away from the stimulus is **negative taxis**. Notable stimuli include light (PHOTOTAXIS) and chemicals (chemotaxis). Various types of algae, for example, exhibit positive phototaxis – they swim towards a light source in order to increase photosynthesis.

taxon
General term for any unit of CLASSIFICATION of plants and animals; taxonomic units include PHYLUM, CLASS, ORDER and so on.

taxonomy
Organization of organisms into categories based on similarities of either morphology and anatomy (**classical taxonomy**), protein and nucleic acid structure (**biochemical taxonomy**), the behaviour and morphology of chromosomes (**cytotaxonomy**), or the analysis of numerical data (**numerical taxonomy**). Carolus LINNAEUS developed the first taxonomic system during the 1750s. *See also* BINOMIAL NOMENCLATURE; CLASSIFICATION; Ready Reference, pages 462–63

◀ **tea** The evergreen shrub *Camellia sinensis* is the commercial source of tea. The leathery, oblong leaves grow to a maximum of 25cm (10in) in length. It takes about 40 days for a tea plant to produce a full "flush" of leaves ready for picking. Many different varieties are cultivated.

tayberry
Cultivated fruit tree produced from a cross between a RASPBERRY and an American BLACKBERRY. The tayberry is one of several hybrid berries originating from crosses between the raspberry and a member of the BRAMBLE group. The bright crimson soft fruits have good flavour and are used in desserts, freezing and jam-making. Family Rosaceae; genus *Rubus*.

tayra
MARTEN with a short body and long legs. It is native to the forests of South America, where it feeds on small animals and fruits. It has a short, dark brown coat, with a cream-coloured throat patch. The sexes are similar in size. Tayras live in small family groups. Three kittens are born in May after a 65-day gestation. Head-body length: 90–115cm (35–45in); tail: 35–45cm (14–18in). Family Mustelidae; species *Eira barbata*.

tchagra (bush-shrike)
Any of several species of ground-dwelling birds with heavily hooked bills. The tchagra has mainly brown plumage, with a striped head pattern or black cap. It is difficult to see as it creeps around the bottom of bushes in reedy swamps, dry bush and woodlands, but it reveals its presence with a distinctive call. Length: 81–23cm (7–9in). Family Laniidae; genus *Tchagra*.

tea
Any member of a family of trees and shrubs with leathery, undivided leaves and five-petalled blossoms. *Camellia sinensis* is the commercial source of tea. Cultivated in moist, tropical regions, tea plants can reach 9m (30ft) in height but are kept low by frequent picking of the young shoots for tea leaves. The leaves are dried immediately to produce green tea and are fermented before drying for black tea. Family Theaceae; there are *c*.500 species.

teak
Tree, native to s India, Burma and Indonesia, that is valued for its hard, yellowish-brown wood. Teak wood is water-resistant and takes a high polish; it is widely used for furniture and in shipbuilding. Height: 45m (150ft). Family Verbenaceae; species *Tectona grandis*.

teal
Any member of a large group of small dabbling DUCKS. Most species graze on plants growing along water margins, but some up-end and graze from the bottom. The male is often richly coloured, usually with an iridescent coloured patch (the speculum) on each wing. Length: *c*.40cm (*c*.16in). Family Anatidae.

tear fault (lateral fault, wrench fault)
Geological FAULT in which the movement is along the horizontal. Tear faults occur frequently in areas of TECTONIC activity. The amount of movement may only be a few metres, but it can be several kilometres in some cases. The San Andreas Fault in California is a well-known example of a tear fault.

T

tears

Salty fluid secreted by the lachrymal glands; it moistens the surface of the EYE. Having antibacterial properties, tears cleanse and disinfect the surface of the eye and also bring nutrients to the CORNEA.

teasel

Any of several species of plants that grow in Europe, the Middle East and North America. They are prickly plants with cup-like leaf bases that trap water. Species include fuller's teasel (*Dipsacus fullonum*), the purple flowers heads of which were used for carding wool. Family Dipsacaceae.

tectonics

Deformation within the Earth's CRUST and the geological structures produced by deformation, including FOLDS, FAULTS and the development of mountain chains. PLATE TECTONICS originates from the study of the main structural features of the Earth's crust, such as MID-OCEAN RIDGES, major TEAR FAULTS, ocean TRENCHES, continental blocks and earthquake belts, but it is now used to describe a theory that can explain the distribution and evolution of these features.

teeth

Hard, bone-like structures embedded in the JAWS of vertebrates, used for chewing food, defence or other purposes. The teeth of all vertebrates have a similar structure, consisting of three layers. Mammalian teeth have an outer layer of hard enamel. The middle layer consists of dentine, which is a bone-like substance capable of regeneration. The core of a tooth contains pulp, which is softer and has a blood supply and nerves; it provides nutrients for the dentine.

tef

Annual GRASS native to Ethiopia, where red- and white-seeded forms are cultivated for the grain, which is ground into a brownish flour and made into pancakes. Elsewhere in Africa tef is grown as a fodder crop. The straw is used in brick manufacture. Height: to 1m (39in). Family Poaceae/Gramineae; species *Eragrostis tef*.

tektite

Generally dark, glassy objects, ranging in diameter from 40 micrometres to 2mm (microtektites) and larger (to 10cm), believed to be of either lunar origin or formed from splashes of liquefied rock during meteorite impact on Earth. Tektites occur in limited areas, called strewn-fields, on continents and ocean floors.

teleost

Member of a very large group, *c*.22,000 species, of bony FISH, such as COD, SALMON and EEL. Teleosts evolved in late Triassic times; in Tertiary times they became the dominant fish of marine and fresh waters.

telophase

Stage in CELL DIVISION, following ANAPHASE. It is the final phase of MITOSIS and MEIOSIS. In **mitosis**, telophase involves the division of the CYTOPLASM to form two daughter cells with the same number of CHROMOSOMES as the original cell nucleus. The separated CHROMATIDS accumulate at the poles of the SPINDLE and a nuclear membrane forms to separate the two groups. In **meiosis**, there are two stages of telophase. In the first stage, two daughter cells are produced when a membrane forms between the separated chromatids. In the second telophase, these daughter cells divide to produce four cells, which are HAPLOID.

temperate zone

Either of two regions of the Earth. The northern temperate zone lies between the Arctic Circle and the Tropic of Cancer, and the southern zone lies between the Tropic of Capricorn and the Antarctic Circle. A **temperate climate** is a moderate CLIMATE, as occurs in most temperate zones. The summers tend to be warm, but the winters are cool. Temperate climates have neither very high nor very low temperatures.

temperature

Measure of the hotness or coldness of an object. Strictly, it describes the number of energy states available to a substance or system. Two objects placed in thermal contact exchange heat energy initially, but eventually arrive at thermal equilibrium, where both are said to have the same temperature – each is losing and gaining heat at equal rates so that neither has a net gain or loss of heat. At equilibrium, the most probable distribution of energy states of the

▲ **tench** The tench (*Tinca tinca*) is usually found in slow-moving muddy waters with plentiful vegetation. It feeds mainly on insect larvae and small crustaceans, which it finds amongst the plants. It is an adaptable fish, noted for its ability to live in conditions of low oxygen.

atoms and molecules composing the objects has been attained. At high temperatures, the number of energy states available to the atoms and molecules of a system is large; at lower temperatures, fewer states are available (molecules become locked into position and liquids change to solids). At a sufficiently low temperature, all parts of the system are at their lowest energy levels, the absolute zero of temperature. *See also* TEMPERATURE SCALE

temperature inversion

Anomalous increase in TEMPERATURE with height. Normally the temperature of the air decreases from ground level upwards. The average rate of decrease is 1°C (1.8°F) for every 160m (525ft). In certain meteorological conditions, this situation is reversed. On a clear, calm, anticyclonic night, the cool air may roll downhill and accumulate in valleys, and the air temperature will be lower near the valley bottom than it is 100m to 200m (328–656ft) higher. Above the cold layer there will be warmer air, which is likely to form cloud or haze. Evidence of a temperature inversion can be seen if there is smoke rising from a bonfire. The smoke will rise vertically and then bend horizontally when it reaches the "inversion layer". If this situation develops on a larger scale, dust and dirt rising into the atmosphere are trapped and unable to escape, causing serious pollution.

temperature scale

Graduated scale of degrees for measuring TEMPERATURE. The establishment of any temperature scale requires: a thermometric parameter that varies linearly with temperature (such as the volume of a gas at constant pressure, or the expansion of a liquid in a tube); two or more fixed points (readily reproducible reference points such as the boiling and the freezing points of water); and the assignment of arbitrary divisions (called degrees) between the fixed points. Gas, alcohol, mercury, electrical resistance and wavelength of light have been used as thermometric parameters. Common temperature scales include the FAHRENHEIT, CELSIUS (formerly centigrade) and KELVIN (or absolute) scales; these are abbreviated to °F, °C and K. The Fahrenheit scale originally used as fixed points the freezing point of water (taken to be 32°F) and the human body temperature (96°F, although later found to be 98.6°F). The interval between these was divided into 64 degrees; by extrapolation, the boiling point of water is 212°F. The Celsius scale uses 0°C and 100°C as the freezing and the boiling point of water, respectively; the interval is divided into 100 degrees. Zero on the Kelvin (or thermodynamic)

◀ **tenrec** The common tenrec (*Tenrec ecaudatus*) of Madagascar, like other members of the Tenrecidae family, has a very variable body temperature. It saves energy while resting by allowing its body temperature to become very low. The common tenrec's eyesight is poor but it has powerful senses of smell and hearing.

T

scale ($-273.15°$C, $-459.67°$F) coincides with absolute zero, the lower limit of temperature; the kelvin represents the same temperature difference as the degree Celsius. To convert Fahrenheit to Celsius: $C = 5(F-32)/9$; to convert Celsius to Fahrenheit, $F = (9C/5) + 32$.

tench

Freshwater food and sport fish of Europe and Asia, belonging to the CARP family. It has a stout, golden-yellow body, with small scales. Length: to 71cm (28in). Family Cyprinidae; species *Tinca tinca*.

tendon

In vertebrates, strong, flexible band of CONNECTIVE TISSUE that joins MUSCLE to BONE.

tendril

Coiling part of STEM or LEAF, a slender, thread-like structure used by climbing plants, such as *Clematis*, for support.

tenrec

Any member of the family Tenrecidae, a group of burrowing, insectivorous mammals native to Madagascar and the Comoros Islands. The common

▶ **tern** The arctic tern (*Sterna paradisaea*) feeds on small fish, which it catches by diving into the water, sometimes becoming completely submerged. Sociable birds, arctic terns nest in large colonies, which can number up to a thousand pairs of birds. They will fiercely defend these colonies. Relatively long-lived birds, most terns mate for life.

tenrec (*Tenrec ecaudatus*) is a nocturnal, highly prolific animal; the female bears up to 20 young at a time. The tenrec has a spiny coat like that of a hedgehog and is the size of a small domestic cat. Family Tenrecidae.

tentacle

Any slender, flexible organ of an animal, most notably those of the OCTOPUS and some other CEPHALOPODS. It is capable of feeling and grasping.

tent caterpillar

Medium-sized, hairy, dark-brown moth CATERPILLAR that, in early spring, spins a large communal nest of silk, usually in a tree crotch. Tent caterpillars defoliate many shrubs and trees and are serious pests in North America and Eurasia. The eastern tent caterpillar (*Malacosoma americanum*), native to North America, has a white stripe down its back and blue and white spots on its sides. Family Lasiocampidae; genus *Malacosoma*.

termite

See feature article

tern

Any of several species of graceful, gull-like water birds. Most species of tern are white with a strongly forked tail, buoyant flight and a thin, pointed bill. Some, such as the sooty tern (*Sterna fuscata*), are blackish above and white below. Many species are long distance migrants; the arctic tern (*Sterna paradisaea*) migrates from pole to pole and back each year. The little tern (*Sterna albifrons*) is the smallest species and the Caspian tern (*Sterna caspia*) the largest species. Length: 22–54cm (9–21in); wingspan: 48–145cm (19–57in). Family Laridae; subfamily Sterninae.

tern, arctic

Sea bird whose migrations are the longest of any bird: it flies from its summer breeding areas in the far north to wintering areas in Antarctica, a round trip of about 35,500km (22,000mi). It has grey, black and white feathers and a reddish bill and feet. It nests in colonies, laying between one and four eggs in a sandy scrape nest. Length: 38cm (15in). Subfamily Sterninae; species *Sterna paradisaea*.

terracing

In geology, process of DEPOSITION or EROSION that produces step-like formations on a slope. Alluvial terracing is usually caused by periodic reductions in the area of the floodplain of a river.

terrane

Small crustal PLATE, or a FAULT-bounded fragment of a larger plate, that can be displaced a considerable distance from its original geological context and added to another plate during PLATE TECTONIC movement.

TERMITE

Social insect found worldwide. It lives in subterranean nests and above-ground mounds. Termites have a complicated caste system, with a king and queen guarded and tended by soldiers, workers and nymphs. Wood is a common component of their diet, which is digested with the help of symbiotic protozoa or bacteria that live in the termites' intestines. Length: 0.2–2.3cm (0.08–0.9in); queens: to 10cm (4in). Order Isoptera.

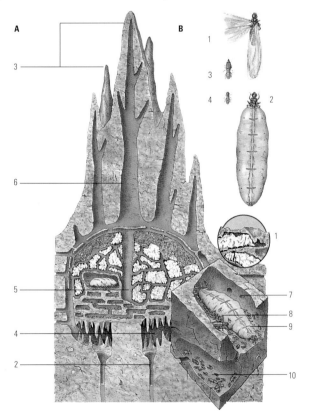

▶ **Built of saliva** and soil particles, termite mounds (A) dominate the African savanna. Most termites prefer to eat dead plant material that has been partly softened by fungus. This food supply is limited in dry conditions because fungi need moisture. For this reason *Macrotermes* termites create fungus chambers (1). These are combs of carton (a mixture of saliva and faecal pellets), which provide a large surface area on which the fungus grows. The fungus flourishes in the humid atmosphere of the nest as it breaks down the faeces in the carton walls. Some termite species dig deep tunnels (2) to find underground water to ensure that the nest is moist. The peaks of the mound (3) act as lungs. Air seeps into the main nest from an air cellar below (4). As the fungus breaks down the faecal comb, heat is generated. The hot air rises, via a large central air space (5), into the chimneys (6). The walls of the nest are porous, so carbon dioxide diffuses into the chimneys. The newly oxygenated air loses heat to the air outside and cools, sinking back to the cellar. The royal cell (7) is in the centre of the nest, where the king (8) and the queen (9) can be protected. The workers, as well as feeding the royal couple, remove the eggs to the brood chambers (10). There the workers lick the eggs to keep them clean. Most termite species have a variety of castes (B) or types. These include: the temporarily winged reproductives (male and female) called alates (1), responsible for setting up colonies; the queen (2), whose enlarged abdomen contain thousands of eggs; the soldier termites (3), which protect the colony; and the workers (4), which collect food, care for the queen and serve as builders.

T

terrapin

Any of several species of fresh or brackish water TURTLES. In North America the term refers only to the diamondback TERRAPIN, but elsewhere it is applied to other aquatic turtles of the families Bataguridae, Emydidae and Pelomedusidae.

terrapin, diamondback

Small terrapin. Its dark, smooth-edged CARAPACE has a central keel and a pattern of concentric grooves on each scute. Its head and neck are usually pale grey, with black spots or flecks. Diamondback terrapins are residents of brackish waters along the E coast of the United States, where their meat was formerly prized. Length: to 23cm (9in). Family Emydidae; species *Malaclemys terrapin*.

terrapin, helmeted

Common, side-necked TURTLE found in most of sub-Saharan Africa and Madagascar. Its carapace is smooth and oval, and its toes are webbed. Helmeted terrapins occupy temporary water bodies and can travel widely between ponds. They produce a foul musky odour if disturbed. Length: to 30cm (12in). Family Pelomedusidae; species *Pelomedusa subrufa*.

terrestrial life

Life on land. The emergence of life on land from life in the seas is thought to have begun early in PALAEOZOIC times, but the fossil record of land-living organisms does not begin until ORDOVICIAN times. The spores of MOSSES and LIVERWORTS are known from Ordovician strata; these BRYOPHYTES were probably the first macroscopic forms of plant life. The fossil footprints (TRACE FOSSILS) of small millipede-like ARTHROPODS are known from some freshwater Ordovician deposits, and it is highly likely that arthropods, with their tough exoskeletons, were the first visible animals to live on dry land. Higher plants did not appear until SILURIAN times and were very small, simple stems, with forked branches and terminal spore-bearing capsules for reproduction. Tree-sized plants did not evolve until DEVONIAN times.

▲ **theropod** The *Tarbosaurus*, shown above, was one of the larger theropod dinosaurs. As with other theropods, it was bipedal and used its large tail to aid balance. Fossil remains of theropods have been found on all continents except Antarctica.

▶ **thistle** The creeping thistle (*Cirsium arvense*) is a weed, commonly found on waste and cultivated land. There are *c.*150 species belonging to the genus *Cirsium*, the flowers of which may be violet, mauve, pink, yellow or white.

terrigenous deposits

Accumulations of sand, silt or mud that form in the sea near land as a result of EROSION.

territory

Restricted life space of an organism. It is an area selected for mating, nesting, roosting, hunting or feeding; it may be occupied by one or more organisms and defended against others of the same or a different species. The area may be defended or indicated by noise-making, chemical scent, physical displays or aggression. Many invertebrates and most vertebrates display territorial behaviour.

Tertiary

Earlier period of the CENOZOIC era, lasting from 65 million to *c.*2 million years ago. It is divided into five epochs, starting with the PALAEOCENE, followed by the EOCENE, OLIGOCENE, MIOCENE and PLIOCENE. Early Tertiary times were marked by great mountain-building activity (the Rockies, Andes, Alps and Himalayas). Both marsupial and placental mammals diversified greatly. Archaic forms of carnivores and herbivores flourished, along with early primates, bats, rodents and whales. *See also* GEOLOGICAL TIME

tertiary consumer

In a FOOD CHAIN, a CARNIVORE that preys on other carnivores (SECONDARY CONSUMERS). Secondary consumers are also carnivores, but they prey on PRIMARY CONSUMERS.

testis (pl. testes)

Male SEX gland, found as a pair located in a pouch, the scrotum, which is external to the body. The testes are made up of seminiferous tubules in which SPERM are formed and mature, after which they drain into ducts and are stored in the epididymis prior to being discharged.

testosterone

Steroid HORMONE secreted mainly by the mammalian TESTIS. It is responsible for the growth and development of male sex organs and male SECONDARY SEXUAL CHARACTERISTICS, such as voice change and growth of facial hair.

tetra

Any of numerous, diverse species of colourful, freshwater fish found in South America. They are egg layers. Tetras are popular aquarium fish. Family Characidae; genera include *Hemigrammus*, *Hyphessobrycon* and *Mimagoniates*.

tetrahedrite

Sulphide mineral composed of varying amounts of copper, iron, zinc, silver, antimony and arsenic sulphides. It is found in medium- to low-temperature ore veins. Tetrahedrite displays cubic system, well-formed, tetrahedral crystals and also appears as masses. it is metallic grey to black. It is an important ore of copper. Hardness 3–5–4; r.d. 4.9.

tetraploid

Having four sets of CHROMOSOMES, each chromosome being represented four times.

tetrapod

Any animal that has four limbs. Tetrapods include most mammals, amphibians and reptiles (except snakes). Some authorities include also bats and birds (because their forelimbs have become adapted into wings) as well as whales and snakes (because they evolved from ancestors that once had four limbs). **Quadrupeds** use all four limbs for walking.

Thallophyta

Obsolete term for a subkingdom of plants that lack clearly differentiated roots, stems or leaves. Thallophytes range in size from one-celled plants to large 60m (200ft) SEAWEEDS. Asexual reproduction is by spores and sexual reproduction is by fusion of gametes. Chlorophyll-containing thallophytes include ALGAE, DINOFLAGELLATES and LICHENS. Thallophytes also included chlorophyll-lacking organisms formerly considered plants, such as BACTERIA, FUNGI and SLIME MOULDS. *See also* THALLUS

thallus

Nonvascular plant body of a SEAWEED. Usually flat or ribbon-shaped, it is not differentiated into root, stem or leaves.

therapsid

Any member of a group of reptile-like, SYNAPSID tetrapods that evolved in late Permian times; the group includes the DICYNODONTS and the CYNODONTS. They died out in early Jurassic times.

thermal

Small-scale, rising current of air produced by local heating of the Earth's surface. Thermals are often used by gliding birds and human-built gliders.

thermocline

Middle layers of OCEAN water, between surface and deep waters, which are defined by differing densities and temperatures. The thermocline is up to 1000m (3300ft) thick and has a temperature only a few degrees above freezing. It is important as a stable boundary that prevents interchange between layers.

thermosphere

Shell of light gases between the MESOSPHERE and the EXOSPHERE, between 100km (60mi) and 400km (250mi) above the Earth's surface. The temperature steadily rises with height in the thermosphere.

theropod

Member of a diverse subgroup of SAURISCHIAN DINOSAURS that included *c.*40% of known kinds of dinosaurs. They evolved in late Triassic times, finally becoming extinct at the end of the Cretaceous. Theropods were mostly large, bipedal and carnivorous, including such groups as the TYRANNOSAURS.

thick-knee

See STONE-CURLEW

thistle

Any of many species of herbaceous plant, usually with prickly leaves or stems and purple, blue, white or yellow flower heads. Some species are cultivated in gardens, such as the globe thistles (*Echinops* spp.). Other species have become weeds, for example the

T

creeping thistle (*Cirsium arvense*) and the sowthistles (*Sonchus* spp.). *Centaurea iberica* is the thistle of the Bible. Family Asteraceae; genera include *Carduus*, *Centaurea*, *Cirsium*, *Echinops* and *Sonchus*.

Thomson, Sir Charles Wyville (1830–82)
Scottish naturalist. He was appointed director of the Challenger expedition (1872–76), which sailed nearly 128,000km (69,000 nautical mi) making studies of the life, water and seafloor in the three main oceans. Thomson published *The Depths of the Sea* (1873) and an account of his expedition, *The Voyage of the Challenger* (1877).

Thomson's gazelle
See GAZELLE, THOMSON'S

thongweed
Olive-green, perennial SEAWEED found in deep pools of the lower shores of the North Sea and Atlantic coasts from Norway to Portugal. The vegetative plant resembles a mushroom, with a trumpet-shaped disc on a short stalk. Its narrow, once- or twice-branched, strap-like fruiting bodies develop from this stalk and reach lengths of up to 2m (6.6ft). Family Himanthaliaceae; species *Himanthalia elongata*.

thorax
In anatomy, part between the neck and the abdomen. In mammals it is enclosed by the ribcage and contains the lungs, heart and oesophagus. It is separated from the abdomen by the diaphragm. In arthropods the thorax consists of several segments to which legs and other appendages are attached.

thornbill
Any of several species of very small Australian songbirds. The thornbill is mostly buff or yellow below, with a reddish-brown or yellow rump. It flits constantly through vegetation, snapping-up insects, and is a strong songster and mimic. The brown thornbill (*Acanthiza pusilla*) is the familiar brown garden bird of coastal SE Australia. Length: 9–11cm (*c*.4in). Family Acanthizidae; genus *Acanthiza*.

thorny devil
See MOLOCH

thrasher
Any of many species of thrush-like songbirds found in North and Central America; they belong to the MOCKINGBIRD family. The thrasher has a longish, curved bill and a long, graduated tail. The brown thrasher (*Toxostoma rufum*) has reddish-brown plumage, with a heavily spotted breast; other thrasher species are mainly olive green. Its song is noted for its volume and rich variety of phrases; some

species mimic the songs of others. Length: 22–31cm (9–12in). Family Mimidae.

threadworm (pinworm)
Small parasitic worm common in moist tropical regions. It resembles a short length of hair or thread. The threadworm may inhabit the intestines of animals but can live and breed freely in soil. Phylum Aschelminthes; species *Oxyurus vermicularis*.

thrift
See SEA PINK

thrip
Any of numerous species of slender, sucking insects found throughout the world. Most species have long, narrow wings, but some are wingless. They vary in colour, according to species. Most feed on plant sap and some transmit plant diseases. Length: to 8mm (0.3in). Order Thysanoptera.

thrush
Any of a large group of small to medium-sized songbirds. Some species are entirely ground living. All feed mainly on insects and berries. Many species, such as the song thrush (*Turdus philomelos*), are brown above and spotted below. White's (scaly) thrush (*Zoothera dauma*) has a boldly scaled pattern. The rock thrushes (species of the genera *Pseudocossyphus* and *Monticola*) have a blue head and back and an orange belly. Length: 17–27cm (7–11in). Family Turdidae.

thrush, hermit
North American songbird. It is brownish, with a spotted breast and reddish-brown tail. It is a fine singer. Length: to 18cm (7in). Family Turdidae; species *Hylocichla guttata*.

thunder fly (thunder bug)
Any of *c*.5000 species of small, brown or black flies. They have slender bodies and usually two pairs of narrow, fringed wings. Thunder flies are often found in flowers, where they feed on sap. They are very common in mid-summer and are associated with thundery weather. Order Thysanoptera; families Phlaeothripidae, Aeolothripidae and Thripidae; species include *Haplothrips tritici*.

thunderstorm
Electrical storm, commonly experienced as LIGHTNING and thunder. Thunderstorms are caused by the separation of electrical charges in CLOUDS. Water drops are carried by updrafts to the top of a cloud, where they become ionized and accumulate into positive charges – the base of the cloud being negatively charged. An electrical discharge (a spark) between clouds, or a cloud and the ground, is accompanied by light (seen as a lightning stroke) and heat, which expands the air explosively and causes it to reverberate and produce sounds and echoes called thunder. Thunderstorms are usually accompanied by heavy rain; OZONE and the oxides of NITROGEN are produced in the air.

thylacine
See TASMANIAN WOLF

thyme
Aromatic garden herb of the MINT family. It is planted as an ornamental and has purple flowers. Its fragrant leaves are used in cooking. Thyme yields an oil from which the drug thymol is prepared. Height: 15–20cm (6–8in). Family Lamiaceae/Labiatae; species *Thymus vulgaris*.

◄ **thyme** The herb thyme (*Thymus vulgaris*) has a pungent aroma and retains much of its flavour when dried. It is a favourite herb for Mediterranean cooking and is an essential ingredient of bouquet garni.

thymine
In molecular biology, one of the four nitrogen-containing organic bases in the NUCLEIC ACID DNA (the other bases are ADENINE, GUANINE and CYTOSINE). In RNA thymine is replaced by URACIL in the base sequence.

tibia (shinbone)
Inner and larger of the two lower leg bones. It articulates with the FEMUR, or upper leg bone, at the knee and extends to the ankle, where its lower end forms the projecting ankle bone on the inside of the leg. *See also* FIBULA

tick
Any of *c*.600 species of blood-sucking insects. Ticks differ from MITES in that they are larger and have a pair of breathing pores (spiracles) behind the third or fourth pair of legs. The tick's gnathosoma (head) comprises a base, a pair of palps and a rigid, toothed structure to anchor it to the host. Several species transmit diseases: the fowl tick carries spirochaetosis; and *Dermacentor andersoni* carries Colorado tick fever. Other diseases carried by ticks include lyme disease and Rocky Mountain fever. Adult body length: 2mm (0.08in). There are two families: Argasidae (soft ticks) and Ixodidae (hard ticks, including the ticks of humans and cattle). Order Parasitiformes; subclass Acari (part).

tick, sheep
See SHEEP KED

tidal bore
Flow of tidal water from the ocean into a funnel-shaped river mouth or estuary, which, opposing outflowing river water, builds into a surface "wall" that accelerates upstream. Notable bores occur in the rivers Amazon, in South America, and Severn, in the United Kingdom. Three bores have been observed in North America – at the heads of the Bay of Fundy in New Brunswick, Canada; the Gulf of California; and Cook Inlet, Alaska. The world's largest known tidal bore is in Tsientang Kiang, China. *See also* TIDE

tidal flat
Extensive, nearly flat, barren land area that is alternately covered and uncovered by the action of the tide. It consists of mud and sand. A tidal marsh has a covering of salt-tolerant plants and grasses.

tidal wave
See TSUNAMI

tide
Periodic rise and fall of the OCEAN caused by the pull exerted on Earth by the Moon, and, to a lesser extent, by the Sun. In most parts of the world there are two high tides and two low tides every day. The time of each high tide is 12 hours 20–25 minutes later than

► **thrip** A tiny pest, thrips (order Thysanoptera) are significant for the damage they do to crops and for carrying disease. They have simple, fringed wings – or none at all – and unusual mouthparts with which they suck plant juices. The onion thrips, in both adult and nymphal stages, infest a number of hosts to which they may transmit the tomato spotted wilt virus.

T

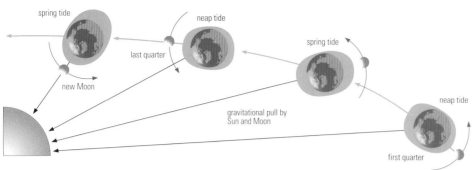

the preceding tide, because the position of the Moon relative to the Earth will have changed by a small amount after 12 hours have elapsed.

tiger
Large, powerful CAT found, in decreasing numbers, in forested areas throughout Asia. It has a characteristic striped coat of yellow, orange, white and black, with the chin and underparts white. Relying on keen hearing, it hunts for birds, deer, cattle and reptiles. An adult tiger will eat up to 25kg (55lb) of meat in one meal. The largest tiger is the Siberian race. Length: to 4m (13ft); weight: to 230kg (500lb). Family Felidae; species *Panthera tigris*.

tiger cat
See MARSUPIAL CAT

tigerfish
Largest of the characiform fish (those belonging to the order Characiformes); the several species of tigerfish make up the genus *Hydrocynus*. The tigerfish has massively developed canine teeth and striped markings. It occurs in African fresh waters, where it is an important sport fish. Length: to 1.3m (4.3ft). Family Characidae; species include *Hydrocynus vittatus*.

tiger lily (devil lily)
LILY that usually has orange-red or purple flowers, spotted deep purple, although there is a yellow variety. The flowers grow in clusters of between 12 and 20. Height: to 150cm (59in). Family Liliaceae; species *Lilium lancifolium*.

tilapia
Any member of the genus *Tilapia*, a group of freshwater fish native to the Middle East and Africa. They are mouth brooders. Family Cichlidae; species include *Tilapia mossambica*.

tilefish (blanquillos)
Tropical marine fish of some commercial value. It has an elongated olive-green or blue body, with yellow and rose markings. Length: 61cm (24in). Family Branchiostegidae; there are 15 species, including *Malacanthus plumieri* (Atlantic sand tilefish).

till (boulder clay)
In geology, SEDIMENT consisting of an unsorted mixture of clay, sand, gravel and boulders deposited directly by the ice of GLACIERS. It is not deposited in layers. **Tillite** is till that has become solid rock.

tillite
See TILL

tinamou
Any member of the family Tinamidae, a group of plump, slender-necked, small-headed, ground–living birds found in the forests of Central and South America. The tinamou has brown, leaf-like plumage.

Furtive in habits, it prefers to slip away quietly when disturbed, rather than fly. The sex roles are reversed, with the male incubating the eggs and rearing the young. Length: 23–46cm (9–18in). Family Tinamidae; species include *Crypturellus noctivagus* (yellow-legged tinamou).

◀ **tide** The daily rise and fall of the ocean's tides are the result of the gravitational pull of the Moon and that of the Sun, although the effect of the latter is less than half as strong as that of the Moon. The effect is greatest on the hemisphere facing the Moon and causes a tidal "bulge". When the Sun, Earth and Moon are in line, tide-raising forces are at a maximum, and spring tides occur. At a spring tide, high tide reaches the highest values, and low tide falls to low levels. When lunar and solar forces are least coincidental, with the Sun and Moon at an angle (near the Moon's first and third quarters), neap tides occur, which have a small tidal range.

Tinbergen, Nikolaas (1907–88)
Dutch ethologist. He shared with Konrad LORENZ and Karl von FRISCH the 1973 Nobel Prize for physiology or medicine for his pioneering work in ETHOLOGY. Tinbergen studied how in animals certain stimuli evoke specific responses. He empha-

Siberian tiger

Sumatran tiger

albino Bengal tiger

Bengal tiger

Caspian tiger

◀ **tiger** The various races or subspecies of tiger are distinguished by different coat lengths and markings and by size. The large Siberian or Manchurian tiger (*Panthera tigris altaica*) occupies forests and grasslands of central Asia, China and Korea. It is extremely rare. The Sumatran tiger (*Panthera tigris sumatrae*) exists in the wild only on the island of Sumatra. The albino Bengal tiger and the non-albino Bengal tiger (both *Panthera tigris tigris*) occur in forests and grasslands from India, Nepal and Bangladesh into China. Albino tigers are thought only occur in this subspecies. The Caspian tiger (*Panthera tigris virgata*) used to be found from Iran and Afghanistan through central Asia to Mongolia but is now believed to be extinct. All tiger races are threatened with extinction due to habitat loss; their survival is also threatened by demand for tiger parts in traditional E Asian remedies.

sized the importance of observing animals under natural conditions.

tinkerbird

Any member of the genus *Pogoniulus*, a group of forest songbirds found in central and E Africa; they belong to the BARBET family. The tinkerbird is often boldly coloured, with black, white and yellow stripes. It sticks to the tree canopy and is best located and identified by its distinctive, loud, whistling and hooting calls. Length: 8–10cm (3–4in). Family Capitonidae; species *Pogoniulus scolopaceus* (speckled tinkerbird).

tissue

Material of a living body consisting of a group of similar and often interconnected CELLS, usually supporting a similar function. Tissues vary greatly in structure and complexity. In animals, they may be loosely classified according to function into epithelial, connective, skeletal, muscular, nervous and glandular tissues, although each of these categories contains more than one different type of cell.

tit

Any of several species of small, active, acrobatic, insect-eating birds. Some species are specialized for life in cool conifer forests, others live in temperate broad-leaved woodlands and gardens. Many species have black caps and are pale brown or greenish-yellow, with black markings. In North America the tit is called a CHICKADEE after its calls. True tits belong to the family Paridae.

tit, blue

Small, active bird with mainly blue plumage. It is familiar in gardens and woodlands through most of Europe, as far as W Russia. The blue tit feeds mainly on insects and spiders. It breeds in holes in trees and readily uses nest-boxes. Length 12cm (5in). Family Paridae; species *Parus caeruleus*.

tit, coal

Smallest true tit found in Europe. It usually has dull, greyish-brown plumage, a distinctive white patch on its nape and a black head with white cheeks. The coal tit's preferred habitat is coniferous trees, with a favoured food being spruce seeds. It is found through Europe into Russia and also in Japan and the Himalayan region. Length: 11cm (4in). Family Paridae; species *Parus ater*.

tit, great

Large and familiar tit found through Europe into Asia, including Japan and Sri Lanka. It is green above and bright yellow with a black central stripe below. It has a characteristic two-note repetitive call. The great tit is one of the most intensively studied of all bird species. Length: 14cm (6in). Family Paridae; species *Parus major*.

tit, long-tailed

Small, active tit found through Europe and into Asia, as far as Japan and China. It has a tiny bill and a very long tail. Its plumage is mainly black and white, with a pinkish tinge. It makes remarkable oval nests, incorporating feathers, lichens and spider webs. Long-tailed tits are sociable birds, which often roam about in loose flocks, especially in winter. Length: 14cm (6in), of which 9cm (3.5in) is the tail. Family Aegithalidae; species *Aegithalos caudatus*.

tit, bearded (bearded reedling)

Brownish, sociable bird that is now classified in the

▲ **tinamou** The variegated tinamou (*Crypturellus variegatus*) is found in humid forests east of the Andes, up to an altitude of 1300m (4300ft), notably in Colombia, Venezuela and the Amazon region. As with other tinamou species, it is a fast runner, but flies only rarely and for short distances.

BABBLER family. It nests in extensive reedbeds, where it is often seen flitting about in or above the reeds. The male has a bluish head with a black moustache. Its contact call is a sharp, metallic "*zing*". The bearded tit is found scattered throughout Europe and through Asia to N China. Length: 12cm (5in), of which 7cm (3in) is the tail. Family Timaliidae; species *Panurus biarmicus*.

tit, penduline

Very small bird that is found mainly in S and E Europe and into Asia. It has a reddish back, a grey head and a black face patch. It takes its name from

its remarkable, free-hanging nests, which have an entrance tube near the top. The penduline tit's preferred habitat is wetlands with woodland and reeds. Length: 11cm (4in). Family Remizidae; species *Remiz pendulinus*.

titmouse

See CHICKADEE

tit-warbler

Any of several species of very small birds belonging to the WARBLER family, native to Asia. The tit-warbler is very distinctive, with purplish plumage, a white rump and an eye stripe. It lives in conifer forest and low scrub above the tree line. It is shy and can be difficult to see. Length: 10cm (4in). Family Sylviidae; genus *Leptopoecile*.

tityra

Aggressive, fruit-eating bird found in the forests of South America. Its plumage is silvery-white, with black wings, tail and head markings. It has a strongly hooked beak and red facial patches of bare skin. The tityra is often seen flying rapidly across forest clearings in small groups. Length: 20cm (8in). Family Cotinga; genus *Tityra*; species include the black-tailed tityra (*Tityra cayana*).

tizi

Large bush-CRICKET. It is mainly green or brown in colour and is found in low bushes. Tizi is the French name: it refers to the short, double chirp that the animal makes with its wings. The female's chirp is softer than the male's. Family Tettigoniidae; species *Ephippiger ephippiger*.

T-lymphocyte

See LYMPHOCYTE

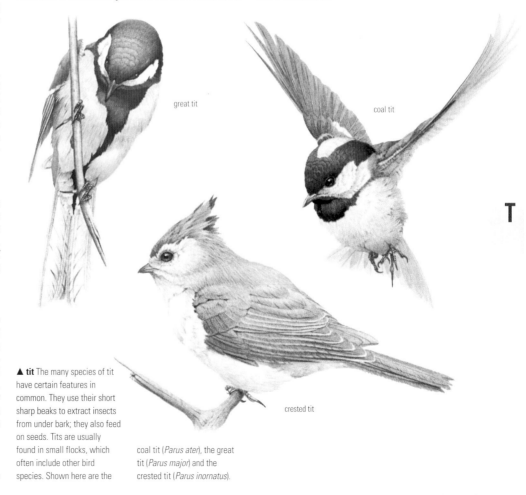

great tit

coal tit

crested tit

▲ **tit** The many species of tit have certain features in common. They use their short sharp beaks to extract insects from under bark; they also feed on seeds. Tits are usually found in small flocks, which often include other bird species. Shown here are the coal tit (*Parus ater*), the great tit (*Parus major*) and the crested tit (*Parus inornatus*).

T

toad

Any of many species of tailless AMPHIBIANS. True toads, which usually have enlarged poison glands on their backs, are in the family Bufonidae. Many frogs, particularly those with squat, rotund bodies, relatively short legs and warty or bumpy skin, are also called toads, regardless of their taxonomic placement. Because of their limb and body proportions, most toad species walk or hop rather than jump. Length: 2–24cm (0.8–9in).

toad, cane (marine toad)

Very large toad with huge poison glands (parotoids). Cane toads are native to the Americas, where they are found from S Texas to N South America. They have been introduced in Australia and elsewhere. Where they have been introduced, cane toads may displace native amphibians, eat beneficial insects and poison pets and native wildlife that attempt to prey upon them. Length: 10–24cm (4–9in). Family Bufonidae; species *Bufo marinus*.

toad, crucifix

Small, yellow or olive, round-bodied toad. It has black warts and red, yellow and white spots that form a cross pattern on its back. The crucifix toad is a burrowing species native to arid and semiarid SE Australia. It is capable of storing large amounts of water in its bladder. Length: *c*.5cm (*c*.2in). Family Myobatrachidae; species *Notaden bennetti*.

toad, fire-bellied

Any of several species of flattened toad found in Europe and temperate regions of Asia. They live and breed in shallow waters. Fire-bellied toads have drab, warty backs, but bright yellow, orange or red and black bellies. When disturbed, fire-bellied toads arch their backs to expose the ventral colour, which warns predators that they are distasteful. Length: to 7cm (3in). Family Bombinatoridae; genus *Bombina*.

toad, golden

Brilliantly coloured toad native to high elevations in Costa Rica. The male is bright uniform orange; the larger female is dark and has red spots with yellow margins. Although the golden toad used to congregate in large numbers to breed, it has not been seen since 1989 and may be extinct. Length: to 5cm (2in). Family Bufonidae; species *Bufo periglenes*.

▶ **toad** The spadefoot toad (*Scaphiopus* spp.) has adapted to life in dry climates. Its kidneys produce a concentrated solution of urea that can be released into its tissues in order to raise the concentration of the body fluids. The difference in concentration between the animal's body fluid and the surrounding soil causes water to enter the toad's body across its skin. The horned frog (*Ceratophrys ornata*) is found in Argentina. Its horns are outgrowths of the upper eyelids. It uses its large pointed teeth to attack other frogs, which it eats. The green toad (*Bufo viridis*) is common in coastal areas of Europe. Green toads sometimes gathers in very large groups, particularly after heavy rain.

toad, green

Widespread toad found in Europe, temperate Asia and North Africa from sea level to elevations of more than 4600m (15,000ft). It has a distinctive pattern of green spots and blotches on a pale background. More than 10,000 eggs are laid at a time in breeding ponds. Length: to 10cm (4in). Family Bufonidae; species *Bufo viridis*.

toad, horned

Any member of the genus *Ceratophrys*, a group of large, terrestrial FROGS native to South America. They have very wide heads and fleshy "horns" over the eyes. These aggressive frogs can eat very large prey, including small mammals and reptiles. The name is sometimes incorrectly applied to horned lizards, a type of iguanid lizard from North America. Length: to 20cm (8in). Family Leptodactylidae; genus *Ceratophrys*.

toad, Mexican burrowing toad

Fat-bodied toad native to S United States, Mexico and Central America. It digs using its powerful forelegs and feeds on termites, which it catches with its slender, sticky tongue, protruding through a slot in the small, pointed snout. The toads emerge on the surface after heavy rains to breed. Length: 5–8cm (2–3in). Family Rhinophryidae; species *Rhinophrynus dorsalis*.

toad, marine

See TOAD, CANE

toad, oak

Tiny, partly diurnal toad found in the pine woods of SE United States. It has a pale stripe down the middle of its back flanked by several pairs of black or brown spots. Its call, a high-pitched peeping, can be heard after warm rains near the shallow ponds and ditches that serve as breeding sites. Length: to 3cm (1in). Family Bufonidae; species *Bufo quercicus*.

toad, spadefoot

Any of several species of toads that have vertical pupils, relatively smooth skin and no enlarged poison glands. They are native to North America. On each hindfoot they have a dark, sharp-edged tubercle (the "spade"), which they use to burrow downwards into the cooler, moister soil. Although seldom seen, spadefoot toads can emerge from underground in large numbers to forage and breed on warm, rainy

spadefoot toad

green toad

horned frog

▲ **toadfish** Found in the waters of Japan, this toadfish (*Pterophryne histrio*) is one of a group of fish that live in coastal waters. Toadfish are voracious predators, feeding on crabs, squid and worms, which they catch with their large mouths and sharp teeth. They are able to make a wide range of sounds.

nights. Length: to 9cm (4in). Family Pelobatidae; genera *Scaphiopus* and *Spea*.

toadfish

Any member of the family Batrachoididae, comprising *c*.40 species of bottom-dwelling fish found in temperate and tropical seas. The toadfish has a large mouth and head, a tapered body and a long ventral fin. Most species are grey, green, yellow or brown, with dark speckled markings. The dorsal fin spines of some species are venomous. Length: to 30cm (12in). Family Batrachoididae.

toadflax

Any of several species of annual and perennial plants, the leaves of which resemble those of flax plants. Some species are grown as ornamentals. The common toadflax (*Linaria vulgaris*), also known as butter-and-eggs, has dense clusters of two-lipped, pale yellow flowers. Family Scrophulariaceae.

tobacco

Cultivated, herbaceous, annual plant native to tropical America. Its stems and large leaves are covered in sticky hairs and clusters of trumpet-shaped flowers. The most important constituent is the alkaloid nicotine, used as an insecticide as well as a component of tobacco. Flowering tobacco, *Nicotiana x sanderae*, originated as a cross between two South American species. It is grown for its colourful flowers, which are fragrant in the evening. Family Solanaceae; species *Nicotiana tabacum*.

tody

Any of several species of tiny FLYCATCHERS found in South America. The tody has a large head and a large bill. Plumage patterns vary according to species, from black and white to reddish-brown, olive and yellow. The tody is shy and difficult to see. It makes short sallies from a perch to catch insects in dense undergrowth. Length: 9cm (4in). Family Todidae.

tolerance

Ability to endure or resist circumstances that might ordinarily be expected to be harmful to an organism. HALOPHYTES, for example, can tolerate soil salt concentrations that would kill most other plants.

tomato

Fruit plant native to the Americas. It was cultivated in Europe as early as 1544 but was not eaten until the 16th century because it was believed to be poisonous. Family Solanaceae; species *Lycopersicum esculentum*. The small cherry tomato is a variety (*Lycopersicum esculentum cerasiforme*).

tombolo

Bar connecting an island with the mainland. It is usually formed by a sand spit that grows until it reaches the island.

T

tongue

In most vertebrates, muscular organ usually rooted to the floor of the mouth. The tongue contains the TASTE buds, groups of cells that distinguish the four basic tastes: bitter, tasted on the back of the tongue; sweet and salty, tasted on the tip and front of the tongue; and sour, tasted mainly on the sides of the tongue. The tongue helps to move food around the mouth for chewing and swallowing; animals also use it for lapping fluids and for grooming. In human beings, the tongue is vital for the production of speech. *See also* SENSES

tongue worm (pentastomid)

Any member of the phylum Pentastomida, which comprises parasitic worms. Most species of tongue worm live in the respiratory tracts of reptiles, but some species are found in birds and mammals. The worm attaches itself to respiratory tissues by means of four appendages which surround the mouth. Phylum Pentastomida.

toothcarp

Any member of the suborder Cyprinodontoide, which contains small freshwater fish, including the KILLIFISH and MOSQUITOFISH. They are so named because of their small teeth. Many toothcarp species are live bearers; the eggs of other species can survive harsh conditions, including drought.

topaz

Any of several species of tiny HUMMINGBIRD. The topaz has an almost straight bill. It is found in South America and the Caribbean region. The male has a glittering, topaz-orange throat and upper breast. The dingy female is easily confused with other species. Some species are migratory. Length: 7.5cm (3in). Family Trochilidae.

topaz

Transparent, glassy mineral, aluminium fluosilicate, $Al_2SiO_4(F,OH)_2$, found in pegmatites. Its crystals are orthorhombic system, columnar prisms; it occurs as granular masses. Topaz is colourless, white, blue or yellow, and some large crystals are of gem quality. Hardness 8; r.d. 3.5.

tope

Small SHARK that lives in British waters. It has a grey-brown body and is often found in schools. It is

▲ **tobacco** Tobacco is produced mainly from the plant *Nicotiana tabacum*, which is cultivated worldwide. The leaves are removed and dried. Native Americans smoked tobacco leaves and used them medicinally long before the arrival of Europeans in the New World.

▲ **tortoise, giant** The largest of the giant tortoises are found on Aldabra, shown here. The survival of the species has been threatened by the introduction of rats, cats and pigs to its native environment. Rats and cats eat the eggs and young of the tortoise; pigs remove the vegetation on which it feeds.

found near the ocean bottom, where it feeds on small fish. Length: to 2m (6.5ft). Family Carcharinidae; species *Galeorhinus galeus*.

topi

ANTELOPE, the most numerous species of Africa. Various races of topi are known as the tsessebe, sassaby, tiang, damalisc, korrigum or bastard hartebeest. The topi grazes on savanna and swampland, living in small herds led by a single male, who marks his territory with dung and scent. The topi's coat is usually glossy red, with bold black patches. Each female produces a single calf after about eight months' gestation. Head-body length: 1.5–2m (4.9–6.6ft); tail: 40–60cm (16–24in). Family Bovidae; subfamily Hippotraginae; species *Damaliscus lunatus*.

topknot

Flatfish found in the NE Atlantic Ocean. It is related to the FLOUNDER. Its oval body is dark with a marbled appearance. Order Pleuronectiformes; species *Zeugopterus punctatus*.

topography

Study of surface features such as hills, valleys, rivers, roads and lakes. It is also the representation of such features on a relief map or a plan for construction. The terrain of a region is explored using surveyors' instruments or aerial photogrammetry (plotting elevations from photographs).

top shell

Any member of the family Trochidae, comprising marine SNAILS with short, conical, spiral shells. The patterns on some of these shells, when taken with their shape, make the shells resemble toy spinning tops. They are found most frequently in shallow waters along rocky coastlines. Phylum Mollusca; class Gastropoda; order Archaeogastropoda; family Trochidae; genera include *Trochus* and *Gibbula*.

tornado (twister)

Funnel-shaped, violently rotating storm extending downwards from the cumulonimbus CLOUD in which it forms. At the ground its diameter may be only about 100m (300ft). Rotational wind speeds range from 150 to 500km/h (100–300mph). The centre of a tornado is an area of extreme low pressure, which sucks up dust to form a blackish funnel rising to the

sky. Around this funnel of rising air are very strong winds that destroy crops and sometimes buildings. Tornadoes occur in deep low-pressure areas, associated with FRONTS or other instabilities. They are associated with intense heating in continental areas in late summer, when land masses are at their hottest. Tornadoes are most common in the interior of the United States, but they also occur in India and many other countries. When tornadoes cross over water they become WATERSPOUTS. The average life of a tornado or a waterspout is four minutes. The violent storms that occur at the start of the rainy season in w Africa are also called tornadoes. They bring strong winds and torrential rain, which is caused by mild air coming in from the sea and meeting dry air from the Sahara Desert.

Torrey, John (1796–1873)

US botanist and chemist. He conducted major studies of North American plant life and amassed one of the most valuable botanical libraries and herbariums of his time. His works include *Flora of the Northern and Middle Sections of the United States* (1824) and *Flora of the State of New York* (1843), which he wrote after being appointed state botanist (1836).

tortoise

Any of *c*.50 species of terrestrial TURTLES. They are usually characterized by high-domed CARAPACES (shells), short heads, rounded feet lacking webs, and other adaptations for life away from water. Tortoises occur in Africa, Asia, s Europe, South America and s North America. Giant species occur on the Galápagos Islands and Aldabra Atoll. Family Testudinidae. In some countries both land and freshwater turtles are referred to as tortoises.

tortoise, Galápagos

See TORTOISE, GIANT

tortoise, giant (Galápagos tortoise)

Very large tortoise native to the Galápagos Islands and Aldabra Atoll in the Indian Ocean. Other insular

T

giant tortoises have become extinct due to human predation. It has a small head and a very long neck. Its limbs are thick and its carapace is high-domed or saddle-shaped. Length: to 1.4m (4.6ft); weight: to 261kg (575lbs). Family Testudinidae; species *Geochelone elephantopus*.

tortoise, gopher

Any member of the genus *Gopherus*, comprising several species of tortoise native to SE and SW United States and Mexico. The gopher tortoise has a brownish-tan, high-domed shell. It has stumpy legs and powerful forelimbs for digging burrows. Length: 15in (38cm). Family Testudinae; genus *Gopherus*.

tortoise, Hermann's

Tortoise that is found in S Europe. Its carapace is rounded, with a lumpy surface. The plastron (bony plate on the tortoise's underside) is dark with a yellow margin; it lacks thigh tubercles. Like most of its relatives, Hermann's tortoise is almost exclusively vegetarian. Length: to 20cm (8in). Family Testudinidae; species *Testudo hermanni*.

tortoise, hingeback

Any of four species of African tortoises with a distinctive, movable hinge on the back of the carapace. The carapace is elongate and has sloping sides. Hingeback tortoises live in a variety of habitats from dense forest to open savanna. Most species are omnivorous. Length: 12–32cm (5–13in). Family Testudinidae; genus *Kinixys*.

tortoise, leopard

Large tortoise; it has a yellowish plastron and a high-domed carapace with dark spots that fade with age. It lives in the savannas, thickets and grasslands of Africa, where it feeds on a variety of plants. Leopard tortoises are capable of travelling great distances, but they generally maintain home ranges. Length: to 75cm (30in); weight: to 40kg (88lbs). Family Testudinidae; species *Geochelone pardalis*.

tortoise, pancake

Very flattened tortoise found in the savannas, thickets and thornbush of E Africa. It has a flexible carapace, which enables it to wedge itself into cracks and crevices in order to escape predators or to shelter from the intense heat. The pancake tortoise is also a good climber. It lays a single large egg at a time. Length: to 18cm (7in). Family Testudinidae; species *Malacochersus tornieri*.

tortoise, spur-thighed

Smooth-shelled, blunt-headed tortoise found in dry habitats of the Mediterranean region. Its shell is yellow or tan with large dark blotches, but in some individuals it may be a uniform grey or black. There is a large conical tubercle on each thigh. Spur-thighed tortoises are no longer found in some areas of their range due to collecting for the pet trade. Length: to 30cm (12in). Family Testudinidae; species *Testudo graeca*.

tortoiseshell butterfly

Any of a widespread group of medium-sized BUTTERFLIES native to Europe and temperate regions of Asia. Their wings have tortoise-shell-like markings of orange, black, brown and yellow. Family Nymphalidae.

toucan

Any of numerous species of conspicuous and well-known birds found in Central and South America. The toucan has an enormous, colourful, banana-

▲ **toucan** The New World counterparts of the hornbills, toucans are found in forests of tropical America. There are *c*.35 species. The large, bright bill of the Toco toucan (*Ramphastos toco*) is typical. Members of the family nearly all have similar plumage, but the bill colour varies from species to species.

shaped bill. Its red, yellow or white bib and cheeks contrast with its black body. Despite its large size the bill is porous and very light. The toucan feeds on fruit supplemented by nestlings and the eggs of other birds. Length: 50cm (20in). Family Ramphastidae.

toucanet

Any of several species of birds with predominantly green plumage. The toucanet is closely related to, but smaller than, the TOUCAN. It does not perch in the open as do toucans. It feeds in noisy, active, small parties, which move through the tree canopy in a follow-my-leader fashion. The toucanet is omnivorous and often robs bird nests. Length: 37cm (15in). Family Ramphastidae.

touch

One of the five SENSES, functioning by means of specialized nerve receptors in the SKIN.

tourmaline

Silicate mineral, sodium or calcium aluminium borosilicate, found in IGNEOUS and METAMORPHIC rocks. Its crystals are hexagonal system and glassy, either opaque or transparent. Tourmaline may be black, red, green, brown or blue. Some crystals are prized as gems. Hardness 7.5; r.d. 3.1.

towhee

Any of several species of small, mostly dull brown songbirds found in North and Central America. The towhee is named after its call note. Most species nest and forage on the ground for seeds and insects. The rufous-sided towhee (*Pipilo erythrophthalmus*) of North America has several colour variations; some races are black with orange-red underparts and yellow undertail feathers. Length: 19–24cm (7–9in). Family Fringillidae; genus *Pipilo*.

toxin

Poisonous substance produced by a living organism. The unpleasant symptoms of many bacterial diseases are due to the release of toxins into the body by the BACTERIA. The toxins may be secreted into the bloodstream or they may be released when the bacteria die. Many moulds, some larger FUNGI (such as the DEATH CAP) and the seeds of some higher plants (such as LABURNUM and castor oil) produce toxins. The VENOMS of many SNAKES contain powerful toxins.

trace element

Chemical element that is essential to life but only in small quantities normally obtainable from the diet. Trace elements include boron, cobalt, copper,

iodine, magnesium, manganese, molybdenum and zinc. They are essential to the reactions of ENZYMES and HORMONES.

trace fossil

See FOSSIL, TRACE

trachea (windpipe)

Airway that extends from the LARYNX to about the middle of the STERNUM (breastbone). Reinforced with rings of CARTILAGE, the trachea is lined with hair-like CILIA that prevent dirt and other substances from entering the LUNGS. At its lower end, the trachea splits into two branches, the bronchi, which lead to the lungs.

tracheophyte

In certain classification systems, any VASCULAR PLANT of the phylum Tracheophyta, defined by having some kind of vascular tissue. Within this phylum are: psilopsids (leafless, rootless primitive forms, such as whisk fern), sphenopsids (such as HORSETAIL), lycopsids (such as CLUB MOSS), pteropsids (such as FERN), CONIFEROPHYTES and ANGIOSPERMS. In the Five KINGDOMS classification, these groups now constitute separate phyla in their own right, and the Tracheophyta is no longer considered to be a separate entity.

trachyte

Uncommon, fine-grained, extrusive IGNEOUS ROCK of volcanic origin. Usually light-coloured, it is rich in alkali feldspar and contains small amounts of quartz, nepheline and other minerals; its silica content is up to 60%. Trachyte is formed, along with basalt, in lava flows from island volcanoes, and it also occurs in small sills and dykes.

Tradescant, John

Either of two British botanists and travellers, father and son, who became successive gardeners to Charles I. John (*c*.1570–1638) travelled to Russia and Algeria gathering plants, among them the "Algiers Apricot", and established a garden of exotic plants at his Lambeth home. His son, also named John (1608–62), travelled to Virginia for plants for the Lambeth garden. He wrote a book about the Lambeth collection, *Musaeum Tradescantium* (1656). Their collection, which was transferred to Oxford after their deaths, formed the nucleus of the Ashmolean Museum.

trade winds

Steady winds that blow from the tropical high-pressure zones (the HORSE LATITUDES) to the equatorial low-pressure zones (the DOLDRUMS). In the Northern Hemisphere, the air moving from the Tropic of Cancer towards the Equator is deflected to the right, making it a northeasterly wind. In the Southern Hemisphere, the air moving from the Tropic of Capricorn to the Equator is turned to the left to become a southeasterly wind. The trade winds are persistent winds – all are easterly and tropical – blowing from the deserts towards the tropical forest zone.

tragopan

Any of several species of beautiful, pheasant-like birds found in sub-alpine forests of Southeast Asia. The tragopan is extremely shy and skulking. It feeds on the forest floor in the early mornings and late evenings. The male's head and breast are a rich blood red, blue and yellow, with intricately speckled back and breast patterns. Length: 58–72cm (23–28in). Family Phasianidae; genus *Tragopan*.

T

trainbearer

Any of several species of short-billed HUMMING-BIRD found in South America. It is named after its extremely long, forked tail, which can be up to 17cm (7in) in length. Its plumage is glittering green, and the tail can be all-black or emerald green. It is noisy and aggressive. It hovers from below eye level to the top of the canopy, weaving in and out like a bee. Length: 10–16cm (4–6in). Family Trochilidae, genus *Lesbia*.

transcription (DNA transcription)

Stage in PROTEIN SYNTHESIS within a EUKARYOTE cell in which the GENETIC CODE, represented by NUCLEOTIDES on DNA, is copied into single-stranded MESSENGER RNA (mRNA). It takes place in the cell nucleus (because the DNA-containing chromosomes are located there). RNA polymerase enzymes make an RNA copy from the original unwound strand of DNA that forms the template. The section to be copied is indicated on the DNA template strand by start and termination "signals". The mRNA then migrates to the RIBOSOMES, where actual protein synthesis takes place. Different RNA polymerase ENZYMES synthesize different types of RNA. *See also* TRANSLATION

transduction

Natural process by which genetic material is transferred between one host CELL and another by a VIRUS.

transfer RNA

See RNA

transform fault

Special class of strike-slip FAULT characteristic of MID-OCEAN RIDGES. Because of the transform faults, which are at right angles to the ridge itself, the MID-ATLANTIC RIDGE does not run in a straight line but in offset steps. Some geologists think that the four major structures of the Earth's crust are mountains, deep-sea trenches, mid-ocean ridges and strike-slip faults, and that they form continuous networks.

transgenic

Describing an organism whose GENOME contains GENES artificially transferred from another species. Using GENETIC ENGINEERING techniques, transgenic organisms are created by inserting isolated DNA from another species into the fertilized egg or early embryo. Transgenic animals and plants are usually created for commercial purposes. For example, it is possible to insert the genes for extra growth hormone into the genomes of livestock in order to increase meat production.

translation

Part of the process of PROTEIN SYNTHESIS that takes place in living cells. MESSENGER RNA (mRNA) carries a genetic code, in the form of a series of **codons** (triplets of NUCLEOTIDES), which ultimately determines the correct sequence for AMINO ACIDS to form protein. RIBOSOMES in the cell cytoplasm scan the mRNA for its codons, relaying the information to amino acid-bearing transfer RNA (tRNA). The strands of tRNA have their own **anti-codons**, which form pairs with the codons of the mRNA. In effect, the tRNA (along with its amino acid), by pairing and attaching to the mRNA, "translates" the mRNA code to form the correct sequence of amino acids to form peptides, polypeptides and eventually proteins. As the polypeptide chain grows, the tRNA falls away.

translocation

In botany, movement of food materials in solution through the tissues of VASCULAR PLANTS from one part to another. It includes the passage upwards of minerals and other inorganic salts from the soil and roots to the XYLEM tissue, and the movement of sugars and other organic compounds from the leaves to other parts of the plant in the PHLOEM tissue.

translocation

In genetics, process that alters the genetic makeup of a CHROMOSOME. A section of a chromosome breaks off, leaving it with less genetic information. The fragment joins onto another chromosome, also altering its genetic makeup. Rearrangement of genes within a single chromosome is also called translocation.

transpiration

See feature article, page 386

traveller's tree

Palm-like plant native to Madagascar. It is so-called because each cup-shaped leaf base holds about one litre (1.75 pints) of drinkable water. The traveller's tree has large clusters of white blossoms and blue seeds. Height: to 28m (92ft). Family Strelitziaceae; species *Ravenala madagascariensis*.

travertine

SEDIMENTARY ROCK consisting almost entirely of crystals of CALCITE (calcium carbonate, $CaCO_3$). It has a very light colour, unless stained yellowish by iron compounds, and is often porous. It usually forms in hot springs from water rich in dissolved calcium carbonate. *See also* TUFA

► **tragopan** One of the most beautiful of the tragopan species, Temminck's tragopan (*Tragopan temmincki*), also known as the crimson-bellied tragopan, is native to W China, Tibet, NE Burma and N Vietnam. It is found in rainforests at high altitudes, usually between 900 and 2700m (3000–9000ft). As with most other pheasant species, the female has much duller plumage than the male. Tragopans are the most arboreal of pheasants.

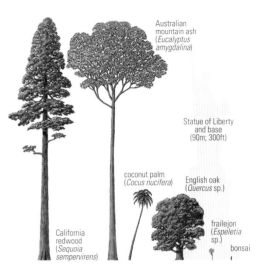

▲ **tree** Trees grow taller than any other living thing but can still survive in miniature form. If the roots are restricted, either artificially, such as the cultivation of bonsai in Japan, or by natural means, as when a seed germinates in thin soil on a mountain, a fully formed tree only a few centimetres high will result. The California redwood, the tallest tree, is closely rivalled by a eucalyptus, such as the mountain ash of Australia. The coconut palm reaches its height of 27m (90ft) in a few years. The English oak enlarges slowly – c.4.5m (15ft) in ten years – but produces wood of prodigious strength. The small frailejon grows on snowy ledges above 400m (1300ft) in the Sierra Nevada.

tree

Woody, perennial plant with one main trunk and smaller branches. The trunk increases in diameter each year; the leaves are EVERGREEN or DECIDUOUS. The largest trees, SEQUOIAS, can grow to more than 100m (330ft); the bristlecone pine can live for more than 5000 years.

tree-babbler

Any member of the genus *Stachyris*, a group of birds belonging to the BABBLER family. The tree-babbler is a small woodland bird found in Southeast Asia. It is more olive green and golden yellow than other babblers, often with a reddish-brown cap. Its preferred habitat is deep undergrowth, forest edges and ravines. Length: 10–12cm (4–5in). Family Timaliidae; genus *Stachyris*.

treecreeper

Any of several species of small woodland birds that habitually creep, mouse-like, about tree trunks and branches. It is brown streaked above and paler below. It has a longish, stiff tail, which it presses against the trunk as support. It has a curved beak. In winter the treecreeper often joins mixed flocks of tits. Length: 12cm (5in). Family Certhiidae and Climacteridae; genus *Certhia*.

tree fern

Tree-like FERN of the family Cyatheaceae. It grows in tropical and sub-tropical regions, particularly in moist, mountainous areas. Height: 3–25m (10–80ft). Phylum Filicinophyta; genus *Cyathea*; there are c.600 species.

tree frog

See FROG

treehopper

Any member of the family Membracidae, comprising numerous species of HOMOPTERAN insects that suck plant juices. Most species are found in tropical regions. They have an enlarged THORAX, which extends over the head and forms a spine over the body. Treehopper species can be green, blue or bronze, sometimes with spots or stripes. Many species are considered to be pests because their feeding habits cause damage to growing crops and help to spread plant diseases. Order Homoptera; family Membracidae; there are *c*.2600 species.

tree of heaven (Ailanthus, paradise tree)

Any of nine species of deciduous tree native to China and naturalized in America and Europe. It is weed-

TRANSPIRATION

Transpiration is the loss of moisture from plants as water vapour from leaf surfaces or other plant parts. Most of the water entering plant roots is lost by transpiration. The process is speeded up in light, warm and dry conditions. The flow of water from the roots to the leaf pores (STOMATA) is called the **transpiration stream**. Several forces drive this flow. As moisture evaporates from the stomata in the leaves, water moves in by OSMOSIS from adjacent cells, setting up a flow of water by

osmosis across the leaf from the XYLEM tubes to the stomata, pulling water out of the xylem. The force of attraction between the water molecules as they pass up the xylem tubes from the root to the leaves makes it difficult to break the water column. These tubes are also very narrow, so water rises in them by capillary action. In the roots, water being drawn into the xylem creates a lower concentration of water in adjacent root cells; thus water is drawn across the root from the root hairs by osmosis.

▶ **The diagram of** a plant (A) shows the tube-like cells used for transporting water and nutrients. The cells form the vascular bundles, which begin near the root tip, and run up the length of the stem and into the leaves. They consist of two main elements – the xylem and the phloem. The xylem carries water and dissolved mineral salts up through the plant to the leaf tissue, while the phloem carries sugars up and down the plant. The leaf of a dicotyledonous plant consists of two distinct parts – the petiole, or leaf stalk, which prevents the leaves bunching on the stem, and the blade. The cross-section of the leaf (B) shows how the veins, themselves vascular bundles, apart from carrying water and nutrients, also support the rest of the blade including mesophyll tissue, which contains chloroplasts vital for photosynthesis. The stem supports the plant and contains many vascular bundles (C). The roots (D) have thousands of tiny root hairs growing from them. As well as anchoring the plant in the soil, the root hairs also increase the surface area of the root system, thereby enabling the plant to absorb as much water and as many minerals as possible. The root tip (E) is divided into three sections. The root cap protects and lubricates the tip of the root, giving the growing roots a smooth passage through the soil. It is also the region in the root that perceives gravity and thereby controls the direction the root grows. The meristematic zone is where

cells divide, adding new cells to the root cap below it, which is being permanently worn down; and to the zone of elongation above it, the zone that aids rapid growth in root length.

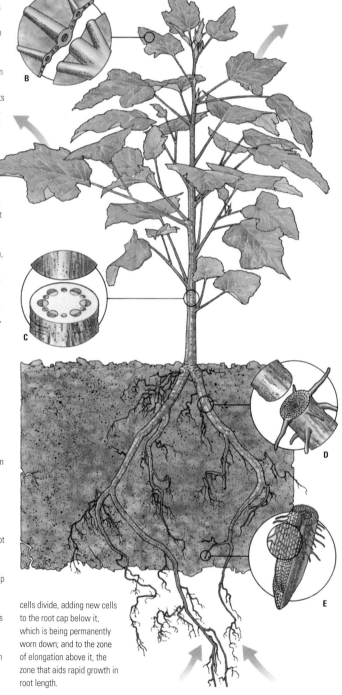

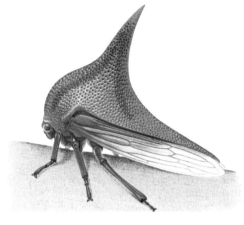

▲ **treehopper** Members of the treehopper family are distinguished by their large thoraxes, which resemble spines. The treehopper shown here (*Umbonia spinosa*) has a spine that resembles the thorn of the plants on which it feeds. It is found in Central and South America.

like in its native country. The tree of heaven is tolerant of air pollution, thrives in any soil or climate and resists most insects and diseases. Greenish-yellow male and female flowers are borne on separate trees. Height: 15–23m (49–75ft). Family Simaroubaceae; species include *Ailanthus altissima*.

tree-porcupine
See PORCUPINE, TREE-

tree shrew
Small, tree-dwelling mammal found from India throughout Southeast Asia to Indonesia. It looks like a long-snouted, whiskerless squirrel, but it is classified as a primitive PRIMATE. The tree shrew is grey-brown in colour and feeds on insects and fruit. Family Tupaiidae; species *Tupaia glis*.

trefoil
Any of numerous species of plants, such as CLOVER, with leaves divided into three parts. Bird's-foot trefoil (*Lotus corniculatus*) is a perennial used as forage. Family Fabaceae/Leguminosae.

trematode
Any member of the class of invertebrates Trematoda, which includes nearly 6000 species of parasitic FLATWORMS and FLUKES. Parasitic trematodes have a thick outer cuticle and one or more suckers for attaching to the tissues of the host. They are bilaterally symmetrical. Trematodes are commonly found as endoparasites or ectoparasites in all classes of vertebrates, including human beings. Length: to 10cm (4in).

trench
Deep, V-shaped depression of the SEAFLOOR. In PLATE TECTONIC theory ocean trenches are places where one plate is being pushed under another. They are the deepest – to 11km (7mi) – formations on Earth and are found primarily along the borders of the Pacific Ocean.

trepang
Any of several large species of SEA CUCUMBER. They are fished along the warm coasts of the w Pacific Ocean. Trepangs are dried and sold for use in Chinese soups. Phylum Echinodermata; class Holothuroidea; order Dendrochirotida; family Cucumariidae.

Triassic
First period of the MESOZOIC era, lasting from 248 to 213 million years ago. Following a wave of

T

extinctions at the close of the PERMIAN period, many new kinds of animals developed. On land lived the first DINOSAURS. MAMMAL-like reptiles were common and by the end of the Triassic period the first true mammals existed. In the seas lived the first ICHTHYOSAURS, placodonts and nothosaurs. The first FROGS, TURTLES, CROCODILIANS and LIZARDS also appeared. Plant life consisted mainly of primitive non-flowering plants, with FERNS and CONIFERS predominating.

clown triggerfish

decorated triggerfish

triggerfish

Any of several species of tropical marine fish found in warm, shallow, Pacific waters. The triggerfish is identified by a dorsal fin spine that can be erected to lodge the fish in a coral cavity, as a protection against predators. Most species are brightly coloured. Length: to 60cm (24in). Family Balistidae; typical genus *Balistoides*.

triglyceride

See LIPID

triller

Any of several species of small, tree-loving birds found in Southeast Asia and Australia. The triller is black above and white or barred below; it has a white stripe above the eye. It feeds mainly on insects and nectar. Its distinctive call reveals its presence: first one bird trills then others join in like a chorus. Length: 17cm (7in). Family Corvidae; genus *Lalage*; species include *Lalage suerii* (the white-winged triller).

trillium (wake-robin)

Any member of the genus *Trillium*, a group of herbaceous, perennial plants native to North America and Asia. Trillium has three leaves in a whorl at the top of the stem and a solitary flower composed of three outer green segments and three large inner petals of white, yellow or pink to purple. It is grown as an ornamental in shady gardens. Family Liliaceae; genus *Trillium*.

trilobite

Any of an extinct group of ARTHROPODS found as fossils in marine deposits, ranging in age from Cambrian through Permian times. The body is mostly oval, tapering towards the rear; it was covered by a skeleton made of chitin. The name refers to the division of the body into three – a central axis and two lateral lobes. Transverse divisions show segmentation, with each segment bearing a pair of jointed limbs. Most species were bottom-crawling, shallow-water forms. They ranged in size from 6mm (0.2in) to 75cm (30in).

triose sugar

MONOSACCHARIDE that comprises three carbon atoms. Biologically important trioses include glyceraldehyde, which is the first formed sugar in PHOTOSYNTHESIS and an intermediate in GLYCOLYSIS.

triplet code

See CODON

tripod fish

Deep sea (abyssal), bottom-dwelling fish. It sits on the seabed balanced on its two extended pelvic fin rays, with its tail fin forming a tripod. Family Ipnopidae; genus *Bathypterois*.

trisomic

Describing a DIPLOID organism that has three of one type of chromosome instead of two. Trisomy is the cause of several human genetic disorders, notably Down's syndrome.

tritium (symbol T)

Radioactive isotope of hydrogen, the nucleus of which consists of one proton and two neutrons. Only one atom in 10^{17} of natural hydrogen is tritium. Tritium compounds are used in radioactive tracing. Properties: half-life 12.3 yr.

trochus shell

TOP SHELL of the genus *Trochus*.

trogon

Any member of the family Trogonidae, a group of brightly coloured, short-necked birds found in dense tropical forests around the world. The trogon has a long tail, short wings and a short, broad bill. It sits motionless then swoops with a brief hover to snatch a fruit or a passing insect before alighting on a new perch. Length: 24–33cm (9–13in). Family Trogonidae. The various QUETZAL species belong to the trogon family.

trophic level

Position that an organism occupies in a FOOD CHAIN. It is usually defined in terms of the food supply. The first trophic level is occupied by PRIMARY PRODUC-

▲ **triggerfish** The clown triggerfish (*Balistoides nigeri*), left, and the decorated triggerfish (*Pseudobalistes fuscus*) are typical members of this family. They appear oval from the side and are extremely thin. The front dorsal spine can be erected and locked into place by the second spine.

ERS, which are green plants that use photosynthesis to obtain energy from sunlight. Herbivores (PRIMARY CONSUMERS), which eat the plants, occupy the second level. SECONDARY CONSUMERS, on the third trophic level, are carnivores, which eat the herbivores. There may be a fourth level (TERTIARY CONSUMERS) occupied by other carnivores that eat those on the third level.

tropics

Area between the Tropic of CANCER and the Tropic of CAPRICORN where maximum heating from the Sun occurs. Around 21–22 June the Sun's rays are perpendicular to the ground surface along the Tropic of Cancer (latitude 23 degrees and 30 minutes North); it thus exerts its maximum heating effect in that region. By 22–23 December the motion of the Earth has brought the Sun's vertical rays south to the Tropic of Capricorn (latitude 23 degrees and 30 minutes South).

tropicbird

Beautiful, white seabird found in tropical regions. It has immensely long central tail feathers and a bright red or yellow bill. It ranges far out to sea and twists and turns sharply to plunge into the water for food. It feeds mainly on squid, which rise to the surface at night. Length: 40–60cm (16–24in); tail streamers 35–45cm (14–18in). Family Phaethontidae; genus *Phaethon*; species include *Phaethon rubricauda* (the red-tailed tropicbird).

tropism (tropic response)

Response in growth and orientation of a plant or a part of it in relation to a directional, external stimulus. Such stimuli include light (PHOTOTROPISM), gravity (GEOTROPISM) or water (HYDROTROPISM).

troposphere

Lowest part of the Earth's ATMOSPHERE. In the troposphere, temperature decreases with height, and it is within this region that clouds and other weather phenomena occur. The troposphere extends to about 16km (10mi) above the Earth's surface.

trout

Any of several species of freshwater sport fish of North America and Europe. Also a food fish, trout is commonly propagated in hatcheries. Trout move upstream to spawn. Those species that migrate to the ocean between spawnings are called steelheads. Members of the *Salvelinus* genus include: the high mountain golden trout (*Salvelinus aquakonita*) of W North America, which is marked by vertical side

T

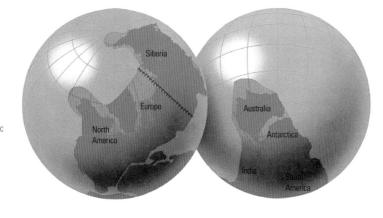

▶ **Triassic** During the Triassic period, the collision between the North America-Europe landmass and the Siberian plate pushed up the Ural Mountains.

Siberia

Europe

North America

Australia

Antarctica

India

South America

► **trout** The brook trout (*Salvelinus fontinalis*) inhabits cold, clean waters. It is a popular game fish. The lake trout (*Salvelinus namaycush*) is widely distributed in cold waters of N North America and has been introduced elsewhere. The brown trout (*Salmo trutta*) is native to Europe. It inhabits slightly warmer waters than its North American relations. It is also prized as a game fish. Trout feed on insects, crustaceans and small fish.

brook trout

lake trout

brown trout

bars; and the brook trout (CHAR) (*Salvelinus fontinalis*) of E North America. The *Oncorhynchus* genus includes rainbow trout (*Oncorhynchus mykiss*), which are marked by a longitudinal red stripe. Other species include the large European brown trout (*Salmo trutta*). Length: to 100cm (39in). Family Salmonidae.

truffle
Any of several species of fungi that grow underground, mostly among tree roots. Most species are edible and are highly prized delicacies. Found in Europe, particularly France, and in parts of the United States, truffles are hunted with pigs and dogs that are trained to scent them out. Phylum Ascomycota; family Tuberaceae.

trumpeter
Any of several species of ground bird found in the Amazon region. The trumpeter has a long neck, long legs, a rounded body and a short bill. It has a hunchbacked gait. The feathers of the trumpeter's head and neck are very short and velvety-black. It is kept as a pet and prized for its habit of "sounding the alarm". Length: to 56cm (22in). Family Psophiidae; genus *Psophia*; species include *Psophia crepitans* (common trumpeter).

trunkfish (boxfish)
Marine fish that lives in temperate and tropical waters. Its body is almost triangular when seen from the front, with a broad, flat ventral region tapering to a narrow dorsal region. Length: to 50cm (20in). Family Ostraciontidae; genus *Lactophrys*.

trypsin
Digestive ENZYME secreted by the PANCREAS. It is secreted in an inactive form (so it does not damage tissues en route to the intestine), which is converted into active trypsin by an enzyme in the small intestine. It breaks down peptide bonds on the AMINO ACIDS lysine and arginine. *See also* ALIMENTARY CANAL; DIGESTION; DIGESTIVE SYSTEM

tsetse fly
See feature article

tsunami
WAVE caused by a submarine EARTHQUAKE, subsidence or volcanic eruption. Tsunamis spread radially from their source in ever-widening circles. In mid-ocean they are shallow, 30–60cm (1–2ft) high, and are

rarely detected. In shallower water they build up in force and height, occasionally reaching 30m (100ft), crashing on shore and causing enormous damage. Such waves are also called seismic sea waves; tidal wave is an erroneous term for them, as tsunamis are never the result of the activity of the TIDES.

tuatara
One of two species of nocturnal, lizard-like reptiles found in New Zealand. They are remarkable for being active at quite low temperatures and for being the sole surviving members of the primitive order Rhynchocephalia. Tuataras are brownish in colour and have an exceptionally well-developed pineal body on their heads. Length: to 70cm (28in). Order Rhynchocephalia; species *Sphenodon punctatus* and *Sphenodon guntheri*.

tuber
In plants, short, swollen, sometimes edible underground STEM (modified for the storage of food as in the POTATO) or swollen ROOT (such as the DAHLIA). In stem tubers, new plants develop from the buds (or eyes), growing in the AXILS of the scale leaves. Tubers are propagated by sections containing at least one eye. In the wild, tubers enable the plant to survive an adverse season (winter or dry season), providing food for the development of new shoots and roots later.

tubeworm
Any of many hundreds of species of tube-dwelling, marine POLYCHAETES. They construct the tubes within the substratum or from sediments. The tubes are thus predominantly made from calcium carbonate, accumulated organic detritus, or mucous and silt. Phylum Annelida; class Polychaeta.

tubulidentate
Any member of the order Tubulidentata. Tubulidentates are insectivorous mammals found in central and s Africa. The AARDVARK is the only member of the order.

tuco-tuco
Rodent that lives on the grasslands of Argentina. It has huge front teeth, which it uses to dig the complex burrow systems in which it lives. It has a brown coat with pale underparts, small ears, a long tail and strongly clawed toes. Tuco-tucos spend most of their lives underground, feeding on roots and tubers. In winter or spring between two and five young are born after a gestation of 15 weeks. Head-body length: 17–25cm (7–10in); tail 6–11cm (2–4in). Family Ctenomyidae; species *Ctenomys talarum*.

tucuxi
DOLPHIN that inhabits the Amazon river system. Its torpedo-shaped body is grey, with a pale-grey or yellow-ochre underside. It has a small, triangular dorsal fin and large, spoon-shaped flippers. The tucuxi has a pronounced beak and a rounded forehead. A gregarious animal, it often swims in groups that roll in tight formation. The tucuxi is regarded by local people as sacred and is therefore not exploited. However, its habitat is being destroyed or polluted, and it is becoming rare. Head-tail length: 1.4m (4.6ft). Family Delphinidae; species *Sotalia fluviatilis*.

tufa
SEDIMENTARY ROCK composed mainly of CALCITE (calcium carbonate, $CaCO_3$). It is a porous, non-bedded rock, similar to but less dense than TRAVERTINE. It forms when dissolved calcium carbonate precipitates from lime-rich water in limestone caves. It may rapidly encrust small growing plants or it may contain embedded sediment grains and pebbles. The presence of iron oxides gives it a yellow or red colour.

tuff
SEDIMENTARY ROCK that is made up of particles of

TSETSE FLY
Any of several species of blood-sucking flies that are found in Africa. Larger than a HOUSEFLY, the tsetse fly has a grey thorax and a yellow to brown abdomen. Its mouthparts are designed to pierce skin and suck blood. Staying close to the ground, they find their victims by sight. Females transmit a cattle disease. Almost 80% of the flies that bite humans are males, which carry sleeping sickness. Length: to 16mm (0.6in). Order Diptera; family Muscidae; genus *Glossina*.

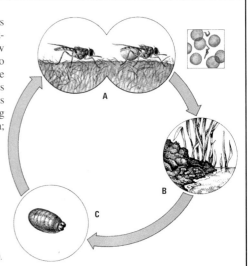

► **The life cycle** of the tsetse fly *Glossina palpalis* is shown above. The abdomen of the adult fly fills with blood as it feeds on the human arm (A). Trypanosomes, which cause sleeping sickness, are transmitted by an infected fly's saliva into the human's blood. The female tsetse fly produces one egg at a time, which hatches inside her body. The larva is deposited on damp, shaded soil (B), where it becomes a pupa (C).

T

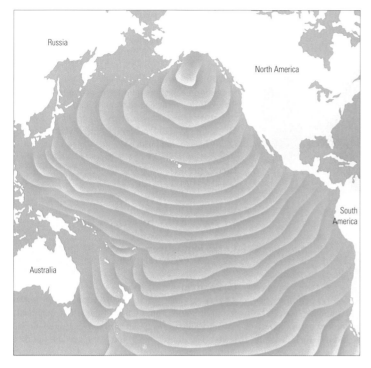

▲ **tsunami** When a submarine earthquake causes a sudden shift in the seafloor along a fault line, a tsunami is produced. The upheaval creates a bulge that breaks down into a series of waves travelling at speeds of up to 750km/h (450mph). The maps shows the hourly position of a tsunami that originated just south of Alaska.

IGNEOUS ROCK from volcanic eruptions. The particles vary in size from fine to coarse but are generally smaller than 4mm (0.2in). They may be either stratified or heterogeneous in their arrangement. *See also* PYROCLASTIC FLOW

tui
Perching bird that is common in New Zealand, the only country in which it is found. Its plumage is all-dark, with a purple sheen, two white throat tufts and a lacy collar of fine white feathers. It is an energetic feeder on nectar and fruit. It flies with whirring wing beats. Length: 30cm (12in). Family Meliphagidae; species *Prosthemadera novaeseelandiae*.

tulip
Any member of the genus *Tulipa*, a group of hardy, bulb-forming plants native to Europe, Asia and North Africa. Tulips have long, pointed leaves growing from the base and elongated, cup-shaped flowers that can be almost any colour or combination of colours. Family Liliaceae; genus *Tulipa*.

tumbleweed
Any of several species of AMARANTH plant that charactcristically break off near the ground in the autumn and are rolled along by the wind. Height: to 51cm (20in). Family Amaranthaceae; genus *Amaranthus*; species include *Amaranthus albus*.

tumbu-fly
Fly found in Africa that is closely related to the FLESH-FLY group. It lays its eggs in dry soil that is contaminated with urine and faeces. The larvae penetrate human skin, to the subcutaneous layers, where they feed and grow. The larval chambers appear boil-like and inflamed on the skin. Family Sarcophagidae; species *Cordylobia anthropophaga*.

tuna (tunny)
Any of several species of marine fish, related to MACKEREL, found in tropical and temperate seas. An important commercial fish, the tuna has a blue-black and silvery streamlined body with a large, deeply divided tail. Length: to 4.3m (14ft). Family Scombridae; genus *Thunnus*; species include *Thunnus thynnus* (bluefin tuna) and *Thunnus albacares* (yellowfin tuna).

tundra
Treeless, level or gently undulating plain characteristic of Arctic and sub-Arctic regions. The main swath of tundra occurs in the Northern Hemisphere, running across N North America and Eurasia. Summer days are quite long and often sunny, but average temperatures for July do not rise above 10°C (50°F). During winter, temperatures can fall to −30°C (−86°F). For six to nine months the average temperature is below freezing point, and there is a thick layer of PERMAFROST, of which only the top few centimetres thaw out in the summer. Where melting occurs, the land is wet and marshy, an ideal breeding ground for mosquitoes. The wet tundra soils are **gleys**, and waterlogging is characteristic. Generally, trees cannot grow in the tundra because of the unfavourable conditions. Mosses and lichens are common, and there are many small flowering plants in the summer. *See also* MUSKEG

tunicate (Urochordate)
Any member of the subphylum Tunicata, a large group of marine invertebrate chordates. Tunicates can be sessile or free-living. There are more than 2000 species. Perhaps the best-known tunicates are the sea squirts (the ASCIDIANS).

tunny
See SKIPJACK; TUNA

tun shell
Any marine SNAIL of the genus *Dolium*. It is so called because of its squat, cask-like shape. Phylum Mollusca; class Gastropoda; order Caenogastropoda; family Tonnidae.

tupelo (black gum)
Any of several species of deciduous tree found in moist forests in North America. Its fine-textured wood is used for furniture, mallets and so on. It has lustrous leaves and tiny, greenish-white flowers. Its dark blue fruit clusters are relished by birds. Height: to 30m (100ft). Family Cornaceae; species include *Nyssa sylvatica* (sour gum) and *Nyssa aquatica* (water tupelo or cotton gum).

tur
Either of two species of GOAT-ANTELOPE that inhabit the Caucasus mountains. Well-adapted to living on cliffs, the tur is very sure-footed and can leap from crag to crag. It is dark brown in winter and moults to red in summer. Turs are gregarious and live in small social herds. Both sexes have backwards-coiling cylindrical horns; in males the horns grow continuously through life, becoming large and heavy. Gestation is *c.*160 days and twins are often born. Head-tail length: 1.2–1.5m (4–5ft). Family Bovidae; species *Capra cylindricornis* and *Capra caucasica*.

turaco
Any of several species of large African birds found in woodlands, especially near streams. The turaco has a small head, a thick bill, a long tail and a crested head. Its plumage is mainly blue, as in the great blue turaco (*Corythaeola cristata*), or green with blue wings. Most species have a bare facial patch of red skin around the eyes. Length: 40–75cm (16–30in). Family Musophagidae; genera include *Tauraco*.

turban shell
Any marine SNAIL of the family Turbinidae. The shape of the shell is squat and rounded, with a turban-like spiral at the end opposite to the aperture. It can grow very large and always has a big aperture. Phylum Mollusca; class Gastropoda; order Archaeogastropoda; family Turbinidae.

turbellarian
Any member of the class Turbellaria, comprising the PLANARIANS.

turbidite
Layer of SEDIMENT deposited under the influence of gravity from a type of fluid density current (turbidity current). The currents can flow downslope at high

T

◀ **tuatara** Surviving only on a few small islands off the coast of New Zealand, the tuatara (*Sphenodon puncatatus* shown here) is a rare example of a "living fossil". Tuataras resemble lizards in appearance but belong to an entirely separate order, members of which were abundant millions of years ago over much of the world. Tuataras live in burrows, from which they emerge at night to forage for the invertebrates, and sometimes birds' eggs, on which they feed.

▶ **turbot** The turbot (*Scophthalmus maximus*) is an important food fish. It lives on the seafloor in the continental shelf region of European seas. It can adjust its coloration to be camouflaged against the sand or gravel of the sea bed.

speed, carrying large volumes of sediment in turbulent suspension over tens of kilometres before losing their energy, spreading out and allowing the load to settle out. In marine environments, turbidity currents are initiated at the outer shelf and flow via SUBMARINE CANYON down to the ocean floor before depositing the turbidite.

turbidity current
See TURBIDITE

turbot
Scaleless, bottom-dwelling, marine FLATFISH of European waters. It has a broad, flat body with both eyes on its grey-brown, mottled upper surface, which may also be covered in bony knobs. Length: to 100cm (39in). Family Scophthalmidae; species *Scophthalmus maximus*.

turgor pressure
See PRESSURE POTENTIAL

turkey
Either of two bird species. The common turkey (*Meleagris gallopavo*) is the largest gamebird in North America. It is the origin of the domestic turkey but is more slender. It forages on the ground for seeds, nuts and acorns. It roosts in trees at night. In spring the male's gobbling call can be heard more than a mile away. Length: male 120cm (47in); female 90cm (35in). The ocellated turkey (*Agriocharis ocellata*) of Central America has a blue head with red "warts"; its call has a bell-like sound. Length: 80–100cm (32–40in). Family Meleagrididae.

turkey vulture
See VULTURE, TURKEY

turmeric
Herbaceous perennial plant originally native to India; it is widely cultivated in Southeast Asia. The dried rhizome is powdered for use as seasoning, a yellow dye and in medicines. Family Zingiberaceae; species *Curcuma longa*.

turnip
Garden vegetable best grown in cool climates. The edible leaves are large and toothed with thick midribs. A biennial, the turnip has a large, bulbous, white or yellow, fleshy root, which can be cooked and eaten. Height: to 55cm (20in). Family Brassicaceae/Cruciferae; species *Brassica rapa*.

turnstone
Either of two species of short-billed wading birds that

breed on arctic tundra and winter south, worldwide, on rocky coasts. In summer the more common species, the ruddy turnstone (*Arenaria interpres*), has a distinctive, chestnut, harlequin plumage. It feeds by turning over seaweed and stones, looking for insects and crustaceans. Length: 23cm (9in). Family Scolopacidae; genus *Arenaria*.

turquoise
Blue mineral, hydrated basic copper aluminium phosphate, found in aluminium-rich rocks in deserts. Its crystal system is triclinic and it occurs as tiny crystals and dense masses. Its colour ranges from sky-blue and blue-green to a greenish grey. It is a popular gemstone. Turquoise occurs as a secondary mineral in veins in association with aluminium IGNEOUS or SEDIMENTARY rocks that have undergone considerable alteration. Hardness 6; r.d. 2.7.

turret shell
Any of several SNAIL species, the shells of which have turret-like square invaginations in the otherwise uniform outline of their apertures. Phylum Mollusca; class Gastropoda.

turtle
Reptile found on land or in marine and fresh waters. Turtles have the most ancient lineage of all reptiles, preceding even the DINOSAURS. Fossils have been found from 200 million years ago. They have a bony, horn-covered, box-like CARAPACE (shell) that encloses shoulder and hip girdles and all internal organs. All species lay eggs on land. Terrestrial turtles are usually called TORTOISES, and some edible species found in brackish waters are called TERRAPINS. SEA TURTLES usually have smaller, lighter shells. Length: 10–200cm (4–80in). Order Chelonia.

turtle, alligator snapping
Largest freshwater turtle of North America. It has a huge head, with a powerful hooked beak, and a long tail. The carapace has three prominent keels and the plastron (bony plate on the turtle's underside) is reduced. Alligator snapping turtles spend most of their time underwater. They use a pink, worm-like growth on the floor of their mouths to lure fish into biting range. Length: to 80cm (31in); weight: to 140kg (300lbs) but usually less than 60kg (130lbs). Family Chelydridae; species *Macroclemys temminckii*.

turtle, box
Terrestrial North American turtle. It has a high domed carapace. A hinge across the plastron allows the turtle to close its shell completely around the withdrawn head and appendages. Box turtles eat both plant and

animal matter and pass cold periods or exceptionally hot, dry spells by burrowing beneath logs or vegetation. Length: 12–19cm (5–7in). Family Emydidae; genus *Terrapene*.

turtle, chicken
Very long-necked, aquatic turtle native to SE United States. It has vertical stripes on its hindlegs. It prefers still waters, but often comes on to land. Length: 10–25cm (4–10in). Family Emydidae; species *Deirochelys reticularia*.

turtle, green
See SEA TURTLE, GREEN

turtle, leatherback
See SEA TURTLE, LEATHERBACK

turtle, loggerhead
See SEA TURTLE, LOGGERHEAD

turtle, map (sawback)
Any of several species of lake and river turtles found in N and central United States. The map turtle is flat-shelled; many species have ridged dorsal keels. The limbs, head and carapace are marked with numerous whorls and lines. The females of most species are larger than the males. The map turtle feeds on molluscs. Length: to 28cm (11in). Family Emydidae; genus *Graptemys*.

turtle, mud
Any of 12 species of freshwater turtles found in the Americas. It dwells in the mud in areas of shallow water. The mud turtle has a short tail and fleshy chin barbels. It has hinged, protective flaps at the front and rear of its undershell. Length: 15cm (6in). Family Kinosternidae; genus *Kinosternon*.

turtle, musk
Any of several species of small aquatic turtles native to the United States. The musk turtle is abundant in sluggish streams. It has a high-domed carapace, and its reduced plastron is hinged. Its musky secretion gives it the nickname "stinkpot". Family Kinosternidae; genus *Sternotherus*.

turtle, painted
Freshwater turtle of the United States. It has bright orange or red markings around the periphery of its smooth, dark-olive shell. Males have long front claws. Length: to 15cm (5.9in). Family Emydidae; species *Chrysemys picta*.

turtle, pond
Any of several species of freshwater turtles belong-

▲ **turnip** The edible part of the turnip (*Brassica rapa*), shown here, is a modification of the stem base together with the swollen root. The turnip probably originated in central Asia and is now grown in cool temperate regions worldwide.

T

ing to the Emydidae family. Pond turtles are found in Europe and America. The European pond turtle (*Emys orbicularis*) is blackish with many small yellow markings. It occurs throughout much of continental Europe and the Mediterranean region. The Pacific pond turtle (*Clemmys marmorata*) is the only freshwater turtle in much of w North America. Pond turtles are chiefly carnivorous. Length: 15–22cm (6–9in). Family Emydidae.

turtle, side-necked
Turtle that can bend its neck sideways under its shell to hide its head. There are two families: hidden-necked turtles (Pelomedusidae) of Africa and South America; and snake-necked turtles (Chelidae) of Australia and South America. Several species of side-necked turtles inhabit fresh water. Length: 15–80cm (6–31in). *See also* MATAMATA; TERRAPIN, HELMETED

turtle, slider
See SLIDER, RED-EARED

turtle, snapping
Large aquatic turtle found in North and South America. It has a large head, broad neck and powerful limbs. Its long, saw-toothed tail is too bulky to be retracted into its shell. It belongs to the same family as the alligator snapping TURTLE. Length: 38cm (15in). Family Chelydridae; genus *Chelydra*.

turtle, softshelled
Any member of the family Trionychidae, a group of freshwater turtles widely distributed in Africa, Asia and North America. The turtle has a soft, leathery shell, a beak with fleshy lips, and a snorkel-like proboscis. Length: to 76cm (30in). Family Trionychidae; the most common of the seven genera is *Trionyx*.

turtle, wood
Medium-sized turtle of NE North America. It has a relatively flattened, very rough-textured carapace and orange skin on its legs and neck. Wood turtles

spiny
soft-shelled
turtle

box turtle

▲ **turtle** The North American box turtle (*Terrapene carolina*) spends most of its time on land. As with other turtles, it has a massive bony shell made of plates of keratin that are fused to the backbone and ribs. It can pull back its head under the shell when danger threatens. The spiny soft-shelled turtle (*Trionyx spiniferus*) is found in North America. It is so called because of the small spiny tubercles that project from its leathery carapace. It has a large shell, which is flat and almost circular.

spend much of their time on land and can be found in woods or on farms far from water. Hatchlings have a round shell and a very long, slender tail. Length: 14–20cm (6–8in). Family Emydidae; species *Clemmys insculpta*.

turtle dove
See DOVE, TURTLE

tusk shell
Any of *c*.400 species of MOLLUSC. The tusk shell is found in ocean depths, where it feeds on microorganisms in the sediments. Its body is encased in a tubular shell that is open at both ends. A muscular foot for digging is located near the anterior mouth. Phylum Mollusca; class Scaphopoda.

typhoon
Name given in the NW Pacific Ocean to a HURRICANE, a violent tropical cyclonic storm.

tyrannosaur
Member of an extinct group of large-headed THEROPOD dinosaurs that lived in late Cretaceous times and were distributed throughout North America and E Asia. They were bipedal predators or scavengers, with unusually short arms and two-fingered hands. The tyrannosaur group included some of the largest-known, land-living carnivores, such as *Tyrannosaurus rex*, which grew to 15m (49ft) in length, stood up to 6m (20ft) high, and weighed as much as 7 tonnes.

tyrannulet
Any of *c*.50 species of FLYCATCHER native to Central and South America. The tyrannulet is a tiny bird, which is found in every habitat from coastal to tropical forests right up to the snowline. The species are confusingly similar. Most tyrannulets are brownish above and buff-yellow below. Some species have different combinations of wing bars and eye stripes. Length: 8–13cm (3–5in). Family Tyrannidae (part).

tyrant
Any of many species that are similar in appearance to, but slightly larger than, the TYRANNULET; the tyrant is a member of the diverse group of tyrant flycatchers. Some tyrant species are confusingly similar in appearance and are best identified by call and habitat. Length: 10–23cm (4–9in). Family Tyrannidae (part).

◀ **tyrannosaur** The tyrannosaurs were the dominant land-living predators of the Northern Hemisphere. Their fossil remains are often found near those of the ceratopsians on which they probably preyed. The tyrannosaurs' teeth were serrated front and back in order to slice easily through flesh.

T

U

ultrafiltration

Filtration under pressure such as that created by blood pressure. It occurs in the KIDNEY, where the afferent arteriole bringing blood into the GLOMERULUS is wider than the efferent arteriole taking blood away. The resultant high blood pressure forces substances up to a relative molecular mass of 68,000 into the BOWMAN'S CAPSULE. Ultrafiltration also occurs in blood capillaries, where the pressure of blood forces tissue fluid out of the vessels.

ultraviolet radiation

Type of electromagnetic radiation of shorter wavelength and higher frequency than visible light. Typical wavelengths range from roughly 4–400nm (nanometres), and those of visible light range from 400nm (violet) to 700nm (red). Ultraviolet radiation affects living matter in a number of important ways: it kills bacteria and many other parasites (and so is used medically to sterilize equipment); it tans the skin by stimulating the formation of the pigment melanin; and it helps to make VITAMIN D in the body, which plays a part in the prevention of rickets. Ultraviolet light also causes certain materials to fluoresce (emit visible light), notably the brighteners added to some detergents. Sunlight contains ultraviolet rays, most of which are filtered by the OZONE LAYER. If the ozone layer is weakened, enough ultraviolet can reach the ground to harm living things. Excessive exposure to sunlight can cause sunburn and skin cancer.

umbilical cord

In placental mammals, long, thick cord that connects a developing FETUS with the PLACENTA. The umbilical cord contains two large arteries and one vein. In human beings, the cord is clamped at birth and cut from the placenta; the part of the cord remaining on the baby's abdomen dries and falls off, leaving the scar known as the navel.

umbrellabird

Any of several species of strange, woodpecker-like birds found in the humid forests of South America. It belongs to the COTINGA family. It has a distinctive, umbrella-shaped feather crest. Its plumage is all black, and it has black wattles, up to 33cm (13in) long, that hang down from the breast. Its crest and wattles can be extended during courtship displays. Length: 50cm (20in). Family Cotingidae; genus *Cephalopterus.*

unconformity

In geology, break in the time sequence of rocks layered one above the other. The time gap may be caused by interruptions in the deposition of sediment, ancient erosion, earth movements or other activity. An angular uncomformity occurs when successive strata (*see* STRATUM) dip at different angles.

ungulate

MAMMAL with hoofed feet. Most ungulates, including cattle (*see* OX), SHEEP, PIGS and DEER, are members of the order ARTIODACTYLA (with an even number of toes). The order PERISSODACTYLA (ungulates with an odd number of toes) consists of HORSES, TAPIRS and RHINOCEROSES. The orders Proboscidea and Hyracoidea, collectively known as subungulates, contain ELEPHANTS and HYRAXES.

unicorn plant

Any of several species of herbaceous annual or perennial plants found in tropical and subtropical South America and Mexico. Its fruit capsules bear curved "horns", formed from the persistent style, which aid in dispersal by animals. The plant is grown for these fruits, which can be pickled and eaten. Family Martyniaceae; genera *Martynia* and *Proboscidea.*

upas tree

Evergreen tree of the FIG family; it is native to Java. Its milky juice is used to poison the tips of arrows. The reddish-brown fruit is pear-shaped. Height: to 30m (100ft). Family Moraceae; species *Antiaris toxicaria.*

upper atmosphere

Region of the ATMOSPHERE, extending upwards from about 50km (30mi), which is free of disturbances caused by the WEATHER. It includes the MESOSPHERE, THERMOSPHERE and IONOSPHERE. At this altitude the air is rarefied, with temperatures ranging from $-110°C$ ($-170°F$) in the lower regions to 250–1500°C (500–2700°F) higher up. The behaviour of the upper atmosphere is greatly affected by such extraterrestrial phenomena as solar and cosmic radiation, which cause the gas molecules to produce the ionosphere, and atmospheric tides, which cause turbulence.

uracil

One of the four nitrogen-containing organic bases in the NUCLEOTIDES that make up RNA (ribonucleic acid). A PYRIMIDINE derivative, uracil accounts for the major difference between RNA and DNA: in DNA uracil is replaced by THYMINE (the other three bases, ADENINE, CYTOSINE and GUANINE, are common to both RNA and DNA). In forming associations with DNA and other RNA molecules, uracil pairs with adenine.

uraninite (pitchblende)

Dense radioactive mineral form of uranium oxide, UO_2, the chief ore of uranium and the most important source for uranium and radium. The blackish and lustrous ore occurs in several varieties: crystallized varieties are called uraninite, massive varieties are called pitchblende. They usually contain small amounts of radium, lead, thorium, polonium, and sometimes the gases helium and argon. Both varieties are found around the world in veins (often quartz and silver), especially in the United States, Canada, Britain, Europe, Australia, Congo and South Africa. Hardness 5–6; r.d. 6.5–8.5 (pitchblende), 8–10 (uraninite).

urea

Organic compound ($CO(NH_2)_2$), a white crystalline solid excreted in URINE. Most vertebrate species excrete the majority of their nitrogen wastes as urea; human urine contains about 25 grams of urea to a litre. Because it is so high in nitrogen, urea is a good fertilizer. It is also used to make urea-formaldehyde resins and barbiturates.

ureter

In vertebrates, the long, narrow duct that connects the KIDNEY to the urinary BLADDER. The ureters transport URINE from the kidneys to the bladder, where it is stored until it is discharged by way of the URETHRA.

urethra

Duct through which URINE is discharged from the bladder in mammals. Urine is produced in the KIDNEY, stored in the BLADDER until pressure in the bladder triggers specific neural responses that cause urine, under voluntary control, to be released through the urethra. In males the urethra is also the tube through which SEMEN is ejaculated.

urial

Wild SHEEP of central Asia. It is reddish-brown in colour. Ewes have small horns; the rams have massive horns that form a complete arch. Height: to 90cm (35in) at the shoulder. Family Bovidae; species *Ovis ammon orientalis.*

uric acid

Insoluble end product of protein METABOLISM. It is the main excretory substance in birds, insects and reptiles, but only small quantities of it are normally produced by humans (who, like most mammals, mainly excrete soluble UREA). An excessive buildup of uric acid in human blood causes gout, which is the deposition of urate salts around the joints.

urine

Fluid filtered out from the bloodstream by the KIDNEY. It consists mainly of water, salts and waste products such as UREA. From the kidneys it passes through the URETERS to the BLADDER for discharging by way of the URETHRA. In diabetes, urine contains glucose, and to diagnose the disease urine is tested for glucose.

urticale

Any member of the Urticales order of dicotyledonous plants; it includes such families as Moraceae (MULBERRY and FIGS, among others), Ulmaceae (ELMS) and Urticaceae (stinging NETTLES).

U-shaped valley

Glaciated trough with a characteristic U-shaped cross-section. It is usually formed by the overdeepening of an original river VALLEY through EROSION by a flowing GLACIER.

uterus (womb)

Hollow muscular organ located in the pelvis of female mammals. It protects and nourishes the growing FETUS until birth. The upper part is broad and branches out on each side into the FALLOPIAN TUBES. The lower uterus narrows into the CERVIX, which leads to the VAGINA. Its muscular walls are lined with mucous membrane (ENDOMETRIUM), to which the egg attaches itself after fertilization. *See also* MENSTRUAL CYCLE

utricle

Fluid-filled chamber in the mammalian inner EAR. The three SEMICIRCULAR CANALS, the organs of balance, loop out from the utricle. Sensory cells within the utricle detect changes in the direction of movement of the ear (and hence the head). They also sense how fast the fluid in the canals is moving. All the information passes along part of the auditory nerve to the brain, which processes it to provide the sense of balance. *See also* EQUILIBRIUM SENSE

V

vacuole
Membrane-bounded cavity within the CYTOPLASM of a CELL. Depending on the organism, vacuoles contain either liquid, gas or food particles. Vacuoles perform various functions. In single-celled organisms, such as an amoeba, **contractile vacuoles** fill with water before rapidly contracting and expelling excess water or wastes. In this way vacuoles perform OSMOREGULATION and excretion. In plants, vacuoles allow individual cells to increase in size without amassing bulk that would hinder cell METABOLISM.

vagina
In mammals, portion of the female reproductive tract, running from the CERVIX of the UTERUS to the exterior of the body. Tube-like in shape, it receives the erect PENIS during sexual intercourse. The muscular walls of the vagina enable it to dilate massively to allow the passage of the offspring during birth. *See also* SEXUAL REPRODUCTION

valence (valency)
Measure of the "combining power" of a particular element. It is equal to the number of (individual) CHEMICAL BONDS one ATOM can form. The valence of an atom is determined by the number of ELECTRONS in the outermost (valence) shell. The valence of many elements is determined by their ability to combine with hydrogen or to displace it in compounds (hydrogen has a valence of one). For example, one carbon atom combines with four hydrogen atoms to make methane (CH_4) so the valence of carbon is given as four. *See also* COVALENT BOND; OXIDATION-REDUCTION

valerian
Any member of the family Valerianaceae. Common valerian (*Valeriana officinalis*) is a perennial plant native to Europe and N Asia, naturalized in North America. It has been used medicinally for centuries for its sedative and anti-spasmodic properties. Other species of *Valeriana* are grown as ornamentals for their decorative foliage. Red valerian (*Centranthus ruber*) is a perennial plant native to Europe, North Africa and Asia Minor. It has branching rootstock and heads of small pink, white or deep red flowers. It is frequently grown in gardens. The leaves are eaten as salad or vegetable greens, but the plant has none of the medicinal properties of common valerian. Greek valerian, not a true valerian, is better known as JACOB'S LADDER. Family Valerianaceae; genera include *Centranthus* and *Valeriana*.

valley
Elongated, gently sloping depression of the Earth's surface, commonly situated between mountains or hills. It often contains a stream or river that receives the drainage from the surrounding heights. A U-SHAPED VALLEY was probably formed by a glacier, a V-shaped valley by a stream. The term may also be applied to a broad, generally flat area that is drained by a river, such as the Mississippi Valley in the United States.

valves
In anatomy, structures that prevent the backflow of blood in the HEART and VEINS. Heart valves separate and connect the two atria and ventricles, the right ventricle and the pulmonary artery, and the left ventricle and the aorta.

vampire bat
See BAT, VAMPIRE

Van Allen radiation belts
Two doughnut-shaped regions of radiation trapped by Earth's MAGNETIC FIELD in the upper ATMOSPHERE, named after the US physicist James Van Allen (1914–), who discovered them in 1958. The belts contain particles carrying energies of 10,000 to several million electron volts. Artificial satellites are insulated against this radiation. The inner belt (of ELECTRONS and PROTONS) extends from 1000km to 4000km (600–2500mi) above the Equator. The outer belt (of electrons) extends from 15,000 to 25,000km (9000–15,000mi) above the Equator. It is thought that the particles come from SOLAR FLARES and are carried by the SOLAR WIND.

vanilla
Climbing ORCHID native to Mexico. The vines bear greenish-yellow flowers that produce seed pods – the source of the flavouring vanilla. Family Orchidaceae; species *Vanilla planifolia*.

variation
Differences between members of the same SPECIES. Variation occurs naturally due to HEREDITY and to differences in the environment during development. The difference may be in physical appearance, behaviour or fertility. *See also* ADAPTATION; EVOLUTION

variegation
Term used to describe parts of plants, especially leaves, that display different colours. It occurs naturally, mostly as the result of a lack of the green pigment CHLOROPHYLL, the most common effect being yellow, cream or white patches, streaks or spots on green leaves. Variegation is exploited for ornamental purposes, but such decorative plants are usually weaker than the uniformly coloured plants. The variegated petals of some flowers can often be the result of mutation or viral infection.

variscite
Glassy, white to green phosphate mineral, hydrous aluminium phosphate with iron impurities, found in aluminium-rich rocks near the Earth's surface. It occurs as crystals in the orthorhombic system. It resembles turquoise but is greener. It is used in jewellery. Hardness 3.5–4.5; r.d. 2.5.

varve
Term applied to a layer of SEDIMENT deposited in a single year in a body of still water. Specifically a varve consists of two layers of sediment, a coarse layer deposited in the summer and a fine layer deposited in the winter in glacial meltwater lakes. Varves have been used to date the age of Pleistocene glacial deposits.

vascular bundle
Strand of conductive tissue that transports water and dissolved mineral salts and nutrients throughout a VASCULAR PLANT. Vascular bundles are the equivalent of the blood and lymph vessels found in animals. They extend from the ROOTS, through the STEM, and out to the LEAVES. They consist of two types of tissue: XYLEM, which conducts water from the roots to the shoot and is located towards the centre of the bundle; and PHLOEM, which conducts salts and nutrients and forms the outer regions of the bundle. In plants that exhibit SECONDARY THICKENING, the xylem and phloem are separated by a thin layer of CAMBIUM, from which new vascular tissue is generated.

vascular plant
Plant with vessels or tubes to carry water and nutrients within it. All higher plants – FERNS, CONIFERS and FLOWERING PLANTS – have a vascular system (XYLEM and PHLOEM). This system exists in ROOTS, STEMS and LEAVES.

vascular system
Network of vessels through which fluids circulate in the body of an animal or plant. They include BLOOD VESSELS (ARTERIES, VEINS and CAPILLARIES) in the blood vascular system and lymph vessels in the LYMPHATIC SYSTEM. The network of tubes that carries fluid and nutrients in the PHLOEM and XYLEM of plants is called a vascular system or VASCULAR BUNDLE.

vector
In disease, any agent that carries an infectious agent from one host to another. It may be an insect, such as a MOSQUITO or FLEA, or an inanimate object such as a cup. It also may serve as an intermediate host for the infectious agent.

◀ **valley** Tasmania is a mountainous and forested island. In the southwest of the island is an area of wilderness known as the Tasmanian Wilderness, which is a World Heritage Site. Parallel mountain ranges divided by wide valleys run through this region. The River Weld, a tributary of the River Huon, rises in the mountains shown in this photograph.

► **velvet ant** The wingless female velvet ant is found on the ground, often in leaf litter. In spring she enters the nest of a wasp or bee, paralyses the larvae and then lays her eggs. The hatched velvet ant larvae feed on the larvae of the wasp or bee.

vegetable marrow (vegetable spaghetti)
Herbaceous annual cultivated for its large, fleshy, edible fruits. One of the oldest domesticated plants, it is thought to have originated in Mexico. It was a staple in the diet of Native Americans. The whole plant is roughly hairy, with separate male and female yellow flowers. Many varieties have been developed. Height: to 2m (6.6ft). Family Cucurbitaceae; species *Cucurbita pepo*.

vegetable spaghetti
See VEGETABLE MARROW

vegetative reproduction (vegetative propagation)
Form of ASEXUAL REPRODUCTION in higher plants. It involves an offshoot or a piece of the original plant (from leaf, stem or root) separating and giving rise to an entire new plant. It may occur naturally, as in STRAWBERRIES reproducing by RUNNERS, or artificially, as in a houseplant cutting yielding a new plant. The reproductive structure may include a food store, as in a BULB, CORM or TUBER.

vein
In mammals, vessel that carries deoxygenated BLOOD to the HEART. An exception is the pulmonary vein, which carries oxygenated blood from the lungs to the left upper chamber of the heart. Veins have VALVES on their inner walls to prevent any backflow of blood. *See also* ARTERY

velvet ant
Any member of the family Mutillidae, a group of solitary WASPS. The velvet ant is so called because the female is wingless and covered in soft hair, resembling an ANT. The male is winged. The larvae are parasites of the pupae and grubs of wasps and bees. *Mutilla europaea* is the largest and most common of the three British species. Order Hymenoptera; superfamily Scolioidea; family Mutillidae.

velvet worm (onychophoran)
Any member of the phylum Onychophora, comprising *c*.70 species of worm-like, terrestrial invertebrates. They are found mainly in tropical forests. In evolutionary terms, the velvet worm is seen as an intermediate stage between the ANNELIDS and the ARTHROPODS. It has about 20 pairs of legs, which end in tiny claws. The velvet worm preys on other invertebrates, which it captures by coating them with slime. Length: 15cm (6in). Phylum Onychophora; there are 10 genera, of which one of the most common is *Peripatus*.

Vening Meinesz, Felix Andries (1887–1966)
Dutch geophysicist and geodesist. He developed (1923) a method of measuring gravity in ocean basins. He is also noted for research on the effect of solar movements on the Earth's surface and studies of convection currents within the Earth.

venom, snake
Toxic substance produced in the poison glands of SNAKES and injected into the victim through ducts in or along their fangs. Many venoms are dangerous to people, and some can be lethal unless counteracted by antiserums. The effects of snake venom vary according to the species and the constituents of the poison. Blood coagulation, respiratory effects and haemorrhage are the commonest effects.

ventilation
Process by which air or water is taken into and expelled from the body of an animal and passed over a surface across which GAS EXCHANGE takes place. Ventilation mechanisms include: BREATHING, by which air is drawn into the LUNGS for gas exchange across the wall of the alveoli; the movements of the floor of a FISH's mouth, coupled with those of its GILL covers, which draw water across the gills; and the pumping movements of the ABDOMEN of some insects, which draw air through SPIRACLES that carry it to the tissues.

ventral
Describing that part of an organism that normally faces the ground. In plants, the ventral surface of a leaf is the under surface (which usually faces away from the light). In fish, the ventral fin is the fin pointing downwards. In four-legged animals, it is the lower or under surface. In humans and other bipedal animals, it is the forward-facing surface, more usually described as anterior. *See also* DORSAL

ventricle
Either of the two lower chambers of the HEART. The term is also used for the four fluid-filled cavities within the BRAIN.

Venus' comb
Marine SNAIL found in the Indo-Pacific region. It belongs to the murex group, comprising species belonging to the family Muricidae. Venus' comb bears elongate projections on its shell, which give it the appearance of a hair comb. Length: to 15cm (6in). Class Gastropoda; family Muricidae; species *Murex pecten*.

Venus' flower-basket
Any of several species of SPONGE within the genus *Euplectella*. Venus' flower basket is found in deep marine waters. Its long cylindrical skeleton is formed from separate silica spicules within a latticed silica framework. Length: 25cm (10in). Phylum Porifera; species include *Euplectella aspergillum*.

Venus' flytrap
INSECTIVOROUS PLANT that belongs to the same family as the SUNDEWS. It is native to swampy habitats in the pine barrens of the SE United States. Its leaves are modified into a two-lobed, hinged trap, which is sprung when an insect, or other small animal, lands on the surface and touches the sensitive hairs. Venus' flytrap is sometimes grown as a novelty house plant. Family Droseraceae; species *Dionaea muscipula*.

Venus' girdle
See COMB JELLY

verbena
Any member of the genus *Verbena*, a large group of herbaceous, annual or perennial plants. Verbenas are native to tropical and temperate America, but many species are cultivated elsewhere as ornamentals. *Verbena x hybrida* is a complex group of hybrids of garden origin. They are grown for their heads of ornate, often fragrant flowers and are used as bedding, edging and window-box plants. Family Verbenaceae; genus *Verbena*.

verdin
Small, sprightly, insect- and seed-eating bird. Its plumage is grey, with a chestnut shoulder patch, a yellow head and throat and a fine bill. It is found in arid scrub country in the s United States and in Central America. Length: 11cm (4in). Family Remizidae; species *Auriparus flaviceps*.

vermiculite
Clay mineral. Its flakes are light and are used in plaster and insulation, and as a packing material. The mineral is also used widely for conditioning soil and as a starting medium for seeds.

veronica
See SPEEDWELL

vertebra
One of the bones making up the SPINE (backbone) or vertebral column. Each vertebra is composed of a large, solid body from the top of which wing-like projections jut to either side. It has a hollow centre through which the SPINAL CORD passes. The human backbone is composed of 26 vertebrae (the five sacral and four vertebrae of the coccyx fuse together to form two solid bones), which are held together by ligaments and INTERVERTEBRAL DISCS.

vertebrate
Animal with individual discs of bone or cartilage, called VERTEBRAE, which surround or replace the embryonic NOTOCHORD to form a jointed backbone that encloses the SPINAL CORD. The principal division within the vertebrates is between the aquatic, fish-like forms and partly land-adapted forms (AMPHIBIANS) and the wholly land-adapted forms (REPTILES, BIRDS and MAMMALS), although some mammals, such as whales, have adapted for a totally

▲ **vetch** These scrambling plants support one another by means of many twining tendrils. Common vetch (*Vicia sativa*), shown here, is frequently grown in temperate climates by farmers as a fodder crop. It is also found wild on waste ground and along roadsides.

V

aquatic existence. Birds and mammals are the only warm-blooded vertebrates to have circulatory, respiratory and excretory systems that allow for constant high body temperatures. Phylum CHORDATA; subphylum Vertebrata.

vervet monkey
See MONKEY, VERVET

vestigial structure
Organ or limb that is deformed or degenerate in appearance and no longer has any recognizable function. Human vestigial structures include the tonsils and the appendix. *See also* DEGENERATION

vesuvianite
See IDOCRASE

vetch
Any annual or perennial plant of the genus *Vicia*, native to temperate and warm areas of the world. Most vetches are tendril climbers, with pea-like flowers. Many species are grown for food, green manure or forage. Family Fabaceae/Leguminosae.

viburnum
Any member of the genus *Viburnum*, a group of flowering shrubs and small trees native to North America and Eurasia. All species have small, fleshy fruits containing single, flat seeds. Many species are grown as ornamentals for their fragrant flowers and decorative foliage. Family Caprifoliaceae; there are *c*.120 species.

viceroy butterfly
See BUTTERFLY, VICEROY

vicuña
Graceful, even-toed, hoofed mammal of South America. It is the smallest member of the CAMEL family. The vicuña is humpless and resembles the LLAMA. Its silky coat is tawny brown, with a yellowish bib under the neck. Vicuña wool was used by the Inca kings and is still expensive and rare. Height: 86cm (34in) at the shoulder; weight: 45kg (100lb). Family Camelidae; species *Vicugna vicugna*.

vine
Term loosely applied to numerous species of climbing plants. To aid their climb, vines develop modifications, such as TENDRILS, disc-like holdfasts, ADVENTITIOUS ROOTS and RUNNERS. One of the most common species of vine is the European GRAPE plant (*Vitis vinifera*), the fruits of which may be eaten fresh or dried to give currants or raisins.

vinegar-fly
Any of several species of FRUIT FLY belonging to the genus *Drosophila*. The vinegar-fly is a small fly that is attracted to fermenting materials and rotting fruit. *Drosophila melanogaster* has been used extensively in genetic and developmental biology studies. Its life-cycle takes approximately two weeks. Length: *c*.3mm (*c*.0.1in). Order Diptera; family Drosophilidae.

violet
Any of many species of herbs and shrublets belonging to the genus *Viola*. Violets may be annual or perennial and are found worldwide. The five-petalled flowers, which may be blue, violet, lilac, yellow or white, grow singly on stalks. Family Violaceae. *See also* PANSY

viper
Any of *c*.200 species of venomous SNAKES with hol-

low, erectile fangs that inject venom into prey. Vipers often eat very large prey, which the venom helps to digest. Most viper species are thick-bodied and many have wide, triangular heads. Length: to 3m (10ft). Family Viperidae; species include ADDER, PUFF ADDER, RATTLESNAKE and SIDEWINDER.

viperfish
Any of several species of fish found in tropical marine waters worldwide. The viperfish is a deep-sea fish, with bioluminescent organs to attract its prey. It gets its common name from its large teeth. Length: to 30cm (12in). Family Chauliodontidae; species include *Chauliodus sloani*.

viper's bugloss
See BUGLOSS

Virchow, Rudolf (1821–1902)
German pathologist. His discovery that all CELLS arise from other cells completed the formulation of the cell theory and repudiated theories of SPONTANEOUS GENERATION. Virchow also studied the nature of disease at a cellular level and established the science of cellular pathology.

vireo
Any member of the family Vireonidae, a group of small woodland songbirds of the Americas. The vireo resembles the warbler but is chunkier and less active. Its short, sturdy bill is slightly hooked at the tip. Most species are similar in appearance, with dull plumage. Some species, such as the red-eyed vireo (*Vireo olivaceus*), have eyebrow stripes; other species, such as the grey vireo (*Vireo vicinior*), have faint wing bars. Length: 11–16cm (4–6in). Family Vireonidae.

Virginia creeper (woodbine or American ivy)
Climbing plant native to North America, found mainly in E United States. It is a tendril climber with leaves divided into five parts. Virginia creeper produces green flower clusters and blue-black inedible berries. Family Vitaceae; species *Parthenocissus quinquefolia*.

Virtanen, Artturi Ilmari (1895–1973)
Finnish biochemist who was awarded the 1945 Nobel Prize for chemistry for his work on fodder preservation. During the 1920s Virtanen discovered

that fermentation in green fodder, which ruins silage stores, could be prevented by the addition of hydrochloric and sulphuric acids. He also found that this technique, known as the AIV method, had no detrimental effects on the nutritional qualities or edibility of the fodder.

virus
See feature article, page 396

viscacha
South American rodent closely related to the CHINCHILLA. Its fur is not commercially valuable. The plains viscacha lives in burrows on the Argentine pampas. The mountain viscacha (mountain chinchilla) lives in crevices in the rocks. Both species feed on plants. Family Chinchilla; species *Lagostomus maximus* (plains viscacha) and *Lagidium peruanum* (mountain viscacha).

vision
See SIGHT

visual purple
See RHODOPSIN

vitamin
Organic compound that is essential in small amounts to the maintenance and healthy growth of all animals. Vitamins are classified as either water-soluble (B and C) or fat-soluble (A, D, E and K). They are usually found in a healthy diet, but today most can be made synthetically. Some are synthesized in the body. Many vitamins act as coenzymes, helping ENZYMES in RESPIRATION and other metabolic processes such as the synthesis of cell components and the detoxification of body wastes. Lack of a particular vitamin can lead to a deficiency disease. **Vitamin E** is important in reproduction and many other biological processes. **Vitamin D** helps the body absorb phosphorus and calcium. It is essential for the normal growth of bone and teeth. Existing in human skin (activated by sunlight), vitamin D is also found in fish-liver oil, yeast and egg yolk. Deficiency causes such bone diseases as rickets, while an excess could cause kidney damage. **Vitamin C** or ascorbic acid is commonly found in many fruits and vegetables. It helps the body resist infection and stress and is essential to normal

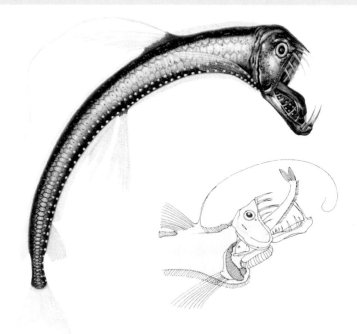

◀ **viperfish** The viperfish *Chauliodus sloani* lives at depths of between 500 and 2000m (1600–6600ft) in the Atlantic Ocean. At night, it makes vertical migrations towards the surface to feed. Its prey is attracted by a light organ on the end of the first ray of its dorsal fin. Prey may also be attracted by phosphorescent organs along the sides of its body, and on the eyeball and the roof of its mouth. When the viper fish moves in to attack, its head is thrown back, the lower jaw, which is armed with needle-sharp teeth, is shot forward and the prey is swallowed and digested extremely rapidly.

V

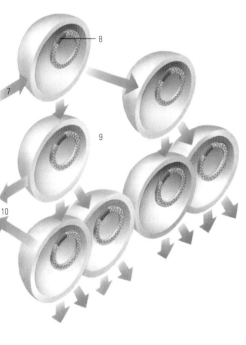

Viruses are submicroscopic infectious organisms, varying in size from 10 to 300 nanometres. They consist of packets of genetic material – DNA, or the closely related RNA – surrounded by a protective coating (known as a capsid) of proteins. Viruses are most familiar to us as the cause of human, animal and plant diseases. Smallpox (now eradicated), rabies and polio are ancient examples. Other viruses, such as the human immunodeficiency virus (HIV), the cause of AIDS, seem to have arisen in more recent times.

Viruses are incapable of independent existence. They can grow and reproduce only when they enter another cell, such as a bacterium or animal cell, because they lack energy-producing and protein-synthesizing functions. Viruses often gain entry to cells by latching onto proteins on the cell surface – proteins that are normally used by the cells for quite different purposes. The AIDS virus, for example, attacks only a particular set of leucocytes (white blood cells), T-LYMPHOCYTES. These carry a special protein on their surface to which the virus sticks. Once attached to its "receptor" protein, the virus is then taken into the cell.

Upon entering a cell, a virus discards its proteins and replicates itself by copying and translating its genetic material. Then the cell begins copying and translating the virus' NUCLEIC ACID instead of its own. The genes encoded in viral nucleic acid direct the manufacture of more virus-coating protein, and the nucleic acid itself is also copied many times. Thus the cell is tricked into making new virus particles that are eventually shed from the cell, sometimes destroying the cell in the process. Most viruses have relatively few genes, all of which are directed to replicating it.

Control of viruses is difficult because harsh measures are required to kill them. The animal body has, however, evolved some protective measures, such as production of interferon and of ANTIBODIES directed against specific viruses. In most cases, one attack of a viral disease confers lifelong immunity. Where the specific agent can be isolated vaccines can be developed, but some viruses (such as those responsible for causing influenza) change so rapidly that vaccines become ineffective. There are few antiviral drugs. *See also* PATHOGEN

▲ ▶ **Bacteriophages are viruses** that infect bacteria. They achieve this by injecting DNA through the cell wall. Bacteriophage *lambda* (A), which infects *E. coli* bacteria in the human intestine, has a simple structure. The DNA (1) is stored in a polyhedral protein head (2) attached to a hollow tail (3) with a single tail fibre (4). The phage attaches itself to a bacterium (B) at the tail (1), and injects its DNA (2). This can result in an infection that causes the cell to lyse (break open), releasing replica phages. During such a lytic infection, the phage DNA remains separate from the bacterial DNA (3), and manipulates the cell's enzymes to synthesize the proteins that form the components of new phages (4). The phage DNA replicates and large numbers of phages are assembled (5). In the process, the bacterial DNA is used, and by the time the cell lyses (6), the

phage DNA may be completely destroyed. In some cases, the injection of phage DNA results in a lysogenic infection (7), when the phage DNA becomes part of the bacterial chromosome (8). Cell division (9) then produces numerous replicas of the phage DNA. During the course of lysogenic growth, damage to the cell may result in a lytic infection (10) by causing the phage DNA to be ejected from the bacterial chromosome.

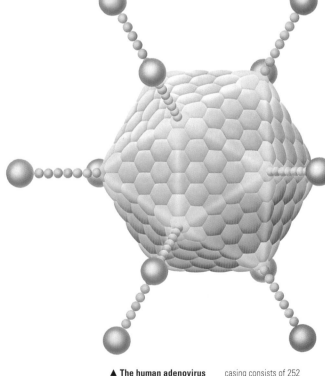

▲ **The human adenovirus** (C) is of the type responsible for colds and sore throats. The virus is colour coded for ease of identification. The casing consists of 252 protein molecules (capsomeres) arranged into a regular icosahedron (20 faces). This structure occurs in many viruses, representing the most economical packing arrangement around the DNA inside. Twelve of the capsomeres, located at the points of the icosahedron, are five-sided pentagon bases (yellow). The remaining 240 are six-sided hexons (green). Five of these (green-yellow) adjoin each penton base, from which extends a single fibre (red) tipped with a terminal structure (blue) that begins cell entry.

V

metabolism. A deficiency causes scurvy. Vitamin C is destroyed by heating, and much is lost during cooking. **Vitamin B** is actually a group of 12 vitamins, known collectively as the **vitamin B complex**, important in assisting the process by which energy is produced in the body (RESPIRATION). Vitamin B_1 or thiamine occurs in yeast and cereals. Lack of it causes a disease called beriberi. Another B vitamin is **niacin** (nicotinic acid) found in milk, meat and green vegetables. Lack of this vitamin causes pellagra. **Vitamin B_{12}** is needed for the formation of blood cells. It is found especially in meat, liver and eggs. Deficiency causes anaemia. **Vitamin A** (retinol) is important for healthy eyes, and shortage of the vitamin caused night-blindness. It is found in fish-liver oil, but the body can convert carotene, the red pigment in carrots, mangoes and red peppers, into Vitamin A.

vitreous humour

Transparent, jelly-like medium that fills the eyeball between the lens and the retina. It constitutes the vitreous body, which serves to hold the retina in position and combines with the lens to ensure the clear passage of light to the receptor cells of the retina. *See also* AQUEOUS HUMOUR; EYE

viviparity

Process or trait among animals of giving birth to live young. Placental mammals show the highest development of viviparity, in which the offspring develops inside the body within the mother's UTERUS. The young receive nutrition via the mother's PLACENTA. *See also* OVOVIPARITY

volcanic bomb

See BOMB, VOLCANIC

volcanic plug

Hard mass of solidified LAVA in the vent of a VOLCANO. Over a period of millions of years the volcano will erode, but the hard plug will survive as a small isolated hill in the CRATER.

volcanism

Volcanic activity. The term includes all aspects of the process: the eruption of molten and gaseous matter, the building up of cones and mountains, and the formation of LAVA flows, GEYSERS and hot springs.

volcano

See feature article, page 398

vole

Any of *c*.100 species of short-tailed, small-eared, plant-eating rodents. Voles usually live in sociable colonies, often in shallow tunnels. They can remain active in winter by burrowing under snow for insulation. Population numbers fluctuate in cycles: they breed prolifically when conditions are favourable, but numbers crash when they have exhausted their food supply. Family Muridae (part).

vole, field

Any member of the genus *Microtus*, a group of voles found in North America, Eurasia and North Africa.

► **vole, water** The European water vole (*Arvicola terrestris*) is a burrowing, colonial rodent. It feeds on aquatic plants and some invertebrates. Very shy, it digs its burrow complexes in areas with plenty of ground cover.

The field vole can reproduce at the rate of more than 100 offspring per female per year. Head-body length: 9–12cm (4–5in); tail: 3–6cm (1–2in). Family Muridae; species include *Microtus pennsylvanicus* (meadow vole).

vole, mountain

Any member of the genus *Alticola*, comprising voles that inhabit the upland areas of Asia. Family Muridae; species include *Alticola macrotis*.

vole, red-backed (bank vole)

Any member of the genus *Clethrionomys*, comprising voles that inhabit the forests of Eurasia and North America. It has red fur on its back. Head-body length: 8–11cm (3–4in); tail: 3–6cm (1–2in). Family Muridae; species include *Clethrionomys rutilus* (northern red-backed vole).

vole, water

Any member of the genus *Arvicola*, comprising voles that lives in burrows, often along river banks. They are native to Eurasia. Head-body length: 14–19cm (6–7in); tail: 4–10cm (2–4in). Family Muridae; species include *Arvicola terrestris* (European water vole).

voluntary muscle

In human beings and other mammals, the most plentiful of the three types of MUSCLE, comprising the bulk of the body. It is also known as **skeletal muscle** or **striated muscle** because of its characteristic striped appearance under the microscope. Mostly attached to BONE, either directly or through TENDONS, it includes FLEXORS to bend joints and EXTENSORS to straighten them. *See also* INVOLUNTARY MUSCLE

vortex

Eddy or WHIRLPOOL observed in fluid motion. Vortices cannot occur in ideal (nonviscous) fluid motion, but they are important in the study of real fluids. In particular, the vortices occurring behind airfoils are of great interest in aerodynamic design. The study of turbulence shows that energy is dissipated most efficiently in smaller vortices.

vulture

Very large BIRD OF PREY found in mountainous areas worldwide except for Australia and New Zealand. It is adapted to soaring and feeding on carrion. A vulture can soar at a great height watching for a carcass then plummet, many thousands of feet, in large numbers to feed on the corpse. Order Falconiformes.

vulture, bearded (lammergeier)

Large vulture found in remote mountains of s Europe and Asia. It has long, narrow wings and a long, wedge-shaped tail. It has a moustache-like tuft of feathers at the base of its bill. The bearded vulture

◄ **vulture, turkey** The red-headed turkey vulture (*Cathartes aura*) is a New World vulture, which is found in mountainous regions from Canada south to the Magellan Strait. It has a sharply hooked bill, with fleshy seres across the top, through which the nostrils open. A scavenger, the turkey vulture is not as strong as other birds of prey and relies on its keen eyesight to spot carrion.

cracks bones, by dropping them onto rocks, in order to eat the marrow. Length: 100–120cm (39–47in); wingspan: 266–282 (105–111in). Family Accipitridae; species *Gypaetus barbatus*.

vulture, black

Any of three different, mainly all-black, species of vulture. The black vulture of Europe (*Aegypius monachus*) is the largest European bird. It has a wingspan of up to 3m (9.8ft). The Asian black vulture (*Sarcogyps calvus*) has bare red skin on its head and neck. The South American species (*Coragyps atratus*) is more eagle-like. It has conspicuous white patches on its under wing.

vulture, griffon

Vulture that is widespread in s Europe and Asia. It has pale brown plumage with dark flight feathers. Its head and neck are covered in grey down. The griffon vulture breeds in colonies on cliff ledges. It gives way to the larger black vulture at carcasses but takes precedence over smaller vultures. Length: 95–105cm (37–41in); wingspan: 240–280cm (94–110in). Subfamily Aegypiinae; species *Gyps fulvus*.

vulture, king

Solitary vulture found in the forests of South America. It has a bare head and neck, wattled orange, yellow and purple. In flight it appears white, with thick, black wing edges. It has a short, black tail. Length: 70–80cm (28–31in); wingspan: to 200cm (80in). Family Cathartidae; species *Sarcoramphus papa*.

vulture, palm-nut

Vulture of central Africa. It feeds and breeds in stands of oil palms, and it forages around the edges of lakes. Its plumage is white, with black trailing edges to the wings; the head and neck are feathered. The palm-nut vulture spends long periods perched. Unlike other vultures, it does not soar. Length: 60cm (24in). Subfamily Aegypiinae; species *Gypohierax angolensis*.

vulture, turkey

Common vulture of North and South America; it is familiar around garbage tips near settlements. The turkey vulture is often misnamed "buzzard". It has a bare red head and distinctive, silver-grey flight feathers, with dark underwing linings. It can detect carrion by smell from a great distance. Length: 70cm (28in); wingspan: 175cm (69in). Family Cathartidae; species *Cathartes aura*.

vulva

In human anatomy, the external genitalia of females. Extending downwards from the clitoris (a sensitive, erectile organ), a pair of fleshy lips (*labia majora*) surround the vulvar orifice. Within them two smaller folds of skin (*labia minora*) surround a small depression called the vestibule, within which are the urethral and vaginal openings.

V

A volcano is a vent from which molten rock or LAVA, solid rock debris and gases issue. The term is also applied to the pile of rock around the vent. Volcanoes may be of the **central vent type**, where the material erupts from a single pipe, or of the **fissure type**, where material is extruded along an extensive fracture, building plains and plateaus. Volcanoes are usually classed as active, dormant or extinct.

Volcanoes occur when the Earth's surface is breached and MAGMA either flows out as lava or explodes into the air as TUFF. All volcanic eruptions are driven by rapidly expanding gases within the magma, so the two factors that determine the violence of an eruption are the amount of dissolved gases and how easily they can escape. It is the magma's viscosity or fluidity that controls how the gas escapes, and it is the composition of the magma that determines its viscosity.

When the magma has low viscosity and is mainly composed of basalt, with a low content of dissolved gas that rises slowly through the crust, the gas escapes slowly and gradually as the magma rises. Near the surface, perhaps a few metres away, the magma may start to foam; this is what causes lava fountains.

Magma that has a high silica content with high viscosity and high dissolved gas content behaves very differently. As the magma rises, the gas starts to escape from solution, but the high viscosity of the melt holds the bubbles back, so that they have an internal pressure that can be as high as several hundred atmospheres. When enough bubbles form, or the external pressure decreases, the gas pressure blows the rock apart and starts an explosive eruption. Violent eruptions that throw dust and rock fragments into the air are called PYROCLASTIC eruptions. These eruptions alternate with lava flows to produce cone-shaped, crater-topped mountains, sloping up at angles of about 30°, such as seen at Mount Fuji in Japan. Such mountains are called stratovolcanoes.

The gases produced by volcanoes consist of water vapour – the most prevalent component – carbon dioxide, sulphur dioxide, hydrochloric acid and nitrogen. In fact the ratios of these volcanic gases are extraordinarily close to the ratios of water, carbon, chlorine and nitrogen in the air, oceans and surface rocks of the Earth. The main difference is that volcanoes produce too much sulphur. Nevertheless, it may be that the volcanoes, expelling the Earth's gases throughout the millennia of geological time, were what created the atmosphere, oceans and rocks. *See also* Ready Reference, page 454

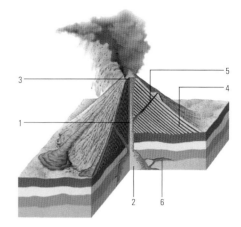

▲ **Volcanoes are formed** when molten lava (1) from a magma chamber (2) in the Earth's crust forces its way to the surface (3). The classic, cone-shaped volcano is formed of alternating layers of cooled lava and cinders (4) thrown out during an eruption. Side vents (5) can occur and when offshoots of lava are trapped below the surface, laccoliths (6) are formed.

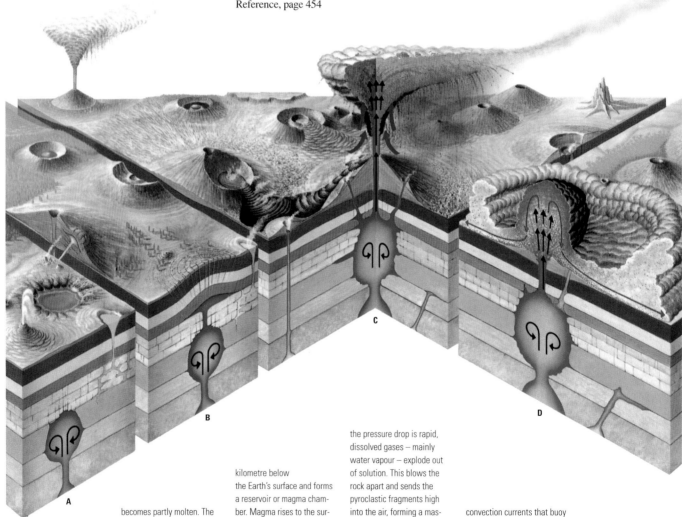

▲ **The forces that** lie behind a volcano are born deep in the Earth. Mantle material upwells and becomes partly molten. The decrease in pressure as it rises causes it to melt even more and to melt the surrounding rock. The magma then ponds (A) about a kilometre below the Earth's surface and forms a reservoir or magma chamber. Magma rises to the surface (B) and erupts (C) when the pressure in the magma chamber exceeds the pressure of the surrounding rock. If the magma is viscous and the pressure drop is rapid, dissolved gases – mainly water vapour – explode out of solution. This blows the rock apart and sends the pyroclastic fragments high into the air, forming a massive eruption column composed of hot gases and incandescent pumice and ash. The particles heat up the surrounding air, causing convection currents that buoy them even higher – up to 50km (30mi). When the column can no longer be supported by the surrounding air (D) it collapses to create incandescent pyroclastic flows that race outwards at velocities of up to 100m/s (more than 200 mph).

W

wadi (arroyo)

Narrow, steep-sided VALLEY found in deserts and semiarid regions. As rainfall is infrequent in desert areas, wadis are dry for much of the year. When it does rain, however, it falls in heavy showers. Because much of the land has no vegetation, surface runoff is rapid. The water carries away sand and small rock fragments, which cause EROSION. Vertical CORRASION forms the narrow, steep-sided wadis, which can be several hundred metres in depth and extend for long distances.

waggle dance (bee dance)

Method of communication performed by worker HONEYBEES to indicate to other worker BEES the exact position and richness of sources of pollen and nectar. The dances rely on a knowledge of the position of the Sun.

▶ **wallaby** The pretty-faced wallaby (*Macropus parryi*) is also known as the whip-tailed wallaby after its long tail. It has distinctive white cheeks. It inhabits the hills and woodlands of Queensland and New South Wales, Australia. The ring-tailed rock wallaby (*Petrogale xanthopus*) has a yellow and brown tail and brightly coloured feet. It inhabits the Flinders mountains of s Australia.

pretty-faced wallaby

ring-tailed rock wallaby

wagtail

Any of several species of bird, most belonging to the genus *Motacilla*, so called because they continually wag their tails up and down. The Eurasian wagtails are medium-sized, insect-eating birds. Their long tails bob up and down as they walk and run. Several birds from other groups are also called wagtails for their tail-flicking habits. Family Motacillidae.

wagtail, grey

Wagtail found across Europe and Asia, usually near water. It has grey-blue upperparts and pale yellow underparts. It has a white eyebrow and "moustache" stripes. Length: 18cm (7in). Family Motacillidae; species *Motacilla cinerea*.

wagtail, pied (white wagtail)

Wagtail with black and white upperparts and a long black tail. There are distinct races, with different plumage patterns, of both pied and yellow wagtails. Length: 18cm (7in). Family Motacillidae; species *Motacilla alba*.

wagtail, Willie

Wagtail found in Australia and Southeast Asia. It resembles the pied wagtail. It is familiar in parks and gardens. Length: 20cm (8in). Family Monarchidae; species *Rhipidura leucophrys*.

wagtail, yellow

Wagtail found in N Europe, Asia and w Alaska in summer; it migrates to tropical Africa and Asia for winter. It is mainly green but has a bright yellow underside. Length: 16cm (6in). Family Motacillidae; species *Motacilla flava*.

wahoo

Marine fish of the MACKEREL family, found in tropical waters worldwide. It is fast-moving with an elongated body. Length: to 1.8m (5.9ft). Family Scombridae; species *Acanthocybium solanedri*.

walking catfish

See CATFISH, WALKING

wallaby

Common name often given to small KANGAROOS of the family Macropodidae.

wallaby, forest

Any member of the genus *Dorcopsis*. The forest wallaby is a small kangaroo found in the rainforests of New Guinea. Head-body length: 34–80cm (13–31in); tail: 27–55cm (11–22in). Family Macropodidae; genus *Dorcopsis*.

wallaby, hare

Any member of the genus *Lagorchestes*, comprising several species of rare, fast-moving kangaroos found in parts of Australia. The hare wallaby feeds on leaves and fruit on open grassy plains. Head-body length: 32–50cm (13–20in); tail: 27–45cm (11–18in). Family Macropodidae; genus *Lagorchestes*.

wallaby, rock

Any member of the genus *Petrogale*, a group of small kangaroos that are adept at climbing. The rock wallaby has a long cylindrical tail and rough-soled feet for gripping rocks. Head-body length: 29–80cm (11–31in); tail: 25–70cm (10–28in). Family Macropodidae; genus *Petrogale*.

wallaby, scrub (pademelon)

Any member of the genus *Thylogale*, comprising several species of small kangaroos found in rainforest, woodland and grassland in Australia and Tasmania; it

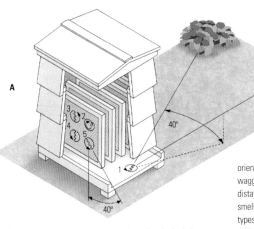

A

sun light

40°

40°

▲▼ **waggle dance** Inside a dark hive, foraging worker honeybees perform complex dances on combs, using touch (conveyed to bee "dance-followers" via their antennae), air vibrations and smell to communicate nectar and pollen locations to others. Nectar and pollen provide carbohydrates and protein – both vital to a colony. The round dance (B) indicates food *c*.50–100m (*c*.150–300ft) from the hive, the dance's length and vigour showing the source's richness. A waggle dance (C) consists of a figure of eight with a waggle in the middle and indicates more distant sources (waggle orientation shows direction; waggle frequency shows distance). The dancing bee's smell may indicate flower types. To communicate and utilize the information requires a knowledge of the Sun's position (even if hidden in a blue sky, the Sun's position can be detected by light-polarization levels), a sense of time and wind speed, the use of visual landmarks and perhaps some sort of magnetic sensory device. Bee dances (A) usually take place in the darkness of the hive on the comb sides. They are interpreted mainly by touch and smell. However, the bees are essentially communicating visual directions based on the Sun's position. This is apparent when the waggle dance is performed on the horizontal entrance board of a hive (1). The angle of the waggle indicates a nectar source 40° to the left of the Sun. Inside the hive, the vertical surfaces do not affect the round dance (2), but a downwards (3) waggle indicates a direction away from the Sun, and an upwards one (4) towards the Sun. The dance (5) is a vertical representation of (1).

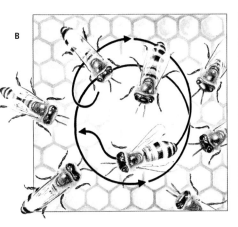

B

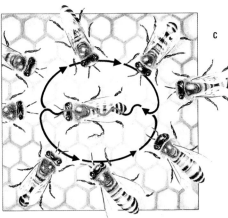

C

W

▶ **walnut** Walnut trees are commercially valuable for their wood and nuts. Before the fruits harden into nuts they can be used for pickling, but once mature, they burst from their green casing and the edible nuts can be removed from the hard outer shell.

is common in some areas. The scrub wallaby can be seen grazing at dusk and dawn. Gregarious species use foot thumping as an alarm signal. Head-body length: 50–78cm (20–31in); tail: 32–47cm (13–19in). Family Macropodidae; genus *Thylogale*.

wallaby, tammar (scrub wallaby, dama wallaby)
Small kangaroo that lives in relatively dry areas and drinks very little. The tammar wallaby is rabbit-sized. Head-body length: 40–50cm (16–20in); tail: 40–54cm (16–21in). Family Macropodidae; species *Macropus eugenii*.

Wallace, Alfred Russel (1823–1913)
British naturalist and evolutionist. Wallace developed a theory of NATURAL SELECTION independently of but at the same time as Charles DARWIN. He wrote *Contributions to the Theory of Natural Selection* (1870), which, with Darwin's *The Origin of Species*, comprised the fundamental explanation and understanding of the theory of EVOLUTION.

Wallace's line
Imaginary line dividing the islands of Borneo and Bali from Sulawesi and Lombok. It was drawn by Alfred Russel WALLACE to demarcate animal populations that live close to each other and yet are extraordinarily different. Earlier this observation had influenced Wallace to state his theory of NATURAL SELECTION, which was coincident with that of Charles DARWIN. He argued that homogeneous animal populations could, for various reasons, divide and diversify gradually until they had evolved into separate species.

wallaroo (euro)
Large, stocky KANGAROO found in mountainous regions of Australia, where it grazes on grasses and shrubs. It has shaggy, dark fur, which is paler underneath. It is distinguished by a bare, black snout. Head-body length: 55–110cm (22–43in); tail: 53–90cm (21–35in). Family Macropodidae; species *Macropus robustus*. There are two other species of

▶ **walrus** The walrus (*Odobenus rosmarus*) is the only living member of the family Odobenidae. A gregarious animal, it has a tough hide and a thick fat layer, which helps protect against the tusks of other walruses as well as providing insulation from the cold.

wallaroo, the black wallaroo (*Macropus bernadus*) and the antilopine wallaroo (*Macropus antilopinus*).

wallcreeper
Agile bird found in mountains and rocky scrub across Europe and Asia to China. It can grip the vertical stone faces of cliffs while foraging for insects. The wallcreeper has a long, slim, sharp bill, a grey body and red patches on its rounded wings. Length: 16cm (6in). Family Sittidae, species *Tichodroma muraria*.

walleye (walleyed pike)
Freshwater game fish of E North America; it is particularly common in Lake Erie. It is closely related to the PIKE PERCH. The walleye has a mottled greenish-brown body and large opaque eyes. Length: to 91cm (36in). Family Percidae; species *Stizostedion vitreum*.

wallflower
Any of several species of perennial plants belonging to the genera *Cheiranthus* and *Erysimum*. They are so called for their habit of growing on old walls. Some of the sweet-scented species are widely cultivated in Europe and the United States. The European wallflower (*Cheiranthus cheiri*) has lance-shaped leaves and red, orange, yellow or purple flowers. Height: to 90cm (35in). Family Brassicaceae/Cruciferae.

walnut (English walnut)
Tall, spreading tree, native to SE Europe and central Asia. It has silvery-grey bark. The walnut is grown for ornament as well as for its globular, green fruits, which contain the thin-shelled walnut of commerce. The hardwood timber is valued for furniture and interior decoration. Height: to 24m (79ft). Family Juglandaceae; species *Juglans regia*.

walrus
Large mammal found in Arctic waters of Eurasia and North America. It has a massive body and a large head. Its tusks, which develop from upper canine teeth, can reach 1m (39in) in length. They are used to rake up the seafloor in search of molluscs and to climb on to ice floes. Length: to 3.7m (12ft). Family Odobenidae; species *Odobenus rosmarus*.

wapiti (American elk)
Large DEER found in North America, central Asia and China; it has been introduced in New Zealand. It is known as "elk" only in North America. The wapiti's favoured habitat is grassland and the edges of forests. It is grey-brown, with a whitish rump and brown-black legs, head and neck. Male wapiti develop large, branched antlers. Shoulder height: c.145cm (c.57in). Family Cervidae; species *Cervus canadensis*.

warble-fly
Any of several species of large, hairy, bee-like flies. The warble-fly lays its eggs on the feet of animals

▲ **wapiti** The second-largest deer (after the moose), the wapiti (*Cervus canadensis*) is closely related to the red deer. The female is usually darker than the male. The male sheds his antlers annually in March or April. The new ones are fully grown by August, just before the breeding season begins.

such as cattle and deer. The larvae work their way through the skin into the animal's body, causing painful swellings, known as warbles, through which the larvae eventually emerge shortly before maturing into adult flies. Warble-flies are common in Europe and North America. Family Hypodermatidae, species include *Hypoderma lineatum* and *Hypoderma bovis*.

warbler
Any of numerous species of birds with attractive songs. The main groups are the Old World warblers (family Sylviidae) and the American wood warblers (family Parulidae).

warbler, black and white
Warbler that spends the summer in forests, parks and gardens of S Canada and the United States, migrating to S United States for winter. It has striking, black and white, almost zebra-like, striped plumage. The female has a white throat; the male's throat is black. The warbler searches tree bark for insects. Length: 13cm (5in). Family Parulidae; species *Mniotilta varia*.

warbler, reed
Small, brown, inconspicuous warbler commonly found among reeds or other waterside vegetation. It migrates from Africa to Europe each summer to breed. The reed warbler feeds on insects. It builds, from grass blades and stems, a strong, deep, tightly woven, cup-shaped nest slung among the reeds. Length: 12cm (5in). Family Sylviidae; species *Acrocephalus scirpaceus*.

warbler, Sardinian
Warbler found in the Mediterranean region. It has brownish wings and grey-white underparts. The Sardinian warbler has a glossy black head, which is slightly greyer in the female, and bright red-brown eyes. Length: 13cm (5in). Family Sylviidae; species *Sylvia melanocephala*.

warbler, subalpine
Warbler that breeds around the Mediterranean area and migrates south of the Sahara for winter. It has grey-brown upperparts, a white belly and a whitish "moustache" stripe. It frequents bushes and thickets, where it feeds almost exclusively on insects. Length: 11cm (4in). Family Sylviidae; species *Sylvia cantillans*.

warbler, yellow-rumped (yellow warbler)
Insectivorous warbler that breeds in most of North and Central America; some populations fly south for the winter. It thrives in scattered woodland, parks and gardens. The male is yellow, with bright yellow spots and a dusky olive back and wings. The female is a

W

paler yellow with less conspicuous spots on the underparts. Length: 12cm (5in). Family Parulidae; species *Dendroica coronata*.

warbler, yellow-throated
Warbler that breeds in the woodlands and river valleys of E North America; most populations fly south to Central America for winter. It has brown-grey plumage, with black wing stripes and a yellowish throat. Its song is loud and melodic. It feeds high in branches on insects. Length: 12cm (5in). Family Parulidae; species *Dendroica dominica*.

Warburg, Otto Heinrich (1883–1970)
German biochemist who was awarded the 1931 Nobel Prize for physiology or medicine for his discovery of respiratory enzymes. He made significant contributions to the understanding of the mechanisms of cellular respiration and energy transfer, and of photosynthesis.

warm blooded
See ENDOTHERMIC

warm front
See FRONT

warning coloration
Markings of an animal that warn potential predators that it is dangerous. It may indicate that the animal tastes bad or is poisonous. Red, yellow and black are common warning colours, as in some venomous insects and snakes. Some nonpoisonous animal species mimic the warning colours of other animals in order to trick potential predators into thinking they are not suitable prey. *See also* MIMICRY

wart-biter
Large species of bush-CRICKET. Found only on chalk grassland, it is an endangered species in the British Isles. It is a major predator of other ORTHOPTERANS. Family Tettigoniidae; species *Decticus verrucivorus*.

warthog
Member of the PIG family found in savanna and woodland in sub-Saharan Africa. Warthogs are active in the daytime. They feed mainly on grasses, which they gather using their strong lips and sharp incisors. The warthog's tusks are used mainly in display and in fights between rivals. Length: 125cm (49in). Family: Suidae; species *Phacochoerus aethiopicus*.

wasp
Any of thousands of species of stinging HYMENOPTERAN insects. The common wasp (*Vespa vulgaris*) has a yellow body ringed with black. Adults feed on nectar, tree sap and fruit. Order Hymenoptera; families include Agaonidae, Chrysididae, Cynipidae, Siricidae, Sphecidae and Vespidae. *See also* BRACONID

wasp, cuckoo
Any of numerous species of metallic-coloured wasps that lay eggs in the nests of other insects, usually those of solitary WASPS or BEES. The larvae then eat the host's larvae. A hard cuticle protects the adults from the stings of the host. Many species can roll themselves up for added protection. Adult body length: 3–18mm (0.1–0.7in). Family Chrysididae; genera *Chrysis*, *Stilbum* and *Parnopes*.

wasp, digger (hunting wasp)
Any of many species of solitary wasps that nest in the ground. The female has a spiny comb on her front legs for digging. She uses her sting to paralyse other

insects, which she then places in the burrow where she lays her eggs. The developing grubs rely on the store of food until they pupate. Adult body length: 2–44mm (0.08–2in). Family Sphecidae; genera include *Argogorytes*, *Sceliphron* and *Philanthus*.

wasp, fig
Any member of the family Agaonidae, a group of small hymenopterans with a remarkable life cycle. The male is wingless and never leaves the gall of the fig fruit. The female is winged and mates before she leaves the gall. On leaving the fig, she is covered in fig pollen and thus fertilizes other figs as she lays her eggs. The fig wasp *Blastophaga psenes* was introduced into the United States to pollinate the Smyrna fig (*Ficus carica*); *Blastophaga nota* was introduced from the Philippines to pollinate *Ficus nota*. Adult body length: 1.5mm (0.06in). Family Agaonidae.

wasp, gall
Any member of a family of small, brown wasps found worldwide. The female lays eggs in plant tissues and a gall develops as the larvae hatch and mature. The abnormal plant tissues provide the larvae with food and shelter. The galls are usually found on oak trees, where they are known as oak apples, and on roses, known as robin's pincushions. Length 6–8mm (0.2–0.3in). Family Cynipidae.

wasp, German
Social wasp that nests annually in buildings or the ground. Nests are built from paper, which the wasps make from wood. The adults feed on nectar or other sweet substances, and the larvae are reared on other insects that the workers collect. The colony disintegrates in autumn and a few mated females hibernate. Adult body length: 20–25mm (0.8–1in). Family Vespidae; species *Vespula germanica*.

wasp, hunting
See WASP, DIGGER

wasp, jewel
Any of many species of beautiful metallic-coloured wasps, which are often blue, green or red in colour. The jewel wasp's body is extremely hard as a protection from the stings of other wasps and bees. Its abdomen is concave, allowing it to curl up if attacked. The female lays her eggs in the nests of solitary bees or wasps; the hatched larvae eat the host larvae. Adult body length: 3–18mm (0.1–0.7in). Family Chrysididae; genus *Chrysis*.

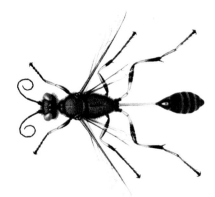

▲ **wasp, mud-dauber** Mud-dauber wasps of the genus *Sceliphron* are found worldwide but abound in the tropics. The female builds nest cells under rocks and overhanging roofs and stocks them with spiders; a single egg is laid in each nest. The developing larva consumes the spiders and then pupates.

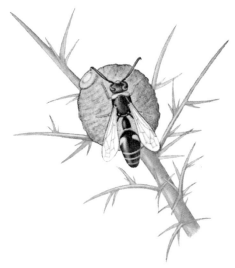

▲ **wasp, potter** The potter wasp (*Eumenes coartica* shown here) builds clay pots, attached to plants, in which she lays an egg. After stocking the pot with caterpillars, which she paralyses with her sting, she seals the pot with a mud pellet. The amount of food provided by the mother is thought to determine the gender of the offspring.

wasp, mason
Any of many wasp species of the genus *Ancistrocerus*. The solitary adult females use sand and mud to build numerous egg cells in cavities and crevices. Each cell receives an egg and is then packed with small caterpillars. Old walls and hollow stems are favoured for nest sites. Adult body size: *c*.11mm (*c*.0.4in). Subfamily Eumeninae; genus *Ancistrocerus*.

wasp, mud dauber
Any of many species of solitary wasps that are black with yellow markings. Mud dauber wasps are found worldwide. They construct nests in the form of short mud tubes attached to building walls and ceilings. The larvae feed on spiders. Length: 19–25mm (0.7–1in). Family Sphecidae; genera *Sceliphron* and *Chalybion*.

wasp, Norwegian
Any member of the genus *Dolichovespula*, a group of social wasps that live in annual colonies founded and ruled by a queen. The larvae are fed chewed insects and other animal matter by worker wasps. Only newly mated females survive the winter, often found hibernating in houses. Adult body size: *c*.7mm (*c*.0.3in). Family Vespidae; genus *Dolichovespula*.

wasp, paper
Any member of the wasp genus *Polistes*. The adult female masticates wood pulp with adhesive saliva to make the egg cells of the nests. Fertilized eggs produce worker females who raise extra offspring. Unfertilized eggs laid nearer the end of the year produce males; this is a typical wasp trait. It is said that the paper wasp inspired the Chinese inventor of paper. Adult body size: *c*.12mm (*c*.0.5in). Family Vespidae; genus *Polistes*.

wasp, potter
Any of many species of solitary wasps with characteristically narrow waists. The female builds vase-shaped mud nests into which she lay an egg. The vase is then stocked with caterpillars and sealed; another vase is then built, usually attached to the first. Adult body size: *c*.15mm (0.6in). Family Eumeninae; genus *Eumenes*.

wasp, ruby-tailed
Any of many species of small cuckoo wasps with bright, metallic colours. They are parasitic in some

W

▲ **waterfall** The spectacular Iguaçu waterfalls on the border between Brazil and Argentina occur on the River Iguaçu near its confluence with the River Paraná. The waters of the Iguaçu cascade over the edge of the Paraná plateau into a narrow gorge. There are hundreds of separate waterfalls, with drops of up to 70m (230ft), separated by rocky islands.

bees' and wasps' nests. The ruby-tailed wasp is commonly seen in the sunshine flying extremely actively. Adult body size: *c*.10mm (*c*.0.4in). Family Chrysidae; genera *Chrysis* and *Stilbum*.

wasp, sand

Any of many wasp species that dig their nests on beaches and other sandy sites, provisioning the nest with a caterpillar. Once caterpillar and egg are inserted, the entrance is sealed. Family Sphecoidea; genus *Ammophila*; species include *Ammophila pubescens* and *Ammophila sabulosa*.

wasp, social

Any of numerous wasp species that live in fairly large colonies. They all have a worker caste, except a few of the "cuckoo" species. There are seven British species, including the HORNET. Superfamily Vespoidea; family Vespidae; species include *Vespa crabro*.

wasp, solitary

Any of a group of non-colonial wasps. Solitary wasps

▲ **water beetle** The great silver water beetle (*Hydrophilus piceus*) is one of the largest European beetles. It inhabits marshy freshwater, where it feeds on decaying plant and animal matter. The larvae are carnivorous.

do not live in colonies, and most species do not defend their nests from intruders. A female wasp digs a hole and places a paralysed host in it, for example a caterpillar. Many species are very selective in their prey choice. An egg is laid on this host and the hole sealed. The larva feeds on the host until cocoon formation. Families include Evaniidae, Sphecidae, Scoliidae and Vespidae.

wasp, spider-hunting

Solitary wasp, generally orange and black. It is commonly ground-dwelling and inhabits sandy areas. After mating, the female hunts for spiders to provision her young. She paralyses the host and places it into a self-made burrow, where she oviposits on it before sealing it in. Superfamily Pompiloidea; family Pompilidae; species include *Cryptocheilus comparatus*.

wasp, tree

Social wasp that builds its spherical, communal nest hanging from the branches of a tree or bush. Its thorax has pale hairs at the sides, with two yellow spots at the rear. Family Vespidae; species *Dolichovespula sylvestris*.

wasp, wood (horntail)

Large hymenopteran insect with wasp-like markings. Its long, powerful ovipositor can penetrate wood, although it usually lays its eggs in leaves or stems. Cocoons are either attached to the host plant or pupation may be on the soil or in leaf litter. Suborder Symphyta; family Siricidae; species *Urocerus gigas*.

waste disposal, nuclear

Nuclear fission reactors and their fuel preparation plants produce waste residues containing highly radioactive substances. After uranium, plutonium and any other useful fission products have been removed some long-lived radioactive products remain, such as caesium-137 and strontium-90. These wastes have to be disposed of so that they will not contaminate the soil, seas or atmosphere. International regulations exist for disposing of the wastes, with separate regulations applying to liquids, gases and solids. In general, disposal consists of burying the materials under controlled conditions in underground tanks, in disused mines and in the ocean.

water

Odourless, colourless liquid (H_2O) that covers more than 70% of the Earth's surface and is the most widely used solvent. Essential to life, it makes up about 60–70% of the human body. It is a compound of hydrogen and oxygen with the two H-O links of the molecule forming an angle of 105°. This asymmetry results in polar properties and a force of attraction (hydrogen bond) between opposite ends of neighbouring water molecules. These forces maintain the substance as a liquid, in spite of its low molecular weight, and account for its unusual property of having its maximum density at 4°C (39.2°F). Properties: r.d. 1.000; m.p. 0.0°C (32°F); b.p. 100°C (212°F).

water-bear (tardigrade)

Any member of the phylum Tardigrada. Water-bears are herbivorous animals found in damp places such as in the mosses and liverworts surrounding freshwater ponds. Their legs are short and stumpy, resembling those of bears. They feed by sucking plant cell contents via piercing mouthparts. Water-bears can survive long periods of desiccation and cold by contracting into a barrel shape, known as the tun, which is then revived by contact with more favourable damp conditions. Adult body length: 1mm (0.04in). Phylum Tardigrada.

water beetle

Aquatic BEETLE. There are several families of water beetle. **Whirligig beetles** (family Gyrinidae) skim around the surface of water, feeding on small insects. **Water scavenger beetles** (family Hydrophilidae) feed on water plants; their larvae are fierce predators. Predacious **diving beetles** are the most numerous water beetles. They are black, brown or greenish, prey on snails and fish and can remain underwater for long periods. Order Coleoptera. *See also* BEETLE, DIVING; BEETLE, WATER SCAVENGER; BEETLE, WHIRLIGIG

water boatman (water bug)

Any insect of the HEMIPTERAN family Corixidae, a group of aquatic insects found worldwide. The water boatman's body is grey to black, oval and flat, with fringed, oar-like hind legs. Length: *c*.15mm (*c*.0.6in). Family Corixidae. The carnivorous "backswimmers" of the family Notonectidae are sometimes known as water boatmen.

waterbuck (waterbok)

Any of six species of large, gregarious, coarse-haired ANTELOPES. The waterbuck is native to sub-Saharan Africa and the Nile Valley. Length: 1.4–2.1m (4.6–6.9ft); shoulder height: 1.1–1.5m (3.6–4.9ft). Family Bovidae; genus *Kobus*.

▲ **water flea** Microscopic crustaceans, water fleas of the genus *Daphnia* are found in streams and ponds throughout Europe and North America. They use their antennae to swim, often in a hopping motion, hence their common name. They are a vital part of the food chain.

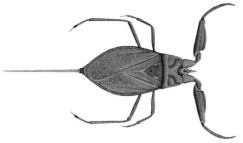

▲ **water scorpion** Members of the genus *Nepa*, such as the species shown above, have a more oval body shape than other water scorpions. The long tail acts as a "snorkel", allowing the animal to breathe under water. It feeds on small aquatic animals, which it seizes with its scorpion-like front legs.

water chestnut

Floating, aquatic plant found in Asia, Europe and Africa. It has diamond-shaped leaves and edible, spiny, chestnut-like fruit. Family Trapaceae; species *Trapa natans*. The water chestnut of Chinese cookery is the succulent corm of a Chinese sedge, *Eleocharis tuberosus*. Family Cyperaceae.

water-cock (kora)

RAIL found in swamps and paddies from India to the Philippines. The male has slaty black breeding plumage and red legs; the female's plumage has a yellowish-brown pattern. Family Rallidae; species *Gallicrex cinerea*.

watercress

Floating or creeping plant found in running or spring waters. The succulent leaves, divided into small, oval leaflets, have a pungent flavour and are used in salads and soups. The clustered flowers are white. Height: 25cm (10in). Family Brassicaceae/Cruciferae; species *Nasturtium officinale*.

water cycle

See HYDROLOGICAL CYCLE

water dragon

Any of several species of crest-bearing, partly aquatic, agamid LIZARDS found in Southeast Asia and Australia. Although they spend much of their time in trees or on the ground, water dragons are accomplished swimmers and divers, capable of remaining under water for more than an hour. Length: 50–90cm (20–35in). Family Agamidae; genus *Physignathus*.

waterfall

Steep or vertical descent of the water of a stream or river. Where there is a change of rock type on the bed of a stream or river, there are different rates of EROSION. The softer rock is eroded more quickly than the harder rock, causing an abrupt change in the gradient. If there is a vertical or nearly vertical STRATUM of hard rock, only a small waterfall will be created. If the harder rock is horizontal, a much larger waterfall can form.

water flea

Any of numerous species of small, chiefly freshwater, branchiopod CRUSTACEANS. They are so called because of their jerky jumping movement through the water. Some of the best-known species belong to the genus *Daphnia*, which is widespread in Europe and North America. Water fleas are an important food source for many freshwater fish. Length (*Daphnia* spp.): to 3mm (0.1in). Class Branchiopoda; order Cladocera.

water hyacinth

Aquatic herb native to the American tropics. It has swollen petioles that float in water. It produces spikes of violet flowers. Family Pontederiaceae; species *Eichhornia crassipes*.

water lily

Any of *c*.90 species of freshwater plants, widely distributed in temperate and tropical regions. They have leaves that float at the surface and showy flowers of white, pink, red, blue or yellow. Family Nymphaeaceae; genera *Nymphaea*, *Nuphar*, *Nelumbo* and *Victoria*. *See also* LOTUS

water measurer

Slender HEMIPTERAN bug with a greatly elongated head and very small wings. It is found on still and slow-moving water, where it spears food through the water film. The water measurer's rostrum is then used to hold the food. Its main food sources are water fleas and mosquito larvae. Family Hydrometridae; species *Hydrometra stagnorum*.

watermelon

Trailing annual VINE; it is native to tropical Africa and Asia and is cultivated in warm areas worldwide. Its edible fruit has a greenish rind, red flesh and many seeds. Family Cucurbitaceae; species *Citrullus lanatus*. *See also* GOURD

water moccasin

See COTTONMOUTH

water-rat

See RAT, WATER-

water scorpion

Any of numerous species of freshwater insects belonging to the family Nepidae. They are found found worldwide. The water scorpion has a long breathing tube at the end of its body and front legs modified for grasping, giving it a scorpion-like appearance. Some species can inflict a painful bite. Order Hemiptera; family Nepidae.

watershed (water divide, water parting)

High ground that forms the boundary or dividing line between two river basins. On one side of the boundary line the water will drain in one direction; on the other side of the boundary line it will drain in the opposite direction. The watershed is normally a ridge or a piece of ground that is higher than the surrounding areas. It is often a very irregular line. The **Continental Divide** is the US watershed that separates westward- and eastward-flowing rivers; it largely follows the spine of the Rocky Mountains.

▶ **water table** Artesian springs and wells are found where groundwater is under pressure. The water table (1) in the confined aquifer (2) lies near the top of the dipping layers. A well (4) drilled through the top impervious layer (3) is not an artesian well because the head of the hydrostatic pressure (6) is not sufficient to force water to the surface. In such wells, the water must be pumped or drawn to the surface. The top of an artesian well (5) lies below the level of the head of hydrostatic pressure and so water gushes to the surface.

Artesian springs (8) may occur along joints or faults (7), where the head of hydrostatic pressure is sufficient to force the water

up along the fault. Areas with artesian wells are called artesian basins. In the London and Paris artesian basins, the

water has been so heavily tapped that the water level has dropped below the level of the well heads.

water slater (hog-louse)

Any of many species of freshwater ISOPOD crustaceans. The water slater resembles an aquatic woodlouse. It is active at night, hiding in cracks, crevices and under debris in the day. It feeds mainly on plant material. It is widely distributed and relatively abundant. The water slater has a rough texture, with an oval body shape and a grey-greenish colour. Adult body length: 24mm (0.9in). Order Isopoda; family Asellidae; species include *Asellus aquaticus*.

waterspout

Funnel-shaped mass of water, which is similar in formation to a TORNADO. It occurs over water when a heated patch of air rises and whirls around in a circular or corkscrew fashion. Waterspouts are mostly seen in tropical areas, especially in late summer. When waterspouts go on to land they become tornadoes, and when tornadoes go over lakes or the ocean, they become waterspouts. Waterspouts are generally less than 30m (98ft) in height and can last for about half an hour. They can cause great damage to shipping and coastal installations.

water stick insect

Large water bug that resembles a STICK INSECT. It has long legs and an elongated body. It often remains motionless when out of the water. When submerged it captures passing aquatic creatures. Water stick insects are found by weedy ponds and lakes. Length: 50mm (0.2in). Order Hemiptera; family Nepidae; species *Ranatra linearis*.

water strider (pond skater)

Any member of the HEMIPTERAN family Gerridae, a group of dark-brown to black aquatic insects found worldwide. The water strider has long legs with which it glides on the surface of calm waters. Members of the genus *Halobates* are often found far out at sea. Many water strider species travel in groups. Length: 8–25mm (0.3–1in). Order Hemiptera; family Gerridae.

water table

In geology, level below which the rock is saturated. After rain has fallen, the water trickles downwards through the pores in the rocks. The level at which all pores are full is the water table. The height of the water table gradually changes, moving up or down depending on the recent rainfall. Water located below the water table is called GROUNDWATER.

water vapour

Water in its gaseous state. It occurs in the atmosphere and determines humidity and the formation of CLOUDS as it condenses. Most of the atmosphere's

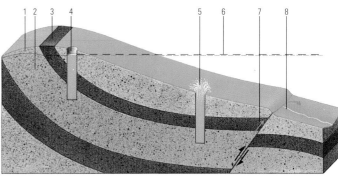

W

water vapour is found in the TROPOSPHERE, mainly below an altitude of 8km (5mi). Water vapour absorbs infrared radiation and holds it in the atmosphere, because of the GREENHOUSE EFFECT, thus playing a vital role in the transfer of energy and the Earth's heat balance.

Watson, James Dewey (1928–)
US geneticist and biophysicist. He is known for his role in the discovery of the double-helix molecular structure of deoxyribonucleic acid (DNA), for which he shared the 1962 Nobel Prize for physiology or medicine with Francis CRICK and Maurice WILKINS. Watson later helped to break the GENETIC CODE of the DNA base sequences. He found the ribonucleic acid messenger (MESSENGER RNA) that carries the DNA code to the cell's protein-forming structures.

wattle
Any of a number of ACACIAS found in Australia. The wattle group comprises trees and shrubs, with or without thorns. The leaves are made up of many small leaflets, and the yellow flowers have numerous stamens in small round or cylindrical heads. Wattles are grown for timber, shelter, hedges and as ornamentals. The black wattle (*Acacia mearnsii*) is used as a source of tanning material. Family Mimosaceae; genus *Acacia*.

wattlebird
Any of several species of stout bird found in dry forests of Australia. The wattlebird has grey plumage. Its black bill has a distinctive blue wattle (fleshy flap) on either side. It takes a variety of foods, including fruits and insects. Length: 45cm (18in). Family Meliphagidae; genus *Anthochaera*.

wattle-eye
Any of a group of birds related to the MONARCH flycatcher. The wattle-eye is found in woods and farms in Africa. It is named after the bright red fleshy flap over each eye. It feeds in pairs on insects and other small prey. Length: 13cm (5in). Family Monarchidae; genus *Platysteira*.

▶ **weathering** The breakdown of rock in place is called weathering. It occurs in two main ways: physical (A and C) and chemical (B). They usually occur in combination. At the surface, plant roots and animals such as worms break down rock, turning it into soil (A). In chemical weathering (B), soluble rocks such as limestone (1) are dissolved by groundwater, which is a very mild solution of carbonic acid. Acid rain caused by sulphate pollution (2) also attacks the rock. The water can create cave systems deep below the surface. Both heat and cold can cause physical weathering (C). When temperatures drop below freezing, freeze-thaw weathering can split even the hardest rocks, such as granite (4). Water that settles in cracks and joints during the day expands as it freezes at night (5). The expansion cleaves the rock along the naturally occurring joints (6). In deserts, rock expands and contracts due to the extremes of cooling and heating, resulting in layers of rock splitting off.

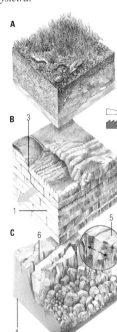

wave
In oceanography, moving disturbance travelling on or through water that does not move the water itself. Wind causes waves by frictional drag. The strength and size of the waves depends on the wind speed and the distance of open water across which the wind blows. Waves not under pressure from strong winds are called swells. Waves begin to break on shore or "feel bottom" when they reach a depth shallower than half the wave's length. When the water depth is about 1.3 times the wave height, the wave front is so steep that the top falls over and the wave breaks.

waxbill
Any member of the genus *Estrilda*, a small group of birds found in tropical regions. The waxbill has a bright crimson, glossy beak that merges with its crimson eye stripe. It has brownish upperparts and a grey to buff underside. The common waxbill (*Estrilda astrild*) is found across Africa, s of the Sahara. It forms busy, twittering flocks. It forages among grass for seeds, with its tail constantly flicking from side to side. Length: 11cm (4in). Family Estrildidae; genus *Estrilda*.

waxwing
Brown-grey bird found in conifer woods of the Northern Hemisphere. It has a head crest and black and white face stripes. It is named after the distinctive, waxy-looking, droplet-shaped tips of its secondary wing feathers. It eats fruits, berries and occasionally insects. Some populations migrate south in winter. Length: 17cm (7in). Family Bombycillidae; species *Bombycilla garrulus*.

wayfaring tree
Deciduous tree-like shrub native to Europe, North Africa and w Asia; it is widely grown as an ornamental. It has oval leaves and creamy flowers. The flowers are followed by red berries, which turn black upon maturity. Height: to 6m (20ft). Family Caprifoliaceae; species *Viburnum lantana*.

weakfish (squeteague)
Common marine fish of the CROAKER family. It is found in tropical and temperate waters of the w Atlantic Ocean. It is dark grey and blue, with black spots. A commercial and game fish, it has a soft mouth that is easily torn by a fishing hook. Length: to 60cm (24in). Family Sciaenidae; species *Cynoscion regalis*.

weasel
Any of several species of small, carnivorous, mostly terrestrial mammals of Eurasia, North Africa and North and South America. Most species have small heads, long necks, slender bodies, short legs and long tails. Weasels are reddish-brown with light-coloured underparts; some species turn completely white in winter. Weasels are fierce predators, eating eggs and rodents and often attacking much larger animals and domestic poultry. Length: 50cm (20in) overall. Family Mustelidae; genus *Mustela*.

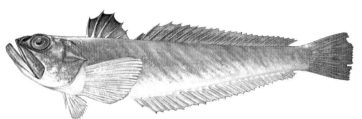

◀ **weever** The greater weever (*Trachinus draco*) inhabits shallow water up to depths of 100m (330ft) in the Mediterranean Sea and NE Atlantic Ocean. It often buries itself in the sand. The spines on its gill covers and on the first dorsal fin are associated with venom glands.

weather
State of the ATMOSPHERE at a given locality or over a broad area, particularly as it affects human activity. Weather refers to short-term states (days or weeks) as opposed to long-term CLIMATE conditions. Weather involves such elements as atmospheric temperature, pressure, humidity, precipitation, cloudiness, brightness, visibility and wind.

weathering
In geology and physical geography, the breakdown and chemical disintegration of rocks and minerals at the Earth's surface by physical, chemical and organic processes. Weathering is important in the formation of soil and plays a major part in shaping landscapes. In **mechanical weathering** (physical weathering) in cold, wet climates, water seeping into cracks in the rock expands on freezing, thus causing the rock to crack further and to crumble. Extreme temperature changes in drier regions, such as deserts, also cause rocks to fragment. Cracks opened by the weather can be exploited by plants, the roots of which place further stress on the rock. **Chemical weathering** can lead to a weakening of the rock structure by altering the minerals of a rock and changing their size, volume and ability to hold shape. The best-known example is the dissolution of limestone in acid rainwater. Chemical weathering processes include oxidation, hydration, silication, desilication and carbonation. **Organic weathering** describes the breakdown of rock and soil by plants, such as by root action, and animals, such as worms, which are important for the breaking up of soil. Unlike EROSION, weathering does not involve the transportation of broken-down material.

weaver
Any of many species belonging to the family Ploceidae. The weaver is a sparrow-like bird, named after its habit of making complex nests by intertwining stems and leaves. Family Ploceidae.

weaver, sociable
Weaver with a grey crown, a black bib and scaly-look-

▲ **weevil** The apple blossom weevil (*Anthonomus pomorum*) causes great damage to the flowers and buds of apple and pear trees. Eggs are laid in the fruit tree buds, and the larvae destroy the flowers before they open.

W

ing back plumage. It lives in large flocks of up to 100 pairs in the dry scrub of s Africa. It builds huge communal tree nests for roosting and breeding. It feeds on the ground on seeds and insects. Length: 15cm (6in). Family Ploceidae; species *Philetirus socius*.

weaver, village
Weaver with a black head, a yellow body, and black and yellow mottled wings. It is found in mixed habitats of sub-Saharan Africa. Village weavers build many, but separate, hanging nests in the same tree. Length: 18cm (7in). Family Ploceidae; species *Ploceus cucullatus*.

web-spinner
Any of *c.*140 mostly tropical species of insect of the order Embioptera. They have fragile, yellow or brown bodies, biting mouthparts, short, stout legs and, in the male, two pairs of narrow wings. Larvae and adults have silk-producing glands, but web-spinners are not of great economic importance. Length: to 20mm (0.8in). Order Embioptera.

webworm (sod worm)
CATERPILLAR of various species of pyralid MOTH. The webworm is found worldwide in meadows and lawns, where it feeds on grass stems, crowns and roots. It lives on webs at the base of the grasses. The white to yellow-brown adult moth flies in the evening. Length: 7–13mm (0.3–0.5in). Family Pyralidae.

weebill (brown weebill, southern weebill, short-billed scrub-tit)
Smallest bird native to Australia. It varies widely in plumage, being dull brown with dusty yellow in the north, and more olive-green in the south, with pale yellow-white underparts. It flits in pairs or small flocks through woods, searching for tiny insects. Length: 9cm (4in). Family Acanthizidae; species *Smicrornis brevirostris*.

weeping willow
See WILLOW

weever
Any of four species of small fish that commonly bury themselves in sand in European and Mediterranean coastal waters. Poison spines on the dorsal fin and gill covers can inflict a painful sting. Family Trachinidae; genus *Trachinus*.

weevil (snout beetle)
Any of numerous species of BEETLE belonging to the family Curculionidae (the largest family in the animal kingdom). Weevils are pests to crops, with many species having long, down-curved beaks for boring into plants. Order Coleoptera; family Curculionidae; species include the BEAN WEEVIL, BOLL WEEVIL and GRAIN WEEVIL.

Wegener, Alfred Lothar (1880–1930)
German geologist, meteorologist and explorer. In *The Origin of Continents and Oceans* (1915) Wegener was the first to use well-presented evidence and scientific argument in support of a theory of CONTINENTAL DRIFT.

weigela
Any member of the genus *Weigela*, a group of flowering shrubs native to E Asia and now grown in many parts of the world. They have narrow, oval leaves. The flowers are white to red, tubular and borne in clusters. The long, narrow seed pods split to disperse the seeds. Height: to 4m (13ft). Family Caprifoliaceae; there are 12 species.

Weismann, August (1834–1914)
German biologist. His essay discussing the germ plasm theory, *The Continuity of the Germ Plasm* (1885), proposed the immortality of the germ line cells as opposed to body cells. It was influential in the development of modern genetic study.

weka (flightless rail)
Inconspicuous, flightless RAIL native to New Zealand. It usually has brown plumage, barred and flecked with black, although some forms are almost black. The weka is a fast runner and swimmer. It lives in scrub and along wood and town edges, where it eats a wide variety of foods, raids rubbish dumps and farmyards, and also pecks at bright inedible objects. Length: 52cm (20in). Family Rallidae; species *Gallirallus australis*.

well
Shaft sunk vertically in the Earth's CRUST through which water, oil, natural gas, brine, sulphur or other mineral substances can be extracted. ARTESIAN WELLS are sunk into water-bearing rock strata, the so-called AQUIFERS, from which water rises under pressure in the wells to the surface.

wels
One of the largest species of CATFISH in the world; it is the only catfish native to w Europe. The wels is green or black with a pale underside. It is found in large rivers and lakes, where its prey includes fish, water birds and frogs. It is an important food and sport fish. Length: to 5m (16ft). Family Siluridae; species *Silurus glanis*.

westerlies
WINDS which frequently blow from a westward direction and often occur in mid-latitudes. In the Northern Hemisphere they blow from the southwest and in the Southern Hemisphere from the northwest.

◄ **whale, blue** The largest animal in the history of the Earth is the blue whale (*Balaenoptera musculus*). Its stomach can hold about two tonnes of food. It is a rather solitary animal and is rarely encountered in schools. It is sometimes known as the sulphur-bottom whale because of the film of yellowish microscopic algae that often forms on its undersurface. The blue whale is a critically endangered species.

weta
Large, nocturnal GRASSHOPPER found only in New Zealand. It has very long antennae. It inhabits holes, such as dry crevices, that have been used by other creatures. It is predated on by rats and birds. The giant weta (*Deinacrida* spp.) is solitary; the tree weta (*Hemideina* spp.) is gregarious. Order Orthoptera.

wetland
Marshy ground in an intertidal zone with prolific vegetation. Coastal wetlands are said to contain a greater concentration of living matter, both flora and fauna, than any other kind of terrain.

wet rot fungus
Any of many fungal species that cause wet rot of wood, both indoors and outdoors, in very damp to wet conditions. The timber cracks longitudinally and becomes dark brown to black in colour. The most common wet rot fungus is the cellar fungus (*Coniophora puteana*), which is identified by dark brown threads spreading over the surface of the timber. Phylum Basidiomycota. **Wet rot fungus**, also known as blossom blight or whisker rot, is also the name of a fungal disease of flower parts and fruit. It affects vegetable crops in wet weather. The fungus infects spent sepals and petals and invades injured fruit tissues, setting up a wet rot. Family Choanephoraceae; species *Choanephora cucurbitarum*.

whale
Any of *c.*76 species of large marine mammal, entirely specialized for life in the open ocean. There are two subdivisions: the baleen whales and the toothed whales. The latter group also contains the DOLPHINS and PORPOISES. Order Cetacea; suborders Odontoceti (toothed whales) and Mysticeti (baleen whales).

whale, blue
Largest animal that has ever existed. Blue whales can weigh up to 150 tonnes, but, despite their bulk, they are streamlined and graceful. Like all the family Balaenopteridae (rorqual whales), they have throat grooves that allow the skin of the lower jaw to expand as they take in water to feed. Blue whales have fringed baleen plates inside their mouths to filter tiny planktonic animals from the water. In summer, while in polar seas, they take over four tonnes of food a day. In winter they migrate to the Equator, where they fast, give birth and mate. Though protected, blue whales are still in danger of extinction. Head-tail length: 25–32m (82–105ft). Family Balaenopteridae; species *Balaenoptera musculus*.

whale, bowhead (Greenland right whale)
Whale that is found in coastal waters of the Arctic Ocean. It has a massive head, and its curved jaws contain the longest baleen plates of any whale, up to 4.5m (15ft) long. These plates are used to filter the smallest planktonic organisms from the water. Mating takes place in spring, and a single calf or

W

twins are born about one year later and suckled for another year. Head-tail length: 15–20m (49–66ft). Family Balaenidae; species *Balaena mysticetus*.

whale, fin

Whale found in all the world's oceans. It is grey above and white below, with up to 100 throat grooves. Its dorsal fin, though small, is larger than that of other members of the family Balaenopteridae (rorqual whales). As in all rorqual whales, the female is larger than the male. The number of fin whales has been severely reduced by whaling; consequently the age of sexual maturity had fallen from 10 years old in the 1930s to six years old by the end of the century. Fin whales are vulnerable to extinction. Head-tail length: 25m (83ft). Family Balaenopteridae; species *Balaenoptera physalus*.

whale, grey

Whale that lives in coastal waters of the N Pacific Ocean. It feeds at the bottom of the sea, stirring up the sediment and filtering shellfish through fringed horny baleen plates hanging from its upper jaw. It spends the summer months feeding in the Arctic Ocean and migrates thousands of kilometres south to breed in winter. Its mottled grey skin is covered with barnacles and it has a row of humps along its back in place of a dorsal fin. Grey whales are vulnerable to extinction. Head-tail length: 12–15m (40–50ft). Family Eschrichtidae; species *Eschrichtius robustus*.

whale, humpback

Whale with characteristically knobbly skin around its mouth and over its very long, scalloped flippers. It is a gregarious animal, living in groups of three or four and using "songs" to communicate with others. Like other baleen whales, humpback whales are filter feeders: Southern Hemisphere populations take planktonic crustaceans, whereas Northern Hemisphere populations take fish. They migrate from polar feeding grounds to tropical breeding grounds in winter. Humpback whales are endangered. Head-tail length: 14.6–19m (48–62ft). Family Balaenopteridae; species *Megaptera novaeangliae*.

whale, killer (orca)

Whale found in cool coastal waters worldwide. It is the largest member of the DOLPHIN family. It is strikingly marked, black above and white below. In the male the dorsal fin can be up to 2m (6.6ft) high and straight; in the female the fin is shorter and curved in the more typical dolphin shape. Killer whales live in large family groups or pods and hunt cooperatively for fish, squid, sea birds and other marine mammals. Head-tail length: 7–9.7m (23–32ft). Family Delphinidae; species *Orcinus orca*. The closely related **pygmy killer whale** is found in all tropical and subtropical seas. Head-tail length: 2.1–2.4m (7–8ft). Family Delphinidae; species *Feresa attenuata*.

whale, false killer

Large, toothed whale found in warm waters of all oceans. It hunts fish and squid by ECHOLOCATION. The false killer whale is black, with a patch of grey on its belly. It has long, narrow flippers, which are bent backwards. False killer whales are occasionally involved in mass-strandings, in which a group of individuals fatally beach themselves for reasons that are still unclear. Head-tail length: 5–5.5m (16.4–18ft). Family Delphinidae; species *Pseudorca crassidens*.

whale, melon-headed (many-toothed blackfish)

Whale found in all tropical seas. It is black all over apart from small areas of grey on its belly and white around its lips and anal region. It has pointed flippers, a sickle-shaped dorsal fin (characteristic of dolphins), a pointed head and an underslung jaw. Since the 1960s mass-strandings of melon-headed whales have increased, which is thought to be due to an increase in their numbers. Head-tail length: 2.1m (7ft). Family Delphinidae; species *Peponocephala electra*.

whale, minke

Smallest member of the family Balaenopteridae (rorqual whales). It is found in shallow water and estuaries of temperate and polar regions of all oceans. It feeds by filtering planktonic animals from cold water using its baleen plates; in warmer water it eats fish and squid. The minke whale has a narrow, pointed snout and between 60 and 70 throat grooves. It has a gestation period of between 10 and 11 months; the single calves are suckled for six months. Head-tail length: 8–10m (26–33ft). Family Balaenopteridae; species *Balaenoptera acutorostrata*.

whale, pilot

Either of two species of whale – the long-finned pilot whale (pothead whale) and the short-finned pilot whale – found in coastal waters of tropical and temperate oceans. Pilot whales are mainly black, with a white patch between their long, narrow, front flippers. They have the bulging forehead common to other members of the DOLPHIN family. Pilot whales live in small groups with strong social bonds. They communicate using a wide range of sounds and use ECHOLOCATION to hunt squid and fish. Head-tail length: 4.8–8.5m (16–28ft). Family Delphinidae; species include *Globicephala melaena* (long-finned pilot whale).

whale, right

Whale that is so called because it was considered the "right" whale to catch. It suffered greatly at the hands of the whaling industry and, although it has now had many years of protection, there are only a few thousand individuals alive. The right whale is black or grey above with white patches below; the large head has warty areas that are infested with barnacles and other parasites. It lives in small groups in temperate waters and has a repertoire of vocalizations. It feeds by skimming through the plankton, straining off crustaceans with its 2.5m (8ft) long baleen plates. Head-tail length: 5–18m (16–59ft). Family Balaenidae; species *Balaena glacialis*. The **pygmy right whale** is a slim whale with throat grooves more like those of a rorqual than a right whale. Head-tail length: 1.8–6.5m (6–21ft). Family Balaenidae; species *Caperea marginata*.

whale, sei

Fast, streamlined whale found in open water of all temperate and tropical oceans. It can reach speeds of up to 50km/hour (31mph). It feeds near the sur-

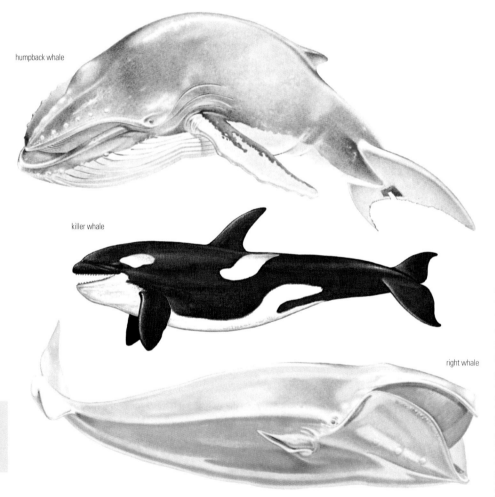

humpback whale

killer whale

right whale

▲ **whale** The humpback whale (*Megaptera novaeangliae*) is one of the most acrobatic of whale species, sometimes somersaulting out of the water. It is also the most vocal. Its long and complex songs vary from group to group and between different areas. The killer whale (*Orcinus Orca*) is found mostly in polar seas and is generally considered to be the most ferocious of whales. Almost any creature in the sea is considered food by the killer whale. The right whale (*Balaena glacialis*) was considered the "right" whale to catch because it was a relatively slow swimmer, it was rich in blubber and it floated when dead. It is noted for the large size of its head, which sometimes accounts for up to 40% of the whale's body length.

W

▶ **wheat** Along with rice, wheat is the world's most important food crop. Originating in the Middle East, it is thought to have been cultivated since the Neolithic period (from *c.*8000 BC). The kernels of the plant are ground into flour, which can then be used to make a variety of foods. Wheat remains green in colour until it ripens, when it becomes golden-brown.

face on fish and squid and by filtering planktonic animals. Sei whales live in small groups, within which pair bonds are strong and may last for years. Females are pregnant for 12 months and suckle their single calves for six months. Head-tail length: 15–20m (49–66ft). Family Balaenopteridae; species *Balaenoptera borealis.*

whale, sperm

Largest of the toothed whales. About one-third of the sperm whale's length is its massive head. The head contains a waxy substance called spermaceti, which helps to control buoyancy when the whale dives to 3000m (9900ft) or more to hunt for squid. Sperm whales have a series of humps on their backs, large tail flukes and short flippers. They migrate between the Equator and temperate waters of all the oceans, some reaching as far as the ice caps. Head-tail length: 11–20m (36–66ft). Family Physeteridae; species *Physeter macrocephalus.* The **pygmy sperm whale** lives in warm waters and feeds on both mid-water and deep-water squid and fish. Head-tail length: 3.4m (11ft). Family Physeteridae; species *Kogia breviceps.*

whale, white (beluga)

Whale that has a more flexible "neck" than other species and no dorsal fin. It uses echolocation to hunt fish and shellfish on the bottom of shallow water. It often swims under the pack-ice, which it breaks to come up for air. Sociable animals, white whales gather in huge herds for their annual migrations from the Arctic to warmer water for the winter months, communicating using a wide range of sounds. One calf is born after 14 months' gestation. Head-tail length: 4–6m (13–20ft). Family Monodontidae; species *Delphinapterus leucas.*

whale louse

Any of a small group of specialized, host-specific ectoparasites of whales. The whale louse's body is

▶ **whelk** The whelk shown here (*Baccinum* sp.) is found in temperate waters. Like all whelks, it is a scavenger and a carnivore. It holds on to its victim, usually a crab or lobster, using its large muscular foot. It then bores a hole through the shell using an extensible proboscis tipped with an abrasive radula, through which it feeds.

dorsoventrally compressed in order to hold fast to the whale. It attaches itself by means of numerous spinules and strategically placed hooks on the underside of its body and uses special portions of its body as suction cups. Despite the whale louse's ungainly appearance, it has not lost the ability to swim freely for mating purposes. Adult body length: 25mm (1in). Order Amphipoda; main genus *Cyamus. See also* AMPHIPOD

wheat

Any of a small group of robust grasses belonging to the genus *Triticum.* The wheat plant has flat leaves and spike-like flowerheads. Common or breadwheat (*Triticum aestivum*) is of hybrid origin and has been cultivated since ancient times. Wheat is still one of the most important cereal crops in the world, producing the grain that is ground into flour for breads and bakery goods. The many types of wheat include spring or winter, hard or soft, bearded or non-bearded, red or white, depending upon characteristics of growth, flowerhead or starch type. Other species of *Triticum* used for human food now or in the past include macaroni wheat (*Triticum durum*), spelt wheat (*Triticum spelta*), emmer wheat (*Triticum dicoccon*) and einkorn wheat (*Triticum monococcum*). Family Poaceae; genus *Triticum.*

wheatear

THRUSH found on moors, heaths and other open habitats throughout the Northern Hemisphere. The wheatear feeds on the ground, eating insects and other small creatures. The male has distinctive breeding plumage of a grey crown and nape, black cheek patches ringed with white, a pale yellow chest, grey underparts, black wings, and a white rump, which he displays to the female. Length: 13cm (5in). Family Turdidae; species include *Oenanthe oenanthe.*

wheat jointworm

Black, ant-like, CHALCID wasp. It attacks the stems of wheat and is found in most of the wheat-growing regions of North America. Length: 2–3mm (0.08–0.12in). Order Hymenoptera; superfamily Chalcidoidea; family Eurytomidae, species *Harmolita tritici.*

wheel animalcule (rotifer)

Any of the *c.*2000 species that belong to the class Rotifera. The wheel animalcule is a microscopic METAZOAN found mainly in freshwater. Although it resembles ciliate protozoa, it is many-celled with a general body structure similar to that of a simple WORM. Wheel animalcules may be elongated or round. They are identified by a crown of cilia around the mouth. Class Rotifera.

whelk

Any member of the family Buccinidae, a group of edible, marine GASTROPODS found on seashores. The whelk has a coiled shell with a smooth rim and a notch at the end. Length: 13–18cm (5–7in). Class Gastropoda; family Buccinidae.

whipbird (Eastern whipbird)

Insect-eating bird native to E Australia. It stays near thick vegetation, where it feeds in leaf litter. The whipbird runs and climbs well but rarely flies. It has mostly dark or black plumage, with a tall head crest, long tail, white cheeks and variable chest mottling. Length: 28cm (11in). Family Orthonychidae; species *Psophodes olivaceus.*

whip-poor-will

NIGHTJAR that inhabits woodlands of Central

▲ **whip-poor-will** Named after its distinctive call, which it sometimes repeats hundreds of times without stopping, the whip-poor-will (*Caprimulgus vociferus*) breeds in E North America and winters in Central America. The male, shown here, has a white collar and tail markings. The female is plainer.

America and E North America. It is seldom seen, due to its plumage, which is mottled in soft browns and greys for excellent camouflage on the forest floor. It rests on the forest floor by day and hunts at night. It keeps its wide-gaped beak open to catch flying insects. Its name comes from its loud incessant call. Length: 25cm (10in). Family Caprimulgidae; species *Caprimulgus vociferus.*

whip scorpion (vinegaroon)

Any member of the ARACHNID order Uropygi, consisting of *c.*75 species found in tropical or warm temperate regions of Asia and the Americas. The whip scorpion has an elongate, flattened body. Its front pair of thickened pedipalps, which contain spines, are used to capture and crush insect prey. The first pair of legs are modified feelers, and the abdomen ends in a slender, whip-like flagellum. Whip scorpions are non-venomous, nocturnal creatures, with cryptic coloration. They can give a nasty bite. *Mastigoproctus giganteus* secretes ethanoic acid from a gland at the base of its tail, hence the american name "vinegaroon". Adult body length: 65mm (2.6in). Class Arachnida; order Uropygi; families include Thelyphonidae.

whip-scorpion, micro

See MICRO WHIP-SCORPION

whip-scorpion, tailless (whip-spider)

Any of many species of flattened, red-brown, tropi-

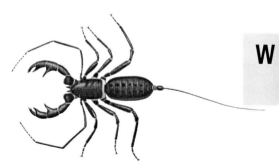

▲ **whip scorpion** The largest whip scorpion species, the giant vinegaroon (*Mastigoproctus giganteus*) is found in S United States and Mexico, usually in desert areas. It is nocturnal and is thought to locate its prey by sensing vibrations.

W

cal ARACHNIDS. A tailless whip-scorpion has a whip-like first pair of legs (sense organs). It captures insects with its strong, spiny pedipalps. All species are nocturnal and non-venomous, with cryptic coloration. The cephalothorax and segmented abdomen are narrowly attached. Around 60 eggs are laid in a flexible sac, with the young being carried until the first moult. Class Arachnida; subclass Amblypygi; there are *c*.130 species

whirlpool

Circular motion of a fluid. Whirlpools in rivers occur in regions where waterfalls or sharp breaks in topographic continuity make steady flow impossible. *See also* VORTEX

whistler (golden whistler)

Bird found across Southeast Asia and Australia; the more than 80 geographic races of this species vary enormously in appearance. Whistlers usually have a black head, white bib, yellow underparts, mottled yellow-black wings and an olive tail. They feed in woods and scrub on insects and berries. Length: 17cm (7in). Family Pachycephalidae; species *Pachycephala pectoralis*.

whitebait

Tropical marine fish found in Australian waters. It has an elongated body, with its dorsal fin set far back. Length: to 10cm (5in). Family Galaxiidae; species *Galaxias attentuatus*. The name **whitebait** is also given to the young of several species of European HERRING. Length: to 5cm (2in). Family Clupeidae.

whitebeam

Tree found in mountainous regions of s and central Europe. The undersides of the leaves have a white felt of hairs. The scented flowers are dull white in colour. It bears bright red fruits. Family Rosaceae; species *Sorbus aria*.

white blood cell

See LEUCOCYTE

white butterfly

See BUTTERFLY, WHITE

▲ **whistler** The golden whistler (*Pachycephala pectoralis*) is found in many different forms on islands round the Australian coast. Bill shape, as shown above, varies considerably between the island races, reflecting the way in which each race has adapted to feed in different kinds of forest.

▲ **whiting** The European whiting (*Merlangus merlangus*) congregates in large shoals and is common in shallow, inshore waters. It is found mainly in areas with sandy or gravel bottoms and feeds on crabs, shrimps, molluscs and small fish. It is an important commercial food fish.

whitecurrant

Small shrub and its round, seedless berry, which is less acid than the redcurrant or blackcurrant. It is now grown in Europe, Asia and North America. The currants may be made into preserves or dried. Family Grossulariaceae; genus *Ribes*.

white-eye

Any member of the family Zosteropidae, a group of short-tailed birds named after the distinctive ring of small white feathers around the eye. Most species are small and short-legged, with a yellow underside and greenish upperparts. Family Zosteropidae.

white-eye, African yellow

White-eye found in open bush country of sub-Saharan Africa. It is greenish-yellow above with bright yellow underparts and a narrow white eye ring. Length: 10cm (4in). Family Zosteropidae; species *Zosterops senegalensis*.

white-eye, Japanese

Grey-bellied white-eye found in the woods and scrub of Southeast Asia. It flits actively between trees in search of insects, fruits, berries and other foods. Length: 12cm (5in). Family Zosteropidae; species *Zosterops japonica*.

white-eye, pale

White-eye that inhabits islands off the N coast of Australia. Length: 12cm (5in). Family Zosteropidae; species *Zosterops citrinella*.

whitefly

Any member of the HEMIPTERAN family Aleyrodidae, a group of small, aphid-like bugs most abundant in the tropics. The whitefly is covered with a fine, white, waxy powder, hence its common name. The flat, oval larvae are active in the first stage, but the legs and antennae are lost after the first moult and the second and third stages are motionless. It feeds as larvae and in the early stages of the pupal phase, but feeding ceases when the adult stage develops inside the body. Several introduced species are pests in greenhouses. Length: to *c*.5mm (*c*.0.2in). Order Hemiptera; super family Aleyrodoidea; family Aleyrodidae; species include *Trialeurodes vaporariorum*.

whiting

Several unrelated food fish. The European whiting is a haddock-like fish of the COD family. It is found primarily in the North Sea, where it feeds on invertebrates and small fish. It is silver with distinctive black markings at the base of the pectoral fin. Length: to 70cm (28in). Family Gadidae; species *Merlangus merlangus*. Other fish commonly called whitings include the kingfish (family Sciaenidae; species *Menticirrhus saxatilis*), found in the Atlantic Ocean, and the freshwater whitefish (family Salmonidae; species *Coregonus clupeaformis*), found in the Great Lakes of North America.

whortleberry

See BILBERRY

whydah

Any of several species of African birds. They whydah is a brood-parasite of other small birds. The male has spectacular breeding plumage, with long tail streamers. Family Ploceidae.

whydah, paradise

Whydah of E and S Africa. The male has spectacular, long, black tail feathers, up to 38cm (15in) in length. It has a black head, face and bib, reddish-brown chest and buff underparts. The female is similar but duller and lacks the long tail. The paradise whydah forages in flocks for seeds on the ground. Family Ploceidae; subfamily Viduinae; species *Vidua paradisaea*.

whydah, pin-tailed

Black and white whydah with a bright red beak. It eats mainly grass seeds. It is a brood parasite of the waxbill. The male is distinctive for its long tail, which is twice the length of the female's. Length: 10–13cm (3.9–5.1in). Family Ploceidae; subfamily Viduinae; species *Vidua macroura*.

widowbird

Any of eight species closely related to the BISHOP and found in varied habitats in Africa. It gets its common name from the black plumage of many of the long-tailed males. The females are more brown, streaked with grey and buff. The widowbird sometimes forages in flocks for grass and similar seeds. Length: 15cm (6in). Family Ploceidae; genus *Euplectes*.

Wieland, Heinrich Otto (1877–1957)

German chemist who was awarded the 1927 Nobel

▲ **whydah, paradise** The plumage of the paradise whydah (*Vidua paradisaea*) is much more spectacular in the male (shown here) than the female. In the breeding season, the males display to the females on a clear patch of ground, fanning and twisting their long tail feathers. After the display the females mate with the males of their choice. Eggs are usually laid in the nests of weavers or waxbills. Young whydahs closely resemble the young of the host and are reared by the other birds.

Prize for chemistry for his research into bile acids. In 1912 he discovered that the three bile acids then known were closely related in structure. He showed them to have a steroid skeleton and thus found that they were also structurally related to CHOLESTEROL. Wieland also did research into oxidation reactions (*see* OXIDATION-REDUCTION) occurring in living tissues and discovered that such oxidation consisted of dehydrogenation (removal of hydrogen atoms) rather than the addition of oxygen.

wigeon
DUCK that breeds in Europe and Asia, with the northern populations moving south for winter. The wigeon prefers shallow, still, inland waters, where it dabbles for water plants and insects. It also grazes meadows, like geese, and moves to coasts in winter. The male wigeon has a pale yellow crown, chestnut head and a mainly grey body; the female is flecked brown. Length: 45cm (18in). Family Anatidae; species *Anas penelope*.

wild boar
See BOAR, WILD

wildebeest
See GNU

wild rice
Annual GRASS native to the wetlands of North America. Its stems are crowned with large, open flower clusters. The rod-like grains are dark brown or black. Wild rice was an important food for Native North Americans. Height: to 3m (10ft). Family Gramineae; species *Zizania aquatica*.

Wilkins, Maurice Hugh Frederick (1916–)
British biophysicist, b. New Zealand. During World War 2 he worked on the separation of uranium isotopes for the Manhattan Project. Wilkins is celebrated for his work in molecular biology, in particular the structure of NUCLEIC ACID. While working at King's College, London, he extracted some fibres from a gel

◀ **willow** Members of the willow family are fairly small trees: the European willow (*Salix caprea*), shown here, grows to a maximum height of 10m (35ft). The seeds are light and wind dispersed. Willows often grow by water, where rapid germination is effected.

of deoxyribonucleic acid (DNA). Using X-ray diffraction, he noted the helical structure of the strands. Francis CRICK and James WATSON used this research to build a model of the structure of DNA and to describe its action. For this work the three men shared the 1962 Nobel Prize for physiology or medicine.

willow
Any of a large group of trees or shrubs widely distributed in the Northern Hemisphere. The male and female flowers are produced in catkins on separate plants. Trees are widely grown as ornamentals (for example, weeping willow or PUSSY WILLOW) and for uses such as cricket bats (cricket bat willow) and OSIERS for basketry and biomass production (basket willow). Willow bark was the origin of aspirin. Family Salicaceae; genus *Salix*.

willow herb
Any of several species of perennial plants with willow-like leaves, especially fireweed or rosebay willowherb (*Epilobium angustifolium*). Fireweed has a long, unbranched stem, with narrow leaves and purple red flowers. Height: to 1m (3.3ft). Family Onagraceae; genus *Epilobium*.

Wilson, Edmund Beecher (1856–1939)
US biologist whose research mainly concerned embryology and cytology. He traced the formation of different kinds of tissues from individual precursor cells. He also studied the relationship of CHROMOSOMES to sex determination and the hereditary function of chromosomes.

Wilson, John Tuzo (1908–93)
Canadian geophysicist and geologist who determined global patterns of faulting and the structure of the continents. His investigations have influenced theories of CONTINENTAL DRIFT, SEAFLOOR SPREADING and convection currents within the Earth.

wilt disease
Any of a group of plant diseases characterized by yellowing and wilting of leaves and young stems, often followed by death of the plant. Wilt diseases are caused by bacteria or fungi that grow in the sapwood, plugging the water-conducting tissues or disrupting the plant's water balance in some other way.

wilting
Drooping of the herbaceous parts of a plant due to lack of turgor. It occurs when TRANSPIRATION exceeds the supply of water to these parts. Wilting may be due to drought, excessive salt concentration in the soil or disease. *See also* PRESSURE POTENTIAL

wind
Air current that moves rapidly parallel to the Earth's surface. (Air currents in vertical motion are called updrafts or downdrafts.) Wind direction is indicated by wind or weather vanes, wind speed by anemometers and wind force by the BEAUFORT WIND SCALE. Steady winds in the tropics, such as those in the DOLDRUMS, are called TRADE WINDS. MONSOONS are seasonal winds that bring predictable rains in Asia. **Foehns** (föhns) are warm, dry winds produced by adiabatic compression (compression accompanied by temperature rise) as air descends the lee of mountainous areas in the Alps; they are called **chinooks** in the Rockies. **Siroccos** are hot, dry Mediterranean winds. The MISTRAL is a cold, northerly wind that sweeps from the Massif Central of France down the Rhône Valley during winter.

windchill factor
Perceived cooling effect of WIND in low-temperature conditions. The air temperature feels much

W

► **whirlpool** The rivers and creeks in the Tasmanian Wilderness, now a World Heritage Site, often have the topographical discontinuity necessary for the creation of whirlpools. The shape of the rocks on the river bed can make steady flow impossible, as can the meeting of two different currents.

▲ **wolf, maned** The shy, nocturnal maned wolf (*Chrysocyon brachyurus*) is found in deciduous forests and plains of South America. As with other plains' predators, it feeds on almost anything, from small animals to fruit. Opposite sex pairs share territory, but only associate closely with each other in the breeding season.

colder if there is a wind blowing, so the windchill factor is obtained by the relationship between the temperature and the windspeed. If the wind reaches speeds around 40km/h (25mph) temperatures of 5°C can feel very cold, and in sub-zero weather even moderate winds of 10km/h (6mph) can significantly reduce effective temperatures. With a wind speed of 80km/h (50mph), a zero temperature would feel like –20°C (–4°F).

window midge
MIDGE that takes its common name from the fact that it is often found inside houses. The larvae inhabit decaying matter and sewage beds or similar sites. Order Diptera; family Anisopodidae; species include *Sylvicola fenestralis*.

wingnut (Caucasian wingnut)
Deciduous tree native to the Caucasus and Iran. It has a thick trunk and is occasionally planted for timber or ornament in Europe. Male and female flowers are produced in separate catkins, and the fruits are surrounded by green wings. Height: to 30m (98ft). Family Juglandaceae; species *Pterocarya fraxinifolia*.

wings
Specialized organs for flight that are possessed by most BIRDS, many INSECTS, and certain mammals and reptiles. The forelimbs of a bird have developed into such structures. BATS have membranous tissue supported by the digits ("fingers") of the forelimbs. Insects may have one or two pairs of veined or membranous wings.

W

winkle (periwinkle)
Any member of the family Littorinidae, a group of small, aquatic, gastropod MOLLUSCS. The winkle's unsegmented body is soft and is protected by a hard, univalve shell. It has a distinct head and a muscular foot. Winkles feed on rock algae in the intertidal zone. The common marine species *Littorina littorea* is edible. Family Littorinidae.

winter aconite
Herbaceous perennial native to Europe and naturalized in North America. It has underground tubers and deeply palmately lobed basal leaves. Its solitary, yel-

low flowers, produced very early in the spring, are surrounded by a whorl of three leaf-like bracts. It is common in gardens and naturalizes readily into woods and parks. Family Ranunculaceae; species *Eranthis hymalis*.

winter gnat
Fly that is often seen dancing and swarming, especially in the winter. The larvae inhabit decaying matter. The swarms are mostly made up of males. Winter gnats do not bite. Order Diptera; family Trichoceridae; species *Trichocera annulata*.

wintergreen
Any of various woody, evergreen plants, especially *Gaultheria procumbens*, the teaberry of the United States, Canada and Britain. It produces pale pink flowers followed by red fruits. The name evergreen also refers to the aromatic oil derived from its leaves. Family Ericaceae.

winter jasmine
Deciduous, scrambling shrub native to China, commonly grown as an ornamental. It has long, green, trailing stems, which root along their length. Leaves are simple and arranged in threes. The solitary yellow, trumpet-shaped flowers are produced in winter and spring in the absence of leaves. Family Oleaceae; species *Jasminum nudiflorum*.

wiretail
See SPINETAIL

wireworm
Long, cylindrical larva of a click BEETLE. It is found in temperate woodlands of the Northern Hemisphere. The wireworm is generally brown or yellow and is distinctly segmented. Most species live in the soil and can cause serious damage to the roots of cultivated crops. Order Coleoptera; family Elateridae.

wisent
See BISON, EUROPEAN

wisteria
Any member of the genus *Wisteria*, a group of hardy, woody vines native to North America, Japan and China. Wisteria plants have showy, fragrant, pendulous flower clusters of purplish-white, pink or blue. Family Fabaceae/Leguminosae; species include *Wisteria floribunda* (Japanese wisteria).

▲ **wolverine** The wolverine (*Gulo gulo*) is primarily a scavenger, feeding on carrion, mainly deer and sheep, and often chasing large predators away from their kills. Its strong, sharp teeth and long claws mean that it is rarely preyed upon. It secretes from its anal glands an unpleasant-smelling liquid, which it uses to mark its territory and in defence.

witches' broom
Abnormal growth of closely bunched, slender twigs at the ends of branches of woody plants, giving the appearance of a broomhead. It a symptom of infection by a fungus, virus or bacteria. Some are of widespread occurrence and may be serious pests of agricultural trees.

witch hazel
Any of several species of shrubs and small trees of the genus *Hamamelis*, native to temperate regions, mostly in Asia. Witch hazel blooms in late autumn or early spring. The common witch hazel (*Hamamelis virginiana*) has yellow flowers. Family Hamamelidaceae.

Withering, William (1741–99)
British doctor who introduced the use of DIGITALIS (a drug obtained from the leaves of the FOXGLOVE) to treat cardiac disorders, giving details of his work in *An Account of the Foxglove* (1785). He was the first to establish a connection between dropsy and heart disease. Also a keen botanist, Withering published *Botanical Arrangement* (1776).

wobbegong
Any of six species of dorso-ventrally flattened, benthic SHARKS of the w Pacific Ocean. The wobbegong has a camouflaged appearance, with abundant fringe-like appendages, barbles around its mouth and fang-like teeth in the middle of its upper and lower jaws. Length: to 3.5m (11.5ft). Family Orectolobidae.

wolf
Largest member of the DOG family. It is an adaptable opportunist, taking a wide range of plant and small animal food and scavenging if the opportunity arises. Wolves live in well-organised family groups or packs, with a complex hierarchy. The pack defends a sizeable territory and hunts large prey together. Wolves pair for life and every winter produce a litter of four to five pups, which are cared for in a den. Order Carnivora; family Canidae.

wolf, grey
Wolf that once lived in forests across N Europe and North America. Due to persecution, it is vulnerable to extinction and its range is now severely restricted. Head-body length: 1–1.5m (39–59in); tail: 31–51cm (12–20in). Family Canidae; species *Canis lupus*.

wolf, maned
Wolf that inhabits the grassland and scrub of South America. It has a fox-like face and very long legs. It is vulnerable to extinction. Head-body length: 1m (39in); tail: 45cm (18in). Family Canidae; species *Chrysocyon brachyurus*.

wolf, red
Wolf that once lived on the plains of SE United States. It is now thought to be extinct in the wild. It is smaller than the grey wolf. Family Canidae; species *Canis rufus*.

wolffia (water meal)
Any of a small group of minute aquatic plants found in tropical and warm to temperate waters. The wolffia rarely flowers, instead budding off new growths vegetatively. The tiny *Wolffia angusta* at 0.6 × 0.33mm (0.02 × 0.01in) is possibly the smallest flowering plant in the world. *Wolffia brasiliensis* is distributed on bird's feathers. Family Lemnaceae; genus *Wolffia*.

wolffish
Voracious fish that lives in the N Atlantic Ocean. It is

▲ **wombat** The wombat's teeth, like those of rodents, grow continuously so that they are not worn away by the constant gnawing required for the wombat's diet of grasses and roots. The common wombat (*Vombatus ursinus*), shown here, occupies forests and heathlands of SE Australia.

brown or grey, with long fins along its back and belly. It has powerful jaws and teeth. The wolffish is valued as a food fish in Iceland, where its skin is made into leather. Length: 91cm (36in). Family Anarhichadidae; species *Anarhichas lupus*.

wolf spider
See SPIDER, WOLF

wolverine
Solitary, ferocious mammal, native to pine forests of the United States and Eurasia; it is the largest member of the WEASEL family. The wolverine is dark brown, with lighter bands along its sides and neck. It has a bushy tail and large feet. Length: 91cm (36in); weight: 30kg (66lb). Family Mustelidae; species *Gulo gulo*.

womb
See UTERUS

wombat
Short-legged, bear-shaped MARSUPIAL that inhabits Australia and Tasmania. Its long claws are adapted for digging, and it excavates large burrow systems. The wombat is herbivorous and nocturnal. Its preferred habitat is semi-arid woodland and grassland. Head-body length: 80–100cm (31–39in); tail: 3–5cm (1–2in). Family Vombatidae; genera *Vombatus* and *Lasiorhinus*; there are three species.

wood
Hard substance that forms the trunks of TREES; it is the XYLEM (the vascular tissue of a woody plant) that comprises the bulk of the STEMS and ROOTS, supporting the plant. It consists of fine cellular tubes arranged vertically within the trunk, which accounts for the grain found in all wood. The relatively soft, light-coloured wood is called **sapwood**. The nonconducting, older, darker wood is called **heartwood**, and is generally filled with RESIN, GUMS, mineral salts and tannin (tannic acid). Easily worked softwood, generally from a CONIFER such as PINE, is composed of simple tracheids that provide support and conduct water and food. More durable hardwood, generally from a DECIDUOUS species such as OAK, derives support from woody fibres; water and food are conducted through separate vessels.

woodbine
See HONEYSUCKLE

woodchuck (groundhog)
MARMOT found in North America from Canada to the SE United States. It has grizzled black-brown hair. Using its sharp front teeth and short, strong legs, it

digs burrows. It feeds heavily in autumn before hibernating. The woodchuck eats plants, often becoming a garden pest. Length: 61cm (24in); Weight: to 6kg (13lb). Family Sciuridae; species *Marmota monax*.

woodcock
Any of six species of unusual birds, related to the SNIPES, found in woods and forests of North America and Eurasia. The woodcock feeds on worms, grubs and other soil creatures, probing with its long, tube-like beaks. It is shy and extremely well camouflaged, with mottled brown plumage. Length: 27cm (11in). Family Scolopacidae; genus *Scolopax*.

woodcreeper
Any of c.50 species of mainly insect-eating forest birds found in Central and South America. The barred woodcreeper (*Dendrocolaptes certhia*) is a stout bird with a long, powerful beak. It has an olive head and upper back, with lighter lengthways bars, and a brownish body and tail. It climbs trunks in the manner of a WOODPECKER, using its strongly clawed toes, with stiff tail feathers for support. Length: 20–38cm (8–15in). Family Dendrocolaptidae.

wood-hoopoe
Any of eight species of birds found in the woods and forests of central and s Africa. The most distinctive is the green wood-hoopoe (*Phoeniculus purpureus*), which has a very long, thin, down-curved, red bill. It has a glossy dark green head and back, and a purple neck, underside and tail. Its tail is longer than its slender body. Wood-hoopoes forage as noisy flocks in trees, searching for grubs, caterpillars and other small creatures. Length: 22–38cm (9–15in). Family Phoeniculidae.

woodland
Area of land where trees are the dominant vegetation. Often divided into DECIDUOUS woodland (trees are broad-leaved ANGIOSPERMS), CONIFEROUS woodland (trees are narrow-leaved CONIFEROPHYTES) and mixed woodland (comprising both types of trees). *See also* FOREST

woodlouse (sowbug)
Any member of the genus *Oniscus*, a group of terrestrial, ISOPOD crustaceans found in damp conditions worldwide. The woodlouse has an oval, segmented body. It feeds mainly on vegetable matter. It retains its eggs in a brood pouch. Length: 20mm (0.8in). Order Isopoda; genus *Oniscus*.

woodnymph
HUMMINGBIRD that is widespread in the forests of South America. Its needle-like bill makes up one-quarter of its length. It usually has a gleaming green

head, purple chest, green-bronze wings and a blue-black, deeply forked tail. Several other colour forms exist. The woodnymph feeds on nectar, pollen and tiny insects from flowers. Length: 10cm (4in). Family Trochilidae; species *Thalurania furcata*.

wood-partridge
Bird that frequents thick forest and bamboo clumps in Southeast Asia. It feeds on seeds, fruits, shoots and small creatures. The male has a red crest, scarlet facial skin and a blue-black head and neck; its body is mainly green, with dark brown, orange-tipped wings. The female lacks the crest and is generally duller. Length: 25cm (10in). Family Phasianidae, species *Rollulus roulroul*.

woodpecker
Tree-climbing bird found worldwide. With two toes pointing forwards and two pointing backwards, it is well adapted to climbing. It has stiff supporting tail feathers. Family Picidae; there are c.200 species.

woodpecker, acorn
Woodpecker of North and Central America. It has a scarlet head crown, patches of white and black on its body, and glossy black on its back, wings and tail. It lives in small groups, which peck holes in their central "larder tree" to fill with excess acorns and similar food. Length: 22cm (9in). Family Picidae; subfamily Picinae; species *Melanerpes formicivorus*.

woodpecker, black
Largest European woodpecker. It is completely black and resembles a CROW. It feeds on ants as well as wood-boring insects and their larvae. Length: 45cm (18in). Family Picidae; subfamily Picinae; species *Dryocopus martius*.

woodpecker, great spotted
Europe's most common and adaptable woodpecker; it is also found in North Africa and across Asia. It is not so much spotted, as black with white cheeks and wing bars. The male of this species also has a red band around the rear of its neck. The great spotted woodpecker hammers at trees with a rapid drumming sound to extract grubs and other prey. Length: 22cm (9in). Family Picidae; subfamily Picinae; species *Dendrocopus major*.

woodpecker, green
Large-billed, powerful woodpecker. It has bright green wings, a yellow rump and a pale neck and chest. The head has a red cap and black face, with a red "moustache" stripe on the male. It hammers trees for wood-boring grubs and also pecks at the ground for ants, worms and occasionally fruits and seeds. Length: 32cm (13in). Family Picidae; subfamily Picinae; species *Picus viridis*.

◄ **woodcock** The Eurasian woodcock (*Scolopax rusticola*) breeds in temperate regions of Europe and Asia. It prefers woodlands with moist, fertile soil, in which it can easily find its favoured food - earthworms. The woodcock's eyes are set unusually far back on the head, giving it all-round vision. In the breeding season, the male displays by flying just above the treetops in a particular route; this display, known as roding, is accompanied by distinctive mating calls.

W

411

acorn woodpecker

red-headed woodpecker

▲ **woodpecker** The acorn woodpecker (*Melanerpes formicivorus*) drills holes in trees to store acorns and berries, with which it supplements its insect diet. It also feeds on sap, and groups of acorn woodpeckers are known to use the same sap holes year after year. Unlike other woodpecker species, the red-headed woodpecker (*Melanerpes erythrocephalus*) rarely drills holes in trees, preferring to catch insects on the wing. It takes insects, worms, spiders and small birds' eggs, as well as nuts and berries. Both species nest in cavities in trees.

woodpecker, pileated

Large, strong woodpecker of North America. It has a massive, sword-like bill and a red forehead that sweeps up into a tall head crest. Most of its body is dark brown, apart from a white stripe on each side of the neck and chest. The face is white, with a black eye stripe and red "moustache". Length: 50cm (20in). Family Picidae; subfamily Picinae; species *Dryocopus pileatus*.

woodpecker, red-cockaded

Small, mainly barred black and white woodpecker. It is found in pine and oak woods in the SE United States. The red-cockaded woodpecker is a threatened species because of the loss of its preferred habitat. Length: 22cm (9in). Family Picidae; subfamily Picinae; species *Picoides borealis*.

wood sorrel

See OXALIS

W

woodstar

Any of a group of small HUMMINGBIRDS. It includes the amethyst woodstar (*Calliphlox amethystina*), which is one of the smallest of all hummingbirds. Its fast-beating wings create a distinct buzzing. Length: 7cm (3in). Family Trochilidae.

woodswallow

Any of *c*.10 species of swallow-like birds found in E and W Australia. The woodswallow flies rather like a miniature eagle, soaring in flocks. The dusky woodswallow (*Artamus cyanopterus*) is also called the bee bird from its habit of roosting in compact huddles. It is slate-grey, with a black-tipped blue bill and white-edged, blue-black wings and tail. The woodswallow feeds on nectar, flowers and insects. Length: 17cm (7in). Family Artamidae.

woodworm

Larva of the FURNITURE BEETLE.

woody nightshade

See NIGHTSHADE

woolly bear

CATERPILLAR of many tiger MOTH species. Its body is densely covered with long hairs. The larva of the North American Isabella tiger moth (*Isia isabella*) is known as the banded woolly bear. It is black in front and behind, with a rusty-coloured middle band of variable width. Family Arctiidae.

woolly rhinoceros

One of the extinct, cold-adapted mammals that existed during the Quaternary ICE AGE. It had a thick coat of insulating hair and a pair of large horns on its snout, the front one growing to lengths of more than 1m (39in) in males. Woolly rhinoceros remains are occasionally found frozen in the PERMAFROST of Siberia. It was depicted by early modern humans before becoming extinct *c*.10,000 years ago. Genus *Coelodonta*.

worm

Any of a large variety of wriggling, limbless creatures with soft bodies. Most worms belong to one or other of four main groups: ANNELIDS, FLATWORMS, NEMATODES (roundworms) and BOOTLACE WORMS (ribbon worms).

wormwood

Any member of the genus *Artemisia*, a group of aromatic bitter shrubs and herbs. It includes common wormwood (*Artemisia absinthium*), a European shrub that yields a dark green oil used to make absinthe. It bears clusters of small, yellowish flower heads. Family Asteraceae/Compositae.

woylie

See BETTONG

wrack (tang)

Any of a group of SEAWEEDS with tough, narrow, strap- or ribbon-like fronds that branch dichotomously in one plane; in several species the fronds are supported by gas bladders. Wrack is widely distributed from Norway to Iberian Atlantic coasts. It has been used to improve soil or as grazing for sheep and cattle on the shore. Family Fucaceae; genera include *Fucus*, *Ascophyllum* and *Pelvetia*.

wrasse

Any of *c*.600 species of usually brilliantly coloured marine fish found in tropical and temperate waters, often among coral reefs; many of the smaller species are popular aquarium species. Wrasses have protrusible mouths and sleep on their sides. Some, such as the

▲ **woolly rhinoceros** During the glacial periods of the Pleistocene era, the woolly rhinoceros was found in N Europe. Herbivorous, it is thought to have grazed on a wide range of vegetation, from conifer twigs to coarse grasses. It was about the size of a modern-day African rhinoceros.

cleaner wrasse (*Labroides dimidiatus*), remove parasites from larger fish. Other species include the rainbow wrasse (*Coris julis*). Length: 8–300cm (3–118in). Family Labridae.

wren

Any member of the family Troglodytidae, a group of tiny insectivorous birds with camouflaged plumage. Most species have loud, trilling songs. Family Troglodytidae; there are *c*.70 species.

wren, northern

Tiny, plump-bodied, active, brownish bird. It hops in dense vegetation for small insects and grubs, with its tail held almost vertical. It is found in undergrowth in varied habitats across all northern continents. Length: 8cm (3in). Family Troglodytidae; species *Troglodytes troglodytes*.

wren, house

Wren with plain brown upperparts and grey underparts. It is found in parks, gardens and woods in much of North America; it migrates south for winter. The house wren feeds on large insects, spiders and snails, Length: 12cm (5in). Family Troglodytidae; species *Troglodytes aedon*.

wren, cactus

Largest species of wren in North America. It inhabits dry scrub and semi-desert in the SW United States. Its plumage is flecked grey and brown, with a distinctive white eye stripe. Length: 22cm (9in). Family Troglodytidae; species *Campylorhynchus brunneicapillus*.

wren-babbler

Any of several species of BABBLER found mainly in lowland forests in Southeast Asia. The wren-babbler is a rather dumpy bird with a whistling call. Length: 20cm (8in). Family Timaliidae; genus *Napothera*.

wren-tit

Only species of the BABBLER family to be found in

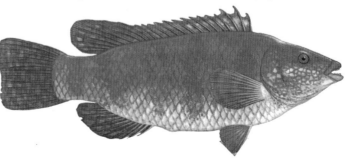

◄ **wrasse** The large ballan wrasse (*Labrus bergylta*) is found in the Mediterranean Sea and the NE Atlantic Ocean. Its dull coloration is unusual for a member of the wrasse family. It uses the sharp teeth at the front of its mouth to grasp molluscs and crustaceans. The hard shells of its prey are then crushed by the wrasse's strong throat teeth.

North America. The wren-tit pairs and mates for life. It seldom leaves its territory, which it aggressively defends against intruders. Both the male and female are dark brown above, pale brown below, with a long tail held semi-upright. It inhabits dry scrub and bush in w North America, where it forages in bushes and shrubs for insects, spiders and similar food. Length: 16cm (6in). Family Timaliidae; species *Chamaea fasciata*.

Wright, Sewall (1889–1988)

US geneticist, best known for his studies of GENETIC DRIFT. He produced a mathematical description of EVOLUTION from observation of the selective breeding methods used to improve livestock. He showed how genetically controlled characteristics could be lost if the few animals having them did not pass them on to the next generation. This suggested that evolution could occur without the influence of NATURAL SELECTION.

wrybill

Small PLOVER that is found in the marshes, estuaries and rivers of New Zealand. It gets its common name from its sharp beak, which has a tip angled to the right. It turns its head and sweeps its bill over mud to find small creatures to eat. The wrybill has light brown upperparts, a white underside and a black frontal neck collar. Length: 20cm (8in). Family Charadriidae; species *Anarhynchus frontalis*.

wryneck

Either of two species of birds belonging to the WOODPECKER family. The wryneck is found in Europe, North Africa and Asia. It is named after its habit of twisting its head and neck into contorted

◄ **wren** Wrens are songbirds, and the northern wren (*Troglodytes troglodytes*), shown here, is one of the best singers. It is the only wren species native to the Old World, but it is also found widely in North America. The male uses its impressive singing skills to mark and defend its territory.

positions when it is feeding and courting. The wryneck has mottled brown plumage. Using its long tongue, it gathers insects and other small creatures from bark and foliage. Some populations migrate to more southerly regions for winter. Length: 18cm (7in). Family Picidae; species *Jynx torquilla* and *Jynx ruficollis*.

W

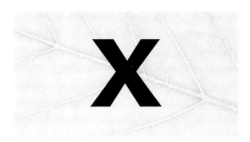

xanthine

Yellow substance found in plants, in most body tissues and fluids, and in urinary tract stones; it can be oxidized to form URIC ACID. It is a muscle stimulant, particularly of cardiac muscle, and its synthetic derivatives are used as diuretics and to dilate blood vessels and bronchi.

xanthophyll

PLANT PIGMENT responsible for the yellow and brown colours of leaves in autumn. Chemically it is a carotenoid, a group of compounds that includes CAROTENE, a pigment that gives the red colour to carrots and tomatoes. All carotenoids, including xanthophyll, play a part in PHOTOSYNTHESIS.

X-chromosome

Sex CHROMOSOME appearing singly in the heterogametic (XY) sex (males in humans, female in birds) and paired in the homogametic (XX) sex. *See also* SEX DETERMINATION

xenops

Any member of the genus *Xenops*, comprising several species of small, active birds found in the damp forests of South America. The xenops is usually brown, with rusty red, black-edged wings and tail. Most species have white stripes above and below each eye. Length: *c*.12cm (*c*.5in). Family Furnariidae; genus *Xenops*.

xerophyte

Any plant that is adapted to survive in dry conditions, in areas subject to drought or in physiologically dry areas such as saltmarshes and acid bogs, where saline or acid conditions make the uptake of water difficult. SUCCULENTS, such as cacti, have thick fleshy leaves and stems for storing water. Other adaptations include the ability to reduce water loss by shedding leaves during drought, having waxy or hairy leaf coatings or reduced leaf area.

xylem

Transport TISSUE of a plant; it conducts water and minerals from the roots to the rest of the plant and provides support for it. The most important cells are long, thin tapering cells called xylem vessels. These cells are dead and have no cross-walls; they are arranged in columns to form long tubes, up which water is drawn. As water evaporates from the leaves (TRANSPIRATION), water is drawn across the leaf by OSMOSIS to replace it, drawing water out of the xylem. This process creates PRESSURE POTENTIAL in the xylem vessels, which, along with rings of LIGNIN that reinforce side walls and prevent them from collapsing, provides support to the plant. Tiny holes in the walls of the xylem vessels, called **pits**, allow water to cross from one tube to another. FERNS and CONIFERS do not have xylem vessels. Instead they have similar cells called **tracheids**, which do not lose their end walls, so water has to travel through the pits, which slows the flow. The lignin makes the walls of vessels and tracheids strong and rigid, an important support as the plant grows bigger. Xylem tissue also contains non-conducting fibres, dead cells thickened with lignin for extra support. In trees, the xylem becomes blocked with age, and new xylem forms towards the outside of the trunk to replace it. The core of dead, non-functioning xylem remains an essential part of the support system. *See also* PHLOEM; VASCULAR BUNDLE

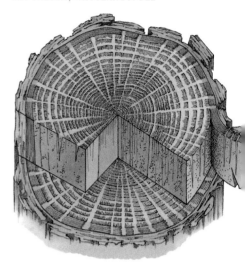

▲ **xylem** Wood is made of the old xylem of previous years' growth, the walls of which have become heavily impregnated with lignin. The cells die and are embalmed in tannins and resins, forming the strong, dark heartwood. The heartwood is surrounded by sapwood, which is weaker and makes up most of the thickness of the trunk in young trees. A layer of new sapwood is added to the outer edge of the column of wood with each year's growth, so forming a ring visible among others in the trunk. The rings are most apparent in trees growing in temperate regions, where patterns of growth vary from season to season.

Y

▲ **yapok** The yapok (*Chironectes minimus*) frequents freshwater streams and lakes. Its hind feet are webbed, making it a strong swimmer, and the female's pouch can be closed tightly to keep the young dry. It is nocturnal.

yak

Large, powerful, long-haired OX. It is native to Tibet, with domesticated varieties found throughout central Asia. It inhabits barren heights up to 6000m (20,000ft). Domesticated varieties are generally smaller and varied in colour; they breed freely with domestic cattle. Wild yaks have coarse, black hair, except on the tail and flanks, where it hangs as a long fringe. The horns curve upwards and outwards. Height: to 1.8m (6ft) at the shoulder. Family Bovidae; species *Bos grunniens*.

yam

Any of several species of herbaceous vines that grow in warm and tropical regions; also the edible, large, tuberous roots of several tropical species. The yam plant is an annual with a long, climbing stem. It has lobed or unlobed leaves and small clusters of greenish, bell-shaped flowers. The SWEET POTATO is also sometimes called a yam. Family Dioscoreaceae; genus *Dioscorea*.

yapok (water opossum)

Only MARSUPIAL to be highly adapted to living in water; it has webbed hind feet and thick fur. It is found in tropical regions of Central and South America. The yapok feeds on crustaceans, fish, frogs and insects. Head-body length: 27–40cm (11–16in); tail: 31–43cm (12–17in). Family Didelphidae; species *Chironectes minimus*.

yardang

Elongated ridge formed by wind EROSION in arid areas. Rock is eroded into a series of ridges and furrows lying parallel to the prevailing wind direction.

yarrow

See MILFOIL

Y-chromosome

Sex CHROMOSOME found only in the heterogametic (XY) sex. Differs from the X-chromosome in size and shape and usually carries very few genes. *See also* SEX DETERMINATION

▲ **yak** The wild yak (*Bos grunniens*) is considered a vulnerable species: there are perhaps only a few hundred individuals left in the wild, in remote parts of the Tibetan plateau and adjacent highlands. They are threatened mainly by poaching. Domesticated varieties are vital to the traditional Tibetan lifestyle, being used in farming and also for their meat, milk, hair, hide and horns.

yeast

Any of a group of single-celled, microscopic FUNGI found worldwide in the soil and in organic matter. Yeasts reproduce asexually by BUDDING or FISSION. Yeasts are also produced commercially for use in baking, brewing and wine-making. They occur naturally as a bloom (white-covering) on grapes and other fruit. See also ASEXUAL REPRODUCTION; RESPIRATION

yellow-green algae

Variety of flagellate ALGAE (division Xanthophyta). They differ from GREEN ALGAE by their characteristically motile bodies and unequal FLAGELLA.

yellow jack

Tropical marine fish of the JACK family, found in the Indo-Pacific region. It has a golden body, with 8–12 dark bands. It is a food fish. Length: to 91cm (36in). Family Carangidae; species *Caranx bartholomaei*.

yellowlegs

Either of two species of medium-sized wading birds, characterized by a long bill and long, yellow legs. The greater yellowlegs (*Tringa melanoleuca*) breeds across the northern tundra of North America and winters to southern coasts. The lesser yellowlegs (*Tringa flavipes*) breeds in E and central Canada and Alaska. Length: 25–36cm (10–14in). Family Scolopacidae.

yellowtail (California yellowtail)

Marine fish found in the Sea of Cortez off the s California coast. It is a solid-bodied fish, with large eyes and a scimitar-shaped tail. It is yellow, green and silver. The yellowtail is a popular game fish. Family Carangidae; species *Seriola dorsalis*.

yellowthroat

Common songbird of damp habitats in North and Central America. Its plumage is olive green above, with bright yellow beneath, especially on the throat. The male has a black mask across its forehead and face, and a loud, distinctive song. Length: 12cm (5in). Family Parulidae; species *Geothlypis trichas*.

Yerkes, Robert Mearns (1876–1956)

US biologist and psychologist. He was a pioneer in the comparative study of apes and the development of methods to test the abilities of lower animals and humans. His publications include *The Mind of a Gorilla* (1927) and *Chimpanzees: A Laboratory Colony (1943)*.

yew

Any of a number of evergreen shrubs and trees of the genus *Taxus*, which are native to temperate regions of the Northern Hemisphere. They have stiff, narrow, dark green needles, often with pale undersides, and poisonous, red, berry-like fruits. Height: to 25m (80ft). Family Taxaceae.

ylang-ylang

Fast-growing tree from s India, Java and the Philippines. It has drooping branches and large, fragrant, bell-shaped, yellowish-green flowers. Aromatic oil (cananga oil) obtained by distillation of the petals is used in hairdressing and is one of the most important oils used in perfume production. Family Annonaceae; species *Cananga odorata*.

yolk

Rich substance found in the EGGS or OVA of most ANIMALS, except those of placental mammals. It consists of fats and proteins and serves as a store of food for the developing EMBRYO.

yolk sac

Membranous, sac-like structure in the EGGS of most animals. It is attached directly to the ventral surface or gut of the developing EMBRYO in the eggs of birds, reptiles and some fish; it contains YOLK. The term also refers to an analogous, sac-like membrane that develops below the mammalian embryo. It contains no yolk but is connected to the UMBILICAL CORD.

yucca

Any member of the genus *Yucca*, comprising *c*.40 species of succulent plants native to the s United States, Mexico and the West Indies. Most species are stemless, forming a rosette of leaves, or have a trunk. The clusters of flowers are white, tinged with yellow or purple. The leaves are poisonous. Height: to 10m (33ft). Family Liliaceae; species include *Yucca aloifolia* and *Yucca brevifolia* (the JOSHUA TREE).

yuhina

Any of eight species of mostly dark brown BABBLERS found in India and Southeast Asia. The yuhina tends to be found in mountain forests and scrub, where it flits about actively after insects and berries. Length: *c*.15cm (*c*.6in). Family Timaliidae; genus *Yuhina*.

◀ **yam** Various species and varieties of yam are cultivated in tropical regions, where they are an important food crop. *Dioscorea alata*, shown here, is native to Southeast Asia and is one of the most important and widely cultivated species of yam. The tuber is edible cooked in a variety of ways. Starch extracted from the tuber is used as an ingredient in ice cream and confectionery.

Y

zander

Elongate, predatory fish found in oxygen-rich fresh waters of Central and E Europe. It is a type of PIKE PERCH. It is grey or green with dark markings. The zander is an important food fish. Length: to 1.3m (4.3ft). Family Percidae; species *Stizostedion lucioperca*.

zebra

Any of three species of strikingly patterned, striped, black-and-white, equine mammals of the grasslands of Africa; the stripes are arranged in various patterns, according to species. The zebra has long ears, a tufted tail and narrow hooves. Height: to 140cm (55in) at the shoulder. Family Equidae; genus *Equus*.

zebrafish

Any member of the genus *Danio*, a group of striped freshwater MINNOWS. *Danio rerio* is a major model species for the investigation of fundamental patterns and mechanisms of vertebrate development. Length: to 4cm (2in). Family Cyprinidae; genus *Danio*.

zinnia

Any member of the genus *Zinnia*, a group of annual and perennial herbs and shrubs from North, Central and South America. The zinnia plant has hairy stems, roughly hairy leaves, which clasp the stem, and solitary, daisy-like flowers. Many garden forms have been developed with single or double flowers of scarlet, crimson, rose, white or striped. Family Asteraceae; genus *Zinnia*.

zeolite

Group of alumino-silicates containing loosely held water that can be continuously expelled on heating. They also contain sodium, calcium or barium. Some members occur as fibrous aggregates, whereas others form robust, non-fibrous crystals. There are many zeolites varying in hardness from 3 to 5 and in specific gravity from 2 to 2.4. Zeolites include analcime ($NaAlSi_2O_6.H_2O$), stilbite ($NaCa_2(Al_5Si_{13}36.14H_2O$) and natrolite ($Na_2Al_2Si_3O_{10}.2H_2O$).

zircon

Orthosilicate mineral, zirconium silicate ($ZrSiO_4$), found in IGNEOUS and METAMORPHIC ROCKS and in sand and gravel. It displays tetragonal system prismatic crystals. Its colour is variable: it is usually light or reddish brown but can be colourless, grey, yellow or green. It is used widely as a gemstone because of its hardness and high refractive index. Hardness 7.5; r.d. 4.6.

zoisite

Orthosilicate mineral, hydrous calcium aluminum silicate ($Ca_2Al_3Si_3O_{12}(OH)$), found in METAMORPHIC ROCKS. It occurs as orthorhombic system prismatic crystals and masses. It can be glassy, transparent grey, white, brown, green or pink. A vivid blue variety from Tanzania, called tanzanite, is a gemstone. Hardness 6–6.5; r.d. 3.2.

zokor

Rodent from the grasslands of China. It has large front feet and very long claws. It digs burrows amongst roots and tubers, which it eats or stores underground for winter use. The zokor digs rapidly, leaving behind "mole-hills" on the surface. It rarely comes above ground, but it has not lost its eyes and ears as other underground-dwellers have done. Head-body length: 15–27cm (6–11in); tail: 3–7cm (1–3in). Family Myospalacinae; species *Myospalax fontanieri*.

zonation

See feature article

▲ **zebra** The plains zebra (also known as Burchell's zebra, *Equus burchelli*) is the most common of the zebra species. The subspecies shown here, Chapmann's zebra (*Equus burchelli chapmani*), is found on the savannas of S and SE Africa, where, like other zebras, it lives in permanent groups.

zoogeography (animal geography)

Study of the geographic distribution of animals. Formerly, the approach of this science was descriptive; today it utilizes various data, including isotope dating and ocean-bottom core sampling.

zoological garden

Place where animals are kept in captivity, originally for viewing but increasingly as places where endangered species may be conserved and bred in a protected environment. When numbers have been sufficiently increased they are reintroduced into the wild. Zoos often freeze ova, sperm and embryos for later use.

zoology

Study of animals; combined with BOTANY, it comprises the science of BIOLOGY. It is concerned with the structure of the animal and the way in which animals behave, reproduce and function, their evolution and their role in interactions with humankind and

◀ **zorilla** A zorilla (*Ictonyx striatus*) feeds on its rodent prey. If threatened, the zorilla will erect its dorsal hairs and raise and curve forward its tail. It will also make a high-pitched scream. Any creature that is hit by the zorilla's defensive anal secretion retains the foul odour for several days.

their environment. There are various subdivisions of the discipline, including: TAXONOMY; ECOLOGY; PALAEONTOLOGY; anatomy; and ZOOGEOGRAPHY. Anthropology is an extension of zoology. *See also* EMBRYOLOGY; GENETICS; MORPHOLOGY

zooplankton

Animal portion of the PLANKTON. It consists of a wide variety of microorganisms, such as COPEPOD and larval forms of higher animals. It is a central constituent of the oceans' FOOD CHAINS. There are few levels or areas of the ocean that have no zooplankton. *See also* PHYTOPLANKTON

zoospore

Asexual reproductive cell found in ALGAE and FUNGI. It swims using one or more flagella. *See also* ASEXUAL REPRODUCTION

zorapteran (angel insect)

Any member of the order Zoraptera, a group of minute, rarely seen insects that live in organic debris and sawdust. The scientific name means purely wingless but there are some winged forms. Zorapterans spin silken tunnels along the inside of wood. They feed mostly on mites, smaller insects and fungal spores. They are found in most regions, except Europe and Australia, living in colonies beneath the bark of rotting trees and in humus. Order Zoraptera.

zorilla (African polecat, striped polecat)

Small carnivore that inhabits semiarid areas of sub-Saharan Africa. It is strikingly marked with white and black bands along its body. It has long hair and a bushy tail. It is nocturnal and feeds on small animals and eggs. If disturbed the zorilla produces a very unpleasant secretion from its anal glands. Burrows, borrowed or self-made, are used to hide in by day and also to give birth to litters of two to three young. Head-body length: 28–38cm (11–15in); tail: 20–30cm (8–12in). Family Mustelidae; species *Ictonyx striatus*.

zucchini (courgette)

Cultivated variety of the VEGETABLE MARROW. It is widely grown as a greenhouse crop in temperate regions. It belongs to the CUCUMBER family, which includes a number of important food plants, such as GOURDS, MELONS, SQUASHES and PUMPKINS. Family Cucurbitaceae; cultivar of the species *Cucurbita pepo*.

zwitterion

IONS that are dipolar, that is they have a positive and a negative pole. In nature AMINO ACIDS form zwitterions when a hydrogen ion from the carboxyl group (COOH) is lost, making it negatively charged (COO−). The association of the hydrogen ion with the amino group on the same molecule makes it positive (NH+). Amino acids therefore exhibit both acidic and basic properties, that is they are amphoteric.

zygomycota

Phylum of the FUNGUS kingdom. Members of the group produce zygospores when SEXUAL REPRODUCTION by CONJUGATION takes place. They also reproduce asexually by means of SPORES, which are produced inside a SPORANGIUM. The HYPHAE are non-septate, that is they lack cell walls. Examples include *Mucor* and *Rhizopus*.

ZONATION

In ecology, occurrence of bands of characteristic FLORA and FAUNA in an area. Examples include the bands of different types of SEAWEED that occur progressively up a shore from the low-tide to high-tide levels. Species from the low-tide zone would dry out and die at the high-tide level, whereas high-tide species could not withstand prolonged immersion in seawater in the low-tide zone.

▲ As levels of rainfall, temperature and soil type vary within an area, different groups of plants will grow. Thus, different habitats are produced, which attract a variety of animals. This zonation effect is most marked in areas where conditions are changed by moving from one level to another. On a mountain, for example Mount Kilimanjaro (A), zones range from dry savanna (1) through rainforest (2), bamboo (3) and cloud forest (4) to reach an area below the snow line, where lobelias have evolved in isolation to giant proportion (5). These habitats arise because each level has a different amount of rain, a different temperature and will encourage a different group of animals. In (B) experiments have shown how quickly plants will adapt to different zones. California yarrow was grown at different altitudes, the higher the zone the shorter the stem that grew. When all the plants were replanted at sea level the difference in stem height was maintained.

zygote

In SEXUAL REPRODUCTION, a CELL formed by fusion of a male and a female GAMETE. It contains a DIPLOID number of CHROMOSOMES, half contributed by SPERM, half by the OVUM. Through successive CELL DIVISIONS, a zygote will develop into an EMBRYO.

Z

CHRONOLOGY

This chronology traces the history of science over thousands of years, from 10,000 BC to the present day. It is organized into five categories – food and farming, biology, chemistry, physics and medicine – in which the major discoveries and events are clearly summarized. The history of science and the people that shaped it can be followed easily through the centuries.

Dates are much more than isolated markers of events. Organized into a chronology, dates establish sequence and synchronicity. In creating this chronology of science, every care has been taken to use accurate and informative dates. It is impossible, however, to achieve "definitive" dates when referring to events that occurred many thousands of years ago. Virtually all dates before AD 1 are based on archaeology – the dating of objects dug from the ground. The most useful and widespread method of dating such material is by measuring the decay of the isotope carbon-14 (radiocarbon dating). This method is reliable but not strictly precise. Even when correlated with dendrochronology (tree-ring dating) radiocarbon dates are at best accurate to within 50–100 years, and the further back the method is applied, the wider the margin for error. To spare the reader any confusion between correlated and uncorrelated dates, we have often selected a single date, prefixed by the abbreviation *c.* (circa) to indicate a date-range. In more recent times, *c.* indicates a degree of uncertainty owing to the fact that definitive written records are rare.

PREHISTORY

15,000 mya (million years ago)
According to the Big Bang theory, the Universe is formed

4600 mya
The Earth is formed

3800 mya
Simple single-celled life appears

1200 mya
Complex single-celled plants and animals appear

600 mya
Multi-cellular plants and animals appear

560 mya
Beginning of Cambrian period of geological timescale, during which animals evolve eyes and jointed legs

400 mya
The first land plants and animals appear

220 mya
A massive extinction event wipes out 90% of species

65 mya
An extinction event, probably caused by an asteroid impact, kills the land-living dinosaurs

***c.*4 mya**
Australopithecines appear in s Africa

***c.*1.8 mya**
The most recent ice age starts; *Homo habilis* appears in SE Africa

***c.*1.5 mya**
Homo erectus appears in E Africa

***c.*250,000 BC**
Archaic *Homo sapiens* appears in E Africa

***c.*200,000 BC**
Homo neanderthalensis appears in Europe and Asia

***c.*150,000 BC**
Modern *Homo sapiens* appears in E Africa

***c.*55,000 BC**
Modern *Homo sapiens* moves into Europe and Australia

***c.*35,000 BC**
Neanderthals become extinct in Europe

FARMING AND FOOD	BIOLOGY	CHEMISTRY	PHYSICS	MEDICINE
	c.10,000 BC Dog is domesticated in Mesopotamia.			
	c.9000 BC Einkorn wheat is domesticated in Palestine; sheep and goats are domesticated in Persia (for food).			
c.7500 BC Beer is brewed in Mesopotamia.	**c.8000** Pumpkins and squashes are domesticated in Central America.			
	c.7500 BC Potatoes and chile peppers are domesticated in Peru.			
	c.7000 BC Water buffalo and chickens are domesticated in Asia; cattle are domesticated in Asia Minor.			
	c.6000 BC Durum wheat is domesticated in Asia Minor.			
	c.5000 BC Horse is domesticated (for food) in Russia and millet is domesticated in China.			
	c.4500 BC Guinea pig is domesticated in Peru (for food); maize is domesticated in Central America.			
c.4000 BC Primitive ox-drawn plough is used in China and later (c.3500 BC) in Sumeria.	**c.4000 BC** Pigs are domesticated in Southeast Asia.			
c.3500 BC Wine is made in the Middle East.	**c.3500 BC** Alpaca and llama are domesticated in Peru; donkeys are domesticated in Palestine.			
c.3000 BC Barley is grown as a main crop in Sumeria.	**c.3000 BC** Peanuts are domesticated in Peru; camels are domesticated in Arabia; wild boar are domesticated in Europe.			**c.3000 BC** Filling of teeth is practised in Sumeria.
c.2500 BC Bees are kept for honey in Egypt.	**c.2500 BC** Yak is domesticated in Tibet.			**c.2500 BC** Contraception is practised by the ancient Egyptians.
c.1600 BC Wooden ploughshare is invented in Mesopotamia; grape vines and olives are cultivated in Crete.				**c.1550 BC** Central control function of the brain is discovered by physicians in Egypt.
c.1500 BC Seed drill (a vertical tube with a funnel at the top) is invented in Sumeria.				
c.1100 BC Iron ploughshare is invented in the Middle East.				
	c.1000 BC Reindeer are domesticated in Siberia; oats are domesticated in Europe.	**c.600 BC** Three-element theory – that all matter consists of a combination of mist, earth and water – is introduced by Greek natural philosopher Thales of Miletus (c.620–c.555 BC).		**c. 535 BC** Human dissection (for medical study) is introduced by Greek physician Alcmaeon of Croton.
	c.520 BC Behaviour and structure of animals (using dissection) are studied by Greek physician Alcmaeon of Croton.	**c.530 BC** Fact that air is the primary substance is proposed by Greek natural philosopher Anaximenes of Miletus (d.c.500 BC).		
	c.450 BC Detailed studies of human anatomy are made by Greek physician Hippocrates of Kos.	**c.450 BC** Four-element theory – that all matter is made of a combination of earth, air, fire and water – is introduced by Greek natural philosopher Empedocles (d.c.430 BC).		**c.450 BC** Fact that disease has natural causes is recognized by Greek physician Hippocrates of Cos (d.c.485 BC).
350 BC Rice is cultivated in western Africa.	**c.350 BC** Animals and plants (about 500 known species) are classified into eight classes by the Greek philosopher Aristotle (384–322 BC).	**c.400 BC** Atomic theory – that all matter consists of atoms – is developed by Greek natural philosopher Democritus of Abdera (c.460–c.370 BC), probably based on previous (c.450 BC) ideas of Leucippus of Miletus.	**c.340 BC** Fact that heavier objects fall faster than lighter ones (which is incorrect) is proposed by Greek philosopher Strato of Lampsacus (d.c.270 BC).	
	c.340 BC Arteries and veins are distinguished by Greek physician Praxagoras of Cos (who thought that arteries carry air and veins carry blood from the liver).	**306 BC** Democritus' atomic theory gains support from Greek philosopher Epicurus (c.342–270 BC).		
290 BC Chest harness for horses is invented in China.	**c.300 BC** First detailed studies of plants (more than 550 species) are made by Greek natural philosopher Theophrastus of Eresus.	**c.270 BC** Five-element theory – that all matter is made of a combination of earth, fire, water, wood and metal – is introduced by Chinese philosopher Zou Yan.		**c.300 BC** First Greek treatise on medicine is written by Greek physician Diocles of Carystus.
				c.290 BC Human dissection to aid understanding how the body works is undertaken by Greek physician Herophilus of Alexandria (c.335–c.280 BC), who identifies the brain as the centre of thought and divides the nervous system into motor and sensory systems.
200 BC Archimedes' screw is used to pump water for irrigation.	**c.190 BC** Duodenum and prostate gland are discovered (and named) by Greek physician Herophilus of Chalcedon (c.330–260 BC).			
100 BC Oysters are raised (for food) in heated seawater tanks by the Romans near Naplestea; water wheels are used to drive mills for grinding grain in Albania.				

FARMING AND FOOD

AD 80 Chain pumps are used for lifting water for irrigation in China.

90 Fan-like winnowing machine is invented in China.

110 Hand-operated multi-tube seed drill is invented in China.

530 Water-powered machine for shaking and sifting flour is invented in China.

600 Windmills are used to grind grain in Iran.

630 Cotton (imported from the east) is grown in Arabia and, later (775), Spain.

700 Tea (for making a hot drink) is grown in China.

800 Open fields, using three-crop rotation, are used in Europe.

900 Wheeled ploughs are used in Europe.

1000 Coffee is used (initially as a medicine) in Arabia.

1100s Hunting for whales is begun in the Western Atlantic by Spanish fishermen.

1100 Wine is distilled to make brandy in Italy.

1275 A whisky distillery is built in Ireland.

BIOLOGY

AD c.40 Medicinal properties of 600 plants are described by Greek physician Pedanius Dioscorides of Anazarbus.

77 Encyclopedic 37-volume work Historia Naturalis (Natural History) is completed by Roman scholar Pliny the Elder (Gaius Plinius Secundus) (23–79).

c.100 Dried chrysanthemum flowers are used as an insecticide by Chinese farmers.

c.175 Principles of human anatomy and physiology are established by Greek physician Galen (c.130–201).

c.1260 Pulmonary circulation (of the blood, through the lungs) is discovered by Arab physician Ibn al-Nafis (1200–88), although the discovery is forgotten until re-made in 1546.

1333 Botanical garden is established in Venice, Italy.

CHEMISTRY

AD 250 Mica is used for making windows in China.

750 Preparation of several acids and their salts, including ethanoic (acetic) acid, is described by Arab alchemist Geber (Jabir ibn-Hayyan) (c.721–c.815).

c.880 Ethanol (alcohol) is distilled from wine (by alchemists) in Arabia, and later (1150) in Europe; its preparation is described (1300) by Spanish alchemist Arnau de Villanova (c.1235–1312).

c.1242 Gunpowder is introduced into Europe from the East.

c.1250 Semimetallic element arsenic (symbol As) is probably discovered by German scholar Albertus Magnus (Albert von Bollstädt) (1193–1280).

c.1300 Sulphuric acid is first described by Spanish alchemist known as the False Geber, later (1775) rediscovered by British chemist Joseph Priestley (1733–1804).

1300 Alum is discovered in Rocca, Spain, and later (1470) in Tuscany, Italy.

1315 Ammonia is described by Spanish philosopher Raymond Lully (Ramón Lull) (c.1235–1315).

PHYSICS

1010 How lenses work is described by Arab mathematician Alhazen (Abu al-Hassan ibn al Haytham) (c.965–1039).

1180 Magnetic compass is first described in Europe by English scholar Alexander Neckam (1157–1217), although already known for two centuries in China.

1269 Properties of magnetic poles are described by French scholar Petrus Peregrinus (b.c.1240).

1275 Scientific explanation of the rainbow (in terms of reflections within a raindrop) is given by German scientist and ecclesiastic Theodoric of Freiburg (c.1250–1310). Much later (1611), a similar explanation is offered by Italian ecclesiastic Marco de Dominis (1566–1624).

MEDICINE

AD c.30 First Latin treatise on medicine is written by Roman author Aulus Celsus; 500 years later his name was partly adopted by Swiss alchemist and physician Paracelsus, real name Theophrastus von Hohenheim (c.1493–1541).

c.70 Use of liver from a mad dog to protect against rabies is suggested by Roman scholar Pliny the Elder (Gaius Plinius Secundus) (23–79).

116 Major work on gynaecology is published by Greek physician Soranus of Ephesus, who practised in Alexandria.

c.175 The use of the human pulse as an aid to medical diagnosis is introduced by Claudius Galenus (Galen) c.130–201).

c.640 Symptoms of diabetes are noted by Chinese physician Chen Ch'uan.

c.650 Symptoms of lead poisoning are described by Greek physician Paul of Aegina.

c.900 Measles and smallpox are recognized as different diseases by Persian-born Arab physician Rhazes (850–923).

c.1000 The Canon of Medicine, a five-volume seminal book on general medicine, is written by Arab physician Avicenna (ibn-Sina) (980–1037).

1067 Hospital for lepers is founded by Spanish soldier El Cid (Ruy Diaz de Vivar) (c.1043–99).

1150 Bloodletting as a treatment for disease is advocated by Arab physician Avenzoar (abu-Mervan ibn-Zuhr) (c.1091–1162).

1170 First European textbook on surgery, Practica chirurgiae, is written by Roger of Solerno.

1320 Benefit of stitching wounds is discovered by French physician Henri de Mondeville (1260–1320).

1340 Black Death (plague) breaks out in Asia; by 1352 it reaches northern Europe.

AD 1
250
500
600
700
800
900
1000
1050
1100
1150
1200
1250
1300

FARMING AND FOOD	BIOLOGY	CHEMISTRY	PHYSICS	MEDICINE

1400

1400 Coffee is made into a beverage in Ethiopia.

1400 Beer is imported into England from Belgium.

1410 Drift nets are used by Dutch fisherman, who also use salt to preserve the catch.

1450

1495 Whiskey is distilled in Scotland by Friar John Cor.

1414 Influenza is first described (in France).

1490 Capillary action is discovered by Italian scientist and artist Leonardo da Vinci (1452–1519).

1493 Medicinal use of tobacco (by Native Americans) is recorded by Italian explorer Christopher Columbus (1451–1506).

1493 Syphilis occurs in Spain and later (1495) Italy (following the return of Christopher Columbus and his sailors from North America); it is described and named by Italian physician Fracastorius (Girolamo Fracastoro) (1478–1553), who used mercury as a treatment.

1497 Surgical treatment of gunshot wounds is introduced by Hieronymus Brunschwygk (c.1452–1512).

1500

c.1500 Human anatomy is studied by Italian artist Leonardo da Vinci (1452–1519).

1517 Fact that fossils are the remains of once-living organisms is proposed by Italian scientist Girolamo Fracastoro (c.1478–1553).

1517 Homologies between bones in various types of vertebrates are discovered by French naturalist Pierre Belon (1517–64).

1538 Optic nerves are discovered by Italian anatomist and surgeon Constanzo Varoli (c.1543–75).

1546 Lesser (pulmonary) circulation of the blood (from the heart to the lungs and back) is rediscovered by Italian anatomist Realdo Colombo (c.1516–59) and, independently (c.1553), Spanish biologist Michael Servetus (1511–53).

1546 Term fossil is introduced by German mineralogist Georgius Agricola (Georg Bauer) (1494–1555).

1504 Iron prosthetic hand is made in Germany, for mercenary knight Götz von Berlichingen (1480–1562).

1518 Smallpox occurs in the Americas, later (1520) decimating the Aztecs.

1530 Laudanum (tincture of opium) is first used in treatment (and named) by Swiss physician and alchemist Paracelsus (Theophrastus von Hohenheim) (1493–1541).

1542 Appendicitis is first described by French physician Jean Fernel (1497–1558).

1543 Eight-volume Fabrica (in full De humani corporis fabrica), the first book on human anatomy based entirely on observation, is published by Flemish anatomist Andreas Vesalius (Andreas van Wesele) (1514–64).

1546 Fact that microbes, or germs, cause disease is proposed by Italian physician Fracastorius (Girolamo Fracastoro) (1478–1553).

1550

1565 First potatoes are imported into Spain from South America.

1566 First seed drill in Europe is invented by Italian agriculturalist Camillo Torello.

1575 Commercial production of gin is introduced by Dutch distiller Lucas Bols.

1552 Eustachian tube (connecting the middle ear to the throat) is discovered by Italian anatomist Bartolommeo Eustachio (c.1520–74), although it had earlier (1546) been described by Italian physician Giovanni Ingrassia (1510–80) and much earlier (c.520 BC) by Greek physician Alcmaeon of Crotona.

c.1555 Fallopian tubes (connecting the ovaries to the uterus) are discovered by Italian anatomist Gabriele Falloppio (1523–62).

1558 Historia Animalium, the basis of modern zoology, is completed by Swiss naturalist Konrad non Gestner (1516–65).

1573 Pons Varolii (a nerve tract in the brain) is discovered by Italian anatomist Constanzo Varolio (c.1543–75).

1574 Valves in veins are discovered by Italian anatomist Hieronymus Fabricius ab Aquapendente (Girolamo Fabrici) (1537–1619).

1580 Existence of male and female flowers (on different plants) is discovered by Italian botanist Prospero Alpini (1553–1616).

1583 Method of classifying plants by their structure is introduced by Italian botanist Andrea Cesalpino (1519–1603).

1592 First European description of the coffee plant is given by Italian botanist Prospero Alpini (1553–1617).

1599 First comprehensive book on zoology is written by Italian naturalist Ulisse Aldrovani (1522–1605).

1597 Preparation of hydrochloric acid is first described by German alchemist Andreas Libavius (Andreas Libau) (c.1540–1616), later (1775) rediscovered by British chemist Joseph Priestley (1733–1804).

1576 Magnetic dip is discovered by English navigator Robert Norman (b.c.1560).

1577 Principle of the siphon is discovered by Scottish mathematician William Wellwood (d.c.1622).

1586 Fact that different weights dropped from the same height fall at the same rate (in vacuum) is demonstrated by Dutch mathematician Stevinus (Simon Stevin) (1548–1620), and later (after 1610) taken up by Galileo Galilei (1564–1642).

1550 Ligature for stopping arterial bleeding during surgery is introduced by French surgeon Ambroise Paré (c.1510–90), much later (1674) extended to the exterior of a limb as the tourniquet by his compatriot Morel.

1597 Rhinoplasty (plastic surgery to reconstruct the nose by grafting tissue) is perfected by Italian surgeon Gaspare Taglacozzi (1545–99).

FARMING AND FOOD

1610 First tea is imported into Europe from Asia.

1635 Iron cooking range is patented by British inventor John Sibthorpe.

1666 Cheddar cheese is invented in England.

1668 Champagne is invented by French Benedictine monk Dom Pierre Pérignon (1638–1715).

BIOLOGY

1622 Lacteal vessels are discovered (in a dog) by Italian anatomist and physician Gasparo Aseli (Gaspar Asellius) (1581–1626).

1627 Aurochs, the ancestor of domestic cattle, becomes extinct.

1628 Circulation of the blood, with the heart as a pump, is discovered by English physician William Harvey (1578–1657).

1641 African chimpanzee is first described by Dutch anatomist Claes Tulp (Nicolaes Pieterszoon) (c.1593–c.1674).

1642 Pancreatic duct, which carries digestive juices from the pancreas to the common bile duct (and thence to the duodenum) is discovered by German anatomist Georg Wirsung (1600–43).

1647 Thoracic duct (which carries lymph from the legs, abdomen and left side of the body) is discovered by French anatomist Jean Pecquet (1622–74).

1649 Capillary blood vessels linking arteries and veins are discovered by English physician Henry Power (1623–68).

1653 Lymphatic vessels are discovered by Swedish naturalist Olof Rudbeck (1630–1702) and, independently, Danish physician Thomas Bartholin (1616–80).

1658 Erythrocytes (red blood cells) are discovered by Dutch naturalist Jan Swammerdam (1637–80).

1660 Blind spot (where the optic nerve joins the retina of the eye) is discovered by French physicist Edmé Marriotte (c.1620–84).

1661 Blood capillaries linking the arterial and venous circulation in the lungs are discovered by Italian anatomist Marcello Malpighi (1628–94).

1662 Parotid duct (Stensen's duct), which carries saliva from the parotid gland below the ear into the mouth, is discovered by Danish physician Nils Stensen (1638–86).

1664 Circle of Willis (blood vessels in the brain) are discovered by English physician Thomas Willis (1621–75).

1665 Word "cell" is coined, based on his microscope studies of plants, by English scientist Robert Hooke (1635–1703).

1667 Fact that the essential feature of respiration is the modification of blood in the lungs is demonstrated by English scientist Robert Hooke (1635–1703).

1668 Spontaneous generation (of living organisms) is first disproved by Italian physician Francesco Redi (1626–97).

1669 Metamorphosis in insects is discovered by Dutch naturalist Jan Swammerdam (1637–80).

1672 Human ovaries are discovered by Dutch naturalist Jan Swammerdam (1637–80).

1672 Graafian follicle (surrounding the developing egg in the ovary) is discovered by Dutch anatomist Reinier de Graaf (1641–73).

CHEMISTRY

1620 Word "gas" (from "chaos") is coined by Flemish alchemist Jan (Jean, Johannes) van Helmont (1577–1644).

c.1625 Method of making hydrochloric acid from sodium chloride (common salt) and sulphuric acid is discovered by German chemist Johann Glauber (1604–68), who also produced sodium sulphate, known as Glauber's salt.

1644 Water glass is discovered by German chemist Johann Glauber (1604–68).

1649 Atomic theory is proposed by French philosopher Pierre Gassendi (1592–1655), after studying the works of the Greek Epicurus (c.342–270 BC) who in turn adopted the idea from Democritus.

c.1650 Coal gas (made by distilling coal) is discovered by English scientist John Clayton.

1661 Definition of an element (as a substance that cannot be broken down into simpler substances) is given in his book The Sceptical Chemist by Irish scientist Robert Boyle (1627–1691).

1669 Nonmetallic element phosphorus (symbol P) is discovered by German alchemist Hennig Brand (c.1630–c.92), later (1680) described independently by Irish scientist Robert Boyle (1627–91).

1677 Ammonia solution is prepared by German alchemist Johann Kunckel (c.1630–1702).

1695 Epsom salts (magnesium sulphate) are discovered in natural mineral water by English physician and botanist Nehemiah Grew (1641–1712).

1697 Phlogiston theory (that all flammable substances contain phlogiston, which is released on burning) is proposed by German chemist Georg Stahl (1660–1734), developed from the ideas of his tutor Johann Becher (1635–81).

PHYSICS

1600 Magnetic properties of the Earth are explained by English physician William Gilbert (1544–1603).

1602 Constancy of the period of a swinging pendulum is discovered by Italian scientist Galileo Galilei (1564–1642).

c.1610 Law of falling bodies (that all objects fall to Earth at the same speed) is proposed by Italian scientist Galileo Galilei (1564–1642), although not published until 1638.

1621 Snell's law, or law of refraction (in modern form that, during refraction of light by a transparent medium, the ratio of the sines of the angles of incidence and refraction is a constant equal to the refractive index of the medium), is discovered by Dutch scientist Willebrod van Roijen Snell (or Snellus) (1591–1626).

1635 Gradual shift in the position of the north magnetic pole is discovered by English astronomer Henry Gellibrand (1597–1636).

c.1640 Fermat's principle (that light travels the shortest path between two points, i.e. in straight lines) is discovered by French mathematician Pierre de Fermat (1601–65).

1645 Torricellian vacuum (in the space above a column of mercury) is discovered by Italian physicist Evangelista Torricelli (1608–47).

1647 Pascal's law or principle (that external pressure on a liquid is transmitted equally in all directions) is discovered by French scientist Blaise Pascal (1623–62).

1650 Fact that sound will not travel in a vacuum is discovered by German scientist Athanasius Kircher (1601–80), later (1705) elaborated by English physicist Francis Hawksbee (or Hauksbee) (c.1670–c.1713).

1662 Boyle's law (that the pressure of a gas is inversely proportional to its volume, at constant temperature) is formulated by Irish scientist Robert Boyle (1627–91), and later (1676) independently discovered by French physicist Edme Mariotte (1620–84) – hence the alternative name Mariotte's law.

c.1665 Law of gravity is formulated by English scientist Isaac Newton (1642–1727).

1665 Wave theory of light is proposed by English scientist Robert Hooke (1635–1703).

1665 Diffraction of light is discovered by Italian physicist Francesco Grimaldi (1618–63).

1668 Principle of conservation of momentum is discovered by English mathematician John Wallis (1616–1703).

1669 Double refraction of light (by a crystal of Iceland spar) is discovered by Danish physician Erasmus Bartholin (1625–98).

1671 Ability of a glass prism to disperse white light into a spectrum is discovered by English scientist Isaac Newton (1642–1727).

1675 Corpuscular theory of light (that light consists of a stream of particles) is proposed by English scientist Isaac Newton (1642–1727).

1676 Finite speed of light is discovered by Danish astronomer Ole Römer (1644–1710).

1678 Hooke's law (that in a stretched elastic solid stress is proportional to strain) is discovered by English scientist Robert Hooke (1635–1703).

MEDICINE

1645 Clinical description of rickets is given by English physician Daniel Whistler (1619–84) and later (1650), independently, by his compatriot anatomist Francis Glisson (1597–1677).

1658 Fact that apoplexy (stroke) is caused by a brain haemorrhage is discovered by Swiss pathologist Johann Wepfer (1620–1695).

1659 Symptoms and progress of typhoid fever are first described by English physician Thomas Willis (1621–75).

c.1660 Laudanum (tincture of opium) is rediscovered by English physician Thomas Sydenham (1624–89).

1666 Blood transfusion (between two dogs) is first demonstrated by English physician Richard Lower (1631–91); later (1667) transfusion from a sheep to a boy is made by French physician Jean Denis (or Denys) (d.1704).

1666 Use of iron to treat anaemia and cinchona bark (containing quinine) for malaria are discovered by English physician Thomas Sydenham (1624–89).

1670 Fact that the urine of a diabetic contains sugar (glucose) is discovered by English physician Thomas Willis (1621–75), although this was also known to the ancients.

1677 Peyer's patches (lymphatic glands in the small intestine) are discovered by Swiss anatomist Johann Peyer (1653–1712).

1683 Clinical description of gout is given by English physician Thomas Sydenham (1624–89).

c.1695 Bartholin's glands (greater vestibular glands in the vagina) are discovered by Danish physician Kasper Bartholin Jr (1655–1738).

FARMING AND FOOD	BIOLOGY	CHEMISTRY	PHYSICS	MEDICINE
	1672 Studies of chick embryos by Italian anatomist Marcello Malphigi (1628–94) establishes the science of embryology.		**1678** Wave theory of light is proposed by Dutch physicist Christiaan Huygens (1629–95).	
	1677 Human sperm are discovered by Dutch scientist Anton van Leeuwenhoek (1632–1723), who called them "human larvae".		**1684** Law of universal gravitation (which states that the gravitational force of attraction between any two objects is proportional to the product of their masses divided by the square of the distance between them) is finalized by English scientist Isaac Newton (1642–1727).	
	1680 Bacteria are discovered by Dutch scientist Anton van Leeuwenhoek (1632–1723), using a microscope of his own invention.		**1685** Concept of centre of gravity (mass) – that an object behaves as if all of its mass is concentrated at its centre – is proposed by English scientist Isaac Newton (1642–1727).	
	1681 Dodo becomes extinct on the island of Mauritius.		**1687** Principia Mathematica, summarizing many original ideas in mathematics and physics (including the laws of motion and the theory of gravitation), is published by English scientist Isaac Newton (1642–1727).	
	1682 Male and female parts of a flower are discovered by English botanist Nehemiah Grew (1641–1712), later (1694) confirmed by German botanist Rudolf Camerarius (1665–1721).		**1690** Huygen's principle (that every point on a wavefront can act as a source of secondary waves) is discovered by Dutch physicist Christiaan Huygens (1629–95).	
	c.1690 Plants are divided into monocotyledons and dicotyledons by English naturalist John Ray (1627–1705).		**1699** Expansion of gases – specifically that all gases increase in volume by the same amount for the same rise in temperature – is discovered by French physicist Guillaume Amontons (1663–1705).	
	1690 Angiosperms are defined by Paul Hermann.			
	1691 Haversian canals (in bone) are discovered by English physician Clopton Havers (c.1655–1702).			
1700				
1701 Mechanical seed drill and horse-drawn hoe are invented by British agricultural engineer Jethro Tull (1674–1741).	**1711** Fact that corals are animals (not plants, as previously thought) is discovered by Italian naturalist Luigi Marsigli (1658–1730).	**1701** Boric acid (boracic acid) is discovered by Dutch chemist Willem Homberg (1652–1715).	**1701** Term "acoustics" is coined by French physicist Joseph Sauveur (1653–1716).	**1701** Vaccination of children with smallpox (in an attempt to prevent the disease in later life) is performed by Italian physician Giacomo Pylarini (1659–1715); the practice is already carried out in Turkey (and elsewhere) and introduced into England (1714) by John Woodward and, independently, Mary Wortley (1689–1762).
1701 Nougat is invented at Montelimar, France.		**1722** Role of carbon in the hardness of steel is discovered by French physicist René Réaumur (1683–1757).	**1709** Electrical discharges in low-pressure air are described by English physicist Francis Hawksbee (or Hauksbee) (c.1670–c.1713), who in the same year studied capillarity in narrow glass tubes.	
1715 Method of producing cognac commercially is invented by Jersey-born Jean Martell.				**1702** Cowper's glands (bulboutherial glands at the base of the penis) are discovered by English surgeon William Cowper (1666–1709).
				1721 Vaccination against smallpox is introduced (in Boston, USA) by US physician Zabdiel Boylston (1679–1766).
1720				
	1734 Science of entomology is established by French scientist René Réaumur (1683–1757) in his book in insects.	**1727** Fact that some silver salts turn black on exposure to light – a phenomenon that was to become the key to photography – is discovered by German chemist Johann Schulze.	**1729** Difference between electrical insulators and conductors is discovered by English scientist Stephen Gray (1696–1736).	**1726** First blood pressure measurement (of a horse) is made by English scientist Stephen Hales (1677–1761).
	1735 Binomial classification of plants is introduced by Swedish botanist Carolus Linnaeus (Carl von Linné) (1707–78) in his book Systema Naturae, thus establishing the science of taxonomy.	**1730** Ethoxyethane is discovered by German chemist Frobenius.	**1733** Existence of two types of static electricity (positive and negative) is discovered by French physicist Charles du Fay (1698–1739).	**1730** Tracheostomy (for treating diphtheria) is first performed by Scottish physician George Martine (1702–41); it is later (1825) used routinely by French physician Pierre Bretonneau (1771–1862).
		1732 Gold-coloured copper-zinc alloy (for making watches) is invented by English clockmaker Christopher Pinchbeck (c.1670–1732).	**1738** Kinetic theory of gases is proposed by Swiss mathematician Daniel Bernoulli (1700–1782).	**1732** Sedative effect of ipecac and opium mixture (Dover's powder) is discovered by English naval officer and physician Thomas Dover (1660–1743).
		1736 Potassium and sodium salts are distinguished by French chemist Henri Duhamel du Monceau (1700–82).		**1736** Scarlet fever is first described by US physician William Douglass.
		1737 Metallic element cobalt (symbol Co) is discovered by Swedish chemist Georg Brandt (1694–1768).		**1738** Caesarian section to deliver a baby is performed by Irish midwife Mary Donally (although the procedure was first described in 1500).
1740				
1741 Artificial mineral water, made by aerating spring water with carbon dioxide gas, is made by British physician William Brownrigg (1711–1800); commercial production of soda water begins later (1767) by Richard Bewley, with the soda siphon invented (1813) by Charles Plinth; fruit-flavoured carbonated drinks are introduced (1807) in the USA by Townsend Speakman; tonic water is patented (1858) by Englishman Erasmus Bond.	**1740** Parthenogenesis (reproduction by means of unfertilized eggs) is discovered in aphids by Swiss naturalist Charles Bonnet (1720–93).	**c.1740** Curare is discovered by French chemist Marie de Lacondamine (1701–74).	**1742** Celsius temperature scale is devised by Swedish astronomer Anders Celsius (1701–44).	**1747** Value of citrus fruits in combating scurvy is discovered by Scottish physician James Lind (1716–94) and later (1795) confined to lime juice by British physician Gilbert Blane (1749–1834).
	1740 Freshwater hydra is discovered by Swiss naturalist Abraham Trembley (1710–84), who later (1744) discovers their ability to regenerate tissue.	**1741** Platinum (symbol Pt) is identified as an element by British chemist William Brownrigg (1711–1800), although known 200 years previously as the native metal in Spain and described in 1557 by the Italian physician Julius Scaliger (1484–1558); it is later (1748) also described by Spanish scientist and soldier Antonio de Ulloa (1716–95).	**1746** Leyden jar (the original electrical condenser) is discovered independently by Dutch physicist Pieter van Musschenbroek (1692–1761) and Polish cleric Ewald von Kleist.	**1748** Clinical description of diphtheria is given by British physician John Fothergill (1712–80).
1747 Process for extracting sugar from sugar beet is invented by German chemist Andreas Marggraf (1709–82).	**1751** Reflex response (of contraction of the pupil when light is shone into the eye) is discovered by Scottish physician Robert Whytt (1714–66).		**1752** Electrical nature of lightning is discovered by US scientist and politician Benjamin Franklin (1706–90).	**1752** Role of gastric juices in digestion is discovered by French scientist René de Réaumur (1683–1757).
1750 Incubator for chickens' eggs is invented by French physicist René Réaumur (1683–1757); later (1609) reinvented in England by Dutch engineer Cornelis van Drebbel (1572–1634).		**1746** Metallic element zinc (symbol Zn), which has been known since antiquity in the Orient and described by the Swiss alchemist Paracelsus (1493–1541), is rediscovered by German chemist Andreas Marggraf (1709–82).	**1758** Method of making achromatic lenses (by using a combination of crown and flint glass) is discovered by English optician John Dolland (1706–61) and his son Peter (1730–1820), although the principle had earlier (1733) been discovered independently by English scientist Chester Hall (1703–71).	**1756** Method of taking a mould of a patient's mouth for making false teeth is introduced by German dentist Philipp Pfaff (1715–67).

FARMING AND FOOD

1750 Plain chocolate bars are produced by British physician and typefounder Joseph Fry (1728–87); eating chocolate is later (1819) popularized in Switzerland by François Cailler.

1756 Mayonnaise is invented by French nobleman Louis de Richelieu (1696–1788).

1760 Soft liquorice candy (Pontefract cake) is invented by British confectioner George Dunhill.

1762 Sandwiches are invented by John Montagu, 4th Earl of Sandwich (1718–92) (who also gave his name to the Sandwich Islands, Hawaii).

1765 Preserving food using a hermetic seal is proposed by Italian biologist Lazzaro Spallanzani (1729–99).

1768 Mechanical flail for dressing (threshing) grain is invented by Scottish engineer Andrew Maikle (1719–1811), who later (1788) patented an efficient drum threshing machine.

BIOLOGY

1760s New breeds of farm animals, such as Longhorn cattle and Leicestershire sheep, result from selective breeding experiments of British agriculturist Robert Bakewell (1725–95).

1765 Fact that heat and hermetical sealing (to achieve proper sterilization) prevents the growth of microbes is discovered by Italian biologist Lazzaro Spallanzani (1729–99).

1766 Fact that nerve impulses control muscle action is discovered by Swiss physiologist Albrecht von Haller (1708–77).

1770 Fact that phosphorus is an essential constituent of bone is discovered by Swedish mineralogist Johann Gahn (1745–1818).

1771 Blood-clotting protein fibrin is discovered by British physician William Henson.

1772 Labyrinth of the ear is discovered by Italian anatomist Antonio Scarpa (1747–1832).

1773 Digestive action of saliva is discovered by Italian biologist Lazzaro Spallanzani (1729–99).

1779 Plant respiration and photosynthesis are discovered by Dutch scientist Jan Ingenhousz (1730–99), later (1782) demonstrated by Swiss botanist Jean Senebier (1742–1809).

CHEMISTRY

1747 Sugar (sucrose) is discovered in beet by German chemist Andreas Marggraf (1709–82).

1751 Metallic element nickel (symbol Ni) is discovered by Swedish industrial chemist Alex Cronstedt (1722–65) and later (1775) isolated in pure form by his compatriot Torbern Bergman (1735–84).

1753 Metallic element bismuth (symbol Bi), probably discovered as its compounds by Valentine in 1450, is isolated and shown to be different from lead by French chemist Claud Geoffroy.

1755 Metallic element magnesium (symbol Mg) is identified by Scottish chemist Joseph Black (1728–99), and later (1808) isolated by British chemist Humphry Davy (1778–1829).

1758 Flame tests (for identifying metallic elements) are introduced by German chemist Andreas Marggraf (1709–82).

1766 Gaseous element hydrogen (symbol H) is discovered by British chemist Henry Cavendish (1731–1810), who called it "inflammable air".

1769 Tartaric acid is discovered by Swedish chemist Karl Scheele (1742–1786).

1770 Phosphorus in bones is discovered by Karl Scheele and mineralogist Johan Gahn (1745–1818).

1770 Mercury fulminate, later used as a detonator for firearms, is discovered by German chemist Johann Kunckel (1630–1703).

1771 Gaseous element fluorine (symbol F) is discovered by Karl Scheele and later (1886) isolated by French chemist Ferdinand Moissan (1852–1907).

1771 Picric acid, originally used as a yellow dye and not an explosive, is discovered by French chemist Pierre Woulfe.

1772 Gaseous element oxygen (symbol O) is discovered by Karl Scheele, although his discovery was not announced until 1777. It was independently discovered in 1774 by British chemist Joseph Priestley (1733–1804) and named in 1777 by French chemist Antoine Lavoisier (1749–94). As early as 1727 it was observed in plant respiration, but not recognized as an element, by English physiologist Stephen Hales (1677–1761).

1772 Gaseous element nitrogen (symbol N) is discovered by Scottish physician Daniel Rutherford (1749–1819) and later (1790) named by French chemist Jean Chaptal (1756–1832).

1772 Fact that diamond is pure carbon is discovered by Antoine Lavoisier, who obtains carbon dioxide by burning a diamond.

1772 Rubber is so named by Joseph Priestley, because it rubs out (erases) pencil marks.

1774 Gaseous element chlorine (symbol Cl) is discovered by Karl Scheele, and later (1810) shown to be an element and named by British chemist Humphry Davy (1778–1829).

1774 Ammonia gas is discovered by Joseph Priestley.

1774 Methanoic (formic) acid is discovered by Karl Scheele.

1774 Metallic element manganese (symbol Mn) is discovered by Swedish mineralogist Johan Gahn (1745–1818).

1775 Pure nickel is prepared by Swedish chemist Torbern Bergman (1735–84).

1776 Uric acid is discovered by Karl Scheele and, independently, by his compatriot Torbern Bergman.

PHYSICS

1760 Lambert's laws (concerning luminance and luminous intensity) are discovered by German scientist Johann Lambert (1728–77).

1762 Compressibility of water is discovered by British physicist John Canton (1718–72).

1763 Latent heat (the heat needed to produce a change of state from a solid to a liquid or a liquid to a vapour) is discovered by Scottish physicist Joseph Black (1728–99).

1772 Latent heat of fusion (of ice) is discovered by Swedish physicist Johan Wilcke (1732–96).

MEDICINE

1760 Extrauterine pregnancy is first discovered by US physician John Bard (1716–99).

1761 Technique of percussion of the chest as an aid to diagnosis (ausculation) is discovered by Austrian physician Leopold Auenbrugger (1722–1809); it is later pioneered by French physician Jean Corvisart (1755–1821).

1768 Heart condition angina pectoris is described by British physician William Heberden (1710–1801).

1768 Experimental pathology is established by Scottish surgeon John Hunter (1728–93).

1775 Fact that repeated exposure to soot can cause cancer of the scrotum in chimney sweeps is discovered by British physician Percivall Pott (1714–88).

1776 Trigeminal neuralgia (Fothergill's disease) is discovered by British physician John Fothergill (1712–80).

FARMING AND FOOD

1783 Mechanized flour mill is built by US inventor Oliver Evans (1775–1819).

1785 Cast-iron ploughshare is invented by British engineer Robert Ransome (1753–1830).

1786 Gypsum-based fertilizer is invented by US farmer John Binns (c.1761–1813).

1789 Bourbon whisky is first made (from maize) in Kentucky by clergyman Elijah Craig.

1793 Cotton gin is invented by US engineer Eli Whitney (1765–1825).

1797 First cast-iron plough in the USA is patented by US inventor Charles Newbold.

1799 Wool-carding machine is invented in Belgium by British engineer William Cockerill (1759–1832).

BIOLOGY

1780 Artificial insemination is discovered (using dogs) by Italian biologist Lazaro Spallanzani (1729–99).

1790 Shorthorn cattle are created by selective breeding by British farmers Robert (1749–1820) and Charles (1750–1836) Colling.

1793 Role of insects in pollination of flowers is discovered by German botanist Christian Sprengel (1750–1816).

1793 Fact that fossils are the remains of once-living organisms is proposed by French naturalist Jean Baptiste Lamarck (1744–1829).

1793 Dichogamy (the maturing of male and female parts of the same flower at different times to prevent self-fertilization) is discovered by German botanist Christian Sprengel (1750–1816).

1794 Zoonomia (proposing a Lamarckian-type theory of evolution) is published by British physician Erasmus Darwin (1731–1802).

1795 Fossil bones (Mosasaurus, found in the Netherlands in 1766) are identified as being those of an extinct reptile by French anatomist Georges Cuvier (1769–1832), who went on to found the science of palaeontology.

1798 Correlation between food supply and human population growth is discovered (and published anonymously) by British economist Thomas Malthus (1766–1834).

CHEMISTRY

1780 Lactic acid and casein are discovered by Swedish chemist Karl Scheele (1742–86).

1781 Water is shown to be a compound by British scientist Henry Cavendish (1731–1810).

1781 Metallic element tungsten (symbol W) is discovered by Karl Scheele, who called it wolfram. It is later (1783) isolated by Spanish mineralogists Don Juan and Don Fausto d'Elhuyer (1755–1833).

1781 Metallic element molybdenum (symbol Mo) is isolated by Swedish chemist Peter Hjelm (1760–1813), following its discovery in 1778 by his compatriots Torbern Bergman and Karl Scheele, who named it.

1782 Metallic element tellurium (symbol Te) is discovered by Austrian chemist Franz Müller (1740–1825) who sent a sample for confirmation to German chemist Martin Klaproth (1743–1817), who named it.

1782 Hydrocyanic (prussic) acid is discovered by Karl Scheele, and its composition later (1787) found by French chemist Claude Berthollet (1748–1822), who in the same year also determined the compositions of ammonia and hydrogen sulphide.

1783 Fact that the atmosphere has a constant composition (at different places) is discovered by Henry Cavendish.

1783 Citric acid and glycerol (glycerine) are discovered by Karl Scheele.

1784 Bleaching action of chlorine is discovered by Claude Berthollet, who produces a chemical bleach called Eau de Javelle.

1785 Fact that water is a compound (of hydrogen and oxygen) is discovered by Henry Cavendish.

1789 Metallic element zirconium (symbol Zr) is discovered in the mineral zirconia (its oxide) by German chemist Martin Klaproth (1743–1817), later (1824) isolated by Swedish chemist Jöns Berzelius (1779–1848).

1789 Radioactive element uranium (symbol U) is discovered (as its oxide) by Martin Klaproth, later (1841) isolated by French chemist Eugène Péligot (1811–90).

1791 Mineral dolomite (calcium magnesium carbonate) is discovered by French mineralogist Déodat de Dolmieu (1750–1801), who gave his name to both the mineral and the mountains where it was first found.

1791 Metallic element titanium (symbol Ti) is discovered by British amateur mineralogist (and minister) William Gregor (1761–1817), who called it "menanchinite"; the element is later (1795) named titanium by Martin Klaproth.

1794 Metallic element yttrium (symbol Y) is identified by Finnish chemist Johan Gadolin, later (1828) isolated by German chemist Friedrich Wöhler (1800–82).

1796 Carbon disulphide is discovered by German chemist Wilhelm Lampadius (1772–1842); its composition is later (1802) determined by French scientists Charles Désormes (1777–1862) and Nicolas Clément (1779–1841).

1797 Metallic element chromium (symbol Cr) is discovered by Martin Klaproth and, independently, by French chemist Louis Vauquelin (1763–1829), who named it.

1798 Liquid ammonia, the first gas to be liquefied by cooling alone, is produced by French chemist Louis Guyton de Morveau (1737–1816).

PHYSICS

1781 Concept of specific heat is proposed by German physicist Johan Wilcke (1732–96).

1784 Sulphur dioxide is liquefied (the first gas to be liquefied) by French mathematician and physicist Gaspard Monge (1746–1818).

1785 Coulomb's law (that the force of attraction or repulsion between two electric charges is proportional to the product of their magnitudes divided by the square of the distance between them) is formulated by French physicist Charles de Coulomb (1736–1806).

c.1787 Charles' law (that the volume of an ideal gas increases by 1/273 for each Celsius degree rise in temperature) is discovered by French physicist Jacques Charles (1746–1823), and is later (1802) accurately defined by his compatriot Joseph Gay-Lussac (1778–1850).

1787 Ammonia is liquefied by Dutch physicists Martinus van Marum (1750–1837) and Pars van Troostwijk (1752–1837).

1788 Blagden's law (that the decrease in freezing point of a liquid when a solute is added is proportion to the concentration of the solute) is discovered by British chemist Charles Blagden (1748–1820).

1791 Prévost's theory of exchange (that, at equilibrium, an object emits and absorbs radiant energy at equal rates) is discovered by Swiss physicist Pierre Prévost (1751–1839).

1791 Fact that heat can only travel from a hot object to a cooler object (and not the other way round) is discovered by Pierre Prévost.

1798 Density of the Earth is accurately determined by British scientist Henry Cavendish (1731–1810), although it had been estimated earlier (1774) by British astronomer Nevil Maskelyne (1732–1811).

1798 Relationship between mechanical work and heat is discovered by US scientist Count Rumford (Benjamin Thompson) (1753–1814).

MEDICINE

1785 Use of digitalis (foxglove) in treating dropsy (oedema) is discovered by British physician William Withering (1741–99); active ingredient (digitalin) is not isolated until 1904.

1793 Link between cirrhosis of the liver and excessive drinking (of alcohol) is discovered by British physician Matthew Baillie (1761–1823).

1794 Colour blindness is first described by British chemist John Dalton (1766–1844) who, like his brother Jonathan, was colour blind.

1795 Fact that puerperal fever is contagious is discovered by Scottish physician Alexander Gordon (1752–99). This was later (1843) rediscovered by US physician Oliver Wendell Holmes (1809–94), and later still (1848) confirmed by Hungarian physician Ignaz Semmelweiss (1818–65), who died of the disease.

1796 Vaccination against smallpox is pioneered by British physician Edward Jenner (1749–1823), independently of Zabdiel Boylston (1721).

1799 Anaesthetic effect of dinitrogen oxide (nitrous oxide, or laughing gas) is discovered by British chemists Thomas Beddoes (1760–1808) and Humphry Davy (1778–1829).

CHEMISTRY

1798 Metallic element strontium (symbol Sr) is identified by German chemist Martin Klaproth (1743–1817) and, independently, Scottish chemist Thomas Hope (1766–1844); it was later (1808) isolated by British chemist Humphry Davy (1778–1829).

1798 Metallic element beryllium (symbol Be) is identified (as its oxide) by French chemist Louis Vauquelin (1763–1829), later (1828) isolated by French chemist Antoine Bussy and, independently, German chemist Friedrich Wöhler (1785–1867), who called it glucinium.

1798 Bleaching powder is discovered by British industrial chemists Charles Tennant (1761–1815) and Charles Macintosh (1766–1843).

1799 Proust's law, or law of constant composition (that chemical compounds contain elements in definite proportions), is discovered by French chemist Joseph Proust (1754–1826).

1799 Urea is discovered by French chemist Antoine de Fourcroy (1755–1809).

1799 Fructose (grape sugar) is discovered by French chemist Joseph Proust (1754–1826).

1800 Electrolysis (of water) is discovered by British chemists William Nicholson (1753–1815) and Anthony Carlisle (1768–1840).

1800 Dinitrogen monoxide (nitrous oxide) is discovered by Humphry Davy, who suggests its possible use as an anaesthetic.

1800 Quinoline synthesis is discovered by Hungarian-born Austrian chemist Zdenko Skraup (1850–1910).

1801 Carbon monoxide is discovered by French scientist Charles Désormes (1777–1862) and his son-in-law Nicolas Clément (1779–1841).

1801 Metallic element niobium (symbol Nb) is discovered by British chemist Charles Hatchett (c.1765–1847) and first isolated (1864) by Swedish chemist Christian Blomstrand (1826–97), both of whom originally called it columbium; it was named niobium by German chemist Heinrich Rose (1795–1864).

1801 Metallic element vanadium (symbol V) is discovered by Spanish-born Mexican mineralogist Andrés del Rio (1764–1849), who called it erythronium; the discovery went unacknowledged until vanadium was rediscovered (1831) and named by Swedish chemist Nils Sefström (1787–1854).

1802 Metallic element tantalum (symbol Ta) is discovered by Swedish chemist Anders Ekeberg (1767–1813), later (1820) isolated by his compatriot Jöns Berzelius (1779–1848).

1803 Atomic theory of matter is proposed by British chemist John Dalton (1766–1844), who compiled a list of atomic weights.

1803 Henry's law (that the mass of gas dissolved in a liquid is proportional to the pressure of the gas) is discovered by British chemist William Henry (1774–1836).

1803 Metallic element cerium (symbol Ce) is discovered by Swedish chemists Jöns Berzelius (1779–1848) and Wilhelm von Hisinger (1766–1852) and, independently, by Martin Klaproth.

1803 Metallic elements palladium (symbol Pd) and rhodium (symbol Rh) are discovered by British scientist William Wollaston (1766–1828).

1804 Metallic elements iridium (symbol Ir) and osmium (symbol Os) are discovered by British chemist Smithson Tennant (1761–1815).

FARMING AND FOOD

1802 Wheeled threshing machine is invented by Englishman Thomas Wigful.

1802 Factory for making sugar from sugar beet is established by German chemist Karl Archard.

1806 Coffee percolator is invented (in Germany) by US-born scientist Benjamin Thompson (Count Rumford) (1753–1814).

BIOLOGY

1802 Term "biology" is coined by French naturalist Jean-Baptiste de Lamarck (1744–1829).

1804 Fact that plants require carbon dioxide (from air) and nitrogen (from the soil) for proper growth is discovered by Swiss chemist and naturalist Nicholas de Saussure (1767–1845), who first used saltpetre (potassium nitrate) as a nitrogenous fertilizer.

1809 Lamarckism (an erroneous theory of evolution that acquired characteristics can be inherited) is proposed by French biologist Jean-Baptiste de Lamarck (1744–1829).

PHYSICS

1800 Infrared radiation (from the Sun) is discovered by British astronomer William Herschel (1738–1822).

1801 Henry's law (that the equilibrium amount of gas that dissolves in a liquid at constant temperature is proportional to the partial pressure of the gas) is discovered by British chemist and physician William Henry (1775–1836).

1801 Interference of light is discovered by British physicist and physician Thomas Young (1773–1829).

1801 Ultraviolet light is discovered by German scientist Johann Ritter (1776–1810).

1802 Charles' law (that, at constant pressure, all gases increase in volume by the same amount with the same rise in temperature) – also known as Gay-Lussac's law, who independently discovered it – is formulated by French physicist Jacques Charles (1746–1823). The work of both scientists was anticipated in 1699 by Guillaume Amontons.

1807 Wave theory of light (to explain the phenomenon of interference) is proposed by British physicist and physician Thomas Young (1773–1829).

1807 Young's modulus, a measure of a material's elasticity, is discovered by Thomas Young.

1800 Polarized light is discovered by French physicist Étienne Malus (1775–1812).

MEDICINE

1801 Cause of astigmatism (irregular curvature of the cornea of the eye) is discovered by British physicist and physician Thomas Young (1773–1829); treatment with corrective spectacles is later (1827) introduced by British astronomer George Airy (1831–81).

1803 Haemophilia is discovered by US physician John Otto (1774–1844) and later (1829), independently, by German physician Johann Schönlein (1793–1864).

1803 Painkilling drug morphine is discovered in opium by French chemist Charles Derosne (1780–1846) and later (1806) German chemist Friedrich Sertürner (1783–1841).

1809 Successful ovariotomy (to remove a cyst from the ovary) is performed by US surgeon Ephraim McDowell (1771–1830).

1800

CHEMISTRY

1805 Morphine is discovered by German apothecary Friedrich Sertürner (1783–1841), although his discovery is not recognized until 1817.

1806 Amino acid asparagine (the first to be found) is discovered by French chemists Louis Vauquelin (1763–1829) and Pierre Robiquet (1780–1840).

1806 Role of nitrogen monoxide (nitric oxide) in the lead-chamber process for producing sulphuric acid is discovered by French scientists Charles Désormes (1777–1862) and Nicolas Clément (1779–1841).

1807 Metallic elements potassium (symbol K) and sodium (symbol Na) are isolated by British chemist Humphry Davy (1778–1829).

1808 Metallic elements barium (symbol Ba), calcium (symbol Ca), magnesium (symbol Mg) and strontium (symbol Sr) are isolated (using electrolysis) by Humphry Davy. He also isolates the non-metallic element boron (symbol B), which is discovered independently by French chemists Joseph Gay Lussac (1778–1850) and Louis Thénard (1777–1857).

1808 Gay Lussac's law (that gases combine in simple proportions by volume) is discovered by Joseph Gay Lussac.

1810

FARMING AND FOOD

1810 Preservation of pre-cooked food by canning (rather than by bottling, which had been used commercially since 1790) is invented by French confectioner Nicolas Appert (1752–1841).

1812 Combined heat sterilization and canning process for foods is invented by British engineer Bryan Donkin (1768–1855); tin cans are later (1818) introduced into the USA by Peter Durant.

1813 Soda siphon is invented in England by Charles Plinth.

1818 Primitive combine harvester is invented by US blacksmith John Lane; it is improved by Moore and Hascall in 1838.

1819 Cast-iron plough is invented by Stephen McCormick (with replaceable parts and a wrought-iron point) and, independently, (with a shaped mouldboard) by Jethro Wood (1774–1834).

1819 Canned sardines are manufactured by Frenchman Joseph Colin.

BIOLOGY

1811 Fossil bones of an ichthyosaur, the first of their kind to be found, are discovered by British naturalist Mary Anning (1799–1847) when she was still a child; she later (1821) discovered the first complete ichthyosaur in England.

1811 Separate functions of motor and sensory nerves are discovered by Scottish anatomist Charles Bell (1774–1842).

1813 System of plant classification is introduced by Swiss botanist Augustin de Candolle (1778–1841), who also coins the term "taxonomy".

1815 Arachnids are given family status by French naturalist Jean-Baptiste de Lamarck (1744–1829).

1817 Pander layers, found originally in chick embryos, are discovered by Latvian anatomist Christian Pander (1794–1865).

1819 Alternation of generations is discovered by French poet and biologist Adelbert von Chamisso (1781–1838).

CHEMISTRY

1810 Amino acid cystine is discovered by British scientist William Wollaston (1766–1828).

1811 Glucose is prepared (by heating starch with sulphuric acid) by German-born Russian chemist Gottlieb Kirchhoff (1764–1833).

1811 Highly explosive nitrogen trichloride is discovered by French scientist Pierre Dulong (1785–1838) – who was blinded in one eye as a result.

1811 Nonmetallic element iodine (symbol I) is discovered by French chemists Bernard Courtois (1777–1838) and, independently (1813), Charles Désormes (1777–1862) and Nicolas Clément (1779–1841).

1813 Modern system of chemical symbols and formulae is devised by Swedish chemist Jöns Berzelius (1779–1848).

1815 Prout's hypothesis, that all relative atomic masses are whole-number multiples of that of hydrogen, is proposed by British chemist William Prout (1785–1850).

1815 Cyanogen is discovered by Joseph Gay-Lussac.

1815 Oleic acid (a constituent of fats) is discovered by French chemist Michel Chevreul (1786–1889).

1817 Chlorophyll is discovered and named by French chemists Pierre Pelletier (1788–1842) and Joseph Caventou (1795–1877).

1817 Alkaloid emetine is discovered (in ipecacuanha) by French physiologist François Magendie (1783–1855) and his compatriot chemist Joseph Pelletier (1788–1842).

1817 Metalloid element selenium (symbol Se) is discovered by Swedish chemist Jöns Berzelius (1779–1848).

1817 Metallic element cadmium (symbol Cd) is discovered by German chemist Friedrich Strohmeyer (1776–1835).

1817 Metallic element lithium (symbol Li) is discovered by Swedish chemistry student Johan Arfwedson (1792–1841) and later (1818) isolated and named by his tutor Jöns Berzelius (1779–1848).

1818 Hydrogen peroxide is discovered by French chemist Louis Thénard (1777–1857).

PHYSICS

1811 Avogadro's law (hypothesis), that equal volumes of all gases – at the same temperature and pressure – contain the same number of molecules, is discovered by Italian physicist Amedeo Avogadro (1770–1856) and later (1814), independently, by French physicist André Ampère (1775–1836).

1811 Polarization of light (in quartz crystals) is discovered by French physicist Dominique Arago (1786–1853).

1812 "Two-fluid" (i.e. positive and negative) characteristics of static electricity, and the inverse square law describing attraction between unlike charges, are proposed by French physicist Siméon Poisson (1781–1840).

c.1814 Fraunhofer diffraction (in which the light source and the receiving screen are infinitely far apart) is discovered by German physicist Joseph von Fraunhofer (1787–1826).

1815 How light is refracted is discovered by French physicist Augustin Fresnel (1788–1827).

1815 Brewster's law (that the polarization of reflected light is maximized when the reflected and refracted rays are at right angles) is formulated by Scottish physicist David Brewster (1781–1868).

1815 Optical activity (the ability of certain molecules to rotate the plane of polarized light) is discovered in vegetable oils by French physicist Jean Biot (1774–1862). He later discovered the optical activity of sugar (1818) and tartaric acid (1832).

1819 Ratio of the specific heats of gases (by adiabatic expansion) is discovered by French scientists Charles Désormes (1777–1862) and his son-in-law Nicolas Clément (1779–1841).

1819 Dulong and Petit's law (that the product of an element's relative atomic mass and specific heat – its atomic heat – is approximately constant) is discovered by French scientists Pierre Dulong (1785–1838) and Alexis-Thérèse Petit (1791–1820).

MEDICINE

1811 Colles' fracture (of the wrist) is described by Irish surgeon Abraham Colles (1773–1843).

1817 Parkinsonism (shaking palsy, paralysis agitans or Parkinson's disease) is discovered by British surgeon and palaeontologist James Parkinson (1755–1824).

1818 Method of treating goitre with iodine is discovered by French physician Jean Dumas (1800–84).

1818 Homeopathy is founded by German physician Samuel Hahnemann (1755–1843).

FARMING AND FOOD

1820 Hygrometer for measuring moisture in the air in hothouses is invented by British physicist John Daniell (1790–1845).

1820s Nitrates (for fertilizers) are imported into Europe from South America.

1822 Method of decolourizing crude sugar using charcoal is invented by French chemist Anselme Payen (1795–1871).

1825 Canned salmon is manufactured by Scotsman John Moir.

1827 First mechanical reaper is invented by Scottish clergyman Patrick Bell (1799–1869).

1828 Cocoa (drinking chocolate) is popularized by Dutchman Coenrad van Houten, although it was originally introduced into Europe from Spanish colonies in America in 1615.

BIOLOGY

1821 Systematic classification of fungi is produced by Swedish botanist Elias Fries (1794–1878).

1825 Fossil teeth are discovered to be those of a "giant lizard" (Iguanadon dinosaur) by British palaeontologist Gideon Mantell (1790–1852).

1827 Mammalian ovum is discovered by Estonian-born German biologist Karl von Baer (1792–1876).

1828 Role of the semicircular canals (in the ear) in the sense of balance is discovered by French physician Jean Flourens (1794–1867).

1829 Gill arches and gill slits are discovered in embryo birds and mammals by German biologist Martin Rathke (1793–1860).

CHEMISTRY

1818 Alkaloid strychnine is discovered by French chemists Pierre Pelletier (1788–1842) and Joseph Caventou (1795–1877).

1819 Amino acid leucine is discovered by French chemist Joseph Proust (1754–1826).

1819 Naphthalene is discovered (in coal tar) by British chemist and physician John Kidd (1775–1851).

1820 Alkaloid quinine is discovered by French chemist Joseph Caventou (1795–1877) and Joseph Pelletier (1788–1842), who went on to discover the alkaloids brucine and cinchonine.

1820 Amino acid glycine is discovered by French naturalist Henri Braconnot (1781–1855).

1820 Isomorphism (the existence of two or more compounds with the same crystal structure) is discovered by German chemist Eilhard Mitscherlich (1794–1863).

1822 Use of animal charcoal as a decolourizing agent (originally for impure sugar) is discovered by French chemist Anselme Payen (1795–1871).

1822 Potassium hexacyanoferrate(III) (potassium ferricyanide, known as Gmelin's salt) is discovered by German chemist Leopold Gmelin (1788–1853).

1822 Alkaloid caffeine is discovered (in coffee) by French chemist Joseph Caventou (1795–1877).

1822 Triiodomethane (iodoform) is discovered by French chemist Georges Serrulas (1744–1832).

1823 Fact that animal fats are esters of glycerol and a fatty acid is discovered by French chemist Michel Chevreul (1786–1889), who in the same year discovers stearin.

1823 Nonmetallic element silicon (symbol Si) is isolated by Swedish chemist Jöns Berzelius (1779–1848), having been detected earlier (1817) and named by Scottish chemist Thomas Thomson (1773–1852).

1823 Monoclinic sulphur is discovered by German chemist Eilhardt Mitscherlich (1794–1863).

1824 Metallic element aluminium (symbol Al) is discovered by Danish physicist Hans Oersted (1777–1851), later (1827) isolated by German chemist Friedrich Wöhler (1800–82); the name aluminum was suggested by British Humphry Davy (1778–1829) but afterwards changed to "aluminium" in everywhere but North America. Quantity extraction was first achieved (1855) by French chemist Henri Sainte-Claire Deville (1818–81).

1825 Benzene and benzene hexachloride (BHC) – used a century later as an insecticide – are discovered by British scientist Michael Faraday (1791–1867).

1826 Osmosis is rediscovered by French physiologist René Dutrochet (1776–1847), having been earlier (1748) described by his compatriot Jean Nollet (1700–70).

1826 Liquid non-metallic element bromine (symbol Br) is discovered by French chemist Antoine Balard (1802–76) and, independently, German chemist Carl Löwig.

1826 Phenylamine (aniline) is discovered by German chemist Otto Unverdorben (1806–73), later (1834) investigated by his compatriot Friedlieb Runge (1795–1867).

1827 Selenic(IV) (selenous) acid is discovered by German chemist Eilhard Mitscherlich (1794–1863).

PHYSICS

1820 Electromagnetism – the production of a magnetic field by an electric current flowing in a conductor – is discovered by Danish physicist Hans Oersted (1777–1851).

1820 Biot-Savart law (that the magnetic field strength near a current-carrying conductor is proportional to the current and inversely proportional to the distance from the conductor) is discovered by French physicists Jean Biot (1774–1862) and Félix Savart (1791–1841).

c.1820 Positions of dark lines in the Sun's spectrum – first observed (1802) by British scientist William Wollaston (1766–1828) – are identified by German spectroscopist Josef von Fraunhofer (1787–1826).

c.1820 Fresnel diffraction (in which the light source and receiving screen are at a finite distance from the refracting object) is discovered by French physicist Augustin Fresnel (1788–1827).

1822 Critical state of liquids (at which vapour and liquid phases become indistinguishable) is discovered by French physicist Charles Cagniard de la Tour (1777–1859).

1824 Magnetic induction is first demonstrated by French physicist Dominique Arago (1786–1853).

1824 Carnot's theorem (that all reversible heat engines working between the same pair of temperatures have the same efficiency), based on the ideal Carnot cycle, is formulated by French physicist Nicolas Carnot (1796–1832).

1827 Ohm's law (that the voltage across a current-carrying conductor is equal to the product of the current and the conductor's resistance) is discovered by German physicist Georg Ohm (1789–1854).

1827 Brownian movement (the random movement of microscopic particles suspended in a fluid) is discovered (while studying pollen grains) by British botanist Robert Brown (1773–1858).

1827 That the unit of length should be based on the wavelength of a particular colour of light is proposed by French physicist Jacques Babinet (1794–1872), a suggestion which was finally adopted in 1960.

1828 Term "potential" for electric voltage is coined by British mathematician and physicist George Green (1793–1841).

1829 Poisson's ratio (of lateral strain to longitudinal stress in a stretched elastic object) is discovered by French physicist Siméon Poisson (1781–1840).

1829 Coriolis effect (then called the Coriolis force) is postulated and explained by French mathematician Gaspard de Coriolis (1792–1843).

MEDICINE

1824 Carbon dioxide gas is used as an anaesthetic (on animals) by British physician Henry Hickman (1800–30).

1827 Bright's disease (a type of non-bacterial nephritis) is discovered by British physician Richard Bright (1798–1858).

CHEMISTRY

1828 Wöhler's synthesis (of urea by heating ammonium isocyante) is discovered by German chemist Friedrich Wöhler (1800–82), the first synthesis of an organic compound from an inorganic one.

1828 Radioactive element thorium (symbol Th) is discovered by Swedish chemist Jöns Berzelius (1779–1848).

1829 Graham's law (that the rate of diffusion of a gas is inversely proportional to the square root of its density) is discovered by Scottish chemist Thomas Graham (1805–69).

1829 Existence of sets of three chemically similar elements ("triads") is discovered by German chemist Johann Döbereiner (1780–1849).

FARMING AND FOOD

1830

1830 Cast steel plough for bulk manufacture is invented by US industrialist John Deere (1804–86).

1830 Angostura bitters, named after the town of Angostura (since 1846 Cuidad Bolivar), Venezuela, is invented by German Johann Siegert.

1831 Improved still for manufacturing whisky is invented by Irish distiller Aeneas Coffrey (1779–1852).

1833 Reaping machine is invented by US engineer Obed Hussey (1792–1860).

1833 Plough with steel-clad mouldboard and share is invented by US blacksmith John Lane.

1834 Improved reaping and binding machine is invented by US engineer Cyrus McCormick (1809–1884).

1837 All-steel plough is invented by US engineer John Deere (1804–86).

1837 Worcester sauce is invented by British pharmacists John Lea and William Perrins.

1839 Commercial process for making superphosphate fertilizer is invented by agriculturalists Englishman John Lawes (1814–1900) and, independently, Irishman James Murray (who had invented it in 1817).

BIOLOGY

1830 Mechanism of pollination is discovered by Italian microscopist Giovanni Amici (1786–1863).

c.1830 Proteins are discovered by German physiologist Johannes Müller (1801–58).

1831 Nucleus of plant cells is discovered (and named) by Scottish botanist Robert Brown (1773–1858).

1832 Reflex nerve action is discovered by British physician Marshall Hall (1790–1857), although its is not correctly explained until much later (1906) by British neurophysiologist Charles Sherrington (1857–1952).

1833 Diastase, the first known enzyme, is discovered (in malt extract) by French chemists Anselme Payen (1795–1871) and Jean-François Persoz.

1834 Nitrogen fixation in plants is discovered by French chemist Jean Boussingault (1802–87).

1835 Schwann cells (which form the myelin sheath surrounding a nerve fibre) are discovered by German biologist Theodor Schwann (1810–82); the myelin sheath was later (1838) discovered independently by Polish-born German anatomist Robert Remak (1815–65).

1835 Protoplasm in bodies of unicellular animals is discovered by French zoologist Félix Dujardin (1801–60).

1836 Digestive enzyme pepsin is discovered by German physiologist Theodor Schwann (1810–82).

1836 Method of classifying plants by their fruits is introduced by US botanist Asa Gray (1810–88).

1836 Epic round-the-world voyage on HMS Beagle is completed by British naturalist Charles Darwin (1809–82).

1837 Von Baer's law of biogenesis, that the embryos of very different species are similar, is discovered by Estonian-born German biologist Karl von Baer (1792–1876).

1838 Purkinje cells in the cortex of the brain are discovered by Czech histologist Johannes Purkinje (1787–1869).

1839 Fact that all living matter is made up of cells is proposed by German physiologist Theodor Schwann (1810–1882).

CHEMISTRY (continued)

1830 Manganic(VII) (permanganic) acid is discovered by German chemist Eilhard Mitscherlich (1794–1863).

1831 Trichloromethane (chloroform) is discovered by French pharmacist Eugène Soubeiran (1797–1858) and, independently, by US chemist Samuel Guthrie (1782–1848) and German chemist Justus von Liebig (1803–73).

1831 Red dye alizarin is discovered by French chemists Pierre Robiquet (1780–1840) and Jean Colin (1784–1865).

1832 Nitrobenzene is discovered by German chemist Eilhardt Mitscherlich (1794–1863).

1832 Pain-killing drug codeine is discovered by French chemist Pierre Robiquet (1780–1840).

1832 Anthracene is discovered in coal tar by French chemists Auguste Larent (1807–53) and Jean Dumas (1800–84).

1833 Ethyl radical is discovered by Irish chemist Robert Kane (1809–90) and, independently (1834), German chemist Justus von Liebig (1803–73).

1833 Alkaloid atropine is discovered by German chemist Philipp Geiger.

1833 Creosote is discovered (in coal tar) by German industrial chemist Karl von Reichenbach (1788–1869).

1834 Laws of electrolysis are discovered by British scientist Michael Faraday (1791–1867).

1834 Quinoline is discovered by German chemist Friedlieb Runge (1795–1867).

1834 Dichlorine oxide (chlorine monoxide) is discovered by French chemist Antoine Balard (1802–76).

1834 Phenol (carbolic acid) is discovered by German chemist Friedlieb Runge (1795–1867).

1834 Cellulose is extracted from wood (and named) by French chemist Anselme Payen (1795–1871).

1834 Law of substitution (that chlorine, e.g., can replace hydrogen in hydrocarbons) is discovered by French chemist Jean Baptiste Dumas (1800–84).

1835 Methanol is discovered by French chemist Jean Dumas (1800–84).

1835 Pyruvic acid is discovered by Swedish chemist Jöns Berzelius (1779–1848).

1836 Catalysis is discovered by Swedish chemist Jöns Berzelius (1779–1848).

1836 Ethyne (acetylene) is discovered by British chemist Edmund Davy.

1838 Method of making nitric acid by oxidizing ammonia in the presence of a platinum catalyst is discovered by French chemist Charles Kuhlmann (1803–81).

PHYSICS

c.1832 Gauss' law (that electric flux is proportional to the sum of the electric charges within a surface) is discovered by German physicist Karl Gauss (1777–1855).

1834 Peltier effect (that an electric current passing through a junction between two different metals causes a change in temperature) is discovered by French physicist Jean Peltier (1785–1845).

1831 Electromagnetic induction (the production of a voltage in a conductor in a changing magnetic field) is discovered by British scientist Michael Faraday (1791–1867).

1833 Lenz's law (that the direction of an induced electric current is such as to oppose the change producing it) is discovered by German physicist Heinrich Lenz (1804–65).

MEDICINE

1830 Bloodletting as a treatment for disease is reintroduced by British physician Marshall Hall (1790–1857).

1831 Dupuytren's contracture (curling of the fingers caused by thickening of ligaments in the palm, usually associated with ageing) is discovered by French surgeon Guillaume Dupuytren (1777–1835).

1832 Hodgkin's disease (a progressive disorder involving enlargement of the lymph glands and spleen) is discovered by British physician Thomas Hodgkin (1798–1866).

1833 Peripheral neuritis (later found to be caused by a deficiency of vitamin B) is described by French neurologist Jules Dejerine (1849–1917).

1835 Graves' disease (thyrotoxicosis or exophthalmic goitre) is discovered by Irish physician Robert Graves (1796–1853) and, later (1840) independently, by German physician Karl von Basedow (1799–1854), after whom it was also called Basedow's disease.

1835 Trichina (or Trichinella), a nematode parasite in humans, is discovered in undercooked meat by British surgeon James Paget (1814–99).

1837 Correct distinction between typhus and typhoid fever is made by US physician William Gerhard (1809–72) and, later (1849) British physician William Jenner (1815–98).

1838 Stokes-Adams syndrome (loss of consciousness caused by irregular heartbeat) is discovered by Irish physician William Stokes (1804–78) and late (1842) by his compatriot Robert Adams (1791–1875).

1839 Microscopic fungus that causes favus (a kind of ringworm) is discovered by Swiss physician Johann Schönlein (1793–1864).

FARMING AND FOOD

840 Gin-based Pimms No. 1 cocktail is invented by British restaurant-owner James Pimm.

845 Self-raising flour is introduced by British baker Henry Jones.

845 Fruit jelly dessert is invented by US engineer Peter Cooper (1791–1883); it is later (1897) marketed as Jell-O by manufacturer Pear Wait.

846 Wine containing the astringent drug quinine is invented by French pharmacist Joseph Dubonnet.

847 Ring-shaped doughnuts are invented by US baker Hanson Gregory.

848 Chewing gum (based on spruce gum) is invented in the USA by John Curtis; gum based on chicle is not introduced commercially until 1871, although the American Mayans had been chewing chicle since AD 900.

850s First sugar refineries (for sugar cane) are built in the USA by US sugar planter Valcour Aime (1798–1867).

851 Process for the commercial production of ice cream is invented in the USA by Jacob Fussel.

851 Meat biscuit is invented by US food technologist Gail Borden (1801–74).

853 Potato chips are invented by Native American chef George Crum.

BIOLOGY

1840 Fact that plants obtain nitrogen from nitrates in the soil is discovered by French agricultural chemist Jean-Baptiste Boussingault (1802–87).

1841 Word "dinosaur" ("fearful lizard") is coined by British anti-Darwinian palaeontologist Richard Owen (1804–92).

1841 Digestive enzyme ptyalin is discovered (in saliva) by French biologist Louis Mialhe (1807–86).

1842 Alternation of generations in certain animals (such as jellyfish and some worms) is discovered by Danish zoologist Johannes Steenstrup (1813–97).

1842 Concept of cranial index (ratio of the width of a person's skull to its length), as a means of classifying human races, is introduced by Swedish anatomist Anders Retzius (1796–1860).

1842 Bowman's capsule (on a kidney nephron) is discovered by British physician William Bowman (1816–92); Bowman's glands and Bowman's membranes are also named after him.

1843 Penetration of the ovum by a spermatazoan is discovered by British physician Martin Barry (1802–55).

1843 Electrical nature of nerve impulses is discovered by German biologist Emil du Bois-Reymond (1818–96).

1844 Fact that an ovum is a cell and that embryos develop by division of this cell is discovered by Swiss anatomist Rudolf von Kölliker (1817–1905).

1845 Standard three germ layers in an embryo are discovered by Polish-born German anatomist Robery Remak (1815–65).

1846 Protoplasm is discovered (and named) by German botanist Hugo von Mohl (1805–72).

1846 Fact that protists are single cells is discovered by German biologist Karl von Siebold (1804–85).

1849 Cellular nature of nerve cells is discovered by Swiss anatomist Rudolf von Kölliker (1817–1905).

1851 Vasomotor nerves are discovered by French biologist Claude Bernard (1813–78).

1852 Parathyroid glands are discovered (in a rhinoceros) by British zoologist Richard Owen (1804–92).

1852 Meissner's corpuscles (sense organs of touch in the skin) are discovered by German physiologists George Meissner (1829–1905) and Rudolf Wagner (1805–64).

CHEMISTRY

1838 1-hydroxybenzoic (salicylic) acid is discovered by Italian chemist Rafaelle Piria (1815–65).

1838 Methylbenzene (toluene) is discovered by Polish chemist Philippe Walter (1810–47) and French chemist Joseph Pelletier (1788–1842).

1839 Metallic element lanthanum (symbol La) is discovered by Swedish chemist Carl Mosander (1797–1858).

1840 Ozone is discovered by German chemist Christian Schönbein (1799–1868).

c.1840 Fehling's test (for reducing sugars) is discovered by German chemist Hermann von Fehling (1812–85).

1840 Dichloroethene (dichloroethylene) is discovered by French chemist Henri Regnault (1810–78).

1841 Nitroprussides (nitrosopentacyanoferrate(III)) are discovered by Scottish chemist Lyon Playfair (1818–98).

1843 Metallic elements erbium (symbol Er) and terbium (symbol Tb) are discovered by Swedish chemist Carl Mosander (1797–1858). In the same year he also discovered "didymium", which later turned out to be a mixture of two elements, neodymium and praseodymium.

1844 Metallic element ruthenium (symbol Ru) is discovered by German chemist Karl Claus (1796–1864).

1845 Explosive properties of cellulose nitrate (nitrocellulose, guncotton) are discovered by German chemist Christian Schönbein (1799–1868).

1845 Ethanoic (acetic) acid is synthesized (from inorganic compounds) by German chemist Hermann Kolbe (1818–84).

1846 Glyceryl trinitrate (nitroglycerine) is discovered by Italian chemist Ascanio Sobrero (1812–88).

1846 Collodion is discovered by French chemist Louis Menard (1822–1901).

1846 Amino acid tyrosine is discovered by German chemist Justus von Liebig (1803–73).

1847 Babo's law (that the decrease in vapour pressure of a liquid when a solute is added is proportional to the amount of solute) is discovered by German chemist Lambert Babo (1818–99).

1848 Optical activity (of tartaric acid) is discovered by French scientist Louis Pasteur (1822–95).

1848 Accurate relative atomic mass (atomic weight) of carbon is determined by French chemist Jean Dumas (1800–84).

1849 Kolbe's method of making an alkane (by electrolytically decomposing a dissolved carboxylic acid salt) is discovered by German chemist Herman Kolbe (1818–84).

1849 Pentanol (amyl alcohol) is discovered by British chemist Edward Frankland (1825–99).

c.1850 Barfoed's test (for reducing sugars) is discovered by Swedish physician C. Barfoed (1815–99).

1850 Williamson's synthesis (for making ethers by reacting a haloalkane with an alkoxide) is discovered by British chemist Alexander Williamson (1824–1904).

1850 Red phosphorus is discovered by Austrian chemist Anton Schrötter (1802–75).

PHYSICS

1840 Joule's law (that the rate of heating by an electric current flowing in a conductor is equal to the product of the conductor's resistance and the square of the current) is discovered by British physicist James Joule (1818–89).

1842 Principle of conservation of energy is discovered by German physicist Julius von Meyer (1814–78) and, independently, by James Joule.

1842 Doppler effect (the apparent change in frequency of a wave motion with the change in relative velocity of the observer and the source) is discovered by Austrian physicist Christian Doppler (1805–53). Applied initially only to sound waves, the effect was later (1848) applied also to light waves by French physicist Armand Fizeau (1819–96).

1843 Mechanical equivalent of heat is discovered by James Joule.

1843 Poiseuille's formula or law (that the volume of flow of a liquid through a tube is determined by the pressure and the dimensions of the tube) is discovered by French physician Jean Poiseuille (1799–1869).

1844 Significance of the critical temperature in the liquefaction of gases is discovered by Irish chemist Thomas Andrews (1813–85).

1845 Kinetic theory of gases is proposed by Scottish physicist John Waterson (1811–83), although his work is overlooked for nearly 30 years.

1845–47 Kirchhoff's laws (concerning electric currents in circuits and networks) are discovered by German physicist Gustav Kirchhoff (1824–87).

1846 Magnetostriction, the shortening of a bar of ferromagnetic metal when it is magnetized, is discovered by James Joule.

1847 Principle of conservation of energy is formulated by German scientist Hermann Helmholtz (1821–94).

1847 Draper point (the temperature, about 525°C, at which all substances glow a dull red colour) is discovered by British-born US chemist John Draper (1811–82).

1848 Absolute temperature scale, and the concept of absolute zero, is proposed by British physicist William Thomson (Lord Kelvin) (1824–1907).

1849 First fairly accurate value for the speed of light is obtained by French physicist Armand Fizeau (1819–96).

1849 Stokes' law (that defines the force acting on an object as it falls through a viscous fluid) is discovered by Irish physicist George Stokes (1819–1903).

1850 Second law of thermodynamics (that heat cannot flow by itself from one object to a hotter object) is formulated by German physicist Rudolf Clausius (1822–88) and, independently (1851), by British physicist William Thomson (Lord Kelvin) (1824–1907).

1850 Foucault's pendulum, which demonstrates the rotation of the Earth, is devised by French physicist Léon Foucault (1819–68).

MEDICINE

1840 Theory that infectious diseases are caused by parasitic organisms is proposed by German pathologist Friedrich Henle (1809–85).

1842 Bell's palsy (paralysis of the facial nerve) is discovered by Scottish surgeon Charles Bell (1774–1842).

1842 Anaesthetic effect of ethoxyethane (ether) is discovered by US physician Crawford Long (1815–78), although he did not report the fact until 1849.

1844 Anaesthesia using dinitrogen oxide (nitrous oxide, laughing gas) is discovered by US dentist Horace Wells (1815–48).

1846 Anaesthesia using ethoxyethane (ether) is demonstrated in the USA by dentist Thomas Morton (1819–68) and in Britain by physician John Snow (1813–58).

1847 Anaesthetic effect of trichloromethane (chloroform) is discovered independently by Scottish physician James Simpson (1811–70) and British physician John Snow (1813–58).

1847 Leukemia is recognized by German physician Rudolf Verchow (1821–1902) and, independently, Scottish physician John Bennet (1812–75).

1847 Silver amalgam for filling teeth is introduced by US dentist Thomas Evans (1823–97).

1848 Terms "thrombosis" and "embolus" for blood clots are coined by German pathologist Rudolph Virchow (1821–1902).

1849 Pernicious anaemia (at first called Addisonian anaemia) is discovered by British physician Thomas Addison (1793–1860); later (1872) called "pernicious" (or Biermer's) anaemia after its description by German physician Anton Biermer (1827–92).

1849 Bacterium that causes anthrax is discovered by French bacteriologist Aloys Pollender, and later (1863) by his compatriot Casimir Davaine (1812–82).

1849 Clinical description of multiple sclerosis is given by German physician Friedrich von Frerichs (1819–85).

1850 Use of the hypodermic syringe is introduced by British physician Alfred Higginson (1808–84).

1854 Fact that cholera is linked to contaminated drinking water is discovered by British physician John Snow (1813–53).

1854 Quick-drying plaster of Paris is introduced as a cast for broken bones by Dutch physician Anthonius Mathijsen (1805–78).

FARMING AND FOOD

1855 Self-propelled rotary cultivator is invented by Canadian engineer Robert Romaine.

1856 Condensed milk is invented by US food technologist Gail Borden (1801–74) and, independently, German-born Swiss Henri Nestlé (1814–90).

1857 Steam plough is invented by British engineer John Fowler (1826–64).

1858 Self-binding machine is invented by US engineer John Appleby (1840–1917).

1858 Can opener is invented by US Ezra Warner (previously food cans were opened using a chisel).

1858 Concentrated meat extract is invented by German chemist Justus von Liebig (1803–73).

BIOLOGY

1852 Term "evolution" is coined by British philosopher Herbert Spencer (1820–1903).

1856 X- and Y-chromosomes in mammals are discovered by US biologist Edmund Wilson (1856–1939).

1856 Remains of Neanderthal man are found by French anatomist Pierre Broca (1824–80).

1856 Method of keeping animal organs alive in vitro is discovered by German physiologist Carl Ludwig (1816–95).

1857 Glycogen ("animal starch") is discovered by French physiologist Claude Bernard (1813–78) and, independently, German physiologist Victor Hensen (1835–1924); it is (1875) isolated by US chemist Russell Chittenden (1856–1943).

1859 The Origin of Species by Means of Natural Selection, outlining the theory of evolution, is published by British naturalist Charles Darwin (1809–82); similar conclusions had been reached independently by his compatriot Alfred Russel Wallace (1823–1913) and communicated to Darwin in 1858. Wallace's own book, Contributions to the Theory of Natural Selection, was published in 1870.

CHEMISTRY

c.1850 Barfoed's test (for reducing sugars) is discovered by Swedish physician C. Barfoed (1815–99).

1851 Pyridine is discovered by Scottish chemist Thomas Anderson (1819–74).

1852 Deviations from Boyle's law by real gases is discovered by French chemist Henri Regnault (1810–78).

1852 Concept of valence is introduced by British chemist Edward Frankland (1825–99).

1852 Kerosene is discovered by Canadian geologist Abraham Gesner (1797–1864).

1853 Cannizzaro reaction (in which an aldehyde disproportionates into an alcohol and a carboxylic acid) is discovered by Italian chemist Stanislao Cannizzaro (1826–1910).

1853 Transport number (which acknowledges that not all ions travel at the same speed during electrolysis) is discovered by German physical chemist Johann Hittorf (1824–1914).

1853 Aspirin (acetylsalicylic acid), although not its analgesic action, is discovered by French chemist Charles (Karl) Gerhardt (1816–56).

1853 Dye rosaniline is discovered by German chemist August Hofmann (1818–92).

1854 Fact that each element has its own characteristic spectrum is discovered by US physicist David Alter (1807–81).

1855 Theory of types in organic chemistry, including homologous and heterologous series, is proposed by French chemist Charles (Karl) Gerhardt (1816–56).

c.1855 Wurtz reaction (between a haloalkane and sodium to form an alkane) is discovered by French chemist Charles-Adolphe Wurtz (1817–84).

c.1855 Fact that ozone is an allotrope of oxygen is discovered by Irish physical chemist Thomas Andrews (1813–85).

1856 Mauvine, the first synthetic aniline dye, is discovered by British chemist William Perkin (1848–1907).

1857 Photochemical reaction (of hydrogen with chlorine) is discovered by German chemist Robert Bunsen (1811–99) and British chemist Henry Rosco (1833–1915).

1857 Silicon nitride is discovered by German chemist Friedrich Wöhler (1800–82) and, independently, French chemist Henri Sainte-Claire Deville (1818–81).

1857 Reversible dissociation of chemical compounds is discovered by Henri Sainte-Claire Deville.

1857 Glycogen is discovered by French physiologist Claude Bernard (1813–78).

1858 Fact that carbon atoms are tetravalent and can combine with each other to form chains (thus introducing the concept of chemical bonds in organic compounds) is discovered by Scottish chemist Archibald Couper (1831–92), but his findings remain unpublished until after German chemist Friedrich Kekulé von Stradonitz (1829–96) independently announces reaching the same conclusion in the same year.

1858 Distinction between atomic and molecular weights (masses) is made by Stanislao Cannizzaro.

1858 Composition of silica (silicon dioxide) is discovered by Swiss chemist Jean de Marignac (1817–94).

1859 Cocaine is prepared (from coca leaves) by German chemist Albert Niemann (1834–61).

PHYSICS

1851 Weber's constant (the ratio of the electrostatic and electromagnetic units of quantity of electricity, which equals the speed of light) is discovered by German physicist Wilhelm Weber (1804–91).

1852 Joule-Thomson (Joule-Kelvin) effect (the cooling that accompanies the expansion of a gas into a region of lower pressure) is discovered by British physicists James Joule (1818–89) and William Thomson (Lord Kelvin) (1824–1907).

1852 Regnault's method (of measuring the density of a gas) is discovered by French chemist Henri Regnault (1810–78).

1853 Mechanism of formation of absorption and emission spectra is explained by Swedish physicist Anders Ångström (1814–74).

1853 Magnus effect, which causes a spinning ball to swerve in flight, is discovered by German physicist Heinrich Magnus (1802–70).

1856 Term "kinetic energy" is coined by British physicist William Thomson (Lord Kelvin) (1824–1907).

1857 Lissajous figures (curves produced by combining two harmonic motions) are discovered by French physicist Jules Lissajous (1822–80).

1858 Fact that electric discharges in a low-pressure gas (cathode rays) are deflected by a magnetic field is discovered by German physicist Julius Plücker (1801–68).

MEDICINE

1859 Muscle relaxant properties of curare are discovered by French physiologist Claude Bernard (1813–78).

1855 Addison's disease (caused by excessive activity of the adrenal glands) is discovered by British physician Thomas Addison (1793–1860).

1855 Fact that cells arise only by division of other cells is discovered by German pathologist Rudolf Virchow (1821–1902).

1858 Clinical description of tabes dorsalis (locomotor ataxia), a long-term effect of syphilis, is given by French physician Guillaume Duchenne (1806–75).

1858 Fact that farsightedness is often caused by eyeballs that are too short front-to-back is discovered by Dutch physician Franciscus Donders (1818–89).

1859 Chemical test (on urine) for gout is discovered by French physician Alfred Garod (1819–1907).

FARMING AND FOOD

1860 Hydroponics (the cultivation of plants without soil) is introduced by German scientist Julius von Sachs (1832–97).

1863 Pasteurization (originally for wine) is invented by French chemist Louis Pasteur (1822–95).

1863 Starch-free slimming diet ("Bantingism") is invented by British undertaker William Banting (1797–1878).

1867 Baby food mimicking mother's milk is invented by German chemist Justus von Liebig (1803–73).

1868 Refrigerated railway freight cars for transporting perishable foods are invented by US engineer William Davis (1812–68).

1868 Plough with hardened cast-iron edge to the share is invented by Scottish engineer James Oliver (1823–1908).

1869 Commercial margarine production (from tallow) is patented by French chemist Hippolyte Mergé-Mouriès; the original discovery of margarine was made 30 years earlier by Michel Chevreul (1786–1889) and the process later (1872) improved, by using also skimmed milk, by French inventor F. Boudet.

1869 Chewing gum (based on chicle) is invented by US photographer Thomas Adams (patented 1871).

BIOLOGY

1860 Damaging criticism of Charles Darwin's theory of natural selection (as the mechanism for evolution) is published anonymously by British palaeontologist Richard Owen (1804–92).

1861 Broca's area (the speech centre in the cortex of the brain) is discovered by French anatomist Pierre Broca (1824–80).

1861 Batesian mimicry (in which a harmless animal gains protection by mimicking the coloration of an animal that is harmful to predators) is discovered by British naturalist Henry Bates (1825–92).

1862 Spontaneous generation of life (actually bacteria from inorganic material) is finally disproved by French scientist Louis Pasteur (1822–95).

1865 Laws of heredity – the foundation of genetics – are published (but go unnoticed) by Moravian monk Gregor Mendel (1822–84).

1865 "Germ theory" of fermentation (that each type of fermentation depends on a specific microorganism) is proposed by French bacteriologist Louis Pasteur (1822–93).

1865 Chloroplasts (chlorophyll-containing structures in plant cells) are discovered by German botanist Julius von Sachs (1833–97).

1866 Lichens are discovered to be symbiotes (algae and fungi living together) by German botanist Heinrich de Barry (1831–1888).

1866 Recapitulation theory (that an animal's embryonic development mirrors its evolutionary history) is proposed by German biologist Ernst Haeckel (1834–1919), after having been first suggested (1864) by his compatriot Fritz Müller (1821–97). Haeckel also coins the term "ecology" (German Oecologie).

1866 Difference between rods and cones in the retina of the eye is discovered by German zoologist Max Schultze (1825–74).

1867 Method of gold-staining of tissue samples and the role of white blood cells in inflammation are discovered by German pathologist Julius Cohnheim (1839–84).

1868 Fossils of Cro-Magnon Man (the earliest in Europe) are discovered in France by French palaeontologist Edouard Lartet (1801–71).

1869 Islets of Langerhans (groups of cells in the pancreas which produce insulin) are discovered by German physiologist Paul Langerhans (1847–88).

1869 Nucleic acid DNA is discovered by German biochemist Friedrich Mieschler.

CHEMISTRY

1860 Spectrum analysis for identifying elements is introduced by German physicist Gustav Kirchhoff (1824–87) and chemist Robert Bunsen (1811–99), who in that year used the technique to discover the metallic element caesium (symbol Cs).

1861 Isomerism (in organic compounds) is discovered by Russian chemist Alexander Butlerov (1828–86).

1860 Method of making synthetic ruby (a form of corundum) is discovered by French chemist Edmond Frémy (1814–94).

1861 Azo dyes are discovered by German chemist Peter Griess (1829–88).

1861 Term "colloid" is coined by Scottish chemist Thomas Graham (1805–69).

1861 Metallic element thallium (symbol Tl) is discovered (spectroscopically) by British physicist William Crookes (1832–1919) and, independently, French chemist C. Lamy (1820–78).

1861 Metallic element rubidium (symbol Ru) is discovered (spectroscopically) by Robert Bunsen and Gustav Kirchhoff.

1862 Chemical elements are plotted in order of atomic weights around a cylinder, creating a primitive periodic table with elements arranged in vertical groups, by French geologist Alexandre Beguyer de Chancourtois (1820–86).

1862 Crystalline haemoglobin is prepared by German biochemist Ernst Hoppe-Segler (1825–95).

1863 Law of mass action (that the rate of a chemical reaction, at a given temperature, is proportional to the product of the active masses of the reactants) is discovered by Norwegian physicist Cato Guldberg (1836–1902) and his brother-in-law Peter Waage (1833–1900) and, independently (1864), by British chemists William Harcourt (1789–1871) and W. Esson (1839–1916).

1863 Metallic element indium (symbol In) is discovered spectroscopically by German physicist Ferdinand Reich (1799–1882) and German chemist Hieronymus Richter (1824–98).

1863 Trinitrotoluene (TNT) is discovered by German chemist T. Wilbrand.

1863 Two optical isomers of lactic acid are discovered by German chemist Johannes Wislicenus (1835–1902).

1863 Law of octaves, an early attempt at a periodic classification of the elements, is formulated by British chemist John Newlands (1837–98).

1864 Existence of tertiary alcohols is predicted by Russian chemist Alexander Butlerov (1828–86).

1864 Microstructure of steel is discovered by British geologist Henry Sorby (1826–1908).

1865 First modern table of relative atomic masses is drawn up by Belgian chemist Jean Stas (1813–91).

1865 Kekulé structure of benzene (a structure with alternate single and double bonds) is proposed by German chemist Friedrich Kekulé von Stradonitz (1829–69).

1866 Method of extracting aluminium electrolytically is discovered by US chemist Charles Hall (1863–1914) and, independently, French chemist Paul Héroult (1863–1914).

1867 Methanal (formaldehyde) is discovered by German chemist August Hofmann (1818–92), who in the same year discovers methyl violet dyes.

PHYSICS

1860 Thomson (Kelvin) effect (the evolution of heat by an electric current flowing along a conductor whose ends are at different temperatures) is discovered by William Thomson (Lord Kelvin).

c.1860 Kirchhoff's laws of radiation (that the emissivity of an object is equal to its absorptance at the same temperature) is discovered by German physicist Gustav Kirchhoff (1824–87).

1864 Velocity of electromagnetic waves is predicted to be the same as that of light by Scottish physicist James Clerk Maxwell (1831–79).

1865 Term "entropy" is coined by German mathematician and physicist Rudolf Clausius (1822–88).

1866 Boltzmann's law (concerning the equipartition of energy) is formulated by Austrian physicist Ludwig Boltzmann (1844–1906).

1869 Tyndall effect (the scattering of light by fine particles suspended in a fluid) is discovered by Irish physicist John Tyndall (1820–93), who also showed that the effect is responsible for the blue colour of the daytime sky.

MEDICINE

1863 Antiseptic surgery, using phenol (carbolic acid), is introduced by British surgeon Joseph Lister (1827–1912), using the disinfectant properties of phenol as previously advocated by British chemist Frederick Calvert (1819–73).

1863 Barbituric acid is discovered by German chemist Johann von Baeyer (1835–1917), later (1903) used to produce barbiturate drugs by Emil Fischer (1852–1919).

1864 International Red Cross is founded by Swiss banker Jean Dunant (1828–1910).

1865 Fact that tuberculosis is infectious is discovered by German physician Wilhelm Wundt (1832–1920), later (1867) confirmed by polish pathologist Julius Cohnheim (1839–84) and French physician Jean Villemin (1827–92).

1866 Trypanosome that causes filariasis (elephantiasis) is discovered by British physician Joseph Bancroft (1836–94) and, a year later, by Welsh physician Timothy Lewis (1841–86).

1867 Amyl nitrite as a treatment for angina pectoris is discovered by Scottish physician Thomas Brunton (1844–1916).

1867 Cholecystotomy, an operation to remove gallstones, is introduced by US surgeon John Bobbs (1809–70).

1867 Use of an incubator for premature babies is introduced by US gynaecologist Theodore Thomas (1831–1903).

FARMING AND FOOD	BIOLOGY	CHEMISTRY	PHYSICS	MEDICINE

CHEMISTRY (continued from top, pre-1870)

1867 Bismark brown dye is discovered by German naturalist Karl Martinus (1794–1868).

1868 Phase rule is discovered by US chemist Josiah Gibbs (1839–1903).

1868 Composition and method of synthesizing alizarin (used to make dyes) are discovered by German chemists Karl Graebe (1841–1927) and Karl Liebermann (1842–1914), and, independently, British chemist William Perkin (1838–1907), who in the same year synthesizes coumarin.

1868 Gaseous element helium (symbol He) is discovered in the spectrum of the Sun by French physicist Jules Janssen (1824–1907) and, independently, British astronomer Norman Lockyer (1836–1920) and British chemist Edward Frankland (1825–99). It is later (1895) discovered in mineral deposits on Earth by Swedish chemist Per Cleve (1840–1905) and in air by Scottish chemist William Ramsay (1825–1916).

1868 Periodic law (relating to properties of the elements and leading to the Periodic Table, based on relative atomic masses), is proposed by Russian chemist Dmitri Mendeléev (1834–1907). A similar table was later (1870) independently drawn up by German chemist Julius Lothar Meyer (1830–95).

1870

FARMING AND FOOD

1870 Differential gears for reaping machines are invented by German-born US engineer Rudolf Eickemeyer (1831–95).

1875 Refrigerated cold store for meat and dairy produce is constructed by Australian Thomas Mort.

1875 Large-scale meat processing and canning is introduced by US industrialist Philip Armour (1832–1901).

1875 Baked beans are first canned by the US Burnham and Morrill company (for the crews of their fishing boats); they became know as "Boston beans" and were later (1891) marketed in the USA canned in tomato sauce.

1876 Mass-produced canned foods are first marketed by US retailer Henry Heinz (1844–1919).

1876 Ship with refrigerated hold, the Paraguay, is used by French engineer Charles Tellier (1828–1913) to carry perishable foods across the Atlantic Ocean.

1876 Vanilla essence, the first artificial flavouring, is synthesized by German chemists William Haarman and Karl Reimer.

1877 Centrifugal cream separator is invented by Swedish engineer Carl de Laval (1845–1913).

1878 Grain binding machine is invented by US engineer John Appleby (1840–1917).

1878 Frozen mutton is sent from Argentina to France on SS Paraguay.

BIOLOGY

1871 Enzyme invertase, which mediates the conversion of sucrose (table sugar) into glucose and fructose, is discovered by German biochemist Ernst Hoppe-Seyler (1825–95).

1873 Blood cells called platelets are discovered by Canadian physician William Osler (1849–1919).

1873 Staining technique that allows microscopic study of nerve cells is discovered by Italian histologist Camillo Golgi (1843–1926).

1875 Knee-jerk reflex is discovered by German physiologists Wilhelm Erb (1840–1921) and, independently, Carl Westphal (1833–90).

1875 Method of classifying proteins is devised by German biochemist Ernst Hoppe-Seyler (1825–95).

1876 Centrosomes (structures within a cell) are discovered by Belgian cytologist Édouard van Beneden (1846–1910); the term "centrosome" was later (1888) coined by German cytologist Theodor Boveri (1862–1915).

1878 Okapi is discovered by Russian-born German explorer Wilhelm Junker (1840–92).

1878 Chromosomes are discovered by German cytologist Walther Flemming (1843–1915), who later (1879) identifies chromatin.

1878 Word "enzyme" is introduced by German physiologist Willy Kuhne (1837–1900).

CHEMISTRY

1870 Markovnikov's rule (which predicts the principal product in a mixture produced by reacting an acid with an unsymmetrical alkene) is discovered by Russian chemist Vladimir Markovnikov (1837–1904).

c.1870 Fittig synthesis (for making aromatic hydrocarbons from their halogen compounds, using sodium) is discovered by German chemist Rudolph Fittig (1835–1910).

1871 Phenolphthalein (used as a dye and in medicine) is discovered by German chemist Adolf von Baeyer (1835–1917).

1872 Nitromethane is discovered by German chemist Hermann Kölbe (1818–84).

1874 Stereochemistry is established by Dutch chemist Jacobus van't Hoff (1852–1911), who discovers the tetrahedral arrangement of carbon's valences.

1874 Fact that optical activity in organic compounds is due to an asymmetrical carbon atom is discovered by French chemist Joseph Le Bel (1847–1930).

1874 Nitrosyl chloride is discovered by British chemist William Tilden (1842–1926).

1874 DDT is discovered by German chemist Othmar Zeidler, who does not recognize its insecticidal properties.

1875 Metallic element gallium (symbol Ga) is discovered by French chemist Paul Lecoq Boisbaudran (c.1838–c.1912).

1875 Eosin scarlet dye is discovered by Adolf von Baeyer.

1875 Phenylhydrazine (an important chemical in organic analysis) is discovered by German chemist Emil Fischer (1852–1919).

1876 Idea of chemical potential (extending thermodynamics into chemistry) is proposed by US chemist Josiah Gibbs (1839–1903).

1876 Tiemann-Reimer reaction (for synthesizing hydroxy-aldehydes) is discovered by German chemists Johann Tiemann (1848–99) and, independently, C. Reimer (1856–1921).

1877 Friedel-Crafts reaction (in which an alkyl or acyl group is substituted into a benzene ring) is discovered by French chemist Charles Friedel (1832–99) and US chemist James Crafts (1839–1917).

PHYSICS

1871 Method of measuring the conductivity of electrolytes (using alternating current) is discovered by German physicist Friedrich Kohlrausch (1840–1910), leading to Kohlrausch's law (that ions migrate independently during electrolysis).

1873 Electromagnetic theory of light is published by Scottish physicist James Clerk Maxwell (1831–79).

1873 Equation of state or Van der Waals' equation (relating pressure and volume of a gas and making due allowance for the force of attraction between gas molecules – the Van der Waals' force) is discovered by Dutch physicist Johannes Van der Waals (1837–1923).

1874 Term "electron" is coined by Irish physicist George Stoney (1826–1911) – later (1897) to be adopted instead of J.J. Thomson's term "corpuscle".

c.1874 Mach's principle (that the inertia of an object results from its interaction with the rest of the Universe) is discovered by Austrian physicist and philosopher Ernst Mach (1838–1916),

1875 Photoelectric properties of selenium are discovered by British physicist Willoughby Smith (1828–91).

1875 Kerr effect (the differential refraction of light by some materials when they are in a strong electric field) is discovered by Scottish physicist John Kerr (1824–1907).

1876 Cathode rays – emitted by the cathode of a discharge tube – are described and named by German physicist Eugen Goldstein (1850–1930), who went on (1886) to identify "canal rays" (positive ions emitted by the anode).

1877 Theory of sound (as consisting of vibrations in an elastic medium) is proposed by British physicist Lord Rayleigh (John William Strutt) (1842–1919).

1877 Method of liquefying oxygen by compression and cooling is devised by Swiss physicist Raoul Pictet (1846–1929) and, independently, French physicist Louis Cailletet (1832–1913), who went on to liquefy also air, hydrogen and nitrogen.

1878 Properties of "molecular rays" (cathode rays, i.e. electrons), produced in high-voltage discharge ("Crookes") tubes, are described by British physicist William Crookes (1832–1919).

MEDICINE

1870 Nephrotomy, an operation to remove a kidney, is introduced by German surgeon Gustav Simon (1824–76).

1874 Osteopathy is founded by US physician Andrew Still (1828–1917).

1876 Bacterium that causes anthrax is isolated by German bacteriologist Robert Koch (1843–1910).

1877 Paget's disease (a form of osteitis causing bone thickening) is discovered by British surgeon James Paget (1814–99).

1877 Lancereaux's diabetes (diabetes mellitus with pancreatic disease) is discovered by French physician Étienne Lancereaux (1829–1910).

1877 Role of the gnat Culex in carrying the nematode worms (Filaria) that cause elephantiasis (filariasis) in humans is discovered by Scottish physician Patrick Manson (1844–1922).

1878 Cause of "the bends" in divers who have breathed compressed air (nitrogen dissolved in the blood) is discovered by French physiologist Paul Bert (1833–86).

1879 Electrocardiograph for studying the electrical activity of the brain is introduced by British physician Augustus Waller (1816–80).

1879 Bacterium (gonococcus) that causes gonorrhea is discovered by German bacteriologist Albert Niesser (1855–1916).

CHEMISTRY

1878 Metallic element ytterbium (symbol Yb) is discovered by Swiss chemist Jean de Marignac (1817–94), although his "element" is later (1907) found by French chemist Georges Urbain (1872–1938) to be a mixture of two elements, which he called neoytterbium and lutetium; in the event, the name ytterbium was retained for neoytterbium.

1879 Saccharin is discovered by US chemists Ira Remsen (1846–1927) and Constantin Fahlberg (1850–1910).

1879 Nucleic acids are discovered by German biochemist Albrecht Kossel (1853–1927), later (1929) to be rediscovered by Russian-born US chemist Phoebus Levene (1869–1940).

1879 Four-carbon ring compounds are discovered by Russian chemist Vladimir Markovnikov (1837–1904).

1879 Metallic elements holmium (symbol Ho), detected spectroscopically a year earlier by Swiss chemist J.L. Soret, and thulium (symbol Tm) are isolated by Swedish chemist Per Cleve (1840–1905).

1879 Metallic element samarium (symbol Sm) is discovered by French chemist Paul Lecoq Boisbaudran (c.1838–1912).

1879 Metallic element scandium (symbol Sc) is discovered (as its oxide) by Swedish physicist Lars Nilson (1840–99).

1880 Wallach rearrangement (of organic azo compounds) is discovered by German chemist Otto Wallach (1847–1931).

1880 Étard reaction – the oxidation of methylbenzene (toluene) to benzenecarbaldehyde (benzaldehyde) by chromium oxychloride (chromyl chloride) – is discovered by French chemist Alexandre Étard (1852–1910).

1880 Method of synthesizing indigo is discovered by German chemist Adolf von Baeyer (1835–1917), who later (1883) works outs its structure.

PHYSICS

1879 Stefan's law (that the radiation emitted by a hot object – per unit area per unit time – is proportional to the fourth power of its absolute temperature) is discovered by Austrian physicist Joseph Stefan (1835–93). It was later (1884) proved theoretically by his compatriot Ludwig Boltzmann (1844–1906) and is now usually termed the Stefan-Boltzmann law.

FARMING AND FOOD

1880 Frozen beef is sent from Australia to England on SS Strathleven.

1881 petrol-engined farm tractor is built by US engineer John Froelich.

1882 Frozen meat is sent from New Zealand to England on SS Dunedin.

1884 Method of making evaporated milk is patented in the USA by John Mayenberg, who later (1885) manufactures it with his Helvetia Milk Condensing Company.

1885 Bordeaux mixture is introduced as a fungicide for use on grape vines by French horticulturist P.M. Millarder.

1885 Canned treacle (sold as "Golden Syrup") is marketed by Scottish sugar refiner Abram Lyle III.

1886 Coca-Cola is invented by US physician John Pemberton, later (1894) bottled commercially by Joseph Biedenham.

1887 Malted milk drink is marketed by British-born US industrialist William Horlick (1846–1936).

1889 Simple milking machine is invented by Scottish farmer William Murchland.

1889 Machines for knotting cord round bales in a binder is invented by US engineer La Verne Noyes (1849–1919).

BIOLOGY

1880 Fact that starch acts as an energy store in plants is discovered by German botanist Andreas Schimper (1856–1901).

c.1880 Golgi apparatus (body), in the protoplasm of cells, is discovered by Italian biologist Camillo Golgi (1843–1926).

1882 Process of cell division is discovered by German cytologist Walther Flemming (1843–1915), who named it "mitosis".

1883 Phagocytes (cells that devour foreign "invaders") are discovered by Russian-born French biologist Ilya Mechnikov (1845–1916).

1883 Term "eugenics" is coined (for the improvement of human characteristics through selective breeding) by British scientist Francis Galton (1822–1911).

1883 Quagga becomes extinct.

1884 Method of staining, and therefore classifying, bacteria is discovered by Danish bacteriologist Hans Gram (1853–1938).

1884 Fact that the energy content of foods, as made use of by the body, is exactly the same as the energy produced when the same foods are burned (the calorie content) is discovered by german physiologist Max Rubner (1854–1932).

1886 Weismannism (or "germ plasm" theory, that only the contents of sperm and ova are passed unchanged to offspring – but not acquired characteristics) is proposed by German biologist August Weismann (1834–1914).

CHEMISTRY

1880 Metallic element gadolinium (symbol Gd) is discovered by Swiss chemist Jean de Marignac (1817–94), later (1886) rediscovered by Paul Lecoq Boisbaudran (1838–1912).

1882 Raoult's law (that, at a given temperature, the relative lowering of vapour pressure of a solution is proportional to the concentration of solute) is discovered by French chemist François Raoult (1830–1901).

1882 Oximes are discovered by German chemist Viktor Meyer (1848–97).

1883 Thiophene is discovered by German chemist Viktor Meyer (1848–97).

1883 Method of analyzing the amount of nitrogen in organic compounds is discovered by Danish chemist Johan Kjeldahl (1849–1900).

c.1883 Ostwald's dilution law (that the degree of dissociation of a weak electrolyte is proportional to the square root of the dilution) is discovered by Latvian-born German chemist Friedrich Ostwald (1853–1932).

1884 Amino acid cysteine is discovered by German chemist Eugen Baumann (1846–96).

1884 Sandmeyer reaction (for making aromatic halides using diazonium compounds) is discovered by German chemist Traugott Sandmeyer (1854–1922).

1884 Dissociation of ionic compounds in aqueous solution (to form an electrically-conducting electrolyte) is discovered by Swedish chemist Svante Arrhenius (1859–1927), later (1893) reaffirmed by German physical chemist Hermann Nernst (1864–1941).

PHYSICS

1880 Piezoelectric effect (that pressure across a crystal of quartz produces a voltage) is discovered by French physicist Pierre Curie (1859–1906).

1883 Method of large-scale liquefaction of nitrogen is discovered by Polish physicist Zygmunt Wróblewski (1845–88).

1884 Convergent series of lines in the atomic spectrum of hydrogen (subsequently of great importance in the development of quantum theory) is discovered by Swiss physicist Johann Balmer (1825–98).

1886 Nernst effect (in which a difference in temperature between the ends of a conductor in a magnetic field results in a voltage between the opposite faces of the conductor) is discovered by German physical chemist Walter Nernst (1864–1941).

1886 Canal rays are discovered by German physicist Eugen Goldstein (1850–1931).

1887 Non-existence of the ether (a medium through which light was supposed to travel) is proved experimentally by US physicists Albert Michelson (1852–1931) and Edward Morley (1838–1923).

1887 Photoelectric effect and the existence of electromagnetic (radio) waves – first called Hertzian waves – are confirmed by German physicist Heinrich Hertz (1857–94).

1888 Liquid crystals are discovered by Austrian botanist Friedrich Reinitzer, although not utilized until much later (1964) by Scottish chemist George Gray (1926–), who made stable liquid crystals for electronic displays.

MEDICINE

1880 Bacterium that causes typhoid fever is discovered by German bacteriologist Karl Eberth (1835–1926) and, independently, his compatriot Robert Koch (1843–1910) and, later (1884), by German bacteriologist Georg Gaffky (1850–1918).

1881 Fact that the mosquito is the vector of yellow fever is discovered by Cuban physician Carlos Finlay (1833–1915), although his discovery attracted little attention at the time.

1881 Pneumococcus bacterium that causes pneumonia is discovered by US physician George Sternberg (1838–1915).

1882 Bacterium that causes tuberculosis is discovered by German bacteriologist Robert Koch (1843–1910).

1882 Cholecystectomy, an operation to remove the gall bladder, is introduced by German surgeon Carl Langenbuch (1846–1901).

c.1883 Down's syndrome (trisomy 21) is discovered by British physician John Haydon-Down (1828–96).

1883 Association between myxoedema and thyroid function is discovered by Swiss surgeon Emil Kocher (1841–1917).

1883 Analgesic and fever-reducing drug antipyrene is discovered by German chemist Ludwig Knorr (1859–1921).

1883 Ringer's solution (used for keeping tissues alive outside the body) is devised by British physician Sydney Ringer (1835–1910).

1883 Bacterium that causes diphtheria is discovered by German bacteriologist Edwin Klebs (1834–1913), later (1884) isolated by his compatriot Friedrich Löffler (1852–1915).

1880

FARMING AND FOOD	BIOLOGY	CHEMISTRY	PHYSICS	MEDICINE

BIOLOGY

1887 Fact that in all species the body cells, whatever their type, contain a fixed number of chromosomes is discovered by Belgian cytologist Édouard van Beneden (1846–1910).

1887 Nitrogen fixation (the conversion of nitrogen in the soil into nitrates and nitrites by bacteria in plant roots) is discovered by German agricultural chemist Hermann Hellriegel (1831–95).

1887 Centrosomes (bodies within cells) are discovered by German biologist Theodor Boveri (1862–1915) and, independently, Belgian cytologist Édouard van Beneden (1846–1910).

1888 Fact that there are different kinds of yeast (some of which are better than others for fermentation processes such as brewing and wine-making) is discovered by Danish botanist Emil Hansen (1842–1909).

1888 Word "chromosome" (for chromatin threads formed during cell division) is coined by German anatomist Heinrich von Waldeyer (1836–1921).

1888 Fixation of atmospheric nitrogen by nodules of the roots of leguminous plants is discovered by German chemist Hermann Hellriegel (1831–95).

CHEMISTRY

1884 Van't Hoff factor (the ratio of the number of particles in an electrolyte to the number of undissociated particles) is discovered by Dutch chemist Jacobus van't Hoff (1852–1911).

1885 Mélinite explosive (ammonium picrate) is discovered by French chemist Eugène Turpin.

1885 Metallic elements neodymium (symbol Nd) and praseodymium (symbol Pr) are discovered by Austrian chemist Carl von Welsbach (1856–1929).

1886 Beckman rearrangement (of oximes of ketones into amides) is discovered by German chemist Ernst Beckmann (1853–1923).

1886 Metalloid element germanium (symbol Ge) is discovered by German chemist Clemens Winkler (1838–1904).

1886 Metallic element dysprosium (symbol Dy) is discovered by French chemist Paul Lecoq Boisbaudran (1838–1912).

1887 Hydrazine is discovered by German chemist Theodor Curtius (1875–1928).

1887 Fructose is synthesized by German chemist Emil Fischer (1852–1919), who founds the science of biochemistry.

1887 Rhodamine dyes are discovered by German chemist Adolf von Baeyer (1835–1917).

1887 Gabriel's synthesis (of primary amines from potassium phthalimide and haloalkanes) is discovered by German chemist Siegmund Gabriel (1851–1924).

1888 Le Chatelier's principle, that if a constraint is imposed on a system in equilibrium the system adjusts itself to minimize the effects of the constraint, is discovered by French chemist Henry le Chatelier (1850–1936).

1889 Arrhenius equation (for the rate of a chemical reaction) is discovered by Swedish chemist Svante Arrhenius (1859–1927).

1889 Seven-carbon ring compounds are discovered by Russian chemist Vladimir Markovnikov (1837–1904).

1889 Metallic element europium (symbol Eu) is discovered spectroscopically by British scientist William Crookes (1832–1919) and, later (1896), isolated by French chemist Eugène Demarçay (1852–1903).

1889 Method of making pure nickel by heating nickel carbonyl is discovered by German-born British chemist Ludwig Mond (1839–1909).

PHYSICS

1888 Hallwachs effect (a type of photoelectric effect) is discovered by German physicist Wilhelm Hallwachs (1859–1922).

MEDICINE

1883 Bacterium that causes cholera is discovered by German bacteriologist Robert Koch (1843–1910) who, in the same year, developed a vaccine against anthrax.

1883 Fact that the trypanasome that transmits filariasis is carried by a mosquito is discovered by Scottish physician Patrick Manson (1844–1922).

1884 Cocaine is first used as a local anaesthetic (in eye surgery) by Austrian-born US physician Carl Koller (1857–1944).

1884 Operation for the removal of a brain tumour is first carried out by British surgeon Rickman Godlee (1849–1925).

1885 Vaccine against rabies is developed by French bacteriologist Louis Pasteur (1822–1895).

1885 Acromegaly (overgrowth of bones after adulthood) is discovered by French neurologist Pierre Marie (1853–1940); its cause (a defect in the pituitary gland) is later (1909) discovered by US physician Harvey Cushing (1869–1939).

1885 Method of treating goitre by removing the thyroid gland is introduced by Swiss surgeon Emil Kocher (1841–1917).

1886 Appendicitis (and appendicetomy, the surgical treatment of it) is described by US physician Reginald Fitz (1843–1913). Appendicetomy is later (1880) perfected by British surgeon Robert Tait (1845–99) and (1886) German surgeon Ulrich Krönlein (1847–1910).

1886 Use of steam for sterilizing surgical instruments is introduced by Latvian-born German brain surgeon Ernst von Bergmann (1836–1907).

1886 Muscular dystrophy is described by French neurologist Jules Dejerine (1849–1917).

1886 Bacterium that causes glanders in horses and the bacterium that causes rinderpest in cattle are discovered by German bacteriologist Friedrich Löffler (1852–1915).

1886 Cause of Weil's disease (infectious jaundice, later called leptospirosis) in sewer workers is shown to be due to contact with rat's urine by German physician Adolf Weil (1848–1916).

1887 Bacterium that causes undulant fever (Malta fever or brucellosis) is discovered by Scottish bacteriologist David Bruce (1855–1931).

1888 Bacterium that causes salmonella (food poisoning) is discovered by German bacteriologist August Gärtner (1848–1934), later named by US veterinary surgeon Daniel Salmon (1850–1914).

1890

FARMING AND FOOD

1890 Agricultural tractor is patented by US inventor G. Edwards.

1890 Method of measuring the butterfat content of milk is invented by US agricultural chemist Stephen Babcock (1843–1931).

1890s Stationary steam engines are used for ploughing in Europe and North America.

1891 Crown cork bottle top is invented in the USA by William Painter.

1891 Process for manufacturing chewing gum is set up by US industrialist William Wrigley (1861–1932).

1892 First commercially produced petrol-driven agricultural tractor is built in the USA by John Froelich.

1893 Shredded wheat breakfast cereal is invented by US lawyer Henry Perky.

1895 Wheat flakes are invented by US physician John Kellog (1852–1943).

BIOLOGY

1891 Mechanism of the knee-jerk reflex is discovered by British physiologist Charles Sherrington (1857–1952), also described by British chemist Stephen Hales (1677–1761) and Scottish neurologist Robert Whytt (1714–1766).

1891 Fossil bones of Pithecanthropus (later Homo) erectus ("Java man", a link in human evolution) are discovered by Dutch palaeontologist Marie Eugène Dubois (1858–1940).

1893 Dollo's law (of irreversibility in evolution) is formulated by French palaeontologist Louis Dollo (1857–1931).

1894 Hormone adrenaline (epinephrine) is discovered by British endocrinologist Edward Sharpey-Schafer (1850–1935) and physiologist George Oliver (1841–1915), later (1897) isolated by US biochemist John Abel (1857–1938) and crystallized in pure form (1901) by Japanese-born US chemist Jokichi Takamine (1854–1922).

CHEMISTRY

1890 Tautomerism (in which two isomers are in equilibrium) is discovered by German chemist Ludwig Claisen (1851–1930), who called it pseudomerism, and, independently, by his compatriot Johannes Wislicenus (1835–1902).

1890 Gattermann reaction (for making aromatic halides using diazonium compounds) is discovered by German chemist Ludwig Gattermann (1860–1920).

1890 Babcock test for the amount of fat in milk is discovered by US agricultural chemist Stephen Babcock (1843–1931).

1890 Guldberg's law (relating critical temperature to boiling point) is discovered by Swedish chemist Cato Guldberg (1836–1902) and, independently, P. Guye (1862–1922).

1890 Dye base acridine is discovered by German chemists Karl Graebe (1841–1927) and Heinrich Caro (1834–1910).

PHYSICS

1890 Guldberg's law (relating critical temperature to boiling point) is discovered by Norwegian physicist Cato Guldberg (1836–1902), also discovered independently by P. Guye (1862–1922).

1890 Fleming's rules (relating the relative directions of the magnetic field, electric current and motion in electric machines) are proposed by British physicist John Fleming (1849–1945).

1890 Magnetic hysteresis is discovered by Scottish physicist Alfred Ewing (1855–1935) and, later (1892), by German-born electrical engineer Charles (Karl) Steinmetz (1865–1923).

1890 Rydberg formula (for calculating the frequency of spectral lines, which includes a term later called the Rydberg constant) is discovered by Swedish physicist Johannes Rydberg (1854–1919).

1891 Gravitational constant is determined by British physicist John Poynting (1852–1914).

MEDICINE

1890 Bacterium that causes phthisis (pulmonary tuberculosis) is discovered by German bacteriologist Robert Koch (1843–1910).

1890 Antitoxins (for diphtheria and tetanus) are discovered by German bacteriologist Emil von Behring (1854–1914).

1890 Antituberculosis serum is first used on humans by French physiologist Charles Richet (1850–1935).

1891 Injection of thyroid extract as a treatment for myxoedema is discovered by German physiologist Moritz Schiff (1823–96).

1891 Technique of lumbar puncture is introduced by German physician Heinrich Quincke (1834–1924).

1892 Guarnieri bodies, cell inclusions that are diagnostic of smallpox and cowpox, are discovered by Italian pathologist Giuseppi Guarnieri (1856–1918).

FARMING AND FOOD

1895 Health food called Postum is marketed in the USA by Charles Post (1854–1914); he later (1897) introduces a breakfast cereal called Grape Nuts.

1895 Practical "pulsating" milking machine is invented by Scottish physician Alexander Shields.

1898 Pepsi-Cola (for treating dyspepsia) is invented by US pharmacist Caleb Bradman.

1898 Corn flakes are invented by William Kellog (1860–1951).

1899 Oxo cubes (beef stock cubes) are manufactured in Fray Bentos, Uruguay.

BIOLOGY

1895 Fact that gas exchange in plants occurs through "pores" (stomata) in the leaves is discovered by British plant physiologist Frederick Blackman (1866–1947).

1896 Medelian ratio of 3:1 in the first generation in plant-breeding experiments (first discovered by Gregor Mendel in 1866) is rediscovered by Dutch physiologist Hugo de Vries (1848–1935) and, independently, Karl Correns (1864–1933) and E. von Tschermak (1871–1962).

1897 Plant viruses are discovered by Dutch botanist Martinus Beijerinck (1851–1931).

1898 Golgi body (apparatus) in cells is discovered by Italian histologist Camillo Golgi (1844–1926).

1899 Natural pacemaker of the heart (the sino-atrial node) is discovered by Scottish anatomist and anthropologist Arthur Keith (1866–1955) and Englishman Martin Flack (1882–1931).

1899 "Lock-and-key" mechanism of enzyme action is proposed by German chemist Emil Fischer (1852–1919).

CHEMISTRY

c.1890 Claisen condensation (in which two molecules of an ester combine to form a keto ester) is discovered by German chemist Ludwig Claisen (1851–1930).

1891 Silicon carbide (Carborundum) is discovered by US chemist Edward Acheson (1856–1931).

1891 Nature of coordination compounds (complexes) is discovered by German-born Swiss chemist Alfred Werner (1866–1919).

1892 Polymerization of isoprene to form a synthetic rubber is discovered by British chemist William Tilden (1842–1926).

1892 Crum Brown rule (for aromatic substitution) is discovered by Scottish chemist Alexander Crum Brown (1838–1922).

1893 Dissociation of ionic compounds in aqueous solution (to form an electrically-conducting electrolyte) is discovered by German physical chemist Hermann Nernst (1864–1941).

1893 Formula of camphor is discovered by German chemist Julius Bredt (1855–1937), later (1903) synthesized by G. Komppa (1867–1949).

1894 Gaseous element argon (symbol Ar) is discovered by British scientist Lord Rayleigh (1842–1919) and Scottish chemist William Ramsay (1852–1916).

1896 Iron-nickel alloy invar (which has a very low coefficient of expansion) is discovered by Swiss-born French physicist Charles Guillaume (1861–1938).

1896 Amino acid histidine is discovered by German biochemist Albrecht Kossel (1853–1927) and Swede Sven Hedin (1865–1952).

1896 Cell-free fermentation of sugar (i.e., using ground-up yeast cells) is discovered by German chemist Eduard Buchner (1860–1917).

1896 Walden inversion (the interconversion of two optical isomers) is discovered by Russian chemist Paul Walden (1863–1957).

1897 Ability of finely divided nickel to catalyze the hydrogenation of unsaturated hydrocarbons (an important reaction in organic synthesis) is discovered by French chemists Paul Sabatier (1854–1941) and Jean-Baptiste Senderens (1856–1937).

1897 Method of manufacturing pure aspirin (acetylsalicylic acid) is discovered by German chemist Felix Hoffman, later (1899) marketed by the Bayer company.

1898 Purine is discovered by German chemist Emil Fischer (1852–1919).

1898 Radioactive elements polonium (symbol Po) and radium (symbol Ra) are discovered (in pitchblende) by Polish-born French chemists Marie (1867–1934) and Pierre (1859–1906) Curie.

1898 Gaseous elements krypton (symbol Kr), neon (symbol Ne) and xenon (symbol Xe) are discovered by Scottish chemists William Ramsay (1852–1916) and Morris Travers (1872–1961).

1899 Radioactive element actinium (symbol Ac) is discovered by French chemist André Debierne (1874–1949).

1899 Radioactive gas "thoron" (actually an isotope of radon) is discovered by New Zealand-born British physicist Ernest Rutherford (1871–1937).

PHYSICS

1892 Properties of cathode rays (then called Lenard rays) outside a discharge tube are investigated by German physicist Philipp von Lenard (1862–1947).

1893 Wien's law (that the wavelength of maximum energy radiated by a black body is inversely proportional to its absolute temperature) is discovered by German physicist Wilhelm Wien (1864–1928).

1894 Physical properties of radio ("Hertzian") waves are discovered by British physicist Oliver Lodge (1851–1940).

1895 X-rays (Röntgen rays) are discovered by German physicist William Röntgen (1845–1923).

1895 Explanation for the negative result of the 1887 Michelson-Morley experiment (to determine the existence of the "ether", a medium through which light was supposed to travel) is given by Irish physicist George Fitzgerald (1851–1901), who proposed that at speeds approaching the speed of light objects shorten in length. Because of a similar conclusion by Dutch physicist Hendrik Lorentz (1853–1928), the phenomenon became known as the Fitzgerald-Lorentz contraction.

1895 Curie point or temperature (at which ferromagnetic substances become paramagnetic) is discovered by French physicist Pierre Curie (1859–1906).

1895 Fact that cathode rays are negatively charged is discovered by French physicist Jean Perrin (1870–1942).

1895 Curie's law (that the magnetic susceptibility of a ferromagnetic substance is proportional to its absolute temperature) is discovered by French physicist Pierre Curie (1859–1906).

1895 Method of liquefying air in quantity is discovered by German engineer Carl von Linde (1842–1934).

1896 Alpha and beta rays are discovered by New Zealand-born British physicist Ernest Rutherford (1871–1937).

1896 Radioactivity (of uranium) is discovered by French physicist Antoine Becquerel (1852–1908).

1896 Zeeman effect (the splitting of spectral lines in a strong magnetic field) is discovered by Dutch physicist Pieter Zeeman (1865–1943); the theoretical explanation of the phenomenon is later given by Dutch physicist Hendrik Lorentz (1853–1928).

1896 Fact that X-rays are a type of electromagnetic radiation is discovered by Irish physicist George Stokes (1819–1903).

1897 Electron is discovered by British physicist J.J. (Joseph John) Thompson (1856–1940), who called it a "corpuscle".

1897 Charge on a single gas ion is determined by Irish physicist John Townsend (1868–1957).

1897 Hall effect (the generation of a voltage across a current-carrying conductor at right angles to a magnetic field) is discovered by US physicist Edwin Hall (1855–1938).

1897 Electric field emission is discovered by US physicist Robert Wood (1868–1955).

1897 Larmor progression (of charged particles in a magnetic field) is discovered by Joseph Larmor (1857–1942).

1898 Method of producing liquid hydrogen in quantity is discovered by Scottish physicist James Dewar (1842–1923).

MEDICINE

1892 Vaccine against typhoid fever is discovered by British bacteriologist Almoth Wright (1861–1947).

1892 Clostridium bacterium which causes gas gangrene is discovered by US pathologists William Welch (1850–1934) and G. Nuttall (1862–1937).

1893 Fact that Texas cattle fever is caused by a protozoan parasite and spread by cattle ticks is discovered by US microbiologist Theobald Smith (1859–1934).

1893 Inoculation against cholera is developed by Russian bacteriologist Waldemar Haffkine (1860–1930).

1894 Bacterium that causes bubonic plague is discovered by Swiss-born French bacteriologist Alexandre Yersin (1863–1943) and, independently, Japanese bacteriologist Shibasaburo Kitasato (1856–1931).

1894 Bacteriolysis – the destruction of bacteria by vaccine-induced antibodies – is discovered by Polish bacteriologist Richard Pfeiffer (1858–1945).

1894 Anaphylaxis – a fatal allergic reaction – is discovered by French physiologist Charles Richet (1850–1935).

1894 Reaction for detecting cholera is discovered by German bacteriologist Richard Pfeiffer (1879–1945).

1895 Tse-tse fly is identified as the carrier of sleeping sickness by Australian-born British bacteriologist David Bruce (1855–1931).

1895 Parasite that causes malaria is discovered by British physician Ronald Ross (1857–1932).

1896 Diagnostic X-ray photographs are first taken by Hungarian-born US physicist Michael Pupin (1858–1935).

1896 Bacterium that causes Bang's disease (infectious abortion in cattle) is discovered by Danish veterinary surgeon Bernhard Bang (1848–1932).

1896 Vaccine against rinderpest in cattle is developed by German bacteriologist Robert Koch (1843–1910).

1896 Fact that the disease beriberi is caused by the lack of some factor in food is discovered by Dutch physician Christiaan Eijkman (1858–1930).

1897 Inoculation against plague is developed by Russian bacteriologist Waldemar Haffkine (1860–1930).

1897 Use of ultraviolet light as a treatment for skin disorders, such as lupus vulgaris, is discovered by Danish physician Niels Finsen (1860–1904).

1897 Barium meal, which can be swallowed to make the stomach and intestines opaque to X-rays (and therefore show up on an X-ray photograph), is introduced by US physician Walter Cannon (1871–1945).

1898 Fact that mosquitoes transmit malaria to humans by biting is discovered by Italian parisitologists Giovanni Grassi (1854–1925), Arnico Bignami (1862–1929) and Giuseppi Bastianelli (1862–1959).

1898 Tobacco mosaic virus (the first known virus) is discovered by Dutch botanist Martinus Beijerinck (1851–1931).

1898 Fact that hoof-and-mouth disease is caused by a virus is discovered by German bacteriologists Friedrich Löffler (1852–1915) and Paul Frosch.

1898 Causative agent of one type of dysentery is discovered by Japanese bacteriologist Shibasaburo Kitasato (1856–1931).

PHYSICS

1898 Sabine's law of acoustics (that, for a given room, the product of the reverberation time and the absorptivity equals the volume) is discovered by US physicist Wallace Sabine (1868–1919).

1899 Identity between a beam of electrons and cathode rays is established by Dutch physicist Hendrik Lorentz (1853–1928), who also coined the word electron.

MEDICINE

1898 Chiropractic is established in the USA by Canadian osteopath Daniel Palmer (1845–1939).

1899 Vaccine against foot-and-mouth disease is developed by German bacteriologist Friedrich Löffler (1852–1915).

1899 Toxin produced by the diphtheria bacterium is discovered by French bacteriologist Pierre Roux (1853–1933) and Swiss-born French bacteriologist Alexandre Yersin (1863–1943).

1899 Aspirin (acetylsalicylic acid) is marketed (as a prescription drug, in powder form) by the German Bayer company, later (1915) as tablets.

1900

FARMING AND FOOD

1900 Hamburger is invented in the USA by Louis Lassen.

1901 Commercially successful petrol-engined tractor is produced in the USA by Charles Hart and Charles Parr.

1902 Tea-making machine (with an alarm clock) is invented by British gunsmith Frank Smith.

1903 Agricultural tractor is marketed by the British Petter company.

1903 Processed cheese is marketed by US manufacturer James Kraft.

1903 Decaffeinated coffee, trade-marked Sanka, is introduced by German coffee dealer Ludwig Roselius.

1904 Ovaltine (then called Ovamaltine) is patented in Switzerland by George Wander.

1906 Freeze-drying to preserve food is invented by French biophysicists Jacques Arsène d'Arsonval (1851–1940) and Georges Bordas.

1908 Caterpillar farm tractor is manufactured by US engineer Benjamin Holt, using track designs purchased from the British Hornsby company.

1909 Electric toaster is marketed by US General Electric Company.

BIOLOGY

1900 Mendel's laws of inheritance are rediscovered by German botanist Karl Correns (1864–1933) and, independently, Dutch botanist Hugo de Vries (1848–1935).

1902 Hormone secretin (produced in the walls of the small intestine to stimulate the production of digestive juices by the pancreas and liver) is discovered by British physiologists Ernest Starling (1866–1927) and William Bayliss (1860–1924).

1903 Enzyme zymase is discovered by German biologist Eduard Buchner (1860–1917).

1904 Conditioned reflexes are discovered by Russian biologist Ivan Pavlov (1849–1936).

1904 Breeding ground of the European eel is found to be in the western Atlantic by Danish biologist Johannes Schmidt (1877–1933).

1904 Coenzymes are discovered by British biochemist Arthur Harden (1865–1940).

c. 1905 Nissl bodies (particles in nerve cells) are discovered by German neurologist Franz Nissl (1860–1919).

1905 Mammalian sex chromosomes (XX for females and XY for males) are discovered by US biologist Clarence McClung.

1905 Technique for growing tissue cells in vitro (outside the body) is discovered by US biologist Ross Harrison (1870–1959).

1907 Fact that proteins are composed of amino acids is discovered by German chemist Emil Fischer (1852–1919).

1908 Phagocytes (digestive white blood cells) are discovered by Russian biologist Ilya Metchnikoff (1845–1916).

1909 Pituitary hormone oxytocin (which stimulates contractions of the womb during childbirth) is discovered by British physiologist Henry Dale (1875–1968).

1909 Word "gene" is coined by Danish botanist Wilhelm Johannsen (1857–1927).

CHEMISTRY

1900 Grignard reagents (organo-metallic compounds of magnesium used in organic synthesis) are discovered by French chemist François Grignard (1871–1935).

1900 Fulvene (a red hydrocarbon) is discovered by German chemist Friedrich Thiele (1865–1918).

1900 Radioactive gaseous element radon (symbol Rn) is discovered by German chemist Ernst Dorn (1848–1916), and later (1908) extracted by Scottish chemist William Ramsay (1852–1916) and British chemists Frederick Soddy (1877–1956) and Robert Whytlaw-Gray (1877–1958), who initially named it niton.

1900 Basic process for cracking crude oil to make petrol is discovered by US chemist Charles Palmer (1858–1939).

1900 Absorption chromatography (for separating petroleum mixtures) is discovered by US chemist David Day (1859–1925).

1900 Triphenylmethyl, the first free radical to be isolated, is discovered by Russian-born US chemist Moses Gomberg (1866–1947).

1901 Amino acid proline is discovered by German chemist Emil Fischer (1852–1919).

1901 First essential amino acid, tryptophan, is discovered by British chemists Frederick Gowland Hopkins (1861–1947) and S. Cole.

1902 Amino acid hydroxyproline is discovered by Emil Fischer.

1902 Optically active inorganic compounds (previously all such compounds were organic) are discovered by British chemist William Pope (1870–1939).

1902 Method of making artificial corundum (aluminium oxide) is discovered by French chemist Auguste Verneuil (1856–1913).

1903 Buffer solutions, for stabilizing pH, are discovered by German physical chemist Hermann Nernst (1864–1941).

1903 Amino acid isoleucine is discovered by German bacteriologist Paul Ehrlich (1854–1915).

1904 Abegg's "rule of eight" (that an outer atomic shell containing eight electrons confers extra stability on an atom or ion) is discovered by German chemist Richard Abegg (1869–1910).

1904 Highly toxic chemical divinylchloroarsine, later (World War 1) used as the war gas Lewisite, is discovered by Belgian-born US chemist Julius Nieuwland (1878–1936).

1905 Fact that radioactive metals all eventually decay to (an isotope of) lead is discovered by US chemist Bertram Boltwood (1870–1927), who later (1907) discovered "ionium", thought to be a new element but now known to be a radioactive isotope of thorium.

PHYSICS

1900 Quantum theory is proposed by German physicist Max Planck (1858–1947).

1900 Gamma rays are discovered by French physicist Paul Villard (1860–1934).

1901 Fact that light exerts a pressure is discovered, and the pressure measured, by Russian physicist Pyotr Lebedev (1866–1912).

1902 Heaviside-Kennelly layer (of ionized gas in the upper atmosphere that reflects radio signals) is discovered independently by British physicist Oliver Heaviside (1850–1925) and US electrical engineer Arthur Kennelly (1861–1939).

1902 Photoelectric effect (the emission of electrons from the surface of a metal exposed to light or other electromagnetic radiation) is quantified by German physicist Philipp von Lenard (1862–1947).

1902 Claude process (for the bulk liquefaction of air) is discovered by French scientist George Claude (1870–1960).

1904 Model of the atom as a "pudding" of positive charges containing negatively charged electrons (the "plums" in the pudding) is proposed by British physicist J.J. Thomson (1856–1940).

1905 Special Theory of Relativity is proposed by German-born US physicist Albert Einstein (1879–1955).

1905 Third law of thermodynamics (that entropy change tends to zero at absolute zero) is formulated by German physical chemist Hermann Nernst (1864–1941).

1905 Explanation of paramagnetism (as being caused by electron charges within an atom) is given by French physicist Paul Langevin (1872–1946).

1906 X-rays characteristic of the element that scatters them – related to the element's atomic number – are discovered by British physicist Charles Barkla (1877–1944).

1906 Lines in the ultraviolet region of the hydrogen spectrum (the Lyman series) are discovered by US physicist Theodore Lyman (1874–1954).

1907 Theory that explains ferromagnetism in terms of magnetic domains within the material is proposed by French physicist Pierre Weiss (1865–1940).

1908 Method of liquefying helium is discovered by Dutch physicist Heike Kamerlingh Onnes (1853–1926).

1909 Avogadro's number (the number of molecules in 1 cubic centimetre of gas at normal temperature and pressure) is determined by French physicist Jean Perrin (1870–1942).

MEDICINE

1900 A, B and O blood groups are discovered by Austrian pathologist Karl Landsteiner (1868–1943).

1900 Bacterium that causes one kind of dysentery is discovered by US microbiologist Simon Flexner (1863–1946); another type is isolated later (1915) by US biochemist Edward Kendall (1886–1972).

1900 Microorganism (a protozoan) that causes kala-azar (leishmaniasis) is discovered by Scottish physician William Leishman (1865–1926).

1901 Role of white blood cells in combating infection is discovered by Russian biologist Ilya Metchnikoff (1845–1916).

1901 Fact that yellow fever is caused by a virus is discovered by US surgeon Walter Reed (1851–1902).

1902 Anaphylaxis (a life-threatening allergic reaction) is discovered by French physician Charles Richet (1850–1935).

1903 X-ray treatment for cancerous tumours is discovered by German physician Georg Perthes (1869–1927).

1904 Local anaesthetic novocaine is discovered by US physician J. Leonard Corring.

1905 Successful direct blood transfusion between humans is performed by US physician George Coile (1864–1943).

1905 Bacterium (a spirochete) that causes syphilis is discovered by German bacteriologists Erich Hoffman (1868–1959) and Fritz Schaudinn (1871–1906).

1906 Allergies are discovered by Austrian physician Clement von Pirquet (1874–1929).

1906 Bacterium that causes whooping cough (pertusis) is discovered by Belgian physician Jules Bordet (1870–1961).

1906 Fact that Rocky Mountain spotted fever is spread by cattle ticks is discovered by US pathologist Howard Ricketts (1871–1910), who went on to discover the microorganisms (rickettsia) that cause the disease.

1906 Corneal transplant operation is introduced by French surgeon Edouard Zirm (1863–1944).

1906 Wassermann test (for syphilis) is discovered by German bacteriologist August von Wassermann (1866–1925).

1906 Atoxyl, the first synthetic drug (for treating sleeping sickness), is discovered by German physician Paul Ehrlich (1854–1915).

1907 Role of protozoans in causing various tropical diseases is discovered by French physician Charles Laveran (1845–1922).

1907 Serum for treating cerebrospinal meningitis is discovered by US microbiologist Simon Flexner (1863–1946).

FARMING AND FOOD	BIOLOGY	CHEMISTRY	PHYSICS	MEDICINE

CHEMISTRY

1905 Cyclooctatetraene (an 8-carbon cyclic compound) is discovered by German chemist Richard Willstätter (1872–1942).

1906 Tricarbon dioxide (carbon suboxide) is discovered by German chemist Otto Diels (1876–1954).

1906 Metallic element lutetium (symbol Lu) is discovered by French chemist George Urbain (1872–1938) and, independently (1907), Austrian chemist Carl von Welsbach (1858–1929).

1906 Isotope thorium-230 is discovered by US chemist Bertram Boltwood (1870–1927), who calls it "ionium".

1908 Food additive monosodium glutamate (MSG) is discovered by Japanese food technologist Ikeda Kikunae (1864–1936).

1909 Concept of pH (as a measure of acidity/alkalinity) is introduced by Danish biochemist Sören Sörensen (1868–1939).

1909 Identity of the sugar component (D-ribose) in the nucleic acid RNA is discovered by Russian-born US biochemist Phoebus Levene (1869–1940), who went on (1929) to identify the sugar (deoxyribose) in DNA.

MEDICINE

1907 Full clinical description of pre-senile dementia (Alzheimer's disease) is given by German neuropathologist Alois Alzheimer (1864–1915).

1907 AB blood group is discovered by Czech physician Jan Jansky (1873–1921) and, independently, later (1910) by US physician William Moss.

1908 Vaccine against tuberculosis is developed by French physicians Albert Calmette (1863–1933) and Charles Guérin, later (1923) used as BCG (bacille Calmette Guérin) vaccine.

1909 First cancer-causing virus (Rous chicken sarcoma) is discovered by US physician Francis Rous (1879–1970).

FARMING AND FOOD

1910 Petrol-driven combine harvester is invented in the USA.

1910 Coffee-making machine is invented by Englishman Alfred Cohn.

1912 Process for making sugar from wood is invented by German chemist Friedrich Bergius (1884–1949).

1913 Vacuum milking machine is invented by Swede Carl de Laval (1845–1913).

1917 Uncooked quick-frozen foods are invented by US food technologist Clarence Birdseye (1886–1956).

1918 Domestic mechanical refrigerator is marketed in the USA by the Kelvinator Company.

1919 Paper tea bags are invented and mass-produced in the USA by Joseph Krieger; silk tea bags were made earlier (1904) by tea importer Thomas Sullivan.

1919 First supermarket, called Piggly-Wiggly, is opened in Memphis, Tennessee, by US retailer Clarence Saunders (1881–1953).

1920 Steam-powered rotary hoe (called a Rotovator) is invented by Australian blacksmiths Albert and Cliff Howard.

1921 Aeroplanes are first used for dusting crops with pesticides in the USA.

1925 First successful hydroponics experiments (growing plants without soil) are carried out in the USA.

1926 Artificial PKN (phosphorus, potash and nitrogen) fertilizers are first produced in Britain.

1927 Improved machine for picking cotton is invented in the USA by the brothers John (1892–1954) and Mack (1900–66) Rust.

1928 Wrapped sliced bread is invented by US jeweller Otto Rohwedder.

BIOLOGY

1910 Role of chromosomes in inheritance (and occurrence of genes along chromosomes) is discovered by US geneticist Thomas Hunt Morgan (1866–1945).

1911 Histamine (which can cause allergies) is discovered by British physiologist Henry Dale (1875–1968).

1911 Gradient theory of regeneration, that the dominant part of a regenerating organ develops first, is proposed by US biologist Charles Child (1869–1954).

1912 Fossil remains of Piltdown man are "discovered" by British naturalist Charles Dawson (1864–1916), later (1953) shown to fraudulent.

1913 Chromosome mapping is devised by US geneticist Alfred Sturtevant (1891–1970).

1914 Role of ATP (adenosine triphosphate) in cell metabolism is discovered by Russian-born US biochemist Fritz Lipmann (1899–1986).

1914 Amino acids in blood are discovered by US physiologist John Abel (1857–1938).

1915 Bacteriophages (viruses that attack bacteria) are discovered by British bacteriologist Frederick Twort (1877–1950) and later (1966), independently, by Canadian bacteriologist Felix D'Hérelle (1873–1949), who named them.

1915 Thyroid hormone thyroxine is discovered by US biochemist Edward Kendall (1886–1972).

1917 Role of calories (in food) as an energy source is discovered by US physiologist Graham Lusk (1866–1932) and British bacteriologist Frederick Twort (1877–1950).

1918 Fact that humans have 48 chromosomes in all body cells is discovered by US embryologist Herbert Evans (1882–1971).

1919 Acetylcholine is discovered by British physiologist Henry Dale (1875–1968), although its role as a neurotransmitter is not established until later (1921) by German physiologist Otto Loewi (1873–1961).

1919 Communication among honeybees by means of body movements (the "bee's dance") is discovered by Austrian-born German biologist Karl von Frisch (1886–1982), who later (1947) discovers that the bees use the polarization of light for orientation.

CHEMISTRY

1910 Amino acid tryptophan is discovered by British chemist Frederick Gowland Hopkins (1861–1947).

1910 Histamine is synthesized by British physiologists George Barker (1878–1939) and Henry Dale (1875–1968).

1911 Method of making propanone (acetone) by the bacterial fermentation of grain is discovered by Russian-born Israeli chemist Chaim Weizmann (1874–1952).

1911 Metallic element hafnium (symbol Hf) is discovered by French chemist Georges Urbain (1872–1932), and first extracted (1923) by Dutch physicist Dirk Coster (1889–1950) and Hungarian-born Swedish chemist Georg von (or George de) Hevesy (1886–1966).

1912 Existence of two forms of uranium (now known to be isotopes) is discovered by German physicist Hans Geiger (1882–1945) and British physicist J. Nuttall (1890–1958).

1912 Use of radioactive tracers in chemical analysis is established by Austrian chemist Friedrich Paneth (1887–1958) and Hungarian-born Swedish chemist Georg von (or George de) Hevesy (1886–1966).

1913 Fact that lead from different natural sources can have different relative atomic masses (now known to be due to their having different combinations of isotopes) is discovered by US chemist Theodore Richards (1868–1928).

1913 Isotopes are discovered by British chemist Frederick Soddy (1877–1956).

1913 Presence of ozone in the upper atmosphere is discovered by French physicist Charles Fabry (1867–1945).

1913 Composition of chlorophyll is discovered by German chemist Richard Willstätter (1872–1942).

1914 Phenarsazine chloride (Adamsite), a potential war gas that causes sneezing, is discovered by US chemist Roger Adams (1889–1971).

1914 Xylyl bromide (Cyclite, T-Stoff) is developed as a toxic war gas in World War 1 by German chemist von Tappen.

1915 Carbonyl chloride (phosgene, Collognite or D-Stoff) is developed as a toxic war gas by Germany, and later used by other combatants in World War 1.

PHYSICS

1911 Atomic nucleus is discovered by New Zealand-born British physicist Ernest Rutherford (1871–1937).

1911 Cosmic rays (although not named as such until 1925 by US physicist Robert Millikan) are discovered by Austrian physicist Victor Hess (1883–1964), who also showed that they come from outer space, not from the Sun.

1911 Superconductivity at very low temperatures is discovered by Dutch physicist Kamerlingh Onnes (1853–1926).

1912 X-ray diffraction by crystals is discovered by French physicist Max von Laue (1879–1960).

1912 Bragg's law (relating the diffraction of X-rays by crystals to the spacing of the atoms in the crystal) is formulated by British physicist William Henry Bragg (1862–1942), assisted by his son William Lawrence Bragg (1890–1971).

1912 Electric charge on an electron is determined by US physicist Robert Millikan (1868–1953).

1912 Born-Haber cycle (for calculating the lattice energy of an ionic crystal) is discovered by German-born British physicist Max Born (1882–1970) and German chemist Fritz Haber (1868–1934).

1912 Paschen-Back effect (the splitting of spectral lines in a strong magnetic field) is discovered by German physicists Louis Paschen (1865–1947) and Ernest Back (1881–1959).

1913 Stark effect (the splitting of spectral lines in a strong electric field) is discovered by German physicist Johannes Stark (1874–1957).

1913 Atom is conceived as having a central nucleus surrounded by orbiting electrons by Danish physicist Niels Bohr (1885–1962).

1913 Atomic number is equated with the positive charge on the atomic nucleus by British physicist Henry Moseley (1887–1915).

1914 Relationship between the atomic number of an element and the frequency of the lines in its X-ray spectrum (Moseley's law) is discovered by British physicist Henry Moseley (1887–1915).

1915 Elliptical (rather than circular) orbits of electrons in atoms is proposed by German physicist Arnold Sommerfield (1868–1951) and, independently, W. Wilson (1875–1965).

MEDICINE

1910 Bacterium that causes typhus is discovered by US pathologist Howard Ricketts (1871–1910), who also showed, independently of French physician Charles Nicolle (1866–1936), that the disease is transmitted by body lice.

1910 Chagas' disease, the South American form of trypanosomiasis, is discovered by Brazilian bacteriologist Carlos Chagas (1879–1934).

1910 Antiseptic and disinfectant properties of iodine are discovered by US physician F. Woodbury.

1910 Antitoxin against botulism is discovered by German physician L. Leuchs.

1910 Sickle-cell anaemia is discovered by US physician James Herrick (1861–1954) and, later (1917), his compatriot V. Emmel (1878–1928).

1910 Antisyphilis drug Salvarsan (arsphenamine) is discovered by German physician Paul Ehrlich (1854–1915); its synthesis is aided by US dermatologist Jay Shamberg (1870–1934).

1911 Plasma transfusion to treat haemophilia is discovered by US physician Thomas Addis (1881–1949).

1911 Vitamin B1 (thiamine) – the first vitamin to be found – is discovered by Polish-born biochemist Casimir Funk (1884–1967) and its deficiency shown to be the cause of beriberi.

1912 Nicotinic acid (niacin), a B vitamin, is discovered in rice polishings by Polish-born biochemist Casimir Funk (1884–1967); in the same year he coined the word "vitamine", later shortened to "vitamin".

1913 Vitamin A (retinol), soluble in fats, is discovered by US biochemist Elmer McCollum (1879–1967), who distinguished it from water-soluble compounds, which he classified as B vitamins. Vitamin A is simultaneously, and independently, discovered by his biochemist compatriots Thomas Osborne (1859–1929) and Lafayette Mendel (1872–1935).

1913 Cancer is produced artificially in experimental animals by Danish physician Johannes Fibiger (1867–1928), first using nematodes to produce tumours in rats and later (1920) using coal tar as a carcinogen.

1913 Schick test (for immunity to diphtheria) is discovered by Hungarian-born US physician Béla Schick (1877–1967).

CHEMISTRY

1916 Explanation that a covalent bond involves the sharing of electrons between two atoms is given by US chemist Gilbert Lewis (1875–1946).

1916 Bromacetone (Martonite, BA or B-Stoff) is developed as a tear gas by Germany, and later used by other combatants in World War 1.

1916 Chloropicrin (nitrochloroform) is developed as a tear gas by Russia, and later used (sometimes mixed with chlorine as Yellow Star gas) by other combatants in World War 1.

1916 Powerfully magnetic cobalt-tungsten steel is discovered by Japanese metallurgist Kotaro Honda (1870–1954).

1916 Dichloroethyl sulphide (mustard gas, a toxic and blinding gas) is developed by Germany.

1917 Toxic war gases diphenylchlorarsine (Clark I, a sneezing gas), diphenylcyanarsine (Clark II, a lethal gas) and phenyldichlorarsine (Sternite, a tear gas) – the so-called Blue Cross gases – are developed by Germany.

1917 Isotope of the radioactive element protactinium (Pa-234) is discovered and named by German physicists Lise Meitner (1878–1968) and Otto Hahn (1879–1968), although another isotope had been found earlier (1913) by Polish-born physical chemist Kasimir Fajans (1887–1975).

1918 Chemical chain reactions are discovered by German physical chemist Hermann Nernst (1864–1941).

1918 Lewisite poison gas (for warfare) is developed by US chemist Winford Lewis (1878–1943).

1918 Toxic gas bromobenzoyl cyanide (BBC, Camite) is developed in France as a tear gas for warfare.

1919 Whole-number rule (that isotopes have integral atomic masses) is discovered by British physicist Francis Aston (1877–1945).

PHYSICS

1915 Rectifying effect (ability to convert alternating current into direct current) of germanium is discovered by Swedish physicist Carl Benedicks (b.1875).

1916 General Theory of Relativity is proposed by German-born US physicist Albert Einstein (1879–1955).

1919 Proton is discovered by New Zealand-born British physicist Ernest Rutherford (1871–1937).

1919 Atomic fission – splitting of an atom – (by alpha-ray bombardment of nitrogen to convert it into oxygen) is achieved by New Zealand-born British physicist Ernest Rutherford (1871–1937).

1919 First separation of isotopes (of neon) is achieved by British physicist Francis Aston (1877–1945), using his mass spectroscope.

1919 Barkhausen effect (the discontinuity of magnetization of a ferromagnetic substance) is discovered by German physicist Heinrich Barkausen (1881–1956).

MEDICINE

1913 Vaccine against diphtheria is developed by German bacteriologist Emil von Behring (1854–1917).

1914 Successful open-heart surgery is first performed (on a dog) by French surgeon Alexis Carrel (1873–1944).

1914 Anticoagulant properties of sodium citrate (used in stored blood for transfusions) is discovered by US physician Richard Lewisohn.

1914 Dakin's solution (0.5% sodium hypochlorite), an antiseptic for treating war wounds, is developed by British chemist Henry Dakin (1880–1952) and French biologist Alexis Carrel (1873–1944).

1914 Fact that Brill's disease (named after US physician Nathan Brill (1860–1925) is actually typhus is discovered by US bacteriologist Harry Plotz (1890–1947), who went on to produce a vaccine against it.

1915 Fact that pellagra is a dietary deficiency disease is discovered by Austrian-born US physician Joseph Goldberger (1874–1929); the vitamin concerned (nicotinic acid, or niacin) is later (1937) used in the treatment of pellagra by US biochemist Conrad Elvehjem (1901–62).

1915 Streptomyces bacterium is discovered by Russian-born US microbiologist Selman Waksman (1888–1973).

1917 Vaccine against Rocky Mountain spotted fever is developed by US bacteriologist Ralph Parker (1888–1949).

1917 Bacteriophages (viruses that attack bacteria) are discovered by French bacteriologist Félix d'Hérelle (1873–1949).

1917 Treatment for general paralysis by deliberately infecting the patient with malaria – a precursor of shock therapy – is introduced by Austrian neurologist Julius von Wagner-Jauregg (1857–1940).

1918 Anticoagulant drug heparin is discovered by US physiologists William Howell (1860–1945) and Luther Holt (1855–1924).

1919 Fact that there are two strains of botulism (each requiring a different antitoxin) is discovered by US physician Georgiana Burke.

1919 Drug tryparsamide is introduced as a treatment for sleeping sickness by US physician Louise Pearce (1885–1959).

1920

FARMING AND FOOD

BIOLOGY

1921 Insulin is discovered by Canadian physiologists Frederick Banting (1891–1941) and Charles Best (1899–1978) and Scotsman John Macleod (1876–1935).

1921 Chemical mechanism for the transmission of nerve impulses is discovered by German-born US pharmacologist Otto Loewi (1873–1961).

1922 Lysozyme (an enzyme that destroys bacteria) is discovered by Scottish bacteriologist Alexander Fleming (1881–1955).

1923 Method of studying tissue respiration is discovered by German botanist Otto Warburg (1859–1938).

1924 Electric currents in the brain are discovered by German physiologist Hans Berger (1873–1941).

1924 Role of ultraviolet light in increasing vitamin D from food is discovered by US chemist Harry Steenbock (1886–1967).

1924 Fossils of Australopithecus (an apelike link in human evolution) are discovered by Australian-born South African anthropologist Raymond Dart (1893–1988).

CHEMISTRY

1920 Electronic nature of organic chemical reactions is discovered by Scottish chemist Arthur Lapworth (1872–1941).

1921 Glutathione, a tripeptide (combination of three amino acids) involved in cell metabolism, is discovered by British biochemist Frederick Gowland Hopkins (1861–1947).

1922 Natural polymers (in rubber) are discovered by German chemist Hermann Staudinger (1881–1965); he later (1926) identified the polymeric nature of all plastics.

1923 Unified theory of acids and bases is proposed by Danish chemist Johannes Bronsted (1879–1947) and, independently, British chemist Thomas Lowry (1874–1936).

1924 Parachor (the molecular volume of a substance with unit surface tension, a useful quantity in organic chemistry) is discovered by British chemist Samuel Sugden (1892–1950).

1925 Metallic element rhenium (symbol Re) is discovered by German chemists Walter Noddack (1893–1960) and Ida Tacke (later Noddack) (1896–1979).

PHYSICS

1920 Existence of the neutron is postulated by New Zealand-born British physicist Ernest Rutherford (1871–1937).

1923 Compton effect – the scattering of X-rays, with an increase in wavelength (reduction in energy), by collisions with matter – is discovered by US physicist Arthur Compton (1892–1962).

1924 Existence of the ionosphere is proved by British physicist Edward Appleton (1892–1965).

1924 Exclusion principle (that no two subatomic particles can have the same set of quantum numbers) is discovered by Austrian physicist Wolfgang Pauli (1900–58).

1924 Fact that moving subatomic particles have an associated wavelength (i.e., that they can behave as both particles and waves) is discovered by French physicist Louis de Broglie (1892–1987).

1924 Method of refracting X-rays (and thereby measuring their wavelength) is discovered by Swedish physicist Karl Siegbahn (1886–1978).

MEDICINE

1920 Ergotamine treatment for migraine is discovered by German chemist Karl Spiro (1867–1932).

1920 Band-Aid sterile first-aid dressings are marketed by the US Johnson & Johnson company; its British equivalent (Elastoplast) did not appear until 1928.

1922 Vitamin D (calciferol) is discovered by US biochemist Elmer McCollum (1879–1967).

1922 Vitamin E (tocopherol) is discovered by US embryologist Herbert Evans (1882–1971).

1922 Cod liver oil or sunlight as a treatment for rickets is discovered by Austrian physician H. Chick, later shown to be effective because of the formation of vitamin D in the body.

1922 Insulin is first used successfully to treat a diabetic patient (in Toronto, Canada); it is later (1925) used on children in England.

1923 Dick test, for determining a person's susceptibility to scarlet fever, is discovered by US bacteriologists Gladys (1881–1963) and George (1881–1967) Dick.

BIOLOGY

1925 Fact that iron is an important component of erythrocytes (red blood cells) is discovered by US biologist George Whipple (1878–1976).

1925 Cytochrome, an enzyme that acts as a respiratory catalyst in cells, is discovered by Russian-born Polish (later British) chemist David Keilin (1887–1963).

1926 Crystalline urease (the first enzyme to be crystallized) is produced by US chemist James Sumner (1877–1955), who also shows that it is a protein.

1926 Crystalline insulin is produced by US biochemist John Abel (1857–1938), who also shows that it is a protein.

1927 Mutations in fruit flies (Drosophila) are produced using X-rays by US geneticist Hermann Muller (1890–1967).

1929 Female sex hormone oestrogen is discovered by German chemist Adolf Butenandt (1903–95) and, independently, US biologist Edward Doisy (1893–1986).

1929 Structure of haem (the non-protein part of haemoglobin) is discovered by German chemist Hans Fischer (1881–1945), who also synthesized it.

CHEMISTRY

1925 Structure of morphine is discovered by British chemist Robert Robinson (1886–1975).

1927 Modern theory of valence – that valence depends on the number of electrons in an atom's outer shells – is proposed by British chemist Nevil Sidgwick (1873–1952).

1927 Quantum theory of chemical bonding is developed by German physicists Fritz London (1900–54) and Walter Heitler.

1927 Zyklon-B, a solid fumigant that gives off toxic hydrogen cyanide gas when exposed to air, is developed by German chemist Bruno Tesch (1946–); it is later (World War 2) used in Nazi extermination camps.

1928 Diels-Alder reaction (in which two double-bonded organic molecules join to form a ring compound) is discovered by German chemists Otto Diels (1876–1954) and Kurt Alder (1902–58).

1929 Short-life free radicals (e.g. methyl radical) are discovered by Austrian chemist Friedrich Paneth (1887–1958).

1929 Polymerization of ethyne (acetylene) is discovered by Belgian-born US chemist Julius Nieuwland (1878–1936).

1929 Fact that oxygen consists of three different isotopes (O-16, O-17 and O-18) is discovered by US chemist William Giauque (1895–1982).

1929 Goldschmidt's law, relating crystal structure to the properties of the component ions, is discovered by Swiss chemist Victor Goldschmidt (1888–1947).

PHYSICS

1925 Fact that electrons spin is discovered by Dutch-born US physicists Samuel Goudsmit (1901–78) and fellow research student George Uhlenbeck (1900–88).

1925 Auger effect (the emission of an electron from an atom with accompanying X-rays or gamma rays) is discovered by French physicist Pierre Auger (1899–1993).

1926 Wave equation for the hydrogen atom (which describes the distribution of electrons) is discovered by Austrian physicist Erwin Schrödinger (1887–1961), thus founding wave mechanics.

1926 Method of attaining temperatures within a thousandth of a degree of absolute zero is discovered by US chemist William Giauque (1895–1982).

1926 Term "photon" for a quantum of light is coined by US chemist Gilbert Lewis (1875–1946).

1927 Fact that parity is conserved in nuclear reactions is discovered by Hungarian-born US physicist Eugene Wigner (1901–95).

1927 Method of diffracting a beam of electrons (thus proving their wave nature) using a nickel crystal is discovered by US physicists Clinton Davisson (1881–1958) and Lester Germer (1896–1971) and, independently, using gold foil by British physicist George Thomson (1892–1975).

1927 First X-ray crystallographic analysis of proteins (animal fibres) is carried out by British physicist William Astbury (1898–1961).

1928 Existence of the positron is postulated by US physicist Julius Oppenheimer (1904–67) and, independently, British physicist Paul Dirac (1902–84).

1928 Raman effect or scattering (the scattering of electromagnetic radiation by the molecules of a medium through which it passes) is discovered by Indian physicist Chandrasekhara Raman (1888–1970).

1929 Unified Field Theory, which combines electromagnetism with gravitation, is proposed by German-born US physicist Albert Einstein (1879–1955).

MEDICINE

1924 Use of liver in the diet as a treatment for pernicious anaemia is discovered by US physicians George Minot (1885–1950) and William Murphy (1892–1987).

1924 Bacterium that causes scarlet fever is discovered by US bacteriologists Gladys (1881–1963) and George (1881–1967) Dick.

1925 Carcinogenetic effect of ultraviolet radiation is discovered by US biologist Ernest Just (1883–1941).

1925 Use of parathyroid gland extract as a treatment for pernicious anaemia is discovered by Canadian biochemist James Collip (1892–1965).

1928 Antibiotic penicillin is discovered by Scottish bacteriologist Alexander Fleming (1881–1955), later (1935) developed by Australian-born British pathologist Howard Florey (1898–1968) and German-born British bacteriologist Ernst Chain (1906–79).

1928 Vitamin C (ascorbic acid) is discovered by Hungarian biochemist Albert Szent-Györgyi (1893–1986) and later (1932), independently, by US biochemist Glen King (1896–1988).

1929 Technique of diagnosing heart conditions by passing a catheter into the heart (via an artery in the arm) is introduced by German surgeon Werner Forssmann (1904–1979), and developed by French physician André Cournard (1895–1988) and US physician Dickinson Richards (1895–1973).

1930

FARMING AND FOOD

1935 Canned beer is first marketed in the USA by the Krueger Brewing company.

1937 Instant coffee (Nescafé, produced by freeze drying) is marketed by the Swiss Nestlé company.

1939 Precooked frozen foods are marketed by the US Birds Eye company.

BIOLOGY

1930 Enzyme pepsin is crystallized (and shown to be a protein) by US biochemist John Northrop (1891–1987), who later (1932) also crystallizes trypsin.

1931 Male sex hormone androsterone is discovered by German chemist Adolf Butenandt (1903–95); androsterone is later (1934) synthesized by Croation-born Swiss chemist Leopold Ruzicka (1887–1976).

1932 Muscle protein myoglobin is crystallized by Swedish biochemist Hugo Theorell (1903–82); its structure is later (1957) determined by British biochemist John Kendrew (1917–97).

1932 Concept of homeostasis (the automatic self-regulation of the body's internal environment in such a way that biochemical process proceed in the best way) is proposed by US physiologist Walter Cannon (1871–1945).

1933 Role of rhodopsin in the reina of the eye, and its relation to vitamin A, is discovered by US biochemist George Wald (1906–97).

1933 Tasmanian wolf probably becomes extinct.

1934 Female sex hormone progesterone is discovered and isolated by German chemist Adolf Butenandt (1903–95).

CHEMISTRY

1930 Refrigerant gas Freon (dichlorodifluoromethane, the first of the CFCs) is discovered by US chemist Thomas Midgley (1889–1944).

1930 Electrophoresis (as a method of separating proteins) is developed by Swedish chemist Arne Tiselius (1902–1971).

1930 Sedative drug sodium pentothal (Nembutal) is discovered by US pharmacologists Ernest Volwiler (1893–1992) and Donalee Tabern (1900–74).

1930 Method of catalytic cracking of crude oil is introduced by French-born US engineer Eugene Houdry (1892–1962).

1931 Synthetic rubber neoprene is developed by Belgian-born US chemist Julius Nieuwland (1878–1936).

1932 Deuterium (heavy hydrogen, isotope of mass 2) is discovered by US chemist Harold Urey (1893–1981) and, independently (1933), by his compatriot Gilbert Lewis (1875–1946).

1933 Molecular orbital theory, which explains chemical bonding, is developed by British mathematician Charles Coulson (1910–1974) and, independently, German theoretical chemist Erich Hückel (1896–1980).

PHYSICS

1930 Fact that cosmic rays consist of protons (and other positively charged particles) is discovered by Italian-born US physicist Bruno Rossi (1905–94).

1930 Value of Van der Waals' (or London) forces between molecules is discovered by German physicist Fritz London (1900–54).

c.1930 Néel temperature (above which an antiferromagnetic material becomes paramagnetic) is discovered by French physicist Louis Néel (1904–2000).

1931 Existence of neutrino is postulated by Hungarian-born US physicist Wolfgang Pauli (1900–58).

1932 Neutron is discovered by British physicist James Chadwick (1891–1974); its existence had been predicted earlier (1920) by US physicist William Harkins (1873–1951).

1932 Positron is discovered (in cosmic rays) by US physicist Carl Anderson (1905–91).

1932 Atoms (of lithium and boron) are split by fast protons that are accelerated in a machine devised by British physicist John Cockroft (1897–1967) and Irish physicist Ernest Walton (1903–95).

MEDICINE

1930 Vaccine against typhus is developed by US bacteriologist Hans Zinsser (1878–1940).

1930 Vaccine against yellow fever is developed by South African bacteriologist Max Theiler (1899–1972).

1931 Method of culturing viruses (for making vaccines) in chick embryos is discovered by US pathologist Ernest Goodpasture (1886–1960).

1931 Structure of vitamin A (retinol) is determined by German chemist Paul Karrer (1889–1971).

1931 Vitamin D2 (cholecalciferol) is crystallized by German chemist Adolf Windaus (1876–1959).

1932 First sulpha drug, Prontosil, is discovered by German biochemist Gerhard Domagk (1895–1964); it is later (1935) used to treat streptococcal infections.

1933 Natural childbirth, without the use of anaesthetics, is advocated by British gynaecologist Grantly Dick-Read (1890–1959).

1934 Vitamin K is discovered by Danish biochemist Carl Dam (1895–1976) and, independently, US biochemist Edward Doisy (1893–1986), who later (1939) determines its structure.

FARMING AND FOOD	BIOLOGY	CHEMISTRY	PHYSICS	MEDICINE

BIOLOGY

1935 Adrenal hormone cortisone is discovered by US biochemist Edward Kendall (1886–1972) and later (1936) isolated by Polish-born Swiss chemist Tadeus Reichstein (1897–1996), who determines its structure.

1935 Hormone-like prostaglandin is discovered by Swedish physiologist Ulf von Euler (1905–83), later isolated by his compatriots Sune Bergström (1916–) and Bengt Samuelsson (1934–).

1935 Imprinting in young animals is discovered by Austrian biologist Konrad Lorenz (1903–89), who establishes the science of ethology.

1935 Term "ecosystem" is coined by British botanist and ecologist Arthur Tansley (1871–1955).

1935 Tobacco mosaic virus is produced in crystalline form (the first virus to be crystallized) by US biochemist Wendell Stanley (1904–71) and later (1936), independently, by British biochemists Frederick Bawden (1908–72) and Norman Pirie (1907–97), who also showed that it contains RNA, establishing this nucleic acid as a basic component of life.

1936 Fact that a virus can cause cancer (in mice) is established by US biologist John Bittner (1904–61).

1937 Essential amino acids (which cannot be made in the body and must therefore be supplied by foods) are discovered by US biochemist William Rose (1887–1984).

1937 Electrical nature of nerve transmission is discovered by US physiologist Joseph Erlanger (1874–1965).

1937 Mutations produced by polyploidy (multiplication of chromosomes) are discovered by US botanist Albert Blakeslee (1874–1954).

1938 First bacteriophage (virus that attacks bacteria) is isolated by US biochemist John Northrop (1891–1987).

1938 Coelacanth (a "living fossil" fish) is discovered and identified by South African biologist J.-L.-B. Smith; the fish is later (1953) found to be relatively common near the Comoro Islands.

1939 Plant growth hormone gibberellin is discovered by Japanese biologist Teijiro Yabuta.

CHEMISTRY

1933 Vitamin C is synthesized by Polish-born Swiss chemist Tadeus Reichstein (1897–1996) and later (1934), independently, by British chemist Walter Haworth (1883–1950), who names it ascorbic (meaning "anti-scurvy") acid.

1933 Thyroid hormone thyroxine is synthesized by British chemist Charles Harington (1897–1972).

1934 Tritium (hydrogen isotope of mass 3) is discovered by Australian physicist Mark Oliphant (1901–2000).

1934 Male sex hormone androsterone is synthesized by Swiss chemist Leopold Ruzicka (1887–1976), who later (1954) also synthesizes oxytocin.

1935 Amino acid threonine, the last essential amino acid to be found, is discovered by US biochemist William Rose (1887–1984).

1935 Physostygmine (an alkaloid drug used to treat the eye disorder glaucoma) is synthesized by US chemist Percy Julian (1899–1975).

1935 Fissionable uranium-235 isotope is discovered by US physicist Arthur Dempster (1886–1950).

1936 Tabun, the first nerve gas, is discovered by German chemist Gerhard Schracher.

1937 Radioactive element technetium (symbol Tc) is discovered by Italian physicists Emilio Segrè (1905–89) and Carlo Perrier, who first called it masurium.

1939 Radioactive metallic element francium (symbol Fr) is discovered by French chemist Marguérite Perey (1909–75).

1939 Insecticidal properties of DDT are discovered by Swiss chemist Paul Müller (1899–1965), who also synthesized it; DDT is first used on a large scale in Italy in 1944.

PHYSICS

1933 Meissner effect (the absence of magnetism in a superconductor cooled below its critical temperature in a magnetic field) is discovered by Walther Meissner and R. Ochsenfeld.

1934 Radioisotopes are produced artificially (by alpha-particle bombardment) by French physicists Irène (1897–1956) and Jean-Frédéric Joliot (1900–58) and, independently, (by neutron bombardment) by Italian-born US physicist Enrico Fermi (1901–54). In the same year US physicist Ernest Lawrence (1901–58) used a cyclotron to produce useful amounts of radioisotopes, which were later used to treat cancer.

1934 Cherenkov radiation (produced by charged particles moving through a medium faster than the speed of light through that medium) is discovered by Soviet physicist Pavel Cherenkov (1904–90), later (1937) explained by his compatriots Ilya Frank (1908–90) and Igor Tamm (1895–1971).

1934 Dislocations in crystal structures, a common cause of failure in metals, are discovered by British physicist Geoffrey Taylor (1886–1975).

1934 First general theory of superconductivity is proposed by Dutch physicist Hendrik Casimir (1909–2000).

1935 Interference effect of sunspot activity on radio communications is discovered by US physicist John Dellinger (1886–1962).

1935 London equations, which explain superconductivity, are discovered by German-born US physicists Fritz (1900–54) and Heinz (1907–70) London.

1936 Wigner effect (the storage in a crystal of energy from irradiation) is discovered by Hungarian-born US physicist Eugene Wigner (1902–95).

1937 Muon (mu-meson) is discovered in cosmic rays by US physicist Carl Anderson (1905–91), and by US physicists Jabez Street (1906–89) and Edward Stevenson.

1938 Nuclear fission (by means of neutron bombardment) is achieved unknowingly by Austrian-born Swedish physicist Lise Meitner (1878–1968) and German physical chemists Otto Hahn (1879–1968) and Fritz Strassmann (1902–80).

1939 Fact that the Earth's magnetic field is produced by eddy currents in its rotating liquid metallic core is proposed by German-born US physicist Walter Elsasser (1904–91).

MEDICINE

1934 Method of extracting vitamin B1 (thiamine, deficiency of which causes beriberi) from rice polishings is discovered by US chemist Robert Williams (1886–1965), who later (1936) works out its structure and a method of synthesizing it.

1935 Structure and synthesis of vitamin B2 (riboflavin) are discovered by German chemist Paul Karrer (1889–1971) and, independently, Austrian-born German chemist Richard Kuhn (1900–67).

1935 Prefrontal lobotomy (leucotomy), as a treatment of mental illness, is introduced by Portuguese surgeon António Egaz Moniz (1874–1955).

1936 Crystalline tobacco mosaic virus (the first virus to be crystallized) is produced by British biochemists Norman Pirie (1907–97) and Frederick Bawden (1908–72).

1937 First antihistamine, pyrilamine (mepyramine), is discovered by Swiss physiologist Daniel Bovet (1907–92).

1938 Vitamin B6 (pyridoxine) is isolated by Austrian-born German biochemist Richard Kuhn (1900–67), who later (1939) determines its structure.

1938 Vitamin E (tocopherol) is synthesized by German chemist Paul Karrer (1889–1971).

1939 Antibiotic tyrothricin (gramicidin), the first to be produced commercially, is discovered by French-born US microbiologist René Dubos (1901–82).

1939 Sulphapyridine (M & B 693 or sulphadiazine, a sulpha drug) is discovered by British chemist Arthur Ewins (1882–1957) and, independently, US chemist Richard Roblin (1907–).

1940

FARMING AND FOOD

1946 Espresso coffee machine is produced by Italian inventor Achille Gaggia.

BIOLOGY (cont.)

1940 Krebs cycle, also called tricarboxylic acid (TCA) or citric acid cycle, is discovered by German-born British physiologist Hans Krebs (1900–81).

1940 Rhesus factor (in blood) is discovered by Austrian-born US biologist Karl Landsteiner (1868–1943).

1940 Role of iodine in thyroid function is discovered by US anatomist Herbert Evans (1882–1971).

1940 Paedomorphism, the fact that adult animals retain some ancestral juvenile features, is proposed by British zoologist Gavin de Beer (1899–1972), thus refuting Haeckel's recapitulation theory of 1866.

1941 Role of ATP (adenosine triphosphate) in cellular energy release is discovered by German-born US biochemist Fritz Lipmann (1899–1986).

1941 Role of genes in controlling chemical reactions in cells is discovered by US biologists George Beadle (1903–89) and Edward Tatum (1909–75).

1942 Electron microscope is first used in biological research by Belgian-US biologist Albert Claude (1898–1983).

CHEMISTRY (cont.)

1940 Radioactive carbon-14 isotope is discovered by Canadian-born US biochemist Martin Kamen (1913–).

1940 Radioactive element plutonium (symbol Pu) is discovered by US chemist Glenn Seaborg (1912–99) et al.

1940 Radioactive element astatine (symbol At) is discovered by Italian-born US physicist Emilio Segrè (1905–89) et al.

1940 Radioactive element neptunium (symbol Np) is discovered by US physical chemists Edwin McMillan (1907–91) and Philip Abelson (1913–).

1943 Silicones are first manufactured by the US Dow Corning company.

1944 Quinine is synthesized by US chemists Robert Woodward (1917–79) and William Doering.

1945 Radioactive elements americium (symbol Am) and curium (symbol Cm) are discovered by Glenn Seaborg (1912–99) et al.

1945 Structure of penicillin is discovered by British chemist Dorothy Hodgkin (1910–94).

PHYSICS (cont.)

1940 Decay of a cosmic-ray meson into an electron is discovered by Welsh physicist Evan Williams (1903–45).

1940 Fact that it is the uranium-235 isotope (not the much more common uranium-238) that undergoes nuclear fission, as carried out earlier (1938) by Lise Meitner (1878–1968), is discovered by US physicist John Dunning (1907–75).

1940 Method of separating the two uranium isotopes (U-235 and U-238), by thermal diffusion of gaseous uranium hexafluoride, is proposed by US physical chemist Philip Abelson (1913–).

1940 Fact that beryllium will slow down fast neutrons (and therefore act as a moderator in a nuclear reactor) is discovered by Austrian-born US physicist Maurice Goldhaber (1911–).

1941 Spontaneous fission of uranium is discovered by Soviet physicist Georgii Flerov (1913–).

1942 First nuclear reactor ("atomic pile") is completed in the USA under the direction of Italian-born US physicist Enrico Fermi (1901–54).

MEDICINE (cont.)

1940 Vitamin H (biotin) is discovered by Hungarian biochemist Albert Szent-Györgyi (1893–1986) and US biochemist Vincent Du Vigneaud (1901–78), who later (1942) determines its structure and then (1943) synthesizes it.

1940 Structure of the B vitamin pantothenic acid is determined by US chemist Robert Williams (1886–1965).

1940 Fact that blood plasma can be used instead of whole blood for transfusion and a method of storing plasma in blood banks are discovered by US physician Charles Drew (1904–50).

1941 Use of female sex hormones to treat prostate cancer is discovered by US physician Charles Huggins (1901–97).

1941 Connection between birth defects and German measles (rubella) during pregnancy is discovered by Australian physician Norman Gregg (1892–1966).

1941 Term "antibiotic" is coined by Russian-born US microbiologist Selman Waksman (1888–1973).

1943 Antibiotic streptomycin (effective against tuberculosis) is discovered in soil by Selman Waksman.

BIOLOGY

1943 Formation of enzyme-substrate complexes (the key to how enzymes work) is discovered by US biochemist Britton Chance (1913–).

1944 Structure of the bile pigment bilirubin is discovered by German chemist Hans Fischer (1881–1945), who also synthesized it.

1946 Fact that viruses can combine to form new viruses is discovered by German-born US biologist Max Delbrück (1906–81) and US biologist Alfred Hershey (1908–97).

1946 Noradrenaline (norepinephrine) is discovered by Swedish physiologist Ulf von Euler (1905–83).

1947 Coenzyme A is discovered by German-born US biochemist Fritz Lipmann (1899–1986).

1947 Nerve growth factor (in embryos) is discovered by Italian neurophysiologist Rita Levi-Montalcini (1909–).

1948 Fossils of Proconsul africanus, a 20 million-year-old ape, are found in Kenya by British archaeologist Mary Leakey (1913–96).

1949 Barr bodies (condensed X-chromosomes in nondividing nuclei of cells of female animals) are discovered by Canadian geneticist Murray Barr (1908–95).

CHEMISTRY

1946 Radiocarbon dating (based on the amount of the isotope carbon-14 in an organic sample) is discovered by US chemist Willard Libby (1908–80).

1946 Structure of strychnine is discovered by British chemist Robert Robinson (1886–1975); it is later (1954) synthesized by US chemist Robert Woodward (1917–79).

1947 ADP (adenosine diphosphate) and ATP (adenosine triphosphate), important energy-containing chemicals involved in cell metabolism, are synthesized by Scottish chemist Alexander Todd (1907–97).

1947 Radioactive element promethium (symbol Pm) is discovered by J. Marinsky et al.

1949 Method of studying ultrafast chemical reactions is discovered by British physical chemists George Porter (1920–) and Ronald Norrish (1897–1978).

1949 Radioactive element berkelium (symbol Bk) is discovered by US chemist Glenn Seaborg (1912–99) et al.

PHYSICS

1942 Existence of magnetohydrodynamic waves (Alfvén waves) in plasmas is predicted by Swedish physicist Hannes Alfvén (1908–95).

1946 Proton linear accelerator is developed by US physicist Luis Alvarez (1911–88).

1946 First fast nuclear reactor (called Clementine) is built at Los Alamos, New Mexico, USA.

1946 Nuclear magnetic resonance (NMR) spectroscopy is developed by Swiss-born US physicist Felix Bloch (1905–83) and, independently, US physicist Edward Purcell (1912–97).

1947 Pion (pi-meson) is discovered in cosmic rays by British physicist Cecil Powell (1903–69).

1947 Lamb shift (between two energy levels in the hydrogen spectrum) is discovered by US physicist Willis Lamb (1913–).

1948 Basic concept of holography is discovered by Hungarian-born British physicist Dennis Gabor (1900–79).

1948 "Shell" structure for the protons and neutrons in the atomic nucleus is proposed by German-born US physicist Marie Goeppert-Mayer (1906–72) and, independently, German physicist Hans Jensen (1907–73).

1948 Quantum electrodynamics, which deals with the interactions of charged subatomic particle, is formulated by US physicists Richard Feynman (1918–88) and Julian Schwinger (1918–94), and, independently, Japanese physicist Sin-Itiro Tomonaga (1906–79).

MEDICINE

1943 Hallucinogenic drug LSD (lysergic acid diethylamide, in German Lyserg-Saure-Diathylamid) is discovered by German chemist Albert Hofmann.

1943 Pap smear test (for uterine cancer) is discovered by Greek-born US physician George Papanicolaou (1883–1962).

1944 Antibiotic Aureomycin (chlortetracycline, the first of the tetracyclines) is discovered by US botanist Benjamin Dugger (1872–1956).

1944 Surgical treatment of the heart defect in newborn "blue babies" is developed by US physicians Helen Taussig (1899–1986) and Alfred Blalock (1899–1964).

1944 Method of making viruses visible under the electron microscope (by "shadowing" them with a thin layer of metal) is discovered by US biophysicists Robley Williams (1908–) and Ralph Wyckoff (1897–1994).

1947 Powerful antibiotic chloramphenicol is discovered in a Streptomyces bacillus in a sample of soil from Venezuela.

1948 Operation to enlarge the mitral valve in the heart (which can malfunction because of narrowing called mitral stenosis) is introduced by US physician Dwight Harken (1910–) and, independently, British surgeon Russell Brock (1903–80).

1948 Cortisone treatment for rheumatoid arthritis is discovered by US physician Philip Hench (1896–1965) and biochemist Edward Kendall (1886–1972).

1948 Use of ultrasound to scan the fetus in pregnant women is pioneered by Scottish physician Ian Donald (1910–87).

1948 Structure of antibiotic streptomycin is determined by US biochemists Karl Folkers (1906–97) et al. of the US Merck company. In the same year they isolated vitamin B12 (cyanocobalamin), whose structure was later (1956) determined by the British biochemist Dorothy Hodgkin (1910–94).

1949 Role of the immune system in tissue rejection (in skin grafts) is discovered by Australian biologist Frank Burnet (1899–1985).

1949 Cause of sickle-cell anaemia is discovered by US biochemist Linus Pauling (1901–94).

1949 Method of growing poliomyelitis virus in a tissue culture (treated with antibiotic) is discovered by US microbiologist John Enders (1897–1985).

FARMING AND FOOD

1953 Edible synthetic protein made from soya beans is patented by US scientist Robert Boyer (who first made it when looking for a substitute for natural leather).

1954 Non-stick cooking pans are invented by French research engineer Marc Grégoire.

1959 Tab-opening aluminium drinks can is invented in the USA by Ermal Fraze (patented in 1963).

BIOLOGY

1950 Fact that a single organism has many different kinds of RNA (but only one kind of DNA) is discovered by Czech-born US biochemist Erwin Chargaff (1905–).

1950 Alpha-helix structure of proteins is discovered by US biochemist Linus Pauling (1901–94).

1950 Parasexual cycle in fungi is discovered by Italian geneticist Guido Pontecorvo (1907–93).

1951 "Jumping genes" are discovered by US geneticist Barbara McClintock (1902–92).

1952 Fact that DNA carries genetic information is discovered by US biologists Alfred Hershey (1908–97) and M. Chase.

1952 "Sodium pump" mechanism of nerve transmission is discovered by British physiologists Alan Hodgkin (1914–98) and Andrew Huxley (1917–), and, independently, Australian physiologist John Eccles (1903–97).

1952 Plasmids, mobile rings of DNA found in bacteria, are discovered by US geneticist Joshua Lederberg (1925–).

CHEMISTRY

1950 Element Californium (Cf) is discovered by US chemist Glenn Seaborg (1912–99)

1951 Cholesterol and cortisone are synthesized by US chemist Robert Woodward (1917–79).

1952 Radioactive elements einsteinium (symbol Es) and fermium (symbol Fm) are discovered by US chemists Glenn Seaborg (1912–99), Albert Ghiorso and others.

1953 Ziegler process (for making high-density polyethene) is discovered by German chemist Karl Ziegler (1898–1973), later (1954) improved by Italian chemist Giulio Natta (1903–79).

1954 Method of studying the progress of very rapid chemical reactions is discovered by German chemist Manfred Eigen (1927–).

1954 Series of reactions by which the body synthesizes cholesterol are discovered by German-born US chemist Konrad Bloch (1912–2000).

1955 Method of making synthetic diamonds is discovered by US physicist Percy Bridgman (1882–1961).

PHYSICS

1950 "Shell" and "liquid drop" models of the atomic nucleus are combined in a single theory by US physicist Leo Rainwater (1917–86) with Aage Bohr (1922–) and Ben Mottelson (1926–).

1955 Antiproton is discovered by US physicists Emilio Segrè (1905–89) and Owen Chamberlain (1920–).

1956 Neutrino is discovered by US physicists Clyde Cowan (1919–) and Frederick Reines (1918–).

1956 Continuous emission maser is developed by Dutch-born US physicist Nicolaas Bloembergen (1920–).

1956 Cooper pairs (bound pairs of electrons that carry electric current in superconductors) are discovered by US physicist Leon Cooper (1930–).

1956 Use of colliding-beam storage-rings for increasing the energy of particle accelerators is proposed by US physicist Gerard O'Neill (1927–92).

1957 Tunnel effect (in which electrons penetrate a narrow potential barrier) is discovered by Japanese physicist Leo Esaki (1925–).

MEDICINE

1950 Statistical correlation between cigarette smoking and the incidence of lung cancer is discovered by British physicians William Doll (1912–) and Austin Hill (1897–1991).

1950 Reserpine treatment for hypertension is discovered by US physician Robert Wilkins (1906–), who later (1952) also discovers the sedative effect of the drug, which becomes the first tranquilizer.

1952 Apgar score test for newborns is introduced by US physician Virginia Apgar (1909–74).

1952 Sex-change operation is first performed by Danish surgeon Karl Hamburger, when US soldier George Jorgensen becomes Christine Jorgensen.

1953 Salk oral vaccine against poliomyelitis is developed by US microbiologist Jonas Salk (1914–95).

1953 Carcinogenic properties of tars from tobacco are discovered by US surgeon Evarts Graham (1883–1957).

1954 Human kidney transplant (between identical twins) is first performed by US surgeon Joseph Murray (1919–).

1950

FARMING AND FOOD	BIOLOGY	CHEMISTRY	PHYSICS	MEDICINE

BIOLOGY

1952 Rapid eye movement (REM) sleep, which occurs when a person is dreaming, is discovered by Russian-born US physiologist Nathaniel Kleitman (1895–).

1953 Structure of DNA is discovered by British biophysicist Francis Crick (1916–) and US biologist James Watson (1928–), using measurements made by New Zealand-born British physicist Maurice Wilkins (1916–).

1953 Structures of vasopressin and oxytocin (two hormones from the pituitary gland) are discovered by US biochemist Vincent Du Vigneaud (1901–78), who also synthesizes them.

1954 Fact that triplets of nucleotides (in nucleic acids) act as the genetic code in enzyme formation is discovered by Russian-born US physicist George Gamov (1909–68).

1955 Lysosomes (structures within cells) are discovered by British-born Belgian biochemist Christian de Duve (1917–78).

1955 Method of synthesizing RNA is discovered by Spanish-born US molecular biologist Severo Ochoa (1905–93).

1955 Amino-acid sequence of insulin is discovered by British biochemist Frederick Sanger (1918–).

1956 Ribosomes, and the fact that they are mostly RNA, are discovered by Romanian-born US physiologist George Palade (1912–).

1956 Transfer RNA (tRNA) is discovered by Mahlon Haogland and Paul Zamecnick.

1956 Enzyme that catalyzes DNA synthesis is discovered by US biochemist Arthur Kornberg (1918–).

1957 Interferons (which attack viruses) are discovered by British biologists Alick Isaacs and Jean Lindermann.

1957 Mechanism by which glycogen is synthesized in the body is discovered by French biochemist Luis Leloir (1906–).

1957 Details of how the DNA double helix carries genetic information are discovered by US molecular biologists Matthew Meselson (1930–) and Franklin Stahl (1929–).

1957 Crystalline prostaglandins are isolated by Swedish biochemist Sune Bergström (1916–).

1958 All-female species of lizard that reproduces parthenogenetically (without the intervention of a male) is discovered in Armenia by Soviet biologist J. Darevsky.

1958 Human histocompatibility system is discovered by French biologist J. Dausset.

1959 Method of staining and sorting human chromosomes is discovered by British biologist C. Ford.

CHEMISTRY

1955 Radioactive element mendelevium (symbol Md) is discovered by US chemist Albert Ghiorso et al.

1956 Structure of vitamin B12 is discovered by British chemist Dorothy Hodgkin (1910–94).

1958 Method of identifying the amino acids and their sequence in proteins and nucleic acids is developed by US biochemists Stanford Moore (1913–82) and William Stein (1911–80).

1958 Radioactive element nobelium (symbol No) is discovered by US chemists Albert Ghiorso and Glenn Seaborg (1912–99) and, independently, scientists in the Soviet Union.

PHYSICS

1957 Mössbauer effect (the recoil-less emission of gamma rays by the nuclei of atoms in a crystal) is discovered by German physicist Rudolf Mössbauer (1929–).

1959 Xi-zero subatomic particles is discovered by US physicist Luis Alvarez (1911–88) et al.

MEDICINE

1954 Contraceptive pill is developed by Chinese biologist Min-Chueh Chang (1909–91), US physiologist Gregory Pincus (1903–67) and Polish-born US chemist Frank Colton (1923–), who patented the first pill Enovid.

1955 Fact that some viruses can be split into a protein and a nucleic acid (the infective part) is discovered by German-born US biochemist Heinz Fraenkel-Conrat (1910–).

1955 Structure of vitamin B12 (cyanocobalamin) is determined by British biochemist Dorothy Hodgkin (1910–94).

1956 Successful bone marrow transplant is carried out by US physician Edward Thomas (1920–).

1957 Sabin vaccine against poliomyelitis is developed by Polish-born US microbiologist Albert Sabin (1906–93).

1957 Interferon is discovered by Scottish virologist Alick Isaacs (1921–67).

1958 Vaccine against measles is developed by US bacteriologist John Enders (1897–1985), and later (1962) put into quantity production.

1958 Sedative drug thalidomide is introduced in West Germany; later (1961) it is withdrawn because it causes fetal deformities.

1959 Abnormal chromosome responsible for Down's syndrome (trisomy 21) is discovered by French geneticist Jérôme Lejeune (1926–94).

1959 Cause of Burkitt's lymphoma (a cancer of the lymphatic system) is discovered by Irish physician Denis Burkitt (1911–93).

1959 External heart massage (as a first-aid technique) is introduced by US engineer William Kouwenhoven (1886–1975).

1960

FARMING AND FOOD

1963 Process for preserving food using radiation is developed in Britain.

1967 Domestic microwave oven is marketed by the Raytheon Company.

BIOLOGY (1960s)

1960 Sequence of amino acids (124 of them) in ribonuclease is discovered by biochemists Stanford Moore (1913–82) and William Stein (1911–80).

1960 Structure of haemoglobin is discovered by British biochemist John Kendrew (1917–97).

1960 Hormone parathormone is isolated by Lyman Craig (1906–).

1960 Operons (genes that regulate other genes) are discovered by French bacteriologists Jacques Monod (1910–76) and François Jacob (1920–).

1961 Messenger RNA (mRNA) is discovered by Sydney Brenner (1927–) and François Jacob (1920–).

CHEMISTRY (1960s)

1960 Chlorophyll is synthesized by US chemist Robert Woodward (1917–79).

1961 Radioactive element lawrencium (symbol Lr, formerly Lw)) is discovered by US chemist Albert Ghiorso and others.

1962 First compound of a rare gas, xenon heptafluoroplatinate, is made by British chemist Neil Bartlett (1932–).

1962 Solid phase method of synthesizing peptides and proteins (from amino acids) is discovered by US chemist Bruce Merrifield (1921–).

1962 Structure of human immunoglobulin is discovered by British biochemist Rodney Porter (1917–85).

PHYSICS (1960s)

1962 Muon neutrino is discovered by US physicists Leon Lederman (1922–), Melvin Schwartz (1932–) and Jack Steinberger (1921–).

1964 Existence of the quark is proposed by US physicists Murray Gell-Mann (1929–) and George Zweig.

1964 Existence of an elementary particle (the Higgs boson) that accounts for the mass of other particles is proposed by British physicists Peter Higgs (1929–) and Thomas Kibble (1932–).

1964 Non-conservation of parity in certain reactions involving subatomic particles is discovered by US nuclear physicists James Cronin (1931–) and Val Fitch (1923–).

MEDICINE (1960s)

1960 Metal-and-plastic artificial hip joints are fitted by British orthopaedic surgeon John Charnley (1911–82), who later (1963) settled on a combination of polished stainless steel and high molecular weight polyethylene (HMWP).

1962 Killed-virus vaccine against German measles (rubella) is developed by US biologist Thomas Weller (1915–).

1962 Successful kidney transplant from an unrelated donor is first performed by US surgeon Joseph Murray (1919–) and between nonidentical twins by French physician Jean Hamberger (1909–92), who later (1963) pioneered immunosuppressive therapy and the use of donor kidneys from cadavers.

FARMING AND FOOD	BIOLOGY	CHEMISTRY	PHYSICS	MEDICINE

BIOLOGY

1961 Genetic code of DNA is discovered by British biophysicist Francis Crick (1916–) and South-African born molecular biologist Sydney Brenner (1927–).

1961 Role of ATP in energy transfer in chloroplasts (in plant cells) and mitochondria (in animal cells) is discovered by British biochemist Peter Mitchell (1920–92).

1962 Role of the thymus gland in establishing the immune system in young animals is discovered by French-born Australian physician Jacques Miller (1931–).

1962 Fact that natural selection applies to both K type and R type animal species is discovered by Canadian ecologist Robert Macarthur (1930–71).

1965 Nucleotide sequence of transfer-RNA is discovered by US biochemist Robert Holley (1922–93).

1965 Insulin is first synthesized.

1966 Human growth hormone is discovered by Chinese-born US biochemist Choh Hao Li (1913–).

1967 Method of synthesizing biologically active DNA is discovered by US biochemist Arthur Kornberg (1918–).

1968 Enzyme (produced by bacteria) that selectively cuts viral DNA is discovered by Swiss microbiologist Werner Arber (1929–).

1969 Amino acid sequence of immunoglobulin is discovered by US Biochemist Gerald Edelman (1929–).

1970 Hormone LRF (luteinizing releasing factor) from the hypothalamus is discovered by French physiologist Roger Guillemin (1924–) and, independently, Polish-born US physiologist Andrew Schally (1926–).

1970 Enzyme reverse transcriptase (which transcribes RNA into DNA in some viruses) is discovered by US virologists Howard Temin (1934–94) and David Baltimore (1938–).

1970 Restriction enzymes are discovered by US molecular biologist Hamilton Smith (1931–).

1971 Theory of punctuated equilibrium (that evolution takes place in short "bursts") is proposed by US palaeontologist Stephen Gould (1941–).

1972 Hybrid DNA is made by splicing bacterial and viral DNA by US molecular biologist Paul Berg (1926–).

1973 Technique of using restriction enzymes to "cut and splice" DNA (that is, using recombinant DNA in genetic engineering) is discovered by US biochemists Stanley Cohen (1935–) and Herbert Boyer (1936–).

1974 Fossils of Australopithecus afarensis, the oldest humanoid fossil yet found, are discovered in Ethiopia by US palaeoanthropologist Donald Johanson (1943–).

1976 Endorphins are discovered by French physiologist Roger Guillemin.

1976 First functional artificial gene is made by Indian-born US chemist Har Khorana (1922–) et al.

1977 Full sequences of bases in DNA is discovered by British biochemist Frederick Sanger (1918–).

1977 Introns (DNA sequences that do not code for proteins) are discovered by British biochemists Alec Jeffreys (1950–) and R. Flavell (1945–).

1979 Gaia hypothesis, which regards the whole Earth as a single organism, is proposed by British scientist James Lovelock (1919–).

CHEMISTRY

1962 Crown ethers and cryptate metal complexes are discovered by Korean-born US chemist Charles Pedersen (1904–89).

1969 Structure of insulin is discovered by British chemist Dorothy Hodgkin (1910–94).

1969 Woodward-Hoffmann rules (concerning the behaviour of molecular orbitals during some organic reactions) are discovered by US chemist Robert Woodward (1917–79) and Polish-born US Roald Hoffmann (1937–)

PHYSICS

1964 Test to detect an interconnection between two widely separated subatomic particles that were once connected is devised by British physicist John Bell (1928–90).

1967 Fact that the electromagnetic force and the weak nuclear force are variations of a single force (the electroweak force) is proposed by US physicists Steven Weinberg (1933–) and Sheldon Glashow (1932–) and, independently, Pakistani physicist Abdus Salam (1926–).

1974 J-psi particle (a type of meson) is discovered by US physicists Samuel Ting (1936–) and, independently, Burton Richter (1931–).

1977 Upsilon particle is discovered by US physicist Leon Lederman (1922–).

1977 Mechanism of the quantum Hall effect is discovered by German physicist Klaus von Klitzing (1943–).

MEDICINE

1963 Liver transplant is first performed by US surgeons Thomas Starzl (1926–) and Francis Moore (1913–).

1964 Beta-blocker drug propranalol, used to treat heart disorders, is discovered by British pharmacologist James Black (1924–).

1964 First medical tests in space are carried out in orbiting Soviet spacecraft Voskod 1 by Soviet physician Boris Yegorov (1937–94).

1966 Live-virus vaccine against German measles (rubella) is developed by US bacteriologists Harry Meyer Jr (1928–) and Paul Parkman (1932–).

1967 Successful human heart transplant is carried out by South African surgeon Christiaan Barnard (1922–) and, later (1968), US surgeon Norman Shumway (1923–).

1967 Coronary bypass operation is introduced by US cardiovascular surgeon Rene Favaloro (1923–).

FARMING AND FOOD

1972 Perrier mineral water, from Vergèze, France, is marketed internationally.

1970

1972 Drug cimetridine, which blocks acid-producing sites in the stomach and thereby aids healing of ulcers, is discovered by British pharmacologist James Black (1924–).

1975 Technique for large-scale production of monoclonal antibodies is discovered by Argentinian-born British molecular biologist César Milstein (1927–) and Georges Köhler (1926–95).

1976 Legionnaire's disease is recognized for the first time, in Philadelphia, USA.

1976 Mechanism by which dormant oncogenes initiate the development of cancer is discovered by US virologists John Bishop (1936–) and Harold Varmus (1939–).

1977 Smallpox virus becomes extinct in the wild; World Health Organization later (1979) announces that smallpox has been eliminated worldwide.

1977 Balloon angioplasty (for dilating and thereby unblocking a constricted artery) is introduced by German surgeon Andreas Grüntzig (1939–85).

1978 World's first test-tube baby, Louise Brown, is born in England.

1979 AIDS (acquired immune deficiency syndrome) is first diagnosed, in the USA.

1980

FARMING AND FOOD

1981 Aspartame is introduced as an artificial sweetener in soft drinks in the USA.

1987 Process for making artificial milk from soya beans is invented by French Agrotechnic Company.

BIOLOGY

1981 Genes are transplanted between different organisms by geneticists at Ohio University.

1982 Bacteria that live in very hot (105°C) sea water are discovered by German biologist Karl Setter.

1984 Fossil skeleton of *Homo erectus* is found in Africa by British archaeologist Richard Leaky (1944–).

1984 Clone of a lamb is produced.

1984 Human Genone Project is proposed by Robert Sinsheimer of the University of California; it is launched in 1989.

1985 Genetic fingerprinting technique is devised by British biochemist Alec Jeffreys (1950–).

1985 Retinoblastoma, the first human cancer gene, is isolated in the United States.

1987 Fossilized dinosaur eggs containing embryos are discovered by Canadian palaeontologist Kevin Aulenback.

CHEMISTRY

1985 Buckminsterfullerenes, allotropes of carbon whose molecules consist of spherical structures of 60 or more carbon atoms, are discovered by Harold Kroto and David Walton.

PHYSICS

1983 W and Z particles ("weakons") are discovered by Italian physicist Carlo Rubbia (1934–) and Dutch physicist Simon van der Meer (1925–).

1986 Superconductors that work at relatively high temperatures (-243°C) are discovered by German physicist Georg Bednorz (1950–) and Swiss physicist Karl Müller (1927–); later (1987) a higher temperature (-196°C) is achieved by Chinese physicist Ching-Wu Chu (1941–).

1986 Brief controlled production of energy by laser-induced nuclear fusion is achieved by the Nova device at the Lawrence Livermore National Laboratory.

1989 Large Electron Positron Collider (LEP) particle accelerator comes into operation at the CERN laboratories near Geneva, Switzerland, and proves the existence of the Z particle.

1989 Production of energy by cold nuclear fusion is announced by US physicists Martin Fleischmann (1927–) and Stanley Pons (1943–), but the results were not substantiated and were refuted by Austrian-born US physicist Harold Furth (1930–).

MEDICINE

1980 Device to break up kidney stones using ultrasound is introduced by the German Dornier Medical Systems company.

1982 Prions (virus-like infective agents consisting simply of proteins) are discovered by US molecular biologist Stanley Prusiner.

1982 Genetically-engineered human insulin (for treating diabetes) is marketed by the US Eli Lilly company.

1983 Human immunodeficiency virus (HIV), responsible for AIDS, is discovered by French virologist Luc Montagnier (1932–) and, independently (1984), US Robert Gallo (1937–).

1984 Vaccine against leprosy becomes available.

1986 Defective gene responsible for Duchenne muscular dystrophy is discovered by US geneticist Louis Kunkel (1949–) et al.

1990

FARMING AND FOOD

1993 Genetically engineered tomato is devised by the US Calgene Company.

1995 Bovine spongiform encephalopathy (BSE) reaches epidemic proportions among beef cattle in Britain; its spread is associated with the inclusion in cattle feed of nerve tissue from slaughtered cattle.

1997 Based on the amount of carbon dioxide in the atmosphere (365 parts/million), US scientists predict that the greenhouse effect and possible resultant global warming will favour agriculture in higher latitudes.

1997 Edible packaging for food (based on the seaweed product carrageenan) is introduced in the USA.

BIOLOGY

1994 Technique of DNA recombination is devised to produce new "synthetic" genes from different parent genes.

1997 Fossil of early bird-like animal, *Proarchaeopteryx*, is discovered in China.

1997 Adult sheep Dolly is cloned by a team of researchers in Scotland.

1998 Adult sheep Dolly gives birth.

CHEMISTRY

1995 Structure of a protein fundamental for metabolism is determined.

1996 Ban on the manufacture and use of chlorofluorocarbons (CFCs) is imposed by US government.

PHYSICS

1991 Brief controlled production of energy by nuclear fusion is achieved by the JET (Joint European Torus) project in England; later (1993) fusion energy is also briefly produced by the Tokamak Fusion Test Reactor in the USA.

1995 Top quark is discovered by scientists at the US Fermi National Accelerator Laboratory.

1996 Atoms of antihydrogen (each consisting of a positron and antiproton) – the first example of antimatter – are observed by scientists at CERN, Geneva.

1997 Exotic meson, a new particle probably made up of four quarks, is discovered independently by US and Russian physicists.

1997 Atom laser beam (consisting of supercooled sodium atoms) is produced by US physicist Wolfgang Ketterle and colleagues.

1997 Quantum action at a distance is confirmed by Swiss physicist Nicolas Gisin (1952–).

MEDICINE

1993 Gene therapy to treat cystic fibrosis is introduced in the USA.

1994 New type of Ebola virus is discovered in Côte d'Ivoire (Ivory Coast), leading to further outbreaks in 1995 (Gabon and Zaire) and in 1996 (again in Gabon).

1995 Experimental transgenic organ transplants (of animal organs into humans) are investigated by US researchers; in 1997 a UK government report states that technique is acceptable in principle.

1996 Link is suggested between Creutzfeld-Jakob disease (CJD) in humans and bovine spongiform encephalopathy (BSE) in cattle.

1996 Epidemic of food-borne gastrointestinal illness (caused by the bacterium *E. coli*) occurs in Japan; the bacterium is identified with other outbreaks of "food poisoning" elsewhere in the world.

1996 Do-it-yourself AIDS testing kit is marketed in the USA.

1998 Laser for treating gum disease and ulcers is introduced by US dentists.

READY REFERENCE

PHYSICAL CONSTANTS

universal constant	symbol	value	Unit
speed of light in vacuum	c	299,792,458	ms^{-1}
permeability of vacuum	μ_0	12.566370614	$10^{-7}NA^{-2}$
permittivity of vacuum	ϵ_0	8.854187817	$10^{-12}Fm^{-1}$
Newtonian constant of gravitation	G	6.67259	$10^{-11}m^3kg^{-1}s^{-2}$
Planck constant	h	6.6260755	$10^{-34}Js$

electromagnetic constants

elementary charge	e	1.60217733	$10^{-19}C$

electron

electron mass	m_e	9.1093897	$10^{-31}kg$
electron specific charge	$-e/m_e$	−1.75881962	$10^{11}Ckg^{-1}$

muon, proton and neutron

muon mass	m_μ	1.8825327	$10^{-28}kg$
proton mass	m_p	1.6726231	$10^{-27}kg$
neutron mass	m_n	1.6749286	$10^{-27}kg$

physico-chemical constants

Avogadro constant	N_A,L	6.0221367	$10^{23}mol^{-1}$
atomic mass constant	m_u	1.6605402	$10^{-27}kg$
Faraday constant	F	96,485.309	$Cmol^{-1}$
molar gas constant	R	8.314510	$Jmol^{-1}K^{-1}$
Boltzmann constant	k	1.380658	$10^{-23}JK^{-1}$

SI DERIVED UNITS

measurement	unit	symbol
area	square metre	m^2
volume	cubic metre	m^3
velocity	metre per second	$m\,s^{-1}$
acceleration	metre per second squared	$m\,s^{-2}$
angular velocity	radian per second	$rad\,s^{-1}$
angular acceleration	radian per second squared	$rad\,s^{-2}$
density	kilogram per cubic metre	$kg\,m^{-3}$
momentum	kilogram metre per second	$kg\,m\,s^{-1}$
angular momentum	kilogram metre squared per second	$kg\,m^2\,s^{-1}$
mass rate of flow	kilogram per second	$kg\,s^{-1}$
volume rate of flow	cubic metre per second	$m^3\,s^{-1}$
torque	newton metre	$N\,m$
surface tension	newton per metre	$N\,m^{-1}$
dynamic viscosity	newton second per metre squared	$N\,s\,m^{-2}$
kinematic viscosity	metre squared per second	$m^2\,s^{-1}$
thermal coefficient	per °Celsius, or per kelvin	$°C^{-1}$, or K^{-1}
thermal conductivity	watt per metre °C	$W\,m^{-1}\,°C^{-1}$
heat capacity	joule per kelvin	$J\,K^{-1}$
specific latent heat	joule per kilogram	$J\,kg^{-1}$
specific heat capacity	joule per kilogram kelvin	$J\,kg^{-1}\,K^{-1}$
velocity of light	metre per second	$m\,s^{-1}$
permeability	henry per metre	$H\,m^{-1}$
permittivity	farad per metre	$F\,m^{-1}$
electric force	volt per metre	$v\,m^{-1}$
electric flux density	coulomb per metre squared	$C\,m^{-2}$

SYMBOLS FOR UNITS, CONSTANTS AND QUANTITIES

a	semi-major axis	L	luminosity	t	time		
Å	angstrom unit	L_n	Lagrangian points	T	temperature (absolute),		
AU	astronomical unit		(n = 1 to 5)	epoch	(time of perihelion		
c	speed of light	l.y.	light year		passage)		
d	distance	m	metre, minute	T_{eff}	effective temperature		
e	eccentricity	m	apparent magnitude,	v	velocity		
E	energy		mass	W	watt		
eV	electron-volt	m_{bol}	bolometric magnitude	y	year		
f	following	m_{pg}	photographic magnitude	z	redshift		
F	focal length, force	m_{pv}	photovisual magnitude	a	constant of aberration,		
g	acceleration due to gravity	m_v	visual magnitude		right ascension		
		M	absolute magnitude,	d	declination		
G	gauss		mass (stellar)	l	wavelength		
G	gravitational constant	N	newton	m	proper motion		
h	hour	p	preceding	n	frequency		
h	Planck constant	P	orbital period	p	parallax		
H_0	Hubble constant	pc	parsec	w	longitude of perihelion		
Hz	hertz	q	perihelion distance	W	observed/critical density		
i	inclination	q_0	deceleration parameter	ratio, longitude of			
IC	Index Catalogue	Q	aphelion distance		ascending node		
Jy	jansky	r	radius, distance	°	degree		
k	Boltzmann constant	R	Roche limit	'	arc minute		
K	degrees kelvin	s	second	"	arc second		

ROMAN NUMERALS

Arabic	Roman
1	I
2	II
3	III
4	IV
5	V
6	VI
7	VII
8	VIII
9	IX
10	X
11	XI
12	XII
13	XIII
14	XIV
15	XV
16	XVI
17	XVII
18	XVIII
19	XIX
20	XX
30	XXX
40	XL
50	L
60	LX
70	LXX
80	LXXX
90	XC
100	C
200	CC
300	CCC
400	CD
500	D
1000	M
5000	V̄
10,000	X̄
100,000	C̄

CONVERSIONS

length

1 inch (in)	= 2.54 centimetres (cm)
	= 25.4 millimetres (mm)
1 foot (ft)	= 0.3048 metre (m)
1 yard (yd)	= 0.9144 metre
1 mile (mi)	= 1.6093 kilometres (km)
1 centimetre	= 0.3937 inch
1 metre	= 3.2808 feet = 1.0936 yards
1 kilometre	= 0.6214 mile

area

1 square inch	= 6.4516 square centimetres
1 square foot	= 0.0929 square metre
1 acre	= 0.4047 hectare
1 sq mile	= 2.5899 square kilometres
1 square centimetre	= 0.155 square inch
1 square metre	= 10.7639 square feet
1 hectare	= 2.471 acres
1 square kilometre	= 0.3861 square mile

volume

1 cubic inch	= 16.3871 cubic centimetres
1 cubic foot	= 0.0283 cubic metre
1 cubic yard	= 0.7646 cubic metre
1 cubic centimetre	= 0.061 cubic inch
1 cubic metre	= 35.3147 cubic feet
1 cubic metre	= 1.3030 cubic yards

capacity

1 UK fluid ounce (fl oz)	= 0.02841 litre (l)
1 US fluid ounce	= 0.02961 litre
1 UK pint (pt)	= 0.56821 litre
1 US pint	= 0.47321 litre
1 UK gallon	= 4.546 litres
1 US gallon	= 3.7854 litres
1 litre	= 35.1961 fluid ounces (UK)
	= 33.814 fluid ounces (US)
	= 1.7598 pints (UK)
	= 2.1134 pints (US)
	= 0.22 gallon (UK)
	= 0.2642 gallon (US)
1 US cup	= 8 fluid ounces
1 UK pint	= 1.2 US pints
1 UK gallon	= 1.2009 US gallons
1 US pint	= 0.83 UK pint
1 US gallon	= 0.8327 UK gallon

weight*

1 ounce (oz)	= 28.3495 grams (g)
1 pound (lb)	= 0.454 kilograms (kg)
1 UK ton	= 1.016 tonnes
1 US ton	= 0.9072 tonne
1 gram	= 0.0353 ounce
1 kilogram	= 2.205 pounds
1 tonne	= 0.9842 UK ton = 1.1023 US tons
1 UK ton	= 1.1199 US tons
1 US ton	= 0.8929 UK ton

temperature

°Celsius to °Fahrenheit: ×9, ÷5, +32
°Fahrenheit to °Celsius: −32, ×5, ÷9

energy†

1000 British thermal units (Btu)	= 0.293 kilowatt hour
100,000 British thermal units	= 1 therm
1 UK horsepower	= 550 ft-lb per second
	= 745.7 watts
1 US horsepower	= 746 watts

nautical length and speed

UK nautical mile	= 6,080 feet
international nautical mile	= 6,076.1 feet
	= 0.9994 UK nautical mile

1 knot = 1 UK nautical mile per hour = 1.15 mph

petroleum

1 barrel	= 34.97 UK gallons = 42 US gallons
	= 0.159 cubic metres

precious stones

1 troy ounce	= 480 grains
1 metric carat	= 200 milligrams

type sizes

72 1/4 points = 1 inch
1 didot point = 0.376 mm
1 pica em = 12 points

*Avoirdupois † work, heat

BASIC MATHEMATICAL SYMBOLS

+	plus; positive
−	minus; negative
±	plus or minus; positive or negative; degree of accuracy
×	multiplied by ("times") (3×2)
÷	divided by (6 ÷ 2)
/	divided by; ratio of (2:1)
!	factorial (4! = 4×3×2×1)
=	equal to
≠	not equal to
≡	identical with
≢	not identical with
≙	corresponds to
:	ratio of (2:1)
::	proportionately equals (2:3 :: 4:6)
≈	approximately equal to; equivalent to; similar to
>	greater than
≫	much greater than
≯	not greater than
<	less than
≪	much less than
≮	not less than
≥	greater than or equal to
≤	less than or equal to
∝	directly proportional to
( )	parentheses
[ ]	brackets
{ }	braces
∞	infinity
→	approaches the limit
√	square root
³√, ⁴√	cube root, fourth root, etc
%	per cent
′	prime; minute(s) of arc; foot/feet
″	double prime; second(s) of arc; inch(es)
∩	arc of circle
°	degree of arc
⊻	equiangular
⊥	perpendicular
∥	parallel
∴	therefore
∵	because
Δ	increment
Σ	summation
Π	product
∫	integral sign

SI PREFIXES

prefix	symbol	power	multiple in full
exa-	E	10^{18}	1,000,000,000,000,000,000
peta-	P	10^{15}	1,000,000,000,000,000
tera-	T	10^{12}	1,000,000,000,000
giga-	G	10^{9}	1,000,000,000
mega-	M	10^{6}	1,000,000
kilo-	k	10^{3}	1000
hecto-	h	10^{2}	100
deca-	da	10^{1}	10
deci-	d	10^{-1}	0.1
centi-	c	10^{-2}	0.01
milli-	m	10^{-3}	0.001
micro-	μ	10^{-6}	0.000001
nano-	n	10^{-9}	0.000000001
pico-	p	10^{-12}	0.000000000001
femto-	f	10^{-15}	0.000000000000001
atto-	a	10^{-18}	0.000000000000000001

GEOMETRIC FIGURES

shape	circumference	area
circle	$2\pi r$	πr^2
parallelogram		lh
(l = length, h = perpendicular distance to side parallel to l)		
rectangle		lw
(l = length, w = width)		
triangle		1/2 lh

shape	volume	surface area
cone	$1/3\pi r^2 h$	$\pi r^2 + \pi rl$
(h = perpendicular height)		
cylinder	$\pi r^2 h$	$\pi r^2 + 2\pi rh$
pyramid	1/3Bh	
(B = area of base)		
sphere	$4/3\pi r^3$	$4\pi r^2$

Pythagoras' theorem: $a^2 = b^2 + c^2$
$\pi = 3.1415926...$
r = radius

POWER OF NUMBERS

factor	number	name
10^2	100	hundred
10^3	1,000	thousand
10^6	1,000,000	million
10^9	1,000,000,000	billion
10^{12}	1,000,000,000,000	trillion
10^{15}	1,000,000,000,000,000	quadrillion
10^{18}	1,000,000,000,000,000,000	quintillion
10^{100}	1 with 100 zeros	googol

In Britain, one billion was traditionally used for a million million (US trillion), whereas in the USA the billion represented a thousand million. From 1 January 1975, the UK has employed the US system in its finances, with a billion standing for £1000 million. Since then, the American system has been adopted throughout the English-speaking world.

PRIME NUMBERS

These are whole numbers that have only two factors – the number itself and the number one. The only even prime number is two: all other prime numbers are odd. These are the prime numbers below 100.

2	3	5	7	11	13	17	19	23	29	31	37	41
43	47	53	59	61	67	71	73	79	83	89	97	

POLYGONS

name	number of sides	each internal angle	sum of internal angles
triangle	3	60°	180°
square	4	90°	360°
pentagon	5	108°	540°
hexagon	6	120°	720°
heptagon	7	128.6°	900°
octagon	8	135°	1080°
nonagon	9	140°	1260°
decagon	10	144°	1440°
undecagon	11	147.3°	1620°
dodecagon	12	150°	1800°

SI UNITS

The *Système International d'Unités* is the worldwide standard system of units used by scientists. Originally proposed in 1960, it is based on seven basic units.

measurement	unit	symbol
basic units		
length	metre	m
mass	kilogram	kg
time	second	s
electric current	ampere	A
thermodynamic temperature	kelvin	K
amount of substance	molc	mol
luminous intensity	candela	cd
supplementary units		
plane angle	radian	rad
solid angle	steradian	sr
derived units		
frequency	hertz	Hz
force	newton	N
pressure, stress	pascal	Pa
work (energy, heat)	joule	J
power	watt	W
electric charge	coulomb	C
electromotive force	volt	V
electric resistance	ohm	Ω
electric conductance	siemens	S
electric capacitance	farad	F
inductance	henry	H
magnetic flux	weber	Wb
magnetic flux density	tesla	T
illuminance	lux	lx
luminous flux	lumen	lm
radiation exposure	roentgen	r
radiation activity	becquerel	Bq
radiation absorbed dose	gray	Gy
radiation dose equivalent	sievert	Sv
Celsius temperature	°Celsius	°C

SQUARES, CUBES AND ROOTS

no.	square	cube	square root	cube root
1	1	1	1	1
2	4	8	1.414	1.260
3	9	27	1.732	1.442
4	16	64	2	1.587
5	25	125	2.236	1.710
6	36	216	2.449	1.817
7	49	343	2.646	1.913
8	64	512	2.828	2
9	81	729	3	2.080
10	100	1000	3.162	2.154
11	121	1331	3.317	2.224
12	144	1728	3.464	2.289
13	169	2197	3.606	2.351
14	196	2744	3.742	2.410
15	225	3375	3.873	2.466
16	256	4096	4	2.520
17	289	4913	4.123	2.571
18	324	5832	4.243	2.621
19	361	6859	4.359	2.668
20	400	8000	4.472	2.714
25	625	15,625	5	2.924
30	900	27,000	5.477	3.107
40	1600	64,000	6.325	3.420
50	2500	125,000	7.071	3.684

GREEK ALPHABET

α	A	alpha
β	B	beta
γ	Γ	gamma
δ	Δ	delta
ε	E	epsilon
ζ	Z	zeta
η	H	eta
θ	Θ	theta
ι	I	iota
κ	K	kappa
λ	Λ	lambda
μ	M	mu
ν	N	nu
ξ	Ξ	xi
o	O	omicron
π	Π	pi
ρ	P	rho
σ, ς	Σ	sigma
τ	T	tau
υ	Υ	upsilon
φ	Φ	phi
χ	X	chi
ψ	Ψ	psi
ω	Ω	omega

In mathematics, π (pi) equals 3.1415926....

CHEMICAL ELEMENTS

name	symbol	atomic number	relative atomic mass*	valency	melting point °C	boiling point °C	date of discovery
actinium	Ac	89	(227)	–	1230	3200	1899
aluminium	Al	13	26.98154	3	660.2	2350	1827
americium	Am	95	(243)	3, 4 ,5, 6	995	2600	1944
antimony	Sb	51	121.75	3.5	630.5	1750	c.1000BC
argon	Ar	18	39.948	0	−189.4	−185.9	1894
arsenic	As	33	74.9216	3.5	613	–	1250
astatine	At	85	(210)	1, 3 ,5, 7	302	377	1940
barium	Ba	56	137.34	2	725	1640	1808
berkelium	Bk	97	(247)	3, 4	986	–	1949
beryllium	Be	4	9.01218	2	1285	2470	1798
bismuth	Bi	83	208.9804	3, 5	271.3	1560	1753
boron	B	5	10.81	3	2079	3700	1808
bromine	Br	35	79.904	1, 3, 5, 7	−7.2	58.8	1826
cadmium	Cd	48	112.40	2	320.9	765	1817
caesium	Cs	55	132.9054	1	28 4	678	1860
calcium	Ca	20	40.08	2	839	1484	1808
californium	Cf	98	(251)	–	–	–	1950
carbon	C	6	12.011	2.4	3550	4200	–
cerium	Ce	58	140.12	3, 4	798	3257	1803
chlorine	Cl	17	35.453	1, 3, 5, 7	−101	−34.6	1774
chromium	Cr	24	51.996	2, 3, 6	1890	2672	1797
cobalt	Co	27	58.9332	2, 3	1495	2870	1735
copper	Cu	29	63.546	1, 2	1083	2567	c.8000BC
curium	Cm	96	(247)	3	1340	–	1944
dubnium‡	Db	104	(261)	–	–	–	1969
dysprosium	Dy	66	162.50	3	1409	2335	1896
einsteinium	Es	99	(254)	–	–	–	1952
erbium	Er	68	167.26	3	1522	2863	1843
europium	Eu	63	151.96	2, 3	822	1597	1896
fermium	Fm	100	(257)	–	–	–	1952
fluorine	F	9	18.9984	1	−219.6	−188.1	1886
francium	Fr	87	(223)	1	30	650	1939
gadolinium	Gd	64	157.25	3	1311	3233	1880
gallium	Ga	31	69.72	2, 3	29.78	2403	1875
germanium	Ge	32	72.59	4	937.4	2830	1886
gold	Au	79	196.9665	1, 3	1063	2800	–
hafnium	Hf	72	178.49	4	2227	4602	1923
helium	He	2	4.0026	0	−272	268.9	1895
holmium	Ho	67	164.9304	3	1470	2300	1878
hydrogen	H	1	1.0079	1	−259.1	−252.9	1766
indium	In	49	114.82	3	156.6	2080	1863
iodine	I	53	126.9045	1, 3, 5, 7	113.5	184.4	1811
iridium	Ir	77	192.22	3, 4	2410	4130	1804
iron	Fe	26	55.847	2, 3	1540	2760	c.4000BC
krypton	Kr	36	83.80	0	−156.6	−152.3	1898
lanthanum	La	57	138.9055	3	920	3454	1839
lawrencium	Lr	103	(256)	–	–	–	1961
lead	Pb	82	207.2	2, 4	327.5	1740	–
lithium	Li	3	6.941	1	180.5	1347	1817
lutetium	Lu	71	174.97	3	1656	3315	1907
magnesium	Mg	12	24.305	2	648.8	1090	1808
manganese	Mn	25	54.9380	2, 3, 4, 6, 7	1244	1962	1774
mendelevium	Md	101	(258)	–	–	–	1955
mercury	Hg	80	200.59	1, 2	−38.9	356.6	c.1500BC
molybdenum	Mo	42	95.94	3, 4, 6	2610	5560	1778
neodymium	Nd	60	144.24	3	1010	3068	1885
neon	Ne	10	20.179	0	−248.7	−246.1	1898
neptunium	Np	93	237.0482	4, 5, 6	640	3902	1940
nickel	Ni	28	58.70	2, 3	1453	2732	1751
niobium	Nb	41	92.9064	3, 5	2468	4742	1801
nitrogen	N	7	14.0067	3, 5	−210	−195.8	1772
nobelium	No	102	(255)	–	–	–	1958
osmium	Os	76	190.2	2, 3, 4, 8	3045	5027	1903
oxygen	O	8	15.9994	2	−218.4	−183	1774
palladium	Pd	46	106.4	2, 4, 6	1552	3140	1803
phosphorus	P	15	30.97376	3, 5	44.1	280	1669
platinum	Pt	78	195.09	2, 4	1772	3800	1735
plutonium	Pu	94	(244)	3, 4, 5, 6	641	3232	1940
polonium	Po	84	(209)	–	254	962	1898
potassium	K	19	39.098	1	63.2	777	1807
praseodymium	Pr	59	140.9077	3	931	3512	1885
promethium	Pm	61	(145)	3	1080	2460	1941
protactinium	Pa	91	231.0359	–	1200	4000	1913
radium	Ra	88	226.0254	2	700	1140	1898
radon	Rn	86	(222)	0	−71	−61.8	1899
rhenium	Re	75	186.207	–	3180	5627	1925
rhodium	Rh	45	102.9055	3	1966	3727	1803
rubidium	Rb	37	85.4678	1	38.8	688	1861
ruthenium	Ru	44	101.07	3, 4, 6, 8	2310	3900	1827
samarium	Sm	62	150.35	2, 3	1072	1791	1879
scandium	Sc	21	44.9559	3	1539	2832	1879
selenium	Se	34	78.96	2, 4, 6	217	684.9	1817
silicon	Si	14	28.086	4	1410	2355	1823
silver	Ag	47	107.868	1	961.9	2212	c.4000BC
sodium	Na	11	22.98977	1	97.8	882	1807
strontium	Sr	38	87.62	2	769	1384	1808
sulphur	S	16	32.06	2, 4, 6	112.8	444.7	–
tantalum	Ta	73	180.9479	5	2996	5425	1802
technetium	Tc	43	(97)	6, 7	2172	4877	1937
tellurium	Te	52	127.60	2, 4, 6	449.5	989.8	1782
terbium	Tb	65	158.9254	3	1360	3041	1843
thallium	Tl	81	204.37	1, 3	303.5	1457	1861
thorium	Th	90	232.0381	4	1750	4790	1828
thulium	Tm	69	168.9342	3	1545	1947	1879
tin	Sn	50	118.69	2, 4	232	2270	c.3500BC
titanium§	Ti	22	47.90	3, 4	1660	3287	1791
tungsten§	W	74	183.85	6	3410	5660	1783
unnilpentium†	Unp	105	(262)	–	–	–	1970
uranium	U	92	238.029	4, 6	1132	3818	1789
vanadium	V	23	50.9414	3, 5	1890	3380	1801
xenon	Xe	54	131.30	0	−111.9	−107.1	1898
ytterbium	Yb	70	173.04	2, 3	824	1193	1907
yttrium	Y	39	88.9059	3	1510	3300	1828
zinc	Zn	30	65.38	2	419.6	907	1800
zirconium	Zr	40	91.22	4	1852	4377	1789

* relative atomic mass: values given in parentheses are for radioactive elements, the relative atomic masses of which cannot be given precisely without knowledge of origin; it is the atomic mass number of the isotope of longest known half-life
† also called hahnium, nielsbohrium, rutherfordium or element 105
‡ also called unnilquadium (Unq) or element 104
§ also called wolfram

INSIDE THE EARTH

	density	% of Earth's mass	temperature at top	state	thickness
continental crust	2.7	0.37	*	solid	25–90km (15–55mi)
oceanic crust	3.0	0.01		solid	6–11km (4–7mi)
upper mantle	3.5	18	1400°C (2550°F)	solid, flowing slowly	660km (410mi)
lower mantle	5.0	49	1600°C (2850°F)	solid, flowing slowly	2230km (1390mi)
outer core	11.0	31	4500°C (8070°F)	liquid	2255km (1410mi)
inner core	12.8	1.7	4700°C (8430°F)	solid	1215km (760mi)

* near the top of the crust the temperature increases at a rate of about 30°C per km

COMPOSITION OF THE EARTH

The table shows the abundances of the most common elements in the Earth, estimated by weight percent. Uncertainties are greatest in the estimates for the whole Earth, because although it is fairly certain that the core is mostly iron the proportions of other elements there are unknown.

crust	mantle	whole Earth	
iron	5	6	35
oxygen	47	44	29
silicon	27	21	14
magnesium	2.3	2.5	14
sulphur	0.04	0.12	2–4
nickel	0.008	0.24	1.6–2.0
aluminium	8.1	1.5	1.9
calcium	5.0	1.8	1.7
sodium	2.1	0.22	0.03–0.15
potassium	1.3	0.10	0.013–0.019

SELECTED EARTH RECORDS

greatest tides	Bay of Fundy, Nova Scotia, Canada, 16.3m (53.5ft)
deepest gorge*	Colca River, Peru, 3205m (10,515ft)
longest gorge	Grand Canyon, Arizona, USA, 350km (217mi)
deepest lake	Lake Baikal, Siberia, Russia, 1620m (5315ft)
highest navigable lake	Lake Titicaca, Peru/Bolivia, 3812m (12,506ft)
deepest cave	Réseau Jean Bernard, Haute-Savoie, France, 1602m (5256ft)
longest cave system	Mammoth Cave, Kentucky, USA, 560km (348mi)
deepest valley*	Kali Gandaki, Nepal, 5883m (19,300ft)
longest glacier	Lambert-Fisher Ice Passage, Antarctica, 515km (320mi)
deepest depression	Dead Sea, Israel/Jordan, 395m (1296ft)
largest volcano	Mauna Loa, Hawaii, USA, 16km (10mi) above 120km (75mi) wide base (on floor of Pacific ocean)

* a gorge is a type of valley found in areas of hard rock and having particularly steep sides

PLANET EARTH

mean distance from the Sun	149,500,000km (92,860,000mi)
average speed around the Sun	108,000km/h (66,600mph)
age	c.4,500,000,000 years
mass	5975 million million million tonnes
density	5515 times that of water
volume	1,083,207,000,000cu km (260,000,000,000cu mi)
area	509,450,000sq km (196,672,000sq mi)
land surface	149,450,000sq km (57,688,000sq mi) – 29.3% of total area
water surface area	360,000,000sq km (138,984,000sq mi) – 70.7% of total
equatorial circumference	40,075km (24,902mi)
polar circumference	40,008km (24,860mi)
equatorial diameter	12,756km (7926mi)
polar diameter	12,714km (7900mi)

RIVER DRAINAGE BASINS

The table shows the size of the area drained (the "catchment area") by the major rivers of each continent.

	sq km	sq mi
Europe		
Volga	1,380,000	533,000
Danube	815,000	315,000
Rhine	869,000	225,000
Asia		
Yenisey-Angara [5]	2,700,000	1,042,000
Ob-Irtysh [6]	2,430,000	938,000
Lena [7]	2,420,000	934,000
Amur [9]	1,840,000	710,000
Ganges-Brahmaputra	1,730,000	668,000
Yangtze	1,175,000	454,000
Huang He	980,000	378,000
Indus	960,000	371,000
Africa		
Congo (Zaïre) [2]	3,700,000	1,428,000
Nile [8]	1,900,000	733,400
Zambezi	1,330,000	513,000
Niger	1,200,000	463,000
Orange	1,020,000	394,000
North America		
Mississippi-Missouri [3]	3,250,000	1,255,000
Mackenzie [10]	1,765,000	681,000
Yukon	855,000	330,000
South America		
Amazon [1]	7,050,000	2,721,000
Paraná-Plata [4]	3,100,000	1,197,000
Orinoco	945,000	365,000
Australia		
Murray-Darling	910,000	351,000

CLIMATE RECORDS

temperature
highest recorded temperature: Al Aziziyah, Libya, 58°C (136.4°F), 13 September 1922
highest mean annual temperature: Dallol, Ethiopia, 34.4°C (94°F), 1960–66
longest heatwave: Marble Bar, w Australia, 162 days over 38°C (100°F), 23 October 1923 to 7 April 1924
lowest recorded temperature (outside poles): Verkhoyansk, Siberia, −68°C (−90°F), 6 February 1933
lowest mean annual temperature: Polus Nedostupnosti (Pole of Cold) Antarctica, −57.8°C (−72°F)

precipitation
driest place: Arica, N Chile, 0.8mm (0.03in) per year (60-year average)
longest drought: Calama, N Chile; no recorded rainfall in 400 years to 1971
wettest place (average): Tututendo, Colombia; mean annual rainfall 11,770mm (463.4in) wettest place (12 months): Cherrapunji, Meghalaya, NE India, 26,470mm (1040in), August 1860 to August 1861[†]
wettest place (24-hour period): Cilaos, Réunion, Indian Ocean, 1870mm (73.6in), 15–16 March 1952
heaviest hailstones: Gopalganj, Bangladesh, up to 1.02kg (2.25lb), 14 April 1986[‡]
heaviest snowfall (continuous): Bessans, Savoie France, 1730mm (68in) in 19 hours, 5–6 April 1969
heaviest snowfall (season/year): Paradise Ranger Station, Mt Rainier, Washington, USA, 31,102mm (1224.5in), 19 February 1971 to 18 February 1972

pressure and winds
highest barometric pressure: Agata, Siberia, 1083.8mb (32in) at altitude 262m (862ft), 31 December 1968
lowest barometric pressure: Typhoon Tip, 480km (300mi) w of Guam, Pacific Ocean, 870mb (25.69in), 12 October 1979
highest recorded wind speed: Mt Washington, New Hampshire, USA, 371km/h (231mph), 12 April 1934[§]
windiest place: Commonwealth Bay, George V Coast, Antarctica, where gales reach over 320km/h (200mph)

* Verkhoyansk also registered the greatest annual range of temperature: −70°C to 37°C (−94°F to 98°F)
† Cherrapunji also holds the record for rainfall in one month: 930mm (37in) fell in July 1861
‡ killed 92 people
§ three times as strong as hurricane force on the Beaufort scale

LARGEST INLAND LAKES AND SEAS

	location	sq km	sq mi
Europe			
Lake Ladoga	Russia	17,700	6800
Lake Onega	Russia	9600	3700
Saimaa system	Finland	8000	3100
Vänern	Sweden	6500	2100
Asia			
Caspian Sea [1]	Central Asia	371,000	143,000
Aral Sea* [6]	Kazakstan/Uzbekistan	33,640	13,000
Lake Baikal [9]	Russia	31,500	12,200
Tonlé Sap	Cambodia	20,000	7700
Lake Balkhash	Kazakstan	18,400	7100
Africa			
Lake Nyanza [3]	East Africa	68,000	26,000
Lake Tanganyika [7]	Central Africa	33,000	12,700
Lake Malawi [10]	East Africa	29,600	11,400
Lake Chad**	Central Africa	26,000	10,000
Lake Turkana	Ethiopia/Kenya	8500	3300
Lake Volta[†]	Ghana	8480	3250
North America			
Lake Superior [2]	Canada/USA	82,400	31,800
Lake Huron [4]	Canada/USA	59,600	23,010
Lake Michigan [5]	USA	58,000	22,300
Great Bear Lake [8]	Canada	31,800	12,280
Great Slave Lake	Canada	28,400	11,000
Lake Erie	Canada/USA	25,700	9900
Lake Winnipeg	Canada	24,500	9500
Lake Ontario	Canada/USA	19,700	7600
Lake Nicaragua	Nicaragua	8000	3100
South America			
Lake Titicaca[‡]	Bolivia/Peru	8300	3200
Lake Poopó	Peru	2800	1100
Australia			
Lake Eyre[§]	Australia	9300	3600
Lake Torrens[§]	Australia	5800	2200
Lake Gairdner[§]	Australia	4800	1900

* shrinking in area due to environmental factors; until the 1980s it was the world's 4th largest
** shallow lake, with area fluctuating naturally with the seasons. The area quoted is the usual wet-season area prior to 1963. The lake's area was only a twentieth of this by 2000, mainly because of water extraction from rivers for irrigation
† artificial lake created by Akosombo Dam (1966)
‡ Lake Maracaibo, in Venezuela, is far larger at 13,260 sq km (5120 sq mi), but it is linked to the Caribbean by a narrow channel and therefore not an "inland" lake
§ salt lakes that vary in size with rainfall

LARGEST ISLANDS

	sq km	sq mi
Europe		
Great Britain [8]	229,900	88,700
Iceland	103,000	39,800
Ireland	84,400	32,600
Novaya Zemlya (N)	48,200	18,600
Sicily	25,700	9900
Sardinia	24,090	9300
Asia		
Borneo [3]	743,000	287,400
Sumatra [6]	425,000	164,000
Honshu [7]	230,800	89,100
Sulawesi	189,200	73,000
Java	126,500	48,800
Luzon	104,700	40,400
Mindanao	95,000	36,600
Hokkaido	83,500	32,200
Sakhalin	76,400	29,500
Sri Lanka	65,600	25,300
Africa		
Madagascar [4]	587,000	226,700
Socotra	3100	1200
Réunion	2510	969
North America		
Greenland [1]	2,175,000	840,000
Baffin Island [5]	507,500	195,900
Victoria Island [9]	212,200	81,900
Ellesmere Island [10]	196,200	75,800
Cuba	110,860	42,800
Newfoundland	96,000	37,100
Hispaniola	76,500	29,500
Jamaica	11,000	4200
Puerto Rico	8900	3400
South America		
Tierra del Fuego	47,000	18,100
Falkland Island (E)	6800	2600
Oceania*		
New Guinea [2]	885,800	342,000
New Zealand (S)	150,500	58,100
New Zealand (N)	114,700	44,300
Tasmania	68,300	26,400
Hawaii	10,450	4000

* geographers consider Australia to be a continental landmass

LONGEST RIVERS

	outflow	km	mi
Europe			
Volga	Caspian Sea	3750	2330
Danube	Black Sea	2859	1770
Ural*	Caspian Sea	2535	1575
Asia			
Yangtze [3]	Pacific Ocean	6300	3900
Yenisey-Angara [5]	Arctic Ocean	5550	3445
Huang He [6]	Pacific Ocean	5500	3400
Ob-Irtysh [7]	Arctic Ocean	5410	3360
Amur [10]	Pacific Ocean	4400	2730
Mekong [9]	Pacific Ocean	4180	2600
Africa			
Nile[†] [1]	Mediterranean	6700	4160
Congo (Zaïre) [8]	Atlantic Ocean	4670	2900
Niger	Atlantic Ocean	4180	2600
Zambezi	Indian Ocean	2740	1700
North America			
Mississippi-Missouri [4]	Gulf of Mexico	6050	3760
Mackenzie	Arctic Ocean	4240	2630
Missouri	Mississippi	4120	2560
Mississippi	Gulf of Mexico	3780	2350
Yukon	Pacific Ocean	3185	1980
Rio Grande	Gulf of Mexico	3030	1880
Arkansas	Mississippi	2335	1450
Colorado	Pacific Ocean	2333	1450
South America			
Amazon [2]	Atlantic Ocean	6430	3990
Paraná-Plata [4]	Atlantic Ocean	4480	3032
Purus	Amazon	3350	2080
Madeira	Amazon	3200	1990
São Francisco	Atlantic Ocean	2900	1800
Australia			
Murray-Darling	Southern Ocean	3750	2830
Darling	Murray	3070	1905
Murray	Southern Ocean	2575	1600
Murrumbidgee	Murray	1690	1050

* flows through Europe and Asia
† although the Nile is the world's longest river, it discharges less water than the Amazon, which drains a larger area

CONTINENTS

continent	area			highest point above sea level				lowest point below sea level		
	sq km	sq mi	%			m	ft		m	ft
Asia	44,391,000	17,139,000	29.8	Mt Everest (China/Nepal)		8848	29,029	Dead Sea, Israel/Jordan	−396	−1302
Africa	30,000,000	11,700,000	20.3	Mt Kilimanjaro, Tanzania		5895	19,340	Lake Assal, Djibouti	−153	−502
North America	24,454,000	9,442,000	16.2	Mt McKinley, Alaska		6194	20,321	Death Valley, California, USA	−86	−282
South America	17,793,000	6,868,000	11.9	Mt Aconcagua, Argentina		6960	22,834	Peninsular Valdés, Argentina	−40	−131
Antarctica	14,200,000	5,500,000	9.4	Vinson Massif		4897	16,066	*		
Europe	10,360,000	4,000,000	6.7	Mt Elbrus, Russia		5633	18,481	Caspian Sea, Central Asia	−28	−92
Oceania	8,945,000	3,454,000	5.7	Puncak Jaya (Ngga Pulu), Indonesia		5029	16,499	Lake Eyre (N), South Australia	−15	−50

The Bentley trench (−2540m/−8333ft) is englacial and therefore not a surface point

OCEANS

ocean	area					greatest known depth			
	sq km	sq mi	%	m	ft			m	ft
Pacific	166,000,000	69,356,000	49.9	4300	14,100	Mariana Trench		11,033	36,198
Atlantic	82,000,000	32,000,000	25.7	3700	12,100	Puerto Rico Trench*		8650	28,370
Indian	73,600,000	28,400,000	20.5	4000	13,000	Java Trench		7725	25,344
Arctic	13,986,000	5,400,000	3.9	1330	4300	Molloy Deep		5608	18,399

7th deepest trench in the world; 8 of the deepest 10, including 1–6, are in the Pacific Ocean

ATMOSPHERIC COMPOSITION

gas	% of total
nitrogen (N_2)	77
oxygen (O_2)	21
water vapour (H_2O)	1
argon (Ar)	0.16
carbon dioxide (CO_2)	0.035

HIGHEST MOUNTAINS

	location	m	ft
Europe			
Elbrus*	Russia	5633	18,481
Mont Blanc† ‡	France/Italy	4810	15,781
Monte Rosa‡	Italy/Switzerland	4634	15,203
also			
Matterhorn (Cervino)‡	Italy/Switzerland	4478	14,691
Jungfrau	Switzerland	4158	13,642
Grossglockner	Austria	3797	12,457
Mulhacen	Spain	3478	11,411
Etna	Italy (Sicily)	3340	10,958
Zugspitze	Germany	2962	9718
Olympus	Greece	2917	9570
Galdhopiggen	Norway	2468	8100
Ben Nevis	UK (Scotland)	1343	4406
Asia§			
Everest	China/Nepal	8848	29,029
K2 (Godwin Austen)	China/Kashmir	8611	28,251
Kanchenjunga‡	India/Nepal	8586	28,169
Lhotse‡	China/Nepal	8516	27,939
Makalu‡	China/Nepal	8481	27,824
Cho Oyu	China/Nepal	8201	26,906
Dhaulagiri‡	Nepal	8172	26,811
Manaslu (Kutang)‡	Nepal	8156	26,758
Nanga Parbat	Kashmir	8126	26,660
Annapurna‡	Nepal	8078	26,502
also			
Kommunizma Pik	Tajikistan	7495	24,590
Ararat	Turkey	5165	16,945
Gunong Kinabalu	Malaysia (Borneo)	4101	13,455
Fujiyama (Fuji-san)	Japan	3776	12,388
Africa			
Kilimanjaro	Tanzania	5895	19,340
Mt Kenya	Kenya	5200	17,058

	location	m	ft
Ruwenzori	Uganda/Zaire	5109	16,763
North America			
Mt McKinley (Denali)‡	USA (Alaska)	6194	20,321
Mt Logan	Canada	6050	19,849
Citlaltépetl (Orizaba)	Mexico	5700	18,701
Mt St Elias	USA/Canada	5489	18,008
Popocatépetl	Mexico	5452	17,887
also			
Mt Whitney	USA	4418	14,495
Tajumulco	Guatemala	4220	13,845
Chirripo Grande	Costa Rica	3837	12,589
Pico Duarte	Dominican Republic	3175	10,417
South America			
Aconcagua#	Argentina	6960	22,834
Ojos del Salado**	Argentina/Chile	6863	22,516
Pissis	Argentina	6779	22,241
Mercedario	Argentina/Chile	6770	22,211
Huascarán‡	Peru	6768	22,204
Oceania			
Puncak Jaya	Indonesia (w Irian)	5029	16,499
Puncak Trikora	Indonesia (w Irian)	4750	15,584
Puncak Mandala	Indonesia (w Irian)	4702	15,427
Mt Wilhelm	Papua New Guinea	4508	14,790
also			
Mauna Kea	USA (Hawaii)	4205	13 796
Mauna Loa	USA (Hawaii)	4169	13,678
Mt Cook (Aorangi)	New Zealand	3764	12,349
Mt Kosciusko	Australia	2228	7310
Antarctica			
Vinson Massif	–	4897	16,066
Mt Tyree	–	4965	16,289

* Caucasus Mountains include 14 other peaks higher than Mont Blanc, the highest point in non-Russian Europe
† highest point is in France; the highest point wholly in Italian territory is 4760m (15,616ft)
‡ many mountains, especially in Asia, have two or more significant peaks; only the highest ones are listed here
§ the ranges of Central Asia have more than 100 peaks over 7315m (24,000ft); thus the first 10 listed here constitute the world's 10 highest mountains
# highest mountain outside Asia
** highest active volcano

THE EARTH'S DRYLANDS

Drylands are areas with very low rainfall that nonetheless support life: around 20% of the world's population live in drylands. These areas cover around 60 million square kilometres, or about 40% of the total land area. Of this some 10 million square kilometres are true desert areas. Desertification of drylands areas is a serious threat: the current rate is around 60,000sq km (23,000sq mi) annually (or 0.1% per year).

continent	% of global area
Asia 32%	
Africa	32%
North America	12%
Australia	11%
South America	8%
Europe	5%

CLOUDS

name	description	height range* (metres)
high-level clouds		
cirrus	white, thread-like	+6000
cirrocumulus	thin sheets	+6000
cirrostratus	white, transparent	+6000
medium-level clouds		
altocumulus	greyish-white	2000–6000
altostratus	grey, streaky	2000–6000
low-level clouds		
stratocumulus	large masses	below 2000
stratus	low, grey	below 850
nimbostratus	thick, dark	below 850
heap clouds		
cumulus	white, fluffy	850–9000
cumulonimbus	dark, towering	up to 18,000

* in temperate regions

HIGHEST WATERFALLS

name	total height		location	river	highest fall	
	m	ft			m	ft
Angel	980	3212	Venezuela	Carrao	807	2648
Tugela	947	3110	Natal, South Africa	Tugela	410	1350
Utigård	800	2625	Nesdale, Norway	Jostedal Glacier	600	1970
Mongefoseen	774	2540	Mongebekk, Norway	Monge	–	–
Yosemite	739	2425	California, USA	Yosemite Creek	739	2425
Østre Mardøla Foss	656	2154	Eikisdal, Norway	Mardals	296	974
Tyssestrengane	646	2120	Hardanger, Norway	Tysso	289	948
Cuquenán	610	2000	Venezuela	Arabopó	–	–
Sutherland	580	1904	Otago, New Zealand	Arthur	248	815
Takkakaw	502	1650	British Columbia, Canada	Daly Glacier	365	1200
Ribbon	491	1612	California, USA	Ribbon Fall Stream	491	1612

The greatest waterfalls by volume are the Boyoma (formerly Stanley) Falls on the Congo (Zaïre) River, with a mean annual flow of 17,000 cu m/sec (600,000 cu ft/sec). The Niagara Falls and the Victoria Falls (*Mosi oa Tunya*, "the smoke that thunders") are 4th and 9th respectively, in terms of volume; though both are relatively modest in height.

LARGEST DESERTS

desert	country	sq km	sq mi
Sahara	Africa	8,600,000	3,320,000
Arabian	Asia	2,230,000	900,000
Gobi	Mongolia, China	1,166,000	450,000
Patagonian	Argentina	673,000	260,000
Great Victoria	Australia	647,000	250,000
Great Basin	USA	492,000	190,000
Chihuahuan	Mexico	450,000	175,000
Great Sandy	Australia	400,000	150,000
Sonoran	USA	310,000	120,000
Kyzyl Kum	Kazakstan	300,000	115,000
Takla Makan	China	270,000	105,000
Kara Kum	Turkmenistan	260,000	100,000
Kavir	Iran	260,000	100,000
Syrian	Middle East	260,000	100,000

LAYERS IN THE ATMOSPHERE

The four lower layers in the atmosphere are bounded by reversals of the temperature gradient. The lowest and densest part of the atmosphere is the troposphere. Temperature decreases with height throughout the troposphere until a level, known as the tropopause, is reached, beyond which the temperature increases with height. This new layer is called the stratosphere, the top of which, the stratopause, marks the height above which temperature once again decreases with height in another layer called the mesosphere. Above the mesopause temperature increases with height throughout both the thermosphere and the exosphere. These are both exceedingly tenuous, the difference between the two being simply that gas molecules in the exosphere (which has no well-defined top) are not securely bound to the Earth and can leak away slowly to interplanetary space.

	height	temperature
troposphere	0–6km (0–4mi) near poles 0–17km (0–11mi) near tropics	decreasing with height to −50 °C at top
stratosphere	6–50km (4–30mi) near poles 17–50km (11–30mi) near tropics	increasing with height to 10 °C
ozone layer (part of stratosphere)	16–32km (10–20mi)	−20°C
mesosphere	50–80km (30–50mi)	decreasing with height to −90°C at top
thermosphere	80–450km (50–280mi)	increasing with height to >1000°C
exosphere	>450km (>280mi)	1200°C

BEAUFORT SCALE

Named after the 19th-century British naval officer who devised it, the Beaufort scale assesses wind speed according to its effects. Originally designed in 1806 as an aid for sailors, it has since been adapted for use on land and was internationally recognized in 1874.

scale	wind speed km/h	mph	name
0	0–1	0–1	calm
1	1–5	1–3	light air
2	6–11	4–7	light breeze
3	12–19	8–12	gentle breeze
4	20–28	13–18	moderate
5	29–38	19–24	fresh
6	39–49	25–31	strong
7	50–61	32–38	near gale
8	62–74	39–46	gale
9	75–88	47–54	strong gale
10	89–102	55–63	storm
11	103–117	64–72	violent storm
12	118+	73+	hurricane

WIND-CHILL FACTORS

A combination of cold and wind makes the human body feel cooler than the actual air temperature. The charts below give approximate equivalents for combinations of wind speed and temperature. In sub-zero temperatures, even moderate winds will significantly reduce effective temperatures: if human skin was exposed to winds of 48km/h (30mph) in a temperature of −34°C (−30°F) it would freeze solid in 30 seconds.

Temp. °C	Wind speed (km/h) 16	32	48	64*	Temp. °F	Wind speed (mph) 10	20	30	40*
15	11	9	8	6	30	16	4	−2	−5
10	6	3	2	−1	20	3	−10	−18	−21
5	1	4	−5	−8	10	−9	−24	−33	−37
0	−8	−14	−17	−19	0	−2	−39	−49	−53
−5	−14	−21	−25	−27	−10	−34	−53	−6	−69
−10	−20	−28	−33	−35	−20	−46	−67	−79	−84
−15	−26	−36	−40	−43	−30	−58	−81	−93	−100
−20	−32	−42	−48	−51	−40	−71	−95	−109	−115

*wind speeds of more than about 64km/h (40mph) have only a marginally greater cooling effect

MERCALLI INTENSITY SCALE

The Mercalli intensity scale measures the intensity of earthquakes by evaluating the damage done at a particular place. It is a subjective guide to the degree of shaking caused by an earthquake.

I	not felt
II	felt by persons at rest, indoors or favourably placed
III	felt indoors; hanging objects swing; vibration like the passing of light trucks; may not be recognized as an earthquake
IV	hanging objects swing; windows, dishes, doors rattle; vibration like the passing of heavy trucks; wooden walls and frames may creak
V	felt outdoors; sleepers wakened; liquids disturbed; small, unstable objects displaced or upset; doors, shutters, pictures move
VI	felt by all; people walk unsteadily; windows, dishes, glassware break; objects fall from shelves and pictures from walls; furniture moves; plaster and weak masonry crack; trees and bushes shake visibly and are heard to rustle
VII	difficult to stand; noticed by drivers; furniture breaks; weak chimneys crack at roof-line; plaster, loose bricks, tiles, stones fall; some cracks in ordinary, unre inforced masonry; waves visible on ponds; sand and gravel banks slide
VIII	steering of cars affected; damage to ordinary masonry and to partially reinforced masonry but not to masonry designed to resist lateral forces; fall of chimneys, towers, monuments, elevated water tanks; branches broken from trees; springs and wells affected; cracks appear in wet ground and on steep slopes
IX	general panic; general damage to foundations and frames of buildings; weak masonry destroyed and ordinary masonry seriously damaged or destroyed; reinforced masonry damaged; underground pipes break; cracks in ground; serious damage to reservoirs
X	most masonry and frame structures destroyed; serious damage to dams and dykes; large landslides; rails bent slightly; some bridges destroyed
XI	rails bent severely; underground pipelines destroyed
XII	total destruction of land-based objects; large rock masses displaced

RICHTER SCALE

The Richter scale, devised in 1935, uses seismic readings to measure the magnitude of earthquakes. It is logarithmic: each unit represents a 10-fold increase in the amplitude of the waves. The higher the number, the stronger the earthquake; the most destructive earthquake recorded so far in terms of human casualties had a value of 8.2, and the largest earthquakes are around 8.9.

magnitude	number per year	example (5 and above)
8 and above	2	San Francisco, USA, 1906
7.0–7.9	20	Kobe, Japan, 1995
6.0–6.9	100	Los Angeles, USA, 1989
5.0–5.9	3000	Cook Strait, New Zealand, 1995
4.0–4.9	15,000	
3.0–3.9	+100,000	
less than 3	millions	

VOLCANIC EXPLOSIVITY INDEX

The Volcanic Explosivity Index (VEI) is a way to compare the sizes of explosive eruptions. It is analogous to the Richter scale used for earthquakes. There are about 60 eruptions (of all kinds) per year, but the largest eruptions are much rarer.

VEI	number per thousand years	volume of fragmental material erupted	typical eruption column height
8	0.01–0.001	>1000 cubic km	>25km
7	1	100–1000 cubic km	>25km
6	10	10–100 cubic km	> 25km
5	100	1–10 cubic km	>25km
4	<1000	0.1–1 cubic km	10–25km
3	>1000	0.01–0.1 cubic km	3–15km
2	>1000	0.001–0.01 cubic km	1–5km
1	>1000	10,000–1 million cubic m	0.1–1km
0	>1000	<10,000 cubic m	<0.1km

MOST DEADLY EARTHQUAKES

An earthquake is manifested at the surface by shaking of the ground. It happens when subterranean masses suddenly slide past one another, on either side of a fault. Earthquakes occur only in the rigid outer part of the Earth, which includes the crust and the uppermost part of the underlying mantle.

The deepest-known earthquake had a source at a depth of 720km (450mi). Most occur at depths of less than 200km (120mi). The strength of an earthquake at its source is measured on the Richter scale. This scale does not equate to the violence of the ground shaking, because the deeper the source the less the effect at the surface. The amount of shaking also depends on the mechanical properties of the soil and shallow rock layers. The violence of an earthquake as experienced at any point on the surface is therefore measured on the Mercalli intensity scale. This generally reveals a concentric pattern of decreasing violence away from a point, known as the epicentre, directly above the source.

This table lists the all the earthquakes known to have killed 50,000 or more people.

year	location	magnitude*	deaths
1556	Shanxi, China–		830,000
1976	Tangshan, China	8.0	†255,000
1138	Aleppo, Syria –		230,000
1927	Nan Xian, China	8.3	200,000
856	Damghan, Iran	–	200,000
1920	Gansu, China	8.6	200,000
893	Ardabil, Iran –		150,000
1923	Yokohama, Japan	8.3	143,000
1948	Ashgabat, Turkmenistan	7.3	110,000
1908	Messina, Italy	7.5	83,000
1290	Chihli, China –		100,000
1667	Shemakha, Azerbaijan	–	80,000
1727	Tabriz, Iran –		77,000
1755	Lisbon, Portugal	8.7	70,000
1932	Gansu, China	7.6	70,000
1970	Casma, Peru	7.8	66,000
1268	Cilicia, Turkey	–	60,000
1693	Sicily, Italy –		60,000
1935	Quetta, Pakistan	7.5	60,000
1783	Calabria, Italy–		50,000
1990	w Iran	7.7	50,000

* on the Richter scale; this value is unknown for most earthquakes before 1900
† the official value; some estimates are as high as 655,000

MAJOR VOLCANIC ERUPTIONS

Most, but not all, volcanoes are near boundaries between tectonic plates. Volcanic eruptions occur when molten rock (magma), usually generated below the Earth's crust, rises to the surface. If magma oozes out quietly it produces lava flows. Lava flows can destroy any property in their path, but they are not very dangerous because they move slowly. However, magma that has a high content of dissolved gases is more likely to result in an explosive eruption. Explosive eruptions can generate pyroclastic flows (consisting of fragmented material) that sweep across the terrain at speeds in excess of 100 km per hour, and eruption columns that rise tens of kilometres into the atmosphere. These are much more dangerous, and the usual way of recording the strength of an eruption is by its Volcanic Explosivity Index (VEI).

The numbers of deaths caused by some of the greatest eruptions of the past two thousand years are listed in this table. Only one of these had a VEI as high as 7. Note that it is not necessarily the largest eruptions that take the most lives.

year	volcano	VEI*	deaths	main cause(s) of death
79 AD	Vesuvius, Italy	5	>3500	pyroclastic flows
1598	Asama, Japan	3	800	religious pilgrims killed by explosion at summit
1631	Vesuvius, Italy	4	>4000	mostly pyroclastic flows
1672	Merapi, Indonesia	3	?3000	pyroclastic flows
1783	Laki, Iceland	4	c.10,000	famine
1783	Asama, Japan	4	1500	mudflows, pyroclastic flows
1792	Unzen, Japan	0	14,300	debris avalanche, tsunami
1815	Tambora, Indonesia	7	60,000	famine, disease, pyroclastic flows, airfall
1822	Galungung, Indonesia	5	3600	mudflows
1877	Cotopaxi, Ecuador	4	1000	mudflows
1883	Krakatoa, Indonesia	6	36,000	tsunami, pyroclastic flows
1902	Mount Pelée, Martinique	4	29,000	pyroclastic flows
1902	Soufrière, St Vincent	4	1680	pyroclastic flows
1911	Taal, Philippines	4	>1335	pyroclastic flows
1919	Kelut, Indonesia	4	5100	mudflows
1929	Santa Maria, Guatemala	3	5000	pyroclastic flows
1930	Merapi, Indonesia	3	1369	pyroclastic flows
1951	Lamington, Papua New Guinea	4	2900	pyroclastic flows
1953	Ruapehu, New Zealand	2	151	mudflows
1977	Niyaragongo, Democratic Republic of Congo	1	60–300	lava flows
1979	Iliwerung, Indonesia	0	?539	tsunami
1980	St Helens, Washington, USA	5	57	directed blast
1982	El Chichón, Mexico	5	1900	pyroclastic flows
1985	Ruiz, Colombia	3	23,000	lahar
1986	Lake Nyos, Cameroon	0	>1700	asphyxiation by gases
1991	Pinatubo, Philippines	6	1200	disease, roof collapses, mud flows
1997	Soufrière Hills, Montserrat	3	19	pyroclastic flow
1998	Casita, Nicaragua	0	1600	mudflows

* Volcanic Explosivity Index

MAJOR EARTHQUAKES SINCE 1900

The table lists some of the most notable earthquakes since 1900, showing how many people died as a result of each. The damage to buildings depends on their response to the shaking. In the 1985 Mexico City earthquake, 70% of buildings between ten and twenty stories high in the most severely effected part of the city were badly damaged, but most buildings less than five or more than twenty stories high escaped relatively unscathed.

Death and damage attributed to earthquakes are sometimes caused by their after effects rather than by the immediate effect of collapsing buildings. For example, many of the deaths resulting from the 1908 Messina earthquake were caused by tsunamis. In the 1906 San Francisco and 1923 Yokohama earthquakes, most of the damage was caused by fires that broke out after the quake. In earthquakes in Iran in 1990 and in El Salvador in 2001 most of the damage was caused by landslides.

year	location	magnitude*	deaths
1902	Turkistan	6.4	4500
1905	Kangra, India	8.6	19,000
1905	Calabria, Italy	7.9	2500
1906	San Francisco, USA	8.3	503
1906	Valparaíso, Chile	8.6	20,000
1908	Messina, Italy	7.5	83,000
1920	Gansu, China	8.6	200,000
1923	Yokohama, Japan	8.3	143,000
1927	Nan Xian, China	8.3	200,000
1929	Iran	7.4	3300
1931	Nicaragua	5.6	2400
1932	Gansu, China	7.6	70,000
1933	Sanriku, Japan	8.9	2990
1934	Bihar, India	8.4	10,700
1935	Quetta, Pakistan	7.5	60,000
1939	Chillán, Chile	8.3	28,000
1939	Erzincan, Turkey	8.0	30,000
1944	San Juan, Argentina	7.8	5000
1948	Ashgabat, Turkmenistan	7.3	110,000
1950	Assam, India	8.7	1530
1954	Ech-Cheliff, Algeria	6.8	1250
1960	Agadir, Morocco	5.9	15,000
1960	Valdivia, Chile	9.5†	5000
1962	Qazvin, Iran	7.3	12,230
1963	Skopje, Macedonia	6.0	1100
1964	Anchorage, Alaska	8.4	131
1970	Casma, Peru	7.8	66,000
1976	Guatemala	7.5	23,000
1976	Tangshan, China	8.0	255,000
1978	Tabas, Iran	7.8	15,000
1980	Ech-Cheliff, Algeria	7.7	3500
1985	Mexico City, Mexico	8.1	9500
1988	Spitak, Armenia	6.8	25,000
1989	San Francisco, USA	6.7	61
1990	w Iran	7.7	50,000
1993	Maharastra, India	6.3	9748
1995	Kobe, Japan	6.9	5502
1999	Bilecik, Turkey	7.4	17,118
1999	Taiwan	7.6	2297
2001	El Salvador	7.6	1246
2001	Bhuj, Gujarat, India‡	7.7	20,000

* on the Richter scale
† highest ever recorded
‡ shallow earthquake; 167,000 injured; 600,000 homeless

CALDERA-FORMING ERUPTIONS

Eruptions of Volcanic Explosivity Index (VEI) 7 and above are capable of seriously disrupting the global climate, by injecting ash particles and sulphuric acid aerosols into the stratosphere. It is thought that the Toba eruption of 75,000 years ago reduced the human population of the globe to a few thousand individuals, from whom we are all descended.

date*	volcano	VEI†	caldera‡ diameter (km)	volume of magma erupted (cubic km)
1883 AD	Krakatoa, Indonesia	6	8	10
1815 AD	Tambora, Indonesia	7	6	40
180 AD	Taupo, New Zealand	7	35	35
1620 BC	Thíra (Santoríni), Aegean Sea	6	7 × 10	25
7.7 ka	Crater Lake, Oregon	7	8 × 10	55
35 ka	Campi Flegrei, Italy	7	13	80
75 ka	Toba, Indonesia	8	30 × 80	1500
160 ka	Kos, Greece	7	20 × 15	150
600 ka	Yellowstone, Wyoming, USA	8	60	1000–2000
760 ka	Long Valley, California, USA	8	15 × 30	600
1.1 Ma	Valles, New Mexico, USA	8	20 × 22	300
2.2 Ma	Cerro Galan, Argentina	8	25 × 35	2000
4.6 Ma	La Pacana, Chile	8	65 × 35	>2000

* ka = thousand years ago, Ma = million years ago
† Volcanic Explosivity Index
‡ a caldera is a large crater-like depression created by the eruption of a large volume of magma

ROCK TYPES

	igneous	sedimentary	metamorphic
origin	crystallized from magma	compaction of rock and mineral particles, or precipitation from solution	recrystallization of other rock types when subjected to heat or pressure
texture	interlocking crystals, usually in random orientations	usually fragmental and often arranged in layers	interlocking crystals, often aligned or layered
ease of breaking	usually hard	crumbly, but sometimes difficult to break	hard, sometimes splits into layers
notes	usually, larger crystals denote slower cooling; lava may contain bubbles; explosive volcanic eruptions make fragmental rocks that can be mistaken for sediments	deposited by wind or water; finer grains denote gentler conditions; may contain fossils	larger crystals denote high temperatures of metamorphism; good layering denotes high pressures of metamorphism
examples	granite, basalt, gabbro, andesite, pumice, obsidian	sandstone, shale, conglomerate, clay, limestone, chalk, coal	slate, schist, gneiss, marble, quartzite hornfels

ECOSYSTEMS

The Earth supports an astonishing variety of lifeforms. There is a wide variety of ecosystems, in which organic life forms and inorganic habitat exist in a delicate balance.

habitat	typical inhabitant	typical plant life
fresh water	beaver, trout, carp, duck	bulrush, pondweed, algae
salt water	whale, squid, tuna, krill	seaweed, sea lettuce
temperate grassland	hedgehog, bison	grass
tropical grassland	lion, coyote	grass
temperate forest	wolf, fox, owl, wood mouse	conifers, deciduous trees, wildflowers
tropical forest	fruit bat, spider monkey, opossum, hummingbird	trees, epiphytes, fungi
desert	camel, kangaroo rat, lizard	cacti
arctic	polar bear, arctic hare, puffin	moss, lichen, arctic poppy
tundra	caribou, wolf, sea eagle arctic fox	saxifrage, mountain aven

ECOSYSTEM CONVERSION

Converted land represents cropland, permanent pasture and man-made forest. Data for selected countries.

	land area (million hectares)	area converted (%)
Asia-Pacific		
Australia	764.4	60
Bangladesh	13.0	81
Cambodia	17.7	25
India	297.3	65
Indonesia	181.2	27
Malaysia	39.9	15
Philippines	29.8	36
Thailand	51.1	43
Vietnam	32.5	26
Africa		
Ivory Coast	31.8	53
Madagascar	58.2	47
Mozambique	78.4	60
Nigeria	91.1	80
South Africa	122.1	78
Sudan	237.1	52
Tanzania	88.4	44
Democratic Republic of Congo	226.7	10
Zambia	74.3	48
North America		
Mexico	190.9	52
United States*	957.3	45
South America		
Argentina	273.7	62
Bolivia	108.4	27
Brazil	845.7	28
Colombia	103.9	44
Ecuador	27.7	19
Paraguay	39.7	60
Venezuela	88.2	25

* excludes man-made forest

ZONE FOSSILS

Fossils may be used to provide an indication of the age of the rocks in which they occur, and to provide correlations between rocks of the same age over a wide geographic area. Certain fossils, known as zone fossils or index fossils, are key indicators for their period.

period	fossil type
Cambrian	trilobites, brachiopods
Ordovician	graptolites, trilobites
Silurian	graptolites
Devonian	goniatites, freshwater fish, plants
Carboniferous	corals, brachiopods, foraminifera (microscopic plankton), goniatites, freshwater bivalves and plant spores
Permian	foraminifera, goniatites, plant spores
Triassic	ammonites, plant spores
Jurassic	ammonites, ostracods
Cretaceous	ammonites, foraminifera, ostracods, echinoderms, bivalves, belemnites, brachiopods, gastropods, plant spores
Cenozoic	foraminifera, bivalves, gastropods

FOSSIL FUEL RESERVES

Fossil fuels are coal, oil and natural gas, the energy content of which is essentially stored sunlight from millions of years ago. Fossil fuels are being used much faster than they are being replaced by natural processes. Thus, fossil fuels are non-renewable energy sources, as distinct from renewable energy sources like wind-, wave- and solar-power. The table gives some estimates of how long the world supply of fossil fuels is likely to last. The term "resources" means the total amount of a commodity available in the world, whereas "reserves" refers to the smaller quantity of these resources that can be extracted profitably and legally under present conditions. Traditionally, when reserves become scarce the price goes up, which makes it viable to extract resources in ways that were previously uneconomical or environmentally unacceptable.

fuel	proven reserves (1990) (GTOE)*	ratio: reserves to current annual use (years)	ultimately recoverable resources[†] (GTOE*)
coal	496	197	
lignite	110	293	3400
conventional oil	137	40	200
unconventional oils (heavy crude, natural bitumen, oil shale)	–	–	600
natural gas	108	56	220

* Gtoe = thousand million tonnes of oil equivalent
† estimates of reserves that are potentially recoverable at high but not prohibitive costs under current conditions

GLOBAL WARMING

Calculating the average temperature of the globe is very complex, but it has been made easier by the use of satellites. Most scientists now agree that the average temperature of the globe has increased by about 0.6°C (1.1°F) since the late 19th century, and that the rate of global warming increased during the final quarter of the 20th century. Increasing temperatures mean more violent storms. Increasing temperatures also lead to sea-level rise because water expands as it warms up. Global sea-level has been rising by 1–2mm/yr during the past 100 years. Changes in global temperature and sea-level occur naturally over geological time, but the current rates of change are much faster, and are almost certainly caused by human-induced release of gases into the atmosphere. This table shows the difference in average annual global temperatures relative to the recent time-averaged values.

year	land surface	sea surface	whole globe
1880	−0.27°C (0.49°F)	−0.15°C (0.27°F)	−0.18°C (0.32°F)
1890	−0.19°C (0.34°F)	−0.23°C (0.41°F)	−0.22°C (0.40°F)
1900	−0.03°C (0.05°F)	−0.02°C (0.04°F)	−0.03°C (0.05°F)
1910	−0.22°C (0.40°F)	−0.33°C (0.59°F)	−0.29°C (0.52°F)
1920	−0.16°C (0.29°F)	−0.09°C (0.16°F)	−0.11°C (0.20°F)
1930	+0.08°C (0.14°F)	−0.02°C (0.04°F)	+0.01°C (0.02°F)
1940	+0.11°C (0.20°F)	0.00°C (0.00°F)	+0.04°C (0.07°F)
1950	−0.17°C (0.31°F)	0.00°C (0.00°F)	−0.05°C (0.09°F)
1960	+0.04°C (0.07°F)	+0.13°C (0.23°F)	+0.10°C (0.18°F)
1970	+0.05°C (0.09°F)	+0.08°C (0.14°F)	+0.07°C (0.13°F)
1980	+0.25°C (0.45°F)	+0.16°C (0.29°F)	+0.19°C (0.34°F)
1990	+0.69°C (1.24°F)	+0.30°C (0.54°F)	+0.41°C (0.74°F)
1991	+0.55°C (0.99°F)	+0.28°C (0.50°F)	+0.36°C (0.65°F)
1992	+0.30°C (0.54°F)	+0.18°C (0.32°F)	+0.21°C (0.38°F)
1993	+0.34°C (0.61°F)	+0.17°C (0.31°F)	+0.22°C (0.40°F)
1994	+0.58°C (1.04°F)	+0.22°C (0.40°F)	+0.33°C (0.59°F)
1995	+0.69°C (1.24°F)	+0.30°C (0.54°F)	+0.42°C (0.76°F)
1996	+0.38°C (0.68°F)	+0.26°C (0.47°F)	+0.30°C (0.54°F)
1997	+0.64°C (1.15°F)	+0.44°C (0.79°F)	+0.50°C (0.90°F)
1998	+1.00°C (1.80°F)	+0.50°C (0.90°F)	+0.65°C (1.17°F)
1999	+0.73°C (1.31°F)	+0.25°C (0.45°F)	+0.40°C (0.72°F)
2000	+0.59°C (1.06°F)	+0.30°C (0.54°F)	+0.39°C (0.70°F)

GASES IMPLICATED IN CLIMATE CHANGE

The gases in this table are all implicated in climate change, either through contributing to the greenhouse effect, which leads to global warming, or through attacking the ozone layer. Recent increases in their concentrations in the atmosphere are caused by human activities. CO_2 = carbon dioxide, CH_4 = methane, N_2O = nitrous oxide, CFCs = chlorofluorocarbons, CF_4 = perfluorocarbon, SF_6 = carbon hexafluoride. Concentrations are shown as parts per million (ppm), parts per billion (ppb) or parts per trillion (ppt) measured by volume in the atmosphere. The rates of increase for CO_2, CH_4 and N_2O are the average over ten years up to 1994. For the other gases the rates are for the 1990s.

	CO_2	CH_4	N_2O	CFCs	CF_4	SF_6
pre-industrial level	280 ppm	700 ppb	275ppb	zero	zero	zero
1994 concentration	358 ppm	1720 ppb	312 ppb	268 ppt	72 ppt	4 ppt
annual rate of increase	0.4%	0.6%	0.25%	5%	2%	5%

GREENHOUSE GAS EMISSIONS

Carbon dioxide and methane are the two gases released as a result of human activities that contribute most to global warming. They add to the greenhouse effect. Note that carbon dioxide emissions in the industrialized world are dominantly from industrial processes, but in the developing world a far greater proportion comes from land-use change, especially the burning of forests. The values in the table are for 1991.

	CO_2 emissions from industrial processes	from land use change	methane from man-made sources					
			solid waste	coal mining	oil and gas production	wet rice agriculture	livestock	total
				'000 metric tonnes				
world	22,339,408	4,100,000	43,000	36,000	44,000	69,000	81,000	270,000
Africa	715,773	730,000	1700	1700	6000	2400	9000	21,000
Europe	6,866,494	11,000	17,000	6600	15,000	420	14,000	53,000
North and Central America	5,715,466	190,000	11,000	6100	8200	590	9200	35,000
South America	605,029	1,800,000	2200	280	2200	870	15,000	21,000
Asia	7,118,317	1,300,000	9900	20,000	12,000	65,000	30,000	140,000
Oceania	297,246	38,000	690	1400	310	75	3300	5800

HUMAN-GENERATED CO_2 EMISSIONS

The table shows the carbon dioxide emissions from selected industrialized countries estimated for the year 2000, together with the percentage change in the annual rate since 1990. Positive values represent an increase, negative values a decrease. The numbers reveal some remarkable contrasts in the willingness of the worst-polluting nations to change their practices in order to respond responsibly to the threat posed by global warming. The emissions shown here exclude any caused by land-use change and forestry.

country	2000 emission (million tonnes)	% change since 1990
Australia	311	+19
Belgium	125	+8
Bulgaria	75	−11
Canada	501	+8
Czech Republic	139	−17
Denmark	54	−9
Estonia	20	−47
Finland	59	+10
France	373	−2
Germany	894	−12
Greece	89	+12
Hungary	64	−23
Ireland	35	+14
Italy	421	+5
Japan	1200	+8
New Zealand	31	+22
Norway	44	+22
Poland	425	−12
Portugal	50	+35
Russian Federation	1750	−26
Slovak Republic	45	−24
Spain	258	+14
Sweden	60	+3
Switzerland	44	−7
Ukraine	530	−25
United Kingdom	550	−5
United States	5627	+13

PER CAPITA CO_2 EMISSIONS

The industrialized countries are responsible for far greater emissions of carbon dioxide per head of population than non-industrialized nations. This table shows per capita CO_2 emissions for ten indicative countries during 1995.

country	tonnes
Brazil	1.6
China	2.7
Czech Republic	10.9
Japan	9.0
Russian Federation	12.2
Swaziland	0.5
India	1.0
Malaysia	5.3
United Kingdom	9.3
United States	20.5

HOLES IN THE OZONE LAYER

A small amount of ozone concentrated in the stratosphere plays a vital role in protecting the surface of the Earth from the harmful effects of ultraviolet radiation. This layer has been attacked by chlorine-bearing molecules, notably CFCs (which used to be used as coolants in refrigerators and air-conditioning systems). Release of many chlorine-bearing molecules into the atmosphere is now banned by international treaty.

The greatest depletion of ozone has taken place over the poles, where the effect has been described as an "ozone hole". These holes are a partly natural, seasonally variable phenomenon, and are affected by volcanic eruptions as well as by industrial pollution. Provided treaties are adhered to, the ozone layer is now expected to regenerate to something like its pre-industrial state.

The largest ozone hole on record occupied 25 million square km (10 million square miles) over Antarctica in September 1998. Within this hole the amount of ozone has on average less than 70% of its pre-1980 concentration. The 1999 Antarctic ozone hole is the second largest on record.

The table shows the extra ultraviolet radiation (UV-B) reaching ground level in 2000 relative to the 1970s, at different latitudes, and is a measure of how much protection we have lost because of the thinning of the ozone layer.

latitude	UV-B in 2000 relative to 1970s
Arctic	+22%
25–65° N	+7% (winter and spring)
25–65° N	+4% (summer and autumn)
25–65° S	+6%
Antarctic	+130%

NUMBERS OF THREATENED SPECIES OF ANIMALS AND PLANTS

The table below shows the threatened status categories for major taxonomic groups of animals in 2000.

class	EX	EW	subtotal	CR	EN	VU	subtotal	LR/cd	LR/nt	DD	total
vertebrates											
Mammalia	83	4	**87**	180	340	610	**1130**	74	602	240	**2133**
Aves	128	3	**131**	182	321	680	**1183**	3	727	79	**2123**
Reptilia	21	1	**22**	56	79	161	**296**	3	74	59	**454**
Amphibia	5	0	**5**	25	38	83	**146**	2	25	53	**231**
Cephalaspidomorphi	1	0	**1**	0	1	2	**3**	0	5	3	**12**
Elasmobranchii	0	0	**0**	3	17	19	**39**	4	35	17	**95**
Actinopterygii	80	11	**91**	152	126	431	**709**	12	96	251	**1159**
Sarcopterygii	0	0	**0**	1	0	0	**1**	0	0	0	**1**
subtotal	**318**	**19**	**337**	**599**	**922**	**1986**	**3507**	**98**	**1564**	**702**	**6208**
invertebrates											
Echinoidea	0	0	**0**	0	0	0	**0**	0	1	0	**1**
Arachnida	0	0	**0**	0	1	9	**10**	0	1	7	**18**
Chilopoda	0	0	**0**	0	0	1	**1**	0	0	0	**1**
Crustacea	8	1	**9**	56	72	280	**408**	9	1	32	**459**
Insecta	72	1	**73**	45	118	392	**555**	3	76	40	**747**
Merostomata	0	0	**0**	0	0	0	**0**	0	1	3	**4**
Onychophora	3	0	**3**	1	3	2	**6**	0	1	1	**11**
Hirudinoidea	0	0	**0**	0	0	0	**0**	0	1	0	**1**
Oligochaeta	0	0	**0**	1	0	4	**5**	0	1	0	**6**
Polychaeta	0	0	**0**	1	0	0	**1**	0	0	1	**2**
Bivalvia	31	0	**31**	52	28	12	**92**	5	60	7	**195**
Gastropoda	260	12	**272**	170	209	467	**846**	14	177	513	**1822**
Enopla	0	0	**0**	0	0	2	**2**	0	1	3	**6**
Turbellaria	1	0	**1**	0	0	0	**0**	0	0	0	**1**
Anthozoa	0	0	**0**	0	0	2	**2**	0	0	1	**3**
subtotal	**375**	**14**	**389**	**326**	**431**	**1171**	**1928**	**31**	**321**	**608**	**3277**
total	**693**	**33**	**726**	**925**	**1353**	**3157**	**5435**	**129**	**1885**	**1310**	**9485**

Source: 2000 IUCN Red List of Threatened Animals (www.redlist.org)

The table below shows the threatened status categories for major taxonomic groups of plants in 2000.

class	EX	EW	subtotal	CR	EN	VU	subtotal	LR/cd	LR/nt	DD	total
mosses											
Bryopsida	2	0	**2**	10	15	11	**36**	0	0	0	**38**
Anthocerotopsida	0	0	**0**	0	1	1	**2**	0	0	0	**2**
Marchantiopsida	1	0	**1**	12	16	14	**42**	0	0	0	**43**
subtotal	**3**	**0**	**3**	**22**	**32**	**26**	**80**	**0**	**0**	**0**	**83**
gymnosperms											
Coniferopsida	0	1	**1**	17	40	83	**140**	24	52	33	**250**
Ginkgoopsida	0	0	**0**	0	1	0	**1**	0	0	0	**1**
subtotal	**0**	**1**	**1**	**17**	**41**	**83**	**141**	**24**	**52**	**33**	**251**
dicotyledons											
Magnoliopsida	69	14	**83**	896	1110	3093	**5099**	203	610	298	**6293**
monocotyledons											
Liliopsida	1	2	**3**	79	83	129	**291**	17	45	39	**395**
total	**73**	**17**	**90**	**1014**	**1266**	**3331**	**5611**	**244**	**707**	**370**	**7022**

Source: 2000 IUCN Red List of Threatened Species (www.unep-wcmc.org)

categories:
EX – extinct: a taxon is extinct when there is no reasonable doubt that the last individual has died.
EW – extinct in the wild: a taxon is extinct in the wild when it is known only to survive in cultivation, in captivity or as a naturalized population (or populations) well outside the past range. A taxon is presumed extinct in the wild when exhaustive surveys in known and/or expected habitat, at appropriate times (diurnal, seasonal, annual), throughout its historic range have failed to record an individual. Surveys should be over a time frame appropriate to the taxon's life cycle and life form.
CR – critically endangered: a taxon is critically endangered when it is facing an extremely high risk of extinction in the wild in the immediate future.
EN – endangered: a taxon is endangered when it is not critically endangered but is facing a very high risk of extinction in the wild in the near future.
VU – vulnerable: a taxon is vulnerable when it is not critically endangered or endangered but is facing a high risk of extinction in the wild in the medium-term future.
LR – lower risk: a taxon is lower risk when it has been evaluated, does not satisfy the criteria for any of the categories critically endangered, endangered or vulnerable. Taxa included in the lower risk category can be separated into three subcategories:
1. conservation dependent (**cd**): taxa that are the focus of a continuing taxon-specific or habitat-specific conservation programme targeted towards the taxon in question, the cessation of which would result in the taxon qualifying for one of the threatened categories above within a period of five years.
2. near threatened (**nt**): taxa that do not qualify for conservation dependent, but that are close to qualifying for vulnerable.
3. least concern (**lc**): taxa that do not qualify for conservation dependent or near threatened.
DD – data deficient: a taxon is data deficient when there is inadequate information to make a direct, or indirect, assessment of its risk of extinction based on its distribution and/or population status. A taxon in this category may be well studied, and its biology well known, but appropriate data on abundance and/or distribution are lacking. Data deficient is therefore not a category of threat or lower risk. Listing of taxa in this category indicates that more information is required and acknowledges the possibility that future research will show that threatened classification is appropriate. It is important to make positive use of whatever data are available. In many cases great care should be exercised in choosing between DD and threatened status. If the range of a taxon is suspected to be relatively circumscribed, if a considerable period of time has elapsed since the last record of the taxon, threatened status may well be justified.

WORLD'S RAREST TREES

The table lists some of the world's most threatened trees.

species name	family	distribution	further information
Abies nebrodensi	Pinaceae	Sicily, Italy	Endemic to Sicily, this species is known from a small population containing fewer than 20 individuals. Only a fraction of them appear to be reproductively capable. A propagation programme is under way.
Aloe helenae	Aloaceae	Madagascar	This arborescent aloe is endemic to s Madagascar, where two or three populations are known to occur in thorny bush on sandy shores in the Fort Dauphin region. Each population consists of fewer than 10 adult individuals. No regeneration has been observed. The species is listed in Appendix I of *CITES.
Aloe suzannae	Aloaceae	Madagascar	This arborescent aloe is confined to thorny bush on sandy shores in the Amboasary region and Itampolo in s and sw Madagascar. Only a few adult individuals are known in each population and there is no evidence of regeneration. The species has been cultivated from wild seed, but fewer than six reared plants exist in nurseries in Madagascar. The species is listed in *CITES Appendix I.
Attalea crassispatha	Palmae	Haiti	This palm tree, found in lowland forest in river valleys, is confined to the sw peninsula of Haiti. In 1996 fewer than 30 individuals were found, all in two adjacent river valleys. The species is threatened by encroaching agriculture and local exploitation of the edible seeds. It is in cultivation at the Fairchild Tropical Garden, but the mature palms do not flower.
Betula uber	Betulaceae	Virginia, USA	Described in 1918 and subsequently thought to have become extinct, this species was rediscovered along the banks of Cressy Creek in 1975. The population is found in highly disturbed second-growth forest along a one-km stretch of the river owned by private and federal government parties. The number of individuals has been reduced from 41 to 11. Protective measures are in place and a large-scale replanting programme has resulted in the establishment of 20 populations of sub-adult trees. The species is interfertile with *Betula lenta* and introduced populations contain hybrids. It is listed as threatened in the US Endangered Species Act.
Carpinus putoensi	Corylaceae	Zhejiang, China	A single fenced tree is left in the wild on Mount Froding on Putuo Island in the Zhoushan Archipelago. Originally occurring in evergreen broad-leaved forest, the remaining tree now exists at the edge of a sparse mixed forest. The species is monoecious.
Cyanea procera	Campanulaceae	Hawaii, USA	This palm-like tree, formerly found in the Kamalo region on Molokai, was thought to be extinct until it was recently rediscovered at Puu O Kaeha, west of Kamalo. A total of eight individuals have been found in three populations in an area known to harbour feral goats. The species is classified as endangered by the US Endangered Species Act.
Diospyros katendei	Ebenaceae	Uganda	At present this species is known from a single population of about 20 trees in upland evergreen rainforest in central Kasyoha-Kitomi. The area is designated as a forest reserve and timber is being extracted.
Holmskioldia gigas	Verbenaceae	Kenya and Tanzania	Formerly known from a single individual in Kenya, which was felled in the 1980s, this species is now known to occur in a 0.1ha patch of forest near Ngarama Forest Reserve in Tanzania. Only a single individual exists.
Picea martinezii	Pinaceae	Nuevo León, Mexico	This species has been treated as a synonym of *Picea chihuahuana*. It is a timber tree confined to just two sites of montane forest near streams in Nuevo León. Timber has been extracted in recent years in the larger of the two populations. The other population has fewer than 15 individuals. Fire is the main threat.
Sorbus wilmottiana	Rosaceae	Great Britain, UK	Known from both sides of the Avon Gorge in Somerset and Gloucestershire, this species is one of the rarest *Sorbus* species in the UK. As few as 20 trees may remain in woodland margins and on cliff edges with other rare *Sorbus* species. The area is managed so as to conserve the rare plants. There have, however, been reports of the illegal collection and cutting down of trees.
Voanioala gerardii	Palmae	Madagascar	This tree is a Madagascan endemic, inhabiting primary forest on gentle slopes at an altitude of about 400m (1300ft) on the Masoala Peninsula. Fewer than 10 trees are known to exist in the wild. Deforestation and palm heart exploitation are the main threats. Unless effective protection can be given to areas of forest on the Masoala Peninsula and the trees are safeguarded against exploitation, the species is unlikely to survive.

* CITES Appendix I includes species threatened with extinction; only in exceptional circumstances is trade in these species permitted

Source: extract from: Oldfield, S., Lusty, C., MacKinven, A. (1998). *The World List of Threatened Trees*. World Conservation Press, Cambridge, UK, 650pp.^

FOREST AREA CHANGE

The table shows how forest areas, by region and type, have changed in the period between 1990 and 1995.

forest type and region	total forest 1990 (1000 ha)	total forest 1995 (1000 ha)	total change 1990–95 (1000 ha)	annual change rate (%)
total tropical Africa	523,376	504,901	−18,475	−0.7
total non-tropical Africa	15,602	15,336	−266	−0.3
total tropical Asia	295,041	279,766	−15,275	−1.1
total temperate Asia	222,464	223,235	771	0
total tropical Oceania	42,659	41,903	−756	−0.4
total temperate Oceania	48,490	48,792	302	0.1
Northern Europe	52,498	52,538	40	n.s.
Western Europe	57,688	59,479	1791	0.6
Eastern Europe	820,546	821,309	763	0
total temperate North and Central America	453,270	457,086	3816	0.2
total tropical and subtropical North and Central America	84,628	79,443	−5185	−1.3
total tropical South America	851,223	827,946	−23,277	−0.6
total temperate South America	43,243	42,648	−595	−0.3
world total	**3,510,728**	**3,454,382**	**256,346**	**20.3**

Source: Based on FAO – State of the World's Forests (www.fao.org/forestry/fo/sofo/sofo99/pdf/sofo_e/coper_en.pdf)

DISTRIBUTION OF THE WORLD'S WATER

The table indicates how the world's water is distributed across the various resources; the area of the Earth's surface is provided for comparison.

	area (million km^2)	% of total area	volume (million km^3)	% of total water	% of fresh water
Earth surface	510				
land	149	29			
water					
world ocean	361	71	1338	96.5	
fresh water	–	–	35	2.5	
ice	16	–	24	1.75	69
ground water	–	–	10.5	1.7	30
wetlands*	2.6	–	0.1	0.0008	0.03
lakes†	1.5	–	0.09	0.007	0.26
rivers	–	–	0.02	0.0002	0.006

All estimates are approximations and vary according to the methods used to derive them; for consistency the data are taken from a single source

* marshes, swamps, mires, lagoons, floodplains
† excluding saline lakes

Source: Anon, USSR Committee for the International Hydrological Decade, 1978.

GLOBAL FOREST TYPES AND COVERAGE

The table shows the area covered by certain types of forest and how much of that area is protected.

forest type	total forest (km^2)	total protected (km^2)	% forests protected
temperate and boreal			
evergreen needleleaf forest	8,045,880.3	1,116,784.9	13.9
deciduous needleleaf forest	3,615,991.3	36,708.0	1.0
mixed broadleaf/needleleaf forest	2,020,162.5	195,387.0	9.7
broadleaf evergreen forest	345,776.8	82,795.7	23.9
deciduous broadleaf forest	3,873,399.1	355,865.2	9.2
freshwater swamp forest	125,556.8	9656.1	7.7
sclerophyllous dry forest	754,497.2	146,195.6	19.4
disturbed natural forest	60,080.5	3419.6	5.7
sparse trees/parkland	5,823,171.6	469,594.8	8.1
exotic species plantations	65,338.3	5745.2	8.8
native species plantations	0.0	0.0	–
unspecified forest plantation	8073.1	105.9	1.3
unclassified forest data	264,541.6	14,529.8	5.5
tropical			
lowland evergreen broadleaf rainforest	7,296,908.0	1,006,690.4	13.8
lower montane forest	622,225.0	71,791.8	11.5
upper montane forest	717,294.8	119,613.5	16.7
freshwater swamp forest	532,390.0	40,691.8	7.6
semi-evergreen moist broadleaf forest	1,109,626.8	92,717.8	8.4
mixed needleleaf/broadleaf forest	17,731.3	898.5	5.1
needleleaf forest	56,027.5	5317.8	9.5
mangrove	216,431.4	29,907.4	13.8
disturbed natural forest	838,901.5	29,853.5	3.6
deciduous/semi-deciduous broadleaf forest	3,178,576.0	397,837.3	12.5
sclerophyllous dry forest	435,098.3	49,171.6	11.3
thorn forest	257,116.5	15,335.7	6.0
sparse trees/parkland	5,082,842.3	404,558.9	8.0
exotic species plantations	18,260.3	845.7	4.6
native species plantations	398.3	22.5	5.7
total	**45,382,296.4**	**4,702,042.0**	**10.4**

Source: Based on UNEP-WCMC website 2001 (www.unep-wcmc.org/forest/world.htm)

NUMBERS OF DESCRIBED SPECIES

The table lists the estimated numbers of described species*, together with the possible global total.

kingdom	phyla	estimated described species†	estimated possible total‡
Bacteria		4000	1,000,000
Protoctista		80,000	600,000
Animalia	Craniata (vertebrates) total	52,000	55,000
	mammals	4630	
	birds	9946	
	reptiles	7400	
	amphibians	4950	
	fish	25,000	
	Mandibulata (insects and myriapods)	963,000	8,000,000
	Chelicerata (which includes arachnids)	75,000	750,000
	Mollusca	70,000	200,000
	Crustacea	40,000	150,000
	Nematoda	25,000	400,000
Fungi		72,000	150,000
Plantae		270,000	320,000
total		**1,750,000**	**14,000,000**

* described species are those species that have been discovered, described and given a taxonomic name
† estimates are incomplete but should not vary considerably
‡ estimated possible totals are based on the numbers of described species and provisional working estimates of undescribed species; they may vary considerably

Sources: World Conservation Monitoring Centre 2000. Groombridge, B., Jenkins, M.D. *Global Biodiversity: Earth's living resources in the 21st century*. World Conservation Press, Cambridge, UK.

PROTECTED AREAS

The table shows the amount of land that is protected in various regions of the world.

region*	total area of region	total no.PAs[†]	total area of PAs	% of total area protected
Antarctica	14,245,000	55	3028	0.02
Europe	25,156,389	19,062	4,233,426	16.8
Asia	24,993,681	7154	3,472,674	13.9
Middle East and North Africa	12,735,896	1490	2,088,684	16.4
sub-Saharan Africa	24,110,670	2538	4,149,436	17.2
North America	19,313,574	13,230	5,887,376	30.5
Central America and Caribbean	2,739010	2118	705,572	25.8
South America	18,013,270	2936	3,677,874	20.4
Oceania	8,503,714	12,062	2,243,452	26.4
total	**149,811,204**	**60,645**	**26,461,522**	**17.7**

* regions based on definitions by the World Resources Institute (WRI), 2000
† a Protected Area (PA) is an area of more than 1000 hectares of land and/or sea that is dedicated to the protection and maintenance of biological diversity, and of natural and associated cultural resources, and managed through legal or other effective means (IUCN, 1997)

Source: Based on the 1997 UN List of Protected Areas

MEGADIVERSE COUNTRIES

The table shows the seventeen most diverse countries of the world, according to levels of biodiversity.

rank	country
1	Brazil
2	Colombia
3	Indonesia
4	China
5	Mexico
6	South Africa
7	Venezuela
8	Ecuador
9	Peru
10	United States
11	Papua New Guinea
12	India
13	Australia
14	Malaysia
15	Madagascar
16	Democratic Republic of the Congo
17	Philippines

Source: Based on list by Conservation International (www.conservation.org/web/fieldact/megadiv/list.htm)

CORAL REEF AREAS

region	area of coral reef (10km)
Caribbean	20,000
Atlantic	1600
Red Sea and Gulf of Aden	17,400
Arabian Gulf and Arabian Sea	4200
Indian Ocean	32,000
Southeast Asia	94,700
Pacific	115,900
Eastern Pacific	1600
total	**287,400**

Source: Spalding M.D.,Ravilious C.and Green E.P. (in press), *World Atlas of Coral Reefs*. University of California Press, Berkeley, USA.

MILESTONES IN CONSERVATION HISTORY

year	event
1840	"The Great Slaughter"; time of mass slaughter of buffalo, USA (1)
1872–74	Height of slaughter on Great Plains, USA (1)
1872	President Ulysses S. Grant signs a bill that leads to the creation of Yellowstone National Park, the world's first national park. It is preceded by the introduction of a new bill in congress – the National Park Act in the House of Representatives, USA (1)
1884	President Kruger proposes a game reserve in South Africa. Two are created in 1898; 28 years later they become part of Kruger National Park, South Africa (1)
1890	Royal Society for the Protection of Birds (RSPB) formed as the Didsbury Group, UK (16)
1894	Significant decline in buffalo after the slaughter of 1840. Theodore Roosevelt and President Grover Cleveland sign the Lacey Act, which forbids the killing of buffalo under penalty of $1000 fine or imprisonment, USA.
1895	National Trust formed, UK (1)
1903	Fauna and Flora International (FFI) founded as Society for the Preservation of the Wild Fauna of the British Empire, UK (3)
1916	Congress create a National Park Service, USA (1)
1922	BirdLife International founded as the International Committee for Bird Protection, UK (4)
1945	United Nations Educational, Scientific and Cultural Organization (UNESCO) founded, Paris, France (17)
1948	The World Conservation Union (IUCN) founded as the International Union for the Protection of Nature (IUPN), Gland, Switzerland (5)
1961	World Wide Fund for Nature (WWF) founded as World Wildlife Fund, Gland, Switzerland (6)
1962	First publication of Rachel Carson's *Silent Spring*, USA (10)
1963	Production of the first Red List of Threatened Animals and Plants, Gland, Switzerland
1968	UNESCO Conference on the Conservation and Rational Use of the Biosphere leads to foundation of Man and Biosphere Programme (MAB), which runs overseas biosphere reserves, London, UK
1971	Convention on Wetlands (Ramsar) opens for signature; it enters into force in 1975, Ramsar, Iran (13, 19)
1972	Stockholm Conference on the Human Environment leads to the foundation of United Nations Environment Programme (UNEP), Stockholm, Sweden (7)
1972	Convention Concerning the Protection of the World Cultural and Natural Heritage (World Heritage Convention) opens for signature; it enters into force in 1975, Paris, France (15, 19)
1973	Convention on International Trade in Endangered Species of Fauna and Flora (CITES) opens for signature; it enters into force in 1975, Washington, USA (11, 19)
1979	The Convention on the Conservation of European Wildlife and Natural Habitats (Bern) opens for signature; it enters into force in 1982, Bern, Switzerland (18, 19)
1983	The "Brundtland Commission" World Commission on Environment and Development founded, Geneva, Switzerland (9)
1983	The Bonn Convention or Convention on Migratory Species (CMS) opens for signature; it enters into force in 1983, Bonn, Germany (12, 19)
1992	Rio Earth Summit leads to Agenda 21 and the UN Commission on Sustainable Development (CSD). The Convention on Biological Diversity (CBD) opens for signature; it enters into force in 1993. UN Framework Convention on Climate Change (UNFCCC) opens for signature; it enters into force in 1994. Rio de Janeiro, Brazil (8, 19)
1994	UN Convention on Combating Desertification (UNCCD) opens for signature, Paris, France (14, 19)
1995	Agreement on the Conservation of African-Eurasian Migratory Waterbirds (AWEA) opens for signature, The Hague, The Netherlands (20, 19)

references:
1) Willock, C., 1991. *Wildfight; a history of conservation.* Jonathan Cape, UK, 143pp.
2) Holdgate, M., 1996. *From care to action; making a sustainable world.* Earthscan Publications Ltd, UK, 346pp.
3) www.fauna-flora.org
4) www.wing-wbsj.or.jp/birdlife
5) www.iucn.org
6) www.panda.org
7) www.un.org
8) iisd.ca/rio+5/agenda/default.htm
9) www.earthsummit2002.org
10) www.rachelcarson.org
11) www.cites.org
12) www.unep-wcmc.org/cms
13) www.ramsar.org
14) www.unccd.org
15) www.unesco.org/whc/nwhc/pages/home/pages/homepage.htm
16) www.rspb.org.uk
17) www.unesco.org/general/eng/about/index.shtml
18) www.nature.coe.int/english/cadres/berne.htm
19) sedac.ciesin.org/entri/entri-toc.html
20) www.wcmc.org.uk/AEWA/agreement.htm

WORLD'S MOST INVASIVE PLANTS

The table shows some of the world's most invasive plants. The order in which the plants appear is not indicative of the severity of their invasive effect.

habitat	common name	scientific name	native country	invaded area and nature of problem
aquatic	caulerpa seaweed	*Caulerpa taxifolia*	Germany	Mediterranean [1]
	common cord-grass	*Spartina anglica*	North America	worldwide [1]
	wakame seaweed	*Undaria pinnatifida*	Japan	worldwide [1]
	water hyacinth	*Eichhornia crassipes*	Amazon basin	worldwide [1]
terrestrial	African tulip tree	*Spathodea campanulata*	Africa	worldwide [1]
	black wattle	*Acacia mearnsii*	Australia, Papua New Guinea, E Indonesia	worldwide [1]
	Brazilian pepper tree	*Schinus terebinthifolius*	Argentina	worldwide [1]
	cogon grass	*Imperata cylindrica*	Southeast Asia	worldwide [1]
	cluster pine	*Pinus pinaster*	Mediterranean basin	temperate regions [1]
	erect pricklypear	*Opuntia stricta*	SE North America	arid regions [3]
	fire tree	*Myrica faya*	Azores, Madeira, Canary Islands	Hawaii [1]
	giant reed	*Arundo donax*	India	temperate regions [1]
	gorse	*Ulex europaeus*	Central and W Europe	worldwide [1]
	hiptage	*Hiptage benghalensis*	India, Southeast Asia, Philippines	La Réunion, Mauritius [1]
	Japanese knotweed	*Polygonum cuspidatum*	Japan	worldwide [1]
	kahili ginger	*Hedychium gardnerianum*	E Himalayas	South Pacific islands [1]
	koster's curse	*Clidemia hirta*	Central America	tropical islands, Southeast Asia [1]
	kudzu	*Pueraria montana*	Asia	worldwide, especially E North America [1]
	lantana	*Lantana camara*	Central America	tropics to temperate [1]
	leafy spurge	*Euphorbia esula*	Europe, temperate Asia	worldwide except Australia [1]
	leucaena	*Leucaena leucocephala*	tropical America	Pacific Islands [1]
	melaleuca	*Melaleuca quinquenervia*	E Australia, New Guinea	open swamps worldwide [1]
	mesquite	*Prosopis glandulosa*	North America	Australia [1]
	miconia	*Miconia calvescens*	tropical America	Tahiti, Hawaii, Australia [1]
	mile-a-minute weed	*Mikania micrantha*	Central and South America	South Pacific islands, Indian Ocean islands [1]
	mimosa	*Mimosa pigra*	tropical America	tropical and subtropical wetlands [1]
	privet	*Ligustrum robustum*	Eurasia, Malaysia, Australia	La Réunion, Mauritius [1]
	pumpwood	*Cecropia peltata*	tropical America	Cameroon, Ivory Coast, Malaysia [1]
	purple loosestrife	*Lythrum salicaria*	Eurasia	North America [1]
	quinine tree	*Cinchona pubescens*	Costa Rica, Venezuela	Tahiti, Galápagos Islands, Hawaii [1]
	shoebutton ardisia	*Ardisia elliptica*	Asia	wet lowlands [1]
	Siam weed	*Chromolaena odorata*	tropical America	tropical Africa and Asia [1,3]
	strawberry guava	*Psidium cattleianum*	tropical America	Florida, Hawaii, Mauritius [1]
	tamarisk	*Tamarix ramosissima*	Asia, SE Europe	North America [3]
	wedelia	*Wedelia trilobata*	Central America	Micronesia, American Samoa, Australia [1]
	yellow Himalayan raspberry	*Rubus ellipticus*	S Asia	Hawaii [1]

1 *competition*
2 *predation*
3 *economic pest*

Source: Based on *100 of the World's Worst Invasive Alien Species*, IUCN SSC Invasive Species Specialist Group

WORLD'S MOST INVASIVE ANIMALS

The table shows some of the world's most invasive animals. The order in which the animals appear is not indicative of the severity of their invasive effect.

kingdom	common name	scientific name	native country	invaded area and nature of problem
amphibians	bullfrog	*Rana catesbeiana*	Central and E North America	W North America [1,2]
	cane toad	*Bufo marinus*	North and South America	Oceanic, Atlantic, Pacific and Indian Ocean islands, Australia [1,2]
	Caribbean tree frog	*Eleutherodactylus coqui*	Puerto Rico	Hawaii, Virgin Islands [2]
reptiles	brown tree snake	*Boiga irregularis*	N Australia, Papua New Guinea	Guam [1,2]
	red-eared slider	*Trachemys scripta*	North America	worldwide [1]
fish	brown trout	*Salmo trutta*	Europe, N Africa, W Asia	cold water worldwide [1,2]
	carp	*Cyprinus carpio*	Eurasia	temperate freshwater worldwide [1]
	large-mouth bass	*Micropterus salmoides*	North America	worldwide [2]
	Mozambique tilapia	*Oreochromis mossambicus*	tropical and subtropical Africa	worldwide [1]
	Nile perch	*Lates niloticus*	freshwater and river systems of tropical Africa	Lake Victoria, Africa [1,2]
	rainbow trout	*Oncorhynchus mykiss*	North America	cold water worldwide [1,2]
	walking catfish	*Clarias batrachus*	Southeast Asia	North America [1,2]
	western mosquito fish	*Gambusia affinis*	North America	worldwide [2]
birds	Indian mynah bird	*Acridotheres tristis*	India	worldwide [1,2]
	red-vented bulbul	*Pycnonotus cafer*	Asia	Pacific islands [1]
	starling	*Sturnus vulgaris*	Eurasia, N Africa	worldwide [3]
mammals	brushtail possum	*Trichosurus vulpecula*	Australia	New Zealand [1,2]
	domestic cat	*Felis catus*	all breeds possibly derived from an African cat	worldwide except Australasia and Oceanic islands [1]
	goat	*Capra hircus*	—	worldwide [1]
	grey squirrel	*Sciurus carolinensis*	North America	United Kingdom, Italy, South Africa [1]
	macaque monkey	*Macaca fascicularis*	Southeast Asia	Mauritius [1,2]
	mouse	*Mus musculus*	—	worldwide [3]
	nutria	*Myocastor coypus*	South America	North America, Europe, Asia [1,3]
	pig	*Sus scrofa*	—	worldwide [3]
	rabbit	*Oryctolagus cuniculus*	—	worldwide except Antarctica and Asia [3]
	red deer	*Cervus elaphus*	—	worldwide [1]
	red fox	*Vulpes vulpes*	—	worldwide [2]
	ship rat	*Rattus rattus*	India	worldwide [3]
	small Indian mongoose	*Herpestes javanicus*	Asia	Mauritius, Fiji, West Indies, Hawaii [2]
	stoat	*Mustela erminea*	—	worldwide [1,2]

1 *competition*
2 *predation*
3 *economic pest*

Source: Based on *100 of the World's Worst Invasive Alien Species*, IUCN SSC Invasive Species Specialist Group

TWO-KINGDOM CLASSIFICATION SYSTEM

Taxonomy is the study of the principles of organizing groups (or taxa) into hierarchies.

So far more than 1.5 million different species have been identified and this is estimated to be only a tiny fraction of the total number; there are perhaps somewhere between 10 million and 50 million different species. For this reason a system of classification is essential.

The first real attempt to classify organisms into groups was made by Aristotle in the fourth century BC, and the system he devised was used into the 1600s. He recognized two groups – plants and animals. He subdivided the animals according to whether or not they had blood and how they moved. For example, all flying organisms were grouped together, meaning that a bat, a bird and a butterfly would be placed in the same group regardless of the differences between them.

In the 18th century the Swedish botanist Carolus Linnaeus also recognized plants and animals as being the two main groups, and he named these groups kingdoms. He subdivided the plant and animal kingdoms into smaller and smaller groups based on the similarities of form shown. A sequence of taxa was devised from kingdom through phylum, class, order, family, genus and species. The further down the hierarchy the fewer different organisms there are in each taxa and the greater the number of similarities between them.

The dendrogram below shows the relationships between the major taxa:

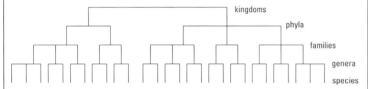

In this two-kingdom classification system the human and the meadow buttercup would be classified as shown below:

taxonomic rank	human	meadow buttercup
kingdom	Animalia	Plantae
phylum	Chordata	Angiospermophyta
class	Mammalia	Dicotyledonae
order	Primates	Ranales
family	Hominidae	Ranunculaceae
genus	*Homo*	*Ranunculus*
species	*Homo sapiens*	*Ranunculus acris*

The table below shows how the grizzly bear is classified in this system. Several other animals are listed in the table in order to show how the taxonomic levels become less and less inclusive. Towards the left of the table, the categories are the broadest; moving towards the right they become more specific, narrowing to the bear family and finally the unique species name of the grizzly bear.

	phylum Chordata	class Mammalia	order Carnivora	family Ursidae	genus *Ursus*	species *Ursus arctos*
trout	√					
cow	√	√				
tiger	√	√	√			
brown bear	√	√	√	√	√	
grizzly bear	√	√	√	√	√	√
polar bear	√	√	√	√		
hyena	√	√	√			
baboon	√	√				
finch	√					
python	√					

Linnaeus' system of taxonomy still forms the basis of the classification systems in use today, although technological advances have shown the two-kingdom system to be oversimplified. It is no longer widely accepted.

FIVE-KINGDOM CLASSIFICATION SYSTEM

The problems with the two-kingdom scheme can be exemplified by fungi, bacteria and *Euglena*, none of which fit neatly into either kingdom. *Euglena* species are single-celled organisms which, like plants, can photosynthesize. However, they can also, like animals, use their flagella to move from place to place. Fungal cells resemble plants in that they have rigid cell walls, but, unlike plants, they are unable to photosynthesize and so feed heterotrophically. Fungi and bacteria are very different from both plants and animals.

In the past it was only possible to use gross structural features, such as the presence or absence of a backbone, to classify organisms. Nowadays, however, many other techniques are available. Advances in microscopy have meant that detailed cellular structure can be observed and this has been vital in sorting prokaryotic bacterial cells from eukaryotes, as well as enabling the chromosomes of different species to be counted. It is possible to compare the amino acid sequences in the proteins of different organisms or the order of bases in their DNA. This work gives valuable information, not only about the relationships between various species, but also about their evolutionary origins. In 1959, partly as a result of some of these modern techniques, R.H.Whittaker suggested a scheme based on five kingdoms:

prokaryotes	prokaryotic cells (simple cells without membrane-surrounded structures) with a variety of feeding mechanisms
protists	unicellular eukaryotes (cells with a membrane-bound nucleus) with a variety of feeding mechanisms
fungi	multicellular eukaryotes feeding heterotrophically by absorption
plants	multicellular eukaryotes feeding by photosynthesis
animals	multicellular eukaryotes feeding heterotrophically by ingestion

Although this system solved the problem of the fungi not being plants and *Euglena* species being neither plants nor animals, it did have other problems, notably that the algae were split between two different kingdoms.

Margulis and Schwartz proposed a modification of Whittaker's scheme, suggesting that the multicellular algae should be removed from the kingdom Plantae and placed with all the unicellular eukaryotes in the kingdom Protoctista (which replaced Whittaker's Protista). This modification makes the plant kingdom a more "natural" group, but it does leave the Protoctista as the least homogeneous group. The Protoctista kingdom contains all eukaryotes that cannot be defined as plants, animals or fungi; it therefore lacks clearly defined features of its own. Incorporating Margulis' and Schwartz's modification, the five-kingdom system can be summarized as shown in the table below:

kingdom	features
Prokaryotae	prokaryotic organisms, for example bacteria and cyanobacteria
Protoctista	eukaryotic organisms not included in other kingdoms
Fungi	eukaryotic; multicellular with little or no tissue differentiation; feed by heterotrophic absorptive nutrition
Plantae	eukaryotic; multicellular organisms with tissue differentiation; feed by photosynthesis
Animalia	eukaryotic; multicellular organisms with tissue differentiation; feed by heterotrophic ingestive nutrition

This scheme has been criticized by some taxonomists because the kingdoms of plants, animals and fungi have been largely determined by their nutritional modes, which, it can be argued, should be considered adaptations rather than a sound basis for revealing evolutionary relationships.

Although the five-kingdom scheme has serious flaws it is still the scheme in most widespread use. The kingdoms and major phyla only are shown in the following table:

kingdom	phyla
Prokaryotae	Cyanobacteria; Bacteria
Protoctista	Rhizopoda; Zoomastigina; Apicomplexa; Ciliophora; Euglenophyta; Oomycota; Chlorophyta;Rhodophyta; Phaeophyta
Fungi	Zoomycota; Ascomycota; Basidiomycota
Plantae	Bryophyta; Lycopodophyta; Sphenophyta; Filicinophyta; Coniferophyta; Angiospermophyta
Animalia	Cnidaria; Platyhelminthes; Nematoda; Annelida; Mollusca; Arthropoda; Echinodermata; Chordata

EIGHT-KINGDOM CLASSIFICATION SYSTEM

The most recently proposed classification scheme is the most controversial. The eight-kingdom system has led to the reorganization of many groups in an attempt to represent more accurately their evolutionary relationships to other groups. The system also tries to deal with the most difficult areas of taxonomy – the prokaryotic and microscopic eukaryotic organisms.

In the eight-kingdom system there are two kingdoms of prokaryotic organisms, the Eubacteria and the Archaebacteria. The latter are thought to have diverged from the main evolutionary line early on. The Eubacteria gave rise to the Archezoa, the eukaryotic cells of which lack mitochondria, peroxisomes and Golgi bodies; they contain ribosomes similar to those in prokaryotes. From the Archezoa arose the Protista and then the four higher eukaryotic kingdoms – Chromista, Fungi, Plantae and Animalia.

The diagram below illustrates the relationships between the eight kingdoms:

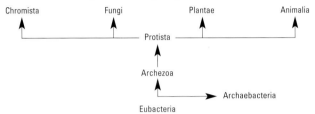

In another version of this scheme a category known as a domain is recognized; it is higher than a kingdom. All eukaryotic organisms are grouped together in the domain Eukarya, and the prokaryotes are divided into the domains Archaea and the Bacteria. The Archaea are "living fossils" – anaerobic bacteria that are genetically and metabolically different from other organisms and that may have survived since before the Earth's atmosphere had free oxygen. The three-domain scheme recognizes dozens of kingdoms.

EIGHT-KINGDOM CLASSIFICATION SYSTEM

1 Kingdom Eubacteria
    Proteobacteria
    Prochlorophyta
    Cyanobacteria
    green sulphur bacteria
    spirochaetes
    gram-positive bacteria

2 Kingdom Archaebacteria
    methanogens
    halophiles
    thermoacidophiles
    sulphur reducers

3 Kingdom Archezoa
    Metamonada
    Microsporidia
    Archeamoeba

4 Kingdom Protista
    Subkingdom Kinetoplatid
      Parabasala
      Euglenozoa
      Heterolobosea
      Rhizopoda
      Amoebozoa
      Granuloreticulosea
    Subkingdom Actinopoda
      Heliozoa
      Polycystinea
    Subkingdom Aveolata
      Dinoflagellata
      Apicomplexa
      Ciliophora
    Subkingdom aerobic Zooflagelate
      Choanoflagellata
      Opalozoa
    Subkingdom Mycetozoa
      Mycetozoa

5 Kingdom Chromista
    Subkingdom Cryptista
      Cryptista
    Subkingdom Heterokonta
      Sagenista
      Pseudofungi
      Ochrista
    Subkingdom Haptophyta
      Haptophyta

6 Kingdom Plantae
    Subkingdom Biliphyta
      Rhodophyta
      Glaucophta
    Subkingdom Viridiplantae
      Section Chlorophyta
        Chlorophyta
      Section Streptophyta
        Subsection Charophyta
          Charophata
        Subsection Embyophyta
          Bryophyta
          Tracheophyta

7 Kingdom Fungi
    Chytridiomycota
    Zygomycota
    Ascomycota
    Basidiomycota

8 Kingdom Animalia
    Subkingdom Parazoa
      Porifera
    Subkingdom Eumetazoa
      Section Radiate
        Cnidaria
        Placozoa
        Ctenophora
      Section Myxozoa
        Myxozoa
      Section Protostomia
        Platyhelminthes
        Gnathostomulida
        Nemertea
        Acanthocephala
        Mesozoa
        Rotifera
        Gastrotricha
        Kinorhyncha
        Nemata
        Nematomorpha
        Chaetognatha
        Entoprocta
        Loricifera
        Priapulida
        Bryozoa
        Phoronida
        Brachiopoda
        Mollusca
        Pogonophora
        Sipuncula
        Echiura
        Annelida
        Onychophora
        Tardigrada
        Arthropoda
      Section Deuterostomia
        Echinodermata
        Hemichordata
        Chordata

NOBEL PRIZEWINNERS

year	chemistry	physics	physiology or medicine
1901	J.H. van't Hoff	W.C. Roentgen	E.A. von Behring
1902	Emil Fischer	H.A. Lorentz	Sir Ronald Ross
		Pieter Zeeman	
1903	S.A. Arrhenius	A.H. Becquer	N.R. Finsen
		Pierre Curie	
		Marie S. Curie	
1904	Sir William Ramsay	J.W.S. Rayleigh	Ivan P. Pavlov
1905	Adolf von Baeyer	Philipp Lenard	Robert Koch
1906	Henri Moissan	Sir Joseph Thomson	Camillo Golgi
			S. Ramón y Cajal
1907	Eduard Buchner	A.A. Michelson	C.I.A. Laveran
1908	Sir Ernest Rutherford	Gabriel Lippman	Paul Ehrlich
			Élie Metchnikoff
1909	Wilhelm Ostwald	Guglielmo Marconi	Emil T. Kocher
		C.F. Braun	
1910	Otto Wallach	J.D. van der Waals	Albrecht Kossel
1911	Marie S. Curie	Wilhelm Wien	Allvar Gullstrand
1912	Victor Grignard	N.G. Dalen	Alexis Carrel
	Paul Sabatier		
1913	Alfred Werner	Heike Kamerlingh Onnes	C.R. Richet
1914	T.W. Richards	Max von Laue	Robert Barany
1915	Richard Willstätter	Sir William H. Bragg	
		Sir William L. Bragg	
1916			
1917		C.G. Barkla	
1918	Fritz Haber	Max Planck	
1919		Johannes Stark	Jules Bordet
1920	Walther Nernst	C.E. Gauillaume	S.A.S. Krogh
1921	Frederick Soddy	Albert Einstein	
1922	F.W. Aston	Niels Bohr	A.V. Hill
			Otto Meyerhof
1923	Fritz Pregl	Robert A. Millikan	Sir Frederick G. Banting
			J.J.R. Macleod
1924		K.M.G. Siegbahn	William Einthoven
1925	Richard Zsigmondy	James Franck	
		Gustav Hertz	
1926	Theodor Svedberg	J.B. Perrin	Johannes Fibiger
1927	Heinrich Wieland	A.H. Compton	Julius Wagner-Jauregg
		C.T.R. Wilson	
1928	Adolf Windaus	Sir Owen W. Richardson	C.J.H. Nicolle
1929	Sir Arthur Harden	L.V. de Broglie	Christian Eijkman
	Hans von Euler-Chelpin		Sir Frederick G. Hopkins
1930	Hans Fischer	Sir Chandrasekhara V. Raman	Karl Landsteiner
1931	Carl Bosch		Otto H. Warburg
	Friedrich Bergius		
1932	Irving Langmuir	Werner Heisenberg	E.D. Adrian
			Sir Charles Sherrington
1933		Paul Dirac	Thomas H. Morgan
		Erwin Schrödinger	
1934	Harold C. Urey		G.H. Whipple
			G.R. Minot
			W.P. Murphy
1935	Frédéric Joliot-Curie	Sir James Chadwick	Hans Spemann
	Irène Joliot-Curie		
1936	P.J.W. Debye	C.D. Anderson	Sir Henry H. Dale
		V.F. Hess	Otto Loewi
1937	Sir Walter N. Haworth	C.J. Davisson	Albert von Szent-Gyorgyi
	Paul Karrer	Sir George P. Thomson	
1938		Enrico Fermi	Corneille Heymans
1939	Adolf Butenandt	E.O. Lawrence	Gerhard Domagk
	Leopold Ruzicka		
1943	Georg von Hevesy	Otto Stern	E.A. Doisy
			Henrik Dam
1944	Otto Hahn	I.I. Rabi	Joseph Erlanger
			H.S. Gasser
1945	A.I. Virtanen	Wolfgang Pauli	Sir Alexander Fleming
			E.B. Chain
			Sir Howard W. Florey
1946	J.B. Sumner	P.W. Bridgman	H.J. Muller
	J.H. Northrop		
	W.M. Stanley		
1947	Sir Robert Robinson	Sir Edward V. Appleton	C.F. Cori
			Gerty T. Cori
			B.A. Houssay
1948	Arne Tiselius	P.M.S. Blackett	Paul H. Mueller
1949	W.F. Giauque	Hideki Yukawa	W.R. Hess
			Egas Moniz
1950	Otto Diels	C.F. Powell	Philip S. Hench
	Kurt Alder		Edward C. Kendall
			Tadeus Reichstein
1951	Edwin M. McMillan	Sir John D. Cockcroft	Max Theiler
	Glenn T. Seaborg	Ernest T.S. Walton	

NOBEL PRIZEWINNERS continued

year	chemistry	physics	physiology or medicine
1952	A.J.P. Martin	Felix Bloch	S.A. Waksman
	R.L.M. Synge	E.M. Purcell	
1953	Herman Staudinger	Frits Zernike	F.A. Lipmann
			Sir Hans A. Krebs
1954	Linus C. Pauling	Max Born	J.F. Enders
		Walter Bothe	F.C. Robbins
			T.H. Weller
1955	Vincent du Vigneaud	Willis E. Lamb, Jr.	A.H.T. Theorell
		Polykarp Kusch	
1956	Sir Cyril N.Hinshelwood	W.B. Shockley	D.W. Richards, Jr.
	Nikolai N.Semenov	W.H. Brattain	A.F. Cournand
		John Bardeen	Werner Forssmann
1957	Sir Alexander R. Todd	Tsung-Dao Lee	Daniele Bovet
		Chen Ning Yang	
1958	Frederick Sanger	P.A. Cherenkov	Joshua Lederberg
		Igor Y. Tamm	G.W. Beadle
		Ilya M. Frank	E.L. Tatum
1959	Jaroslav Heyrovsky	Emilio Segrè	Severo Ochoa
		Owen Chamberlain	Arthur Kornberg
1960	W.F. Libby	D.A. Glaser	Sir Macfarlane Burnet
			P.B. Medawar
1961	Melvin Calvin	Robert Hofstadter	Georg von Bekesy
		R.L. Moessbauer	
1962	M.F. Perutz	L.D. Landau	J.D. Watson
	J.C. Kendrew		F.H.C. Crick
			M.H.F. Wilkins
1963	Giulio Natta	Eugene Paul Wigner	Sir John Carew Eccles
	Karl Ziegler	Maria Goeppert Mayer	Alan Lloyd Hodgkin
		J. Hans D. Jensen	Andrew Fielding Huxley
1964	Dorothy Mary Crowfoot Hodgkin	Charles Hard Townes	Konrad E. Bloch
		Nikolai Gennadyevich Basov	Feodor Lynen
		Alexander Mikhailovich Prokhorov	
1965	Robert Burns Woodward	Richard Phillips Feynman	François Jacob
		Shinichiro Tomonaga	André Lwoff
		Julian Seymour Schwinger	Jacques Monod
1966	Robert S. Mulliken	Alfred Kastler	Francis Peyton Rous
			Charles Brenton Huggins
1967	Manfred Eigen	Hans Albrecht Bethe	Ragnar Granit
	Ronald George Wreyford Norrish		Haldan Keffer Hartline
	George Porter		George Wald
1968	Lars Onsager	Luis W. Alvarez	Robert W. Holley
			H. Gobind Khorana
			Marshall W. Nirenberg
1969	Derek H.R. Barton	Murray Gell-Mann	Max Delbrück
	Odd Hassel		Alfred D. Hershey
			Salvador E. Luria
1970	Luis Federico Leloir	Louis Eugène Néel	Julius Axelrod
		Hans Olof Alfven	Bernard Katz
			Ulf von Euler
1971	Gerhard Herzberg	Dennis Gabor	Earl W. Sutherland
1972	Stanford Moore	John Bardeen	Gerald M. Edelman
	William Howard Stein	Leon N. Cooper	Rodney R. Porter
	Christian B. Anfinsen	John Robert Schreiffer	
1973	Ernst Otto Fischer	Leo Esaki	Konrad Lorenz
	Geoffrey Wilkinson	Ivan Giaever	Nikolaas Tinbergen
		Brian D. Josephson	Karl von Frisch
1974	Paul J. Flory	Martin Ryle	Albert Claude
		Antony Hewish	George Emil Palade
			Christian de Duve
1975	John Warcup Comforth	Aage N. Bohr	David Baltimore
		Ben Roy Mottelson	Renato Dulbecco
	Vladimir Prelog	James Rainwater	Howard M. Temin
1976	William Nunn Lipscomb	Burton Richter	Baruch Samuel Blumberg
		Samuel Chao Chung Ting	Daniel Carleton Gajdusek
1977	Ilya Prigogine	Philip W. Anderson	Rosalyn S. Yalow
		Sir Nevill F. Mott	Roger C.L. Guillemin
		John H. Van Vleck	Andrew V. Schally
1978	Peter Mitchell	Peter Kapitza	Werner Arber
		Arno A. Penzias	Daniel Nathans
		Robert W. Wilson	Hamilton O. Smith
1979	Herbert C. Brown	Steven Weinberg	Allan Macleod Cormack
	Georg Witting	Sheldon L. Glashow	Godfrey Newbold Hounsfield
		Abdus Salam	
1980	Paul Berg	James W. Cronin	Baruj Benacerraf
	Walter Gilbert	Val F.Fitch	George D. Snell
	Frederick Sanger		Jean Dausset
1981	Kenichi Fukui	Nicolaas Bloembergen	Roger W. Sperry
	Roald Hoffmann	Arthur Schawlow	David H. Hubel
		Karl M. Siegbahn	Torsten N. Wiesel
1982	Aaron Klug	Kenneth G. Wilson	Sune K. Bergström
			Bengt I. Samuelsson
			John R. Vane

NOBEL PRIZEWINNERS continued

year	chemistry	physics	physiology or medicine
1983	Henry Taube	Subrahmanyan Chandrasekhar William A. Fowler	Barbara McClintock
1984	R. Bruce Merrifield	Carlo Rubbia Simon van der Meer	Cesar Milstein George J.F. Kohler Niels K. Jerne
1985	Herbert A. Hauptman Jerome Karle	Klaus von Klitzing	Michael S. Brown Joseph L. Goldstein
1986	Dudley R. Herschbach Yuan T. Lee John C. Polyani	Ernst Ruska Gerd Binnig Heinrich Rohrer	Rita Levi-Montalcini Stanley Cohen
1987	Donald J. Cram Charles J. Pedersen Jean-Marie Lehn	K. Alex Müller J. Georg Bednorz	Susumu Tonegawa
1988	Johann Deisenhofer Robert Huber Hartmut Michel Nikolai N. Semenov	Leon M. Lederman Melvin Schwartz Jack Steinberger	Gertrude B. Elion George H. Hitchings James Black
1989	Thomas R. Cech Sidney Altman	Norman F. Ramsey Hans G. Dehmelt Wolfgang Pauli	J. Michael Bishop Harold E. Varmus
1990	Elias James Corey	Richard E. Taylor Jerome I. Friedman Henry W. Kendall	Joseph E. Murray E. Donnall Thomas
1991	Richard R. Ernst	Pierre-Gilles de Gennes	Edwin Neher Bert Sakmann
1992	Rudolph A. Marcus	George Charpak	Edmond H. Fisher Edwin G. Krebs
1993	Kary Mullis Michael Smith	Joseph Taylor Russell Hulse	Phillip Sharp Richard Roberts
1994	George A. Olah	Clifford G. Shull Bertram N. Brockhouse	Alfred Gilman Martin Rodbell
1995	Paul Crutzen Mario Molina F. Sherwood Rowland	Martin L. Perl Frederick Reines	Edward B. Lewis Christiane Nüsslein-Volhard Eric F. Wieschaus
1996	Robert F. Curl Harold W. Kroto Richard E. Smalley	David M. Lee Douglas D. Osheroff Robert C. Richardson	Peter C. Doherty Rolf M. Zinkernagel
1997	Paul D. Boyer John E. Walker Jens C. Skou	Steven Chu Claude Cohen-Tannoudji William D. Phillips	Stanley B. Prusiner
1998	Walter Kohn John Pople	Robert Laughlin Daniel Tsui Horst Stoermer	Robert F. Furchgott Louis J. Ignarro Ferid Murad
1999	Ahmed Zewail	Gerhardus Hooft Martinus Veltman	Günter Blobel
2000	Alan J. Heeger Alan G. MacDiarmid Hideki Shirakawa	Zhores I. Alferov Herbert Kroemer Jack S. Kilby	Arvid Carlsson Paul Greengard Eric Kandel

reference: www.nobel.se

NATURAL HISTORY MUSEUMS

name and location	website	exhibits
AUSTRALIA		
Macleay Museum Gosper Lane, off Science Road University of Sydney Sydney	www.usyd.edu.au/su/macleay	invertebrates, vertebrates, ethnography, historic scientific instruments, historic photographs
Queen Victoria Museum Wellington Street Launceston	www.qvmag.tased.edu.au	Australian minerals, flora and fauna, planetarium
AUSTRIA		
Haus der Natur Museumsplatz 5 Salzburg	www.salzburg.co.at/hausdernatur	aquarium, reptiles, astronomy
Sternwarte Kremsmünster Stift Kremsmünster Kremsmünster	members.magnet.at/stewar/english.htm	geological, palaeontological, prehistoric, mineralogical, physics and zoological collections; folklore, ethnology
Vorarlberger Naturschau Marktstrasse 33 Dornbirn	www.naturschau.at	palaeontological and biological collections; zoology, botany and earth sciences exhibits
BELGIUM		
Museum of the Royal Belgian Institute of Natural Sciences Chaussée de Wavre 260 Brussels	www.naturalsciences.be	evolution, mammals, birds, invertebrates, sea life, minerals
CANADA		
Canadian Museum of Nature Victoria Memorial Museum Building 240 McLeod Street Ottawa	www.nature.ca	animal behaviour, birds, dinosaurs, insects, reptiles, rodents, mammals, plants and herbs, rocks and minerals, the Earth, exploration station
Lynn Canyon Ecology Centre Lynn Canyon Park North Vancouver	www.dnv.org/ecology	interactive displays about the environment and the temperate rainforest; film screenings
Nova Scotia Museum of Natural History 1747 Summer Street Halifax Nova Scotia	museum.gov.ns.ca/mnh	nature centre, seasonal live displays, zoological displays
Ecomuseum 21, 125 Chemin Ste-Marie Ste-Anne-de-Bellevue	www.agrenv.mcgill.ca/EXTENSION/ECOMUSE/ECOMUSE.HTM	live collections of wildlife native to the St Lawrence Valley
Provincial Museum of Alberta 12845-102nd Avenue Edmonton Alberta	www.pma.edmonton.ab.ca	botany, geology, ichthyology, invertebrate zoology, mammalogy, ornithology, palaeontology
CROATIA		
Croatia Natural History Museum Demetrova 1 Zagreb	mahpm.hpm.hr	minerals, precious stones, zoology
DENMARK		
Museums of Natural History Faculty of Science Copenhagen University Copenhagen	www.nathimus.ku.dk	botanical, geological and zoological museums
FINLAND		
Finnish Museum of Natural History Pohjoinen Rautatiekatu 13 Helsinki	www.fmnh.helsinki.fi	botanical, zoological, geological and palaeontological specimens
GERMANY		
Naturmuseum Senckenberg Senckenberganlage 25 Frankfurt am Main	www.senckenberg.uni-frankfurt.de	evolution, embryology, dinosaurs, planets, rainforest, geology, fossils, mammals, reptiles, fish, amphibians, birds, insects, crustaceans
HUNGARY		
Hungarian Natural History Museum Ludovika tér 6 Budapest	www.nhmus.hu	zoology, mineralogy and petrology, anthropology, botany, geology and palaeontology
INDIA		
Natural History Museum FICCI Building Barakhamba Road New Delhi	www.envfor.nic.in/nmnh/nmnh.html	natural history and conservation displays, interactive activities
ITALY		
Museo di Storia Naturale Certosa di Calci Calci Pisa	astrpi.difi.unipi.it/Museo_di_Calci/MusSN-e.html	mineralogy, palaeontology, zoology, cetacean gallery
Museo di Storia Naturale di Firenze Via G. La Pira, 4 Florence	www.unifi.it/unifi/msn	botany, geology, palaeontology, mineralogy
JAPAN		
Lake Biwa Museum Lakeshore Road Lake Biwa Shiga Prefecture	www.lbm.go.jp/english/index-e.html	geological and human history of Lake Biwa; aquarium
Osaka Museum of Natural History Nagai Park Osaka	www.mus-nh.city.osaka.jp/english/omnh-e-home.html	fish, reptile, amphibian and insect collections; local history, evolution, conservation exhibits
NETHERLANDS		
Natural History Museum De Bosquetplein 6-7 Maastricht	www.nhmmaastricht.nl	geology, palaeontology, entomology, botany

continued...

NATURAL HISTORY MUSEUMS continued

name and location	website	exhibits
NEW ZEALAND **Museum of New Zealand** Te Papa Tongarewa Cable Street Wellington	www.tepapa.govt.nz	art, birds, botany, entomology, fish, history, mammals, molluscs, Pacific cultures, photography, reptiles, amphibians, Maori culture
NORWAY **Museum of Natural History** Sars' gt. 1 Oslo	www.toyen.uio.no/toyensider/engelsk.html	arboretum, zoological, mineralogical-geological and palaeontological museums
RUSSIA **State Darwin Museum of Natural History** 57/1 Vavilova st. Moscow	www.darwin.museum.ru	history of biology and biodiversity displays; mammal, bird and butterfly collections
SOUTH AFRICA **Albany Museum** Somerset Street Grahamstown	www.ru.ac.za/affiliates/am	freshwater invertebrates, terrestrial insects, freshwater fish, plants, birds, fossils, rocks and minerals, ethnography
Transvaal Museum Paul Kruger Street Pretoria	www.nfi.org.za/tmpage.html	vertebrates, invertebrates, human origins, palaeontology
SPAIN **Museo Nacional de Ciencas Naturales** José Gutiérrez Abascal, 2 Madrid	www.mncn.csix.es	mineralogy and petrology, palaeontology, palaeobotany, entomology, ichthyology, herpetology, birds, mammals
SWEDEN **Naturhistoriska riksmuseet** Frescativägen 40 Stockholm	www.nrm.se	animals, plants, minerals, fossils, environments, astronomy
SWITZERLAND **Natural History Museum** Bernastrasse 15 Berne	www.nmbe.ch	Swiss and other birds and mammals; minerals, zoological and geological exhibits
Natural History Museum Chemin du Musée 6 Fribourg	www.etatfr.ch/mhn/en	botany, geography, mineralogy, zoology and geology
UNITED KINGDOM **Hancock Museum** Barras Bridge Newcastle-upon-Tyne	www.ncl.ac.uk/~nhancock	insects, birds, aquaria, Egyptology, geology, ecology
Kendal Museum Station Road Kendal Cumbria	www.kendalmuseum.org.uk	archaeology, geology, natural and social history, Lakeland flora and fauna
Leicester City Museums **(New Walk Museum)** 53 New Walk Leicester	www.leicestermuseums.ac.uk	Egyptology, dinosaurs, rocks and fossils
Natural History Museum Cromwell Road London	www.nhm.ac.uk	botany, entomology, mineralogy, palaeontology, zoology; Darwin centre, dinosaurs, fossils
Oxford University Museum of Natural History Parks Road Oxford	www.oum.ox.ac.uk	entomology, geology, mineralogy, zoology
Royal Albert Memorial Museum Queen Street Exeter	www.exeter.gov.uk/tourism	ethnography, natural history, botany, geology, zoology
Royal Cornwall Museum River Street Truro	www.royalcornwallmuseum.org.uk	minerals, archaeology and local history
Towneley Hall Art Gallery and Museums Burnley Lancashire	www.burnley.gov.uk/towneley	aquarium, insect, rock and mineral collections
Tunbridge Wells Museum and Art Gallery Civic Centre, Mount Pleasant Tunbridge Wells	www.tunbridgewells.gov.uk/museum	British birds, local butterflies and moths, insects, fauna, rocks, fossils and minerals
Walter Rothschild Zoological Museum Akeman Street Tring Hertfordshire	www.nhm.ac.uk/museum/tring	mammals, amphibians, marsupials, reptiles, fish, invertebrates, ornithological collection and library
UNITED STATES **American Museum of Natural History** Central Park West at 79th Street New York	www.amnh.org	astronomy, Earth, fossils, biodiversity, mammals, birds, reptiles, minerals
Barrick Museum of Natural History University of Las Vegas Las Vegas	hrcweb.lv-hrc.nevada.edu	entomology, herpetology, ornithology, arboretum
Bell Museum of Natural History University of Minnesota Minneapolis	www1.umn.edu/bellmuse	Minnesota's wildlife; collections of amphibians, reptiles, birds, fish, fungi, lichens, molluscs, mammals, plants
Burke Museum of Natural History University of Washington Seattle	www.washington.edu/burkemuseum	geology, anthropology, zoology
California Academy of Natural History 5 Concourse Drive Golden Gate Park San Francisco	www.calacademy.org	evolution, earthquakes, anthropology, minerals and gems, insects; Morrison Planetarium; Steinhart Aquarium
Carnegie Museum of Natural History 4400 Forbes Avenue Pittsburgh	www.clpgh.org/cmnh	dinosaurs, fossils, geology, minerals and gems, botany, African wildlife, insects, amphibians, reptiles, Native American culture

continued...

NATURAL HISTORY MUSEUMS continued

name and location	website	exhibits
UNITED STATES continued		
Cincinnati Museum Center Union Terminal 1301 Western Avenue Cincinnati	www.cincymuseum.org	anthropology, palaeontology, zoology
Cleveland Museum of Natural History 1 Wade Oval Drive, University Circle Cleveland Ohio	www.cmnh.org	archaeology, astronomy, botany, anthropology, palaeontology, invertebrate zoology, mineralogy, palaeobotany
Colorado University Museum of Natural History Broadway Boulder Colorado	www.Colorado.EDU/CUMUSEUM	anthropology, biology, fossils
Dallas Museum of Natural History 3535 Grand Avenue, Fair Park Dallas Texas	www.dallasdino.org	lagoon nature walk, palaeontology, prehistory, wildlife dioramas
Denver Museum of Natural History 2001 Colorado Boulevard Denver	www.dmnh.org	prehistory, Colorado's wildlife, Native American culture, ancient Egypt, minerals, mammals, birds, astronomy
Field Museum of Natural History Museum Campus Chicago	www.fieldmuseum.org	animals, plants, ecosystems, rocks and fossils, anthropology
Florida Museum of Natural History University of Florida Gainesville Florida	www.flmnh.ufl.edu	amphibians, birds, butterflies, fish, mammals, molluscs, reptiles, vertebrates, invertebrates, fossils
Franklin and Marshall College's North Museum 400 College Avenue Lancaster Pennsylvania	www.northmuseum.org	astronomy, dinosaurs, planetarium, Native American culture
Great Valley Museum of Natural History Modesto Junior College Modesto California	mjc.yosemite.cc.ca.us/greatvalley	Great Central Valley flora and fauna, mammals, Native American culture
Hastings Museum 1330 N Burlington Ave Hastings Nebraska	www.hastingsnet.com/museum	natural history and people of the Great Plains, birds, insects, seashells and corals, rocks and minerals, fossils
Idaho Museum of Natural History Idaho State University Pocatello Idaho	www.isu.edu/departments/museum	anthropology, botany, geology, palaeontology and zoology of Idaho and the surrounding region
Illinois State Museum Spring & Edwards Streets Springfield Illinois	www.museum.state.il.us	anthropology, botany, geology, zoology, natural and cultural history of Illinois
International Wildlife Museum Speedway Boulevard Tucson Arizona	www.arizonaguide.com/iwm	mammals, birds, insects and prehistoric animals
Kansas City Museum 3218 Gladstone Boulevard Kansas City Missouri	www.kcmuseum.com	planetarium, astronomy (Challenger Learning Center), Native American culture
Las Vegas Natural History Museum 900 N Las Vegas Boulevard Las Vegas	www.vegaswebworld.com/lvnathistory	dinosaurs, mammals, plants, marine life
Lafayette Natural History Museum & Planetarium 637 Girard Park Drive Lafayette Louisiana	www.lnhm.org	Native American culture, collection of fossils, meteorites, planetarium
McClung Museum University of Tennessee Knoxville Tennessee	mcclungmuseum.utk.edu	geology, anthropology, archaeology, Egyptology, local history
Milwaukee Public Museum 800 West Wells Street Milwaukee Wisconsin	www.mpm.edu	anthropology, botany, geology, history and zoology, rainforest exhibit, dinosaurs, free-flying butterflies, marine life
Museum of Anthropology & Cormack Planetarium Roger Williams Park Providence Rhode Island	www.osfn.org/museum	plants, insects, molluscs, birds, mammals, rocks, minerals, fossils
Natural History Museum of Los Angeles County 900 Exposition Boulevard, Exposition Park Los Angeles California	www.lam.mus.ca.us	mammals, dinosaurs, birds, marine life, minerals and gems, fossils, insects
New Mexico Museum of Natural History & Science 1801 Mountain Road NW Albuquerque New Mexico	www.nmmnh-abq.mus.nm.us	dinosaurs, fossils, archaeology, evolution, geology
New York State Museum Empire State Plaza Albany New York	www.nysm.nysed.gov	birds, anthropology, biology, geology, local history, fossils, minerals
North Carolina State Museum of Natural Sciences 11 W Jones St. Raleigh North Carolina	www.naturalsciences.org	geography, geology, plants and animals, dinosaurs
Oklahoma Museum of Natural History 2401 Chautauqua Avenue Norman Oklahoma	www.snomnh.ou.edu	herpetology, ichthyology, invertebrates, mammalogy, ornithology, archaeology, ethnology, minerals collections
Peabody Museum of Natural History 170 Whitney Avenue Yale University New Haven	www.peabody.yale.edu	fossils, dinosaurs, mammalian evolution

continued...

name and location	website	exhibits
UNITED STATES continued		
San Bernardino County Museum Orange Tree Lane Redlands California	www.co.san-bernardino.ca.us/museum	anthropology, herpetology, ornithology, mammalogy, botany, palaeontology, mineralogy
San Diego Natural History Museum Balboa Park San Diego California	www.sdnhm.org	regional exhibits, entomology, desert ecology, snakes, reptiles
Santa Barbara Museum of Natural History 2559 Puesta del Sol Road Santa Barbara California	www.sbnature.org	mammals, birds, amphibians and reptiles, invertebrates, marine life, geology and palaeontology, astronomy
South Carolina State Museum 301 Gervais Street Columbia South Carolina	www.museum.state.sc.us	prehistoric fossils, sharks, habitat dioramas, science and technology, cultural history
The Schiele Museum of Natural History 1500 East Garrison Blvd Gastonia North Carolina	www.schielemuseum.org	planetarium, nature trail, regional wildlife and habitats, pre-historic animals, ethnography, human origins, marine life
University of Kansas Natural History Museum Jayhawk Blvd Lawrence Kansas	ron.nhm.ukans.edu	fossils, dinosaurs, dioramas of birds, mammals and plants, working bee hive
University of Nebraska State Museum 307 Morrill Hall University of Nebraska Lincoln Nebraska	www-museum.unl.edu	planetarium, fossils, dinosaurs, biodiversity, Encounter Center
University of Oregon Museum of Natural History University of Oregon Eugene Oregon	natural-history.uoregon.edu	archaeology and fossil history of Oregon, animals, plants, environmental topics, traditional human cultures, anthropology
University of Wisconsin Stevens Point Museum of Natural History 900 Reserve Street Stevens Point Wisconsin	www.uwsp.edu/museum	eggs, fossils, rocks and minerals, Earth and the solar system, wildlife and ecosystems
Utah Museum of Natural History Presidents Circle University of Utah Salt Lake City Utah	www.umnh.utah.edu	anthropology, minerals, vertebrates, biology, palaeontology
Virginia Museum of Natural History 1001 Douglas Avenue Martinsville Virginia	www.vmnh.org	rocks, mammals, reptiles, dinosaurs

BOTANIC GARDENS AND ARBORETUMS

name and location	website
AUSTRALIA	
Australian National Botanic Gardens Clunies Ross Street Acton (Black Mountain)	www.anbg.gov.au/anbg
Brisbane Botanic Gardens Mt Coot-tha Brisbane	users.bit.net.au/~bcc.bbg
Royal Botanic Gardens Melbourne South Yarra Melbourne	www.rbgmelb.org.au
Royal Botanic Gardens Sydney Mrs Macquaries Road Sydney	www.rbgsyd.gov.au
National Rhododendron Gardens The Georgian Road Olinda Victoria	www.yarranet.swin.edu.au/Melb-E-REDO/tourism/pages/rhodo/ rhodo.html
Norfolk Island Botanic Gardens	www.anbg.gov.au/norfolk.gardens
AUSTRIA	
Botanical Garden of the University of Vienna Rennweg 14 Vienna	www.botanik.univie.ac.at/hbv/hbv.htm
BELGIUM	
Flemish Show Gardens Houtmarkt 1 Hoegaarden	www.innet.net/toontuinen/en/indexen.htm
National Botanic Garden of Belgium Domein van Bouchout Meise Brussels	www.br.fgov.be/index.html
CANADA	
Butchart Gardens Victoria Vancouver Island British Columbia	www.butchartgardens.com
Dr Sun Yat-Sen Classical Chinese Garden 578 Carrall Street Vancouver British Columbia	www.vancouverattractions.com/sunyatsengardens.htm
Montréal Botanical Garden and Insectarium 4101 Sherbrooke East Montréal	www.ville.montreal.qc.ca/jardin
Niagara Parks Botanical Gardens Niagara Parks Ontario	www.niagaraparks.com/hort/botanical.html
Royal Botanical Gardens 680 Plains Road West Burlington Ontario	www.rbg.ca
Devonian Botanic Garden University of Alberta Edmonton Alberta	www.discoveredmonton.com/devonian
University of British Columbia Botanic Gardens 6804 SW Marine Drive Vancouver British Columbia	www.hedgerows.com/UBCBotGdn
CHINA	
Shanghai Botanic Garden 1100 Long Wu Road Shanghai	sinosource.com/SH/PUB/SHBG
COSTA RICA	
Lankester Botanical Garden Cartago	cariari.ucr.ac.cr/~jbl
DENMARK	
Royal Horticultural Garden The Royal Veterinary and Agricultural University Grönnegaardsvej 15 Copenhagen	www.lbh.kvl.dk/uk/index.htm
ESTONIA	
Botanical Garden of the University of Tartu Lai 38/40 Tartu	www.ut.ee/BGBA/botanic.html
Tallinn Botanic Garden Kloostrimetsa tee 52 Tallinn	www.tba.ee/TBGeng.htm
FINLAND	
Botanical Garden, University of Helsinki Unioninkatu 44 Kaisaniemi Helsinki	www.helsinki.fi/ml/botgard
Botanical Gardens of the University of Oulu Kaitoväylä 5 Oulu	cc.oulu.fi/~biolwww/puutarha/eindex.htm
FRANCE	
Jardin Botanique Terrasse du Jardin Public Place Bardineau Bordeaux	www.mairie-bordeaux.fr/jardin-botanique/gb/Index.html
Tête d'Or Park Lyon	www.mairie-lyon.fr/en/tour_parc.html

continued...

BOTANIC GARDENS AND ARBORETUMS continued

name and location	website
GERMANY	
Arboretum Stadt Freiburg Municipal Forest District of Freiburg	www.biologie.uni-ulm.de/extern/guenterstal/ukarbtxt.htm
Botanical Garden and Botanical Museum Berlin-Dahlem Königin-Luise-Str. 6-8 Freie Universität Berlin Berlin	www.bgbm.fu-berlin.de
Bonn University Botanic Garden Meckenheimer Allee 171 Bonn	www.botanik.uni-bonn.de/botgart
Botanic Garden Greifswald Grimmer Str. 88 Greifswald	www.uni-greifswald.de/~botanik/botgar.htm
Botanischer Garten Menzinger Str. 61–65 Munich	www.botanik.biologie.uni-muenchen.de/botgart
Palmengarten Siesmayerstraße Frankfurt	www.stadt-frankfurt.de/palmengarten
IRELAND	
National Botanic Gardens Glasnevin Glasnevin Dublin	www.irelandseye.com/visit/IG/glasnevin.html
Talbot Botanic Gardens Malahide Dublin	www.castlesireland.com/the-talbot.html
NETHERLANDS	
Botanical Garden of Nijmegen University of Nijmegen Toernooiveld 1 Nijmegen	www-sci.sci.kun.nl/bgard
NEW ZEALAND	
Christchurch Botanic Gardens Christchurch	canterbury.cyberplace.org.nz/community/botanic.html
NORWAY	
University of Oslo Botanical Garden Tøyen Oslo	www.toyen.uio.no/botanisk/bothage/garden_intro.html
PORTUGAL	
Jardim Botânico da Madeira Caminho do Meio Bom sucesso Funchal Madeira	www.uma.pt/jb/jb_eng.html
SOUTH AFRICA	
Pretoria National Botanical Garden 2 Cussonia Avenue Brummeria Pretoria	www.nbi.ac.za/pretoria/mainpage.htm
SWEDEN	
Göteborg Botanical Gardens Göteborg	w3.goteborg.se/botaniska/engelska/e_index.htm
Uppsala University Botanical Garden Villavägen 8 Uppsala	www.linnaeus.uu.se/hortuseng.html
SWITZERLAND	
University of Zürich Botanic Garden Zollikerstraße 107 Zürich	www.unizh.ch/bguz
UNITED KINGDOM	
Birmingham Botanical Gardens & Glasshouses Westbourne Road Edgbaston Birmingham	www.bham-bot-gdns.demon.co.uk
Borde Hill Garden Balcombe Road Haywards Heath West Sussex	www.bordehill.co.uk
Cambridge University Botanic Garden Bateman Street Cambridge	www.botanic.cam.ac.uk
Durham University Botanic Garden Hollingside Lane Durham	www.dur.ac.uk/~deb0www/dubg/bghomep.html
Eden Project Bodelva St Austell Cornwall	www.edenproject.com
National Botanic Garden of Wales Middleton Hall Llanarthne Carmarthenshire	www.gardenofwales.org.uk
Ness Botanic Gardens University of Liverpool Environmental & Horticultural Research Station Neston South Wirral Cheshire	www.merseyworld.com/nessgardens

continued...

BOTANIC GARDENS AND ARBORETUMS continued

name and location	website
Royal Botanic Gardens Kew London	www.rbgkew.org.uk
Royal Botanic Garden Edinburgh Inverleith Row Edinburgh	www.rbge.org.uk
Sir Harold Hillier Gardens and Arboretum Jermyns Lane Ampfield Hampshire	www.hillier.hants.gov.uk
Ventnor Botanic Garden Undercliff Drive Ventnor Isle of Wight	www.botanic.co.uk
Westonbirt Arboretum Tetbury Gloucestershire	www.forestry.gov.uk/westonbirt

UNITED STATES

name and location	website
Arboretum of Los Angeles County 301 North Baldwin Avenue Arcadia California	www.arboretum.org
Brooklyn Botanic Garden 1000 Washington Avenue Brooklyn New York	www.bbg.org
California Living Museum 10500 Alfred Harrell Highway Bakersfield California	www.calmzoo.org
Cedar Valley Arboretum and Botanic Gardens 1927 East Orange Road Waterloo Iowa	www.cedarnet.org/gardens
Chicago Botanic Garden 1000 Lake Cook Road Glencoe Illinois	www.chicago-botanic.org
Cincinnati Zoo and Botanical Garden Dury Avenue Cincinnati Ohio	www.cincyzoo.org
Desert Botanical Garden 1201 North Galvin Parkway Phoenix Arizona	www.dbg.org
Missouri Botanical Garden 4344 Shaw Boulevard St Louis Missouri	www.mobot.org
Mitchell Park Horticultural Conservatory 524 S. Layton Blvd Milwaukee Wisconsin	www.countyparks.com/horticulture
New York Botanical Garden 200th St & Kazimiroff Boulevard New York	www.nybg.org
North Carolina Botanical Garden The University of North Carolina Chapel Hill North Carolina	www.unc.edu/depts/ncbg
San Antonio Botanical Garden 555 Funston Place San Antonio Texas	www.sabot.org/bg
Santa Barbara Botanic Garden 1212 Mission Canyon Road Santa Barbara California	www.santabarbarabotanicgarden.org
State Botanical Garden of Georgia 2450 South Milledge Avenue Athens Georgia	www.uga.edu/~botgarden
United States National Arboretum New York Avenue Washington, DC	www.usna.usda.gov

NATURE-RELATED WEBSITES

organizations specializing in animals

www.bornfree.org.uk	BornFree Foundation, an international wildlife charity dedicated to conservation of species in situ
www.orangutan.org	Orangutan Foundation International, an international wildlife charity dedicated to conservation of orangutans in situ and caring for former captives
www.pinnipeds.fsnet.co.uk	Seal Conservation Society, a UK-based, non-profit charitable organization dedicated to protecting and conserving pinnipeds worldwide
www.rspb.org.uk	Royal Society for the Protection of Birds, a UK-based, non-profit charitable organization dedicated to protecting birds and other UK wildlife
www.awf.org	African Wildlife Foundation, an international wildlife charity dedicated to conservation of habitats and species in Africa
www.birdlife.net	BirdLife International, an international Non-Governmental Organization (NGO) dedicated to conserving birds

websites and networks specializing in animals

www.ultimateungulate.com	The Ultimate Ungulate, a searchable website on hoofed mammals
www.ex.ac.uk/MEDASSET	EuroTurtle, a searchable website on turtles
www.fishbase.org/home.htm	Fishbase, an online database of the World's fish

organizations specializing in marine life

www.cgiar.org/iclarm	The World Fish Centre, an international, non-profit NGO dedicated to improving the productivity, management and conservation of aquatic resources for the benefit of users and consumers in developing countries
www.unep.ch/seas/rshome.html	UNEP Regional Seas, a United Nations Environment Programme (UNEP) for regional seas concerned with implementation of Agenda 21 in oceans

websites and networks specializing in marine life

www.reefbase.org	ReefBase, a global information system on coral reefs
www.unep.ch/coral/icran.htm	International Coral Reef Action Network, an international network dedicated to reversing the decline in the health of coral reefs

general organizations

www.iucn.org	The World Conservation Union, an international, intergovernmental organization dedicated to conserving biodiversity
www.panda.org	WWF (World Wildlife Fund) International, an international NGO dedicated to conserving biodiversity
www.fws.gov	US Fish and Wildlife Service, a US governmental organization dedicated to conserving biodiversity in the USA
www.greenpeace.org	Greenpeace International, an international campaigning NGO dedicated to preserving biodiversity
www.tnc.org	The Nature Conservancy, an international NGO dedicated to conserving biodiversity
www.conservation.org	Conservation International, an international, field-based NGO dedicated to conserving biodiversity
www.si.edu	Smithsonian Institute, a US trust and research centre for education in humanities and science
www.fauna-flora.org	Fauna and Flora International, an international NGO providing support to conservation initiatives
www.unep-wcmc.org	UNEP World Conservation Monitoring Centre, an International NGO providing support with biodiversity data
www.rgs.org	Royal Geographic Society, a society representing geographers providing support and research
www.igc.org/wri	World Resources Institute, an international institute dedicated to conserving natural resources
www.traffic.org	Traffic International, the Wildlife Trade Monitoring Programme of the WWF
www.eea.eu.int	European Environment Agency, a European governmental organization dedicated to improving Europe's environment
www.worldbank.org	The World Bank, an international association dedicated to fighting poverty

United Nations (UN) organizations and committees

www.un.org	United Nations
www.fao.org	Food and Agriculture Organization, a UN agency dedicated to improving nutrition, agricultural productivity and living standards
www.unep.org	United Nations Environment Programme, a UN agency dedicated to conserving the environment
www.undp.org	United Nations Development Programme, a UN agency dedicated to combating poverty
www.un.org/esa/sustdev	UN Commission on Sustainable Development, a UN commission dedicated to overseeing the implementation of the Rio Declaration on Environment and Development and Agenda 21
www.unesco.org	United Nations Educational, Scientific and Cultural Organization, a UN agency dedicated to promoting peace and security through education, science and culture
www.wmo.ch/index-en.html	World Meteorological Organization, a UN convention dedicated to improving international development of meteorology and hydrology

UN websites

www.gefweb.org	Global Environment Facility, an international network providing support in combating biodiversity loss, climate change and degradation of water and ozone
www.unep.net	UNEP.Net, a portal for global environmental information

organizations specializing in plants

www.cgiar.org	Consultative Group on International Agricultural Research, an association dedicated to ensuring food security and poverty eradication in the developing world
iopi.csu.edu.au/iopi	International Organization for Plant Information, an international NGO for plant information through databases
www.rbgkew.org.uk	Royal Botanic Gardens, Kew, a UK botanical gardens dedicated to conserving plants and fungi

websites and networks specializing in plants

www.ipni.org	International Plant Name Index, an online database of plant names and bibliographic references
155.187.10.12/index.html	Australian National Botanic Gardens Biodiversity Server

organizations specializing in forestry

www.cifor.cgiar.org	Centre for International Forestry Research, an international NGO dedicated to enhancing the benefits of forests for people in the tropics
www.efi.fi	European Forestry Institute, an international NGO dedicated to helping conserve forests through capacity building
www.fscoax.org/principal.htm	Forestry Stewardship Council, an international NGO that certifies forests according to their management
www.icraf.cgiar.org	International Centre for Research in Agroforestry, an international research centre in agroforestry dedicated to improving human welfare

websites and networks specializing in forestry

www.ran.org	Rainforest Action Network, a portal for global rainforest information
www.unep-wcmc.org/forest/homepage.htm	UNEP-WCMC Forestry Programme, a portal for global forest information and provision of global data

organizations and websites specializing in environmental law

www.ecolex.org	Ecolex, a non-governmental organization and governmental organization collaboration dedicated to providing legal material used for conservation management
www.ecnc.nl	European Centre for Nature Conservation, an association of national and intergovernmental organizations and scientific research centres dedicated to conserving Europe's biodiversity through capacity building

organizations specializing in protected areas (PAs)

www.unesco.org	United Nations Educational, Scientific and Cultural Organization, a UN agency dedicated to promoting peace and security through education, science and culture
www.wetlands.agro.nl	Wetlands International, an international NGO dedicated to conserving global wetlands and their species

websites and networks specializing in protected areas (PAs)

www.nationalgeographic.com/wildworld/global.html	Global 200, 200 globally threatened areas, identified by the WWF, hosted by National Geographic

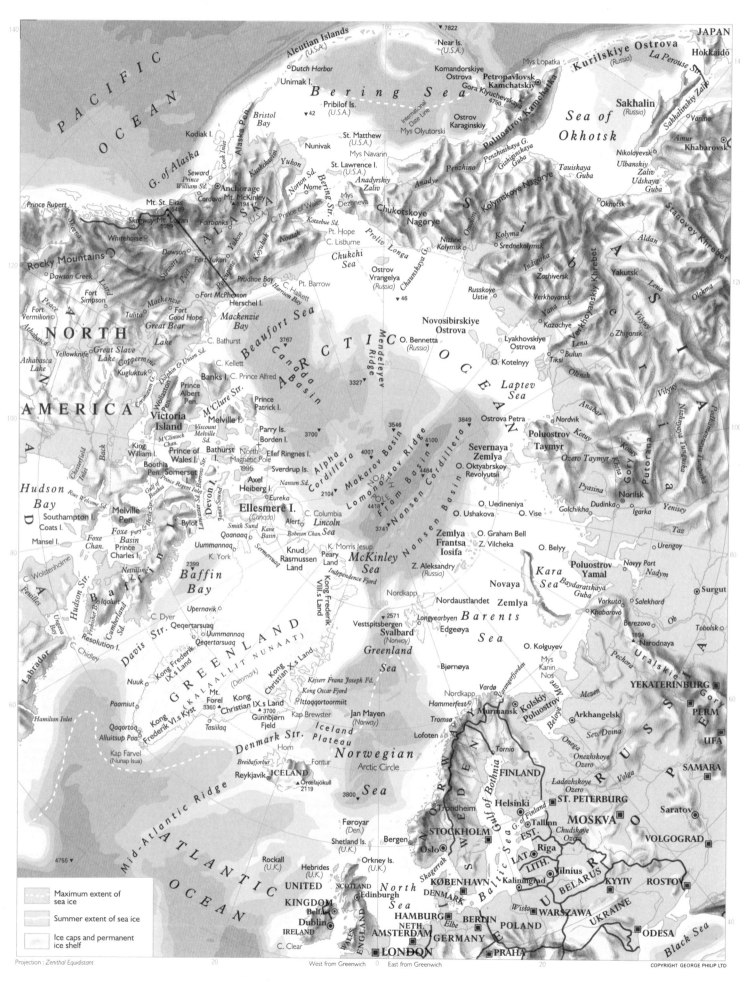

ARCTIC OCEAN 1:35 000 000